P8-2B No check figure
P8-3B Allow. for Uncollect. Accts. $5,099
P8-4B Allow. for Doubtful Accts. $3,809
P8-5B No check figure
P8-6B Accrued interest revenue $398
P8-7B 19X6 Inventory turnover 7.5 times
DP 1 Net income, 19X3, $61,800
DP 2 No check figure
FSP 1 1. Cash collections $866,796,000
FSP 2 No check figure

P9-1A Cost of goods sold, $1,590
P9-2A LIFO end. inventory $18,269
P9-3A FIFO inventory profit $500
P9-4A Gross margin: Weighted-average $2,435; FIFO $2,587; LIFO $2,289
P9-5A FIFO gross margin $5,445
P9-6A FIFO end. inventory $360
P9-7A Net income: 19X1 $27 million; 19X2 $9 million; 19X3 $11 million
P9-8A Est. cost of end. inventory $340,000
P9-1B Cost of goods sold $3,906
P9-2B Wtd.-avg. COGS $11,482
P9-3B FIFO inventory profit $263
P9-4B Gross margin: Weighted-average $61,686; FIFO $62,195; LIFO $61,255
P9-5B FIFO gross margin $2,766 million
P9-6B FIFO end. inventory $540
P9-7B Net income: 19X4 $11 million; 19X5 $63 million; 19X6 $65 million
P9-8B Est. cost of end. inventory $175,000
DP-1 Net income without purchase: FIFO $249,000; LIFO $213,000 Net income with purchase: FIFO $249,000; LIFO $120,000
DP-2 No check figure
FSP 1 4. COGS (FIFO) $510,701,000
FSP 2 No check figure

P10-1A Depr. -Land improv. $3,990; Home office bldg. $30,503; Garage $2,175; Furniture $11,700
P10-2A No check figure
P10-3A Depr. 19X6 - SL $9,000; UOP $7,560; DDB $0; SYD $2,571
P10-4A Depr. Exp. 19X5, before closing $7,938
P10-5A No check figure
P10-6A Cost of truck no. 103, $20,390
P10-7A Part 1: Depletion $1,118,480
P10-1B Depr.-Land improve. $2,217; Office bldg. $16,286; Storage bldg. $1,013; Furniture $9,075
P10-2B No check figure
P10-3B Depr. 19X5: SL $36,000; UOP $27,000; DDB $5,920; SYD $12,000

P10-4B Depr. Exp. 19X3, before closing, $6,166
P10-5B No check figure
P10-6B Cost of truck no. 182, $17,533
P10-7B Part 1: Depletion $525,000
DP 1 Net Income: Blue Bonnet $79,000; Bavarian $41,000
DP 2 No check figure
FSP 1 4. Loss on sale $684,000
FSP 2 No check figure

P11-1A No check figure
P11-2A No check figure
P11-3A Total employee earnings $23,345
P11-4A Total annual cost of employee $87,082
P11-5A Total liab. $304,614
P11-6A Net pay $2,231
P11-7A No check figure
P11-1B No check figure
P11-2B No check figure
P11-3B Wage exp. $17,207
P11-4B Total annual cost of employee $83,714
P11-5B Total liab. $378,146
P11-6B Net pay $2,022
DP 1 No check figure
DP 2 No check figure
FSP 1 No check figure
FSP 2 No check figure

P12-1A No check figure
P12-2A No check figure
P12-3A Net income year 2, $30,260
P12-4A Income, percentage-completion method, 19X8, $903,000
P12-5A Correct net inc. 19X4, $46,700
P12-1B No check figure
P12-2B No check figure
P12-3B Net inc. year 2, $32,450
P12-4B Income, percentage-completion method 19X5, $1,116,000
P12-5B Correct net inc. 19X7, $66,650
DP 1 Net income $42,800
DP 2 No check figure
CP 1 Branson total assets, revised $2,237,900; Branson net income, revised $184,500
CP 2 No check figure

P13-1A No check figure
P13-2A 2. Ringle, Capital $48,560; LaBlanc, Capital $48,560
P13-3A 2. Net income: Dewey $35,333; Karlin $30,333; DeCastro $25,334
P13-4A 4. Debit: Koehn, Capital $38,000; Neiman, Capital $1,143; Marcus, Capital $857

P13-5A 1. b. Cash to: Whitney $20,700; Kosse $52,800; Itasca $11,500
P13-1B No check figure
P13-2B 2. Axtell, Capital $40,450; 2. Riesel, Capital $40,450
P13-3B 2. Net income: Collins $69,750; Davis $53,500; Chiu $56,750
P13-4B 4. Debit: Lark, Capital $50,000; Smythe, Capital $13,548; Spahn, capital $16,452
P13-5B 1. b. Cash to: Monet $19,000; Blair $ 33,000; Trippi $26,000
DP 1 No check figure
DP 2 No check figure

P14-1A No check figure
P14-2A Total stock. equity $323,900
P14-3A Total stock. equity: Millett $650,000; Structural $695,000
P14-4A 6. b. Com. div. $15,000,000
P14-5A Total assets $743,000; Return on common equity $0.067
P14-6A 2. 19X3 Div. pay.: Pfd. $2,500; Com. $28,500
P14-7A BV per share: Pfd. $28.20; Com. $7.16
P14-8A 1. Taxable income: 19X7, $215,000; 19X8, $265,000 3. Net income: 19X7, $149,500; 19X8, $162,500
P14-1B No check figure
P14-2B Total stock. equity $470,300
P14-3B Total stock. equity: Premier $738,000; Ensenada $461,000
P14-4B 6. b. Com. div. $25,840
P14-5B Total assets $478,000; Return on common equity 0.091
P14-6B 2. 19X3 Div. Pay.: Pfd. $35,000; Com. $180,000
P14-7B BV per share: Pfd. $52.55; Com. $8.43
P14-8B 1. Taxable income: 19X3, $200,000; 19X4, $230,000 3. Net income: 19X3, $136,500; 19X4, $143,000
DP 1 Total stock. equity: Plan 1, $415,900; Plan 2, $400,900
DP 2 No check figure
FSP 1 No check figure
FSP 2 No check figure

P15-1A No check figure
P15-2A Total stock. equity: Dec. 31, 19X6, $395,500; Dec. 31, 19X7, $473,100
P15-3A No check figure
P15-4A Total stock. equity $688,680
P15-5A Total stock. equity $557,000

(continued on back cover)

PRENTICE HALL SERIES IN ACCOUNTING

Charles T. Horngren, Consulting Editor

Third Edition

ACCOUNTING

Charles T. Horngren
Stanford University

Walter T. Harrison, Jr.
Baylor University

Michael A. Robinson
Baylor University

PRENTICE HALL, Upper Saddle River, New Jersey 07458

Library of Congress Cataloging-in-Publication Data
Horngren, Charles T.
    Accounting / Charles T. Horngren, Walter T. Harrison, Jr., Michael
A. Robinson. —3rd ed.
        p. cm.
    Includes indexes.
    ISBN 0-13-305822-0
    1. Accounting.   I. Harrison, Walter T.   II. Robinson, Michael A.
III. Title.
HF5635.H8125   1996
657—dc20   94-48751
                                                             CIP

Senior Development Editor: Karen Karlin
Editor in Chief, Development: Steve Deitmer
Assistant Editor: Diane deCastro
Senior Project Manager: Carol Burgett
Design Director: Patricia Wosczyk
Interior Art: Tony Mikolajczyk/Steve Frim
Cover Art: Illustration by Don Baker
Cover Design: Maria Lange
Interior Design: Jeannette Jacobs/Rosemarie Votta
Dummy Artists: Jeannette Jacobs/Meryl Poweski
Electronic Assistance: Lorraine Patsco/John Nestor
Photo Editor: Lorinda Morris-Nantz
Photo Researcher: Fran Antmann
Copy Editor: Margo Quinto
Buyer: Vincent Scelta
Marketing Manager: Deborah Hoffman Emry
Editorial Assistants: Linda Albelli, Amy Hinton, Renee Pelletier

For our wives—Joan, Nancy, and Roberta

© 1995, 1993, 1992, 1989 by Prentice-Hall, Inc.
A Simon & Schuster / A Viacom Company
Upper Saddle River, New Jersey 07458

Printed in the United States of America

10 9 8 7 6 5 4

ISBN 0-13-305822-0

PRENTICE-HALL INTERNATIONAL (UK) LIMITED, *London*
PRENTICE-HALL OF AUSTRALIA PTY. LIMITED, *Sydney*
PRENTICE-HALL CANADA INC., *Toronto*
PRENTICE-HALL HISPANOAMERICANA, S.A., *Mexico*
PRENTICE-HALL OF INDIA PRIVATE LIMITED, *New Delhi*
PRENTICE-HALL OF JAPAN, INC., *Tokyo*
SIMON & SCHUSTER ASIA PTE, LTD., *Singapore*
EDITORA PRENTICE-HALL DO BRASIL, LTDA., *Rio de Janeiro*

Photo Credits

FINANCIAL ACCOUNTING

MANAGEMENT ACCOUNTING

Brief Contents

Contents

---

*In each chapter, Problems include Group A and Group B sets.
**Extending Your Knowledge includes Decision Problems, an Ethical
Issue, and Financial Statement Problems.

APPENDIXES

GLOSSARY

INDEXES

Preface

Accounting, third edition, provides full introductory coverage of financial and management accounting. We have written the book for use in a two-semester course. *Accounting* is in the mainstream for courses in introductory accounting. This book focuses on the most widely used accounting theory and practice.

Mission of the Book

Our mission is to present the fundamentals of financial and management accounting by challenging students to think and to make decisions. We emphasize the importance of connecting accounting to the business world and provide the student with the best support available for studying and learning accounting.

All the features of *Accounting* have been extensively tested in the market. Professor focus groups, student focus groups, reviewer conferences, dozens of reviewers, solutions checkers, an English-as-a-Second-Language student reviewer, and two development editors have critiqued all aspects of this book.

Helping Students Become Decision Makers

Beginning with page 1 we create a business context for the student. The real-world environment promotes student interest. We integrate actual companies and their data into the text narrative and assignment material. Familiar companies enliven the material and illustrate the role of accounting in business. Sometimes, however, "live" data drawn from real companies are too advanced for introductory students. In those situations, we illustrate the accounting with realistic examples to build a framework that invites students to participate in the learning process.

In this edition, we start the development of decision-making skills even before the first chapter—in a section called *Accounting's Role in Business*. Students are challenged to develop their own plan for running a business. By piecing together a business plan, students start to see how accounting serves an organization. Students are thus motivated to integrate the details into a broad view of accounting.

Each chapter opens with an actual business situation and provides a quotation by a company manager, investor, or owner that gives insight into the chapter topic. Each chapter-opening story is illustrated with a photograph that draws students into the story. Students then revisit this story throughout the chapter, connecting accounting to a real business decision.

New or Expanded Features of the Third Edition

The third edition presents a number of new features:

- *Stop & Think* "speedbumps" ask students to do just that—stop and think about an application of accounting or an extension of the basic material—at various points in each chapter. These are not "boxes," which typically fall outside the running text and can be bypassed. They are part of the text, complete with answers to show students "how to do it," and they are identified by the icon you see here in the margin.
- Our *Putting Skills to Work* features illustrate how particular businesses or individuals use accounting. These features also serve as a summary of major concepts in the chapter. In Chapter 2 (page 46) Bill Neely, the founder of B. G. Graphics, discusses how accounting helps him manage his business.

- A new category of exhibits called *Concept Highlights* contains tabular or visual summaries. The Concept Highlights give students another way to review the material. Exhibit 1-7 (page 18) and Exhibit 2-6 (page 52) are examples of Concept Highlights.
- There are many *new exhibits* in this edition. Most exhibits now use diagrams to illustrate concepts and relationships, helping students visualize accounting concepts and principles. Examples include Exhibit 1-1 (page 5) and Exhibit 2-3 (page 48).
- *Highlighted photographs* with excerpts from the text emphasize accounting's role in business. In Chapter 3, for example, this feature calls attention to the role of accounting at Four Seasons Hotels and Resorts (page 91) and J.C. Penney (page 92).
- *Concept links* are margin notes that refer students to important topics studied in earlier chapters. Indicated by a red arrow in the margin ◀‖‖ and in the accompanying text, they will help students see how the details of accounting come together.
- *Student annotations* in the margins provide a self-check or offer additional material of interest. Three types of student annotations are included. *Key Points* highlight concepts or topics that often cause students to stumble. *Short Exercises*—complete with solutions—give students immediate practice in applying new material. *Real-World Examples* illustrate the use of accounting in actual business situations.
- Each of the seven Parts of *Accounting* ends with a *Video Case* based on a real company. An accompanying video clip is available. Each Video Case includes *Case Questions* that require critical-thinking skills and a basic understanding of the concepts and principles covered in the text.
- An *all-new design* enhances learning. From the use of color to the addition of photos and exciting diagrams, the design has been thoughtfully created to bring accounting to today's visually oriented students. Different colors identify internal and external financial statements. Red corner marks identify the pages of assignment material.
- Each chapter has one or more new *Challenge Exercises*, which go beyond the ordinary coverage to develop students' critical-thinking skills and offer instructors more variety in assignment material.
- Chapters 2 through 5 include a *Serial Exercise*. A single running example builds in complexity as it illustrates the accounting cycle.
- All-new *Financial Statement Problems* are based on the financial statements of Lands' End, Inc. The Lands' End annual report appears in Appendix A.
- *Group Projects* are recommended to begin the course and are at the end of each of the seven Parts of the book, within the Comprehensive Problems. These Group Projects challenge students to develop a plan for managing a business. The intent is for students to participate in the learning process by creating a familiar context. As students move through the course, they incorporate new material to refine the plan.
- *Decision-oriented assignment materials* have been expanded in this edition.
  1. Basic exercises and problems include ratios for decision making in the context of actual business practice. For example, the classified balance sheet is accompanied by the current ratio and the debt ratio. With inventories we introduce inventory turnover and gross profit percentage.
  2. Decision Problems ask students to make decisions that go beyond mere number crunching, such as determining the price to pay to acquire an existing business or whether a company is poised for a business expansion.
  3. We want students to step back and ponder the use of accounting information for decision making. To reach this target, selected problems now include this new requirement: "How will what you learned in this problem help you manage a business (or evaluate an investment)?"
- Assignment material has been updated. This includes the *Mid-Chapter Summary Problems for Your Review, Summary Problems for Your Review, Self-Study Questions* (with Answers), *Questions, Exercises, Challenge Exercises, Problems* (sets A and B), and

Extending Your Knowledge. Many exercises and problems can be worked with a computer. Those that are coordinated with the Lotus Templates have a spreadsheet icon, and those that can be worked with the Prentice Hall Accounting Software (PHAS) are marked with a disk icon.

- Each chapter *Summary* is now organized by Chapter Objective.

Chapter-by-chapter revisions include the following:

- A new appendix to Chapter 1 discusses the accounting profession.
- Chapter 3 has a new appendix on alternate accounting treatments for prepaid expenses and unearned revenues. This material promotes the development of critical-thinking skills and illustrates that accounting is not so "cut and dried."
- In Chapter 4, reversing entries have been moved to an appendix.
- Chapter 5 uses a modern perpetual inventory system to illustrate accounting for inventory. More intuitive to students, the perpetual system helps them learn income measurement and the matching principle. At the same time, Chapter 5 maintains the strengths of the periodic inventory system—such as the computation of cost of goods sold—and offers a chapter supplement on the periodic system.
- Chapter 6 expands the coverage of computer information systems. Also, throughout the book we discuss computer applications in context to reinforce the fact that accountants use the computer as a tool. These sections are identified in the margin by a computer terminal icon.

- Chapter 7 has a new section on ethical decision making in accounting.
- Chapter 9 shows how to convert a LIFO company's income to the FIFO basis. This material is especially helpful for investment analysis and for credit decisions when companies are using different methods and the analyst must make a comparison. New sections of the chapter briefly discuss the LIFO liquidation problem and LIFO's potential use for manipulating income.
- To make room for more decision-relevant material, Chapters 12 (The Foundation for Generally Accepted Accounting Principles) and 13 (Accounting for Partnerships) have been streamlined, and stock subscriptions have been deleted from Chapter 14.
- Chapter 16's appendix now includes future value as we introduce the present-value techniques used to value bonds and amortize bond premium or to discount by the effective-interest method. This section of the appendix can be bypassed if instructors so desire.
- Chapter 20 includes a new discussion of management's planning and control functions and managers' uses of accounting information. It combines an introduction to management accounting, manufacturing accounting, and job order costing.
- Chapter 21 is entirely devoted to process costing to help students sharpen their focus on this challenging material. Both the FIFO and weighted-average methods are presented.
- Chapter 22 derives the cost-volume-profit formula from the contribution margin income statement and includes a new section on the difference between operating income computed under absorption costing and under variable costing.
- Chapter 23 is a new chapter that discusses cost behavior in depth, contrasting committed and discretionary fixed costs and engineered and discretionary variable costs.
- Chapter 24 combines the master budget and responsibility accounting to emphasize the natural link between the two.
- Chapter 25 discusses the role of continuous improvement and perfection goals in the standard-setting process and includes a new section on three-variance overhead analysis to help students understand what causes overhead variances.
- Chapter 26 is a new chapter that places activity-based costing (ABC) in the context of activity-based *management*. It contrasts traditional production systems with just-in-time systems and demonstrates how companies use target costing and kaizen costing to improve their operations.
- Chapter 27 includes a new section on the equipment-replacement decision.

Recommendations of the Accounting Education Change Commission (AECC)

The recommendations of the AECC have inspired us in several ways.

- *Critical-Thinking Skills*—Each chapter includes Stop & Think "speedbumps" and new Challenge Exercises and places more emphasis on the Decision Problems, which require critical thinking.
- *User Perspective*—Most introductory students are not accounting majors. We motivate discussions on the basis of the experience of people who use accounting information.
- *Decision Making*—Chapter-opening stories, summaries of the material covered, and the assignment materials focus on decision making.
- *Group Learning Activities*—We propose a Group Project in *Accounting's Role in Business*, which precedes Chapter 1. In addition, each of the seven Parts of the text includes a Group Project that asks students to devise their own business plan for financing, promoting, and operating a business.
- *Business Context for Accounting*—Students need a context for learning new material, and we have created Group Projects, chapter-opening stories, real-company examples, Putting Skills to Work, margin annotations, and company and product photographs. All of these serve to build a picture of the real business world for students. These features are especially helpful to students who have little or no previous experience in business.
- *Ethical Issues in Business*—Chapter 7 includes a new section on ethical decision making. Also, each chapter includes an *Ethical Issue* among the assignment materials.
- *International Accounting*—Chapter 9 (Merchandise Inventory) and Chapter 10 (Plant Assets, Intangible Assets, and Related Expenses) include new discussions of international accounting for these assets. The second half of Chapter 17 is devoted to accounting for international operations.
- *Communication Skills*—Each chapter includes assignment materials that require students to write business memoranda to explain the rationale for business decisions. Selected problems require students to explain how those problems will help them to, among other things, manage a business or evaluate an investment. The Group Projects can be presented orally in class.

Supplements

Supplements for the Instructor

ANNOTATED INSTRUCTOR'S EDITION   The *Annotated Instructor's Edition* includes the text plus margin notes for the instructor to use during his/her lecture. The following annotations are included:

- *Teaching Tips*, which suggest interesting new ways of presenting the material;
- *Applications*, which show how accounting is applied;
- *Class Exercises* (with full solutions), which are provided to give students immediate practice in applying concepts and implementing procedures;
- *Discussion Questions*, which introduce topics for group thinking and provide immediate feedback on how well students understand the material.

COURSE MANAGER   The *Course Manager* is a three-hole-punched copy of the Annotated Instructor's Edition in a binder. Instructors can use the Course Manager to organize their lectures by including all the necessary supplementary material for the lecture, along with the text chapter(s), in the order that the instructor prefers.

INSTRUCTOR'S MANUAL AND MEDIA GUIDE   The *Instructor's Manual and Media Guide* contains the following elements for each chapter of the text: Chapter Overview, Chapter Outline, Assignment Grid, Suggested Readings, Ten-Minute Quiz, Answer Key to the Ten-Minute Quiz, Supplement Grid, and Video Write-Ups.

SOLUTIONS MANUAL   The *Solutions Manual* contains answers to all questions, exercises, and problems in the text. The pages have been designed so that they can also be used as transparency masters.

SOLUTIONS MANUAL ON DISK   All numerical exercises and problems are available on disk in Lotus 2.2 format.

TRANSPARENCIES OF SOLUTIONS   Every page from the *Solutions Manual* has been recreated as an acetate for use on the overhead projector.

TEST ITEM FILE   Completely new for this edition of the text, this *Test Item File* contains 2,835 test items. Each chapter consists of 105 questions: 20 true/false, 70 multiple choice, 10 exercises/problems, 5 critical thinking/essay. Each chapter has been content-reviewed for clarity and solution-checked for accuracy.

TEACHING TRANSPARENCIES   Approximately 80 two-color acetates have been created to provide overviews and outlines of chapter topics, summarize compare/contrast concepts, show actual exhibits such as a balance sheet, provide additional numerical examples, and give step-by-step explanations of complicated topics.

ABC News/PH Video Library for Accounting

Video is the most dynamic of all the supplements you can use to enhance your class. The quality of the video material and how well it relates to your course can make all the difference. For these reasons, Prentice Hall and ABC News are working together to bring you the best and most comprehensive video ancillaries available in the college market.

Through its award-winning programs—*Nightline, Business World, On Business, This Week with David Brinkley,* and *World News Tonight*—ABC offers a resource for feature and documentary-style videos related to text concepts and applications. The programs have extremely high production quality, present substantial content, and are hosted by well-versed, well-known anchors. Prentice Hall, its authors, and its editors provide the benefit of having selected videos on topics that will work well with this course and give the instructor teaching notes on how to use them in the classroom.

The ABC News/PH Video Library offers video material for selected topics in the text. A video guide is provided to integrate the videos into your lecture. Some of the topics covered include PepsiCo's use of bar coding in processing accounts receivable transactions; the introduction of Frito Lay's automated accounting information system to track sales, inventory, and the development of new markets; and frequent-flier miles as current liabilities.

Supplements for Students

STUDY GUIDE   Each *Study Guide* chapter contains the following parts: Chapter Overview, Chapter Review, and Test Yourself (with Matching, Multiple-Choice, and Completion Exercises and Critical-Thinking and Demonstration Problems).

WORKING PAPERS   *Working Papers* is a set of tear-out forms that students can use to solve all exercises and problems in the text. Because T-accounts, general journals, cash receipts journals, purchases journals, and so on are already set up, students can focus on accounting concepts by filling in the necessary calculations to solve their assignments.

The forms are numbered in the same way as the textbook exercises and problems and are arranged in the same order.

PRACTICE SETS   The *Runners Corporation Practice Set* is a merchandising corporation practice set for a complete, one-year accounting cycle. It includes narrative of transactions and is available in both manual and computerized formats.

The *Galleria Leathergoods, Inc., Practice Set* is a merchandising corporation practice set with payroll, in business paper format. It is available only in a manual format.

***THE NEW YORK TIMES* SUPPLEMENTS FOR FINANCIAL AND MANAGE-MENT ACCOUNTING**   *The New York Times* and Prentice Hall are sponsoring "A Contemporary View," a program designed to enhance student access to current information of relevance to the classroom. Through this program, the core subject matter provided in the text is supplemented by a collection of time-sensitive articles from one of the world's most distinguished newspapers, *The New York Times*. These articles demonstrate the connection between what is learned in the classroom and what is happening in the world around us.

Prentice Hall and *The New York Times* are proud to co-sponsor "A Contemporary View." We hope it will make the reading of both textbooks and newspapers a dynamic learning process.

Software Supplements

PRENTICE HALL ACCOUNTING SOFTWARE (PHAS)—GENERAL LEDGER PACKAGE   *Prentice Hall Accounting Software* is a user-friendly general ledger package covering the accounting cycle. The student will be able to use existing exercises or problems from the textbook, create new problems or companies, enter journal entries, change or delete journal entries, print journal and other reports, post journal entries in batch mode, backup data files, and close the period. PHAS is available in both DOS and Windows versions.

COMPACT d/SEC ACADEMIC EDITION   *Compact d/SEC* is a financial disclosure package that can be used in various accounting courses. It contains complete financial information for either 30 or 100 companies. Financial information for Lands' End, Inc., the company whose annual report is included in ***Accounting,*** can be found on this software as well.

PH RE-ENFORCER   An interactive *Tutorial* consists of multiple-choice questions, problems, and case problems for each chapter of the text.

PH PROFESSOR   The *Classroom Presentation Package* on PowerPoint 3.0 can be used to present chapter material using graphics and innovative ways of explaining concepts from the text. Other publishers provide this type of software but call it electronic transparencies.

LOTUS TEMPLATES   *Lotus Templates* can be used to solve selected exercises and problems in the text. The documentation includes a short tutorial on how to use Lotus, and a "walk-through" for each template is provided. Students are not required to have an in-depth knowledge of Lotus programming techniques. Instead, the templates are designed to focus on the accounting concepts presented in each template.

TEST MANAGER   Prentice Hall's *Test Manager* 2.0 can be used to generate tests of up to 200 questions. Instructors can select the questions they want to use or allow questions to be randomly selected by chapter section, level of difficulty, or question type. The existing question bank can be edited on-screen, and instructors can create and insert their own questions as well.

Entire tests can be previewed on-screen before printing. Tests can be saved to one of three word processing file formats: WordPerfect, Microsoft Word, or ASCII. Test Manager can print multiple variations of the same test, scrambling the order of questions and multiple-choice answers. A comprehensive, fully indexed desktop reference guide is included.

Acknowledgments

The authors and publisher wish to thank our many reviewers and focus group participants. Their contributions have meant a great deal to this project.

Reviewers

Salvador D. Aceves, Napa Valley College
Diane Adcox, University of North Florida
John Blahnick, Lorain County Community College
Nina Brown, Tarrant County Junior College
Kurt H. Buerger, Angelo State University
Glenn Bushnell, DeAnza College
Eric Carlson, Kean College of New Jersey
Wallace P. Carroll, J. Sargeant Reynolds Community College
Donna Chadwick, Sinclair Community College
Darrel W. Davis, University of Northern Iowa
S. T. Desai, Cedar Valley College
James Emig, Villanova University
Kevin Feeney, Southern Connecticut State University
Carl J. Fisher, Foothill College
Jessica Frazier, Eastern Kentucky University
Marilyn Fuller, Paris Junior College
Roger Gee, San Diego Mesa College
Lucille Genduso, Nova University
James Genseal, Joliet Junior College
Barbara Gerrity, Berkeley School of Westchester
Gloria Grayless, Sam Houston State University
Ann Gregory, South Plains College
Debby Halik, Ivy Technical College
Jim Hansen, North Dakota State University
Saad Hassanein, Marymount University
Jimmie Henslee, El Centro College
Cynthia Holloway
Andrew Hrechek, Seton Hall University
Jean Insinga, Middlesex Community College
Tyronne James, Southern University of New Orleans
Fred Jex, Macomb Community College
Mary Thomas Keim, California State University—Bakersfield
Nancy L. Kelly, Middlesex Community College
Randy Kidd, Penn Valley Community College
Raymond L. Larson, Appalachian State University
Cathy Larson, Middlesex Community College
Linda Lessing, SUNY College of Technology—Farmingdale
Lola Locke, Tarrant County Junior College
Cathy Lumbattis, Southern Illinois University
Paul Mihalek, University of Hartford
Graham Morris
Bruce Neumann, University of Colorado—Denver
Alfonso R. Oddo, Niagara University
Linda Overstreet, Hillsborough Community College
Robert Palmer, Troy State University
Patrick M. Premo, St. Bonaventure University
Karen Russom, North Harris College
Sherry Shively, Johnson County Community College

Kathleen Simione, Quinnipiac College
Dorothy Steinsapir, Middlesex Community College
Gracelyn Stuart, Palm Beach Community College
Kathy Terrell, University of Central Oklahoma
Cynthia Thomas, Central Missouri State University
John Vaccaro, Bunker Hill Community College
Paul Waite, Niagara Community College
Martin Ward, DeVry Institute of Technology
Jim Weglin, North Seattle Community College
Bill Wempe, Wichita State University
Dale Westfall, Midland College
Joe Zernick, Ivy Technical College

English-as-a-Second-Language Reviewer

Zhu Zhu, Phoenix College

Focus Group Participants

Richard Ahrens, Los Angeles Pierce College
Charles Alvis, Winthrop University
Juanita Ardavant, Los Angeles Valley College
Patricia Ayres, Arapahoe Community College
Carl Ballard, Central Piedmont Community College
Maria Barillas, Phoenix College
Dorcus Berg, Wingate College
Angela Blackwood, Belmont Abbey College
Gary R. Bower, Community College of Rhode Island
Jack Brown, Los Angeles Valley College
Virginia Brunell, Diablo Valley College
James Carriger, Ventura College
Stan Carroll, New York City Technical College
Janet Cassagio, Nassau Community College
Les Chadwick, University of Delaware
Stanley Chu, Borough of Manhattan Community College
Kerry Colton, Aims Community College
Shaun Crayton, New York City Technical College
Susan Crosson, Santa Fe Community College
Don Daggett, Mankato State University
Joneal W. Daw, Los Angeles Valley College
Lyle E. Dehning, Metropolitan State College
Wanda Deleo, Winthrop University
Jim Donnelly, Bergen Community College
Bruce England, Massasoit Community College
Dave Fellows, Red Rocks Community College
Roger Gee, San Diego Mesa College
Marty Ginsberg, Rockland Community College
Earl Godfrey, Gardner Webb University
Edward S. Goodhart, Shippensburg University
Jean Gutmann, University of Southern Maine

Ralph W. Hernandez, New York City Technical College

Carl High, New York City Technical College

Mary Hill, University of North Carolina—Charlotte

Jean Insinga, Middlesex Community College

Bernard Johnson, Santa Monica College

Diane G. Kanis, Bergen Community College

John Keelan, Massachusetts Bay Community College

Mary Thomas Keim, California State University—Bakersfield

Cynthia Kreisner, Austin Community College

Raymond L. Larson, Appalachian State University

Cathy Larson, Middlesex Community College

Linda Lessing, SUNY College of Technology—Farmingdale

Angela LeTourneau, Winthrop University

Frank Lordi, Widener University

Audra Lowray, New York City Technical College

Grace Lyons, Bergen Community College

Ed Malmgren, University of North Carolina—Charlotte

Paola Marocchi, New York City Technical College

Larry McCarthy, Slippery Rock University

Linda Spotts Michael, Maple Woods Community College

Greg Mostyn, Mission College

Kitty Nessmith, Georgia Southern University

Lee Nicholas, University of Northern Iowa

Terry Nunnelly, University of North Carolina—Charlotte

Alfonso R. Oddo, Niagara University

Al Partington, Los Angeles Pierce College

Lynn Mazzola Paluska, Nassau Community College

Juan Perez, New York City Technical College

Ron Pierno, University of Missouri

Geraldine Powers, Northern Essex Community College

Harry Purcell, Ulster County Community College

John Ribezzo, Community College of Rhode Island

Rosemarie Ruiz, York University

Steve Schaefer, Contra Costa College

Parmar Sejal, Bergen Community College

Lynn Shoaf, Belmont Abbey College

Walter J. Silva, Roxbury Community College

Leon Jo Singleton, Santa Monica College

David Skougstad, Metropolitan State College

Paul Sunko, Olive-Harvey College

Chandra Taylor, New York City Technical College

Phillip Thornton, Metropolitan State College

John L. Vaccaro, Bunker Hill Community College

The authors wish to thank Betsy Willis and Becky Jones for their assistance with the annotations and links; Eric Carlson, Jean Insinga, Roger Gee, and Steve Schaefer for their assistance with the computer sections of this text; and W. Morley Lemon for his contributions to the Decision Problems. We also wish to thank Judith Cassidy, J. R. Dietrich, Barbara Gerrity, Carl High, Jean Marie Hudson, Alfonso R. Oddo, and Beverly Terry for a variety of helpful suggestions. Each chapter-opening story has benefited from the comments of real people in business, so we want to thank them as well.

Among the many people at Prentice Hall who helped to publish this book are Linda Albelli, Carol Burgett, Patti Dant, Diane deCastro, Steve Deitmer, Rob Dewey, Debbie Emry, Katherine Evancie, Patrice Fraccio, David Gillespie, Joe Heider, Amy Hinton, Joanne Jay, Karen Karlin, Michelle Martin, Charlotte Morrissey, Rosemarie Votta, Lorraine Patsco, Renee Pelletier, Judy Perkinson, Vincent Scelta, Amy Smith, Ben Smith, Joyce Turner, Grace Walkus, and Pat Wosczyk. In addition, we want to thank Fran Antmann, Judy Block, Nancy Brandwein, Jeannette Jacobs, Jeffrey Kirk, Pat McCabe, Tony Mikolajczyk, Meryl Poweski, Margo Quinto, Rhoda Sidney, Stuart Weiss, and Joe Wesselkamper for their contributions.

Charles T. Horngren
Walter T. Harrison, Jr.
Michael A. Robinson

Accounting's Role in Business

The Primary Mission of Business

Every organization has a primary mission. Hospitals provide health care. Law firms advise clients on legal matters. Automobile manufacturers produce cars. Auto dealers sell cars.

Consider a Ford automobile dealership, Pearson Ford. Most car dealerships are complex organizations that bring together the activities of a diverse group of people. The owners operate the business to earn a profit. They probably have to borrow money from the bank and other creditors. The Pearson dealership purchases automobiles from Ford Motor Company and sells the cars to customers such as you. Along the way, the business hires employees, buys and uses supplies, and pays bills for its building, insurance, and electric power. The following diagram shows these relationships, with the business at the center interacting with various parties.

The primary mission of the Ford dealership is to sell cars to customers. For the Ford Motor Company, headquartered in Dearborn, Michigan, the mission is to manufacture the cars. But let's return to Pearson Ford. It must buy the cars that the public wants. It must hire productive employees and pay its bills to stay in business.

A dealership needs support services to accomplish its primary mission. For example, Pearson needs employees—salespersons, mechanics, and accountants. The dealership's personnel officer hires these employees. Someone else or some group must manage the overall business. We call this support function *administration* or *management.* The managers need information to make wise business decisions. Accountants produce much of this information. If the dealership borrows money (and most do), the lenders demand reports on how well the business is doing. Accountants supply much of this information, too. Virtually all businesses have an accounting function. Depending on the size and complexity of the organization, it may need additional support services. For now, however, let's focus on a business that has the functions we have mentioned.

Primary Mission of the Business—to Provide a Product or a Service

Functions directly related to the primary mission:	**Support functions:**
• Production (or purchasing)	• Personnel
• Sales	• Administration
	• Accounting

Accounting as a Business Function

Accounting is a support function in business. Unlike the sale of automobiles, which brings in money to the dealership, accounting by itself generates no cash. To earn its way, accounting must provide more benefit for the organization than the cost of operating the accounting department. What benefits does an accounting department bring to a car dealership? Simply, better decisions. For example, the owner must decide how many salespersons to hire and how to pay them: straight salary, commission, or salary plus commission. Accounting information aids these and many other decisions. Operating without an accounting department would be like driving blind from Los Angeles to a remote village.

Business activity is complex. Suppose that Ford sales have been down for the past five years. Pearson is considering adding a Nissan dealership. If you were Pearson, how would you decide whether to invest? You probably would seek the advice of other people in the organization. The salespersons have valuable opinions about their ability to sell Nissans. The mechanics can predict the training they will need in order to work on foreign cars. The general manager may be reluctant to make so drastic a change. The accountant can answer the question, "How much will this changeover cost us?"

There is abundant evidence that groups can make better decisions than an individual can. "Two heads are better than one." That is why most business activity occurs in groups. In fact, more people fail in business because they cannot get along with others than because they are incompetent.

Innovations in Accounting Education

Over the past several years, an organization known as the Accounting Education Change Commission (AECC) has suggested innovations in the way accounting is taught at the college level. The authors, one of whom was a charter member of the AECC, believe that some key changes can enrich the teaching—and the learning—of accounting. This book incorporates several innovations that are a direct result of the work of the AECC.

Accounting in Context

The key innovation of this book is that accounting is presented in its business context. Throughout, we set the context before we launch into how to do accounting procedures. We want you to know *why* the accounting is done. In this way you will learn the subject better.

Accounting and Decision Making

Another innovation is that we present accounting as a tool for *decision making*. Every chapter has exercises and problems that ask you to make decisions. You will learn how accounting generates information for decision making. You will also learn to use the information to make business decisions. We ask questions that lead you to think about what you will do with accounting information. As you progress through the book—specifically, as you finish each exercise and each problem in the assignment material—we encourage you to answer these questions:

1.   What did you learn from working this exercise or problem?
2.   How will what you learned help you manage a business?

To illustrate what we mean, consider Exercise 1-7. That exercise asks you to account for the transactions of Dr. Allison LaChappelle, a physician who is starting a pediatric medical practice. The exercise determines the amount of cash, medical supplies, and so on that LaChappelle's medical practice has at the end of the first month. For this exercise, let's address our two key questions.

1.   What did you learn from working this exercise or problem? Possible answers (there can be many):
  a. A business should account for its affairs separately from those of its owners.
  b. A business begins by raising money from its owners.
  c. To know where it stands, the business must account for its buying and selling transactions.
  d. Each business transaction, such as the purchase of land, has at least two effects.
2.   How will what you learned help you manage a business?
  a. By keeping my personal affairs separate from those of my business, I am better able to evaluate the business. If I mix my personal finances with those of my business, I will not be able to tell how well the business is doing.
  b. If I go into business, I will probably have to invest some of my own money. Therefore, I should save. I will probably have to borrow, so I will need a good credit record.
  c. Accounting is necessary if I want to know how my business is doing.
  d. It makes sense that buying and selling have two effects on an organization because it takes two parties—a buyer and a seller—to complete a business transaction, such as the purchase of land.

To Instructors—A Group Project

To emphasize that accounting is best learned in the context of business decision making, the authors recommend that you begin the course with the following group activity (or some similar project). Divide the class into groups of four or five students. Allow 15 to 30 minutes for each group to list the decisions they must make to plan, promote, and present a **rock concert.** Each group's goal is to earn a profit. Instruct them to be as specific and as detailed as they can in describing the decisions for this business endeavor. At the end of the allotted time, have them report their business plan to the class. Your class can engage in this project at any time. It works particularly well as a structure builder at the beginning of the course. At the end of the term, you can revisit the exercise to summarize what the students have learned.[1] There are several benefits from beginning the study of accounting with the students' own business plan:

1.   Starting a business is a stimulating endeavor that should capture student interest.
2.   This strategy provides a context for illustrating the relevance of accounting.
3.   The broad exercise helps students to think critically—beyond the details of accounting.
4.   Student goals form the structure of learning.

---

[1]The authors thank J. R. Dietrich for suggesting this Group Project.

5. The project develops group skills and communication skills—both oral and written.

6. Students become active participants in the learning process. The project is student-centered and learning-centered rather than instructor-centered and teaching-centered.

7. The exercise is decision-oriented.

We hope students will understand why accountants rise to leadership positions in their organizations in greater numbers than businesspersons trained in any other field.

The possibilities for implementation are virtually endless. Instructors may wish to have students refine their business plans as they cover new material in each chapter. The book includes a Comprehensive Problem at the end of each Part (after Chapters 6, 12, 17, 19, 21, 25, and 27) to challenge students to incorporate and synthesize the material they learned in the preceding chapters. Students can write short memoranda or formal reports, as desired. Either individuals or groups can make class presentations. The authors encourage instructors to relay to us your experiences with this project. If you prefer to use e-mail, you can contact us at the following addresses:

Charles T. Horngren
fhorngren@GSB-lira.stanford.edu

Walter T. Harrison, Jr.
tom_harrison@baylor.edu

Michael A. Robinson
mike_robinson@baylor.edu

PART ONE

The Basic Structure of Accounting

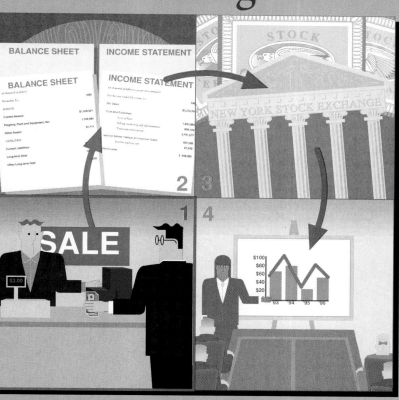

Chapter 1
Accounting and Its Environment

1. Develop an accounting vocabulary for decision making

2. Apply accounting concepts and principles to analyze business transactions

3. Use the accounting equation to describe an organization's financial position

4. Use the accounting equation to analyze business transactions

5. Prepare the financial statements

6. Evaluate the performance of a business

"Accounting may not be what you think it is. You are probably already using basic accounting skills without even knowing it!"

JULIE DEFILIPPO, OWNER OF AN EXTRA HAND

Can you start a successful business with $50 or less? Believe it or not, you can. Like many college students, Julie DeFilippo of Armonk, New York, needed to earn some extra money. A business major at Fairfield University in Connecticut, she was having trouble making the payments on her used car. Although she had only $50 to work with, DeFilippo chose to start her own business in March 1992. With the experience she gained working for a catering firm, she decided to offer her services as a helping hand at parties. She would set up for a party, serve the food, and clean up afterward—do everything but supply and cook the food—for $10 an hour. DeFilippo named her company An Extra Hand. She spent $20 to have 250 fliers printed and $18 to purchase red aprons. By May 1992 she had acquired enough clients to take on a partner. She and her partner assisted at different parties, and both took full pay for the parties they worked. With a total of eight jobs in May, DeFilippo earned $200, and her partner made $100. They bought matching red skirts and white shirts to complete their work uniforms.

During the summer of 1992, DeFilippo averaged 10 jobs a month. She hired two high school students at $8 an hour and earned $300 a month that summer. By September she had paid $200 in business expenses and had earned $900—enough to pay off her car and have $100 left over. And she gained valuable experience from advertising her services, dealing with both clients and employees, and maintaining the finances of her business. *Source: Adapted from Peter C. T. Elsworth, Andrée Brooks, "Earning and Learning: How a Student Built a Small Business," The New York Times, July 3, 1993, Section 1, p. 32.*

• • • • •

What role does accounting play in this real situation? DeFilippo had to decide how to organize her company. An Extra Hand started out as a proprietorship—a single-owner company—with DeFilippo as the owner. Later she joined forces with a fellow student and formed a partnership. If she wanted to continue the business after graduation, she could choose to incorporate—that is, to form a corporation. In this chapter we discuss all three forms of business organizations: proprietorship, partnership, and corporation.

DeFilippo needed a certain amount of money to start An Extra Hand. That is, she had to *finance* the business. She had $50 personal cash to invest. This chapter covers owner investments to start a business.

How did DeFilippo know the total revenues the company earned? Her accounting records provided the amount. Without records, DeFilippo would have had to guess. *Revenue* is an accounting term that people use in everyday conversation. This chapter explains the concept of revenue more precisely.

Finally, An Extra Hand earned $900 during 1992. What are *earnings*? In common usage, we might say that during 1992 An Extra Hand "made" $900. This means that for 1992 An Extra Hand earned a profit of $900 after all expenses for the year were subtracted. *Earnings* and *profit* are accounting terms that mean the same thing. *Expenses* is another key accounting term. This chapter covers all these terms and introduces the financial statements that businesses use to report their financial affairs.

You may already know many accounting terms and relationships, because accounting affects people's behavior in many ways. This first accounting course will sharpen your focus by explaining how accounting works. As you progress through this course, you will see how accounting helps people like Julie DeFilippo—and you—achieve business goals.

What Is Accounting?

OBJECTIVE 1

Develop an accounting vocabulary for decision making

Accounting is the system that measures business activities, processes that information into reports, and communicates the results to decision makers. For this reason it is called "the language of business." The better you understand the language, the better you can manage the financial aspects of living. A recent survey indicates that business managers believe it is more important for college students to learn accounting than any other business subject. Personal financial planning, education expenses, loans, car payments, income taxes, and investments are based on the *information system* that we call accounting. A key product of an accounting information system, financial statements allow people to make informed business decisions. **Financial statements** are the documents that report on an individual's or an organization's business in monetary amounts.

Is my business making a profit? Should I hire assistants? Am I earning enough money to pay my rent? Intelligent answers to business questions like these are based on accounting information.

Please don't mistake bookkeeping for accounting. *Bookkeeping* is a procedural element of accounting, just as arithmetic is a procedural element of mathematics. Increasingly, people are using computers to do detailed bookkeeping—in households, businesses, and organizations of all types. Exhibit 1-1 illustrates the role of accounting in business. The process starts and ends with people making decisions.

Users of Accounting Information: Decision Makers

Decision makers need information. The more important the decision, the greater the need for accurate information. Virtually all businesses and most individuals keep accounting records to aid in making decisions. Most of the material in this book describes business situations, but the principles of accounting apply to the financial affairs of other organizations and individuals as well. The following sections discuss some of the people and groups who use accounting information.

EXHIBIT 1-1
The Accounting System: The Flow of Information

INDIVIDUALS   People such as you use accounting information in day-to-day affairs to manage bank accounts, to evaluate job prospects, to make investments, and to decide whether to rent or to buy a house.

BUSINESSES   Managers of businesses use accounting information to set goals for their organizations, to evaluate progress toward those goals, and to take corrective action if necessary. Decisions based on accounting information may include which building to purchase, how much merchandise inventory to keep on hand, and how much cash to borrow. Julie DeFilippo needed to know how much she could spend on advertising and on supplies for her catering business.

INVESTORS AND CREDITORS   Investors provide the money a business needs to begin operations. To decide whether to help start a new venture, potential investors evaluate what income they can expect on their investment. This means analyzing the financial statements of the new business. Those people who do invest monitor the progress of the business by analyzing the company's financial statements. They also keep up with developments in the business press—for example, *The Wall Street Journal*, *Business Week*, *Forbes*, and *Fortune*. Before making a loan, banks determine the borrower's ability to meet scheduled payments. This evaluation includes a projection of future operations, which is based on accounting information.

GOVERNMENT REGULATORY AGENCIES   Most organizations face government regulation. For example, the *Securities and Exchange Commission (SEC)*, a federal agency, requires businesses to disclose certain financial information to the investing public. Like many government agencies, the SEC bases its regulations in part on the accounting information it receives from firms.

TAXING AUTHORITIES   Local, state, and federal governments levy taxes on individuals and businesses. The amount of the tax is figured using accounting information. Businesses determine their sales tax from accounting records that show how much they have sold. Individuals and businesses compute income tax from their recorded earnings.

NONPROFIT ORGANIZATIONS   Nonprofit organizations—such as churches, hospitals, government agencies, and colleges, which operate for purposes other than profit—use accounting information in much the same way that profit-oriented businesses do. Both profit organizations and nonprofit organizations deal with budgets, payrolls, rent payments, and the like—all from the accounting system.

OTHER USERS   Employees and labor unions make wage demands based on their employer's reported income. Consumer groups and the general public are also interested in the amount of income businesses earn. For example, during fuel shortages consumer groups have charged that oil companies have earned "obscene profits." And newspapers report "improved profit pictures" of companies as the nation emerges from economic recession. Such news, based on accounting information, is related to our standard of living.

Users of accounting information are a diverse population, but they may be categorized as external users or internal users. This distinction allows us to classify accounting into two fields—financial accounting and management accounting.

Financial accounting provides information to people outside the firm. Creditors and stockholders, for example, are not part of the day-to-day management of the company. Likewise, government agencies, such as the SEC, and the general public are external users of a firm's accounting information. Chapters 2 through 19 of this book deal primarily with financial accounting.

Management accounting generates confidential information for internal decision makers, such as top executives, department heads, college deans, and hospital administrators. Chapters 20 through 27 cover management accounting.

The Development of Accounting

Accounting has a long history. Some scholars claim that writing arose in order to record accounting information. Account records date back to the ancient civilizations of China, Babylonia, Greece, and Egypt. The rulers of these civilizations used accounting to keep track of the costs of labor and materials used in building structures such as the great pyramids. The need for accounting has existed as long as there has been business activity.

In the nineteenth century, the growth of corporations spurred the development of accounting. Corporation owners—the stockholders—were no longer the managers of their business. Managers had to create accounting systems to report to the owners how well their business was doing. Because managers want their performance to look good, society needs a way to ensure that business information is reliable.

In the United States, the *Financial Accounting Standards Board (FASB)* determines how accounting is practiced. The FASB works with the SEC and the *American Institute of Certified Public Accountants (AICPA)*, the largest professional organization of accountants. **Certified public accountants,** or **CPAs**, are licensed accountants who serve the general public rather than one particular company. The relationships among the SEC, the FASB, and the AICPA and the rules that govern them (generally accepted accounting principles, or GAAP) are diagrammed in Exhibit 1-2. (Start with the public sector at the top.) The appendix at the end of this chapter explains their work, and the work of other accounting organizations, in more detail.

Computers have revolutionized accounting in the late twentieth century. Tasks that are time-consuming when done by hand are handled quickly and easily by computer. In addition to helping with accounting itself, microcomputers—personal computers, such as Apples, IBMs, and Compaqs—assist with many financial applications of accounting information and in business correspondence. Also, thanks to telecommunications, microcomputers can tap into the information stored in larger computers across the globe. As we progress through the study of accounting, we will consider computer applications that fit the topics under discussion.

Like other segments of society, accounting must be practiced in an ethical manner. We look next at the ethical dimension of accounting.

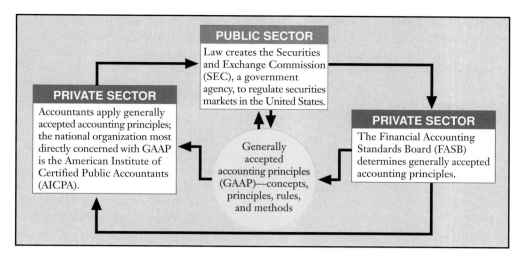

EXHIBIT 1-2
Key Accounting Organizations

PUBLIC SECTOR
Law creates the Securities and Exchange Commission (SEC), a government agency, to regulate securities markets in the United States.

PRIVATE SECTOR
Accountants apply generally accepted accounting principles; the national organization most directly concerned with GAAP is the American Institute of Certified Public Accountants (AICPA).

Generally accepted accounting principles (GAAP)—concepts, principles, rules, and methods

PRIVATE SECTOR
The Financial Accounting Standards Board (FASB) determines generally accepted accounting principles.

Ethical Considerations in Accounting and Business

Ethical considerations pervade all areas of accounting and business. Consider a situation that challenged the ethical conduct of the accountant.

In 1984 Texaco, Inc., was the defendant in a major lawsuit that threatened to put the company out of business. The managers of Texaco had reason to downplay this lawsuit for fear that customers would stop buying the company's products, which include gasoline, motor oil, and antifreeze; that Texaco's stock price would fall; and that banks would stop loaning money to the company. Should Texaco have disclosed this sensitive information? Accounting guidelines required Texaco to

"In 1984 Texaco, Inc., was the defendant in a major lawsuit that threatened to put the company out of business."

describe this situation in its financial statements. And the company's auditor was required to state whether the Texaco disclosure was adequate.

By what criteria do accountants address questions that challenge their ethical conduct? The AICPA, other professional accounting organizations, and most large companies have codes of ethics that bind their members and employees to high levels of ethical conduct.

Standards of Professional Conduct

The Code of Professional Conduct was adopted by the members of the AICPA to provide guidance in performing their professional duties. The preamble to the Code states: "[A] certified public accountant assumes an obligation of self-discipline above and beyond the requirements of laws and regulations...[and] an unswerving commitment to honorable behavior, even at the sacrifice of personal advantage." Key terms in the Code include *self-discipline, honorable behavior, moral judgments, the public interest, professionalism, integrity*, and *technical and ethical standards*.

Types of Business Organizations

A business takes one of three forms of organization, and in some cases the accounting procedures depend on which form the organization takes. Therefore, you should understand the differences among the three types of business organizations: a proprietorship, a partnership, and a corporation.

PROPRIETORSHIPS A **proprietorship** has a single owner, called the proprietor, who is generally also the manager. Julie DeFilippo's company, An Extra Hand, started out as a proprietorship. Proprietorships tend to be small retail establishments or individual professional businesses, such as those of physicians, attorneys, and accountants. From the accounting viewpoint each proprietorship is distinct from its proprietor. Thus the accounting records of the proprietorship do *not* include the proprietor's personal financial records.

PARTNERSHIPS A **partnership** joins two or more individuals together as co-owners. Each owner is a partner. An Extra Hand became a partnership when DeFilippo took on a partner. Many retail establishments, as well as some professional organizations of physicians, attorneys, and accountants, are partnerships. Most partnerships are small or medium-sized, but some are gigantic, exceeding 2,000 partners. Accounting treats the partnership as a separate organization, distinct from the personal affairs of each partner.

CORPORATIONS A **corporation** is a business owned by **stockholders**, or *shareholders*, people who own stock, or shares of ownership, in the business. A business becomes a corporation when the state approves its articles of incorporation. A corporation is a legal entity, an "artificial person" that conducts its business in its own name. Like the proprietorship and the partnership, the corporation is an organization with existence separate from its owners.

From a legal standpoint, however, corporations differ significantly from proprietorships and partnerships. If a proprietorship or a partnership cannot pay its debts, lenders can take the owner's personal assets—cash and belongings—to satisfy the business's obligations. But if a corporation goes bankrupt, lenders cannot take the personal assets of the stockholders. This limited personal liability of stockholders for corporate debts partly explains why corporations are the dominant form of business organization: People can invest in corporations with limited personal risk.

Another factor in corporate growth is the division of ownership into individual shares. The Coca-Cola Company, for example, has 1.3 billion shares of stock owned by some 559,000 stockholders. An investor with no personal relationship either to the corporation or to any other stockholder can become a co-owner by buying 30, 100, 5,000, or any number of shares of its stock. For many corporations, the investor can sell the stock at any time. It is usually harder to sell out of a proprietorship or a partnership than to sell out of a corporation.

"The Cola-Cola Company, for example, has 1.3 billion shares of stock owned by some 559,000 stockholders."

Exhibit 1-3 shows how the three types of business organizations compare.

Accounting for corporations includes some unique complexities. For this reason, we initially focus on proprietorships. Partnerships are covered in Chapter 13, and discussion of corporations begins in Chapter 14.

Accounting Concepts and Principles

OBJECTIVE 2

Apply accounting concepts and principles to analyze business transactions

Accounting practices follow certain guidelines. The rules that govern how accountants measure, process, and communicate financial information fall under the heading GAAP, which stands for **generally accepted accounting principles**.

The term *accounting principles* is broader than you might think. Generally accepted accounting principles include not only principles but also concepts and methods that identify the proper way to produce accounting information. GAAP

	Proprietorship	Partnership	Corporation
1. Owner(s)	Proprietor—one owner	Partners—two or more owners	Stockholders—generally many owners
2. Life of entity	Limited by owner's choice or death	Limited by owners' choices or death	Indefinite
3. Personal liability of owner(s) for business debts	Proprietor is personally liable	Partners are personally liable	Stockholders are not personally liable
4. Accounting status	Accounting entity is separate from proprietor	Accounting entity is separate from partners	Accounting entity is separate from stockholders

comprises all conventions, rules, and procedures that constitute accepted accounting practice at any given time. Generally accepted accounting principles are like the law—rules for conducting behavior in a way acceptable to the majority of people.

GAAP rests on a conceptual framework written by the FASB. *The primary objective of financial reporting is to provide information useful for making investment and lending decisions.* To be useful, information must be relevant, reliable, and comparable. Accountants strive to meet those goals in the information they produce. This course will expose you to the generally accepted methods of accounting; we discuss GAAP fully in Chapter 12. First, however, you need to understand several basic concepts.

Key Point: Think of GAAP as the rules or guidelines that accountants must follow when they prepare financial statements.

The Entity Concept

The most basic concept in accounting is that of the **entity**. An accounting entity is an organization or a section of an organization that stands apart from other organizations and individuals as a separate economic unit. From an accounting perspective, sharp boundaries are drawn around each entity so as not to confuse its affairs with those of other entities.

Consider Julie DeFilippo, the owner of the catering firm An Extra Hand. Suppose that her bank account shows a $2,000 balance at the end of the year. Only $1,200 of that amount grew from the business's operations. The other $800 was a gift from her grandparents. If DeFilippo follows the entity concept, she will account for the money generated by the business—one economic unit—separately from the money she received from her family, a second economic unit. This separation makes it possible to view An Extra Hand's financial position clearly.

Suppose DeFilippo disregards the entity concept and treats the full $2,000 as a product of An Extra Hand's operations. She will be misled into believing that the business has produced more cash than it has. Any steps needed to make the business more successful may not be taken.

Consider Toyota, a huge organization made up of several divisions. Toyota management evaluates each division as a separate accounting entity. If sales in the Lexus division were dropping drastically, Toyota would do well to identify the reason. But if sales figures from all divisions of the company were analyzed as a single amount, then management would not even know that the company was not selling enough Lexus automobiles. Thus the entity concept also applies to the parts of a large organization—in fact, to any entity that needs to be evaluated separately.

"If sales in the Lexus division were dropping drastically, Toyota would do well to identify the reason."

In summary, the transactions of different entities should not be accounted for together. Each entity should be evaluated separately.

The Reliability (or Objectivity) Principle

Accounting records and statements are based on the most reliable data available so that they will be as accurate and as useful as possible. This guideline is the *reliability principle*, also called the *objectivity principle*. Reliable data are verifiable. They may be confirmed by any independent observer. For example, Julie DeFilippo's $18 purchase of aprons is supported by a paid invoice. This is objective evidence of her cost of the aprons. Ideally, accounting records are based on information that flows from activities documented by objective evidence. Without the reliability principle, accounting records would be based on whims and opinions and subject to dispute.

Suppose that you want to open a stereo shop. To have a place for operations, you transfer a small building to the business. You believe the building is worth $155,000. To confirm its cost to the business, you hire two real estate professionals, who appraise the building at $147,000. Is $155,000 or $147,000 the more reliable estimate of the building's value? The real estate appraisal of $147,000 is, because it is supported by external, independent, objective observation. The business should record the building at cost of $147,000, the cost of acquiring the building.

The Cost Principle

The *cost principle* states that acquired assets and services should be recorded at their actual cost (also called historical cost). Even though the purchaser may believe the price paid is a bargain, the item is recorded at the price paid in the transaction and not at the "expected" cost. Suppose your stereo shop purchases stereo equipment from a supplier who is going out of business. Assume that you get a good deal on this purchase and pay only $2,000 for merchandise that would have cost you $3,000 elsewhere. The cost principle requires you to record this merchandise at its actual cost of $2,000, not the $3,000 that you believe the equipment to be worth.

The cost principle also holds that the accounting records should maintain the historical cost of an asset for as long as the business holds the asset. Why? Because cost is a reliable measure. Suppose your store holds the stereo equipment for six months. During that time, stereo prices increase, and the equipment can be sold for $3,500. Should its accounting value—the figure "on the books"—be the actual cost of $2,000 or the current market value of $3,500? According to the cost principle, the accounting value of the equipment remains at actual cost, $2,000.

Short Exercise: You are considering the purchase of land for future expansion. The seller is asking $50,000 for land that cost him $35,000. An appraisal shows a value of $47,000. You first offer $44,000; the seller counter-offers with $48,000, and you agree on $46,000. What dollar value is reported on your financial statements? *A:* The land's "historical cost," $46,000.

The Going-Concern Concept

Another reason for measuring assets at historical cost is the *going-concern concept*, which holds that the entity will remain in operation for the foreseeable future. Most assets—that is, the firm's resources, such as supplies, land, buildings, and equipment—are acquired to use rather than to sell. Under the going-concern concept, accountants assume that the business will remain in operation long enough to use existing assets for their intended purpose. The market value of an asset—the price for which the asset can be sold—may change during the asset's life. Therefore, an asset's current market value may not be relevant for decision making. Moreover, historical cost is a more reliable accounting measure for assets than is market value.

To understand the going-concern concept better, consider the alternative, which is to *go out of business*. A store that is holding a Going-Out-of-Business Sale is trying to sell all its assets. In that case, the relevant measure of the assets is their current market value. Going out of business, however, is the exception rather than the rule, and for this reason accounting records list assets at their historical cost.

The Stable-Monetary-Unit Concept

We think of a loaf of bread and a month's rent in terms of their dollar value. In the United States accountants record transactions in dollars because the dollar is the medium of exchange. British accountants record transactions in pounds sterling, and in Japan transactions are recorded in yen.

Unlike the value of a liter, a mile, or an acre, the value of a dollar or of a Mexican peso changes over time. A rise in prices is called *inflation*. During inflation a dollar will purchase less milk, less toothpaste, and less of other goods. When prices are stable—when there is little inflation—a dollar's purchasing power is also stable.

Accountants assume that the dollar's purchasing power is relatively stable. The *stable-monetary-unit concept* is the basis for ignoring the effect of inflation in the accounting records. It allows accountants to add and subtract dollar amounts as though each dollar has the same purchasing power as any other dollar at any other time. In South America, where inflation rates are high, accountants make adjustments to report monetary amounts in units of current buying power—a very different concept.

The Accounting Equation

Financial statements tell us how a business is performing and where it stands. They are the final product of the accounting process. But how do we arrive at the items and amounts that make up the financial statements?

The most basic tool of accounting is the **accounting equation.** This equation presents the resources of the business and the claims to those resources. **Assets** are the economic resources of a business that are expected to be of benefit in the future. Cash, office supplies, merchandise, furniture, land, and buildings are examples. Claims to those assets come from two sources.

Liabilities are "outsider claims," which are economic obligations—debts—payable to outsiders. These outside parties are called *creditors*. For example, a creditor who has loaned money to a business has a claim—a legal right—to a part of the assets until the business pays the debt. "Insider claims" are called **owner's equity,** or **capital.** These are the claims held by the owners of the business. An owner has a claim to the entity's assets because he or she has invested in the business. The $50 that Julie DeFilippo invested in An Extra Hand is an example. Owner's equity is measured by subtracting liabilities from assets.

The accounting equation in Exhibit 1-4 shows the relationship among assets, liabilities, and owner's equity. Assets appear on the left-hand side of the equation. The legal and economic claims against the assets—the liabilities and owner's equity—appear on the right-hand side of the equation. The two sides must be equal:

EXHIBIT 1-4
The Accounting Equation

Assets   Liabilities

Owner's Equity

Assets = **Liabilities + Owner's Equity**

Economic Resources		*Claims to Economic Resources*
Assets	=	Liabilities + Owner's Equity

Let's take a closer look at the elements that make up the accounting equation. Suppose you run a business that supplies meat to McDonald's and other restaurants. Some customers pay you in cash when you deliver the meat. Cash is an asset. Other customers buy on credit and promise to pay you within a certain time after delivery. This promise is also an asset because it is an economic resource that will benefit you in the future when you receive cash from the customer. To you (the meat supplier), this promise is an **account receivable.** If the promise that entitles you to receive cash in the future is formally written out, it is called a **note receivable.** All receivables are assets.

"Suppose you run a business that supplies meat to McDonald's and other restaurants."

McDonald's promise to pay you for the meat it purchases on credit creates a debt for the restaurant. This liability is an **account payable** of McDonald's, which means that the debt is not formally written out. Instead it is backed up by the reputation and the credit standing of McDonald's. A written promise of future payment is called a **note payable.** All payables are liabilities.

EXHIBIT 1-5
Transactions That Increase or
Decrease Owner's Equity

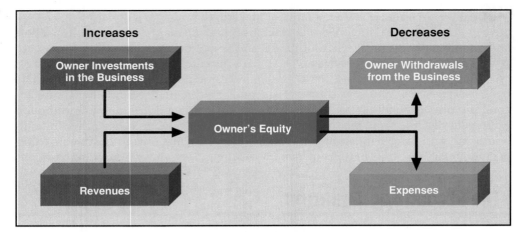

Short Exercises: (1) If the assets of a business are $174,300 and the liabilities are $82,000, how much is the owner's equity? (2) If the owner's equity in a business is $22,000 and the liabilities are $36,000, how much are the assets? *A:* (1) $92,300 (2) $58,000

Key Point: Increases in cash are not always revenues. Cash also increases when a company borrows money, but borrowing money creates a liability—not a revenue. Revenue results from rendering a service or selling a product, not necessarily from the receipt of cash.

Key Point: Decreases in cash are not always expenses. Cash decreases when land is purchased, for example, but the purchase also increases the asset land, which is not an expense. Expenses result from using goods or services in the course of earning revenue, not necessarily from the payment of cash.

Owner's equity is the amount of the assets that remains after the liabilities are subtracted. For this reason, owner's equity is often referred to as *net assets*. We often write the accounting equation to show that the owner's claim to business assets is a residual:

$$\text{Assets} - \text{Liabilities} = \text{Owner's Equity}$$

The purpose of business is to increase assets and owner's equity through **revenues,** which are amounts earned by delivering goods or services to customers. Revenues increase owner's equity because they increase the business's assets but not its liabilities. As a result, the owner's share of the assets of the business increases. Exhibit 1-5 shows that owner investments and revenues increase the owner's equity of the business.

Exhibit 1-5 also indicates the types of transactions that decrease owner's equity. Owner withdrawals are those amounts removed from the business by the owner. Withdrawals are the opposite of owner investments. **Expenses** are decreases in owner's equity that occur in the course of delivering goods and services to customers. Expenses are the cost of doing business and are the opposite of revenues. Expenses include office rent, salaries of employees, newspaper advertisements, and utility payments for light, electricity, gas, and so forth.

Accounting for Business Transactions

OBJECTIVE 4
Use the accounting equation to analyze business transactions

In accounting terms, a **transaction** is any event that *both* affects the financial position of the business entity *and* can be reliably recorded. Many events may affect a company, including (1) elections, (2) economic booms and recessions, (3) purchases and sales of merchandise inventory, (4) payment of rent, (5) collection of cash from customers, and so on. But an accountant records only events with effects that can be measured reliably as transactions.

Which of the above five events would an accountant record? The answer is events (3), (4), and (5) because their dollar amounts can be measured reliably. The dollar effects that elections and economic trends have on a particular entity cannot be measured reliably. Therefore, an accountant would not record a key election or a trend even though it might affect the business more than events (3), (4), and (5).

To illustrate accounting for business transactions, let's assume that Gary Lyon has recently become a CPA and opens his own accounting practice. Because the business has a single owner, it is called a proprietorship.

We now consider 11 events and analyze each in terms of its effect on the accounting equation of Gary Lyon's accounting practice. Transaction analysis is the essence of accounting.

TRANSACTION 1 Gary Lyon invests $50,000 of his money to begin the business. Specifically, he deposits $50,000 in a bank account entitled Gary Lyon, CPA. The effect of this transaction on the accounting equation of the Gary Lyon, CPA, business entity is

Assets		Liabilities + Owner's Equity	Type of Owner's Equity Transaction
Cash	=	Gary Lyon, Capital	
(1) +50,000		+50,000	Owner investment

The amount on the left side of the equation must equal the amount on the right side for every transaction. The first transaction increases both the assets (in this case, Cash) and the owner's equity of the business (Gary Lyon, Capital). The transaction involves no liabilities of the business because it creates no obligation for Lyon to pay an outside party. To the right of the transaction we write "Owner investment" to keep track of the reason for the effect on owner's equity. This transaction is identical to Julie DeFilippo's $50 investment in An Extra Hand. Most businesses start with an investment by an owner, *not* with borrowed money. Why not? Because a lender usually requires the owner to have some of his or her own money in the business.

TRANSACTION 2 Lyon purchases land for a future office location, paying cash of $40,000. The effect of this transaction on the accounting equation is

Assets				Liabilities + Owner's Equity	Type of Owner's Equity Transaction
Cash	+	Land	=	Gary Lyon, Capital	
(1)	50,000			50,000	Owner investment
(2)	−40,000	+ 40,000			
Bal.	10,000	40,000		50,000	
	50,000			50,000	

The cash purchase of land increases one asset, Land, and decreases another asset, Cash, by the same amount. After the transaction is completed, Lyon's business has cash of $10,000, land of $40,000, no liabilities, and owner's equity of $50,000. Note that the sums of the balances (which we abbreviate Bal.) on both sides of the equation are equal. This equality must always exist.

STOP & THINK Gary Lyon's realtor assures Lyon that the land is worth $75,000. Could Lyon ethically record the land at $75,000?

Answer: No, because generally accepted accounting principles require a buyer to record an asset at its actual cost. This is the cost principle in action.

TRANSACTION 3 Lyon buys stationery and other office supplies, agreeing to pay $500 within 30 days. This transaction increases both the assets and the liabilities of the business. Its effect on the accounting equation is

	Assets				Liabilities + Owner's Equity	
	Cash +	Office Supplies +	Land	=	Accounts Payable +	Gary Lyon, Capital
Bal.	10,000		40,000			50,000
(3)		+500			+500	
Bal.	10,000	500	40,000		500	50,000
		50,500			50,500	

The asset affected is Office Supplies, and the liability is called an account payable. The term *payable* signifies a liability. Because Lyon is obligated to pay $500 in the future but signs no formal promissory note, we record the liability as an Account Payable, not as a Note Payable. We say that purchases supported by the general credit standing of the buyer are made on an *open account*.

TRANSACTION 4   Gary Lyon earns service revenue by providing professional accounting services for his clients. Assume he earns $5,500 and collects this amount in cash. The effect on the accounting equation is an increase in the asset Cash and an increase in Gary Lyon, Capital, as follows:

	Assets				Liabilities +	Owner's Equity	Type of Owner's Equity Transaction
	Cash	+ Office Supplies	+ Land		Accounts Payable +	Gary Lyon, Capital	
Bal.	10,000	500	40,000	=	500	50,000	
(4)	+ 5,500					+ 5,500	Service revenue
Bal.	15,500	500	40,000		500	55,500	
		56,000				56,000	

This revenue transaction caused the business to grow, as shown by the increase in total assets and in total liabilities plus owner's equity. A company that sells goods to customers is a merchandising business. Its revenue is called *sales revenue*. By contrast, Gary Lyon and Julie DeFilippo perform services for clients; their revenue is called *service revenue*.

TRANSACTION 5   Lyon performs services for a client who does not pay immediately. In return for his accounting services, Lyon receives the client's promise to pay the $3,000 amount within one month. This promise is an asset to Lyon, an account receivable because he expects to collect the cash in the future. In accounting, we say that Lyon performed this service *on account*. When the business performs service for a client or a customer, the business earns revenue regardless of whether it receives cash immediately or expects to collect cash later. This $3,000 of service revenue is as real to Lyon's business as the $5,500 of revenue that he collected immediately in the preceding transaction. Lyon records an increase in the asset Accounts Receivable and an increase in Owner's Equity as follows:

	Assets					Liabilities +	Owner's Equity	Type of Owner's Equity Transaction
	Cash	+ Accounts Receivable	+ Office Supplies	+ Land		Accounts Payable +	Gary Lyon, Capital	
Bal.	15,500		500	40,000	=	500	55,500	
(5)		+3,000					+ 3,000	Service revenue
Bal.	15,500	3,000	500	40,000		500	58,500	
			59,000				59,000	

Again, this revenue transaction caused the business to grow.

TRANSACTION 6   During the month, Lyon pays $2,700 in cash expenses: office rent, $1,100; employee salary, $1,200 (for a part-time assistant); and total utilities, $400. The effect on the accounting equation is

	Assets						Liabilities +	Owner's Equity Gary Lyon, Capital	Type of Owner's Equity Transaction
	Cash	+ Accounts Receivable	+ Office Supplies	+ Land			Accounts Payable +		
Bal.	15,500	3,000	500	40,000		=	500	58,500	
(6)	– 2,700							– 1,100	Rent expense
								– 1,200	Salary expense
								– 400	Utilities expense
Bal.	12,800	3,000	500	40,000			500	55,800	
		56,300						56,300	

Because expenses have the opposite effect of revenues, they cause the business to shrink, as shown by the smaller amounts of total assets and total owner's equity.

Each expense should be recorded in a separate transaction. Here, for simplicity, they are recorded together. Note that even though the figure $2,700 does not appear on the right-hand side of the equation, the three individual expenses add up to $2,700 total. As a result, the "balance" of the equation holds, as we know it must.

Businesspeople, Gary Lyon included, run their businesses with the objective of having more revenues than expenses. An excess of total revenues over total expenses is called **net income, net earnings,** or **net profit.** If total expenses exceed total revenues, the result is called a **net loss.**

Short Exercise: A company reported monthly revenues of $77,600 and expenses of $81,300. What is the result of operations for the month? *A:* Net loss of $3,700, because expenses exceed revenues.

TRANSACTION 7 Lyon pays $400 to the store from which he purchased $500 worth of office supplies in Transaction 3. In accounting, we say that he pays $400 *on account.* The effect on the accounting equation is a decrease in the asset Cash and a decrease in the liability Accounts Payable as follows:

	Assets						Liabilities +	Owner's Equity Gary Lyon, Capital
	Cash	+ Accounts Receivable	+ Office Supplies	+ Land			Accounts Payable +	
Bal.	12,800	3,000	500	40,000		=	500	55,800
(7)	– 400						–400	
Bal.	12,400	3,000	500	40,000			100	55,800
		55,900						55,900

The payment of cash on account has no effect on the asset Office Supplies because the payment does not increase or decrease the supplies available to the business.

TRANSACTION 8 Lyon remodels his home at a cost of $30,000, paying cash from his personal funds. This event is *not* a transaction of Gary Lyon's business. It has no effect on Lyon's accounting practice and therefore is not recorded by the business. It is a transaction of the Gary Lyon *personal* entity, not the Gary Lyon, CPA, *business* entity. We are focusing now solely on the business entity, and this event does not affect it. This transaction illustrates the application of the *entity concept.*

Julie DeFilippo and her partner purchased matching clothing to use as uniforms in their party business. They used company funds for this business expense, so they had to record the transaction. But the $100 that DeFilippo paid for car insurance was a personal transaction, not a business transaction and would not have been recorded by An Extra Hand.

TRANSACTION 9 In Transaction 5, Gary Lyon performed service for a client on account. Lyon now collects $1,000 from the client. We say that Lyon collects the cash *on account*. Lyon will record an increase in the asset Cash. Should he also record an increase in service revenue? No, because Lyon already recorded the revenue when he earned it in Transaction 5. The phrase "collect cash on account" means to record an increase in Cash and a decrease in the asset Accounts Receivable. The effect on the accounting equation is

		Assets				Liabilities +	Owner's Equity
	Cash	+ Accounts Receivable	+ Office Supplies	+ Land	=	Accounts Payable +	Gary Lyon, Capital
Bal.	12,400	3,000	500	40,000		100	55,800
(9)	+ 1,000	−1,000					
Bal.	13,400	2,000	500	40,000		100	55,800
			55,900				55,900

Total assets are unchanged from the preceding transaction's total. Why? Because Lyon merely exchanged one asset for another. Also, total liabilities and owner's equity are unchanged.

TRANSACTION 10 An individual approaches Lyon about selling a parcel of land owned by the Gary Lyon, CPA, business entity. Lyon and the other person agree to a sale price of $22,000, which is equal to Lyon's cost of the land. Lyon's business sells the land and receives $22,000 cash, and the effect on the accounting equation is

		Assets				Liabilities +	Owner's Equity
	Cash	+ Accounts Receivable	+ Office Supplies	+ Land	=	Accounts Payable +	Gary Lyon, Capital
Bal.	13,400	2,000	500	40,000		100	55,800
(10)	+22,000			−22,000			
Bal.	35,400	2,000	500	18,000		100	55,800
			55,900				55,900

TRANSACTION 11 Lyon withdraws $2,100 cash from the business for personal use. The effect on the accounting equation is

		Assets				Liabilities +	Owner's Equity	Type of Owner's Equity Transaction
	Cash	+ Accounts Receivable	+ Office Supplies	+ Land	=	Accounts Payable +	Gary Lyon, Capital	
Bal.	35,400	2,000	500	18,000		100	55,800	
(11)	− 2,100						− 2,100	Owner withdrawal
Bal.	33,300	2,000	500	18,000		100	53,700	
			53,800				53,800	

Key Point: When the owner makes a withdrawal from the business, it is generally in the form of cash. The withdrawal reduces the owner's investment or equity in the business, but it is not a business expense because the assets are not being used to produce revenue.

Lyon's withdrawal of $2,100 cash decreases the asset Cash and also the owner's equity of the business. The double underlines below each column indicate a final total.

Does this withdrawal decrease the business entity's holdings? The answer is yes, because the cash withdrawn is unavailable for business use after Lyon spends it for personal use. The withdrawal does *not* represent a business expense because the cash is used for personal affairs unrelated to the business. We record this decrease in owner's equity as Withdrawals or as Drawings.

Evaluating Business Transactions

Exhibit 1-6 summarizes the 11 preceding transactions. Panel A of the exhibit lists the details of the transactions, and Panel B presents the analysis. As you study the exhibit, note that every transaction maintains the equality

EXHIBIT 1-6 *Analysis of Transactions of Gary Lyon, CPA*

Assets = Liabilities + Owner's Equity

PANEL A—Details of transactions

(1) Lyon invested $50,000 cash in the business.
(2) Paid $40,000 cash for land.
(3) Bought $500 of office supplies on account.
(4) Received $5,500 cash from clients for accounting service revenue earned.
(5) Performed accounting service for a client on account, $3,000.
(6) Paid cash expenses: rent, $1,100; employee salary, $1,200; utilities, $400.
(7) Paid $400 on the account payable created in Transaction 3.
(8) Remodeled his personal residence. This is *not* a business transaction.
(9) Received $1,000 on the account receivable created in Transaction 5.
(10) Sold land for cash at its cost of $22,000.
(11) Withdrew $2,100 cash for personal expenses.

PANEL B—Analysis of transactions

	Cash	+ Accounts Receivable	+ Office Supplies	+ Land		Accounts Payable	+ Gary Lyon, Capital	Type of Owner's Equity Transaction
(1)	+50,000						+50,000	Owner investment
Bal.	50,000						50,000	
(2)	−40,000			+40,000				
Bal.	10,000			40,000			50,000	
(3)			+500			+500		
Bal.	10,000		500	40,000		500	50,000	
(4)	+ 5,500						+ 5,500	Service revenue
Bal.	15,500		500	40,000		500	55,500	
(5)		+3,000					+ 3,000	Service revenue
Bal.	15,500	3,000	500	40,000	=	500	58,500	
(6)	− 2,700						− 1,100	Rent expense
							− 1,200	Salary expense
							− 400	Utilities expense
Bal.	12,800	3,000	500	40,000		500	55,800	
(7)	− 400					−400		
Bal.	12,400	3,000	500	40,000		100	55,800	
(8)	Not a transaction of the business							
(9)	+ 1,000	−1,000						
Bal.	13,400	2,000	500	40,000		100	55,800	
(10)	+22,000			−22,000				
Bal.	35,400	2,000	500	18,000		100	55,800	
(11)	− 2,100						− 2,100	Owner withdrawal
Bal.	33,300	2,000	500	18,000		100	53,700	

53,800 = 53,800

STOP & THINK Why does Gary Lyon, or anyone else, go into business? If you could identify only one reason, what would it be? How will accounting serve to meet this need?

Answer: Gary Lyon went into business to earn a profit—and thereby to make a living. Lyon hopes his accounting revenues exceed his expenses to provide an excess—a net income. Lyon hopes he can withdraw cash from the business to pay his personal bills. Accounting tells him how much income he has earned and how much cash and other assets his business has. Lyon also needs to know how much in liabilities the business owes. The financial statements help answer these questions.

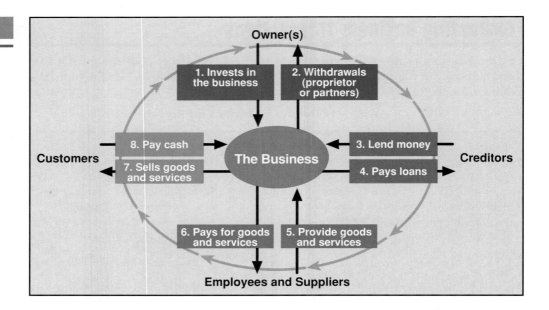

Summary of Business Activities

Exhibit 1-7 summarizes (in clockwise fashion) the business activities that we have accounted for in this chapter. For a new entity such as Gary Lyon, CPA, the process begins when the owner supplies financial resources to start the business. The entity may also borrow from creditors. These are the two ways of *financing* a business with money received from owner(s) and with money lent by creditors.

Most businesses *invest* in long-term assets, such as the land that Gary Lyon purchased. There are other transactions between the business and its employees and suppliers—salary paid to employees (an expense) and the purchase of office supplies (an asset)—for the services and goods provided.

The *operations* of a business center on the sale of services and goods to customers and the collection of cash—items 7 and 8 in Exhibit 1-7. After a period the business pays off its loans and, if it is profitable, distributes money to its owner (withdrawals) or owners (dividends, for a corporation).

Financial Statements

OBJECTIVE 5

Prepare the financial statements

Once the analysis of the transactions is complete, what is the next step in the accounting process? How does a business present the results of the analysis? We now look at the *financial statements*, which are formal reports of financial information about the entity. The primary financial statements are the (1) *income statement*, (2) *statement of owner's equity*, (3) *balance sheet*, and (4) *statement of cash flows*.

The **income statement** presents a summary of the *revenues* and *expenses* of an entity for a specific period of time, such as a month or a year. The income statement, also called the **statement of earnings** or **statement of operations**, is like a video of the entity's operations during the period. The income statement holds perhaps the most important single piece of information about a business—its *net income*, revenues minus expenses. If expenses exceed revenues, a net loss results for the period.

The **statement of owner's equity** presents a summary of the changes that occurred in the *owner's equity* of the entity during a specific time period, such as a month or a year. Increases in owner's equity arise from investments by the owner and from net income earned during the period. Decreases result from withdrawals by the owner and from a net loss for the period. Net income or net loss comes directly from the income statement. Investments and withdrawals by the owner are capital transactions between the business and its owner, so they do not affect the income statement.

The **balance sheet** lists all the *assets, liabilities,* and *owner's equity* of an entity as of a specific date, usually the end of a month or a year. The balance sheet is like a snapshot of the entity. For this reason, it is also called the **statement of financial position**.

The **statement of cash flows** reports the amount of cash coming in—*cash receipts*—and the amount of cash going out—*cash payments* or *disbursements*—during a period. Business activities result in a net cash inflow (receipts greater than payments) or a net cash outflow (payments greater than receipts). The statement of cash flows shows the net increase or decrease in cash during the period and the cash balance at the end of the period. We will cover the statement of cash flows in greater depth in Chapter 18.

Computers and software programs for use in accounting have had a significant impact on the preparation of the financial statements. Financial statements can be produced instantaneously after the data from the financial records are entered into the computer. Of course, any errors that exist in the financial records will be passed on to the financial statements. For this reason, the person responsible for analyzing the accounting data is critical to the accuracy of the financial statements.

Each financial statement has a heading that gives the name of the business (in our discussion, Gary Lyon, CPA), the name of the particular statement, and the date or time period covered by the statement. A balance sheet taken at the end of year 19X4 would be dated December 31, 19X4. A balance sheet prepared at the end of March 19X7 is dated March 31, 19X7.

An income statement or a statement of owner's equity covering an annual period ending in December 19X5 is dated For the Year Ended December 31, 19X5. A monthly income statement or statement of owner's equity for September 19X9 has in its heading For the Month Ended September 30, 19X9, Month Ended September 30, 19X9, or For the Month of September 19X9. Income is meaningless unless identified with a particular time period.

Relationships among the Financial Statements

Exhibit 1-8 illustrates all four statements. Their data come from the transaction analysis in Exhibit 1-6. We are assuming the transactions occurred during the month of April 19X1. Study the exhibit carefully, because it shows the relationships among the four financial statements.

Observe the following in Exhibit 1-8:

1. The *income statement* for the month ended April 30, 19X1
    a. Reports all *revenues* and all *expenses* during the period. Revenues and expenses are reported only on the income statement.
    b. Reports *net income* of the period if total revenues exceed total expenses, as in the case of Gary Lyon's accounting practice for April. If total expenses exceed total revenues, a *net loss* is reported instead.
2. The *statement of owner's equity* for the month ended April 30, 19X1
    a. Opens with the owner's capital balance at the beginning of the period.
    b. Adds *investments by the owner* of the business and also adds *net income* (or subtracts *net loss,* as the case may be). Net income (or net loss) comes directly from

EXHIBIT 1-8

*Financial Statements of Gary
Lyon, CPA*

GARY LYON, CPA
INCOME STATEMENT
MONTH ENDED APRIL 30, 19X1

Revenue:		
Service revenue		$8,500
Expenses:		
Salary expense	$1,200	
Rent expense	1,100	
Utilities expense	400	
Total expenses		2,700
Net income		$5,800

① ②

GARY LYON, CPA
STATEMENT OF OWNER'S EQUITY
MONTH ENDED APRIL 30, 19X1

Gary Lyon, capital, April 1, 19X1	$ 0
Add: Investments by owner	50,000
Net income for the month	5,800
	55,800
Less: Withdrawals by owner	2,100
Gary Lyon, capital, April 30, 19X1	$53,700

GARY LYON, CPA
BALANCE SHEET
APRIL 30, 19X1

Assets		**Liabilities**	
Cash	$33,300	Accounts payable	$ 100
Accounts receivable	2,000	**Owner's Equity**	
Office supplies	500		
Land	18,000	Gary Lyon, capital	53,700
		Total liabilities and	
Total assets	$53,800	owner's equity	$53,800

③

GARY LYON, CPA
STATEMENT OF CASH FLOWS*
MONTH ENDED APRIL 30, 19X1

Cash flows from **operating** activities:		
Receipts:		
Collections for customers ($5,500 + $1,000)		$ 6,500
Payments:		
To suppliers ($1,100 + $400 + $400)	$ (1,900)	
To employees	(1,200)	(3,100)
Net cash inflow from operating activities		3,400
Cash flows from **investing** activities:		
Acquisition of land	$(40,000)	
Sale of land	22,000	
Net cash outflow from investing activities		(18,000)
Cash flows from **financing** activities:		
Investment by owner	$ 50,000	
Withdrawal by owner	(2,100)	
Net cash inflow from financing activities		47,900
Net increase in cash		$33,300
Cash balance, April 1, 19X1		0
Cash balance, April 30, 19X1		$33,300

*The statement of cash flows is included here merely for completeness. Chapter 18 will explain how to
prepare this statement.

the income statement, which includes the effect of all the revenues and all the expenses for the period (see arrow 1 in Exhibit 1-8).

    c. Subtracts *withdrawals by the owner.*

    d. Ends with the owner's capital balance at the end of the period.

3. The *balance sheet* at April 30, 19X1, the end of the period

    a. Reports all *assets*, all *liabilities*, and *owner's equity* of the business at the end of the period. No other statement reports assets and liabilities.

    b. Reports that total assets equal the sum of total liabilities plus total owner's equity. This balancing feature gives the balance sheet its name. It is based on the accounting equation.

    c. Reports the owner's ending capital balance, taken directly from the statement of owner's equity (see arrow 2).

4. The *statement of cash flows* for the month ended April 30, 19X1

    a. Reports cash flows from three types of business activities (*operating*, *investing*, and *financing* activities) during the month. Each category results in a net cash inflow or a net cash outflow for the period.

    b. Reports a net increase in cash during the month and ends with the cash balance at April 30, 19X1. This is the amount of cash to report on the balance sheet (see arrow 3).

STOP & THINK How well did Lyon's accounting practice perform during April?

Answer: Rather well. Business net income was $5,800—very good in relation to service revenue of $8,500. Lyon was able to withdraw cash of $2,100 for personal use. The business ended April with cash of $33,300 (after Lyon's withdrawals had been subtracted). The total assets of $53,800 far exceed the total liabilities of $100. The owner's equity of $53,700 provides a good cushion against which Lyon can borrow. The business's financial position at April 30, 19X1, is strong. What identifies a strong financial position? Plenty of cash and assets far in excess of liabilities—hence a large amount of owner's equity. Lenders like to see these features before making a loan: "Those most able to borrow money need it the least."

Now read the chapter appendix to become familiar with accounting organizations and the structure of the profession.

SUMMARY PROBLEM FOR YOUR REVIEW

Jill Smith opens an apartment-location business near a college campus. She is the sole owner of the proprietorship, which she names Campus Apartment Locators. During the first month of operations, July 19X1, Smith engages in the following transactions:

a. Smith invests $35,000 of personal funds to start the business.

b. She purchases on account office supplies costing $350.

c. Smith pays cash of $30,000 to acquire a lot next to the campus. She intends to use the land as a future building site for her business office.

d. Smith locates apartments for clients and receives cash of $1,900.

e. She pays $100 on the account payable she created in Transaction (b).

f. She pays $2,000 of personal funds for a vacation.

g. She pays cash expenses for office rent, $400, and utilities, $100.

h. The business sells office supplies to another business for its cost of $150.

i. Smith withdraws cash of $1,200 for personal use.

Required

1. Analyze the preceding transactions in terms of their effects on the accounting equation of Campus Apartment Locators. Use Exhibit 1-6 as a guide, but show balances only after the last transaction.
2. Prepare the income statement, statement of owner's equity, and balance sheet of the business after recording the transactions. Use Exhibit 1-8 as a guide.

SOLUTION TO REVIEW PROBLEM

PANEL A—Details of transactions

a. Smith invested $35,000 cash to start the business.
b. Purchased $350 of office supplies on account.
c. Paid $30,000 to acquire land as a future building site.
d. Earned service revenue and received cash of $1,900.
e. Paid $100 on account.

f. Paid for a personal vacation, which is not a business transaction.
g. Paid cash expenses for rent, $400, and utilities, $100.
h. Sold office supplies for cost of $150.
i. Withdrew $1,200 cash for personal use.

PANEL B—Analysis of transactions

	Assets				Liabilities +	Owner's Equity	Type of Owner's Equity Transaction
	Cash	+	Office Supplies +	Land	Accounts Payable +	Jill Smith, Capital	
(a)	+35,000					+35,000	Owner investment
(b)			+350		+350		
(c)	−30,000			+30,000			
(d)	+ 1,900					+ 1,900	Service revenue
(e)	− 100				−100		
(f)	Not a transaction of the business						
(g)	− 500					− 400	Rent expense
						− 100	Utilities expense
(h)	+ 150		−150				
(i)	− 1,200					− 1,200	Owner withdrawal
Bal.	5,250		200	30,000	250	35,200	

35,450 = 35,450

SUMMARY

1. Develop an accounting vocabulary for decision making. Accounting is a system for measuring, processing, and communicating financial information. As the "language of business," accounting helps a wide range of decision makers. Accounting dates back to ancient civilizations, but its importance to society has been greatest since the Industrial Revolution.

2. Apply accounting concepts and principles to analyze business transactions. The three basic forms of business organization are the proprietorship, the partnership, and the corporation. Whatever the form, accountants use the entity concept to keep the business's records separate from the personal records of the people who run it. Accountants at all levels must be ethical to serve their intended purpose. *Generally accepted accounting principles (GAAP)* guide accountants in their work.

Among these guidelines are the *entity concept*, the *reliability principle*, the *cost principle*, the *going-concern concept*, and the *stable-monetary-unit concept*.

3. Use the accounting equation to describe an organization's financial position. In its most common form, the accounting equation is

Assets = Liabilities + Owner's Equity

4. Use the accounting equation to analyze business transactions. Transactions affect a business's assets, liabilities, and owner's equity. Therefore, transactions are analyzed in terms of their effect on the accounting equation.

FINANCIAL STATEMENTS OF CAMPUS APARTMENT LOCATORS

CAMPUS APARTMENT LOCATORS
INCOME STATEMENT
MONTH ENDED JULY 31, 19X1

Revenue:		
Service revenue		$1,900
Expenses:		
Rent expense	$400	
Utilities expense	100	
Total expenses		500
Net income		$1,400

CAMPUS APARTMENT LOCATORS
STATEMENT OF OWNER'S EQUITY
MONTH ENDED JULY 31, 19X1

Jill Smith, capital, July 1, 19X1	$ 0
Add: Investments by owner	35,000
Net income for the month	1,400
	36,400
Less: Withdrawals by owner	1,200
Jill Smith, capital, July 31, 19X1	$35,200

CAMPUS APARTMENT LOCATORS
BALANCE SHEET
JULY 31, 19X1

Assets		Liabilities	
Cash	$ 5,250	Accounts payable	$ 250
Office supplies	200	**Owner's Equity**	
Land	30,000		
		Jill Smith, capital	35,200
		Total liabilities and	
Total assets	$35,450	owner's equity	$35,450

---

5. ***Prepare the financial statements.*** The *financial statements* communicate information for decision making by the entity's managers, owners, and creditors and by government agencies. The *income statement* presents a video of the entity's operations in terms of revenues earned and expenses incurred during a specific period. Total revenues minus total expenses equal net income. Net income or net loss answers the question, How much income did the entity earn, or, How much loss did it incur during the period? The *statement of owner's equity* reports the changes in owner's equity during the period. The *balance sheet* provides a photograph of the entity's financial standing in terms of its assets, liabilities, and owner's equity at a specific time. It answers the question, What is the entity's financial position? The *statement of cash flows* reports the cash coming in and the cash going out during the period. It answers, Where did cash come from, and, Where did it go?

6. ***Evaluate the performance of a business.*** High net income indicates success in business; net loss indicates a bad year.

SELF-STUDY QUESTIONS

Test your understanding of the chapter by marking the best answer for each of the following questions:

1. The organization that formulates generally accepted accounting principles is *(p. 6)*
    a. American Institute of Certified Public Accountants (AICPA)
    b. Internal Revenue Service
    c. Financial Accounting Standards Board (FASB)
    d. Institute of Management Accountants (IMA)

2. Which of the following forms of business organization is an "artificial person" and must obtain legal approval from a state to conduct business? *(p. 8)*
    a. Law firm
    b. Proprietorship
    c. Partnership
    d. Corporation

3. You have purchased some unclaimed freight for $10,000 and can sell it immediately for $15,000. What accounting concept or principle governs the amount at which to record the goods you purchased? *(p. 10)*

a. Entity concept
b. Reliability principle
c. Cost principle
d. Going-concern concept

4. The economic resources of a business are called *(p. 11)*
   a. Assets
   b. Liabilities
   c. Owner's Equity
   d. Receivables

5. A business has assets of $140,000 and liabilities of $60,000. How much is its owner's equity? *(p. 12)*
   a. $0
   b. $80,000
   c. $140,000
   d. $200,000

6. The purchase of office supplies on account will *(p. 13)*
   a. Increase an asset and increase a liability
   b. Increase an asset and increase owner's equity
   c. Increase one asset and decrease another asset
   d. Increase an asset and decrease a liability

7. The performance of service for a customer or client and immediate receipt of cash will *(p. 14)*
   a. Increase one asset and decrease another asset

b. Increase an asset and increase owner's equity
c. Decrease an asset and decrease a liability
d. Increase an asset and increase a liability

8. The payment of an account payable will *(p. 15)*
   a. Increase one asset and decrease another asset
   b. Decrease an asset and decrease owner's equity
   c. Decrease an asset and decrease a liability
   d. Increase an asset and increase a liability

9. The report of assets, liabilities, and owner's equity is called the *(p. 19)*
   a. Financial statement
   b. Balance sheet
   c. Income statement
   d. Statement of owner's equity

10. The financial statements that are dated for a time period (rather than a specific time) are the *(pp. 18–19)*
    a. Balance sheet and income statement
    b. Balance sheet and statement of owner's equity
    c. Income statement, statement of owner's equity, and statement of cash flows
    d. All financial statements are dated for a time period.

Answers to the Self-Study Questions follow the Accounting Vocabulary.

ACCOUNTING VOCABULARY

Accounting, like many other subjects, has a special vocabulary. It is important that you understand the following terms. They are explained in the chapter and also in the glossary at the end of the book.

Account payable. A liability backed by the general reputation and credit standing of the debtor *(p. 11)*.

Account receivable. An asset, a promise to receive cash from customers to whom the business has sold goods or for whom the business has performed services *(p. 11)*.

Accounting. The system that measures business activities, processes that information into reports and financial statements, and communicates the findings to decision makers *(p. 4)*.

Accounting equation. The most basic tool of accounting: Assets = Liabilities + Owner's Equity *(p. 11)*.

Asset. An economic resource that is expected to be of benefit in the future *(p. 11)*.

Auditing. The examination of financial statements by outside accountants, the most significant service that CPAs perform. The conclusion of an audit is the accountant's professional opinion about the financial statements *(p. 39)*.

Balance sheet. List of an entity's assets, liabilities, and owner's equity as of a specific date. Also called the statement of financial position *(p. 19)*.

Capital. Another name for the owner equity of a business *(p. 11)*.

Certified public accountant (CPA). A licensed accountant who serves the general public rather than one particular company *(p. 6)*.

Corporation. A business owned by stockholders that begins when the state approves its articles of incorporation. A corporation is a legal entity, an "artificial person," in the eyes of the law *(p. 8)*.

Entity. An organization or a section of an organization that, for accounting purposes, stands apart from other organizations and individuals as a separate economic unit. This is the most basic concept in accounting *(p. 9)*.

Expense. Decrease in owner's equity that occurs in the course of delivering goods or services to customers or clients *(p. 12)*.

Financial accounting. The branch of accounting that provides information to people outside the business *(p. 6)*.

Financial statements. Business documents that report financial information about an entity to persons and organizations outside the business *(p. 4)*.

Generally accepted accounting principles (GAAP). Accounting guidelines, formulated by the Financial Accounting Standards Board, that govern how businesses report their financial statements to the public *(p 8)*.

Income statement. List of an entity's revenues, expenses, and net income or net loss for a specific period. Also called the statement of operations or the statement of earnings *(p. 18)*.

Liability. An economic obligation (a debt) payable to an individual or an organization outside the business *(p. 11)*.

Management accounting. The branch of accounting that generates information for internal decision makers of a business, such as top executives *(p. 6)*.

Net earnings. Another name for net income or net profit *(p. 15)*.

Net income. Excess of total revenues over total expenses. Also called net earnings or net profit *(p. 15)*.

Net loss. Excess of total expenses over total revenues *(p. 15)*.

Net profit. Another name for net income or net earnings *(p. 15)*.

Note payable. A liability evidenced by a written promise to make a future payment *(p. 11)*.

Note receivable. An asset evidenced by another party's written promise that entitles you to receive cash in the future *(p. 11)*.

Owner's Equity. The claim of an owner of a business to the assets of the business. Also called capital *(p. 11)*.

Partnership. A business with two or more owners (*p. 8*).

Proprietorship. A business with a single owner (*p. 8*).

Revenue. Increase in owner's equity that is earned by delivering goods or services to customers or clients (*p. 12*).

Statement of cash flows. Reports cash receipts and cash disbursements classified according to the entity's major activities: operating, investing, and financing (*p. 19*).

Statement of earnings. Another name for income statement (*p. 18*).

Statement of operations. Another name for income statement (*p. 18*).

Statement of owner's equity. Summary of the changes in the owner's equity of an entity during a specific period (*p. 18*).

Stockholder. A person who owns stock in a corporation (*p. 8*).

Transaction. An event that affects the financial position of a particular entity and can be reliably recorded (*p. 12*).

ANSWERS TO SELF-STUDY QUESTIONS

1. c	**3.** c	**5.** b	**7.** b	**9.** b
2. d	**4.** a	**6.** a	**8.** c	**10.** c

QUESTIONS

1. Distinguish between accounting and bookkeeping.
2. Identify five users of accounting information, and explain how they use it.
3. Name two important reasons for the development of accounting.
4. What organization formulates generally accepted accounting principles? Is this organization a government agency?
5. Identify the owner(s) of a proprietorship, a partnership, and a corporation.
6. Why do ethical standards exist in accounting? Which organization directs its standards toward independent auditors? Which organization directs its standards more toward management accountants?
7. Why is the entity concept so important to accounting?
8. Give four examples of accounting entities.
9. Briefly describe the reliability principle.
10. What role does the cost principle play in accounting?
11. If *assets = liabilities + owner's equity*, then how can liabilities be expressed?
12. Explain the difference between an account receivable and an account payable.
13. What role do transactions play in accounting?
14. Give a more descriptive title for the balance sheet.
15. What feature of the balance sheet gives this financial statement its name?
16. Give another title for the income statement.
17. Which financial statement is like a snapshot of the entity at a specific time? Which financial statement is like a video of the entity's operations during a period of time?
18. What information does the statement of owner's equity report?
19. Give two synonyms for the owner's equity of a proprietorship.
20. What piece of information flows from the income statement to the statement of owner's equity? What information flows from the statement of owner's equity to the balance sheet? What balance sheet item is explained by the statement of cash flows?

EXERCISES

E1-1 Gao and Yi Huan want to open a Chinese restaurant in Baltimore. In need of cash, they ask City Bank & Trust for a loan. The bank's procedures require borrowers to submit financial statements to show likely results of operations for the first year and likely financial position at the end of the first year. With little knowledge of accounting, Gao and Yi don't know how to proceed. Explain to them the information provided by the statement of operations (the income statement) and the statement of financial position (the balance sheet). Indicate why a lender would require this information.

*Explaining the income statement and the balance sheet (**Obj. 1**)*

E1-2 For each of the following items, give an example of a business transaction that has the described effect on the accounting equation:

*Business transactions (**Obj. 2**)*

a. Decrease an asset and decrease a liability.
b. Increase an asset and increase owner's equity.
c. Increase an asset and increase a liability.
d. Increase one asset and decrease another asset.
e. Decrease an asset and decrease owner's equity.

E1-3 Blaine Controls, a proprietorship, or Derrick Blaine, the owner, experienced the following events. State whether each event (1) increased, (2) decreased, or (3) had no effect on the total assets of the business. Identify any specific asset affected.

*Transaction analysis (**Obj. 2**)*

a. Borrowed money from the bank.
b. Cash purchase of land for a future building site.
c. Blaine increased his cash investment in the business.
d. Paid cash on accounts payable.
e. Purchased machinery and equipment for a manufacturing plant; signed a promissory note in payment.
f. Performed service for a customer on account.
g. Blaine withdrew cash from the business for personal use.
h. Received cash from a customer on account receivable.
i. Blaine used personal funds to purchase a swimming pool for his home.
j. Sold land for a price equal to the cost of the land; received cash.

Accounting equation
(Obj. 3)

E1-4 Compute the missing amount in the accounting equation for each entity:

	Assets	Liabilities	Owner's Equity
Entity A	$?	$41,800	$84,400
Entity B	95,900	?	34,000
Entity C	81,700	29,800	?

Accounting equation
(Obj. 4, 5)

E1-5 Obenosky Travel Agency balance sheet data at May 31, 19X2, and June 30, 19X2, follow:

	May 31, 19X2	**June 30, 19X2**
Total assets	$150,000	$195,000
Total liabilities	109,000	131,000

Required

Below are three assumptions about investments and withdrawals by the owner of the business during June. For each assumption, compute the amount of net income or net loss of the business during June 19X2.

1. The owner invested $20,000 in the business and made no withdrawals.
2. The owner made no additional investments in the business but withdrew $16,000 for personal use.
3. The owner invested $39,000 in the business and withdrew $6,000 for personal use.

Transaction analysis
(Obj. 4)

E1-6 Indicate the effects of the following business transactions on the accounting equation. Transaction *a* is answered as a guide.

a. Received cash of $20,000 from the owner, who was investing in the business.
   Answer: Increase asset (Cash)
               Increase owner's equity (Capital)
b. Paid $300 cash to purchase office supplies.
c. Performed legal service for a client and received cash of $780.
d. Paid monthly office rent of $500.
e. Performed legal service for a client on account, $2,000.
f. Purchased on account office furniture at a cost of $500.
g. Received cash on account, $900.
h. Paid cash on account, $250.
i. Sold land for $12,000, which was our cost of the land.

Transaction analysis; accounting
equation
(Obj. 2, 4)

E1-7 Allison LaChappelle opens a medical practice to specialize in child care. During the first month of operation, January, her practice, entitled Allison LaChappelle, M.D., experienced the following events:

Jan. 6   LaChappelle invested $100,000 in the business by opening a bank account in the name of Allison LaChappelle, M.D.
     9   LaChappelle paid cash for land costing $65,000. She plans to build an office building on the land.

Jan. 12   She purchased medical supplies for $2,000 on account.
15   LaChappelle officially opened for business.
15–31   During the rest of the month she treated patients and earned service revenue of $8,000, receiving cash.
15–31   She paid cash expenses: employee salaries, $1,400; office rent, $1,000; utilities, $300.
28   She sold supplies to another physician for cost of $500.
31   She paid $1,500 on account.

Required

Analyze the effects of these events on the accounting equation of the medical practice of Allison LaChappelle, M.D. Use a format similar to that of Exhibit 1-6, with headings for Cash; Medical Supplies; Land; Accounts Payable; and Allison LaChappelle, Capital.

E1-8   The analysis of the transactions in which Krannig Leasing engaged during its first month of operations follows. The company buys equipment that it leases out to earn revenue. The owners of the business made only one investment to start the business and no withdrawals.

Business organization, transactions, and net income (Obj. 2, 3, 4)

	Cash	+ Accounts Receivable	+ Lease Equipment	= Accounts Payable	+ Partners' Capital
a.	+50,000				+50,000
b.			+100,000	+100,000	
c.	– 750		+ 750		
d.		+500			+ 500
e.	– 1,000				– 1,000
f.	+ 3,600				+ 3,600
g.	+ 150	–150			
h.	–10,000			– 10,000	

Required

1.   What type of business organization is Krannig Leasing? How can you tell?
2.   Describe each transaction.
3.   If these transactions fully describe the operations of Krannig Leasing during the month, what was the amount of net income or net loss?

E1-9   Presented below are the balances of the assets and liabilities of High-and-Dry Delivery Service as of September 30, 19X2. Also included are the revenue and expense figures of the business for September.

Business organization, balance sheet (Obj. 2, 5)

Delivery service revenue	$4,100	Delivery equipment	$15,500
Accounts receivable	1,900	Supplies	600
Accounts payable	1,750	Note payable	6,000
H. Dry, capital	?	Rent expense	500
Salary expense	2,000	Cash	750

Required

1.   What type of business organization is High-and-Dry Delivery Service? How can you tell?
2.   Prepare the balance sheet of High-and-Dry Delivery Service as of September 30, 19X2.

E1-10   Presented below are the balance of the assets, liabilities, owner's equity, revenues, and expenses of Albeitz Import Service at December 31, 19X3, the end of its first year of business. During the year, V. Albeitz, the owner, invested $15,000 in the business.

Income statement (Obj. 2, 5)

Note payable	$ 30,000	Office furniture	$45,000
Utilities expense	6,800	Rent expense	24,000
Accounts payable	3,300	Cash	3,600
V. Albeitz, capital	27,100	Office supplies	4,800
Service revenue	151,200	Salary expense	49,000
Accounts receivable	9,000	Salaries payable	2,000
Supplies expense	4,000	Property tax expense	1,200

Required

1. Prepare the income statement of Albeitz Import Service for the year ended December 31, 19X3.
2. What was the amount of the proprietor's withdrawals during the year?

CHALLENGE EXERCISES

Transaction analysis, effects on financial statements
(Obj. 4)

E1-11   Opportunity Associates conducts summer camps for children with disabilities. Because of the nature of its business, Opportunity experiences many unusual transactions. Evaluate each of the following transactions in terms of its effect on Opportunity Associates' income statement and balance sheet.

a. A camper suffered an injury that was not covered by insurance. Opportunity paid $320 for the child's medical care. How does this transaction affect the income statement and the balance sheet?

b. Opportunity sold land adjacent to the camp for $190,000, receiving cash of $50,000 and a note receivable for $140,000. When purchased five years earlier, the land cost Opportunity $120,000. How should Opportunity account for the sale of the land?

c. Some campers cannot pay their fees, so Opportunity solicits donations for camp scholarships. Because Opportunity Associates is organized to earn a profit, donation receipts are treated as revenue. How should Opportunity account for a donation receipt of a small building valued at $45,000?

d. One camper's mother is a physician. Opportunity allows this child to attend camp in return for the mother's serving part-time in the camp infirmary for the two-week term. The standard fee for a camp term is $600. The physician's salary for this part-time work would be $600. How should Opportunity account for this arrangement?

e. Camp counselors build playground equipment during their off-duty hours. If Opportunity had purchased this equipment, it would have cost $2,000. But counselors are paid only their room, board, and transportation to and from camp. Should this equipment be included in Opportunity's financial statements? If so, where, and at what dollar amount?

Using the financial statements
(Obj. 5)

E1-12   Compute the missing amounts for each of the following companies.

	Green Co.	White Co.	Black Co.
Beginning:			
Assets	$ 50,000	$ 90,000	$110,000
Liabilities	20,000	60,000	50,000
Ending:			
Assets	$ 70,000	$?	$160,000
Liabilities	35,000	80,000	70,000
Owner's Equity:			
Investments by owner	$ 0	$ 10,000	$?
Withdrawals by owner	40,000	70,000	100,000
Income Statement:			
Revenues	$210,000	$400,000	$430,000
Expenses	?	300,000	320,000

PROBLEMS (GROUP A)

Analyzing a loan request
(Obj. 1, 3)

P1-1A   As an analyst for First National Bank, it is your job to write recommendations to the bank's loan committee. Curry Company has submitted these summary data at the top of page 29 to support Curry's request for a $100,000 loan.

Required

Analyze these financial statement data to decide whether the bank should lend $100,000 to Curry Company. Write a one-paragraph recommendation to the loan committee.

Income Statement Data:	19X5	19X4	19X3
Total revenues	$850,000	$770,000	$720,000
Total expenses	640,000	570,000	540,000
Net income	$210,000	$200,000	$180,000

Statement of Owner's Equity Data:	19X5	19X4	19X3
Beginning capital	$450,000	$390,000	$330,000
Add: Net income	210,000	200,000	180,000
	660,000	590,000	510,000
Less: Withdrawals	160,000	140,000	120,000
Ending capital	$500,000	$450,000	$390,000

Balance Sheet Data:	19X5	19X4	19X3
Total assets	$740,000	$670,000	$590,000
Total liabilities	$240,000	$220,000	$200,000
Total owner's equity	500,000	450,000	390,000
Total liabilities and owner's equity	$740,000	$670,000	$590,000

P1-2A Clarence Graff practiced law with a large firm, a partnership, for five years after graduating from law school. Recently he resigned his position to open his own law office, which he operates as a proprietorship. The name of the new entity is Clarence Graff, Attorney. Graff experienced the following events during the organizing phase of his new business and its first month of operations. Some of the events were personal and did not affect his law practice. Others were business transactions and should be accounted for by the business. *Entity concept, transaction analysis, accounting equation (Obj. 2, 4)*

Feb. 4 Graff received $80,000 cash from his former partners in the law firm from which he resigned.

5 Graff deposited $60,000 cash in a new business bank account entitled Clarence Graff, Attorney.

6 Graff paid $300 cash for letterhead stationery for his new law office.

7 Graff purchased office furniture for his law office. He agreed to pay the account payable, $7,000, within six months.

10 Graff sold 500 shares of IBM stock, which he and his wife had owned for several years, receiving $75,000 cash from his stockbroker.

11 Graff deposited the $75,000 cash from sale of the IBM stock in his personal bank account.

12 A representative of a large company telephoned Graff and told him of the company's intention to transfer its legal business to the new entity of Clarence Graff, Attorney.

18 Graff finished court hearings on behalf of a client and submitted his bill for legal services, $4,000. Graff expected to collect from this client within two weeks.

25 Graff paid office rent, $1,000.

28 Graff withdrew $2,000 cash from the business for personal living expenses.

Required

1. Classify each of the preceding events as one of the following:
   a. A business transaction to be accounted for by the proprietorship of Clarence Graff, Attorney.
   b. A business-related event but not a transaction to be accounted for by the proprietorship of Clarence Graff, Attorney.
   c. A personal transaction not to be accounted for by the proprietorship of Clarence Graff, Attorney.
2. Analyze the effects of the above events on the accounting equation of the proprietorship of Clarence Graff, Attorney. Use a format similar to that in Exhibit 1-6.

P1-3A The bookkeeper of Murtz Auction Co. prepared the balance sheet of the company while the accountant was ill. The balance sheet contains numerous errors. In particular, the bookkeeper knew that the balance sheet should balance, so he plugged in the owner's equity amount needed to achieve this balance. The owner's equity amount, however, is not correct. All other amounts are accurate. *Balance sheet (Obj. 2, 5)*

```
                    MURTZ AUCTION CO.
                     BALANCE SHEET
                 MONTH ENDED JULY 31, 19X3
```

Assets		Liabilities	
Cash	$ 3,000	Accounts receivable	$ 3,000
Office supplies	1,000	Service revenue.............................	59,000
Land...	44,000	Property tax expense.....................	800
Advertising expense......................	2,500	Accounts payable	9,000
Office furniture............................	10,000	**Owner's Equity**	
Note payable................................	16,000		
Rent expense...............................	4,000	Owner's equity	8,700
Total assets..................................	$80,500	Total liabilities	$80,500

Required

1. Prepare the correct balance sheet, and date it correctly. Compute total assets, total liabilities, and owner's equity.

2. Identify the accounts listed above that should *not* be presented on the balance sheet and state why you excluded them from the correct balance sheet you prepared for Requirement 1.

Balance sheet, entity concept
(Obj. 2, 3, 5)

P1-4A Charlotte Braun is a realtor. She buys and sells properties on her own, and she also earns commission as a real estate agent for buyers and sellers. She organized her business as a proprietorship on November 24, 19X4. Consider the following facts as of November 30, 19X4:

a. Braun owed $85,000 on a note payable for some undeveloped land that had been acquired by her business for a total price of $140,000.

b. Braun's business had spent $20,000 for a Century 21 real estate franchise, which entitled her to represent herself as a Century 21 agent. Century 21 is a national affiliation of independent real estate agents. This franchise is a business asset.

c. Braun owed $120,000 on a personal mortgage on her personal residence, which she acquired in 19X1 for a total price of $170,000.

d. Braun had $10,000 in her personal bank account and $12,000 in her business bank account.

e. Braun owed $1,800 on a personal charge account with Neiman-Marcus Department Store.

f. Braun acquired business furniture for $17,000 on November 25. Of this amount, her business owed $6,000 on open account at November 30.

g. Office supplies on hand at the real estate office totaled $1,000.

Required

1. Prepare the balance sheet of the real estate business of Charlotte Braun, Realtor, at November 30, 19X4.

2. Identify the personal items given in the preceding facts that would not be reported on the balance sheet of the business.

Business transactions and analysis
(Obj. 4)

P1-5A Campanelli Company was recently formed. The balance of each item in the company's accounting equation is shown below for June 10 and for each of the nine following business days.

	Cash	Accounts Receivable	Supplies	Land	Accounts Payable	Owner's Equity
June 10	$ 8,000	$4,000	$1,000	$ 8,000	$4,000	$17,000
11	13,000	4,000	1,000	8,000	4,000	22,000
12	6,000	4,000	1,000	15,000	4,000	22,000
15	6,000	4,000	3,000	15,000	6,000	22,000
16	5,000	4,000	3,000	15,000	5,000	22,000
17	7,000	2,000	3,000	15,000	5,000	22,000
18	16,000	2,000	3,000	15,000	5,000	31,000
19	13,000	2,000	3,000	15,000	2,000	31,000
22	11,000	2,000	5,000	15,000	2,000	31,000
23	5,000	2,000	5,000	15,000	2,000	25,000

Required

Assuming that a single transaction took place on each day, describe briefly the transaction that was most likely to have occurred, beginning with June 11. Indicate which accounts were affected and by what amount. No revenue or expense transactions occurred on these dates.

Income statement, statement of owner's equity, balance sheet (Obj. 5)

P1-6A Presented below are the amounts of (a) the assets and liabilities of Wilke Hardware as of December 31 and (b) the revenues and expenses of the company for the year ended on that date. The items are listed in alphabetical order.

Accounts payable	$ 19,000	Note payable	$ 85,000
Accounts receivable	12,000	Property tax expense	4,000
Advertising expense	13,000	Rent expense	23,000
Building	170,000	Salary expense	63,000
Cash	10,000	Salary payable	1,000
Furniture	20,000	Service revenue	200,000
Interest expense	9,000	Supplies	3,000
Land	58,000		

The beginning amount of Chris Wilke, capital, was $150,000, and during the year Wilke withdrew $70,000 for personal use.

Required

1. Prepare the entity's income statement for the year ended December 31 of the current year.
2. Prepare the statement of owner's equity of the company for the year ended December 31.
3. Prepare the balance sheet of the company at December 31.

Transaction analysis, accounting equation, financial statements (Obj. 4, 5)

P1-7A Lisa Owen owns and operates an interior design studio called Owen Interiors. The following amounts summarize the financial position of her business on August 31, 19X2:

	Assets				= Liabilities	+ Owner's Equity
	Cash +	Accounts Receivable +	Supplies +	Land =	Accounts Payable +	Lisa Owen, Capital
Bal.	1,250	1,500		12,000	8,000	6,750

During September 19X2 the following events occurred:

a. Owen inherited $20,000 and deposited the cash in the business bank account.
b. Performed services for a client and received cash of $700.
c. Paid off the beginning balance of accounts payable.
d. Purchased supplies on account, $1,000.
e. Collected cash from a customer on account, $1,000.
f. Invested personal cash of $1,000 in the business.
g. Consulted on the interior design of a major office building and billed the client for services rendered, $2,400.
h. Recorded the following business expenses for the month:
   (1) Paid office rent—$900.
   (2) Paid advertising—$100.
i. Sold supplies to another business for $150 cash, which was the cost of the supplies.
j. Withdrew cash of $1,800 for personal use.

Required

1. Analyze the effects of the above transactions on the accounting equation of Owen Interiors. Adapt the format of Exhibit 1-6.
2. Prepare the income statement of Owen Interiors for the month ended September 30, 19X2. List expenses in decreasing order by amount.
3. Prepare the entity's statement of owner's equity for the month ended September 30, 19X2.
4. Prepare the balance sheet of Owen Interiors at September 30, 19X2.
5. What did you learn from working this problem?
6. How will what you learned help you manage a business?

Analyzing a loan request
(Obj. 1, 3)

P1-1B   As an analyst for Guaranty Bank, it is your job to write recommendations to the bank's loan committee. Shamrock Enterprises has submitted these summary data to support the company's request for a $400,000 loan:

Income Statement Data:	19X5	19X4	19X3
Total revenues	$890,000	$830,000	$820,000
Total expenses	640,000	570,000	540,000
Net income	$250,000	$260,000	$280,000

Statement of Owner's Equity Data:	19X5	19X4	19X3
Beginning capital	$380,000	$400,000	$390,000
Add: Net income	250,000	260,000	280,000
	630,000	660,000	670,000
Less: Withdrawals	290,000	280,000	270,000
Ending capital	$340,000	$380,000	$400,000

Balance Sheet Data:	19X5	19X4	19X3
Total assets	$730,000	$700,000	$660,000
Total liabilities	$390,000	$320,000	$260,000
Total owner's equity	340,000	380,000	400,000
Total liabilities and owner's equity	$730,000	$700,000	$660,000

Required

Analyze these financial statement data to determine whether the bank should lend $400,000 to Shamrock Enterprises. Write a one-paragraph recommendation to the loan committee.

Entity concept, transaction
analysis, accounting equation
(Obj. 2, 4)

P1-2B   Carol Thompson practiced law with a large firm, a partnership, for 10 years after graduating from law school. Recently she resigned her position to open her own law office, which she operates as a proprietorship. The name of the new entity is Carol Thompson, Attorney and Counselor. Thompson experienced the following events during the organizing phase of her new business and its first month of operations. Some of the events were personal and did not affect the law practice. Others were business transactions and should be accounted for by the business.

July 1	Thompson sold 1,000 shares of Eastman Kodak stock, which she had owned for several years, receiving $88,000 cash from her stockbroker.
2	Thompson deposited in her personal bank account the $88,000 cash from sale of the Eastman Kodak stock.
3	Thompson received $150,000 cash from her former partners in the law firm from which she resigned.
5	Thompson deposited $140,000 cash in a new business bank account entitled Carol Thompson, Attorney and Counselor.
6	A representative of a large company telephoned Thompson and told her of the company's intention to transfer its legal business to the new entity of Carol Thompson, Attorney and Counselor.
7	Thompson paid $550 cash for letterhead stationery for her new law office.
9	Thompson purchased office furniture for the law office, agreeing to pay the account payable, $9,500, within three months.
23	Thompson finished court hearings on behalf of a client and submitted her bill for legal services, $3,000. She expected to collect from this client within one month.
30	Thompson paid office rent, $1,900.
31	Thompson withdrew $3,500 cash from the business for personal living expenses.

Required

1.   Classify each of the preceding events as one of the following:

    a.   A business transaction to be accounted for by the proprietorship of Carol Thompson, Attorney and Counselor.

    b.   A business-related event but not a transaction to be accounted for by the proprietorship of Carol Thompson, Attorney and Counselor.

c. A personal transaction not to be accounted for by the proprietorship of Carol Thompson, Attorney and Counselor.

2. Analyze the effects of the above events on the accounting equation of the proprietorship of Carol Thompson, Attorney and Counselor. Use a format similar to Exhibit 1-6.

P1-3B The bookkeeper of Jackson Travel Agency prepared the balance sheet of the company while the accountant was ill. The balance sheet contains numerous errors. In particular, the bookkeeper knew that the balance sheet should balance, so he plugged in the owner's equity amount needed to achieve this balance. The owner's equity amount, however, is not correct. All other amounts are accurate.

Balance sheet
(Obj. 2, 5)

JACKSON TRAVEL AGENCY
BALANCE SHEET
MONTH ENDED OCTOBER 31, 19X7

Assets		Liabilities	
Cash...	$ 3,400	Notes receivable	$14,000
Advertising expense	300	Interest expense	2,000
Land	40,500	Office supplies	800
Salary expense	3,300	Accounts receivable	2,600
Office furniture	6,700	Note payable................................	30,000
Accounts payable	3,000	**Owner's Equity**	
Utilities expense...........................	2,100		
		Owner's equity	9,900
Total assets	$59,300	Total liabilities	$59,300

Required

1. Prepare the correct balance sheet, and date it correctly. Compute total assets, total liabilities, and owner's equity.

2. Identify the accounts listed above that should *not* be presented on the balance sheet and state why you excluded them from the correct balance sheet you prepared for Requirement 1.

P1-4B James Renfro is a realtor. He buys and sells properties on his own, and he also earns commission as a real estate agent for buyers and sellers. He organized his business as a proprietorship on March 10, 19X2. Consider the following facts as of March 31, 19X2:

Balance sheet, entity concept
(Obj. 2, 3, 5)

a. Renfro had $5,000 in his personal bank account and $9,000 in his business bank account.

b. Office supplies on hand at the real estate office totaled $1,000.

c. Renfro's business had spent $15,000 for an Electronic Realty Associates (ERA) franchise, which entitled him to represent himself as an ERA agent. ERA is a national affiliation of independent real estate agents. This franchise is a business asset.

d. Renfro owed $33,000 on a note payable for some undeveloped land that had been acquired by his business for a total price of $70,000.

e. Renfro owed $65,000 on a personal mortgage on his personal residence, which he acquired in 19X1 for a total price of $90,000.

f. Renfro owed $950 on a personal charge account with Sears.

g. He had acquired business furniture for $12,000 on March 26. Of this amount, Renfro's business owed $6,000 on open account at March 31.

Required

1. Prepare the balance sheet of the real estate business of James Renfro, Realtor, at March 31, 19X2.

2. Identify the personal items given in the preceding facts that would not be reported on the balance sheet of the business.

P1-5B ClayDesta Oil Company was recently formed. The balance of each item in the company's accounting equation follows for August 4 and for each of the nine business days given:

Business transactions and analysis
(Obj. 4)

	Cash	Accounts Receivable	Supplies	Land	Accounts Payable	Owner's Equity
Aug. 4	$3,000	$7,000	$ 800	$11,000	$3,800	$18,000
9	4,000	6,000	800	11,000	3,800	18,000
14	2,000	6,000	800	11,000	1,800	18,000
17	2,000	6,000	1,100	11,000	2,100	18,000
19	3,000	6,000	1,100	11,000	2,100	19,000
20	1,900	6,000	1,100	11,000	1,000	19,000
22	7,900	6,000	1,100	5,000	1,000	19,000
25	7,900	6,200	900	5,000	1,000	19,000
26	7,700	6,200	1,100	5,000	1,000	19,000
28	2,600	6,200	1,100	10,100	1,000	19,000

Required

Assuming that a single transaction took place on each day, describe briefly the transaction that was most likely to have occurred beginning with August 9. Indicate which accounts were affected and by what amount. No revenues or expense transactions occurred on these dates.

Income statement, statement of owner's equity, balance sheet (Obj. 5)

P1-6B Presented below are the amounts of (a) the assets and liabilities of Shelby Delivery Service as of December 31 and (b) the revenues and expenses of the company for the year ended on that date. The items are listed in alphabetical order.

Accounts payable	$12,000	Note payable	$ 31,000
Accounts receivable	6,000	Property tax expense	2,000
Building	26,000	Rent expense	14,000
Cash	4,000	Salary expense	38,000
Equipment	21,000	Service revenue	120,000
Interest expense	4,000	Supplies	17,000
Interest payable	1,000	Utilities expense	3,000
Land	8,000		

The beginning amount of Chris Shelby, Capital, was $11,000, and during the year Shelby withdrew $32,000 for personal use.

Required

1. Prepare the income statement of Shelby Delivery Service for the year ended December 31 of the current year.
2. Prepare the statement of owner's equity of the company for the year ended December 31 .
3. Prepare the balance sheet of the company at December 31.

Transaction analysis, accounting equation, financial statements (Obj. 4, 5)

P1-7B K. T. Barr owns and operates an interior design studio called Barr Designers. The following amounts summarize the financial position of her business on April 30, 19X5:

	Assets				=	Liabilities	+	Owner's Equity
	Cash +	Accounts Receivable +	Supplies +	Land	=	Accounts Payable	+	K. T. Barr, Capital
Bal.	1,720	2,240		24,100		5,400		22,660

During May 19X5 the following events occurred:

a. Barr received $12,000 as a gift and deposited the cash in the business bank account.
b. Paid off the beginning balance of accounts payable.
c. Performed services for a client and received cash of $1,100.
d. Collected cash from a customer on account, $750.
e. Purchased supplies on account, $720.
f. Consulted on the interior design of a major office building and billed the client for services rendered, $5,000.
g. Invested personal cash of $1,700 in the business.
h. Recorded the following business expenses for the month:
   (1) Paid office rent—$1,200.
   (2) Paid advertising—$660.

i. Sold supplies to another interior designer for $80 cash, which was the cost of the supplies.

j. Withdrew cash of $2,400 for personal use.

Required

1. Analyze the effects of the above transactions on the accounting equation of Barr Designers. Adapt the format of Exhibit 1-6.

2. Prepare the income statement of Barr Designers for the month ended May 31, 19X5. List expenses in decreasing order by amount.

3. Prepare the statement of owner's equity of Barr Designers for the month ended May 31, 19X5.

4. Prepare the balance sheet of Barr Designers at May 31.

5. What did you learn from working this problem?

6. How will what you learned help you manage a business?

EXTENDING YOUR KNOWLEDGE

DECISION PROBLEMS

1. The proprietors of two businesses, Benet Drug Store and Andrea Arnold, Consulting Psychologist, have sought business loans from you. To decide whether to make the loans, you have requested their balance sheets.

Using financial statements to evaluate a request for a loan (Obj. 1, 2, 6)

BENET DRUG STORE
BALANCE SHEET
AUGUST 31, 19X4

Assets		Liabilities	
Cash	$ 9,000	Accounts payable	$ 12,000
Accounts receivable	14,000	Note payable	18,000
Merchandise inventory...............	85,000	Total liabilities	30,000
Store supplies	500	**Owner's Equity**	
Furniture and fixtures.................	9,000		
Building	82,000	Bob Benet, capital	183,500
Land...	14,000	Total liabilities	
Total assets.................................	$213,500	and owner's equity	$213,500

ANDREA ARNOLD, CONSULTING PSYCHOLOGIST
BALANCE SHEET
AUGUST 31, 19X4

Assets		Liabilities	
Cash	$11,000	Accounts payable	$ 3,000
Accounts receivable	4,000	Note payable	18,000
Office supplies	1,000	Total liabilities	21,000
Office furniture	6,000	**Owner's Equity**	
Land...	19,000		
		Andrea Arnold, capital	20,000
		Total liabilities	
Total assets.................................	$41,000	and owner's equity	$41,000

Required

1. Solely on the basis of these balance sheets, to which entity would you be more comfortable lending money? Explain fully, citing specific items and amounts from the balance sheets.

2. In addition to the balance sheet data, what other financial statement information would you require? Be specific.

2. A friend learns that you are taking an accounting course. Knowing that you do not plan a career in accounting, the friend asks you why you are "wasting your time." Explain to the friend:

1. Why you are taking the course.
2. How accounting information is used and will be used:
   a. In your personal life.
   b. In the business life of your friend, who plans to be a farmer.
   c. In the business life of another friend who plans a career in sales.

ETHICAL ISSUE

The board of directors of Abrahamson Corporation is meeting to discuss the past year's results before releasing financial statements to the public. The discussion includes this exchange:

Mark Abrahamson, company president: "Well, this has not been a good year! Revenue is down and expenses are up—way up. If we don't do some fancy stepping, we'll report a loss for the third year in a row. I can temporarily transfer some land that I own into the company's name, and that will beef up our balance sheet. Gwen, can you shave $500,000 from expenses? Then we can probably get the bank loan that we need."

Gwen Netherton, company chief accountant: "Mark, you are asking too much. Generally accepted accounting principles are designed to keep this sort of thing from happening."

Required

1. What is the fundamental ethical issue in this situation?
2. Discuss how the company president's proposals violate generally accepted accounting principles. Identify the specific concept or principle involved, and also refer to specifics from the AICPA Code of Professional Conduct.

FINANCIAL STATEMENT PROBLEMS

1. This and similar problems in succeeding chapters focus on the financial statements of a real company—Lands' End, Inc., a catalog merchandising company. As you study each problem, you will gradually build the confidence that you can understand and use actual financial statements.

Refer to the Lands' End financial statements in Appendix A.

Required

1. How much in cash (including cash equivalents) did Lands' End, Inc., have on January 28, 1994?
2. What were total assets at January 28, 1994? At January 29, 1993?
3. Write the company's accounting equation at January 28, 1994, by filling in the dollar amounts:

ASSETS = LIABILITIES + STOCKHOLDERS' EQUITY

4. Identify net sales (revenue) for the year ended January 28, 1994. (Net sales means sales revenue after certain subtractions.)
5. How much net income or net loss did Lands' End, Inc., experience for the year ended January 28, 1994? Was the year ended January 28, 1994, a good year or a bad year compared to the preceding year? State your reasons.

2. Obtain the annual report of a real company of your choosing. Annual reports are available in various forms, including the original document in hard copy and computerized databases such as that provided by Disclosure, Inc.

Required

Answer the following questions about the company. Concentrate on the current year in the annual report you select, except as directed for particular questions.

1. How much in cash (which may include cash equivalents) did the company have at the end of the current year? At the end of the preceding year? Did cash increase or decrease during the current year? By how much?

2. What were total assets at the end of the current year? At the end of the preceding year?

3. Write the company's accounting equation at the end of the current year by filling in the dollar amounts:

$$\textbf{ASSETS = LIABILITIES + } \begin{array}{c} \textbf{OWNERS' OR} \\ \textbf{STOCKHOLDERS'} \end{array} \textbf{EQUITY}$$

4. Identify net sales revenue for the current year. The company may label this as *Net sales, Sales, Net revenue*, or other title. How much was the corresponding revenue amount for the preceding year?

5. How much net income or net loss did the company experience for the current year? For the preceding year? Evaluate the current year's operations in comparison with the preceding year.

Appendix

The Accounting Profession: Career Opportunities

This appendix discusses the accounting profession in a sequence that does not interrupt the flow of the text material. It discusses the work of accountants and the organizations that influence the accounting profession. Study it either before you cover the main text material or after.

The Work of Accountants

Positions in the field of accounting may be divided into several areas. Two general classifications are *private accounting* and *public accounting.*

Private accountants work for a single business, such as a local department store, the McDonald's restaurant chain, or the Eastman Kodak Company. Charitable organizations, educational institutions, and government agencies also employ private accountants. The chief accounting officer usually has the title of controller, treasurer, or chief financial officer. Whatever the title, this person usually carries the status of a vice-president.

Public accountants are those who serve the general public and collect professional fees for their work, much as doctors and lawyers do. Their work includes auditing, income tax planning and preparation, and management consulting. These specialized accounting services are discussed in a later section. Public accountants are a small fraction (about 10 percent) of all accountants. Those public accountants who have met certain professional requirements are designated as *certified public accountants (CPAs).*

Some public accountants pool their talents and work together within a single firm. Most public accounting firms are called *CPA firms* because most of their professional employees are CPAs. CPA firms vary greatly in size. Some are small businesses, and others are large partnerships. The largest CPA firms are worldwide partnerships with more than 2,000 partners. The six largest U.S. accounting firms, often called the Big Six, are, in alphabetical order,

Arthur Andersen & Co.	Ernst & Young
Coopers & Lybrand	KPMG Peat Marwick
Deloitte & Touche	Price Waterhouse

Although these firms employ only about 12 percent of the 350,000 CPAs in the United States, they audit the financial statements of approximately 85 percent of the 2,600 largest corporations. The top partners in the large accounting firms earn about the same amount as the top managers of other large businesses.

Exhibit 1A-1 shows the accounting positions within public accounting firms and other organizations. Of special interest in the exhibit is the upward movement of accounting personnel, as the arrows show. In particular, note how accountants may move from positions in public accounting firms to similar or higher positions in industry and government. This is a frequently traveled career path. Because accounting deals with all facets of an organization—such as purchasing, manufacturing, marketing, and distribution—it provides an excellent basis for gaining broad business experience.

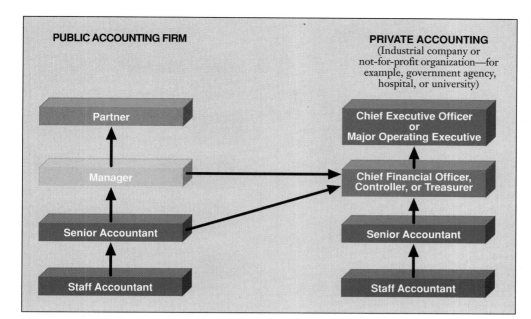

PUBLIC ACCOUNTING FIRM

PRIVATE ACCOUNTING
(Industrial company or not-for-profit organization—for example, government agency, hospital, or university)

Partner

Manager

Senior Accountant

Staff Accountant

Chief Executive Officer or Major Operating Executive

Chief Financial Officer, Controller, or Treasurer

Senior Accountant

Staff Accountant

Specialized Accounting Services

Because accounting affects people in many different fields, public accounting and private accounting include specialized services.

Public Accounting

Auditing is one of the accounting profession's most significant services to the public. An audit is the independent examination that ensures the reliability of the reports that management submits to investors, creditors, and others outside the business. In carrying out an audit, CPAs from outside a business examine the business's financial statements. If the CPAs believe that these documents are a fair presentation of the business's operations, the CPAs give a professional opinion stating that the firm's financial statements are in accordance with generally accepted accounting principles, which is the standard. Why is the audit so important? Creditors considering loans want assurance that the facts and figures the borrower submits are reliable. Stockholders, who have invested in the company, need to know that the financial picture management shows them is complete. Government agencies need accurate information from businesses.

Tax accounting has two aims: complying with the tax laws and minimizing the taxes to be paid. Because federal income tax rates range as high as 39.6 percent for individuals and 35 percent for corporations, reducing income tax is an important management consideration. Tax work by accountants consists of preparing tax returns and planning business transactions to minimize taxes. CPAs advise individuals on what type of investments to make and on how to structure their transactions.

Management consulting is the catchall term that describes the wide scope of advice CPAs provide to help managers run a business. As CPAs conduct audits, they look deep into a business's operations. With the insight they gain, they often make suggestions for improvements in the business's management structure and accounting systems. Management consulting is the fastest-growing service provided by accountants.

Private Accounting

Cost accounting analyzes a business's costs to help managers control expenses. Good cost accounting records guide managers in pricing their products and services to

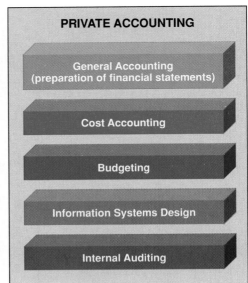

PUBLIC ACCOUNTING

Auditing

Tax Planning and Preparation

Management Consulting
(cost accounting, budgeting,
information systems design)

PRIVATE ACCOUNTING

General Accounting
(preparation of financial statements)

Cost Accounting

Budgeting

Information Systems Design

Internal Auditing

achieve greater profits. Also, cost accounting information shows management when a product is not profitable and should be dropped.

Budgeting sets sales and profit goals and develops detailed plans—called budgets—for achieving those goals. Some of the most successful companies in the United States have been pioneers in the field of budgeting—Procter & Gamble and General Electric, for example.

Information systems design identifies the organization's information needs, both internal and external. Using flow charts and manuals, designers develop and implement the system to meet those needs.

Internal auditing is performed by a business's own accountants. Large organizations—Motorola, Bank of America, and 3M among them—maintain a staff of internal auditors. These accountants evaluate the firm's own accounting and management systems to improve operating efficiency and ensure that employees follow management's policies.

Exhibit 1A-2 summarizes these accounting specializations.

Accounting Organizations and Designations

The position of accounting in today's business world has created the need for control over the professional, educational, and ethical standards for accountants.

The *American Institute of Certified Public Accountants (AICPA)* is the national professional organization of CPAs. A CPA is a professional accountant who earns this title through a combination of education, qualifying experience, and an acceptable score on a written national examination that takes approximately three days. The AICPA prepares and grades the examination and gives the results to the individual states, which then issue licenses that enable qualifying people to practice accounting as CPAs. CPAs must also be of high moral character and must conduct their professional practices according to a code of professional conduct.

The Auditing Standards Board of the AICPA formulates generally accepted auditing standards, which govern the way CPAs perform audits. The AICPA publishes a monthly professional journal, the *Journal of Accountancy*.

The *Financial Accounting Standards Board (FASB)* formulates *generally accepted accounting principles (GAAP)*. These principles are the most important accounting guidelines. The FASB issues documents called *financial accounting standards*, which are to financial accounting what government laws are to our general conduct. The

FASB, composed of seven members, is governed by the Financial Accounting Foundation and is an independent organization.

The *Institute of Management Accountants (IMA)*, formerly the *National Association of Accountants (NAA)*, focuses on the practice of management accounting, which is designed to help manage a business. A *CMA—certified management accountant—*earns this designation under the direction of the IMA. The IMA publishes the journal *Management Accounting.*

The *American Accounting Association (AAA)* focuses on the academic and research aspect of accounting. A high percentage of its members are professors. The AAA publishes quarterly journals, *The Accounting Revue, Accounting Horizons,* and *Issues in Accounting Education.*

The *Securities and Exchange Commission (SEC)* is an agency of the U.S. government with the legal power to set and enforce accounting and auditing standards. The SEC has delegated much of this authority to the FASB and the AICPA.

The *Internal Revenue Service (IRS)*, another federal agency, enforces the tax laws and collects the revenue needed to finance the government.

IMA Standards of Ethical Behavior

The opening paragraph of the IMA Standards of Ethical Conduct states: "Management accountants have an obligation to the organizations they serve, their profession, the public, and themselves to maintain the highest standards of ethical conduct." The Ethical Standards include sections on competence, confidentiality, integrity, objectivity, and resolution of ethical conflict. The requirements for a high level of professional conduct are similar to those in the AICPA code.

The Boeing Company's Business Conduct Guidelines

Most corporations set standards of ethical conduct for their employees. The Boeing Company, a leading manufacturer of aircraft, has a highly developed set of business conduct guidelines. In the introduction to those guidelines, the chairperson of the board and chief executive officer state: "We owe our success as much to our reputation for integrity as we do to the quality and dependability of our products and services. This reputation is fragile and can easily be lost." For example, Boeing could be ruined if shoddy work led to plane crashes.

Chapter 2
Recording Business Transactions

1. Define and use key accounting terms: *account, ledger, debit,* and *credit*

2. Apply the rules of debit and credit

3. Record transactions in the journal

4. Post from the journal to the ledger

5. Prepare a trial balance

6. Set up a chart of accounts for a business

7. Analyze transactions without a journal

"I had to create financial statements to generate more business. I hired an accountant to organize and present the information. This helped me run the business better. My accountant calls accounting the 'thermometer of business'—it tells you not just hot or cold, but how hot or how cold."

RENATO NAHAS,
DIRECTOR OF COMPACTA

Renato Antonio Nahas graduated with a degree in engineering from the university in Sao Paulo, Brazil. After graduation, Nahas took a job with his brother Raul's building renovation firm. Within a couple of years, he had learned the business of cleaning and polishing the concrete exteriors of buildings and had made enough contacts in Rio de Janeiro to launch his own renovation company there. He called the company Compacta—Central de restauracao e revestimentos Ltda. Early on, the business had only a few clients. Expenses consisted of Nahas's withdrawals, the salary of a small construction crew, and supplies. For several months Nahas kept his accounting records in a notebook.

At the end of the first year, Nahas tallied his revenue: 50 million cruzeiros (approximately $80,000). To expand the business, he needed to convince the owners of larger buildings, such as the Copacabana Palace Hotel, to hire him. The larger the deal, the more Nahas had to prove the strength of Compacta. Nahas was forced to consider the financial statements that customers required before they would accept his bid. He had to hire an accountant (a *contador*, in Portuguese) to prepare the statements to show how well Compacta had performed and where it stood financially.

• • • • •

Renato Nahas sounds a lot like Julie DeFilippo, the entrepreneur in the beginning of Chapter 1. Both appear headed for success. It takes several qualities to succeed in business: a product or service that customers demand, the ability to deliver the product or service at a competitive price, and the perseverance to keep working when it would be easier to quit.

At some point most businesses must keep score to measure the results of operations, cash flows, and financial position. Renato Nahas has an immediate need for accounting information. His potential clients require financial statements to learn how stable his business is. The statements include income information by which to predict Compacta's likely income over the next year or two, what resources Nahas has to work with (assets), and how much he already owes (liabilities). Overall, the clients want to predict the likelihood that Nahas can handle their renovation projects, and accounting information helps make the prediction.

Chapter 1 introduced accounting by analyzing the effects of transactions on the accounting equation. That approach emphasizes analysis, but it becomes unwieldy if many transactions occur. In practice, accountants do most of their work by computer. This chapter focuses on processing accounting information as it is done in practice. The illustrations show what is going on behind the scenes to help a business like Compacta operate more efficiently.

The Account

OBJECTIVE 1

Define and use key accounting terms: account, ledger, debit, and credit

◄▮▮▮ ◄▮▮▮ ◄▮▮▮ Recall that in Chapter 1, p. 11, we learned that the accounting equation is the most basic tool of the accountant. It measures the assets of the business and the claims to those assets.

The basic summary device of accounting is the **account.** This is the detailed record of the changes that have occurred in a particular asset, liability, or owner's equity during a period of time. For convenient access to the information, accounts are grouped in a record called the **ledger.** In the phrases "keeping the books" and "auditing the books," *books* refers to the ledger. Today the ledger usually takes the form of a computer listing.

Accounts are grouped in three broad categories, according to the accounting equation: ◄▮▮▮

ASSETS = LIABILITIES + OWNER'S EQUITY

Assets

Assets are the economic resources that benefit the business and will continue to do so in the future. Most firms use the following asset accounts.

CASH   The Cash account shows the cash effects of a business's transactions. Cash means money and any medium of exchange that a bank accepts at face value, such as bank account balances, paper currency, coins, certificates of deposit, and checks. Most business failures result from a shortage of cash.

NOTES RECEIVABLE   A business may sell its goods or services in exchange for a promissory note, which is a written pledge that the customer will pay the business a fixed amount of money by a certain date. The Notes Receivable account is a record of the promissory note the business expects to collect in cash. Renato Nahas may demand a note receivable when he completes a job because a note receivable offers more security for collection than a mere account receivable does.

Key Point: A receivable is always an asset. A payable is always a liability.

ACCOUNTS RECEIVABLE   A business may sell its goods or services in exchange for an oral or implied promise for future cash receipt. Such sales are made on credit ("on account"). The Accounts Receivable account contains these amounts. Most sales in the United States and in other developed countries are made on account receivable.

PREPAID EXPENSES   A business often pays certain expenses in advance. A prepaid expense is an asset because the business avoids having to pay cash in the future for the specified expense. The ledger holds a separate asset account for each prepaid expense. Prepaid Rent, Prepaid Insurance, and Office Supplies are accounted for as prepaid expenses.

LAND   The Land account is a record of the cost of land a business owns and uses in its operations. Land held for sale is accounted for separately—in an investment account.

BUILDING The cost of a business's buildings—office, warehouse, garage, and the like—appear in the Building account. Buildings held for sale are separate assets accounted for as investments.

EQUIPMENT, FURNITURE, AND FIXTURES A business has a separate asset account for each type of equipment—Office Equipment and Store Equipment, for example. The Furniture and Fixtures account shows the cost of this asset, which is similar to equipment.

Other asset categories and accounts will be discussed as needed. For example, many businesses have an Investments account for their investments in the stocks and bonds of other companies.

Liabilities

Recall that a *liability* is a debt. A business generally has fewer liability accounts than asset accounts because a business's liabilities can be summarized under relatively few categories.

NOTES PAYABLE The Notes Payable account is the opposite of the Notes Receivable account. Notes Payable represents the amounts that the business must pay because it signed a promissory note to borrow money or to purchase goods or services.

ACCOUNTS PAYABLE The Accounts Payable account is the opposite of the Accounts Receivable account. The oral or implied promise to pay off debts arising from credit purchases appears in the Accounts Payable account. Such a purchase is said to be made on account.

ACCRUED LIABILITIES Liability categories and accounts are added as needed. Taxes Payable, Interest Payable, and Salary Payable are liability accounts of most companies.

Owner's Equity

The owner's claim to the assets of the business is called *owner's equity*. In a proprietorship or a partnership, owner's equity is often split into separate accounts for the owner's capital balance and the owner's withdrawals.

CAPITAL The Capital account shows the owner's claim to the assets of the business. After total liabilities are subtracted from total assets, the remainder is the owner's capital. The owner's investments in the business are recorded directly in the Capital account. As we shall see, the Capital balance equals the owner's investments in the business plus its net income and minus net losses and owner withdrawals over the entire life of the business.

WITHDRAWALS When Renato Nahas withdraws cash or other assets from the business for personal use, the business's assets and owner's equity decrease. The amounts taken out of the business appear in a separate account entitled Withdrawals, or Drawing. If withdrawals were recorded directly in the Capital account, the amount of owner withdrawals would not be highlighted and decision making would be more difficult. The Withdrawals account shows a *decrease* in owner's equity.

REVENUES The increase in owner's equity created by delivering goods or services to customers or clients is called *revenue*. The ledger contains as many revenue accounts as needed. Renato Nahas's renovation business would need a Service Revenue account for amounts earned by providing cleaning services for clients. If a business loans money to an outsider, it will need an Interest Revenue account for the interest earned on the loan. If the business rents a building to a tenant, it will need a Rent Revenue account.

Short Exercise: Name two things that (1) increase owner's equity; (2) decrease owner's equity. *A:* (1) Investments by owner and net income (revenue greater than expenses). (2) Withdrawals by owner and net loss (expenses greater than revenue).

EXPENSES   The cost of operating a business is called *expense*. Expenses have the opposite effect of revenues, so they decrease owner's equity. A business needs a separate account for each type of expense, such as Salary Expense, Rent Expense, Advertising Expense, and Utilities Expense. Businesses strive to minimize their expenses to maximize net income.

Exhibit 2-1 shows how asset, liability, and owner's equity accounts can be grouped into the ledger.

EXHIBIT 2-1

The Ledger (Asset, Liability, and Owner's Equity Accounts)

Double-Entry Accounting

Accounting is based on a *double-entry system*, which means that we record the *dual effects* of a business transaction. *Each transaction affects at least two accounts*. For example, Gary Lyon's $50,000 cash investment in his accounting practice increased both the Cash account and the Capital account of the business. It would be incomplete to record only the increase in the entity's cash without recording the increase in its owner's equity.

Consider a *cash purchase of supplies*. What are the dual effects of this transaction? The purchase (1) decreases cash and (2) increases supplies. A *purchase of supplies on credit* (1) increases supplies and (2) increases accounts payable. A *cash payment on account* (1) decreases cash and (2) decreases accounts payable. All transactions have at least two effects on the entity.

The T-Account

How do we record transactions? The account format used most widely in this book is called the *T-account* because it takes the form of the capital letter "T." The vertical line in the letter divides the account into its left and right sides. The account title rests on the horizontal line. For example, the Cash account of a business appears in the following T-account format:

Key Point: A T-account is a quick way to show the effect of transactions on a particular account—a useful shortcut in accounting.

Cash	
(Left side)	(Right side)
Debit	Credit

The left side of the account is called the **debit** side, and the right side is called the **credit** side. Often beginners in the study of accounting are confused by the words *debit* and *credit*. To become comfortable using them, remember that

> Debit = Left side
> Credit = Right side

Even though *left side* and *right side* are more descriptive, the terms *debit* and *credit* are deeply entrenched in business.[1]

Increases and Decreases in the Accounts

The type of an account determines how increases and decreases in it are recorded. For any given account, all increases are recorded on one side, and all decreases are recorded on the other side. Increases in *assets* are recorded in the left (debit) side of the account. Decreases in assets are recorded in the right (credit) side. Conversely, increases in *liabilities* and *owner's equity* are recorded by *credits*. Decreases in liabilities and owner's equity are recorded by *debits*. These are the *rules of debit and credit*.

In everyday conversation, we may praise someone by saying, "She deserves credit for her good work." In your study of accounting forget this general usage. Remember only that *debit means left side* and *credit means right side*. Whether an account is increased or decreased by a debit or credit depends on the type of account (Exhibit 2-2).

OBJECTIVE 2

Apply the rules of debit and credit

---

[1]The words *debit* and *credit* have a Latin origin (*debitum* and *creditum*). Pacioli, the Italian monk who wrote about accounting in the fifteenth century, used these terms.

EXHIBIT 2-2

The Accounting Equation and the Rules of Debit and Credit (The Effects of Debits and Credits on Assets, Liabilities, and Owner's Equity)

Accounting Equation:	Assets	=	Liabilities	+	Owner's Equity
Rules of Debit and Credit:	Debit + / Credit −		Debit − / Credit +		Debit − / Credit +

In a computerized accounting system, the computer interprets debits and credits as increases or decreases by account type. For example, a computer reads a debit to Cash as an increase to that account. But *debit* and *credit* are so deeply ingrained in accounting vocabulary that we use them even for computerized systems.

This pattern of recording debits and credits is based on the accounting equation:

ASSETS = LIABILITIES + OWNER'S EQUITY

Key Point: The accounting equation must balance after every transaction. But verifying that total assets = total liabilities + owner's equity is no longer necessary after every transaction. The equation will balance as long as the debits in each transaction equal the credits in the transaction.

Assets are on the opposite side of the equation from liabilities and owner's equity. Therefore increases and decreases in assets are recorded in the opposite manner from those in liabilities and owner's equity. And liabilities and owner's equity, which are on the same side of the equal sign, are treated in the same way. Exhibit 2-2 shows the relationship between the accounting equation and the rules of debit and credit.

To illustrate the ideas diagrammed in Exhibit 2-2, reconsider the first transaction from Chapter 1. Gary Lyon invested $50,000 in cash to begin his accounting practice. Which accounts of the business are affected? By what amounts? On what side (debit or credit)? The answer is that Assets and Capital would increase by $50,000, as the following T-accounts show:

ASSETS = LIABILITIES + OWNER'S EQUITY

Cash	Gary Lyon, Capital
Debit for Increase, 50,000	Credit for Increase, 50,000

Notice that Assets = Liabilities + Owner's Equity *and* that total debit amounts = total credit amounts. Exhibit 2-3 illustrates the accounting equation and Gary Lyon's first three transactions.

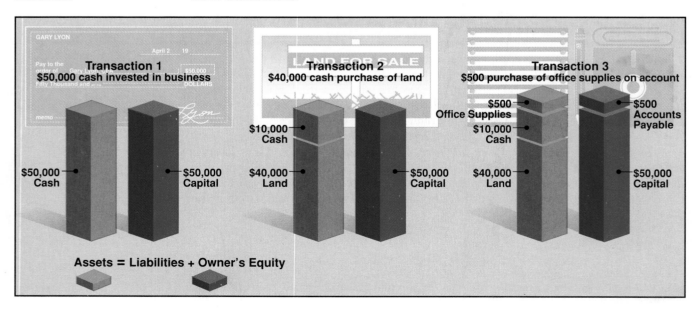

Transaction 1
$50,000 cash invested in business
$50,000 Cash / $50,000 Capital

Transaction 2
$40,000 cash purchase of land
$10,000 Cash / $40,000 Land / $50,000 Capital

Transaction 3
$500 purchase of office supplies on account
$500 Office Supplies / $10,000 Cash / $40,000 Land / $500 Accounts Payable / $50,000 Capital

Assets = Liabilities + Owner's Equity

The amount remaining in an account is called its *balance*. This initial action gives Cash a $50,000 debit balance and Gary Lyon, Capital a $50,000 credit balance.

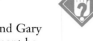

STOP & THINK Can you prepare a balance sheet and an income statement for Gary Lyon's accounting practice at this point? What would Lyon's financial statements report?

Answer: You could prepare a balance sheet that would report Cash, an asset, of $50,000 and Gary Lyon, Capital, an owner's equity, of $50,000. You would not yet prepare an income statement because the business has experienced no revenues or expenses.

The second transaction is a $40,000 cash purchase of land. This transaction affects two assets: Cash and Land. It decreases (credits) Cash and increases (debits) Land, as shown in the T-accounts:

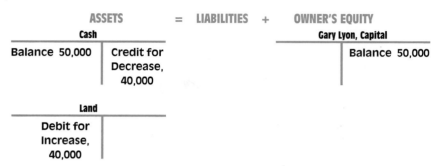

After this transaction, Cash has a $10,000 debit balance ($50,000 debit balance minus $40,000 credit amount), Land has a debit balance of $40,000, and Capital has a $50,000 credit balance, as shown in Exhibit 2-3.

Transaction 3 is a $500 purchase of office supplies on account. This transaction increases the asset Office Supplies and the liability Accounts Payable, as shown in the following accounts and in Exhibit 2-3:

We can create accounts as needed. The process of creating a new T-account in preparation for recording a transaction is called *opening the account*. For Transaction 1, we opened the Cash account and the Gary Lyon, Capital account. For Transaction 2, we opened the Land account and for Transaction 3, Office Supplies and Accounts Payable.

We could record all transactions directly in the accounts, as we have shown for the first three transactions. However, that way of accounting is not practical because it does not leave a clear record of each transaction. Suppose you need to know what accounts were affected by a particular transaction. Looking at each account in the ledger does not answer this question because double-entry accounting always affects at least two accounts. Therefore, you may have to search through all the accounts to find both sides of a particular transaction. To save time, accountants keep a record of each transaction in a journal and then transfer this information into the accounts.

Recording Transactions in Journals

OBJECTIVE 3

Record transactions in the journal

In practice, accountants record transactions first in a **journal**, which is a chronological record of the entity's transactions. The journalizing process follows these five steps:

1. Identify the transaction from source documents, such as bank deposit slips, sale receipts, and check stubs.

2. Specify each account affected by the transaction and classify it by type (asset, liability, or owner's equity).

3. Determine whether each account is increased or decreased by the transaction.

4. Using the rules of debit and credit, determine whether to debit or credit the account to record its increase or decrease.

5. Enter the transaction in the journal, including a brief explanation for the journal entry. The debit side of the entry is entered first and the credit side next.

We have discussed steps 1, 2, 3, and 4. Step 5, "Enter the transaction in the journal," means to record the transaction in the journal. This step is also called "making the journal entry" or "journalizing the transaction."

These five steps are completed in a computerized accounting system as well as in a manual system. In step 5, however, the journal entry is generally entered into the computer by account number, and the account name is then listed automatically. Most computer programs replace the explanation in the journal entry with some other means of tracing the entry back to its source documents.

Let's apply the five steps to journalize the first transaction of the accounting practice of Gary Lyon, CPA—the $50,000 cash investment in the business.

Step 1. The source documents are Lyon's bank deposit slip and $50,000 check, which is drawn on his personal bank account.

Step 2. *Cash* and *Gary Lyon, Capital* are the accounts affected by the transaction. Cash is an asset account, and Gary Lyon, Capital is an owner's equity account.

Step 3. Both accounts increase by $50,000. Therefore, Cash is the asset account that is increased, and Gary Lyon, Capital is the owner's equity account that is increased.

Step 4. Debit Cash to record an increase in this asset account. Credit Gary Lyon, Capital to record an increase in this owner's equity account.

Step 5. The journal entry is

Date	Accounts and Explanation	Debit	Credit
Apr. 2[a]	Cash[b]...	50,000[d]	
	Gary Lyon, Capital[c]...		50,000[e]
	Initial investment by owner.[f]		

Short Exercise: Prepare the journal entry to record a $1,600 payment on account. (1) Identify the accounts. (2) Are they increased or decreased? (3) Debit or credit? (4) Enter transaction, debit first. *A:* (1) Cash and Accounts Payable. (2) Both are decreased. (3) Debit Accounts Payable; reductions in liabilities are debits. Credit Cash; reductions in assets are credits. (4) Accounts Payable... 1,600
   Cash 1,600

The journal entry includes (a) the date of the transaction, (b) the title of the account debited (placed flush left), (c) the title of the account credited (indented slightly), the dollar amounts of the (d) debit (left) and (e) credit (right)—dollar signs are omitted in the money columns—and (f) a short explanation of the transaction.

A helpful hint: To get off to the best start when analyzing a transaction, first pinpoint its effects (if any) on cash. Did cash increase or decrease? Then find its effect on other accounts. Typically, it is easier to identify the cash effect of a transaction than to identify the effects on other accounts.

The journal offers information that the ledger accounts do not provide. Each journal entry shows the complete effect of a business transaction. Let's examine Gary Lyon's initial investment. The Cash account shows a single figure, the $50,000 debit. We know that every transaction has a credit, so in what account will we find the cor-

Journal				Page 6
Date	Accounts and Explanation	Debit	Credit	
Apr. 2	Cash	50,000		
	Gary Lyon, Capital...................		50,000	
	Initial investment by owner.			

EXHIBIT 2-4
The Journal

Key Point: In a journal entry, such as Exhibit 2-4, the account debited is always written first (not indented). The account credited is indented on the line below, and the explanation is not indented on the next line. Journal entries should always be recorded in this format.

responding $50,000 credit? In this simple illustration, we know that the Capital account holds this figure. But imagine the difficulties you would face trying to link debits and credits for hundreds of daily transactions—without a separate record of each transaction. The journal solves this problem and presents the full story for each transaction. Exhibit 2-4 shows how a journal page might look after the first transaction is recorded.

In these introductory discussions we temporarily ignore the date of each transaction to focus on the accounts and their dollar amounts.

Regardless of the accounting system in use, an accountant must analyze every business transaction in the manner we are presenting in these opening chapters. Once the transaction has been analyzed, a computerized accounting package performs the same actions as accountants do in a manual system. For example, when a sales clerk runs your MasterCard through the credit card reader, the underlying accounting system records the store's sales revenue and receivable from MasterCard. The computer automatically records the transaction as a journal entry, but an ac-

> *"When a sales clerk runs your MasterCard through the credit card reader, the underlying accounting system records the store's sales revenue and receivable from MasterCard."*

countant had to program the computer to do so. A computer's ability to perform routine tasks and mathematical operations fast and without error frees accountants for decision making.

Transferring Information (Posting) from the Journal to the Ledger

Posting means transferring the amounts from the journal to the appropriate accounts in the ledger. Debits in the journal are posted as debits in the ledger, and credits in the journal as credits in the ledger. The initial investment transaction of Gary Lyon is posted to the ledger, as shown in Exhibit 2-5. Computers perform this tedious task quickly and without error.

OBJECTIVE 4
Post from the journal to the ledger

EXHIBIT 2-5
Journal Entry and Posting to the Ledger

PANEL A—Journal Entry:

Accounts and Explanation	Debit	Credit
Cash	50,000	
Gary Lyon, Capital..............		50,000
Initial investment by owner.		

PANEL B—Posting to the Ledger:

Cash	Gary Lyon, Capital
50,000	50,000

Flow of Accounting Data

Exhibit 2-6 summarizes the flow of accounting data from the business transaction to the ledger. We continue the example of Gary Lyon, CPA, and account for six of his early transactions. Transactions that affect cash are the easiest to analyze. Therefore, when a transaction affects cash, we account for the cash effect first.

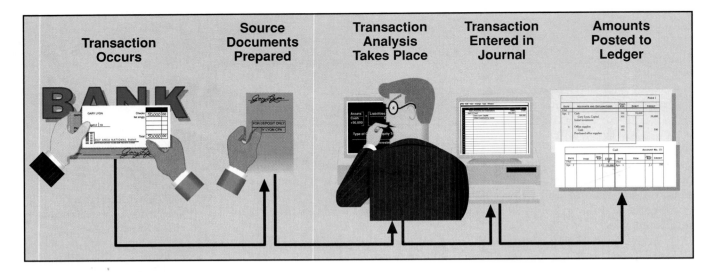

| Transaction Occurs | Source Documents Prepared | Transaction Analysis Takes Place | Transaction Entered in Journal | Amounts Posted to Ledger |

Transaction Analysis, Journalizing, and Posting

1. *Transaction:* Lyon invested $50,000 to begin his accounting practice.
   Analysis: Lyon's investment in the business increased its asset cash; to record this increase, debit Cash. His investment also increased the owner's equity of the entity; to record this increase, credit Gary Lyon, Capital.

   Journal Entry:

Cash	50,000	
Gary Lyon, Capital		50,000
Initial investment by owner.		

   Ledger Accounts:

Cash	Gary Lyon, Capital
(1) 50,000	(1) 50,000

 STOP & THINK Suppose you are a lender and Gary Lyon asks you for a $10,000 business loan. After his initial investment of $50,000, how would you evaluate Lyon as a credit risk? Would your evaluation differ if Lyon had invested $5,000 of his own money and owed $25,000 to another bank?

Answer: You would probably view the loan request favorably. Lyon has invested $50,000 of his own money in the business. The CPA practice has no debts, so Lyon should be able to repay you. However, if he had invested only $5,000 in the business and owed others $25,000, he would be a less attractive credit risk.

2. *Transaction:* He paid $40,000 cash for land as a future office location.
   Analysis: The purchase decreased cash; therefore, credit Cash. The purchase increased the entity's asset land; to record this increase, debit Land.

   Journal Entry:

Land	40,000	
Cash		40,000
Paid cash for land.		

   Ledger Accounts:

Cash		Land	
(1) 50,000	(2) 40,000	(2) 40,000	

3. *Transaction:* He purchased $500 office supplies on account payable.
   Analysis: The credit purchase of office supplies increased this asset; to record this increase, debit Office Supplies. The purchase also increased the

liability accounts payable; to record this increase, credit Accounts Payable.

Journal Entry:

Office Supplies 500
        Accounts Payable 500
Purchased office supplies on account.

Ledger Accounts:

Office Supplies	Accounts Payable
(3) 500	(3) 500

4. *Transaction:* He paid $400 on the account payable created in Transaction 3.
   Analysis: The payment decreased the asset cash; therefore, credit Cash. The payment also decreased the liability, accounts payable; to record this decrease, debit Accounts Payable.

Journal Entry:

Accounts Payable 400
        Cash 400
Paid cash on account.

Ledger Accounts:

Cash		Accounts Payable	
(1) 50,000	(2) 40,000	(4) 400	(3) 500
	(4) 400		

5. *Transaction:* He remodeled his personal residence. This is not a transaction of the accounting practice, so no journal entry is made.
6. *Transaction:* Lyon withdrew $2,100 cash for personal living expenses.
   Analysis: The withdrawal decreased the entity's cash; therefore, credit Cash. The transaction also decreased the owner's equity of the entity and must be recorded by a debit to an owner's equity account. Decreases in the owner's equity of a proprietorship that result from owner withdrawals are debited to a separate owner's equity account entitled Withdrawals. Therefore, debit Gary Lyon, Withdrawals.

Journal Entry:

Gary Lyon, Withdrawals 2,100
        Cash 2,100
Withdrawal of cash by owner.

Ledger Accounts:

Cash		Gary Lyon, Withdrawals
(1) 50,000	(2) 40,000	(6) 2,100
	(4) 400	
	(6) 2,100	

Each journal entry posted to the ledger is keyed by date or by transaction number. In this way, any transaction can be traced from the journal to the ledger and, if need be, back to the journal. This linking allows you to locate efficiently any information needed.

Accounts after Posting

We next illustrate how the accounts look when the amounts of the preceding transactions have been posted. The accounts are grouped under the accounting equation's headings.

Each account has a balance, denoted as Bal. This amount is the difference between the account's total debits and its total credits. For example, the balance in the Cash account is the difference between the debits, $50,000, and the credits, $42,500 ($40,000 + $400 + $2,100). Thus the cash balance is $7,500. The balance amounts are not journal entries posted to the accounts, so we set an account balance apart by horizontal lines.

ASSETS			=	LIABILITIES			+	OWNER'S EQUITY		
Cash				**Accounts Payable**				**Gary Lyon, Capital**		
(1) 50,000	(2)	40,000		(4) 400	(3)	500			(1)	50,000
	(4)	400			Bal.	100			Bal.	50,000
	(6)	2,100								
Bal. 7,500										

Office Supplies		**Gary Lyon, Withdrawals**	
(3) 500		(6) 2,100	
Bal. 500		Bal. 2,100	

Land	
(2) 40,000	
Bal. 40,000	

If the sum of an account's debits is greater than the sum of its credits, that account has a debit balance, as the Cash account does here. If the sum of its credits is greater, that account has a credit balance, as Accounts Payable does.

OBJECTIVE 5
Prepare a trial balance

Trial Balance

A **trial balance** is a list of all accounts with their balances—assets first, followed by liabilities and then owner's equity. It provides a check on accuracy by showing whether the total debits equal the total credits. A trial balance may be taken at any time the postings are up to date, but the most common time is at the end of the period. Exhibit 2-7 is the trial balance of the ledger of Gary Lyon's accounting practice after the first six transactions have been journalized and posted.

CORRECTING TRIAL BALANCE ERRORS The title *trial balance* is well chosen. The list is prepared to *test* the accounts' balances by showing whether the total debits and total credits are equal. If they are not equal, then accounting errors exist. Most computerized accounting systems prohibit the recording of unbalanced journal entries. Because the journal amounts are posted precisely as they have been journalized, trial balances will always balance. Hence computers minimize accounting errors. But they cannot *eliminate* errors, because human operators might input the amounts incorrectly.

Many out-of-balance conditions can be detected by computing the difference between total debits and total credits on the trial balance. Then perform one or more of the following:

1. Search the trial balance for a missing account. Trace each account and its balance from the ledger to the trial balance.

EXHIBIT 2-7
Trial Balance

GARY LYON, CPA TRIAL BALANCE APRIL 30, 19X1		
	Balance	
Account Title	**Debit**	**Credit**
Cash	$ 7,500	
Office supplies	500	
Land	40,000	
Accounts payable		$ 100
Gary Lyon, capital		50,000
Gary Lyon, withdrawals	2,100	
Total	$50,100	$50,100

2. Search the journal for the amount of difference. For example, suppose the total credits on Gary Lyon's trial balance equal $50,100 and total debits are $49,900. A $200 transaction may have been recorded incorrectly in the journal or posted incorrectly to the ledger. Search the journal for a $200 transaction.

3. Divide the difference between total debits and total credits by two. A debit treated as a credit, or vice versa, doubles the amount of error. Suppose Gary Lyon debited $300 to Cash instead of crediting the Cash account, or assume he posted a $300 credit as a debit. Total debits contain the $300, and total credits omit the $300. The out-of-balance amount is $600, and dividing by two identifies the $300 of the transaction. Then search the journal for a $300 transaction and trace to the account affected.

4. Divide the out-of-balance amount by nine. If the result is evenly divisible by nine, the error may be a *slide* (example: writing $61 as $610) or a *transposition* (example: treating $61 as $16). Suppose Gary Lyon wrote his $2,100 Withdrawals balance as $21,000 on the trial balance—a slide-type error. Total debits would differ from total credits by $18,900 ($21,000 – $2,100 = $18,900). Dividing $18,900 by 9 yields $2,100, the correct amount of withdrawals. Trace this amount through the ledger until you reach the Gary Lyon, Withdrawals account with a balance of $2,100. Computer-based systems avoid such errors.

Do not confuse the trial balance with the balance sheet. Accountants prepare a trial balance for their internal records. The company reports its financial position—both inside and outside the business—on the balance sheet, a formal financial statement. And remember that the financial statements are the focal point of the accounting process; the trial balance is merely a step in the preparation of the financial statements.

Short Exercise: Assume that Gary Lyon, Withdrawals, $2,100, is erroneously listed in the credit column on the trial balance in Exhibit 2-7. (1) Recompute the trial balance totals. (2) To find the mistake, calculate the difference between the column totals. (3) Then divide the difference by two. *A:* (1) Debit = $48,000; Credit = $52,200. (2) $52,200 – $48,000 = $4,200. (3) $4,200 ÷ 2 = $2,100.

If you find that amount somewhere on the trial balance, you may have entered it in the wrong column. This is one easy way to find an error if your trial balance does not balance.

SUMMARY PROBLEM FOR YOUR REVIEW — MID-CHAPTER

On August 1, 19X5, Liz Shea opens Shea's Research Service. She will be the owner of the proprietorship. During the entity's first 10 days of operations, these transactions take place:

a. To begin operations, Shea deposits $50,000 of personal funds in a bank account entitled Shea's Research Service.

b. Shea pays $40,000 cash for a small house to be used as an office.

c. Shea purchases office supplies for $500 on account.

d. Shea pays cash of $6,000 for office furniture.

e. Shea pays $150 on the account payable she created in Transaction (c).

f. Shea withdraws $1,000 cash for personal use.

Required

1. Journalize these transactions. Key the journal entries by letter.
2. Post the entries to the ledger.
3. Prepare the trial balance of Shea's Research Service at August 10, 19X5.

SOLUTION TO REVIEW PROBLEM

Requirement 1

	Accounts and Explanation	Debit	Credit
a.	Cash	50,000	
	Liz Shea, Capital		50,000
	Initial investment by owner.		
b.	Building	40,000	
	Cash		40,000
	Purchased building for an office.		

c. Office Supplies 500

        Accounts Payable 500

    Purchased office supplies on account.

d. Office Furniture 6,000

        Cash 6,000

    Purchased office furniture.

e. Accounts Payable 150

        Cash 150

    Paid cash on account.

f. Liz Shea, Withdrawals 1,000

        Cash 1,000

    Withdrew cash for personal use.

Requirement 2

ASSETS				LIABILITIES		OWNER'S EQUITY	

ASSETS

Cash

(a)	50,000	(b)	40,000
		(d)	6,000
		(e)	150
		(f)	1,000
Bal.	2,850		

Office Furniture

(d)	6,000	
Bal.	6,000	

Office Supplies

(c)	500	
Bal.	500	

Building

(b)	40,000	
Bal.	40,000	

LIABILITIES

Accounts Payable

(e)	150	(c)	500
		Bal.	350

OWNER'S EQUITY

Liz Shea, Capital

		(a)	50,000
		Bal.	50,000

Liz Shea, Withdrawals

(f)	1,000	
Bal.	1,000	

Requirement 3

SHEA'S RESEARCH SERVICE
TRIAL BALANCE
AUGUST 10, 19X5

	Balance	
Account Title	Debit	Credit
Cash	$ 2,850	
Office supplies	500	
Office furniture	6,000	
Building	40,000	
Accounts payable		$ 350
Liz Shea, capital		50,000
Liz Shea, withdrawals	1,000	
Total	$50,350	$50,350

Details of Journals and Ledgers

To focus on the main points of journalizing and posting, we purposely omitted certain essential data. In practice, the journal and the ledger provide additional details that create a "trail" through the accounting records for future reference. For example, a supplier may bill us twice for the same item we purchased on account. To prove we paid the bill, we would search the accounts payable records and work backward to the journal entry that recorded our payment. To see how this works, let's take a closer look at the journal and the ledger.

JOURNAL Exhibit 2-8, Panel B, presents a widely used journal format. The journal page number appears in the upper right corner. As the column headings indicate, the *journal* displays the following information:

1. The *date*, which indicates when the transaction occurred. The year appears only when the journal is started or when the year has changed. For our purposes, the

EXHIBIT 2-8
Details of Journalizing and Posting

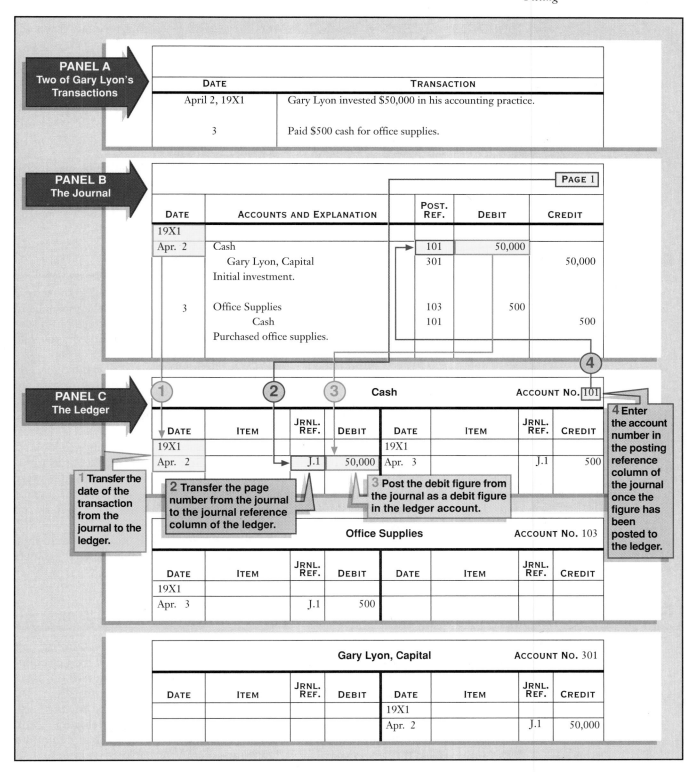

year appears with an X in the third, or decade's, position. Thus, 19X1 is followed by 19X2, and so on. The date of the transaction is recorded for every transaction.

2. The *account title* and explanation of the transaction, as in Exhibit 2-4.
3. The *posting reference*, abbreviated Post. Ref. How this column helps the accountant will become clear when we discuss the details of posting.
4. The *debit* column, which shows the amount debited.
5. The *credit* column, which shows the amount credited.

LEDGER Exhibit 2-8, Panel C, presents the *ledger* in T-account format. Each account has its own record in the illustrative ledger. Our example shows Gary Lyon's Cash account. This account maintains the basic format of the T-account but offers more information—for example, the account number at the upper right corner. Each account has its own identification number.

The column headings identify the ledger account's features:

1. The date.
2. The item column. This space is used for any special notation.
3. The journal reference column, abbreviated Jrnl. Ref. The importance of this column will become clear when we discuss the mechanics of posting.
4. The debit column, with the amount debited.
5. The credit column, with the amount credited.

Posting

We know that posting means transferring information from the journal to the ledger accounts. But how do we handle the additional details that appear in the journal and the ledger formats that we have just seen? Exhibit 2-8 illustrates the steps in full detail. Panel A lists two transactions of Gary Lyon, CPA; Panel B presents the journal; and Panel C shows the ledger.

Because the flow of accounting data moves from the journal to the ledger, you would first record the journal entry, as shown in Panel B. The transaction data are given in Panel A, except for the Post Ref. number. The journal's page number, Page 1, is copied from the journal to the journal reference column, Jrnl. Ref., of the ledger. Why bother with this detail? If you are using the Cash account and need to locate the original journal entry, the journal page number tells you where to look.

Once a dollar figure is posted to the appropriate account, that account's number is entered in the journal's Post. Ref. column (Arrow 4 of Exhibit 2-8). This step indicates that the information for that account has been transferred from the journal to the ledger. A blank Post Ref. column for a journal entry means that the entry has not yet been posted to the ledger account.

Having performed these steps for the debit amount of $50,000, you would then post the credit entry to the ledger. After posting, you can draw up the trial balance, as we discussed earlier.

Four-Column Account Format

The ledger accounts illustrated in Exhibit 2-8 are in two-column T-account format, with the debit column on the left and the credit column on the right. The T-account clearly distinguishes debits from credits and is often used for illustrative purposes that do not require much detail.

Another standard format has four amount columns, as illustrated for the Cash account in Exhibit 2-9. The first pair of amount columns are for the debit and credit amounts posted from individual entries, as just discussed. The second pair of amount columns are for the account's balance. This four-column format keeps a running bal-

Account Cash					Account No. 101	
Date	Item	Jrnl. Ref.	Debit	Credit	Balance Debit	Balance Credit
19X1 Apr. 2		J.1	50,000		50,000	
3		J.1		500	49,500	

EXHIBIT 2-9
Account in Four-Column Format

ance in the account. For this reason, it is used more often in practice than the two-column format. In Exhibit 2-9, Cash has a debit balance of $50,000 after the first transaction is posted and a debit balance of $49,500 after the second transaction.

Chart of Accounts

As you know, the ledger contains the business's accounts grouped under these headings:

1. Balance Sheet Accounts: Assets, Liabilities, and Owner's Equity
2. Income Statement Accounts: Revenues and Expenses.

To keep track of their accounts, organizations have a **chart of accounts,** which lists all the accounts and their account numbers. These account numbers are used as posting references, as illustrated by Arrow 4 in Exhibit 2-8. It is easier to input the account number, 101, in the posting reference column of the journal than to input the account title, Cash. Also, this numbering system makes it easy to locate individual accounts in the ledger.

Accounts are identified by account numbers with two or more digits. Assets are often numbered beginning with 1, liabilities with 2, owner's equity with 3, revenues with 4, and expenses with 5. The second, third, and higher digits in an account number indicate the position of the individual account within the category. For example, Cash may be account number 101, which is the first asset account. Accounts Receivable may be account number 111, the second asset account. Accounts Payable may be number 201, the first liability account. All accounts are numbered by this system.

Organizations with many accounts use lengthy account numbers. For example, the chart of accounts of Yankelovich-Clancy-Shulman, a leading marketing research firm, uses five-digit account numbers. Exhibit 2-10 lists some of Yankelovich's asset accounts. Clorox Corporation, maker of Clorox beach and Kingsford charcoal, uses account numbers

"Clorox Corporation, maker of Clorox bleach and Kingsford Charcoal, uses account numbers that are 35 digits long."

that are 35 digits long. The assignment material reflects the variety found in practice.

Account Number	Account Title
10100	Cash Chase [cash in Chase Manhattan Bank]
10130	Cash—Petty Cash [cash on hand]
10200	Accounts Receivable—Trade
10300	Accounts Receivable— Rent
10520	Prepaid Insurance
10530	Prepaid Rent
11110	Furniture & Fixtures
11140	Machinery & Equipment

EXHIBIT 2-10
Partial Chart of Accounts of Yankelovich-Clancy-Shulman

Balance Sheet Accounts:		
Assets	**Liabilities**	**Owner's Equity**
101 Cash	201 Accounts Payable	301 Gary Lyon, Capital
111 Accounts Receivable	231 Notes Payable	311 Gary Lyon, Withdrawals
141 Office Supplies		
151 Office Furniture		Income Statement Accounts (part of Owner's Equity):
191 Land		

Revenues	**Expenses**
401 Service Revenue	501 Rent Expense
	502 Salary Expense
	503 Utilities Expense

EXHIBIT 2-11

Chart of Accounts—Accounting Practice of Gary Lyon, CPA

◀▥◀▥◀▥ We learned in Chapter 1, p. 19, that balance sheet amounts report the assets, liabilities, and owner's equity of an entity as of a specific date; the income statement amounts report the revenues and expenses of the entity for a specific period of time.

The chart of accounts for Gary Lyon, CPA, appears in Exhibit 2-11. ◀▥ Notice the gap in account numbers between 111 and 141. Gary Lyon realizes that at some later date he may need to add another category of receivables—for example, Notes Receivable, numbered 121.

The chapter appendix gives two expanded charts of accounts that you will find helpful as you work through this course. The first chart lists the typical accounts of a large service proprietorship, such as Gary Lyon's accounting practice after a period of growth. The second chart is for a merchandising corporation, one that sells a product rather than a service. Study the service proprietorship chart of accounts now, and refer to the second chart of accounts as needed later.

Normal Balance of an Account

Key Point: The normal balance of an account is the side on which increases are recorded.

Short Exercise: Compute the missing amounts:

(1)	Capital	
		Bal. ?
22,000		56,000
		15,000
		Bal. 73,000

(2)	Cash	
Bal. 10,000		
20,000		13,000
Bal. ?		

(3)	Accounts Payable	
		Bal. 12,800
?		45,600
		Bal. 23,500

A: (1) $24,000; (2) $17,000; (3) $34,900

An account's *normal balance* is on the side of the account—debit or credit—where *increases* are recorded. That is, the normal balance is on the side that is positive. For example, Cash and other assets usually have a debit balance (the debit side is positive and the credit side negative), so the normal balance of assets is on the debit side, and assets are called *debit-balance accounts*. Conversely, liabilities and owner's equity usually have a credit balance, so their normal balances are on the credit side, and they are called *credit-balance accounts*. Exhibit 2-12 illustrates the normal balances of assets, liabilities, and owner's equity.

An account that normally has a debit balance may occasionally have a credit balance, which indicates a negative amount of the item. For example, Cash will have a temporary credit balance if the entity overdraws its bank account. Similarly, the liability Accounts Payable—normally a credit-balance account—will have a debit balance if the entity overpays its account. In other instances, the shift of a balance amount away from its normal column indicates an accounting error. For example, a credit balance in Office Supplies, Office Furniture, or Buildings indicates an error because negative amounts of these assets cannot exist.

Assets		=	**Liabilities**	+	**Owner's Equity**
Normal Bal. Debit			Normal Bal. Credit		Normal Bal. Credit

EXHIBIT 2-12

Normal Balances of Balance Sheet Accounts

As we have explained, owner's equity usually contains several accounts. In total, these accounts show a normal credit balance for the owner's equity of the business. Each owner's equity account has a normal credit balance if it represents an *increase* in owner's equity (for example, the Capital account in Exhibit 2-14). However, if the individual owner's equity account represents a *decrease* in owner's equity, the account will have a normal debit balance (for example, the Withdrawals account in Exhibit 2-14).

Additional Owner's Equity Accounts: Revenues and Expenses

The owner's equity category includes the two income statement accounts Revenues and Expenses. As we have discussed, *revenues* are increases in owner's equity that result from delivering goods or services to customers. *Expenses* are decreases in owner's equity due to the cost of operating the business. Therefore, the accounting equation may be expanded as shown in Exhibit 2-13. Revenues and expenses appear in parentheses because their net effect—revenues minus expenses—equals net income, which increases owner's equity. If expenses are greater, the net effect is a net loss, which decreases owner's equity.

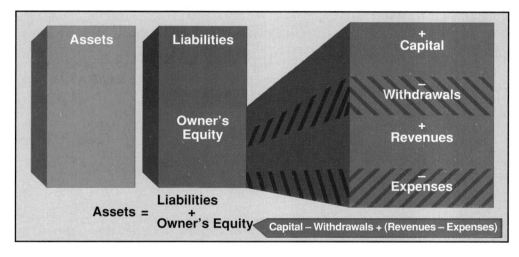

EXHIBIT 2-13
Expansion of the Accounting Equation

Key Point: Because withdrawals reduce capital, the Withdrawals account is sometimes referred to as a *contra equity* account, meaning that it has the opposite balance of capital.

We can now express the rules of debit and credit in final form, as shown in Exhibit 2-14, Panel A (page 62). Panel B shows the *normal* balances of the five types of accounts: *Assets; Liabilities;* and *Owner's Equity* and its subparts, *Revenues* and *Expenses*. All of accounting is based on these five types of accounts. You should not proceed until you have learned the rules of debit and credit and the normal balances of the five types of accounts.

Expanded Problem Including Revenues and Expenses

Let's account for the revenues and expenses of the law practice of Sara Nichols, Attorney, for the month of July 19X1. We follow the same steps illustrated earlier: Analyze the transaction, journalize, post to the ledger, and prepare the trial balance. Revenue accounts and expense accounts work just like asset, liability, and owner's equity accounts.

EXHIBIT 2-14

Rules of Debit and Credit and Normal Balances of Accounts

PANEL A—Rules of Debit and Credit:

Assets		=	Liabilities		+	Capital	
Debit for Increase	**Credit for** Decrease		**Debit for** Decrease	**Credit for** Increase		**Debit for** Decrease	**Credit for** Increase

Withdrawals	
Debit for Increase	**Credit for** Decrease

Revenues	
Debit for Decrease	**Credit for** Increase

PANEL B—Normal Balances:

Assets	Debit
Liabilities	Credit
Owner's Equity—overall	Credit
Capital	Credit
Withdrawals	Debit
Revenues	Credit
Expenses	Debit

Expenses	
Debit for Increase	**Credit for** Decrease

Transaction Analysis, Journalizing, and Posting

1. *Transaction:* Sara Nichols invested $10,000 cash in a business bank account to open her law practice.

   Analysis: The asset cash is increased; therefore, debit Cash. The owner's equity of the business increased; therefore, credit Sara Nichols, Capital.

   Journal Entry:

Cash	10,000	
Sara Nichols, Capital		10,000
Invested cash in the business.		

   Ledger Accounts:

Cash		Sara Nichols, Capital	
(1) 10,000			(1) 10,000

2. *Transaction:* Nichols performed service for a client and collected $3,000 cash.

   Analysis: The asset cash is increased; therefore, debit Cash. The revenue account Service Revenue is increased; credit Service Revenue.

   Journal Entry:

Cash	3,000	
Service Revenue		3,000
Performed service and received cash.		

   Ledger Accounts:

Cash		Service Revenue	
(1) **10,000**			(2) 3,000
(2) 3,000			

3. *Transaction:* Nichols performed service for a client and billed the client for $500 on account receivable. This means the client owes the business $500 even though the client signed no formal promissory note.

   Analysis: The asset accounts receivable is increased; therefore, debit Accounts Receivable. Service revenue is increased; credit Service Revenue.

Sara Nichols must keep track of the revenues and expenses of her law practice, Sara Nichols, Attorney.

Journal	Accounts Receivable	500	
Entry:	Service Revenue		500
	Performed service on account.		

Ledger
Accounts:

Accounts Receivable			Service Revenue	
(3) 500			(2) 3,000	
			(3) 500	

4. *Transaction:* Nichols performed legal service of $700 for a client, who paid $300 cash immediately. Nichols billed the remaining $400 to the client on account receivable.

   Analysis: The assets cash and accounts receivable are increased; therefore, debit both of these asset accounts. Service revenue is increased; credit Service Revenue for the sum of the two debit amounts.

Journal	Cash	300	
Entry:	Accounts Receivable	400	
	Service Revenue		700
	Performed service for cash and on account.		

   Note: Because this transaction affects more than two accounts at the same time, the entry is called a *compound entry*. No matter how many accounts a compound entry affects—there may be any number—total debits must equal total credits.

Ledger
Accounts:

Cash		Accounts Receivable		Service Revenue	
(1) 10,000		(3) 500		(2) 3,000	
(2) 3,000		(4) 400		(3) 500	
(4) 300				(4) 700	

5. *Transaction:* Nichols paid the following cash expenses: office rent, $900; employee salary, $1,500; and utilities, $500.

   Analysis: The asset cash is decreased; therefore, credit Cash for the sum of the three expense amounts. The following expenses are increased: Rent Expense, Salary Expense, and Utilities Expense. Each should be debited.

Journal	Rent Expense	900	
Entry:	Salary Expense	1,500	
	Utilities Expense..	500	
	Cash...		2,900
	Paid cash expenses.		

Ledger
Accounts:

Cash		Rent Expense	
(1) 10,000	(5) 2,900	(5) 900	
(2) 3,000			
(4) 300			

Salary Expense		Utilities Expense	
(5) 1,500		(5) 500	

6. *Transaction:* Nichols received a telephone bill for $120 and will pay this expense next week.

   Analysis: Utilities expense is increased; therefore, debit this expense. The liability accounts payable is increased; credit this account.

Journal   Utilities Expense...   120
Entry: Accounts Payable   120
         Received utility bill.

Key Point: Recording an expense does not necessarily involve a credit to cash. In Transaction 6 the expense is recorded now, but the cash will be paid later. Likewise, a debit to cash does not always reflect revenue. Transaction 7 records cash collected on a receivable (the revenue was recorded in Transaction 3).

Ledger Accounts:

Accounts Payable		Utilities Expense	
	(6) 120	(5) 500	
		(6) 120	

7. *Transaction:* Nichols collected $200 cash from the client established in Transaction 3.

Analysis: The asset cash is increased; therefore, debit Cash. The asset accounts receivable is decreased; therefore, credit Accounts Receivable.

Journal   Cash   200
Entry: Accounts Receivable   200
         Received cash on account.

Note: This transaction has no effect on revenue; the related revenue is accounted for in Transaction 3.

Ledger Accounts:

Cash		Accounts Receivable	
(1) 10,000	(5) 2,900	(3) 500	(7) 200
(2) 3,000		(4) 400	
(4) 300			
(7) 200			

8. *Transaction:* Nichols paid the telephone bill that was received and recorded in Transaction 6.

Analysis: The asset cash is decreased; credit Cash. The liability accounts payable is decreased; therefore, debit Accounts Payable.

Journal   Accounts Payable...   120
Entry: Cash...   120
         Paid cash on account.

Note: This transaction has no effect on expense because the related expense was recorded in Transaction 6.

Ledger Accounts:

Cash		Accounts Payable	
(1) 10,000	(5) 2,900	(8) 120	(6) 120
(2) 3,000	(8) 120		
(4) 300			
(7) 200			

9. *Transaction:* Nichols withdrew $1,100 cash for personal use.

Analysis: The asset cash decreased; credit Cash. The withdrawal decreased owner's equity; therefore, debit Sara Nichols, Withdrawals.

Journal   Sara Nichols, Withdrawals...............................   1,100
Entry: Cash...   1,100
         Withdrew for personal use.

Ledger Accounts:

Cash		Sara Nichols, Withdrawals	
(1) 10,000	(5) 2,900	(9) 1,100	
(2) 3,000	(8) 120		
(4) 300	(9) 1,100		
(7) 200			

Ledger Accounts after Posting

	ASSETS				LIABILITIES					OWNER'S EQUITY				

ASSETS

Cash

(1)	10,000	(5)	2,900
(2)	3,000	(8)	120
(4)	300	(9)	1,100
(7)	200		
Bal.	9,380		

Accounts Receivable

(3)	500	(7)	200
(4)	400		
Bal.	700		

LIABILITIES

Accounts Payable

(8)	120	(6)	120
		Bal.	0

OWNER'S EQUITY

Sara Nichols, Capital

		(1)	10,000
		Bal.	10,000

Sara Nichols, Withdrawals

(9)	1,100		
Bal.	1,100		

REVENUE

Service Revenue

		(2)	3,000
		(3)	500
		(4)	700
		Bal.	4,200

EXPENSES

Rent Expense

(5)	900	
Bal.	900	

Salary Expense

(5)	1,500	
Bal.	1,500	

Utilities Expense

(5)	500	
(6)	120	
Bal.	620	

Trial Balance

SARA NICHOLS, ATTORNEY
TRIAL BALANCE
JULY 31, 19X1

Account Title	Balance Debit	Balance Credit
Cash	$ 9,380	
Accounts receivable	700	
Accounts payable		$ 0
Sara Nichols, capital........................		10,000
Sara Nichols, withdrawals...............	1,100	
Service revenue.................................		4,200
Rent expense.....................................	900	
Salary expense...................................	1,500	
Utilities expense	620	
Total...	$14,200	$14,200

STOP & THINK Review the chapter-opening story and concentrate on Renato Nahas's need for financial statement information. How will the procedures you have applied in this chapter help Compacta convince potential customers that the business is stable?

Answer: The end product of the accounting process is a set of financial statements. Compacta's accounting records will generate the income statement and balance sheet that customers require of contractors before accepting a bid.

Use of Accounting Information for Quick Decision Making

What dominates the accountant's analysis of transactions: the accounting equation, the journal, or the ledger? The accounting equation is most fundamental. And the ledger is more useful than the journal in providing an overall model of the organization. The ledger includes all the accounts, which represent all the entity's assets, liabilities, owner's equity, revenues, and expenses. The journal is merely a record of transactions.

OBJECTIVE 7
Analyze transactions without a journal

Businesspeople must often make quick decisions without the benefit of a complete accounting system. For example, Norman Erickson, a barber in New Preston, Connecticut, may be renegotiating the rental of his shop. He may not have the time for a thorough recording of the effects of all the transactions. One who knows accounting can skip the journal and go directly to the ledger, compressing transaction analysis, journalizing, and posting into one step. This type of analysis saves time that may make the difference between a good business decision and a lost opportunity.

"Norman Erickson, a barber in New Preston, Connecticut, may be renegotiating the rental of his shop."

Erickson may be comparing the expense of renting the shop for $800 per month with the $75,000 cost of buying his own building. In the heat of negotiation, he doesn't have time to journalize and post all the likely transactions and prepare a trial balance. But if he knows some accounting, he can make this quick comparison:

Rent the Shop		Buy the Building	
Cash	**Rent Expense**	**Cash**	**Building**
800	800	75,000	75,000

Immediately Erickson can see that buying the building will require more cash. But he can also see that he will obtain the building as an asset. This may motivate him to borrow cash and buy the building.

Companies do not actually keep their records in this short-cut fashion. But a decision maker who needs information immediately need not perform all the accounting steps to analyze the effect of a set of transactions on the company's financial statements.

SUMMARY PROBLEM FOR YOUR REVIEW

The trial balance of Tomassini Computer Service Center on March 1, 19X2, lists the entity's assets, liabilities, and owner's equity on that date.

	Balance	
Account Title	**Debit**	**Credit**
Cash	$26,000	
Accounts receivable	4,500	
Accounts payable		$ 2,000
Larry Tomassini, capital		28,500
Total	$30,500	$30,500

During March the business engaged in the following transactions:

a. Borrowed $45,000 from the bank. He signed a note payable in the name of the business.
b. Paid cash of $40,000 to a real estate company to acquire land.
c. Performed service for a customer and received cash of $5,000.
d. Purchased supplies on credit, $300.
e. Performed customer service and earned revenue on account, $2,600.
f. Paid $1,200 on account.
g. Paid the following cash expenses: salaries, $3,000; rent, $1,500; and interest, $400.
h. Received $3,100 on account.

i. Received a $200 utility bill that will be paid next week.

j. Withdrew $1,800 for personal use.

Required

1. Open the following accounts, with the balances indicated, in the ledger of Tomassini Computer Service Center. Use the T-account format.

   Assets—Cash, $26,000; Accounts Receivable, $4,500; Supplies, no balance; Land, no balance

   Liabilities—Accounts Payable, $2,000; Note Payable, no balance

   Owner's Equity—Larry Tomassini, Capital, $28,500; Larry Tomassini, Withdrawals, no balance

   Revenues—Service Revenue, no balance

   Expenses—(none have balances) Salary Expense, Rent Expense, Utilities Expense, Interest Expense

2. Journalize the preceding transactions. Key journal entries by transaction letter.

3. Post to the ledger.

4. Prepare the trial balance of Tomassini Computer Service Center at March 31, 19X2.

5. Compute the net income or net loss of the entity during the month of March. List expenses in order from the largest to the smallest.

SOLUTION TO REVIEW PROBLEM

Requirement 1

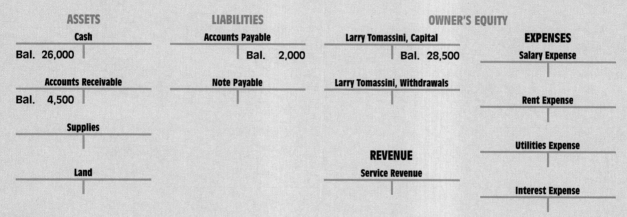

Requirement 2

Accounts and Explanation	Debit	Credit
a. Cash	45,000	
Note Payable...		45,000
Borrowed cash on note payable.		
b. Land..	40,000	
Cash		40,000
Purchased land for cash.		
c. Cash	5,000	
Service Revenue...		5,000
Performed service and received cash.		
d. Supplies...	300	
Accounts Payable		300
Purchased supplies on account.		
e. Accounts Receivable...	2,600	
Service Revenue...		2,600
Performed service on account.		
f. Accounts payable	1,200	
Cash		1,200
Paid on account.		

g.	Salary Expense..	3,000	
	Rent Expense..	1,500	
	Interest Expense...	400	
	Cash		4,900
	Paid cash expenses.		
h.	Cash	3,100	
	Accounts Receivable		3,100
	Received on account.		
i.	Utilities Expense	200	
	Accounts Payable		200
	Received utility bill.		
j.	Larry Tomassini, Withdrawals..	1,800	
	Cash		1,800
	Withdrew for personal use.		

Requirement 3

ASSETS

Cash

Bal.	26,000	(b)	40,000
(a)	45,000	(f)	1,200
(c)	5,000	(g)	4,900
(h)	3,100	(j)	1,800
Bal.	31,200		

Accounts Receivable

Bal.	4,500	(h)	3,100
(e)	2,600		
Bal.	4,000		

Supplies

(d)	300		
Bal.	300		

Land

(b)	40,000		
Bal.	40,000		

LIABILITIES

Accounts Payable

(f)	1,200	Bal.	2,000
		(d)	300
		(i)	200
		Bal.	1,300

Note Payable

		(a)	45,000
		Bal.	45,000

OWNER'S EQUITY

Larry Tomassini, Capital

		Bal.	28,500

Larry Tomassini, Withdrawals

(j)	1,800		
Bal.	1,800		

REVENUE

Service Revenue

		(c)	5,000
		(e)	2,600
		Bal.	7,600

EXPENSES

Salary Expense

(g)	3,000		
Bal.	3,000		

Rent Expense

(g)	1,500		
Bal.	1,500		

Utilities Expense

(i)	200		
Bal.	200		

Interest Expense

(g)	400		
Bal.	400		

Requirement 4

TOMASSINI COMPUTER SERVICE CENTER
TRIAL BALANCE
MARCH 31, 19X2

	Balance	
Account Title	Debit	Credit
Cash..	$31,200	
Accounts receivable.............................	4,000	
Supplies	300	
Land	40,000	
Accounts payable..................................		$ 1,300
Note payable		45,000
Larry Tomassini, capital.......................		28,500
Larry Tomassini, withdrawals..............	1,800	
Service revenue		7,600
Salary expense	3,000	
Rent expense	1,500	
Utilities expense	200	
Interest expense....................................	400	
Total..	$82,400	$82,400

Net income for the month of March

Revenue:		
Service revenue................		$7,600
Expenses:		
Salary expense	$3,000	
Rent expense....................	1,500	
Interest expense...............	400	
Utilities expense	200	
Total expenses		5,100
Net income		$2,500

SUMMARY

1. *Define key accounting terms:* account, ledger, debit, *and* credit. The *account* can be viewed in the form of the letter "T." The left side of each T-account is its *debit* side. The right side is its *credit* side. The *ledger*, which contains a record for each account, groups and numbers accounts by category in the following order: assets, liabilities, and owner's equity (and its subparts, revenues and expenses).

2. *Apply the rules of debit and credit.* *Assets* and *expenses* are increased by debits and decreased by credits. *Liabilities, owner's equity*, and *revenues* are increased by credits and decreased by debits. The side—debit or credit—of the account in which increases are recorded is that account's normal balance. Thus the normal balance of assets and expenses is a debit, and the normal balance of liabilities, owner's equity, and revenues is a credit. The Withdrawals account, which decreases owner's equity, normally has a debit balance. *Revenues*, which are increases in owner's equity, have a normal credit balance. *Expenses*, which are decreases in owner's equity, have a normal debit balance.

3. *Record transactions in the journal.* The accountant begins the recording process by entering the transaction's information in the *journal*, a chronological list of all the business's transactions.

4. *Post from the journal to the ledger.* The information is then posted—transferred—to the *ledger* accounts. Posting references are used to trace amounts back and forth between the journal and the ledger. Businesses list their account titles and numbers in a chart of accounts.

5. *Prepare a trial balance.* The *trial balance* is a summary of all the account balances in the ledger. When *double-entry accounting* has been done correctly, the total debits and the total credits in the trial balance are equal.

6. *Set up a chart of accounts for a business.* The first step in accounting is to set up the chart of accounts.

7. *Analyze transactions without a journal.* Decision makers must often make decisions without a complete accounting system. They can analyze the transactions without a journal.

We can now trace the flow of accounting information through these steps:

Business Transaction → Source Documents →
Journal Entry → Posting to Ledger → Trial Balance

SELF-STUDY QUESTIONS

Test your understanding of the chapter by marking the best answer for each of the following questions.

1. An account has two sides called the *(pp. 47–48)*
   - a. Debit and credit
   - b. Asset and liability
   - c. Revenue and expense
   - d. Journal and ledger

2. Increases in liabilities are recorded by *(pp. 47–48)*
   - a. Debits
   - b. Credits

3. Why do accountants record transactions in the journal? *(pp. 50–51)*
   - a. To ensure that all transactions are posted to the ledger
   - b. To ensure that total debits equal total credits
   - c. To have a chronological record of all transactions
   - d. To help prepare the financial statements

4. Posting is the process of transferring information from the *(p. 51)*
   - a. Journal to the trial balance
   - b. Ledger to the trial balance
   - c. Ledger to the financial statements
   - d. Journal to the ledger

5. The purchase of land for cash is recorded by a *(p. 52)*
   - a. Debit to Cash and a credit to Land
   - b. Debit to Cash and a debit to Land
   - c. Debit to Land and a credit to Cash
   - d. Credit to Cash and a credit to Land

6. The purpose of the trial balance is to *(p. 54)*
   - a. List all the accounts with their balances
   - b. Ensure that all transactions have been recorded
   - c. Speed the collection of cash receipts from the customers
   - d. Increase assets and owner's equity

7. What is the normal balance of the Accounts Receivable, Office Supplies, and Rent Expense accounts? *(p. 60)*
   - a. Debit
   - b. Credit

8. A business has Cash of $3,000, Notes Payable of $2,500, Accounts Payable of $4,300, Service Revenue of $7,000, and Rent Expense of $1,800. On the basis of these data, how much are its total liabilities? *(p. 61)*
   - a. $5,500
   - b. $6,800
   - c. $9,800
   - d. $13,800

9. Farber Company earned revenue on account. The journal entry to record this transaction is a *(pp. 62–63)*
   a. Debit to Cash and a credit to Revenue
   b. Debit to Accounts Receivable and a credit to Revenue
   c. Debit to Accounts Payable and a credit to Revenue
   d. Debit to Revenue and a credit to Accounts Receivable

10. The account credited for a receipt of cash on account is *(p. 64)*
    a. Cash
    b. Accounts Payable
    c. Service Revenue
    d. Accounts Receivable

Answers to the Self-Study Questions follow the Accounting Vocabulary.

ACCOUNTING VOCABULARY

Account. The detailed record of the changes that have occurred in a particular asset, liability, or owner's equity during a period *(p. 44)*.

Chart of accounts. List of all the accounts and their account numbers in the ledger *(p. 59)*.

Credit. The right side of an account *(p. 47)*.

Debit. The left side of an account *(p. 47)*.

Journal. The chronological accounting record of an entity's transactions *(p. 50)*.

Ledger. The book of accounts *(p. 44)*.

Posting. Transferring of amounts from the journal to the ledger *(p. 51)*.

Trial balance. A list of all the ledger accounts with their balances *(p. 54)*.

ANSWERS TO SELF-STUDY QUESTIONS

1. a
2. b
3. c
4. d
5. c
6. a
7. a
8. b ($6,800 = $2,500 + $4,300)
9. b
10. d

QUESTIONS

1. Name the basic summary device of accounting. What letter of the alphabet does it resemble? Name its two sides.
2. Is the following statement true or false? Debit means decrease and credit means increase. Explain your answer.
3. Write two sentences that use the term *debit* differently.
4. What are the three *basic* types of accounts? Name two additional types of accounts. To which one of the three *basic* types are these two additional types of accounts most closely related?
5. Suppose you are the accountant for Smith Courier Service. Keeping in mind double-entry bookkeeping, identify the *dual effects* of Mary Smith's investment of $10,000 cash in her business.
6. Briefly describe the flow of accounting information.
7. To what does the *normal balance* of an account refer?
8. Indicate the normal balance of the five types of accounts.

Account Type	Normal Balance
Assets	_____
Liabilities	_____
Capital	_____
Revenues	_____
Expenses	_____

9. What does posting accomplish? Why is it important? Does it come before or after journalizing?
10. Label each of the following transactions as increasing owner's equity (+), decreasing owner's equity (–), or as having no effect on owner's equity (0). Write the appropriate symbol in the space provided.
    ___ a. Investment by owner
    ___ b. Revenue transaction
    ___ c. Purchase of supplies on credit
    ___ d. Expense transaction
    ___ e. Cash payment on account
    ___ f. Withdrawal by owner
    ___ g. Borrowing money on a note payable
    ___ h. Sale of service on account

11. What four steps does posting include? Which step is the fundamental purpose of posting?
12. Rearrange the following accounts in their logical sequence in the ledger:

Notes Payable	Cash
Accounts Receivable	Jane East, Capital
Sales Revenue	Salary Expense

13. What is the meaning of the statement, Accounts Payable has a credit balance of $1,700?
14. Jack Brown Campus Cleaners launders the shirts of customer Bobby Baylor, who has a charge account at the cleaners. When Bobby picks up his clothes and is short of cash, he charges it. Later, when he receives his monthly statement from the cleaners, Bobby writes a check on Dear Old Dad's bank account and mails the check to Jack Brown. Identify the two business transactions described here. Which transaction increases Jack Brown's owner's equity? Which transaction increases Jack Brown's cash?
15. Explain the difference between the ledger and the chart of accounts.
16. Why do accountants prepare a trial balance?
17. What is a compound journal entry?
18. The accountant for Bower Construction Company mistakenly recorded a $500 purchase of supplies on account as a $5,000 purchase. He debited Supplies and credited Accounts Payable for $5,000. Does this error cause the trial balance to be out of balance? Explain your answer.
19. What is the effect on total assets of collecting cash on account from customers?
20. What is the advantage of analyzing transactions without the use of a journal? Describe how this "journal-less" analysis works.
21. Briefly summarize the similarities and differences between manual and computer-based accounting systems in terms of journalizing, posting, and the preparation of a trial balance.

EXERCISES

E2-1 Your employer, Metric Devices, Inc., has just hired an office manager who does not understand accounting. Metric's trial balance lists Cash of $43,900. Write a short memo to the office manager, explaining the accounting process that produced this listing on the trial balance. Mention *debits, credits, journals, ledgers, posting,* and so on.

Using accounting vocabulary
(Obj. 1)

E2-2 Analyze the following transactions in the manner shown for the December 1 transaction. Also record each transaction in the journal.

Analyzing and journalizing transactions
(Obj. 2, 3)

Dec. 1 Paid utilities expense of $1,200. (*Analysis:* The expense utilities expense is increased; therefore, debit Utilities Expense. The asset cash is decreased; therefore, credit Cash.)

```
  1   Utilities Expense..............................................................    1,200
          Cash......................................................................             1,200
```

```
  4   Borrowed $12,000 cash, signing a note payable.
  8   Performed service on account for a customer, $1,600.
 12   Purchased office furniture on account, $810.
 19   Sold for $74,000 land that had cost this same amount.
 24   Purchased building for $140,000; signed a note payable.
 27   Paid the liability created on December 12.
```

E2-3 Refer to Exercise 2-2.

Applying the rules of debit and credit
(Obj. 2)

Required

1. Open the following T-accounts with their December 1 balances: Cash, debit balance $6,000; Land, debit balance $74,000; Zack Beaty, Capital, credit balance $80,000.
2. Record the transaction of Exercise 2-2 directly in the T-accounts affected. Use the dates as posting references.
3. Compute the December 31 balance in each account, and prove that total debits equal total credits.

E2-4 Chin Consulting Service engaged in the following transactions during March 19X3, its first month of operations:

Journalizing transactions
(Obj. 3)

Mar. 1 Rudy Chin invested $59,000 of cash to start the business.
  2 He purchased office supplies of $200 on account.
  4 He paid $40,000 cash for a building to use as a future office.
  6 He performed service for customers and received cash, $2,000.
  9 He paid $100 on accounts payable.
 17 He performed service for customers on account, $1,600.
 23 He received $1,200 cash from a customer on account.
 31 He paid the following expenses: salary, $1,200; rent, $500.

Required

Record the preceding transactions in the journal of Chin Consulting Service. Key transactions by date and include an explanation for each entry, as illustrated in the chapter. Use the following accounts: Cash; Accounts Receivable; Office Supplies; Building; Accounts Payable; Rudy Chin, Capital; Service Revenue; Salary Expense; Rent Expense.

E2-5 Refer to Exercise 2-4.

Posting to the ledger and preparing a trial balance
(Obj. 4, 5)

Required

1. After journalizing the transactions of Exercise 2-4, post the entries to the ledger, using T-account format. Key transactions by date. Date the ending balance of each account Mar. 31.
2. Prepare the trial balance of Chin Consulting Service at March 31, 19X3.

E2-6 The journal of Benesh Company follows:

	Journal			Page 5
Date	**Accounts and Explanation**	**Post. Ref.**	**Debit**	**Credit**
Aug. 2	Cash		6,000	
	Dana Benesh, Capital			6,000
5	Cash		15,000	
	Note Payable..			15,000
9	Supplies...		270	
	Accounts Payable			270
11	Accounts Receivable..................................		2,630	
	Sales Revenue			2,630
14	Rent Expense...		4,200	
	Cash			4,200
22	Cash		1,400	
	Accounts Receivable			1,400
25	Advertising Expense		350	
	Cash			350
27	Accounts Payable.......................................		270	
	Cash			270
31	Utilities Expense		220	
	Accounts Payable			220

Required

1. Describe each transaction.
2. Post the transactions to the ledger using the following account numbers: Cash, 110; Accounts Receivable, 120; Supplies, 130; Accounts Payable, 210; Note Payable, 230; Dana Benesh, Capital, 310; Sales Revenue, 410; Rent Expense, 510; Advertising Expense, 520; Utilities Expense, 530. Use dates, journal references, and posting references as illustrated in Exhibit 2-8. You may write the account numbers as posting references directly in your book unless directed otherwise by your instructor.
3. Compute the balance in each account after posting. Prepare Benesh Company's trial balance at August 31, 19X6.

E2-7 The first five transactions of Sloan Security Company have been posted to the company's accounts as follows:

Cash				Supplies		Equipment		Land	
(1) 60,000	(3) 42,000		(2) 400			(5) 6,000		(3) 42,000	
(4) 7,000	(5) 6,000								

Accounts Payable		Note Payable		Robert Sloan, Capital	
	(2) 400		(4) 7,000		(1) 60,000

Required

Prepare the journal entries that served as the sources for the five transactions. Include an explanation for each entry as illustrated in the chapter.

E2-8 Prepare the trial balance of Sloan Security Company at April 30, 19X4, using the account data from Exercise 2-7.

E2-9 The accounts of Vito Realty Company follow with their normal balances at October 31, 19X4. The accounts are listed in no particular order.

Account	Balance
Giorgi Vito, capital	$48,800
Advertising expense	650
Accounts payable	4,300
Sales commission revenue	22,000
Land	29,000
Note payable	25,000
Cash	5,000
Salary expense	6,000
Building	45,000
Rent expense	2,000
Giorgi Vito, withdrawals	6,000
Utilities expense	400
Accounts receivable	5,500
Supplies expense	300
Supplies	250

Required

Prepare the company's trial balance at October 31, 19X4, listing accounts in proper sequence, as illustrated in the chapter. For example, Supplies comes before Building and Land. List the expense with the largest balance first, the expense with the next largest balance second, and so on.

E2-10 The trial balance of Mississippi Enterprises at February 28, 19X9, does not balance:

Correcting errors in a trial balance
(Obj. 5)

Cash	$ 4,200	
Accounts receivable	2,000	
Supplies	600	
Land	46,000	
Accounts payable		$ 3,000
Emily Johns, capital		41,600
Service revenue		9,700
Salary expense	1,700	
Rent expense	800	
Utilities expense	300	
Total	$55,600	$54,300

Investigation of the accounting records reveals that the bookkeeper:

a. Recorded a $400 cash revenue transaction by debiting Accounts Receivable. The credit entry was correct.

b. Posted a $1,000 credit to Accounts Payable as $100.

c. Did not record utilities expense or the related account payable in the amount of $200.

d. Understated Emily Johns, Capital, by $400.

Required

Prepare the correct trial balance at February 28, complete with a heading. Journal entries are not required.

E2-11 Open the following T-accounts: Cash; Accounts Receivable; Office Supplies; Office Furniture; Accounts Payable; Dolores Trevino, Capital; Dolores Trevino, Withdrawals; Service Revenue; Salary Expense; Rent Expense.

Recording transactions without a journal
(Obj. 7)

Record the following transactions directly in the T-accounts without using a journal. Use the letters to identify the transactions.

a. Dolores Trevino opened an accounting firm by investing $7,200 cash and office furniture valued at $5,400.

b. Paid monthly rent of $1,500.

c. Purchased office supplies on account, $800.

d. Paid employee salary, $1,800.

e. Paid $400 of the account payable created in Transaction (c).

f. Performed accounting service on account, $1,700.

g. Withdrew $2,000 for personal use.

Preparing a trial balance
(Obj. 5)

E2-12 After recording the transactions in Exercise 2-11, prepare the trial balance of Dolores Trevino, CPA, at May 31, 19X7.

SERIAL EXERCISE

Exercise 2-13 begins an accounting cycle that is completed in Chapter 5.

Recording transactions and preparing a trial balance
(Obj. 2, 3, 4, 5)

E2-13 Emily Schneider completed these transactions during the first half of December:

Dec. 2 Invested $12,000 to start an accounting practice, Emily Schneider, Accountant.
 2 Paid monthly office rent, $500.
 3 Paid cash for a Macintosh computer, $3,000. The computer is expected to remain in service for five years.
 4 Purchased office furniture on account, $3,600. The furniture should last for five years.
 5 Purchased supplies on account, $300.
 9 Performed tax service for a client and received cash for the full amount of $800.
 12 Paid utility expenses, $200.
 18 Performed consulting service for a client on account, $1,700.

Required

1. Open T-accounts in the ledger: Cash; Accounts Receivable; Supplies; Equipment; Furniture; Accounts Payable; Emily Schneider, Capital; Emily Schneider, Withdrawals; Service Revenue; Rent Expense; Utilities Expense; and Salary Expense.

2. Journalize the transactions. Explanations are not required.

3. Post to the T-accounts. Key all items by date, and denote an account balance as *Bal*. Formal posting references are not required.

4. Prepare a trial balance at December 18. In the Serial Exercise of Chapter 3, we will add transactions for the remainder of December and will require a trial balance at December 31.

CHALLENGE EXERCISES

Identifying the accounts of a new business
(Obj. 6)

E2-14 Jack Grimestad asks your advice in setting up the accounting records for his new business. The business will be a photography studio and will operate in a rented building. Grimestad will need office equipment, cameras, tripods, lights, backdrops, and so on. The business will borrow money to buy the needed equipment. Grimestad will purchase on account photographic supplies, such as film, paper, and developing solution, and office supplies. Each asset needs its own expense account, some of which have not yet been discussed. For example, equipment wears out (depreciates) and thus needs a depreciation account. As supplies are used up, the business must record a supplies expense.

Grimestad owns the land on which the studio building stands. He will contribute the land to the business, which will then pay the property tax on the land. A gas station located on a corner of the property will start paying its monthly rent to the photography studio. The studio will need an office manager to arrange appointments, keep the books, design advertisements, and pay the rent and the insurance in advance and the utility bills as they come due. Grimestad anticipates paying this person a weekly salary of $300.

He will want to know which aspects of the business are the most, and the least, profitable, so he will account for each category of service revenue separately: portraits, school pictures, and weddings. He will let his better customers open accounts with the business and expects to collect cash over a three-month period. The studio will carry an inventory of picture frames for sale to customers—a separate category of revenue.

Required

List all the accounts the photography studio will need, starting with the assets and ending with the expenses. Indicate which accounts will be reported on the balance sheet and which accounts will appear on the income statement.

E2-15   The owner of McBee Technical Services is an engineer with little understanding of accounting. He needs to compute the following summary information from the accounting records:

Computing financial statement amounts without a journal (Obj. 7)

a. Net income for the month of March.
b. Total cash paid during March.
c. Cash collections from customers during March.
d. Cash paid on a note payable during March.

The quickest way to compute these amounts is to analyze the following accounts:

	Balance		Additional Information for the Month of March
Account	**Feb. 28**	**Mar. 31**	
1. Owner, Capital....................	$9,200	$10,100	Withdrawals, $3,800
2. Cash.....................................	4,600	3,400	Cash receipts, $61,200
3. Accounts Receivable	24,300	26,700	Sales on account, $53,500
4. Note Payable.......................	13,900	17,400	New borrowing, $6,300

The net income for March can be computed as follows:

Owner, Capital			
March Withdrawals	**3,800**	Feb. 28 Bal.	9,200
		March Net income	x = $4,700
		March 31 Bal.	10,100

Use a similar approach to compute the other three items.

E2-16   Klutz Accountant has trouble keeping his debits and credits equal. During a recent month he made the following errors:

Analyzing accounting errors (Obj. 2, 3, 4, 5)

a. In journalizing a cash sale, Klutz debited Cash for $900 but accidentally credited Accounts Receivable.
b. Klutz posted a $700 utility expense as $70. The credit posting to Cash was correct.
c. In preparing the trial balance, Klutz omitted a $20,000 note payable.
d. Klutz recorded a $120 purchase of supplies on account by debiting Supplies and crediting Accounts Payable for $210.
e. In recording a $400 payment on account, Klutz debited Supplies and credited Accounts Payable.

Required

1. For each of these errors, state whether the total debits equal total credits on the trial balance.
2. Identify any accounts with misstated balances, and indicate the amount and direction of the error (account balance too high or too low).

PROBLEMS

(GROUP A)

P2-1A   The owner of Lamplighter Service Company is selling the business. She offers the trial balance shown on page 76 to prospective buyers.

Analyzing a trial balance (Obj. 1)

Your best friend is considering buying Lamplighter Service Company. He seeks your advice in interpreting this information. Specifically, he asks whether this trial balance is the same as a balance sheet and an income statement. He also wonders whether Lamplighter must be a sound company. After all, the accounts are in balance.

```
              LAMPLIGHTER SERVICE COMPANY
                     TRIAL BALANCE
                   DECEMBER 31, 19XX

    Cash...............................................   $ 12,000
    Accounts receivable........................    27,000
    Prepaid expenses ...........................     4,000
    Land.............................................    81,000
    Accounts payable...........................                    $ 35,000
    Note payable ................................                      32,000
    Jolyn Grant, capital ......................                      30,000
    Jolyn Grant, withdrawals ..............    18,000
    Service revenue .............................                    104,000
    Rent expense ................................    26,000
    Advertising expense......................     3,000
    Wage expense...............................    23,000
    Supplies expense...........................     7,000
                                                  $201,000         $201,000
```

Required

Write a short note to answer your friend's questions. To aid his decision, state how he can use the information on the trial balance to compute Lamplighter's net income or net loss for the current period. State the amount of net income or net loss in your note.

Analyzing and journalizing transactions (Obj. 2, 3)

P2-2A High View Theater Company owns movie theaters in the shopping centers of a major metropolitan area. Its owner, Crystal Stryker, engaged in the following business transactions:

Feb. 1 Stryker invested $60,000 personal cash in the business by depositing that amount in a bank account entitled High View Theater Company.
      2 Paid $40,000 cash to purchase land for a theater site.
      5 Borrowed $220,000 from the bank to finance the construction of the new theater. Stryker signed a note payable to the bank in the name of High View Theater Company.
      7 Received $20,000 cash from ticket sales and deposited that amount in the bank. (Label the revenue as Sales Revenue.)
     10 Purchased theater supplies on account, $1,700.
     15 Paid employee salaries, $2,800, and rent on a theater building, $1,800.
     15 Paid property tax expense on theater building, $1,200.
     16 Paid $800 on account.
     17 Withdrew $3,000 from the business for personal use.

High View uses the following accounts: Cash; Supplies; Land; Accounts Payable; Notes Payable; Crystal Stryker, Capital; Crystal Stryker, Withdrawals; Sales Revenue; Salary Expense; Rent Expense; Property Tax Expense.

Required

1. Analyze each business transaction of High View Theater Company, as shown for the February 1 transaction:

Feb. 1 The asset Cash is increased. Increases in assets are recorded by debits; therefore, debit Cash. The owner's equity of the entity is increased. Increases in owner's equity are recorded by credits; therefore, credit Crystal Stryker, Capital.

2. Journalize each transaction. Explanations are not required.

P2-3A Lane Fuselier opened a law office on September 3 of the current year. During the first month of operations, the business completed the following transactions:

Journalizing transactions, posting to T-accounts, and preparing a trial balance
(Obj. 2, 3, 4, 5)

Sep. 3 Fuselier transferred $25,000 cash from his personal bank account to a business account entitled Lane Fuselier, Attorney.

4 Purchased supplies, $200, and furniture, $1,800, on account.

6 Performed legal services for a client and received $1,000 cash.

7 Paid $15,000 cash to acquire land for a future office site.

10 Defended a client in court, billed the client, and received her promise to pay the $600 within one week.

14 Paid for the furniture purchased September 4 on account.

15 Paid secretary salary, $600.

16 Paid the telephone bill, $120.

17 Received partial payment from client on account, $500.

20 Prepared legal documents for a client on account, $800.

24 Paid the water and electricity bills, $110.

28 Received $1,500 cash for helping a client sell real estate.

30 Paid secretary salary, $600.

30 Paid rent expense, $500.

30 Withdrew $2,400 for personal use.

Required

Open the following T-accounts: Cash; Accounts Receivable; Supplies; Furniture; Land; Accounts Payable; Lane Fuselier, Capital; Lane Fuselier, Withdrawals; Service Revenue; Salary Expense; Rent Expense; Utilities Expense.

1. Record each transaction in the journal, using the account titles given. Key each transaction by date. Explanations are not required.

2. Post the transactions to the ledger, using transaction dates as posting references in the ledger. Label the balance of each account *Bal.*, as shown in the chapter.

3. Prepare the trial balance of Lane Fuselier, Attorney, at September 30 of the current year.

4. How will what you learned in this problem help you manage a business?

P2-4A The trial balance of the accounting practice of Wendi Threlkeld, CPA, is dated February 14, 19X3:

Journalizing transactions, posting to accounts in four-column format, and preparing a trial balance
(Obj. 2, 3, 4, 5)

Account Number	Account	Debit	Credit
	WENDI THRELKELD, CPA		
	TRIAL BALANCE		
	FEBRUARY 14, 19X3		
11	Cash	$ 2,000	
12	Accounts receivable	8,000	
13	Supplies	800	
14	Land	18,600	
21	Accounts payable		$ 3,000
31	Wendi Threlkeld, capital		25,000
32	Wendi Threlkeld, withdrawals	1,200	
41	Service revenue		7,200
51	Salary expense	3,600	
52	Rent expense	800	
53	Utilities expense	200	
	Total	$35,200	$35,200

During the remainder of February, Threlkeld completed the following transactions:

Feb. 15   Threlkeld collected $2,000 cash from a client on account.

16   Performed tax services for a client on account, $900.

18   Paid utilities, $300.

20   Paid on account, $1,000.

21   Purchased supplies on account, $100.

21   Withdrew $1,200 for personal use.

21   Paid for a swimming pool for private residence, using personal funds, $13,000.

22   Received cash of $2,100 for audit work just completed.

28   Paid rent, $800.

28   Paid employees' salaries, $1,600.

Required

1. Record the transactions that occurred during February 15 through 28 in *Page 3* of the journal. Include an explanation for each entry.

2. Open the ledger accounts listed in the trial balance, together with their balances at February 14. Use the four-column account format illustrated in the chapter. Enter *Bal.* (for previous balance) in the Item column, and place a check mark (✓) in the journal reference column for the February 14 balance in each account. Post the transactions to the ledger, using dates, account numbers, journal references, and posting references.

3. Prepare the trial balance of Wendi Threlkeld, CPA, at February 28, 19X3.

Correcting errors in a trial balance
(Obj. 2, 5)

P2-5A   The following trial balance for Christian Counseling Center does not balance:

CHRISTIAN COUNSELING CENTER TRIAL BALANCE JUNE 30, 19X2		
Cash...	$ 2,000	
Accounts receivable.................................	10,000	
Supplies	900	
Office furniture	3,600	
Land	25,000	
Accounts payable.......................................		$ 4,000
Note payable		14,000
Wallace Christian, capital		18,600
Wallace Christian, withdrawals	2,000	
Counseling service revenue		6,500
Salary expense	1,600	
Rent expense	1,000	
Advertising expense..................................	500	
Utilities expense..	300	
Property tax expense	100	
Total...	$47,000	$43,100

The following errors were detected:

a. The cash balance is overstated by $300.

b. Property tax expense of $500 was omitted from the trial balance.

c. Land should be listed in the amount of $23,000.

d. A $200 purchase of supplies on account was neither journalized nor posted.

e. A $2,800 credit to Counseling Service Revenue was not posted.

f. Rent expense of $200 was posted as a credit rather than a debit.

g. The balance of Advertising Expense is $600, but it was listed as $500 on the trial balance.

h. A $300 debit to Accounts Receivable was posted as $30.

i. The balance of Utilities Expense is overstated by $70.

j. A $900 debit to the Withdrawal account was posted as a debit to Wallace Christian, Capital.

Required

Prepare the correct trial balance at June 30. Journal entries are not required.

P2-6A Diana Filner started a consulting service and during the first month of operations completed the following selected transactions:

Recording transactions directly in the ledger, preparing a trial balance
(Obj. 2, 5, 7)

a. Filner began the business with an investment of $7,000 cash and a building valued at $60,000.
b. Borrowed $30,000 from the bank; signed a note payable.
c. Purchased office supplies on account, $1,300.
d. Paid $18,000 for office furniture.
e. Paid employee salary, $2,200.
f. Performed consulting service on account for client, $2,100.
g. Paid $800 of the account payable created in Transaction (c).
h. Received a $600 bill for advertising expense that will be paid in the near future.
i. Performed consulting service for customers and received cash, $1,600.
j. Received cash on account, $1,200.
k. Paid the following cash expenses:
  (1) Rent on land, $700.
  (2) Utilities, $400.
l. Withdrew $3,500 for personal use.

Required

1. Open the following T-accounts: Cash; Accounts Receivable; Office Supplies; Office Furniture; Building; Accounts Payable; Note Payable; Diana Filner, Capital; Diana Filner, Withdrawals; Service Revenue; Salary Expense; Advertising Expense; Rent Expense; Utilities Expense.
2. Record each transaction directly in the T-accounts without using a journal. Use the letters to identify the transactions.
3. Prepare the trial balance of Filner Consulting Service at June 30, 19X3.

(GROUP B)

P2-1B The owner of Electrix Company is selling the business. She offers the following trial balance to prospective buyers:

Analyzing a trial balance
(Obj. 1)

ELECTRIX COMPANY
TRIAL BALANCE
DECEMBER 31, 19XX

Cash	$ 7,000	
Accounts receivable	11,000	
Prepaid expenses	4,000	
Land	31,000	
Accounts payable		$ 31,000
Note payable		20,000
Lonnie Ray, capital		33,000
Lonnie Ray, withdrawals	21,000	
Service revenue		47,000
Rent expense	14,000	
Advertising expense	3,000	
Wage expense	33,000	
Supplies expense	7,000	
	$131,000	$131,000

Your best friend is considering buying Electrix Company. He seeks your advice in interpreting this information. Specifically, he asks whether this trial balance is the same as a balance sheet and an income statement. He also wonders whether Electrix must be a sound company. After all, the accounts are in balance.

Required

Write a short note to answer your friend's questions. To aid his decision, state how he can use the information on the trial balance to compute Electrix's net income or net loss for the current period. State the amount of net income or net loss in your note.

Analyzing and journalizing transactions
(Obj. 2, 3)

P2-2B Jacob Folsom practices medicine under the business title Jacob Folsom, M.D. During May his medical practice engaged in the following transactions:

May 1 Folsom deposited $50,000 cash in the business bank account.
     5 Paid monthly rent on medical equipment, $700.
     9 Paid $42,000 cash to purchase land for an office site.
    10 Purchased supplies on account, $1,200.
    19 Paid $1,000 on account.
    22 Borrowed $20,000 from the bank for business use. Folsom signed a note payable to the bank in the name of the business.
    30 Revenues earned during the month included $6,000 cash and $5,000 on account.
    30 Paid employee salaries ($2,400), office rent ($1,500), and utilities ($400).
    30 Withdrew $4,000 from the business for personal use.

Folsom's business uses the following accounts: Cash; Accounts Receivable; Supplies; Land; Accounts Payable; Notes Payable; Jacob Folsom, Capital; Jacob Folsom, Withdrawals; Service Revenue; Salary Expense; Rent Expense; Utilities Expense.

Required

1. Analyze each transaction of Jacob Folsom, M.D., as shown for the May 1 transaction:

May 1 The asset Cash is increased. Increases in assets are recorded by debits; therefore, debit Cash. The owner's equity is increased. Increases in owner's equity are recorded by credits; therefore, credit Jacob Folsom, Capital.

2. Journalize each transaction. Explanations are not required.

Journalizing transactions, posting to T-accounts, and preparing a trial balance
(Obj. 2, 3, 4, 5)

P2-3B Dee Matthias opened a law office on January 2 of the current year. During the first month of operations the business completed the following transactions:

Jan. 2 Matthias deposited $30,000 cash in the business bank account Dee Matthias, Attorney.
      3 Purchased supplies, $500, and furniture, $2,600, on account.
      4 Performed legal service for a client and received cash, $1,500.
      7 Paid cash to acquire land for a future office site, $22,000.
     11 Defended a client in court and billed the client for $800.
     15 Paid secretary salary, $650.
     16 Paid for the furniture purchased January 3 on account.
     17 Paid the telephone bill, $110.
     18 Received partial payment from client on account, $400.
     19 Prepared legal documents for a client on account, $900.
     22 Paid the water and electricity bills, $130.
     29 Received $1,800 cash for helping a client sell real estate.
     31 Paid secretary salary, $650.
     31 Paid rent expense, $700.
     31 Withdrew $2,200 for personal use.

Required

Open the following T-accounts: Cash; Accounts Receivable; Supplies; Furniture; Land; Accounts Payable; Dee Matthias, Capital; Dee Matthias, Withdrawals; Service Revenue; Salary Expense; Rent Expense; Utilities Expense.

1. Record each transaction in the journal, using the account titles given. Key each transaction by date. Explanations are not required.
2. Post the transactions to the ledger, using transaction dates as posting references in the ledger. Label the balance of each account *Bal.*, as shown in the chapter.
3. Prepare the trial balance of Dee Matthias, Attorney, at January 31 of the current year.
4. How will what you learned in this problem help you manage a business?

P2-4B The trial balance of the law practice of Damon Reed, Attorney, at November 15, 19X3, follows.

DAMON REED, ATTORNEY
TRIAL BALANCE
NOVEMBER 15, 19X3

Account Number	Account	Debit	Credit
11	Cash	$ 3,000	
12	Accounts receivable	8,000	
13	Supplies	600	
14	Land	35,000	
21	Accounts payable		$ 4,400
31	Damon Reed, capital		40,000
32	Damon Reed, withdrawals	2,100	
41	Service revenue		7,100
51	Salary expense	1,800	
52	Rent expense	700	
53	Utilities expense	300	
	Total	$51,500	$51,500

During the remainder of November, Reed completed the following transactions:

Nov. 16 Collected $4,000 cash from a client on account.
17 Performed tax service for a client on account, $1,700.
19 Paid utilities, $100.
21 Paid on account, $2,600.
22 Purchased supplies on account, $200.
23 Withdrew $2,100 for personal use.
23 Used personal funds to pay for the renovation of private residence, $55,000.
24 Received $1,900 cash for legal work just completed.
30 Paid rent, $700.
30 Paid employees' salaries, $1,800.

Required

1. Record the transactions that occurred during November 16 through 30 in *Page 6* of the journal. Include an explanation for each entry.
2. Post the transactions to the ledger, using dates, account numbers, journal references, and posting references. Open the ledger accounts listed in the trial balance together with their balances at November 15. Use the four-column account format illustrated in the chapter. Enter *Bal.* (for previous balance) in the Item column, and place a check mark (✓) in the journal reference column for the November 15 balance of each account.
3. Prepare the trial balance of Damon Reed, Attorney, at November 30, 19X3.

P2-5B The trial balance for Woodway Copy Center, shown on page 82, does not balance. The following errors were detected:

a. The cash balance is overstated by $400.
b. Office maintenance expense of $200 is omitted from the trial balance.
c. Rent expense of $200 was posted as a credit rather than a debit.
d. The balance of Advertising Expense is $300, but it is listed as $400 on the trial balance.
e. A $600 debit to Accounts Receivable was posted as $60.
f. The balance of Utilities Expense is understated by $60.
g. A $1,300 debit to the Withdrawal account was posted as a debit to Anna Newport, Capital.
h. A $100 purchase of supplies on account was neither journalized nor posted.

i. A $5,600 credit to Service Revenue was not posted.

j. Office furniture should be listed in the amount of $1,300.

```
┌─────────────────────────────────────────────────────────────┐
│                    WOODWAY COPY CENTER                        │
│                      TRIAL BALANCE                            │
│                    OCTOBER 31, 19X1                           │
├─────────────────────────────────────────────────────────────┤
```

Cash	$ 3,800	
Accounts receivable	2,000	
Supplies...	500	
Office furniture....................................	2,300	
Land..	46,000	
Accounts payable		$ 2,000
Note payable...		18,300
Anna Newport, capital		29,500
Anna Newport, withdrawals	3,700	
Service revenue.....................................		4,900
Salary expense.......................................	1,000	
Rent expense..	600	
Advertising expense.............................	400	
Utilities expense	200	
Property tax expense	100	
Total..	$60,600	$54,700

Required

Prepare the correct trial balance at October 31. Journal entries are not required.

Recording transactions directly in the ledger, preparing a trial balance
(Obj. 2, 5, 7)

P2-6B Jeff Obenosky started Clearview Cable TV Service and during the first month of operations completed the following selected transactions:

a. Obenosky began the business with an investment of $15,000 cash and a building valued at $50,000.

b. Borrowed $25,000 from the bank; signed a note payable.

c. Paid $32,000 for transmitting equipment.

d. Purchased office supplies on account, $400.

e. Paid employee salary, $1,300.

f. Received $500 for cable TV service performed for customers.

g. Sold cable service to customers on account, $2,300.

h. Paid $100 of the account payable created in Transaction (d).

i. Received a $600 bill for utility expense that will be paid in the near future.

j. Received cash on account, $1,100.

k. Paid the following cash expenses:
   (1) Rent on land, $1,000.
   (2) Advertising, $800.

l. Withdrew $2,600 for personal use.

Required

1. Open the following T-accounts: Cash; Accounts Receivable; Office Supplies; Transmitting Equipment; Building; Accounts Payable; Note Payable; Jeff Obenosky, Capital; Jeff Obenosky, Withdrawals; Service Revenue; Salary Expense; Rent Expense; Advertising Expense; Utilities Expense.

2. Record the following transactions directly in the T-accounts without using a journal. Use the letters to identify the transactions.

3. Prepare the trial balance of Clearview Cable TV Service at January 31, 19X7.

EXTENDING YOUR KNOWLEDGE

DECISION PROBLEMS

1. You have been requested by a friend named Alice Ogden to give advice on the effects that certain business transactions will have on the entity she plans to start. Time is short, so you will not be able to do all the detailed procedures of journalizing and posting. Instead, you must analyze the transactions without the use of a journal. Ogden will continue the business only if she can expect to earn monthly net income of $3,500. The following transactions have occurred:

Recording transactions directly in the ledger, preparing a trial balance, and measuring net income or loss (Obj. 2, 5, 7)

a. Ogden deposited $5,000 cash in a business bank account.
b. Borrowed $4,000 cash from the bank and signed a note payable due within one year.
c. Paid $300 cash for supplies.
d. Purchased advertising in the local newspaper for cash, $800.
e. Purchased office furniture on account, $2,500.
f. Paid the following cash expenses for one month: secretary salary, $1,400; office rent, $400; utilities, $300; interest, $50.
g. Earned revenue on account, $5,300.
h. Earned revenue and received $2,500 cash.
i. Collected cash from customers on account, $1,200.
j. Paid on account, $1,000.
k. Withdrew $900 for personal use.

Required

1. Open the following T-accounts: Cash; Accounts Receivable; Supplies; Furniture; Accounts Payable; Notes Payable; Alice Ogden, Capital; Alice Ogden, Withdrawals; Service Revenue; Salary Expense; Advertising Expense; Rent Expense; Utilities Expense; Interest Expense.
2. Record the transactions directly in the accounts without using a journal. Key each transaction by letter.
3. Prepare a trial balance at the current date. List expenses with the largest amount first, the next largest amount second, and so on. The business name will be Ogden Apartment Locators.
4. Compute the amount of net income or net loss for this first month of operations. Would you recommend that Ogden continue in business?

2. Although all the following questions deal with the accounting equation, they are not related:

Using the accounting equation (Obj. 2)

1. Explain the advantages of double-entry bookkeeping over single-entry bookkeeping to a friend who is opening a used book store.
2. When you deposit money in your bank account, the bank credits your account. Is the bank misusing the word *credit* in this context? Why does the bank use the term *credit* to refer to your deposit, and not *debit*?
3. Your friend asks, "When revenues increase assets and expenses decrease assets, why are revenues credits and expenses debits and not the other way around?" Explain to your friend why revenues are credits and expenses are debits.

ETHICAL ISSUE

Community Chest, a charitable organization in Mojave, New Mexico, has a standing agreement with Encino State Bank. The agreement allows Community Chest to overdraw its cash balance at the bank when donations are running low. In the past, Community Chest managed funds wisely and rarely used this privilege. Greg Osborn has recently become the president of Community Chest. To expand operations, Osborn is acquiring office equipment and spending large amounts for fundraising. During his presidency, Community Chest has maintained a negative bank balance of approximately $1,000.

Required

What is the ethical issue in this situation? State why you approve or disapprove of Osborn's management of Community Chest funds.

FINANCIAL STATEMENT PROBLEMS

Journalizing transactions for an actual company
(Obj. 2, 3)

1. This problem helps to develop skill in recording transactions by using an actual company's account titles. Refer to the Lands' End, Inc., financial statements in Appendix A. Assume that Lands' End completed the following selected transactions during October 1996:

Oct. 5 Earned sales revenue on account, $60,000.
9 Borrowed $500,000 by signing a note payable (long-term debt).
12 Purchased equipment on account, $50,000.
17 Paid $100,000, a current maturity of a long-term debt, plus interest expense of $8,000.
19 Earned sales revenue and immediately received cash of $16,000.
22 Collected the cash on account that was earned on October 5.
24 Paid rent of $24,000 for three months in advance.
28 Received a home-office electricity bill for $1,000, which will be paid in November (this is a general and administrative expense).
30 Paid off half the account payable created on October 12.

Required

Journalize these transactions, using the following account titles taken from the financial statements of Lands' End, Inc.: Cash; Receivables; Prepaid Expenses; Equipment; Current Maturities of Long-Term Debt; Accounts Payable; Long-Term Debt; Sales Revenue; Selling, General and Administrative Expense; Interest Expense. Explanations are not required.

Journalizing transactions for an actual company
(Obj. 2, 3)

2. Obtain the annual report of a real company of your choosing. Assume that the company completed the following selected transactions during May of the current year:

May 3 Borrowed $350,000 by signing a short-term note payable (may be called *short-term debt* or other account title).
5 Paid rent for six months in advance, $4,600.
9 Earned revenue on account, $74,000.
12 Purchased equipment on account, $33,000.
17 Paid a telephone bill, $300 (this is Selling Expense).
19 Paid $90,000 of the money borrowed on May 3.
26 Collected half the cash on account from May 9.
30 Paid the account payable from May 12.

Required

1. Journalize these transactions, using the company's actual account titles taken from its annual report. Explanations are not required.
2. Open a ledger account for each account that you used in journalizing the transactions. (For clarity, insert no actual balances in the accounts.) Post the transaction amounts to the accounts, using the dates as posting references. Take the balance of each account.
3. Prepare a trial balance.

Appendix

Typical Charts of Accounts for Different Types of Businesses

(FOR BUSINESSES DISCUSSED IN CHAPTERS 1-13)

SERVICE PROPRIETORSHIP

ASSETS	LIABILITIES	OWNER'S EQUITY
Cash	Accounts Payable	Owner, Capital
Accounts Receivable	Notes Payable, Short-Term	Owner, Withdrawals
Allowance for Uncollectible Accounts	Salary Payable	**Revenues and Gains**
Notes Receivable, Short-Term	Wage Payable	Service Revenue
Interest Receivable	Employee Income Tax Payable	Interest Revenue
Supplies	FICA Tax Payable	Gain on Sale of Land (Furniture, Equipment, or Building)
Prepaid Rent	State Unemployment Tax Payable	
Prepaid Insurance	Federal Unemployment Tax Payable	**Expenses and Losses**
Notes Receivable, Long-Term	Employee Benefits Payable	Salary Expense
Land	Interest Payable	Payroll Tax Expense
Furniture	Unearned Service Revenue	Insurance Expense for Employees
Accumulated Depreciation— Furniture	Notes Payable, Long-Term	Rent Expense
Equipment		Insurance Expense
Accumulated Depreciation— Equipment		Supplies Expense
Building		Uncollectible Account Expense
Accmulated Depreciation— Building		Depreciation Expense— Furniture
		Depreciation Expense— Equipment
		Depreciation Expense— Building
		Property Tax Expense
		Interest Expense
		Miscellaneous Expense
		Loss on Sale (or Exchange) of Land (Furniture, Equipment, or Building)

SERVICE PARTNERSHIP

Same as Service Proprietorship, except for Owners' Equity:

OWNERS' EQUITY

Partner 1, Capital
Partner 2, Capital
Partner N, Capital
Partner 1, Drawing
Partner 2, Drawing
Partner N, Drawing

MERCHANDISING CORPORATION

ASSETS	LIABILITIES	STOCKHOLDERS' EQUITY

ASSETS

Cash
Short-Term Investments
(Trading Securities)
Accounts Receivable
Allowance for Uncollectible
Accounts
Notes Receivable, Short-
Term
Interest Receivable
Inventory
Supplies
Prepaid Rent
Prepaid Insurance
Notes Receivable, Long-Term
Investments in Subsidiaries
Investments in Stock
(Available-for-Sale
Securities)
Investments in Bonds (Held-
to-Maturity Securities)
Other Receivables, Long-
Term
Land
Land Improvements
Furniture and Fixtures
Accumulated Depreciation—
Furniture and Fixtures
Equipment
Accumulated Depreciation—
Equipment
Buildings
Accumulated Depreciation—
Buildings
Organization Cost
Franchises
Patents
Leaseholds
Goodwill

LIABILITIES

Accounts Payable
Notes Payable, Short-Term
Current Portion of Bonds
Payable
Salary Payable
Wage Payable
Employee Income Tax
Payable
FICA Tax Payable
State Unemployment Tax
Payable
Federal Unemployment Tax
Payable
Employee Benefits Payable
Interest Payable
Income Tax Payable
Unearned Sales Revenue
Notes Payable, Long-Term
Bonds Payable
Lease Liability
Minority Interest

STOCKHOLDERS' EQUITY

Preferred Stock
Paid-in Capital in Excess of
Par—Preferred
Common Stock
Paid-in Capital in Excess of
Par—Common
Paid-in Capital from Treasury
Stock Transactions
Paid-in Capital from
Retirement of Stock
Retained Earnings
Foreign Currency Translation
Adjustment
Treasury Stock

Revenues and Gains

Sales Revenue
Interest Revenue
Dividend Revenue
Equity-Method Investment
Revenue
Unrealized Holding Gain on
Trading Investments
Gain on Sale of Investments
Gain on Sale of Land
(Furniture and Fixtures,
Equipment, or Buildings)
Discontinued Operations—
Gain
Extraordinary Gains

Expenses and Losses

Cost of Goods Sold
Salary Expense
Wage Expense
Commission Expense
Payroll Tax Expense
Insurance Expense for
Employees
Rent Expense
Insurance Expense
Supplies Expense
Uncollectible Account
Expense
Depreciation Expense—
Land Improvements
Depreciation Expense—
Furniture and Fixtures
Depreciation Expense—
Equipment
Depreciation Expense—
Buildings
Organization Expense
Amortization Expense—
Franchises
Amortization Expense—
Leaseholds
Amortization Expense—
Goodwill
Income Tax Expense
Unrealized Holding Loss on
Trading Investments
Loss on Sale of Investments
Loss on Sale (or Exchange) of
Land (Furniture and Fix-
tures, Equipment, or Build-
ings)
Discontinued Operations—
Loss
Extraordinary Losses

MANUFACTURING CORPORATION

Same as Merchandising Corporation, except for
Assets and Expenses:

ASSETS	Expenses (Contra Expenses if Credit Balance)
Inventories:	Direct Materials Price Variance
Materials Inventory	Direct Materials Efficiency Variance
Work in Process Inventory	Direct Labor Price Variance
Finished Goods Inventory	Direct Labor Efficiency Variance
Factory Wages	Overhead Flexible Budget Variance
Factory Overhead	Overhead Production Volume Variance
	Overhead Spending Variance
	Overhead Efficiency Variance

Chapter 3
Measuring Business Income:
The Adjusting Process

After studying this chapter, you should be able to

1. Distinguish accrual-basis accounting from cash-basis accounting

2. Apply the revenue and matching principles

3. Make adjusting entries at the end of the accounting period

4. Prepare an adjusted trial balance

5. Prepare the financial statements from the adjusted trial balance

A1. Account for a prepaid expense recorded initially as an expense

A2. Account for an unearned (deferred) revenue recorded initially as a revenue

66 1993 was a difficult year; factors such as flat retail sales, low consumer confidence levels, and conservative buying by our retail customers contributed to a drop in the company's gross margin. We are combating these issues in 1994 by refocusing the three divisions in our core sportswear business to provide increased clarity among product lines as well as improving gross margins, shortening product cycle time, and planning conservatively. 99

SAMUEL MILLER, SENIOR
VICE-PRESIDENT/CHIEF
FINANCIAL OFFICER OF
LIZ CLAIBORNE, INC.

During the booming 1980s, Liz Claiborne, Inc., was the high flier among women's designer clothing manufacturers. Liz Claiborne sportswear consistently outsold competitors, such as Bernard Chaus and Leslie Fay. But the Liz Claiborne brand is not wearing so well in the 1990s. Consumer demand for the brand is falling, and retail stores are cutting back on new orders of Liz Claiborne merchandise.

According to one major retail chain, which declined to be identified, the slow sales of Liz Claiborne sportswear provided the reason for not ordering Claiborne's new autumn line. Said an executive at the chain, "The styling doesn't have the freshness fashion-wise, compared to some of the other brands out there."

Liz Claiborne, Inc., reported that second-quarter net income fell from $39.5 million in 1992 to $31.1 million in 1993, a drop of 21 percent. And the seemingly invincible company expected a 30-percent decline in 1993 earnings for the year as a whole. All this bad news resulted in a 23-percent drop in the price of Liz Claiborne, Inc., stock on the New York Stock Exchange. *Source: Adapted from Teri Agine, "Liz Claiborne Seems to Be Losing Its Invincibility," The Wall Street Journal, July 19, 1993, p. B4.*

• • • • •

This story shows how accounting income affects people's behavior—from fashion designers to top executives to retail stores and Wall Street investors. A high-flying company like Liz Claiborne, Inc., finds it difficult to stay on top forever.

When Liz Claiborne clothing appeals to consumers, its revenues and profits soar. The company's reported income figures spur competitors to match its progress.

Other companies' clothing designers are now beating Claiborne at "fashion freshness." The result? Consumers start buying more clothing from competitors and less from Liz Claiborne. Department stores allocate less floor space to Liz Claiborne displays, and sales and profits slip a bit. Investors sell their Liz Claiborne stock, and the company's stock price falls. There is a shake-up in top management as Claiborne executives try to regain their magic touch for increasing sales and high income. The quest for profits continues.

The primary goal of business is to earn a profit. Virtually all companies want to earn increasing amounts of profit each year, but, as the Liz Claiborne story indicates, that is not always possible.

Gary Lyon, the CPA whose accounting practice we discussed in the earlier chapters, earns business income by providing accounting services for clients. Whether the entity is Gary Lyon, CPA, or Liz Claiborne, Inc., the profit motive increases the owner's drive to carry on the business. As you read this chapter, consider how important accounting income is to a business and how the pursuit of income affects people's behavior.

At the end of each accounting period, the entity prepares its financial statements. The period may be a month, three months, six months, or a full year. Liz Claiborne is typical. The company reports on a quarterly basis—at the end of every three months, with audited financial statements only at the end of the year.

Whatever the length of the period, the end accounting product is the financial statements. And the most important single amount in these statements is the net income or net loss—the profit or loss—for the period. Net income captures much information: total revenues minus total expenses for the period. In essence, net income—or net loss—measures the ability of the business to generate revenues from its outputs (products or services) that exceed the costs of its inputs (merchandise, employee labor, supplies, utilities, and so on). A business that consistently earns net income adds value to its owners, its employees, its customers, and society. The business is able to pay its debts. Net income captures these important aspects of a business.

An important step in financial statement preparation is the trial balance. ◀▥ The account balances in the trial balance include the effects of the transactions that occurred during the period—cash collections, purchases of assets, payments of bills, sales of assets, and so on. To measure its income, however, a business must do some additional accounting at the end of the period to bring the records up to date before preparing the financial statements. This process is called *adjusting the books*, and it consists of making special entries called *adjusting entries*. This chapter focuses primarily on these adjusting entries to help you better understand the nature of business income.

The accounting profession has concepts and principles to guide the measurement of business income. Chief among these are the concepts of accrual-basis accounting, the accounting period, the revenue principle, and the matching principle. In this chapter, we apply these (and other) concepts and principles to measure the income and prepare the financial statements of Gary Lyon's business for the month of April.

Short Exercise: All parts of the financial statements are important in describing the financial condition of a business. Which statement would be most helpful to Liz Claiborne's management in evaluating the company's performance for the past year? *A:* The income statement, because it reports how profitable the company has been for that period.

◀▥ ◀▥ ◀▥ The trial balance, introduced in Chapter 2, p. 54, lists the ledger accounts and their balances.

Accrual-Basis Accounting versus Cash-Basis Accounting

OBJECTIVE 1
Distinguish accrual-basis accounting from cash-basis accounting

There are two widely used bases of accounting: the accrual basis and the cash basis. In **accrual-basis accounting,** an accountant recognizes the impact of a business event as it occurs. When the business performs a service, makes a sale, or incurs an expense, the accountant enters the transaction into the books, whether or not cash has been received or paid. In **cash-basis accounting,** however, the accountant does not record a transaction until cash is received or paid. Cash receipts are treated as revenues, and cash payments are handled as expenses.

Suppose a client paid the Four Seasons Hotel in New York City $15,000 on October 1, 1995, for a six-month stay in a suite to begin October 1, 1995. Exhibit 3-1 shows how hotel revenues would be recorded by the two methods of accounting over the six-month period October 1, 1995, through March 31, 1996. In actuality, the Four Seasons Hotels and Resorts, which operates nearly 40 luxury properties worldwide and serves 3.1 million guests a year, uses accrual-basis accounting to match the expenses and related revenues in a given fiscal period.

"The Four Seasons Hotels and Resorts . . . uses accrual-basis accounting to match the expenses and related revenues in a given fiscal period."

GAAP requires that a business use the accrual basis. This means that the accountant records revenues as they are *earned* and expenses as they are *incurred*—not necessarily when cash changes hands.

Using accrual-basis accounting, Liz Claiborne, Inc., records revenue when it sells goods to a store, not when it collects cash later. Gary Lyon records revenue when he performs services for a client on account. Lyon has earned the revenue at that time because his efforts have generated an account receivable, a legal claim against the client for whom he did the work. By contrast, if Gary Lyon used cash-basis accounting, he would not record revenue at the time he performed the service. He would wait until he received cash.

Why does GAAP require that businesses use the accrual basis? What advantage does accrual-basis accounting offer? Suppose Gary Lyon's accounting period ends after he earned some revenue but before he has collected the money. If he used the cash-basis method, his financial statements would not include this revenue or the related account receivable. As a result, the financial statements would be misleading. Revenue and the asset Accounts Receivable would be understated, and thus his business would look less successful than it actually is. If he wants to get a bank loan to expand his practice, the understated revenue and asset figures might hurt his chances.

Using accrual-basis accounting, Gary Lyon treats expenses in a like manner. For instance, salary expense includes amounts paid to employees plus any amount owed to employees but not yet paid. Lyon's use of an employee's service, not the payment of cash to the employee, brings about the expense.

Under cash-basis accounting, a business records salary expense only when it actually pays the employee. Suppose Gary Lyon owed his secretary a salary, and the financial statements were drawn up before Lyon paid. Expenses and liabilities would be understated, so the business would look more successful than it really is. This incomplete information would not give potential creditors an accurate accounting.

EXHIBIT 3-1
Accrual-Basis Accounting versus Cash-Basis Accounting

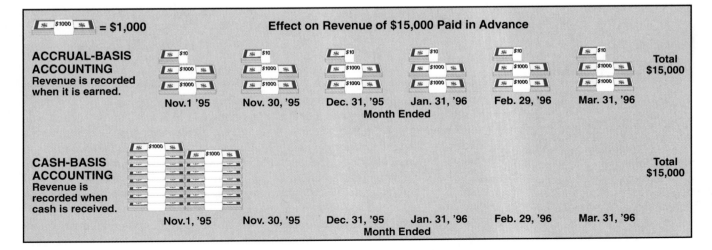

As these examples show, accrual-basis accounting provides more complete information than does cash-basis accounting. This difference is important because the more complete the data, the better equipped decision makers are to reach conclusions about the firm's financial health and future prospects. Three concepts used in accrual-basis accounting are the accounting period, the revenue principle, and the matching principle.

The Accounting Period

The only way to know for certain how successfully a business has operated is to close its doors, sell all its assets, pay the liabilities, and return any leftover cash to the owners. This process, called *liquidation*, is the same as going out of business. Obviously, it is not practical for accountants to measure business income in this manner. Instead, businesses need periodic reports on their progress. Accountants slice time into small segments and prepare financial statements for specific periods. Until a business sells all its assets for cash and pays all its liabilities, the amounts reported in its financial statements must be regarded as estimates.

The most basic accounting period is one year, and virtually all businesses prepare annual financial statements. For about 60 percent of large companies in a recent survey, the annual accounting period runs the calendar year from January 1 through December 31. Other companies use what is called a *fiscal year*, which ends on some date other than December 31. The year-end date is usually the low point in business activity for the year. Depending on the type of business, the fiscal year may end on April 30, July 31, or some other date. Retailers are a notable example. For instance, J.C. Penney Company uses a fiscal year ending on January 31 because the low point in Penney's business activity falls during January after the Christmas sales. J.C. Penney does more than 30 percent of its yearly sales during November and December but only 5 percent in January.

"*J.C. Penney does more than 30 percent of its yearly sales during November and December but only 5 percent in January.*"

Managers and investors cannot wait until the end of the year to gauge a company's progress. Companies prepare financial statements for *interim* periods, which are less than a year. Publicly owned companies must issue quarterly financial statements. Managers want financial information more often, so monthly statements are common. A series of monthly statements can be combined for quarterly and semiannual periods. Most of the discussions in this book are based on an annual accounting period, but the procedures and statements can be applied to interim periods as well.

Revenue Principle

OBJECTIVE 2

Apply the revenue and matching principles

◀▥▥◀▥▥◀▥▥   Revenue, defined in Chapter 1, p. 12, is the increase in owner's equity from delivering goods and services to customers in the course of operating a business.

The **revenue principle** tells accountants (1) *when* to record revenue by making a journal entry and (2) the *amount* of revenue to record. ◀▥▥ When we speak of "recording" something in accounting, the act of recording (or recognizing) the item naturally leads to posting to the ledger accounts and preparing the trial balance and the financial statements. Although the financial statements are the end product of accounting and what accountants are most concerned about, our discussions often focus on recording the entry in the journal because that is where the accounting process starts.

The general principle guiding *when* to record revenue says to record revenue once it has been earned—but not before. In most cases, revenue is earned when the

EXHIBIT 3-2
Recording Revenue

business has delivered a completed good or service to the customer. The business has done everything required by the agreement, including transferring the item to the customer. Exhibit 3-2 shows two situations that provide guidance on when to record revenue. The first situation illustrates when *not* to record revenue. Situation 2 illustrates when revenue should be recorded. If the client pays for Gary Lyon's service immediately, Lyon will debit Cash. If the service is performed on account, Lyon will debit Accounts Receivable. In either case, Lyon should record revenue by crediting the Service Revenue account.

The general principle guiding the *amount* of revenue says to record revenue equal to the cash value of the goods or the service transferred to the customer. Suppose that in order to obtain a new client, Gary Lyon performs accounting service for the price of $500. Ordinarily, Lyon would have charged $600 for this service. How much revenue should Lyon record? The answer is $500 because that was the cash value of the transaction. Lyon will not receive the full value of $600, so that is not the amount of revenue to record. He will receive only $500 cash, and that pinpoints the amount of revenue earned.

Short Exercise: A client pays Lyon $900 on March 15 for service to be performed April 1 to June 30. Has he earned revenue on March 15? *A:* No. He has received the cash but will not perform the service until later. Under the *accrual method*, Lyon will record Unearned Service Revenue on March 15. It is a liability because he has an obligation to perform a service in the future.

Matching Principle

The **matching principle** is the basis for recording expenses. ◀▥ Recall that expenses, such as rent, utilities, and advertising, are the costs of operating a business. Expenses are the costs of assets that are used up in the earning of revenue. The matching principle directs accountants (1) to identify all expenses incurred during the accounting period, (2) to measure the expenses, and (3) to match the expenses against the revenues earned during that same span of time. To match expenses against revenues means to subtract the expenses from the revenues in order to compute net income or net loss. Exhibit 3-3 illustrates the matching principle.

▥◀ ▥◀ ▥◀ An expense, defined in Chapter 1, p. 12, is a decrease in owner's equity that occurs in the course of operating a business.

EXHIBIT 3-3
The Matching Principle

There is a natural link between revenues and some types of expenses. Accountants follow the matching principle by first identifying the revenues of a period and the expenses that can be linked to particular revenues. For example, a business that pays sales commissions to its sales personnel will have commission expense if the employees make sales. If they make no sales, the business has no commission expense. *Cost of goods sold* is another example. If there are no sales of suits, Liz Claiborne, Inc., has no cost of goods sold—that is, no cost of producing those suits.

Other expenses are not so easy to link with particular sales. Monthly rent expense occurs, for example, regardless of the revenues earned during the period. The matching principle directs accountants to identify those types of expenses with a particular time period, such as a month or a year. If Gary Lyon employs a secretary at a monthly salary of $1,900, the business will record salary expense of $1,900 at the end of each month. Because financial statements appear at definite intervals, there must be some cutoff date for the necessary information. Most entities engage in so many transactions that some are bound to spill over into more than a single accounting period. Gary Lyon prepares monthly statements for his business at April 30. How does he account for a transaction that begins in April but ends in May? How does he bring the accounts up to date for preparing the financial statements? To answer these questions, accountants use the time-period concept.

Short Exercise: Lyon pays $4,500 on July 31 for office rent for the next three months. Has he incurred an expense on July 31? *A:* No. He has paid cash, but the rent will not expire for three months. Under the *accrual method*, Lyon will record Prepaid Rent on July 31. It is an asset because he has paid in advance for the use of an office in the future.

Time-Period Concept

Managers, investors, and creditors are making decisions daily and need periodic readings on the business's progress. To meet this need for information, accountants prepare financial statements at regular intervals. Virtually all companies report net income for an annual period and their assets, liabilities, and owner's equity at the end of the year. Most companies also prepare monthly and quarterly financial statements.

The **time-period concept** ensures that accounting information is reported at regular intervals. It interacts with the revenue principle and the matching principle to underlie the use of accruals. To measure income accurately, companies update the revenue and expense accounts immediately before the end of the period. Hawaiian Airlines, Inc., provides a real example of an expense accrual. At December 31, 1992, Hawaiian Airlines recorded employee compensation of $2.7 million that the company owed its workers for unpaid services performed before year end. The company's accrual entry was

"*Hawaiian Airlines, Inc., provides a real example of an expense accrual.*"

1992			
Dec. 31	Salary and Wage Expense.................................	2,700,000	
	Salary and Wage Payable		2,700,000

This entry serves two purposes. It assigns the expense to the proper period. Without the accrual entry at December 31, total expenses of 1992 would be understated, and as a result net income would be overstated. Incorrectly, the expense would fall in 1993 when the company makes the next payroll disbursement. The accrual entry also records the liability for reporting on the balance sheet at December 31, 1992. Without the accrual entry, total liabilities would be understated.

At the end of the accounting period, companies also accrue revenues that have been earned but not collected. The remainder of the chapter discusses how to make the necessary adjustments to the accounts.

Adjustments to the Accounts

At the end of the period, the accountant prepares the financial statements. This end-of-period process begins with the trial balance that lists the accounts and their balances after the period's transactions have been recorded in the journal and posted to the accounts in the ledger. Exhibit 3-4 is the trial balance of Gary Lyon's accounting practice at April 30, 19X1.

OBJECTIVE 3
Make adjusting entries at the end of the accounting period

This *unadjusted trial balance* includes some new accounts that will be explained in this section. It lists most, but not all, of the revenue and the expenses of Lyon's accounting practice for the month of April. These trial balance amounts are incomplete because they omit certain revenue and expense transactions that affect more than one accounting period. That is why it is called an *unadjusted* trial balance. In most cases, however, we refer to it simply as the trial balance, without the label "unadjusted."

Under cash-basis accounting, there would be no need for adjustments to the accounts because all April cash transactions would have been recorded. The accrual basis requires adjusting entries at the end of the period in order to produce correct balances for the financial statements. To see why, consider the Supplies account in Exhibit 3-4.

Lyon's accounting practice uses supplies in providing accounting services for clients during the month. This use reduces the quantity of supplies on hand and thus constitutes an expense, just like salary expense or rent expense. Gary Lyon does not bother to record this expense daily, and it is not worth his while to record supplies expense more than once a month. It is time-consuming to make hourly, daily, or even weekly journal entries to record the expense for the use of supplies. So how does he account for supplies expense?

By the end of the month, the Supplies balance is not correct. The balance represents the amount of supplies on hand at the start of the month plus any supplies purchased during the month. This balance fails to take into account the supplies used (supplies expense) during the accounting period. It is necessary, then, to subtract the month's expenses from the amount of supplies listed on the trial balance. The resulting new adjusted balance measures the cost of supplies that are still on hand at April 30. This is the correct amount of supplies to report on the balance sheet. Adjusting the entries in this way will bring the accounts up to date.

Adjusting entries assign revenues to the period in which they are earned and expenses to the period in which they are incurred. Adjusting entries also update the asset and liability accounts. They are needed (1) to measure properly the period's in-

GARY LYON, CPA UNADJUSTED TRIAL BALANCE APRIL 30, 19X1		
Cash	$24,800	
Accounts receivable	2,250	
Supplies	700	
Prepaid rent	3,000	
Furniture	16,500	
Accounts payable		$13,100
Unearned service revenue		450
Gary Lyon, capital		31,250
Gary Lyon, withdrawals	3,200	
Service revenue		7,000
Salary expense	950	
Utilities expense	400	
Total	$51,800	$51,800

EXHIBIT 3-4
Unadjusted Trial Balance

come and (2) to bring related asset and liability accounts to correct balances for the financial statements. For example, an adjusting entry is needed to transfer the amount of supplies used during the period from the asset account Supplies to the expense account Supplies Expense. The adjusting entry updates both the Supplies asset account and the Supplies Expense account. This adjustment achieves accurate measures of assets and expenses. Adjusting entries, which are the key to accrual-basis accounting, are made before the financial statements are prepared. The end-of-period process of updating the accounts is called *adjusting the accounts, making the adjusting entries,* or *adjusting the books.*

A large company would use accounting software to print out a trial balance. At Occidental Petroleum ("OXY"), a multidivisional company that locates, produces,

"At Occidental Petroleum ("OXY"), a multidivisional company that locates, produces, and transports oil and natural gas, each division has its own accounting software that prints a monthly trial balance."

and transports oil and natural gas, each division has its own accounting software that prints a monthly trial balance. The accountants then analyze the amounts on the trial balance, testing them for reasonableness and tracing the balances back to the ledger. If necessary, the accountants might go back to the supporting documents that generated the transactions. This analysis results in the adjusting entries. Posting the adjusting entries updates the ledger accounts. The trial balance has now become the adjusted trial balance. At Occidental, the adjusted trial balances from all divisions are consolidated.

Prepaids (Deferrals) and Accruals

A helpful way to categorize adjusting entries is based on the timing of recording an expense or a revenue relative to the payment or receipt of cash. In a *prepaid*-type adjustment, the cash transaction occurs before the related expense or revenue is recorded. Prepaids are also called *deferrals* because the recording of the expense or the revenue is deferred until after cash is paid or received. *Accrual*-type adjustments are the opposite of prepaids. For accruals we record the expense or revenue before the related cash settlement. Adjusting entries can be further divided into five categories:

1. Prepaid expenses
2. Depreciation of plant assets
3. Accrued expenses
4. Accrued revenues
5. Unearned revenues

Prepaid Expenses

Key Point: Prepaid expenses are assets, not expenses.

Prepaid expenses is a category of miscellaneous assets that typically expire or are used up in the near future. Prepaid rent and prepaid insurance are prepaid expenses. They are called prepaid expenses because they are expenses that are paid in advance. Salary expense and utilities expense, among others, are typically *not* prepaid expenses because they are not paid in advance. All companies, large and small, must make adjustments regarding prepaid expenses. For example, McDonald's Corporation must contend with such prepayments as rents, packaging supplies, and insurance.

PREPAID RENT Landlords usually require tenants to pay rent in advance. This prepayment creates an asset for the renter because that person has purchased the future benefit of using the rented item. Suppose Gary Lyon prepays three months' rent on April 1, 19X1, after negotiating a lease for his business office. If the lease specifies monthly rental amounts of $1,000 each, the entry to record the payment for three months is a debit to the asset account, Prepaid Rent, as follows:

Apr. 1	Prepaid Rent ($1,000 × 3)...	3,000	
	Cash..		3,000
	Paid three months' rent in advance.		

After posting, Prepaid Rent appears as follows:

Prepaid Rent	
Apr. 1	3,000

The trial balance at April 30, 19X1, lists Prepaid Rent as an asset with a debit balance of $3,000. Throughout April, the Prepaid Rent account maintains this beginning balance as shown in Exhibit 3-4.

At April 30 Prepaid Rent should be adjusted to remove from its balance the amount of the asset that has expired, which is one month's worth of the prepayment. By definition, the amount of an asset that has expired is *expense*. The adjusting entry transfers one-third, or $1,000 ($3,000 × 1/3), of the debit balance from Prepaid Rent to Rent Expense. The debit side of the entry records an increase in Rent Expense, and the credit records a decrease in the asset Prepaid Rent:

Apr. 30	Rent Expense ($3,000 × 1/3)	1,000	
	Prepaid Rent..		1,000
	To record rent expense.		

After posting, Prepaid Rent and Rent Expense appear as follows:

Prepaid Rent				Rent Expense	
Apr. 1	3,000	Apr. 30 1,000	⟶	Apr. 30 1,000	
Bal.	2,000			Bal. 1,000	

Correct asset amount: $2,000 → **Total accounted for: $3,000** ← **Correct expense amount: $1,000**

The full $3,000 has been accounted for: Two-thirds measures the asset, and one-third measures the expense. Recording this expense illustrates the matching principle. The same analysis applies to a prepayment of three months' insurance premiums. The only difference is in the account titles, which would be Prepaid Insurance and Insurance Expense instead of Prepaid Rent and Rent Expense. In a computerized system, the adjusting entry crediting the prepaid account and debiting the expense account could be established to recur automatically in each subsequent accounting period until the prepaid account has a zero balance.

The chapter appendix shows an alternate treatment of prepaid expenses. The end result on the financial statements is the same as that for the method given here.

SUPPLIES   Supplies are accounted for in the same way as prepaid expenses. On April 2 Gary Lyon paid cash of $700 for office supplies:

Apr. 2	Supplies	700	
	Cash..		700
	Paid cash for supplies.		

Assume that Lyon purchased no additional supplies during April. The April 30 trial balance, therefore, lists Supplies with a $700 debit balance, as shown in Exhibit 3-4.

During April, Lyon used supplies in performing services for clients. The cost of the supplies used is the measure of *supplies expense* for the month. To measure his firm's supplies expense during April, Gary Lyon counts the supplies on hand at the

Short Exercise: At the beginning of the month, supplies were $5,000. During the month, $7,800 of supplies were purchased. At month's end, it was determined that $3,600 of supplies were still on hand. What are the adjusting entry and the ending balance in the Supplies account? *A:*
Supplies Expense   9,200
    Supplies...........   9,200
Ending balance = $5,000 + $7,800 – $9,200 = $3,600

end of the month. This is the amount of the asset still available to the business. Assume that the count indicates that supplies costing $400 remain. Subtracting the entity's $400 supplies on hand at the end of April from the cost of supplies available during April ($700) measures supplies expense during the month ($300).

Cost of asset available during the period	–	Cost of asset on hand at the end of the period	=	Cost of asset used (expense) during the period
$700	–	$400	=	$300

The April 30 adjusting entry to update the Supplies account and to record the supplies expense for the month debits the expense and credits the asset:

Apr. 30	Supplies Expense ($700 - $400)...	300	
	Supplies..		300
	To record supplies expense.		

After posting, the Supplies and Supplies Expense accounts appear as follows:

The Supplies account then enters the month of May with a $400 balance, and the adjustment process is repeated each month.

Depreciation of Plant Assets

The logic of the accrual basis is probably best illustrated by how businesses account for plant assets. **Plant assets** are long-lived tangible assets, such as land, buildings, furniture, machinery, and equipment used in the operations of the business. As one accountant said, "All assets but land are on a march to the junkyard." That is, all plant assets but land decline in usefulness as they age. This decline is an *expense* to the business. Accountants systematically spread the cost of each plant asset, except land, over the years of its useful life. This process of allocating cost to expense is called **depreciation**.

SIMILARITY TO PREPAID EXPENSES   The concept underlying accounting for plant assets and depreciation expense is the same as for prepaid expenses. In a sense, plant assets are large prepaid expenses that expire over a number of periods. For both prepaid expenses and plant assets, the business purchases an asset that wears out or is used up. As the asset is used, more and more of its cost is transferred from the asset account to the expense account. The major difference between prepaid expenses and plant assets is the length of time it takes for the asset to lose its usefulness. Prepaid expenses usually expire within a year, whereas most plant assets remain useful for a number of years.

Consider Gary Lyon's accounting practice. Suppose that on April 3 Lyon purchased furniture on account for $16,500:

Apr. 3	Furniture...	16,500	
	Accounts Payable..		16,500
	Purchased office furniture on account.		

After posting, the Furniture account appears as follows:

Furniture	
Apr. 3 16,500	

In accrual-basis accounting, an asset is recorded when the furniture is acquired. Then, a portion of the asset's cost is transferred from the asset account to Depreciation Expense each period that the asset is used. This method matches the asset's expense to the revenue of the period, which is an application of the matching principle. In many computerized systems, the adjusting entry for depreciation is programmed to occur automatically each month for the duration of the asset's life.

Lyon believes the furniture will remain useful for five years and will be virtually worthless at the end of its life. One way to compute the amount of depreciation for each year is to divide the cost of the asset ($16,500 in our example) by its expected useful life (five years). This procedure—called the straight-line method—gives annual depreciation of $3,300 ($16,500/5 years = $3,300 per year). Depreciation for the month of April is $275 ($3,300/12 months = $275 per month). Chapter 10 covers depreciation in more detail.

THE ACCUMULATED DEPRECIATION ACCOUNT Depreciation expense for April is recorded by the following entry:

Apr. 30	Depreciation Expense—Furniture	275	
	Accumulated Depreciation—Furniture		275
	To record depreciation on furniture.		

Accumulated Depreciation is credited instead of Furniture because the original cost of the plant asset (the furniture) is an objective measurement, and that amount remains in the original asset account as long as the business uses the asset. Accountants may refer to that account if they need to know how much the asset cost. This information may be useful in a decision about whether to replace the furniture and the amount to pay. The amount of depreciation, however, is an *estimate*. Accountants use the **Accumulated Depreciation** account to show the cumulative sum of all depreciation expense from the date of acquiring the asset. Therefore, the balance in this account increases over the life of the asset.

Accumulated Depreciation is a *contra asset* account, which means an asset account with a normal credit balance. ◄▓▓ A **contra account** has two distinguishing characteristics: (1) It always has a companion account, and (2) its normal balance is opposite that of the companion account. In this case, Accumulated Depreciation accompanies Furniture. It appears in the ledger directly after Furniture. Furniture has a debit balance, and therefore Accumulated Depreciation, a contra asset, has a credit balance. All contra asset accounts have credit balances.

A business carries an accumulated depreciation account for each depreciable asset. If a business has a building and a machine, for example, it will carry the accounts Accumulated Depreciation—Building, and Accumulated Depreciation—Machine.

After the depreciation entry has been posted, the Furniture, Accumulated Depreciation, and Depreciation Expense accounts of Gary Lyon, CPA, are

Furniture		Accumulated Depreciation—Furniture		Depreciation Expense—Furniture	
Apr. 3 16,500			Apr. 30 275	Apr. 30 275	
Bal. 16,500			Bal. 275	Bal. 275	

BOOK VALUE The balance sheet shows the relationship between Furniture and Accumulated Depreciation. The balance of Accumulated Depreciation is subtracted from the balance of Furniture. The net amount of a plant asset (cost minus accumulated depreciation) is called its **book value**, or *net book value*, as shown here for Furniture:

Key Point: Use a separate Depreciation Expense account and Accumulated Depreciation account for each type of asset (Depreciation Expense—Furniture, Depreciation Expense—Buildings, and so on). You must know the amount of depreciation recorded for each asset.

◄▓▓◄▓▓◄▓▓ Recall from Chapter 2, p. 60, that the normal balance of an account marks the side of the account where increases are recorded.

Short Exercise: (1) What is the book value of Lyon's furniture at the end of May? (2) Is that what the furniture could be sold for then? (3) What is the asset's book value at the end of its life?
A: (1) $16,500 − $275 − $275 = $15,950. (2) Not necessarily. *Book value* represents the part of the asset's *cost* that has not yet been depreciated. (3) $0.

Plant Assets:

Furniture	$16,500
Less Accumulated Depreciation	275
Book value	$16,225

Because Accumulated Depreciation is reported with its companion account to determine the asset's book value, Accumulated Depreciation is called a *valuation account*.

Suppose Lyon's accounting practice owns a building that cost $48,000 and on which annual depreciation is $2,400 ($48,000/20 years). The amount of depreciation for one month would be $200 ($2,400/12), and the following entry records depreciation for April:

Apr. 30	Depreciation Expense—Building	200	
	Accumulated Depreciation—Building		200
	To record depreciation on building.		

The balance sheet at April 30 reports Lyon's plant assets as shown in Exhibit 3-5.

EXHIBIT 3-5

Plant Assets on the Balance Sheet of Gary Lyon, CPA (April 30)

Plant assets:

Furniture	$16,500	
Less Accumulated depreciation	275	$16,225
Building	48,000	
Less Accumulated depreciation	200	47,800
Book value of plant assets		$64,025

"Johnson & Johnson has real-estate holdings around the world."

Exhibit 3-6 shows how Johnson & Johnson—makers of Band-Aids, Tylenol, and other health-care products—displayed Property, Plant, and Equipment in its annual report. Johnson & Johnson has real-estate holdings around the world; they are reported in line 1 of Exhibit 3-6. Line 2 includes the cost of buildings used for office space, manufacturing, and research as well as the air conditioners, elevators, plumbing, and so on in those buildings. The company's manufacturing machinery, office equipment, and furniture are given in line 3, and line 4 represents assets that are under construction.

Now, however, let's return to Gary Lyon's situation.

Accrued Expenses

Businesses often incur expenses before they pay cash. Payment is not due until later. Consider an employee's salary. The employer's salary expense and salary payable

EXHIBIT 3-6

Johnson & Johnson's Reporting of Property, Plant, and Equipment (Amounts in Millions)

Land and land improvements	$ 262
Buildings and building equipment	2,226
Machinery and equipment	3,143
Construction in progress	672
	6,303
Less Accumulated depreciation	2,188
	$4,115

grow as the employee works, so the liability is said to *accrue*. Another example is interest expense on a note payable. Interest accrues as the clock ticks. The term **accrued expense** refers to a liability that arises from an expense that the business has incurred but has not yet paid.

It is time-consuming to make hourly, daily, or even weekly journal entries to accrue expenses. Consequently, the accountant waits until the end of the period. Then an adjusting entry brings each expense (and related liability) up to date just before the financial statements are prepared.

SALARY EXPENSE   Most companies pay their employees at set times. Suppose Gary Lyon pays his employee a monthly salary of $1,900, half on the 15th and half on the last day of the month. Here is a calendar for April that has paydays circled:

			APRIL			
Sun.	Mon.	Tue.	Wed.	Thur.	Fri.	Sat.
					1	2
3	4	5	6	7	8	9
10	11	12	13	14	(15)	16
17	18	19	20	21	22	23
24	25	26	27	28	29	(30)

Assume that if either payday falls on the weekend, Lyon pays the employee on the following Monday. During April Lyon paid his employee's first half-month salary of $950 on Friday, April 15, and recorded the following entry:

Apr. 15   Salary Expense 950
                    Cash   950
              To pay salary.

Short Exercise: What is the adjusting entry for this situation? Weekly salaries for a five-day week total $3,500, payable on Friday. April 30 falls on a Tuesday. *A:* $3,500 × 2/5 = $1,400. The adjusting entry is:
Salary Expense...... 1,400
    Salary Payable...   1,400

After posting, the Salary Expense account is

Salary Expense

Apr. 15	950

The trial balance at April 30 (Exhibit 3-4) includes Salary Expense, with its debit balance of $950. Because April 30, the second payday of the month, falls on a Saturday, the second half-month amount of $950 will be paid on Monday, May 2. Without an adjusting entry, this second $950 amount is not included in the April 30 trial balance amount for Salary Expense. Therefore, at April 30 Lyon adjusts for additional *salary expense* and *salary payable* of $950 by recording an increase in each of those accounts as follows:

Apr. 30   Salary Expense 950
                    Salary Payable   950
              To accrue salary expense.

After posting, the Salary Expense and Salary Payable accounts appear as follows:

Salary Expense				Salary Payable		
Apr. 15	950				Apr. 30	950
Apr. 30	950				Bal.	950
Bal.	1,900					

The accounts at April 30 now contain the complete salary information for the month. The expense account has a full month's salary, and the liability account shows the portion that the business still owes.

Lyon will record the payment of this liability on May 2 by debiting Salary Payable and crediting Cash for $950. This payment entry will not affect April or May expenses because the April expense was recorded on April 15 and April 30. May expense will be recorded in a like manner. All accrued expenses are recorded with similar entries—a debit to the appropriate expense account and a credit to the related liability account.

 Many computerized systems contain a payroll module, or functional unit. The adjusting entry for accrued salaries is automatically journalized and posted at the end of each accounting period.

Accrued Revenues

Businesses often earn revenue before they receive the cash because collection occurs later. A revenue that has been earned but not yet received in cash creates an asset called an **accrued revenue.** Assume that Gary Lyon is hired on April 15 by Guerrero Construction Company to perform services on a monthly basis. Under this agreement, Guerrero will pay Lyon $500 monthly, with the first payment on May 15. During April, Lyon will earn half a month's fee, $250, for work performed April 15 through April 30. On April 30 he makes the following adjusting entry in the journal of Gary Lyon, CPA, to record an increase in Accounts Receivable and Service Revenue:

Apr. 30	Accounts Receivable ($500 × 1/2)..	250	
	Service Revenue...		250
	To accrue service revenue.		

Recall that Accounts Receivable has an unadjusted balance of $2,250, and the Service Revenue unadjusted balance is $7,000 (Exhibit 3-4). Posting this adjusting entry has the following effects on these two accounts:

Accounts Receivable				Service Revenue		
	2,250					7,000
Apr. 30	250				Apr. 30	250
Bal.	2,500				Bal.	7,250

Short Exercise: Suppose Lyon held a note receivable from a client. At the end of April, there is $125 of interest due. Prepare the adjusting entry: *A:* Interest Receivable 125
    Interest Revenue .   125

This adjusting entry illustrates accrual-basis accounting and the revenue principle in action. Without the adjustment, Lyon's financial statements would be misleading—they would understate Accounts Receivable and Service Revenue by $250 each. All accrued revenues are accounted for similarly—by debiting a receivable and crediting a revenue.

Unearned Revenues

Key Point: An unearned revenue is a liability, not a revenue.

Some businesses collect cash from customers in advance of doing work for the customer. Doing so creates a liability called **unearned revenue,** which is an obligation arising from receiving cash in advance of providing a product or a service. Only when the job is completed will the business have earned the revenue. Suppose Baldwin Computing Service Center engages Lyon's services, agreeing to pay him $450 monthly, beginning immediately. If Baldwin makes the first payment on April 20, Lyon records this increase in the liabilities of Gary Lyon, CPA, as follows:

Apr. 20   Cash   450
              Unearned Service Revenue   450
           Received revenue in advance.

After posting, the liability account appears as follows:

Unearned Service Revenue

	Apr. 20	450

Unearned Service Revenue is a liability because it represents Lyon's obligation to perform service for the client. The April 30 unadjusted trial balance (Exhibit 3-4) lists this account with a $450 credit balance prior to the adjusting entries. During the last 10 days of the month—April 21 through April 30—Lyon will have *earned* one-third (10 days divided by April's total 30 days) of the $450, or $150. Therefore, he makes the following adjustment to decrease the liability, Unearned Service Revenue, and to record an increase in Service Revenue:

Apr. 30   Unearned Service Revenue ($450 × 1/3)   150
              Service Revenue   150
           To record unearned service revenue that has been earned.

This adjusting entry shifts $150 of the total amount from the liability account to the revenue account. After posting, the balance of Service Revenue is increased by $150, and the balance of Unearned Service Revenue is reduced to $300:

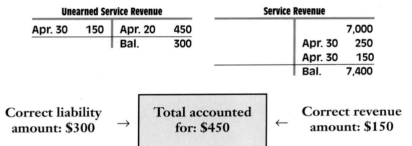

Unearned Service Revenue			
Apr. 30	150	Apr. 20	450
		Bal.	300

Service Revenue	
	7,000
Apr. 30	250
Apr. 30	150
Bal.	7,400

Correct liability amount: $300 → **Total accounted for: $450** ← **Correct revenue amount: $150**

All types of revenues that are collected in advance are accounted for similarly.

An unearned revenue to one company can be a prepaid expense to the company that made the payment. For example, suppose that two months in advance Xerox Corporation paid American Airlines $1,800 for the airfare of Xerox executives. To Xerox the payment is Prepaid Travel Expense. To American Airlines, the receipt of cash creates Unearned Service Revenue. After the executives take the trip, American Airlines records the revenue.

The chapter appendix shows an alternate treatment of unearned revenues.

STOP & THINK   Consider the tuition you pay. Assume that one semester's tuition costs $500 and that you make a single payment at the start of the term. Can you make the journal entries to record the tuition transactions on your own books and on the books of your college or university?

Answer:

	Your Entries			**Your College's Entries**		
Start of semester:	Prepaid Tuition...............	500		Cash	500	
	Cash		500	Unearned Tuition		
	Paid semester tuition			Revenue		500
				Received revenue in advance.		
End of semester:	Tuition Expense..............	500		Unearned Tuition		
	Prepaid Tuition..........		500	Revenue	500	
	To record tuition expense			Tuition Revenue		500
				To record unearned tuition revenue that has been earned.		

Short Exercise: In which, if any, of the five categories of adjusting entries would the following transactions fall? (1) Paid one year's insurance in advance. (2) Recorded part of a building's cost as an expense for the current period. (3) Recorded revenue from renting a building before receiving cash. (4) Paid a bill for maintenance of company automobiles. *A:* (1) Prepaid expense. (2) Depreciation. (3) Accrued revenue. (4) No adjusting entry necessary.

Short Exercise: What is the result on the financial statements of omitting this adjusting entry? *A:* Liabilities are overstated by $150; revenues, net income, and owner's equity are understated by $150.

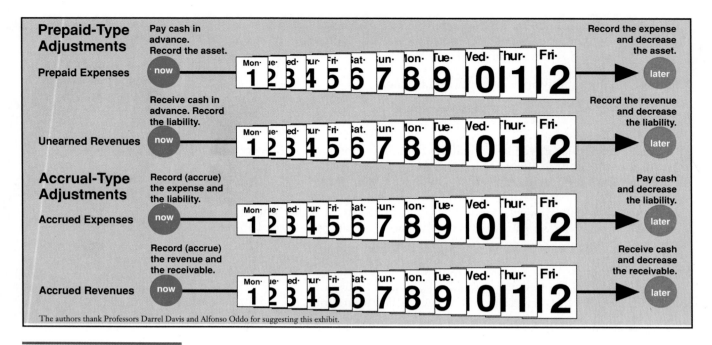

The authors thank Professors Darrel Davis and Alfonso Oddo for suggesting this exhibit.

EXHIBIT 3-7
Prepaid- andAccrual-Type Adjustments

Exhibit 3-7 diagrams the timing of prepaid-type and accrual-type adjusting entries.

Summary of the Adjusting Process

One purpose of the adjusting process is to measure business income, so each adjusting entry affects at least one income statement account—a revenue or an expense. The other purpose of the adjusting process is to update the balance sheet accounts. Therefore, the other side of the entry—a debit or a credit—affects an asset or a liability. No adjusting entry debits or credits Cash because the cash transactions are recorded at other times. The end-of-period adjustment process is reserved for the noncash transactions that are required by accrual-basis accounting. Exhibit 3-8 summarizes the adjusting entries.

EXHIBIT 3-8
Summary of Adjusting Entries

Type of Account Debited	Category of Adjusting Entries	Type of Account Credited
Expense	Prepaid expense	Asset
Expense	Depreciation	Contra asset
Expense	Accrued expense	Liability
Asset	Accrued revenue	Revenue
Liability	Unearned revenue	Revenue

Adapted from Beverly Terry.

Overview of the Adjusting Entries

◄▥▥ ◄▥▥ ◄▥▥ Recall from Chapter 2, p. 51, that posting is the process of transferring amounts from the journal to the ledger.

Exhibit 3-9 summarizes the adjusting entries of Lyon's business at April 30. Panel A briefly describes the data for each adjustment, Panel B gives the adjusting entries, and Panel C shows the accounts after they have been posted. ◄▥▥ The adjustments are keyed by letter.

PANEL A—Information for Adjustments at April 30, 19X1

a. Accrued service revenue, $250.
b. Supplies on hand, $400.
c. Prepaid rent expired, $1,000.

d. Depreciation on furniture, $275.
e. Accrued salary expense, $950.
f. Amount of unearned service revenue that has been earned, $150.

PANEL B—Adjusting Entries

a.	Accounts Receivable	250	
	Service Revenue		250
	To accrue service revenue.		
b.	Supplies Expense	300	
	Supplies...		300
	To record supplies used.		
c.	Rent Expense	1,000	
	Prepaid Rent..		1,000
	To record rent expense.		
d.	Depreciation Expense—Furniture..................................	275	
	Accumulated Depreciation—Furniture................		275
	To record depreciation on furniture.		
e.	Salary Expense	950	
	Salary Payable..		950
	To accrue salary expense.		
f.	Unearned Service Revenue	150	
	Service Revenue		150
	To record unearned revenue that has been earned.		

PANEL C—Ledger Accounts

ASSETS

Cash

Bal. 24,800	

Accounts Receivable

2,250	
(a) 250	
Bal. 2,500	

Supplies

700	(b)	300	
Bal. 400			

Prepaid Rent

3,000	(c)	1,000	
Bal. 2,000			

Furniture

Bal. 16,500	

Accumulated Depreciation— Furniture

	(d)	275
	Bal.	275

LIABILITIES

Accounts Payable

	Bal. 13,100

Salary Payable

	(e)	950
	Bal.	950

Unearned Service Revenue

(f)	150		450
		Bal.	300

OWNER'S EQUITY

Gary Lyon, Capital

	Bal. 31,250

Gary Lyon, Withdrawals

Bal. 3,200	

REVENUE

Service Revenue

		7,000
	(a)	250
	(f)	150
	Bal.	7,400

EXPENSES

Rent Expense

(c)	1,000	
Bal.	1,000	

Salary Expense

	950	
(e)	950	
Bal.	1,900	

Supplies Expense

(b)	300	
Bal.	300	

Depreciation Expense—Furniture

(d)	275	
Bal.	275	

Utilities Expense

Bal. 400	

Adjusted Trial Balance

Key Point: The differences between the amounts in the trial balance and in the adjusted trial balance of Exhibit 3-10 result from the adjusting entries. If the adjusting entries were not given, you could obtain them by computing the differences between the adjusted and unadjusted amounts.

This chapter began with the trial balance before any adjusting entries—the unadjusted trial balance (Exhibit 3-4). After the adjustments are journalized and posted, the accounts appear as shown in Exhibit 3-9, Panel C. A useful step in preparing the financial statements is to list the accounts, along with their adjusted balances, on an **adjusted trial balance**. This document has the advantage of listing all the accounts and their adjusted balances in a single place. Exhibit 3-10 shows the preparation of the adjusted trial balance.

The format of Exhibit 3-10 is called a *work sheet*. We will consider the work sheet further in Chapter 4. For now simply note how clearly this format presents the data. The information in the Account Title column and in the Trial Balance columns is drawn directly from the trial balance. The two Adjustments columns list the debit and credit adjustments directly across from the appropriate account title. Each adjusting debit is identified by a letter in parentheses that refers to the adjusting entry. For example, the debit labeled (a) on the work sheet refers to the debit adjusting entry of $250 to Accounts Receivable in Panel B of Exhibit 3-9. Likewise for adjusting credits, the corresponding credit—labeled (a)—refers to the $250 credit to Service Revenue.

The Adjusted Trial Balance columns give the adjusted account balances. Each amount on the adjusted trial balance of Exhibit 3-10 is computed by combining the amounts from the unadjusted trial balance plus or minus the adjustments. For example, Accounts Receivable starts with a debit balance of $2,250. Adding the $250 debit amount from adjusting entry (a) gives Accounts Receivable an adjusted balance of

EXHIBIT 3-10

Preparation of Adjusted Trial Balance

GARY LYON, CPA
PREPARATION OF ADJUSTED TRIAL BALANCE
APRIL 30, 19X1

Account Title	Trial Balance Debit	Trial Balance Credit	Adjustments Debit	Adjustments Credit	Adjusted Trial Balance Debit	Adjusted Trial Balance Credit
Cash	24,800				24,800	
Accounts receivable	2,250		(a) 250		2,500	
Supplies	700			(b) 300	400	
Prepaid rent	3,000			(c) 1,000	2,000	
Furniture	16,500				16,500	
Accumulated depreciation				(d) 275		275
Accounts payable		13,100				13,100
Salary payable				(e) 950		950
Unearned service revenue		450	(f) 150			300
Gary Lyon, capital		31,250				31,250
Gary Lyon, withdrawals	3,200				3,200	
Service revenue		7,000		(a) 250		7,400
				(f) 150		
Rent expense			(c) 1,000		1,000	
Salary expense	950		(e) 950		1,900	
Supplies expense			(b) 300		300	
Depreciation expense			(d) 275		275	
Utilities expense	400				400	
	51,800	51,800	2,925	2,925	53,275	53,275

$2,500. Supplies begins with a debit balance of $700. After the $300 credit adjustment, its adjusted balance is $400. More than one entry may affect a single account, as is the case for Service Revenue. If an account is unaffected by the adjustments, it will show the same amount on both the adjusted and the unadjusted trial balances. This is true for Cash, Furniture, Accounts Payable, the Capital account, and the Withdrawals account.

Key Point: Because an adjusting entry never affects Cash, Withdrawals, or Capital, these accounts' balances on the adjusted trial balance should be the same as on the unadjusted trial balance.

Preparing the Financial Statements from the Adjusted Trial Balance

The April financial statements of Gary Lyon, CPA, can be prepared from the adjusted trial balance. Exhibit 3-11 shows how the accounts are distributed from the adjusted trial balance to these three financial statements. The income statement (Exhibit 3-12) comes from the revenue and expense accounts. The statement of owner's equity (Exhibit 3-13) shows the reasons for the change in the owner's capital during the period. The balance sheet (Exhibit 3-14) reports the assets, liabilities, and owner's equity.

OBJECTIVE 5
Prepare the financial statements from the adjusted trial balance

Financial Statements

The financial statements are best prepared in the order shown: the income statement first, followed by the statement of owner's equity, and then the balance sheet. The essential features of all financial statements are (1) the name of the entity, (2) the title of the statement, (3) the date or the period covered by the statement, and (4) the body of the statement.

It is customary to list expenses in descending order by amount, as shown in Exhibit 3-12. However, Miscellaneous Expense, a catchall account for expenses that do not fit another category, is usually reported last regardless of its amount.

Account Title	Adjusted Trial Balance Debit	Adjusted Trial Balance Credit	
Cash	24,800		
Accounts receivable	2,500		
Supplies	400		
Prepaid rent	2,000		
Furniture	16,500		**Balance Sheet** (Exhibit 3-14)
Accumulated depreciation		275	
Accounts payable		13,100	
Salary payable		950	
Unearned service revenue		300	**Statement of Owner's Equity** (Exhibit 3-13)
Gary Lyon, capital		31,250	
Gary Lyon, withdrawals	3,200		
Service revenue		7,400	
Rent expense	1,000		**Income Statement** (Exhibit 3-12)
Salary expense	1,900		
Supplies expense	300		
Depreciation expense	275		
Utilities expense	400		
	53,275	53,275	

EXHIBIT 3-11
Preparing the Financial Statements of Gary Lyon, CPA, from the Adjusted Trial Balance

EXHIBIT 3-12

Income Statement

GARY LYON, CPA
INCOME STATEMENT
FOR THE MONTH ENDED APRIL 30, 19X1

Revenue:		
Service revenue		$7,400
Expenses:		
Salary expense	$1,900	
Rent expense	1,000	
Utilities expense	400	
Supplies expense	300	
Depreciation expense	275	
Total expenses		3,875
Net income		$3,525

EXHIBIT 3-13

Statement of Owner's Equity

GARY LYON, CPA
STATEMENT OF OWNER'S EQUITY
FOR THE MONTH ENDED APRIL 30, 19X1

Gary Lyon, capital, April 1, 19X1	$31,250
Add: Net income	3,525
	34,775
Less: Withdrawals	3,200
Gary Lyon, capital, April 30, 19X1	$31,575

①

EXHIBIT 3-14

Balance Sheet

GARY LYON, CPA
BALANCE SHEET
APRIL 30, 19X1

Assets			Liabilities		
Cash		$24,800	Accounts payable		$13,100
Accounts receivable		2,500	Salary payable		950
Supplies		400	Unearned service		
Prepaid rent		2,000	revenue		300
Furniture	$16,500		Total liabilities		14,350
Less Accumulated					
depreciation	275	16,225	**Owner's Equity**		
			Gary Lyon, capital		31,575
			Total liabilities and		
Total assets		$45,925	owner's equity		$45,925

②

Relationships among the Three Financial Statements

◀▦◀▦◀▦ The relationships among the financial statements were introduced in Chapter 1, p. 19.

The arrows in Exhibits 3-12, 3-13, and 3-14 illustrate the relationships among the income statement, the statement of owner's equity, and the balance sheet. ◀▦ Consider why the income statement is prepared first and the balance sheet last.

1. The income statement reports net income or net loss, figured by subtracting expenses from revenues. Because revenues and expenses are owner's equity accounts, their net amount is then transferred to the statement of owner's equity. Note that net income in Exhibit 3-12, $3,525, increases owner's equity in Exhibit 3-13. A net loss would decrease owner's equity.

2. Capital is a balance sheet account, so the ending balance in the statement of owner's equity is transferred to the balance sheet. This amount is the final balancing element of the balance sheet. To solidify your understanding of this relationship, trace the $31,575 figure from Exhibit 3-13 to Exhibit 3-14.

You may be wondering why the total assets on the balance sheet ($45,925 in Exhibit 3-14) do not equal the total debits on the adjusted trial balance ($53,275 in Exhibit 3-11). Likewise, the total liabilities and owner's equity do not equal the total credits on the adjusted trial balance. The reason for these differences is that Accumulated Depreciation and Owner's Withdrawals are *subtracted* from their related accounts on the balance sheet but *added* in their respective columns on the adjusted trial balance.

STOP & THINK Examine Gary Lyon's adjusted trial balance in Exhibit 3-10. If Lyon forgot to record the $950 accrual of salary expense at April 30, what net income would his accounting practice have reported for April? What total assets, total liabilities, and total owner's equity would the balance sheet have reported at April 30?

Answer: Omission of the salary accrual would produce these effects:

1. Net income would have been reported on the income statement (Exhibit 3-12) as $4,475 ($3,525 + $950).
2. Total assets would have been unaffected by the error—$45,925, as reported on the balance sheet (Exhibit 3-14).
3. Total liabilities would have been reported as $13,400 ($14,350 - $950) on the balance sheet (Exhibit 3-14).
4. Owner's equity (Gary Lyon, capital) would have been reported at $32,525 ($31,575 + $950) on the balance sheet (Exhibit 3-14).

This specific example addresses an accounting-error question. But the analysis needed to compute these amounts is important to marketing, finance, statistics, and management personnel in business—because everyone is affected by the amount of the net income that a business reports.

SUMMARY PROBLEM FOR YOUR REVIEW

The trial balance of State Service Company pertains to December 31, 19X3, which is the end of its year-long accounting period. Data needed for the adjusting entries include:

a. Supplies on hand at year end, $2,000.
b. Depreciation on furniture and fixtures, $20,000.
c. Depreciation on building, $10,000.
d. Salaries owed but not yet paid, $5,000.
e. Accrued service revenue, $12,000.
f. Of the $45,000 balance of unearned service revenue, $32,000 was earned during the year.

Required

1. Open the ledger accounts with their unadjusted balances. Show dollar amounts in thousands, as shown for Accounts Receivable:

Accounts Receivable

370

2. Journalize State Service Company's adjusting entries at December 31, 19X3. Key entries by letter as in Exhibit 3-9.

3. Post the adjusting entries.
4. Write the trial balance on a work sheet, enter the adjusting entries, and prepare an adjusted trial balance, as shown in Exhibit 3-10.
5. Prepare the income statement, the statement of owner's equity, and the balance sheet. Draw arrows linking these three financial statements.

STATE SERVICE COMPANY TRIAL BALANCE DECEMBER 31, 19X3		
Cash	$ 198,000	
Accounts receivable	370,000	
Supplies	6,000	
Furniture and fixtures	100,000	
Accumulated depreciation—furniture and fixtures		$ 40,000
Building	250,000	
Accumulated depreciation—building		130,000
Accounts payable		380,000
Salary payable		
Unearned service revenue		45,000
Capital		293,000
Owner's withdrawals	65,000	
Service revenue		286,000
Salary expense	172,000	
Supplies expense		
Depreciation expense—furniture and fixtures		
Depreciation expense—building		
Miscellaneous expense	13,000	
Total	$1,174,000	$1,174,000

SOLUTION TO REVIEW PROBLEM

Requirements 1 and 3

ASSETS

Cash

Bal.	198	

Accounts Receivable

	370	
(e)	12	
Bal.	382	

Supplies

	6	(a)	4
Bal.	2		

Furniture and Fixtures

Bal.	100	

Accumulated Depreciation— Furniture and Fixtures

		40
	(b)	20
	Bal.	60

Building

Bal.	250	

Accumulated Depreciation— Building

		130
	(c)	10
	Bal.	140

LIABILITIES

Accounts Payable

	Bal.	380

Salary Payable

	(d)	5
	Bal.	5

Unearned Service Revenue

(f)	32		45
		Bal.	13

OWNER'S EQUITY

Capital

	Bal.	293

Owner's Withdrawals

Bal.	65	

REVENUE

Service Revenue

			286
	(e)		12
	(f)		32
		Bal.	330

EXPENSES

Salary Expense

	172	
(d)	5	
Bal.	177	

Supplies Expense

(a)	4	
Bal.	4	

Depreciation Expense— Furniture and Fixtures

(b)	20	
Bal.	20	

Depreciation Expense— Building

(c)	10	
Bal.	10	

Miscellaneous Expense

Bal.	13	

Requirement 2

19X1

a. Dec. 31 Supplies Expense ($6,000 – $2,000) 4,000
　　　　　　　　Supplies .... 　　4,000
　　　　　　To record supplies used.

b. 　31 　Depreciation Expense—Furniture and Fixtures................. 20,000
　　　　　　　　Accumulated Depreciation—Furniture and Fixtures 　　20,000
　　　　　　To record depreciation expense on furniture and fixtures.

c. 　31 　Depreciation Expense—Building.. 10,000
　　　　　　　　Accumulated Depreciation—Building .... 　　10,000
　　　　　　To record depreciation expense on building.

d. 　31 　Salary Expense... 5,000
　　　　　　　　Salary Payable .... 　　5,000
　　　　　　To accrue salary expense.

e. 　31 　Accounts Receivable 12,000
　　　　　　　　Service Revenue .... 　　12,000
　　　　　　To accrue service revenue.

f. 　31 　Unearned Service Revenue 32,000
　　　　　　　　Service Revenue .... 　　32,000
　　　　　　To record unearned service revenue that has been earned.

Requirement 4

STATE SERVICE COMPANY
PREPARATION OF ADJUSTED TRIAL BALANCE
DECEMBER 31, 19X3
(AMOUNTS IN THOUSANDS)

	Trial Balance		Adjustments		Adjusted Trial Balance	
	Debit	Credit	Debit	Credit	Debit	Credit
Cash	198				198	
Accounts receivable	370		(e) 12		382	
Supplies	6			(a) 4	2	
Furniture and fixtures	100				100	
Accumulated depreciation— furniture and fixtures		40		(b) 20		60
Building	250				250	
Accumulated depreciation— building		130		(c) 10		140
Accounts payable		380				380
Salary payable				(d) 5		5
Unearned service revenue		45	(f) 32			13
Capital		293				293
Owner's withdrawals	65				65	
Service revenue		286		(e) 12		330
				(f) 32		
Salary expense	172		(d) 5		177	
Supplies expense			(a) 4		4	
Depreciation expense—furniture and fixtures			(b) 20		20	
Depreciation expense— building			(c) 10		10	
Miscellaneous expense	13				13	
	1,174	1,174	83	83	1,221	1,221

Requirement 5

STATE SERVICE COMPANY
INCOME STATEMENT
FOR THE YEAR ENDED DECEMBER 31, 19X3
(AMOUNTS IN THOUSANDS)

Revenue:		
Service revenue		$330
Expenses:		
Salary expense	$177	
Depreciation expense—furniture and fixtures	20	
Depreciation expense—building	10	
Supplies expense	4	
Miscellaneous expense	13	
Total expenses		224
Net income		$106

STATE SERVICE COMPANY
STATEMENT OF OWNER'S EQUITY
FOR THE YEAR ENDED DECEMBER 31, 19X3
(AMOUNTS IN THOUSANDS)

Capital, January 1, 19X3	$293
Add: Net income	106
	399
Less: Withdrawals	65
Capital, December 31, 19X3	$334

STATE SERVICE COMPANY
BALANCE SHEET
DECEMBER 31, 19X3
(AMOUNTS IN THOUSANDS)

Assets			Liabilities		
Cash		$198	Accounts payable		$380
Accounts receivable		382	Salary payable		5
Supplies		2	Unearned service		
Furniture and fixtures	$100		revenue		13
Less Accumulated			Total liabilities		398
depreciation	60	40			
Building	$250		**Owner's Equity**		
Less Accumulated			Capital		334
depreciation	140	110	Total liabilities and		
Total assets		$732	owner's equity		$732

SUMMARY

1. Distinguish accrual-basis accounting from cash-basis accounting. In *accrual-basis accounting*, business events are recorded as they affect the entity. In *cash-basis accounting*, only those events that affect cash are recorded. The cash basis omits important events such as purchases and sales of assets on ac- count. It also distorts the financial statements by labeling as expenses those cash payments that have long-term effects, such as the purchases of buildings and equipment. Some small organizations use cash-basis accounting, but the generally accepted method is the accrual basis.

2. Apply the revenue and matching principles. Businesses divide time into definite periods—such as a month, a quarter, and a year—to report the entity's financial statements. The year is the basic *accounting period*, but companies prepare financial statements as often as they need the information. Accountants have developed the *revenue principle* to determine when to record revenue and the amount of revenue to record. The *matching principle* guides the accounting for expenses.

3. Make adjusting entries at the end of the accounting period. *Adjusting entries* are a result of the accrual basis of accounting. These entries, made at the end of the period, update the accounts for preparation of the financial statements. One of the most important pieces of business information is net income or net loss, and the adjusting entries help to measure the

net income of the period. Adjusting entries can be divided into five categories: *prepaid expenses, depreciation, accrued expenses, accrued revenues,* and *unearned revenues.*

4. Prepare an adjusted trial balance. To prepare the *adjusted trial balance,* enter the adjusting entries next to the *unadjusted trial balance* and compute each account's balance.

5. Prepare the financial statements from the adjusted trial balance. The adjusted trial balance can be used to prepare the financial statements. The three financial statements are related as follows: Income, shown on the *income statement,* increases the owner's capital, which also appears on the *statement of owner's equity.* The ending balance of capital is the last amount reported on the *balance sheet.*

SELF-STUDY QUESTIONS

Test your understanding of the chapter by marking the best answer for each of the following questions.

1. Accrual-basis accounting (*pp. 90–92*)
   a. Results in higher income than cash-basis accounting
   b. Leads to the reporting of more complete information than does cash-basis accounting
   c. Is not acceptable under GAAP
   d. Omits adjusting entries at the end of the period

2. Under the revenue principle, revenue is recorded (*pp. 92–93*)
   a. At the earliest acceptable time
   b. At the latest acceptable time
   c. After it has been earned, but not before
   d. At the end of the accounting period

3. The matching principle provides guidance in accounting for (*p. 93*)
   a. Expenses
   b. Owner's equity
   c. Assets
   d. Liabilities

4. Adjusting entries (*pp. 95–96*)
   a. Assign revenues to the period in which they are earned
   b. Help to properly measure the period's net income or net loss
   c. Bring asset and liability accounts to correct balances
   d. All of the above

5. A law firm began November with office supplies of $160. During the month, the firm purchased supplies of $290. At November 30 supplies on hand total $210. Supplies expense for the period is (*pp. 97–98*)
   a. $210
   b. $240
   c. $290
   d. $450

6. A building that cost $120,000 has accumulated depreciation of $50,000. The book value of the building is (*p. 100*)

   a. $50,000   c. $120,000
   b. $70,000   d. $170,000

7. The adjusting entry to accrue salary expense (*p. 101*)
   a. Debits Salary Expense and credits Cash
   b. Debits Salary Payable and credits Salary Expense
   c. Debits Salary Payable and credits Cash
   d. Debits Salary Expense and credits Salary Payable

8. A business received cash of $3,000 in advance for service that will be provided later. The cash receipt entry debited Cash and credited Unearned Revenue for $3,000. At the end of the period, $1,100 is still unearned. The adjusting entry for this situation will (*p. 103*)
   a. Debit Unearned Revenue and credit Revenue for $1,900
   b. Debit Unearned Revenue and credit Revenue for $1,100
   c. Debit Revenue and credit Unearned Revenue for $1,900
   d. Debit Revenue and credit Unearned Revenue for $1,100

9. The links between the financial statements are (*p. 108*)
   a. Net income from the income statement to the statement of owner's equity
   b. Ending capital from the statement of owner's equity to the balance sheet
   c. Both a and b
   d. None of the above

10. Accumulated Depreciation is reported on the (*p. 108*)
    a. Balance sheet   c. Statement of owner's equity
    b. Income statement   d. Both a and b

Answers to the Self-Study Questions follow the Accounting Vocabulary.

ACCOUNTING VOCABULARY

Accrual-basis accounting. Accounting that recognizes (records) the impact of a business event as it occurs, regardless of whether the transaction affected cash (*p. 90*).

Accrued expense. An expense that has been incurred but not yet paid in cash (*p. 101*).

Accrued revenue. A revenue that has been earned but not yet received in cash (*p. 102*).

Accumulated depreciation. The cumulative sum of all depreciation expense from the date of acquiring a plant asset (*p. 99*).

Adjusted trial balance. A list of all the

ledger accounts with their adjusted balances (*p. 106*).

Adjusting entry. Entry made at the end of the period to assign revenues to the period in which they are earned and expenses to the period in which they are incurred. Adjusting entries help measure the period's income and bring the related asset and liability accounts to correct balances for the financial statements (p. 95).

Book value of a plant asset. The asset's cost less accumulated depreciation (p. 99).

Cash-basis accounting. Accounting that records only transactions in which cash is received or paid (p. 90).

Contra account. An account that always has a companion account and whose normal balance is opposite that of the companion account (p. 99).

Depreciation. Expense associated with spreading (allocating) the cost of a plant asset over its useful life (p. 98).

Matching principle. The basis for recording expenses. Directs accountants to identify all expenses incurred during the period, to measure the expenses, and to match them against the revenues earned during that same span of time (p. 93).

Plant asset. Long-lived assets, such as land, buildings, and equipment, used in the operation of the business (p. 98).

Prepaid expense. A category of miscellaneous assets that typically expire or get used up in the near future. Examples include prepaid rent, prepaid insur-

ance, and supplies (p. 96).

Revenue principle. The basis for recording revenues; tells accountants when to record revenue and the amount of revenue to record (p. 92).

Time-period concept. Ensures that accounting information is reported at regular intervals (p. 94).

Unearned revenue. A liability created when a business collects cash from customers in advance of doing work for the customer. The obligation is to provide a product or a service in the future. Also called deferred revenue (p. 102).

ANSWERS TO SELF-STUDY QUESTIONS

1.	b	4.	d	7.	d	9.	c
2.	c	5.	b ($160 + $290 − $210 = $240)	8.	a ($3,000 received − $1,100 unearned = $1,900 earned)	10.	a
3.	a	6.	b ($120,000 − $50,000 = $70,000)				

QUESTIONS

1. Distinguish accrual-basis accounting from cash-basis.
2. How long is the basic accounting period? What is a fiscal year? What is an interim period?
3. What two questions does the revenue principle help answer?
4. Briefly explain the matching principle.
5. What is the purpose of making adjusting entries?
6. Why are adjusting entries made at the end of the accounting period, not during the period?
7. Name five categories of adjusting entries, and give an example of each.
8. Do all adjusting entries affect the net income or net loss of the period? Include the definition of an adjusting entry.
9. Why must the balance of Supplies be adjusted at the end of the period?
10. Manning Supply Company pays $1,800 for an insurance policy that covers three years. At the end of the first year, the balance of its Prepaid Insurance account contains two elements. What are the two elements, and what is the correct amount of each?
11. The title Prepaid Expense suggests that this type of account is an expense. If it is, explain why. If it is not, what type of account is it?

12. What is a contra account? Identify the contra account introduced in this chapter, along with the account's normal balance.
13. The manager of a Quickie-Pickie convenience store presents his entity's balance sheet to a banker to obtain a loan. The balance sheet reports that the entity's plant assets have a book value of $135,000 and accumulated depreciation of $65,000. What does *book value* of a plant asset mean? What was the cost of the plant assets?
14. Give the entry to record accrued interest revenue of $800.
15. Why is an unearned revenue a liability? Give an example.
16. Identify the types of accounts (assets, liabilities, and so on) debited and credited for each of the five types of adjusting entries.
17. What purposes does the adjusted trial balance serve?
18. Explain the relationship among the income statement, the statement of owner's equity, and the balance sheet.
19. Bellevue Company failed to record the following adjusting entries at December 31, the end of its fiscal year: (a) accrued expenses, $500; (b) accrued revenues, $850; and (c) depreciation, $1,000. Did these omissions cause net income for the year to be understated or overstated, and by what overall amount?

EXERCISES

Cash basis versus accrual basis (Obj. 1)

E3-1 The Oak Lodge had the following selected transactions during August:

Aug. 1	Prepaid rent for three months, $3,000.
5	Paid electricity expenses, $700.
9	Received cash for the day's room rentals, $1,400.
14	Purchased six television sets, $3,000.
23	Served a banquet, receiving a note receivable, $1,200.
31	Made the adjusting entry for rent (from Aug. 1).
31	Accrued salary expense $900.

Show how each transaction would be handled using the cash basis and the accrual basis. Under each column give the amount of revenue or expense for August. Journal entries are not required. Use the following format for your answer, and show your computations:

Oak Lodge—Amount of Revenue or Expense for August

Date	Cash Basis	Accrual Basis

E3-2 Identify the accounting concept or principle that gives the most direction on how to account for each of the following situations:

Applying accounting concepts and principles (Obj. 2)

a. A customer states her intention to switch travel agencies. Should the new travel agency record revenue based on this intention?

b. The owner of a business desires monthly financial statements to measure the progress of the entity on an ongoing basis.

c. Expenses of the period total $6,100. This amount should be subtracted from revenue to compute the period's income.

d. Expenses of $2,800 must be accrued at the end of the period to measure income properly.

E3-3 Write a short paragraph to explain in your own words the concept of depreciation as it is used in accounting.

Applying accounting concepts (Obj. 2)

E3-4 Compute the amounts indicated by question marks for each of the following Prepaid Insurance situations. For situations 1 and 2, journalize the needed entry. Consider each situation separately.

Allocating prepaid expense to the asset and the expense (Obj. 2, 3)

	Situation			
	1	2	3	4
Beginning Prepaid Insurance	$ 300	$ 500	$ 600	$ 900
Payments for Prepaid Insurance during the year..........	1,100	?	?	1,100
Total amount to account for	?	?	1,300	2,000
Ending Prepaid Insurance	200	600	500	?
Insurance Expense	$?	$ 400	$ 800	$1,400

E3-5 Journalize the entries for the following adjustments at December 31, the end of the accounting period.

Journalizing adjusting entries (Obj. 3)

a. Prepaid insurance expired, $600.

b. Interest revenue accrued, $4,100.

c. Unearned service revenue earned, $800.

d. Depreciation, $6,200.

e. Employee salaries owed for two days of a five-day workweek; weekly payroll, $9,000.

E3-6 Suppose the adjustments required in Exercise 3-5 were not made. Compute the overall overstatement or understatement of net income as a result of the omission of these adjustments.

Analyzing the effects of adjustments on net income (Obj. 3)

E3-7 Journalize the adjusting entry needed at December 31 for each of the following independent situations.

Journalizing adjusting entries (Obj. 3)

a. The business owes interest expense of $1,400 that it will pay early in the next period.

b. Interest revenue of $900 has been earned but not yet received. The business holds a $20,000 note receivable.

c. On July 1, when we collected $6,000 rent in advance, we debited Cash and credited Unearned Rent Revenue. The tenant was paying for two years' rent.

d. Salary expense is $1,000 per day—Monday through Friday—and the business pays employees each Friday. This year December 31 falls on a Thursday.

e. The unadjusted balance of the Supplies account is $3,100. The total cost of supplies on hand is $1,200.

f. Equipment was purchased last year at a cost of $10,000. The equipment's useful life is four years. Record the year's depreciation.

g. On September 1, when we prepaid $1,800 for a one-year insurance policy, we debited Prepaid Insurance and credited Cash.

Recording adjustments in T-accounts (Obj. 3)

E3-8   The accounting records of Dimitri Plesek, Artist, include the following unadjusted balances at May 31: Accounts Receivable, $1,200; Supplies, $600; Salary Payable, $0; Unearned Service Revenue, $400; Service Revenue, $4,700; Salary Expense, $1,200; Supplies Expense, $0. Plesek's accountant develops the following data for the May 31 adjusting entries:

a. Supplies on hand, $400.

b. Salary owed to employee, $400.

c. Service revenue accrued, $350.

d. Unearned service revenue that has been earned, $250.

Open the foregoing T-accounts and record the adjustments directly in the accounts, keying each adjustment amount by letter. Show each account's adjusted balance. Journal entries are not required.

Adjusting the accounts (Obj. 3, 4)

E3-9   The adjusted trial balance of Ship-n-Go Service is incomplete. Enter the adjustment amounts directly in the adjustment columns of the text. Service Revenue is the only account affected by more than one adjustment.

	Trial Balance		Adjustments		Adjusted Trial Balance	
SHIP-N-GO SERVICE **PREPARATION OF ADJUSTED TRIAL BALANCE** **OCTOBER 31, 19X2**						
	Debit	**Credit**	**Debit**	**Credit**	**Debit**	**Credit**
Cash	3,000				3,000	
Accounts receivable	6,500				7,400	
Supplies	1,040				800	
Office furniture	29,300				29,300	
Accumulated depreciation		11,060				11,420
Salary payable						600
Unearned revenue		900				690
Capital		26,340				26,340
Owner's withdrawals	6,200				6,200	
Service revenue		11,830				12,940
Salary expense	2,690				3,290	
Rent expense	1,400				1,400	
Depreciation expense					360	
Supplies expense					240	
	50,130	50,130			51,990	51,990

Journalizing adjustments (Obj. 3, 4)

E3-10   Make journal entries for the adjustments that would complete the preparation of the adjusted trial balance in Exercise 3-9. Include explanations.

Preparing the financial statements (Obj. 5)

E3-11   Refer to the adjusted trial balance in Exercise 3-9. Prepare Ship-n-Go Service's income statement and statement of owner's equity for the three months ended October 31, 19X2, and its balance sheet on that date. Draw the arrows linking the three statements.

E3-12   The accountant for Charles Holcomb, M.D., has posted adjusting entries (a) through (e) to the accounts at May 31, 19X2. Selected balance sheet accounts and all the revenues and expenses of the entity follow in T-account form.

Preparing the financial statements
(Obj. 5)

Accounts Receivable		Supplies		Accumulated Depreciation—Furniture	
23,000		4,000	(a) 2,000		5,000
(e) 4,500					(b) 4,000

Accumulated Depreciation—Building		Salary Payable		Service Revenue	
	33,000		(d) 1,500		135,000
(c)	5,000				(e) 4,500

Salary Expense		Supplies Expense		Depreciation Expense—Furniture		Depreciation Expense—Building	
28,000		(a) 2,000		(b) 4,000		(c) 5,000	
(d) 1,500							

Required

Prepare the income statement of Charles Holcomb, M.D., for the year ended May 31, 19X2. List expenses in order from the largest to the smallest.

E3-13   A. J. Hawari Company began the year with capital of $90,000. On July 9 the owner invested $12,000 cash in the business. On September 26 he transferred to the company land valued at $70,000. The income statement for the year ended September 30, 19X5, reported a net loss of $28,000. During this fiscal year, the owner withdrew $1,500 monthly for personal use. Prepare the company's statement of owner's equity for the year ended September 30, 19X5.

Preparing the statement of owner's equity
(Obj. 5)

SERIAL EXERCISE

Exercise 3-14 continues the Emily Schneider, Accountant, situation begun in Exercise 2-13 of Chapter 2.

E3-14   Refer to Exercise 2-13 of Chapter 2. Start from the trial balance and the posted T-accounts that Emily Schneider, Accountant, prepared for her accounting practice at December 18. Later in December, Schneider's business completed these transactions:

Adjusting the accounts, preparing an adjusted trial balance, and preparing the financial statements.
(Obj. 3, 4, 5)

Dec. 21   Received $900 in advance for tax work to be performed evenly over the next 30 days.
21   Hired a secretary to be paid $1,500 on the 20th day of each month.
26   Paid for the supplies purchased on December 5.
28   Collected $600 from the consulting client on December 18.
30   Withdrew $1,600 for personal use.

Required

1. Open these T-accounts: Accumulated Depreciation—Equipment; Accumulated Depreciation—Furniture; Salary Payable; Unearned Service Revenue; Depreciation Expense—Equipment; Depreciation Expense—Furniture; Supplies Expense.
2. Journalize the transactions of December 21 through 30.
3. Post to the T-accounts, keying all items by date.
4. Prepare a trial balance at December 31. Also set up columns for the adjustments and for the adjusted trial balance, as illustrated in Exhibit 3-10.
5. At December 31, Emily Schneider gathers the following information for the adjusting entries:
   a.   Accrued service revenue, $400.
   b.   Earned a portion of the service revenue collected in advance on December 21.
   c.   Supplies on hand, $100.
   d.   Depreciation expense—equipment, $50; furniture, $60.
   e.   Accrued expense for secretary salary.

Make these adjustments directly in the adjustments columns, and complete the adjusted trial balance at December 31.

6. Journalize and post the adjusting entries. Denote each adjusting amount as *Adj.* and an account balance as *Bal.*

7. Prepare the income statement and the statement of owner's equity of Emily Schneider, Accountant, for the month ended December 31, and prepare the balance sheet at that date.

CHALLENGE EXERCISES

Computing the amount of revenue
(Obj. 3)

E3-15 Lei Ma Enterprises aids Singaporean students upon their arrival in the United States. Paid by the Singaporean government, Lei Ma collects some service revenue in advance. In other cases he receives cash after performing relocation services. At the end of August—a particularly busy period—Lei Ma's books show the following:

	July 31	August 31
Accounts receivable	$1,900	$2,200
Unearned service revenue	1,200	300

During August Lei Ma Enterprises received cash of $6,100 from the Singaporean government. How much service revenue did the business earn during August? Show your work.

Computing cash amounts
(Obj. 3)

E3-16 For the situation of Exercise 3-15, take the service revenue of Lei Ma Enterprises as $5,700 during August. How much cash did the business collect from the Singaporean government that month? Show your work.

PROBLEMS

(GROUP A)

Cash basis versus accrual basis
(Obj. 1, 2)

P3-1A Albritton Counseling Service had the following selected transactions during October:

Oct. 1	Prepaid insurance for October through December, $450.
4	Purchased office equipment for cash, $800.
5	Performed counseling service and received cash, $700.
8	Paid advertising expense, $300.
11	Performed counseling service on account, $1,200.
19	Purchased office furniture on account, $150.
24	Collected $400 on account for the October 11 service.
26	Paid account payable from October 19.
29	Paid salary expense, $900.
31	Recorded adjusting entry for October insurance expense (see Oct. 1).
31	Debited unearned revenue and credited revenue to adjust the accounts, $600.

Required

1. Show how each transaction would be handled using the cash basis and the accrual basis. Under each column give the amount of revenue or expense for October. Journal entries are not required. Use the following format for your answer, and show your computations:

Albritton Counseling Service—Amount of Revenue or Expense for October

Date	Cash Basis	Accrual Basis

2. Compute October net income or net loss under each method.
3. Indicate which measure of net income or net loss is preferable. Give your reason.

Applying accounting principles
(Obj. 2, 3)

P3-2A As the controller of Binswanger Auto Glass Company, you have hired a new bookkeeper, whom you must train. He objects to making an adjusting entry for accrued salaries at the end of the period. He reasons, "We will pay the salaries soon. Why not wait until payment to record the expense? In the end, the result will be the same." Write a reply to explain to the bookkeeper why the adjusting entry for accrued salary expense is needed.

Journalizing adjusting entries
(Obj. 3)

P3-3A Journalize the adjusting entry needed on December 31, end of the current accounting period, for each of the following independent cases affecting Brunansky Consulting Company.

a. Each Friday Brunansky pays its employees for the current week's work. The amount of the payroll is $3,500 for a five-day work week. The current accounting period ends on Thursday.

b. Brunansky has received notes receivable from some clients for professional services. During the current year, Brunansky has earned accrued interest revenue of $9,575, which will be received next year.

c. The beginning balance of Engineering Supplies was $3,800. During the year the entity purchased supplies costing $12,530, and at December 31 the inventory of supplies on hand is $2,970.

d. Brunansky is conducting tests of the strength of the steel to be used in a large building, and the client paid Brunansky $36,000 at the start of the project. Brunansky recorded this amount as Unearned Engineering Revenue. The tests will take several months to complete. Brunansky executives estimate that the company has earned three-fourths of the total fee during the current year.

e. Depreciation for the current year includes: Office Furniture, $5,500; Engineering Equipment, $6,360; Building, $3,790. Make a compound entry.

f. Details of Prepaid Insurance are shown in the account:

Prepaid Insurance	
Jan. 1 Bal.	1,200
Apr. 30	1,800
Oct. 31	1,800

Brunansky pays semiannual insurance premiums (the payment for insurance coverage is called a *premium*) on April 30 and October 31. At December 31, part of the last payment is still in force.

P3-4A Henderson Commission Company's unadjusted and adjusted trial balances at December 31, 19X7, follow:

Analyzing and journalizing adjustments (Obj. 3)

HENDERSON COMMISSION COMPANY
ADJUSTED TRIAL BALANCE
DECEMBER 31, 19X7

Account Title	Trial Balance Debit	Trial Balance Credit	Adjusted Trial Balance Debit	Adjusted Trial Balance Credit
Cash	4,120		4,120	
Accounts receivable	11,260		14,090	
Supplies	1,090		780	
Prepaid insurance	2,600		1,330	
Office furniture	21,630		21,630	
Accumulated depreciation		8,220		10,500
Accounts payable		6,310		6,310
Salary payable				960
Interest payable				480
Note payable		12,000		12,000
Unearned commission revenue		1,840		1,160
Deanne Henderson, capital		13,510		13,510
Deanne Henderson, withdrawals	29,370		29,370	
Commission revenue		72,890		76,400
Depreciation expense			2,280	
Supplies expense			310	
Utilities expense	4,960		4,960	
Salary expense	26,660		27,620	
Rent expense	12,200		12,200	
Interest expense	880		1,360	
Insurance expense			1,270	
	114,770	114,770	121,320	121,320

Journalize the adjusting entries that account for the differences between the two trial balances.

Journalizing and posting adjustments to T-accounts, preparing the adjusted trial balance
(Obj. 3, 4)

P3-5A The trial balance of Pettit Realty at August 31 of the current year and the data needed for the month-end adjustments follow.

PETTIT REALTY TRIAL BALANCE AUGUST 31, 19X6		
Cash	$ 3,100	
Accounts receivable	23,780	
Prepaid rent	2,420	
Supplies	1,180	
Furniture	19,740	
Accumulated depreciation		$ 3,630
Accounts payable		3,310
Salary payable		
Unearned commission revenue		2,790
Tom Pettit, capital		39,510
Tom Pettit, withdrawals	4,800	
Commission revenue		11,700
Salary expense	3,800	
Rent expense		
Utilities expense	550	
Depreciation expense		
Advertising expense	1,570	
Supplies expense		
Total	$60,940	$60,940

Adjustment data:

a. Unearned commission revenue still unearned at August 31, $1,670.
b. Prepaid rent still in force at August 31, $620.
c. Supplies used during the month, $700.
d. Depreciation for the month, $400.
e. Accrued advertising expense at August 31, $610. (Credit Accounts Payable.)
f. Accrued salary expense at August 31, $550.

Required

1. Open T-accounts for the accounts listed in the trial balance, inserting their August 31 unadjusted balances.
2. Journalize the adjusting entries and post them to the T-accounts. Key the journal entries and the posted amounts by letter.
3. Prepare the adjusted trial balance.

Preparing an adjusted trial balance and the financial statements
(Obj. 3, 4, 5)

P3-6A The adjusted trial balance of Blitz Delivery Services at December 31, 19X8 follows at the top of page 121.

Required

1. Prepare Blitz's 19X8 income statement, statement of owner's equity, and balance sheet. List expenses in decreasing order on the income statement and show total liabilities on the balance sheet. Draw arrows linking the three financial statements.
2. How will what you learned in this problem help you manage a business?

```
                    BLITZ DELIVERY SERVICES
                    ADJUSTED TRIAL BALANCE
                      DECEMBER 31, 19X8

Cash ..................................................................  $   2,340
Accounts receivable ...........................................      41,490
Prepaid rent .......................................................       1,350
Supplies.............................................................         970
Equipment ..........................................................      75,690
Accumulated depreciation—equipment .....................                        $  22,240
Office furniture..................................................      24,100
Accumulated depreciation—office furniture .............                            18,670
Accounts payable ...............................................                    13,600
Unearned service revenue ...................................                        4,520
Interest payable..................................................                  2,130
Salary payable ....................................................                   930
Note payable.......................................................                45,000
Andrew Taylor, capital.........................................                    32,380
Andrew Taylor, withdrawals .................................      48,000
Service revenue ..................................................                195,790
Depreciation expense—equipment.........................      11,300
Depreciation expense—office furniture...................       2,410
Salary expense....................................................     102,800
Rent expense ......................................................      12,000
Interest expense ..................................................       4,200
Utilities expense..................................................       3,770
Insurance expense ...............................................       3,150
Supplies expense .................................................       1,690
Total ..................................................................  $335,260     $335,260
```

P3-7A Consider the unadjusted trial balance of Lori Morgan, Speech Therapist, at October 31, 19X2, and the related month-end adjustment data.

Preparing an adjusted trial balance and the financial statements
(Obj. 3, 4, 5)

```
                LORI MORGAN, SPEECH THERAPIST
                        TRIAL BALANCE
                      OCTOBER 31, 19X2

Cash ..................................................  $16,300
Accounts receivable ...........................      8,000
Prepaid rent ......................................      4,000
Supplies.............................................        600
Furniture...........................................     15,000
Accumulated depreciation .................               $ 3,000
Accounts payable .............................                2,800
Salary payable ...................................
Lori Morgan, capital..........................               36,000
Lori Morgan, withdrawals................      3,600
Consulting service revenue................                7,400
Salary expense ...................................      1,400
Rent expense ......................................
Utilities expense................................        300
Depreciation expense........................
Supplies expense ...............................
Total .................................................  $49,200     $49,200
```

Adjustment data:

a. Accrued consulting service revenue at October 31, $2,000.
b. Prepaid rent expired during the month. The unadjusted prepaid balance of $4,000 relates to the period October 19X2 through January 19X3.
c. Supplies on hand October 31, $200.
d. Depreciation on furniture for the month. The furniture's expected useful life is five years.
e. Accrued salary expense at October 31 for one day only. The five-day weekly payroll is $2,000.

Required

1. Write the trial balance on a work sheet, using Exhibit 3-10 as an example, and prepare the adjusted trial balance of Lori Morgan, Speech Therapist, at October 31, 19X2. Key each adjusting entry by letter.
2. Prepare the income statement, the statement of owner's equity, and the balance sheet. Draw arrows linking the three financial statements.

(GROUP B)

Cash basis versus accrual basis
(Obj. 1, 2)

P3-1B   Selective Placement Services experienced the following selected transactions during January:

Jan. 1   Prepaid insurance for January through March, $600.
      4   Purchased office equipment for cash, $1,400.
      5   Received cash for services performed, $900.
      9   Paid gas bill, $400.
     12   Performed services on account, $1,500.
     14   Purchased office equipment on account, $300.
     28   Collected $500 on account from January 12.
     29   Paid salary expense, $1,100.
     30   Paid account payable from January 14.
     31   Recorded adjusting entry for January insurance expense (see Jan. 1).
     31   Debited unearned revenue and credited revenue in an adjusting entry, $700.

Required

1. Show how each transaction would be handled using the cash basis and the accrual basis. Under each column give the amount of revenue or expense for January. Journal entries are not required. Use the following format for your answer, and show your computations:

Selective Placement Services—Amount of Revenue or Expense for January

Date	Cash Basis	Accrual Basis

2. Compute January net income or net loss under each method.
3. Indicate which measure of net income or net loss is preferable. Give your reason.

Applying accounting principles
(Obj. 1, 2)

P3-2B   Write a short memo to a new bookkeeper to explain the difference between the cash basis of accounting and the accrual basis. Mention the roles of the revenue principle and the matching principle in accrual-basis accounting.

Journalizing adjusting entries
(Obj. 3)

P3-3B   Journalize the adjusting entry needed on December 31, end of the current accounting period, for each of the following independent cases affecting Peters Construction Contractors.

a. Details of Prepaid Rent are shown in the account:

Prepaid Rent	
Jan. 1 Bal.	600
Mar. 31	1,200
Sept. 30	1,200

Peters pays office rent semiannually on March 31 and September 30. At December 31, part of the last payment is still an asset.

b. Peters pays its employees each Friday. The amount of the weekly payroll is $2,000 for a five-day work week, and the daily salary amounts are equal. The current accounting period ends on Monday.

c. Peters has loaned money, receiving notes receivable. During the current year the entity has earned accrued interest revenue of $737 that it will receive next year.

d. The beginning balance of Supplies was $2,680. During the year the entity purchased supplies costing $6,180, and at December 31 the cost of supplies on hand is $2,150.

e. Peters is servicing the air conditioning system in a large building, and the owner of the building paid Peters $12,900 as the annual service fee. Peters recorded this amount as Unearned Service Revenue. Dan Peters, the owner, estimates that the company has earned one-fourth the total fee during the current year.

f. Depreciation for the current year includes: Office Furniture, $850; Equipment, $3,850; Trucks, $10,320. Make a compound entry.

P3-4B Glenda Shaw Court Reporting Company's unadjusted and adjusted trial balances at November 30, 19X1, follow.

Analyzing and journalizing adjustments
(Obj. 3)

	GLENDA SHAW COURT REPORTING COMPANY ADJUSTED TRIAL BALANCE NOVEMBER 30, 19X1			
	Trial Balance		**Adjusted Trial Balance**	
Account Title	**Debit**	**Credit**	**Debit**	**Credit**
Cash	8,180		8,180	
Accounts receivable	6,360		6,540	
Interest receivable			300	
Note receivable	4,100		4,100	
Supplies	980		290	
Prepaid rent	2,480		720	
Building	66,450		66,450	
Accumulated depreciation		16,010		17,110
Accounts payable		6,920		6,920
Wages payable				320
Unearned service revenue		670		110
Glenda Shaw, capital		60,790		60,790
Glenda Shaw, withdrawals	3,600		3,600	
Service revenue		9,940		10,680
Interest revenue				300
Wage expense	1,600		1,920	
Rent expense			1,760	
Depreciation expense			1,100	
Insurance expense	370		370	
Supplies expense			690	
Utilities expense	210		210	
	94,330	94,330	96,230	96,230

Required

Journalize the adjusting entries that account for the differences between the two trial balances.

Journalizing and posting adjustments to T-accounts, preparing the adjusted trial balance (Obj. 3, 4)

P3-5B   The trial balance of Fidelity Insurors at October 31, 19X2, and the data needed for the month-end adjustments follow.

FIDELITY INSURORS TRIAL BALANCE OCTOBER 31, 19X2		
Cash	$ 1,280	
Accounts receivable	14,750	
Prepaid rent	3,100	
Supplies	780	
Furniture	22,370	
Accumulated depreciation		$11,640
Accounts payable		1,940
Salary payable		
Unearned commission revenue		2,290
J. W. Bailes, capital		24,140
J. W. Bailes, withdrawals	2,900	
Commission revenue		8,400
Salary expense	2,160	
Rent expense		
Utilities expense	340	
Depreciation expense		
Advertising expense	730	
Supplies expense		
Total	$48,410	$48,410

Adjustment data:

a. Prepaid rent still in force at October 31, $700.

b. Supplies used during the month, $640.

c. Depreciation for the month, $900.

d. Accrued advertising expense at October 31, $320. (Credit Accounts Payable.)

e. Accrued salary expense at October 31, $180.

f. Unearned commission revenue still unearned at October 31, $2,000.

Required

1. Open T-accounts for the accounts listed in the trial balance, inserting their October 31 unadjusted balances.
2. Journalize the adjusting entries and post them to the T-accounts. Key the journal entries and the posted amounts by letter.
3. Prepare the adjusted trial balance.

Preparing the financial statements from an adjusted trial balance (Obj. 5)

P3-6B   The adjusted trial balance of Sunkist Travel Designers at December 31, 19X6, follows at the top of page 125.

Required

1. Prepare Sunkist's 19X6 income statement, statement of owner's equity, and balance sheet. List expenses in decreasing order on the income statement and show total liabilities on the balance sheet. Draw arrows linking the three financial statements.
2. How will what you learned in this problem help you manage a business?

```
                    SUNKIST TRAVEL DESIGNERS
                     ADJUSTED TRIAL BALANCE
                       DECEMBER 31, 19X6

Cash .....................................................................    $   1,320
Accounts receivable ................................................        8,920
Supplies................................................................        2,300
Prepaid rent ..........................................................        1,600
Office equipment.....................................................       20,180
Accumulated depreciation—office equipment ..............                          $   4,350
Office furniture......................................................       17,710
Accumulated depreciation—office furniture .................                          4,870
Accounts payable ...................................................                          3,640
Property tax payable ...............................................                          1,100
Interest payable......................................................                            830
Unearned service revenue .......................................                            620
Note payable..........................................................                       25,500
Cookie Lapp, capital...............................................                          6,090
Cookie Lapp, withdrawals........................................       44,000
Service revenue......................................................                       127,910
Depreciation expense—office equipment.....................        6,680
Depreciation expense—office furniture ......................        2,370
Salary expense........................................................       39,900
Rent expense..........................................................       17,400
Interest expense......................................................        3,100
Utilities expense ....................................................        2,670
Insurance expense...................................................        3,810
Supplies expense ....................................................        2,950
Total .....................................................................    $174,910      $174,910
```

P3-7B The unadjusted trial balance of Phillip Heider, Attorney, at July 31, 19X2, and the related month-end adjustment data are as follows:

Preparing an adjusted trial balance and the financial statements
(Obj. 3, 4, 5)

```
                   PHILLIP HEIDER, ATTORNEY
                         TRIAL BALANCE
                        JULY 31, 19X2

Cash ......................................    $14,600
Accounts receivable ...........................    11,600
Prepaid rent ..................................     3,600
Supplies.......................................       800
Furniture......................................    16,800
Accumulated depreciation..................                  $ 3,500
Accounts payable .............................                    3,450
Salary payable ................................
Phillip Heider, capital........................                   38,650
Phillip Heider, withdrawals...............     4,000
Legal service revenue ........................                    8,750
Salary expense................................     2,400
Rent expense..................................
Utilities expense .............................       550
Depreciation expense .......................
Supplies expense ............................
Total..........................................    $54,350       $54,350
```

Adjustment data:

a. Accrued legal service revenue at July 31, $900.

b. Prepaid rent expired during the month. The unadjusted prepaid balance of $3,600 relates to the period July through October.

c. Supplies on hand at July 31, $400.

d. Depreciation on furniture for the month. The estimated useful life of the furniture is four years.

e. Accrued salary expense at July 31 for one day only. The five-day weekly payroll is $1,000.

Required

1. Using Exhibit 3-10 as an example, write the trial balance on a work sheet and prepare the adjusted trial balance of Phillip Heider, Attorney, at July 31, 19X2. Key each adjusting entry by letter.

2. Prepare the income statement, the statement of owner's equity, and the balance sheet. Draw arrows linking the three financial statements.

EXTENDING YOUR KNOWLEDGE

DECISION PROBLEMS

Valuing a business on the basis of its net income
(Obj. 4, 5)

1. Alex White has owned and operated White Biomedical Systems, a management consulting firm for physicians, since its beginning 10 years ago. From all appearances the business has prospered. White lives in the fast lane—flashy car, home located in an expensive suburb, frequent trips abroad, and other signs of wealth. In the past few years, you have become friends with him and his wife through weekly rounds of golf at the country club. Recently, he mentioned that he has lost his zest for the business and would consider selling it for the right price. He claims that his clientele is firmly established and that the business "runs itself." According to White, the consulting procedures are fairly simple and anyone could perform the work.

Assume that you are interested in buying this business. You obtain its most recent monthly trial balance, which follows. Revenues and expenses vary little from month to month and April is a typical month. Your investigation reveals that the trial balance does not include the effects of monthly revenues of $1,100 and expenses totaling $2,100. If you were to buy White Biomedical Systems, you would hire a manager so you could devote your time to other duties. Assume that this person would require a monthly salary of $2,000.

WHITE BIOMEDICAL SYSTEMS TRIAL BALANCE APRIL 30, 19XX		
Cash	$ 9,700	
Accounts receivable	4,900	
Prepaid expenses	2,600	
Plant assets	241,300	
Accumulated depreciation		$189,600
Land	158,000	
Accounts payable		13,800
Salary payable		
Unearned consulting revenue		56,700
Alex White, capital		157,400
Alex White, withdrawals	9,000	
Consulting revenue		12,300
Rent expense		
Salary expense	3,400	
Utilities expense	900	
Depreciation expense		
Supplies expense		
Total	$429,800	$429,800

Required

1. Is this an unadjusted or an adjusted trial balance? How can you tell?
2. Assume that the most you would pay for the business is 30 times the monthly net income you could expect to earn from it. Compute this possible price.
3. White states that the least he will take for the business is his ending capital. Compute this amount.
4. Under these conditions, how much should you offer White? Give your reason.

2. The following independent questions are related to accrual-basis accounting:

Understanding the concepts underlying the accrual basis of accounting
(Obj. 1, 2)

1. It has been said that the only time a company's financial position is known for certain is when the company is ended and its only asset is cash. Why is this statement true?
2. A friend suggests that the purpose of adjusting entries is to correct errors in the accounts. Is your friend's statement true? What is the purpose of adjusting entries if the statement is wrong?
3. The text suggested that furniture (and each other plant asset that is depreciated) is a form of prepaid expense. Do you agree? Why do you think some accountants view plant assets this way?

ETHICAL ISSUE

The net income of Adkin's, a department store, decreased sharply during 1995. Mark Adkin, owner of the store, anticipates the need for a bank loan in 1996. Late in 1995 he instructed the accountant to record a $2,600 sale of furniture to the Adkin family, even though the goods will not be shipped from the manufacturer until January 1996. Adkin also told the accountant not to make the following December 31, 1995, adjusting entries:

Salaries owed to employees	$1,800
Prepaid insurance that has expired...............	530

Required

1. Compute the overall effect of these transactions on the store's reported income for 1995.
2. Why did Adkin take this action? Is this action ethical? Give your reason, identifying the parties helped and the parties harmed by Adkin's action.
3. As a personal friend, what advice would you give the accountant?

FINANCIAL STATEMENT PROBLEMS

1. Lands' End, Inc.—like all other businesses—makes adjusting entries prior to year end in order to measure assets, liabilities, revenues, and expenses properly. Examine Lands' End's balance sheet, and pay particular attention to Prepaid Expenses, Accrued Liabilities (which includes Salary Payable and Interest Payable), and Advance Payment on Orders (another title for Unearned Revenue). Assume the following balances at January 29, 1993, the beginning of the current year: Salary Payable, $2,689 thousand; Interest Payable, $81 thousand.

Journalizing and posting transactions and tracing account balances to the financial statements
(Obj. 3, 4, 5)

Required

1. Open T-accounts for these four accounts. Insert Lands' End's balances (in thousands) at January 29, 1993. (Examples: Prepaid Expenses, $5,496; Interest Payable, $81.)
2. Journalize the following for the current year, ended January 28, 1994. Key entries by letter. Explanations are not required.

Cash transactions (amounts in thousands):
a. Paid prepaid expenses, $8,719.
b. Paid the January 29, 1993, salary payable.
c. Paid the January 29, 1993, interest payable.
d. Received $767 cash for customers' advance payments on orders.

Adjustments at January 28, 1994 (amounts in thousands):
e. Prepaid expenses expired: $2,428. (Debit General and Administrative Expense.)
f. Salary Payable, $3,452. (Debit Selling Expense.)

g. Accrued interest payable, $88.

h. Earned sales revenue for which cash has been received from customers in advance, $1,224.

3. After these entries are posted, show that the balances in Prepaid Expenses and Advance Payment on Orders agree with the corresponding amounts reported in the January 28, 1994, balance sheet.

Adjusting the accounts of an actual company
(Obj. 2)

2. Obtain the annual report of a real company of your choosing. Assume that the company accountants *failed* to make four adjustments at the end of the current year. For illustrative purposes, we shall assume that the amounts reported in the company's balance sheet for the related assets and liabilities are *incorrect*.

Adjustments omitted:

a. Depreciation of equipment, $800,000
b. Salaries owed to employees but not yet paid, $230,000
c. Prepaid rent used up during the year, $100,000
d. Accrued sales (or service) revenue, $140,000

Required

1. Compute the correct amounts for the following balance sheet items:
   a. Book value of plant assets
   b. Total liabilities
   c. Prepaid expenses
   d. Accounts receivable

2. Compute the amount of net income or net loss that the company would have reported if the accountants had recorded these transactions properly. Ignore income tax.

Appendix

Alternate Treatment of Accounting for Prepaid Expenses and Unearned Revenues

Chapters 1 through 3 illustrate the most popular way to account for prepaid expenses and unearned revenues. This appendix illustrates an alternate—equally appropriate—approach to handling prepaid expenses and unearned revenues.

Prepaid Expenses

Prepaid expenses are advance payments of expenses. Prepaid Insurance, Prepaid Rent, Prepaid Advertising, and Prepaid Legal Cost are prepaid expenses. Supplies that will be used up in the current period or within one year are also accounted for as prepaid expenses.

When a business prepays an expense—rent, for example—it can debit an *asset* account (Prepaid Rent) as follows:

Aug. 1	Prepaid Rent.....................................	XXX	
	Cash...		XXX

Alternatively, it can debit an *expense* account in the entry to record this cash payment:

Rent Expense	XXX	
Cash...		XXX

Regardless of the account debited, the business must adjust the accounts at the end of the period. Making the adjustment allows the business to report the correct amount of expense for the period and the correct amount of asset at the period's end.

Prepaid Expense Recorded Initially as an Expense

Prepaying an expense creates an asset, as recorded in this chapter. However, the asset may be so short-lived that it will expire in the current accounting period—within one year or less. Thus the accountant may decide to debit the prepayment to an expense account at the time of payment. A $6,000 cash payment for rent (one year, in advance) on August 1 may be debited to Rent Expense:

> **OBJECTIVE A1**
>
> Account for a prepaid expense recorded initially as an expense

19X6				
Aug. 1	Rent Expense		6,000	
	Cash...			6,000

At December 31 only five months' prepayment has expired, leaving seven months' rent still prepaid. In this case, the accountant must transfer 7/12 of the original prepayment of $6,000, or $3,500, to Prepaid Rent. The adjusting entry decreases the balance of Rent Expense to 5/12 of the original $6,000, or $2,500. The December 31 adjusting entry is

Adjusting Entries

19X6			
Dec. 31	Prepaid Rent ($6,000 × 7/12)...........	3,500	
	Rent Expense		3,500

Short Exercise: How does a business record (1) the prepayment of monthly rent in an expense account; (2) utilities expense; (3) the prepayment of three months' rent? *A:*
(1) Rent Expense....... XX
    Cash XX
(2) Utilities Expense . XX
    Cash XX
(3) Rent Expense....... XX
    Cash XX
It is easier to record the payment as an expense than as an asset, like most payments.

After posting, the two accounts appear as follows:

Prepaid Rent			
19X6			
Dec. 31	Adj.	3,500	
Dec. 31	Bal.	3,500	

Rent Expense						
19X6			19X6			
Aug. 1	CP	6,000	Dec. 31	Adj.	3,500	
Dec. 31	Bal.	2,500				

CP = Cash payment entry   Adj. = Adjusting entry

The balance sheet for 19X6 reports Prepaid Rent of $3,500, and the income statement for 19X6 reports Rent Expense of $2,500. Whether the business initially debits the prepayment to an asset account or to an expense account, the financial statements report the same amounts for prepaid rent and rent expense.

Unearned (Deferred) Revenues

Unearned (deferred) revenues arise when a business collects cash in advance of earning the revenue. The recognition of revenue is *deferred* until later when it is earned. Unearned revenues are liabilities because the business that receives cash owes the other party goods or services to be delivered later.

Unearned (Deferred) Revenue Recorded Initially as a Revenue

OBJECTIVE A2
Account for an unearned (deferred) revenue recorded initially as a revenue

Receipt of cash in advance of earning the revenue creates a liability, as recorded in this chapter. Another way to account for the initial transaction is to credit a *revenue* account when the cash is received. If the business has earned all the revenue within the period during which it received the cash, no adjusting entry is necessary. However, if the business earns only a part of the revenue at the end of the period, it must make adjusting entries.

Suppose on October 1, 19X2, a law firm records the receipt of cash for a nine-month advance fee of $7,200 as revenue. The cash receipt entry is

19X2				
Oct. 1	Cash..		7,200	
	Legal Revenue			7,200

Short Exercise: The required adjusting entry depends on the way the transaction was originally recorded. (1) If the receipt of cash is recorded as a liability before it is earned, what adjusting is required? (2) If the receipt of cash is originally recorded as revenue, what adjusting entry is required? *A:*.
(1) Unearned Rev...... XX
    Revenue XX
(2) Revenue XX
    Unearned Rev. . XX
These entries are not interchangeable.

At December 31 the attorney has earned only 3/9 of the $7,200, or $2,400. Accordingly, the firm makes an adjusting entry to transfer the unearned portion (6/9 of $7,200, or $4,800) from the revenue account to a liability account.

Adjusting Entries			
19X2			
Dec. 31	Legal Revenue ($7,200 × 6/9)...................	4,800	
	Unearned Legal Revenue................		4,800

The adjusting entry leaves the earned portion (3/9, or $2,400) of the original amount in the revenue account. After posting, the total amount ($7,200) is properly divided between the liability account ($4,800) and the revenue account ($2,400), as follows:

Short Exercise: Co. X receives $3,000 for magazine subscriptions in advance and records it is as a liability. (1) If $1,600 are unearned at the end of the year, what is the adjusting entry? (2) If the subscriptions were originally recorded as revenue, what is the adjusting entry? *(cont'd)*

Unearned Legal Revenue			
	19X2		
	Dec. 31	Adj.	4,800
	Dec. 31	Bal.	4,800

Legal Revenue						
19X2			19X2			
Dec. 31	Adj.	4,800	Oct. 1	CR	7,200	
			Dec. 31	Bal.	2,400	

CR = Cash receipt entry   Adj. = Adjusting entry

The attorney's 19X2 income statement reports legal revenue of $2,400, and the balance sheet at December 31, 19X2, reports as a liability the unearned legal revenue of $4,800. Whether the business initially credits a liability account or a revenue account, the financial statements report the same amounts for unearned legal revenue and legal revenue.

A:

(1) Unearned Rev. . 1,400
        Revenue........   1,400
(2) Revenue............ 1,600
        Unearned Rev.   1,600
Only $1,400 of the $3,000 had been earned. The revenue account needs a $1,400 balance. That account must be reduced (debited) by $1,600.

APPENDIX EXERCISES

E3A-1   At the beginning of the year, supplies of $1,690 were on hand. During the year, the business paid $3,400 cash for supplies. At the end of the year, the count of supplies indicates the ending balance is $1,360.

Recording supplies transactions two ways
(Obj. A1)

Required

1. Assume that the business records supplies by initially debiting an *asset* account. Therefore, place the beginning balance in the Supplies T-account, and record the above entries directly in the accounts without using a journal.
2. Assume that the business records supplies by initially debiting an *expense* account. Therefore, place the beginning balance in the Supplies Expense T-account, and record the above entries directly in the accounts without using a journal.
3. Compare the ending account balances under both approaches. Are they the same? Explain.

E3A-2   At the beginning of the year, the company owed customers $6,750 for unearned service collected in advance. During the year, the business received advance cash receipts of $10,000. At year end, the unearned revenue liability is $3,700.

Recording unearned revenues two ways
(Obj. A2)

Required

1. Assume that the company records unearned revenues by initially crediting a *liability* account. Open T-accounts for Unearned Service Revenue and Service Revenue, and place the beginning balance in Unearned Service Revenue. Journalize the cash collection and adjusting entries, and post their dollar amounts. As references in the T-accounts, denote a balance by Bal., a cash receipt by CR, and an adjustment by Adj.
2. Assume that the company records unearned revenues by initially crediting a *revenue* account. Open T-accounts for Unearned Service Revenue and Service Revenue, and place the beginning balance in Service Revenue. Journalize the cash collection and adjusting entries, and post their dollar amounts. As references in the T-accounts, denote a balance by Bal., a cash receipt by CR, and an adjustment by Adj.
3. Compare the ending balances in the two accounts. Explain why they are the same or different.

APPENDIX PROBLEM

P3A-1   Diebolt Sales and Service completed the following transactions during 19X4:

Recording prepaid rent and rent revenue collected in advance two ways
(Obj. A1, A2)

Aug. 31   Paid $6,000 store rent covering the six-month period ending February 28, 19X5.
Dec. 1   Collected $3,200 cash in advance from customers. The service revenue will be earned $800 monthly over the period ending March 31, 19X5.

Required

1. Journalize these entries by debiting an asset account for Prepaid Rent and by crediting a liability account for Unearned Service Revenue. Explanations are unnecessary.
2. Journalize the related adjustments at December 31, 19X4.
3. Post the entries to the ledger accounts, and show their balances at December 31, 19X4. Posting references are unnecessary.
4. Repeat Requirements 1 through 3. This time debit Rent Expense for the rent payment and credit Service Revenue for the collection of revenue in advance.
5. Compare the account balances in Requirements 3 and 4. They should be equal.

Chapter 4
Completing the Accounting Cycle

After studying this chapter, you should be able to

1. Prepare an accounting work sheet

2. Use the work sheet to complete the accounting cycle

3. Close the revenue, expense, and withdrawal accounts

4. Correct typical accounting errors

5. Classify assets and liabilities as current or long-term

6. Use the current and debt ratios to evaluate a business

"People often ask, what's the value of closing the books faster? Clearly, the value of information today is greater than the value of that same information tomorrow. The fast close provides time for more important functions, such as planning and analysis, and reduces overtime, thereby improving morale. It is a distinct competitive advantage."

KENNETH J. JOHNSON, CORPORATE VICE-PRESIDENT AND CONTROLLER OF MOTOROLA COMPANY

Motorola Company, best known for its computer chips and cellular telephones, pagers, and other electronic products, was awarded the Malcolm Baldrige National Quality Award for superior management of its quality control processes, or total quality management (TQM). The U.S. Department of Commerce grants this award every year to companies that do exemplary work in each of three categories. Motorola won the Malcolm Baldrige Award in the manufacturing category.

To compete in a swiftly changing economy, companies must get financial data to decision makers fast and at low cost. Motorola accomplishes this goal by rapidly *closing its accounts*, or *closing its books*—the process of preparing the accounts at the end of each period for recording the transactions of the next period. The company amasses detailed financial information in a computerized system that allows its finance division to analyze the information continuously. Motorola can close its accounts in just two days and is working toward the goal of closing its books on a continuous basis. Compared with that of other companies that take two to four weeks to assemble the same type of information, Motorola's statement-preparation process is lightning-fast. This means that Motorola's managers can have up-to-date financial information virtually all the time. *Source: Adapted from Sandy Denarski, "Benchmarking the Best—Summary of Results,"* Financial Management News, *April 1993, p. 4.*

• • • • •

*I*n Chapter 3 we prepared the financial statements from an adjusted trial balance. That approach works well for quick decision making, but organizations of all sizes take the accounting process a step further. Whether it's Motorola or Gary Lyon, CPA, the closing process follows the basic pattern outlined in this chapter. It marks the end of the *accounting cycle* for a given period.

Often included in the accounting process is a document known as the accountant's *work sheet*. There are many different types of work sheets in business—as many as there are needs for summary information. Businesspersons who can visualize a useful summary of relevant information—a work sheet—are valuable because work sheets aid decision making.

Overview of the Accounting Cycle

Key Point: The accounting cycle is repeated each accounting period. The goal of the cycle is the financial statements.

The **accounting cycle** is the process by which companies produce their financial statements for a specific period of time. For a new business, the cycle begins with setting up (opening) the ledger accounts. Gary Lyon started his accounting practice on April 1, 19X1, so the first step in the cycle was to open the accounts. After a business has operated for one period, however, the account balances carry over from period to period. Therefore, the accounting cycle usually starts with the account balances at the beginning of the period, as shown in Exhibit 4-1. The exhibit highlights the new steps that we will be discussing in this chapter.

The accounting cycle is divided into work performed during the period—journalizing transactions and posting to the ledger—and work performed at the end of the period to prepare the financial statements. The end-of-period work also readies the accounts for the next period. The greater number of individual steps at the end of the period may suggest that most of the work is done at the end. But the recording and posting during the period take far more time than the end-of-period work, as is reflected in the organization of this book. We cover the end-of-period accounting in a couple of chapters. The remainder of the book deals with the information needed for decisions on an ongoing basis.

Companies prepare financial statements on a monthly or a quarterly basis, and steps 1 to 6a in Exhibit 4-1 are adequate for statement preparation. Steps 6b through 7 can be performed monthly or quarterly but are necessary only at year's end.

Accounting Work Sheet

OBJECTIVE 1

Prepare an accounting work sheet

Accountants often use a **work sheet,** a multicolumned document, to help move data from the trial balance to the financial statements. The work sheet provides an orderly way to summarize the data for the financial statements. Listing all the accounts and their unadjusted balances helps identify the accounts that need adjustment. Although it is not essential, the work sheet is helpful because it brings together in one place the effects of all the transactions of a particular period. The work sheet aids the closing process by listing the adjusted balances for all accounts. It can also reveal errors.

The work sheet is not part of the ledger or the journal, nor is it a financial statement. Therefore, it is not part of the formal accounting system. Instead, it is a summary device that exists for the accountant's convenience.

Exhibits 4-2 through 4-6 illustrate the development of a typical work sheet for the business of Gary Lyon, CPA. The heading at the top names the business, identifies the document, and states the accounting period. A step-by-step description of its preparation follows.

EXHIBIT 4-1
Steps in the Accounting Cycle

PANEL A

During the Period	End of the Period

1. Start with the account balances in the ledger at the beginning of the period.
2. Analyze and journalize transactions as they occur.
3. Post journal entries to the ledger accounts.
	4. Compute the unadjusted balance in each account at the end of the period.
	5. **(Optional) Enter the trial balance on the work sheet, and complete the work sheet.**
	6. Using the adjusted trial balance or the full work sheet as a guide,
	   a. Prepare the financial statements.
	   b. Journalize and post the adjusting entries.
	   c. Journalize and post the closing entries.
	7. **Prepare the postclosing, or afterclosing, trial balance. This trial balance becomes step 1 for the next period.**

PANEL B

1 Start with the balances in the ledger at the beginning of the period.

Accounts Receivable
2,000

2 Analyze and journalize transactions as they occur.

Accounts Receivable   250
   Sales Revenue   250

3 Post entries to the ledger accounts.

Accounts Receivable
2,000
250

4 Compute the unadjusted balance in each account at the end of the period.

Accounts Receivable
2,000
250
2,250

5 Enter the trial balance on the work sheet, and complete the work sheet. (Optional)

WORK SHEET
Cash   24,800
Accounts receivable   2,250

6 Journalize and post the adjusting entries and the closing entries. Prepare the financial statements.

Adjusting entries

Closing entries

Cash 24,800   Accts. Rec. 2,250

INCOME STATEMENT

BALANCE SHEET

7 Prepare the postclosing trial balance.

POSTCLOSING TRIAL BALANCE
Cash   24,800
Accounts receivable   2,250

134a

EXHIBIT 4-2
Trial Balance

	GARY LYON, CPA ACCOUNTING WORK SHEET FOR THE MONTH ENDED APRIL 30, 19X1									
	Trial Balance		Adjustments		Adjusted Trial Balance		Income Statement		Balance Sheet	
Account Title	Dr.	Cr.	Dr.	Cr.	Dr.	Cr.	Dr.	Cr.	Dr.	Cr.
Cash	24,800									
Accounts receivable	2,250									
Supplies	700									
Prepaid rent	3,000									
Furniture	16,500									
Accumulated depreciation										
Accounts payable		13,100								
Salary payable										
Unearned service revenue		450								
Gary Lyon, capital		31,250								
Gary Lyon, withdrawals	3,200									
Service revenue		7,000								
Rent expense										
Salary expense	950									
Supplies expense										
Depreciation expense										
Utilities expense	400									
	51,800	51,800								
Net income										

Write the account titles and their unadjusted ending balances in the Trial Balance columns of the work sheet, and total the amounts.

EXHIBIT 4-1

Steps in the Accounting Cycle

PANEL A

During the Period

1. Start with the account balances in the ledger at the beginning of the period.
2. Analyze and journalize transactions as they occur.
3. Post journal entries to the ledger accounts.

End of the Period

4. Compute the unadjusted balance in each account at the end of the period.
5. **(Optional) Enter the trial balance on the work sheet, and complete the work sheet.**
6. Using the adjusted trial balance or the full work sheet as a guide,
   a. Prepare the financial statements.
   b. Journalize and post the adjusting entries.
   c. **Journalize and post the closing entries.**
7. **Prepare the postclosing, or afterclosing, trial balance. This trial balance becomes step 1 for the next period.**

PANEL B

1 Start with the balances in the ledger at the beginning of the period.

2 Analyze and journalize transactions as they occur.

3 Post entries to the ledger accounts.

4 Compute the unadjusted balance in each account at the end of the period.

5 Enter the trial balance on the work sheet, and complete the work sheet. (Optional)

6 Journalize and post the adjusting entries and the closing entries. Prepare the financial statements.

7 Prepare the postclosing trial balance.

EXHIBIT 4-2
Trial Balance

GARY LYON, CPA
ACCOUNTING WORK SHEET
FOR THE MONTH ENDED APRIL 30, 19X1

Account Title	Trial Balance		Adjustments		Adjusted Trial Balance		Income Statement		Balance Sheet	
	Dr.	Cr.	Dr.	Cr.	Dr.	Cr.	Dr.	Cr.	Dr.	Cr.
Cash	24,800									
Accounts receivable	2,250									
Supplies	700									
Prepaid rent	3,000									
Furniture	16,500									
Accumulated depreciation										
Accounts payable		13,100								
Salary payable										
Unearned service revenue		450								
Gary Lyon, capital		31,250								
Gary Lyon, withdrawals	3,200									
Service revenue		7,000								
Rent expense										
Salary expense	950									
Supplies expense										
Depreciation expense										
Utilities expense	400									
	51,800	51,800								
Net income										

Write the account titles and their unadjusted ending balances in the Trial Balance columns of the work sheet, and total the amounts.

Steps introduced in Chapter 3 to prepare the adjusted trial balance:◀◀◀

1. Print the account titles and their unadjusted ending balances in the Trial Balance columns of the work sheet, and total the amounts.
2. Enter the adjustments in the Adjustments columns, and total the amounts.
3. Compute each account's adjusted balance by combining the trial balance and adjustment figures. Enter the adjusted amounts in the Adjusted Trial Balance columns.

New steps introduced in this chapter:

4. Extend the asset, liability, and owner's equity amounts from the Adjusted Trial Balance to the Balance Sheet columns. Extend the revenue and expense amounts to the Income Statement columns. Total the statement columns.
5. Compute net income or net loss as the difference between total revenues and total expenses on the income statement. Enter net income or net loss as a balancing amount on the income statement and on the balance sheet, and compute the adjusted column totals.

1. *Print the account titles and their unadjusted balances in the Trial Balance columns of the work sheet, and total the amounts.* Total debits must equal total credits, as shown in Exhibit 4-2. The account titles and balances come directly from the ledger accounts before the adjusting entries are prepared. Accounts are grouped on the work sheet by category and are usually listed in the order they appear in the ledger. By contrast, their order on the financial statements follows a different pattern. For example, the expenses on the work sheet in Exhibit 4-2 indicate no particular order. But on the income statement, expenses can be ordered by amount, with the largest first (see Exhibit 4-7).

Accounts may have zero balances (for example, Depreciation Expense). All accounts are listed on the trial balance because they appear in the ledger. Electronically prepared work sheets can list all the accounts, not just those with a balance.

2. *Enter the adjusting entries in the Adjustments columns, and total the amounts.* Exhibit 4-3 includes the April adjusting entries. These are the same adjustments that we illustrated in Chapter 3 to prepare the adjusted trial balance.

How can we identify the accounts that need to be adjusted? By scanning the trial balance. Cash needs no adjustment because all cash transactions are recorded as they occur during the period. Consequently, Cash's balance is up to date.

Accounts Receivable is listed next. Has Gary Lyon earned revenue that he has not yet recorded? The answer is yes. Lyon provides professional service for a client. At April 30 Lyon has earned $250, which must be accrued because the cash will be received during May. Lyon debits Accounts Receivable and credits Service Revenue on the work sheet in Exhibit 4-3. A letter is used to link the debit and the credit of each adjusting entry. By moving down the trial balance, Lyon identifies the remaining accounts that need adjustment. Supplies is next. The business has used supplies during April, so Lyon debits Supplies Expense and credits Supplies. The other adjustments are analyzed and entered on the work sheet.

The process of identifying accounts that need to be adjusted is aided by listing the accounts in their proper sequence. But suppose one or more accounts are omitted from the trial balance. It can always be written below the first column totals—$51,800. Assume that Supplies Expense was accidentally omitted and thus did not appear on the trial balance. When the accountant identifies the need to update the Supplies account, he or she knows that the debit in the adjusting entry is to Supplies

◀◀◀ We introduced the adjusted trial balance in Chapters 3, p. 106.

Key Point: Remember how posting references help track data from the journal to the ledger. These identifiers are equally important for organizing the adjusting entries on the work sheet.

Expense. In this case, the accountant can write Supplies Expense on the line beneath the amount totals and enter the debit adjustment—$300—on the Supplies Expense line. Keep in mind that the accounting work sheet is not the finished version of the financial statements, so the order of the accounts on the work sheet is not critical. Supplies Expense can be listed in its proper sequence on the income statement. After the adjustments are entered on the work sheet, the amount columns are totaled.

3. *Compute each account's adjusted balance by combining the trial balance and adjustment figures. Enter the adjusted amounts in the Adjusted Trial Balance columns.* Exhibit 4-4 shows the work sheet with the adjusted trial balance added. This step is performed as illustrated in Chapter 3. For example, the Cash balance is up to date, so it receives no adjustment. Accounts Receivable's adjusted balance of $2,500 is computed by adding the trial balance amount of $2,250 to the $250 debit adjustment. Supplies' adjusted balance of $400 is determined by subtracting the $300 credit adjustment from the unadjusted debit balance of $700. An account may receive more than one adjustment, as does Service Revenue. The column totals must maintain the equality of debits and credits.

4. *Extend (that is, transfer) the asset, liability, and owner's equity amounts from the Adjusted Trial Balance to the Balance Sheet columns. Extend the revenue and expense amounts to the Income Statement columns. Total the statement columns.* Every account is either a balance sheet account or an income statement account. The asset, liability, and owner's equity accounts go to the balance sheet, and the revenues and expenses go to the income statement. Debits on the adjusted trial balance remain debits in the statement columns, and likewise for credits. Each account's adjusted balance should appear in only one statement column, as shown in Exhibit 4-5.

The income statement indicates total expenses in the debit column ($3,875) and total revenues ($7,400) in the credit column. The balance sheet shows total debits of $49,400 and total credits of $45,875. At this stage, the column totals should not necessarily be equal.

STOP & THINK Study Exhibit 4-5. How much was Gary Lyon's net income or net loss during April? How can you compute net income or net loss from the work sheet?

Answer: Net income for April was $3,525: total revenues of $7,400 minus total expenses of $3,875—all from the income statement columns of the work sheet.

Key Point: Net income is the difference between the debit and credit Income Statement columns.

5. *Compute net income or net loss as the difference between total revenues and total expenses on the income statement. Enter net income or net loss as a balancing amount on the income statement and on the balance sheet and compute the adjusted column totals.* Exhibit 4-6 presents the completed accounting work sheet, which shows net income of $3,525, computed as follows:

Revenue (total credits on the income statement) $7,400
Expenses (total debits on the income statement) 3,875
Net income $3,525

Net income of $3,525 is entered in the debit column of the income statement to balance with the credit column of the income statement, which totals $7,400. The net income amount is then extended to the credit column of the balance sheet, because an excess of revenues over expenses increases capital, and increases in capital are recorded by a credit. In the closing process, net income will find its way into the Capital account, as we shall soon see.

If expenses exceed revenues, the result is a net loss. In that event, Net loss is printed on the work sheet. The loss amount should be entered in the credit column of the income statement and in the debit column of the balance sheet, because an excess of expenses over revenues decreases capital, and decreases in capital are recorded by a debit. After completion, total debits equal total credits in the Income Statement columns and in the Balance Sheet columns. The balance sheet columns are totaled at $49,400.

The trial balance of State Service Company at December 31, 19X1, the end of its fiscal year, is presented below:

STATE SERVICE COMPANY TRIAL BALANCE DECEMBER 31, 19X1		
Cash	$ 198,000	
Accounts receivable	370,000	
Supplies	6,000	
Furniture and fixtures	100,000	
Accumulated depreciation—furniture and fixtures		$ 40,000
Building	250,000	
Accumulated depreciation—building		130,000
Accounts payable		380,000
Salary payable		
Unearned service revenue		45,000
Capital		293,000
Withdrawals	65,000	
Service revenues		286,000
Salary expense	172,000	
Supplies expense		
Depreciation expense—furniture and fixtures		
Depreciation expense—building		
Miscellaneous expense	13,000	
Total	$1,174,000	$1,174,000

Data needed for the adjusting entries include:

a. Supplies on hand at year end, $2,000.
b. Depreciation on furniture and fixtures, $20,000.
c. Depreciation on building, $10,000.
d. Salaries owed but not yet paid, $5,000.
e. Accrued service revenue, $12,000.
f. Of the $45,000 balance of Unearned Service Revenue, $32,000 was earned during 19X1.

Required

Prepare the accounting work sheet of State Service Company for the year ended December 31, 19X1. Key each adjusting entry by the letter corresponding to the data given.

Account Title	Trial Balance Dr.	Cr.	Adjustments Dr.	Cr.	Adjusted Trial Balance Dr.	Cr.	Income Statement Dr.	Cr.	Balance Sheet Dr.	Cr.
				STATE SERVICE COMPANY WORK SHEET FOR THE YEAR ENDED DECEMBER 31, 19X1						
Cash	198,000				198,000				198,000	
Accounts receivable	370,000		(e) 12,000		382,000				382,000	
Supplies	6,000			(a) 4,000	2,000				2,000	
Furniture and fixtures	100,000				100,000				100,000	
Accumulated depreciation— furniture and fixtures		40,000		(b) 20,000		60,000				60,000
Building	250,000				250,000				250,000	
Accumulated depreciation— building		130,000		(c) 10,000		140,000				140,000
Accounts payable		380,000				380,000				380,000
Salary payable				(d) 5,000		5,000				5,000
Unearned service revenue		45,000	(f) 32,000			13,000				13,000
Capital		293,000				293,000				293,000
Withdrawals	65,000				65,000				65,000	
Service revenue		286,000		(e) 12,000 (f) 32,000		330,000		330,000		
Salary expense	172,000		(d) 5,000		177,000		177,000			
Supplies expense			(a) 4,000		4,000		4,000			
Depreciation expense— furniture and fixtures			(b) 20,000		20,000		20,000			
Depreciation expense— building			(c) 10,000		10,000		10,000			
Miscellaneous expense	13,000				13,000		13,000			
	1,174,000	1,174,000	83,000	83,000	1,221,000	1,221,000	224,000	330,000	997,000	891,000
Net income							106,000			106,000
							330,000	330,000	997,000	997,000

Using the Work Sheet

OBJECTIVE 2
Use the work sheet to complete the accounting cycle

The work sheet helps organize accounting data and compute the net income or net loss for the period. It also aids in preparing the financial statements, recording the adjusting entries, and closing the accounts.

Preparing the Financial Statements

Even though the work sheet shows the amount of net income or net loss for the period, it is still necessary to prepare the financial statements. ◀▥ The sorting of accounts to the balance sheet and the income statement eases the preparation of the statements. The work sheet also provides the data for the statement of owner's equity. Exhibit 4-7 presents the April financial statements for the accounting practice of Gary Lyon, CPA (based on data from the work sheet in Exhibit 4-6).

◀▥◀▥◀▥ The financial statements can be prepared directly from the adjusted trial balance; see p. 107. That is why completion of the work sheet is optional.

Recording the Adjusting Entries

The adjusting entries are a key element of accrual-basis accounting. The work sheet helps identify the accounts that need adjustments, which may be conveniently entered directly on the work sheet (Exhibits 4-2 through 4-6). But actual adjustment of the accounts requires journal entries that are posted to the ledger accounts; see Panel

EXHIBIT 4-7
April Financial Statements of Gary Lyon, CPA

GARY LYON, CPA
INCOME STATEMENT
FOR THE MONTH ENDED APRIL 30, 19X1

Revenue:
Service revenue		$7,400
Expenses:		
Salary expense	$1,900	
Rent expense	1,000	
Utilities expense	400	
Supplies expense	300	
Depreciation expense—furniture	275	
Total expenses		3,875
Net income		$3,525

GARY LYON, CPA
STATEMENT OF OWNER'S EQUITY
FOR THE MONTH ENDED APRIL 30, 19X1

Gary Lyon, capital, April 1, 19X1	$31,250
Add: Net income	3,525
	34,775
Less: Withdrawals	3,200
Gary Lyon, capital, April 30, 19X1	$31,575

GARY LYON, CPA
BALANCE SHEET
APRIL 30, 19X1

Assets			**Liabilities**	
Cash		$24,800	Accounts payable	$13,100
Accounts receivable		2,500	Salary payable	950
Supplies		400	Unearned service revenue	300
Prepaid rent		2,000	Total liabilities	14,350
Furniture	$16,500			
Less Accumulated			**Owner's Equity**	
depreciation	275	16,225	Gary Lyon, capital	31,575
			Total liabilities and	
Total assets		$45,925	owner's equity	$45,925

A of Exhibit 4-8. Panel B shows the postings to the accounts, with "Adj." denoting an amount posted from an adjusting entry. Only the revenue and expense accounts are to focus on the closing process, which is discussed in the next section.

The adjusting entries can be recorded in the journal when they are entered on the work sheet, but it is not necessary to journalize them at the same time. Most accountants prepare the financial statements immediately after completing the work sheet. They can wait to journalize and post the adjusting entries just before they make the closing entries. Delaying the journalizing and posting of the adjusting entries illustrates another use of the work sheet. Many companies journalize and post the adjusting entries—as in Exhibit 4-8—only at the end of the year. The need for monthly or quarterly financial statements requires a tool like the work sheet. The entity can use the work sheet for preparing interim statements without entering the adjusting entries in the journal and posting them to the ledger.

Short Exercise: Review: Where is each account extended—Income Statement, debit column; Income Statement, credit column; Balance Sheet, debit column; or Balance Sheet, credit column?

1. Cash *A*: Balance Sheet, debit
2. Supplies *A*: Balance Sheet, debit
3. Supplies Expense *A*: Income Statement, debit
4. Unearned Revenue *A*: Balance Sheet, credit
5. Service Revenue *A*: Income Statement, credit
6. Capital *A*: Balance Sheet, credit

PANEL A—Journalizing: Page 4

Adjusting Entries

Apr. 30	Accounts Receivable	250	
	Service Revenue		250
30	Supplies Expense	300	
	Supplies		300
30	Rent Expense	1,000	
	Prepaid Rent		1,000
30	Depreciation Expense............................	275	
	Accumulated Depreciation		275
30	Salary Expense	950	
	Salary Payable		950
30	Unearned Service Revenue	150	
	Service Revenue		150

PANEL B—Posting the Adjustments to the Revenue and Expense Accounts:

REVENUE

Service Revenue

		7,000
	Adj.	250
	Adj.	150
	Bal.	7,400

EXPENSES

Rent Expense

Adj.	1,000	
Bal.	1,000	

Salary Expense

	950	
Adj.	950	
Bal.	1,900	

Depreciation Expense

Adj.	275	
Bal.	275	

Utilities Expense

	400	
Bal.	400	

Supplies Expense

Adj.	300	
Bal.	300	

Adj. = Amount posted from an adjusting entry   Bal. = Balance

EXHIBIT 4-8 *Journalizing and Posting the Adjusting Entries*

OBJECTIVE 3
Close the revenue, expense, and withdrawal accounts

Closing the Accounts

The term **closing the accounts** refers to the end-of-period step that prepares the accounts for recording the transactions of the next period. Closing the accounts consists of journalizing and posting the closing entries. Closing sets the balances of the revenue and expense accounts back to zero in order to measure the net income of the next period. Closing is a clerical procedure that requires only accounting procedures that we have already covered. Recall that the income statement reports only one period's income. For example, net income for Burger King, Inc., for 1996 relates exclusively to 1996. At December 31, 1996, Burger King's accountants close the company's revenue and expense accounts for that year. Because these accounts' balances relate to a particular accounting period and are therefore closed at the end of the period, the revenue and expense accounts are called **temporary (nominal) accounts.** The owner's withdrawal account—although not a revenue or an expense—is also a temporary account because it measures withdrawals for a specific period. The closing process applies only to temporary accounts.

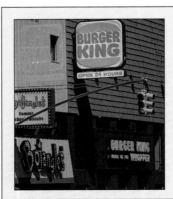

"At December 31, 1996, Burger King's accountants close the company's revenue and expense accounts for that year."

To understand better the closing process, contrast the nature of the temporary accounts with the nature of the **permanent (real) accounts**—the assets, liabilities, and capital. The asset, liability, and owner's capital accounts are *not* closed at the end of the period because their balances are not used to measure income. Consider Cash, Accounts Receivable, Supplies, Buildings, Accounts Payable, Notes Payable, and Gary Lyon, Capital. These accounts do not represent increases and decreases for a single period as do the revenues and expenses, which relate exclusively to only one accounting period. Instead, the permanent accounts represent assets, liabilities, and capital that are on hand at a specific time. This is why their balances at the end of one accounting period carry over to become the beginning balances of the next period. For example, the Cash balance at December 31, 19X1, is also the beginning balance for 19X2.

Briefly, **closing entries** transfer the revenue, expense, and owner withdrawal balances from their respective accounts to the capital account. As you know, revenues increase owner's equity, and expenses and owner withdrawals decrease it. It is when we post the closing entries that the capital account absorbs the impact of the balances in the temporary accounts. As an intermediate step, however, the revenues and the expenses are transferred first to an account entitled **Income Summary,** which collects in one place the total debit for the sum of all expenses and the total credit for the sum of all revenues of the period. The Income Summary account is like a temporary "holding tank" that is used only in the closing process. Then the balance of Income Summary is transferred to capital. The steps in closing the accounts of a proprietorship such as Gary Lyon, CPA, are as follows:

Key Point: There is no account for Net Income, which is the net result of all revenue and expense accounts. The Income Summary combines all revenue and expense amounts into one account.

① Debit each revenue account for the amount of its credit balance. Credit Income Summary for the sum of the revenues. This entry transfers the sum of the revenues to the credit side of Income Summary.

② Credit each expense account for the amount of its debit balance. Debit Income Summary for the sum of the expenses. This entry transfers the sum of the expenses to the debit side of Income Summary.

③ Debit Income Summary for the amount of its credit balance (revenues minus expenses), and credit the Capital account. If Income Summary has a debit balance, then credit Income Summary for this amount, and debit Capital. This entry transfers the net income or loss from Income Summary to the Capital account.

④ Credit the Withdrawals account for the amount of its debit balance. Debit the Capital account of the proprietor. This entry transfers the withdrawal amount to the debit side of the Capital account. Withdrawals are not expenses and do not affect net income or net loss.

To illustrate, suppose Gary Lyon closes the books at the end of April. Exhibit 4-9 presents the complete closing process for Lyon's business. Panel A gives the closing journal entries, and Panel B shows the accounts after the closing entries have been posted.

The amount in the debit side of each expense account is its adjusted balance. For example, Rent Expense has a $1,000 debit balance. Also note that Service Revenue has a credit balance of $7,400 before closing. These amounts come directly from the adjusted balances in Exhibit 4-8, Panel B.

Closing entry ① in Panel B of Exhibit 4-9, denoted in the Service Revenue account by *Clo.*, transfers Service Revenue's balance to the Income Summary account. This entry zeroes out Service Revenue for April and places the revenue on the credit side of Income Summary. Closing entry ② zeros out the expenses and moves their total ($3,875) to the debit side of Income Summary. At this point, Income Summary contains the impact of April's revenues and expenses; hence Income Summary's balance is the month's net income ($3,525). Closing entry ③ closes the Income Sum-

Key Point: It is not necessary to make a separate closing entry for each expense. In one closing entry, record one debit to Income Summary and a separate credit to each expense account.

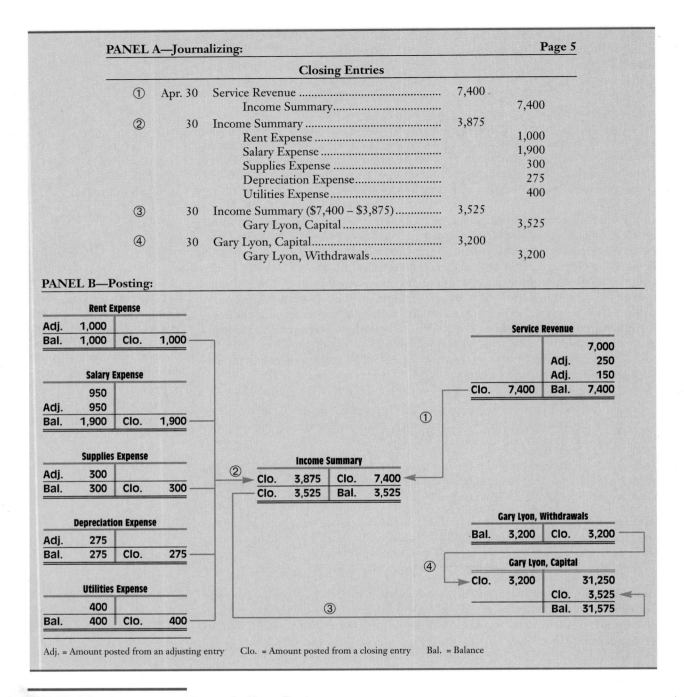

PANEL A—Journalizing: Page 5

Closing Entries

①	Apr. 30	Service Revenue	7,400	
		Income Summary.....................................		7,400
②	30	Income Summary	3,875	
		Rent Expense		1,000
		Salary Expense		1,900
		Supplies Expense		300
		Depreciation Expense........................		275
		Utilities Expense..............................		400
③	30	Income Summary ($7,400 – $3,875)..............	3,525	
		Gary Lyon, Capital		3,525
④	30	Gary Lyon, Capital...	3,200	
		Gary Lyon, Withdrawals......................		3,200

PANEL B—Posting:

Rent Expense

| Adj. | 1,000 | | |
| Bal. | 1,000 | Clo. | 1,000 |

Salary Expense

	950		
Adj.	950		
Bal.	1,900	Clo.	1,900

Supplies Expense

| Adj. | 300 | | |
| Bal. | 300 | Clo. | 300 |

Depreciation Expense

| Adj. | 275 | | |
| Bal. | 275 | Clo. | 275 |

Utilities Expense

| | 400 | | |
| Bal. | 400 | Clo. | 400 |

Service Revenue

			7,000
		Adj.	250
		Adj.	150
Clo.	7,400	Bal.	7,400

Income Summary

| Clo. | 3,875 | Clo. | 7,400 |
| Clo. | 3,525 | Bal. | 3,525 |

Gary Lyon, Withdrawals

| Bal. | 3,200 | Clo. | 3,200 |

Gary Lyon, Capital

Clo.	3,200		31,250
		Clo.	3,525
		Bal.	31,575

Adj. = Amount posted from an adjusting entry   Clo. = Amount posted from a closing entry   Bal. = Balance

EXHIBIT 4-9   *Journalizing and Posting the Closing Entries*

mary account by transferring net income to the credit side of Gary Lyon, Capital.[1] The last closing entry, entry ④, moves the owner withdrawals to the debit side of Gary Lyon, Capital, leaving a zero balance in the Withdrawals account.

After all the closing entries, the revenues, the expenses, and the Withdrawals account are set back to zero for use in the next period. The owner's Capital account includes the full effects of the April revenues, expenses, and withdrawals. These amounts, combined with the beginning Capital balance, give Capital an ending bal-

---

[1]The Income Summary account is a convenience for combining the effects of the revenues and expenses before transferring their income effect to Capital. It is not necessary to use the Income Summary account in the closing process. Another way of closing the revenues and expenses makes no use of this account. In this alternative procedure, the revenues and expenses are closed directly to Capital.

ance of $31,575. Note that this Capital balance agrees with the amount reported on the statement of owner's equity and on the balance sheet in Exhibit 4-7.

CLOSING A NET LOSS What would the closing entries be if Lyon's business had suffered a net *loss* during April? Suppose April expenses totaled $7,700 and all other factors were unchanged. Only closing entries ② and ③ would be altered. Closing entry ② would transfer expenses of $7,700 to the debit side of Income Summary, as follows:

Short Exercise: (1) Would the Income Summary have a debit or a credit balance if the company suffers a net loss? (2) In the event of a loss, how is Income Summary closed? *A:* (1) Expenses would exceed revenues, and Income Summary would have a debit balance. (2) Income Summary is credited, and Capital is debited.

Income Summary			
Clo.	7,700	Clo.	7,400
Bal.	300		

Closing entry ③ would then credit Income Summary to close its debit balance and to transfer the net loss to Capital:

③ Apr. 30   Gary Lyon, Capital 300
                     Income Summary............. 300

After posting, these two accounts would appear as follows:

Income Summary					Gary Lyon, Capital		
Clo.	7,700	Clo.	7,400	→	Clo.	300	31,250
Bal.	300	Clo.	300				

Key Point: The double line in an account means that the account has a zero balance; nothing more will be posted to it in the current period. The double line is drawn immediately after the closing entry is posted. In the general ledger, the account has a zero balance.

Finally, the Withdrawals balance would be closed to Capital, as before.

As outlined, the closing process is fundamentally mechanical and is completely automated in a computerized system. Accounts are identified as either temporary or permanent. The temporary accounts are closed automatically by selecting that option from the software's menu. Posting also occurs automatically.

Postclosing Trial Balance

The accounting cycle ends with the **postclosing trial balance** (see Exhibit 4-10). The postclosing trial balance is the final check on the accuracy of journalizing and posting the adjusting and closing entries. Like the trial balance that begins the work sheet, the postclosing trial balance is a list of the ledger's accounts and balances. This step ensures that the ledger is in balance for the start of the next accounting period. The postclosing trial balance is dated as of the end of the period for which the statements have been prepared.

GARY LYON, CPA POSTCLOSING TRIAL BALANCE APRIL 30, 19X1		
Cash	$24,800	
Accounts receivable	2,500	
Supplies	400	
Prepaid rent	2,000	
Furniture	16,500	
Accumulated depreciation		$ 275
Accounts payable		13,100
Salary payable		950
Unearned service revenue		300
Gary Lyon, capital		31,575
Total	$46,200	$46,200

EXHIBIT 4-10
Postclosing Trial Balance

The postclosing trial balance resembles the balance sheet. It contains the ending balances of the permanent accounts—the balance sheet accounts: the assets, liabilities, and capital. No temporary accounts—revenues, expenses, or withdrawal accounts—are included because their balances have been closed. The ledger is up to date and ready for the next period's transactions.

Correcting Journal Entries

OBJECTIVE 4
Correct typical accounting errors

In Chapter 2 we discussed errors that affect the trial balance: treating a debit as a credit and vice versa; transpositions; and slides. Here we show how to correct errors in journal entries.

When a journal entry contains an error, the entry can be deleted and corrected—if the error is caught immediately. A computerized accounting system makes easy work of retrieving an incorrect entry. When you delete the original entry, the posting is also cancelled. You can then record the correct entry, which is posted automatically.

If the error is detected after posting, the accountant makes a *correcting entry*. Suppose Gary Lyon paid $5,000 cash for furniture and erroneously debited Supplies as follows:

Short Exercise: (1) John Doe recorded the collection of a $1,000 receivable as a debit to Cash and a credit to Service Revenue for $1,000. Prepare the correcting entry.
(2) If Doe's net income before the correction was $26,000, how much is the corrected net income? *A:*
(1) Service Rev. 1,000
         Accounts Rec.   1,000
(2) $25,000 ($26,000 – $1,000)

Incorrect Entry		
May 13 Supplies.......................................	5,000	
Cash		5,000
Bought supplies.		

The debit to Supplies is incorrect, so it is necessary to make a correcting entry as follows:

Correcting Entry		
May 15 Furniture......................................	5,000	
Supplies..............................		5,000
To correct May 13 entry.		

The credit to Supplies in the second entry offsets the incorrect debit of the first entry. The debit to Furniture in the correcting entry places the furniture's cost in the correct account. Now both Supplies and Furniture are correct. Cash was unaffected by the error because Cash was credited correctly in the entry to purchase the furniture.

Classification of Assets and Liabilities

OBJECTIVE 5
Classify assets and liabilities as current or long-term

On the balance sheet, assets and liabilities are classified as either *current* or *long-term* to indicate their relative *liquidity*. **Liquidity** is a measure of how quickly an item can be converted to cash. Cash is the most liquid asset. Accounts receivable is a relatively liquid asset because the business expects to collect the amount in cash in the near future. Supplies are less liquid than accounts receivable, and furniture and buildings are even less so.

Users of financial statements are interested in liquidity because business difficulties often arise from a shortage of cash. How quickly can the business convert an asset to cash and pay a debt? How soon must a liability be paid? These are questions of liquidity. Balance sheets list assets and liabilities in the order of their relative liquidity.

CURRENT ASSETS **Current assets** are assets that are expected to be converted to cash, sold, or consumed during the next 12 months or within the business's normal operating cycle if longer than a year. The **operating cycle** is the time span during which (1) cash is used to acquire goods and services, and (2) these goods and services are sold to customers, who in turn pay for their purchases with cash. For most businesses, the operating cycle is a few months. A few types of businesses have operating cycles longer than a year. Cash, Accounts Receivable, Notes Receivable due within a year or less, and Prepaid Expenses are current assets. Merchandising entities such as Kmart, Sears, and Motorola have an additional current asset, Inventory. This account shows the cost of goods that are held for sale to customers.

"Merchandising entities such as Kmart, Sears, and Motorola have an additional current asset, Inventory."

LONG-TERM ASSETS **Long-term assets** are all assets other than current assets. They are not held for sale, but rather they are used to operate the business. One category of long-term assets is plant assets, often labeled Property, Plant, and Equipment. Land, Buildings, Furniture and Fixtures, and Equipment are plant assets. Of these, Gary Lyon has only Furniture. Other categories of long-term assets include Available-for-Sale Securities and Held-to-Maturity Securities (formerly labeled Investments) and Other Assets (a catchall category for assets that are not classified more precisely).

Financial statement users such as creditors are interested in the due dates of an entity's liabilities. The sooner a liability must be paid, the more current it is. Liabilities that must be paid on the earliest future date create the greatest strain on cash. Therefore, the balance sheet lists liabilities in the order in which they are due. Knowing how many of a business's liabilities are current and how many are long-term helps creditors assess the likelihood of collecting from the entity. Balance sheets usually have at least two liability classifications, *current liabilities* and *long-term liabilities.*

CURRENT LIABILITIES **Current liabilities** are debts that are due to be paid within one year or within the entity's operating cycle if the cycle is longer than a year. Accounts Payable, Notes Payable due within one year, Salary Payable, Unearned Revenue, and Interest Payable owed on notes payable are current liabilities.

LONG-TERM LIABILITIES All liabilities that are not current are classified as **long-term liabilities.** Many notes payable are long-term. Other notes payable are paid in installments, with the first installment due within one year, the second installment due the second year, and so on. In that case, the first installment would be a current liability, and the remainder long-term liabilities.

An Actual Classified Balance Sheet

Exhibit 4-11 is an actual classified balance sheet of International Business Machines Corporation, better known as IBM. IBM labels its balance sheet as the Statement of Financial Position, a more descriptive title. The statement is labeled Consolidated because it reports the accounts of IBM and its component companies as well. Dollar amounts are reported in millions to avoid clutter. IBM reports on a calendar-year basis, ending each December 31. It is customary to present two or more years' statements together to let people compare one year with the other—1992 and 1991 in this case. For your understanding, we have added bracketed explanations for several accounts. The bracketed items do not appear on IBM's balance sheet.

EXHIBIT 4-11

Classified Balance Sheet

INTERNATIONAL BUSINESS MACHINES CORPORATION AND SUBSIDIARY COMPANIES
CONSOLIDATED STATEMENT OF FINANCIAL POSITION

(Dollars in millions) At December 31:	1992	1991
Assets		
Current Assets:		
Cash	$ 1,090	$ 1,171
Cash equivalents [such as money-market accounts]	3,356	2,774
Marketable securities, at cost, which approximates market	1,203	1,206
Notes and accounts receivable—trade	12,829	15,391
Sales-type leases receivable	7,405	7,435
Other accounts receivable	1,370	1,491
Inventories	8,385	9,844
Prepaid expenses and other current assets [such as supplies]	4,054	1,657
	39,692	40,969
Plant, Rental Machines and Other Property	52,786	55,678
Less: Accumulated depreciation	31,191	28,100
	21,595	27,578
Investments and Other Assets:		
Software, less accumulated amortization (1992, $8,531; 1991, $6,950)	4,119	4,483
Investments and sundry assets	21,299	19,443
	25,418	23,926
	$86,705	$92,473
Liabilities and Stockholders' Equity		
Current Liabilities:		
Taxes	$ 979	$ 2,449
Short-term debt	16,467	13,716
Accounts payable	3,147	3,507
Compensation and benefits	3,476	3,241
Deferred income [same as Unearned revenues]	3,316	3,472
Other accrued expenses and liabilities	9,352	7,566
	36,737	33,951
Long-Term Debt [such as long-term notes payable]	12,853	13,231
Other Liabilities [such as unearned revenue, long-term]	7,461	6,685
Deferred Income Taxes	2,030	1,927
Total Liabilities	59,081	55,794
Stockholders' Equity [Capital for a proprietorship]	27,624	36,679
	$86,705	$92,473

You should be familiar with all but a few of IBM's account titles. Among the Current Assets are Marketable securities (now better known as Trading securities), which are investments that IBM expects to sell within one year. These assets are very liquid, which explains why they are listed before the receivables. IBM leases out computer equipment and expects to collect cash on the sales-type leases receivable. These receivables are similar to accounts receivable and notes receivable.

"IBM leases out computer equipment and expects to collect cash on the sales-type leases receivable."

IBM reports plant assets as Plant, Rental Machines, and Other Property on its balance sheet. These assets cost IBM $52,786 million in 1992 and had book value (that is, cost minus accumulated depreciation) of $21,595 million. The final asset category, Investments and Other Assets, includes IBM's Software, reported with its accumulated *amortization*, which is similar to accumulated depreciation on plant assets. At December 31, 1992, IBM had software with book value (cost minus accumulated amortization) of $4,119 million. IBM could have reported the asset software in the same way it reported the assets plant, rental machines, and other property, as follows:

Software..	$12,650
Less: Accumulated amortization................	8,531
	$ 4,119

IBM's Investments are the shares of stock that IBM owns in other companies. These investments are not current assets because IBM does not expect to sell them within one year of the balance sheet date. Sundry assets could be labeled Other Assets, a catchall category for items that are difficult to classify.

You should recognize all of IBM's current liabilities. Taxes could be labeled Taxes Payable. Short-term Debt could be labeled Short-term Notes Payable. Compensation and benefits could be listed as Salary and Wages Payable. IBM collects some revenues in advance from customers. This practice explains the account titled Deferred Income, which is another name for the Unearned Revenues account.

IBM reports a long-term liability for Deferred Income Taxes. These are corporate income tax payables that the company may pay beyond one year in the future. Finally, IBM calls its owners' equity stockholders' equity; other corporations may call it shareholders' equity.

Formats of Balance Sheets

The balance sheet of IBM shown in Exhibit 4-11 lists the assets at the top and the liabilities and owners' equity below. This arrangement is known as the *report format*. The balance sheet of Gary Lyon, CPA, presented in Exhibit 4-7 lists the assets at the left and the liabilities and the owner's equity at the right. That arrangement is known as the *account format*.

Either balance sheet format is acceptable. A recent survey of 600 companies indicated that 69 percent use the report format and that 31 percent use the account format.

STOP & THINK   IBM reported less stockholders' equity at December 31, 1992, than at December 31, 1991. Why might stockholders' equity have decreased?

Answer: The main reasons were that IBM suffered a net loss during 1992 and that the company paid dividends to its stockholders (similar to withdrawals by a proprietor). You may be wondering why a company would pay dividends during a loss year. Suppose Gary Lyon's accounting practice had a bad year and lost money. He would still need to pay household and other personal expenses. If the business had accumulated assets and capital in previous years, Lyon could draw on those resources in a lean year.

It is the same for a large corporation. Prior to 1992, IBM had built up lots of assets and owner's equity, which were available to absorb losses and pay dividends in a bad year. This is why investors and creditors feel comfortable investing in, and lending to, a business with a large amount of owner's equity. It has the capital to survive hard times.

Use of Accounting Information in Decision Making: Accounting Ratios

The purpose of accounting is to provide information for decision making. Chief users of accounting information include managers, investors, and creditors. A creditor considering lending money must predict whether the borrower can repay the loan. If the borrower already has lots of debt, the probability of repayment is lower than if the borrower has a small amount of liabilities. To assess financial position, decision makers use ratios computed from various items drawn from a company's financial statements.

Short Exercise: A company has current assets of $100,000 and current liabilities of $50,000. How will the payment of a $10,000 account payable affect the current ratio? *A:* The payment of an account payable would cause both cash and accounts payable to decrease and thus would increase the current ratio from 2.00 to 2.25.

Current Ratio

One of the most common financial ratios is the **current ratio**, which is the ratio of an entity's current assets to its current liabilities:

$$\text{Current ratio} = \frac{\text{Total current assets}}{\text{Total current liabilities}}$$

The current ratio measures the ability to pay current liabilities with current assets. A company prefers to have a high current ratio, which means that the business has plenty of current assets to pay current liabilities. An increasing current ratio from period to period indicates improvement in financial position.

A rule of thumb: A strong current ratio is 2.00, which indicates that the company has $2.00 in current assets for every $1.00 in current liabilities. A company with a current ratio of 2.00 would probably have little trouble paying its current liabilities. Most successful businesses operate with current ratios between 1.50 and 2.00. A current ratio of 1.00 is considered quite low. Lenders and investors would view a company with a current ratio of 1.50 or 2.00 as substantially less risky. Such a company could probably borrow money on better terms and also attract more investors.

Real-World Example: According to Robert Morris Associates, the median current ratio among computer manufacturers in 3/93 was 1.9, while the top 25% reported a current ratio of 3.0. But for companies with sales over $25 million, the median current ratio was 2.3, and the top 25% reported a current ratio of 3.1.

Debt Ratio

A second aid to decision making is the **debt ratio,** which is the ratio of total liabilities to total assets:

$$\text{Debt ratio} = \frac{\text{Total liabilities}}{\text{Total assets}}$$

The debt ratio indicates the proportion of a company's assets that are financed with debt. This ratio measures a business's ability to pay both current and long-term debts—total liabilities.

A low debt ratio is safer than a high debt ratio. Why? Because a company with a small amount of liabilities has low required payments. Such a company is unlikely to get into financial difficulty. By contrast, a business with a high debt ratio may have trouble paying its liabilities, especially when sales are low and cash is scarce. When a company fails to pay its debts, the creditors can take the business away from its owner. The largest retail bankruptcy in history, Federated Department Stores (parent company of Bloomingdale's), was due largely to high

Real-World Example: The defense contractor McDonnell Douglas, a very capital-intensive company, had a debt ratio of 0.34 in 9/93, while another defense contractor, Northrop Corp., had a debt ratio of only 0.10.

> *"The largest retail bankruptcy in history, Federated Department Stores (parent company of Bloomingdale's) was due largely to high debt during a retail-industry recession."*

debt during a retail-industry recession. Federated was unable to weather the downturn and had to declare bankruptcy.

In general, a *high* current ratio is preferable to a low current ratio. *Increases* in the current ratio indicate improving financial position. By contrast, a *low* debt ratio is preferable to a high debt ratio. Improvement is indicated by a *decrease* in the debt ratio.

Financial ratios are an important aid to decision making. It is unwise, however, to place too much confidence in a single ratio or in any group of ratios. For example, a company may have a high current ratio, which indicates financial strength. It may also have a high debt ratio, which suggests weakness. Which ratio gives the more reliable signal about the company? Experienced managers, lenders, and investors evaluate a company by examining a large number of ratios over several years to spot trends and turning points. These people also consider other factors, such as the company's cash position and its trend in net income. No single ratio gives the whole picture about a company.

As you progress through the study of accounting, we will introduce key ratios used for decision making. Chapter 19 summarizes all the ratios discussed throughout this book and provides a good overview of ratios used in decision making.

PUTTING SKILLS TO WORK

RATIOS: SHOULD A BANK GRANT A LOAN?

Suppose IBM, the company in Exhibit 4-11, needed a bank loan to finance the purchase of a new division. How would a bank evaluate the company's financial position to judge whether to grant the loan? The example above shows just two pieces of information a loan office would consider.

EXCERPTS FROM IBM'S BALANCE SHEET

= $10,000,000

Total Current Assets: $39,692,000

Total Current Liabilities: $36,737,000

Total Assets: $86,705,000

Total Liabilities: $59,081,000

THE CURRENT RATIO

The bank might look first at IBM's current ratio to determine the company's ability to pay current liabilities with current assets.

The bank could use IBM's balance sheet to calculate a current ratio of 1.08 at December 31, 1992:

$$\frac{\text{Current}}{\text{ratio}} = \frac{\$39,692,000}{\$36,737,000} = 1.08$$

The low value of this ratio indicates that IBM has barely enough current assets to pay all its current liabilities - a risky position. One year earlier, at December 31, 1991, IBM's current ratio stood at 1.21 ($40,969,000/$33,951,000 = 1.21), which was somewhat better.

THE DEBT RATIO

The bank would want more information than just the current ratio before making a decision about a loan. It could next compute IBM's debt ratio to measure the company's ability to pay current and long-term debts. From the balance sheet, IBM's debt ratio is calculated to be 0.68 at December 31, 1992:

$$\frac{\text{Debt}}{\text{ratio}} = \frac{\$59,081,000}{\$86,705,000} = 0.68$$

That figure is in line with the debt ratios of other large companies but is somewhat higher than IBM's debt ratio only one year earlier, at December 31, 1991 ($55,794,000/$92,473,000 = 0.60).

THE FINAL DECISION

How would a decision maker use IBM's ratios? IBM's low current ratio would worry the loan officer because it may signal difficulty in paying debts. In fact, IBM has experienced some losses in recent years. If the bank agreed to loan money, it might place restrictions on IBM because of the company's financial standing. For example, the lender might charge a high interest rate and restrict payments to the company's owners. Some potential investors may be reluctant to invest in the company because of its operating losses and rising debt ratio. IBM's managers may feel pressure to reduce the company's debt.

IBM headquarters in Armonk, New York

Refer to the data in the Mid-Chapter Summary Problem for Your Review, presented on pages 137–138.

Required

1. Journalize and post the adjusting entries. (Before posting to the accounts, enter into each account its balance as shown in the trial balance. For example, enter the $370,000 balance in the Accounts Receivable account before posting its adjusting entry.) Key adjusting entries by *letter*, as shown in the work sheet solution to the mid-chapter review problem. You can take the adjusting entries straight from the work sheet on page 138.

2. Journalize and post the closing entries. (Each account should carry its balance as shown in the adjusted trial balance.) To distinguish closing entries from adjusting entries, key the closing entries by *number*. Draw the arrows to illustrate the flow of data, as shown in Exhibit 4-9, page 142. Indicate the balance of the Capital account after the closing entries are posted.

3. Prepare the income statement for the year ended December 31, 19X1. List Miscellaneous Expense last among the expenses, a common practice.

4. Prepare the statement of owner's equity for the year ended December 31, 19X1. Draw the arrow that links the income statement to the statement of owner's equity.

5. Prepare the classified balance sheet at December 31, 19X1. Use the report form. All liabilities are current. Draw the arrow that links the statement of owner's equity to the balance sheet.

SOLUTION TO REVIEW PROBLEM

Requirement 1

a.	Dec. 31	Supplies Expense	4,000	
		Supplies		4,000
b.	31	Depreciation Expense—Furniture and Fixtures.....................	20,000	
		Accumulated Depreciation—		
		Furniture and Fixtures.................................		20,000
c.	31	Depreciation Expense—Building	10,000	
		Accumulated Depreciation—Building.........................		10,000
d.	31	Salary Expense...	5,000	
		Salary Payable		5,000
e.	31	Accounts Receivable...	12,000	
		Service Revenue		12,000
f.	31	Unearned Service Revenue	32,000	
		Service Revenue		32,000

Accounts Receivable		
370,000		
(e) 12,000		

Supplies		
6,000	(a)	4,000

Accumulated Depreciation—Furniture and Fixtures		
		40,000
	(b)	20,000

Accumulated Depreciation—Building		
		130,000
	(c)	10,000

Salary Payable		
	(d)	5,000

Unearned Service Revenue		
(f) 32,000		45,000

Service Revenue		
		286,000
	(e)	12,000
	(f)	32,000
	Bal.	330,000

Salary Expense		
172,000		
(d) 5,000		
Bal. 177,000		

Supplies Expense		
(a)	4,000	
Bal.	4,000	

Depreciation Expense—Furniture and Fixtures		
(b)	20,000	
Bal.	20,000	

Depreciation Expense—Building		
(c)	10,000	
Bal.	10,000	

Requirement 2

1.	Dec. 31	Service Revenue..	330,000	
		Income Summary		330,000
2.	31	Income Summary..	224,000	
		Salary Expense..		177,000
		Supplies Expense		4,000
		Depreciation Expense—Furniture and Fixtures...............		20,000
		Depreciation Expense—Building......................................		10,000
		Miscellaneous Expense..		13,000
3.	31	Income Summary ($330,000 - $224,000).....................................	106,000	
		Capital...		106,000
4.	31	Capital..	65,000	
		Withdrawals..		65,000

Requirement 3

STATE SERVICE COMPANY		
INCOME STATEMENT		
FOR THE YEAR ENDED DECEMBER 31, 19X1		
Revenue:		
Service revenue...		$330,000
Expenses:		
Salary expense..	$177,000	
Depreciation expense—furniture and fixtures...............	20,000	
Depreciation expense—building....................................	10,000	
Supplies expense...	4,000	
Miscellaneous expense	13,000	
Total expenses...		224,000
Net income		$106,000

Requirement 4

STATE SERVICE COMPANY	
STATEMENT OF OWNER'S EQUITY	
FOR THE YEAR ENDED DECEMBER 31, 19X1	
Capital, January 1, 19X1.....................	$293,000
Add: Net income	106,000
	399,000
Less: Withdrawals	65,000
Capital, December 31, 19X1..............	$334,000

Requirement 5

STATE SERVICE COMPANY		
CLASSIFIED BALANCE SHEET		
DECEMBER 31, 19X1		
Assets		
Current assets:		
Cash..		$198,000
Accounts receivable..		382,000
Supplies		2,000
Total current assets		582,000
Plant assets:		
Furniture and fixtures	$100,000	
Less Accumulated depreciation................	60,000	40,000
Building..	250,000	
Less Accumulated depreciation................	140,000	110,000
Total assets		$732,000
Liabilities		
Current liabilities:		
Accounts payable...		$380,000
Salary payable...		5,000
Unearned service revenue...		13,000
Total current liabilities...		398,000
Owner's Equity		
Capital		334,000
Total liabilities and owner's equity.............................		$732,000

SUMMARY

1. Prepare an accounting worksheet. The *accounting cycle* is the process by which accountants produce the financial statements for a specific period of time. The cycle starts with the beginning account balances. During the period, the business journalizes transactions and posts them to the ledger accounts. At the end of the period, the trial balance is prepared, and the accounts are adjusted in order to measure the period's net income or net loss. Completion of the accounting cycle is aided by use of a *work sheet*. This multicolumned document summarizes the effects of all the activity of the period.

2. Use the work sheet to complete the accounting cycle. The work sheet is neither a journal nor a ledger but merely a convenient device for completing the accounting cycle. It has columns for the trial balance, the adjustments, the adjusted trial balance, the income statement, and the balance sheet. It aids the adjusting process, and it is the place where the period's net income or net loss is first computed. The work sheet also provides the data for the financial statements and the *closing entries*. It is not, however, a necessity. The accounting cycle can be completed from the less elaborate adjusted trial balance.

3. Close the revenue, expense, and withdrawal accounts. Revenues, expenses, and withdrawals represent increases and decreases in owner's equity for a specific period. At the end of the period, their balances are closed out to zero, and, for this reason, they are called *temporary accounts*. Assets, liabilities, and capital are not closed because they are the *permanent accounts*. Their balances at the end of one period become the beginning balances of the next period. The final accuracy check of the period is the *postclosing trial balance*.

4. Correct typical accounting errors. Accountants correct errors by making correcting journal entries.

5. Classify assets and liabilities as current or long-term. The balance sheet reports *current* and *long-term assets* and *current* and *long-term liabilities*. It can be presented in *report format* or *account format*.

6. Use the current and debt ratios to evaluate a business. Two decision-making aids are the *current ratio*—total current assets divided by total current liabilities—and the *debt ratio*—total liabilities divided by total assets.

SELF-STUDY QUESTIONS

Test your understanding of the chapter by marking the best answer to each of the following questions.

1. The focal point of the accounting cycle is the (*p. 134*)
   a. Financial statements
   b. Trial balance
   c. Adjusted trial balance
   d. Work sheet

2. Arrange the following accounting cycle steps in their proper order (*p. 134a*)
   a. Complete the work sheet
   b. Journalize and post adjusting entries
   c. Prepare the postclosing trial balance
   d. Journalize and post cash transactions
   e. Prepare the financial statements
   f. Journalize and post closing entries

3. The work sheet is a (*p. 134*)
   a. Journal
   b. Ledger
   c. Financial statement
   d. Convenient device for completing the accounting cycle

4. The usefulness of the work sheet is (*p. 134*)
   a. Identifying the accounts that need to be adjusted
   b. Summarizing the effects of all the transactions of the period
   c. Aiding the preparation of the financial statements
   d. All of the above

5. Which of the following accounts is not closed? (*p. 141*)
   a. Supplies Expense
   b. Prepaid Insurance
   c. Interest Revenue
   d. Owner Withdrawals

6. The closing entry for Salary Expense, with a balance of $322,000, is (*p. 142*)
   a. Salary Expense 322,000
      Income Summary 322,000

   b. Salary Expense 322,000
      Salary Payable............. 322,000

   c. Income Summary 322,000
      Salary Expense............ 322,000

   d. Salary Payable 322,000
      Salary Expense............ 322,000

7. The purpose of the postclosing trial balance is to (*p. 143*)
   a. Provide the account balances for preparation of the balance sheet
   b. Ensure that the ledger is in balance for the start of the next period
   c. Aid the journalizing and posting of the closing entries
   d. Ensure that the ledger is in balance for completion of the work sheet

8. A payment on account was recorded by debiting Inventory and crediting Cash. This entry was posted. The correcting entry is (*p. 144*)
   a. Accounts Payable X
         Inventory X
   b. Inventory X
         Accounts Payable X
   c. Cash X
         Accounts Payable X
   d. Cash X
         Inventory X

9. The classification of assets and liabilities as current or long-term depends on (*p. 144*)
   a. Their order of listing in the ledger
   b. Whether they appear on the balance sheet or the income statement
   c. The relative liquidity of the item
   d. The format of the balance sheet—account format or report format

10. In 19X4, Gary Lyon debited Depreciation Expense for the cost of a computer that he uses in his accounting practice. For 19X4, this error (p. 144)
    a. Overstated net income

    b. Understated net income
    c. Either a or b, depending on the circumstances
    d. Had no effect on net income

Answers to the Self-Study Questions follow the Accounting Vocabulary.

ACCOUNTING VOCABULARY

Accounting cycle. Process by which accountants produce an entity's financial statements for a specific period (*p. 134*).

Closing the accounts. Step in the accounting cycle at the end of the period that prepares the accounts for recording the transactions of the next period. Closing the accounts consists of journalizing and posting the closing entries to set the balances of the revenue, expense, and owner withdrawal accounts to zero (*p. 140*).

Closing entries. Entries that transfer the revenue, expense, and owner withdrawal balances from these respective accounts to the capital account (*p. 141*).

Current asset. An asset that is expected to be converted to cash, sold, or consumed during the next 12 months, or within the business's normal operating cycle if longer than a year (*p. 145*).

Current liability. A debt due to be paid within one year or one of the entity's operating cycles if the cycle is longer than a year (*p. 145*).

Current ratio. Current assets divided by current liabilities. Measures the ability to pay current liabilities from current assets (*p. 148*).

Debt ratio. Ratio of total liabilities to total assets. Tells the proportion of a company's assets that it has financed with debt (*p. 148*).

Income Summary. A temporary "holding tank" account into which the revenues and expenses are transferred prior to their final transfer to the capital account (*p. 141*).

Liquidity. Measure of how quickly an item can be converted to cash (*p. 144*).

Long-term asset. An asset other than a current asset (*p. 145*).

Long-term liability. A liability other than a current liability (*p. 145*).

Nominal account. Another name for a temporary account (*p. 140*).

Operating cycle. Time span during which cash is paid for goods and services that are sold to customers who then pay the business in cash (*p. 145*).

Permanent account. Another name for a real account—asset, liability, and capital—that is *not* closed at the end of the period (*p. 141*).

Postclosing trial balance. List of the ledger accounts and their balances at the end of the period after the journalizing and posting of the closing entries. The last step of the accounting cycle, the postclosing trial balance ensures that the ledger is in balance for the start of the next accounting period (*p. 143*).

Real account. Another name for a permanent account (*p. 141*).

Reversing entry. An entry that switches the debit and the credit of a previous adjusting entry. The reversing entry is dated the first day of the period after the adjusting entry (*p. 172*).

Temporary account. Another name for a Nominal account. The revenue and expense accounts that relate to a particular accounting period and are closed at the end of the period are temporary accounts. For a proprietorship, the owner withdrawal account is also temporary (*p. 140*).

Work sheet. A columnar document designed to help move data from the trial balance to the financial statements (*p. 134*).

ANSWERS TO SELF-STUDY QUESTIONS

1. a	**3.** d	**5.** b	**7.** b	**9.** c
2. d, a, e, b, f, c	**4.** d	**6.** c	**8.** a	**10.** b

QUESTIONS

1. Identify the steps in the accounting cycle; distinguish those that occur during the period from those that are performed at the end.
2. Why is the work sheet a valuable accounting tool?
3. Name two advantages the work sheet has over the adjusted trial balance.
4. Why must the adjusting entries be journalized and posted if they have already been entered on the work sheet?
5. Why should the adjusting entries be journalized and posted before the closing entries are made?
6. Which types of accounts are closed?
7. What purpose is served by closing the accounts?
8. State how the work sheet helps with recording the closing entries.
9. Distinguish between permanent accounts and temporary accounts; indicate which type is closed at the end of the period. Give five examples of each type of account.
10. Is Income Summary a permanent account or a temporary account? When and how is it used?
11. Give the closing entries for the following accounts (bal-

ances in parentheses): Service Revenue ($4,700), Salary Expense ($1,100), Income Summary (credit balance of $2,000), Rhonda McGill, Withdrawals ($2,300).

12. Why are assets classified as current or long-term? On what basis are they classified? Where do the classified amounts appear?

13. Indicate which of the following accounts are current assets and which are long-term assets: Prepaid Rent, Building, Furniture, Accounts Receivable, Merchandise Inventory, Cash, Note Receivable (due within one year), Note Receivable (due after one year).

14. In what order are assets and liabilities listed on the balance sheet?

15. Identify an outside party that would be interested in whether a liability is current or long-term. Why would this party be interested in this information?

16. A friend tells you that the difference between a current liability and a long-term liability is that they are payable to different types of creditors. Is your friend correct? Define these two categories of liabilities.

17. Show how to compute the current ratio and the debt ratio. Indicate what ability each ratio measures, and state whether a high value or a low value is safer for each.

18. Capp Company purchased supplies of $120 on account. The accountant debited Supplies and credited Cash for $120. A week later, after this entry has been posted to the ledger, the accountant discovers the error. How should he correct the error?

EXERCISES

E4-1 The trial balance of Orkin Pest Control Service follows.

Preparing a work sheet
(Obj. 1)

ORKIN PEST CONTROL SERVICE TRIAL BALANCE SEPTEMBER 30, 19X6		
Cash..	$ 3,560	
Accounts receivable	3,440	
Prepaid rent......................................	1,200	
Supplies	3,390	
Equipment...	12,600	
Accumulated depreciation		$ 2,840
Accounts payable		1,600
Salary payable..................................		
Bobby Orkin, capital.........................		16,030
Bobby Orkin, withdrawals...............	3,000	
Service revenue		9,300
Depreciation expense.......................		
Salary expense	1,800	
Rent expense		
Utilities expense..............................	780	
Supplies expense		
Total	$29,770	$29,770

Additional information at September 30, 19X6:

a. Accrued service revenue, $210.

b. Depreciation, $40.

c. Accrued salary expense, $500.

d. Prepaid rent expired, $600.

e. Supplies used, $1,650.

Required

Complete Orkin's work sheet for September 19X6.

Journalizing adjusting and closing entries (Obj. 2)

E4-2 Journalize the adjusting and closing entries in Exercise 4-1.

Posting adjusting and closing entries (Obj. 2)

E4-3 Set up T-accounts for those accounts affected by the adjusting and closing entries in Exercise 4-1. Post the adjusting and closing entries to the accounts; denote adjustment amounts by Adj., closing amounts by Clo., and balances by Bal. Double underline the accounts with zero balances after you close them, and show the ending balance in each account.

Preparing a postclosing trial balance (Obj. 2)

E4-4 Prepare the postclosing trial balance in Exercise 4-1.

Identifying and journalizing entries (Obj. 3)

E4-5 From the following selected accounts that Higginbotham Catering Service reported in its June 30, 19X4, annual financial statements, prepare the entity's closing entries:

A. Higginbotham, capital	$45,600	Interest expense	$ 2,200
Service revenue	96,100	Accounts receivable	30,000
Unearned revenues	1,350	Salary payable	850
Salary expense	12,500	Depreciation expense	10,200
Accumulated depreciation	35,000	Rent expense	5,900
Supplies expense	1,700	A. Higginbotham, withdrawals	40,000
Interest revenue	700	Supplies	1,400

Identifying and journalizing closing entries (Obj. 3)

E4-6 The accountant for Laura Edwards, Attorney, has posted adjusting entries (a) through (e) to the accounts at December 31, 19X2. All the revenue, expense, and owner's equity accounts of the entity are listed here in T-account form.

Accounts Receivable	
26,000	
(a) 3,500	

Supplies	
4,000	(b) 2,000

Accumulated Depreciation— Furniture	
	5,000
	(c) 1,100

Accumulated Depreciation— Building	
	33,000
	(d) 6,000

Salary Payable	
	(e) 700

Laura Edwards, Capital	
	52,400

Laura Edwards, Withdrawals	
52,400	

Service Revenue	
	102,000
	(a) 3,500

Salary Expense	
26,000	
(e) 700	

Supplies Expense	
(b) 2,000	

Depreciation Expense— Furniture	
(c) 1,100	

Depreciation Expense— Building	
(d) 6,000	

Required

Journalize Edwards's closing entries at December 31, 19X2.

Preparing a statement of owner's equity (Obj. 3)

E4-7 From the following accounts of Automatic Door Company, prepare the entity's statement of owner's equity for the year ended December 31, 19X5:

Kristen Heitmiller, Capital			
Dec. 31 42,000	Jan. 1	52,000
	Mar. 9	28,000
	Dec. 31	43,000

Kristen Heitmiller, Withdrawals	
Mar. 31 9,000	Dec. 31 42,000
Jun. 30 7,000	
Sep. 30 9,000	
Dec. 31 17,000	

Income Summary	
Dec. 31 85,000	Dec. 31 128,000
Dec. 31 43,000	

E4-8 The trial balance and income statement amounts from the March work sheet of Dagnan Labeling Company are presented below.

Identifying and recording adjusting and closing entries (Obj. 2, 3)

Account Title	Trial Balance		Income Statement	
Cash...	$ 5,100			
Supplies	2,400			
Prepaid rent......................................	1,100			
Office equipment	30,100			
Accumulated depreciation................		$ 6,200		
Accounts payable..............................		4,600		
Salary payable				
Unearned service revenue................		4,400		
John Dagnan, capital........................		17,800		
John Dagnan, withdrawals...............	1,000			
Service revenue.................................		11,700		$16,000
Salary expense	3,000		$ 3,800	
Rent expense.....................................	1,200		1,400	
Depreciation expense			300	
Supplies expense...............................			400	
Utilities expense	800		800	
	$44,700	$44,700	6,700	16,000
Net income.......................................			9,300	
			$16,000	$16,000

Required

Journalize the adjusting and closing entries of Dagnan Labeling Company at March 31.

E4-9 Refer to Exercise 4-8.

Preparing a classified balance sheet (Obj. 5, 6)

Required

1. After solving Exercise 4-8, use the data in that exercise to prepare Dagnan Labeling Company's classified balance sheet at March 31 of the current year. Use the report format.
2. Compute Dagnan's current ratio and debt ratio at March 31. One year ago the current ratio was 1.20 and the debt ratio was 0.30. Indicate whether Dagnan's ability to pay its debts has improved or deteriorated during the current year.

E4-10 Prepare a correcting entry for each of the following accounting errors:

Correcting accounting errors (Obj. 4)

a. Debited Supplies and credited Accounts Payable for a $2,900 purchase of office equipment on account.
b. Adjusted prepaid rent by debiting Prepaid Rent and crediting Rent Expense for $900. This adjusting entry should have debited Rent Expense and credited Prepaid Rent for $900.
c. Debited Salary Expense and credited Cash to accrue salary expense of $900.
d. Recorded the earning of $3,200 service revenue collected in advance by debiting Accounts Receivable and crediting Service Revenue.
e. Accrued interest revenue of $800 by a debit to Accounts Receivable and a credit to Interest Revenue.
f. Recorded a $600 cash purchase of supplies by debiting Supplies and crediting Accounts Payable.

SERIAL EXERCISE

This exercise continues the Emily Schneider, Accountant, situation begun in Exercise 2-13 of Chapter 2 and extended to Exercise 3-14 of Chapter 3.

Closing the books, preparing a classified balance sheet, and evaluating a business
(Obj. 3, 5, 6)

E4-11   Refer to Exercise 3-14 of Chapter 3. Start from the posted T-accounts and the adjusted trial balance that Emily Schneider, Accountant, prepared for her accounting practice at December 31.

Required

1. Journalize and post the closing entries at December 31. Denote each closing amount as *Clo.* and an account balance as *Bal.*
2. Prepare a classified balance sheet at December 31.
3. Compute the current ratio and the debt ratio of Emily Schneider's accounting practice and evaluate these ratio values as indicative of a strong or weak financial position.
4. If your instructor assigns it, complete the accounting work sheet at December 31.

Optional requirement
(Obj. 2)

CHALLENGE EXERCISE

Computing financial statement amounts
(Obj. 2, 5)

E4-12   The unadjusted trial balance of ElsiMate Company follows:

Cash	$ 1,900	Unearned service revenue	$ 5,300
Accounts receivable	7,200	Note payable, long-term	6,000
Rent receivable		Elsie Sharp, capital	60,100
Supplies	1,100	Elsie Sharp, withdrawals	16,200
Prepaid insurance	2,200	Service revenue	93,600
Furniture	8,400	Rent revenue	1,900
Accumulated depreciation—		Salary expense	32,700
furniture	1,300	Depreciation expense—furniture	
Building	57,800	Depreciation expense—building	
Accumulated depreciation—building	14,900	Supplies expense	
Land	51,200	Insurance expense	
Accounts payable	6,100	Interest expense	
Salary payable		Advertising expense	7,800
Interest payable		Property tax expense	
Property tax payable		Utilities expense	2,700

Adjusting data at the end of the year include:

a. Unearned service revenue that has been earned, $3,600.
b. Accrued rent revenue, $1,200.
c. Accrued property tax expense, $900.
d. Acrrued service revenue, $1,700.
e. Supplies used in operations, $600.
f. Accrued salary expense, $1,400.
g. Insurance expense, $1,800.
h. Depreciation expense—furniture, $800; building, $2,100.
i. Accrued interest expense, $500.

   Elsie Sharp, the owner, has received an offer to sell ElsiMate Company. She needs to know the following information within one hour:

A. Net income for the year covered by these data.
B. Total assets.
C. Total liabilities.

D. Total owner's equity.

E. Proof that total assets equal total liabilities plus total owner's equity after all items are updated.

Required

Without opening any accounts, making any journal entries, or using a work sheet, provide Elsie Sharp with the requested information. Show all computations

PROBLEMS

(GROUP A)

P4-1A   The trial balance of Krup Family Painting Contractors at July 31, 19X3, appears below.

Preparing a work sheet
(Obj. 1)

KRUP FAMILY PAINTING CONTRACTORS TRIAL BALANCE JULY 31, 19X3		
Cash..	$ 1,200	
Accounts receivable	37,820	
Supplies	17,660	
Prepaid insurance.....................................	2,300	
Equipment	32,690	
Accumulated depreciation—equipment..............		$ 26,240
Building...	36,890	
Accumulated depreciation—building.................		10,500
Land	28,300	
Accounts payable		22,690
Interest payable...		
Wage payable		
Unearned service revenue		10,560
Note payable, long-term		22,400
Liz Krup, capital		59,130
Liz Krup, withdrawals	4,200	
Service revenue		14,190
Depreciation expense—equipment		
Depreciation expense—building		
Wage expense...	3,200	
Insurance expense		
Interest expense		
Utilities expense..	270	
Property tax expense.................................	840	
Advertising expense	340	
Supplies expense		
Total	$165,710	$165,710

Additional data at July 31, 19X3:

a.   Depreciation: equipment, $630; building, $370.

b.   Accrued wage expense, $240.

c.   Supplies on hand, $14,740.

d.   Prepaid insurance expired during July, $500.

e.   Accrued interest expense, $180.

f.   Unearned service revenue earned during July, $4,970.

g.   Accrued advertising expense, $100 (credit Accounts Payable).

h.   Accrued service revenue, $1,100.

Required

Complete Krup's work sheet for July.

P4-2A   The adjusted trial balance of Armored Financial Couriers at June 30, 19X1, the end of the company's fiscal year, follows:

ARMORED FINANCIAL COURIERS ADJUSTED TRIAL BALANCE JUNE 30, 19X1		
Cash..	$ 19,350	
Accounts receivable	26,470	
Supplies	1,290	
Prepaid insurance..	3,200	
Equipment	55,800	
Accumulated depreciation—equipment...............		$ 16,480
Building...	144,900	
Accumulated depreciation—building..................		16,850
Accounts payable		38,400
Interest payable..		1,490
Wage payable		770
Unearned service revenue		2,300
Note payable, long-term		97,000
Hugo Naffa, capital		68,390
Hugo Naffa, withdrawals......................................	45,300	
Service revenue		109,860
Depreciation expense—equipment	7,300	
Depreciation expense—building	3,970	
Wage expense...	18,800	
Insurance expense	3,100	
Interest expense	11,510	
Utilities expense...	4,300	
Property tax expense	2,670	
Supplies expense	3,580	
Total	$351,540	$351,540

Adjusting data at June 30, 19X1, which have all been incorporated into the trial balance figures above:

a.   Depreciation for the year: equipment, $7,300; building, $3,970.

b.   Supplies used during the year, $3,580.

c.   Prepaid insurance expired during the year, $3,100.

d.   Accrued interest expense, $690.

e.   Accrued service revenue, $940.

f.   Unearned service revenue earned during the year, $7,790.

g.   Accrued wage expense, $770.

Required

1.   Journalize the adjusting and closing entries.

2.   Prepare Armored Financial's income statement and statement of owner's equity for the year ended June 30, 19X1, and the classified balance sheet on that date. Use the account format for the balance sheet.

3.   Compute Armored Financial's current ratio and debt ratio at June 30, 19X1. One year ago the current ratio stood at 1.01, and the debt ratio was 0.71. Did Armored Financial's ability to pay debts improve or deteriorate during 19X1?

4.   How will what you learned in this problem help you manage a business?

P4-3A The unadjusted T-accounts of Lou Wilson, Psychologist, at December 31, 19X2, and the related year-end adjustment data follow:

Taking the accounting cycle through the closing entries (Obj. 2, 3)

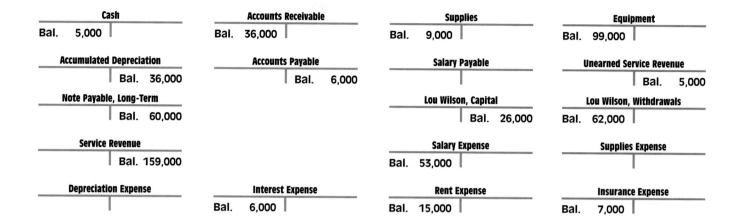

Cash	
Bal. 5,000	

Accounts Receivable	
Bal. 36,000	

Supplies	
Bal. 9,000	

Equipment	
Bal. 99,000	

Accumulated Depreciation	
	Bal. 36,000

Accounts Payable	
	Bal. 6,000

Salary Payable	

Unearned Service Revenue	
	Bal. 5,000

Note Payable, Long-Term	
	Bal. 60,000

Lou Wilson, Capital	
	Bal. 26,000

Lou Wilson, Withdrawals	
Bal. 62,000	

Service Revenue	
	Bal. 159,000

Salary Expense	
Bal. 53,000	

Supplies Expense	

Depreciation Expense	

Interest Expense	
Bal. 6,000	

Rent Expense	
Bal. 15,000	

Insurance Expense	
Bal. 7,000	

Adjustment data at December 31, 19X2, include:

a. Unearned service revenue earned during the year, $5,000.
b. Supplies on hand, $1,000.
c. Depreciation for the year, $9,000.
d. Accrued salary expense, $1,000.
e. Accrued service revenue, $2,000.

Required

1. Write the trial balance on a work sheet, and complete the work sheet. Key each adjusting entry by the letter corresponding to the data given.
2. Prepare the income statement, the statement of owner's equity, and the classified balance sheet in account format.
3. Journalize the adjusting and closing entries.

P4-4A This problem should be used in conjunction with Problem 4-3A. It completes the accounting cycle by posting to T-accounts and preparing the postclosing trial balance.

Completing the accounting cycle (Obj. 2, 3)

Required

1. Using the Problem 4-3A data, post the adjusting and closing entries to the T-accounts, denoting adjusting amounts by *Adj.*, closing amounts by *Clo.*, and account balances by *Bal.*, as shown in Exhibit 4-9. Double underline all accounts with a zero ending balance.
2. Prepare the postclosing trial balance.

P4-5A The trial balance of Wortham Insurance Agency at August 31, 19X9, and the data needed for the month-end adjustments follow.

	WORTHAM INSURANCE AGENCY TRIAL BALANCE AUGUST 31, 19X9		
Account Number	**Account Title**	**Debit**	**Credit**
11	Cash	$ 3,800	
12	Accounts receivable	15,560	
13	Prepaid rent	1,290	
14	Supplies	900	
15	Furniture	15,350	
16	Accumulated depreciation—furniture		$ 12,800
17	Building	89,900	
18	Accumulated depreciation—building		28,600
21	Accounts payable		4,240
22	Salary payable		
23	Unearned commission revenue		8,900
31	M. L. Wortham, capital		71,920
32	M. L. Wortham, withdrawals	4,800	
41	Commission revenue		7,300
51	Salary expense	1,100	
52	Rent expense		
53	Utilities expense	410	
54	Depreciation expense—furniture		
55	Depreciation expense—building		
56	Advertising expense	650	
57	Supplies expense		
	Total	$133,760	$133,760

a. Unearned commission revenue still unearned at August 31, $6,750.

b. Prepaid rent still in force at August 31, $1,050.

c. Supplies used during the month, $340.

d. Depreciation on furniture for the month, $370.

e. Depreciation on building for the month, $130.

f. Accrued salary expense at August 31, $460.

Required

1. Open the accounts listed in the trial balance and insert their August 31 unadjusted balances. Also open the Income Summary account, number 34. Use four-column accounts. Date the balances of the following accounts as of August 1: Prepaid Rent, Supplies, Furniture, Accumulated Depreciation—Furniture, Building, Accumulated Depreciation—Building, Unearned Commission Revenue, and M. L. Wortham, Capital.

2. Write the trial balance on a work sheet and complete the work sheet of Wortham Insurance Agency for the month ended August 31, 19X9.

3. Prepare the income statement, the statement of owner's equity, and the classified balance sheet in report format.

4. Using the work sheet data, journalize and post the adjusting and closing entries. Use dates and posting references. Use 7 as the number of the journal page.

5. Prepare a postclosing trial balance.

P4-6A The accounts of Littlepage Travel Agency at December 31, 19X6, are listed in alphabetical order.

Preparing a classified balance sheet in report format (Obj. 5, 6)

Accounts payable	$ 5,100	Mary Susan Littlepage, capital,		
Accounts receivable	6,600	December 31, 19X5	$50,300	
Accumulated depreciation—		Mary Susan Littlepage,		
building	37,800	withdrawals	47,400	
Accumulated depreciation—		Note payable, long-term	27,800	
furniture	11,600	Note receivable, long-term	4,000	
Advertising expense	2,200	Other assets	3,600	
Building	104,400	Other current assets	1,700	
Cash	6,500	Other current liabilities	4,700	
Commission revenue	93,500	Prepaid insurance	1,100	
Current portion of note payable	2,200	Prepaid rent	6,600	
Current portion of note		Salary expense	24,600	
receivable	1,000	Salary payable	3,900	
Depreciation expense	1,300	Supplies	2,500	
Furniture	22,700	Supplies expense	5,700	
Insurance expense	800	Unearned commission		
Interest payable	600	revenue	5,400	
Interest receivable	200			

Required

1. All adjustments have been journalized and posted, but the closing entries have not yet been made. Prepare the company's classified balance sheet in report format at December 31, 19X6. Use captions for total assets, total liabilities, and total liabilities and owner's equity.

2. Compute Littlepage's current ratio and debt ratio at December 31, 19X6. At December 31, 19X5, the current ratio was 1.52, and the debt ratio was 0.37. Did Littlepage's ability to pay debts improve or deteriorate during 19X6?

P4-7A Accountants for Kitok Catering Service, a proprietorship, encountered the following situations while adjusting and closing the books at December 31. Consider each situation independently.

Analyzing and journalizing corrections, adjustments, and closing entries (Obj. 3, 4)

a. The $39,000 balance of Equipment was entered as $3,900 on the trial balance.
   (1) What is the name of this type of error?
   (2) Assume that this is the only error in the trial balance. Which will be greater, the total debits or the total credits, and by how much?
   (3) How can this type of error be identified?

b. The company bookkeeper made the following entry to record a $600 credit purchase of office equipment:

Nov. 12	Office Supplies	600	
	Accounts Payable		600

   Prepare the correcting entry, dated December 31.

c. A $750 debit to Cash was posted as a credit.
   (1) At what stage of the accounting cycle will this error be detected?
   (2) Describe the technique for identifying the amount of the error.

d. The accountant failed to make the following adjusting entries at December 31:
   (1) Accrued property tax expense, $200.
   (2) Supplies expense, $1,090.
   (3) Accrued interest revenue on a note receivable, $650.
   (4) Depreciation of equipment, $4,000.
   (5) Earned service revenue that had been collected in advance, $5,100.
   Compute the overall net income effect of these omissions.

e. Record each of the adjusting entries identified in item *d*.

f. The revenue and expense accounts, after the adjusting entries had been posted were Service Revenue, $56,800; Interest Revenue, $2,000; Salary Expense, $14,200; Rent Expense, $5,100; Depreciation Expense, $5,550; Supplies Expense, $1,530; and Property Tax Expense, $1,190. Two balances prior to closing were Li Kitok, Capital, $58,600, and Li Kitok, Withdrawals, $30,000. Journalize the closing entries.

(GROUP B)

Preparing a work sheet
(Obj. 1)

P4-1B   The trial balance of Wentworth Learning Center at May 31, 19X2, follows:

WENTWORTH LEARNING CENTER TRIAL BALANCE MAY 31, 19X2		
Cash..	$ 3,670	
Notes receivable...	10,340	
Interest receivable		
Supplies	560	
Prepaid insurance..	1,790	
Furniture	27,410	
Accumulated depreciation—furniture................		$ 1,480
Building..	58,900	
Accumulated depreciation—building..................		34,560
Land	13,700	
Accounts payable		14,730
Interest payable...		
Salary payable		
Unearned service revenue		8,800
Note payable, long-term		18,700
Mike Wentworth, capital....................................		34,290
Mike Wentworth, withdrawals............................	3,800	
Service revenue		11,970
Interest revenue		
Depreciation expense—furniture		
Depreciation expense—building		
Salary expense	2,170	
Insurance expense		
Interest expense		
Utilities expense...	490	
Property tax expense	640	
Advertising expense	1,060	
Supplies expense		
Total	$124,530	$124,530

Additional data at May 31, 19X2:

a. Depreciation: furniture, $480; building, $460.

b. Accrued salary expense, $600.

c. Supplies on hand, $410.

d. Prepaid insurance expired during May, $390.

e. Accrued interest expense, $220.

f. Unearned service revenue earned during May, $4,400.

g. Accrued advertising expense, $60 (credit Accounts Payable).

h. Accrued interest revenue, $170.

Required

Complete Wentworth's work sheet for May.

P4-2B The adjusted trial balance of Martinez Tailoring Service at April 30, 19X2, the end of the company's fiscal year, follows:

Preparing financial statements from an adjusted trial balance; journalizing the adjusting and closing entries
(Obj. 2, 5, 6)

MARTINEZ TAILORING SERVICE ADJUSTED TRIAL BALANCE APRIL 30, 19X2		
Cash	$ 1,370	
Accounts receivable	23,740	
Supplies	3,690	
Prepaid insurance	2,290	
Equipment	63,930	
Accumulated depreciation—equipment		$ 28,430
Building	74,330	
Accumulated depreciation—building		18,260
Accounts payable		19,550
Interest payable		2,280
Wage payable		830
Unearned service revenue		3,660
Note payable, long-term		69,900
Horatio Martinez, capital		44,200
Horatio Martinez, withdrawals	47,500	
Service revenue		98,550
Depreciation expense—equipment	6,900	
Depreciation expense—building	3,710	
Wage expense	29,800	
Insurance expense	5,370	
Interest expense	8,170	
Utilities expense	4,970	
Property tax expense	3,010	
Supplies expense	6,880	
Total	$285,660	$285,660

Adjusting data at April 30, 19X2, which have been incorporated into the trial balance figures above, consist of:

a. Unearned service revenue earned during the year, $4,180.
b. Supplies used during the year, $5,880.
c. Prepaid insurance expired during the year, $5,370.
d. Accrued interest expense, $1,280.
e. Accrued service revenue, $2,200.
f. Depreciation for the year: equipment, $6,900; building, $3,710.
g. Accrued wage expense, $830.

Required

1. Journalize the adjusting and closing entries.
2. Prepare Martinez's income statement and statement of owner's equity for the year ended April 30, 19X2, and the classified balance sheet on that date. Use the account format for the balance sheet.
3. Compute Martinez's current ratio and debt ratio at April 30, 19X2. One year ago the current ratio stood at 1.21, and the debt ratio was 0.82. Did Martinez's ability to pay debts improve or deteriorate during 19X2?
4. How will what you learned in this problem help you manage a business?

Taking the accounting cycle through the closing entries
(Obj. 2, 3)

P4-3B   The unadjusted T-accounts of Brad Upchurch, M.D., at December 31, 19X2, and the related year-end adjustment data follow:

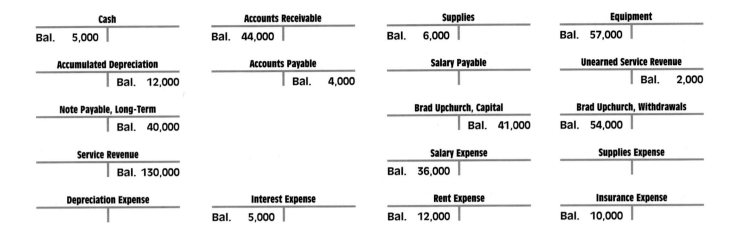

Cash	
Bal. 5,000	

Accounts Receivable	
Bal. 44,000	

Supplies	
Bal. 6,000	

Equipment	
Bal. 57,000	

Accumulated Depreciation	
	Bal. 12,000

Accounts Payable	
	Bal. 4,000

Salary Payable	

Unearned Service Revenue	
	Bal. 2,000

Note Payable, Long-Term	
	Bal. 40,000

Brad Upchurch, Capital	
	Bal. 41,000

Brad Upchurch, Withdrawals	
Bal. 54,000	

Service Revenue	
	Bal. 130,000

Salary Expense	
Bal. 36,000	

Supplies Expense	

Depreciation Expense	

Interest Expense	
Bal. 5,000	

Rent Expense	
Bal. 12,000	

Insurance Expense	
Bal. 10,000	

Adjustment data at December 31, 19X2, include:

a. Depreciation for the year, $5,000.
b. Supplies on hand, $2,000.
c. Accrued service revenue, $4,000.
d. Unearned service revenue earned during the year, $2,000.
e. Accrued salary expense, $4,000.

Required

1. Write the trial balance on a work sheet, and complete the work sheet. Key each adjusting entry by the letter corresponding to the data given.
2. Prepare the income statement, the statement of owner's equity, and the classified balance sheet in account format.
3. Journalize the adjusting and closing entries.

Completing the accounting cycle
(Obj. 2, 3)

P4-4B   This problem should be used in conjunction with Problem 4-3B. It completes the accounting cycle by posting to T-accounts and preparing the postclosing trial balance.

Required

1. Using the Problem 4-3B data, post the adjusting and closing entries to the T-accounts, denoting adjusting amounts by *Adj.*, closing amounts by *Clo.*, and account balances by *Bal.*, as shown in Exhibit 4-9. Double underline all accounts with a zero ending balance.
2. Prepare the postclosing trial balance.

Completing the accounting cycle
(Obj. 2, 3, 5)

P4-5B   The trial balance of Stryker Talent Agency at October 31, 19X0, is at the top of page 167. The data needed for the month-end adjustments are as follows:

Adjustment data:
a. Unearned commission revenue still unearned at October 31, $4,900.
b. Prepaid rent still in force at October 31, $2,000.
c. Supplies used during the month, $770.
d. Depreciation on furniture for the month, $250.
e. Depreciation on building for the month, $580.
f. Accrued salary expense at October 31, $310.

```
                    STRYKER TALENT AGENCY
                       TRIAL BALANCE
                      OCTOBER 31, 19X0
```

Account Number	Account Title	Debit	Credit
11	Cash	$ 1,900	
12	Accounts receivable	15,310	
13	Prepaid rent	2,200	
14	Supplies...	840	
15	Furniture...	26,830	
16	Accumulated depreciation—furniture		$ 3,400
17	Building	68,300	
18	Accumulated depreciation—building		12,100
21	Accounts payable		7,290
22	Salary payable		
23	Unearned commission revenue..........................		5,300
31	Sherman Stryker, capital		84,490
32	Sherman Stryker, withdrawals...........................	3,900	
41	Commission revenue...		9,560
51	Salary expense...	1,840	
52	Rent expense...		
53	Utilities expense	530	
54	Depreciation expense—furniture.......................		
55	Depreciation expense—building........................		
56	Advertising expense	490	
57	Supplies expense		
	Total..	$122,140	$122,140

Required

1. Open the accounts listed in the trial balance, inserting their October 31 unadjusted balances. Also open the Income Summary account, number 33. Use four-column accounts. Date the balances of the following accounts October 1: Prepaid Rent, Supplies, Building, Accumulated Depreciation—Building, Furniture, Accumulated Depreciation—Furniture, Unearned Commission Revenue, and Sherman Stryker, Capital.

2. Write the trial balance on a work sheet and complete the work sheet of Stryker Talent Agency for the month ended October 31, 19X0.

3. Prepare the income statement, the statement of owner's equity, and the classified balance sheet in report format.

4. Using the work sheet data, journalize and post the adjusting and closing entries. Use dates and posting references. Use 12 as the number of the journal page.

5. Prepare a postclosing trial balance.

P4-6B   The accounts of Colin Slagle, CPA, at March 31, 19X3, are listed in alphabetical order.

Preparing a classified balance sheet in report format
(Obj. 5, 6)

Accounts payable	$14,700	Depreciation expense.....................	$ 1,900
Accounts receivable	11,500	Furniture	43,200
Accumulated depreciation—		Insurance expense	600
building	47,300	Interest payable	300
Accumulated depreciation—		Interest receivable	900
furniture	7,700	Colin Slagle, capital,	
Advertising expense	900	March 31, 19X2	42,800
Building	55,900	Colin Slagle,	
Cash..	3,400	withdrawals.................................	31,200
Current portion of note		Note payable, long-term.................	3,200
payable...	800	Note receivable, long-term.............	6,900
Current portion of note		Other assets...................................	2,300
receivable.....................................	3,100	Other current assets.......................	900

Other current liabilities	$ 1,100	Service revenue	$71,100
Prepaid insurance	600	Supplies	3,800
Prepaid rent	4,700	Supplies expense	4,600
Salary expense	17,800	Unearned service revenue	2,800
Salary payable	2,400		

Required

1. All adjustments have been journalized and posted, but the closing entries have not yet been made. Prepare the company's classified balance sheet in report format at March 31, 19X3. Use captions for total assets, total liabilities, and total liabilities and owner's equity.

2. Compute Slagle's current ratio and debt ratio at March 31, 19X3. At March 31, 19X2, the current ratio was 1.28, and debt ratio was 0.32. Did Slagle's ability to pay debts improve or deteriorate during 19X3?

Analyzing and journalizing corrections, adjustments, and closing entries
(Obj. 3, 4)

P4-7B The accountants of Price Septic Service, a proprietorship, encountered the following situations while adjusting and closing the books at February 28. Consider each situation independently.

a. The $1,620 balance of Utilities Expense was entered as $16,200 on the trial balance.

    (1) What is the name of this type of error?

    (2) Assume that this is the only error in the trial balance. Which will be greater, the total debits or the total credits, and by how much?

    (3) How can this type of error be identified?

b. The company bookkeeper made the following entry to record a $950 credit purchase of supplies:

Feb. 26	Equipment	950	
	Accounts Payable		950

    Prepare the correcting entry, dated February 28.

c. A $690 credit to Accounts Receivable was posted as $960.

    (1) At what stage of the accounting cycle will this error be detected?

    (2) Describe the technique for identifying the amount of the error.

d. The accountant failed to make the following adjusting entries at February 28:

    (1) Accrued service revenue, $900.

    (2) Insurance expense, $360.

    (3) Accrued interest expense on a note payable, $520.

    (4) Depreciation of equipment, $3,700.

    (5) Earned service revenue that had been collected in advance, $2,700.

    Compute the overall net income effect of these omissions.

e. Record each of the adjusting entries identified in item *d*.

f. The revenue and expense accounts after the adjusting entries had been posted were Service Revenue, $97,330; Wage Expense, $29,340; Depreciation Expense, $6,180; Interest Expense, $4,590; Utilities Expense, $1,620; and Insurance Expense, $640. Two balances prior to closing were Eva Price, Capital, $75,150, and Eva Price, Drawing, $44,000. Journalize the closing entries.

EXTENDING YOUR KNOWLEDGE

DECISION PROBLEMS

Completing the accounting cycle to develop the information for a bank loan
(Obj. 3, 5)

1. One year ago, Shea Dortch founded Dortch Computing Service. The business has prospered. Dortch, who remembers that you took an accounting course while in college, comes to you for advice. She wishes to know how much net income her business earned during the past year. She also wants to know what the entity's total assets, liabilities, and capital are. Her accounting records consist of the T-accounts of her ledger, which were prepared by an accountant who moved to another city. The ledger at December 31 appears as follows:

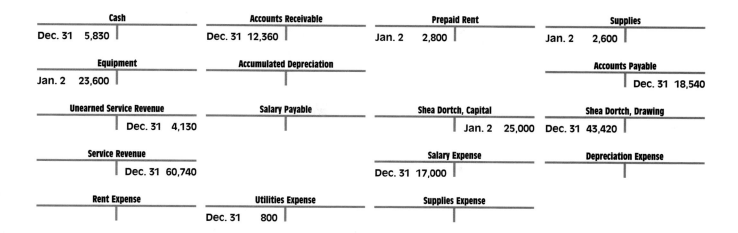

The accounts shown in the T-accounts above are:

Cash		Accounts Receivable		Prepaid Rent		Supplies	
Dec. 31 5,830		Dec. 31 12,360		Jan. 2 2,800		Jan. 2 2,600	

Equipment		Accumulated Depreciation				Accounts Payable	
Jan. 2 23,600							Dec. 31 18,540

Unearned Service Revenue		Salary Payable		Shea Dortch, Capital		Shea Dortch, Drawing	
	Dec. 31 4,130				Jan. 2 25,000	Dec. 31 43,420	

Service Revenue				Salary Expense		Depreciation Expense	
	Dec. 31 60,740			Dec. 31 17,000			

Rent Expense		Utilities Expense		Supplies Expense	
		Dec. 31 800			

Dortch indicates that at the year's end customers owe her $1,600 accrued service revenue, which she expects to collect early next year. These revenues have not been recorded. During the year she collected $4,130 service revenue in advance from customers, but she earned only $600 of that amount. Rent expense for the year was $2,400, and she used up $2,100 in supplies. Dortch estimates that depreciation on her equipment was $5,900 for the year. At December 31 she owes her employee $1,200 accrued salary.

At the conclusion of your meeting, Dortch expresses concern that her withdrawals during the year might have exceeded her net income. To get a loan to expand the business, Dortch must show the bank that her capital account has grown from its original $25,000 balance. Has it? You and Dortch agree that you will meet again in one week. You perform the analysis and prepare the financial statements to answer her questions.

2. You are preparing the financial statements for the year ended October 31, 19X5, for Ambrose Publishing Company, a weekly newspaper. You began with the trial balance of the ledger, which balanced, and then made the required adjusting entries. To save time, you omitted preparing an adjusted trial balance. After making the adjustments on the work sheet, you extended the balances from the trial balance, adjusted for the adjusting entries, and computed amounts for the income statement and balance sheet columns.

Finding an error in the work sheets
(Obj. 1, 4)

a. You added the debits and credits on the income statement and found that the credits exceeded the debits by $X. According to your finding, did Ambrose Publishing have a profit or a loss?

b. You entered the balancing amount from the income statement columns in the balance sheet columns and found that the total debits exceeded the total credits in the balance sheet. The difference between the debits and credits is twice the amount ($2X) you calculated in question *a*. What is the likely cause of the difference? What assumption have you made in your answer?

ETHICAL ISSUE

Stone Associates, a management consulting firm, is in its third year of operations. The company was initially financed by owner's equity as the three partners each invested $30,000. The first year's slim profits were expected because new businesses often start slowly. During the second year, Stone Associates landed a large contract with a paper mill, and referrals from that project brought in several other large jobs. To expand the business, Stone borrowed $100,000 from Texas National Bank of Lufkin, Texas. As a condition for making this loan the bank required that Stone maintain a current ratio of at least 1.50 and a debt ratio of no more than 0.50.

Business during the third year has been good, but slightly below the target for the year. Expansion costs have brought the current ratio down to 1.47 and the debt ratio up to 0.51 at December 15. Emily Stone and her partners are considering the implication of reporting this current ratio to Texas National Bank. One course of action that the partners are considering is to record in December of the third year some revenue on account that Stone Associates will earn in January of their fourth year of operations. The contract for this job has been signed, and Stone will perform the management consulting service for the client during January.

Required

1. Journalize the revenue transaction, and indicate how recording this revenue in December would affect the current ratio and the debt ratio.
2. State whether it is ethical to record the revenue transaction in December. Identify the accounting principle relevant to this situation.
3. Propose for Stone Associates a course of action that is ethical.

FINANCIAL STATEMENT PROBLEMS

Using an actual balance sheet
(Obj. 6)

1. This problem, based on the balance sheet of Lands' End, Inc., in Appendix A, will familiarize you with some of the assets and liabilities of that company. Using the Lands' End balance sheet, answer the following questions.

Required

1. Which balance sheet format does Lands' End, Inc., use?
2. Name the company's largest current asset and largest current liability at January 28, 1994.
3. Compute Lands' End's current ratios and debt ratios at January 28, 1994, and January 29, 1993. Did the ratio values improve, deteriorate, or hold steady during the fiscal year ended January 28, 1994? Refer to the income statement to explain your evaluation of the ratio values.
4. Under what category does Lands' End report land, buildings, machinery, and equipment?
5. What was the cost of the company's plant assets at January 28, 1994? What was the book value of the plant assets?

Using an actual balance sheet
(Obj. 6)

2. Obtain the annual report of a real company of your choosing. Answer the following questions about the company.

Required

1. Which balance sheet format does the company use?
2. Name the company's largest asset and largest liability at the end of the current year and at the end of the preceding year. Name the largest *current* asset and the largest *current* liability at the end of the current year and at the end of the preceding year.
3. Compute the company's current ratio and debt ratio at the end of the current year and the current ratio and debt ratio at the end of the preceding year. Did these ratio values improve, deteriorate, or hold steady during the current year? Does the income statement help to explain why the ratios changed? Give your reason.

Appendix

Reversing Entries: An Optional Step

Reversing entries are special types of entries that ease the burden of accounting after adjusting and closing entries have been made at the end of a period. Reversing entries are used most often in conjunction with accrual-type adjustments such as accrued salary expense and accrued service revenue. GAAP does not require reversing entries. They are used only for convenience and to save time.

REVERSING ENTRIES FOR ACCRUED EXPENSES Accrued expenses accumulate with the passage of time and are paid at a later date. At the end of the period the business makes an adjusting entry to record the expense that has accumulated up to that time.

To see how reversing entries work, return to the adjusting entries (Exhibit 4-8) that Gary Lyon used to update his accounting records for the April financial statements. At April 30—before the adjusting entries—Salary Expense has a debit balance of $950 from salaries paid during April. At April 30 the business owes its employee an additional $950 for service during the last part of the month. Assume for the purpose of this illustration that on May 5, the next payroll date, Lyon will pay the $950 of accrued salary plus $100 in salary that the employee has earned in the first few days of May. The next payroll payment will be $1,050 ($950 + $100). To present the correct financial picture, however, we must include the $950 in salary expense incurred in April in the April statements, not in the May statements. Accordingly, Lyon makes the following adjusting entry on April 30:

Adjusting Entries		
Apr. 30 Salary Expense	950	
Salary Payable		950

After posting, the Salary Payable and Salary Expense accounts appear as follows:[2]

Salary Payable			
	Apr. 30	Adj.	950
	Apr. 30	Bal.	950

Salary Expense			
Paid			
during			
April	CP	950	
Apr. 30	Adj.	950	
Apr. 30	Bal.	1,900	

After the adjusting entry, the April income statement reports salary expense of $1,900, and the balance sheet at April 30 reports Salary Payable, a liability, of $950. The $1,900 debit balance of Salary Expense is eliminated by this closing entry at April 30, 19X1:

Closing Entries		
Apr. 30 Income Summary...............	1,900	
Salary Expense		1,900

Short Exercise: A company pays its employees $1,500 every Friday, the end of a 5-day work week. What journal entry is made each Friday?

Salary Expense 1,500
    Cash................. 1,500

If December 31 falls on a Tuesday, what would be the adjusting entry?

Salary Expense   600
    Salary Payable .   600

What would be the reversing entry on January 1?

Salary Payable   600
    Salary Expense   600

What would be the entry to record the payroll the next Friday?

Salary Expense 1,500
    Cash................. 1,500

---

[2]Entry explanations used throughout this discussion are
Adj. = Adjusting entry   CP = Cash payment entry—includes a credit to Cash
Bal. = Balance   CR = Cash receipt entry—includes a debit to Cash
Clo. = Closing entry   Rev. = Reversing entry

After posting, Salary Expense appears as follows:

			Salary Expense		
Paid during April	**CP**	**950**			
Apr. 30	**Adj.**	**950**			
Apr. 30	**Bal.**	**1,900**	**Apr. 30 Clo.**	**1,900**	

In the normal course of recording salary payments during the year, Gary Lyon makes the standard entry, as follows:

Salary Expense............. XXX	
Cash..................	XXX

But payday usually does not land on the day the accounting period ends, and Lyon has made an adjusting entry to accrue salary payable of $950. On May 5, the next payday, assume the total payroll is $1,050. Lyon credits Cash for $1,050, but what account—or accounts—should he debit? The cash payment entry is

May 5	Salary Payable..............	950	
	Salary Expense.............	100	
	Cash..................		1,050

This method of recording the cash payment is correct but inefficient because Lyon must refer back to the adjusting entries of April 30. Otherwise, he does not know the amount of the required debit to Salary Payable (in this example, $950). Searching the preceding period's adjusting entries takes time, and in business, time is money. To avoid having to separate the debit of a later cash payment entry into two accounts, accountants have devised a technique called reversing entries.

MAKING A REVERSING ENTRY A **reversing entry** switches the debit and the credit of a previous adjusting entry. A reversing entry, then, is the exact opposite of a prior adjusting entry. The reversing entry is dated the first day of the period that follows the adjusting entry.

To illustrate reversing entries, let's return to the Gary Lyon example. Recall that on April 30, Lyon made the following adjusting entry to accrue Salary Payable:

Adjusting Entries			
Apr. 30	Salary Expense...................	950	
	Salary Payable..........		950

The reversing entry simply reverses the position of the debit and the credit:

Reversing Entries			
May 1	Salary Payable....................	950	
	Salary Expense.........		950

The reversing entry is dated the first day of the new period. It is the exact opposite of the April 30 adjusting entry. Ordinarily, the accountant who makes the adjusting entry also prepares the reversing entry at the same time. Lyon postdates—that is, assigns a later date to—the reversing entry to the first day of the next period, however, so that it affects only the new period. Note how the accounts appear after Lyon posts the reversing entry:

Salary Payable					Salary Expense					
May 1 Rev.	950	Apr. 30 Bal.	950		Apr. 30 Bal.	1,900	Apr. 30 Clo.	1,900		
		Zero balance					Zero balance			
							May 1 Rev.	950		

The arrow shows the transfer of the $950 credit balance from Salary Payable to Salary Expense. This credit balance in Salary Expense does not mean that the entity has negative salary expense, as might be suggested by a credit balance in an Expense account. Instead, the odd credit balance is merely a temporary result of the reversing entry. The credit balance is eliminated on May 5, when the $1,050 cash payment for salaries is debited to Salary Expense in the customary manner:

May 5	Salary Expense.............	1,050	
	Cash		1,050

Then this cash payment entry is posted:

Salary Expense			
May 5 CP	1,050	May 1 Rev.	950
May 5 Bal.	100		

Now Salary Expense has its correct debit balance of $100, which is the amount of salary expense incurred thus far in May. The $1,050 cash disbursement also pays the liability for Salary Payable. Thus the Salary Payable account has a zero balance, which is correct, as shown above.

APPENDIX PROBLEM

P4A-1   Refer to the data in Problem 4-5A, page 162.   *Using reversing entries*

Required

1. Open accounts for Salary Payable and Salary Expense. Insert their unadjusted balances at August 31, 19X9.
2. Journalize adjusting entry *f* and the closing entry for Salary Expense at August 31. Post to the accounts.
3. On September 5, Wortham Insurance Agency paid the next payroll amount of $580. Journalize this cash payment, and post to the accounts. Show the balance in each account.
4. Using a reversing entry, repeat Requirements 1 through 3. Compare the balances of Salary Payable and Salary Expense computed by using a reversing entry with those balances computed without using a reversing entry (as appear in your answer to Requirement 3).

Chapter 5

Merchandising and the Accounting Cycle

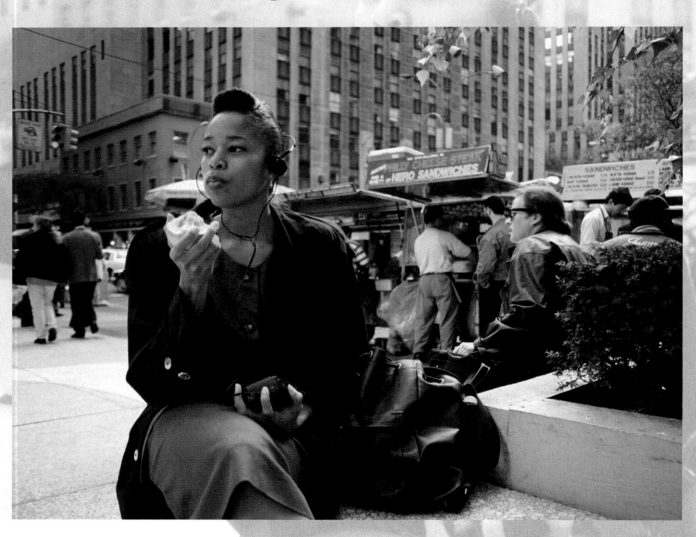

1. Use sales, gross margin, and operating income to evaluate a company

2. Account for the purchase and sale of inventory

3. Compute cost of goods sold and gross margin

4. Adjust and close the accounts of a merchandising business

5. Prepare a merchandiser's financial statements

6. Use the gross margin percentage and the inventory turnover ratio to evaluate a business

S2. Account for the purchase and sale of inventory

S3. Compute cost of goods sold

S4. Adjust and close the accounts of a merchandising business

S5. Prepare a merchandiser's financial statements

"Sales of cassette tapes and tape products have been declining. . . . The industry needed a new, exciting product that would pique consumers' interest and ultimately replace the cassette tape business. Sony is doing just that by selling MiniDisc—a portable, durable, and recordable digital product that meets the needs of today's demanding consumer."

MARK VIKEN, VICE-
PRESIDENT, GENERAL
AUDIO GROUP OF SONY
ELECTRONICS

"When the chips are down, the gambler in Sony invariably comes to the fore. Even by the standards of Japan's battered consumer-electronics industry, Sony has just reported some horrendous results for the year to March 1992. Though its sales worldwide were up by almost 6% to ¥3.8 trillion ($28.5 billion) [¥ is the symbol for the Japanese monetary unit, the yen], its operating profit [total revenues minus all operating expenses] plunged 44% to ¥166 billion. . . . What better time, then, for a high-roller like Sony to announce a spectacular new gadget?

Sony's MiniDisc, long publicized but shown to the public for the first time only on May 26th, is both an impressive feat of engineering and an enormous gamble. It is to be marketed as a recordable version of today's compact discs (CDs)—and one that, like a tape cassette, does not skip beats when jolted in the pocket or on the dashboard of a car.

One reason Sony is pushing its MiniDisc so hard may be that the company badly needs a new money-spinner. . . ." *Source: Quoted from "Sony: Double or Quits,"* The Economist, *May 30, 1992, p. 67.*

• • • • •

How do the operations of Sony Corporation differ from those of the businesses we have studied so far? In the first four chapters Gary Lyon, CPA, provided an illustration of a business that earns revenue by selling its services. Service enterprises include Holiday Inns, American Airlines, physicians, lawyers, CPAs, the Atlanta Braves baseball team, and the 12-year-old who cuts lawns in your neighborhood. A *merchandising entity* earns its revenue by selling products, called *merchandise inventory* or simply *inventory*.

Hershey Foods manufactures and sells its own products and is therefore a merchandising entity.

This chapter shows the central role of inventory in a business that sells merchandise. *Inventory* includes all goods that the company owns and expects to sell in the normal course of their operations. Some businesses, such as department stores, gas stations, and grocery stores, buy their inventory in finished form ready for sale to customers. Others, such as Sony, Hershey Foods, and the Goodyear Tire and Rubber Company, manufacture their own products. Both groups sell products rather than services.

We illustrate accounting for the purchase and sale of inventory plus how to adjust and close the books of a merchandiser. The chapter ends with two ratios that managers, investors, and creditors use to evaluate companies' operations.

Merchandising Operations

OBJECTIVE 1

Use sales, gross margin, and operating income to evaluate a company

Real-World Example: Many businesses use the gross margin percentage (also known as the markup percentage) as a means of determining how well inventory is selling. If too much inventory is purchased and it must be marked down, the gross margin percentage will decline. By monitoring the gross margin percentage, problems can be corrected quickly.

Exhibit 5-1 shows the income statement of Sony Corporation for two recent years. Sony's income statement differs from those of the service businesses discussed in previous chapters. The highlighted items are unique to merchandising operations.

The amount that a business earns from selling merchandise inventory is called **sales revenue**, often abbreviated as **sales**. (Net sales equals sales revenue minus any deductions from sales.) The major revenue of a merchandising entity, sales revenue, represents the increase in owner's equity from delivering inventory to customers. The major expense of a merchandiser is *cost of goods sold*. The title of this expense is well chosen, because it represents the entity's cost of the goods (inventory) it has sold to customers. As long as inventory is held by a business, the inventory is an asset because the goods are an economic resource with future value to the company. When the inventory is sold, however, the inventory's cost becomes an expense to the seller because the goods are no longer available. When Sony sells its MiniDisc to an audio store, the product's cost is expensed as cost of goods sold on Sony's books.

The excess of sales revenue over cost of goods sold is called **gross margin** or **gross profit**. This important business statistic helps measure a business's success. A sufficiently high gross margin is vital to success. Sony's operations were not very successful during the year ended March 31, 1992, despite an increase in sales.

EXHIBIT 5-1
A Real Company's Income Statement

Short Exercise: Calculate (1) Sony's gross margin percentage for 1992 and (2) Sony's COGS as a percentage of sales for 1992. (3) What do these percentages mean to Sony management? *A:* (1) ¥983,238/ ¥3,821,582 = 25.7%; (2) ¥2,838,344/¥3,821,582 = 74.3%; (3) Per yen of sales, Sony spends (on average) ¥0.74 to acquire their products, and they earn (on average) ¥0.26 of gross margin per yen of sales revenue.

	SONY CORPORATION INCOME STATEMENT* YEARS ENDED MARCH 31, 1992 AND 1991			
	In millions of yen (¥)			
	1992		**1991**	
Net sales	¥3,821,582		¥3,616,517	
Cost of sales [same as **Cost of goods sold**]	2,838,344		[2,505,554	
Gross margin	983,238	1.6%	1,110,963	3.1%
Selling, general & administrative expenses [salaries, rent, insurance, depreciation, advertising, delivery, utilities, supplies, and so on]	910,774		887,773	
	72,464		223,190	
[Other] operating revenue	93,814		74,259	
Operating income	166,278		297,449	
Other items summarized	(46,157)		(180,524)	
Net income	¥ 120,121	3.1%	¥ 116,925	3.2%

*Rearranged for instructional purposes.

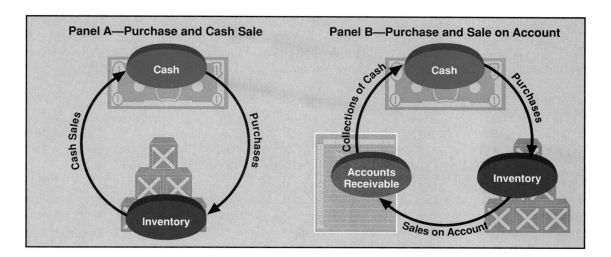

EXHIBIT 5-2
*Operating Cycle of a
Merchandiser*

The following example will clarify the nature of gross margin. Suppose Sony's cost to manufacture a MiniDisc is $500 and Sony sells the product to stores in the United States for $700. Sony's gross margin per unit is $200 ($700 – $500). The gross margin reported on Sony's income statement, ¥983 billion, is the sum of the gross margins on all the products the company sold during its 1992 fiscal year.

The Operating Cycle of a Merchandising Business

A merchandising entity buys inventory, sells the inventory to customers, and uses the cash to purchase more inventory to repeat the cycle. Exhibit 5-2 diagrams the operating cycle for *cash sales* and for *sales on account*. For a cash sale—Panel A—the cycle is from cash to inventory, which is purchased for resale, and back to cash. For a sale on account—Panel B—the cycle is from cash to inventory to accounts receivable and back to cash. In all lines of business, managers strive to shorten the cycle in order to keep assets active. The faster the sale of inventory and the collection of cash, the higher the profits.

Inventory Systems

Two main types of inventory accounting systems exist: the periodic system and the perpetual system. The **periodic inventory system** is used by businesses that sell relatively inexpensive goods. A grocery store without an optical-scanning cash register does not keep a daily running record of every loaf of bread and every can of pineapple that it buys and sells. The cost of record keeping would be overwhelming. Instead, grocers count their inventory periodically—at least once a year—to determine the quantities on hand. The inventory amounts are used to prepare the annual financial statements. Businesses such as office supply outlets, restaurants, and small department stores also use the periodic inventory system. To them, detailed inventory records in the ledger are not necessary for controlling merchandise and managing day-to-day operations. In small businesses, the owner can visually inspect the goods on hand for control purposes. The end-of-chapter supplement covers the periodic inventory system. That system is rapidly decreasing in importance as computers have decreased in price but have greatly increased in processing power.

Under the **perpetual inventory system,** the business maintains a running record of inventory on hand. This system achieves control over expensive goods such as automobiles, jewelry, and furniture. The loss of one item would be significant, and this justifies the cost of a perpetual system. Inventory record keeping is a demanding accounting task, from the paperwork required in purchasing and selling inventory to the job of periodically counting it. Computers have dramatically reduced the time required to manage inventory and have greatly increased a company's ability to control its merchandise. But even under a perpetual system the business counts the inventory on hand annually. The physical count establishes the correct amount of ending inventory and serves as a check on the perpetual records.

The following chart compares the periodic and perpetual systems:

Periodic Inventory System	Perpetual Inventory System
● Does not keep a running record of all goods bought and sold.	● Keeps a running record of all goods bought and sold.
● Inventory counted at least once a year.	● Inventory counted once a year.
● Used for inexpensive goods.	● Used for all types of goods.

A computerized system enhances management control over inventory because the computer can keep accurate, up-to-the-minute records of the number of units purchased, the number of units sold, and the quantities on hand. For a purchase made on account, the goods received are entered in a computer as a debit to Inventory and a credit to Accounts Payable.

Computerized inventory systems are often integrated with accounts receivable and sales. For example, when a prospective customer's order is entered into the computer, the computer checks warehouse records to see if the requested units are in stock. If they are, details of the shipment are entered into the computer, which then multiplies the number of units shipped by the unit sale price. The computer then prints an invoice for the customer and calculates the debit to Accounts Receivable (for that customer), the credit to Sales Revenue, and the decrease in inventory units.

The computer can keep up-to-the-minute records, so managers can call up current inventory information at any time. For example, in a perpetual system the "cash register" at many discount or drug stores is a computer terminal that records the sale and also updates the inventory records. Bar codes, which are scanned by a laser, are an integral part of the perpetual inventory system. The combinations of lines of different widths and lengths represent the data used to keep track of each item. When you ask if a certain item is in stock, the clerk usually consults a computer printout of the perpetual inventory records. Because most businesses today use them, we base our inventory discussions on modern perpetual systems.[1]

"Bar codes, which are scanned by a laser, are an integral part of the perpetual inventory system."

Purchase of Merchandise Inventory in the Perpetual System

OBJECTIVE 2

Account for the purchase and sale of inventory

The cycle of a merchandising entity begins with cash, which is used to purchase inventory, as Exhibit 5-2 shows. For example, a stereo center records the purchase of Sony tape decks, compact disc (CD) players, and other items of inventory acquired for resale by debiting the Inventory account. Most businesses have good credit and can purchase inventory on account, so a $500 purchase on account is recorded as follows:

June 14	Inventory...	500	
	Accounts Payable............................		500
	Purchased inventory on account.		

---

[1]For professors who prefer to concentrate on the periodic inventory system, comprehensive treatment of that system begins on p. 217. Follow Chapter Objectives S2 through S5 instead of 2 through 5.

The Purchase Invoice: A Basic Business Document

Business documents are the tangible evidence of transactions. As we trace the steps that Austin Sound Stereo Center, an actual business in Austin, Texas, takes in ordering, receiving, and paying for inventory, we point out the roles that documents play in carrying on business.

1. Suppose Austin Sound wants to stock JVC brand CD players, cassette decks, and speakers. Austin Sound prepares a *purchase order* and mails it to JVC.

2. On receipt of the purchase order, JVC scans its warehouse for the inventory that Austin Sound ordered. JVC ships the equipment and sends the invoice to Austin the same day. The *invoice* is the seller's request for payment from the purchaser. It is also called the *bill.*

3. Often the purchaser receives the invoice before the inventory arrives. Austin Sound does not pay immediately. Instead, Austin waits until the inventory arrives in order to ensure that it is the correct type, the quantity ordered, and in good condition. After the inventory is inspected and approved, Austin Sound pays JVC the invoice amount.

Exhibit 5-3 is an updated copy of an actual invoice from JVC to Austin Sound Stereo Center. From Austin Sound's perspective, this document is a *purchase invoice* (it is being used to purchase goods), whereas to JVC it is a *sales invoice* (it is being used to sell goods).

Discounts From Purchase Prices

There are two major types of discounts from purchase prices: quantity discounts and cash discounts (called purchase discounts).

EXHIBIT 5-3
An Invoice

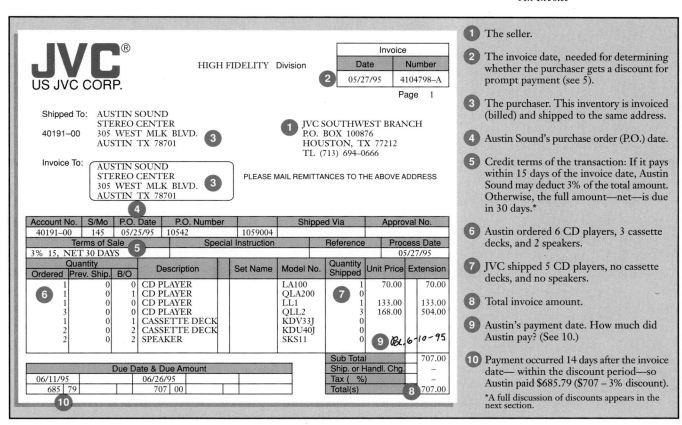

1. The seller.

2. The invoice date, needed for determining whether the purchaser gets a discount for prompt payment (see 5).

3. The purchaser. This inventory is invoiced (billed) and shipped to the same address.

4. Austin Sound's purchase order (P.O.) date.

5. Credit terms of the transaction: If it pays within 15 days of the invoice date, Austin Sound may deduct 3% of the total amount. Otherwise, the full amount—net—is due in 30 days.*

6. Austin ordered 6 CD players, 3 cassette decks, and 2 speakers.

7. JVC shipped 5 CD players, no cassette decks, and no speakers.

8. Total invoice amount.

9. Austin's payment date. How much did Austin pay? (See 10.)

10. Payment occurred 14 days after the invoice date— within the discount period—so Austin paid $685.79 ($707 – 3% discount).

*A full discussion of discounts appears in the next section.

QUANTITY DISCOUNTS A *quantity discount*, which is a type of *trade discount*, works this way: The larger the quantity purchased, the lower the price per item. For example, JVC may offer no discount for the purchase of only one or two CD players and charge the *list price*—the full price—of $200 per unit. However, JVC may offer the following quantity discount terms to persuade customers to buy more CD players.

Quantity	Quantity Discount	Net Price per Unit
Buy minimum quantity, 3 CD players...............	5%	$190[$200 − 0.05($200)]
Buy 4–9 CD players...	10%	$180[$200 − 0.10($200)]
Buy more than 9 CD players...........................	20%	$160[$200 − 0.20($200)]

Suppose that Austin Sound purchases five CD players from this manufacturer. The cost of each CD player is therefore $180. Purchase of five units on account would be recorded by debiting Inventory and crediting Accounts Payable for the total price of $900 ($180 × 5).

There is no Quantity Discount account, and there is no special accounting entry for a quantity discount. Instead, all accounting entries are based on the net price of a purchase after the quantity discount has been subtracted.

PURCHASE DISCOUNTS Many businesses also offer purchase discounts to their customers. A *purchase discount* is a reward for prompt payment. If a quantity discount is also offered, the purchase discount is computed on the net purchase amount after the quantity discount has been subtracted, further reducing the cost of the inventory.

JVC's credit terms of 3% 15, NET 30 DAYS can also be expressed as 3/15 n/30. This means that Austin Sound may deduct 3 percent of the total amount due if Austin pays within 15 days of the invoice date. Otherwise, the full amount—net—is due in 30 days. Terms of simply n/30 indicate that no discount is offered and that payment is due 30 days after the invoice date. Terms of *eom* usually mean that payment is due at the end of the current month. However, a purchase after the 25th of the current month on terms of *eom* can be paid at the end of the next month.

Short Exercise: (1) What is meant by the terms 1/10 n/60? (2) By the terms 2/10 n/eom? (3) By the terms n/30? *A:* (1) 1% discount if paid within 10 days, or the full ("net") amount is due in 60 days. (2) 2% discount if paid within 10 days, or the full amount is due at the end of the month. (3) No discount allowed, and the full amount is due in 30 days.

Let's use the Exhibit 5-3 transaction to illustrate accounting for a purchase discount. Austin Sound records this purchase on account as follows:

May 27	Inventory	707.00	
	Accounts Payable.............................		707.00
	Purchased inventory on account.		

Austin Sound paid within the discount period, so its cash payment entry is

June 10	Accounts Payable.....................................	707.00	
	Cash ($707.00 × 0.97)		685.79
	Inventory ($707.00 × 0.03)		21.21
	Paid on account within discount period.		

In effect, this inventory cost Austin Sound $685.79 ($707.00 - $21.21), as shown in the following Inventory account:

Inventory					Accounts Payable			
May 27	707.00	June 10	21.21		June 10	707.00	May 27	707.00
Bal.	685.79							

The account payable to JVC is zero.

Alternatively, if Austin Sound pays this invoice after the discount period, it must pay the full invoice amount. In that case, the payment entry is

June 29   Accounts Payable 707.00
                   Cash 707.00
               Paid on account after discount period.

Without the discount, Austin Sound's cost of the inventory is the full amount of
$707, as shown in the following T-account:

Inventory	
May 27 707.00	

Purchase Returns and Allowances

Most businesses allow their customers to *return* merchandise that is defective, damaged in shipment, or otherwise unsuitable. Or if the buyer chooses to keep damaged
goods, the seller may deduct an *allowance* from the amount the buyer owes. Because
returns and allowances decrease the cost of inventory, returns and allowances are
recorded by crediting the Inventory account.

Suppose the $70 CD player purchased by Austin Sound (Exhibit 5-3) was not
the CD player ordered. Austin returns the merchandise to the seller and records the
purchase return as follows:

June 3   Accounts Payable 70.00
                  Inventory 70.00
              Returned inventory to seller.

Now assume that one of the JVC CD players was damaged in shipment to Austin
Sound. The damage is minor, and Austin decides to keep the CD player in exchange
for a $10 allowance from JVC. To record this purchase allowance, Austin Sound
makes this entry:

June 4   Accounts Payable 10.00
                  Inventory 10.00
              Received a purchase allowance.

The return and the allowance had two effects. (1) They decreased Austin
Sound's liability, which is why we debit Accounts Payable. (2) They decreased the
net cost of the inventory, which is why we credit Inventory.

Assume that Austin Sound has not paid its debt to JVC. After these return and
allowance transactions are posted, Austin Sound's accounts will show these balances:

Inventory				Accounts Payable			
May 27	707.00	June 3	70.00	June 3	70.00	May 27	707.00
		June 4	10.00	June 4	10.00		
Bal.	627.00					Bal.	627.00

Transportation Costs

The transportation cost of moving inventory from seller to buyer can be significant.
The purchase agreement specifies FOB terms to indicate who pays the shipping
charges. The term *FOB* stands for *free on board* and governs when the legal title—
ownership—to the goods passes from seller to buyer. When FOB *shipping point*
terms are in effect, title passes when the inventory leaves the seller's place of business—the shipping point. The buyer owns the goods while they are in transit and
therefore pays the transportation cost. Under FOB *destination* terms, title passes
when the goods reach the destination, so the seller pays transportation cost. Exhibit
5-4 summarizes FOB terms.

Short Exercise: Austin Sound
purchases $1,000 of merchan-
dise on account, terms 2/10,
n/30 on 9/15; $100 of mer-
chandise is returned for credit
on 9/20. Payment in full is
made on 9/25. Journalize the
transactions.
A:
9/15   Inventory 1,000
            Accts. Pay. .   1,000
9/20   Accts. Pay.   100
            Inventory...   100
9/25   Accts. Pay.
          ($1,000 – $100) 900
          Inventory
             (2% × $900)   18
          Cash
             ($900 – $18)   882
No discount is given on the return.

EXHIBIT 5-4
FOB Terms

	FOB Shipping Point	FOB Destination
When does the title pass to the buyer?	Shipping point	Destination
Who pays the transportation cost?	Buyer	Seller

FOB shipping point terms are most common, so generally, the buyer bears the shipping cost. A freight cost that the buyer pays on an inventory purchase is called *freight in*. In accounting, the cost of an asset includes all costs incurred to bring the asset to its intended use. For inventory, cost includes the net cost after all discounts taken, plus any transportation charges paid. To record the payment for freight in, the buyer debits Inventory and credits Cash or Accounts Payable for the amount. Suppose Austin Sound receives a $60 shipping bill directly from the freight company. Austin Sound's entry to record payment of the freight charge is:

June 1	Inventory....................	60	
	Cash		60
	Paid a freight bill.		

The freight charge increases the cost of the inventory as follows:

Inventory

May 27	707.00	June 3	70.00
June 1	60.00	June 4	10.00
Bal.	687.00		

After the returns, allowances, and transportation costs are considered, this inventory has a cost of $687. Any discounts would be computed only on the account payable to the seller, not on the transportation costs, because the freight company offers no discount.

STOP & THINK Refer to the Accounts Payable account on page 181 (Purchase Returns and Allowances). After all returns, allowances, and transportation charges, what amount of discount can Austin Sound take if it pays JVC on June 9 (within the discount period)? How much should Austin Sound pay JVC on June 9? What is Austin Sound's net cost of this inventory?

Answer: 3% Discount = $18.81 ($707.00 - $70.00 - $10.00) × 0.03
Payment to JVC = $608.19 = $627.00 - $18.81
Net cost of inventory = $668.19 = $608.19 + $60.00 transportation charge

Under FOB shipping point terms, the seller sometimes prepays the transportation cost as a convenience and lists this cost on the invoice. The buyer can debit Inventory for the combined cost of the inventory and the shipping cost because both costs apply to the merchandise. A $5,000 purchase of goods, coupled with a related freight charge of $400, would be recorded as follows:

March 12	Inventory	5,400	
	Accounts Payable...		5,400
	Purchased inventory on account plus freight.		

If the buyer pays within the discount period, the discount will be computed on the $5,000 merchandise cost, not on the $5,400. No discount is offered on transportation cost.

Freight out is the cost of freight charges paid to ship goods sold to customers. It is paid by the seller, not by the purchaser. Freight out, which is also called *delivery expense*, is an operating expense for the seller. It is debited to an account such as Delivery Expense.

Alternative Procedures for Purchase Discounts, Returns and Allowances, and Transportation Costs

Some businesses may want to keep a detailed record of purchase discounts, returns and allowances, and transportation costs. For example, Austin Sound may receive too many defective CD players from an off-brand manufacturer. In recording purchase returns, Austin Sound could credit a special account, Purchase Returns and Allowances, that would serve as a running record of the defective merchandise. The Purchase Returns and Allowances account would carry a credit balance and be treated as a contra account to Inventory. Freight In would be debited for transportation costs. Then for reporting on the financial statements these accounts could be combined with the Inventory account as follows (amounts assumed):

Inventory		$35,000
Less: Purchase discounts	$700	
Purchase returns and allowances	800	1,500
Net purchases of inventory		33,500
Freight in		2,100
Total cost of inventory		$35,600

Key Point: A contra account always has a companion account with the opposite balance. Thus both Purchase Discounts and Purchase Returns and Allowances (credit balances) are reported with Inventory (debit balance) on the balance sheet.

Sale of Inventory and Cost of Goods Sold

The sale of inventory may be for cash or on account, as Exhibit 5-2 shows.

CASH SALE Sales of retailers such as grocery stores, drug stores, gift shops, and restaurants are often for cash. A $3,000 cash sale is recorded by debiting Cash and crediting the revenue account, Sales Revenue, as follows:

Jan. 9	Cash	3,000	
	Sales Revenue		3,000
	Cash sale.		

To update the inventory records, the business also must decrease the Inventory balance. Suppose these goods cost the seller $1,900. An accompanying entry is needed to transfer the $1,900 cost of the goods—not their selling price of $3,000—from the Inventory account (an asset) to Cost of Goods Sold (an expense) as follows:

Jan. 9	Cost of Goods Sold	1,900	
	Inventory		1,900
	Recorded the cost of goods sold.		

Cost of goods sold (also called **cost of sales**) is the largest single expense of most businesses that sell merchandise, such as Sony and Austin Sound. It is the cost of the inventory that the business has sold to customers. ◀▦ The Cost of Goods Sold account keeps a current balance as transactions are journalized and posted.

After posting, the Cost of Goods Sold account holds the cost of the merchandise sold:

◀▦◀▦◀▦ The recording of cost of goods sold along with sales revenue is an example of the matching principle (Chapter 3, p. 93)—matching expense against revenue to measure net income.

Inventory				Cost of Goods Sold	
Purchases 50,000 (amount assumed)	Jan. 9	1,900	↔ Jan. 9	1,900	

The computer automatically records this entry when the cashier keys in the code number of the inventory that is sold. Optical scanners perform this task in most stores.

SALE ON ACCOUNT   Most sales by wholesalers, manufacturers, and retailers are made on account (on credit). A $5,000 sale on account is recorded by a debit to Accounts Receivable and a credit to Sales Revenue, as follows:

Jan. 11	Accounts Receivable	5,000	
	Sales Revenue		5,000
	Sale on account.		

If we assume that these goods cost the seller $2,900, the accompanying inventory entry is

Jan. 11	Cost of Goods Sold.................................	2,900	
	Inventory		2,900
	Recorded the cost of goods sold.		

After the recording of the January 9 and 11 transactions, sales revenue is $8,000 ($3,000 + $5,000). Cost of goods sold totals $4,800 ($1,900 + $2,900).

The related cash receipt on account is journalized as follows:

Jan. 19	Cash	5,000	
	Accounts Receivable		5,000
	Collection on account.		

 STOP & THINK   Why is there no January 19 entry to Sales Revenue, Cost of Goods Sold, or Inventory?

Answer: On January 19 the seller merely receives one asset—Cash—in place of another asset—Accounts Receivable. The sales revenue, the related cost of goods sold, and the decrease in inventory for the goods sold were recorded on January 11.

Sales Discounts and Sales Returns and Allowances

Just as purchase discounts and purchase returns and allowances decrease the cost of inventory purchases, **sales discounts** and **sales returns and allowances**, which are contra accounts to Sales Revenue, decrease the revenue earned on sales. Companies keep close watch on their customers' paying habits and on their own sales of defective and unsuitable merchandise. They maintain separate accounts for Sales Discounts and Sales Returns and Allowances. Let's examine a sequence of the sale transactions of JVC.

On July 7, JVC sells stereo components for $7,200 on credit terms of 2/10 n/30. These goods cost JVC $4,700. JVC's entries to record this credit sale and the cost of the goods sold follow:

July 7	Accounts Receivable	7,200	
	Sales Revenue		7,200
	Sale on account.		

July 7	Cost of Goods Sold.................................	4,700	
	Inventory		4,700
	Recorded the cost of goods sold.		

Assume that the buyer returns goods that sold for $600. JVC's cost of this inventory was $400. JVC records the sales return and the related decrease in Accounts Receivable as follows:

July 12	Sales Returns and Allowances	600	
	Accounts Receivable		600
	Received returned goods.		

JVC would also update the inventory records to include the goods returned by the customer and to decrease cost of goods sold as follows:

"JVC would also update the inventory records to include the goods returned by the customer and to decrease cost of goods sold."

July 12 Inventory 400
      Cost of Goods Sold   400
      Returned goods to inventory.

JVC grants a $100 sales allowance for damaged goods. JVC journalizes this transaction by debiting Sales Returns and Allowances and crediting Accounts Receivable as follows:

July 15 Sales Returns and Allowances.. 100
      Accounts Receivable   100
      Granted a sales allowance for damaged goods.

No inventory entry is needed for a sales allowance transaction because the seller receives no returned goods from the customer. Instead, JVC will receive less cash from the customer.

After the preceding entries are posted, all the accounts have up-to-date balances. Accounts Receivable has a $6,500 debit balance, as follows:

Accounts Receivable			
July 7	7,200	July 12	600
		15	100
Bal.	6,500		

On July 17, the last day of the discount period, JVC collects half ($3,250) of this receivable ($6,500 × ½ = $3,250). The cash receipt is $3,185 [$3,250 − ($3,250 × 0.02)], and the collection entry is

July 17 Cash 3,185
      Sales Discounts ($3,250 × 0.02)................................ 65
        Accounts Receivable   3,250
      Cash collection within the discount period.

Suppose that JVC collects the remainder, $3,250, on July 28. That date is after the discount period, so there is no sales discount. To record this collection on account, JVC debits Cash and credits Accounts Receivable for the same amount, as follows:

July 28 Cash 3,250
        Accounts Receivable   3,250
      Cash collection after the discount period.

Net sales is computed by subtracting the contra accounts as follows:

    Sales Revenue (*credit* balance account)
  − Sales Discounts (*debit* balance account)
  <u>− Sales Returns and Allowances (*debit* balance account)</u>
  = Net sales (a *credit* subtotal, not a separate account)

In Exhibit 5-1, Sony Corporation—like most other businesses—reports to the public only the net sales figure. But Sony managers use the return and allowance data to track customer satisfaction and product quality.

Short Exercise: Best Corp. sold $2,000 of merchandise to Super Sales Co. on 3/1/X2 and granted a 5% quantity discount off that list price. Super Sales returned merchandise on 3/4/X2, and Best Corp. granted Super Sales an allowance of $75. Super Sales pays the balance due on 3/9/X2 and receives a 1% discount for prompt payment. Record Best's collection of the cash. *A:*
Cash 1,806.75
Sales Discount 18.25
  Accounts
    Receivable—
    Super Sales Co ...1,825.00
$2,000 − ($2,000 × 0.05) − $75 = $1,825 Accts. Rec. balance
$1825 − ($1,825 × 0.01) = $1,806.75 cash received

Cost of Goods Sold and Gross Margin

OBJECTIVE 3

Compute cost of goods sold and gross margin

The inventory accounting system illustrated thus far is designed to produce up-to-date records of inventory on hand. This system provides the data for many inventory decisions and for preparation of the financial statements. However, managers have other information needs that the perpetual inventory system does not meet. For example, the owner of Austin Sound plans his operations a year in advance to prepare the budget—a summary of the business strategies—for the coming year. Another computation of cost of goods sold helps managers budget their purchases of inventory. Banks also need another computation of the cost of goods sold because they do not have access to the internal accounting records of their borrowers but must monitor their borrower's financial affairs. We now turn to the alternate computation of cost of goods sold.

Panel A of Exhibit 5-5 gives the computation of cost of goods sold, and Panel B diagrams it.

By studying Exhibit 5-5 you will see that the computation and the diagram tell the same story. That is, a company's goods available for sale during a period come from beginning inventory plus the period's net purchases and freight costs. Either the merchandise is sold during the period or it remains on hand at the end. The merchandise that remains is an asset, Inventory. The cost of the inventory that has been sold is an expense, Cost of Goods Sold. Panel A summarizes the relationship between the expense, Cost of Goods Sold, and the related asset, Inventory, during a period of time. The computation of net purchases is also shown. Panel B reveals that the cost of goods available for sale must wind up either as expense for the period or as an asset.[2]

Exhibit 5-6 summarizes the first half of the chapter by showing Austin Sound's net sales revenue, cost of goods sold, and gross margin on the income statement. (All amounts are assumed.) *Gross margin equals net sales revenue minus cost of goods sold.*

EXHIBIT 5-5

Measurement of Cost of Goods Sold

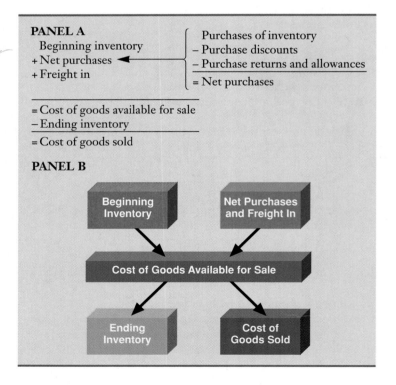

---

[2]This computation of cost of goods sold is based on the periodic inventory system described in the end-of-chapter supplement.

EXHIBIT 5-6
Partial Income Statement

```
AUSTIN SOUND STEREO CENTER
INCOME STATEMENT
FOR THE YEAR ENDED DECEMBER 31, 19X6
```

Sales revenue		$169,300
Less: Sales discounts..............................	$1,400	
Sales returns and allowances.........	2,000	3,400
Net sales revenue.....................................		$165,900
Cost of goods sold		90,800
Gross margin		$ 75,100

Contra accounts—discounts, returns and allowances, and the like—are often netted against their related accounts parenthetically. Austin Sound could report:

Net sales revenue (net of sales discounts, $1,400,
and returns and allowances, $2,000)............................... $165,900

SUMMARY PROBLEM FOR YOUR REVIEW — MID-CHAPTER

Brun Sales Company engaged in the following transactions during June of the current year:

June 3 Purchased inventory on credit terms of 1/10 net eom (end of month), $1,610.
    9 Returned 40 percent of the inventory purchased on June 3. It was defective.
  12 Sold goods for cash, $920 (cost, $550).
  15 Purchased goods of $5,100, less a $100 quantity discount. Credit terms were 3/15 net 30.
  16 Paid a $260 freight bill on goods purchased.
  18 Sold inventory on credit terms of 2/10 n/30, $2,000 (cost, $1,180).
  22 Received damaged goods from the customer of the June 18 sale, $800 (cost, $480).
  24 Borrowed money from the bank to take advantage of the discount offered on the June 15 purchase. Signed a note payable to the bank for the net amount.
  24 Paid supplier for goods purchased on June 15, less all discounts.
  28 Received cash in full settlement of the account from the customer who purchased inventory on June 18.
  29 Paid the amount owed on account from the purchase of June 3.
  30 Purchased inventory for cash, $900, less a quantity discount of $35.

Required

1. Journalize the above transactions. Explanations are not required.
2. Set up T-accounts and post the journal entries to show the ending balances in the Inventory and the Cost of Goods Sold accounts.
3. Assume that the note payable signed on June 24 requires the payment of $95 interest expense. Was the decision wise or unwise to borrow funds to take advantage of the cash discount?

SOLUTION TO REVIEW PROBLEM

Requirement 1

June 3	Inventory...	1,610	
	Accounts Payable...		1,610
9	Accounts Payable ($1,610 × 0.40)..............................	644	
	Inventory...		644
12	Cash..	920	
	Sales Revenue		920
12	Cost of Goods Sold...	550	
	Inventory...		550
15	Inventory ($5,100 – $100)	5,000	
	Accounts Payable...		5,000

June 16	Inventory..	260	
	Cash		260
18	Accounts Receivable	2,000	
	Sales Revenue		2,000
18	Cost of Goods Sold	1,180	
	Inventory		1,180
22	Sales Returns and Allowances	800	
	Accounts Receivable.............................		800
22	Inventory..	480	
	Cost of Goods Sold		480
24	Cash [$5,000 − 0.03($5,000)]	4,850	
	Note Payable		4,850
24	Accounts Payable....................................	5,000	
	Inventory ($5,000 × 0.03).....................		150
	Cash ($5,000 × 0.97)............................		4,850
28	Cash [($2,000 − $800) × 0.98]	1,176	
	Sales Discounts [($2,000 − $800) × 0.02]	24	
	Accounts Receivable ($2,000 − $800)		1,200
29	Accounts Payable ($1,610 − $644)	966	
	Cash		966
30	Inventory ($900 − $35)	865	
	Cash		865

Requirement 2

Inventory						Cost of Goods Sold			
June	3	1,610	June	9	644	June 12	550	June 22	480
	15	5,000		12	550	18	1,180		
	16	260		18	1,180	Bal.	1,250		
	22	480		24	150				
	30	865							
Bal.		5,691							

Requirement 3

The decision to borrow funds was wise because the discount ($150) exceeded the interest paid on the amount borrowed ($95). Thus the entity was $55 better off as a result of its decision.

The Adjusting and Closing Process for a Merchandising Business

A merchandising business adjusts and closes the accounts much as a service entity does. The steps of this end-of-period process are the same: If a work sheet is used, the trial balance is entered, and the work sheet is completed to determine net income or net loss. The work sheet provides the data for journalizing the adjusting and closing entries and for preparing the financial statements.

Adjusting Inventory Based on a Physical Count

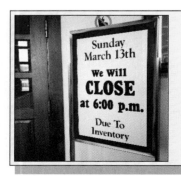

"Virtually all businesses, such as the bookstore chain Barnes & Noble, Inc., take a physical count of inventory at least once each year."

In theory, the Inventory account stays current at all times. However, the actual amount of inventory on hand may differ from what the books show. Theft losses and damage can be significant. Also, accounting errors can cause Inventory's balance to need adjustment. For this reason virtually all businesses, such as the bookstore chain Barnes & Noble, Inc., take a physical count of inventory at least once each year. The most common time for a business to count its inventory is at the end of the fiscal year, before the financial statements are prepared. The business then adjusts the Inventory account to the correct amount on the basis of the physical count.

Exhibit 5-7, Austin Sound's trial balance at December 31, 19X6, lists a $40,500 balance for inventory. With no shrinkage—due to theft or error—the business should have on hand inventory costing $40,500. But on December 31, when Mr. Ernest, the (actual) owner of Austin Sound, counts the merchandise in the store, the total cost of the goods on hand comes to only $40,200. Austin Sound would record the inventory shrinkage with this adjusting entry:

Dec. 31	Cost of Goods Sold	300	
	Inventory ($40,500 – $40,200)............		300

Key Point: As a result of this inventory adjustment, cost of goods sold is higher and gross margin is lower. The cost associated with buying these units is not accompanied by the revenue from a sale. Therefore gross margin shrinks by this amount (cost).

EXHIBIT 5-7
Trial Balance

AUSTIN SOUND STEREO CENTER TRIAL BALANCE DECEMBER 31, 19X6		
Cash...	$ 2,850	
Accounts receivable.............................	4,600	
Note receivable, current	8,000	
Interest receivable		
Inventory.......................................	**40,500**	
Supplies	650	
Prepaid insurance................................	1,200	
Furniture and fixtures	33,200	
Accumulated depreciation		$ 2,400
Accounts payable.................................		47,000
Unearned sales revenue		2,000
Wages payable....................................		
Interest payable		
Note payable, long-term.........................		12,600
C. Ernest, capital.................................		25,900
C. Ernest, withdrawals...........................	54,100	
Sales revenue....................................		**168,000**
Sales discounts	**1,400**	
Sales returns and allowances...............	**2,000**	
Interest revenue..................................		600
Cost of goods sold	**90,500**	
Wage expense.....................................	9,800	
Rent expense	8,400	
Depreciation expense............................		
Insurance expense		
Supplies expense..................................		
Interest expense...................................	1,300	
Total...	$258,500	$258,500

Additional data at December 31, 19X6:

a. Interest revenue earned but not yet collected, $400.
b. Inventory on hand, $40,200.
c. Supplies on hand, $100.
d. Prepaid insurance expired during the year, $1,000.
e. Depreciation, $600.
f. Unearned sales revenue earned during the year, $1,300.
g. Accrued wage expense, $400.
h. Accrued interest expense, $200.

This entry brings Inventory and Cost of Goods Sold to their correct balances. Austin Sound's December 31, 19X6, adjustment data, including this inventory information (item (b)), are given at the bottom of Exhibit 5-7.

The physical count can indicate that more inventory is present than the books show. A search of the records may reveal that Austin Sound made a purchase it did not record. This could be entered the standard way: Debit Inventory and credit Cash or Accounts Payable. If the excess inventory could not be accounted for, the business would adjust the accounts by debiting Inventory and crediting Cost of Goods Sold.

To illustrate a merchandiser's adjusting and closing process, let's use Austin Sound's December 31, 19X6, trial balance in Exhibit 5-7. All the new accounts—Inventory, Cost of Goods Sold, and the contra accounts—are highlighted for emphasis. The additional data item (b) gives the ending inventory figure $40,200.

Accounting Work Sheet of a Merchandising Business

The Exhibit 5-8 work sheet is similar to the work sheets we have seen so far, but a few differences appear. This work sheet does not include adjusted trial balance

EXHIBIT 5-8
Accounting Work Sheet

AUSTIN SOUND STEREO CENTER
ACCOUNTING WORK SHEET
FOR THE YEAR ENDED DECEMBER 31, 19X6

Account Title	Trial Balance Debit	Trial Balance Credit	Adjustments Debit	Adjustments Credit	Income Statement Debit	Income Statement Credit	Balance Sheet Debit	Balance Sheet Credit
Cash	2,850						2,850	
Accounts receivable	4,600						4,600	
Note receivable, current	8,000						8,000	
Interest receivable			(a) 400				400	
Inventory	**40,500**			(b) 300			40,200	
Supplies	650			(c) 550			100	
Prepaid insurance	1,200			(d) 1,000			200	
Furniture and fixtures	33,200						33,200	
Accumulated depreciation		2,400		(e) 600				3,000
Accounts payable		47,000						47,000
Unearned sales revenue		2,000	(f) 1,300					700
Wages payable				(g) 400				400
Interest payable				(h) 200				200
Note payable, long-term		12,600						12,600
C. Ernest, capital		25,900						25,900
C. Ernest, withdrawals	54,100						54,100	
Sales revenue		168,000		(f) 1,300		169,300		
Sales discounts	1,400				1,400			
Sales returns and allowances	2,000				2,000			
Interest revenue		600		(a) 400		1,000		
Cost of goods sold	**90,500**		(b) 300		90,800			
Wage expense	9,800		(g) 400		10,200			
Rent expense	8,400				8,400			
Depreciation expense			(e) 600		600			
Insurance expense			(d) 1,000		1,000			
Supplies expense			(c) 550		550			
Interest expense	1,300		(h) 200		1,500			
	258,500	258,500	4,750	4,750	116,450	170,300	143,650	89,800
Net income					53,850			53,850
					170,300	170,300	143,650	143,650

columns. ◀▥ In most accounting systems, a single operation combines trial balance amounts with the adjustments and extends the adjusted balances directly to the income statement and balance sheet columns. Therefore, to reduce clutter, the adjusted trial balance columns are omitted.

◀▥◀▥◀▥ This work sheet is slightly different from the one introduced in the Chapter 4 acetates—it contains 4 pairs of columns, not 5.

ACCOUNT TITLE COLUMNS The trial balance lists a number of accounts without balances. Ordinarily, these accounts are affected by the adjusting process. Examples include Interest Receivable, Wages Payable, and Depreciation Expense. The accounts are listed in the order they appear in the ledger. If additional accounts are needed, they can be entered at the bottom of the work sheet, above the net income amount.

TRIAL BALANCE COLUMNS Examine the Inventory account, $40,500 in the trial balance. This $40,500 is the ending balance before the physical count. Cost of Goods Sold's balance of $90,500 precedes any adjustment based on the physical count of goods on hand at December 31. We shall assume that any difference between the Inventory amount on the trial balance and the correct amount based on the physical count is unexplained and should be debited or credited directly to Cost of Goods Sold.

Key Point: If you were preparing a work sheet, you could omit the adjusted trial balance columns. Once you understand the mechanics of the work sheet, you can take a trial balance amount, add or subtract the adjustments, and extend the new amount to either the income statement or balance sheet columns.

ADJUSTMENTS COLUMNS The adjustments are similar to those discussed in Chapters 3 and 4. They may be entered in any order desired. The debit amount of each entry should equal the credit amount, and total debits should equal total credits.

INCOME STATEMENT COLUMNS The income statement columns contain adjusted amounts for the revenues and the expenses. Sales Revenue, for example, is $169,300, which includes the $1,300 adjustment.

The income statement column subtotals on the work sheet indicate whether the business earned net income or incurred a net loss. If total credits are greater, the result is net income, as shown in Exhibit 5-8. Inserting the net income amount in the debit column brings total debits into agreement with total credits. If total debits are greater, a net loss has occurred. Inserting a net loss amount in the credit column equalizes total debits and total credits. Net income or net loss is then extended to the opposite column of the balance sheet.

BALANCE SHEET COLUMNS The only new item on the balance sheet is Inventory. The balance listed is the ending amount of $40,200, which is determined by the physical count of inventory on hand at the end of the period.

Financial Statements of a Merchandising Business

Exhibit 5-9 presents Austin Sound's financial statements. The *income statement* through gross margin repeats Exhibit 5-6. This information is followed by the **operating expenses**, which are those expenses other than cost of goods sold that are incurred in the entity's major line of business—merchandising. Austin Sound's operating expenses include wage expense, rent, insurance, depreciation of furniture and fixtures, and supplies expense.

OBJECTIVE 5
Prepare a merchandiser's financial statements

Many companies report their operating expenses in two categories. *Selling expenses* are those expenses related to marketing the company's products—sales salaries; sales commissions; advertising; depreciation, rent, utilities, and property taxes on store buildings; depreciation on store furniture; delivery expense; and so on. *General expenses* include office expenses, such as the salaries of the company president and office employees, depreciation, rent, utilities, property taxes on the home office building, and office supplies.

EXHIBIT 5-9   *Financial Statements of Austin Sound Stereo Center*

AUSTIN SOUND STEREO CENTER
INCOME STATEMENT
FOR THE YEAR ENDED DECEMBER 31, 19X6

Sales revenue		$169,300	
Less: Sales discounts	$ 1,400		
Sales returns and allowances	2,000	3,400	
Net sales revenue			$165,900
Cost of goods sold			90,800
Gross margin			75,100
Operating expenses:			
Wage expense		10,200	
Rent expense		8,400	
Insurance expense		1,000	
Depreciation expense		600	
Supplies expense		550	20,750
Operating income			54,350
Other revenue and (expense):			
Interest revenue		1,000	
Interest expense		(1,500)	(500)
Net income			$ 53,850

AUSTIN SOUND STEREO CENTER
STATEMENT OF OWNER'S EQUITY
FOR THE YEAR ENDED DECEMBER 31, 19X6

C. Ernest, capital, December 31, 19X5	$25,900
Add: Net income	53,850
	79,750
Less: Withdrawals	54,100
C. Ernest, capital, December 31, 19X6	$25,650

AUSTIN SOUND STEREO CENTER
BALANCE SHEET
DECMEBER 31, 19X6

Assets			Liabilities	
Current:			**Current:**	
Cash		$ 2,850	Accounts payable	$47,000
Accounts receivable		4,600	Unearned sales revenue	700
Note receivable		8,000	Wages payable	400
Interest receivable		400	Interest payable	200
Inventory		40,200	Total current liabilities	48,300
Prepaid insurance		200	**Long-term:**	
Supplies		100	Note payable	12,600
Total current assets		56,350	Total liabilities	60,900
Plant:				
Furniture and fixtures	$33,200		**Owner's Equity**	
Less: Accumulated			C. Ernest, capital	25,650
depreciation	3,000	30,200	Total liabilities and	
Total assets		$86,550	owner's equity	$86,550

Gross margin minus operating expenses plus any other operating revenues equals **operating income,** or **income from operations**. As was true for Sony, many people view operating income as the most reliable indicator of a business's success because it measures the entity's major ongoing activities.

The last section of Austin Sound's income statement is **other revenue and expense**. This category reports revenues and expenses that are outside the main operations of the business. Examples include gains and losses on the sale of plant assets (not inventory) and gains and losses on lawsuits. Accountants have traditionally viewed Interest Revenue and Interest Expense as "other" items because they arise from loaning money and borrowing money—financing activities that are outside the operating scope of selling merchandise or, for a service entity, rendering services.

The bottom line of the income statement is net income, which includes the effects of all the revenues and gains less all the expenses and losses. We often hear the term *bottom line* used to refer to a final result. The term originated in the position of net income on the income statement.

A merchandiser's *statement of owner's equity* looks exactly like that of a service business. In fact, you cannot determine whether the entity is merchandising- or service-oriented from looking at the statement of owner's equity.

If the business is a merchandiser, the *balance sheet* shows inventory as a major current asset. In contrast, service businesses usually have minor amounts of inventory.

Adjusting and Closing Entries for a Merchandising Business

Exhibit 5-10 presents Austin Sound's adjusting entries, which are similar to those you have seen previously, except for the inventory adjustment (entry (b)). The closing entries in the exhibit also follow the pattern illustrated in Chapter 4. ◀▥▥ The first closing entry debits the revenue accounts for their ending balances. The offsetting credit of $170,300 transfers their sum to Income Summary. This amount comes directly from the credit column of the income statement on the work sheet (Exhibit 5-8).

The second closing entry includes credits to Cost of Goods Sold and to the contra revenue accounts, Sales Discounts and Sales Returns and Allowances, which are new, and to the other expense accounts. The offsetting $116,450 debit to Income Summary comes from the debit column of the income statement on the work sheet. The last two closing entries close net income from Income Summary and also close owner Withdrawals into the Capital account.

Study Exhibits 5-8, 5-9, and 5-10 carefully because they illustrate the entire end-of-period process that leads to the financial statements. As you progress through this book, you may want to refer to these exhibits to refresh your understanding of the adjusting and closing process for a merchandising business.

◀▥◀▥◀▥ The adjusting and closing entries here are very similar to those discussed in Chapter 4, pp. 138–143. The closing entries also clear the Cost of Goods Sold expense account for accumulating costs in the next period.

Income Statement Format

We have seen that the balance sheet appears in two formats: the report format and the account format. There are also two basic formats for the income statement: *multiple-step* and *single-step*. A recent survey of 600 companies indicated that 64 percent use the multiple-step format and 36 percent use the single-step format.

Multiple-Step Income Statement

The **multiple-step format** contains subtotals to highlight significant relationships. In addition to net income, it also presents gross margin and operating income, or income from operations. This format communicates a merchandiser's results of opera-

EXHIBIT 5-10
Adjusting and Closing Entries

Journal		
Adjusting Entries		
a. Dec. 31 Interest Receivable..	400	
Interest Revenue		400
b. 31 Cost of Goods Sold...................................	300	
Inventory...		300
c. 31 Supplies Expense ($650−$100)...................	550	
Supplies...		550
d. 31 Insurance Expense....................................	1,000	
Prepaid Insurance		1,000
e. 31 Depreciation Expense	600	
Accumulated Depreciation.................		600
f. 31 Unearned Sales Revenue...........................	1,300	
Sales Revenue...................................		1,300
g. 31 Wage Expense	400	
Wages Payable		400
h. 31 Interest Expense....................................	200	
Interest Payable		200
Closing Entries		
Dec. 31 Sales Revenue	169,300	
Interest Revenue	1,000	
Income Summary...............................		170,300
31 Income Summary	116,450	
Cost of Goods Sold.............................		90,800
Sales Discounts		1,400
Sales Returns and Allowances		2,000
Wage Expense....................................		10,200
Rent Expense		8,400
Depreciation Expense.........................		600
Insurance Expense		1,000
Supplies Expense		550
Interest Expense.................................		1,500
31 Income Summary ($170,300−$116,450)	53,850	
C. Ernest, Capital		53,850
31 C. Ernest, Capital....................................	54,100	
C. Ernest, Withdrawals		54,100

Owens-Corning Fiberglas Corporation, known for its building insulation, roofing shingles, and textile yarns, uses the multiple-step format for its income statement.

tions especially well because gross margin and income from operations are two key measures of operating performance. Owens-Corning Fiberglas Corporation and PepsiCo, Inc., use the multiple-step format. The income statements presented thus far in this chapter have been multiple-step. Austin Sound's multiple-step income statement for the year ended December 31, 19X6, appears in Exhibit 5-9.

Single-Step Income Statement

The **single-step format** groups all revenues together and then lists and deducts all expenses together without drawing any subtotals. IBM and Wal-Mart use this format. The single-step format has the advantage of listing all revenues together and all expenses together, as shown in Exhibit 5-11. Thus it clearly distinguishes revenues from expenses. The income statements in Chapters 1 through 4 were single-step. This format works well for service entities because they have no gross margin to report.

Most published financial statements are highly condensed. Appendix A at the end of the book gives the income statement of Lands' End, Inc. Of course, condensed statements can be supplemented with desired details.

AUSTIN SOUND STEREO CENTER **INCOME STATEMENT** **FOR THE YEAR ENDED DECEMBER 31, 19X6**	**EXHIBIT 5-11** *Single-Step Income Statement*

Revenues:
Net sales (net of sales discounts, $1,400, and
    returns and allowances, $2,000) $165,900
  Interest revenue 1,000
  Total revenues.. 166,900
Expenses:
  Cost of goods sold .... $ 90,800
  Wage expense.. 10,200
  Rent expense... 8,400
  Interest expense 1,500
  Insurance expense 1,000
  Depreciation expense 600
  Supplies expense 550
  Total expenses... 113,050
Net income.. $ 53,850

Use of Accounting Information in Decision Making

Merchandise inventory is the most important asset to a merchandising business because it captures the essence of the entity. To manage the firm, owners and managers focus on the best way to sell the inventory. They use several ratios to evaluate operations.

> **OBJECTIVE 6**
> Use the gross margin percentage and the inventory turnover ratio to evaluate a business

Gross Margin Percentage

A key decision-making tool for a merchandiser is related to gross margin, which is net sales minus cost of goods sold. Merchandisers strive to increase the **gross margin percentage**, which is computed as follows:

FOR AUSTIN SOUND STEREO CENTER
(EXHIBIT 5-9)

$$\text{Gross margin percentage} = \frac{\text{Gross margin}}{\text{Net sales revenue}} = \frac{\$75,100}{\$165,900} = 0.453 = 45.3\%$$

The gross margin (or gross profit) percentage is one of the most carefully watched measures of profitability because it is fundamental to a merchandiser. A 45-percent gross margin means that each dollar of sales generates 45 cents of gross profit. On average, the goods cost the seller 55 cents. For most firms, the gross margin percentage changes little from year to year. A small downturn may signal an important drop in income. That was true of Sony, whose gross margin percentage dropped from 30.7 percent in 1991 to 25.7 percent in 1992. A small change in the gross margin percentage usually indicates a sizable shift in profitability.

Austin Sound's gross margin percentage of 45.3 percent compares very favorably with the industry average for electronics retailers, which is 34.9 percent. By contrast, the average gross margin percentage is 14.1 percent for automobile dealers, 22.8 percent for grocery stores, and 55.7 percent for restaurants, according to Robert Morris Associates' *Annual Statement Studies*. Exhibit 5-12 compares Austin Sound's gross margin to that of Wal-Mart.

EXHIBIT 5-12
Gross Margin on $1.00 of Sales for Two Merchandisers

Inventory Turnover

Short Exercise: Calculate inventory turnover given the following data:

Beg. inventory .... $ 2,350
End. inventory 1,980
Purchases 14,550
Freight in 390
A: Cost of goods sold/Avg. inv. turn. = $15,310/$2,165 = 7 times

Owners and managers strive to sell inventory as quickly as possible because it generates no profit until it is sold. The faster the sales occur, the higher the income. The slower the sales, the lower the income. Ideally a business could operate with zero inventory. Most businesses, however, including retailers such as Austin Sound, must keep goods on hand for customers. Successful merchandisers purchase carefully to keep the goods moving through the business at a rapid pace. **Inventory turnover,** the ratio of cost of goods sold to average inventory, indicates how rapidly inventory is sold. Its computation follows:

FOR AUSTIN SOUND STEREO CENTER (EXHIBIT 5-9)

$$\frac{\text{Inventory}}{\text{turnover}} = \frac{\text{Cost of goods sold}}{\text{Average inventory}} = \frac{\text{Cost of goods sold}}{(\text{Beginning inventory} + \text{ending inventory})/2} = \frac{\$90,800}{(\$38,600 + \$40,200)/2} = \begin{array}{c}\text{2.3 times per year}\\ \text{(about every 159 days)}\end{array}$$

Inventory turnover is usually computed for an annual period, and the relevant cost-of-goods sold figure is the amount for the entire year. Average inventory is computed from the beginning and ending amounts. (Austin Sound's beginning inventory would be taken from the business's balance sheet at the end of the preceding year.) The resulting inventory turnover statistic shows how many times the average level of inventory was sold during the year. A high rate of turnover is preferable to a low turnover. An increase in the rate of turnover usually means higher profits.

Inventory turnover varies from industry to industry. Grocery stores, for example, turn their goods over faster than automobile dealers do. Drug stores have higher turnover than furniture stores do. Retailers of electronic products, such as Austin Sound, have an average turnover of 3.6 times per year. Austin Sound's turnover rate of 2.3 times per year suggests that Austin Sound is not very successful. The lower one-fourth of electronics retailers average a turnover rate of 2.7, so Austin Sound's turnover of 2.3 looks rather bad. Exhibit 5-13 compares the inventory turnover rate of Austin Sound and Wal-Mart Stores, Inc.

Financial analysis is complex. Exhibits 5-12 and 5-13 tell an interesting story. Wal-Mart sells lots of inventory at a relatively low gross profit margin. Wal-Mart earns its profits by turning its inventory over rapidly. Austin Sound, a mom-and-pop business, prices inventory to earn a higher gross margin on each dollar of sales. But Austin Sound cannot sell its merchandise nearly as rapidly as Wal-Mart can. Gross margin percentage and rate of inventory turnover do not provide enough information to yield an overall conclusion about either firm, but the example shows how owners and managers may use accounting information to evaluate a company.

EXHIBIT 5-13

Rate of Inventory Turnover for Two Merchandisers

The accompanying trial balance and additional data are related to Jan King Distributing Company.

JAN KING DISTRIBUTING COMPANY
TRIAL BALANCE
DECEMBER 31, 19X3

Cash	$ 5,670	
Accounts receivable	37,100	
Inventory	60,500	
Supplies	3,930	
Prepaid rent	6,000	
Furniture and fixtures	26,500	
Accumulated depreciation		$ 21,200
Accounts payable		46,340
Salary payable		
Interest payable		
Unearned sales revenue		3,500
Note payable, long-term		35,000
Jan King, capital		23,680
Jan King, withdrawals	48,000	
Sales revenue		346,700
Sales discounts	10,300	
Sales returns and allowances	8,200	
Cost of goods sold	171,770	
Salary expense	82,750	
Rent expense	7,000	
Depreciation expense		
Utilities expense	5,800	
Supplies expense		
Interest expense	2,900	
Total	$476,420	$476,420

Additional data at December 31, 19X3:

a. Supplies used during the year, $2,580.
b. Prepaid rent in force, $1,000.
c. Unearned sales revenue still not earned, $2,400. The company expects to earn this amount during the next few months.
d. Depreciation. The furniture and fixtures' estimated useful life is 10 years, and they are expected to be worthless when they are retired from service.
e. Accrued salaries, $1,300.
f. Accrued interest expense, $600.
g. Inventory on hand, $65,800.

Required

1. Enter the trial balance on a work sheet and complete the work sheet.
2. Journalize the adjusting and closing entries at December 31. Post to the Income Summary account as an accuracy check on the entries affecting that account. The credit balance closed out of Income Summary should equal net income computed on the work sheet.
3. Prepare the company's multiple-step income statement, statement of owner's equity, and balance sheet in account format.
4. Compute the inventory turnover for 19X3. Inventory at December 31, 19X2, was $60,500. Turnover for 19X2 was 2.1. Would you expect Jan King Distributing Company to be more profitable or less profitable in 19X3 than in 19X2? Give your reason.

SOLUTION TO REVIEW PROBLEM

Requirement 1

JAN KING DISTRIBUTING COMPANY
ACCOUNTING WORK SHEET
FOR THE YEAR ENDED DECEMBER 31, 19X3

Account Title	Trial Balance Debit	Trial Balance Credit	Adjustments Debit	Adjustments Credit	Income Statement Debit	Income Statement Credit	Balance Sheet Debit	Balance Sheet Credit
Cash	5,670						5,670	
Accounts receivable	37,100						37,100	
Inventory	60,500		(g) 5,300				65,800	
Supplies	3,930			(a) 2,580			1,350	
Prepaid rent	6,000			(b) 5,000			1,000	
Furniture and fixtures	26,500						26,500	
Accumulated depreciation		21,200		(d) 2,650				23,850
Accounts payable		46,340						46,340
Salary payable				(e) 1,300				1,300
Interest payable				(f) 600				600
Unearned sales revenue		3,500	(c) 1,100					2,400
Note payable, long-term		35,000						35,000
Jan King, capital		23,680						23,680
Jan King, withdrawals	48,000						48,000	
Sales revenue		346,700		(c) 1,100		347,800		
Sales discounts	10,300				10,300			
Sales returns and allowances	8,200				8,200			
Cost of goods sold	171,770			(g) 5,300	166,470			
Salary expense	82,750		(e) 1,300		84,050			
Rent expense	7,000		(b) 5,000		12,000			
Depreciation expense			(d) 2,650		2,650			
Utilities expense	5,800				5,800			
Supplies expense			(a) 2,580		2,580			
Interest expense	2,900		(f) 600		3,500			
	476,420	476,420	18,530	18,530	295,550	347,800	185,420	133,170
Net income					52,250			52,250
					347,800	347,800	185,420	185,420

Adjusting Entries

19X3

Dec. 31	Supplies Expense	2,580	
	Supplies..		2,580
31	Rent Expense	5,000	
	Prepaid Rent		5,000
31	Unearned Sales Revenue	1,100	
	Sales Revenue		1,100
31	Depreciation Expense ($26,500/10)...............	2,650	
	Accumulated Depreciation...................		2,650
31	Salary Expense	1,300	
	Salary Payable		1,300
31	Interest Expense	600	
	Interest Payable....................................		600
31	Inventory...	5,300*	
	Cost of Goods Sold		5,300

Closing Entries

19X3

Dec. 31	Sales Revenue	347,800	
	Income Summary		347,800
31	Income Summary	295,550	
	Cost of Goods Sold		166,470
	Sales Discounts..		10,300
	Sales Returns and Allowances		8,200
	Salary Expense...		84,050
	Rent Expense...		12,000
	Depreciation Expense		2,650
	Utilities Expense		5,800
	Supplies Expense		2,580
	Interest Expense		3,500
31	Income Summary ($347,800 - $295,550)...............	52,250	
	Jan King, Capital		52,250
31	Jan King, Capital	48,000	
	Jan King, Withdrawals		48,000

Income Summary			
Clo.	295,550	Clo.	347,800
Clo.	52,250	Bal.	52,250

---

* Excess of inventory on hand over the balance in the Inventory account. This adjustment brings Inventory to its correct balance.

Requirement 3

JAN KING DISTRIBUTING COMPANY
INCOME STATEMENT
FOR THE YEAR ENDED DECEMBER 31, 19X3

Sales revenue			$347,800
Less: Sales discounts	$10,300		
Sales returns and allowances ..	8,200	18,500	
Net sales revenue			$329,300
Cost of goods sold			166,470
Gross margin			162,830
Operating expenses:			
Salary expense		84,050	
Rent expense		12,000	
Utilities expense		5,800	
Depreciation expense		2,650	
Supplies expense		2,580	107,080
Income from operations			55,750
Other expense:			
Interest expense			3,500
Net income			$ 52,250

JAN KING DISTRIBUTING COMPANY
STATEMENT OF OWNER'S EQUITY
FOR THE YEAR ENDED DECEMBER 31, 19X3

Jan King, capital, December 31, 19X2	$23,680
Add: Net income	52,250
	75,930
Less: Withdrawals	48,000
Jan King, capital, December 31, 19X3	$27,930

JAN KING DISTRIBUTING COMPANY
BALANCE SHEET
DECEMBER 31, 19X3

Assets			**Liabilities**		
Current:			Current:		
Cash		$ 5,670	Accounts payable		$ 46,340
Accounts receivable		37,100	Salary payable		1,300
Inventory		65,800	Interest payable		600
Supplies		1,350	Unearned sales revenue ..		2,400
Prepaid rent		1,000	Total current liabilities		50,640
Total current assets		110,920	Long-term:		
Plant:			Note payable		35,000
Furniture and fixtures...	$26,500		Total liabilities		85,640
Less: Accumulated					
depreciation	23,850	2,650	**Owner's Equity**		
			Jan King, capital		27,930
			Total liabilities and		
Total assets		$113,570	owner's equity		$113,570

$$\text{Inventory turnover} = \frac{\text{Cost of goods sold}}{\text{Average inventory}} = \frac{\$166,470}{(\$60,500 + \$65,800)/2} = 2.6$$

The increase in the rate of inventory turnover from 2.1 to 2.6 suggests higher profits in 19X3 than in 19X2.

SUMMARY

1. *Use sales, gross margin, and operating income to evaluate a company.* The major revenue of a merchandising business is *sales revenue*, or *net sales*. The major expense is *cost of goods sold*. Net sales minus cost of goods sold is called *gross margin*, or *gross profit*. This amount measures the business's success or failure in selling its products at a higher price than it paid for them.

The *invoice* is the business document generated by a purchase or sale transaction. Most merchandising entities offer *discounts* to their customers and allow them to *return* unsuitable merchandise. They also grant *allowances* for damaged goods that the buyer chooses to keep. Discounts and Returns and Allowances are contra accounts to Sales Revenue.

2. *Account for the purchase and sale of inventory.* The merchandiser's major asset is *inventory*. In a merchandising entity the accounting cycle is from cash to inventory as the inventory is purchased for resale, and back to cash as the inventory is sold.

3. *Compute cost of goods sold and gross margin.* Cost of goods sold, or *cost of sales*, is the cost of the inventory that the business has sold. It is the largest single expense of most merchandising businesses. Gross margin equals net sales revenue minus cost of goods sold.

4. *Adjust and close the accounts of a merchandising business.* The end-of-period adjusting and closing process of a merchandising business is similar to that of a service business. In addition, a merchandiser adjusts inventory for theft losses, damage, and accounting errors.

5. *Prepare a merchandiser's financial statements.* The income statement may appear in the *single-step format* or the *multiple-step format*. A single-step income statement has only two sections—one for revenues and the other for expenses—and a single income amount for net income. A multiple income statement has subtotals for gross margin and from operations. Both formats are widely used.

6. *Use the gross margin percentage and the i turnover ratio to evaluate a business.* Two key decision a merchandiser are the *gross margin percentage* and the *ventory turnover*. Increases in these measures usually increase in profits.

SELF-STUDY QUESTIONS

Test your understanding of the chapter by marking the best answer for each of the following questions.

1. The major expense of a merchandising business is *(p. 176)*
   a. Cost of goods sold
   b. Depreciation
   c. Rent
   d. Interest

2. Sales total $440,000, cost of goods sold is $210,000, and operating expenses are $160,000. How much is gross margin? *(p. 176)*
   a. $440,000
   b. $230,000
   c. $210,000
   d. $70,000

3. A purchase discount results from *(p. 180)*
   a. Returning goods to the seller
   b. Receiving a purchase allowance from the seller
   c. Buying a large enough quantity of merchandise to get the discount
   d. Paying within the discount period

4. Which one of the following pairs includes items that are the most similar? *(pp. 184–185)*
   a. Purchase discounts and purchase returns
   b. Cost of goods sold and inventory
   c. Net sales and sales discounts
   d. Sales returns and sales allowances

5. Which of the following is *not* an account? *(p. 185)*
   a. Sales revenue
   b. Net sales
   c. Inventory
   d. Supplies expense

6. Cost of goods sold can be computed by adding b inventory and net purchases and subtracting X. W *(p. 186)*
   a. Net sales
   b. Sales discounts
   c. Ending inventory
   d. Net purchases

7. Which account causes the main difference between a merchandiser's adjusting and closing process and that of a service business? *(p. 193)*
   a. Advertising Expense
   b. Interest Revenue
   c. Cost of Goods Sold
   d. Accounts Receivable

8. The major item on a merchandiser's income statement that a service business does not have is *(p. 176)*
   a. Cost of goods sold
   b. Inventory
   c. Salary expense
   d. Total revenue

9. The closing entry for Sales Discounts is *(p. 194)*
   a. Sales Discounts
        Income Summary
   b. Sales Discounts
        Sales Revenue
   c. Income Summary
        Sales Discounts
   d. Not used: Sales Discounts is a permanent account, which is not closed.

10. Which income statement format reports income from operations? *(p. 193)*
   a. Account format
   b. Report format
   c. Single-step format
   d. Multiple-step format

Answers to the Self-Study Questions follow the Accounting Vocabulary.

ACCOUNTING VOCABULARY

Cost of goods sold. The cost of the inventory that the business has sold to customers, the largest single expense of most merchandising businesses. Also called cost of sales (p. 183).

Cost of sales. Another name for cost of goods sold (p. 183).

Gross margin. Excess of sales revenue over cost of goods sold. Also called gross profit (p. 176).

Gross margin percentage. Gross margin divided by net sales revenue. A measure of profitability (p. 195).

Gross profit. Another name for gross margin (p. 176).

Income from operations. Another name for operating income (p. 193).

Inventory turnover. Ratio of cost of goods sold to average inventory. Measures the number of times a company sells its average level of inventory during a year (p. 196).

Multiple-step income statement. Format that contains subtotals to highlight significant relationships. In addition to net income, it presents gross margin and income from operations (p. 193).

Net purchases. Purchases less purchase discounts and purchase returns and allowances (p. 217).

Net sales. Sales revenue less sales discounts and sales returns and allowances (p. 185).

Operating expenses. Expenses, other than cost of goods sold, that are incurred in the entity's major line of business. Examples include rent, depreciation, salaries, wages, utilities, property tax, and supplies expense (p. 191).

Operating income. Gross margin minus operating expenses plus any other operating revenues. Also called income from operations. (p. 193).

Other expense. Expense that is outside the main operations of a business, such as a loss on the sale of plant assets (p. 193).

Other revenue. Revenue that is outside the main operations of a business, such as a gain on the sale of plant assets (p. 193).

Periodic inventory system. Type of inventory accounting system in which the business does not keep a continuous record of the inventory on hand. Instead, at the end of the period the business makes a physical count of the on-hand inventory and applies the appropriate unit costs to determine the cost of the ending inventory (p. 177).

Perpetual inventory system. Type of accounting inventory system in which the business keeps a continuous record for each inventory item to show the inventory on hand at all times (p. 177).

Sales. Another name for sales revenue (p. 176).

Sales discount. Reduction in the amount receivable from a customer, offered by the seller as an incentive for the customer to pay promptly. A contra account to Sales Revenue (p. 184).

Sales returns and allowances. Decrease in the seller's receivable from a customer's return of merchandise or from granting the customer an allowance from the amount the customer owes the seller. A contra account to Sales Revenue (p. 184).

Sales revenue. The amount that a merchandiser earns from selling its inventory, before expenses are subtracted. Also called sales (p. 176).

Single-step income statement. Format that groups all revenues together and then lists and deducts all expenses together without drawing any subtotals (p. 194).

ANSWERS TO SELF-STUDY QUESTIONS

1. a
2. b ($440,000 – $210,000 = $230,000)
3. d
4. d
5. b
6. c
7. c
8. a
9. c
10. d

QUESTIONS

1. Gross margin is often mentioned in the business press as an important measure of success. What does gross margin measure, and why is it important?
2. Describe the operating cycle for (a) the purchase and cash sale of inventory and (b) the purchase and sale of inventory on account.
3. Identify 10 items of information on an invoice.
4. Indicate which accounts are debited and credited for (a) a credit purchase of inventory and the subsequent cash payment and (b) a credit sale of inventory and the subsequent cash collection. Assume no discounts, returns, allowances, or freight.
5. Inventory costing $1,000 is purchased and invoiced on July 28 under terms of 3/10 n/30. Compute the payment amount on August 6. How much would the payment be on August 8? What explains the difference? What is the latest acceptable payment date under the terms of sale?
6. Inventory listed at $35,000 is sold subject to a quantity discount of $3,000 and under payment terms of 2/15 n/45. What is the net sales revenue on this sale if the customer pays within 15 days?
7. Name the new contra accounts introduced in this chapter.
8. Briefly discuss the similarity in computing supplies expense and computing cost of goods sold by the method shown on page 186.
9. Why is the title Cost of Goods Sold especially descriptive? What type of account is Cost of Goods Sold?
10. Beginning inventory is $5,000, net purchases total $30,000, and freight in is $1,000. If ending inventory is $8,000, what is the cost of goods sold?
11. You are evaluating two companies as possible investments. One entity sells its services; the other is a merchandiser. How can you identify the merchandiser by examining the entities' balance sheets and income statements?

12. You are beginning the adjusting and closing process at the end of your company's fiscal year. Does the trial balance carry the final ending amount of inventory? Give your reason.
13. Give the adjusting entry for inventory if shrinkage is $9,100.
14. What is the identifying characteristic of the "other" category of revenues and expenses? Give an example of each.
15. Name and describe the two income statement formats, and identify the type of business to which each format best applies.

16. List eight different operating expenses.
17. Which financial statement reports sales discounts and sales returns and allowances? Show how they are reported, using any reasonable amounts in your illustration.
18. Does a merchandiser prefer a high or a low rate of inventory turnover? Give your reason.
19. In general, what does a decreasing gross margin percentage, coupled with an increasing rate of inventory turnover, suggest about a business's pricing strategy?

EXERCISES

E5-1   IBM recently reported its operations on this income statement:

Evaluating a real company's revenues, gross margin, operating income, and net income
(Obj. 1)

CONSOLIDATED STATEMENT OF EARNINGS
INTERNATIONAL BUSINESS MACHINES CORPORATION
AND SUBSIDIARY COMPANIES

(Dollars in millions) For the year ended December 31:	1992	1991	1990
Revenue:			
Sales	$ 33,755	$ 37,093	$ 43,959
Software	11,103	10,498	9,865
Maintenance	7,635	7,414	7,198
Services	7,352	5,582	4,124
Rentals and financing	4,678	4,179	3,785
	64,523	64,766	68,931
Cost:			
Sales	19,698	18,571	19,401
Software	3,924	3,865	3,118
Maintenance	3,430	3,379	3,302
Services	6,051	4,531	3,315
Rentals and financing	1,966	1,727	1,579
	35,069	32,073	30,715
Gross Profit	29,454	32,693	38,216
Operating Expenses:			
Selling, general and administrative	19,526	21,375	20,709
Research, development and engineering	6,522	6,644	6,554
Restructuring charges	11,645	3,735	—
	37,693	31,754	27,263
Operating Income	(8,239)	939	10,953
Other Income, principally interest	573	602	495
Interest Expense	1,360	1,423	1,324
Earnings before Income Taxes	(9,026)	118	10,124
Provision for Income Taxes	(2,161)	716	4,157
Net Earnings before Changes in Accounting Principles	(6,865)	(598)	5,967
Effect of Changes in Accounting Principles	1,900	(2,263)	—
Net Earnings	$ (4,965)	$ (2,861)	$ 5,967

Required

1. Is IBM a merchandising entity, a service business, or both? How can you tell?
2. Compute IBM's gross margin on sales (not total revenues) for 1992, 1991, and 1990. Compare this trend with the company's trend of total gross margin.

3. Write a brief memo to investors advising them of IBM's two-year trend of sales, total revenues, gross margin, operating income, and net income. In which year did IBM experience the larger change from the preceding year, 1992 or 1991?

Journalizing purchase and sales transactions
(Obj. 2)

E5-2 Journalize, without explanations, the following transactions of Mariposa, Inc., during July:

July 3   Purchased $1,000 of inventory under terms of 2/10 n/eom (end of month) and FOB shipping point.
    7   Returned $300 of defective merchandise purchased on July 3.
    9   Paid freight bill of $110 on July 3 purchase.
   10   Sold inventory for $2,200, collecting cash of $400. Payment terms on the remainder were 2/15 n/30. These goods cost Mariposa $1,300.
   12   Paid amount owed on credit purchase of July 3, less the discount and the return.
   16   Granted a sales allowance of $800 on the July 10 sale.
   23   Received cash from July 10 customer in full settlement of her debt, less the allowance and the discount.

Journalizing transactions from a purchase invoice
(Obj. 2)

E5-3 As the proprietor of Kendrick Tire Company, an actual business, you receive the accompanying invoice from a supplier.

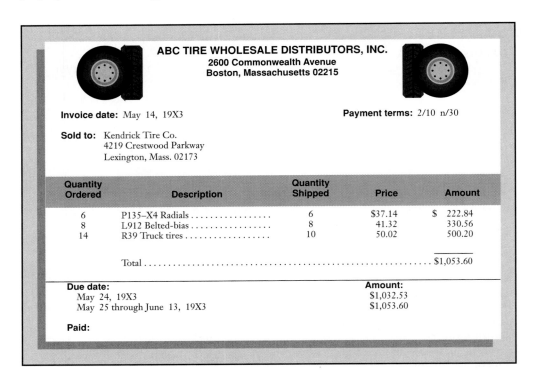

ABC TIRE WHOLESALE DISTRIBUTORS, INC.
2600 Commonwealth Avenue
Boston, Massachusetts 02215

Invoice date: May 14, 19X3   **Payment terms:** 2/10 n/30

Sold to: Kendrick Tire Co.
4219 Crestwood Parkway
Lexington, Mass. 02173

Quantity Ordered	Description	Quantity Shipped	Price	Amount
6	P135–X4 Radials	6	$37.14	$ 222.84
8	L912 Belted-bias	8	41.32	330.56
14	R39 Truck tires	10	50.02	500.20
	Total			$1,053.60

Due date:	Amount:
May 24, 19X3	$1,032.53
May 25 through June 13, 19X3	$1,053.60

Paid:

Required

1. Record the May 15 purchase on account.
2. The R39 truck tires were ordered by mistake and therefore were returned to ABC. Journalize the return on May 19.
3. Record the May 22 payment of the amount owed.

Journalizing purchase transactions
(Obj. 2)

E5-4 On April 30 Corwin Jewelers purchased inventory of $5,300 on account from La Roche Fine Gems, a wholesale jewelry supplier. Terms were 3/15 net 45. On receiving the goods, Corwin checked the order and found $800 of unsuitable merchandise. Therefore, Corwin returned this amount of merchandise to the supplier on May 4.

To pay the remaining amount owed, Corwin had to borrow from the bank because of a temporary cash shortage. On May 14 Corwin signed a short-term note payable to the bank and immediately paid the borrowed funds to La Roche. On May 31 Corwin paid the bank the net amount of the invoice, which Corwin had borrowed, plus $30 interest.

Required

Record the indicated transactions in the journal of Corwin Jewelers. Explanations are not required.

E5-5 Refer to the business situation in Exercise 5-4. Journalize the transactions of La Roche Fine Gems. La Roche's gross margin is 40 percent. Explanations are not required.

Journalizing sales transactions (Obj. 2)

E5-6 Supply the missing income statement amounts in each of the following situations:

Computing the elements of a merchandiser's income statement (Obj. 3)

Sales	Sales Discounts	Net Sales	Beginning Inventory	Net Purchases	Ending Inventory	Cost of Goods Sold	Gross Margin
$94,300	(a)	$92,800	$32,500	$66,700	$39,400	(b)	$33,000
72,400	$2,100	(c)	27,450	43,000	(d)	$44,100	(e)
91,500	1,800	89,700	(f)	54,900	22,600	59,400	(g)
(h)	3,000	(i)	40,700	(j)	48,230	62,500	36,600

E5-7 For the year ended December 31, 19X9, House of Fabrics, a retailer of home-related products, reported net sales of $338 million and cost of goods sold of $154 million. The company's balance sheet at December 31, 19X8 and 19X9, reported inventories of $133 million and $129 million, respectively. What were House of Fabrics' net purchases during 19X9?

Computing cost of goods sold for an actual company (Obj. 3)

E5-8 Selected amounts from the accounting records of Handy Dan Home Products are listed in alphabetical order.

Preparing a merchandiser's multiple-step income statement to evaluate the business (Obj. 3, 5, 6)

Accounts receivable	$48,300	Owner's equity, May 31 ..	$126,070
Accumulated depreciation	18,700	Purchases of inventory....	91,300
Cost of goods sold	?	Purchase discounts	3,000
Freight in	2,200	Purchase returns	2,000
General expenses	23,800	Sales discounts	9,000
Interest revenue	1,500	Sales returns...................	4,600
Inventory, June 30.................	21,870	Sales revenue..................	201,000
Inventory, May 31.................	19,450	Selling expenses	37,840
		Unearned sales revenue..	6,500

Required

Prepare the business's multiple-step income statement for June of the current year. In a separate schedule, show the computation of cost of goods sold. Compute the rate of inventory turnover. Last year the turnover was 3.8 times. Does this two-year trend suggest improvement or deterioration in profitability?

E5-9 Prepare Handy Dan Home Products' single-step income statement for June, using the data from Exercise 5-8. In a separate schedule, show the computation of cost of goods sold. Compute the gross margin percentage, and compare it with last year's value of 58 percent for Handy Dan. Does this two-year trend suggest better or worse profitability during the current year?

Preparing a single-step income statement to evaluate the business (Obj. 3, 5, 6)

E5-10 The trial balance and adjustments columns of the work sheet of Western Detail Supply include the following accounts and balances at March 31, 19X2.

Using work sheet data to prepare a merchandiser's income statement and evaluate the business (Obj. 4, 6)

Account Title	Trial Balance Debit	Trial Balance Credit	Adjustments Debit	Adjustments Credit
Cash	2,000			
Accounts receivable	8,500		(a) 2,100	
Inventory	36,070			(b) 1,170
Supplies	13,000			(c) 8,600
Store fixtures	22,500			
Accumulated depreciation		11,250		(d) 2,250
Accounts payable		9,300		
Salary payable				(e) 1,200
Note payable, long-term		7,500		
K. Brownlee, capital		33,920		
K. Brownlee, withdrawals	45,000			
Sales revenue		213,000		(a) 2,100
Sales discounts	2,000			
Cost of goods sold	111,600		(b) 1,170	
Selling expense	21,050		(c) 5,200	
			(e) 1,200	
General expense	10,500		(c) 3,400	
			(d) 2,250	
Interest expense	2,750			
Total	274,970	274,970	15,320	15,320

Ending inventory at March 31, 19X1, was $34,500.

Required

Prepare the company's multiple-step income statement for the year ended March 31, 19X2. Compute the gross margin percentage and the inventory turnover for the year. Compare these figures with the gross margin percentage of 49 percent and the inventory turnover of 3.16 for 19X1. What does the two-year trend suggest about the company's sales pricing strategy this year?

Using work sheet data to prepare the closing entries of a merchandising business (Obj. 4)

E5-11 Use the data from Exercise 5-10 to journalize Western Detail Supply's closing entries at March 31, 19X2.

SERIAL EXERCISE

This exercise completes the Emily Schneider, Accountant, situation begun in Exercise 2-13 of Chapter 2 and extended to Exercise 3-14 of Chapter 3 and Exercise 4-11 of Chapter 4.

Accounting for merchandising and service transactions (Obj. 2, 4, 5)

E5-12 Emily Schneider's accounting practice now includes a great deal of systems consulting business. In conjunction with the consulting, Schneider has begun selling accounting software. During January the business completed these transactions:

Jan. 2   Completed a consulting engagement and received cash of $5,800.
2   Prepaid three months' office rent, $1,500.
7   Purchased accounting software on account for merchandise inventory, $4,000.
16   Paid employee salary, $1,400.
18   Sold accounting software on account, $1,100 (cost $700).
19   Consulted with a client for a fee of $900 on account.
21   Paid on account, $2,000.
24   Paid utilities, $300.
28   Sold accounting software for cash, $600 (cost $400).
31   Recorded these adjusting entries:
Accrued salary expense, $1,400.
Accounted for expiration of prepaid rent.
Depreciation of office furniture, $200.

Required

1. Open the following T-accounts in the ledger: Cash; Accounts Receivable; Accounting Software Inventory; Prepaid Rent; Accumulated Depreciation—Office Furniture; Accounts Payable; Salary Payable; Emily Schneider, Capital; Income Summary; Service Revenue; Sales Revenue; Cost of Goods Sold; Salary Expense; Rent Expense; Utilities Expense; and Depreciation Expense—Office Furniture.

2. Journalize and post the January transactions. Key all items by date. Compute each account balance, and denote the balance as *Bal.* Journalize and post the closing entries. Denote each closing amount as *Clo.* After posting, prove the equality of debits and credits in the ledger.

3. Prepare the January income statement of Emily Schneider, Accountant. Use the single-step format.

CHALLENGE EXERCISE

E5-13   Pharmacy Management Services, Inc. (PMSI), is a leading provider of products for workers' compensation insurance purposes. The company recently reported these figures.

Evaluating a company's profitability
(Obj. 1, 6)

PHARMACY MANAGEMENT SERVICES, INC., AND SUBSIDIARIES CONSOLIDATED STATEMENTS OF OPERATIONS FOR THE YEARS ENDED JULY 31, 1992 AND 1991		
	1992	**1991**
Sales	$106,115,984	$81,685,715
Cost of sales	76,424,328	60,981,847
Gross margin	29,691,656	20,703,868
Cost and expenses		
Selling, general and administrative	21,801,737	16,576,484
Depreciation and amortization	2,169,196	918,693
Restructuring charges	7,096,774	—
	31,067,707	17,495,177
Operating income (loss)	(1,376,051)	3,208,691
Other items (summarized)	(635,153)	(1,315,490)
Net income (loss)	$ (2,011,204)	$ 1,893,201

Required

Evaluate PMSI's operations during 1992 in comparison with 1991. Consider sales, gross margin, operating income, and net income. Track the gross margin percentage and inventory turnover in both years. PMSI's inventories at December 31, 1992, 1991, and 1990, were $7,766,322, $12,163,053, and $10,176,722, respectively. In the annual report PMSI's management describes the restructuring charges in 1992 as a one-time event. How does this additional information affect your evaluation?

PROBLEMS

(GROUP A)

P5-1A   Wal-Mart Stores, Inc., is the largest retailer in the world. The company has moved past Kmart, Sears, and other retailers by opening very large stores in out-of-the-way places. Another Wal-Mart advantage is its sophisticated perpetual inventory accounting system.

Explaining the accounting for inventory by a retailer
(Obj. 2)

Required

You are the manager of a Wal-Mart store in Columbus, Ohio. Write a memo to a new employee that explains how the company accounts for the purchase and sale of merchandise inventory.

P5-2A The following transactions occurred between Royal Medical Supply and Ridgewood Clinic during February of the current year.

Feb. 6 Royal Medical Supply sold $6,300 worth of merchandise to Ridgewood Clinic on terms of 2/10 n/30, FOB shipping point. Royal prepaid freight charges of $500 and included this amount in the invoice total. (Royal's entry to record the freight payment debits Accounts Receivable and credits Cash.) These goods cost Royal $4,100.

10 Ridgewood returned $900 of the merchandise purchased on February 6. Royal issued a credit memo for this amount and returned the goods to inventory (cost, $590).

15 Ridgewood paid $3,000 of the invoice amount owed to Royal for the February 6 purchase. This payment included none of the freight charge.

27 Ridgewood paid the remaining amount owed to Royal for the February 6 purchase.

Required

Journalize these transactions, first on the books of Ridgewood Clinic and second on the books of Royal Medical Supply.

Computing cost of goods sold and gross margin to evaluate the business
(Obj. 3, 6)

P5-3A Selected amounts from the accounting records of DeGaulle Lock and Safe Company had these balances at November 30 of the current year:

Accumulated depreciation—furniture and fixtures	$ 13,600
Note payable	14,000
Purchase discounts	600
Sales discounts	2,100
General expenses	19,300
Accounts receivable	7,200
Purchases of inventory	132,000
Selling expenses	8,800
Furniture and fixtures	37,200
Purchase returns and allowances	900
Salary payable	300
Charles DeGaulle, capital	52,800
Sales revenue	184,600
Sales returns and allowances	3,200
Inventory: November 30, 19X0	41,700
November 30, 19X1	41,500
Accounts payable	9,500
Cash	3,700
Freight in	1,600

Required

1. Show the computation of DeGaulle's net sales, cost of goods sold, and gross margin for the year ended November 30 of the current year.

2. Charles DeGaulle, owner of DeGaulle Lock and Safe Company, strives to earn a gross margin percentage of 25 percent. Did he achieve this goal?

3. Did the rate of inventory turnover reach the industry average of 3.4?

4. How will what you learned in this problem help you manage a business?

Preparing a merchandiser's financial statements
(Obj. 3, 5)

P5-4A Items from the accounts of Superior Milk Company follow, listed in alphabetical order.

Accounts payable	$ 16,950		Inventory: April 30	$ 69,350
Accounts receivable	43,700		May 31	65,520
Accumulated depreciation—			Note payable, long-term	45,000
office equipment	22,450		Office equipment	58,680
Accumulated depreciation—			Purchases of inventory	364,000
store equipment	16,000		Purchase discounts	1,990
Capital, April 30	74,620		Purchase returns	
Cash	7,890		and allowances	3,400
Cost of goods sold	?		Salary payable	2,840
General expenses	116,700		Sales discounts	10,400
Interest expense	5,400		Sales returns and	
Interest payable	1,100		allowances	18,030

Sales revenue.................................	$731,000	Supplies	$ 5,100
Selling expenses	132,900	Unearned sales revenue..............	13,800
Store equipment	88,000	Withdrawals	9,000

Required

1. Prepare the business's multiple-step income statement for May of the current year. In a separate schedule, show the computation of cost of goods sold.

2. Prepare the income statement in single-step format.

3. Prepare the balance sheet in report format at May 31 of the current year. Show your computation of the May 31 balance of Capital.

P5-5A The trial balance and adjustments columns of the work sheet of Biagonni Development Company include the following accounts and balances at November 30, 19X4:

Using accounting work sheet data to prepare financial statements and evaluate the business (Obj. 3, 5, 6)

Account Title	Trial Balance		Adjustments	
	Debit	Credit	Debit	Credit
Cash..	4,000			
Accounts receivable.........................	14,500		(a) 6,000	
Inventory	46,330		(b) 1,010	
Supplies	2,800			(c) 2,400
Furniture	39,600			
Accumulated depreciation		4,900		(d) 2,450
Accounts payable............................		12,600		
Salary payable.................................				(f) 1,000
Unearned sales revenue		13,570	(e) 6,700	
Note payable, long-term.................		15,000		
L. Biagonni, capital.........................		60,310		
L. Biagonni, drawing	42,000			
Sales revenue		164,000		(a) 6,000
				(e) 6,700
Sales returns	6,300			
Cost of goods sold...........................	72,170			(b) 1,010
Selling expense	28,080		(f) 1,000	
General expense	13,100		(c) 2,400	
			(d) 2,450	
Interest expense..............................	1,500			
Total..	270,380	270,380	19,560	19,560

Required

1. Inventory on hand at November 30, 19X3, was $52,650. Without entering the preceding data on a formal work sheet, prepare the company's multiple-step income statement for the year ended November 30, 19X4, and its November 30, 19X4, balance sheet. Show your computation of the ending balance of L. Biagonni, Capital.

2. Compute the gross margin percentage and the rate of inventory turnover for 19X4. For 19X3, Biagonni's gross margin percentage was 58 percent, and inventory turnover was 1.1. Does the two-year trend in these ratios suggest improvement or deterioration in profitability?

P5-6A Chenot Apparel's trial balance (at the top of page 210) pertains to December 31 of the current year.

Preparing a merchandiser's accounting work sheet (Obj. 4)

Additional data at December 31, 19XX:

a. Rent expense for the year, $10,200.

b. Store fixtures have an estimated useful life of 10 years and are expected to be worthless when they are retired from service.

c. Accrued salaries at December 31, $900.

d. Accrued interest expense at December 31, $360.

e. Inventory on hand at December 31, $73,200.

| CHENOT APPAREL |
| TRIAL BALANCE |
| DECEMBER 31, 19XX |

Cash	$ 1,270	
Accounts receivable	4,430	
Inventory	73,900	
Prepaid rent	4,400	
Store fixtures	22,100	
Accumulated depreciation		$ 8,380
Accounts payable		6,290
Salary payable		
Interest payable		
Note payable, long-term		18,000
Kay Chenot, capital		55,920
Kay Chenot, withdrawals	39,550	
Sales revenue		170,150
Cost of goods sold	67,870	
Salary expense	24,700	
Rent expense	7,700	
Advertising expense	4,510	
Utilities expense	3,880	
Depreciation expense		
Insurance expense	2,770	
Interest expense	1,660	
Total	$258,740	$258,740

Required

Complete Chenot's accounting work sheet for the year ended December 31 of the current year.

Journalizing the adjusting and closing entries of a merchandising business
(Obj. 4)

P5-7A   Refer to the data in Problem 5-6A.

Required

1. Journalize the adjusting and closing entries.
2. Determine the December 31 balance of Kay Chenot, Capital.

(GROUP B)

Explaining the operating cycle of a retailer
(Obj. 2)

P5-1B   EyeMasters is a regional chain of optical shops in the southwestern United States. They specialize in offering a large selection of eyeglass frames, and they provide while-you-wait service. EyeMasters has launched a vigorous advertising campaign promoting its two-for-the-price-of-one frame sales.

Required

EyeMasters expects to grow rapidly and increase its level of inventory. As the chief accountant of this company, you wish to install a perpetual inventory system. Write a memo to the company president to explain how that system would work.

Accounting for the purchase and sale of inventory
(Obj. 2)

P5-2B   The following transactions occurred between Advanced Hospital Supply and Scott & White Medical Clinic during June of the current year.

June 8   Advanced Hospital Supply sold $4,900 worth of merchandise to Scott & White Medical Clinic on terms of 2/10 n/30, FOB shipping point. Advanced Hospital Supply prepaid freight charges of $200 and included this amount in the invoice total. (Advanced's entry to record the freight payment debits Accounts Receivable and credits Cash.) These goods cost Advanced $2,100.

June 11 Scott & White returned $600 of the merchandise purchased on June 8. Advanced issued a credit memo for this amount and returned the goods to inventory (cost, $250).

   17 Scott & White paid $2,000 of the invoice amount owed to Advanced for the June 8 purchase. This payment included none of the freight charge.

   26 Scott & White paid the remaining amount owed to Advanced for the June 8 purchase.

Required

Journalize these transactions, first on the books of Scott & White Medical Clinic and second on the books of Advanced Hospital Supply.

P5-3B Selected amounts from the accounting records of Concord Supply Company at June 30, 19X9, were as follows:

Computing cost of goods sold and gross margin to evaluate the business
(Obj. 3, 6)

Selling expenses	$ 29,800
Equipment	44,700
Purchase discounts	1,300
Accumulated depreciation—equipment	6,900
Note payable	30,000
Sales discounts	3,400
General expenses	16,300
Accounts receivable	22,600
Accounts payable	23,800
Cash	13,600
Purchases of inventory	98,100
Freight in	4,300
Sales revenue	173,100
Purchase returns and allowances	1,400
Salary payable	1,800
John Wilfong, capital	36,000
Sales returns and allowances	12,100
Inventory: June 30, 19X8	33,800
June 30, 19X9	38,500

Required

1. Show the computation of Concord Supply's net sales, cost of goods sold, and gross margin for the year ended June 30, 19X9.

2. John Wilfong, owner of Concord Supply, strives to earn a gross margin percentage of 40 percent. Did he achieve this goal?

3. Did the rate of inventory turnover reach the industry average of 2.8?

4. How will what you learned in this problem help you manage a business?

P5-4B Items from the accounts of McDuff Entertainment Center are listed in alphabetical order:

Preparing a merchandiser's financial statements
(Obj. 3, 5)

Accounts payable	$127,380	Office equipment	$ 79,000
Accounts receivable	31,200	Purchases of inventory	373,100
Accumulated depreciation—		Purchase discounts	4,670
office equipment	9,500	Purchase returns	
Accumulated depreciation—		and allowances	10,190
store equipment	6,880	Salary payable	6,120
Capital, June 30	73,720	Sales discounts	8,350
Cash	12,320	Sales returns and	
Cost of goods sold	?	allowances	17,900
General expenses	75,830	Sales revenue	531,580
Interest expense	7,200	Selling expense	84,600
Interest payable	3,000	Store equipment	47,500
Inventory: June 30	190,060	Supplies	4,350
July 31	187,390	Unearned sales revenue	9,370
Note payable, long-term	160,000	Withdrawals	11,000

Required

1. Prepare the entity's multiple-step income statement for July of the current year. In a separate schedule, show the computation of cost of goods sold.
2. Prepare the income statement in single-step format.
3. Prepare the balance sheet in report format at July 31 of the current year. Show your computation of the July 31 balance of Capital.

Using accounting work sheet data to prepare financial statements and evaluate the business (Obj. 3, 5, 6)

P5-5B The trial balance and adjustments columns of the work sheet of Schweiz Coffee Company include the following accounts and balances at September 30, 19X5:

Account Title	Trial Balance Debit	Trial Balance Credit	Adjustments Debit	Adjustments Credit
Cash	7,300			
Accounts receivable.......................	4,360		(a) 1,800	
Inventory	29,630		(b) 2,100	
Supplies..	10,700			(c) 7,640
Equipment.......................................	79,450			
Accumulated depreciation.............		29,800		(d) 9,900
Accounts payable............................		13,800		
Salary payable				(f) 200
Unearned sales revenue.................		3,780	(e) 2,600	
Note payable, long-term................		10,000		
Lana Schweiz, capital		58,360		
Lana Schweiz, drawing...................	35,000			
Sales revenue		242,000		(a) 1,800
				(e) 2,600
Sales returns	3,100			
Cost of goods sold	125,600			(b) 2,100
Selling expense	40,600		(c) 7,640	
			(f) 200	
General expense	21,000		(d) 9,900	
Interest expense..............................	1,000			
Total..	357,740	357,740	24,240	24,240

Required

1. Inventory on hand at September 30, 19X4, was $32,580. Without entering the preceding data on a formal accounting work sheet, prepare the company's multiple-step income statement for the year ended September 30, 19X5, and its September 30, 19X5, balance sheet. Show your computation of the ending balance of Lana Schweiz, Capital.
2. Compute the gross margin percentage and the inventory turnover for 19X5. For 19X4, Schweiz's gross margin percentage was 57 percent, and the rate of inventory turnover was 4.2. Does the two-year trend in these ratios suggest improvement or deterioration in profitability?

Preparing a merchandiser's accounting work sheet (Obj. 4)

P5-6B Lopez Paint Company's trial balance (at the top of page 213) pertains to December 31 of the current year.

Additional data at December 31, 19XX:

a. Insurance expense for the year, $6,090.
b. Store fixtures have an estimated useful life of 10 years and are expected to be worthless when they are retired from service.
c. Accrued salaries at December 31, $1,260.
d. Accrued interest expense at December 31, $870.
e. Store supplies on hand at December 31, $760.
f. Inventory on hand at December 31, $99,650.

LOPEZ PAINT COMPANY TRIAL BALANCE DECEMBER 31, 19XX		
Cash...	$ 2,910	
Accounts receivable	6,560	
Inventory..	101,760	
Store supplies...................................	1,990	
Prepaid insurance.............................	3,200	
Store fixtures....................................	63,900	
Accumulated depreciation		$ 37,640
Accounts payable		29,770
Salary payable		
Interest payable................................		
Note payable, long-term		37,200
Hector Lopez, capital		63,120
Hector Lopez, withdrawals	36,300	
Sales revenue....................................		286,370
Cost of goods sold	161,090	
Salary expense	46,580	
Rent expense	14,630	
Utilities expense...............................	6,780	
Depreciation expense........................		
Insurance expense	5,300	
Store supplies expense		
Interest expense	3,100	
Total	$454,100	$454,100

Required

Complete Lopez's accounting work sheet for the year ended December 31 of the current year.

P5-7B Refer to the data in Problem 5-6B.

Required

1. Journalize the adjusting and closing entries.
2. Determine the December 31 balance of Hector Lopez, Capital.

Journalizing the adjusting and closing entries of a merchandising business (Obj. 4)

EXTENDING YOUR KNOWLEDGE

DECISION PROBLEMS

1. Nanette Rountree owns Heights Pharmacy, which has prospered during its second year of operation. In deciding whether to open another pharmacy in the area, Rountree has prepared the current financial statements of the business (on page 214).

Using the financial statements to decide on a business expansion (Obj. 5, 6)

Rountree recently read in an industry trade journal that a successful pharmacy meets all of these criteria:

a. Gross margin percentage is at least 50 percent.

b. Current ratio is at least 2.0.

c. Debt ratio is no higher than 0.50.

d. Inventory turnover is at least 4.0. Inventory at December 31, 19X0, was $19,200.

Basing her opinion on the entity's financial statement data, Rountree believes the business meets all four criteria. She plans to go ahead with her expansion plan and asks your advice on preparing the pharmacy's financial statements in accordance with generally accepted accounting principles. She assures you that all amounts are correct.

HEIGHTS PHARMACY
INCOME STATEMENT
FOR THE YEAR ENDED DECEMBER 31, 19X1

Sales revenue		$175,000
Gain on sale of land		24,600
Total revenue		199,600
Cost of goods sold		85,200
Gross margin		114,400
Operating expenses:		
Salary expense	$18,690	
Rent expense	12,000	
Interest expense	6,000	
Depreciation expense	4,900	
Utilities expense	2,330	
Supplies expense	1,400	
Total operating expense		45,320
Income from operations		69,080
Other expense:		
Sales discounts ($3,600) and returns ($7,100)		10,700
Net income		$ 58,380

HEIGHTS PHARMACY
STATEMENT OF OWNER'S EQUITY
FOR THE YEAR ENDED DECEMBER 31, 19X1

N. Rountree, capital, December 31, 19X0	$40,000
Add increases in owner's equity:	
Net income	58,380
N. Rountree, capital, December 31, 19X1	$98,380

HEIGHTS PHARMACY
BALANCE SHEET
DECEMBER 31, 19X1

Assets

Current:		
Cash	$ 5,320	
Accounts receivable	9,710	
Inventory	30,100	
Supplies	2,760	
Store fixtures	63,000	
Total current assets	110,890	
Other:		
Withdrawals	45,000	
Total assets	$155,890	

Liabilities

Current:		
Accumulated depreciation—store fixtures	$ 6,300	
Accounts payable	10,310	
Salary payable	900	
Total current liabilities	17,510	
Other:		
Note payable due in 90 days	40,000	
Total liabilities	57,510	

Owner's Equity

N. Rountree, capital	98,380	
Total liabilities and owner's equity	$155,890	

Required

1. Prepare a correct multiple-step income statement, a statement of owner's equity, and a balance sheet in report format.
2. On the basis of the corrected financial statements, compute correct measures of the four criteria listed in the trade journal.
3. Assuming that the criteria are valid, make a recommendation about whether to undertake the expansion at this time.

2A. Gayle Yip-Chuk has come to you for advice. Earlier this year she opened a record store in a plaza near the university she had attended. The store sells cassettes and compact discs for cash and on credit cards and, as a special feature, on credit to certain students. Many of the students at the university are co-op students who alternate school and work terms. Yip-Chuk allows co-op students to buy on credit while they are on a school term, with the understanding that they will pay their account shortly after starting a work term.

Understanding the operating cycle of a merchandiser **(Obj. 1, 3)**

   Business has been very good. Yip-Chuk is sure it is because of her competitive prices and the unique credit terms she offers. Her problem is that she is short of cash, and her loan with the bank has grown significantly. The bank manager has indicated that he wishes to reduce Yip-Chuk's line of credit because he is worried that she will get into financial difficulties.

Required

1. Explain to Yip-Chuk why you think she is in this predicament.
2. Yip-Chuk has asked you to explain her problem to the bank manager and to assist in asking for more credit. What might you say to the bank manager to assist Yip-Chuk?

B. The employees of Schneider Ltd. made an error when they performed the periodic inventory count at year end, October 31, 19X2. Part of one warehouse was not counted and therefore was not included in inventory.

Required

1. Indicate the effect of the inventory error on cost of goods sold, gross margin, and net income for the year ended October 31, 19X2.
2. Will the error affect cost of goods sold, gross margin, and net income in 19X3? If so, what will the effects be?

ETHICAL ISSUE

Kingston & Barnes, a partnership, makes all sales of industrial conveyor belts under terms of FOB shipping point. The company usually receives orders for sales approximately one week before shipping inventory to customers. For orders received late in December, Lisa Kingston and Meg Barnes, the owners, decide when to ship the goods. If profits are already at an acceptable level, they delay shipment until January. If profits are lagging behind expectations, they ship the goods during December.

Required

1. Under Kingston & Barnes's FOB policy, when should the company record a sale?
2. Do you approve or disapprove of Kingston & Barnes's means of deciding when to ship goods to customers? If you approve, give your reason. If you disapprove, identify a better way to decide when to ship goods. (There is no accounting rule against the Kingston & Barnes practice.)

FINANCIAL STATEMENT PROBLEMS

Closing entries for a merchandising corporation; evaluating ratio data
(Obj. 5)

1. This problem uses both the income statement (statement of income) and the balance sheet of Lands' End, Inc., in Appendix A. It will aid your understanding of the closing process of a business with inventories.

Required

1. Journalize Lands' End's closing entries for the year ended January 28, 1994. You will be unfamiliar with certain revenues and expenses, but treat them as either revenues or expenses. For example, treat "Cumulative effect of change in accounting for income taxes" as a revenue account.
2. What amount was closed to Retained Earnings?
3. Compute Lands' End's gross margin (gross profit) percentages and inventory turnover rates for the years ended January 28, 1994, and January 29, 1993. (In addition to the information in the Lands' End report in Appendix A, you will also need the January 31, 1992, Inventory balance, which was $122,558,000.) Did these ratio values of Lands' End improve, deteriorate, or hold steady during 1994? Summarize these results in a sentence.

Identifying items from an actual company's financial statements
(Obj. 5)

2. Obtain the annual report of a real company of your choosing. *Make sure that the company's balance sheet reports Inventory, Merchandise Inventory, or a similar asset category.* Answer the following questions about the company.

Required

1. What was the balance of total inventories reported on the balance sheet at the end of the current year? At the end of the preceding year? (If you selected a manufacturing company, you may observe more than one category of inventories. If so, name these categories and briefly explain what you think they mean.)
2. Give the company's journal entries to close Income Summary and Dividends.
3. Compute the company's gross margin percentage for the current year and for the preceding year. Did the gross margin percentage increase, decrease, or hold steady during the current year? Is that a favorable signal or an unfavorable signal about the company?
4. Compute the rate of inventory turnover for the current year. Would you expect your company's rate of inventory turnover to be higher or lower than that of a grocery chain such as Safeway or Kroger? Higher or lower than that of an aircraft manufacturer such as Boeing or McDonnell Douglas? State your reasoning.

Supplement

Accounting for Merchandise Inventory in a Periodic System

Purchase of Merchandise Inventory in the Periodic System

Some businesses find it uneconomical to invest in a computerized (perpetual) inventory system that keeps up-to-the-minute records of merchandise on hand and cost of goods sold. For example, a Taco Bell restaurant may experience such rapid inventory turnover that a perpetual inventory system costs more than it is worth. These types of business use a periodic system that relies on visual inspection for inventory control during the period. Accountants make entries to the Inventory account only in response to the physical count at the end of the period.

> *"A Taco Bell restaurant may experience such rapid inventory turnover that a perpetual inventory system costs more than it is worth."*

Purchases of Inventory

The periodic system uses the Inventory account. But purchases, purchase discounts, purchase returns and allowances, and transportation costs are recorded in separate accounts bearing these titles. Let's account for the purchase of the JVC goods in Exhibit 5S-1 by Austin Sound Stereo Center. The following entries record the purchase and payment on account within the discount period:

> **OBJECTIVE 2**
> Account for the purchase and sale of inventory

May 27	Purchases...	707.00	
	Accounts Payable		707.00
	Purchased inventory on account.		
June 10	Accounts Payable	707.00	
	Cash ($707.00 × 0.97)...................................		685.79
	Purchase Discounts ($707.00 × 0.03)...........		21.21
	Paid on account.		

Purchase Returns and Allowances

Suppose instead that prior to payment Austin Sound returned to JVC goods costing $70 and also received from JVC a purchase allowance of $10. Austin Sound would record these transactions as follows:

June 3	Accounts Payable	70.00	
	Purchase Returns and Allowances		70.00
	Returned inventory to seller.		
June 4	Accounts Payable	10.00	
	Purchase Returns and Allowances		10.00
	Received a purchase allowance.		

Key Point: A contra account always has a companion account with the opposite balance. Thus both Purchase Discounts and Purchase Returns and Allowances (credit balances) are reported with Purchases (debit balance) on the income statement.

During the period, the business records the cost of all inventory bought in the Purchases account. The balance of Purchases is a *gross* amount because it does not include subtractions for purchase discounts, returns, or allowances. **Net purchases** is the remainder computed by subtracting the contra accounts from Purchases:

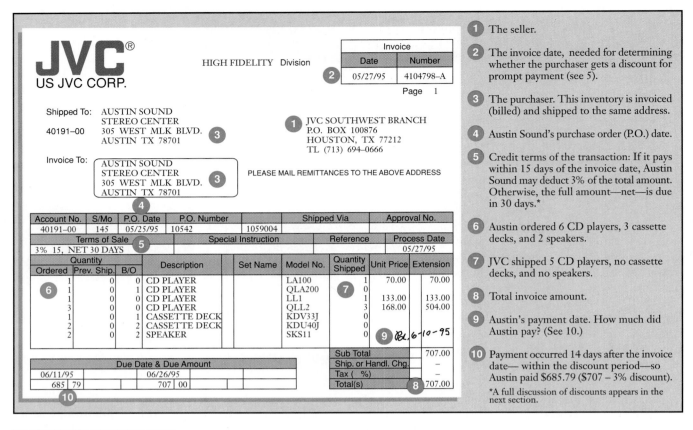

EXHIBIT 5S-1

An Invoice

Purchases (*debit* balance account)
– Purchase Discounts (*credit* balance account)
– Purchase Returns and Allowances (*credit* balance account)

= Net purchases (a *debit* subtotal, not a separate account)

Transportation Costs

Under the periodic system, costs to transport purchased inventory from seller to buyer are debited to a separate account, as shown for payment of a $60 freight bill:

June 1	Freight In	60.00	
	Cash		60.00
	Paid a freight bill.		

Sale of Inventory

Recording sales is streamlined in the periodic system. With no running record of inventory to maintain, we can record a $3,000 sale as follows:

June 1	Accounts Receivable	3,000	
	Sales Revenue		3,000
	Sale on account.		

No accompanying entry to Inventory and Cost of Goods Sold is required. Also, sales discounts and sales returns and allowances are recorded as shown for the perpetual system on page 184, but with no entry to Inventory and Cost of Goods Sold.

OBJECTIVE S3

Compute cost of goods sold

Cost of Goods Sold

Cost of goods sold (also called **cost of sales**) is the largest single expense of most businesses that sell merchandise, such as Sony and Austin Sound. It is the cost of the

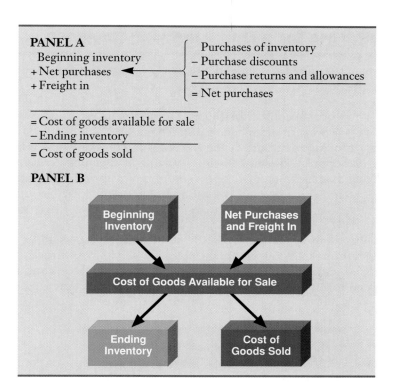

PANEL A

Beginning inventory
+ Net purchases ◄
+ Freight in

{
Purchases of inventory
− Purchase discounts
− Purchase returns and allowances

= Net purchases
}

= Cost of goods available for sale
− Ending inventory

= Cost of goods sold

PANEL B

inventory that the business has sold to customers. In a periodic system, cost of goods sold must be computed as in Exhibit 5S-2 and is *not* a ledger account. It is the residual left when we subtract ending inventory from the cost of goods available for sale.

Exhibit 5S-3 summarizes the first half of the chapter by showing Austin Sound's net sales revenue, cost of goods sold—including net purchases and freight in—and gross margin on the income statement for the periodic system. (All amounts are assumed).

EXHIBIT 5S-3
Partial Income Statement

AUSTIN SOUND STEREO CENTER
INCOME STATEMENT
FOR THE YEAR ENDED DECEMBER 31, 19X6

PANEL A—Detailed Gross Margin Section—Often Required by Management

Sales revenue			$169,300	
Less: Sales discounts		$ 1,400		
Sales returns and allowances		2,000	3,400	
Net sales				$165,900
Cost of goods sold:				
Beginning inventory			$ 38,600	
Purchases		$91,400		
Less: Purchase discounts	$3,000			
Purchase returns and allowances	1,200	4,200		
Net purchases			87,200	
Freight in			5,200	
Cost of goods available for sale			131,000	
Less: Ending inventory			40,200	
Cost of goods sold				90,800
Gross margin				$ 75,100

PANEL B—Summary Gross Margin Section—Most Common in Annual Reports to Outsiders

Net sales	$165,900
Cost of goods sold	90,800
Gross margin	$ 75,100

Short Exercise: Assume:
Purchases $265,000
Sales 463,000
Gross Margin 200,000
Purchase Returns
  and Allowances 2,600
Beginning Inventory.. 12,000
Sales Returns
  and Allowances 4,500
Purchase Discounts ... 2,400
Ending Inventory ...... ?
Sales Discounts.......... 8,500
How much is Ending Inventory? *A:* $22,000. Set up the income statement through gross margin because many of the unknowns will be easier to compute.

The Adjusting and Closing Process for a Merchandising Business

Key Point: Recall that Purchases (not Inventory) was debited for merchandise purchased. In the periodic system, no entries are made to the Inventory account for purchases or sales. Beginning inventory remains on the books and on the trial balance until ending inventory replaces it at the end of the period.

◀▥ ◀▥ ◀▥ This work sheet is slightly different from the one introduced in the Chapter 4 acetates—it contains 4 pairs of columns, not 5.

Key Point: If you were preparing a work sheet, you could omit the adjusted trial balance columns. Once you understand the mechanics of the work sheet, you can take a trial balance amount, add or subtract the adjustments, and extend the new amount to either the income statement or balance sheet columns.

A merchandising business adjusts and closes the accounts much as a service entity does. The steps of this end-of-period process are the same: If a work sheet is used, the trial balance is entered and the work sheet completed to determine net income or net loss. The work sheet provides the data for journalizing the adjusting and closing entries and for preparing the financial statements.

The Inventory account affects the adjusting and closing entries of a merchandiser. At the end of the period, before any adjusting or closing entries, the Inventory account balance is still the cost of the inventory that was on hand at the beginning date. It is necessary to remove this beginning balance and replace it with the cost of the ending inventory. Various techniques might be used to bring the inventory records up to date.

To illustrate a merchandiser's adjusting and closing process under the periodic inventory system, let's use Austin Sound's December 31, 19X6, trial balance in Exhibit 5S-4. All the new accounts—Inventory, Freight In, and the contra accounts—are highlighted for emphasis. Inventory is the only account that is affected by the new closing procedures. The additional data item (h) gives the ending inventory figure $40,200.

Accounting Work Sheet of a Merchandising Business

The Exhibit 5S-5 work sheet is similar to the work sheets we have seen so far, but a few differences appear. This work sheet does not include adjusted trial balance columns. ◀▥ In most accounting systems, a single operation combines trial balance amounts with the adjustments and extends the adjusted balances directly to the income statement and balance sheet columns. Therefore, to reduce clutter, the adjusted trial balance columns are omitted.

ACCOUNT TITLE COLUMNS The trial balance lists a number of accounts without balances. Ordinarily, these accounts are affected by the adjusting process. Examples include Interest Receivable, Interest Payable, and Depreciation Expense. The accounts are listed in the order they appear in the ledger. If additional accounts are needed, they can be written in at the bottom, above net income.

TRIAL BALANCE COLUMNS Examine the Inventory account, $38,600 in the trial balance. This $38,600 is the cost of the beginning inventory. The work sheet is designed to replace this outdated amount with the new ending balance, which in our example is $40,200 (additional data item (h) in Exhibit 5S-4). As we shall see, this task is accomplished later in the columns for the income statement and the balance sheet.

ADJUSTMENTS COLUMNS The adjustments are similar to those discussed in Chapters 3 and 4. They may be entered in any order desired. The debit amount of each entry should equal the credit amount, and total debits should equal total credits.

INCOME STATEMENT COLUMNS The income statement columns contain adjusted amounts for the revenues and the expenses. Sales Revenue, for example, is $169,300, which includes the $1,300 adjustment.

You may be wondering why the two inventory amounts appear in the income statement columns. The reason is that both beginning inventory and ending inventory enter the computation of cost of goods sold. *Placement of beginning inventory*

AUSTIN SOUND STEREO CENTER
TRIAL BALANCE
DECEMBER 31, 19X6

Cash	$ 2,850	
Accounts receivable	4,600	
Note receivable, current	8,000	
Interest receivable		
Inventory	**38,600**	
Supplies	650	
Prepaid insurance	1,200	
Furniture and fixtures	33,200	
Accumulated depreciation		$ 2,400
Accounts payable		47,000
Unearned sales revenue		2,000
Wages payable		
Interest payable		
Note payable, long-term		12,600
C. Ernest, capital		25,900
C. Ernest, withdrawals	54,100	
Sales revenue		**168,000**
Sales discounts	**1,400**	
Sales returns and allowances	**2,000**	
Interest revenue		600
Purchases	**91,400**	
Purchase discounts		**3,000**
Purchase returns and allowances		**1,200**
Freight in	**5,200**	
Wage expense	9,800	
Rent expense	8,400	
Depreciation expense		
Insurance expense		
Supplies expense		
Interest expense	1,300	
Total	$262,700	$262,700

Additional data at December 31, 19X6:

a. Interest revenue earned but not yet collected, $400.
b. Supplies on hand, $100.
c. Prepaid insurance expired during the year, $1,000.
d. Depreciation, $600.
e. Unearned sales revenue earned during the year, $1,300.
f. Accrued wage expense, $400.
g. Accrued interest expense, $200.
h. Inventory on hand, $40,200.

($38,600) in the work sheet's income statement debit column has the effect of adding begin-
ning inventory in computing cost of goods sold. Placing ending inventory ($40,200) in the
credit column has the opposite effect.

Purchases and Freight In appear in the debit column because they are added in
computing cost of goods sold. Purchase Discounts and Purchase Returns and Allowances appear as credits because they are subtracted. All these items are used to
compute cost of goods sold—$90,800 on the income statement in Exhibit 5S-6.

Account Title	Trial Balance Debit	Trial Balance Credit	Adjustments Debit	Adjustments Credit	Income Statement Debit	Income Statement Credit	Balance Sheet Debit	Balance Sheet Credit
Cash	2,850						2,850	
Accounts receivable	4,600						4,600	
Note receivable, current	8,000						8,000	
Interest receivable			(a) 400				400	
Inventory	**38,600**				38,600	40,200	40,200	
Supplies	650			(b) 550			100	
Prepaid insurance	1,200			(c) 1,000			200	
Furniture and fixtures	33,200						33,200	
Accumulated depreciation		2,400		(d) 600				3,000
Accounts payable		47,000						47,000
Unearned sales revenue		2,000	(e) 1,300					700
Wages payable				(f) 400				400
Interest payable				(g) 200				200
Note payable, long-term		12,600						12,600
C. Ernest, capital		25,900						25,900
C. Ernest, withdrawals	54,100						54,100	
Sales revenue		168,000		(e) 1,300		169,300		
Sales discounts	1,400				1,400			
Sales returns and allowances	2,000				2,000			
Interest revenue		600		(a) 400		1,000		
Purchases	**91,400**				91,400			
Purchase discounts		**3,000**				3,000		
Purchase returns and allowances		**1,200**				1,200		
Freight in	**5,200**				5,200			
Wage expense	9,800		(f) 400		10,200			
Rent expense	8,400				8,400			
Depreciation expense			(d) 600		600			
Insurance expense			(c) 1,000		1,000			
Supplies expense			(b) 550		550			
Interest expense	1,300		(g) 200		1,500			
	262,700	262,700	4,450	4,450	160,850	214,700	143,650	89,800
Net income					53,850			53,850
					214,700	214,700	143,650	143,650

EXHIBIT 5S-5
Accounting Work Sheet

The income statement column subtotals on the work sheet indicate whether the business earned net income or incurred a net loss. If total credits are greater, the result is net income, as shown in Exhibit 5S-5. If total debits are greater, a net loss has occurred.

BALANCE SHEET COLUMNS The only new item on the balance sheet is inventory. The balance listed is the ending amount of $40,200, which is determined by a physical count of inventory on hand at the end of the period.

Financial Statements of a Merchandising Business

OBJECTIVE S5

Prepare a merchandiser's financial statements

Exhibit 5S-6 presents Austin Sound's financial statements. The *income statement* through gross margin repeats Exhibit 5S-3. This information is followed by the *operating expenses*, expenses other than cost of goods sold that are incurred in the entity's major line of business—merchandising. Wage expense is Austin Sound's cost of

AUSTIN SOUND STEREO CENTER
INCOME STATEMENT
FOR THE YEAR ENDED DECEMBER 31, 19X6

Sales revenue			$169,300
Less: Sales discounts		$ 1,400	
Sales returns and allowances		2,000	3,400
Net sales revenue			$165,900
Cost of goods sold:			
Beginning inventory		$ 38,600	
Purchases		$ 91,400	
Less: Purchase discounts	$ 3,000		
Purchase returns and allowances	1,200	4,200	
Net purchases		87,200	
Freight in		5,200	
Cost of goods available for sale		131,000	
Less: Ending inventory		40,200	
Cost of goods sold			90,800
Gross margin			75,100
Operating expenses:			
Wage expense		10,200	
Rent expense		8,400	
Insurance expense		1,000	
Depreciation expense		600	
Supplies expense		550	20,750
Income from operations			54,350
Other revenue and (expense):			
Interest revenue		1,000	
Interest expense		(1,500)	(500)
Net income			$ 53,850

AUSTIN SOUND STEREO CENTER
STATEMENT OF OWNER'S EQUITY
FOR THE YEAR ENDED DECEMBER 31, 19X6

C. Ernest, capital, December 31, 19X5	$25,900
Add: Net income	53,850
	79,750
Less: Withdrawals	54,100
C. Ernest, capital, December 31, 19X6	$25,650

AUSTIN SOUND STEREO CENTER
BALANCE SHEET
DECEMBER 31, 19X6

Assets			Liabilities		
Current:			**Current:**		
Cash		$ 2,850	Accounts payable		$47,000
Accounts receivable		4,600	Unearned sales revenue		700
Note receivable		8,000	Wages payable		400
Interest receivable		400	Interest payable		200
Inventory		40,200	Total current liabilities		48,300
Prepaid insurance		200	**Long-term:**		
Supplies		100	Note payable		12,600
Total current assets		56,350	Total liabilities		60,900
Plant:					
Furniture and fixtures	$33,200		**Owner's Equity**		
Less: Accumulated			C. Ernest, capital		25,650
depreciation	3,000	30,200	Total liabilities and		
Total assets		$86,550	owner's equity		$86,550

employing workers. Rent is the cost of obtaining store space. Insurance helps to protect the inventory. Store furniture and fixtures wear out; the expense is depreciation. Supplies expense is the cost of stationery, mailing, and the like, used in operations.

Many companies report their operating expenses in two categories. *Selling expenses* are those expenses related to marketing the company's products—sales salaries; sales commissions; advertising; depreciation, rent, utilities, and property taxes on store buildings; depreciation on store furniture; delivery expense; and so on. *General expenses* include office expenses, such as the salaries of office employees; and depreciation, rent, utilities, and property taxes on the home office building.

Gross margin minus operating expenses and plus any other operating revenues equals *operating income*, or *income from operations*. As was true for Sony, many businesspeople view operating income as the most reliable indicator of a business's success because it measures the entity's major ongoing activities.

The last section of Austin Sound's income statement is *other revenue and expenses*, which is handled the same way in both inventory systems.

Adjusting and Closing Entries for a Merchandising Business

◀▥▥ ◀▥▥ ◀▥▥ The adjusting and closing entries here are very similar to those discussed in Chapter 4, pp. 138–143. The closing entries also clear the Purchases, Purchase Discounts, and Purchase Returns and Allowances accounts for accumulating costs in the next period.

Exhibit 5S-7 presents Austin Sound's adjusting entries. ◀▥ The closing entries in the exhibit include two new effects. The first closing entry debits Inventory for the ending balance of $40,200 and also debits the revenue and expense accounts that have credit balances. For Austin Sound these accounts are Sales Revenue, Interest Revenue, Purchase Discounts, and Purchase Returns and Allowances. The offsetting credit of $214,700 transfers their sum to Income Summary. This amount comes from the credit column of the income statement on the work sheet (Exhibit 5S-5).

The second closing entry includes a credit to Inventory for its beginning balance and credits to the revenue and expense accounts with debit balances. These are Sales Discounts, Sales Returns and Allowances, Purchases, Freight In, and the expense accounts. The offsetting $160,850 debit to Income Summary comes from the debit column of the income statement on the work sheet. Some accountants prefer to include these Inventory entries among the adjustments.

The entries to the Inventory account deserve additional explanation. Recall that before the closing process Inventory still has the period's beginning balance. At the end of the period, this balance is one year old and must be replaced with the ending balance in order to prepare the financial statements at December 31, 19X6. The closing entries give Inventory its correct ending balance of $40,200, as shown here:

Inventory					
Jan. 1	Bal.	38,600	Dec. 31	Clo.	38,600
Dec. 31	Clo.	40,200			
Dec. 31	Bal.	40,200			

The inventory amounts for these entries are taken directly from the income statement columns of the work sheet. The offsetting debits and credits to Income Summary in these entries also serve to record the dollar amount of cost of goods sold in the accounts. Income Summary contains the cost of goods sold amount after Purchases and its related contra accounts and Freight In are closed.[1]

---

[1]Some accountants make the inventory entries as adjustments rather than as part of the closing process. The adjusing-entry approach adds these adjustments (shifted out of the closing entries):

Adjusting Entries

Dec. 31	Income Summary...	38,600	
	Inventory (beginning balance)...............		38,600
31	Inventory (ending balance).............................	40,200	
	Income Summary...................................		40,200

When these entries are posted, the Inventory account will look exactly as shown above, except that the journal references will be "Adj." instead of "Clo." The financial statements are unaffected by the approach used for these inventory entries.

Journal

Adjusting Entries

a.	Dec. 31	Interest Receivable	400	
		Interest Revenue		400
b.	31	Supplies Expense ($650 - $100)	550	
		Supplies		550
c.	31	Insurance Expense	1,000	
		Prepaid Insurance		1,000
d.	31	Depreciation Expense	600	
		Accumulated Depreciation		600
e.	31	Unearned Sales Revenue	1,300	
		Sales Revenue		1,300
f.	31	Wage Expense	400	
		Wages Payable		400
g.	31	Interest Expense	200	
		Interest Payable		200

Closing Entries

	Dec. 31	Inventory (ending balance)...................................	40,200	
		Sales Revenue	169,300	
		Interest Revenue	1,000 ·	
		Purchase Discounts	3,000	
		Purchase Returns and Allowances........................	1,200	
		Income Summary		214,700
	31	Income Summary	160,850	
		Inventory (beginning balance)......................		38,600
		Sales Discounts		1,400
		Sales Returns and Allowances.......................		2,000
		Purchases..		91,400
		Freight In		5,200
		Wage Expense		10,200
		Rent Expense		8,400
		Depreciation Expense....................................		600
		Insurance Expense		1,000
		Supplies Expense..		550
		Interest Expense...		1,500
	31	Income Summary ($214,700 - $160,850)	53,850	
		C. Ernest, Capital		53,850
	31	C. Ernest, Capital...	54,100	
		C. Ernest, Withdrawals		54,100

finance Kit effectul

Key Point: Closing entries for a merchandising company accomplish the same tasks as in Chapter 4 and also replace beginning inventory with the ending inventory balance. The debit and credit to Income Summary match the Income Statement column totals from the work sheet.

Study Exhibits 5S-5, 5S-6, and 5S-7 carefully because they illustrate the entire end-of-period process that leads to the financial statements. As you progress through this book, you may want to refer to these exhibits to refresh your understanding of the adjusting and closing process for a merchandising business.

Net sales, cost of goods sold, operating income, and net income are unaffected by the choice of inventory system. You can prove this by comparing Austin Sound's financial statements given in Exhibit 5S-6 with the corresponding statements in Exhibit 5-9. The only differences appear in the cost-of-goods-sold section of the income statement, and those differences are unimportant. In fact, virtually all companies report cost of goods sold in streamlined fashion, as shown for Sony in Exhibit 5-1 and for Austin Sound in Exhibit 5-9.

The accompanying trial balance pertains to Jan King Distributing Company.

JAN KING DISTRIBUTING COMPANY
TRIAL BALANCE
DECEMBER 31, 19X3

Cash	$ 5,670	
Accounts receivable	37,100	
Inventory	60,500	
Supplies	3,930	
Prepaid rent	6,000	
Furniture and fixtures	26,500	
Accumulated depreciation		$ 21,200
Accounts payable		46,340
Salary payable		
Interest payable		
Unearned sales revenue		3,500
Note payable, long-term		35,000
Jan King, capital		23,680
Jan King, withdrawals	48,000	
Sales revenue		346,700
Sales discounts	10,300	
Sales returns and allowances	8,200	
Purchases	175,900	
Purchase discounts		6,000
Purchase returns and allowances		7,430
Freight in	9,300	
Salary expense	82,750	
Rent expense	7,000	
Depreciation expense		
Utilities expense	5,800	
Supplies expense		
Interest expense	2,900	
Total	$489,850	$489,850

Additional data at December 31, 19X3:
a. Supplies used during the year, $2,580.
b. Prepaid rent in force, $1,000.
c. Unearned sales revenue still not earned, $2,400. The company expects to earn this amount during the next few months.
d. Depreciation. The furniture and fixtures' estimated useful life is 10 years, and they are expected to be worthless when they are retired from service.
e. Accrued salaries, $1,300.
f. Accrued interest expense, $600.
g. Inventory on hand, $65,800.

Required

1. Enter the trial balance on an accounting work sheet and complete the work sheet.
2. Journalize the adjusting and closing entries at December 31. Post to the Income Summary account as an accuracy check on the entries affecting that account. The credit balance closed out of Income Summary should equal net income computed on the work sheet.
3. Prepare the company's multiple-step income statement, statement of owner's equity, and balance sheet in account format.
4. Compute the inventory turnover for 19X3. Turnover for 19X2 was 2.1 Would you expect Jan King Distributing Company to be more profitable or less profitable in 19X3 than in 19X2? Give your reason.

SOLUTION TO REVIEW PROBLEM

Requirement 1

JAN KING DISTRIBUTING COMPANY
ACCOUNTING WORK SHEET
FOR THE YEAR ENDED DECEMBER 31, 19X3

Account Title	Trial Balance Debit	Trial Balance Credit	Adjustments Debit	Adjustments Credit	Income Statement Debit	Income Statement Credit	Balance Sheet Debit	Balance Sheet Credit
Cash	5,670						5,670	
Accounts receivable	37,100						37,100	
Inventory	60,500				60,500	65,800	65,800	
Supplies	3,930			(a) 2,580			1,350	
Prepaid rent	6,000			(b) 5,000			1,000	
Furniture and fixtures	26,500						26,500	
Accumulated depreciation		21,200		(d) 2,650				23,850
Accounts payable		46,340						46,340
Salary payable				(e) 1,300				1,300
Interest payable				(f) 600				600
Unearned sales revenue		3,500	(c) 1,100					2,400
Note payable, long-term		35,000						35,000
Jan King, capital		23,680						23,680
Jan King, withdrawals	48,000						48,000	
Sales revenue		346,700		(c) 1,100		347,800		
Sales discounts	10,300				10,300			
Sales returns and allowances	8,200				8,200			
Purchases	175,900				175,900			
Purchase discounts		6,000				6,000		
Purchase returns and allowances		7,430				7,430		
Freight in	9,300				9,300			
Salary expense	82,750		(e) 1,300		84,050			
Rent expense	7,000		(b) 5,000		12,000			
Depreciation expense			(d) 2,650		2,650			
Utilities expense	5,800				5,800			
Supplies expense			(a) 2,580		2,580			
Interest expense	2,900		(f) 600		3,500			
	489,850	489,850	13,230	13,230	374,780	427,030	185,420	133,170
Net income					52,250			52,250
					427,030	427,030	185,420	185,420

Requirement 2

Adjusting Entries

19X3

			Debit	Credit
Dec. 31	Supplies Expense		2,580	
	Supplies			2,580
31	Rent Expense		5,000	
	Prepaid Rent			5,000
31	Unearned Sales Revenue		1,100	
	Sales Revenue			1,100
31	Depreciation Expense ($26,500/10)		2,650	
	Accumulated Depreciation			2,650
31	Salary Expense		1,300	
	Salary Payable			1,300
31	Interest Expense		600	
	Interest Payable			600

Closing Entries

19X3

			Debit	Credit
Dec. 31	Inventory (ending balance)		65,800	
	Sales Revenue		347,800	
	Purchase Discounts		6,000	
	Purchase Returns and Allowances		7,430	
	Income Summary			427,030
31	Income Summary		374,780	
	Inventory (beginning balance)			60,500
	Sales Discounts			10,300
	Sales Returns and Allowances			8,200
	Purchases			175,900
	Freight In			9,300
	Salary Expense			84,050
	Rent Expense			12,000
	Depreciation Expense			2,650
	Utilities Expense			5,800
	Supplies Expense			2,580
	Interest Expense			3,500
31	Income Summary ($427,030 − $374,780)		52,250	
	Jan King, Capital			52,250
31	Jan King, Capital		48,000	
	Jan King, Withdrawals			48,000

Income Summary

Clo.	374,780	Clo.	427,030
Clo.	52,250	Bal.	52,250

Requirement 3

JAN KING DISTRIBUTING COMPANY
INCOME STATEMENT
FOR THE YEAR ENDED DECEMBER 31, 19X3

Sales revenue			$347,800
Less: Sales discounts		$ 10,300	
Sales returns and allowances		8,200	18,500
Net sales revenue			$329,300
Cost of goods sold:			
Beginning inventory			$ 60,500
Purchases		$175,900	
Less: Purchase discounts	$6,000		
Purchase returns and allowances	7,430	13,430	
Net purchases			162,470
Freight in			9,300
Cost of goods available for sale			232,270
Less: Ending inventory			65,800
Cost of goods sold			166,470
Gross margin			162,830
Operating expenses:			
Salary expense			84,050
Rent expense			12,000
Utilities expense			5,800
Depreciation expense			2,650
Supplies expense			2,580 107,080
Income from operations			55,750
Other expense:			
Interest expense			3,500
Net income			$ 52,250

JAN KING DISTRIBUTING COMPANY
STATEMENT OF OWNER'S EQUITY
FOR THE YEAR ENDED DECEMBER 31, 19X3

Jan King, capital, December 31, 19X2	$23,680
Add: Net income	52,250
	75,930
Less: Withdrawals	48,000
Jan King, capital, December 31, 19X3	$27,930

JAN KING DISTRIBUTING COMPANY
BALANCE SHEET
DECEMBER 31, 19X3

Assets			**Liabilities**	
Current:			Current:	
Cash	$ 5,670		Accounts payable	$ 46,340
Accounts receivable	37,100		Salary payable	1,300
Inventory	65,800		Interest payable	600
Supplies	1,350		Unearned sales revenue	2,400
Prepaid rent	1,000		Total current liabilities	50,640
Total current assets	110,920		Long term:	
Plant:			Note payable	35,000
Furniture and fixtures	$26,500		Total liabilities	85,640
Less: Accumulated depreciation	23,850	2,650	**Owner's Equity**	
			Jan King, capital	27,930
			Total liabilities and	
Total assets		$113,570	owner's equity	$113,570

$$\text{Inventory turnover} = \frac{\text{Cost of goods sold}}{\text{Average inventory}} = \frac{\$166,470}{(\$60,500 + \$65,800)/2} = 2.6$$

The increase in the rate of inventory from 2.1 to 2.6 suggests higher profits in 19X3 than in 19X2.

SUPPLEMENT PROBLEMS

Accounting for the purchase and sale of inventory
(Obj. S2)

P5S-1 The following transactions occurred between Glendale Medical Supply and HealthCare Clinic during February of the current year.

Feb. 6 Glendale Medical Supply sold $5,300 worth of merchandise to HealthCare Clinic on terms of 2/10 n/30, FOB shipping point. Glendale prepaid freight charges of $300 and included this amount in the invoice total. (Glendale's entry to record the freight payment debits Accounts Receivable and credits Cash.)

10 HealthCare returned $900 of the merchandise purchased on February 6. Glendale issued a credit memo for this amount.

15 HealthCare paid $3,000 of the invoice amount owed to Glendale for the February 6 purchase. This payment included none of the freight charge.

27 HealthCare paid the remaining amount owed to Glendale for the February 6 purchase.

Required

Journalize these transactions, first on the books of HealthCare Clinic and second on the books of Glendale Medical Supply.

Preparing a merchandiser's accounting work sheet, financial statements, and adjusting and closing entries
(Obj. S3, S4, S5)

P5S-2 The year-end trial balance of Bliss Sales Company (at the top of page 231) pertains to March 31 of the current year.

Additional data at March 31, 19XX:

a. Accrued interest revenue, $1,030.

b. Insurance expense for the year, $3,000.

c. Furniture has an estimated useful life of 6 years. Its value is expected to be zero when it is retired from service.

d. Unearned sales revenue still unearned, $8,200.

e. Accrued salaries, $1,200.

f. Accrued sales commissions, $1,700.

g. Inventory on hand, $133,200.

Required

1. Enter the trial balance on an accounting work sheet, and complete the work sheet for the year ended March 31 of the current year.

2. Prepare the company's multiple-step income statement and statement of owner's equity for the year ended March 31 of the current year. Also prepare its balance sheet at that date. Long-term notes receivable should be reported on the balance sheet between current assets and plant assets in a separate section labeled Investments.

3. Journalize the adjusting and closing entries at March 31.

4. Post to the Mark Bliss, Capital account and to the Income Summary account as an accuracy check on the adjusting and closing process.

```
                BLISS SALES COMPANY
                  TRIAL BALANCE
                  MARCH 31, 19XX
```

Cash	$ 7,880	
Notes receivable, current	12,400	
Interest receivable....................................		
Inventory	130,050	
Prepaid insurance	3,600	
Notes receivable, long-term.....................	62,000	
Furniture	6,000	
Accumulated depreciation.........................		$ 4,000
Accounts payable		12,220
Sales commission payable..........................		
Salary payable		
Unearned sales revenue............................		9,610
Mark Bliss, capital		172,780
Mark Bliss, withdrawals...........................	66,040	
Sales revenue		440,000
Sales discounts...	4,800	
Sales returns and allowances	11,300	
Interest revenue.......................................		8,600
Purchases	233,000	
Purchase discounts		3,100
Purchase returns and allowances..............		7,600
Freight in	10,000	
Sales commission expense	78,300	
Salary expense..	24,700	
Rent expense..	6,000	
Utilities expense	1,840	
Depreciation expense		
Insurance expense.....................................		
Total..	$657,910	$657,910

Chapter 6
Accounting Information Systems

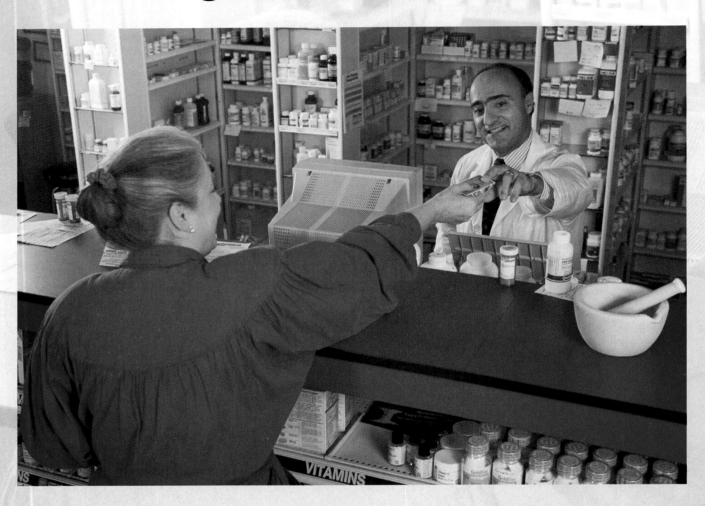

After studying this chapter, you should be able to

1. Describe the features of an effective accounting information system

2. Understand how computerized and manual accounting systems are used

3. Understand how spreadsheets are used in accounting

4. Use the sales journal, the cash receipts journal, and the accounts receivable subsidiary ledger

5. Use the purchases journal, the cash disbursements journal, and the accounts payable subsidiary ledger

> *After 30 years in the pharmacy business, our office is finally organized, our account receivable figures are at our fingertips, our payroll is simple to compute, and our bills go out promptly—all thanks to this new computer system!*

BOB AND MAUREEN HALLISEY, OWNERS OF HALLISEY'S PHARMACY

Bob and Maureen Hallisey, owners of Hallisey's Pharmacy in Old Saybrook, Connecticut, computerized their business 10 years ago. For 20 years they had used a manual accounting system. When asked, "Why did you computerize?" they replied, "For efficiency and speed."

The Halliseys began with a now-obsolete computerized accounting software package. Four years ago, their hardware failed. When they replaced it, they switched to the Business Works Accounting System. The ease of use and of generating accounting reports sold them on the new package.

Now they can analyze cash requirements and track slow-paying customers on a daily basis. The new software also generates the end-of-year information for their financial statements and income tax return. A key report shows sales by product. The Halliseys can identify which products they need to advertise, and they can set prices to achieve a target gross profit percentage on each product. By saving time and helping the Halliseys make better business decisions, their new accounting system has paid for itself many times over.

• • • • •

Hallisey's Pharmacy has more than an accounting system. It has an accounting *information* system. An **accounting information system** is the combination of personnel, records, and procedures that a business uses to meet its need for financial data. The word *information* in the title indicates that the Halliseys can get more than the routine financial statements from their system. Special management reports, such as sales by product and cash-flow projections, provide valuable information for their business decisions.

We have already been using an accounting information system in this text. That simple accounting system consists of two basic components:

● A general journal
● A general ledger

The journal and the ledger we have been using are the *general* journal and the *general* ledger. Every accounting system has these components, but this simple system can efficiently handle only a few transactions per period. Accounting systems cope with heavy transaction loads in two ways: computerization and specialization. We *computerize* to journalize, post, and prepare reports faster and more reliably. *Specialization* comes when we deal with similar transactions in groups to speed the process. We will explore special journals in the second half of this chapter.

Features of an Effective Accounting Information System

OBJECTIVE 1

Describe the features of an effective accounting information system

Several design features make accounting systems run efficiently. A good system—whether computerized or manual—includes four features: control, compatibility, flexibility, and a favorable cost/benefit relationship.

Control

Real-World Example: Computers can make an information system less controllable because many employees have access to a terminal. At a Bloomingdale's store, it would be risky for all employees who use the computer to gain access to customer accounts. An unauthorized employee could change a customer's account or learn confidential information about the customer. Hence, access codes limit access to certain information. Source documents should support all sensitive changes to computer files.

Managers need *control* over operations. *Internal controls* are the methods and procedures used to authorize transactions and safeguard assets. For example, in companies such as Coca-Cola, Dow Chemical, and Kinko's, managers exert tight control over cash disbursements to avoid theft through unauthorized payments. Also, keeping accurate records of accounts receivable is the only way for VISA, MasterCard, Discover, and other credit-card companies to ensure that customers are billed and collections are received on time.

Compatibility

A *compatible* system is one that works smoothly with the business's operations, personnel, and organizational structure. An example is Bank of America, which is organized into a network of branch offices. Bank of America's top managers want to know revenues in each region where the bank does business. They also want to analyze the bank's loans in different geographic regions. If revenues and loans in California or Nevada are lagging, the managers can concentrate their efforts in that region. They may relocate some branch offices, hire new personnel, or purchase a successful local bank to increase their revenues and net income. A compatible accounting *information* system conforms to the particular needs of the business.

Flexibility

Organizations evolve. They develop new products, sell off unprofitable operations and acquire new ones, and adjust employee pay scales. Changes in the business often call for changes in the accounting system. A well-designed system meets the *flexibility* guideline by accommodating changes without needing a complete overhaul. Consider Monsanto Company's acquisition of the pharmaceuticals firm Searle, including Searle's Nutrasweet division. Monsanto's accounting system had the flexibility to fold Searle's/Nutrasweet's financial statements into those of itself, the parent company.

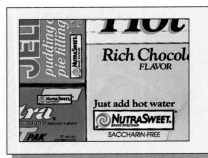

"Monsanto's accounting system had the flexibility to fold Searle's/Nutrasweet's financial statements into those of itself, the parent company."

Favorable Cost/Benefit Relationship

Achieving control, compatibility, and flexibility costs money. These costs reduce a company's net income, so managers often must settle for less than the perfect accounting information system. They strive for a system that offers maximum benefits at a minimum cost—that is, a favorable *cost/benefit relationship*. Most small companies, such as Hallisey's Pharmacy, use off-the-shelf computerized accounting packages, and the very smallest businesses might not computerize at all. But large companies, such as the brokerage firm Merrill Lynch, have specialized needs for information. For them, customized programming is a must because the benefits—in terms of information tailored to the company's needs—far outweigh the cost of the system. The result? Better decisions.

Components of a Computerized Accounting System

Three components form the heart of a computerized accounting system:

1. Hardware
2. Software
3. Company personnel

Each component is critical to the system's success.

Hardware is the electronic equipment that includes computers, disk drives, monitors, printers, and the network that connects them. Most modern accounting systems require a **network,** the system of electronic linkages that allow different computers to share the same information. In a networked system many computers can be connected to the main computer, or **server,** which stores the program and the data. With the right communications hardware and software, a Price Waterhouse auditor in London can access the data of a client located in Sydney, Australia. The result is a speedier audit for the client, often at lower cost than if the auditor had to perform all the work on site in Sydney.

Software is the set of programs that cause the computer to perform the work desired. Accounting software accepts, edits (alters), and stores transaction data and generates the reports managers use to run the business. Many accounting software packages operate independently from the other computing activities of the system. For example, a company that is only partly computerized may use software programs to account for employee payrolls and sales and accounts receivable. The other parts of the accounting system may not be fully automated.

For large enterprises, such as Hershey Foods and Caterpillar Tractor, the accounting software is integrated within the overall company *database*, or computerized storehouse of information. Many business databases, or *management information systems*, include both accounting and nonaccounting data. In negotiating a union contract, the Union Pacific Railroad often needs to examine the relationship between the service time and salary levels of company employees. Union Pacific's database will provide the needed data and enable managers to negotiate effectively with their unions and to develop impact statements, which show the possible effects of union demands on the company. During Union Pacific negotiations, both parties carry laptop computers so that they can access the database and continue to analyze the effects of decisions under consideration.

"During Union Pacific negotiations, both parties . . . can access the database and continue to analyze the effects of decisions under consideration."

Personnel are critical to the success of any endeavor because people operate the system. Modern accounting systems give nonaccounting personnel access to parts (but not all) of the system. For example, a Frito-Lay marketing manager (a nonaccountant) may use a microcomputer and regional sales data (accounting information) to identify the territory that needs a promotional campaign. Management of a computerized accounting system requires careful consideration of data security and screening of the people in the organization who will have access to the data. Security is usually achieved with *passwords*, codes that permit access to computerized records.

EXHIBIT 6-1
The Three Stages of Data Processing

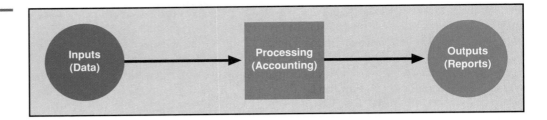

The Three Stages of Data Processing: A Comparison of Computerized and Manual Accounting Systems

OBJECTIVE 2

Understand how computerized and manual accounting systems are used

Computerized accounting systems have replaced manual systems in many organizations—even small businesses such as Hallisey's Pharmacy. As we discuss the three stages of data processing, observe the differences between a computerized system and a manual system. The relationship among the three stages of data processing is shown in Exhibit 6-1.

Inputs represents data from source documents, such as sales receipts and bank deposit slips, and electronically generated data from fax orders and other telecommunications. Inputs are usually grouped by type. For example, a firm would enter cash sale transactions separately from credit sales and purchase transactions.

Computerized accounting systems require that data inputs be arranged in specific formats. Transactions that are missing dates, account numbers, or other critical information are not accepted by the system. Transactions for which debits do not equal credits are also rejected.

Key Point: The output (financial reports) can be only as reliable as the input. If the input is incorrect or incomplete, the output will be flawed.

In a manual system, *processing* includes journalizing transactions, posting to the accounts, and preparing the financial statements. A computerized system also processes but without the intermediate steps (journal, ledger, and trial balance).

Outputs are the reports used for decision making, including the financial statements (income statement, balance sheet, and so on). The Halliseys in the opening story are making better decisions—and prospering—because of the reports their accounting system produces. From the computer's point of view, a trial balance is also a report. But a manual system would treat the trial balance as a processing step leading to the statements. Exhibit 6-2 is an expanded diagram of the relationship between

EXHIBIT 6-2
Overview of a Computerized Accounting System

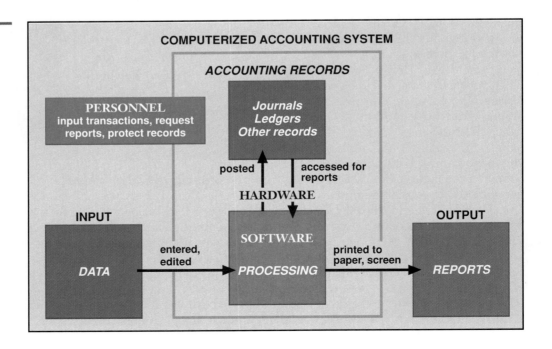

the components of a computerized accounting system and the three stages of data processing.

In a computerized accounting system, the software controls how the hardware operates. Input enters the system, subject to editing for the balancing of debits and credits, numerical limits, and so on. Accounting records, or files, are accessed by the computer and updated (posted). Reports are displayed on the screen and printed in response to operator command, which requires access to the computerized accounting records. All steps are under the control of the software and the operator (accountant).

Accounting Systems Design: The Chart of Accounts

Design of the accounting system begins with the chart of accounts. ◀▏◀▏◀▏ In the accounting system of a company such as Eastman Kodak, account numbers take on added importance. It is efficient to represent a complex account title, such as Accumulated Depreciation—Photographic Equipment, with a concise account number (for example, 16570).

◀▏◀▏◀▏ Recall from Chapter 2, p. 59, that the chart of accounts lists all accounts and their account numbers in the ledger.

Recall that asset accounts generally begin with the digit 1, liabilities with the digit 2, owner equity accounts with the digit 3, revenues with 4, and expenses with 5. Exhibit 6-3 diagrams one structure for computerized accounts. Assets are divided into current assets, fixed assets (property, plant, and equipment), and other assets. Among the current assets we illustrate only three general ledger accounts: Cash in Bank (Account No. 111), Accounts Receivable (No. 112), and Prepaid Insurance (No. 115). Accounts Receivable holds the *total* dollar amount receivable from all customers. To ensure collection and follow-up, companies also keep records of the amount receivable from each customer. (We discuss the individual customer records in the second half of the chapter.)

The account numbers in Exhibit 6-3 get more detailed as you move from top to bottom. For example, Customer A's account number is 1120001, in which 112 represents Accounts Receivable and 0001 refers to Customer A.

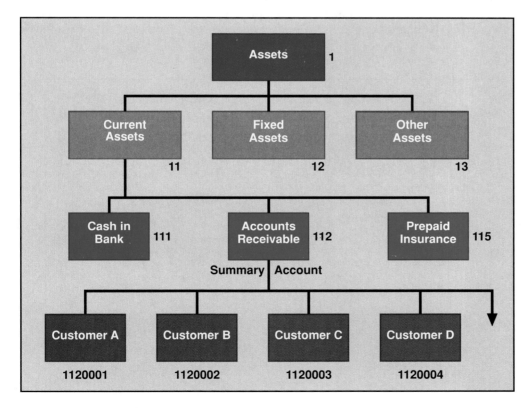

EXHIBIT 6-3
Structure for Computerized Accounts

The choice of number groups for account categories is not as critical in a manual system as it is in a computerized system, except for the ease of looking up accounts in the accounting records. Computerized accounting systems rely instead on *number ranges* to translate accounts and their balances into properly organized financial statements and other reports. For example, the accounts numbered 101–399 (assets, liabilities, and owner equity) are sorted to the balance sheet; the accounts numbered 401–599 (revenues and expenses) go to the income statement.

Classifying Transactions: Computerized and Manual Systems

Recording transactions in an actual accounting system requires an additional step that we have skipped thus far. A business of any size must *classify* transactions by type for efficient handling. In a manual system, credit sales, purchases on account, cash receipts, and cash payments are treated as four separate categories, with each type entered into its own special journal. For example, credit sales are recorded in a special journal called a sales journal. Cash receipts are entered into a cash receipts journal, and so on. Transactions that do not fit any of the special journals, such as the adjusting entries at the end of the period, are recorded in the general journal, which serves as the "journal of last resort."

Computerized systems also require you to preclassify transactions. Suppose you are accruing salary expense (debit Salary Expense; credit Salary Payable). In a manual system, you record the data in the general journal and post to the general ledger. But there is no "set of books" in a computerized system. To record this entry, you choose within the system software the appropriate processing environment from a menu. A **menu** is a list of options for choosing computer functions.

Menu-Driven Accounting Systems

Computerized systems are organized by function, or task. Access to functions is arranged in terms of menus. In such a *menu-driven* system, you first access the most general group of functions, called the *main menu*. You then choose from one or more submenus until you finally reach the function you want. Most computerized systems have similar functions, but their menu structures differ.

Exhibit 6-4 illustrates one type of menu structure. The row at the top of the exhibit shows the main menu. The computer operator (or accountant) had chosen the

Key Point: The general journal will have the fewest entries. Most transactions fall into one of these four categories: credit sales, cash receipts, credit purchases, or cash disbursements.

EXHIBIT 6-4

Main Menu of a Computerized Accounting System

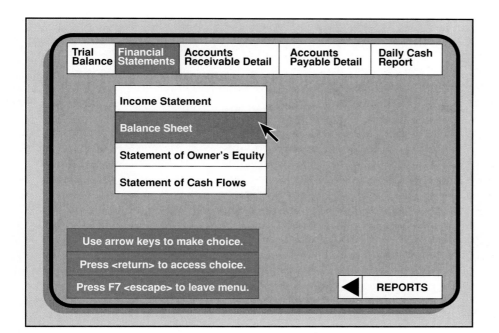

EXHIBIT 6-5
Reports Menu of a Computerized Accounting System

General option (short for General Ledger), as shown by the highlighting. This action opened a submenu of four items—Transactions, Posting, Account Maintenance, and Closing. The Transactions option was then chosen (highlighted).

Posting in a computerized system can be performed continuously as transactions are being recorded—**on-line processing**—or later for a group of similar transactions—**batch processing.** In either case posting is automatic. Batch processing of accounting data allows accountants to check the entries for accuracy before posting them. In effect, the transaction data are "parked" in the computer to await posting, which simply updates the account balances.

Accounting Reports

Outputs—accounting reports—are the final stage of data processing. In a computerized system the financial statements can be printed automatically. For example, the Reports option in the main menu gives the operator various report choices, which are expanded in the Reports submenu of Exhibit 6-5. In the exhibit the operator is working with the financial statements, specifically the balance sheet, as shown by the highlighting.

STOP & THINK Why does every business need an accounting information system? Give several reasons.

Answer: Managers and owners of businesses must make decisions, and they need information to run the organization. The business's accounting system provides much of this information. Likewise, lenders and outside investors use accounting information in their lending and investment decisions. And most businesses are subject to some form of taxation. An accounting system provides tax information as well.

Summary of the Accounting Cycle: Computerized and Manual

Exhibit 6-6 summarizes the accounting cycle in a computerized system and in a manual system. As you study the exhibit, compare and contrast the two types of systems.

Computerized System	Manual System
1. Start with the account balances in the ledger at the beginning of the period.	1. Same.
2. Analyze and classify business transactions by type. Access appropriate menus for data entry.	2. Analyze and journalize transactions as they occur.
3. Computer automatically posts transactions as a batch or when entered on-line.	3. Post journal entries to the ledger accounts.
4. The unadjusted balances are available immediately after each posting.	4. Compute the unadjusted balance in each account at the end of the period.
5. The trial balance, if needed, can be accessed as a report.	5. Enter the trial balance on the work sheet, and complete the work sheet.
6. Enter and post adjusting entries. Print the financial statements. Run automatic closing procedure after backing up the period's accounting records.	6. Prepare the financial statements. Journalize and post the adjusting entries. Journalize and post the closing entries.
7. The next period's opening balances are created automatically as a result of closing.	7. Prepare the postclosing trial balance. This trial balance becomes step 1 for the next period.

Key Point: A computerized system performs all the steps a manual system does, except for the work sheet. Even if you never keep a manual set of books, you still need to understand the entire accounting system.

Integrated Accounting Software

Computerized accounting packages are organized by **modules,** separate but *integrated* units—compatible units that function together. Changes affecting one module will affect others. For example, entry and posting of a sales transaction will update two modules: Accounts Receivable/Sales and Inventory/Cost of Goods Sold. Accounting packages, such as Business Works, Peachtree, DacEasy, One-Write Plus, and RealWorld Accounting, come as a complete set of accounting modules to form an integrated system. The Halliseys in the opening story chose Business Works.

Spreadsheets

OBJECTIVE 3
Understand how spreadsheets are used in accounting

You may have been preparing homework assignments manually. Imagine preparing a work sheet for General Motors. Each adjustment changes the company's financial statement totals. Consider computing General Motors's revenue amounts by hand. The task would be overwhelming. For even a small business with only a few departments, the computations are tedious, time-consuming, and therefore expensive. Furthermore, errors are likely.

Spreadsheets are computer programs that link data by means of formulas and functions. These electronic work sheets were invented to automate budget updates. Spreadsheets are organized as a rectangular grid composed of hundreds or thousands of grid points called *cells*, each defined by a row number and a column number. A cell can contain words (called labels), numbers, or formulas (relationships among cells). The *cursor*, or electronic highlighter, indicates which cell is active, and it can be moved around the spreadsheet. When the cursor is placed over any cell, information can be entered there for processing.

Exhibit 6-7 shows a simple income statement on a spreadsheet screen. The words were entered in cells A1 through A4. The dollar amount of revenues was entered in cell B2 and expenses in cell B3. A formula was placed in cell B4 as follows: +B2–B3. This formula subtracts expenses from revenues to compute net income in cell B4. If revenues in cell B2 increase to $105,000, net income in B4 automatically increases to $45,000. No other cells will change.

Spreadsheets are ideally suited to preparing a budget, the financial goal of a business. Consider Procter & Gamble, whose Health-Care Sector has an annual

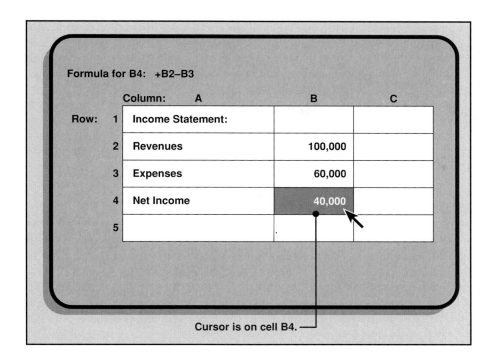

Formula for B4: +B2−B3

Column:	A	B	C
Row: 1	Income Statement:		
2	Revenues	100,000	
3	Expenses	60,000	
4	Net Income	40,000	
5			

Cursor is on cell B4.

EXHIBIT 6-7
A Spreadsheet Screen

advertising budget of $300–$400 million. Procter & Gamble allocates $40–$50 million for its Crest Complete toothbrush and $2 million for a new stand-up tube for Crest toothpaste. Procter & Gamble's advertising expenses will increase in both cases. The company will also forecast an increase in sales revenue, cost of goods sold, and other expenses. A spreadsheet computes all these changes automatically in response to the advertising. The spreadsheet lets Procter & Gamble's managers track relative profitability of each product. Their budget can stay abreast of the latest developments. Armed with current data, the managers can make informed decisions. The result is higher profits.

"The spreadsheet lets Procter & Gamble's managers track relative profitability of each product."

We can add or delete whole rows and columns of data and move blocks of numbers and words on a spreadsheet. The power and versatility of spreadsheets are apparent when enormous amounts of data are entered on the spreadsheet with formula relationships. Change only one number, and save hours of manual recalculation. Exhibit 6-8 shows the basic arithmetic operations in some popular spreadsheet programs such as Lotus 1-2-3.

Operation	Symbol
Addition	+
Subtraction	−
Multiplication	*
Division	/
Addition of a range of cells	@SUM(beginning cell..ending cell)
	or
	=SUM(beginning cell:ending cell)
Examples:	
Add the contents of cells A2 through A9	@SUM(A2..A9)
Divide the contents of cell C2 by the contents of cell D1	+C2/D1

EXHIBIT 6-8
Basic Arithmetic Operations in Spreadsheets

Computerized accounting packages often come with the ability to export data to spreadsheets. For example, the western branch office of the BFGoodrich Company in Los Angeles may export a list of accounts receivable (thousands of customers and their balances) as a spreadsheet to the home office in Akron, Ohio. The spreadsheet can sort the BFGoodrich customers by name, size of balance, sales to the customer during the last quarter, and so on. Other software called **database programs** organize information so that it can be summarized in a variety of report forms. A database program can merge information from various sources to generate even more complex reports than spreadsheets can handle. Some of the common database programs are dBase, Access, and Paradox.

Overview of an Accounting Information System

The purpose of an accounting system is to provide information for decision making. The financial statements and other reports are used by managers, creditors, and others who evaluate the businesses. Each entity designs its accounting system to meet its own needs for information while keeping the cost of the system within its budget. Exhibit 6-9 diagrams a typical accounting system for a merchandising business. The remainder of this chapter describes some of the more important aspects of the system described in Exhibit 6-9.

Special Accounting Journals

Key Point: Transactions are recorded in either the general journal or a special journal, but not in both.

The journal entries illustrated so far in this book have been made in the general journal. The **general journal** is used to record all transactions that do not fit one of the special journals. In practice, it is inefficient to record all transactions in the general journal, so we use special journals. A **special journal** is an accounting journal designed to record one specific type of transaction, such as credit sales, which would be recorded in the special journal called the sales journal.

Both manual systems and computerized systems must specialize by organizing transaction entry by type. Special journals and accounting modules accomplish that task. In a computerized system, accountants do not enter transaction data in these journals. Instead, they input data through various modules, such as the Accounts Receivable module for credit sales. But the underlying accounting principles are the same in manual and computerized systems.

EXHIBIT 6-9

Overview of an Accounting System with Special Journals

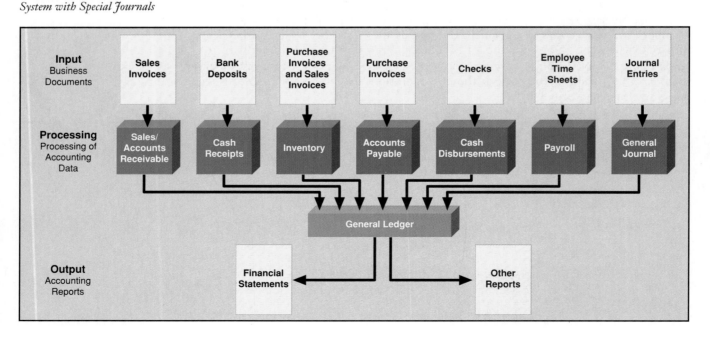

In all likelihood, you will be working with a computerized system. We would rather you *not* view the process as a black box. To help you understand the basic accounting, we take you through the steps in a manual system.

Most of a business's transactions fall into one of four categories, so accountants use special journals to record these transactions. This system reduces the time and cost otherwise spent journalizing, as we will see. The four categories of transactions, the related special journal, and the posting abbreviations follow:

Transaction	Special Journal	Posting Abbreviation
1. Sale on account	Sales journal	S
2. Cash receipt	Cash receipts journal	C R
3. Purchase on account	Purchases journal	P
4. Cash disbursement	Cash disbursements journal	C D

Adjusting and closing entries are entered in the general journal. Its posting abbreviation is J.

Sales Journal

OBJECTIVE 4
Use the sales journal, the cash receipts journal, and the accounts receivable subsidiary ledger

Most merchandisers sell at least some of their inventory on account. These *credit sales* are entered in the **sales journal.** Credit sales of assets other than inventory—for example, buildings—occur infrequently and are recorded in the general journal.

Key Point: Only credit sales are recorded in the sales journal. Cash sales are recorded in the cash receipts journal.

Exhibit 6-10 illustrates a sales journal (Panel A) and the related posting to the ledgers (Panel B) of Austin Sound Stereo Center, the stereo shop introduced in Chapter 5. Each entry in the Accounts Receivable/Sales Revenue column of the sales journal in Exhibit 6-10 is a debit (Dr.) to Accounts Receivable and a credit (Cr.) to Sales Revenue, as the heading above this column indicates. For each transaction, the accountant enters the date, invoice number, and customer account along with the transaction amount. This streamlined way of recording sales on account saves a vast amount of time that, in a manual system, would be spent entering account titles and dollar amounts in the general journal.

In recording credit sales in previous chapters, we did not keep a record of the names of credit-sale customers. In practice, the business must know the amount receivable from each customer. How else can the company keep track of who owes it money, when payment is due—and how much?

Consider the first transaction in Panel A. On November 2 Austin Sound sold stereo equipment on account to Maria Galvez for $935. The invoice number is 422. All this information appears on a single line in the sales journal. No explanation is necessary. The transaction's presence in the sales journal means that it is a credit sale—debited to Accounts Receivable—Maria Galvez and credited to Sales Revenue. To gain additional information about the transaction, we would look up the actual invoice.

In a computerized system, accountants do not enter credit sales in a sales journal. The transaction data may be input through point-of-sales terminals, as in a Sears or J.C. Penney store. When managers wish to review credit sales, they can print a report that resembles the sales journal. The report may show the date and amount of each transaction, the invoice number, and the customer name. The other special journals discussed in this chapter are likewise similar to the reports generated by a computerized system.

Recall from Chapter 5 that Austin Sound uses a *perpetual* inventory system. At the time of recording the sale, Austin Sound also records the cost of the goods sold and the decrease in inventory. Many computerized accounting systems are programmed to read both the sales amount (from the bar code on the package of the item sold) and the cost of goods sold. A separate column of the sales journal holds the cost of goods sold and inventory amount—$505 for the sale to Maria Galvez. If Austin Sound used a *periodic* inventory system, it would not record cost of goods sold

Panel A—Sales Journal:

		Sales Journal			Page 3
Date	Invoice No.	Account Debited	Post. Ref.	Accounts Receivable Dr. Sales Revenue Cr.	Cost of Goods Sold Dr. Inventory Cr.
19X6					
Nov. 2	422	Maria Galvez	✓	935	505
13	423	Brent Harmon	✓	694	361
18	424	Susan Levy	✓	907	517
27	425	Clay Schmidt	✓	1,783	431
30		Total		4,319	1,814
				(112/410)	(511/131)

Individual accounts receivable are posted daily.

Totals can be posted at the end of the month.

Totals can be posted at the end of the month.

Panel B—Posting to Ledgers:
Accounts Receivable Ledger

General Ledger

Maria Galvez

Date	Jrnl. Ref.	Debit	Credit	Balance
Nov. 2	S.3	935		935

Brent Harmon

Date	Jrnl. Ref.	Debit	Credit	Balance
Nov. 13	S.3	694		694

Susan Levy

Date	Jrnl. Ref.	Debit	Credit	Balance
Nov. 18	S.3	907		907

Clay Schmidt

Date	Jrnl. Ref.	Debit	Credit	Balance
Nov. 27	S.3	1,783		1,783

Accounts Receivable   No. 112

Date	Jrnl. Ref.	Debit	Credit	Balance
Nov. 30	S.3	4,319		4,319

Inventory   No. 131

Date	Jrnl. Ref.	Debit	Credit	Balance
Nov. 30	Bal.			3,885
30	S.3		1,814	2,071

Sales Revenue   No. 410

Date	Jrnl. Ref.	Debit	Credit	Balance
Nov. 30	S.3		4,319	4,319

Cost of Goods Sold   No. 511

Date	Jrnl. Ref.	Debit	Credit	Balance
Nov. 30	S.3	1,814		1,814

EXHIBIT 6-10

Sales Journal and Posting to Ledgers

and the decrease in inventory at the time of sale. The sales journal would need only one column to debit Accounts Receivable and to credit Sales Revenue for the amount of the sale.

POSTING TO THE GENERAL LEDGER   The ledger we have used so far is the **general ledger,** which holds the accounts reported in the financial statements. We will soon introduce other ledgers.

Posting from the sales journal to the general ledger can be done *monthly*. In Exhibit 6-10 (Panel A), the total credit sales for November are $4,319. This column has two headings, Accounts Receivable and Sales Revenue. When the $4,319 is posted to these accounts in the general ledger, their account numbers are written beneath the total in the sales journal. In Panel B of Exhibit 6-10, the account number for Accounts Receivable is 112 and the account number for Sales Revenue is 410. These account numbers are entered beneath the credit sales total in the sales journal to signify that the $4,319 has been posted to the two accounts.

The debit to Cost of Goods Sold and the credit to Inventory for the monthly total of $1,814 can also be posted at the end of the month. After posting, these accounts' numbers are entered beneath the total to show that Cost of Goods Sold and Inventory have been updated.

POSTING TO THE SUBSIDIARY LEDGER   The $4,319 sum of the November debits to Accounts Receivable does not identify the amount receivable from any specific customer. Most businesses would find keeping a separate Accounts Receivable account in the general ledger for each customer to be unmanageable. A business may have thousands of customers. Consider the Consumers Digest Company, a Chicago-based firm that publishes the bimonthly magazine *Consumers Digest*. The Consumers Digest Company has 1.2 million customer accounts—one for each subscriber.

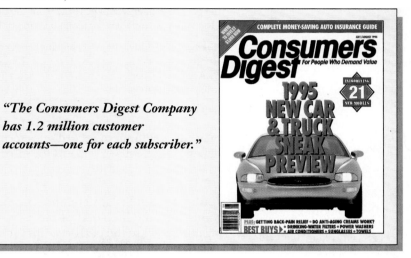

"The Consumers Digest Company has 1.2 million customer accounts—one for each subscriber."

To streamline operations, businesses place the accounts of their individual credit customers in a subsidiary ledger, called the Accounts Receivable ledger. A **subsidiary ledger** is a book of accounts that provides supporting details on individual balances, the total of which appears in a general ledger account. The customer accounts are arranged in alphabetical order.

Amounts in the sales journal are posted to the subsidiary ledger *daily* to keep a current record of the amount receivable from each customer. The amounts are debits. Daily posting allows the business to answer customer inquiries promptly. Suppose Maria Galvez telephones Austin Sound on November 11 to ask how much money she owes. The subsidiary ledger readily provides that information.

When each transaction amount is posted to the subsidiary ledger, a check mark or some other notation is entered in the posting reference column of the sales journal.

Key Point: In a manual system, the dates recorded in the subsidiary ledger and the general ledger must reflect the date of the transaction, not the date on which the transaction was posted. In a computerized system, the computer will automatically record the date entered by the computer operator.

JOURNAL REFERENCES IN THE LEDGERS   When amounts are posted to the ledgers, the journal page number is printed in the account to identify the source of the data. All transaction data in Exhibit 6-10 originated on page 3 of the sales journal, so all journal references in the ledger accounts are S.3. The "S." indicates sales journal.

Trace all the postings in Exhibit 6-10. The most effective way to learn about accounting systems and special journals is to study the flow of data. The arrows indicate the direction of the information. The arrows also show the links between the individual customer accounts in the subsidiary ledger and the Accounts Receivable account. These links are summarized as follows:

Accounts Receivable debit balance	$4,319

Customer Accounts Receivable

Customer	Balance
Maria Galvez ...:..	$ 935
Brent Harmon	694
Susan Levy..	907
Clay Schmidt...	1,783
Total accounts receivable	$4,319

Accounts Receivable in the general ledger is a **control account,** an account whose balance equals the sum of the balances of a group of related accounts in a subsidiary ledger. The individual customer accounts are subsidiary accounts. They are "controlled" by the Accounts Receivable account in the general ledger.

STOP & THINK Suppose Austin Sound had 400 credit sales for the month. How many postings to the general ledger would be made from the sales journal? (Ignore Cost of Goods Sold and Inventory.) How many would there be if all sales transactions were routed through the general journal?

Answer: There are only two postings from the sales journal to the general ledger: one to Accounts Receivable and one to Sales Revenue. There would be 800 postings from the general journal: 400 to Accounts Receivable and 400 to Sales Revenue. This difference clearly shows the benefit of using a sales journal.

Additional data can be recorded in the sales journal. For example, a company may add a column to record sales terms, such as 2/10 n/30. The design of the journal depends on managers' needs for information.

Cash Receipts Journal

Cash transactions are common in most businesses because cash receipts from customers are the lifeblood of business. To record repetitive cash receipt transactions, accountants use the **cash receipts journal.**

Key Point: Every entry in the cash receipts journal includes a debit to Cash. Cash sales are recorded here rather than in the sales journal.

Exhibit 6-11, Panel A, illustrates the cash receipts journal. The related posting to ledgers is shown in Panel B. The exhibit illustrates November transactions for Austin Sound Stereo Center.

Every transaction recorded in this journal is a cash receipt, so the first column is for debits to the Cash account. The next column is for debits to Sales Discounts on collections from customers. In a typical merchandising business, the main sources of cash are collections on account and cash sales. Thus the cash receipts journal has credit columns for Accounts Receivable and Sales Revenue. The journal also has a credit column for Other Accounts, which lists sources of cash other than cash sales and collections on account. This Other Accounts column is also used to record the names of customers from whom cash is received on account.

In Exhibit 6-11, cash sales occurred on November 6, 19, and 28. Observe the debits to Cash and the credits to Sales Revenue ($517, $853, and $1,802). Each sale entry is accompanied by an entry that debits Cost of Goods Sold and credits Inventory for the cost of the merchandise sold. The column for this entry is at the far right side of the cash receipts journal. Some companies may record this entry separately.

On November 11 Austin Sound borrowed $1,000 from First Bank. Cash is debited, and Note Payable to First Bank is credited in the Other Accounts column because no specific credit column is set up to account for borrowings. For this transaction, it is necessary to print the account title, Note Payable to First Bank, in the Other Accounts/Account Title column to record the source of cash.

On November 25 Austin Sound collected $762 of interest revenue. The account credited, Interest Revenue, would be printed in the Other Accounts column. The November 11 and 25 transactions illustrate a key fact about business. Different entities have different types of transactions; they design their special journals to meet

EXHIBIT 6-11 *Cash Receipts Journal and Posting to Ledgers*

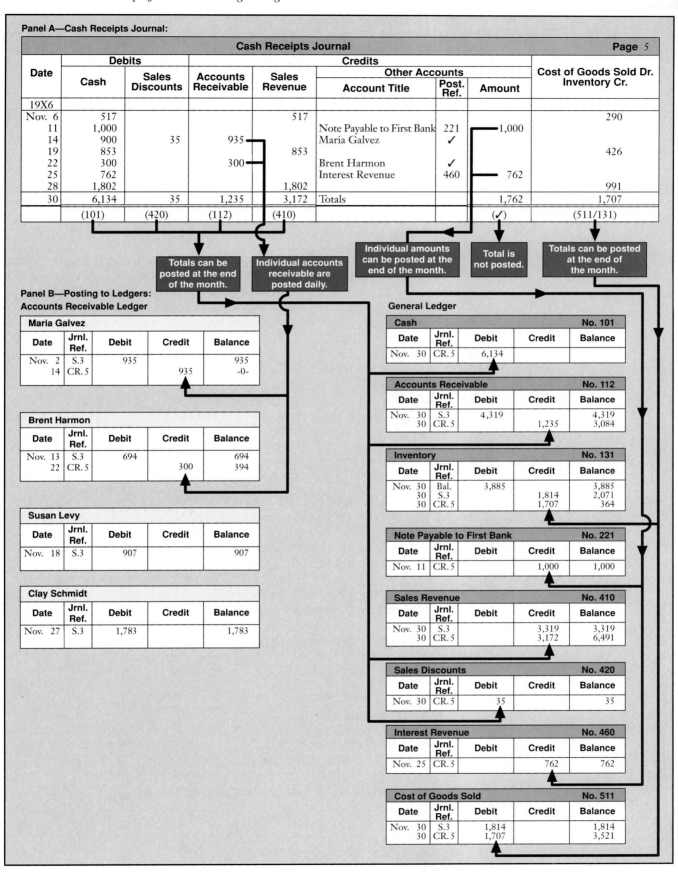

Panel A—Cash Receipts Journal:

	Debits			Credits				Cost of Goods Sold Dr.
Date	**Cash**	**Sales Discounts**	**Accounts Receivable**	**Sales Revenue**	**Other Accounts**			**Inventory Cr.**
					Account Title	**Post. Ref.**	**Amount**	
19X6								
Nov. 6	517			517				290
11	1,000				Note Payable to First Bank	221	1,000	
14	900	35	935		Maria Galvez	✓		
19	853			853				426
22	300		300		Brent Harmon	✓		
25	762				Interest Revenue	460	762	
28	1,802			1,802				991
30	6,134	35	1,235	3,172	Totals		1,762	1,707
	(101)	(420)	(112)	(410)			(✓)	(511/131)

Cash Receipts Journal — Page 5

> Totals can be posted at the end of the month.

> Individual accounts receivable are posted daily.

> Individual amounts can be posted at the end of the month.

> Total is not posted.

> Totals can be posted at the end of the month.

Panel B—Posting to Ledgers:
Accounts Receivable Ledger

Maria Galvez

Date	Jrnl. Ref.	Debit	Credit	Balance
Nov. 2	S.3	935		935
14	CR.5		935	-0-

Brent Harmon

Date	Jrnl. Ref.	Debit	Credit	Balance
Nov. 13	S.3	694		694
22	CR.5		300	394

Susan Levy

Date	Jrnl. Ref.	Debit	Credit	Balance
Nov. 18	S.3	907		907

Clay Schmidt

Date	Jrnl. Ref.	Debit	Credit	Balance
Nov. 27	S.3	1,783		1,783

General Ledger

Cash No. 101

Date	Jrnl. Ref.	Debit	Credit	Balance
Nov. 30	CR.5	6,134		

Accounts Receivable No. 112

Date	Jrnl. Ref.	Debit	Credit	Balance
Nov. 30	S.3	4,319		4,319
30	CR.5		1,235	3,084

Inventory No. 131

Date	Jrnl. Ref.	Debit	Credit	Balance
Nov. 30	Bal.	3,885		3,885
30	S.3		1,814	2,071
30	CR.5		1,707	364

Note Payable to First Bank No. 221

Date	Jrnl. Ref.	Debit	Credit	Balance
Nov. 11	CR.5		1,000	1,000

Sales Revenue No. 410

Date	Jrnl. Ref.	Debit	Credit	Balance
Nov. 30	S.3		3,319	3,319
30	CR.5		3,172	6,491

Sales Discounts No. 420

Date	Jrnl. Ref.	Debit	Credit	Balance
Nov. 30	CR.5	35		35

Interest Revenue No. 460

Date	Jrnl. Ref.	Debit	Credit	Balance
Nov. 25	CR.5		762	762

Cost of Goods Sold No. 511

Date	Jrnl. Ref.	Debit	Credit	Balance
Nov. 30	S.3	1,814		1,814
30	CR.5	1,707		3,521

their particular needs for information. In this case, the Other Accounts credit column is the catchall used to record all nonroutine cash receipt transactions.

On November 14 Austin Sound collected $900 from Maria Galvez. Referring to Exhibit 6-10, we see that on November 2 Austin Sound sold merchandise for $935 to Galvez. The terms of sale allowed a $35 discount for prompt payment, and she paid within the discount period. Austin's cash receipt is recorded by debiting Cash for $900 and Sales Discounts for $35 and by crediting Accounts Receivable for $935. The customer's name appears in the Other Accounts/Account Title column. This procedure enables the business to keep track of each customer's account in the subsidiary ledger.

On November 22, the business collected $300 on account from Brent Harmon, who was paying for part of the November 13 purchase. No discount applied to this collection.

Total debits should equal total credits in the cash receipts journal. This equality holds for each transaction and for the monthly totals. For example, the first transaction has a $517 debit and an equal credit. For the month, total debits ($6,134 + $35 = $6,169) equal total credits ($1,235 + $3,172 + $1,762 = $6,169).

POSTING TO THE GENERAL LEDGER The column totals can be posted monthly. To indicate their posting, the account number is written below the column total in the cash receipts journal. Note the account number for Cash (101) below the column total $6,134, and trace the posting to Cash in the general ledger. Likewise, the Sales Discounts, Accounts Receivable, and Sales Revenue column totals also are posted to the general ledger.

The column total for *Other Accounts* is not posted. Instead, these credits are posted individually. In Exhibit 6-11, the November 11 transaction reads "Note Payable to First Bank." This account's number (221) in the Post. Ref. column indicates that the transaction amount was posted individually. The check mark instead of an account number below the column indicates that the column total was not posted. The November 25 collection of interest revenue is also posted individually. These amounts can be posted to the general ledger at the end of the month. But they should be dated in the ledger accounts on the basis of their actual date in the journal so that it is easy to trace the amounts back to the journal.

POSTING TO THE SUBSIDIARY LEDGER Amounts from the cash receipts journal are posted to the subsidiary accounts receivable ledger daily to keep the individual balances up to date. The postings to the accounts receivable ledger are credits. Trace the $935 posting to Maria Galvez's account. It reduces her balance to zero. The $300 receipt from Brent Harmon reduces his accounts receivable balance to $394.

After posting, the sum of the individual balances that remain in the accounts receivable ledger equals the general ledger balance in Accounts Receivable ($3,084). Austin Sound may prepare a November 30 list of account balances from the subsidiary ledger to follow up on slow-paying customers:

Customer Accounts Receivable

Customer	Balance
Brent Harmon	$ 394
Susan Levy	907
Clay Schmidt	1,783
Total accounts receivable	$3,084

Good accounts receivable records help a business manage its cash.

Purchases Journal

OBJECTIVE 5

Use the purchases journal, the cash disbursements journal, and the accounts payable subsidiary ledger

A merchandising business purchases inventory and supplies frequently. Such purchases are usually made on account. The **purchases journal** is designed to account for all purchases of inventory, supplies, and other assets *on account*. It can also be used to record expenses incurred on account. Cash purchases are recorded in the cash disbursements journal.

Exhibit 6-12 illustrates Austin Sound's purchases journal (Panel A) and posting to ledgers (Panel B).[1] This purchases journal has amount columns for credits to Accounts Payable and debits to Inventory, Supplies, and Other Accounts. A periodic inventory system would replace the Inventory column with a column titled "Purchases." The Other Accounts columns accommodate purchases of items other than inventory and supplies. Each business designs its journals to meet its own needs for information and efficiency. Accounts Payable is credited for all transactions recorded in the purchases journal.

On November 2 Austin Sound purchased from JVC Corporation stereo inventory costing $700. The creditor's name (JVC Corporation) is entered in the Account Credited column. The purchase terms of 3/15 n/30 are also printed to help identify the due date and the discount available. Accounts Payable is credited and Inventory is debited for the transaction amount. On November 19 a credit purchase of supplies is entered as a debit to Supplies and a credit to Accounts Payable.

Key Point: Every transaction in the purchases journal will include a credit to Accounts Payable.

Note the November 9 purchase of fixtures from City Office Supply. The purchases journal contains no column for fixtures, so the Other Accounts debit column is used. Because this was a credit purchase, the accountant enters the creditor name (City Office Supply) in the Account Credited column and Fixtures in the Other Accounts/Account Title column.

The total credits in the purchases journal ($2,876) equal the total debits ($1,706 + $103 + $1,067 = $2,876). This equality proves the accuracy of the entries in the purchases journal.

To pay debts efficiently, a company must know how much it owes particular creditors. The Accounts Payable account in the general ledger shows only a single total, however, and therefore does not indicate the amount owed to each creditor. Companies keep an accounts payable subsidiary ledger. The accounts payable subsidiary ledger lists the creditors in alphabetical order, along with the amounts owed to them. Exhibit 6-12, Panel B, shows Austin Sound's accounts payable subsidiary ledger, which includes accounts for Audio Electronics, City Office Supply, and others. After posting, the total of the individual balances in the subsidiary ledger equals the balance in the Accounts Payable control account in the general ledger. This system is like the accounts receivable system discussed earlier in the chapter.

POSTING FROM THE PURCHASES JOURNAL   Posting from the purchases journal is similar to posting from the sales journal and the cash receipts journal. Exhibit 6-12, Panel B, illustrates the posting process.

Individual accounts payable in the *accounts payable subsidiary ledger* are posted daily, and column totals and other amounts can be posted to the *general ledger* at the end of the month. In the ledger accounts, P.8 indicates the source of the posted amounts—that is, page 8 of the purchases journal.

Key Point: The posting procedure is the same as for the other special journals: Column totals can be posted to the general ledger at the end of the month; other accounts are posted individually to the general ledger; and individual accounts payable amounts are posted daily to the subsidiary ledger.

---

[1]This is the only special journal that we illustrate with the credit column placed to the left and the debit columns to the right. This arrangement of columns focuses on Accounts Payable, which is credited for each entry to this journal, and on the individual supplier to be paid.

STOP & THINK Contrast the number of general ledger postings from the purchases journal in Exhibit 6-12 with the number that would be required if the general journal were used to record the same seven transactions.

Answer: Use of the purchases journal requires only five general ledger postings—$2,876 to Accounts Payable, $1,706 to Inventory, $103 to Supplies, $440 to Fixtures, and $627 to Furniture. Without the purchases journal, there would have been 14 postings, two for each of the seven transactions.

EXHIBIT 6-12

Purchases Journal and Posting to Ledgers

Cash Disbursements Journal

Businesses make most cash disbursements by check. All payments by check are recorded in the **cash disbursements journal.** Other titles of this special journal are the *check register* and the *cash payments journal.* Like the other special journals, it has multiple columns for recording cash payments that occur frequently.

Exhibit 6-13, Panel A, illustrates the cash disbursements journal, and Panel B shows the postings to the ledgers of Austin Sound. This cash disbursements journal has two debit columns—for Accounts Payable and Other Accounts—and two credit

EXHIBIT 6-13

Cash Disbursements Journal and Posting to Ledgers

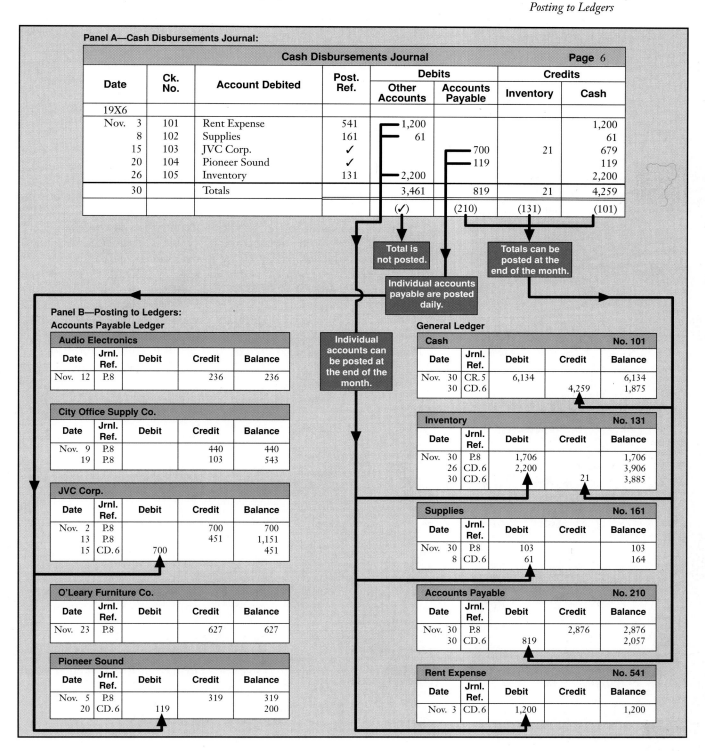

Panel A—Cash Disbursements Journal:

Cash Disbursements Journal							Page 6
Date	Ck. No.	Account Debited	Post. Ref.	Debits		Credits	
				Other Accounts	Accounts Payable	Inventory	Cash
19X6							
Nov. 3	101	Rent Expense	541	1,200			1,200
8	102	Supplies	161	61			61
15	103	JVC Corp.	✓		700	21	679
20	104	Pioneer Sound	✓		119		119
26	105	Inventory	131	2,200			2,200
30		Totals		3,461	819	21	4,259
				(✓)	(210)	(131)	(101)

Total is not posted.

Individual accounts payable are posted daily.

Totals can be posted at the end of the month.

Individual accounts can be posted at the end of the month.

Panel B—Posting to Ledgers:
Accounts Payable Ledger

Audio Electronics

Date	Jrnl. Ref.	Debit	Credit	Balance
Nov. 12	P.8		236	236

City Office Supply Co.

Date	Jrnl. Ref.	Debit	Credit	Balance
Nov. 9	P.8		440	440
19	P.8		103	543

JVC Corp.

Date	Jrnl. Ref.	Debit	Credit	Balance
Nov. 2	P.8		700	700
13	P.8		451	1,151
15	CD.6	700		451

O'Leary Furniture Co.

Date	Jrnl. Ref.	Debit	Credit	Balance
Nov. 23	P.8		627	627

Pioneer Sound

Date	Jrnl. Ref.	Debit	Credit	Balance
Nov. 5	P.8		319	319
20	CD.6	119		200

General Ledger

Cash No. 101

Date	Jrnl. Ref.	Debit	Credit	Balance
Nov. 30	CR.5	6,134		6,134
30	CD.6		4,259	1,875

Inventory No. 131

Date	Jrnl. Ref.	Debit	Credit	Balance
Nov. 30	P.8	1,706		1,706
26	CD.6	2,200		3,906
30	CD.6		21	3,885

Supplies No. 161

Date	Jrnl. Ref.	Debit	Credit	Balance
Nov. 30	P.8	103		103
8	CD.6	61		164

Accounts Payable No. 210

Date	Jrnl. Ref.	Debit	Credit	Balance
Nov. 30	P.8		2,876	2,876
30	CD.6	819		2,057

Rent Expense No. 541

Date	Jrnl. Ref.	Debit	Credit	Balance
Nov. 3	CD.6	1,200		1,200

columns—for Cash and purchase discounts, which are credited to the Inventory account in a perpetual inventory system. This special journal also has columns for the date and for the check number of each cash payment.

Suppose a business makes numerous cash purchases of inventory. What additional column would its cash disbursements journal need to be most useful? A column for Inventory, which would appear under the Debits heading, would streamline the information in the journal.

All entries in the cash disbursements journal include a credit to Cash. Payments on account are debits to Accounts Payable. On November 15 Austin Sound paid JVC on account, with credit terms of 3/15 n/30 (for details, see the first transaction in Exhibit 6-12). Therefore, Austin took the 3-percent discount and paid $679 ($700 less the $21 discount). The discount is credited to the Inventory account.

The Other Accounts column is used to record debits to accounts for which no special column exists. For example, on November 3 Austin Sound paid rent expense of $1,200 and on November 8 the business purchased supplies for $61.

As with all other journals, the total debits ($3,461 + $819 = $4,280) should equal the total credits ($21 + $4,259 = $4,280).

POSTING FROM THE CASH DISBURSEMENTS JOURNAL   Posting from the cash disbursements journal is similar to posting from the cash receipts journal. Individual creditor amounts are posted daily, and column totals and Other Accounts can be posted at the end of the month. Exhibit 6-13, Panel B, illustrates the posting process.

Observe the effect of posting to the Accounts Payable account in the general ledger. The first posted amount in the Accounts Payable account (credit $2,876) originated in the purchases journal, page 8 (P.8). The second posted amount (debit $819) came from the cash disbursements journal, page 6 (CD.6). The resulting credit balance in Accounts Payable is $2,057. Also, see the Cash account. After posting, its debit balance is $2,175.

Amounts in the Other Accounts column are posted individually (for example, Rent Expense—debit $1,200). When each Other Accounts amount is posted to the general ledger, the account number is entered in the Post. Ref. column of the journal.

To review their accounts payable, companies list the individual creditor balances in the accounts payable subsidiary ledger:

Creditor Accounts Payable

Creditor	Balance
Audio Electronics	$ 236
City Office Supply	543
JVC Corp.	451
O'Leary Furniture	627
Pioneer Sound	[[]200
Total accounts payable	$2,057

This total agrees with the Accounts Payable balance in the general ledger in Exhibit 6-13. Agreement of the two amounts indicates that the resulting account balances are correct.

Balancing the Ledgers

At the end of the period, after all postings have been made, equality should exist between:

1. Total debits and total credits of the account balances in the general ledger. These amounts are used to prepare the trial balance that we have been working with throughout Chapters 3 through 5.

2. The balance of the Accounts Receivable control account in the general ledger and the sum of individual customer accounts in the accounts receivable subsidiary ledger.

3. The balance of the Accounts Payable control account in the general ledger and the sum of the individual creditor accounts in the accounts payable subsidiary ledger.

This process is called *balancing the ledgers*, or proving the ledgers. It is an important control procedure because it helps ensure the accuracy of the accounting records.

Documents as Journals in a Manual Accounting System

Many small businesses streamline their accounting systems to save money by using their business documents as the journals. For example, Austin Sound could let its sales invoices serve as its sales journal and keep all invoices for credit sales in a loose-leaf binder. At the end of the period, the accountant simply totals the sales on account and posts that amount to Accounts Receivable and Sales Revenue. Also, the accountant can post directly from invoices to customer accounts in the accounts receivable ledger. This "journal-less" system reduces accounting cost because the accountant does not have to write in journals the information already in the source documents.

Computers and Special Journals

Computerizing special journals to create accounting modules requires no drastic change in the accounting system's design. Systems designers create a special screen for each accounting application (module)—credit sales, cash receipts, credit purchases, and cash payments. The special screen for credit sales would ask the computer operator to enter the following information: date, customer number, customer name, invoice number, and the dollar amount of the sale. These data can generate debits to the subsidiary accounts receivable and files from which are generated monthly customer statements that show account activity and ending balance. For purchases on account, additional computer files keep the subsidiary ledger information on individual vendors.

SUMMARY PROBLEM FOR YOUR REVIEW

A company completed the following selected transactions during March:

Mar.   4   Received $500 from a cash sale to a customer (cost, $319).
       6   Received $60 on account from Brady Lee. The full invoice amount was $65, but Lee paid within the discount period to gain the $5 discount.
       9   Received $1,080 on a note receivable from Beverly Mann. This amount includes the $1,000 note receivable plus interest revenue.
      15   Received $800 from a cash sale to a customer (cost, $522).
      24   Borrowed $2,200 by signing a note payable to Interstate Bank.
      27   Received $1,200 on account from Lance Albert. Payment was received after the discount period lapsed.

The general ledger showed the following balances at February 28: Cash, $1,117; Accounts Receivable, $2,790; Note Receivable—Beverly Mann, $1,000; and Inventory, $1,819. The accounts receivable subsidiary ledger at February 28 contained debit balances as follows: Lance Albert, $1,840; Melinda Fultz, $885; Brady Lee, $65.

Required

1. Record the transactions in the cash receipts journal, page 7.
2. Compute column totals at March 31. Show that total debits equal total credits in the cash receipts journal.
3. Post to the general ledger and the accounts receivable subsidiary ledger. Use complete posting references, including the account numbers illustrated: Cash, 11; Accounts Receivable, 12; Note Receivable—Beverly Mann, 13; Inventory, 14; Note Payable—Interstate Bank, 22; Sales Revenue, 41; Sales Discounts, 42; Interest Revenue, 46; and Cost of Goods Sold, 51. Insert a check mark (√) in the posting reference column for each February 28 account balance.
4. Show that the total of the customer balances in the subsidiary ledger equals the general ledger balance in Accounts Receivable.

SOLUTION TO REVIEW PROBLEM

Requirements 1 and 2

					Cash Receipts Journal				Page 7
	Debits		**Credits**						
					Other Accounts			**Cost of Goods Sold Debit Inventory Credit**	
Date	**Cash**	**Sales Discounts**	**Accounts Receivable**	**Sales Revenue**	**Account Title**	**Post. Ref.**	**Amount**		
Mar. 4	500			500				319	
6	60	5	65		Brady Lee	√			
9	1,080				Note Receivable—				
					Beverly Mann	13	1,000		
					Interest Revenue	46	80		
15	800			800				522	
24	2,200				Note Payable—				
					Interstate Bank	22	2,200		
27	1,200		1,200		Lance Albert	√			
31	5,840	5	1,265	1,300	Total		3,280	841	
	(11)	(42)	(12)	(41)			(√)	(51/14)	

Total Dr. = 5,845   Total Cr. = 5,845

Requirement 3

ACCOUNTS RECEIVABLE LEDGER

Lance Albert

Date	Jrnl. Ref.	Debit	Credit	Balance
Feb. 28	✓			1,840
Mar. 27	CR.7		1,200	640

Melinda Fultz

Date	Jrnl. Ref.	Debit	Credit	Balance
Feb. 28	✓			885

Brady Lee

Date	Jrnl. Ref.	Debit	Credit	Balance
Feb. 28	✓			65
Mar. 6	CR.7		65	—

GENERAL LEDGER

Cash   No. 11

Date	Jrnl. Ref.	Debit	Credit	Balance
Feb. 28	✓			1,117
Mar. 31	CR.7	5,840		6,957

Accounts Receivable   No. 12

Date	Jrnl. Ref.	Debit	Credit	Balance
Feb. 28	✓			2,790
Mar. 31	CR.7		1,265	1,525

Note Receivable—Beverly Mann   No. 13

Date	Jrnl. Ref.	Debit	Credit	Balance
Feb. 28	✓			1,000
Mar. 9	CR.7		1,000	—

Inventory   No. 14

Date	Jrnl. Ref.	Debit	Credit	Balance
Mar. 31	✓			1,819
31	CR.7		841	978

Note Payable—Interstate Bank   No. 22

Date	Jrnl. Ref.	Debit	Credit	Balance
Mar. 24	CR.7		2,200	2,200

Sales Revenue   No. 41

Date	Jrnl. Ref.	Debit	Credit	Balance
Mar. 31	CR.7		1,300	1,300

Sales Discounts   No. 42

Date	Jrnl. Ref.	Debit	Credit	Balance
Mar. 31	CR.7	5		5

Interest Revenue   No. 46

Date	Jrnl. Ref.	Debit	Credit	Balance
Mar. 9	CR.7		80	80

Cost of Goods Sold   No. 51

Date	Jrnl. Ref.	Debit	Credit	Balance
Mar. 31	CR.7	841		841

Requirement 4

Customer balances in the Accounts Receivable subsidiary ledger:

Lance Albert	$ 640
Melinda Fultz	885
Total accounts receivable	$1,525

This total agrees with the balance in Accounts Receivable.

SUMMARY

1. *Describe the features of an effective accounting information system.* An effective *accounting information system* should capture and summarize transactions quickly, accurately, and usefully. It should generate a variety of accounting reports, including financial statements and trial balances, that aid management in operating a business. The four major aspects of a good accounting system are (1) control over operations, (2) compatibility with the particular features of the business, (3) flexibility in response to changes in the business, and (4) a favorable cost/benefit relationship such that benefits outweigh costs.

2. *Understand how computerized and manual accounting systems are used.* Computerized accounting systems process inputs faster than do manual systems and can generate more types of reports. The key components of a computerized accounting system are *hardware*, *software*, and company personnel. Account numbers play a bigger role in the operation of computerized systems than they do in manual systems, because computers classify accounts by account numbers. Both computerized and manual accounting systems require transactions to be classified by type.

Computerized systems use a *menu* structure to organize accounting functions. Posting, trial balances, financial statements, and closing procedures are carried out automatically in a computerized accounting system. Computerized accounting systems are integrated so that the different *modules* of the system are updated together.

3. *Understand how spreadsheets are used in accounting.* *Spreadsheets* are electronic work sheets whose grid points, or cells, are linked by means of formulas. The numerical relationships in the spreadsheet are maintained whenever changes are made to the spreadsheet. Spreadsheets are ideally suited to detailed computations as in budgeting.

4. *Use the sales journal, the cash receipts journal, and the accounts receivable subsidiary ledger.* Manual accounting systems use *special journals* to record transactions by category. Credit sales are recorded in a *sales journal*, and cash receipts in a *cash receipts journal*. Posting goes to the *general ledger* and to the accounts receivable *subsidiary ledger*, which lists each customer and the amount receivable from that customer. The accounts receivable subsidiary ledger is the main device for ensuring that the company collects from customers.

5. *Use the purchases journal, the cash disbursements journal, and the accounts payable subsidiary ledger.* Credit purchases in a manual system are recorded in a *purchases journal*, and cash payments in a *cash disbursements journal*. Posting from these journals is to the general ledger and to the accounts payable subsidiary ledger. The accounts payable subsidiary ledger helps the company stay current in payments to suppliers.

SELF-STUDY QUESTIONS

Test your understanding of the chapter by marking the best answer for each of the following questions.

1. Why does a pharmacy need a different kind of accounting system than a physician uses? *(p. 234)*
   a. They have different kinds of employees.
   b. They have different kinds of journals and ledgers.
   c. They have different kinds of business transactions.
   d. They work different hours.

2. Which feature of an effective information system is most concerned with safeguarding assets? *(p. 234)*
   a. Control   c. Flexibility
   b. Compatibility   d. Favorable cost/benefit relationship

3. The account number 211031 most likely refers to *(p. 237)*
   a. Liabilities
   b. Current liabilities
   c. Accounts payable
   d. An individual vendor

4. If the amount of total revenues is in cell E7 of a spreadsheet and the amount for total expenses is in cell E20, then net income would be computed by the formula *(p. 240)*
   a. +E7+E20
   b. +E7–E20
   c. +E20–E7
   d. None of the above formulas will work

5. Special journals help most by *(p. 242)*
   a. Limiting the number of transactions that have to be recorded
   b. Reducing the cost of operating the accounting system
   c. Improving accuracy in posting to subsidiary ledgers
   d. Easing the preparation of the financial statements

6. Galvan Company recorded 523 credit-sale transactions in the sales journal. Ignoring Cost of Goods Sold and Inventory, how many postings would be required if these transactions were recorded in the general journal? *(p. 244)*
   a. 523   c. 1,569   b. 1,046   d. 2,092

7. Which two dollar-amount columns in the cash receipts journal will be used the most by a department store that makes half its sales for cash and half on credit? *(p. 247)*
   a. Cash Debit and Sales Discounts Debit
   b. Cash Debit and Accounts Receivable Credit
   c. Cash Debit and Other Accounts Credit
   d. Accounts Receivable Debit and Sales Revenue Credit

8. Entries in the purchases journal are posted to the *(p. 249)*
   a. General ledger only
   b. General ledger and the accounts payable ledger
   c. General ledger and the accounts receivable ledger
   d. Accounts receivable ledger and the accounts payable ledger

9. Every entry in the cash disbursements journal includes a *(p. 252)*
   a. Debit to Accounts   c. Credit to Inventory
      Payable
   b. Debit to an Other   d. Credit to Cash
      Account

10. Balancing the ledgers at the end of the period is most closely related to *(p. 253)*
   a. Control   c. Flexibility
   b. Compatibility   d. Favorable cost/benefit relationship

Answers to the Self-Study Questions follow the Accounting Vocabulary.

ACCOUNTING VOCABULARY

Accounting information system. The combination of personnel, records, and procedures that a business uses to meet its need for financial data (p. 233).

Batch processing. Computerized accounting for similar transactions in a group or batch (p. 239).

Cash disbursements journal. Special journal used to record cash payments by check (p. 251).

Cash receipts journal. Special journal used to record cash receipts (p. 246).

Control account. An account whose balance equals the sum of the balances in a group of related accounts in a subsidiary ledger (p. 246).

Database program. Computer program that organizes information so that it can be systematically accessed in a variety of report forms (p. 242).

General journal. Journal used to record all transactions that do not fit one of the special journals (p. 244).

General ledger. Ledger of accounts that are reported in the financial statements (p. 244).

Hardware. Electronic equipment that includes computers, disk drives, monitors, printers, and the network that connects them (p. 235).

Menu. A list of options for choosing computer functions (p. 238).

Module. Separate compatible units of an accounting package that are integrated to function together (p. 240).

Network. The system of electronic linkages that allow different computers to share the same information (p. 235).

On-line processing. Computerized processing of related functions, such as the recording and posting of transactions, on a continuous basis (p. 239).

Purchases journal. Special journal used to record all purchases of inventory, supplies, and other assets on account (p. 249).

Sales journal. Special journal used to record credit sales (p. 243).

Server. The main computer in a network, where the program and data are stored (p. 235).

Software. Set of programs or instructions that cause the computer to perform the work desired (p. 235).

Special journal. An accounting journal designed to record one specific type of transaction (p. 242).

Spreadsheet. A computer program that links data by means of formulas and functions; an electronic work sheet (p. 240).

Subsidiary ledger. Book of accounts that provides supporting details on individual balances, the total of which appears in a general ledger account (p. 245).

ANSWERS TO SELF-STUDY QUESTIONS

1. c
2. a
3. d
4. b
5. b
6. c [523 × 3 (one debit, one credit, and one to the accounts receivable ledger) = 1,569]
7. b
8. b
9. d
10. a

QUESTIONS

1. Describe the four criteria of an effective accounting system.
2. Distinguish batch computer processing from on-line computer processing.
3. What accounting categories correspond to the account numbers 1, 2, 3, 4, and 5 in a typical computerized accounting system?
4. Why might the number 112 be assigned to Accounts Receivable and the number 1120708 to Carl Erickson, a customer?
5. Describe the function of menus in a computerized accounting system.
6. How do formulas in spreadsheets speed the process of budget preparation and revision?
7. Name four special journals used in accounting systems. For what type of transaction is each designed?
8. Describe the two advantages that special journals have over recording all transactions in the general journal.
9. What is a control account, and how is it related to a subsidiary ledger? Name two common control accounts.
10. Graff Company's sales journal has one amount column headed Accounts Receivable Dr. and Sales Revenue Cr. In this journal, 86 transactions are recorded. How many posting references appear in the journal? State what each posting reference represents.
11. The accountant for Bannister Company posted all amounts correctly from the cash receipts journal to the general ledger. However, she failed to post three credits to customer accounts in the accounts receivable subsidiary ledger. How would this error be detected?
12. At what two times is posting done from a special journal? What items are posted at each time?
13. What is the purpose of balancing the ledgers?
14. Posting from the journals of McKedrick Realty is complete. But the total of the individual balances in the accounts payable subsidiary ledger does not equal the balance in the Accounts Payable control account in the general ledger. Does this discrepancy necessarily indicate that the trial balance is out of balance? Give your reason.
15. Assume that posting is completed. The trial balance shows no errors, but the sum of the individual accounts payable does not equal the Accounts Payable control balance in the general ledger. What two errors could cause this problem?

EXERCISES

Assigning account numbers
(Obj. 2)

E6-1   Assign account numbers (from the list that follows) to the accounts of LP Gas Company. Identify the headings, which are *not* accounts and would not be assigned an account number.

Assets	Joseph Jacobson, Capital
Current Assets	Joseph Jacobson, Withdrawals
Property, Plant, and Equipment	Revenues
Accounts Payable	Selling Expenses

Numbers from which to choose:

1	14
2	21
3	31
4	32
5	33
11	121
12	131
13	411

Using a trial balance
(Obj. 2)

E6-2   The following accounts in the computerized accounting system of FAX Supply Company show some of the company's adjusted balances before closing:

Total assets	?
Current assets	5,600
Plant assets	13,400
Total liabilities	?
Current liabilities	1,100
Long-term liabilities	?
Jaime Cortez, capital	8,600
Jaime Cortez, withdrawals	2,000
Total revenues	18,000
Total expenses	11,000

Compute the missing amounts.

Using a spreadsheet to compute depreciation
(Obj. 3)

E6-3   An asset listed on a spreadsheet has a cost of $60,000; this amount is located in cell E7. The number of years of the asset's useful life is found in cell E9. Write the spreadsheet formula to express annual depreciation expense for this asset.

Computing financial statement amounts with a spreadsheet
(Obj. 3)

E6-4   Suppose the values of the following items are stored in the cells of a spreadsheet:

Item	Cell
Total assets	E7
Current assets	E8
Fixed assets	E9
Total liabilities	E10
Current liabilities	E11
Long-term liabilities	E12

Write the spreadsheet formula to calculate:

a.   Current ratio
b.   Total owner equity
c.   Debt ratio

E6-5 The sales and cash receipts journals of Alta Design Company include the following entries: *Using the sales and cash receipts journals* *(Obj. 4)*

Sales Journal

Date	Account Debited	Post. Ref.	Accounts Receivable Dr. Sales Revenue Cr.	Cost of Goods Sold Dr. Inventory Cr.
Oct. 7	C. Carlson	✓	930	550
10	T. Muecke	✓	3,100	1,970
10	E. Lovell	✓	690	410
12	B. Goebel	✓	5,470	3,340
31	Total		10,190	6,270

Cash Receipts Journal

	Debits			Credits				Cost of Goods
						Other Accounts		Sold Debit
Date	Cash	Sales Discounts	Accounts Receivable	Sales Revenue	Account Title	Post. Ref.	Amount	Inventory Credit
Oct. 16					C. Carlson	✓		
19					E. Lovell	✓		
24	300			300				190
30					T. Muecke	✓		

Alta Design makes all credit sales on terms of 2/10 n/30. Complete the cash receipts journal for those transactions indicated. Also, total the journal and show that total debits equal total credits. Each cash receipt was for the full amount of the receivable.

E6-6 The cash receipts journal of Threlkeld, Inc., follows: *Classifying postings from the cash receipts journal* *(Obj. 4)*

Cash Receipts Journal — Page 7

	Debits			Credits			
						Other Accounts	
Date	Cash	Sales Discounts	Accounts Receivable	Sales Revenue	Account Title	Post. Ref.	Amount
Dec. 2	794	16	810		Magna Co.	(a)	
9	1,291		1,291.		Kamm, Inc.	(b)	
14	3,904			3,904		(c)	
19	4,480				Note Receivable	(d)	4,000
					Interest Revenue	(e)	480
30	314	7	321		J. T. Franz	(f)	
31	4,235			4,235		(g)	
31	15,018	23	2,422	8,139	Totals		4,480
	(h)	(i)	(j)	(k)			(l)

Required

Identify each posting reference (a) through (l) as (1) a posting to the general ledger as a column total, (2) a posting to the general ledger as an individual amount, (3) a posting to a subsidiary ledger account, or (4) an amount not posted.

Identifying transactions from postings to the accounts receivable ledger
(Obj. 4)

E6-7   A customer account in the accounts receivable ledger of Zobal Freight Company follows:

Bradley Carpenter

Date		Jrnl. Ref.	Dr.	Cr.	Balance Dr.	Balance Cr.
July 1	....				403	
10	....	S.5	1,180		1,583	
15	....	J.8		191	1,392	
21	....	CR.9		703	689	

Required

Describe the three posted transactions.

Recording purchase transactions in the general journal and in the purchases journal
(Obj. 5)

E6-8   During April, Castlebury, Inc., completed the following credit purchase transactions:

    April 4   Purchased inventory, $1,904, from Hillshire Co. Castlebury uses a
                perpetual inventory system.
        7   Purchased supplies, $107, from JJ Maine Corp.
       19   Purchased equipment, $1,903, from Liston-Fry Co.
       27   Purchased inventory, $2,210, from Milan, Inc.

Record these transactions first in the general journal—with explanations—and then in the purchases journal. Omit credit terms and posting references. Which procedure for recording transactions is quicker?

Posting from the purchases journal, balancing the ledgers
(Obj. 5)

E6-9   The purchases journal of Venable Company follows:

Purchases Journal   Page 7

Date	Account Credited	Terms	Post. Ref.	Account Payable Cr.	Inventory Dr.	Supplies Dr.	Other Accounts Dr. Acct. Title	Other Accounts Dr. Post. Ref.	Other Accounts Dr. Amt. Dr.
Sep. 2	Donahoe Company	n/30		1,300	1,300				
5	Rolf Office Supply	n/30		175		175			
13	Donahoe Company	2/10 n/30		847	847				
26	Marks Equipment Company	n/30		916			Equipment		916
30	Totals			3,238	2,147	175			916

Required

1. Open ledger accounts for Supplies, Equipment, Accounts Payable, and Inventory. Post to these accounts from the purchases journal. Use dates and posting references in the ledger accounts.

2. Open accounts in the accounts payable subsidiary ledger for Donahoe Company, Marks Equipment Company, and Rolf Office Supply. Post from the purchases journal. Use dates and journal references in the ledger accounts.

3. Balance the Accounts Payable control account in the general ledger with the total of the balances in the accounts payable subsidiary ledger.

E6-10   During April, Crest Products had the following transactions:

Using the cash disbursements journal
(Obj. 5)

April 3   Paid $892 on account to Ballast Corp. net of an $8 discount for an earlier purchase of inventory.
        6   Purchased inventory for cash, $1,267.
       11   Paid $375 for supplies.
       15   Purchased inventory on credit from Monroe Corporation, $774.
       16   Paid $8,062 on account to LaGrange Associates; there was no discount.
       21   Purchased furniture for cash, $960.
       26   Paid $3,910 on account to Graff Software for an earlier purchase of inventory. The discount was $90.
       31   Made a semiannual interest payment of $800 on a long-term note payable. The entire payment was for interest.

Required

1. Prepare a cash disbursements journal similar to the one illustrated in this chapter. Omit the check number (Ck. No.) and posting reference (Post. Ref.) columns.
2. Record the transactions in the journal. Which transaction should not be recorded in the cash disbursements journal? In what journal does it belong?
3. Total the amount columns of the journal. Determine that the total debits equal the total credits.

E6-11   The following documents describe two business transactions:

Using business documents to record transactions
(Obj. 5)

Invoice				Debit Memo		
Date: March 14, 19X0				**Date:** March 20, 19X0		
Sold to: Tailwind Bicycle Shop				**Issued to:** Schwinn Company		
Sold by: Schwinn Company				**Issued by:** Tailwind Bicycle Shop		
Terms: 2/10 n/30						
Items Purchased Bicycles				**Items Returned** Bicycles		
Quantity	**Price**	**Total**		**Quantity**	**Price**	**Total**
4	$95	$380		1	$95	$ 95
2	70	140		1	70	70
5	60	300		**Total**		$165
Total		$820		**Reason:** Wrong sizes		

Use the general journal to record these transactions and Tailwind's cash payment on March 21. Record the transactions first on the books of Tailwind Bicycle Shop and, second, on the books of Schwinn Company, which makes and sells bicycles. Both Tailwind and Schwinn use a perpetual inventory system as illustrated in Chapter 5. Schwinn's cost of the bicycles sold to Tailwind was $400. Schwinn's cost of the returned merchandise was $80. Round to the nearest dollar. Explanations are not required. Set up your answer in the following format:

Date	Tailwind Journal Entries	Schwinn Journal Entries

Using a spreadsheet to prepare an
income statement and evaluate
operations
(Obj. 3)

P6-1A The following spreadsheet shows the income statement of DeGraff Wholesale Grocery Co.:

Column

Row Number	A	B
5	Revenues:	
6	Service revenue ————————————→	
7	Rent revenue ——————————————→	
8		————————
9	Total revenue ——————————————→	
10		
11	Expenses:	
12	Salary expense ——————————————→	
13	Supplies expense ——————————————→	
14	Rent expense ——————————————→	
15	Depreciation expense ——————————→	
16		————————
17	Total expenses ——————————————→	
18		————————
19	Net income ——————————————→	
20		════════

Required

1. Write the word *number* in the cells (indicated by arrows) where numbers will be entered.

2. Write the appropriate formula in each cell that will need a formula. Symbols from which to choose are:

+	add
–	subtract
*	multiply
/	divide

@SUM (beginning cell..ending cell)

3. Last year DeGraff Wholesale Grocery Co. used this spreadsheet to prepare the company's budgeted income statement—which shows the company's net income goal—for the current year. It is now one year later, and DeGraff has prepared its actual income statement for the year. State how the president of the company can use this income statement in decision making.

Using the sales, cash receipts, and
general journals
(Obj. 4)

P6-2A The general ledger of Roberson, Inc., includes the following accounts, among others:

Cash	11
Accounts Receivable	12
Inventory	13
Notes Receivable	15
Supplies	16
Land	18
Sales Revenue	41
Sales Discounts	42
Sales Returns and Allowances	43
Interest Revenue	47
Cost of Goods Sold	51

All credit sales are on the company's standard terms of 2/10 n/30. Transactions in May that affected sales and cash receipts were as follows:

May 2 Sold inventory on credit to Wadkins Co., $1,700. Roberson's cost of these goods was $1,200.
4 As an accommodation to a competitor, sold supplies at cost, $85, receiving cash.
7 Cash sales for the week totaled $1,890 (cost, $1,640).
9 Sold merchandise on account to A. L. Prince, $7,320 (cost $5,110).
10 Sold land that cost $10,000 for cash of $10,000.
11 Sold goods on account to Sloan Electric, $5,104 (cost $3,520).
12 Received cash from Wadkins Co. in full settlement of its account receivable from May 2.
14 Cash sales for the week were $2,106 (cost $1,530).
15 Sold inventory on credit to the partnership of Wilkie & Blinn, $3,650 (cost $2,260).
18 Received inventory sold on May 9 to A. L. Prince for $600. The goods shipped were unsatisfactory. These goods cost Roberson $440.
20 Sold merchandise on account to Sloan Electric, $629 (cost $450).
21 Cash sales for the week were $990 (cost, $690).
22 Received $4,000 cash from A. L. Prince in partial settlement of his account receivable.
25 Received cash from Wilkie & Blinn for its account receivable from May 15.
25 Sold goods on account to Olsen Co., $1,520 (cost $1,050).
27 Collected $5,125 on a note receivable, of which $125 was interest.
28 Cash sales for the week totaled $3,774 (cost $2,460).
29 Sold inventory on account to R. O. Bankston, $242 (cost, $170).
30 Received goods sold on May 25 to Olsen Co. for $40. The inventory was damaged in shipment. The salvage value of these goods was $10.
31 Received $2,720 cash on account from A. L. Prince.

Required

1. Roberson records sales returns and allowances in the general journal. Use the appropriate journal to record the above transactions in a sales journal (omit the Invoice No. column), a cash receipts journal, and a general journal.

2. Total each column of the cash receipts journal. Show that the total debits equal the total credits.

3. Show how postings would be made from the journals by writing the account numbers and check marks in the appropriate places in the journals.

P6-3A The following cash receipts journal contains five entries. All five entries are for legitimate cash receipt transactions, but the journal contains some errors in recording the transactions. In fact, only one entry is correct, and each of the other four entries contains one error.

Correcting errors in the cash receipts journal (Obj. 4)

Cash Receipts Journal   Page 13

| | Debits | | Credits | | | | | Cost of Goods Sold Debit Inventory Credit |
| | | | | | Other Accounts | | | |
Date	Cash	Sales Discounts	Accounts Receivable	Sales Revenue	Account Title	Post. Ref.	Amount	
5/6		600		600				290
7	429	22			Marvin Trent	✓	451	
12	2,160				Note Receivable	15	2,000	
					Interest Revenue	45	160	
18				330				150
24	1,100		770					
	3,689	622	770	930	Totals		2,611	440
	(11)	(42)	(12)	(41)			(✓)	(51/13)

Total Dr. = $4,311   Total Cr. = $4,311

Required

1. Identify the correct entry.
2. Identify the error in each of the other four entries.
3. Using the following format, prepare a corrected cash receipts journal.

Cash Receipts Journal   Page 13

Date	Debits		Credits					Cost of Goods Sold Debit Inventory Credit
	Cash	Sales Discounts	Accounts Receivable	Sales Revenue	Other Accounts			
					Account Title	Post. Ref.	Amount	
5/6								
7					Marvin Trent	✓		
12					Note Receivable	15		
					Interest Revenue	45		
18								
24								
	4,289	22	1,221	930	Totals		2,160	
	(11)	(42)	(12)	(41)			(✓)	

Total Dr. = $4,311   Total Cr. = $4,311

Using the purchases, cash disbursements, and general journals
(Obj. 5)

P6-4A The general ledger of Gibbs, Inc., includes the following accounts:

Cash... 111
Inventory... 131
Prepaid Insurance 161
Supplies.. 171
Furniture.. 187
Accounts Payable 211
Rent Expense 564
Utilities Expense... 583

Transactions in August that affected purchases and cash disbursements were as follows:

Aug. 1   Purchased inventory on credit from Cowtown Co., $3,900. Terms were 2/10 n/30.
     1   Paid monthly rent, debiting Rent Expense for $2,000.
     5   Purchased supplies on credit terms of 2/10 n/30 from Ross Supply, $450.
     8   Paid electricity bill, $588.
     9   Purchased furniture on account from A-1 Office Supply, $4,100. Payment terms were net 30.
    10   Returned the furniture to A-1 Office Supply. It was the wrong color.
    11   Paid Cowtown Co. the amount owed on the purchase of August 1.
    12   Purchased inventory on account from Wynne, Inc., $4,400. Terms were 3/10 n/30.
    13   Purchased inventory for cash, $655.
    14   Paid a semiannual insurance premium, debiting Prepaid Insurance, $1,200.
    15   Paid our account payable to Ross Supply, from August 5.
    18   Paid gas and water bills, $196.
    21   Purchased inventory on credit terms of 1/10 n/45 from Software, Inc., $5,200.

Aug. 21 Paid account payable to Wynne, Inc. from August 12.
  22 Purchased supplies on account from Office Sales, Inc., $274. Terms were net 30.
  25 Returned to Software, Inc., $1,200 of the inventory purchased on August 21.
  31 Paid Software, Inc., the net amount owed from August 21, less the return, on August 25.

Required

1. Gibbs, Inc., records purchase returns in the general journal. Use the appropriate journal to record the above transactions in a purchases journal, a cash disbursements journal (omit the Check No. column), and a general journal.

2. Total each column of the special journals. Show that the total debits equal the total credits in each special journal.

3. Show how postings would be made from the journals by writing the account numbers and check marks in the appropriate places in the journals.

(GROUP B)

P6-1B The following spreadsheet shows the assets section of the Quartz Products Company balance sheet:

Using a spreadsheet to prepare a partial balance sheet and evaluate financial positions (Obj. 3)

	Column	
Row Number	A	B
5	Assets:	
6	Current assets:	
7	Cash ———————→	
8	Receivables ——————→	
9	Inventory ——————→	
10		
11	Total current assets ————→	
12		
13	Equipment ——————→	
14	Accumulated depreciation ———→	
15		
16	Equipment, net ————→	
17		
18	Total assets ——————→	
19		

Required

1. Write the word *number* in the cells (indicated by arrows) where numbers will be entered.

2. Write the appropriate formula in each cell that will need a formula. Symbols from which to choose are:

+	add
–	subtract
*	multiply
/	divide

@SUM (beginning cell..ending cell)

3. Last year Quartz Products Company used this spreadsheet to prepare the company's budgeted balance sheet for the current year. The budgeted balance sheet shows the company's goal for total current assets at the end of the year. It is now one year later, and Quartz Products Company has prepared its actual year-end balance sheet. State how the company president can use this balance sheet in decision making.

P6-2B The general ledger of Vasquez Supply Company includes the following accounts:

Cash..	111
Accounts Receivable	112
Notes Receivable	115
Inventory..	131
Equipment	141
Land	142
Sales Revenue..	411
Sales Discounts	412
Sales Returns and Allowances	413
Interest Revenue	417
Gain on Sale of Land................................	418
Cost of Goods Sold...................................	511

All credit sales are on the company's standard terms of 2/10 n/30. Transactions in February that affected sales and cash receipts were as follows:

Feb. 1   Sold inventory on credit to Ruth Lott, $300. Vasquez's cost of these goods was $214.

    5   As an accommodation to another company, sold new equipment for its cost of $770, receiving cash in this amount.

    6   Cash sales for the week totaled $2,107 (cost, $1,362).

    8   Sold merchandise on account to McNair Co., $2,830 (cost $1,789).

    9   Sold land that cost $22,000 for cash of $40,000.

   11   Sold goods on account to Nickerson Builders, $6,099 (cost $3,853).

   11   Received cash from Ruth Lott in full settlement of her account receivable from February 1.

   13   Cash sales for the week were $1,995 (cost $1,286).

   15   Sold inventory on credit to Montez and Montez, a partnership, $800 (cost, $517).

   18   Received inventory sold on February 8 to McNair Co. for $120. The goods we shipped were unsatisfactory. These goods cost Vasquez $73.

   19   Sold merchandise on account to Nickerson Builders, $3,900 (cost, $2,618).

   20   Cash sales for the week were $2,330 (cost, $1,574).

   21   Received $1,200 cash from McNair Co. in partial settlement of its account receivable. There was no discount.

   22   Received cash from Montez and Montez for its account receivable from February 15.

   22   Sold goods on account to Diamond Co., $2,022 (cost, $1,325).

   25   Collected $4,200 on a note receivable, of which $200 was interest.

   27   Cash sales for the week totaled $2,970 (cost, $1,936).

   27   Sold inventory on account to Littleton Corporation, $2,290 (cost, $1,434).

   28   Received goods sold on February 21 to Diamond Co. for $680. The goods were damaged in shipment. The salvage value of these goods was $96.

   28   Received $1,510 cash on account from McNair Co. There was no discount.

Required

1. Use the appropriate journal to record the above transactions in a sales journal (omit the Invoice No. column), a cash receipts journal, and a general journal. Vasquez records sales returns and allowances in the general journal.

2. Total each column of the cash receipts journal. Determine that the total debits equal the total credits.

3. Show how postings would be made from the journals by writing the account numbers and check marks in the appropriate places in the journals.

P6-3B The cash receipts journal below contains five entries. All five entries are for legitimate cash receipt transactions, but the journal contains some errors in recording the transactions. In fact, only one entry is correct, and each of the other four entries contains one error. *Correcting errors in the cash receipts journal (Obj. 4)*

Cash Receipts Journal   Page 5

| | Debits | | Credits | | | | | Cost of Goods |
| | | | | | Other Accounts | | | |
Date	Cash	Sales Discounts	Accounts Receivable	Sales Revenue	Account Title	Post. Ref.	Amount	Sold Debit Inventory Credit
7/5	711	34	745		Meg Davis	✓		
9			346	346	Carl Ryther	✓		
10	8,000			8,000	Land	19		
19	73							44
31	1,060			1,133				631
	9,844	34	1,091	9,479	Totals			675
	(11)	(42)	(12)	(41)			(✓)	

Total Dr. = $9,878   Total Cr. = $10,570

Required

1. Identify the correct entry.
2. Identify the error in each of the other four entries.
3. Using the following format, prepare a corrected cash receipts journal.

Cash Receipts Journal   Page 5

| | Debits | | Credits | | | | | Cost of Goods |
| | | | | | Other Accounts | | | |
Date	Cash	Sales Discounts	Accounts Receivable	Sales Revenue	Account Title	Post. Ref.	Amount	Sold Debit Inventory Credit
7/5					Meg Davis	✓		
9					Carl Ryther	✓		
10					Land	19		
19								
31								
	10,190	34	1,091	1,133	Totals		8,000	
	(11)	(42)	(12)	(41)			(✓)	(51/13)

Total Dr. = $10,224   Total Cr. = $10,224

Using the purchases, cash
disbursements, and general
journals
(Obj. 5)

P6-4B The general ledger of Westernhouse Custom Frames includes the following accounts:

Cash..	111
Inventory..	131
Prepaid Insurance	161
Supplies	171
Equipment	189
Accounts Payable	211
Rent Expense	562
Utilities Expense	565

Transactions in March that affected purchases and cash disbursements were as follows:

Mar. 1   Paid monthly rent, debiting Rent Expense for $1,350.
3   Purchased inventory on credit from Loveton Co., $4,900. Terms were 2/15 n/45.
4   Purchased supplies on credit terms of 2/10 n/30 from Harmon Sales, $800.
7   Paid gas and water bills, $406.
10   Purchased equipment on account from Lancer Co., $1,050. Payment terms were 2/10 n/30.
11   Returned the equipment to Lancer Co. It was defective.
12   Paid Loveton Co. the amount owed on the purchase of March 3.
12   Purchased inventory on account from Lancer Co., $1,100. Terms were 2/10 n/30.
14   Purchased inventory for cash, $1,585.
15   Paid an insurance premium, debiting Prepaid Insurance, $2,416.
16   Paid our account payable to Harmon Sales from March 4.
17   Paid electricity bill, $165.
20   Paid account payable to Lancer Co., less the discount, from March 12.
21   Purchased supplies on account from Master Supply, $754. Terms were net 30.
22   Purchased inventory on credit terms of 1/10 n/30 from Linz Brothers, $3,400.
26   Returned inventory purchased for $500 on March 22, to Linz Brothers.
31   Paid Linz Brothers the net amount owed from March 22, less the return on March 26.

Required

1. Use the appropriate journal to record the above transactions in a purchases journal, a cash disbursements journal (omit the Check No. column), and a general journal. Westernhouse records purchase returns in the general journal.

2. Total each column of the special journals. Show that the total debits equal the total credits in each special journal.

3. Show how postings would be made from the journals by writing the account numbers and check marks in the appropriate places in the journals.

EXTENDING YOUR KNOWLEDGE

DECISION PROBLEMS

Reconstructing transactions from
amounts posted to the accounts
receivable ledger
(Obj. 4)

1.   A fire destroyed some accounting records of Richards Company. The owner, Ann Richards, asks for your help in reconstructing the records. *She needs to know the beginning and ending balances of Accounts Receivable and the credit sales and cash receipts on account from customers during March.* All Richards Company's sales are on credit, with payment terms of 2/10 n/30. All cash receipts on account reached Richards within the 10-day discount period, except as noted. The only accounting record preserved from the fire is the accounts receivable subsidiary ledger, which follows:

Adam Cline

Date	Item	Jrnl. Ref.	Debit	Credit	Balance
Mar. 8		S.6	2,378		2,378
16		S.6	903		3,281
18		CR.8		2,378	903
19		J.5		221	682
27		CR.8		682	–0–

Lou Gross

Date	Item	Jrnl. Ref.	Debit	Credit	Balance
Mar. 1	Balance				1,096
5		CR.8		1,096	–0–
11		S.6	396		396
21		CR.8		396	–0–
24		S.6	1,944		1,944

Norris Associates

Date	Item	Jrnl. Ref.	Debit	Credit	Balance
Mar. 1	Balance				883
15		S.6	2,635		3,518
29		CR.8		883*	2,635

---

*Cash receipt did not occur within the discount period.

Suzuki, Inc.

Date	Item	Jrnl. Ref.	Debit	Credit	Balance
Mar. 1	Balance				440
3		CR.8		440	–0–
25		S.6	3,655		3,655
29		S.6	1,123		4,778

Understanding an accounting system (Obj. 4, 5)

2. The external auditor must ensure that the amounts shown on the balance sheet for Accounts Receivable represent actual amounts that customers owe the company. Each customer account in the accounts receivable subsidiary ledger must represent an actual credit sale to the person indicated, and the customer's balance must not have been collected. This auditing concept is called *validity* or *validating the accounts receivable.*

The auditor must also ensure that all amounts that the company owes are included in Accounts Payable and other liability accounts. For example, all credit purchases of inventory made by the company—and not yet paid—should be included in the balance of the Accounts Payable account. This auditing concept is called *completeness.*

Required

Suggest how an auditor might test a customer's account receivable balance for validity. Indicate how the auditor might test the balance of the Accounts Payable account for completeness.

ETHICAL ISSUE

On a recent trip to Russia, Brian Dodd, sales manager of Micro-electronic Devices, took his wife at company expense. Erika Schwartz, vice-president of sales and Dodd's boss, thought his travel and entertainment expenses seemed excessive. Schwartz approved the reimbursement, however, because she owed Dodd a favor. Schwartz, well aware that the company president routinely reviewed all expenses recorded in the cash disbursements journal, had the accountant record Dodd's wife's expenses in the general journal as follows:

Sales Promotion Expense	3,500	
Cash.......................................		3,500

Required

1. Does recording the transaction in the general journal rather than in the cash disbursements journal affect the amounts of cash and total expenses reported in the financial statements?
2. Why did Schwartz want this transaction recorded in the general journal?
3. What is the ethical issue in this situation? What role does accounting play in the ethical issue?

COMPREHENSIVE PROBLEMS FOR PART ONE

1. COMPLETING A MERCHANDISER'S ACCOUNTING CYCLE

The end-of-month trial balance of Lake Placid Building Materials at January 31 of the current year follows:

LAKE PLACID BUILDING MATERIALS
TRIAL BALANCE
JANUARY 31, 19XX

Account Number	Account	Balance Debit	Balance Credit
11	Cash...	$ 6,430	
12	Accounts receivable...	19,090	
13	Inventory...	65,400	
14	Supplies...	2,700	
15	Building...	188,170	
16	Accumulated depreciation—building...............		$ 36,000
17	Fixtures..	45,600	
18	Accumulated depreciation—fixtures.................		5,800
21	Accounts payable..		28,300
22	Salary payable...		
23	Interest payable		
24	Unearned sales revenue		6,560
25	Note payable, long-term.....................................		87,000
31	Meg Louder, capital...		144,980
32	Meg Louder, withdrawals	9,200	
41	Sales revenue...		177,970
42	Sales discounts..	7,300	
43	Sales returns and allowances............................	8,140	
51	Cost of goods sold..	103,000	
54	Selling expense	21,520	
55	General expense	10,060	
56	Interest expense...		
	Total..	$486,610	$486,610

Additional data at January 31, 19XX:

a. Supplies consumed during the month, $1,500. Half is selling expense, and the other half is general expense.

b. Depreciation for the month: building, $4,000; fixtures, $4,800. One-fourth of depreciation is selling expense, and three-fourths is general expense.

c. Unearned sales revenue still unearned, $1,200.

d. Accrued salaries, a general expense, $1,150.

e. Accrued interest expense, $780.

f. Inventory on hand, $63,720.

Required

1. Using four-column accounts, open the accounts listed on the trial balance, inserting their unadjusted balances. Date the balances of the following accounts January 1: Supplies; Building; Accumulated Depreciation—Building; Fixtures; Accumulated Depreciation—Fixtures; Unearned Sales Revenue; and Meg Louder, Capital. Date the balance of Meg Louder, Withdrawals, January 31.

2. Enter the trial balance on an accounting work sheet, and complete the work sheet for the month ended January 31 of the current year. Lake Placid groups all operating expenses under two accounts, Selling Expense and General Expense. Leave two blank lines under Selling Expense and three blank lines under General Expense.

3. Prepare the company's multiple-step income statement and statement of owner's equity for the month ended January 31 of the current year. Also prepare the balance sheet at that date in report form.

4. Journalize the adjusting and closing entries at January 31, using page 3 of the journal.

5. Post the adjusting and closing entries, using dates and posting references.

6. Compute Lake Placid's current ratio and debt ratio at January 31, and compare these values with the industry averages of 1.9 for the current ratio and 0.57 for the debt ratio. Compute the gross margin percentage and the rate of inventory turnover for the month (the inventory balance at the end of December was $67,100), and compare these ratio values with the industry average of 0.26 for the gross margin ratio and 1.0 for inventory turnover. Does Lake Placid Building Materials appear to be stronger or weaker than the average company in the building materials industry?

2. COMPLETING THE ACCOUNTING CYCLE FOR A MERCHANDISING ENTITY

Note: This problem can be solved with or without special journals. See Requirement 2.

Firestone Company closes its books and prepares financial statements at the end of each month. The company completed the following transactions during August:

Aug.		
1	Issued check no. 682 for August office rent of $2,000. (Debit Rent Expense.)
2	Issued check no. 683 to pay salaries of $1,240, which includes salary payable of $930 from July 31. Firestone does *not* use reversing entries.
2	Issued invoice no. 503 for sale on account to R. T. Loeb, $600. Firestone's cost of this merchandise was $190.
3	Purchased inventory on credit terms of 1/15 n/60 from Grant Publishers, $1,400.
4	Received net amount of cash on account from Fullam Company, $2,156, within the discount period.
4	Sold inventory for cash, $330 (cost, $104).
5	Received from Park-Hee, Inc., merchandise that had been sold earlier for $550 (cost, $174)
5	Issued check no. 684 to purchase supplies for cash, $780.
6	Collected interest revenue of $1,100.
7	Issued invoice no. 504 for sale on account to K. D. Skipper, $2,400 (cost, $759).
8	Issued check no. 685 to pay Federal Company $2,600 of the amount owed at July 31. This payment occurred after the end of the discount period.
11	Issued check no. 686 to pay Grant Publishers the net amount owed from August 3.
12	Received cash from R. T. Loeb in full settlement of her account receivable from August 2.
16	Issued check no. 687 to pay salary expense of $1,240.
19	Purchased inventory for cash, $850, issuing check no. 688.
22	Purchased furniture on credit terms of 3/15 n/60 from Beaver Corporation, $510.
23	Sold inventory on account to Fullam Company, issuing invoice no. 505 for $9,966 (cost, $3,152).
24	Received half the July 31 amount receivable from K. D. Skipper—after the end of the discount period.
25	Issued check no. 689 to pay utilities, $432.
26	Purchased supplies on credit terms of 2/10 n/30 from Federal Company, $180.
30	Returned damaged inventory to company from whom Firestone made the cash purchase on August 19, receiving cash of $850.
30	Granted a sales allowance of $175 to K. D. Skipper.
31	Purchased inventory on credit terms of 1/10 n/30 from Suncrest Supply, $8,330.
31	Issued check no. 690 to Peter Firestone, owner of the business, for personal withdrawal, $1,700.

Required

1. Open these accounts with their account numbers and July 31 balances in the various ledgers.

General Ledger:

101	Cash	$ 4,490
102	Accounts Receivable	22,560
104	Interest Receivable	
105	Inventory	41,800
109	Supplies	1,340
117	Prepaid Insurance	2,200
140	Note Receivable, Long-term	11,000
160	Furniture	37,270
161	Accumulated Depreciation	10,550
201	Accounts Payable	12,600
204	Salary Payable	930
207	Interest Payable	320
208	Unearned Sales Revenue	
220	Note Payable, Long-term	42,000
301	Peter Firestone, Capital	54,260
302	Peter Firestone, Withdrawals	
400	Income Summary	
401	Sales Revenue	
402	Sales Discounts	
403	Sales Returns and Allowances	
410	Interest Revenue	
501	Cost of Goods Sold	
510	Salary Expense	
513	Rent Expense	
514	Depreciation Expense	
516	Insurance Expense	
517	Utilities Expense	
519	Supplies Expense	
523	Interest Expense	

Accounts Receivable Subsidiary Ledger: Fullam Company, $2,200; R. T. Loeb; Park-Hee, Inc., $11,590; K. D. Skipper, $8,770.
Accounts Payable Subsidiary Ledger: Beaver Corporation; Federal Company, $12,600; Grant Publishers; Suncrest Supply.

2. Ask your professor for directions. Journalize the August transactions either in the general journal (page 9; explanations not required) or, as illustrated in Chapter 6, in a series of special journals: a sales journal (page 4), a cash receipts journal (page 11), a purchases journal (page 8), a cash disbursements journal (page 5), and a general journal (page 9). Firestone makes all credit sales on terms of 2/10 n/30 and uses a perpetual inventory system as illustrated in Chapter 5.
3. Post daily to the accounts receivable subsidiary ledger and the accounts payable subsidiary ledger. On August 31, post to the general ledger.

4. Prepare a trial balance in the Trial Balance columns of a work sheet, and use the following information to complete the work sheet for the month ended August 31:
   a. Accrued interest revenue, $100.
   b. Supplies on hand, $990.
   c. Prepaid insurance expired, $550.
   d. Depreciation expense, $230.
   e. Accrued salary expense, $1,030.
   f. Accrued interest expense, $320.
   g. Unearned sales revenue, $450.*
   h. Inventory on hand, $46,700.

   ---

   *On August 2, Firestone Company sold inventory to R. T. Loeb and collected in full on August 12. Upon learning that the shipment to Loeb was incomplete, Firestone plans to ship the goods to her during September. At August 31, $450 of unearned sales revenue needs to be recorded. The cost of this merchandise is $142.

5. Prepare Firestone's multiple-step income statement and statement of owner's equity for August. Prepare the balance sheet at August 31.

6. Journalize and post the adjusting and closing entries.

7. Prepare a postclosing trial balance at August 31. Also, balance the total of the customer accounts in the accounts receivable subsidiary ledger against the Accounts Receivable balance in the general ledger. Do the same for the accounts payable subsidiary ledger and Accounts Payable in the general ledger.

3. GROUP PROJECT: PREPARING A BUSINESS PLAN FOR A SERVICE ENTITY

List what you have learned thus far in the course. On the basis of what you have learned, refine your plan for promoting a rock concert to include everything you believe you must do to succeed in this business venture.

4. GROUP PROJECT: PREPARING A BUSINESS PLAN FOR A MERCHANDISING ENTITY

As you work through Part 2 of this book (Chapters 7–12), you will be examining in detail the current assets, current liabilities, and plant assets of a business. Most of the organizations that form the context for business activity in the remainder of the book are merchandising entities. Therefore, in a group or individually—as directed by your instructor—develop a plan for beginning and operating an audio/video store or other type of business. Develop your plan in as much detail as you can. Remember that the business manager who attends to the most details delivers the best product at the lowest price for customers!

At the end of each Part (after Chapters 12, 17, and 19), we will revisit this plan. Each time we will ask you to refine your plan on the basis of what you learned in that Part. At the end of the course, you will have a good idea of how to plan and operate a business. That is what accounting is all about.

Lawless Container Corporation—Business Analysis

Many of the durable goods we purchase come in boxes—whether they be plain brown corrugated or elaborate color-printed boxes. Although our intent is to pay for what is inside, someone is in the business of producing and selling the containers.

Lawless Container Corporation, headquartered in upstate New York, is one such company. Started in 1946 by the Lawless family to manufacture brown corrugated boxes, the company has grown to more than 375 employees and has broadened its product line to include full-color packaging and store displays for customers such as Fisher Price toys and Royal Dirt Devil vacuum cleaners. Now operating in four plants in New York and one in Ohio, the company has sales exceeding $50 million annually.

In 1986, the company was purchased from the Lawless family by members of management, with the help of an outside investment firm. Management then initiated an employee stock-ownership plan (ESOP). As a result of the ESOP, which awards to employees shares of stock in Lawless Container, 30% of the company's stock is now owned by workers.

Lawless Container Corporation's operations are organized into two main components: brown corrugated boxes and color-process printing, or "value-added" packaging and displays. Because the brown-box business is intensely competitive, each manufacturer serves a market covering only a 150–200-mile radius, and the marketing effort is based on long-term personal relationships between sales staff and customers. In contrast, Lawless is one of only ten U.S. suppliers of color-print boxes. Consequently, this market is national, and marketing techniques include trade shows and advertising in trade magazines to publicize Lawless Container's products to this broader market. Management at Lawless believes that the process-print product line offers the best opportunities for growth in revenues and profits.

Lawless Container's managers work to enhance the company's present and future operations in numerous ways, such as:

- Emphasizing customer satisfaction, with competitive pricing, one-day turnaround on orders, and attention to quality

- Maximizing the use of recycled paper to cut costs, help the environment, and respond to customer demand
- Monitoring revenues and expenses at each plant to evaluate the use of the company's resources
- Implementing quality-control methods that inspect manufactured products at various points during production rather than at the end of production
- Motivating its work force by promoting from within, providing extensive training, listening to workers' suggestions, and giving them an ownership stake in the company
- Using computer-aided design (CAD) to speed up the design process and make design changes easier to implement
- Focusing on long-term growth as well as short-term profits

CASE QUESTIONS

1. On the basis of your knowledge as a consumer, explain why Lawless Container considers color-printed boxes and store displays to be a "value-added" product, whereas brown corrugated boxes are not. What "value" is added?
2. The managers at Lawless Container monitor revenues, expenses, and profits separately at each of its five plants. What information does this analysis provide that analyzing company-wide amounts could not? What changes in the accounting system must be made to permit this type of analysis?
3. Explore the challenges to Lawless Container that result from the following factors. Suggest how the company might respond to each.
   a. Intense competition in brown corrugated box products
   b. Environmental concerns such as recycling and saving forests
   c. Customers who order in small quantities (rather than a few large orders) to minimize their inventory levels

PART TWO

Accounting for Assets and Liabilities

FINANCIAL ACCOUNTING

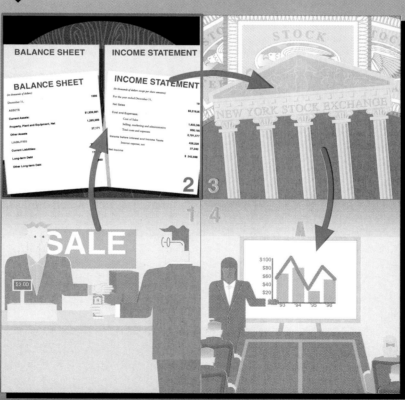

Chapter 7
Internal Control, Cash Transactions, and Ethical Issues

Jan Gibson was a cashier at the Columbia, Missouri, office of the brokerage firm Brown Monroe & Company. Her problems began when appendicitis forced her to miss work and office manager Bruce Ritchie received complaints from customers who had not received credit for their deposits. Ritchie uncovered an elaborate embezzlement scheme that Gibson had begun five years earlier.

The court found that Gibson had stolen a total of $610,934 in a "rob-Peter-to-pay-Paul scheme": She was transferring customer deposits into her personal account and concealing the missing amounts with deposits from other customers. In this way customer accounts always balanced as long as Gibson was present to respond to customer inquiries. She simply explained that the account was temporarily out-of-balance. But while she was recovering in the hospital, her replacement was unable to explain the irregularities in customers' accounts. When all the evidence came to light, it pointed in the direction of the missing employee, who was sentenced to jail. Ritchie then understood why Gibson had never taken a vacation.

• • • • •

What went wrong at the Brown Monroe office? Jan Gibson was able to control not only the cash received from customers, but also part of her company's accounting records. By manipulating the records, she was able to hide her theft for several years. Evidently, no one checked her work on a regular basis. Several procedures that we discuss in this chapter will explain how this embezzlement could have been avoided. How could the embezzlement have been uncovered sooner? By the requirement that employees take vacations. This example illustrates a key feature of control systems in business: They cannot prevent all employee misbehavior, but they can help to detect misbehavior and thereby to limit its effects.

The need for laws requiring internal control has received increased attention since the 1970s. During that time some illegal payments, embezzlements, and other criminal business practices came to light. Concerned citizens wanted to know why the companies' internal controls had failed to

After studying this chapter, you should be able to

1. Define internal control
2. Identify the characteristics of an effective system of internal control
3. Prepare a bank reconciliation and the related journal entries
4. Apply internal controls to cash receipts
5. Apply internal controls to cash disbursements
6. Account for petty cash transactions
7. Weigh ethical judgments in business

A1. Use the voucher system

alert management to these illegalities. To answer these growing worries, the U.S. Congress passed the Foreign Corrupt Practices Act in 1977. This act requires companies under SEC jurisdiction to maintain an appropriate system of internal control whether or not they have foreign operations.[1] Thus its title is misleading.

This chapter discusses *internal control*—the organizational plan and integrated framework that managers use to keep the business under control. The chapter applies these control techniques mainly to transactions of cash, the most liquid asset, and provides a framework for making ethical judgments in business. Later chapters discuss how managers control other assets.

Internal Control

OBJECTIVE 1
Define internal control

A key responsibility of the manager of a business is to keep its operations under control. The owners and the top managers set the entity's goals, the managers lead the way, and the employees carry out the plan. Good managers must decide where the organization is headed for the next several years. But unless they control operations today, they may not remain long enough to put lofty plans into effect. Managers are responsible for the control of their business.

Internal control is the organizational plan and all the related measures adopted by an entity to

1. Safeguard assets,
2. Encourage adherence to company policies,
3. Promote operational efficiency, and
4. Ensure accurate and reliable accounting records.

Internal control is a management priority, not merely a part of the accounting system. Thus it is not a responsibility only of accountants but of managers as well. A business's internal control system is only as effective as the quality of the people in the organization. For example, top managers who expect workers to behave ethically must themselves exhibit ethical behavior. Suppose that the cashier in our opening story had observed unethical behavior by her office manager. Such an act could motivate an employee to take a little money here, a little money there.

"Lee Iacocca, former president of Chrysler Corporation, instilled management's goals in Chrysler employees by getting out of the executive suite and spending time with assembly-line workers."

Internal controls are most effective when employees at all levels adopt the goals and objectives of the organization. Top managers are wise to communicate these goals to workers. Lee Iacocca, former president of Chrysler Corporation, instilled management's goals in Chrysler employees by getting out of the executive suite and spending time with assembly-line workers. (Japanese firms pioneered this style of participative management.) The result? Defects decreased dramatically, and Chrysler products became more competitive. Its sales of cars and trucks increased 14 percent in one year.

"The only thing that is constant in business is that things are going to change." Companies take risks when they move into new industries. Although Brown Monroe & Company is in the investment brokerage business, it also serves as a banker for its clients. Perhaps Brown Monroe's lack of experience in the banking business contributed to the breakdown in internal controls that led to the embezzlement of

---

[1]The Foreign Corrupt Practices Act contains specific prohibitions against bribery and other corrupt practices in addition to requiring the maintenance of accounting records in reasonable detail and accuracy.

Management of Sara Lee Corporation is responsible for the preparation and integrity of the financial information included in this annual report. The financial statements have been prepared in accordance with generally accepted accounting principles, and where required, reflect our best estimates and judgments.

It is the corporation's policy to maintain a *control-conscious environment* through an effective system of *internal accounting controls* supported by formal policies and procedures communicated throughout the corporation. These controls are adequate to provide reasonable assurance that *assets are safe-*

guarded against loss or unauthorized use and to produce the records necessary for the preparation of financial information. There are limits inherent in all systems of internal control based on the recognition that the costs of such systems should be related to the benefits to be derived. We believe the corporation's systems provide this appropriate balance.

The *control environment* is complemented by the corporation's internal auditors who perform extensive audits and evaluate the adequacy of and the adherence to these controls, policies and procedures. In addition, the corporation's independent public accoun-

tants have developed an understanding of our accounting and financial controls and have conducted such tests as they consider necessary to support their report below. . . .

The corporation maintains high standards in selecting, training, and developing personnel to help ensure that management's objectives of maintaining strong, effective internal controls and unbiased, uniform reporting standards are attained. We believe it is essential for the corporation to conduct its business affairs in accordance with the *highest ethical standards* as expressed in Sara Lee Corporation's Code of Conduct.

John H. Bryan
Chairman of the Board and
Chief Executive Officer

Michael E. Murphy
Executive Vice-President and
Chief Financial and
Administrative Officer

Richard G. Rademacher
Senior Vice-President
and Chief Accounting
Officer

Source: Sara Lee Corporation, *1992 Annual Report*, p. 34 (emphasis added).

$610,934. An effective system of internal control is designed to manage change in the organization.

Exhibit 7-1 presents excerpts from the Management Report on Financial Information of Sara Lee Corporation, a manufacturer of frozen foods, Hanes underwear, L'eggs hosiery, and other well-known products. Sara Lee's top managers take responsibility for the financial statements and for the related system of internal control. The second paragraph refers to a *control-conscious environment* and the *safeguarding of assets*. The third paragraph describes the *control environment* further, and the final paragraph states management's intention of conducting business with the *highest ethical standards*. Let's examine in more detail how companies accomplish the goals of an effective system of internal control.

EXHIBIT 7-1
Management Statement about Internal Controls—Sara Lee Corporation

Effective Systems of Internal Control

Whether the business is Brown Monroe, Sara Lee, or a local department store, its system of internal controls, if effective, has the following characteristics.

OBJECTIVE 2
Identify the characteristics of an effective system of internal control

Competent, Reliable, and Ethical Personnel

Employees should be *competent*, *reliable*, and *ethical*. Paying top salaries to attract top-quality employees, training them to do their job well, and supervising their work all help to build a competent staff. A business adds flexibility to its staffing by rotating employees through various jobs. If one employee is sick or on vacation, a second employee is trained to step in and do the job.

Rotating employees through various jobs also promotes reliability. An employee such as Jan Gibson of our opening story is less likely to handle her job improperly if she knows that her misconduct may come to light when a second employee takes over the job. Brown Monroe could have cut its embezzlement losses by rotating two or more employees through the cashier's job. Gibson was able to keep her scam going so long because no one else did her job over a five-year period.

This same reasoning leads businesses to require that employees take an annual vacation. A second employee stepping in to handle the position may uncover any wrongdoing. In Brown Monroe's case, it took a serious illness to place someone else in the cashier's job. Periodic reviews by other employees have a way of keeping workers honest and ethical.

Assignment of Responsibilities

In a business with a good internal control system, no important duty is overlooked. Each employee is assigned certain responsibilities. A model of such *assignment of responsibilities* appears in the corporate organizational chart in Exhibit 7-2. Notice that the corporation has a vice-president of finance and accounting. Two other officers, the treasurer and the controller, report to that vice-president. The treasurer is responsible for cash management. The controller performs accounting duties.

Within this organization, the controller may be responsible for approving invoices for payment, and the treasurer may actually sign the checks. Working under the controller, one accountant may be responsible for property taxes, another accountant for income taxes. In sum, all duties are clearly defined and assigned to individuals who bear responsibility for carrying them out.

EXHIBIT 7-2
Organizational Chart of a Corporation

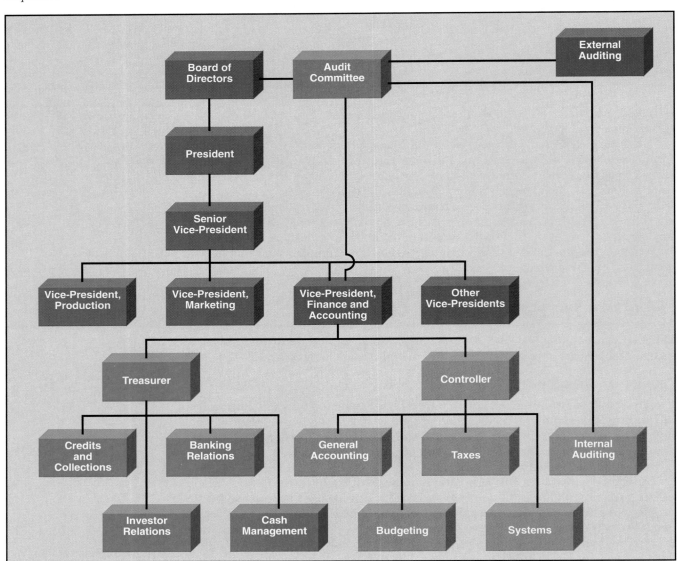

Proper Authorization

An organization generally has a written set of rules that outlines approved procedures. Any deviation from standard policy requires *proper authorization*. For example, managers or assistant managers of retail stores must approve customer checks for amounts above the store's usual limit. Likewise, deans or department chairpersons of colleges and universities must give the authorization for a junior to enroll in courses restricted to seniors.

Separation of Duties

Smart management divides the responsibilities for transactions between two or more people or departments. *Separation of duties* limits the chances for fraud and promotes the accuracy of the accounting records. This crucial component of the internal control system may be divided into four parts.

1. *Separation of operations from accounting.* The entire accounting function should be completely separate from operating departments, such as manufacturing and sales, so that reliable records may be kept. For example, product inspectors, not machine operators, should count units produced by a manufacturing process. Accountants, not salespersons, should keep inventory records. Observe the separation of accounting from production and marketing in Exhibit 7-2.

2. *Separation of the custody of assets from accounting.* Temptation and fraud are reduced if the accountant does not handle cash and if the cashier does not have access to the accounting records. If one employee has both cash-handling and accounting duties, that person can steal cash and conceal the theft by making a bogus entry on the books. We see this component of internal control in Exhibit 7-2. The treasurer has custody of the cash, and the controller accounts for the cash. Neither person has both responsibilities. Jan Gibson was able to apply one customer's cash deposit to another customer's account at Brown Monroe. Apparently the cashier controlled some data entered into the accounting system. This is a serious violation of the separation of duties.

Warehouse employees with no accounting duties should handle inventory. If they were allowed to account for the inventory, they could steal it and write it off as obsolete. In a computerized accounting system, a person with custody of assets should not have access to the computer programs. Similarly, the programmer should not have access to tempting assets such as cash.

3. *Separation of the authorization of transactions from the custody of related assets.* If possible, persons who authorize transactions should not handle the related asset. For example, the same individual should not authorize the payment of a supplier's invoice and also sign the check to pay the bill. With both duties, the person can authorize payments to himself or herself and then sign the checks. When these duties are separated, only legitimate bills are paid.

For another example, an individual who handles cash receipts should not have the authority to write off accounts receivable. (Businesses that sell on credit declare certain of their accounts receivable as uncollectible, realizing that these receivables will never be collected. Chapter 8 looks at uncollectible accounts receivable in detail.) Suppose the company shown in Exhibit 7-2 employs Hien Tho. He works in Credits and Collections (under the treasurer) and handles cash receipts from customers.

Among the business's accounts receivable is Gina Kowalski's $500 balance. Tho could label Kowalski's account as uncollectible, and the business might cease trying to collect from her. When Kowalski mails a $500 check to pay off her balance, Tho forges the endorsement and pockets the money. Kowalski, of course, has no reason to notify anyone else at the business that she has mailed a check, so Tho's crime goes undetected. This theft could have been avoided by denying Tho either the access to cash receipts or the authority to declare customer accounts uncollectible.

4. *Separation of duties within the accounting function.* Independent performance of various phases of accounting helps to minimize errors and the opportunities for fraud. For example, different accountants should be responsible for recording cash receipts and

Short Exercise: What problems can result when a sales clerk can also grant credit approval and record the sale? *A:* The clerk could grant credit approval to friends who do not meet the credit standards, steal merchandise and hide the theft in the accounting records, fail to do all three jobs well and make mistakes, or forget to perform a task when the sales floor is busy.

cash disbursements. The employees who process accounts payable and check requests should have nothing to do with the approval process.

Internal and External Audits

It is not economically feasible for auditors to examine all the transactions during a period, so they must rely on the accounting system to produce accurate records. To gauge the reliability of the company's accounting system, auditors evaluate its system of internal controls. Auditors also spot the weaknesses in the system and recommend corrections. Auditors offer *objectivity* in their reports, while managers immersed in operations may overlook their own weaknesses.

Key Point: External auditors are concerned mainly with the financial statements and the factors affecting them. Internal auditors also want to ensure that the employees adhere to company policies.

Audits are internal or external. Exhibit 7-2 shows *internal auditors* as employees of the business reporting directly to the audit committee. Some organizations have the internal auditors report directly to a vice-president. Throughout the year, they audit various segments of the organization. *External auditors* are entirely independent of the business. Employed by an accounting firm, they are hired by an entity as outsiders to audit the entity as a whole. Both groups of auditors are independent of the operations they examine.

An auditor may find that an employee has both cash-handling and cash-accounting duties or may learn that a cash shortage has resulted from lax efforts to collect accounts receivable. In such cases, the auditor suggests improvements. Auditors' recommendations assist the business in running efficiently.

Documents and Records

Business *documents and records* vary considerably, from source documents such as sales invoices and purchase orders to special journals and subsidiary ledgers. Documents should be prenumbered. A gap in the numbered sequence calls attention to a missing document.

Real-World Example: In a retail business, if a clerk makes a mistake on the sales ticket, the ticket is not destroyed but is marked VOID. Most companies use prenumbered sales receipts, so a missing receipt would be noted.

Prenumbering cash-sale receipts discourages theft by the cashier because the copy retained by the cashier, which lists the amount of the sale, can be checked against the actual amount of cash received. If the receipts are not prenumbered, the cashier can destroy the copy and pocket the cash sale amount. However, if the receipts are prenumbered, the missing copy can easily be identified. In a computerized system, a permanent record of the sale is stored electronically when the transaction is completed.

In a bowling alley, for example, a key document is the score sheet. The manager can check on cashiers by comparing the number of games scored with the amount of cash received. By multiplying the number of games by the price per game and comparing the result with each day's cash receipts, the manager can see whether all the bowling revenue is being collected by the business. If cash on hand is low, the cashier might be stealing.

Electronic and Other Controls

"If a customer tries to remove from the store an item with the sensor attached, an alarm is activated."

Businesses use electronic devices to meet their needs for control over assets and operations. For example, retailers such as Target Stores, Bradlees, and Dillard's control their inventories by attaching an *electronic sensor* to merchandise. The cashier removes the sensor when a sale is made. If a customer tries to remove from the store an item with the sensor attached, an alarm is activated. According to Checkpoint Systems, which manufactures electronic sensors, these devices reduce loss due to theft by as much as 50 percent.

Accounting systems are relying less and less on documents and more and more on digital storage devices. Computers produce accurate records and enhance operational efficiency, but that does not automatically safeguard assets or encourage employees to behave in accordance with company policies. What computers have done is shift the internal controls to the people who write the programs. Programmers carry out the plans of managers and accountants. All the controls that apply to accountants apply to computer programmers as well.

Businesses of all types keep cash and important business documents such as titles to property and contracts in *fireproof vaults*. They use burglar alarms to protect buildings and other property.

Retailers receive most of their cash from customers on the spot. To safeguard cash they use *point-of-sale terminals* that serve as a cash register and record each transaction as it is entered in the machine. Several times each day a supervisor removes the cash for deposit in the bank.

Employees who handle cash are in an especially tempting position. Many businesses purchase *fidelity bonds* on cashiers. The bond is an insurance policy that reimburses the company for any losses due to the employee's theft. Before issuing a fidelity bond, the insurance company investigates the employee's past to ensure a record of ethical conduct.

Within a single company, each department may take steps to maintain control over its assets and accounting records. Consider a large company such as the retailer Saks Fifth Avenue. If Saks's system is well designed, each department can ensure that its transactions are processed correctly. Each department needs to maintain record counts or dollar control totals. For example, the shoe department submits daily credit sales totals for computer processing. The shoe department expects a printout showing a total sales amount agreeing with the control total that was calculated *before* its documents went to the computer operators. This amount is the control figure.

"If Saks's system is well designed, each department can ensure that its transactions are processed correctly."

The accounts receivable department relies on the computer operators to post correctly to the thousands of customer accounts. Proper posting can be ensured by devising customer account numbers so that the last digit is a mathematical function of the previous digits (for example, 1359, where 1 + 3 + 5 = 9). Any miskeying of a customer account number would trigger an error message to the keyboarder, and the computer would not accept the number. Many companies now employ electronic data processing (EDP) auditors to ensure the integrity of the firms' computer databases.

STOP & THINK Ralph works the late movie at Big-Hit Theater. Occasionally Ralph must sell tickets and take the tickets as customers enter the theater. Standard procedure requires that Ralph tear the tickets, give one half to the customer, and keep the other half. To control cash receipts, the theater manager compares each night's cash receipts with the number of ticket stubs on hand.

What is the internal control weakness in this situation? What might a dishonest employee do? What additional steps should the manager take to strengthen the control over cash receipts?

Answer: The internal control weakness is the lack of separation of duties. Ralph receives cash from customers and also controls the tickets. Good internal control would require that Ralph handle either cash or the tickets, but not both. If he were dishonest, he could issue no ticket and keep the customer's cash. To control that dishonest behavior, the manager could physically count the people watching a movie and compare that number with the number of ticket stubs retained. Or a dishonest employee could destroy some ticket stubs and keep the cash received from customers. To catch that dishonest behavior, the manager could account for all ticket stubs by serial number. Missing serial numbers would raise questions that would lead to investigations.

Limitations of Internal Control

Most internal control measures can be overcome. Systems designed to thwart an *individual* employee's fraud can be beaten by two or more employees working as a team—*colluding*—to defraud the firm. Consider the Big-Hit Theater again. Ralph and a fellow employee could put together a scheme in which the ticket seller pockets the cash from 10 customers and the ticket taker admits the customers without tickets. Who would catch them? The manager could take additional control measures, such as matching the number of people in the theater against the number of ticket stubs retained. But that would take time away from other duties. As you see, the stricter the internal control system, the more expensive it becomes.

A system of internal control that is too complex may strangle people in red tape. Efficiency and control are hurt rather than helped. The more complicated the system, the more time and money it takes to maintain. Just how tight should an internal control be? Managers must make sensible judgments. Investments in internal control must be judged in light of the costs and benefits.

The Bank Account as a Control Device

Keeping cash in a *bank account* is part of internal control because banks have established practices for safeguarding cash. Banks also provide depositors with detailed records of cash transactions. To take full advantage of these control features, the business should deposit all cash receipts in the bank account and make all cash payments through it (except petty cash disbursements, which we look at later). We now discuss banking records and documents.

For many businesses, cash is the most important asset. After all, cash is the most common means of exchange, and most transactions ultimately affect cash. But cash is also the most tempting asset for theft. Consequently, internal controls for cash are more elaborate than for most other assets. We consider cash to be not just paper money and coins but also checks, money orders, and money kept in bank accounts. Cash reported on a company's balance sheets may also include *cash equivalents*, liquid investments that can be converted into cash within a few months. Cash equivalents include bank certificates of deposit (CDs), money-market funds, and government treasury bills and notes. We treat cash equivalents as cash. Cash includes neither stamps, because they are supplies, nor IOUs payable to the business, because they are receivables.

The documents used to control a bank account include the signature card, the deposit ticket, the check, the bank statement, and the bank reconciliation.

SIGNATURE CARD Banks require each person authorized to transact business through an account in that bank to sign a *signature card*. The bank compares the signatures on the documents against the signature card to protect the bank and the depositor against forgery.

DEPOSIT TICKET Banks supply standard forms such as *deposit tickets*. The customer fills in the dollar amount and the date of deposit. The customer retains either (1) a duplicate copy of the deposit ticket or (2) a deposit receipt, depending on the bank's practice, as proof of the transaction.

CHECK To draw money from an account, the depositor writes a **check,** which is the document that instructs the bank to pay the designated person or business the specified amount of money. There are three parties to a check: the *maker*, who signs the check; the *payee*, to whom the check is drawn; and the *bank* on which the check is drawn.

Most checks are serially numbered and preprinted with the name and address of the maker and the bank. The checks have places for the date, the name of the

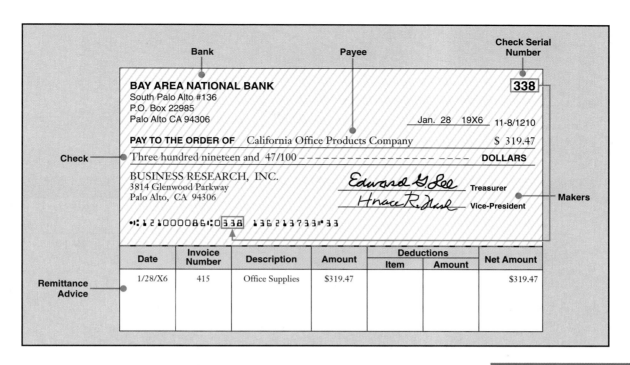

EXHIBIT 7-3
Check with Remittance Advice

payee, the signature of the maker, and the amount. The bank name and bank identification number and the maker account number are usually imprinted in magnetic ink for machine processing.

Exhibit 7-3 shows a check drawn on the bank account of Business Research, Inc. The check has two parts, the check itself and the *remittance advice*, an optional attachment that tells the payee the reason for the payment. The maker (Business Research) retains a duplicate copy of the check for its recording in the check register (cash disbursements journal). Note that internal controls at Business Research require two signatures on checks.

BANK STATEMENT Most banks send monthly **bank statements** to their depositors. The statement shows the account's beginning and ending balance for the period and lists the month's transactions. Included with the statement are the maker's *canceled checks*, those checks that have been paid by the bank on behalf of the depositor. The bank statement also lists any deposits and other changes in the account. Deposits appear in chronological order and checks in a logical order, along with the date each check cleared the bank.

Exhibit 7-4 on page 290 is the bank statement of Business Research, Inc., for the month ended January 31, 19X6. At many banks, some depositors receive their statements on the first of the month, some on the second, and so on. This spacing eliminates the clerical burden of supplying all the statements at one time. Most businesses—like Business Research—receive their bank statement at the end of each calendar month.

Electronic funds transfer (EFT) is a system that relies on electronic impulses—not paper documents—to transfer cash. More and more businesses today rely on EFT for repetitive cash transactions. It is much cheaper for a company to pay employees by EFT (direct deposit) than by issuing hundreds of payroll checks. Also, many people make mortgage, rent, and insurance payments by prior arrangement with their bank and never write checks for those payments. The bank statement lists cash receipts by EFT among the deposits and cash payments by EFT among the checks and other bank charges. The bank statement may be the depositor's only notification of the transaction.

ACCOUNT STATEMENT

BAY AREA NATIONAL BANK
SOUTH PALO ALTO #136 P.O. BOX 22985 PALO ALTO, CA 94306

Business Research, Inc.
3814 Glenwood Parkway
Palo Alto, CA 94306

CHECKING ACCOUNT 136–213733

CHECKING ACCOUNT SUMMARY AS OF 01/31/X6

BEGINNING BALANCE	TOTAL DEPOSITS	TOTAL WITHDRAWALS	SERVICE CHARGES	ENDING BALANCE
6,556.12	4,352.64	4,963.00	14.25	5,931.51

CHECKING ACCOUNT TRANSACTIONS

DEPOSITS	DATE	AMOUNT
Deposit	01/04	1,000.00
Deposit	01/04	112.00
Deposit	01/08	194.60
EFT—Collection of rent	01/17	904.03
Bank Collection	01/26	2,114.00
Interest	01/31	28.01

CHARGES	DATE	AMOUNT
Service Charge	01/31	14.25
Checks:		

CHECKS			BALANCES			
Number	Date	Amount	Date	Balance	Date	Balance
332	01/12	3,000.00	12/31	6,556.12	01/17	5,264.75
656	01/06	100.00	01/04	7,616.12	01/20	4,903.75
333	01/12	150.00	01/06	7,416.12	01/26	7,017.75
334	01/10	100.00	01/08	7,610.72	01/31	5,931.51
335	01/06	100.00	01/12	4,360.72		
336	01/31	1,100.00				

OTHER CHARGES	DATE	AMOUNT
NSF	01/04	52.00
EFT—Insurance	01/20	361.00

MONTHLY SUMMARY

Withdrawals: 8	Minimum Balance: 4,360.00	Average Balance: 6,091.00

EXHIBIT 7-4
Bank Statement

BANK RECONCILIATION   There are two records of the business's cash: its Cash account in its own general ledger and the bank statement, which tells the actual amount of cash the business has in the bank. The balance in the business's Cash account rarely equals the balance shown on the bank statement.

The books and the bank statement may show different amounts, but both are correct. The difference arises because of a time lag in recording certain transactions. When a firm writes a check, it immediately credits its Cash account. The bank, however, will not subtract the amount of the check until the check reaches it for payment. This step may take days, even weeks, if the payee waits to cash the check. Likewise, the business debits Cash for all cash receipts, and it may take a day or so for the bank to add this amount to the business's bank balance.

Good internal control means knowing where a company's money comes from, how it is spent, and the current cash balance. How else can the accountant keep the accurate records management needs to make informed decisions? The accountant must report the correct cash amount on the balance sheet. To ensure accuracy, the accountant explains the reasons for the difference between the firm's records and the bank statement figures on a certain date. This process is called the **bank reconciliation**. Properly done, the bank reconciliation ensures that all cash transactions have been accounted for and that the bank and book records of cash are correct.

Common items that cause differences between the bank balance and the book balance are:

1. Items recorded by the company but not yet recorded by the *bank:*
    a. **Deposits in transit** (outstanding deposits). The company has recorded these deposits, but the bank has not.
    b. **Outstanding checks.** These checks have been issued by the company and recorded on its books but have not yet been paid by its bank.
2. Items recorded by the bank but not yet recorded by the *company:*
    a. **Bank collections.** The bank sometimes collects money on behalf of depositors. Many businesses have their customers pay directly to the company bank account. This practice, called a lock-box system, reduces the possibility of theft and also places the business's cash in circulation faster than if the cash had to be collected and deposited by company personnel. An example is a bank's collecting cash on a note receivable and the related interest revenue for the depositor. The bank may notify the depositor of these bank collections on the bank's statement.
    b. *Electronic funds transfers.* The bank may receive or pay cash on behalf of the depositor. The bank statement will list the EFT and may serve as notification for the depositor to record these transactions.
    c. *Service charge.* The amount is the bank's fee for processing the depositor's transactions. Banks commonly base the service charge on the balance in the account. The depositor learns the amount of the service charge from the bank statement.
    d. *Interest revenue on checking account.* Banks often pay interest to depositors who keep a large enough balance of cash in the account. This is especially true of business checking accounts. The bank notifies the depositor of this interest on the bank statement.
    e. **NSF (nonsufficent funds) checks** received from customers. To understand how to handle NSF checks, also called hot checks, you first need to know the route a check takes. The maker writes the check, credits Cash to record the payment on the books, and gives the check to the payee. On receiving the check, the payee debits Cash on his or her books and deposits the check in the bank. The payee's bank immediately adds the receipt amount to the payee's bank balance on the assumption that the check is good. The check is returned to the maker's bank, which then deducts the check amount from the maker's bank balance. If the maker's bank balance is insufficient to pay the check, the maker's bank refuses to pay the check, reverses this deduction, and sends an NSF notice back to the payee's bank. The payee bank subtracts the receipt amount from the payee's bank balance and notifies the payee of this action. This process may take three to seven days. The company may learn of NSF checks through the bank statement, which lists the NSF check as a charge (subtraction), as shown near the bottom of Exhibit 7-4.
    f. *Checks collected, deposited, and returned to payee by the bank for reasons other than NSF.* Banks return checks to the payee if (1) the maker's account has closed, (2) the date is stale (some checks state "void after 30 days"), (3) the signature is not authorized, (4) the check has been altered, or (5) the check form is improper (for example, a counterfeit). Accounting for all returned checks is the same as for NSF checks.
    g. *The cost of printed checks.* This charge against the company's bank account balance is handled like a service charge.
3. Errors by either the company or the bank. For example, a bank may improperly charge (decrease) the bank balance of Business Research, Inc., for a check drawn by another company, perhaps Business Research Associates. Or a company may mis-

Key Point: Your checking account is a liability on the bank's balance sheet. When the bank reduces your account for a service charge, the bank will debit your account. Banks may send a debit memo to inform you that the deduction has been made. They may send a credit memo to notify you when interest revenue has been added (credited) to your account.

compute its bank balance on its own books. Computational errors are becoming less frequent with the widespread use of computers. Nevertheless, all errors must be corrected, and the corrections will be a part of the bank reconciliation.

OBJECTIVE 3

Prepare a bank reconciliation and the related journal entries

Steps in Preparing the Bank Reconciliation

The steps in preparing the bank reconciliation are

1. Start with two figures, the balance shown on the bank statement (*balance per bank*) and the balance in the company's Cash account (*balance per books*) as in Exhibit 7-5, Panel B. These two amounts will probably disagree because of the differences discussed earlier.

2. Add to, or subtract from, the *bank* balance those items that appear on the books but not on the bank statement:

   a. Add *deposits in transit* to the bank balance. Deposits in transit are identified by comparing the deposits listed on the bank statement with the company list of cash receipts. They show up as cash receipts on the books but not as deposits on the bank statement. As a control measure, the accountant should also ensure that de-

EXHIBIT 7-5

Bank Reconciliation

PANEL A—Reconciling Items:

1. Deposit in transit, $1,591.63.
2. Bank error; add $100 to bank balance.
3. Outstanding checks: no. 337, $286; no. 338, $319.47; no. 339, $83; no. 340, $203.14; no. 341, $458.53.
4. EFT receipt of rent revenue, $904.03.

5. Bank collection, $2,114, including interest revenue of $214.
6. Interest earned on bank balance, $28.01.
7. Book error; add $360 to book balance.
8. Bank service charge, $14.25.
9. NSF check from L. Ross, $52.
10. EFT payment of insurance expense, $361.00.

PANEL B—Bank Reconciliation:

Key Point: Each reconciling item is treated in the same way in every situation. Here is a summary:
Bank Balance—always
- *Add* deposits in transit
- *Subtract* outstanding checks
Book Balance—always
- *Add* bank collection items, interest revenue, and EFT receipts
- *Subtract* service charges, NSF checks, and EFT payments
Errors—adjust the side where the error was made
Entries—only for items on the book side

BUSINESS RESEARCH, INC.
BANK RECONCILIATION
JANUARY 31, 19X6

Bank:			Books:		
Balance, January 31.......................		$5,931.51	Balance, January 31....................		$3,294.21
Add:			Add:		
1. Deposit of January 30 in transit		1,591.63	4. EFT receipt of rent revenue.		904.03
2. Correction of bank error—Business Research Associates check erroneously charged against company account		100.00	5. Bank collection of note receivable, including interest revenue of $214....................		2,114.00
		7,623.14	6. Interest revenue earned on bank balance.........................		28.01
3. Less outstanding checks:			7. Correction of book error—Overstated amount of check no. 333.................................		360.00
					6,700.25
No. 337	$286.00		Less:		
No. 338	319.47		8. Service charge......	$ 14.25	
No. 339	83.00		9. NSF check	52.00	
No. 340	203.14		10. EFT payment of		
No. 341	458.53	(1,350.14)	insurance expense	361.00	(427.25)
Adjusted bank balance		$6,273.00	Adjusted book balance		$6,273.00

Amounts agree.

posits in transit from the preceding month appear on the current month's bank statement. If they do not, the deposits may be lost.

b. Subtract *outstanding checks* from the bank balance. Outstanding checks are identified by comparing the canceled checks returned with the bank statement with the company list of checks in the cash disbursements journal. They show up as cash payments on the books but not as paid checks on the bank statement. This comparison also verifies that all checks paid by the bank were valid company checks and were correctly recorded by the bank and by the company. Outstanding checks are usually the most numerous items on a bank reconciliation.

3. Add to, or subtract from, the *book* balance those items that appear on the bank statement but not on the company books:

a. Add to the book balance (1) *bank collections*, (2) *EFT cash receipts*, and (3) *interest revenue* earned on money in the bank. These items are identified by comparing the deposits listed on the bank statement with the list of cash receipts. They show up as cash receipts on the bank statement but not on the books.

b. Subtract from the book balance (1) *EFT cash payments*, (2) *service charges*, (3) *cost of printed checks*, and (4) *other bank charges* (for example, charges for NSF or stale-date checks). These items are identified by comparing the other charges listed on the bank statement with the cash disbursements recorded on the company books. They show up as subtractions on the bank statement but not as cash payments on the books.

4. Compute the *adjusted bank balance* and the *adjusted book balance*. The two adjusted balances should be equal.

5. Journalize each item in step 3, that is, each item listed on the book portion of the bank reconciliation. These items must be recorded on the company books because they affect cash.

6. Correct all book errors and notify the bank of any errors it has made.

Key Point: Preparing the bank reconciliation does not change the Cash balance on the books; it just shows what the balance should be. An entry is needed for every reconciling item on the *book side* to bring the Cash account to its correct balance.

Key Point: A journal entry is needed for each reconciling item on the book side. There are no entries for items on the bank side.

PUTTING SKILLS TO WORK

BANK RECONCILIATION ILLUSTRATED

The bank statement in Exhibit 7-4 indicates that the January 31 bank balance of Business Research, Inc., is $5,931.51. However, the company's Cash account has a balance of $3,294.21. In following the steps outlined in the text, the accountant finds these reconciling items:

1. The January 30 deposit of $1,591.63 does not appear on the bank statement.

2. The bank erroneously charged to the Business Research, Inc., account a $100 check—number 656—written by Business Research Associates.

3. Five company checks issued late in January and recorded in the cash disbursements journal have not been paid by the bank:

Check No.	Date	Amount
337	Jan. 27	$286.00
338	28	319.47
339	28	83.00
340	29	203.14
341	30	458.53

4. By EFT the bank received $904.03 on behalf of Business Research, Inc. The bank statement serves as initial notification of this receipt of monthly rent revenue on unused office space.

5. The bank collected on behalf of the company a note receivable, $2,114 (including interest revenue of $214). This cash receipt has not been recorded by Business Research, Inc.

6. The bank statement shows interest revenue of $28.01 that the company has earned on its cash balance.

7. Check number 333 for $150 paid to Brown Company on account was recorded in the cash disbursements journal as a $510 amount, creating a $360 understatement of the Cash balance per books.

8. The bank service charge for the month was $14.25.

9. The bank statement shows an NSF check for $52, which was received from customer L. Ross.

10. Business Research, Inc., pays insurance expense monthly by EFT. The company has not yet recorded this $361 payment.

Exhibit 7-5 is the bank reconciliation based on the above data. Panel A lists the reconciling items, which are keyed by number to the reconciliation in Panel B. After the reconciliation, the adjusted bank balance equals the adjusted book balance. This equality is an accuracy check.

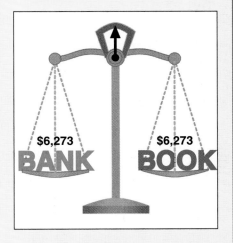

Recording Entries from the Reconciliation

The bank reconciliation does not directly affect the journals or the ledgers. Like the work sheet, the reconciliation is an accountant's tool, separate from the company's books.

The bank reconciliation acts as a control device by signaling the company to record the transactions listed as reconciling items in the Books section of the reconciliation because the company has not yet done so. For example, the bank collected the note receivable on behalf of the company, but the company has not yet recorded this cash receipt. In fact, the company learned of the cash receipt only when it received the bank statement.

STOP & THINK Why does the company *not* need to record the reconciling items on the Bank side of the reconciliation?

Answer: Those items have already been recorded on the company books.

Short Exercise: The bank statement balance is $4,500 and shows a service charge of $15, interest earned of $5, and an NSF check for $300. Deposits in transit total $1,200; outstanding checks are $575. The bookkeeper recorded as $152 a check of $125 in payment of an account payable. (1) What is the adjusted bank balance? (2) What was the book balance of cash before the reconciliation? *A:* (1) $5,125 ($4,500 + $1,200 − $575); (2) $5,408 ($5,125 + $15 + $300 − $5− $27). The adjusted book and bank balances are the same. The answer can be determined by working backward from the adjusted balance.

On the basis of the reconciliation in Exhibit 7-5, Business Research, Inc., makes these entries. They are dated January 31 to bring the Cash account to the correct balance on that date:

Jan. 31	Cash		904.03	
		Rent Revenue		904.03
	Receipt of monthly rent.			
31	Cash		2,114.00	
		Notes Receivable		1,900.00
		Interest Revenue		214.00
	Note receivable collected by bank.			
31	Cash		28.01	
		Interest Revenue		28.01
	Interest earned on bank balance.			
31	Cash		360.00	
		Accounts Payable—Brown Co.		360.00
	Correction of check no. 333.			
31	Miscellaneous Expense		14.25	
		Cash		14.25
	Bank service charge.			
31	Accounts Receivable—L. Ross		52.00	
		Cash		52.00
	NSF check returned by bank.			
31	Insurance Expense		361.00	
		Cash		361.00
	Payment of monthly insurance.			

Short Exercise: Prepare the adjusting journal entry(ies) for the previous Short Exercise.

A:		
Cash	27	
Acct. Payable ...		27
Misc. Exp	15	
Cash		15
Acct. Receivable	300	
Cash		300
Cash	5	
Interest Rev.		5

Note: Miscellaneous Expense is debited for the bank service charge because the service charge pertains to no particular expense category.

These entries bring the business's books up to date.

The entry for the NSF check needs explanation. Upon learning that L. Ross's $52 check was not good, Business Research credits Cash to bring the Cash account up to date. Since Business Research still has a receivable from Ross, it debits Accounts Receivable—L. Ross and pursues collection from him.

The Cash account of Bain Company at February 28, 19X3, follows:

Cash			
Feb. 1 Balance 3,995		Feb. 3	400
6	800	12	3,100
15	1,800	19	1,100
23	1,100	25	500
28	2,400	27	900
Feb. 28 Balance 4,095			

Bain Company receives this bank statement on February 28, 19X3 (as always, negative amounts are in parentheses):

Bank Statement for February 19X3

Beginning balance...		$3,995
Deposits:		
Feb. 7...	$ 800	
15...	1,800	
24...	1,100	3,700
Checks (total per day):		
Feb. 8...	$ 400	
16...	3,100	
23...	1,100	(4,600)
Other items:		
Service charge...		(10)
NSF check from M. E. Crown...		(700)
Bank collection of note receivable for the company..............		1,000*
EFT—monthly rent expense...		(330)
Interest on account balance..		15
Ending balance...		$3,070

---

*Includes interest of $119.

Additional data: Bain Company deposits all cash receipts in the bank and makes all cash disbursements by check.

Required

1. Prepare the bank reconciliation of Bain Company at February 28, 19X3.
2. Record the entries based on the bank reconciliation.

Requirement 1

BAIN COMPANY
BANK RECONCILIATION
FEBRUARY 28, 19X3

Bank:

Balance, February 28, 19X3		$3,070
Add: Deposit of February 28 in transit		2,400
....		5,470
Less: Outstanding checks issued on Feb. 25		
($500) and Feb. 27 ($900)		(1,400)
Adjusted bank balance, February 28, 19X3....................		$4,070

Books:

Balance, February 28, 19X3			$4,095
Add: Bank collection of note receivable,			
including interest of $119			1,000
Interest earned on bank balance			15
....			5,110
Less: Service charge	$ 10		
NSF check...	700		
EFT—Rent expense	330		(1,040)
Adjusted book balance, February 28, 19X3			$4,070

Requirement 2

Feb. 28	Cash..		1,000	
		Note Receivable ($1,000 – $119)		881
		Interest Revenue		119
	Note receivable collected by bank.			
28	Cash..		15	
		Interest Revenue		15
	Interest earned on bank balance.			
28	Miscellaneous Expense		10	
		Cash		10
	Bank service charge.			
28	Accounts receivable—M. E. Crown		700	
		Cash		700
	NSF check returned by bank.			
28	Rent Expense		330	
		Cash		330
	Monthly rent expense.			

Reporting of Cash

Cash is the first current asset listed on the balance sheet of most companies. Even small businesses have several bank accounts and one or more *petty cash* funds—small sums of cash kept on hand for making small disbursements. But companies usually combine all cash amounts into a single total for reporting on the balance sheet. They also include liquid assets such as time deposits and certificates of deposit. These are interest-bearing accounts that can be withdrawn with no penalty after a short period of time. Although they are slightly less liquid than cash, they are sufficiently similar to be reported along with cash. For example, the balance sheet of Sara Lee Corporation recently reported the following (in millions of dollars):

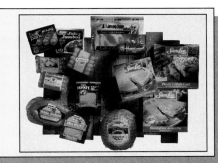

"Of the $198 million reported by Sara Lee as 'cash and equivalents,' $126 million is cash and $72 million is short-term investments."

Assets:

Cash and equivalents	$ 198
Trade accounts receivable	1,180
Inventories	2,160
Other current assets	157
Total current assets	$3,695

Of the $198 million reported by Sara Lee as "cash and equivalents," $126 million is cash and $72 million is short-term investments.

Companies perform the bank reconciliation on the balance sheet date to be assured of reporting the correct amount of cash.

Internal Control over Cash Receipts

Internal control over cash receipts ensures that all cash receipts are deposited in the bank and that the company's accounting record is correct. Many businesses receive cash over the counter and through the mail. Each source of cash receipts calls for *security measures*. Exhibit 7-6 outlines the controls over cash receipts.

OBJECTIVE 4
Apply internal controls to cash receipts

CASH RECEIPTS OVER THE COUNTER The point-of-sale terminal (cash register) offers management control over cash received in a store. Consider a Macy's store. First, the machine should be positioned so that customers can see the amounts the cashier enters into the computer. No person willingly pays more than the marked price for an item, so the customer helps prevent the sales clerk from overcharging and pocketing the excess over actual prices. Also, company policy should require issuance of a receipt to make sure each sale is recorded in the register.

Real-World Example: Stores often give customers a bonus if the clerk fails to give them a receipt.

Second, the cash drawer opens only when the salesclerk enters an amount on the keys, and a roll of tape locked inside the machine records each amount. At the end of the day, a manager proves the cash by comparing the total amount in the cash drawer against the tape's total. This step helps prevent outright theft by the clerk. For security reasons, the clerk should not have access to the tape.

Third, pricing merchandise at "uneven" amounts—say, $3.95 instead of $4.00—means that the clerk generally must make change, which in turn means having to get into the cash drawer. This requires entering the amount of the sale on the keys and so onto the register tape.

At the end of the day, the cashier or other employee with cash-handling duties deposits the cash in the bank. The tape goes to the accounting department as the

EXHIBIT 7-6
Internal Controls over Cash Receipts

Element of Internal Control	Internal Controls over Cash Receipts
Competent, reliable, ethical personnel	Companies carefully screen employees for undesirable personality traits. They also spend large sums for training programs.
Assignment of responsibility	Specific employees are designated as cashiers, supervisors of cashiers, or accountants for cash receipts.
Proper authorization	Only designated employees, such as department managers, can grant exceptions for customers, approve check receipts above a certain amount, and allow customers to purchase on credit.
Separation of duties	Cashiers and mailroom employees who handle cash do not have access to the accounting records. Accountants who record cash receipts have no opportunity to handle cash.
Internal and external audits	Internal auditors examine company transactions for agreement with management policies. External auditors examine the internal controls over cash receipts to determine whether the accounting system produces accurate amounts for revenues, receivables, and other items related to cash receipts.
Documents and records	Customers receive receipts as transaction records. Bank statements list cash receipts for reconciliation with company records (deposit tickets). Customers who pay by mail include a remittance advice showing the amount of cash the company received.
Electronic and other controls	Cash registers serve as transaction records. Cashiers are bonded. Cash is stored in vaults and banks. Each day's receipts are matched with customer remittance advices and with the day's deposit ticket from the bank. Employees are rotated among jobs and are required to take vacations.

Short Exercise: The bookkeeper in your company has stolen cash received from customers. The bookkeeper prepared fake credit memos to indicate that the customers had returned merchandise. What internal control feature could have prevented this theft? *A:* The bookkeeper should not have had access to cash.

basis for an entry in the cash receipts journal. These security measures, coupled with periodic on-site inspection by a manager, discourage fraud.

CASH RECEIPTS BY MAIL All incoming mail should be opened by a mailroom employee. This person should compare the actual enclosed amount of cash or check with the attached remittance advice. If no advice was sent, the mailroom employee should prepare one and enter the amount of each receipt on a control tape. At the end of the day, this control tape is given to a responsible official, such as the controller, for verification. Cash receipts should be given to the cashier, who combines them with any cash received over the counter and prepares the bank deposit.

Having a mailroom employee be the first to handle postal cash receipts is just another application of a good internal control procedure—in this case, separation of duties. If the accountants opened postal cash receipts, they could easily hide a theft.

The mailroom employee forwards the remittance advices to the accounting department. They provide the data for entries in the cash receipts journal and postings to customers' accounts in the accounts receivable ledger. As a final step, the controller compares the three records of the day's cash receipts: (1) the control tape total from the mailroom, (2) the bank deposit amount from the cashier, and (3) the debit to Cash from the accounting department.

CASH SHORT AND OVER A difference often exists between actual cash receipts and the day's record of cash received. Usually the difference is small and results from honest errors. When the recorded cash balance exceeds cash on hand, we have a *cash short* situation. When actual cash exceeds the recorded cash balance, we have a *cash over*. Suppose the cash register tapes of Macy's indicated sales revenue of $25,000, but the cash received was $24,980. To record the day's sales, the store would make this entry:

```
Cash ...................................    24,980
Cash Short and Over.............        20
        Sales Revenue...............              25,000
    Daily cash sales.
```

As the entry shows, Cash Short and Over is debited when sales revenue exceeds cash receipts. This account is credited when cash receipts exceed sales. A debit balance in Cash Short and Over appears on the income statement as Miscellaneous Expense, a credit balance as Other Revenue.

This account's balance should be small. The debits and credits for cash shorts and overs collected over an accounting period tend to cancel each other. A large balance signals the accountant to investigate. For example, too large a debit balance may mean an employee is stealing. Cash Short and Over, then, acts as an internal control device.

Internal Control over Cash Disbursements (Payments)

Cash disbursements are at least as important as cash receipts because how a business spends its money determines the source and amount of cash receipts.

OBJECTIVE 5

Apply internal controls to cash disbursements

Controls over Payment by Check

Payment by *check* is an important control over cash disbursements. First, the check acts as a source document. Second, to be valid the check must be signed by an authorized official, so each payment by check draws the attention of management. Before signing the check, the manager should study the evidence supporting the payment. To illustrate the internal control over cash disbursements, suppose the business is buying inventory for sale to customers. Let's examine the process leading up to the cash payment.

CONTROLS OVER PURCHASING   The purchasing process—outlined in Exhibit 7-7—starts when the sales department identifies the need for merchandise and prepares a *purchase request* (or requisition). A separate purchasing department specializes in locating the best buys and mails a *purchase order* to the supplier, the outside company that sells the needed goods. When the supplier ships the goods to the requesting business, the supplier also mails the *invoice*, or bill, which is a notification of the need to pay. ◀ As the goods arrive, the receiving department checks them for any damage and lists the merchandise received on a document called the *receiving report*. The accounting department attaches all the foregoing documents, checks them for accuracy and agreement, and forwards this disbursement packet to designated officers for approval and payment. The packet includes the invoice, receiving report, purchase order, and purchase request, as shown in Exhibit 7-8.

◀▏▏▏◀▏▏▏◀▏▏▏   Recall from Chapter 5 (p. 179) that purchase orders and invoices are documents that play a key role in the recording of purchases and cash disbursements.

Business Document	Prepared by	Sent to
Purchase request	Sales department	Purchasing department
Purchase order	Purchasing department	Outside company that sells the needed merchandise (supplier, or vendor)
Invoice	Outside company that sells the needed merchandise (supplier, or vendor)	Accounting department
Receiving report	Receiving department	Accounting department
Disbursement packet	Accounting department	Officer who signs the check

EXHIBIT 7-7
Purchasing Process

EXHIBIT 7-8
Disbursement Packet

EXHIBIT 7-8
Disbursement Packet

Short Exercise: You manage a clothing store. The checks are prepared by the bookkeeper and require two signatures—the bookkeeper's and yours. You are leaving on a two-week vacation. To minimize inconvenience, you have pre-signed 20 checks so that only the bookkeeper must sign them in your absence. You have left strict instructions about allowable payments. What internal control feature is being violated? *A:* Never leave signed checks. The bookkeeper can make unauthorized payments. Payments need your approval.

CONTROLS OVER APPROVAL OF PAYMENTS Before approving the disbursement, the controller and the treasurer should examine a sample of transactions to determine that the following control steps have been performed by the accounting department:

1. The invoice is compared with a copy of the purchase order and purchase request to ensure that the business pays cash only for the goods that it ordered.
2. The invoice is compared with the receiving report to ensure that cash is paid only for the goods that are actually received.
3. The mathematical accuracy of the invoice is proved.

Information technology is streamlining cash disbursement procedures in many businesses. For example, the CPA firm of Deloitte & Touche is revamping the payment system of Bank of America. Exhibit 7-9 summarizes the internal controls over cash disbursements. The use of **vouchers**, documents that authorize cash disbursements, improves the internal control over cash disbursements. (See the appendix at the end of this chapter for a discussion of the voucher system.)

CONCEPT HIGHLIGHT

EXHIBIT 7-9
Internal Controls over Cash Disbursements

Element of Internal Control	Internal Controls over Cash Disbursements
Competent, reliable, ethical personnel	Cash disbursements are entrusted to high-level employees, with larger amounts paid by the treasurer or assistant treasurer.
Assignment of responsibility	Specific employees approve purchase documents for payment. Executives examine approvals, then sign checks.
Proper authorization	Large expenditures must be authorized by the company owner or board of directors to ensure agreement with organizational goals.
Separation of duties	Computer operators and other employees who handle checks have no access to the accounting records. Accountants who record cash disbursements have no opportunity to handle cash.
Internal and external audits	Internal auditors examine company transactions for agreement with management policies. External auditors examine the internal controls over cash disbursements to determine whether the accounting system produces accurate amounts for expenses, assets, and other items related to cash disbursements.
Documents and records	Suppliers issue invoices that document the need to pay cash. Bank statements list cash payments (checks and EFT disbursements) for reconciliation with company records. Checks are prenumbered to account for payments in sequence.
Electronic and other controls	Blank checks are stored in a vault and controlled by a responsible official with no accounting duties. Machines stamp the amount on a check in indelible ink. Paid invoices are punched to avoid duplicate payment.

As further security and control over disbursements, many firms require two signatures on a check, as we saw in Exhibit 7-3. To avoid document alteration, some firms also use machines that indelibly stamp the amount on the check. After payment, the check signer can punch a hole through the disbursement packet. This hole denotes that the invoice has been paid and discourages a dishonest employee from running the documents through the system for a duplicate payment.

STOP & THINK Talon Computer Concepts processes payroll checks for small businesses. Clients give their employees' time cards to Talon each week, and Talon programmers write computer programs to meet the clients' payrolls. Talon computer operators process and deliver the checks to the clients for distribution to employees. Identify two employee functions of Talon's cash disbursements system that should be separated. Give your reason.

Answer: The programmers should not also be computer operators. Any person who performed both functions could write the program to process checks to himself or herself or to a fictitious employee and then pocket the printed checks.

Petty Cash Disbursements

OBJECTIVE 6

Account for petty cash transactions

It would be uneconomical for a business to write a separate check for an executive's taxi fare, a box of pencils needed right away, or the delivery of a special message across town. Therefore, companies keep a small amount of cash on hand to pay for such minor amounts. This fund is called **petty cash**.

Even though the individual amounts paid through the petty cash fund may be small, such expenses occur so often that the total amount over an accounting period may grow quite large. Thus the business needs to set up these controls over petty cash: (1) designate an employee to administer the fund as its custodian, (2) keep a specific amount of cash on hand, (3) support all fund disbursements with a petty cash ticket, and (4) replenish the fund through normal cash disbursement procedures.

The petty cash fund is opened when a payment is approved for a predetermined amount and a check for that amount is issued to Petty Cash. Assume that on February 28 the business decides to establish a petty cash fund of $200. The custodian cashes the check and places the currency and coin in the fund, which may be a cash box, safe, or other device. The petty cash custodian is responsible for controlling the fund. Starting the fund is recorded as follows:

Feb. 28	Petty Cash..	200	
	Cash in Bank............................		200
	To open the petty cash fund.		

For each petty cash disbursement, the custodian prepares a *petty cash ticket* like the one illustrated in Exhibit 7-10.

Observe the signatures (or initials, for the custodian) that identify the recipient of petty cash and the fund custodian. Requiring both signatures reduces unauthorized cash disbursements. The custodian keeps all the petty cash tickets in the fund. The sum of the cash plus the total of the ticket amounts should equal the opening

---

PETTY CASH TICKET

Date Mar. 25, 19X4   **No.** 47

Amount $23.00

For Box of floppy diskettes

Debit Office Supplies, Acct. No. 145

Received by *Lewis Wright*   **Fund Custodian** *WAR*

EXHIBIT 7-10
Petty Cash Ticket

balance at all times—in this case, $200. Also, the Petty Cash account keeps its prescribed $200 balance at all times. Maintaining the Petty Cash account at this balance, supported by the fund (cash plus tickets totaling the same amount), is a characteristic of an imprest system. The control feature of an **imprest system** is that it clearly identifies the amount for which the custodian is responsible.

Key Point: No journal entries are made for petty cash disbursements until the fund is replenished. At that time, all petty cash payments will be recorded in a summary entry. This procedure avoids the need to journalize many payments for small amounts.

Disbursements reduce the amount of cash in the fund, so periodically the fund must be replenished. Suppose that on March 31st the fund has $118 in cash and $82 in tickets. A check for $82 is issued, made payable to Petty Cash. The fund custodian cashes this check for currency and coins and puts the money in the fund to return its actual cash to $200. The petty cash tickets identify the accounts to be debited: Office Supplies for $23, Delivery Expense for $17, and Miscellaneous Selling Expense for $42. The entry to record replenishment of the fund is

Mar. 31	Office Supplies	23	
	Delivery Expense	17	
	Miscellaneous Selling Expense	42	
	Cash in Bank		82
	To replenish the petty cash fund.		

If this cash payment exceeds the sum of the tickets—that is, if the fund comes up short, Cash Short and Over is debited for the missing amount. If the sum of the tickets exceeds the payment, Cash Short and Over is credited. Replenishing the fund does *not* affect the Petty Cash account. Petty Cash keeps its $200 balance at all times.

Whenever petty cash runs low, the fund is replenished. It *must* be replenished on the balance sheet date. Otherwise, the reported balance for Petty Cash will be overstated by the amount of the tickets in the fund. The income statement will understate the expenses listed on those tickets.

Petty Cash is debited only when the fund is started (see the February 28 entry) or when its amount is changed. In our illustration, suppose the business decides to raise the fund amount from $200 to $250 because of increased demand for petty cash. This step would require a $50 debit to Petty Cash.

Ethics and Internal Controls

An article in *The Wall Street Journal* (August 2, 1993, page A1) quoted a young entrepreneur in Russia as saying that he was getting ahead in business by breaking laws.

"Ethical practice is, quite simply, good business."

He stated that "Older people have an ethics problem. By that I mean they *have* ethics." Conversely, Roger Smith, former chairman of General Motors, said, "Ethical practice is, quite simply, good business." Which perspective is valid? The latter. There are at least two key differences between these competing perspectives. The young entrepreneur is operating in a country where legal, social, and ethical structures are in tremendous upheaval. In contrast, Smith's environment—the United States—is stable. Businesses in Russia are fledglings with little in the way of internal controls. Apparently, the young entrepreneur has not yet been caught. Smith has been in business long enough to see the danger in unethical behavior. Sooner or later unethical conduct comes to light, as was true in our chapter-opening story.

Corporate and Professional Codes of Ethics

Most large companies have a code of ethics designed to encourage employees to behave ethically and responsibly. A set of general guidelines may not be specific enough to identify misbehavior. A list of do's and don'ts can lead to the false view that anything is okay if it's not specifically forbidden. There is no easy answer. But most businesses are intolerant of unethical conduct by employees. One executive has stated, "I cannot describe all unethical behavior, but I know it when I see it."

Accountants have additional incentives to behave ethically. As professionals, they are expected to maintain higher standards than society in general. Why? The work of professionals such as accountants and physicians is difficult to judge. Their ability to attract business depends entirely on their reputation. Most independent accountants are members of the American Institute of Certified Public Accountants and must abide by the *AICPA Code of Professional Conduct*. Accountants who are members of the Institute of Management Accountants are bound by the *Standards of Ethical Conduct for Management Accountants*. ◀■■■ These documents set minimum standards of conduct for members. Unacceptable actions can result in expulsion from the organization, which makes it difficult for the person to remain in the accounting profession.

◀■■■ ◀■■■ ◀■■■ Refer to the appendix of Chapter 1 (p. 40) for a description of the AICPA and IMA organizations that are concerned about the ethical behavior of their members.

Ethical Issues in Accounting

In many situations the ethical choice is easy. For example, stealing cash as in the chapter opener is illegal and unethical. The cashier's actions landed her in jail. In other cases, the choices are more difficult. But, in every instance, ethical judgments boil down to a personal decision. How should I behave in a given situation? Let's consider three ethical issues in accounting. The first two are easy to resolve. The third issue is more difficult.

OBJECTIVE 7
Weigh ethical judgments in business

SITUATION 1   Sonja Kleberg is preparing the income tax return of a client who has had a particularly good year—higher income than expected. On January 2, the client pays for newspaper advertising and asks Sonja to backdate the expense to the preceding year. The tax deduction would help the client more in the year just ended than in the current year. Backdating would decrease taxable income of the earlier year and save the client a few dollars in tax payments. After all, there is a difference of only two days between January 2 and December 31. This client is important to Kleberg. What should she do? She should refuse the request because the transaction took place in January of the new year. What internal control device could prove that Kleberg behaved unethically if she backdated the transaction in the accounting records? An IRS audit and documents and records: The date of the cash payment could prove that the expense occurred in January rather than in December.

SITUATION 2   Jack Mellichamp's software company owes $40,000 to Bank of America. The loan agreement requires Mellichamp's company to maintain a current ratio (current assets divided by current liabilities) of 1.50 or higher. It is late in the year, and the bank will review Mellichamp's situation early next year. At present, the company's current ratio is 1.40. At this level, Mellichamp is in violation of his loan agreement. He can increase the current ratio to 1.53 by paying off some current liabilities right before year end. Is it ethical to do so? Yes, because the action is a real business transaction. But paying off the liabilities is only a delaying tactic. It will hold off the creditors for now, but time will tell whether the business can improve its underlying operations.

SITUATION 3 Emilia Gomez, an accountant for Hoover Electronics, discovers that her supervisor, Myles Packer, made several errors last year. Overall, the errors overstated net income by 20 percent. It is not clear whether the errors were deliberate or accidental. Gomez is deciding what to do. She knows that Packer evaluates her job performance, and lately her work has been marginal. What should Gomez do? The answer is uncertain.

Framework for Ethical Judgments

Situation 3 poses a difficult question because the best course of action is not clear. Some would consider this an ethical dilemma. Weighing tough ethical judgments requires a decision framework. Consider these six steps as they apply to Emilia Gomez's situation.

1. *Determine the facts.* These are clear from the description of the situation.
2. *Identify the ethical issues.* The root word of ethical is *ethics*, which Webster's dictionary defines as "the discipline dealing with what is good and bad and with moral duty and obligation." Gomez's ethical dilemma is to decide what is the right thing to do with the information she has uncovered.
3. *Specify the alternatives.* Three reasonable alternatives include (a) reporting the errors to Packer, (b) reporting the errors to the owner of the company, and (c) correcting the errors while saying nothing.
4. *Identify the people involved.* Individuals who could be affected include Gomez, Packer, the owner of the company, Gomez's co-workers who observe her behavior, and outsiders who rely on Hoover's financial statements.
5. *Assess the possible consequences.* (a) If Gomez reported the errors to Packer, he might penalize her or reward her for careful work. Her reporting the errors would preserve her integrity and probably would lead to correction of the errors. But Hoover Electronics could suffer embarrassment in notifying users of the changes required to correct the financial statements. (b) If Gomez reported to the company owner—going over Packer's head—her integrity would be preserved. Her relationship with Packer would surely be strained, and it might be difficult for them to work together in the future. The owner might reward Gomez for careful work. But if the owner had colluded with Packer in deliberately overstating income, Gomez could be penalized. If the error was corrected and outsiders were notified, Hoover would be embarrassed. Other accountants who observed this situation would be affected by the outcome. (c) If Gomez quietly corrected the error, she would avoid a confrontation with Packer or the owner. They might or might not discover the error and its correction. If they discovered it, they might or might not notify outsiders. All might criticize Gomez for not bringing the error to their attention. Fellow accountants might or might not learn of the situation.
6. *Make the decision.* The best choice is unclear. Gomez must balance the likely effects on the various people against the dictates of her own conscience. Even though this framework does not provide an easy decision, it identifies the relevant factors. Reporting the error to Packer is preferable because he is Gomez's supervisor. Moreover, Gomez must protect her reputation and consider the interests of outsiders who may be relying on Hoover's financial statements.

Ethics and External Controls

There is another dimension to most ethical issues: external controls, which refer to the discipline on business conduct placed by outsiders who interact with the company. In situation 1, for example, Sonja Kleberg could give in to the client's request to backdate the advertising expense. But because this would be dishonest, it would be risky. To backdate the expense record would be illegal, however insignificant the amount of the transaction. These external controls arise from the business's interaction with the taxing authorities. An IRS audit of Kleberg's client could uncover her action.

In situation 2, the external controls arise from Jack Mellichamp's relationship with the bank that lent money to his software company. As long as the loan agreement is in effect, the company must maintain a current ratio of 1.50 or higher. Paying off current liabilities to improve the current ratio would be a short-term solution to Mellichamp's problem. Over the long run, his business must generate more current assets through operations. Almost certainly his business will need to borrow in the future and will probably face similar loan restrictions. Managers are wise to focus on long-term solutions to their problems if they hope to succeed in business.

The primary external control in situation 3 results from creditors and other outside users of Hoover Electronics' financial statements. If these people suffered a financial loss because they were deceived by Hoover's overstated income, they could file a lawsuit against Hoover. The legal system in the United States places the burden of proof on companies to show that their financial information is accurate. A lender or an investor who can demonstrate that a loss resulted from reliance on fraudulent information can recover damages against the company.

A shifting of income to one year usually causes a corresponding decrease in the income of a later year. Thus Hoover's reporting 20 percent too much income last year may cause the company to report 20 percent too little income the next year. The ethical implication is that companies that are caught manipulating their reported income lose their good reputations very quickly. This loss would make it difficult to attract investors and to borrow money on favorable terms. Honest errors can occur, and lenders and investors can be forgiving, but companies must work hard to keep their reputations clean. That is why they have codes of conduct and why, as Roger Smith put it, "Ethical practice is…good business."

SUMMARY PROBLEM FOR YOUR REVIEW

Grudnitski Company established a $300 petty cash fund. James C. Brown is the fund custodian. At the end of the first week, the petty cash fund contains the following:

a. Cash: $171

b. Petty cash tickets:

No.	Amount	Issued to	Signed by	Account Debited
44	$14	B. Jarvis	B. Jarvis and JCB	Office Supplies
45	9	S. Bell	S. Bell	Miscellaneous Expense
47	43	R. Tate	R. Tate and JCB	—
48	33	L. Blair	L. Blair and JCB	Travel Expense

Required

1. Identify the four internal control weaknesses revealed in the given data.
2. Prepare the general journal entries to record:
    a. Establishment of the petty cash fund.
    b. Replenishment of the fund. Assume that petty cash ticket no. 47 was issued for the purchase of office supplies.
3. What is the balance in the Petty Cash account immediately before replenishment? Immediately after replenishment?

SOLUTION TO REVIEW PROBLEM

Requirement 1   The four internal control weaknesses are:

a. Petty cash ticket no. 46 is missing. Coupled with weakness (b), this omission raises questions about the administration of the petty cash fund and about how the petty cash funds were used.

b. The $171 cash balance means that $129 has been disbursed ($300 − $171 = $129). However, the total amount of the petty cash tickets is only $99 ($14 + $9 + $43 + $33). The fund, then, is $30 short of cash ($129 − $99 = $30). Was petty cash ticket no. 46 issued for $30? The data in the problem offer no hint that helps answer this question. In a real-world setting, management would investigate the problem.

c. The petty cash custodian (JCB) did not sign petty cash ticket no. 45. This omission may have been an oversight on his part. However, it raises the question of whether he authorized the disbursement. Both the fund custodian and the recipient of cash should sign the ticket.

d. Petty cash ticket no. 47 does not indicate which account to debit. What did Tate do with the money, and what account should be debited? At worst, the funds have been stolen. At best, reconstructing the transaction from memory is haphazard. With no better choice available, debit Miscellaneous Expense.

Requirement 2   Petty cash journal entries:

a. Entry to establish the petty cash fund:

Petty Cash..	300	
Cash in Bank......................................		300

b. Entry to replenish the fund:

Office Supplies ($14 + $43)	57	
Miscellaneous Expense	9	
Travel Expense...	33	
Cash Short and Over	30	
Cash in Bank......................................		129

Requirement 3   The balance in Petty Cash is *always* its specified balance, in this case $300, as shown by posting the above entries to the account:

Petty Cash	
(a) 300	

The entry to establish the fund (entry (a)) debits Petty Cash. The entry to replenish the fund (entry (b)) neither debits nor credits Petty Cash.

SUMMARY

1. *Define internal control.* *Internal controls* should safeguard assets, ensure accurate accounting records, promote operational efficiency, and encourage adherence to company policies.

2. *Identify the characteristics of an effective system of internal control.* An effective internal control system includes these features: *reliable personnel, clear-cut assignment of responsibility, proper authorization,* and *separation of duties,* which is the primary element of internal control. Many businesses use security devices, audits, and specially designed documents and records in their internal control systems. Effective computerized internal control systems must meet the same basic standards that good manual systems do.

3. *Prepare a bank reconciliation and the related journal entries.* The *bank account* helps to control and safeguard cash. Businesses use the *bank statement* and the *bank reconciliation* to account for banking transactions.

4. *Apply internal controls to cash receipts.* Different methods are used to control cash receipts over the counter and cash receipts by mail.

5. *Apply internal controls to cash disbursements.* A key control over cash disbursements is payment by check.

6. *Account for petty cash transactions.* An *imprest system* is used to control petty cash disbursements.

7. *Weigh ethical judgments in business.* Ethical judgments can be aided by a process that identifies the ethical issues, specifies the alternative actions, identifies the people involved, and assesses the possible consequences.

Test your understanding of the chapter by marking the best answer for each of the following questions.

1. Which of the following is an element of internal control? *(p. 282)*
   a. Safeguarding assets
   b. Ensuring accurate and reliable accounting records
   c. Promoting operational efficiency
   d. Encouraging adherence to company policies
   e. All the above are elements of internal control

2. Which of the characteristics of an effective system of internal control is violated by allowing the employee who handles inventory to also account for inventory? *(p. 285)*
   a. Competent and reliable personnel
   b. Assignment of responsibilities
   c. Proper authorization
   d. Separation of duties

3. What control function is performed by auditors? *(p. 286)*
   a. Objective opinion of the effectiveness of the internal control system
   b. Assurance that all transactions are accounted for correctly
   c. Communication of the results of the audit to regulatory agencies
   d. Guarantee that a proper separation of duties exists within the business

4. The bank account serves as a control device over *(p. 288)*
   a. Cash receipts
   b. Cash disbursements
   c. Both of the above
   d. None of the above

5. Which of the following items appears on the bank side of a bank reconciliation? *(p. 292)*
   a. Book error
   b. Outstanding check
   c. NSF check
   d. Interest revenue earned on bank balance

6. Which of the following reconciling items requires a journal entry on the books of the company? *(p. 294)*
   a. Book error
   b. Outstanding check
   c. NSF check
   d. Interest revenue earned on bank balance
   e. All of the above but (b)
   f. None of the above

7. What is the major internal control measure over the cash receipts of a Wal-Mart store? *(p. 297)*
   a. Reporting the day's cash receipts to the controller
   b. Preparing a petty cash ticket for all disbursements from the fund
   c. Pricing merchandise at uneven amounts, coupled with use of a cash register
   d. Channeling all cash receipts through the mailroom, whose employees have no cash-accounting responsibilities

8. Before signing a check to pay for goods purchased, the company should determine that the *(p. 299)*
   a. Invoice is for the goods ordered
   b. Merchandise was received
   c. Amount of the bill is correct
   d. All of the above are correct

9. The internal control feature that is specific to petty cash is *(p. 302)*
   a. Separation of duties
   b. Assignment of responsibility
   c. Proper authorization
   d. The imprest system

10. Ethical judgments in accounting and business *(p. 303)*
    a. Require employees to break laws to get ahead
    b. Force decisions about what is good and bad
    c. Always hurt someone
    d. Are affected by internal controls but not by external controls

Answers to the Self-Study Questions follow the Accounting Vocabulary.

ACCOUNTING VOCABULARY

Bank collection. Collection of money by the bank on behalf of a depositor *(p. 291)*.

Bank reconciliation. Process of explaining the reasons for the difference between a depositor's records and the bank's records about the depositor's bank account *(p. 291)*.

Bank statement. Document for a particular bank account showing its beginning and ending balances and listing the month's transactions that affected the account *(p. 289)*.

Check. Document that instructs the bank to pay the designated person or business the specified amount of money *(p. 288)*.

Deposit in transit. A deposit recorded by the company but not yet by its bank *(p. 291)*.

Electronic funds transfer (EFT). System that transfers cash by digital communication rather than paper documents *(p. 289)*.

Imprest system. A way to account for petty cash by maintaining a constant balance in the petty cash account, supported by the fund (cash plus disbursement tickets) totaling the same amount *(p. 302)*.

Internal control. Organizational plan and all the related measures adopted by an entity to safeguard assets, ensure accurate and reliable accounting records, promote operational efficiency, and encourage adherence to company policies *(p. 282)*.

Nonsufficient funds (NSF) check. A "hot" check, one for which the maker's bank account has insufficient money to pay the check *(p. 291)*.

Outstanding check. A check issued by the company and recorded on its books but not yet paid by its bank *(p. 291)*.

Petty cash. Fund containing a small amount of cash that is used to pay minor expenditures *(p. 301)*.

Voucher. Document authorizing a cash disbursement *(p. 300)*.

QUESTIONS

1. Which of the features of effective internal control is the most fundamental? Why?
2. What is the title of the federal act that affects internal control? What requirement does it place on management?
3. Which company employees bear primary responsibility for a company's financial statements and for maintaining the company's system of internal control? How do these persons carry out this responsibility?
4. Identify features of an effective system of internal control.
5. Separation of duties may be divided into four parts. What are they?
6. How can internal control systems be circumvented?
7. Are internal control systems designed to be foolproof and perfect? What is a fundamental constraint in planning and maintaining systems?
8. Briefly state how each of the following serves as an internal control measure over cash: bank account, signature card, deposit ticket, and bank statement.
9. What is the remittance advice of a check? What use does it serve?
10. Each of the items in the following list must be accounted for in the bank reconciliation. Next to each item, enter the appropriate letter from the following possible treatments: (a) bank side of reconciliation—add the item; (b) bank side of reconciliation—subtract the item; (c) book side of reconciliation—add the item; (d) book side of reconciliation—subtract the item.

    _____ Outstanding check
    _____ NSF check
    _____ Bank service charge
    _____ Cost of printed checks
    _____ Bank error that decreased bank balance
    _____ Deposit in transit
    _____ Bank collection
    _____ Customer check returned because of unauthorized signature
    _____ Book error that increased balance of Cash account

11. What purpose does a bank reconciliation serve?
12. Suppose a company has six bank accounts, two petty cash funds, and three certificates of deposit that can be withdrawn on demand. How many cash amounts would this company likely report on its balance sheet?
13. What role does a cash register play in an internal control system?
14. Describe internal control procedures for cash received by mail.
15. What documents make up the disbursement packet? Describe three procedures that use the disbursement packet to ensure that each payment is appropriate.
16. What balance does the Petty Cash account have at all times? Does this balance always equal the amount of cash in the fund? When are the two amounts equal? When are they unequal?
17. Why should accountants adhere to a higher standard of ethical conduct than many other members of society do?
18. "Our managers know that they are expected to meet budgeted profit figures. We don't want excuses. We want results." Discuss the ethical implications of this policy.
19. Why should the same employee not write the computer programs for cash disbursements, sign checks, and mail the checks to payees?

EXERCISES

Identifying internal control strengths and weaknesses (Obj. 2)

E7-1 The following situations suggest either a strength or a weakness in internal control. Identify each as *strength* or *weakness*, and give the reason for your answer.

a. Cash received by mail goes straight to the accountant, who debits Cash and credits Accounts Receivable from the customer.
b. The vice-president who signs checks assumes that the accounting department has matched the invoice with other supporting documents and therefore does not examine the disbursement packet.
c. Top managers delegate all internal control measures to the accounting department.
d. The accounting department orders merchandise and approves vouchers for payment.
e. The operator of a computer has no other accounting or cash-handling duties.
f. Cash received over the counter is controlled by the salesclerk, who rings up the sale and places the cash in the register. The salesclerk has access to the control tape stored in the register.

Identifying internal controls (Obj. 2)

E7-2 Identify the missing internal control characteristic in the following situations:

a. In the course of auditing the records of a company, you find that the same employee orders merchandise and approves invoices for payment.

b. Business is slow at White Water Park on Tuesday, Wednesday, and Thursday nights. To reduce expenses, the owner decides not to use a ticket taker on those nights. The ticker seller (cashier) is told to keep the tickets as a record of the number sold.

c. The manager of a discount store wants to speed the flow of customers through check-out. She decides to reduce the time that cashiers spend making change, so she prices merchandise at round dollar amounts—such as $8.00 and $15.00—instead of the customary amounts—$7.95 and $14.95.

d. Grocery stores such as Kroger and Winn Dixie purchase large quantities of their merchandise from a few suppliers. At another grocery store the manager decides to reduce paperwork. He eliminates the requirement that a receiving department employee prepare a receiving report, which lists the quantities of items received from the supplier.

e. When business is brisk, Stop-n-Shop and many other retail stores deposit cash in the bank several times during the day. The manager at another convenience store wants to reduce the time that employees spend delivering cash to the bank, so he starts a new policy. Cash will build up over Saturdays and Sundays, and the total two-day amount will be deposited on Sunday evening.

E7-3 The following seven items may appear on a bank reconciliation:

Classifying bank reconciliation items
(Obj. 3)

1. Book error: We debited Cash for $200. The correct debit was $2,000.
2. Outstanding checks.
3. Bank error: The bank charged our account for a check written by another customer.
4. Service charge.
5. Deposits in transit.
6. NSF check.
7. Bank collection of a note receivable on our behalf.

Classify each item as (a) an addition to the bank balance, (b) a subtraction from the bank balance, (c) an addition to the book balance, or (d) a subtraction from the book balance.

E7-4 Carol Miller's checkbook lists the following:

Bank reconciliation
(Obj. 3)

Date	Check No.	Item	Check	Deposit	Balance
9/1					$ 525
4	622	Bon Jour Bakery	$ 19		506
9		Dividends		$ 116	622
13	623	General Tire Co.	43		579
14	624	Exxon Oil Co.	58		521
18	625	Cash	50		471
26	626	St. Alban's Lutheran Church	25		446
28	627	Bent Tree Apartments	275		171
30		Paycheck		2,000	2,171

The September bank statement shows:

Balance		$525
Add: Deposits...		116
Deduct checks: <u>No.</u>	<u>Amount</u>	
622	$19	
623	43	
624	68*	
625	<u>50</u>	(180)
Other charges:		
Printed checks...	$ 8	
Service charge	<u>12</u>	<u>(20)</u>
Balance		<u>$441</u>

---

*This is the correct amount of check number 624.

Required

Prepare Miller's bank reconciliation at September 30.

<table>
<tr><td>*Bank reconciliation*
(Obj. 3)</td><td>**E7-5** Dave Green operates four Texaco stations. He has just received the monthly bank statement at October 31 from First National Bank, and the statement shows an ending balance of $3,840. Listed on the statement are an EFT rent collection of $400, a service charge of $12, two NSF checks totaling $74, and a $9 charge for printed checks. In reviewing his cash records, Green identifies outstanding checks totaling $467 and an October 31 deposit in transit of $788. During October he recorded a $290 check for the salary of a part-time employee by debiting Salary Expense and crediting Cash for $29. Green's Cash account shows an October 31 cash balance of $4,117. Prepare the bank reconciliation at October 31.</td></tr>
</table>

Journal entries from a bank reconciliation
(Obj. 3)

E7-6 Using the data from Exercise 7-5, record the entries that Green should make in the general journal on October 31. Include an explanation for each of the entries.

Internal controls and the bank reconciliation
(Obj. 2, 3)

E7-7 A grand jury indicted the treasurer of National Bridge Taxi Company for stealing cash from the company. Over a 10-year period the treasurer allegedly took almost $50,000 and attempted to cover the theft by manipulating the bank reconciliation.

Required

What is the most likely way that a person would manipulate a bank reconciliation to cover a theft? Be specific. What internal control arrangement could have avoided this theft?

Internal control over cash receipts
(Obj. 4)

E7-8 A cash register is located in each department of Winn's Hardware Store. The register shows the amount of each sale, the cash received from the customer, and any change returned to the customer. The machine also produces a customer receipt but keeps no record of transactions. At the end of the day, the clerk counts the cash in the register and gives it to the cashier for deposit in the company bank account.

Required

Write a memo to convince the store manager that there is an internal control weakness over cash receipts. Identify the weakness that gives an employee the best opportunity to steal cash, and state how to prevent such a theft.

Accounting for petty cash
(Obj. 5, 6)

E7-9 The Charity Connection of Thornton, Texas, created a $300 imprest petty cash fund. During the first month of use, the fund custodian authorized and signed petty cash tickets as follows:

Ticket No.	Item	Account Debited	Amount
1	Delivery of pledge cards to donors	Delivery Expense	$22.19
2	Mail package	Postage Expense	52.80
3	Newsletter	Supplies Expense	34.14
4	Key to closet	Miscellaneous Expense	0.85
5	Wastebasket	Miscellaneous Expense	3.78
6	Staples	Supplies Expense	85.37

Required

1. Make general journal entries for creation of the petty cash fund and its replenishment. Include explanations.
2. Immediately before replenishment, describe the items in the fund.
3. Immediately after replenishment, describe the items in the fund.

E7-10 Record the following selected transactions in general journal format (explanations are not required):

Petty cash, cash short and over
(Obj. 4, 5, 6)

April 1 Established a petty cash fund with a $500 balance.
  2 Journalized the day's cash sales. Cash register tapes show a $2,869 total, but the cash in the register is only $2,863.
  10 The petty cash fund has $169 in cash and $271 in petty cash tickets issued to pay for Office Supplies ($61), Delivery Expense ($113), and Entertainment Expense ($97). Replenished the fund.

CHALLENGE EXERCISES

E7-11 Amy Fisk, the owner of Amy's Dress Shop, has delegated management of the business to Micah Floyd, a friend. Fisk drops by the business to meet customers and checks up on cash receipts, but Floyd buys the merchandise and handles cash disbursements. Business has been brisk lately, and cash receipts have kept pace with the apparent level of sales. However, for a year or so the amount of cash on hand has been too low. When asked about this, Floyd explains that designers are charging more for dresses than in the past. During the past year Floyd has taken two expensive vacations, and Fisk wonders how Floyd could afford these trips on his $35,000 annual salary and commissions.

Internal control over cash disbursements, ethical considerations
(Obj. 5, 7)

Required

List at least three ways Floyd could be defrauding the business of cash. In each instance, also identify how Fisk can determine whether Floyd's actions are ethical. Limit your answers to the dress shop's cash disbursements. The business pays all suppliers by check (no EFTs).

E7-12 Approximately 300 current and former members of the U.S. House of Representatives—on a regular basis—wrote a quarter-million dollars of checks without having the cash in their accounts. Later investigations revealed that no public funds were involved. The House bank was a free-standing institution that recirculated House members' cash. In effect, the delinquent check writers were borrowing money from each other on an interest-free, no-service-charge basis. Nevertheless, the House closed its bank after the events became public.

Ethical conduct by government legislators
(Obj. 7)

Required

Suppose you are a new congressional representative from your state. Apply the six-step framework for analysis outlined in the chapter to decide whether you would write NSF checks on a regular basis through the House bank.

PROBLEMS

(GROUP A)

P7-1A An employee of SOS Aircraft Service Company recently stole thousands of dollars of the company's cash. The company has decided to install a new system of internal controls.

Identifying the characteristics of an effective internal control system
(Obj. 1)

Required

As controller of SOS Aircraft Service Company, write a memo to the president explaining how a separation of duties helps to safeguard assets.

P7-2A Each of the following situations has an internal control weakness:

Identifying internal control weaknesses
(Obj. 2, 4, 5)

a. Luann Sorelle employs three professional interior designers in her design studio. She is located in an area with a lot of new construction, and her business is booming. Ordinarily, Sorelle does all the purchasing of furniture, draperies, carpets, fabrics, sewing services, and other materials and labor needed to complete jobs. During the summer she takes a long vacation, and in her absence she allows each designer to purchase materials and labor. At her return, Sorelle reviews operations and notes that expenses are much higher and net income much lower than in the past.

b. Discount stores such as Target and Sam's receive a large portion of their sales revenue in cash, with the remainder in credit card sales. To reduce expenses, a store manager ceases purchasing fidelity bonds on the cashiers.

c. The office supply company from which Champs Sporting Goods purchases cash receipt forms recently notified Champs that the last shipped receipts were not prenumbered. Alex Champion, the owner, replied that he did not use the receipt numbers, so the omission is not important.

d. Flowers Computer Programs is a software company that specializes in programs with accounting applications. The company's most popular program prepares the general journal, cash receipts journal, cash disbursements journal, accounts receivable subsidiary ledger, and general ledger. In the company's early days, the owner and eight employees wrote the computer programs, lined up manufacturers to produce the diskettes, sold the products to stores such as ComputerLand and ComputerCraft, and performed the general management and accounting of the company. As the company has grown, the number of employees has increased dramatically. Recently, the development of a new software program stopped while the programmers redesigned Flowers's accounting system. Flowers's own accountants could have performed this task.

e. Lydia Pink, a widow with no known sources of outside income, has been a trusted employee of Stone Products Company for 15 years. She performs all cash-handling and accounting duties, including opening the mail, preparing the bank deposit, accounting for all aspects of cash and accounts receivable, and preparing the bank reconciliation. She has just purchased a new Lexus and a new home in an expensive suburb. Grant Chavez, the owner of the company, wonders how she can afford these luxuries on her salary.

Required

1. Identify the missing internal control characteristics in each situation.
2. Identify the business's possible problem.
3. Propose a solution to the problem.
4. How will what you learned in this problem help you manage a business?

Identifying internal control weakness (Obj. 2)

P7-3A Tribune Appliance makes all sales on credit. Cash receipts arrive by mail, usually within 30 days of the sale. Brad Copeland opens envelopes and separates the checks from the accompanying remittance advices. Copeland forwards the checks to another employee, who makes the daily bank deposit but has no access to the accounting records. Copeland sends the remittance advices, which show the amount of cash received, to the accounting department for entry in the accounts. Copeland's only other duty is to grant sales allowances to customers. When he receives a customer check for less than the full amount of the invoice, he records the sales allowance and forwards the document to the accounting department.

Required

You are the outside auditor of Tribune Appliance. Write a memo to the company president to identify the internal control weakness in this situation. State how to correct the weakness.

Bank reconciliation and related journal entries (Obj. 3)

P7-4A The May 31 bank statement of Lewiston College has just arrived from Central Bank. To prepare the Lewiston bank reconciliation, you gather the following data:

a. The May 31 bank balance is $4,530.82.

b. The bank statement includes two charges for returned checks from customers. One is an NSF check in the amount of $67.50 received from Harley Doherty, a student, recorded on the books by a debit to Cash, and deposited on May 19. The other is a $195.03 check received from Maria Shell and deposited on May 21. It was returned by Shell's bank with the imprint "Unauthorized Signature."

c. The following Lewiston checks are outstanding at May 31:

Check No.	Amount
616	$403.00
802	74.25
806	36.60
809	161.38
810	229.05
811	48.91

d. A few students pay monthly fees by EFT. The May bank statement lists a $200 deposit for student fees.

e. The bank statement includes two special deposits: $899.14, which is the amount of dividend revenue the bank collected from General Electric Company on behalf of Lewiston, and $16.86, the interest revenue Lewiston earned on its bank balance during May.

f. The bank statement lists a $6.25 subtraction for the bank service charge.

g. On May 31 the Lewiston treasurer deposited $381.14, but this deposit does not appear on the bank statement.

h. The bank statement includes a $410.00 deduction for a check drawn by Marimont Freight Company. Lewiston promptly notified the bank of its error.

i. Lewiston's Cash account shows a balance of $3,521.55 on May 31.

Required

1. Prepare the bank reconciliation for Lewiston College at May 31.

2. Record in general journal form the entries necessary to bring the book balance of Cash into agreement with the adjusted book balance on the reconciliation. Include an explanation for each entry.

3. How will what you learned in this problem help you manage a business?

P7-5A The cash receipts and the cash disbursements of Mobil Resources for March 19X5 appear as follows:

Bank reconciliation and related journal entries (Obj. 3)

Cash Receipts (Posting reference is CR)		Cash Disbursements (Posting reference is CD)	
Date	Cash Debit	Check No.	Cash Credit
Mar. 4	$2,716	1413	$ 1,465
9	544	1414	1,004
11	1,655	1415	450
14	896	1416	8
17	367	1417	775
25	890	1418	88
31	2,038	1419	4,126
Total	$9,106	1420	970
		1421	200
		1422	2,267
		Total	$11,353

The Cash account of Mobil Resources shows the following information on March 31, 19X5:

Cash

Date	Item	Jrnl. Ref.	Debit	Credit	Balance
Mar. 1	Balance				15,188
31		CR. 10	9,106		24,294
31		CD. 16		11,353	12,941

On March 31, 19X5, Mobil Resources received the bank statement at the top of page 314.

Additional data for the bank reconciliation include:

a. The EFT deposit was a receipt of monthly rent. The EFT debit was payment of monthly insurance.

b. The NSF check was received late in February from Jay Andrews.

c. The $1,000 bank collection of a note receivable on March 31 included $122 interest revenue.

d. The correct amount of check number 1419, a payment on account, is $4,216. (The Mobil Resources accountant mistakenly recorded the check for $4,126.)

Bank Statement for March 19X5

Beginning balance			$15,188
Deposits and other Credits:			
Mar. 1	$ 625 EFT		
5	2,716		
10	544		
11	1,655		
15	896		
18	367		
25	890		
31	1,000 BC		8,693
Checks and other Debits:			
Mar. 8	$ 441 NSF		
9	1,465		
13	1,004		
14	450		
15	8		
19	340 EFT		
22	775		
29	88		
31	4,216		
31	25 SC		8,812
Ending balance.......................................			$15,069

Explanation: BC—bank collection, EFT—electronic funds transfer, NSF—nonsufficient fund check, SC—service charge.

Required

1. Prepare the bank reconciliation of Mobil Resources at March 31, 19X5.
2. Record the entries based on the bank reconciliation. Include explanations.

Accounting for petty cash transactions
(Obj. 5, 6)

P7-6A   Suppose that on April 1 Exxon opens a regional office in Omaha and creates a petty cash fund with an imprest balance of $400. During April, Caroline Stump, the fund custodian, signs the following petty cash tickets:

Ticket Number	Item	Amount
101	Office supplies	$86.89
102	Cab fare for executive	25.00
103	Delivery of package across town	37.75
104	Dinner money for sales manager entertaining a customer	80.00
105	Postage for package received	10.00
106	Decorations for office party	19.22
107	Six boxes of floppy disks	44.37

On April 30, prior to replenishment, the fund contains these tickets plus $84.77. The accounts affected by petty cash disbursements are Office Supplies Expense, Travel Expense, Delivery Expense, Entertainment Expense, and Postage Expense.

Required

1. Explain the characteristics and the internal control features of an imprest fund.
2. Make the general journal entries to create the fund and to replenish it. Include explanations. Also, briefly describe what the custodian does on these dates.
3. Make the entry on May 1 to increase the fund balance to $500. Include an explanation, and briefly describe what the custodian does.

P7-7A Tri State Bank in Cairo, Illinois, has a loan receivable from Magellan Manufacturing Company. Magellan is six months late in making payments to the bank, and Sheila Boswell, a Tri State vice-president, is assisting Magellan to restructure its debt. With unlimited access to Magellan's records Boswell learns that the company is depending on landing a manufacturing contract from Loew's Brothers, another Tri State Bank client. Boswell also serves as Loew's loan officer at the bank. In this capacity she is aware that Loew's is considering declaring bankruptcy. No one else outside Loew's Brothers knows this. Boswell has been a great help to Magellan Manufacturing, and Magellan's owner is counting on her expertise in loan workouts to carry the company through this difficult process. To help the bank collect on this large loan, Boswell has a strong motivation to help Magellan survive.

Making an ethical judgment
(Obj. 7)

Required

Apply the ethical judgment framework outlined in the chapter to help Sheila Boswell plan her next action.

(GROUP B)

P7-1B Sadrina Real Estate Development Company prospered during the lengthy economic expansion of the 1980s. Business was so good that the company bothered with few internal controls. The early 1990s' decline in the local real estate market, however, has caused Sadrina to experience a shortage of cash. Diane Sadrina, the company owner, is looking for ways to save money.

Identifying the characteristics of an effective internal control system
(Obj. 1)

Required

As controller of the company, write a memorandum to convince Sadrina of the company's need for a system of internal control. Be specific in telling her how an internal control system could lead to saving money. Include the definition of internal control, and briefly discuss each characteristic, beginning with competent, reliable, and ethical personnel.

P7-2B Each of the following situations has an internal control weakness.

Identifying internal control weaknesses
(Obj. 2, 4, 5)

a. In evaluating the internal control over cash disbursements, an auditor learns that the purchasing agent is responsible for purchasing diamonds for use in the company's manufacturing process, approving the invoices for payment, and signing the checks. No supervisor reviews the purchasing agent's work.

b. Todd Wagoner owns a firm that performs engineering services. His staff consists of 12 professional engineers, and he manages the office. Often his work requires him to travel to meet with clients. During the past six months he has observed that when he returns from a business trip, the engineering jobs in the office have not progressed satisfactorily. He learns that when he is away several of his senior employees take over office management and neglect their engineering duties. One employee could manage the office.

c. Amy Fariss has been an employee of Griffith's Shoe Store for many years. Because the business is relatively small, Fariss performs all accounting duties, including opening the mail, preparing the bank deposit, and preparing the bank reconciliation.

d. Most large companies have internal audit staffs that continuously evaluate the business's internal control. Part of the auditor's job is to evaluate how efficiently the company is running. For example, is the company purchasing inventory from the least expensive wholesaler? After a particularly bad year, Campbell Design Company eliminates its internal audit department to reduce expenses.

e. CPA firms, law firms, and other professional organizations use paraprofessional employees to do some of their routine tasks. For example, an accounting paraprofessional might examine documents to assist a CPA in conducting an audit. In the CPA firm of Dunham & Lee, Cecil Dunham, the senior partner, turns over a significant portion of his high-level audit work to his paraprofessional staff.

Required

1. Identify the missing internal control characteristic in each situation.
2. Identify the business's possible problem.
3. Propose a solution to the problem.
4. How will what you learned in this problem help you manage a business?

Identifying internal control weakness
(Obj. 2)

P7-3B Rocky Mountain Supply Co. makes all sales on credit. Cash receipts arrive by mail, usually within 30 days of the sale. Angela Adkins opens envelopes and separates the checks from the accompanying remittance advices. Adkins forwards the checks to another employee, who makes the daily bank deposit but has no access to the accounting records. Adkins sends the remittance advices, which show the amount of cash received, to the accounting department for entry in the accounts. Her only other duty is to grant sales allowances to customers. When she receives a customer check for less than the full amount of the invoice, she records the sales allowance and forwards the document to the accounting department.

Required

You are the outside auditor of Rocky Mountain Supply Co. Write a memo to the company president to identify the internal control weakness in this situation. State how to correct the weakness.

Bank reconciliation and related journal entries
(Obj. 3)

P7-4B The August 31 bank statement of Security System Company has just arrived from United Bank. To prepare the Security System bank reconciliation, you gather the following data:

a. Security System's Cash account shows a balance of $6,866.14 on August 31.

b. The bank statement includes two charges for returned checks from customers. One is a $395.00 check received from Shoreline Express and deposited on August 20, returned by Shoreline's bank with the imprint "Unauthorized Signature." The other is an NSF check in the amount of $146.67 received from Lipsey, Inc. This check had been deposited on August 17.

c. Security System pays rent ($750) and insurance ($290) each month by EFT.

d. The following Security System checks are outstanding at August 31:

Check No.	Amount
237	$ 46.10
288	141.00
291	578.05
293	11.87
294	609.51
295	8.88
296	101.63

e. The bank statement includes a deposit of $1,191.17, collected by the bank on behalf of Security System. Of the total, $1,011.81 is collection of a note receivable, and the remainder is interest revenue.

f. The bank statement shows that Security System earned $38.19 of interest on its bank balance during August. This amount was added to Security System's account by the bank.

g. The bank statement lists a $10.50 subtraction for the bank service charge.

h. On August 31 the Security System treasurer deposited $316.15, but this deposit does not appear on the bank statement.

i. The bank statement includes a $300.00 deposit that Security System did not make. The bank had erroneously credited the Security System account for another bank customer's deposit.

j. The August 31 bank balance is $7,984.22.

Required

1. Prepare the bank reconciliation for Security System Company at August 31.

2. Record in general journal form the entries necessary to bring the book balance of Cash into agreement with the adjusted book balance on the reconciliation. Include an explanation for each entry.

3. How will what you learned in this problem help you manage a business?

P7-5B The cash receipts and the cash disbursements of Fuddruckers for April 19X4 appear as follows:

Bank reconciliation and related journal entries
(Obj. 3)

Cash Receipts (Posting reference is CR)		*Cash Disbursements* (Posting reference is CD)	
Date	Cash Debit	Check No.	Cash Credit
Apr. 2	$ 4,174	3113	$ 891
8	407	3114	147
10	559	3115	1,930
16	2,187	3116	664
22	1,854	3117	1,472
29	1,060	3118	1,000
30	337	3119	632
Total	$10,578	3120	1,675
		3121	100
		3122	2,413
		Total	$10,924

Assume that the Cash account of Fuddruckers shows the following information at April 30, 19X4:

Cash

Date	Item	Jrnl. Ref.	Debit	Credit	Balance
Apr. 1	Balance				7,911
30		CR. 6	10,578		18,489
30		CD. 11		10,924	7,565

Fuddruckers received the following bank statement on April 30, 19X4:

Bank Statement for April 19X4

Beginning balance		$ 7,911
Deposits and other Credits:		
Apr. 1	$ 326 EFT	
4	4,174	
9	407	
12	559	
17	2,187	
22	1,368 BC	
23	1,854	10,875
Checks and other Debits:		
Apr. 7	$ 891	
13	1,390	
14	903 US	
15	147	
18	664	
21	219 EFT	
26	1,472	
30	1,000	
30	20 SC	6,706
Ending balance......................................		$12,080

Explanation: EFT—electronic funds transfer, BC—bank collection, US—unauthorized signature, SC—service charge.

Additional data for the bank reconciliation include:

a. The EFT deposit was a receipt of monthly rent. The EFT debit was a monthly insurance payment.
b. The unauthorized signature check was received from S. M. Holt.
c. The $1,368 bank collection of a note receivable on April 22 included $185 interest revenue.
d. The correct amount of check number 3115, a payment on account, is $1,390. (Fuddruckers's accountant mistakenly recorded the check for $1,930.)

Required

1. Prepare the bank reconciliation of Fuddruckers at April 30, 19X4.
2. Record the entries based on the bank reconciliation. Include explanations.

Accounting for petty cash transactions
(Obj. 5, 6)

P7-6B   Suppose that on June 1 Pellegrini Electronics opens a district office in Nashville and creates a petty cash fund with an imprest balance of $350. During June, Dana Pellegrini, the fund custodian, signs the following petty cash tickets:

Ticket Number	Item	Amount
1	Postage for package received	$ 8.40
2	Decorations and refreshments for office party	13.19
3	Two boxes of floppy disks	20.82
4	Typewriter ribbons	27.13
5	Dinner money for sales manager entertaining a customer	50.00
6	Plane ticket for executive business trip to Memphis	69.00
7	Delivery of package across town	6.30

On June 30, prior to replenishment, the fund contains these tickets plus $173.51. The accounts affected by petty cash disbursements are Office Supplies Expense, Travel Expense, Delivery Expense, Entertainment Expense, and Postage Expense.

Required

1. Explain the characteristics and the internal control features of an imprest fund.
2. Make the general journal entries to create the fund and to replenish it. Include explanations. Also, briefly describe what the custodian does on these dates.
3. Make the entry on July 1 to increase the fund balance to $500. Include an explanation, and briefly describe what the custodian does.

Making an ethical judgment
(Obj. 7)

P7-7B   Zane Revere is executive vice-president of Costa Mesa Bank in Costa Mesa, California. Active in community affairs, Zane serves on the board of directors of West Point Publishing Company. West Point is expanding rapidly and is considering relocating its plant. At a recent meeting, board members decided to try to buy 15 acres of land on the edge of town. The owner of the property is Amy Gao, a customer of Costa Mesa Bank. Gao is completing a bitter divorce. Revere knows that Gao is eager to sell her local property. In view of Gao's anguished condition, Revere believes she would accept almost any offer for the land. Realtors have appraised the property at $5 million.

Required

Apply the ethical judgment framework outlined in the chapter to help Zane Revere decide what his role should be in West Point's attempt to buy the land from Amy Gao.

EXTENDING YOUR KNOWLEDGE

DECISION PROBLEMS

Using the bank reconciliation to detect a theft
(Obj. 3)

1. Reinli Equipment Company has poor internal control over its cash transactions. Recently Sharon Moore, the owner, has suspected the cashier of stealing. Details of the business's cash position at September 30 follow.

a. The Cash account shows a balance of $19,702. This amount includes a September 30 deposit of $3,794 that does not appear on the September 30 bank statement.

b. The September 30 bank statement shows a balance of $16,624. The bank statement lists a $200 credit for a bank collection, an $8 debit for the service charge, and a $36 debit for an NSF check. The Reinli Equipment accountant has not recorded any of these items on the books.

c. At September 30 the following checks are outstanding:

Check No.	Amount
154	$116
256	150
278	253
291	190
292	206
293	145

d. The cashier handles all incoming cash and makes bank deposits. He also reconciles the monthly bank statement. His September 30 reconciliation follows.

Balance per books, September 30		$19,702
Add: Outstanding checks...........................		560
Bank collection...................................		200
		20,462
Less: Deposits in transit	$3,794	
Service charge......................................	8	
NSF check	36	3,838
Balance per bank, September 30		$16,624

Moore has requested that you determine whether the cashier has stolen cash from the business and, if so, how much. She also asks you to identify how the cashier has attempted to conceal the theft. To make this determination, you perform your own bank reconciliation using the format illustrated in the chapter. There are no bank or book errors. Moore also asks you to evaluate the internal controls and to recommend any changes needed to improve them.

2. The following questions are unrelated except that they all pertain to internal control.

The role of internal control (Obj. 2)

1. Separation of duties is an important consideration if a system of internal control is to be effective. Why is this so?

2. Cash may be a relatively small item on the financial statements. Nevertheless, internal control over cash is very important. Why do you think this is true?

3. Ling Ltd. requires that all documents supporting a check be canceled by the person who signs the check. Why do you think this practice is required? What might happen if it were not?

4. Many managers think that safeguarding assets is the most important objective of internal control systems, whereas auditors emphasize reliable accounting data. Explain why auditors are more concerned about the quality of the accounting records than about safeguarding assets.

ETHICAL ISSUE

Steve Ramm owns apartment buildings in California, Nevada, and Utah. Each property has a manager who collects rent, arranges for repairs, and runs advertisements in the local newspaper. The property managers transfer cash to Ramm monthly and prepare their own bank reconciliations. The manager in Las Vegas has been stealing large sums of money. To cover the theft, he understates the amount of the outstanding checks on the monthly bank reconciliation. As a result, each monthly bank reconciliation appears to balance. However, the balance sheet reports more cash than Ramm actually has in the bank. In negotiating the sale of the Las Vegas property, Ramm is showing the balance sheet to prospective investors.

Required

1. Identify two parties other than Ramm who can be harmed by this theft. In what ways can they be harmed?

2. Discuss the role accounting plays in this situation.

FINANCIAL STATEMENT PROBLEMS

Internal controls and cash
(Obj. 1)

1. Study the Lands' End responsibility statement and the audit opinion of the Lands' End, Inc., financial statement given at the end of Appendix A. Answer the following questions about Lands' End's internal controls and cash position.

Required

1. What is the name of Lands' End's outside auditing firm? What office of this firm signed the audit report? How long after Lands' End's year end did the auditors issue their opinion?
2. Who bears primary responsibility for the financial statements? How can you tell?
3. Does it appear that Lands' End's internal controls are adequate? How can you tell?
4. What standard of auditing did the outside auditors use in examining the Lands' End financial statements? By what accounting standards were the statements evaluated?
5. By how much did Lands' End's cash position change during 1994? The statement of cash flows (discussed in detail in Chapter 18) tells why this change occurred. Which type of activity—operating, investing, or financing—contributed to this change?

Audit opinion, management responsibility, internal controls, and cash
(Obj. 1)

2. Obtain the annual report of a real company of your choosing. Study the audit opinion and the management statement of responsibility (if present) in conjunction with the financial statements. Answer these questions about the company.

Required

1. What is the name of the company's outside auditing firm? What office of this firm signed the audit report? How long after the company's year end did the auditors issue their opinion?
2. Who bears primary responsibility for the financial statements? How can you tell?
3. Does it appear that the company's internal controls are adequate? Give your reason.
4. What standard of auditing did the outside auditors use in examining the company's financial statements? By what accounting standards were the statements evaluated?
5. By how much did the company's cash position (including cash equivalents) change during the current year? The statement of cash flows (discussed in Chapter 18) tells why this increase occurred. Which type of activity—operating, investing, or financing—contributed most to the change in the cash balance?
6. Where is the balance of petty cash reported? Name the financial statement and the account, and identify the specific amount that includes petty cash.

Appendix

The Voucher System

The **voucher system** for recording cash payments improves a business's internal control over cash disbursements by formalizing the process of approving and recording invoices for payment. We will examine the voucher system as it is used by a merchandising business.

The voucher system uses (1) vouchers, (2) a voucher register, (3) an unpaid voucher file, (4) a check register, and (5) a paid voucher file. The merchandising business we discuss has separate departments for purchasing goods, receiving goods, disbursing cash, and accounting.

VOUCHERS   Recall that a *voucher* is a document authorizing a cash disbursement. The accounting department prepares vouchers. Exhibit 7A-1 illustrates the voucher of Bliss Wholesale Company. In addition to places for writing in the *payee*, *due date*, *terms*, *description*, and *invoice amount*, the voucher includes a section for designated officers to sign their approval for payment. The back of the voucher has places for recording the *account debited*, *date paid*, and *check number*. You should locate these nine items in Exhibit 7A-1.

Exhibit 7A-2 lists the various business documents used to ensure that the company receives the goods it ordered and pays only for the goods it has actually received. Exhibit 7A-3 shows how a voucher added to the other documents can provide the evidence for a cash disbursement. The amounts on all these documents should agree.

Key Point: In a voucher system, all expenditures must be approved before payment can be made. This approval takes the form of a voucher. The larger the business, the more likely it is to need strict control over disbursements. The voucher system helps supply this control.

EXHIBIT 7A-1
Voucher

		Voucher No. 326
	BLISS WHOLESALE COMPANY	
Payee	Van Heusen, Inc.	
Address	4619 Shotwell Avenue	
	Brooklyn, NY 10564	
Due Date	March 7	
Terms	2/10, n/30	

Date	Invoice No.	Description	Amount
Mar. 1	6380	144 men's shirts stock no. X14	

Approved *Jane Trent* Controller   **Approved** *Bob Kraft* Treasurer

Front of Voucher

Voucher No. 326
Payee Van Heusen, Inc.
Invoice Amount $1,800
Discount   36
Net Amount $1,764

Due Date   Mar. 7
Date Paid   Mar. 6
Check No.   694

Account Distribution		
Account Debited	**Acct. No.**	**Amount**
Inventory	105	1,800
Store Supplies	145	
Salary Expense	538	
Advertising Expense	542	
Utilities Expense	548	
Delivery Expense	544	
Total		$1,800

Back of Voucher

EXHIBIT 7A-2
Purchasing Process

Business Document	Prepared by	Sent to
Purchase request	Sales department	Purchasing department
Purchase order	Purchasing department	Outside company that sells the needed merchandise (supplier, or vendor)
Invoice	Outside company that sells the needed merchandise (supplier, or vendor)	Accounting department
Receiving report	Receiving department	Accounting department
Voucher	Accounting department	Officer who signs the check

VOUCHER REGISTER After it is approved by the designated officers, the voucher goes to the accounting department, where it is recorded in the **voucher register**. This journal is similar to the purchases journal (discussed in Chapter 6), but the voucher register is more comprehensive. In a voucher system, *all* expenditures are recorded first in the voucher register. This step is a fundamental control feature of the voucher system because it centralizes the initial recording of all expenditures in this one journal. That is, all cash payments must be vouchered and approved prior to payment. For each transaction, the debit is to the account for which payment is being made, and the credit is to Vouchers Payable, the account that replaces Accounts Payable in many voucher systems. Exhibit 7A-4 illustrates the voucher register of Bliss Wholesale Company.

The voucher register has columns to record payment date and check number, which are entered when the voucher is paid. The absence of a payment date and check number means that the voucher is unpaid. In Exhibit 7A-4, for example, Bliss Wholesale has a $2,202 liability at March 31 for vouchers 330 ($369 payable to the *Daily Journal*), 348 ($1,638 payable to Carr Products), and 350 ($195 payable to Consumers Gas Company). If these were the company's only unpaid vouchers at March 31, the balance sheet would report:

Current liabilities:
    Vouchers payable*............. $2,202

---

*Usually reported as Accounts Payable, even by companies that use a voucher system.

UNPAID VOUCHER FILE After recording a voucher in the voucher register, the accountant places the voucher packet in the unpaid voucher file, where it stays until the voucher is paid. The unpaid voucher file acts as the accounts payable subsidiary ledger because each voucher serves as an individual account payable. There is no need for a separate accounts payable ledger.

The unpaid voucher file has 31 slots, one for each day of the month. Each voucher is filed according to its due date. For example, voucher no. 326, in Exhibit 7A-1, was due March 7, so it was filed in the slot marked 7.

CHECK REGISTER The **check register** is the journal in which are recorded all checks issued in a voucher system. It replaces the cash disbursements journal. All entries in the check register debit Vouchers Payable and credit Cash (and Inventory, as appropriate). Exhibit 7A-5 shows a check register. Notice that all the transactions include a credit to the Cash in Bank account.

On or before the due date, the accountant removes the voucher packet from the unpaid voucher file and sends it to the officers for signing. After the checks are signed, the check number and payment date are entered on the back of the voucher, in the check register, and in the voucher register.

EXHIBIT 7A-4
Voucher Register

Voucher Register
Page 16

Date	Voucher No.	Payee	Payment Date	Check No.	Credit Vouchers Payable	Inventory	Store Supplies	Salary Expense	Advertising Expense	Utilities Expense	Delivery Expense	Other Accounts Title	No.	Amount
Mar. 1	326	Van Heusen, Inc.	3/6	694	1,800	1,800								
1	327	Howell Properties	3/2	693	1,500							Rent Expense	547	1,500
4	328	Bell Telephone	3/10	696	128					128				
5	329	Schick Supplies	3/11	697	85		85							
8	330	Daily Journal			369				369					
9	331	Ace Delivery Service	3/9	695	37						37			
26	348	Carr Products			1,638	1,638								
28	349	Petty Cash	3/31	717	82		23				17	Miscellaneous Selling Expense	563	42
29	350	Consumers Gas Co.			195					195				
30	351	City National Bank	3/31	718	360							Interest Expense	546	360
31	352	Ralph Grant	3/31	719	864			864						
31		Totals			12,580	6,209	137	1,781	753	602	185			2,913
					(201)	(105)	(145)	(538)	(542)	(548)	(544)			(✓)

Account numbers in parentheses indicate the accounts to which these amounts have been posted.

				Debit	Credit	
Date	Check No.	Payee	Voucher No.	Vouchers Payable	Inventory	Cash in Bank
Mar. 1	692	Trent Co.	322	600	18	582
2	693	Howell Properties	327	1,500		1,500
6	694	Van Heusen, Inc.	326	1,800	36	1,764
9	695	Ace Delivery Service	331	37		37
10	696	Bell Telephone	328	128		128
11	697	Schick Supplies	329	85		85
31	717	Petty Cash	349	82		82
31	718	City National Bank	351	360		360
31	719	Ralph Grant	352	864		864
31	720	Krasner Supply Co.	336	92		92
31		Totals		11,406	317	11,089
				(201)	(105)	(103)

Check Register — Page 9

Account numbers in parentheses indicate the accounts to which these amounts have been posted.

PAID VOUCHER FILE After payment, the voucher packet is canceled to avoid paying the bill twice. Typically, a hole is punched through the voucher packet. It is then filed alphabetically by payee name. Most businesses also file a copy in numerical sequence by voucher number as a cross-reference. With this dual filing system, a voucher can be located using either classification scheme.

In summary, the voucher system works as follows:

1. The accounting department prepares a *voucher* for each invoice to be paid.
2. Supporting documents (invoice, receiving report, purchase order, and purchase request) are compared in the accounting department for accuracy and attached to the voucher. These documents make up the *voucher packet*.
3. Designated officials examine the supporting documents and approve the voucher for payment.
4. The accounting department enters the voucher payable in the *voucher register*. The entry is a debit to the account of the item purchased (for example, Inventory) and a credit to Vouchers Payable. The voucher remains in the *unpaid voucher file* until payment.
5. Prior to the invoice due date, a check is issued to pay the voucher. The official reviews the supporting documents and signs the check.
6. The accounting department enters the check in the *check register* and updates the voucher and the voucher register to record payment. All checks are debits to Vouchers Payable and credits to Cash.
7. Paid vouchers are canceled and filed by payee name and by voucher number.

To gain a complete understanding of the voucher system, trace voucher no. 326 from Exhibit 7A-1 through the voucher register in Exhibit 7A-4 to the check register in Exhibit 7A-5. Also, trace the check register entries from Exhibit 7A-5 back to Exhibit 7A-4.

APPENDIX PROBLEMS

P7A-1   Assume that a CompuServ store in Boston uses a voucher system. Assume also that the store completed the following transactions during January:

Voucher system entries (Obj. A1)

Jan. 3   Issued voucher no. 135 payable to New England Bell for telephone service of $2,007.
5   Issued voucher no. 136 payable to IBM for the purchase of inventory costing $15,500, with payment terms of 3/10 n/30.
6   Issued voucher no. 137 payable to City Supply Company for inventory costing $350, with payment terms of 2/10 n/45.
7   Issued check no. 404 to pay voucher no. 136.
10   Issued check no. 405 to pay voucher no. 135.
14   Issued check no. 406 to pay voucher no. 137.
15   Issued voucher no. 138 payable to the *Boston Globe* for advertising of $2,990.
17   Issued voucher no. 139 payable to replenish the petty cash fund. The payee is Petty Cash, and the petty cash tickets list Store Supplies ($16), Delivery Expense ($96), and Miscellaneous Expense ($64). Also issued check no. 407 to pay the voucher.
18   Issued voucher no. 140 payable to Apple Computer Company for inventory costing $27,600, with payment terms of 2/10 n/30.
24   Issued voucher no. 141 payable to city of Boston for property tax of $4,235.
27   Issued voucher no. 142 payable to Bay State Bank for payment of a note payable ($10,000) and interest expense ($1,200).
30   Issued check no. 408 to pay voucher no. 140.
31   Issued voucher no. 143 to pay salesperson salary of $2,309 to Lester Gibbs. Also issued check no. 409 to pay the voucher.

Required

1. Record CompuServ transactions in a voucher register and a check register like those illustrated in the appendix. Posting references are unnecessary.
2. Open the Vouchers Payable account and post amounts to that account.
3. Prepare the list of unpaid vouchers at January 31 and show that the total matches the balance of Vouchers Payable.

P7A-2   Assume that Bells, a department-store chain, uses a voucher system. Assume also that a Bells store completed the following transactions during July:

Voucher system entries (Obj. A1)

July 2   Issued voucher no. 614 payable to Hathaway Shirt Company for the purchase of inventory costing $23,000, with payment terms of 2/10 n/30.
3   Issued voucher no. 615 payable to Edison Electric for electricity usage of $2,189.
5   Issued check no. 344 to pay voucher no. 614.
6   Issued voucher no. 616 payable to Baylor Supply Company for inventory costing $850, with payment terms of 2/10 n/45.
7   Issued check no. 345 to pay voucher no. 615.
13   Issued voucher no. 617 payable to replenish the petty cash fund. The payee is Petty Cash, and the petty cash tickets list store supplies ($119), delivery expense ($48), and miscellaneous expense ($36). Also issued check no. 346 to pay the voucher.
14   Issued check no. 347 to pay voucher no. 616.
18   Issued voucher no. 618 payable to *The New York Times* for advertising, $2,800.
19   Issued voucher no. 619 payable to Levi Strauss & Company for inventory costing $65,800, with payment terms of 3/10 n/30.
28   Issued voucher no. 620 payable to city of New York for property tax of $9,165.
30   Issued check no. 348 to pay voucher no. 619.
31   Issued voucher no. 621 payable to Maine Bank for interest expense of $9,000.
31   Issued voucher no. 622 to pay executive salary of $4,644 to Sharon Kratzman. Also issued check no. 349 to pay the voucher.

Required

1. Record Bells's transactions in a voucher register and a check register like those illustrated in the appendix. Posting references are unnecessary.
2. Open the Vouchers Payable account with a zero beginning balance, and post amounts to it.
3. Prepare the list of unpaid vouchers at July 31 and show that the total matches the balance of Vouchers Payable.

Chapter 8
Accounts and Notes Receivable

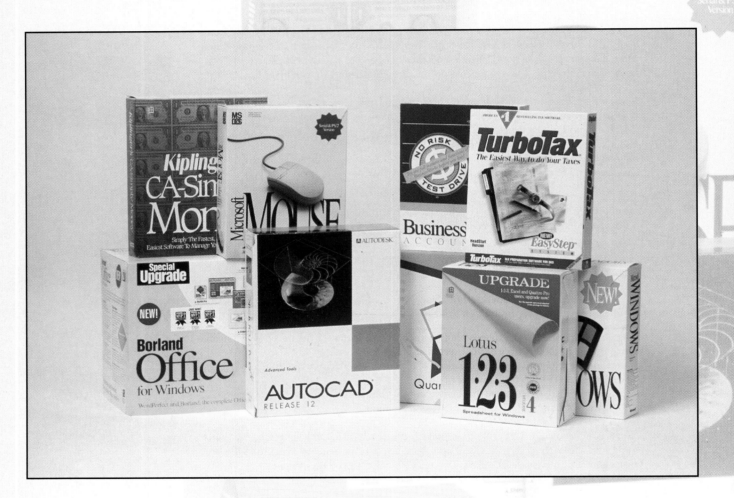

Ultimate Corp. of Lexington, Kentucky, sells computer software packages. The company grew rapidly in the prosperous 1980s, when money was easy. Between 1985 and 1988 sales increased by 93 percent and net income increased by 6 percent, but top managers failed to notice the bulging balances in accounts receivable.

When hard times hit Ultimate, managers took a closer look at operations. They found that the company's receivables had grown 152 percent from 1985 to 1988. They also found that Ultimate's days' sales in receivables—the average number of days it takes to collect receivables—increased from 124 days to 162 days. The results were a cash shortage, more debt, and a drain on profits.

Ultimate instituted a new system for managing receivables, including tougher credit and collection policies. These efforts paid off: In 1991 Ultimate reduced days' sales in receivables to 98 days. *Source: Adapted from T. Pourschine, "No Question, It Looks Bad," Forbes, November 28, 1988, p. 62, and Ultimate Corp., Annual Reports, 10-Ks, 1991–1988.*

• • • • •

*A*ccounts receivable, like most other assets, can represent good news or bad news: Good news because receivables represent a claim to the customer's cash; bad news when the business fails to collect the cash. In the case of Ultimate Corp., receivables got out of hand, and profits suffered. How could the company's sales almost double but its net income increase so modestly? Because Ultimate was not managing its receivables very well. Too much of Ultimate's resources were tied up in accounts receivable—an asset that earns no income. Cash was not flowing into the business quickly enough. To develop profitable computer software packages for sale, Ultimate had to borrow money, and the related interest expense was draining profits.

This chapter discusses the role of the credit department in deciding to which customers the business will sell on account. It explains receivables, including how to account for them when they appear to be uncollectible, and internal control

Chapter Objectives

After studying this chapter, you should be able to

1. Use the allowance method of accounting for uncollectibles

2. Estimate uncollectibles by the percentage of sales and the aging approaches

3. Use the direct write-off method of accounting for uncollectibles

4. Identify internal control weaknesses in accounts receivable

5. Account for notes receivable

6. Report receivables on the balance sheet

7. Use the acid-test ratio and days' sales in receivables to evaluate a company's position over receivables. It also covers notes receivable and introduces several measures that help a business manage customer accounts, including *days' sales in receivables*.

A receivable arises when a business (or person) sells goods or services to a second business (or person) on credit. A receivable is the seller's claim against the buyer for the amount of the transaction. Each credit transaction involves at least two parties—the **creditor**, who sells a service or merchandise and obtains a receivable, and the **debtor**, who makes the purchase and creates a payable. This chapter focuses on accounting for the creditor's receivables. We will discuss the accounts that generally appear on a creditor's balance sheet.

Different Types of Receivables

Receivables are monetary claims against businesses and individuals. They are acquired mainly by selling goods and services and by lending money.

The two major types of receivables are accounts receivable and notes receivable. A business's *accounts receivable* are the amounts that its customers owe it. These accounts receivable are sometimes called *trade receivables*. They are *current assets*.

Accounts receivable should be distinguished from accruals, notes, and other assets because the accounts receivable pertain to sales or service revenue, which represents the lifeblood of a business. Moreover, amounts included as accounts receivable should be collectible according to the business's normal receivables terms (such as net 30, or 2/10 n/30).

Notes receivable are more formal than accounts receivable. The debtor in a note receivable arrangement promises in writing to pay the creditor a definite sum at a specific future date—the date of *maturity*. The terms of these notes usually extend for at least 60 days. A written document known as a *promissory note* serves as evidence of the receivable. A note may require the debtor to pledge *security* for the loan. This means that the borrower promises that the lender may claim certain assets if the borrower fails to pay the amount due at maturity.

Notes receivable due within one year or less are *current assets*. Those notes due beyond one year are *long-term receivables*. Some notes receivable are collected in periodic installments. The portion due within one year is a current asset, and the remaining amount a long-term asset. General Motors may hold a $6,000 note receivable from you, but only the $1,500 you owe on it this year is a current asset to GM.

Other receivables is a miscellaneous category that includes loans to employees and subsidiary companies. Usually these are long-term receivables, but they are current assets if receivable within one year or less. Long-term notes receivable, and other receivables, are often reported on the balance sheet after current assets and before plant assets, as shown in Exhibit 8-1.

Each type of receivable is a separate account in the general ledger and may be supported by a subsidiary ledger if needed.

The Credit Department

A customer who uses a credit card to acquire goods or services is buying on account. This transaction creates a receivable for the seller. Most companies with a high proportion of sales on account have a separate credit department. This department evaluates customers who apply for credit cards by using standard formulas—which include the applicant's income and credit history, among other factors—for deciding which customers the store will sell to on account. After approving a customer, the credit department monitors customer payment records. Customers with a history of paying on time may receive higher credit limits. Those who fail to pay on time have

Assets		Liabilities	
Current:		**Current:**	
Cash	$X,XXX	Accounts payable	$X,XXX
Accounts receivable .... $XXXX		Notes payable, short-term	X,XXX
Less Allowance for		Accrued current liabilities..................	X,XXX
uncollectible accounts . (XXX)	X,XXX	Total current liabilities.......................	X,XXX
Notes receivable, short-term...........	**X,XXX**		
Inventories...	X,XXX		
Prepaid expenses...................................	X,XXX		
Total	X,XXX	**Long-term:**	
		Notes payable, long-term...................	X,XXX
Investments and long-term receivables:		Total liabilities.....................................	X,XXX
Investments in other companies............	X,XXX		
Notes receivable, long-term.............	**X,XXX**		
Other receivables...........................	**X,XXX**		
Total	X,XXX	**Owner Equity**	
Plant assets:			
Property, plant, and equipment.............	X,XXX	Capital	X,XXX
Total assets	$X,XXX	Total liabilities and owner equity.................	$X,XXX

their limits reduced or eliminated. The goal is to collect from customers quickly enough to keep cash circulating, as discussed for Ultimate Corp. in the chapter-opening story. The credit department also assists the accounting department in measuring collection losses on customers who do not pay.

EXHIBIT 8-1
Balance Sheet

Uncollectible Accounts (Bad Debts)

Selling on credit creates both a benefit and a cost. Customers may be unwilling or unable to pay cash immediately and may make a purchase on credit. Revenues and profits rise as sales increase. The cost to the seller of extending credit arises from the failure to collect from some credit customers. Accountants label this cost uncollectible-account expense, doubtful-account expense, or bad-debt expense.

The extent of uncollectible-account expense varies from company to company. In some lines of business, a six-month-old receivable of $1 is worth only 67 cents. A five-year-old receivable of $1 is worth only 4 cents. Uncollectible-account expense depends on the credit risks that managers are willing to accept. At Albany Ladder, a $23 million construction-equipment and supply firm headquartered in Albany, New York, 85 percent of company sales are on account. Albany's receivables grow in proportion to sales. Bad debts cost Albany Ladder about $100,000 a year, or about 1 to 1 1/2 percent of total sales, a figure that has remained fairly constant as a result of careful credit screening and rigorous collection activity. It takes Albany Ladder an average of 70 days to collect its receivables.

Key Point: Selling on credit enables a company to generate more sales revenue. But there is a cost associated with selling on credit; bad-debt expense arises as a result of not collecting from some customers.

"Bad debts cost Albany Ladder about $100,000 a year, or about 1 to 1 1/2 percent of total sales."

Many small retail businesses accept a higher level of risk than do large stores such as Sears. Why? To increase sales. Moreover, small businesses often have personal ties to customers, who are then more likely to pay their accounts.

Measuring Uncollectible Accounts

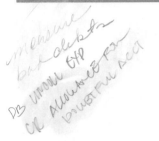

Key Point: The amount of bad-debt expense depends on the volume of credit sales, the effectiveness of the credit department, and the diligence of the collection department.

For a firm that sells on credit, uncollectible-account expense is as much a part of doing business as salary expense and depreciation expense. Uncollectible-Account Expense—an operating expense—must be measured, recorded, and reported. To do so, accountants use the allowance method or the direct write-off method (which will be covered on page 335).

ALLOWANCE METHOD To present the most accurate financial statements possible, accountants in firms with large credit sales use the **allowance method** of measuring bad debts. This method records collection losses on the basis of estimates instead of waiting to see which customers the business will not collect from.

Smart managers know that not every customer will pay in full. But at the time of sale, managers do not know which customers will not pay. If they did, they would not sell on credit to those customers!

Rather than try to guess which accounts will go bad, managers, on the basis of collection experience, estimate the total bad-debt expense for the period. The business debits Uncollectible-Account Expense for the estimated amount and credits **Allowance for Uncollectible Accounts** (or **Allowance for Doubtful Accounts**), a contra account related to Accounts Receivable. This allowance account shows the amount of the receivables that the business expects *not* to collect.

To match expense against revenue properly, the firm estimates the uncollectible-account expense on the basis of past collection experience and records it as an adjusting entry during the period in which sales are made. This expense entry has two effects: (1) *It decreases net income by debiting an expense account*; and (2) *it decreases net accounts receivable by crediting the allowance account*. Allowance for Uncollectible Accounts, the contra account, is subtracted from Accounts Receivable to measure *net* accounts receivable.

Assume that the company's sales for 19X1 are $240,000 and that past collection experience suggests estimated bad-debt expense of $3,100 for the year. The 19X1 journal entries follow, with accounts receivable from customers Rolf and Anderson separated for emphasis:

During the year:

19X1 Accounts Receivable—Rolf	1,300	
Accounts Receivable—Anderson	1,700	
Accounts Receivable—Various Customers	237,000	
Sales Revenue		240,000
To record credit sales.		

End-of-year adjusting entry:

19X1 Uncollectible-Account Expense	3,100	
Allowance for Uncollectible Accounts		3,100
To record estimated bad-debt expense, based on past collection experience.		

The account balances at December 31, 19X1, appear as follows:

Accounts Receivable		Allowance for Uncollectible Accounts		Sales Revenue		Uncollectible-Account Expense	
240,000			3,100		240,000	3,100	

Net accounts receivable = $236,900

The entry to record uncollectible-account expense decreases net accounts receivable.

The 19X1 financial statements will report the following:

Income Statement:	19X1
Revenue:	
Sales revenue..	$240,000
Expense:	
Uncollectible-account expense..............................	3,100

Balance Sheet:	December 31, 19X1
Current assets:	
Accounts receivable..	$240,000
Less: Allowance for uncollectible accounts	3,100
Net accounts receivable...	$236,900

Writing Off Uncollectible Accounts

— No effect on net income (no DR to Exp. Acct)

During 19X2 the company collects on most of the accounts receivable as follows:

19X2	Cash	235,000	
	Accounts Receivable—		
	Various Customers		235,000
	To record collections on account.		

However, the credit department determines that customers Rolf and Anderson cannot pay the amounts they owe. The accountant writes off their receivables with the following entry:

19X2	Allowance for Uncollectible Accounts............................	3,000	
	Accounts Receivable—Rolf...................................		1,300
	Accounts Receivable—Anderson		1,700
	To write off uncollectible accounts.		

The write-off entry has no effect on net income because it includes no debit to an expense account. The entry also has no effect on *net* accounts receivable because both the Allowance account debited and the Accounts Receivable account credited are part of *net* accounts receivable. The account balances at December 31, 19X2, are as follows:

The financial statements for 19X1 and 19X2 will report the following. To highlight the matching of expense and revenue, we are assuming that no sales are made in 19X2.

Income Statement:	19X1	19X2
Revenue:		
Sales revenue...	$240,000	$ 0
Expense:		
Uncollectible-account expense..	3,100	0

Short Exercise: Given:

Accts. Rec.	$90,000
– Allow. for Uncoll.	
Accts.	– 3,500
= Net Accts. Rec.	
(Net Realizable	
Value)	$86,500

If a $700 Account Receivable for Kathy Brown is written off, the journal entry required and Net Accounts Receivable after the write-off are:

Allow. for Uncoll.		
Accts.................	700	
Accts. Rec.—		
K. Brown..		700

Accts. Rec.	
90,000	700
89,300	

Allow. for Uncoll. Accts.	
700	3,500
	2,800

Net accts. rec. (NRV) is the same, $86,500:

Accts. Rec.	$89,300
– Allow. for	
Uncoll. Accts. ...	– 2,800
= Net Accts. Rec.	
(NRV)	$86,500

NRV (the net amount) does not change as a result of writing off a specific customer's account because the same amount is taken out of both Accts. Rec. and the contra account, Allow. for Uncoll. Accts.

According to the matching principle (Chapter 3, p. 93), expenses incurred must be matched against revenue earned during the period.

The matching principle requires that uncollectible-account expense bear a reasonable relationship to sales revenue. This is why there is no expense for 19X2: There was no revenue that year. The comparative balance sheet for 19X1 and 19X2 reports receivables as follows:

Balance Sheet:	December 31, 19X1	December 31, 19X2
Current assets:		
Accounts receivable	$240,000	$2,000
Less: Allowance for uncollectible accounts	3,100	100
Net accounts receivable	$236,900	$1,900

After the accounting, the allowance for uncollectibles should hold the amount of the receivables the business expects *not* to collect ($100). Net accounts receivable is the amount the business *does* expect to collect ($1,900).

Bad-Debt Write-offs Rarely Equal the Allowance for Uncollectibles

The allowance amount is based on estimates because it comes before the determination that any particular customer account receivable is uncollectible. Bad-debt write-offs of customer accounts are actual amounts. Write-offs equal the allowance only if the estimate of bad debts is perfect—a rare occurrence. Usually the difference between write-offs and the allowance is small, as shown in the preceding example. If the allowance is too large for one period, the estimate of bad debts for the next period can be cut back. If the allowance is too low, an adjusting entry can increase it: Debit Uncollectible-Account Expense and credit Allowance for Uncollectible Accounts. This credit brings the Allowance account to a realistic balance. Estimating uncollectibles will be discussed shortly.

Recoveries of Uncollectible Accounts

When an account receivable is written off as uncollectible, the customer still has an obligation to pay. However, the likelihood of receiving cash is so low that the company ceases its collection effort and writes off the account. Some companies turn such accounts over to an attorney for collection in the hope of recovering part of the receivable. To record a recovery, the accountant reverses the write-off and records the collection in the regular manner. The reversal of the write-off is needed to give the customer account receivable a debit balance.

Assume that the write-off of Rolf's account ($1,300) occurs in February 19X2. In August Rolf pays the account in full. The journal entries for this situation follow:

Feb. 19X2	Allowance for Uncollectible Accounts	1,300	
	Accounts Receivable—Rolf		1,300
	To write off Rolf's account as uncollectible (same entry as above).		
Aug. 19X2	Accounts Receivable—Rolf	1,300	
	Allowance for Uncollectible Accounts		1,300
	To reinstate Rolf's account.*		
	Cash	1,300	
	Accounts Receivable—Rolf		1,300
	To record collection from Rolf.		

*This entry places Rolf's account receivable back on the books. It also replaces the $1,300 removed from the Allowance when Rolf's account was written off in February.

OBJECTIVE 2

Estimate uncollectibles by the percentage of sales and the aging approaches

Estimating Uncollectibles

The more accurate the estimate, the more reliable the information in the financial statements. How are bad-debt estimates made? The most logical way to estimate bad debts is to look at the business's past records. Both the *percentage of sales* method and the *aging of accounts receivable* method use the company's collection experience.

PERCENTAGE OF SALES A popular way to estimate uncollectibles, the **percentage of sales approach,** computes the expense as a percentage of net credit sales (or net sales). Uncollectible-account expense is recorded as an adjusting entry at the end of the period.

Basing its decision on figures from the previous four periods, a business estimates that bad-debt expense will be 2.5 percent of credit sales. If credit sales for 19X3 total $500,000, the adjusting entry to record bad-debt expense for the year is:

Key Point: The percentage of sales approach is often referred to as the income statement approach to estimating bad-debt expense because the entry is based on credit sales for the period (an income statement figure).

Adjusting Entries

Dec. 31	Uncollectible-Account Expense ($500,000 × 0.025)	12,500	
	Allowance for Uncollectible Accounts....................		12,500

Under the percentage of sales method, the amount of this entry ignores the prior balance in Allowance for Uncollectible Accounts.

A business may change the percentage rate from year to year, depending on its collection experience. Suppose collections of accounts receivable in 19X4 are greater, and write-offs are less, than expected. The credit balance in Allowance for Uncollectible Accounts would be too large in relation to the debit balance of Accounts Receivable. How would the business change its bad-debt percentage rate in this case? *Decreasing* the percentage rate would reduce the credit entry to the allowance account, and the allowance account balance would not grow too large.

New businesses, with no credit history on which to base their rates, may obtain estimated bad-debt percentages from industry trade journals, government publications, and other sources of collection data.

AGING OF ACCOUNTS RECEIVABLE The second popular way to estimate bad debts is called **aging of accounts receivable**. In this approach, individual accounts receivable are analyzed according to the length of time they have been receivable from the customer. When performed manually, this method is time-consuming. Computers greatly ease the burden. Computerized accounting packages prepare a report for aging accounts receivable. The computer accesses files of customer data and sorts accounts by customer number and date of invoice. Schmidt Home Builders groups its accounts receivable into 30-day periods, as Exhibit 8-2 shows.

Customer Name	Age of Account				
	1–30 Days	31–60 Days	61–90 Days	Over 90 Days	Total Balance
T-Bar-M Co.	$20,000				$ 20,000
Chicago Pneumatic Parts	10,000				10,000
Sarasota Pipe Corp.		$13,000	$10,000		23,000
Oneida, Inc.			3,000	$1,000	4,000
Other accounts*	39,000	12,000	2,000	2,000	55,000
Totals	$69,000	$25,000	$15,000	$3,000	$112,000
Estimated percentage uncollectible	0.1%	1%	5%	90%	
Allowance for Uncollectible Accounts balance	$69	$250	$750	$2,700	$3,769

*Each of the "Other accounts" would appear individually.

EXHIBIT 8-2
Aging the Accounts of Schmidt Home Builders

Key Point: The aging of accounts receivable approach is often referred to as the balance sheet approach to estimating bad debts because the computation focuses on Accounts Receivable (a balance sheet figure).

Schmidt bases the percentage figures on the company's collection experience. In the past, the business has collected all but 0.1 percent of accounts aged from 1 to 30 days, all but 1 percent of accounts aged from 31 to 60 days, and so on.

The total amount receivable in each age group is multiplied by the appropriate percentage figure. For example, the $69,000 in accounts aged 1 to 30 days is multiplied by 0.1 percent (0.001), which comes to $69. The total balance needed in the Allowance for Uncollectible Accounts—$3,769—is the sum of the amounts computed for the various groups ($69 + $250 + $750 + $2,700).

Suppose the Allowance account has a $2,100 *credit* balance from the previous period—that is, before any current-period adjustment:

Allowance for Uncollectible Accounts	
	Unadjusted balance 2,100

Under the aging method, the adjusting entry is designed to adjust this account balance from $2,100 to $3,769, the needed amount determined by the aging schedule. To bring the Allowance balance up to date, Schmidt makes this entry:

Adjusting Entries

Dec. 31	Uncollectible-Account Expense	1,669	
	Allowance for Uncollectible Accounts	
	($3,769 – $2,100)		1,669

Under the aging method, the adjusting entry takes into account the prior balance in Allowance for Uncollectibles. Now the Allowance account has the correct balance:

Allowance for Uncollectible Accounts	
	Unadjusted balance 2,100
	Adjustment amount 1,669
	Adjusted balance 3,769

It is possible for the allowance account to have a *debit* balance at year end prior to the adjusting entry. How can this occur? Bad-debt write-offs during the year could have exceeded the allowance amount. Suppose the unadjusted balance in Allowance for Uncollectible Accounts is a *debit* amount of $1,500:

Allowance for Uncollectible Accounts	
Unadjusted balance 1,500	

In this situation, the adjusting entry is

Adjusting Entries

Dec. 31	Uncollectible-Account Expense ($3,769 + $1,500)..............	5,269	
	Allowance for Uncollectible Accounts........................		5,269

After posting, the allowance account is up-to-date:

Allowance for Uncollectible Accounts	
Unadjusted balance 1,500	Adjustment amount 5,269
	Adjusted balance 3,769

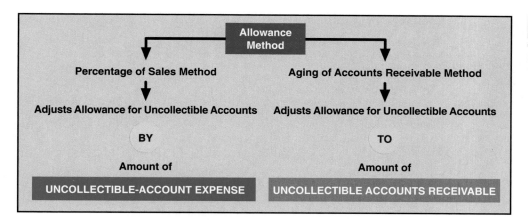

In the final analysis, the balance sheet reports the *expected realizable value* of the accounts receivable—$108,231—$112,000 balance of accounts receivable, minus the $3,769 balance in the allowance account (see the total balance in Exhibit 8-2).

In addition to supplying the information needed for accurate financial reporting, the aging method directs management's attention to the accounts that should be pursued for payment. Ultimate Corp. of the chapter-opening story may not have analyzed accounts receivable this closely.

Using the Percentage of Sales and the Aging Methods Together

In practice, companies use the percentage of sales and the aging of accounts methods together (Exhibit 8-3). For interim statements (monthly or quarterly), companies use the percentage of sales method because it is easier to apply. At the end of the year, these companies use the aging method to ensure that Accounts Receivable is reported at expected realizable value—that is, the expected amount to be collected. The two methods work well together because the percentage of sales approach focuses on measuring bad-debt expense on the income statement, whereas the aging approach is designed to measure net accounts receivable on the balance sheet.

Direct Write-Off Method

Under the **direct write-off method** of accounting for bad debts, the company waits until the credit department decides that a customer's account receivable is uncollectible. Then the accountant debits Uncollectible-Account Expense and credits the customer's account receivable to write off the account.

Assume it is 19X2 and most credit customers have paid for their 19X1 purchases. At this point, the credit department believes that two customers—Jones and Smith—will never pay. The department directs the accountant to write off Jones and Smith as bad debts, using this entry:

19X2	Uncollectible-Account Expense	2,000	
	Accounts Receivable—Jones		800
	Accounts Receivable—Smith		1,200
	To write off uncollectible accounts and record bad-debt expense of $2,000.		

How does the direct write-off method affect the financial statements? The following partial financial statements for 19X1 and 19X2 are based on the assumption of $100,000 credit sales in 19X1 and $0 in 19X2:

OBJECTIVE 3
Use the direct write-off method of accounting for uncollectibles

Key Point: This method is easier to use, but it fails to *match* expenses and revenues properly. It is acceptable only if bad debts are immaterial in amount.

Income Statement:	19X1	19X2
Revenue:		
Sales revenue..	$100,000	$ 0
Expense:		
Uncollectible-account expense...............	0	2,000

	December 31,	
Balance Sheet:	19X1	19X2
Current assets:		
Accounts receivable................................	$100,000	$1,000

STOP & THINK 1. How accurately does the direct write-off method measure income?

Answer: Following generally accepted accounting principles means matching each period's expenses against its revenues. The direct write-off method fails this test: In our example, the full amount of sales revenue appears for 19X1, but the bad-debt expense incurred to generate this revenue appears in 19X2. Consequently, this method gives misleading income figures for both years. The $2,000 bad-debt expense should be matched against the $100,000 sales revenue for 19X1.

2. How accurately does the direct write-off method value accounts receivable?

Answer: The 19X1 balance sheet shows accounts receivable at the full $100,000 figure. But any businessperson knows that bad debts are unavoidable when selling on credit. There are always a few customers who will fail to pay the amount they owe. Is the $100,000 figure, then, the expected realizable value of the accounts? No, showing the full $100,000 in the balance sheet falsely implies that these accounts receivable are worth their full amount.

The direct write-off method is simple to use, and it causes no great error if collection losses are insignificant in amount. However, the resulting accounting records are not as accurate as they could be. The allowance method is a better way to apply the accrual basis for measuring uncollectible-account expense.

Credit Balances in Accounts Receivable

Occasionally, customers overpay their accounts or return merchandise for which they have already paid. The result is a credit balance in the customer's account receivable. Assume that the company's subsidiary ledger contains 213 accounts, with balances as shown:

210 accounts with *debit* balances totaling................	$185,000
3 accounts with *credit* balances totaling...............	2,800
Net total of all balances	$182,200

The company should *not* report the asset Accounts Receivable at the net amount—$182,200. Why not? The credit balance—the $2,800—is a liability. Like any other liability, customer credit balances are debts of the business. A balance sheet that did not indicate to management or to other financial statement users that the company had this liability amount would be misleading if the $2,800 is significant in relation to net income or to total current assets. Therefore, the company would report on its balance sheet:

Assets		**Liabilities**	
Current:		Current:	
Accounts receivable	$185,000	Credit balances in	
		customer accounts.....................	$2,800

Credit-Card Sales

Credit-card sales are common in retailing. American Express, VISA, MasterCard, and Discover are popular. The customer presents the credit card as payment for a purchase. The seller prepares a sales invoice in triplicate. The customer and the seller keep copies as receipts. The third copy goes to the credit-card company, which then pays the seller the transaction amount and bills the customer.

Credit cards offer consumers the convenience of buying without having to pay the cash immediately. Consumers receive a monthly statement from the credit-card company, detailing each credit-card transaction. They can write a single check to cover the entire month's credit-card purchases.

Retailers also benefit from credit-card sales. They do not have to check a customer's credit rating. The company that issues the card has already done so. Retailers do not have to keep an accounts receivable subsidiary ledger account for each customer, and they do not have to collect cash from customers. The copy of the sales invoice that retailers send to the credit-card company signals the card issuer to pursue payment. Further, retailers receive cash more quickly from the credit-card companies than they would from the customers themselves.

Of course, these services to the seller do not come free. The seller receives less than 100 percent of the face value of the invoice. The credit-card company takes a discount ranging between 1 and 5 percent[1] on the sale to cover its services. Suppose a friend treats you to lunch at the Russian Tea Room (the seller) and pays the bill—$100—with a Discover card. The seller's entry to record the $100 Discover Card sale, subject to a 2-percent discount, is

"The credit-card company takes a discount ranging between 1 and 5 percent on the sale to cover its services."

Accounts Receivable—Discover	98	
Credit-Card Discount Expense	2	
Sales Revenue		100

On collection of the discounted value, the seller records:

Cash	98	
Accounts Receivable—Discover		98

Internal Control over Collections of Accounts Receivable

Businesses that sell on credit receive most of their cash receipts by mail. Internal control over collections on account is an important part of the overall internal control system. Chapter 7 detailed control procedures over cash receipts, but a critical element of internal control deserves emphasis here: the separation of cash-handling and cash-accounting duties. Consider the following case.

Butler Supply Co. is a small, family-owned business that takes pride in the loyalty of its workers. Most company employees have been with the Butlers for at least five years. The company makes 90 percent of its sales on account.

The office staff consists of a bookkeeper and a supervisor. The bookkeeper maintains the general ledger and the accounts receivable subsidiary ledger. He also makes the daily bank deposit. The supervisor prepares monthly financial statements

OBJECTIVE 4
Identify internal control weaknesses in accounts receivable

---

[1] The rate varies among companies and over time.

and any special reports the Butlers require. She also takes sales orders from customers and serves as office manager.

Can you identify the internal control weakness? The bookkeeper has access to the general ledger, the accounts receivable subsidiary ledger, and the cash. The bookkeeper could take a customer check and write off the customer's account as uncollectible.[2] Unless the supervisor or some other manager reviews the bookkeeper's work regularly, the theft may go undetected. In small businesses like Butler Supply Co., such a review may not be performed routinely.

How can this control weakness be corrected? The supervisor could open incoming mail and make the daily bank deposit. The bookkeeper should not be allowed to handle cash. Only the remittance advices would be forwarded to the bookkeeper to indicate which customer accounts to credit. By removing cash-handling duties from the bookkeeper and keeping the accounts receivable subsidiary ledger away from the supervisor, the company would separate duties and strengthen internal control. These actions would reduce an employee's opportunity to steal cash and then cover it up with a false credit to a customer account.

Using a bank lock box would achieve the same separation of duties. Customers would send their payments directly to Butler Supply's bank, which would record and deposit the cash into the company's account. The bank would then forward the remittance advice to Butler Supply's bookkeeper to credit the appropriate customer accounts.

Another step should be taken. The bookkeeper should total the amount posted as credits to customer accounts receivable each day. The owner should then compare this total with the day's bank deposit slip. Agreement of the two records would give some assurance that customer accounts were posted correctly and would help avoid accounting errors. Also, the owner should prepare the bank reconciliation.

---

[2]The bookkeeper would need to forge the endorsements of the checks and deposit them in a bank account he controls. This is easier to do than you might imagine.

MID-CHAPTER SUMMARY PROBLEM FOR YOUR REVIEW

CPC International, Inc., is the food-products company that produces Skippy peanut butter, Hellmann's mayonnaise, and Mazola corn oil. The company balance sheet at December 31, 19X7, reported:

	Millions
Notes and accounts receivable [total]	$549.9
Allowances for doubtful accounts	(12.5)

Required

1. How much of the December 31, 19X7, balance of notes and accounts receivable did CPC expect to collect? Stated differently, what was the expected realizable value of these receivables?
2. Journalize, without explanations, 19X8 entries for CPC International, assuming:
   a. Estimated Doubtful-Account Expense of $19.2 million, based on the percentage of sales method.
   b. Write-offs of accounts receivable totaling $23.6 million.
   c. December 31, 19X8, aging of receivables, which indicates that $15.3 million of the total receivables of $582.7 million is uncollectible.
3. Show how CPC International's receivables and related allowance will appear on the December 31, 19X8, balance sheet.
4. What is the expected realizable value of receivables at December 31, 19X8? How much is doubtful-account expense for 19X8?

Requirement 1

	Millions
Expected realizable value of receivables ($549.9 – $12.5)..	$537.4

Requirement 2

	Millions	
a. Doubtful-Account Expense...	19.2	
Allowance for Doubtful Accounts..		19.2
b. Allowance for Doubtful Accounts	23.6	
Accounts Receivable		23.6

Allowance for Doubtful Accounts			
19X8 Write-offs	23.6	Dec. 31, 19X7	12.5
		19X8 Expense	19.2
		19X8 balance prior to December 31, 19X8	8.1

c. Doubtful-Account Expense ($15.3 – $8.1)..	7.2	
Allowance for Doubtful Accounts..		7.2

Requirement 3

	Millions
Notes and accounts receivable	$582.7
Allowance for doubtful acounts..	(15.3)

Requirement 4

	Millions
Expected realizable value of receivables at December 31, 19X8 ($582.7 – $15.3)	$567.4
Doubtful-account expense for 19X8 ($19.2 + $7.2)	26.4

Notes Receivable

As we pointed out earlier, notes receivable are more formal arrangements than accounts receivable. Often the debtor signs a promissory note, which serves as evidence of the debt. Let's define the special terms used to discuss notes receivable.

- **Promissory note:** A written promise to pay a specified amount of money at a particular future date.
- **Maker** of the note: The person or business that signs the note and promises to pay the amount required by the note agreement; the debtor.
- **Payee** of the note: The person or business to whom the maker promises future payment; the creditor.
- **Principal amount,** or **principal:** The amount loaned by the payee and borrowed by the maker of the note.
- **Interest:** The revenue to the payee for loaning out the principal and the expense to the maker for borrowing the principal.
- **Interest period:** The period of time during which interest is to be computed. It extends from the original date of the note to the maturity date. Also called the *note period*, *note term*, or simply *time*.

- **Interest rate:** The percentage rate that is multiplied by the principal amount to compute the amount of interest on the note.
- **Maturity date:** The date on which final payment of the note is due. Also called *due date*.
- **Maturity value:** The sum of principal and interest due at the maturity date of the note.

Exhibit 8-4 illustrates a promissory note. Study it carefully.

Identifying the Maturity Date of a Note

Some notes specify the maturity date, as shown in Exhibit 8-3. Other notes state the period of the note, in days or months. When the period is given in months, the note's maturity date falls on the same day of the month as the date the note was issued. For example, a six-month note dated February 16 matures on August 16. When the period is given in days, the maturity date is determined by counting the days from the date of issue. A 120-day note dated September 14, 19X2, matures on January 12, 19X3, as shown below:

Month	Number of Days	Cumulative Total
Sep. 19X2	30 – 14 = 16	16
Oct. 19X2	31	47
Nov. 19X2	30	77
Dec. 19X2	31	108
Jan. 19X3	12	120

Short Exercise: Calculate the maturity dates of these notes: (1) A 90-day note dated January 4, 19X3. (2) A 150-day note dated September 30, 19X1. (3) A 45-day note dated May 15, 19X2. Begin counting on the day following the date of the note, so that the due date on a 90-day note is day number 90. *A:* (1) April 4, 19X3 (2) February 27, 19X2 (3) June 29, 19X2

Key Point: Here *rate* means interest rate and *time* means interest period.

Key Point: Interest rates are usually stated as an annual rate. Therefore, the time in the formula should also be expressed in terms of a year.

Computing Interest on a Note

The formula for computing interest is

$$\text{Principal} \times \text{Rate} \times \text{Time} = \text{Amount of Interest}$$

Using the data in Exhibit 8-4, Continental Bank computes its interest revenue for one year on its note receivable as:

Principal		Rate		Time		Interest
$1,000	×	**0.09**	×	**1 (yr.)**	=	**$90**

The *maturity value* of the note is $1,090 ($1,000 principal + $90 interest). The time element is one (1) because interest is computed over a one-year period.

EXHIBIT 8-4 *A Promissory Note*

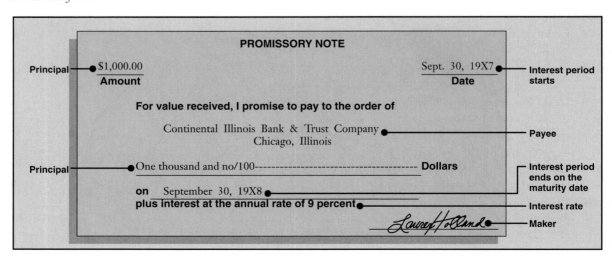

When the interest period of a note is stated in months, we compute the interest based on the 12-month year. Interest on a $2,000 note at 15 percent for three months is computed as:

$$\underset{\$2,000}{\text{Principal}} \times \underset{0.15}{\text{Rate}} \times \underset{3/12}{\text{Time}} = \underset{\$75}{\text{Interest}}$$

When the interest period of a note is stated in days, we sometimes compute interest based on a 360-day year rather than on a 365-day year. The interest on a $5,000 note at 12 percent for 60 days is computed as:

$$\underset{\$5,000}{\text{Principal}} \times \underset{0.12}{\text{Rate}} \times \underset{60/360}{\text{Time}} = \underset{\$100}{\text{Interest}}$$

Short Exercise: Practice calculating interest:
(1) $30,000, 12-1/2%, 180-day note; (2) $8,500, 9%, 6-month note
A: (1) ($30,000 × 0.125 × 180/360) = $1,875 (2) ($8,500 × 0.09 × 6/12) = $383

Recording Notes Receivable

Consider the loan agreement shown in Exhibit 8-4. After Lauren Holland signs the note and presents it to the bank, Continental Bank gives her $1,000 cash. At maturity, Holland pays the bank $1,090 ($1,000 principal plus $90 interest). The bank's entries are

OBJECTIVE 5
Account for notes receivable

Sep. 30, 19X7	Note Receivable—L. Holland	1,000	
	Cash		1,000
	To record the loan.		
Sep. 30, 19X8	Cash	1,090	
	Note Receivable—L. Holland		1,000
	Interest Revenue ($1,000 × 0.09 × 1)		90
	To record collection at maturity.		

Some companies sell merchandise in exchange for notes receivable. This arrangement occurs often when the payment term extends beyond the customary accounts receivable period, which generally ranges from 30 to 60 days.

Suppose that on October 20, 19X3, General Electric sells household appliances for $15,000 to Dorman Builders. Dorman signs a 90-day promissory note at 10 percent annual interest. General Electric's entries to record the sale and collection from Dorman are

Oct. 20, 19X3	Note Receivable—Dorman Builders	15,000	
	Sales Revenue		15,000
	To record sale.		
Jan. 18, 19X4	Cash	15,375	
	Note Receivable—Dorman Builders		15,000
	Interest Revenue ($15,000 × 0.10 × 90/360) .		375
	To record collection at maturity.		

A company may accept a note receivable from a trade customer who fails to pay an account receivable within the customary 30 to 60 days. The customer signs a promissory note—that is, becomes the maker of the note—and gives it to the creditor, who becomes the payee.

Suppose Marlboro, Inc., sees that it will not be able to pay off its account payable to Hoffman Supply that is due in 15 days. Hoffman may accept a one-year, $2,400 note receivable, with 9-percent interest, from Marlboro on October 1, 19X1. Hoffman's entry is:

Oct. 1, 19X1	Note Receivable—Marlboro, Inc.	2,400	
	Accounts Receivable—Marlboro, Inc.		2,400
	To receive a note on account from a customer.		

Why does a company accept a note receivable instead of pressing its demand for payment of the account receivable? The company may pursue receipt but learn that its customer does not have the money. A note receivable gives the company written evidence of the maker's debt, which may aid any legal action for collection. Also, the note receivable may carry a pledge by the maker that gives the payee certain assets if cash is not received by the due date. The company's reward for its patience is the interest revenue that it earns on the note receivable.

Accruing Interest Revenue

Notes receivable may be outstanding at the end of the accounting period. The interest revenue that was accrued on the note up to that point should be recorded as part of that period's earnings. ◄▥ Recall that interest revenue is earned over time, not just when cash is received.

Let's continue with the Hoffman Supply note receivable from Marlboro, Inc. Hoffman Supply's accounting period ends December 31. How much of the total interest revenue does Hoffman earn in 19X1? How much in 19X2?

Hoffman will earn three months' interest in 19X1—for October, November, and December. In 19X2, Hoffman will earn nine months' interest—for January through September. Therefore, at December 31, 19X1, Hoffman Supply will make the following adjusting entry to accrue interest revenue:

Dec. 31, 19X1 Interest Receivable ($2,400 × 0.09 × 3/12).......................... 54
                      Interest Revenue   54
                 To accrue interest revenue earned in 19X1
                 but not yet received.

Then, on the maturity date Hoffman Supply may record collection of principal and interest as follows:

Sep. 30, 19X2 Cash [$2,400 + ($2,400 × 0.09)] 2,616
                    Note Receivable—Marlboro, Inc.......................   2,400
                    Interest Receivable ($2,400 × 0.09 × 3/12)........   54
                    Interest Revenue ($2,400 × 0.09 × 9/12)...........   162
                 To record collection of note receivable on which
                 interest has been previously accrued.

The entries to accrue interest revenue earned in 19X1 and to record collection in 19X2 assign the correct amount of interest to each year.

Discounting a Note Receivable

A payee of a note receivable may need the cash before the maturity date. When this occurs, the payee may sell the note. A note receivable is a *negotiable instrument*, which means that it is readily transferable from one party to another and may be sold. Selling a note is called **discounting a note receivable**. This practice is prevalent with long-term notes receivable secured by real estate as collateral. A bank that has lent money may discount the note receivable to a company such as the Federal National Mortgage Association (known as Fannie Mae). The net result is that the banks and savings and loan institutions can quickly replenish their funds for lending. Moreover, more money is available for people to purchase homes and for businesses to invest in inventory and plant and equipment.

Computers can be used to discount notes. If the company deals with relatively few discounted notes, a spreadsheet may handle the accounting (if the accounting software package does not include a special function for discounting). Companies such as Fannie Mae that discount notes on a regular basis would have a standard program to compute the proceeds.

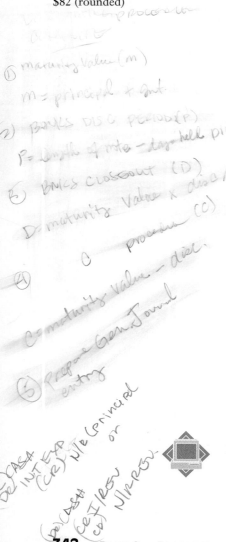

We saw in Chapter 3 (p. 102) that accrued revenue creates an asset for the revenue that has been earned but not received.

Short Exercise: Calculate interest accrued at 12/31 on an 11%, $3,500, 90-day note receivable dated 10/15.
A: $3,500 × 0.11 × 77/360 = $82 (rounded)

The price Fannie Mae pays for a note receivable depends mainly on the interest rate Fannie Mae seeks to earn on its investment. In effect, Fannie Mae pays cash now—at a discounted price—to receive a larger amount at a later date. This is the concept of *present value*: Less money today grows to a larger sum in the future. More advanced accounting courses explore present-value concepts in more detail.

A payee may also discount a short-term note receivable, one with a maturity of one year or less. There are several ways to compute the price to be received. Fundamentally the price is determined by present-value concepts. But the transaction between the seller and the buyer of the note can take any form agreeable to the two parties. We illustrate one procedure used for discounting short-term notes receivable. To receive cash immediately, the seller is willing to accept a significantly discounted price. The purchaser of the note is interested mainly in the margin to be earned on the note—the difference between the purchase price and the amount to be collected at maturity.

Now we return to the example of General Electric (GE) and Dorman Builders from page 341. The maturity date of the Dorman note is January 18, 19X4. Let's assume that GE discounts the Dorman note at First City National Bank on December 9, 19X3. The discount period—the number of days from the date of discounting to the date of maturity (that is, the period the bank will hold the note)—is 40 days; 22 days in December, and 18 days in January. Assume that the bank applies a 12-percent annual interest rate in computing the discounted value of the note. The bank will want to use a discount rate that is higher than the interest rate on the note in order to increase its earnings. GE may be willing to accept this higher rate in order to get cash quickly. The discounted value, called the *proceeds*, is the amount GE receives from the bank. The proceeds can be computed as follows:

Key Point: The discounting procedure follows five steps:

1. Compute the maturity value (principal + interest). $= m$
2. Compute the bank's discount period (length of note – days held prior to discounting). $= P$
3. Compute the bank's discount (maturity value × discount rate × discount period). $= P$
4. Compute the proceeds (maturity value – discount). $= c$
5. Prepare the general journal entry:

Cash (from Step 4) ..	XXX	
Interest Revenue (or expense)		XXX
Note Receivable (principal)		XXX

"*The discounted value, called the* proceeds, *is the amount GE receives from the bank.*"

Principal amount	$15,000		
+ Interest ($15,000 × 0.10 × 90/360)	375		
= Maturity value	15,375	$170	$170
− Discount ($15,375 × 0.12 × 40/360)	(205)		
= Proceeds	$15,170		

At maturity the bank collects $15,375 from the maker of the note, earning $205 interest revenue.

Observe two points in the above computation: (1) The discount is computed on the *maturity value* of the note (principal plus interest) rather than on the original principal amount, and (2) the discount period extends *backward* from the maturity date (January 18, 19X4) to the date of discounting (December 9, 19X3). Follow Exhibit 8-5.

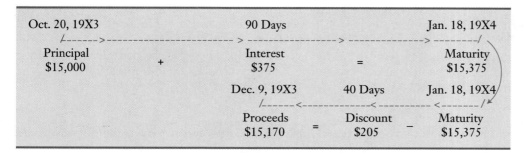

EXHIBIT 8-5
The Timing of Discounting a Note Receivable

Short Exercise: January 5, received a $5,000, 90-day, 10% note from Barney Fife. Sold the Fife note on January 25 by discounting it to a bank at 12%. Prepare the journal entry to record the discounted note on January 25. *A:*

1. Maturity value = $5,000 + ($5,000 × 10% × 90/360) = $5,125
2. Disct. period = 90 − 20 = 70 days
3. Disct. = $5,125 × 12% × 70/360 = $120
4. Proceeds = $5,125 − $120 = $5,005
5. Journal entry:

Cash 5,005
   Interest Revenue ..   5
   Note Receivable—
      Barney Fife   5,000

General Electric's entry to record discounting the note is:

Dec. 9, 19X3	Cash...	15,170	
	Note Receivable—Dorman Builders		15,000
	Interest Revenue ($15,170 − $15,000)		170
	To record discounting a note receivable.		

When the proceeds from discounting a note receivable are less than the principal amount of the note, the payee records a debit to Interest Expense for the amount of the difference. For example, GE could discount the note receivable for cash proceeds of $14,980. The entry to record this transaction is

Dec. 9, 19X3	Cash...	14,980	
	Interest Expense......................................	20	
	Note Receivable—Dorman Builders		15,000

The term *discount* has been used here to distinguish the interest earned by the payee of the note from the interest to be earned by the purchaser of the note. Fundamentally, the discount is interest.

Contingent Liabilities on Discounted Notes Receivable

A **contingent liability** is a potential liability that will become an actual liability only if a potential event does occur. Discounting a note receivable creates a contingent liability for the endorser. If the maker of the note (Dorman, in our example) fails to pay the maturity value to the new payee (the bank), then the original payee (GE, the note's endorser) legally must pay the bank the amount due.[3] Now we see why the liability is "potential." If Dorman pays the bank, then GE can forget the note. But if Dorman dishonors the note—fails to pay it—GE has an actual liability.

This contingent liability of GE exists from the time of the endorsement to the maturity date of the note. In our example, the contingent liability exists from December 9, 19X3—when GE endorsed the note—to the January 18, 19X4, maturity date.

Contingent liabilities are not included with actual liabilities on the balance sheet. After all, they are not real debts. However, financial statement users should be alerted that the business has *potential* debts. Many businesses report contingent liabilities in a footnote to the financial statements. GE's end-of-period balance sheet might carry this note:

As of December 31, 19X3, the Company is contingently liable on notes receivable discounted in the amount of $15,000.

Dishonored Notes Receivable

If the maker of a note does not pay a note receivable at maturity, the maker is said to **dishonor**, or **default on**, the note. Because the term of the note has expired, the note agreement is no longer in force; nor is it negotiable. However, the payee still has a claim against the maker of the note and usually transfers the claim from the note receivable account to Accounts Receivable. The payee records interest revenue earned on the note and debits Accounts Receivable for the full maturity value of the note.

---

[3]The discounting agreement between the endorser and the purchaser may be "without recourse," which means that the endorser has no liability if the note is dishonored at maturity. Under such a condition, there is no contingent liability.

Suppose Rubinstein Jewelers had a six-month, 10-percent note receivable for $1,200 from D. Hatachi, and on the February 3 maturity date Hatachi defaulted. Rubinstein Jewelers would record the default as follows:

Feb. 3   Accounts Receivable—D. Hatachi
        [$1,200 + ($1,200 × 0.10 × 6/12)] 1,260
            Note Receivable—D. Hatachi...................................... 1,200
            Interest Revenue ($1,200 × 0.10 × 6/12) 60
    To record dishonor of note receivable.

Rubinstein would pursue collection from Hatachi as a promissory note default. The company may treat accounts receivable such as this as a special category to highlight them for added collection efforts. If the account receivable later proves uncollectible, the account is written off against Allowance for Uncollectible Accounts in the manner previously discussed.

The maker may dishonor a note after it has been discounted by the original payee. For example, suppose Dorman Builders dishonors its note (maturity value, $15,375) to General Electric (GE) after GE has discounted the note to the bank. On dishonor, the bank adds a *protest fee* to cover the cost of a statement about the facts of the dishonor and requests payment from GE, which then becomes the holder of the dishonored note. Assume that GE pays the maturity value of the note, plus the $25 protest fee, to the bank. This payment creates an obligation for Dorman to pay GE. GE then presents the statement to Dorman and makes the following entry at the maturity date of the note:

Jan. 18, 19X4   Accounts Receivable—Dorman Builders
          ($15,375 + $25) 15,400
            Cash.. 15,400
    To record payment of dishonored note receivable
    that has been discounted, plus a protest fee.

GE's collection of cash, or write-off of the uncollectible account receivable, would be recorded in the normal manner, depending on the ultimate outcome. If GE charges Dorman additional interest, GE's collection entry debits Cash and credits Accounts Receivable and Interest Revenue.

Reporting Receivables and Allowances: Actual Reports

Let's look at how some well-known companies report their receivables and related allowances for uncollectibles on the balance sheet. The terminology and setup vary, but you can understand these real reports by applying what you have learned in this chapter.

OBJECTIVE 6
Report receivables on the balance sheet

Bobbie Brooks, a manufacturer of women's clothing, reported under Current Assets (in thousands):

Accounts receivable, less allowance for doubtful accounts of $602 .... $35,873

To compute the total accounts receivable amount, add the allowance to the net accounts receivable amount: $602 + $35,873 = $36,475.

"Tupperware plastic food-storage containers, Precor exercise equipment, and West Bend kitchen appliances are just some of the products made by divisions of Premark International, Inc."

Tupperware plastic food-storage containers, Precor exercise equipment, and West Bend kitchen appliances are just some of the products made by divisions of Premark International, Inc. Premark combines accounts and notes receivable (amounts in millions):

Accounts and notes receivable, less
   allowances of $19.5 .... $309.9

General Electric Company reports a single amount for its current receivables in the body of the balance sheet and supplements it with a detailed note (amounts in millions):

Current receivables (note 8)	$4,872
Note 8: Current Receivables	
Customers' accounts and notes..	$3,989
Associated companies	49
Nonconsolidated affiliates..	21
Other	927
	4,986
Less allowance for losses	(114)
	$4,872

Nashua Corporation, manufacturer of copying machines and paper products, reported approximately $70 million in net accounts and notes receivable. In addition, the company disclosed a contingent liability for discounted accounts and notes receivable in its Notes to Financial Statements:

Accounts Receivable:
   At December 31, 19X1 and 19X0, the company was contingently liable to third parties as a result of the sale of certain accounts and notes receivable of approximately $19,000,000 and $16,000,000, respectively.

The companies we have featured so far list receivables as *current assets*. National Can Corporation, however, had some long-term receivables that it reported as other assets (amounts in thousands of dollars):

Other Assets:

Notes and accounts receivable, less allowances	$36,970

National Can also disclosed in a note entitled "Notes and Accounts Receivable" that:

Notes and accounts receivable included in other assets are net of allowances for doubtful accounts of $16,772.

Use of Accounting Information in Decision Making

OBJECTIVE 7

Use the acid-test ratio and days' sales in receivables to evaluate a company's position

The balance sheet lists assets in the order of relative liquidity. Cash comes first because it is the medium of exchange and can be used to purchase any item or to pay any bill. Current receivables are less liquid than cash because receivables must be collected. Merchandise inventory is less liquid than receivables because the goods must first be sold; selling the goods creates a receivable that can be collected. Exhibit 8-1 provides an example of a balance sheet showing these accounts.

Acid-Test (or Quick) Ratio

In making decisions, owners and managers use some ratios based on the relative liquidity of assets. In Chapter 4, for example, we discussed the current ratio, which indicates the ability to pay current liabilities with current assets. A more stringent measure of the ability to pay current liabilities is the **acid-test** (or **quick**) **ratio:**◀||| ◀||| ◀|||

The acid-test ratio is similar to the current ratio introduced in Chapter 4 (p. 149) but excludes inventory and prepaid expenses from the numerator.

$$\text{Acid-test ratio} = \frac{\text{Cash + Short-term investments +}}{\text{Net current receivables}} \over \text{Total current liabilities}$$

The acid-test ratio assumes that all current liabilities are payable immediately and that the debtor will convert the most liquid assets to cash. The three most liquid asset categories are cash, short-term investments, and current receivables. Short-term investments (also called *trading securities*, as covered in Chapter 17) are the second most liquid assets because they are readily convertible to cash at the will of the owner. All the owner must do to generate cash is sell these investments.

The higher the acid-test ratio, the better able is the business to pay its current liabilities. An acid-test ratio that increases over time usually indicates improving business operations.

Inventory, although included in the computation of the current ratio, is excluded from the acid-test ratio because it may not be easy to sell the goods. A company may have an acceptable current ratio and a poor acid-test ratio because of a large amount of inventory.

What is an acceptable acid-test ratio value? It depends on the industry. Automobile dealers can operate smoothly with an acid-test ratio of 0.20. Several things make this possible: Car dealers have almost no current receivables. They receive cash from customers, who borrow from banks and other lenders. Dealers carry large inventories, and the manufacturers—GM, Toyota, Mercedes-Benz, for example—allow dealers to pay the cost of automobiles as they are sold at retail prices. In summary, car dealers need little in the way of liquid assets. The average acid-test ratio for women's dress manufacturers is 0.90. Most department stores' ratio values cluster about 0.80, and travel agencies average 1.10. In general, an acid-test ratio of 1.00 is considered safe.

Short Exercise: Compute the current and acid-test ratios for the following selected accounts and their balances at 12/31:

Equipment....................	$4,000
Supplies	500
Interest Payable............	600
Accounts Receivable.....	2,600
Accounts Payable	3,400
Accumulated Deprec....	1,200
Inventory	1,600
Cash.............................	1,300

A: Current ratio = 1.5 ($6,000*/$4,000†)
Acid-test ratio = 0.975 ($3,900/$4,000)
($2,600 + $1,300 = $3,900)

---

*($500 + $2,600 + $1,600 + $1,300 = $6,000)
†($600 + $3,400 = $4,000)

Days' Sales in Receivables

After a business makes a credit sale, the next critical event in the business cycle is collection of the receivable. Several financial ratios center on receivables. **Days' sales in receivables**, also called the *collection period*, indicates how many days it takes to collect the average level of receivables. The shorter the collection period, the more quickly the organization can use cash for operations. The longer the collection period, the less cash is available to pay bills and expand. In the chapter-opening story, Ultimate Corp.'s days' sales in receivables moved from 124 to 162 days, and this increase hurt the company. How could the collection period get so long? Companies enter, and drop out of, the computer sales industry very quickly. Many of these businesses do not succeed, and they cannot pay their bills. Companies like Ultimate may write off lots of receivables as uncollectible. With tougher credit policies—selling to better-paying customers—the collection period dropped to 98 days. Days' sales in receivables can be computed in two steps, as follows:

$$\text{1. One day's sales} = \frac{\text{Net sales}}{365 \text{ days}}$$

$$\text{2. } \frac{\text{Days' sales in}}{\text{average accounts}} = \frac{\text{Average net}}{\text{accounts receivable}} = \frac{\text{(Beginning net receivables}}{\text{+ Ending net receivables})/2} \over \text{One day's sales}$$

Short Exercise: Given:

Net Sales	$48,000
Accts. Rec. (1/1)	10,000
Accts. Rec. (12/31)	14,000

What is the average collection period? *A:* One day's sales = $132 ($48,000/365). Days' sales in average accounts receivable = 91 days ($12,000/$132)

Short Exercise: Refer to the previous Short Exercise. If the company's credit sale terms were 3/10 n/45, how would you evaluate days' sales in receivables? *A:* Far too high; 91 days is nearly twice the allowable credit period of 45 days.

Real-World Example: The average collection period for manufacturers of men's and boys' sport clothing was 47 days in 1993. The top 25% of those companies collected receivables every 26 days. Manufacturers of canned vegetables had an average collection period of 28 days; the top 25% had a 21-day collection period.

The length of the collection period depends on the credit terms of the company's sales. For example, sales on net 30 terms should be collected within approximately 30 days. When there is a discount, such as 2/10 net 30, the collection period may be shorter. Terms of net 45 or net 60 result in longer collection periods. Companies watch their collection period closely. Whenever the collection period lengthens, the business must find other sources of financing, such as borrowing. During recessions, customers pay more slowly, and a longer collection period may be unavoidable.

STOP & THINK Suppose you computed Ultimate Corp.'s acid-test ratio at two dates: In 1988, when the days' sales in receivables stood at 162 days, and in 1991, when the days' sales in receivables was 98 days. Considering only the receivables, which acid-test ratio would look better? Would this appearance be realistic?

Answer: Considering only the receivables, the 1988 acid-test ratio would be higher, and thus look better, because the receivables were much greater in 1988. The 1991 acid-test ratio would be lower, and thus look worse, because of the lower receivables. But appearances can be deceiving. The bloated receivables in 1988 indicated a problem, not a strength.

This situation points to the challenge of financial analysis. Investors and creditors do not evaluate a company on the basis of one or two ratios. Instead they perform a thorough analysis of all the information available on a company. Then they stand back from the data and ask, "What is our overall impression about the strength of this business?"

Computers and Accounts Receivable

Accounting for receivables by a company like M & M Mars requires tens of thousands of postings to customer accounts each month for credit sales and cash collections. Manual accounting methods cannot keep up.

As Chapter 6 explained in more detail, Accounts Receivable can be set up on a computerized system. The order entry and logistics (shipping) systems interface with the billing system, which automatically creates the customers' invoices and debits their accounts in Accounts Receivable. The computer then creates a sales invoice. At the same time, the computer generates records that lead to the printout of sales for the period. The printout is checked and approved. Finally, computerized posting to the general ledger and accounts receivable subledger occurs.

SUMMARY PROBLEM FOR YOUR REVIEW

Suppose Exxon, Inc., engaged in the following transactions:

19X4
Apr. 1   Loaned $8,000 to Bland Co., a service station. Received a one-year, 10-percent note.
June 1   Discounted the Bland note at the bank at a discount rate of 12 percent.
Nov. 30   Loaned $6,000 to Flores, Inc., a regional distributor of Exxon products, on a three-month, 11 percent note.
19X5
Feb. 28   Collected the Flores note at maturity.

Exxon's accounting period ends on December 31.

Required

Explanations are not needed.

1. Record the 19X4 transactions on April 1, June 1, and November 30 on Exxon's books.
2. Make any adjusting entries needed on December 31, 19X4.
3. Record the February 28, 19X5, collection of the Flores note.
4. Which transaction creates a contingent liability for Exxon? When does the contingency begin? When does it end?
5. Write a footnote that Exxon could use in its 19X4 financial statements to report the contingent liability.

SOLUTION TO REVIEW PROBLEM

Requirement 1

19X4

Apr. 1	Note Receivable—Bland Co.	8,000	
	Cash		8,000
June 1	Cash	7,920*	
	Interest Expense	80	
	Note Receivable—Bland Co.		8,000

* Computation of proceeds:

Principal	$8,000
+ Interest ($8,000 × 0.10 × 12/12)	800
= Maturity value...	8,800
− Discount ($8,800 × 0.12 × 10/12)..............	880
= Proceeds	$7,920

Nov. 30	Note Receivable—Flores, Inc.	6,000	
	Cash		6,000

Requirement 2

Adjusting Entries			
19X4			
Dec. 31	Interest Receivable ($6,000 × 0.11 × 1/12)	55	
	Interest Revenue		55

Requirement 3

19X5			
Feb. 28	Cash [$6,000 + ($6,000 × 0.11 × 3/12)]..	6,165	
	Note Receivable—Flores, Inc..		6,000
	Interest Receivable...		55
	Interest Revenue ($6,000 × 0.11 × 2/12)		110

Requirement 4

Discounting the Bland note receivable creates a contingent liability for Exxon. The contingency exists from the date of discounting the note receivable (June 1) to the maturity date of the note (April 1, 19X5).

Requirement 5

Note XX—Contingent liabilities: At December 31, 19X4, the company is contingently liable on notes receivable discounted in the amount of $8,000.

SUMMARY

1. *Use the allowance method of accounting for uncollectibles*. Credit sales create receivables. Accounts receivable are usually current assets, and notes receivable may be current or long-term. Uncollectible receivables are accounted for by the allowance method or the direct write-off method. The *allowance method* matches expenses to sales revenue and also results in a more realistic measure of net accounts receivable.

2. *Estimate uncollectibles by the percentage of sales and the aging approaches*. The *percentage of sales method* and the *aging of accounts receivable method* are the two main approaches to estimating bad debts under the allowance method.

3. *Use the direct write-off method of accounting for uncollectibles*. The *direct write-off* method is easy to apply, but it fails to match the uncollectible-account expense to the corresponding sales revenue. Also, Accounts Receivable are reported at their full amount, which misleadingly suggests that the company expects to collect all its accounts receivable.

In *credit-card* sales, the seller receives cash from the credit-card company (American Express, for example), which bills the customer. For the convenience of receiving cash immediately, the seller pays a fee that is a percentage of the sale.

4. *Identify internal control weaknesses in accounts receivable*. Companies that sell on credit receive most customer collections in the mail. Good *internal control* over mailed-in cash receipts means separating cash-handling duties from cash-accounting duties.

5. *Account for notes receivable*. *Notes receivable* are formal credit agreements. Interest earned by the creditor is computed by multiplying the note's principal amount by the interest rate times the length of the interest period.

Because notes receivable are negotiable, they may be sold. Selling a note receivable—called *discounting a note*—creates a *contingent (possible) liability* for the note's payee.

6. *Report receivables on the balance sheet*. All accounts receivable, notes receivable, and allowance accounts appear in the balance sheet. However, companies use various formats and terms to report these assets.

7. *Use the acid-test ratio and days' sales in receivables to evaluate a company's position*. The *acid-test ratio* measures ability to pay current liabilities from the most liquid current assets. *Days' sales in receivables* indicates how long it takes to collect the average level of receivables.

SELF-STUDY QUESTIONS

Test your understanding of the chapter by marking the best answer for each of the following questions.

1. The party that holds a receivable is called the (p. 328)
   - a. Creditor
   - b. Debtor
   - c. Maker
   - d. Security holder

2. The function of the credit department is to (p. 328)
   - a. Collect accounts receivable from customers
   - b. Report bad credit risks to other companies
   - c. Evaluate customers who apply for credit
   - d. Write off uncollectible accounts receivable

3. Longview, Inc., made the following entry related to uncollectibles:

Uncollectible-Account Expense	1,900	
Allowance for Uncollectible Accounts		1,900

   The purpose of this entry is to (p. 330)
   - a. Write off uncollectibles
   - b. Close the expense account
   - c. Age the accounts receivable
   - d. Record bad-debt expense

4. Longview, Inc., also made this entry:

Allowance for Uncollectible Accounts	2,110	
Accounts Receivable (detailed)		2,100

   The purpose of this entry is to (p. 331)
   - a. Write off uncollectibles
   - b. Close the expense account
   - c. Age the accounts receivable
   - d. Record bad-debt expense

5. The credit balance in Allowance for Uncollectibles is $14,300 prior to the adjusting entries at the end of the period. The aging of accounts indicates that an allowance of $78,900 is needed. The amount of expense to record is (pp. 333–335)
   - a. $14,300
   - b. $64,600
   - c. $78,900
   - d. $93,200

6. The most important internal control over cash receipts is (pp. 338)
   - a. Assigning an honest employee the responsibility for handling cash
   - b. Separating the cash-handling and cash-accounting duties
   - c. Ensuring that cash is deposited in the bank daily
   - d. Centralizing the opening of incoming mail in a single location

7. A six-month, $30,000 note specifies interest of 9 percent. The full amount of interest on this note will be (p. 341)
   - a. $450
   - b. $900
   - c. $1,350
   - d. $2,700

8. The note in Self-Study Question 7 was issued on August 31, and the company's accounting year ends on December 31. The year-end balance sheet will report interest receivable of (p. 342)
   - a. $450
   - b. $900
   - c. $1,350
   - d. $2,700

9. Discounting a note receivable is a way to (p. 342)
   - a. Collect on a note
   - b. Increase interest revenue
   - c. Both of the above
   - d. None of the above

10. Discounting a note receivable creates a (an) (p. 344)
    - a. Cash disbursement
    - b. Interest expense
    - c. Protest fee
    - d. Contingent liability

Answers to the Self-Study Questions follow the Accounting Vocabulary.

ACCOUNTING VOCABULARY

Acid-test ratio. Ratio of the sum of cash plus short-term investments plus net current receivables to total current liabilities. Tells whether the entity could pay all its current liabilities if they came due immediately. Also called the quick ratio (p. 347).

Aging of accounts receivable. A way to estimate bad debts by analyzing individual accounts receivable according to the length of time they have been due (p. 333).

Allowance for Doubtful Accounts. A contra account, related to accounts receivable, that holds the estimated amount of collection losses. Also called Allowance for Uncollectible Accounts (p. 330).

Allowance for Uncollectible Acounts. Another name for Allowance for Doubtful Accounts (p. 330).

Allowance method. A method of recording collection losses based on estimates made before determining that the business will not collect from specific customers (p. 330).

Bad-debt expense. Another name for uncollectible-account expense (p. 329).

Contingent liability. A potential liability that will become an actual liability only if a potential event does occur (p. 344).

Creditor. The party to a credit transaction who sells a service or merchandise and obtains a receivable (p. 328).

Days' sales in receivables. Ratio of average net accounts receivable to one day's sales. Tells how many days' sales remain in Accounts Receivable awaiting collection (p. 347).

Debtor. The party to a credit transaction who makes a purchase and creates a payable (p. 328).

Direct write-off method. A method of accounting for bad debts by which the company waits until the credit department decides that a customer's account receivable is uncollectible and then debits Uncollectible-Account Expense and credits the customer's Account Receivable (p. 335).

Discounting a note receivable. Selling a note receivable before its maturity date (p. 342).

Dishonor of a note. Failure of the maker of a note to pay a note receivable at maturity. Also called default on a note (p. 344).

Doubtful-account expense. Another name for uncollectible-account expense (p. 329).

Interest. The revenue to the payee for loaning out principal and the expense to the maker for borrowing principal (p. 339).

Interest period. The period of time during which interest is to be computed, extending from the original date of a note to the maturity date (p. 339).

Interest rate. The percentage rate that is multiplied by the principal amount to compute the amount of interest on a note (p. 340).

Maker of a note. The person or business that signs the note and promises to pay the amount required by the note agreement; the debtor (p. 339).

Maturity date. The date on which the final payment of a note is due. Also called the due date (p. 340).

Maturity value. The sum of the principal and interest due at the maturity date of a note (p. 340).

Payee of a note. The person or business to whom the maker of a note promises future payment; the creditor (p. 339).

Percentage of sales approach. A method of estimating uncollectible receivables as a percentage of net credit sales (or net sales) (p. 333).

Principal amount. The amount loaned out by the payee and borrowed by the maker of a note (p. 339).

Promissory note. A written promise to pay a specified amount of money at a particular future date (p. 339).

Quick ratio. Another name for the acid-test ratio (p. 347).

Receivable. A monetary claim against a business or an individual, acquired mainly by selling goods and services and by lending money (p. 328).

Uncollectible-account expense. Cost to the seller of extending credit. Arises from the failure to collect from credit customers (p. 329).

ANSWERS TO SELF-STUDY QUESTIONS

1. a
2. c
3. d
4. a
5. b ($78,900 – $14,300 = $64,600)
6. b
7. c ($30,000 × 0.09 × 6/12 = $1,350)
8. b ($30,000 × 0.09 × 4/12 = $900)
9. a
10. d

QUESTIONS

1. Name the two parties to a receivable/payable transaction. Which party has the receivable? Which has the payable? The asset? The liability?
2. List three categories of receivables. State how each category is classified for reporting on the balance sheet.
3. Name the two methods of accounting for uncollectible receivables. Which method is easier to apply? Which method is consistent with generally accepted accounting principles?
4. Which of the two methods of accounting for uncollectible accounts—the allowance method or the direct write-off method—is preferable? Why?
5. Identify the accounts debited and credited to account for uncollectibles under (a) the allowance method and (b) the direct write-off method.
6. What is another term for Allowance for Uncollectible Accounts? What are two other terms for Uncollectible-Account Expense?
7. Which entry decreases net income under the allowance method of accounting for uncollectibles: the entry to

record uncollectible-account expense or the entry to write off an uncollectible account receivable?

8. May a customer pay his or her account receivable after it has been written off? If not, why not? If so, what entries are made to account for reinstating the customer's account and for collecting cash from the customer?

9. Identify and briefly describe the two ways to estimate bad-debt expense and uncollectible accounts.

10. Briefly describe how a company may use both the percentage of sales method and the aging method to account for uncollectibles.

11. How does a credit balance arise in a customer's account receivable? How does the company report this credit balance on its balance sheet?

12. Many businesses receive most of their cash on credit sales through the mail. Suppose you own a business so large that you must hire employees to handle cash receipts and perform the related accounting duties. What internal control feature should you use to ensure that the cash received from customers is not taken by a dishonest employee?

13. Use the terms *maker, payee, principal amount, maturity date, promissory note,* and *interest* in an appropiate sentence or two describing a note receivable.

14. Name three situations in which a company might receive a note receivable. For each situation, show the account debited and the account credited to record receipt of the note.

15. For each of the following notes receivable, compute the amount of interest revenue earned during 19X6:

		Principal	Interest Rate	Interest Period	Maturity Date
a.	Note 1	$ 10,000	9%	60 days	11/30/19X6
b.	Note 2	50,000	10%	3 months	9/30/19X6
c.	Note 3	100,000	8%	1 1/2 years	12/31/19X7
d.	Note 4	15,000	12%	90 days	1/15/19X7

16. Suppose you hold a 180-day, $5,000 note receivable that specifies 10 percent interest. After 60 days you discount the note at 12 percent. How much cash do you receive?

17. How does a contingent liability differ from an ordinary liability? How does discounting a note receivable create a contingent liability? When does the contingency cease to exist?

18. When the maker of a note dishonors the note at maturity, what accounts does the payee debit and credit?

19. Why does the payee of a note receivable usually need to make adjusting entries for interest at the end of the accounting period?

20. Recall the real-world disclosures of receivables the chapter presents. Show three ways to report Accounts Receivable of $100,000 and Allowance for Uncollectible Accounts of $2,800 on the balance sheet or in the related notes.

21. Why is the acid-test ratio a more stringent measure of the ability to pay current liabilities than is the current ratio?

22. Which measure of days' sales in receivables is preferable, 30 or 40? Give your reason.

EXERCISES

Using the allowance method for bad debts
(Obj. 1)

E8-1   On September 30, Rochford Nurseries had a $28,000 debit balance in Accounts Receivable. During October the company had sales of $137,000, which included $90,000 in credit sales. October collections were $91,000, and write-offs of uncollectible receivables totaled $1,070. Other data include:

● September 30 credit balance in Allowance for Uncollectible Accounts, $2,100.
● Uncollectible-account expense, estimated as 2 percent of credit sales.

Required

1. Prepare journal entries to record sales, collections, uncollectible-account expense by the allowance method (using the percentage of sales approach) and write-offs of uncollectibles during October.

2. Show the ending balances in Accounts Receivable, Allowance for Uncollectible Accounts, and *net* accounts receivable at October 31. How much does Rochford expect to collect?

Recording bad debts by the allowance method
(Obj. 1)

E8-2   Prepare general journal entries to record the following transactions under the allowance method of accounting for uncollectibles:

Apr. 2	Sold merchandise for $3,900 on credit terms of 2/10 n/30 to Ithaca Sales Company.
May. 28	Received legal notification that Ithaca Sales Company was bankrupt. Wrote off Ithaca's accounts receivable balance.
Aug. 11	Received $2,200 from Ithaca Sales Company, together with a letter indicating that the company intended to pay its account within the next month.
30	Received the remaining amount due from Ithaca.

E8-3 At December 31, 19X7, the accounts receivable balance of Chung, Limited, is $269,000. The allowance for doubtful accounts has a $3,910 credit balance. Accountants for Chung prepare the following aging schedule for its accounts receivable:

Using the aging approach to estimate bad debts
(Obj. 1, 2)

Total Balance	Age of Accounts			
	1–30 Days	31–60 Days	61–90 Days	Over 90 Days
$269,000	$107,000	$78,000	$69,000	$15,000
Estimated percentage uncollectible	0.3%	1.2%	6.0%	50%

Journalize the adjusting entry for doubtful accounts on the basis of the aging schedule. Show the T-account for the allowance.

E8-4 Refer to the situation of Exercise 8-1.

Using the direct write-off method for bad debts
(Obj. 3)

Required

1. Record uncollectible-account expense for October by the direct write-off method.
2. What amount of *net* accounts receivable would Rochford report on its October 31 balance sheet under the direct write-off method? Does Rochford expect to collect this much of the receivable? Give your reason.

E8-5 As a recent college graduate, you land your first job in the customer collections department of Massey and Ferguson, a partnership. Eddie Massey, the president, has asked you to propose a system to ensure that cash received by mail from customers is handled properly. Draft a short memorandum identifying the essential element in your proposed plan, and state why this element is important. Refer to Chapter 7 if necessary.

Controlling cash receipts from customers
(Obj. 4)

E8-6 Record the following transactions in the general journal:

Nov. 1 Loaned $45,000 cash to Larry Lenamon on a one-year, 9-percent note.
Dec. 3 Sold goods to Lofland, Inc., receiving a 90-day, 12-percent note for $3,750.
16 Received a $2,000, six-month, 12-percent note on account from J. Baker.
31 Accrued interest revenue on all notes receivable.

Recording a note receivable and accruing interest revenue
(Obj. 5)

E8-7 Record the following transactions in the general journal:

Apr. 1, 19X2 Loaned $8,000 to Rhonda Evans on a one-year, 9-percent note.
Dec. 31, 19X2 Accrued interest revenue on the Evans note.
Dec. 31, 19X2 Closed the interest revenue account.
Apr. 1, 19X3 Received the maturity value of the note from Rhonda Evans.

Recording a note receivable and accruing interest revenue
(Obj. 5)

E8-8 Record the following transactions in the general journal, assuming the company uses the allowance method to account for uncollectibles:

May 18 Sold goods to Peterson Office Supply, receiving a 120-day, 12-percent note for $2,900.
Sep. 15 The note is dishonored.
Nov. 30 After pursuing collection from Peterson Office Supply, wrote off the account as uncollectible.

Accounting for a dishonored note receivable
(Obj. 5)

E8-9 Prepare general journal entries to record the following transactions:
Aug. 14 Sold goods on account to V. Moyer, $3,900.
Dec. 2 Received a $3,900, 180-day, 10-percent note from V. Moyer in satisfaction of his past-due account receivable.
30 Sold the Moyer note by discounting it to a bank at 15 percent. (Use a 360-day year, and round amounts to the nearest dollar.)

Write the note to disclose the contingent liability at December 31.

Recording notes receivable, discounting a note, and reporting the contingent liability in a note
(Obj. 5, 6)

Recording bad debts by the allowance method
(Obj. 1, 2, 6)

E8-10   At December 31, 19X5, Knox Builders has an accounts receivable balance of $137,000. Sales revenue for 19X5 is $950,000, including credit sales of $600,000. For each of the following situations, prepare the year-end adjusting entry to record doubtful-account expense. Show how the accounts receivable and the allowance for doubtful accounts are reported on the balance sheet.

a.   Allowance for Doubtful Accounts has a credit balance before adjustment of $1,600. Knox Builders estimates that doubtful-account expense for the year is 1/2 of 1 percent of credit sales.

b.   Allowance for Doubtful Accounts has a debit balance before adjustment of $1,700. Knox Builders estimates that $4,600 of the accounts receivable will prove uncollectible.

Evaluating ratio data
(Obj. 7)

E8-11   Cox's, a department store, reported the following amounts in its 19X8 financial statements. The 19X7 figures are given for comparison.

	19X8		19X7	
Current assets:				
Cash		$ 14,000		$ 9,000
Short-term investments..........................		13,000		11,000
Accounts receivable	$80,000		$74,000	
Less Allowance for				
uncollectibles	7,000	73,000	6,000	68,000
Inventory...		192,000		189,000
Prepaid insurance		2,000		2,000
Total current assets		294,000		279,000
Total current liabilities		114,000		107,000
Net sales..		813,000		762,000

Required

'98 $\dfrac{14K + 13K + 73K}{114K} = .88$

'97 $\dfrac{9K + 11K + 68K}{107K} = .82$

1.   Determine whether the acid-test ratio improved or deteriorated from 19X7 to 19X8. How does Cox's acid-test ratio compare with the industry average of 0.80?

2.   Compare the days' sales in receivables measure for 19X8 with the company's credit terms of net 30.

$\dfrac{9K \times 11K + 68K}{107K} = .82$

Analyzing a real company's financial statements
(Obj. 6, 7)

E8-12   Wal-Mart Stores, Inc., is the largest retailer in the United States. Recently, Wal-Mart reported these figures in millions of dollars:

	19X2	19X1
Net sales	$43,887	$32,602
Receivables at end of year	419	305

The Wal-Mart financial statements include no uncollectible-account expense or allowance for uncollectibles.

1 day sales · NET SALES
365 days

BEG REV + ENDING RU/REC/2

1 days sale

Required

1.   Compute Wal-Mart's average collection period on receivables during 19X2.

2.   How can Wal-Mart have $419 million of receivables at January 31, 19X2, and no significant allowance for uncollectibles?

CHALLENGE EXERCISE

Credit-card sales
(Obj. 2)

E8-13   Village Oaks Men's Store has sold on store credit and managed its own receivables. Average experience for the past three years has been:

	Cash	Credit	Total
Sales	$200,000	$150,000	$350,000
Cost of goods sold	120,000	90,000	210,000
Uncollectible-account expense	—	4,000	4,000
Other expenses	34,000	27,000	61,000

Lou Onassis, the owner, is considering whether to accept bank cards (VISA, MasterCard). Typically, the availability of bank cards increases total sales by 10 percent. But VISA and MasterCard charge approximately 1 percent of sales. If Onassis switches to bank cards, he can save $2,000 on accounting and other expenses. He figures that cash customers will continue buying in the same volume regardless of the type of credit the store offers.

Required

Should Village Oaks Men's Store start selling on bank credit cards? Show the computations of net income under the present plan and under the bank credit-card plan.

PROBLEMS

(GROUP A)

P8-1A On February 28, Hack Branch Co. had a $75,000 debit balance in Accounts Receivable. During March the company had sales revenue of $509,000, which included $445,000 in credit sales. Other data for March include:

Accounting for uncollectibles by the direct write-off and allowance methods
(Obj. 1, 2, 3, 6)

● Collections on accounts receivable, $451,600.
● Write-offs of uncollectible receivables, $3,500.

Required

1. Record uncollectible-account expense for March by the *direct write-off* method. Show all March activity in Accounts Receivable and Uncollectible-Account Expense.

2. Record uncollectible-account expense and write-offs of customer accounts for March by the *allowance* method. Show all March activity in Accounts Receivable, Allowance for Uncollectible Accounts, and Uncollectible-Account Expense. The February 28 unadjusted balance in Allowance for Uncollectible Accounts was $800 (debit). Uncollectible-Account Expense was estimated at 2 percent of credit sales.

3. What amount of uncollectible-account expense would Hack Branch Co. report on its March income statement under the two methods? Which amount better matches expense with revenue? Give your reason.

4. What amount of *net* accounts receivable would Hack Branch Co. report on its March 31 balance sheet under the two methods? Which amount is more realistic? Give your reason.

5. How will what you learned in this problem help you manage a business?

P8-2A Assume that the Kelly Moore Company, a major paint manufacturer, completed the following selected transactions:

Uncollectibles, notes receivable, discounting notes, dishonored notes, and accrued interest revenue
(Obj. 2, 5)

19X4
Dec. 1 Sold goods to Southern Paint Supply, receiving a $17,000, three-month, 10-percent note.
31 Made an adjusting entry to accrue interest on the Southern Paint Supply note.
31 Made an adjusting entry to record doubtful-account expense based on an aging of accounts receivable. The aging analysis indicates that $355,800 of accounts receivable will not be collected. Prior to this adjustment, the credit balance in Allowance for Doubtful Accounts is $346,100.

19X5
Feb. 18 Received a 90-day, 10-percent, $5,000 note from Altex Corp. on account. (This year February has 28 days.)
Mar. 1 Collected the maturity value of the Southern Paint Supply note.
8 Discounted the Altex note to First State Bank at 16 percent.
Apr. 21 Sold merchandise to Logos, Inc., receiving a 60-day, 9-percent note for $4,000.
June 20 Logos, Inc., dishonored its note at maturity; converted the maturity value of the note to an account receivable.
July 12 Loaned $40,000 cash to Consolidated Investments, receiving a 90-day, 13-percent note.
13 Sold merchandise to Pearson Paint Shop, receiving a 4-month, 12-percent, $2,500 note.
Aug. 2 Collected in full from Logos, Inc.
Sep. 13 Discounted the Pearson Paint Shop note to First State Bank at 18 percent.
Oct. 10 Collected the maturity value of the Consolidated Investments note.

Nov. 13 Pearson Paint Shop dishonored its note at maturity; paid First State Bank the maturity value of the note plus a protest fee of $35 and debited an account receivable from Pearson Paint Shop.

Dec. 31 Wrote off as uncollectible the account receivable from Pearson Paint Shop.

Required

Record the transactions in the general journal. Explanations are not required.

Using the percent of sales and aging approaches for uncollectibles (Obj. 2, 6)

P8-3A Planters, Inc., completed the following transactions during 19X1 and 19X2:

19X1

Dec. 31 Began using the allowance method to account for uncollectibles. Estimated that uncollectible-account expense for the year was 1 percent on credit sales of $300,000, and recorded that amount as expense. The accounts receivable balance is $113,500.

31 Made the appropriate closing entry.

19X2

Jan. 17 Sold inventory to D. Lovecky, $652, on credit terms of 2/10 n/30.

June 29 Wrote off the D. Lovecky account as uncollectible after repeated efforts to collect from her.

Aug. 6 Received $250 from D. Lovecky, along with a letter stating her intention to pay her debt in full within 30 days. Reinstated her account in full.

Sep. 4 Received the balance due from D. Lovecky.

Dec. 31 Made a compound entry to write off the following accounts as uncollectible: Bernard Klaus, $837; Louis Mann, $348; and Millie Burnett, $622.

31 Observed that collection losses are lower than expected. Estimated that uncollectible-account expense for the year was 1/2 of 1 percent on credit sales of $420,000, and recorded that amount as expense.

31 Made the appropriate closing entry.

Required

1. Open general ledger accounts for Allowance for Uncollectible Accounts and Uncollectible-Account Expense. Keep running balances.

2. Record the transactions in the general journal, and post to the two ledger accounts.

3. The December 31, 19X2, balance of Accounts Receivable is $130,000. Show how Accounts Receivable would be reported at December 31, 19X1 and 19X2. Why do you think Planters, Inc., decreased its uncollectible accounts percentage from 1 percent to 1/2 of 1 percent in 19X2?

4. Assume that Planters, Inc., begins aging accounts receivable on December 31, 19X2. The balance in Accounts Receivable is $130,000, the credit balance in Allowance for Uncollectible Accounts is $1,193, and the company estimates that $3,293 of its accounts receivable will prove uncollectible.

   a. Make the adjusting entry for uncollectibles.

   b. Show how Accounts Receivable will be reported on the December 31, 19X2, balance sheet. Compare net accounts receivable at December 31, 19X2, with the amount reported in Requirement 3 above. Why do you think the two sets of figures agree or disagree?

Using the percentage of sales and aging approaches for uncollectibles (Obj. 2, 6)

P8-4A The December 31, 19X6, balance sheet of Master Auto Glass reports the following:

Accounts Receivable	$265,000
Allowance for Doubtful Accounts (credit balance)...............	7,100

At the end of each quarter, Master Auto Glass estimates doubtful-account expense to be 2 percent of credit sales. At the end of the year, the company ages its accounts receivable and adjusts the balance in Allowance for Doubtful Accounts to correspond to the aging schedule. During 19X7 Master completes the following selected transactions:

Jan. 31	Wrote off as uncollectible the $955 account receivable from Spinelli Company and the $3,287 account receivable from Vera Delgado.
Mar. 31	Recorded doubtful-account expense based on credit sales of $130,000.
May 2	Received $1,000 from Delgado after prolonged negotiations with Delgado's attorney. Master has no hope of collecting the remainder.
June 15	Wrote off as uncollectible the $1,120 account receivable from Lisa Brown.
June 30	Recorded doubtful-account expense based on credit sales of $166,000.
July 14	Made a compound entry to write off the following uncollectible accounts: C. H. Harris, $766; Graphics Unlimited, $2,413; and Ben McQueen, $134.
Sep. 30	Recorded doubtful-account expense based on credit sales of $141,400.
Nov. 22	Wrote off the following accounts receivable as uncollectible: Monet Corp., $1,345; Blocker, Inc., $2,109; and Main Street Plaza, $755.
Dec. 31	Recorded doubtful-account expense based on the following summary of the aging of accounts receivable:

Total Balance	Age of Accounts			
	1–30 Days	31–60 Days	61–90 Days	Over 90 Days
$296,600	$161,500	$86,000	$34,000	$15,100
Estimated percentage uncollectible	0.2%	0.5%	4.0%	50.0%

Dec. 31	Made the closing entry for Doubtful-Account Expense for the entire year.

Required

1. Record the transactions in the general journal.
2. Open the Allowance for Doubtful Accounts, and post entries affecting that account. Keep a running balance.
3. Most companies report two-year comparative financial statements. If Master's Accounts Receivable balance is $296,600 at December 31, 19X7, show how the company will report its accounts receivable in a comparative balance sheet for 19X7 and 19X6.

P8-5A Oshman's Sporting Goods distributes merchandise to sporting goods stores. All sales are on credit, so virtually all cash receipts arrive in the mail. Pelina Johnson, the company president, has just returned from a trade association meeting with new ideas for the business. Among other things, Johnson plans to institute stronger internal controls over cash receipts from customers.

Controlling cash receipts from customers (Obj. 4)

Required

Outline a set of procedures to ensure that all cash receipts are deposited in the bank and that the total amounts of each day's cash receipts are posted as credits to customer accounts receivable.

P8-6A A company received the following notes during 19X3. Notes (a), (b), and (c) were discounted on the dates and at the rates indicated.

Accounting for notes receivable, including discounting notes and accruing interest revenue (Obj. 5)

Note	Date	Principal Amount	Interest Rate	Term	Date Discounted	Discount Rate
(a)	July 12	$12,000	10%	3 months	Aug. 12	15%
(b)	Sep. 4	8,000	11%	90 days	Sep. 30	13%
(c)	Oct. 21	5,000	15%	60 days	Nov. 3	18%
(d)	Nov. 30	12,000	12%	6 months	—	—
(e)	Dec. 7	6,000	10%	30 days	—	—
(f)	Dec. 23	15,000	9%	1 year	—	—

Required

As necessary in Requirements 1 through 5, identify each note by letter, compute interest using a 360-day year for those notes with terms specified in days or years, round all interest amounts to the nearest dollar, and present entries in general journal form. Explanations are not required.

1. Determine the due date and maturity value of each note.
2. For each discounted note, determine the discount and proceeds from sale of the note.
3. Journalize the discounting of notes (a) and (b).
4. Journalize a single adjusting entry at December 31, 19X3, to record accrued interest revenue on notes (d), (e), and (f).
5. Journalize the collection of principal and interest on note (e).

Using ratio data to evaluate a company's position
(Obj. 7)

P8-7A   The comparative financial statements of Orvis Catalog Merchants for 19X4, 19X3, and 19X2 included the following selected data:

	Millions		
Balance sheet:	19X4	19X3	19X2
Current assets:			
Cash	$ 27	$ 26	$ 22
Short-term investments	73	101	69
Receivables, net of allowance for doubtful accounts of $7, $6, and $4	136	154	127
Inventories	438	383	341
Prepaid expenses	42	31	25
Total current assets	716	695	584
Total current liabilities	440	446	388
Income statement:			
Sales revenue	$2,671	$2,505	$1,944
Cost of sales	1,380	1,360	963

Required

1. For 19X4 and 19X3 compute these ratios:
   a. Current ratio
   b. Acid-test ratio
   c. Inventory turnover
   d. Days' sales in average receivables
2. Explain for top management which ratio values showed improvement from 19X3 to 19X4 and which ratio values showed deterioration. Which item in the financial statements caused some ratio values to improve and others to deteriorate?

(GROUP B)

Accounting for uncollectibles by the direct write-off and allowance methods
(Obj. 1, 2, 3, 6)

P8-1B   On May 31, Don's Humidor, Inc., had a $219,000 debit balance in Accounts Receivable. During June the company had sales revenue of $789,000, which included $640,000 in credit sales. Other data for June include:

● Collections on accounts receivable, $599,400
● Write-offs of uncollectible receivables, $8,900

Required

1. Record uncollectible-account expense for June by the *direct write-off* method. Show all June activity in Accounts Receivable and Uncollectible-Account Expense.
2. Record uncollectible-account expense and write-offs of customer accounts for June by the *allowance* method. Show all June activity in Accounts Receivable, Allowance for Uncollectible Accounts, and Uncollectible-Account Expense. The May 31 unadjusted balance in Allowance

for Uncollectible Accounts was $2,800 (credit). Uncollectible-Account Expense was estimated at 2 percent of credit sales.

3. What amount of uncollectible-account expense would Don's Humidor, Inc., report on its June income statement under the two methods? Which amount better matches expense with revenue? Give your reason.

4. What amount of *net* accounts receivable would Don's Humidor, Inc., report on its June 30 balance sheet under the two methods? Which amount is more realistic? Give your reason.

5. How will what you learned in this problem help you manage a business?

P8-2B Assume that Ralston Purina, manufacturer of pet foods, completed the following selected transactions:

Uncollectibles, notes receivable, discounting notes, dishonored notes, and accrued interest revenue
(Obj. 2, 5)

19X5
Nov. 1   Sold goods to Winn Dixie, Inc., receiving a $24,000, three-month, 12-percent note.
Dec. 31   Made an adjusting entry to accrue interest on the Winn Dixie note.
     31   Made an adjusting entry to record doubtful-account expense based on an aging of accounts receivable. The aging analysis indicates that $197,400 of accounts receivable will not be collected. Prior to this adjustment, the credit balance in Allowance for Doubtful Accounts is $189,900.

19X6
Feb. 1   Collected the maturity value of the Winn Dixie note.
     23   Received a 90-day, 15-percent, $4,000 note from Bliss Company on account. (This year February has 28 days.)
Mar. 31   Discounted the Bliss Co. note to Lakewood Bank at 20 percent.
Apr. 23   Sold merchandise to Lear Corporation, receiving a 60-day, 10-percent note for $9,000.
June 22   Lear Corp. dishonored its note at maturity; converted the maturity value of the note to an account receivable.
July 15   Loaned $8,500 cash to McNeil, Inc., receiving a 30-day, 12-percent note.
     17   Sold merchandise to Grant Corp., receiving a three-month, 10-percent, $8,000 note.
Aug. 5   Collected in full from Lear Corp.
     14   Collected the maturity value of the McNeil, Inc., note.
     17   Discounted the Grant Corp. note to Lakewood Bank at 15 percent.
Oct. 17   Grant Corp. dishonored its note at maturity; paid Lakewood Bank the maturity value of the note plus a protest fee of $50 and debited an account receivable from Grant Corp.
Dec. 15   Wrote off as uncollectible the account receivable from Grant Corp.

Required

Record the transactions in the general journal. Explanations are not required.

P8-3B Lake Air Jewelry Company completed the following selected transactions during 19X1 and 19X2:

Using the percentage of sales and aging approaches for uncollectibles
(Obj. 2, 6)

19X1
Dec. 31   Began using the allowance method to account for uncollectibles. Estimated that uncollectible-account expense for the year was 1 percent on credit sales of $450,000 and recorded that amount as expense. The accounts receivable balance is $142,000.
     31   Made the appropriate closing entry.

19X2
Feb. 4   Sold inventory to Ed Davis, $2,521, on credit terms of 2/10 n/30.
July 1   Wrote off Ed Davis's account as uncollectible after repeated efforts to collect from him.
Oct. 19   Received $521 from Ed Davis, along with a letter stating his intention to pay his debt in full within 30 days. Reinstated his account in full.
Nov. 15   Received the balance due from Ed Davis.
Dec. 31   Made a compound entry to write off the following accounts as uncollectible: Kris Moore, $899; Marie Mandue, $530; and Grant Frycer, $672.
     31   Observed that collection losses are lower than expected. Estimated that uncollectible-account expense for the year was 1/2 of 1 percent on credit sales of $540,000 and recorded the expense.
     31   Made the appropriate closing entry.

Required

1. Open general ledger accounts for Allowance for Uncollectible Accounts and Uncollectible-Account Expense. Keep running balances.

2. Record the transactions in the general journal, and post to the two ledger accounts.

3. The December 31, 19X2, balance of Accounts Receivable is $169,300. Show how Accounts Receivable would be reported at December 31, 19X1 and 19X2. Why do you think Lake Air decreased its uncollectible accounts percentage from 1 percent to 1/2 of 1 percent in 19X2?

4. Assume that Lake Air Jewelry Company begins aging its accounts receivable on December 31, 19X2. The balance in Accounts Receivable is $169,300, the credit balance in Allowance for Uncollectible Accounts is $2,399, and the company estimates that $5,099 of its accounts receivable will prove uncollectible.

   a. Make the adjusting entry for uncollectibles.

   b. Show how Accounts Receivable will be reported on the December 31, 19X2, balance sheet. Compare net accounts receivable at December 31, 19X2, with the amount reported in Requirement 3 above. Why do you think the two sets of figures agree or disagree?

Using the percentage of sales and aging approaches for uncollectibles (Obj. 2, 6)

P8-4B The December 31, 19X4, balance sheet of Ogden Industrial Products reports the following:

Accounts Receivable	$143,000
Allowance for Doubtful Accounts (credit balance)...............	3,200

At the end of each quarter, Ogden estimates doubtful-account expense to be $1\frac{1}{2}$ percent of credit sales. At the end of the year, the company ages its accounts receivable and adjusts the balance in Allowance for Doubtful Accounts to correspond to the aging schedule. During 19X5 Ogden completes the following selected transactions:

Jan. 16 Wrote off as uncollectible the $603 account receivable from Licks, Inc., and the $1,919 account receivable from Johnny's Leather Company.

Mar. 31 Recorded doubtful-account expense based on credit sales of $100,000.

Apr. 15 Received $300 from Johnny's Leather Company after prolonged negotiations with Johnny's Leather Company's attorney. Ogden has no hope of collecting the remainder.

May 13 Wrote off as uncollectible the $2,980 account receivable from M. E. Cate.

June 30 Recorded doubtful-account expense based on credit sales of $114,000.

Aug. 9 Made a compound entry to write off the following uncollectible accounts: Clifford, Inc., $235; Matz Co., $188; and Lew Norris, $706.

Sep. 30 Recorded doubtful-account expense based on credit sales of $130,000.

Oct. 18 Wrote off as uncollectible the $767 account receivable from Bliss Co. and the $430 account receivable from Micro Data.

Dec. 31 Recorded doubtful-account expense based on the following summary of the aging of accounts receivable.

Total Balance	Age of Accounts			
	1–30 Days	31–60 Days	61–90 Days	Over 90 Days
$129,400	$74,600	$31,100	$14,000	$9,700
Estimated percentage uncollectible	0.1%	0.4%	5.0%	30.0%

Dec. 31 Made the closing entry for Doubtful-Account Expense for the entire year.

Required

1. Record the transactions in the general journal.

2. Open the Allowance for Doubtful Accounts, and post entries affecting that account. Keep a running balance.

3. Most companies report two-year comparative financial statements. If Ogden's Accounts Receivable balance is $129,400 at December 31, 19X5, show how the company will report its accounts receivable on a comparative balance sheet for 19X5 and 19X4.

P8-5B Dental Laboratory Service prepares crowns, dentures, and other dental appliances. All work is performed on account, with regular monthly billing to participating dentists. Melany Rank, accountant for Dental Laboratory Service, receives and opens the mail. Company procedure requires her to separate customer checks from the remittance slips, which list the amounts she posts as credits to customer accounts receivable. Rank deposits the checks in the bank. She computes each day's total amount posted to customer accounts and matches this total to the bank deposit slip. This procedure is intended to ensure that all receipts are deposited in the bank.

Controlling cash receipts from customers
(Obj. 4)

Required

As the auditor of Dental Laboratory Service, write a memo to management to evaluate the company's internal controls over cash receipts from customers. If the system is effective, identify its strong features. If the system has flaws, propose a way to strengthen the controls.

P8-6B A company received the following notes during 19X5. Notes (a), (b), and (c) were discounted on the dates and at the rates indicated.

Accounting for notes receivable, including discounting notes and accruing interest revenue
(Obj. 5)

Note	Date	Principal Amount	Interest Rate	Term	Date Discounted	Discount Rate
(a)	July 15	$ 8,000	8%	6 months	Oct. 15	12%
(b)	Aug. 19	12,000	12%	90 days	Aug. 30	15%
(c)	Sep. 1	16,000	15%	120 days	Nov. 2	20%
(d)	Oct. 30	7,000	12%	3 months	—	—
(e)	Nov. 19	15,000	10%	60 days	—	—
(f)	Dec. 1	11,000	9%	1 year	—	—

Required

As necessary in Requirements 1 through 5, identify each note by letter, compute interest using a 360-day year for those notes with terms specified in days or years, round all interest amounts to the nearest dollar, and present entries in general journal form. Explanations are not required.

1. Determine the due date and maturity value of each note.
2. For each discounted note, determine the discount and proceeds from sale of the note.
3. Journalize the discounting of notes (a) and (b).
4. Journalize a single adjusting entry at December 31, 19X5, to record accrued interest revenue on notes (d), (e), and (f).
5. Journalize the collection of principal and interest on note (d).

P8-7B The comparative financial statements of Welch Industries for 19X6, 19X5, and 19X4 included the following selected data:

Using ratio data to evaluate a company's position
(Obj. 7)

	Millions		
	19X6	19X5	19X4
Balance sheet:			
Current assets:			
Cash	$ 59	$ 80	$ 60
Short-term investments	131	174	122
Receivables, net of allowance for doubtful accounts of $6, $6, and $5	237	265	218
Inventories	389	341	302
Prepaid expenses	61	27	46
Total current assets	877	887	748
Total current liabilities	483	528	413
Income statement:			
Sales revenue	$5,189	$4,995	$4,206
Cost of sales	2,734	2,636	2,418

Required

1. For 19X6 and 19X5 compute these ratios:
    a. Current ratio
    b. Acid-test ratio
    c. Inventory turnover
    d. Days' sales in average receivables
2. Explain for top management which ratio values showed improvement from 19X5 to 19X6 and which ratio values showed deterioration. Which item in the financial statements caused some ratio values to improve and others to deteriorate?

EXTENDING YOUR KNOWLEDGE

DECISION PROBLEMS

Uncollectible accounts and evaluating a business (Obj. 1, 2, 3, 5, 6)

1. Chaparral Express performs service either for cash or on notes receivable that earn interest. The business uses the direct write-off method to account for bad debts. Reese Taylor, the owner, has prepared Chaparral's financial statements. The most recent comparative income statements, for 19X3 and 19X2, are as follows:

	19X3	19X2
Total revenue	$220,000	$195,000
Total expenses	157,000	143,000
Net income	$ 63,000	$ 52,000

On the basis of the increase in net income, Taylor seeks to expand his operations. He asks you to invest $50,000 in the business. You and Taylor have several meetings, at which you learn that notes receivable from customers were $200,000 at the end of 19X1 and $400,000 at the end of 19X2. Also, total revenues for 19X3 and 19X2 include interest at 15 percent on the year's beginning notes receivable balance. Total expenses include doubtful-account expense of $2,000 each year, based on the direct write-off basis. Taylor estimates that doubtful-account expense would be 2 percent of sales revenue if the allowance method were used.

Required

1. Prepare for Chaparral Express a comparative single-step income statement that identifies service revenue, interest revenue, doubtful-account expense, and other expenses, all computed in accordance with generally accepted accounting principles.
2. Is Chaparral's future as promising as Taylor's income statement makes it appear? Give the reason for your answer.

Estimating the collectibility of accounts receivable (Obj. 1, 6, 7)

2. Assume that you work in the corporate loan department of Republic Bank. Maria Stones, owner of HD Manufacturing, Inc., a manufacturer of wooden furniture, has come to you seeking a loan for $450,000 to buy new manufacturing equipment to expand her operations. She proposes to use her accounts receivable as collateral for the loan and has provided you with the following information from her most recent audited financial statements:

	19X9	19X8	19X7
Sales	$1,475	$1,589	$1,502
Cost of goods sold	876	947	905
Gross profit	599	642	597
Other expenses	518	487	453
Net profit or (loss) before taxes	$ 81	$ 155	$ 144
Accounts receivable	$ 458	$ 387	$ 374
Allowance for doubtful accounts	23	31	29

Required

1. What analysis would you perform on the information Stones has provided? Would you grant the loan on the basis of this information? Give your reason.

2. What additional information would you request from Stones? Give your reason.

3. Assume that Stones provided you with the information requested in Requirement 2. What would make you change the decision you made in Requirement 1?

ETHICAL ISSUE

Sunshine Finance Company is in the consumer loan business. It borrows from banks and loans out the money at higher interest rates. Sunshine's bank requires Sunshine to submit quarterly financial statements in order to keep its line of credit. Sunshine's main asset is Notes Receivable. Therefore, Uncollectible-Account Expense and Allowance for Uncollectible Accounts are important accounts.

Sunshine's owner, Toby Nugget, likes net income to increase in a smooth pattern rather than increase in some periods and decrease in other periods. To report smoothly increasing net income, Nugget underestimates Uncollectible-Account Expense in some periods. In other periods, Nugget overestimates the expense. He reasons that the income overstatements roughly offset the income understatements over time.

Required

Is Sunshine's practice of smoothing income ethical? Give your reasons.

FINANCIAL STATEMENT PROBLEMS

1. Use data from the balance sheet and income statement of Lands' End, Inc., in Appendix A.

Accounts receivable and related uncollectibles
(Obj. 1)

Required

1. Analyze the Receivables account to compute the amount of cash Lands' End collected from customers during the year ended January 28, 1994.

2. Open the Receivables account, and insert the balance at January 29, 1993. Journalize net sales (all on credit) and cash collections from customers for the year ended January 28, 1994. Post to the Receivables account, and compare its ending balance to the amount reported on the January 28, 1994, balance sheet.

3. Why is Lands' End's Receivables balance so low relative to net sales revenue?

2. Obtain the annual report of a real company of your choosing.

Accounts receivable, uncollectibles, and notes receivable
(Obj. 1, 5)

Required

1. How much did customers owe the company at the end of the current year? Of this amount, how much did the company expect to collect? How much did the company expect *not* to collect?

2. Assume during the current year that the company recorded doubtful-account expense equal to 1 percent of net sales. Starting with the beginning balance, analyze the Allowance for Doubtful Accounts to determine the amount of the receivable write-offs during the current year.

3. If the company does not have notes receivable, you may skip this requirement. If notes receivable are present at the end of the current year, assume that their interest rate is 9 percent. Assume also that no new notes receivable arose during the following year. Journalize these transactions that took place during the following year:

   a. Received cash for 75 percent of the interest revenue earned during the year.

   b. Accrued the remaining portion of the interest revenue earned during the year.

   c. At year end collected half the notes receivable.

4. Suppose the company discounted a $500,000 note receivable. Under what heading in the annual report would the company report the discounting of a note receivable? Show how the company would disclose this fact.

Chapter 9
Merchandise Inventory

> *Over the past few years, we have been focusing on building net income, and our record-breaking 1993 profits show that our efforts have paid off. But when we took a hard look at our standard inventory method, we were amazed to find that we could eventually save millions of dollars in taxes just by switching methods.*
>
> BRAD STREET,
> CONTROLLER OF
> HUNTINGTON GALLERIES

Huntington Galleries, a Maryland-based furniture retailer, reported net income of $3.6 million for 1993, up 20 percent from the previous year. The reported figures continued the company's string of uninterrupted growth in profits. Wall Street responded favorably to the announcement, so Huntington's stock price rose $0.75 and closed at $31.50.

Lori Huntington, chief executive officer (CEO) of Huntington Galleries, attributed the strong performance to a demand for the company's high-end line of furniture during the second half of the year. In a report filed with the SEC, Huntington disclosed that the company switched from the *FIFO method* to the *LIFO method* of accounting for inventories. Brad Street, the controller of Huntington Galleries, explained that the company changed inventory methods to save on income taxes. He estimated that the inventory switch will save Huntington Galleries $1.3 million over the next two years. Not bad for a mere difference in the method of tallying the cost of chairs and sofas.

• • • • •

The Huntington Galleries situation underscores the importance of *merchandise inventory*. It is the lifeblood of a merchandising entity—the entity's major current asset. What is the entity's major expense? It is *cost of goods sold or cost of sales*. For example, Wal-Mart Stores, Inc., reported cost of goods sold at $44.2 billion and operating, selling, and administrative expenses at $8.3 billion. For Wal-Mart, Huntington Galleries, and many other companies, cost of goods sold is greater than all other expenses combined.

If the business buys inventory that is in demand, it will be able to sell the goods at a profit. But there is much more to merchandising than buying and selling.

Accounting plays an important role in merchandising. The most obvious role is the recordkeeping to stay abreast of quantities on hand in order to meet customer demand. Beyond that, there are several different methods of accounting for the cost of inventories. The chapter-opening story refers to

Chapter Objectives

After studying this chapter, you should be able to

1. Account for inventory by the perpetual and periodic systems

2. Apply four inventory costing methods: specific unit cost, weighted-average cost, FIFO, and LIFO

3. Distinguish between the income effects and the tax effects of the inventory costing methods

4. Convert a company's net income from the LIFO basis to the FIFO basis

5. Prepare a perpetual inventory record

6. Apply to inventory the lower-of-cost-or-market rule

7. Compute the effects of inventory errors on cost of goods sold and on net income

8. Estimate inventory by the gross margin method

Real-World Example: Typically, a business's year end coincides with the time of year when inventory is lowest, so that counting the inventory ("taking inventory") will be as simple as possible. Most retailers, such as Wal-Mart Stores, Inc., have a January 31 year end.

the FIFO and LIFO inventory methods, which you will learn about shortly. *FIFO* stands for "first-in, first-out." *LIFO* stands for "last-in, first-out." These popular methods have some peculiar characteristics that managers, investors, and creditors need to understand. For example, FIFO and LIFO result in different amounts of reported income and different amounts of income tax. Huntington Galleries' switch from FIFO to LIFO will save the company $1.3 million in income taxes. In short, accounting for inventory goes far beyond recordkeeping.

This chapter continues where Chapter 5 left off. We begin by reviewing the basic concept of accounting for inventories. Then we go into different inventory systems (perpetual and periodic), the different inventory methods (FIFO, LIFO, and average), and several additional topics.

The Basic Concept of Inventory Accounting

The basic concept of accounting for inventory is simple. Huntington Galleries buys three chairs for $300 each, marks them up $200, and sells two chairs for the retail price of $500 each. Huntington's balance sheet and income statement report the following:

Balance Sheet (partial):			*Income Statement (partial):*	
Current assets:			Sales revenue	$1,000
Cash	$ XXX		**Cost of goods sold**	**600**
Short-term investments	XXX		Gross margin	$ 400
Accounts receivable	XXX			
Inventory	**300**			
Prepaid expenses	XXX			

In practice, the process is not so simple. Complexity arises from several sources. The following sections describe alternate techniques for measuring inventories and how they differ.

Perpetual and Periodic Inventory Systems

OBJECTIVE 1

Account for inventory by the perpetual and periodic systems

Different businesses have different inventory information needs. We begin by reviewing the two main inventory systems that we introduced in Chapter 5:

1. The perpetual system
2. The periodic system

Key Point: Remember the derivation of the balance of every account, including Inventory:

Beg. Bal.
+ Increases (purchases)
– Decreases (COGS)
= End. Bal.

The balance of the Inventory account under the perpetual system should give the cost of inventory on hand at any time.

Perpetual Inventory System

In the **perpetual inventory system**, the business keeps a continuous record for each inventory item. The records thus show the inventory on hand at all times. Perpetual records are useful in preparing monthly, quarterly, or other interim financial statements. The business can determine the cost of ending inventory and the cost of goods sold directly from the accounts without having to count the merchandise.

The perpetual system offers a high degree of control because the inventory records are always up to date. In the past, businesses used the perpetual system mainly for high-unit-cost inventories, such as gemstones and automobiles. Recently, however, most businesses have switched to perpetual systems as accounting software has come down in price.

Computer systems have revolutionized accounting for inventory. Computerized perpetual systems can provide up-to-the-minute inventory data useful for managing the business. They help cut accounting cost by processing large numbers of

$3.00 [handwritten]

Item: Early America[n]			
Date	Quantity Received	Quantity Sold	Quantity on Hand
Nov. 1			10
5		6	4
7	25		29
12		13	16
26	25		41
30		21	20
Totals	50	40	20

transactions without computational error. Computer systems also enhance internal control. They increase efficiency because managers always know the quantity and cost of inventory on hand. Managers can make better decisions about quantities to buy, prices to pay for the inventory, prices to charge customers, and sale terms to offer. Knowing the quantity on hand helps to safeguard the inventory.

Perpetual inventory records can be a computer printout like the Huntington Galleries record shown in Exhibit 9-1. The quantities of goods on hand are updated on a daily basis. Many companies, such as Huntington Galleries, keep their perpetual records in terms of quantities only. We shall soon see how these data can be used to determine the cost of ending inventory and the cost of goods sold. Perpetual inventory records provide information for the following decisions:

1. When customers ask how soon they can get 10 chairs, the salesperson can answer by referring to the perpetual inventory record. Huntington, like most other furniture stores, keeps its goods in warehouses. Employees cannot visually scan the merchandise on hand to answer every customer inquiry. On November 5 the salesperson would reply that the company's stock is low, and the customer may have to wait a few days. On November 7 the salesperson could offer immediate delivery.

2. The perpetual records alert the business to reorder when inventory becomes low. On November 5 the company would be wise to purchase inventory. Sales may be lost if the business cannot promise immediate delivery.

3. At November 30 the company prepares monthly financial statements. The perpetual inventory records show that the company's ending inventory of Early American chairs is 20 units. No physical count is necessary at this time. However, a physical inventory is needed once a year to verify the accuracy of the records.

Computer inventory systems vary considerably. At one extreme are complex systems used by huge retailers such as Sears, J. C. Penney, and Wal-Mart. Purchases of inventory are recorded in perpetual records stored in a central computer. The inventory tags are coded electronically for updating the perpetual records when a sale is recorded on the cash register. Have you noticed a salesclerk passing the inventory ticket over a particular area of the checkout counter? A sensing device in the counter reads the stock number, quantity, cost, and sale price of the item sold. In other systems, the salesclerk passes an electronic device over the inventory tag. The computer records the sale and updates the inventory records. In effect, a journal entry is recorded for each sale, a procedure that is not economical without a computer.

Small companies also use minicomputers and microcomputers to keep perpetual inventory records. These systems may be similar to the systems used by large companies. In less-sophisticated ▮▮▮▮▮ ▮▮▮▮pany may have salesclerks write inventory stock numbers on sale ▮▮▮ ▮▮ock number identifies the particular item of inventory, such as men's s▮▮▮ ▮▮ildren's shoes. The business may accumulate all sales slips for the week. ▮▮ ▮he company has its own computer system, an employee may type the sales information into the computer and store the perpetual records on a magnetic disk. To learn the quantity, cost, or other characteristic of a particular item of inventory, a manager can view the inventory record on the computer monitor. For broader-based decisions affecting the entire inventory, managers use printouts of all items in stock. Many small businesses hire outside computer service centers to do much of the accounting for inventory. Regardless of the arrangement, managers get periodic printouts showing inventory data needed for managing the business. Manual reporting of this information is more time-consuming and expensive.

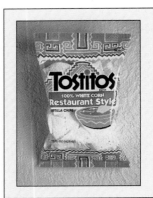

"Frito-Lay identified a drop in sales of tortilla chips by a particular chain of stores. Within two weeks, the company revised its marketing strategy and turned sales up again."

Perpetual inventory systems are becoming so sophisticated that, for example, Frito-Lay's Decision Support System can tell the company president (and other managers) the weekly sales of Ruffles Light potato chips by each route salesperson. In one case, Frito-Lay identified a drop in sales of tortilla chips by a particular chain of stores. Within two weeks, the company revised its marketing strategy and turned sales up again. Without the perpetual system, this process would have taken three months.

ENTRIES UNDER THE PERPETUAL SYSTEM   In the perpetual system, the business records purchases of inventory by debiting the Inventory account. When the business makes a sale, two entries are needed. The company records the sale in the usual manner—debits Cash or Accounts Receivable and credits Sales Revenue for the sale price of the goods. The company also debits Cost of Goods Sold and credits Inventory for cost. The debit to Inventory (for purchases) and the credit to Inventory (for sales) serve to keep an up-to-date record of inventory on hand. The Inventory account and the Cost of Goods Sold account carry a current balance during the period. Exhibit 9-2 illustrates the accounting for inventory transactions in a perpetual system (and in a periodic system as well). Panel A gives the journal entries, and Panel B presents the income statement and balance sheet effects. All amounts are assumed.

Periodic Inventory System

In the **periodic inventory system**, the business does not keep a continuous record of the inventory on hand. Instead, at the end of the period, the business makes a physical count of the inventory on hand and applies the unit costs to determine the cost of ending inventory. This is the inventory figure that appears on the balance sheet. It is also used to compute cost of goods sold. The periodic system is also called the *physical system* because it relies on the actual physical count of inventory. The periodic system is typically used to account for inventory items that have a low unit cost. Low-cost items may not be valuable enough to warrant the cost of keeping a running record of the inventory on hand. To use the periodic system effectively, the owner must be able to control inventory by visual inspection. For example, when a customer inquires about quantities on hand, the owner or manager can eyeball the goods in the store.

Perpetual System			Periodic System		
Panel A—Recording in the Journal					
1. Credit purchases of $560,000:					
Inventory................................	560,000		Purchases	560,000	
Accounts Payable		560,000	Accounts Payable..................		560,000
2. Credit sales of $900,000 (cost $540,000):					
Accounts Receivable	900,000		Accounts Receivable........................	900,000	
Sales Revenue.........................		900,000	Sales Revenue		900,000
Cost of Goods Sold..........................	540,000				
Inventory...............................		540,000			
3. End-of-period entries:			End-of-period entries to update Inventory:		
No entries required. Both			Income Summary	100,000	
Inventory and Cost of Goods			Inventory (beginning balance)		100,000
Sold are up to date.			Inventory (ending balance)..............	120,000	
			Income Summary		120,000

Perpetual System			Periodic System		
Panel B—Reporting in the Financial Statements					
Income Statement (partial):					
Sales revenue	$900,000		Sales revenue		$900,000
Cost of goods sold	540,000		Cost of goods sold:		
Gross margin...................................	$360,000		Beginning inventory	$100,000	
			Purchases	560,000	
			Ending inventory...........................	(120,000)	
			Cost of goods sold...........................		540,000
			Gross margin		$360,000
Ending Balance Sheet (partial):					
Current assets:			Current assets:		
Cash	$XXX,XXX		Cash	$XXX,XXX	
Short-term investments	XXX,XXX		Short-term investments..........	XXX,XXX	
Accounts receivable....................	XXX,XXX		Accounts receivable	XXX,XXX	
Inventories	**120,000**		**Inventories**	**120,000**	
Prepaid expenses	XXX,XXX		Prepaid expenses....................	XXX,XXX	

EXHIBIT 9-2 *Recording and Reporting Inventory Transactions of Huntington Galleries—Perpetual and Periodic Systems (amounts assumed)*

ENTRIES UNDER THE PERIODIC SYSTEM In the periodic system, the business records purchases of inventory in the Purchases account (an expense account). The Inventory account continues to carry the beginning balance left over from the end of the preceding period. At the end of the period, however, the Inventory account must be updated for the financial statements. A journal entry removes the beginning balance, crediting Inventory and debiting Income Summary. A second journal entry sets up the ending balance, based on the physical count. The debit is to Inventory, and the credit to Income Summary. These entries can be made either in the closing process or as an adjustment.

Exhibit 9-2 contrasts the perpetual and periodic inventory systems for one month's operations of Huntington Galleries. Compare the entries under both inventory systems step by step. First study the perpetual system all the way through. On the income statement the perpetual system reports cost of goods sold on a single line. Then study the periodic system, which reports a more detailed computation of cost of goods sold. Both inventory systems report the same amounts for inventory and cost of goods sold. (All amounts are assumed.)

Journal entries for a periodic system were introduced in Chapter 5 (p. 217).

Short Exercise: Which method (1) Uses the Purchases account? (2) Uses the Cost of Goods Sold account? (3) Has the same balance in Inventory all year until closing? (4) Is preferred for high-unit-cost inventory items? (5) Requires a physical count at least once a year? (6) Debits Inventory for goods purchased? *A:* Periodic: 1, 3, 5; Perpetual: 2, 4, 5, 6.

Computing the Cost of Inventory

Under both accounting systems, a physical count establishes the cost of inventory on hand, or the *cost of ending inventory*. The *quantity* of inventory is multiplied by the *unit cost* of inventory to compute the cost of inventory on hand.

Quantity of Inventory on Hand × Unit Cost = Cost of Inventory on Hand

The Huntington Galleries inventory record in Exhibit 9-1 follows the common practice of recording quantities only. The company can multiply the quantity of 20 chairs on hand at November 30 by the unit cost of each chair to compute the value of the ending inventory for the balance sheet.

A physical count of inventory is a good internal control even when the perpetual system is used.

◀▥◀▥◀▥ Recall from Chapter 5 (p. 181) that FOB shipping point and destination determine who is responsible for the freight—buyer or seller.

Key Point: *FOB shipping point* means the goods are placed on board (on the carrier, such as UPS) and the buyer is responsible for paying the freight. *FOB destination* means the freight is paid to the destination by the seller.

DETERMINING THE QUANTITY OF INVENTORY Many businesses—even those that use the perpetual system—physically count their inventory on the last day of the fiscal year. If you have worked at a grocery store or some other type of retail business, you will recall the process of "taking inventory." Some entities shut the business down to get a good count of inventory on hand. Others count the goods on a weekend. Still others inventory the merchandise while business is being conducted.

Complications may arise in determining the inventory quantity. Suppose the business has purchased some goods that are in transit when the inventory is counted. Even though these items are not physically present, they should be included in the inventory count if title to the goods has passed to the purchaser. When title passes from seller to purchaser, the purchaser becomes the legal owner of the goods.

The FOB—free on board—terms of the transaction govern when title passes from the seller to the purchaser.◀▥ **FOB shipping point** indicates that title passes when the goods leave the seller's place of business. **FOB destination** means that title passes when the goods arrive at the purchaser's location. Therefore, goods in transit that Huntington Galleries has purchased FOB shipping point should be included in Huntington's inventory. Goods in transit that it has bought FOB destination should not be included.

Another complication in counting inventory arises from consigned goods. In a **consignment** arrangement, the owner of the inventory (the *consignor*) transfers the goods to another business (the *consignee*). For a fee, the consignee sells the inventory on the owner's behalf. The consignee does *not* take title to the consigned goods and, therefore, should not include them in its own inventory. Consignments are common in retailing. Suppose Huntington Galleries is the consignee for a line of beds in its stores. Should Huntington include this consigned merchandise in its inventory count? No, because Huntington Galleries does not own the beds. Instead, the bed manufacturer—the consignor—includes the consigned goods in its inventory. A rule of thumb is to include in inventory only what the business owns.

DETERMINING THE COST OF INVENTORY Inventories are normally accounted for at historical cost, as the *cost principle* requires. *Inventory cost* is the price the business pays to acquire the inventory—not the selling price of the goods. Suppose Huntington Galleries purchases furniture polish for $10 and offers it for sale at $15. The inventory is reported at its cost of $10 per unit, multiplied by the number of units owned, not at its selling price of $15. Inventory cost includes invoice price, less any purchase discount, plus sales tax, tariffs, transportation charges, insurance while in transit, and all other costs incurred to make the goods ready for sale.

Inventory Costing Methods

Determining the unit cost of inventory is easy when the unit cost remains constant during the period. But the unit cost often changes. For example, during times of inflation, prices rise. The chair that cost Huntington Galleries $300 in January may cost $315 in June and $322 in October. Suppose Huntington sells 40 chairs in November. How many of them cost $300, how many cost $315, and how many cost $322? To compute the cost of goods sold and cost of inventory on hand, the accountant must have some means of assigning the business's cost to each item sold. The four costing methods that GAAP allows are

1. Specific unit cost
2. Weighted-average cost
3. First-in, first-out (FIFO) cost
4. Last-in, first-out (LIFO) cost

A company can use any of these methods. Many companies use several methods—different methods for different categories of inventory.

Specific Unit Cost

OBJECTIVE 2

Apply four inventory costing methods: specific unit cost, weighted-average cost, FIFO, and LIFO

Some businesses deal in inventory items that may be identified individually, such as automobiles, jewels, and real estate. These businesses usually cost their inventory at the **specific unit cost** of the particular unit. For instance, a Chevrolet dealer may have two vehicles in the showroom—a "stripped-down" model that cost $14,000 and a "loaded" model that cost $17,000. If the dealer sells the loaded model for $19,700, cost of goods sold is $17,000, the cost of the specific unit. The gross margin on this sale is $2,700 ($19,700 – $17,000). If the stripped-down auto is the only unit left in inventory at the end of the period, ending inventory is $14,000, the cost to the retailer of the specific unit on hand.

The specific unit cost method is also called the *specific identification* method. This method is not practical for inventory items that have common characteristics, such as bushels of wheat, gallons of paint, or boxes of laundry detergent.

Weighted-Average Cost, FIFO Cost, and LIFO Cost

The weighted-average cost, FIFO (first-in, first-out) cost, and LIFO (last-in, first-out) cost methods are fundamentally different from the specific unit cost method. These methods do not assign to inventory the specific cost of particular units. Instead, they assume different flows of costs into and out of inventory.

WEIGHTED-AVERAGE COST The **weighted-average cost method**, often called the *average cost method*, is based on the weighted-average cost of inventory during the period. This method weighs the cost per unit as the average unit cost during the period—that is, if the unit cost drops or rises over the period, the average of these costs is used. Weighted-average cost is determined as follows: Divide the cost of goods available for sale (beginning inventory plus purchases) by the number of units available. Compute the ending inventory and cost of goods sold by multiplying the number of units by the weighted-average cost per unit. If cost of goods available for sale is $90,000 and 60 units are available, the weighted-average cost is $1,500 per unit ($90,000/60 = $1,500). Ending inventory of 20 units of the same item has an average cost of $30,000 (20 × $1,500 = $30,000). Cost of goods sold (40 units) is $60,000 (40 × $1,500). Panel A of Exhibit 9-3 gives the data in more detail. Panel B shows the weighted-average cost computations.

FIRST-IN, FIRST-OUT (FIFO) COST Under the **first-in, first-out (FIFO) method**, the company must keep a record of the cost of each inventory unit purchased. The unit costs used in computing the ending inventory may be different from the unit costs used in computing the cost of goods sold. Under FIFO, the first costs into inventory are the first costs out to cost of goods sold—hence the name *first-in, first-out*. Ending inventory is based on the costs of the most recent purchases. In our example, the FIFO cost of ending inventory is $36,000. Cost of goods sold is $54,000. Panel A of Exhibit 9-3 gives the data, and Panel B shows the FIFO computations.

Panel A—Illustrative Data

Beginning inventory (10 units @ $1,000 per unit)..................................		$10,000
Purchases:		
No. 1 (25 units @ $1,400 per unit)..	$35,000	
No. 2 (25 units @ $1,800 per unit)..	45,000	
Total		80,000
Cost of goods available for sale (60 units)...........................		90,000
Ending inventory (20 units @ $? per unit)............................		?
Cost of goods sold (40 units @ $? per unit)		$?

Panel B—Ending Inventory and Cost of Goods Sold

Weighted-Average Cost Method

Cost of goods available for sale—see Panel A (60 units @ average cost of $1,500* per unit)..		$90,000
Ending inventory (20 units @ $1,500 per unit)		30,000
Cost of goods sold (40 units @ $1,500 per unit)...........................		$60,000

$$\frac{\text{*Cost of goods available for sale, \$90,000}}{\text{Number of units available for sale, 60}} = \text{Average cost per unit, \$1,500}$$

FIFO Cost Method

Cost of goods available for sale (60 units—see Panel A)		$90,000
Ending inventory (cost of the *last* 20 units available):		
20 units @ $1,800 per unit (from purchase no. 2)...............................		36,000
Cost of goods sold (cost of the *first* 40 units available):		
10 units @ $1,000 per unit (all of beginning inventory)	$10,000	
25 units @ $1,400 per unit (all of purchase no. 1).............................	35,000	
5 units @ $1,800 per unit (from purchase no. 2)................................	9,000	
Total		$54,000

LIFO Cost Method

Cost of goods available for sale (60 units—see Panel A)		$90,000
Ending inventory (cost of the *first* 20 units available):		
10 units @ $1,000 per unit (all of beginning inventory)	$10,000	
10 units @ $1,400 per unit (from purchase no. 1).............................	14,000	
Total		24,000
Cost of goods sold (cost of the *last* 40 units available):		
25 units @ $1,800 per unit (all of purchase no. 2).............................	$45,000	
15 units @ $1,400 per unit (from purchase no. 1).............................	21,000	
Total		$66,000

LAST-IN, FIRST-OUT (LIFO) COST The **last-in, first-out (LIFO) method** also depends on the costs of particular inventory purchases. LIFO is the opposite of FIFO. Under LIFO, the last costs into inventory are the first costs out to cost of goods sold. This method leaves the oldest costs—those of beginning inventory and the earliest purchases of the period—in ending inventory. In our example, the LIFO cost of ending inventory is $24,000. Cost of goods sold is $66,000. Panel A of Exhibit 9-3 gives the data, and Panel B shows the LIFO computations.

Income Effects of FIFO, LIFO, and Weighted-Average Cost

In our discussion and examples, the cost of inventory rose during the accounting period. When inventory unit costs change, the different costing methods produce different cost of goods sold and ending inventory figures, as Exhibit 9-3 shows. When inventory unit costs are increasing, FIFO ending inventory is *highest* because it is priced at the most recent costs, which are the highest. LIFO ending inventory is *lowest* because it is priced at the oldest costs, which are the lowest. When inventory unit costs are decreasing, FIFO ending inventory is lowest, and LIFO is highest.

	FIFO	LIFO	Weighted-Average
Sales revenue (assumed)	$100,000	$100,000	$100,000
Cost of goods sold:			
Goods available for sale (assumed)........................	$90,000	$90,000	$90,000
Ending inventory...	**36,000**	**24,000**	**30,000**
Cost of goods sold..	54,000	66,000	60,000
Gross margin	**$ 46,000**	**$ 34,000**	**$ 40,000**

Summary of Income Effects—When Inventory Unit Costs Are Increasing:

FIFO—Highest ending inventory   LIFO—Lowest ending inventory   Weighted-average—Results fall between the extremes
    Lowest cost of goods sold   Highest cost of goods sold   of FIFO and LIFO
    Highest gross margin   Lowest gross margin

Summary of Income Effects—When Inventory Unit Costs Are Decreasing:

FIFO—Lowest ending inventory   LIFO—Highest ending inventory   Weighted-average—Results fall between the extremes
    Highest cost of goods sold   Lowest cost of goods sold   of FIFO and LIFO
    Lowest gross margin   Highest gross margin

CONCEPT HIGHLIGHT

EXHIBIT 9-4 *Income Effects of FIFO, LIFO, and Weighted-Average Cost Inventory Methods*

Exhibit 9-4 summarizes the income effects of the three inventory methods, using the data from Exhibit 9-3. Study the exhibit carefully, focusing on ending inventory, cost of goods sold, and gross margin.

The Income Tax Advantage of LIFO

When prices are rising, applying the LIFO method results in the *lowest taxable income* and thus the *lowest income taxes*. Let's use the gross margin data of Exhibit 9-4.

OBJECTIVE 3

Distinguish between the income effects and the tax effects of the inventory costing methods

	FIFO	LIFO	Weighted-Average
Gross margin..	$46,000	$34,000	$40,000
Operating expenses (assumed)..............	26,000	26,000	26,000
Income before income tax	$20,000	$ 8,000	$14,000
Income tax expense (40%)....................	$ 8,000	$ 3,200	$ 5,600

Income tax expense is lowest under LIFO ($3,200) and highest under FIFO ($8,000). The most attractive feature of LIFO is reduced income tax payments, which is why Huntington Galleries of our chapter-opening story switched from the FIFO to the LIFO method.

The 1970s and early 1980s were marked by high inflation, so many companies changed to LIFO for its tax advantage. Exhibit 9-5, based on an American Institute of Certified Public Accountants (AICPA) survey of 600 companies, indicates that FIFO and LIFO are the most popular inventory costing methods.

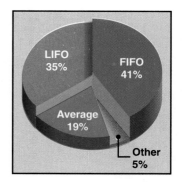

STOP & THINK Why is FIFO so popular if LIFO saves the most in taxes during periods of rising prices?

Answer: Companies in industries with decreasing costs—computers, major appliances, and some agricultural commodities—save taxes by using FIFO. Other companies have inventory turnover rates so high that there is little difference between average cost, FIFO, and LIFO. Still other companies simply want to report higher accounting income under FIFO to attract investors.

EXHIBIT 9-5 *Use of the Various Inventory Methods*

Analysis of Financial Statements—Converting a LIFO Company's Income to the FIFO Basis

OBJECTIVE 4

Convert a company's net income from the LIFO basis to the FIFO basis

The Internal Revenue Service allows companies to use LIFO for income tax purposes only if they use LIFO for financial reporting. But companies may also report an alternative inventory amount in the financial statements. Doing so presents a rare opportunity to convert a company's net income from the LIFO basis to what the income would have been if the business had used FIFO. Why is this conversion so helpful?

Suppose you are a financial analyst, and it is your job to recommend stocks for your clients to purchase as investments. You have narrowed your choice to Wal-Mart Stores, Inc., and The GAP, Inc., the clothing retailer. In your analysis, you observe that Wal-Mart uses the LIFO method to account for its inventories and The GAP uses the FIFO method. The two companies' net incomes are not comparable because they use different inventory methods. To compare the two companies, you need to place them on the same footing. Fortunately, you can convert Wal-Mart's income from the LIFO basis, as reported in the company's financial statements, to the FIFO basis.

"The GAP uses the FIFO method."

Wal-Mart, like many other companies that use LIFO, reports the FIFO cost, a LIFO Reserve, and the LIFO cost of ending inventory. The **LIFO Reserve**[1] is the difference between the LIFO cost of an inventory and what the cost of that inventory would be under FIFO. Wal-Mart reported the following amounts (in millions of dollars):

Short Exercise: Given for the Owens Co. for 1996:

Beg. Inventory	$ 40,000
End. Inventory	30,000
Cost of goods sold	160,000
Net income	45,000
Income tax rate	30%

Owens uses LIFO. If it used FIFO, beginning and ending inventories would be $10,000 and $12,000 higher, respectively. Show the cost of goods sold computation under LIFO and FIFO and the FIFO net income for 1996.

A:

	LIFO	FIFO
Beg. Inv.	$ 40,000*	$ 50,000
+ Purchases	150,000†	150,000
Goods avail. for sale	190,000	200,000
– End. Inv.	30,000*	42,000
= COGS	$160,000*	$158,000

*Given †Derived

Net income under FIFO is $46,400 [$45,000 + ($160,000 – $158,000) × (1 – 0.30)].

WAL-MART USES LIFO

	19X3	19X2
From the Wal-Mart balance sheet:		
Inventories (approximate FIFO cost)	$ 9,780	$7,857
Less LIFO reserve	512	473
LIFO cost	9,268	7,384
From the Wal-Mart income statement:		
Cost of goods sold	$44,175	
Net income	1,995	
Income tax rate	37%	

To convert Wal-Mart's net income to the FIFO basis, first compute the company's cost of goods sold under LIFO. Solve for net purchases, which is the same amount regardless of the inventory method used. Then substitute the FIFO amounts for beginning and ending inventory and recompute cost of goods sold under FIFO. Here are the cost of goods sold figures for Wal-Mart during 19X3:

---

[1]The LIFO Reserve account is widely used in practice even though the term *reserve* is poor terminology.

(Amounts in millions)	19X3 LIFO Amounts as Reported in the Income Statement	LIFO Reserve			19X3 FIFO Amounts
Beginning inventory..........................	$ 7,384	+	$473	=	$ 7,857
Net purchases.................................	46,059				46,059
Cost of goods available for sale........	53,443				53,916
Less: Ending inventory	9,268	+	512	=	9,780
Cost of goods sold...........................	$44,175	–	$ 39	=	$44,136

FIFO cost of goods sold lower by $39

If Wal-Mart had used the FIFO method, cost of goods sold would have been $44,136 million, a decrease of $39 million. Now you can compute Wal-Mart's net income under FIFO, as follows (amounts rounded to the nearest million dollars):

If Wal-Mart Had Used FIFO in 19X3

Lower Cost of goods sold →	Higher pretax income...	$ 39
	Minus income taxes (37%)......................................	14
	Higher net income under FIFO.................................	25
	Actual net income under LIFO.................................	1,995
	Net income Wal-Mart would have	
	reported under FIFO...	$2,020

Finally, you can compare Wal-Mart's net income with that of The GAP. All the ratios used for the analysis—current ratio, inventory turnover, and so on—can be compared between the two companies.

STOP & THINK How much in income taxes did Wal-Mart save during 19X3 by using LIFO?

Answer: $14 million, which can be used to open new stores.

Generally Accepted Accounting Principles and Practical Considerations: A Comparison of Inventory Methods

We may ask three questions to judge the three major inventory costing methods. (1) How well does each method match inventory expense—the cost of goods sold—to sales revenue on the income statement? (2) Which method reports the most up-to-date inventory amount on the balance sheet? (3) What effects do the methods have on income taxes? The weighted-average cost method produces amounts between the extremes of LIFO and FIFO.

LIFO better matches the current value of cost of goods sold with current revenue by assigning to this expense the most recent inventory costs. In contrast, FIFO matches the oldest inventory costs against the period's revenue—a poor matching of current expense with current revenue.

FIFO reports the most current inventory costs on the balance sheet. LIFO can result in misleading inventory costs on the balance sheet because the oldest prices are left in ending inventory.

As shown earlier, LIFO results in the lowest income tax payments when prices are rising. Tax payments are highest under FIFO. When inventory prices are decreasing, tax payments are highest under LIFO and lowest under FIFO.

Key Point: During a period of rising prices—
Advantages of FIFO:
 1. Always reports current cost for ending inventory
 2. Reports higher income
Advantages of LIFO:
 1. Always matches expenses and revenues
 2. Results in lower taxes and higher cash flow (cont.)

Disadvantages of FIFO:
  1. Violates the matching principle (FIFO matches some of the previous year's inventory cost against current revenue)
  2. Results in higher taxes and lower cash flows
  3. Does not adjust cost of goods sold for the effects of inflation
Disadvantages of LIFO:
  1. Reports lower income
  2. Reports understated ending inventory
  3. Can be used to manipulate income

FIFO PRODUCES SO-CALLED INVENTORY PROFITS FIFO is criticized because it overstates income by so-called inventory profit during periods of inflation. Briefly, **inventory profit** is the difference between gross margin figured on the FIFO basis and gross margin figured on the LIFO basis. Exhibit 9-4 illustrates inventory profit. The $12,000 difference between FIFO and LIFO gross margins ($46,000 – $34,000) results from the difference in cost of goods sold. This $12,000 amount is called *FIFO inventory profit*, *phantom profit*, and *illusory profit*. Why? Because to stay in business the company must replace the inventory it has sold. The replacement cost of the merchandise is more closely approximated by the cost of goods sold under LIFO ($66,000) than by the FIFO amount ($54,000).

LIFO ALLOWS MANAGERS TO MANIPULATE REPORTED INCOME—UP OR DOWN LIFO is criticized because it allows managers to manipulate net income. Assume that inventory prices are rising rapidly and that a company wants to show less income for the year (in order to pay less taxes). Managers can buy a large amount of inventory near the end of the year. Under LIFO these high inventory costs immediately become expense—as cost of goods sold. As a result, the income statement reports a lower net income. Conversely, if the business is having a bad year, management may wish to increase reported income. To do so, managers can delay a large purchase of high-cost inventory until the next period. This high-cost inventory is not expensed as cost of goods sold in the current year. Thus management avoids decreasing the current year's reported income. In the process, the company draws down inventory quantities.

LIFO LIQUIDATION When inventory quantities fall below the level of the previous period, the situation is called *LIFO liquidation*. To compute cost of goods sold, the company must dip into older layers of inventory cost. Under LIFO and during a period of rising inventory costs, that action shifts older, lower costs into cost of goods sold. The result is higher net income than the company would have reported if no LIFO liquidation had occurred. Managers try to avoid LIFO liquidation because it increases reported income and income taxes. Owens-Corning Fiberglas Company, the world's leading supplier of glass fiber materials, recently reported that LIFO liquidations added $2.7 million to net income.

INTERNATIONAL PERSPECTIVE Many companies manufacture their inventory in foreign countries to decrease transportation costs and to break down trade barriers. Companies that value inventory by the LIFO method often must use another accounting method for their inventories in foreign countries. What is so special about LIFO? It was first allowed in the United States as the result of tax legislation in 1954. Other countries are not bound by American tax laws or accounting practices. Australia and the United Kingdom, for example, do not permit the use of LIFO. Virtually all countries permit FIFO and the weighted-average method. Exhibit 9-6 lists a sampling of countries and whether or not they permit LIFO.

EXHIBIT 9-6
LIFO Use by Country

Country	LIFO Permitted?	Country	LIFO Permitted?
Australia	No	Netherlands	Yes
Brazil	Yes	Nigeria	No
Canada	Yes	Singapore	No
France	Yes	South Africa	Yes
Germany	Yes	Sweden	No
Hong Kong	No	Switzerland	No
Japan	Yes	United Kingdom	No
Mexico	Yes	United States	Yes

HIGHER INCOME OR LOWER TAXES? A company may want to report the highest income, and FIFO meets this need when prices are rising. But the company must pay the highest income taxes under FIFO. When prices are falling, LIFO reports the highest income.

Which inventory method is better— LIFO or FIFO? There is no single answer to that question. Different companies have different motives for the inventory method they choose. Polaroid Corporation uses FIFO, J. C. Penney Company uses LIFO, and Motorola, Inc., uses weighted-average cost. Still other companies use more than one method. The Black & Decker Corporation, best known for its power tools and small appliances, uses both LIFO and

"The Black & Decker Corporation, best known for its power tools and small appliances, uses both LIFO and FIFO."

FIFO. The following excerpt is from a Black & Decker annual report (amount in millions):

Inventories............... $390

NOTES TO CONSOLIDATED FINANCIAL STATEMENTS
Note 1: Summary of Accounting Policies
Inventories: The cost of United States inventories is based on the last-in, first-out (LIFO) method; all other inventories are based on the first-in, first-out (FIFO) method. The cost of…inventories stated under the LIFO method represents approximately 40% of the value of total inventories.

SUMMARY PROBLEM FOR YOUR REVIEW   MID-CHAPTER

Suppose an IBM division that handles computer components has these inventory records for January 19X6:

Date	Item	Quantity	Unit Cost	Sale Price
Jan. 1	Beginning inventory	100 units	$ 8	
6	Purchase	60 units	9	
13	Sale	70 units		$20
21	Purchase	150 units	9	
24	Sale	210 units		22
27	Purchase	90 units	10	
30	Sale	30 units		25

Company accounting records reveal that related operating expense for January was $1,900.

Required

1. Prepare the January income statement, showing amounts for FIFO, LIFO, and weighted-average cost. Label the bottom line "Operating income." (Round figures to whole dollar amounts.)
2. Suppose you are the financial vice-president of IBM Corporation. Which inventory method will you use if your motive is to
   a. Minimize income taxes?
   b. Report the highest operating income?

c. Report operating income between the extremes of FIFO and LIFO?
d. Report inventory at the most current cost?
e. Attain the best matching of current expense with current revenue?

State the reason for each of your answers.

SOLUTION TO REVIEW PROBLEM

Requirement 1

IBM CORPORATION INCOME STATEMENT FOR COMPONENT MONTH ENDED JANUARY 31, 19X6			
	FIFO	**LIFO**	**Weighted-Average**
Sales revenue......................................	$6,770	$6,770	$6,770
Cost of goods sold:			
Beginning inventory	$ 800	$ 800	$ 800
Net purchases...............................	2,790	2,790	2,790
Cost of goods			
available for sale	3,590	3,590	3,590
Ending inventory	900	720	808
Cost of goods sold.........................	2,690	2,870	2,782
Gross margin	4,080	3,900	3,988
Operating expenses...........................	1,900	1,900	1,900
Operating income.............................	$2,180	$2,000	$2,088

Computations:

Sales revenue:	(70 × $20)	+ (210 × $22) + (30 × $25) = $6,770
Beginning inventory:	100 × $8	= $800
Purchases:	(60 × $9)	+ (150 × $9) + (90 × $10) = $2,790
Ending inventory—FIFO:	90* × $10	= $900
LIFO:	90 × $8	= $720
Weighted-average:	90 × $8.975**	= $808 (rounded from $807.75)

* Number of units in ending inventory = 100 + 60 − 70 + 150 − 210 + 90 − 30 = 90
**$3,590/400 units = $8.975 per unit
  Number of units available = 100 + 60 + 150 + 90 = 400

Requirement 2

a. Use LIFO to minimize income taxes. Operating income under LIFO is lowest when inventory unit costs are increasing, as they are in this case (from $8 to $10). (If inventory costs were decreasing, income under FIFO would be lowest.)

b. Use FIFO to report the highest operating income. Income under FIFO is highest when inventory unit costs are increasing, as in this situation.

c. Use weighted-average cost to report an operating income amount between the FIFO and LIFO extremes. This is true in this problem situation and in others when inventory unit costs are increasing or decreasing.

d. Use FIFO to report inventory at the most current cost. The oldest inventory costs are expensed as cost of goods sold, leaving in ending inventory the most recent (most current) costs of the period.

e. Use LIFO to attain the best matching of current expense with current revenue. The most recent (most current) inventory costs are expensed as cost of goods sold.

Perpetual Inventory Records under FIFO, LIFO, and Weighted-Average Costing

Many companies keep their perpetual inventory records in quantities only, as illustrated in Exhibit 9-1. Other companies keep perpetual records in both quantities and dollar costs.

OBJECTIVE 5
Prepare a perpetual
inventory record

FIFO Huntington Galleries uses the FIFO inventory method. Exhibit 9-7 shows Huntington's perpetual inventory record for the Early American chairs—in both quantities and dollar costs for the month of November.

To prepare financial statements at November 30, Huntington can take the ending inventory cost ($6,400) straight to the balance sheet. Cost of goods sold for the November income statement is $12,350. Some companies combine elements of the perpetual and periodic inventory systems—the perpetual system for control and preparation of the financial statements, and the periodic system for analysis. Here is Huntington's computation of cost of goods sold during November, with data taken from the perpetual record in Exhibit 9-7:

Cost of Goods Sold (Early American Chairs)—November

Beginning inventory	$ 3,000
+ Purchases	15,750
= Cost of goods available for sale	18,750
− Ending inventory	(6,400)
= Cost of goods sold	$12,350

LIFO Few companies keep perpetual inventory records at LIFO cost. The record-keeping is expensive, and LIFO liquidations can occur during the year. To avoid these problems, LIFO companies can keep perpetual inventory records in terms of quantities only, as illustrated in Exhibit 9-1. For financial statements, they can apply LIFO costs at the end of the period. Other companies maintain perpetual inventory

EXHIBIT 9-7
Perpetual Inventory Record—FIFO Cost

HUNTINGTON GALLERIES

Item: Early American Chairs

	Received			Sold			Balance		
Date	**Qty.**	**Unit Cost**	**Total**	**Qty.**	**Unit Cost**	**Total**	**Qty.**	**Unit Cost**	**Total**
Nov. 1							10	$300	$3,000
5				6	$300	$ 1,800	4	300	1,200
7	25	$310	$ 7,750				4	300	1,200
							25	310	7,750
12				4	300	1,200			
				9	310	2,790	16	310	4,960
26	25	320	8,000				16	310	4,960
							25	320	8,000
30				16	310	4,960			
				5	320	1,600	20	320	6,400
Totals	50		$15,750	40		$12,350	20	320	$6,400

records at FIFO cost and convert the FIFO amounts to LIFO costs for the financial statements. Wal-Mart and other companies make this adjustment through the LIFO reserve account illustrated on page 374. This topic is covered in intermediate accounting courses.

WEIGHTED-AVERAGE COST Perpetual inventory records can be kept at weighted-average cost. Most companies that use this method compute the weighted-average cost for the entire period. They apply this cost to both ending inventory and cost of goods sold. These procedures parallel those used in the periodic inventory system (Exhibit 9-3).

The use of computer software to account for inventory eases the computation of the average cost per unit each time additional goods are purchased. The new average unit cost is then applied to each subsequent sale until more goods are purchased, at which time another new average cost is computed.

STOP & THINK Examine Exhibit 9-7. What was Huntington Galleries' weighted-average unit cost during November? How much were ending inventory and cost of goods sold at weighted-average unit cost?

Answer: Weighted-average unit cost $= \dfrac{\$3,000 + \$15,750}{10 \text{ units} + 50 \text{ units}} = \dfrac{\$18,750}{60 \text{ units}} = \$312.50$

Ending inventory	= 20 units × $312.50	=	$ 6,250
Cost of goods sold	= 40 units × $312.50	=	12,500
Cost of goods available for sale		=	$18,750

Consistency Principle

Key Point: The accounting principles used by a company must be consistent from year to year to allow comparison of the financial results from one year to the next. If a company changes its inventory method, the change and its effect must be disclosed in the footnotes.

The **consistency principle** states that businesses should use the same accounting methods and procedures from period to period. Consistency makes it possible to compare a company's financial statements from one period to the next.

Suppose you are analyzing a company's net income pattern over a two-year period. The company switched from LIFO to FIFO during that time. Its net income increased dramatically but only as a result of the change in inventory method. If you did not know of the change, you might believe that the company's income increased because of improved operations, which is not the case.

The consistency principle does not require that all companies within an industry use the same accounting method. Nor does it mean that a company may *never* change its own accounting method. However, a company making an accounting change must disclose the effect of the change on net income. Sun Company, Inc., an oil company, disclosed the following in a note to its annual report:

EXCERPT FROM NOTE 6 OF THE SUN COMPANY FINANCIAL STATEMENTS

…Sun changed its method of accounting for the cost of crude oil and refined product inventories at Suncor from the FIFO method to the LIFO method. Sun believes that the use of the LIFO method better matches current costs with current revenues…. The change decreased the 19X1 net loss…by $3 million….

Disclosure Principle

The **disclosure principle** holds that a company's financial statements should report enough information for outsiders to make knowledgeable decisions about the company. In short, the company should report *relevant*, *reliable*, and *comparable* information about its economic affairs. With respect to inventories, this means to disclose the method or methods in use. Without knowledge of the inventory method, a banker could gain an unrealistic impression of a company and make an unwise lending decision. For example, suppose the banker is comparing two companies—one that uses LIFO and the other, FIFO. The FIFO company reports higher net income, but only because it uses a particular inventory method. Without knowledge of the accounting methods the companies are using, the banker could loan money to the wrong business or could refuse a loan to a promising customer.

In conjunction with the consistency principle, the disclosure principle requires companies to report the net-income effect of a change in accounting method. For example, while considering an investment in Sun Company, Inc., you observe that Sun's net loss was less than expected. Would you be inclined to invest in the company? Perhaps. However, the foregoing note explains that Sun Company's change to the LIFO method reduced the net loss by $3 million. If the company had not changed inventory methods, the net loss would have been $3 million higher. This information casts a different light on Sun's operations and may influence your investment decision. This is the disclosure principle in action.

Materiality Concept

The **materiality concept** states that a company must perform strictly proper accounting *only* for items and transactions that are significant to the business's financial statements. Information is significant—what accountants call *material*—when its inclusion and correct presentation in the financial statements would cause a statement user to change a decision because of that information. Immaterial—nonsignificant—items justify less-than-perfect accounting. The inclusion and proper presentation of *immaterial* items would not affect a statement user's decision. The materiality concept frees accountants from having to compute and report every last item in strict accordance with GAAP. Thus the materiality concept reduces the cost of recording accounting information.

How does a business decide where to draw the line between the material and the immaterial? This decision rests to a great degree on how large the business is. Wendy's, for example, has close to $500 million in assets. Management would likely treat as immaterial a $100 loss of inventory due to spoilage. A loss of this amount is immaterial to Wendy's total assets and net income, so company accountants may ignore the loss. Will this accounting treatment affect anyone's decision about Wendy's? Probably not, so it doesn't matter whether the loss is reported separately.

Large companies may draw the materiality line at a figure as high as $10,000 and expense any smaller amount. Smaller firms may choose to expense only those items less than $50. Materiality varies from company to company. An amount that is material to your local service station may not be material to General Motors.

Accounting Conservatism

Conservatism in accounting means to report items in the financial statements at amounts that lead to the gloomiest immediate financial results. Conservatism comes into play when there are alternative ways to account for the item. What advantage does conservatism give a business? Management often looks on the brighter side of operations and may overstate a company's income and asset values. Many accountants regard conservatism as a counterbalance to management's optimistic tendencies. The goal is for financial statements to present realistic figures.

Conservatism appears in accounting guidelines such as "anticipate no gains, but provide for all probable losses" and "if in doubt, record an asset at the lowest reasonable amount and a liability at the highest reasonable amount."

Accountants generally regard the historical cost of acquiring an asset as its maximum value. Even if the current market value of the asset increases above its cost, businesses do not *write up* (that is, increase) the asset's accounting value. Assume that a company purchased land for $100,000, and its value increased to $300,000. Accounting conservatism dictates that the historical cost, $100,000, be maintained as the accounting value of the land. GAAP makes an exception to this rule for certain investments, as we discuss in Chapter 17.

Conservatism also directs accountants to decrease the accounting value of an asset if it appears unrealistically high—even if no transaction occurs. Assume that a company paid $35,000 for inventory that has become obsolete, and its current value is only $12,000. Conservatism dictates that the inventory be *written down* (that is, decreased) to $12,000.

Lower-of-Cost-or-Market Rule

The **lower-of-cost-or-market rule** (abbreviated as LCM) shows accounting conservatism in action. LCM requires that an asset be reported in the financial statements at whichever is lower—its historical cost or its market value. Applied to inventories, *market value* generally means *current replacement cost* (that is, how much the business would have to pay in the market on that day to purchase the amount of inventory that it has on hand). If the replacement cost of inventory falls below its historical cost, the business must write down the value of its goods because of the likelihood of incurring a loss on the inventory. This departure from historical cost accounting is required by GAAP. The business reports ending inventory at its LCM value on the balance sheet. All this can be done automatically by a computerized accounting system. How is the write-down accomplished?

Suppose a business paid $3,000 for inventory on September 26. By December 31, its value has fallen. The inventory can now be replaced for $2,200. Market value is below cost, and the December 31 balance sheet reports this inventory at its LCM value of $2,200. Usually, the market value of inventory is higher than historical cost, so inventory's accounting value is cost for most companies. Exhibit 9-8 presents the effects of LCM on the income statement and the balance sheet. The exhibit shows that the lower of (a) cost or (b) market value—the replacement cost—is the relevant amount for valuing inventory on both the income statement and the balance sheet. Companies are not required to show both cost and market value amounts. However, they may report the higher amount in parentheses, as shown on the balance sheet in Exhibit 9-8.

LCM states that of the $3,000 cost of ending inventory in Exhibit 9-8, $800 is considered to have expired even though the inventory was not sold during the period. Its replacement cost is only $2,200, and that amount is carried forward to the next period as the cost of beginning inventory. Suppose that during the next period the replacement cost of this inventory increases to $2,500. Accounting conservatism states that it would not be appropriate to write up the book value of inventory. The market value of inventory ($2,200 in this case) is used as its cost in future LCM determinations.

Examine the following income statement effect of LCM summarized from Exhibit 9-8. What expense absorbs the impact of the $800 inventory write-down? Cost of goods sold is increased by $800 because ending inventory is $800 less at market ($2,200) than at cost ($3,000).

	Ending Inventory at		
	Cost	**LCM**	
Cost of goods available for sale	$13,800	$13,800	
Ending inventory:			
Cost	3,000		} $800 Lower
Replacement cost (market value)		2,200	at LCM
Cost of goods sold	$10,800	$11,600 }	$800 Higher at LCM

EXHIBIT 9-8

Lower-of-Cost-or-Market (LCM) Effects

Income Statement:

Sales revenue		$20,000
Cost of goods sold:		
Beginning inventory (LCM = Cost)	$ 2,800	
Net purchases	11,000	
Cost of goods available for sale	13,800	
Ending inventory—		
Cost = $3,000		
Replacement cost (market value) = $2,200		
LCM = Market	2,200	
Cost of goods sold		11,600
Gross margin		$ 8,400

Balance Sheet:

Current assets:		
Cash	$	XXX
Short-term investments		XXX
Accounts receivable		XXX
Inventories, at market (which is lower than $3,000 cost)		2,200
Prepaid expenses		XXX
Total current assets		$ X,XXX

Exhibit 9-8 also reports the application of LCM for inventories in the body of the balance sheet. Companies often disclose LCM in notes to their financial statements, as shown below for CBS, Inc.:

NOTE 1: STATEMENT OF SIGNIFICANT ACCOUNTING POLICIES

Inventories. Inventories are stated at the *lower of cost* (principally based on average cost) *or market value.* [Emphasis added.]

Effects of Inventory Errors

Businesses determine inventory amounts at the end of the period. In the process of counting the items, applying unit costs, and computing amounts, errors may arise. As the period 1 segment of Exhibit 9-9 shows, an error in the ending inventory amount creates errors in the cost of goods sold and gross margin amounts. Compare period 1, when ending inventory is overstated and cost of goods sold is understated, each by $5,000, with period 3, which is correct. Period 1 should look exactly like period 3.

OBJECTIVE 7
Compute the effects of inventory errors on cost of goods sold and on net income

EXHIBIT 9-9

Effects of Inventory Errors

	Period 1 Ending Inventory Overstated by $5,000		Period 2 Beginning Inventory Overstated by $5,000		Period 3 Correct	
Sales revenue		$100,000		$100,000		$100,000
Cost of goods sold:						
Beginning inventory	$10,000		**$15,000**		$10,000	
Net purchases	50,000		50,000		50,000	
Cost of goods available for sale	60,000		65,000		60,000	
Ending inventory	**15,000**		10,000		10,000	
Cost of goods sold		45,000		55,000		50,000
Gross margin		$ 55,000		$ 45,000		$ 50,000
			$100,000			

The authors thank Carl High for this example.

PUTTING SKILLS TO WORK

INVENTORY AND THE GREAT SALAD OIL SCANDAL

In 1963, a scandal rocked the business community and changed forever the way auditors verify inventory. The scandal involved salad oil, on which the financial empire of Anthony DeAngelis was built. As president of Allied Crude Vegetable Oil Refining Corp., DeAngelis was the top dealer in vegetable oils in the United States.

THE SCAM

The "Great Salad Oil Scandal" began when the price of vegetable oil fell dramatically. Unable to pay back creditors who demanded their money, DeAngelis's empire collapsed. Revealed in its wake was a sea of fraudulent inventory claims. The company had pumped water into its vegetable oil storage tanks. Oil floats on water, so inspectors who checked only some of the tanks and only from the top overestimated the quantity of inventory in each tank.

The scam took place on a "tank farm" in Bayonne, New Jersey, where DeAngelis supposedly stored 1.7 billion pounds of oil worth about $150 million. No one believed it was necessary to check the accuracy of the inventory amounts, in part because American Express Warehousing leased the tanks. The American Express name was beyond reproach.

THE DISCOVERY

DeAngelis used the overstated inventory amounts as collateral for loans. When he could not pay the loans, creditors seized the vegetable oil. They then learned that only about 100 million pounds of oil — not 1.7 billion pounds — existed. Some tanks were covered by solid matter, and others contained mixtures of oil, water, and sludge. Four tanks were empty, and eight were filled with sea water. There weren't enough tanks to hold all the oil DeAngelis claimed he owned, even if the tanks *had* been filled with salad oil! The empty or partly filled tanks spelled disaster for DeAngelis's creditors.

The Great Salad Oil Scandal was based on the fact that oil floats on water.

POSTSCRIPT

Among the changes brought about by the Great Salad Oil Scandal was the requirement that independent auditors check the accuracy of the owner's claims. In this case, auditors would have had little trouble uncovering DeAngelis's scam.

Recall that one period's ending inventory is the next period's beginning inventory. Thus the error in ending inventory carries over into the next period; note the highlighted amounts in Exhibit 9-9.

Because the same ending inventory figure that is *subtracted* in computing cost of goods sold in one period is *added* as beginning inventory to compute cost of goods sold in the next period, the error's effect cancels out at the end of the second period. The overstatement of cost of goods sold in period 2 counterbalances the understatement in cost of goods sold in period 1. Thus the total gross margin amount for the two periods is the correct $100,000 figure whether or not an error entered into the computation. These effects are summarized in Exhibit 9-10.

Inventory errors, however, cannot be ignored simply because they counterbalance. Suppose you are analyzing trends in the business's operations. Exhibit 9-9 shows a drop in gross margin from period 1 to period 2, followed by an increase in period 3. But that picture of operations is untrue because of the accounting error. The correct gross margin is $50,000 each period. Providing accurate information for decision making requires that all inventory errors be corrected.

EXHIBIT 9-10

General Effects of Inventory Errors

Inventory Error	Period 1		Period 2	
	Cost of Goods Sold	Gross Margin and Net Income	Cost of Goods Sold	Gross Margin and Net Income
Period 1 Ending inventory overstated	Understated	Overstated	Overstated	Understated
Period 1 Ending inventory understated	Overstated	Understated	Understated	Overstated

Estimating Inventory

Often a business must *estimate* the value of its inventory. Because of cost and inconvenience, few companies physically count their inventories at the end of each month. Yet they may need monthly financial statements. A fire or a flood may destroy inventory, and to file an insurance claim, the business must estimate the value of its loss. In both cases, the business needs to know the value of ending inventory without being able to count it. A widely used method for estimating ending inventory is the *gross margin method*.

OBJECTIVE 8

Estimate inventory by the gross margin method

Gross Margin (Gross Profit) Method

The **gross margin method**, also known as the *gross profit method*, is a way of estimating inventory on the basis of the familiar cost-of-goods-sold model:◀▥

	Beginning inventory
+	Net purchases*
=	Cost of goods available for sale
−	Ending inventory
=	Cost of goods sold

*Here "Net purchases" includes freight in.

◀▥ ◀▥ ◀▥ Recall from Chapter 5 (p. 176) that the gross margin is the excess of the selling price over cost of goods sold.
Selling Price − Cost of Goods Sold = Gross Margin
Selling Price − Gross Margin = Cost of Goods Sold

Rearranging *ending inventory* and *cost of goods sold* makes the model useful for estimating ending inventory and is illustrated in Exhibit 9-11:

	Beginning inventory
+	Net purchases
=	Cost of goods available for sale
−	Cost of goods sold
=	Ending inventory

Suppose a fire destroys your business's inventory. To collect insurance, you must estimate the cost of the ending inventory. If the fire did not also destroy your accounting records, beginning inventory and net purchases amounts may be taken directly from the accounting records. The Sales Revenue, Sales Returns, and Sales Discounts accounts indicate net sales up to the date of the fire. Using the entity's normal *gross margin rate* (that is, gross margin divided by net sales revenue), you can estimate cost of goods sold. The last step is to subtract cost of goods sold from goods available to estimate ending inventory. Exhibit 9-12 illustrates the gross margin method.

Short Exercise: Beginning inventory is $70,000, net purchases total $292,000 and net sales are $480,000. With a normal gross margin rate of 40%, how much is ending inventory?
A: $74,000 [$70,000 + $292,000 − (0.60 × $480,000)]

EXHIBIT 9-11
Estimating Ending Inventory

Beginning inventory......................................		$14,000
Net purchases..		66,000
Cost of goods available for sale..................		80,000
Cost of goods sold:		
Net sales revenue......................................	$100,000	
Less estimated gross margin of 40%.......	40,000	
Estimated cost of goods sold..................		60,000
Estimated cost of *ending inventory*..............		$20,000

Accountants, managers, and auditors use the gross margin method to test the overall reasonableness of an ending inventory amount that has been determined by a physical count for all types of businesses. This method helps to detect large errors.

Internal Control Over Inventory

Internal control over inventory is important because inventory is the lifeblood of a merchandiser. Successful companies take great care to protect their inventory. Elements of good internal control over inventory include:

Inventory must be stored properly so that it will not be damaged, and it must be easily accessible.

1. Physically counting inventory at least once each year no matter which system is used
2. Maintaining efficient purchasing, receiving, and shipping procedures
3. Storing inventory to protect it against theft, damage, and decay
4. Allowing access to inventory only to personnel who do *not* have access to the accounting records
5. Keeping perpetual inventory records for high-unit-cost merchandise
6. Purchasing inventory in economical quantities
7. Keeping enough inventory on hand to prevent shortage situations, which lead to lost sales
8. Not keeping too large an inventory stockpiled, thus avoiding the expense of tying up money in unneeded items

The annual physical count of inventory (item 1) is necessary because the only way to be certain of the amount of inventory on hand is to count it. Errors arise in the best accounting systems, and the count is needed to establish the correct value of the inventory. When an error is detected, the records are brought into agreement with the physical count.

Keeping inventory handlers away from the accounting records (item 4) is an essential separation of duties, discussed in Chapter 7. An employee with access to both inventory and the accounting records can steal the goods and make an entry to conceal the theft. For example, the employee could increase the amount of an inventory write-down to make it appear that goods decreased in value when in fact they were stolen.

Computerized inventory systems allow companies to minimize both the amount of inventory on hand and the chances of running out of stock (items 7 and 8). In an increasingly competitive business environment, companies cannot afford to have cash tied up in too much inventory.

PROBLEM 1

Centronics Data Computer Corporation reported a net loss for the year. In its financial statements, the company noted:

Balance Sheet:
Current assets:
Inventories (notes 1C and 2)... $48,051,000

> Note 1C: Inventories are stated at the lower of cost or market. Cost is determined on a first-in, first-out (FIFO) basis.
>
> Note 2: Declining . . . market conditions during [the] fiscal [year] adversely affected anticipated sales of the Company's older printer products. . . . Accordingly, the statement of loss . . . includes a [debit] of $9,600,000.

Required

1. At which amount did Centronics report its inventory, cost or market value? How can you tell?
2. If the reported inventory of $48,051,000 represents market value, what was the cost of the inventory?

PROBLEM 2

American Hospital Supply Corporation reported using the LIFO inventory method. Its inventory amount was $490.5 million.

Required

1. Suppose that during the period covered by this report, the company made an error that understated its ending inventory by $15 million. What effect would this error have on *cost of goods sold* and *gross margin* of the period? On *cost of goods sold* and *gross margin* of the following period? On *cost of goods sold* and *gross margin* of both periods combined?
2. When American Hospital Supply reported the above amount for inventory, prices were rising. Would FIFO or LIFO have shown a higher gross margin? Why?

SOLUTIONS TO REVIEW PROBLEMS

PROBLEM 1

1. Centronics reported its inventory at *market value*, as indicated by (a) their valuing inventories at LCM and (b) the declining market conditions that caused the company to "include a [debit] of $9,600,000" in "the statement of loss." The company debited the $9,600,000 to a loss account or to cost of goods sold. The credit side of the entry was to Inventory—for a write-down to market value.
2. The cost of inventory before the write-down was $57,651,000 ($48,051,000 + $9,600,000). The $48,051,000 market value is what is left of the original cost. Thus the amount to be carried forward to future periods is $48,051,000.

PROBLEM 2

1. Understating ending inventory by $15 million has the following effects on *cost of goods sold* and *gross margin*:

	Cost of Goods Sold	Gross Margin
Period during which error was made	OVERSTATED by $15 million	UNDERSTATED by $15 million
Following period	UNDERSTATED by $15 million	OVERSTATED by $15 million
Combined total	CORRECTLY STATED	CORRECTLY STATED

2. When prices are rising, FIFO results in higher gross margin than LIFO. FIFO matches against sales revenue the lower inventory costs of beginning inventory and purchases made during the early part of the period.

SUMMARY

1. Account for inventory by the perpetual and periodic systems. Accounting for inventory plays an important part in merchandisers' accounting systems because selling inventory is the heart of their business. Inventory is generally the largest current asset on their balance sheet, and inventory expense—called cost of goods sold—is usually the largest expense on the income statement.

Merchandisers with high-price-tag items generally use the *perpetual inventory system*, which features a running inventory balance. In the past, most merchandisers handling low-price-tag items used the *periodic system*. Recent advances in information technology have led to replacement of periodic inventory systems with perpetual systems. A physical count of inventory is needed in both systems for control purposes.

2. Apply four inventory costing methods: specific unit cost, weighted-average cost, FIFO, and LIFO. Businesses multiply the quantity of inventory items by their unit cost to determine inventory cost. Inventory costing methods are *specific unit cost; weighted-average cost; first-in, first-out (FIFO) cost*; and *last-in, first-out (LIFO) cost*. Only businesses that sell unique items, such as automobiles and jewels, use the specific identification method. Most other companies use the other methods. FIFO reports ending inventory at the most current cost. LIFO reports cost of goods sold at the most current cost.

3. Distinguish between the income effects and the tax effects of the inventory costing methods. When inventory costs increase, LIFO produces the highest cost of goods sold and the lowest income, thus minimizing income taxes. FIFO results in the highest income. The weighted-average cost method avoids the extremes of FIFO and LIFO.

4. Convert a company's net income from the LIFO basis to the FIFO basis. Companies that use LIFO also disclose FIFO inventory amounts that can be used to convert the company's income to the FIFO basis. LIFO liquidation creates a problem because it increases income taxes.

5. Prepare a perpetual inventory record. Some companies combine elements of the perpetual and periodic inventory systems at FIFO cost. Some companies keep perpetual inventory records at weighted-average cost, but few keep such records at LIFO cost.

6. Apply to inventory the lower-of-cost-or-market rule. The *consistency principle* demands that a business stick with the inventory method it chooses. If a change in inventory method is warranted, the company must report the effect of the change on income. The *lower-of-cost-or-market rule*—an example of accounting *conservatism*—requires that businesses report inventory on the balance sheet at the lower of its cost or current replacement value.

7. Compute the effects of inventory errors on the cost of goods sold and on net income. Although inventory overstatements may be counterbalanced by inventory understatements in an adjacent period, effective decision making is aided by accurate inventory information.

8. Estimate inventory by the gross margin method. The *gross margin method* is a technique for estimating the cost of inventory. It comes in handy for preparing interim financial statements and for estimating the cost of inventory destroyed by fire or other casualties.

SELF-STUDY QUESTIONS

1. Which of the following items is the greatest in dollar amount? *(p. 372)*
   a. Beginning inventory
   b. Purchases
   c. Cost of goods available for sale
   d. Ending inventory
   e. Cost of goods sold

2. Sound Warehouse counts 15,000 compact disks, including 1,000 CDs held on consignment, in its Waco, Texas, store. The business has purchased an additional 2,000 units on FOB destination terms. These goods are still in transit. Each CD cost $3.40. The cost of the inventory to report on the balance sheet is *(p. 370)*

   a. $47,600
   b. $51,000
   c. $54,400
   d. $57,800

3. The inventory costing method that best matches current expense with current revenue is *(p. 375)*
   a. Specific unit cost
   b. Weighted-average cost
   c. FIFO
   d. LIFO
   e. FIFO or LIFO, depending on whether inventory costs are increasing or decreasing

4. Why do companies prefer the LIFO inventory method during a period of rising prices? *(p. 377)*

a. Higher reported income

b. Lower income taxes

c. Lower re[...]come

d. Higher en[...]tory

[...]ventory was $35,000, purchases were [...]ales totaled $240,000. With a normal gross [...]5 percent, how much is ending inventory?

a. $25,000   **c.** $97,000

b. $35,000   **d.** $181,000

5. The consistency principle has the most direct impact on *(p. 380)*

   a. Whether to include or exclude an item in inventory

   b. Whether to change from one inventory method to another

   c. Whether to write inventory down to a market value below cost

   d. Whether to use the periodic or the perpetual inventory system

6. Application of the lower-of-cost-or-market rule often results in *(p. 382)*

   a. Higher ending inventory

   b. Lower ending inventory

   c. A counterbalancing error

   d. A change from one inventory method to another

7. An error understated ending inventory of 19X7. This error will *(pp. 383–384)*

   a. Overstate 19X7 cost of sales

   b. Understate 19X8 cost of sales

   c. Not affect owner equity at the end of 19X8

   d. All of the above

9. The year-end entry to close beginning inventory in a perpetual inventory system is *(p. 369)*

   a. Income Summary XXX

         Inventory................................... XXX

   b. Inventory XXX

         Income Summary...................... XXX

   c. Either of the above, depending on whether inventory increased or decreased during the period

   d. Not needed

10. Which of the following statements is true? *(p. 386)*

   a. Separation of duties is not an important element of internal control for inventories.

   b. The perpetual system is used primarily for low-unit-cost inventory.

   c. An annual physical count of inventory is needed regardless of the type of inventory system used.

   d. All the above are true.

Answers to the Self-Study Questions follow the Accounting Vocabulary.

ACCOUNTING VOCABULARY

Conservatism. Concept by which the least favorable figures are presented in the financial statements *(p. 381)*.

Consignment. Transfer of goods by the owner (consignor) to another business (consignee) that, for a fee, sells the inventory on the owner's behalf. The consignee does not take title to the consigned goods *(p. 370)*.

Consistency principle. A business must use the same accounting methods and procedures from period to period *(p. 380)*.

Disclosure principle. A business's financial statements must report enough information for outsiders to make knowledgeable decisions about the business *(p. 380)*.

First-in, first-out (FIFO) method. Inventory costing method by which the first costs into inventory are the first costs out to cost of goods sold. Ending inventory is based on the costs of the most recent purchases *(p. 371)*.

FOB destination. Terms of a transaction that govern when the title to the inventory passes from the seller to the purchaser—when the goods arrive at the purchaser's location *(p. 370)*.

FOB shipping point. Terms of a transaction that govern when the title to the

inventory passes from the seller to the purchaser—when the goods leave the seller's place of business *(p. 370)*.

Gross margin method. A way to estimate inventory on the basis of a rearrangement of the cost-of-goods-sold model: Beginning inventory + Net purchases = Cost of goods available for sale. Cost of goods available for sale – Cost of goods sold = Ending inventory. Also called the gross profit method *(p. 385)*.

Inventory profit. Difference between gross margin figured on the FIFO basis and gross margin figured on the LIFO basis *(p. 376)*.

Last-in, first-out (LIFO) method. Inventory costing method by which the last costs into inventory are the first costs out to cost of goods sold. This method leaves the oldest costs—those of beginning inventory and the earliest purchases of the period—in ending inventory *(p. 372)*.

LIFO reserve. The difference between the LIFO cost of an inventory and what it would be under FIFO *(p. 374)*.

Lower-of-cost-or-market (LCM) rule. Requires that an asset be reported in the financial statements at whichever is lower—its historical cost or its market

value (current replacement cost for inventory) *(p. 382)*.

Materiality concept. A company must perform strictly proper accounting only for items and transactions that are significant to the business's financial statements *(p. 381)*.

Periodic inventory system. The business does not keep a continuous record of the inventory on hand. Instead, at the end of the period, the business makes a physical count of the inventory on hand and applies the appropriate unit costs to determine the cost of the ending inventory *(p. 368)*.

Perpetual inventory system. The business keeps a continuous record for each inventory item to show the inventory on hand at all times *(p. 366)*.

Specific unit cost method. Inventory cost method based on the specific cost of particular units of inventory *(p. 371)*.

Weighted-average cost method. Inventory costing method based on the weighted-average cost of inventory during the period. Weighted-average cost is determined by dividing the cost of goods available for sale by the number of units available. Also called the average cost method *(p. 371)*.

ANSWERS TO SELF-STUDY QUESTIONS

1. c

2. a $(15,000 - 1,000) \times \$3.40 = \$47,600$

3. d

4. b

5. b

6. b

7. d

8. a $\$35,000 + \$146,000 = \$181,000$
   $\$240,000 - (0.35 \times \$240,000) = \$156,000$
   $\$181,000 - \$156,000 = \$25,000$

9. d

10. c

QUESTIONS

1. Why is merchandise inventory so important to a retailer or wholesaler?

2. Suppose your company deals in expensive jewelry. Which inventory system should you use to achieve good internal control over the inventory? If your business is a hardware store that sells low-cost goods, which inventory system would you be likely to use? Why would you choose this system?

3. Identify the accounts debited and credited in the standard purchase and sale entries under (a) the perpetual inventory system and (b) the periodic inventory system.

4. What is the role of the physical count of inventory in (a) the periodic inventory system and (b) the perpetual inventory system?

5. If beginning inventory is $10,000, purchases total $85,000, and ending inventory is $12,700, how much is cost of goods sold?

6. If beginning inventory is $32,000, purchases total $119,000, and cost of goods sold is $127,000, how much is ending inventory?

7. What role does the cost principle play in accounting for inventory?

8. What two items determine the cost of ending inventory?

9. Briefly describe the four generally accepted inventory cost methods. During a period of rising prices, which method produces the highest reported income? Which produces the lowest reported income?

10. Which inventory costing method produces the ending inventory valued at the most current cost? Which method produces the cost-of-goods-sold amount valued at the most current cost?

11. What is the most attractive feature of LIFO? Does LIFO have this advantage during periods of increasing prices or during periods of decreasing prices? Why has LIFO had this advantage recently?

12. Which inventory costing methods are used the most in practice?

13. What is inventory profit? Which method produces it?

14. Identify the chief criticism of LIFO.

15. How does the consistency principle affect accounting for inventory?

16. Briefly describe the influence that the concept of conservatism has on accounting for inventory.

17. Manley Company's inventory has a cost of $48,000 at the end of the year, and the current replacement cost of the inventory is $51,000. At which amount should the company report the inventory on its balance sheet? Suppose the current replacement cost of the inventory is $45,000 instead of $51,000. At which amount should Manley report the inventory? What rule governs your answers to these questions?

18. Gabriel Company accidentally overstated its ending inventory by $10,000 at the end of period 1. Is gross margin of period 1 overstated or understated? Is gross margin of period 2 overstated, understated, or unaffected by the period 1 error? Is total gross margin for the two periods overstated, understated, or correct? Give the reason for your answers.

19. Identify an important method of estimating inventory amounts. What familiar model underlies this estimation method?

20. A fire destroyed the inventory of Olivera Company, but the accounting records were saved. The beginning inventory was $22,000, purchases for the period were $71,000, and sales were $140,000. Olivera's customary gross margin is 45 percent of sales. Use the gross margin method to estimate the cost of the inventory destroyed by the fire.

21. True or false? A company that sells inventory of low unit cost needs no internal controls over the goods. Any inventory loss would probably be small.

EXERCISES

E9-1 Bar-Lev Enterprises' accounting records yield the following data for 19X3:

Inventory, January 1	$ 98,000
Purchases of inventory (on account)..............	1,613,000
Sales of inventory – 1/2 on account;	
1/2 for cash (cost $1,539,000)	2,862,000
Inventory, December 31.................................	?

Recording and reporting transactions under the perpetual and periodic inventory systems
(Obj. 1)

Required

1. Journalize Bar-Lev's inventory transactions for the year—first under the perpetual system, then under the periodic system. Show all amounts in thousands.
2. Report ending inventory, sales, cost of goods sold, and gross margin on the appropriate financial statement (amounts in thousands). Show the computation of cost of goods sold in the periodic system.

E9-2 Baldwin Electric's inventory records for industrial switches indicate the following at October 31:

Computing ending inventory by four methods
(Obj. 2)

Oct. 1	Beginning inventory	10 units @ $160	= 1600
8	Purchase..................................	4 units @ 160	= 640
15	Purchase..................................	11 units @ 170	= 1870
26	Purchase..................................	5 units @ 176	= 880
			4990 –

The physical count of inventory at October 31 indicates that eight units are on hand, and the company owns them.

Required

Compute ending inventory and cost of goods sold, using each of the following methods:

1. Specific unit cost, assuming five $170 units and three $160 units are on hand
2. Weighted-average cost
3. First-in, first-out
4. Last-in, first-out

handwriting:
3×170 =510
5×170 =810
EI FIFO 1390
COGAS 4990
EJ <1390>
3600
8 X 160= 1280   4990 –1280 = 3710
4990 ÷ 30 = 166.33
× 8
1331
ENDING INV   5 @170 + 3 @160 =1330
COST OF GOODS SOLD $4990 –1330= 3660
4990 –1331, 3659

E9-3 Use the data in Exercise 9-2 to journalize, first for the perpetual inventory system, then for the periodic system:

Recording inventory transactions
(Obj. 2)

1. Total October purchases in one summary entry. All purchases were on credit.
2. Total October sales in a summary entry. Assume that the selling price was $300 per unit and that all sales were on credit.
3. October 31 entries for inventory. Baldwin Electric uses LIFO.

E9-4 Use the data in Exercise 9-2 to illustrate the income tax advantage of LIFO over FIFO, assuming that sales revenue is $8,000, operating expenses are $1,100, and the income tax rate is 30 percent.

Computing the tax advantage of LIFO over FIFO
(Obj. 3)

Converting LIFO financial statements to the FIFO basis
(Obj. 4)

E9-5 Hennig Nursery, Inc., reported:

	19X5	19X4
Balance Sheet:		
Inventories—note 4...............	$ 67,800	$ 60,300
Income Statement:		
Cost of goods sold	399,600	381,400
Net income	92,100	86,700
Income tax rate	35%	34%

Note 4. The company determines inventory cost by the last-in, first-out method. If the first-in, first-out method were used, inventories would be $6,100 higher at year end 19X5 and $3,500 higher at year end 19X4.

Required

Show the cost-of-goods-sold computations for 19X5 under LIFO and FIFO. Then compute Hennig's net income for 19X5 if the company had used FIFO.

Change from LIFO to FIFO
(Obj. 4)

E9-6 Walnut Lubricants is considering a change from the LIFO inventory method to the FIFO method. Managers are concerned about the effect of this change on income tax expense and reported net income. If the change is made, it will become effective on March 1. Inventory on hand at February 28 is $63,000. During March, Walnut managers expect sales of $250,000, net purchases between $159,000 and $182,000, and operating expenses, excluding income tax, of $83,000. The income tax rate is 30 percent. Inventories at March 31 are budgeted as follows: FIFO, $85,000; LIFO, $78,000.

Required

Create a spreadsheet model to compute estimated net income for March under FIFO and LIFO. Format your answer as follows:

	A	B	C	D	E
1		**Walnut Lubricants**			
2		**Estimated Income under FIFO and LIFO**			
3		**March 19XX**			
4					
5		FIFO	LIFO	FIFO	LIFO
6					
7	Sales	$250,000	$250,000	$250,000	$250,000
8					
9	Cost of goods sold				
10	Beginning inventory	63,000	63,000	63,000	63,000
11	Net purchases	159,000	159,000	182,000	182,000
12					
13	Cost of goods available				
14	Ending inventory	85,000	78,000	85,000	78,000
15					
16	Cost of goods sold	137,000	144,000	160,000	
17					
18	Gross margin	113,000			
19	Operating expenses	83,000	83,000	83,000	83,000
20					
21	Income from operations	30,000			
22	Income tax expense	9000.00			
23					
24	Net income	$ 45000	$	$	$
25					

E9-7 CPC International, Inc., maker of Hellmann's mayonnaise, Mazola corn oil, and other foods, included the following in its annual report:

Note disclosure of a change in inventory method
(Obj. 3, 4)

> *Inventories* are stated at the lower of cost or market....Outside the United States, inventories generally are valued at average cost. In the United States, vegetable oils and corn are valued at cost on the last-in, first-out method. Other United States inventories are valued at cost on the first-in, first-out method. Had the first-in, first-out method been used for all United States inventories, the carrying value of these inventories would have increased by $20.3 million.

Suppose CPC International were to change to the FIFO method for all its inventories. Write the note to disclose this accounting change in the company's financial statements. Indicate the effect of the change on income before income tax.

E9-8 Reatta String World Music Center carries a large inventory of guitars, keyboards, and other musical instruments. Because each item is expensive, Reatta uses a perpetual inventory system. Company records indicate the following for a particular line of Casio keyboards:

Computing the ending amount of a perpetual inventory
(Obj. 5)

Date	Item	Quantity	Unit Cost
May 1	Balance	5	$90
6	Sale	3	
8	Purchase	11	95
17	Sale	4	
30	Sale	3	

Compute ending inventory and cost of goods sold for keyboards by the FIFO method. Also show the computation of cost of goods sold.

E9-9 From the following inventory records of Bornhauser Corporation for 19X7, prepare the company's income statement through gross margin. Apply the lower-of-cost-or-market rule.

The effect of lower-of-cost-or-market on the income statement
(Obj. 6)

Beginning inventory (average cost)...................... 300 @ $41.63 = $ 12,489
        (replacement cost)............... 300 @ 41.91 =   12,573
Purchases during the year .... 2,600 @ 44.50 = 115,700
Ending inventory (average cost) .... 400 @ 45.07 =   18,028
        (replacement cost).................... 400 @ 42.10 =   16,840
Sales during the year .... 2,500 @ 80.00* = 200,000

*Selling price per unit.

E9-10 Wolk Company's income statement for March reported the following data:

Applying the lower-of-cost-or-market rule
(Obj. 6, 7)

Income Statement:

Sales revenue		$89,000
Cost of goods sold:		
Beginning inventory...............................	$17,200	
Net purchases	51,700	
Cost of goods available for sale	68,900	
Ending inventory...................................	23,800	
Cost of goods sold		45,100
Gross margin		$43,900

Before the financial statements were released, it was discovered that the current replacement cost of ending inventory was $20,400. Correct the above data to include the lower-of-cost-or-market value of ending inventory. Also, show how inventory would be reported on the balance sheet.

Correcting an inventory error
(Obj. 7)

E9-11 Chief Auto Supply reported the following comparative income statement for the years ended September 30, 19X8 and 19X7:

CHIEF AUTO SUPPLY INCOME STATEMENTS FOR THE YEAR ENDED SEPTEMBER 30,				
	19X8		**19X7**	
Sales revenue		$137,300		$121,700
Cost of goods sold:				
Beginning inventory..................	$14,000 12500		$12,800	
Net purchases.............................	72,000		66,000	
Cost of goods available...............	86,000		78,800	
Ending inventory........................	16,600		14,000 12900	
Cost of goods sold		69,400		64,800
Gross margin...............................		67,900		56,900
Operating expenses		30,300		26,100
Net income....................................		$ 37,600		$ 30,800

During 19X8 accountants for the company discovered that ending 19X7 inventory was overstated by $1,500. Prepare the corrected comparative income statement for the two-year period. What was the effect of the error on net income for the two years combined? Explain your answer.

Estimating inventory by the gross margin method
(Obj. 8)

E9-12 Parrish Unpainted Furniture began April with inventory of $42,000. The business made net purchases of $37,600 and had net sales of $60,000 before a fire destroyed the company's inventory. For the past several years, Parrish's gross margin on sales has been 55 percent. Estimate the cost of the inventory destroyed by the fire.

CHALLENGE EXERCISES

Inventory policy decisions
(Obj. 2, 3)

E9-13 For each of the following situations, identify the inventory method that you are using or would prefer to use, or, given the use of a particular method, state the strategy that you would follow to accomplish your goal.

a. Inventory costs are decreasing, and your company's board of directors wants to minimize income taxes.

b. Inventory costs are increasing. Your company uses LIFO and is having an unexpectedly good year. It is near year end, and you need to keep net income from increasing too much.

c. Inventory costs have been stable for several years, and you expect costs to remain stable for the indefinite future. (Give your reason for your choice of method.)

d. Company management, like that of IBM, prefers a middle-of-the-road inventory policy that avoids extremes.

e. Your inventory turns over very rapidly, and the company uses a perpetual inventory system. Inventory costs are increasing, and the company prefers to report high income.

f. Suppliers of your inventory are threatening a labor strike, and it may be difficult for your company to obtain inventory. This situation could increase your income taxes.

LIFO liquidation
(Obj. 2)

E9-14 Whirlpool Corporation, the world's leading manufacturer of major home appliances, reported these figures for 19X1 (in millions of dollars):

Income statement (adapted):

Net revenues...	$6,757
Cost of products sold............................	4,967
Operating expenses................................	1,397
Other expense (net)	93
Earnings before income taxes...............	300
Income taxes	130
Net earnings	$ 170

Note 4 of the financial statements disclosed:

Liquidation of prior years' LIFO inventory layers increased net earnings $8 million.

Required

1. Explain what the LIFO liquidation means and why it affects net earnings.
2. Would Whirlpool management be pleased or displeased at the increase in income due to the LIFO liquidation? Give your reason.
3. Prepare a revised income statement for Whirlpool Corporation if no LIFO liquidation had occurred. The income tax rate was 43.33 percent.

PROBLEMS

(GROUP A)

P9-1A Elsinore Sporting Goods began March with 50 units of inventory that cost $19 each. The sale price of each was $36. During March Elsinore completed these inventory transactions:

Using the perpetual and periodic inventory systems (Obj. 1)

		Units	Unit Cost	Unit Sale Price
March 2	Purchase	12	$20	$37
8	Sale	27	19	36
13	Sale	23	19	36
		1	20	37
17	Purchase	24	20	37
22	Sale	31	20	37
29	Purchase	24	21	39

Required

1. The above data are taken from Elsinore's perpetual inventory records. Which cost method does Elsinore use?
2. Compute Elsinore's cost of goods sold for March under the
   a. Perpetual inventory system
   b. Periodic inventory system
3. Compute gross margin for March.

P9-2A Flostan Vision Center began the year with 140 units of inventory that cost $79 each. During the year Flostan made the following purchases:

Computing inventory by three methods (Obj. 2)

Feb. 3	217 @ $81
Apr. 12	95 @ 82
Aug. 8	210 @ 84
Oct. 24	248 @ 87

The company uses the periodic inventory system, and the physical count at December 31 indicates that ending inventory consists of 229 units.

Required

Compute the ending inventory and cost-of-goods-sold amounts under (1) weighted-average cost, (2) FIFO cost, and (3) LIFO cost. Round weighted-average cost per unit to the nearest cent, and round all other amounts to the nearest dollar.

P9-3A The Hub specializes in men's shirts. The store began operations on January 1, 19X1, with an inventory of 200 shirts that cost $13 each. During the year the store purchased inventory as follows:

Computing inventory, cost of goods sold, and FIFO inventory profits (Obj. 2, 3)

Purchase no. 1	110 @ $14
Purchase no. 2	80 @ 15
Purchase no. 3	320 @ 15
Purchase no. 4	100 @ 17

The ending inventory consists of 150 shirts.

Required

1. Complete the following tabulation, rounding average cost to the nearest cent and all other amounts to the nearest dollar.

	Ending Inventory	Cost of Goods Sold
a. Weighted-average cost	_____	_____
b. FIFO cost	_____	_____
c. LIFO cost	_____	_____

2. Compute the amount of inventory profit under FIFO.
3. Which method produces the most current ending inventory cost? Which method produces the most current cost-of-goods-sold amount? Give the reason for your answers.

Preparing an income statement directly from the accounts (Obj. 2, 3)

P9-4A The records of The Office Depot include the following accounts for one of its products at December 31 of the current year:

Inventory

Jan. 1 Balance	300 units @ $3.00	1,215
	100 units @ 3.15	

Purchases

Feb. 6	800 units @$3.15	2,520
May 19	600 units @ 3.35	2,010
Aug. 12	460 units @ 3.50	1,610
Oct. 4	800 units @ 3.70	2,960
Dec. 31 Balance		9,100

Sales Revenue

Mar. 12	500 units @ $4.10	2,050
June 9	1,100 units @ 4.20	4,620
Aug. 21	300 units @ 4.50	1,350
Nov. 2	600 units @ 4.50	2,700
Dec. 18	100 units @ 4.80	480
Dec. 31 Balance		11,200

Required

1. Compute the quantities of goods in (a) ending inventory and (b) cost of goods sold during the year.
2. Prepare a partial income statement through gross margin under the weighted-average cost, FIFO cost, and LIFO cost methods. Round weighted-average cost to the nearest cent and all other amounts to the nearest dollar.

Converting an actual company's reported income from the LIFO basis to the FIFO basis (Obj. 4)

P9-5A J. C. Penney, Inc., uses the LIFO method for inventories. In a recent annual report, Penney reported these amounts on the balance sheet (in millions):

	End of Fiscal Year	
	19X6	19X5
Merchandise inventories...............	$2,657	$2,613

A note to the financial statements indicated that if another method (assume FIFO) had been used, inventories would have been higher by $405 million at the end of the fiscal year 19X6 and higher by $356 million at the end of 19X5. The income statement reported sales revenue of $16,365 million and cost of goods sold of $10,969 million for 19X6.

Required

1. Show the computation of Penney's cost of goods sold and gross margin for fiscal year 19X6 by the LIFO method as actually reported.
2. Compute Penney's cost of goods sold and gross margin for 19X6 by the FIFO method.
3. Which method makes the company look better in 19X6? Give your reason. If Penney used the FIFO method, what would be the amount of inventory profit for 19X6?
4. Assume an income tax rate of 35 percent. How much in taxes did Penney save by using LIFO?
5. How will what you learned in this problem help you (a) evaluate an investment; (b) manage a business?

P9-6A United Technologies manufactures high-technology products used in the aviation and other industries. Perhaps its most famous product is the Pratt & Whitney aircraft engine. Assume the following data for United Technologies' product SR450:

Using the perpetual inventory system; applying the lower-of-cost-or-market rule (Obj. 5, 6)

	Purchased	Sold	Balance
Dec. 31, 19X1			110 @ $5 = $550
Feb. 10, 19X2	80 @ $6 = $480		
Apr. 7		160	
May 29	110 @ 7 = 770		
July 13		120	
Oct. 4	100 @ 9 = 900		
Nov. 22		80	

Required

1. Prepare a perpetual inventory record for product SR450, using the FIFO method.
2. Assume that United Technologies sold the 160 units on April 7 on account for $13 each. Record the sale and related cost of goods sold in the general journal under the FIFO method.
3. Suppose the current replacement cost of the ending inventory of product SR450 is $305 at December 31, 19X2. Use the answer to Requirement 1 to compute the lower-of-cost-or-market (LCM) value of the ending inventory.

P9-7A The accounting records of the Swick's Barbeque Restaurants chain show these data (in millions):

Correcting inventory errors over a three-year period (Obj. 7)

	19X3		19X2		19X1	
Net sales revenue		$210		$165		$170
Cost of goods sold:						
Beginning inventory	$ 15		$ 25		$ 40	
Net purchases	135		100		90	
Cost of goods available	150		125		130	
Less ending inventory	30		15		25	
Cost of goods sold		120		110		105
Gross margin		90		55		65
Operating expenses		74		38		46
Net income		$ 16		$ 17		$ 19

In early 19X4, a team of internal auditors discovered that the ending inventory of 19X1 had been understated by $8 million. Also, the ending inventory for 19X3 had been overstated by $5 million. The ending inventory at December 31, 19X2, was correct.

Required

1. Prepare corrected income statements for the three years.
2. State whether each year's net income as reported here and the related owners' equity amounts are understated or overstated. For each incorrect figure, indicate the amount of the understatement or overstatement.

Estimating inventory by the gross
margin method; preparing a
multiple-step income statement
(Obj. 8)

P9-8A Assume that Burger King estimates its inventory by the gross margin method when preparing monthly financial statements. For the past two years, gross margin has averaged 25 percent of net sales. Assume further that the company's inventory records for stores in the southeastern region reveal the following data:

Inventory, March 1	$ 392,000
Transactions during March:	
Purchases...	6,585,000
Purchase discounts..........................	149,000
Purchase returns	8,000
Sales..	8,657,000
Sales returns...................................	17,000

Required

1. Estimate the March 31 inventory using the gross margin method.
2. Prepare the March income statement through gross margin for the Burger King stores in the southeastern region. Use the multiple-step format.

(GROUP B)

P9-1B AAdvantage Luggage Company began August 19X8 with 30 units of inventory that cost $40 each. The sale price of these units was $70. During August AAdvantage experienced these inventory transactions:

		Units	Unit Cost	Unit Sale Price
Aug. 3	Sale...	16	$40	$70
8	Purchase...	80	41	72
11	Sale...	14	40	70
	....	16	41	72
19	Sale...	9	41	72
24	Sale...	35	41	72
30	Purchase...	18	42	73
31	Sale...	6	41	72

Required

1. The above data are taken from AAdvantage's perpetual inventory records. Which cost method does AAdvantage use?
2. Compute AAdvantage's cost of goods sold for August under the
    a. Perpetual inventory system
    b. Periodic inventory system
3. Compute gross margin for August.

P9-2B Nemmer Electric Co. began the year with 73 units of inventory that cost $26 each. During the year Nemmer made the following purchases:

March 11	....	113 @ $27
May 2	....	81 @ 29
July 19	....	167 @ 32
Nov. 18	....	44 @ 35

The company uses the periodic inventory system, and the physical count at December 31 indicates that ending inventory consists of 91 units.

Required

Compute the ending inventory and cost-of-goods-sold amounts under (1) weighted-average cost, (2) FIFO cost, and (3) LIFO cost. Round weighted-average cost per unit to the nearest cent, and round all other amounts to the nearest dollar.

P9-3B Sharp Beverage Distributors specializes in soft drinks. The business began operations on January 1, 19X1, with an inventory of 500 cases of drinks that cost $2.01 each. During the first month of operations the store purchased inventory as follows:

Computing inventory, cost of goods sold, and FIFO inventory profits (Obj. 2, 3)

Purchase no. 1	60 @ $2.10
Purchase no. 2	120 @ 2.35
Purchase no. 3	600 @ 2.50
Purchase no. 4	40 @ 2.95

The ending inventory consists of 500 cases of drinks.

Required

1. Complete the following tabulation, rounding average cost to the nearest cent and all other amounts to the nearest dollar:

	Ending Inventory	Cost of Goods Sold
a. Weighted-average cost	_____	_____
b. FIFO cost	_____	_____
c. LIFO cost	_____	_____

2. Compute the amount of inventory profit under FIFO.
3. Which method produces the most current ending inventory cost? Which method produces the most current cost-of-goods-sold amount? Give the reason for your answers.

P9-4B The records of Barton Creek Golf Products include the following accounts for one of its products at December 31 of the current year.

Preparing an income statement directly from the accounts (Obj. 2, 3)

Inventory

Jan.	1 Balance {700 units @ $7.00}	4,900	

Purchases

Jan.	6	300 units @ $7.05	2,115	
Mar.	19	1,100 units @ 7.35	8,085	
June	22	8,400 units @ 7.50	63,000	
Oct.	4	500 units @ 8.50	4,250	
Dec.	31 Balance		77,450	

Sales Revenue

		Feb.	5	1,000 units @ $12.00	12,000
		Apr.	10	700 units @ 12.10	8,470
		July	31	1,800 units @ 13.25	23,850
		Sep.	4	3,500 units @ 13.50	47,250
		Nov.	27	3,100 units @ 14.75	45,725
		Dec.	31	Balance	137,295

Required

1. Compute the quantities of goods in (a) ending inventory and (b) cost of goods sold during the year.
2. Prepare a partial income statement through gross margin under the weighted-average cost, FIFO cost, and LIFO cost methods.

Converting an actual company's reported income from the LIFO basis to the FIFO basis (Obj. 4)

P9-5B Colgate-Palmolive Company uses the LIFO method for inventories. In a recent annual report, Colgate-Palmolive reported these amounts on the balance sheet (in millions):

	December 31,	
	19X9	19X8
Inventories...............	$676	$692

A note to the financial statements indicated that if current cost (approximate FIFO) had been used, inventories would have been higher by $30 million at the end of 19X9 and higher by $28 million at the end of 19X8. The income statement reported sales revenue of $6,060 million and cost of goods sold of $3,296 million for 19X9.

Required

1. Show the computation of Colgate-Palmolive's cost of goods sold and gross margin for 19X9 by the LIFO method as actually reported.
2. Compute Colgate-Palmolive's cost of goods sold and gross margin for 19X9 by the FIFO method.
3. Which method makes the company look better in 19X9? Give your reason. If Colgate-Palmolive used the FIFO method, what would be the amount of inventory profit for 19X9?
4. Assume an income tax rate of 35 percent. How much in taxes did Colgate-Palmolive save by using LIFO?
5. How will what you learned in this problem help you (a) evaluate an investment; (b) manage a business?

Using the perpetual inventory system; applying the lower-of-cost-or-market rule (Obj. 5, 6)

P9-6B Midas is a popular brand of automobile mufflers. Assume the following data for a Midas Muffler store:

	Purchased		Sold	Balance
Dec. 31, 19X3				120 @ $6 = $720
Mar. 15, 19X4	50 @ $7	= $350		
Apr. 10			80	
May 29	100 @ 8.50	= 850		
Aug. 3			130	
Nov. 16	70 @ 9	= 630		
Dec. 12			70	

Required

1. Prepare a perpetual inventory record for Midas, using the FIFO method.
2. Assume that Midas sold the 130 units on August 3 on account for $22 each. Record the sale and related cost of goods in the general journal under the FIFO method.
3. Suppose the current replacement cost of the ending inventory of this Midas store is $750 at December 31, 19X4. Use the answer to Requirement 1 to compute the lower-of-cost-or-market (LCM) value of the ending inventory.

Correcting inventory errors over a three-year period (Obj. 7)

P9-7B The Hillsboro Window Tinting books show these data (in millions):

	19X6		19X5		19X4	
Net sales revenue		$360		$285		$244
Cost of goods sold:						
Beginning inventory.................................	$ 65		$ 55		$ 70	
Net purchases..	195		135		130	
Cost of goods available	260		190		200	
Less ending inventory..............................	70		65		55	
Cost of goods sold....................................		190		125		145
Gross margin...		170		160		99
Operating expenses......................................		113		109		76
Net income		$ 57		$ 51		$ 23

In early 19X7, a team of internal auditors discovered that the ending inventory of 19X4 had been overstated by $12 million. Also, the ending inventory for 19X6 had been understated by $8 million. The ending inventory at December 31, 19X5, was correct.

Required

1. Prepare corrected income statements for the three years.
2. State whether each year's net income and owners' equity amounts are understated or overstated. For each incorrect figure, indicate the amount of the understatement or overstatement.

P9-8B Seiko Appliance Company estimates its inventory by the gross margin method when preparing monthly financial statements. For the past two years, the gross margin has averaged 40 percent of net sales. The company's inventory records for stores in the southwestern region reveal the following data:

Estimating inventory by the gross margin method; preparing a multiple-step income statement (Obj. 8)

Inventory, July 1............................	$ 267,000
Transactions during July:	
Purchases....................................	3,789,000
Purchase discounts.....................	26,000
Purchase returns.........................	12,000
Sales..	6,430,000
Sales returns	25,000

Required

1. Estimate the July 31 inventory, using the gross margin method.
2. Prepare the July income statement through gross margin for the Seiko Appliance Company stores in the southwestern region. Use the multiple-step format.

EXTENDING YOUR KNOWLEDGE

DECISION PROBLEMS

1. Safari Outback is nearing the end of its first year of operations. The company made the following inventory purchases:

Assessing the impact of a year-end purchase of inventory (Obj. 2)

January	1,000 units @	$100	=	$100,000
March	1,000	100		100,000
May	1,000	115		115,000
July	1,000	130		130,000
September	1,000	140		140,000
November	1,000	160		[160,000
Totals	6,000			$745,000

Sales for the year will be 5,000 units for $1,200,000 revenue. Expenses other than cost of goods sold and income taxes will be $200,000. The president of the company is undecided about whether to adopt FIFO or LIFO.

The company has storage capacity for 5,000 additional units of inventory. Inventory prices are expected to stay at $160 per unit for the next few months. The president is considering purchasing 4,000 additional units of inventory at $160 each before the end of the year. He wishes to know how the purchase would affect net income under both FIFO and LIFO. The income tax rate is 40 percent, and income tax is an expense.

Required

1. To aid company decision making, prepare income statements under FIFO and under LIFO, both without and with the year-end purchase of 4,000 units of inventory at $160 per unit.
2. Compare net income under FIFO without and with the year-end purchase. Make the same comparison under LIFO. Under which method does the year-end purchase have the greater effect on net income?
3. Under which method can a year-end purchase be made in order to manipulate net income?

Assessing the impact of the inventory costing method on the financial statements
(Obj. 2, 3, 4)

2. The inventory costing method chosen by a company can affect the financial statements and thus the decisions of the users of those statements.

Required

1. A leading accounting researcher stated that one inventory costing method reports the most recent costs in the income statement, while another method reports the most recent costs in the balance sheet. In this person's opinion, the result is that one or the other of the statements is "inaccurate" when prices are rising. What did the researcher mean?
2. Conservatism is an accepted accounting concept. Would you want management to be conservative in accounting for inventory if you were (a) a shareholder and (b) a prospective shareholder? Give your reason.
3. Elgin Ltd. follows conservative accounting and writes the value of its inventory of bicycles down to market, which has declined below cost. The following year, an unexpected cycling craze results in a demand for bicycles that far exceeds supply, and the market price increases above the previous cost. What effect will conservatism have on the income of Elgin over the two years?

ETHICAL ISSUE

During 19X6, Bigelo-Arnold Company changed to the LIFO method of accounting for inventory. Suppose that during 19X7 Bigelo-Arnold changes back to the FIFO method and the following year switches back to LIFO again.

Required

1. What would you think of a company's ethics if it changed accounting methods every year?
2. What accounting principle would changing methods every year violate?
3. Who can be harmed when a company changes its accounting methods too often? How?

FINANCIAL STATEMENT PROBLEMS

Inventories
(Obj. 2, 3, 4)

1. The notes are an important part of a company's financial statements, giving valuable details that would clutter the tabular data presented in the statements. This problem will help you learn to use a company's inventory notes. Refer to the Lands' End, Inc., statements and related notes in Appendix A. Answer the following questions.

1. How much was Lands' End's merchandise inventory at January 28, 1994? At January 29, 1993?
2. How does Lands' End value its inventories? Which cost method does the company use?
3. By rearranging the cost-of-goods-sold formula, you can solve for net purchases, which are not disclosed in Lands' End's statements. Show how to compute net purchases during the year ended January 28, 1994 (fiscal 1994).
4. Compute the amounts of cost of sales (same as cost of goods sold) and gross margin that Lands' End would have reported for fiscal 1994 if the company had used the FIFO method for inventory. The Inventory note gives relevant information on the difference between LIFO and FIFO costs of beginning and ending inventory. You are a top manager of Lands' End. Which

inventory method would you select if your motive were to report the maximum acceptable gross margin? Which method would you select to minimize income tax?

2.   Obtain the annual report of a real company *that includes Inventories among its current assets.* Answer these questions about the company.

Inventories (Obj. 2, 3, 4)

1. How much were the company's total inventories at the end of the current year? At the end of the preceding year?

2. How does the company value its inventories? Which cost method or methods does the company use?

3. Depending on the nature of the company's business, would you expect the company to use a periodic inventory system or a perpetual system? Give your reason.

4. By rearranging the cost-of-goods-sold formula, you can solve for net purchases, which are not disclosed. Show how to compute the company's net purchases during the current year. Examine the company's note titled *Inventories, Merchandise inventories,* or a similar term. If the company discloses several categories of inventories, including a title similar to Finished Goods, use the beginning and ending balances of Finished Goods for the computation of net purchases. If only one category of Inventories is disclosed, use these beginning and ending balances.

5. If the company does not use the LIFO method for inventories, you can omit this requirement. If the company uses LIFO, convert gross margin from the LIFO basis, as reported, to the FIFO basis, which approximates current cost. For this computation, assume that the entire amount of the excess of FIFO (or current) cost over LIFO cost applies to Finished Goods inventories. If your motive were to maximize reported income, would you prefer LIFO or FIFO? If your goal were to minimize income tax, which method is preferable?

Chapter 10
Plant Assets, Intangible Assets, and Related Expenses

> *"Wal-Mart's aggresive approach to customer service and sales productivity has allowed us to remain a leader in today's marketplace. Capital expenditures in technology and customer-oriented facilities continue to allow us to meet these primary objectives and position ourselves for the future."*

STEPHEN HUNTER,
FINANCIAL OPERATIONS
MANAGER OF WAL-MART
STORES, INC.

A published letter ... ... ecutive of Wal-Mart Stores, Inc., included ... ...ving:

"Wal-Mart Supercenters, ...hich combine a full-line supermarket and Wal-Mart store under one roof, completed their third year of innovation and refinement. These six stores and the additions planned for calendar year 1992 of 12 to 15 new units will put us on track to grow this complete one-stop shopping format more aggressively as the 90's progress. Typically utilizing 160,000 to 180,000 square feet, Supercenters provide a powerful tool for Wal-Mart's continued growth and leading market presence.

We invested $2,500,000,000 in capital expenditures just last year and current plans for fiscal 1993 call for additional capital expenditures of $2,800,000,000. We are carefully building and maintaining systems, distribution and transportation infrastructure capacity to not just sustain growth, but improve our productivity and reduce expenses in existing operations.

Moving more merchandise, faster, further, and less expensively than ever before, is how we describe the Distribution and Transportation group's accomplishments this past year and their challenge for the coming decade. . . ." *Source: 1992 Annual Report, Wal-Mart Stores, Inc., p. 2.*

• • • • •

*W*hat does it take for Wal-Mart to serve its millions of customers? Billions of dollars invested in stores and merchandise. In Chapter 9 we looked at merchandise inventory. In this chapter we consider accounting for the long-term assets used in the operation of a business.

Chapter Objectives

After studying this chapter, you should be able to

1. Identify the elements of a plant asset's cost

2. Explain the concept of depreciation

3. Account for depreciation by four methods

4. Identify the best depreciation method for income tax purposes

5. Account for disposal of plant assets

6. Account for natural resource assets and depletion

7. Account for intangible assets and amortization

8. Distinguish capital expenditures from revenue expenditures

In recent years Wal-Mart has opened stores at a dizzying pace. The company's stated goal is to move "more merchandise, faster, further, and less expensively than ever before." To accomplish this objective, Wal-Mart must continually upgrade its stores and its distribution and transportation facilities—warehouses, truck fleets, and so on.

The chief executive mentioned *capital expenditures*, a term used often in the business press. These are the costs of acquiring and adding to buildings, automobiles, and other long-lived assets. Capital expenditures are a major sign of growth in both businesses and nonprofit organizations such as churches, hospitals, and colleges and universities. Without capital expenditures, an organization falls behind its competitors. Wal-Mart and other leading companies work hard to keep that from happening.

Long-lived assets used in the operation of the business and not held for sale as investments are further divided into plant assets and intangible assets. **Plant assets,** or *fixed assets,* are those long-lived assets that are tangible—for instance, land, buildings, equipment, and oil. Their physical form provides their usefulness. Of the plant assets, land is unique. Its cost is *not* depreciated—expensed over time—because its usefulness does not decrease as does that of other assets. Most companies report plant assets under the heading Property, Plant, and Equipment.

Intangible assets are useful not because of their physical characteristics but because of the special rights they carry. Patents, copyrights, and trademarks are intangible assets. Accounting for intangibles is similar to accounting for plant assets.

Accounting for intangibles has its own terminology. Different names apply to the individual plant assets and their corresponding expense accounts, as shown in Exhibit 10-1.

EXHIBIT 10-1

Terminology Used in Accounting for Plant Assets and Intangible Assets

Asset Account on the Balance Sheet	Related Expense Account on the Income Statement
Plant Assets	
Land	None
Buildings, Machinery and Equipment, Furniture and Fixtures, and Land Improvements	Depreciation
Natural Resources	Depletion
Intangibles	Amortization

The first half of the chapter discusses and illustrates how to identify the cost of a plant asset and how to expense its cost. The second half considers disposing of plant assets and how to account for natural resources, intangible assets, and capital expenditures. Unless stated otherwise, we describe accounting in accordance with generally accepted accounting principles for financial statement reporting, as distinguished from reporting to the IRS for income tax purposes.

The Cost of a Plant Asset

OBJECTIVE 1

Identify the elements of a plant asset's cost

The cost principle directs a business to carry an asset on the balance sheet at the amount paid for the asset. The *cost of a plant asset* is the purchase price, applicable taxes, purchase commissions, and all other amounts paid to acquire the asset and to ready it for its intended use. Because the types of costs differ for various categories of plant assets, we discuss the major groups individually.

Land

The cost of land includes its purchase price (cash plus any note payable given), brokerage commission, survey fees, legal fees, and any back property taxes that the purchaser pays. Land cost also includes any expenditures for grading and clearing the land and for demolishing or removing any unwanted buildings.

The cost of land does *not* include the cost of fencing, paving, sprinkler systems, and lighting. These separate plant assets—called land improvements—are subject to depreciation.

Suppose Wal-Mart signs a $300,000 note payable to purchase 20 acres of land for a new store site. Wal-Mart also pays $10,000 in back property tax, $8,000 in transfer taxes, $5,000 for removal of an old building, a $1,000 survey fee, and $260,000 to pave the parking lot, all in cash. What is the cost of this land?

Purchase price of land		$300,000
Add related costs:		
Back property tax	$10,000	
Transfer taxes	8,000	
Removal of building	5,000	
Survey fee	1,000	
Total incidental costs		24,000
Total cost of land		$324,000

Wal-Mart's entry to record purchase of the land is

Land	324,000	
Note Payable		300,000
Cash		24,000

Buildings

The cost of constructing a building includes architectural fees, building permits, contractors' charges, and payments for material, labor, and overhead. The time between the first expenditure for a new building and its completion can be many months, even years, and the number of separate expenditures numerous. Computers keep track of these details efficiently and assist in monitoring costs as they accumulate.

When an existing building (new or old) is purchased, its cost includes the purchase price, brokerage commission, sales and other taxes, and cash or credit expenditures for repairing and renovating the building for its intended purpose. The Wal-Mart Supercenters mentioned in the chapter-opening story would be classified as buildings.

Machinery and Equipment

The cost of machinery and equipment includes its purchase price (less any discounts), transportation charges, insurance while in transit, sales and other taxes, purchase commission, installation costs, and any expenditures to test the asset before it is placed in service.

Land Improvements

In the Wal-Mart land example, the cost to pave the parking lot ($260,000) is not part of the cost of the land. Instead, the $260,000 would be recorded in a separate account entitled Land Improvements. This account includes costs for such other items

Short Exercise: Which of the following would you include in the cost of machinery: (1) installation charges; (2) testing of the machine; (3) repair to machinery due to installer's error; (4) first-year maintenance cost? *A:* Include 1 and 2, not 3 or 4.

Short Exercise: How would a business divide a $120,000 lump-sum purchase price for land, building, and equipment with estimated market values of $40,000, $95,000, and $15,000, respectively?

A:

	Estimated Market Value	% of Total
Land..........	$ 40,000	26.7
Building	95,000	63.3
Equipment	15,000	10.0
	$150,000	100

	Allocation of Purchase Price
Land	$ 32,000
Building...........	76,000
Equipment	12,000
	$120,000

as driveways, fences, and sprinkler systems. Although these assets are located on the land, they are subject to decay, and therefore their cost should be depreciated. Also, the cost of a new building constructed on the land is a debit to the asset account Building.

Lump-Sum (or Basket) Purchases of Assets

Businesses often purchase several assets as a group, or in a "basket," for a single lump-sum amount. For example, a company may pay one price for land and an office building. The company must identify the cost of each asset. The total cost is divided between the assets according to their relative sales (or market) values. This allocation technique is called the *relative-sales-value method.*

Suppose Xerox Corporation purchases land and a building in Kansas City for a Midwestern sales office. The building sits on two acres of land, and the combined purchase price of land and building is $2,800,000. An appraisal indicates that the land's market (sales) value is $300,000 and that the building's market (sales) value is $2,700,000.

An accountant first figures the ratio of each asset's market value to the total market value. Total appraised value is $3,000,000. Thus land, valued at $300,000, is 10 percent of the total market value. The building's appraised value is 90 percent of the total:

Asset	Market (Sales) Value		Total Market Value		Percentage
Land	$ 300,000	÷	$3,000,000	=	10%
Building	2,700,000	÷	3,000,000	=	90%
Total	$3,000,000				100%

The percentage for each asset is multiplied by the total purchase price to give its cost in the purchase:

Asset	Total Purchase Price		Percentage		Allocated Cost
Land	$2,800,000	×	0.10	=	$ 280,000
Building	$2,800,000	×	0.90	=	2,520,000
Total			1.00		$2,800,000

If Xerox Corporation were to buy land and a building in Kansas City, the company would account for the lump-sum purchase by the relative-sales-value method.

If Xerox pays cash, the entry to record the purchase of the land and building is:

Land	280,000	
Building..................	2,520,000	
Cash		2,800,000

Depreciation of Plant Assets

OBJECTIVE 2
Explain the concept of depreciation

The process of allocating a plant asset's cost to expense over the period the asset is used is called *depreciation.* This process is designed to match the asset's expense against the revenue generated over the asset's life, as the matching principle directs. Exhibit 10-2 shows this process for the purchase of a Boeing 737 jet by United Airlines. The primary purpose of depreciation accounting is to measure income. Of less importance is the need to account for the asset's decline in usefulness.

Suppose Wal-Mart buys a computer for use in its accounting system. Wal-Mart believes it will get four years of service from the computer, which will then be worth-

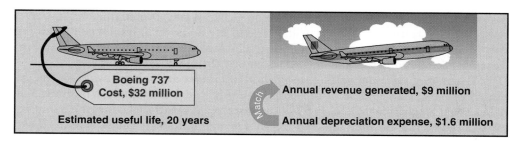

EXHIBIT 10-2
Depreciation and the Matching of Expense to Revenue

less. Using straight-line depreciation (which we discuss later in this chapter), Wal-Mart expenses one-quarter of the asset's cost in each of its four years of use.

Let's contrast what depreciation accounting is with what it is *not*. (1) *Depreciation is not a process of valuation.* Businesses do not record depreciation based on appraisals of their plant assets made at the end of each period. Instead, businesses allocate the asset's cost to the periods of its useful life based on a specific depreciation method. (We discuss these methods in this chapter.) (2) *Depreciation does not mean that the business sets aside cash to replace assets as they become fully depreciated.* Establishing such a cash fund is a decision entirely separate from depreciation. *Accumulated depreciation* is that portion of the plant asset's cost that has already been recorded as an expense. ◀▥▥ Accumulated depreciation does not represent a growing amount of cash.

◀▥▥ ◀▥▥ ◀▥▥ We learned in Chapter 3 (p. 99) that accumulated depreciation is the sum of all depreciation expense from the date a plant asset was acquired. Depreciation expense is the depreciation amount for the current period only.

Determining the Useful Life of a Plant Asset

No asset (other than land) offers an unlimited useful life. For some plant assets physical *wear and tear* from operations and from the elements may be the primary cause of depreciation. For example, physical deterioration takes its toll on the usefulness of trucks that move Wal-Mart merchandise from warehouses to the discount stores. The store fixtures used to display merchandise are also subject to physical wear and tear.

Assets such as computers, other electronic equipment, and airplanes may be *obsolete* before they physically deteriorate. An asset is obsolete when another asset can do the job better or more efficiently. Thus an asset's useful life may be much shorter than its physical life. Accountants usually depreciate computers over a short period of time—perhaps four years—even though they know the computers will remain in working condition much longer. Whether wear and tear or obsolescence causes depreciation, the asset's cost is depreciated over its expected useful life.

Measuring Depreciation

To measure depreciation for a plant asset, we must know the asset's

1. Cost
2. Estimated useful life
3. Estimated residual value

We have already discussed cost, the purchase price of the asset.

Estimated useful life is the length of service the business expects to get from the asset—an estimate of the asset's actual life. Useful life may be expressed in years, units of output, miles, or other measures. For example, the useful life of a building is stated in years. The useful life of a bookbinding machine may be stated as the num-

Key Point: Three essential elements are used in determining depreciation expense: the asset's cost, estimated residual value, and estimated useful life.

ber of books the machine is expected to bind—that is, its expected units of output. A reasonable measure of a delivery truck's useful life is the total number of miles the truck is expected to travel. Companies base such estimates on past experience and information from industry trade magazines and government publications.

Estimated residual value—also called *scrap value* and *salvage value*—is the expected cash value of the asset at the end of its useful life. For example, a business may believe that a machine's useful life will be seven years. After that time, the company expects to sell the machine as scrap metal. The amount the business believes it can get for the machine is the estimated residual value. In computations of depreciation, estimated residual value is *not* depreciated because the business expects to receive this amount from disposing of the asset. The full cost of a plant asset is depreciated if the asset is expected to have no residual value. The plant asset's cost minus its estimated residual value is called the **depreciable cost.**

Of the factors entering the computation of depreciation, only one factor is known—cost. The other two factors—useful life and residual value—must be estimated. Depreciation, then, is an estimated amount.

Depreciation Methods

OBJECTIVE 3

Account for depreciation by four methods

Four basic methods exist for computing depreciation: straight-line, units-of-production, declining-balance, and sum-of-years'-digits. These four methods allocate different amounts of depreciation expense to different periods. However, they all result in the same total amount of depreciation, the asset's depreciable cost over the life of the asset. Exhibit 10-3 presents the data used to illustrate depreciation computations by the four methods for a truck used by Wal-Mart Stores, Inc.

Straight-Line (SL) Method

In the **straight-line (SL) method,** an equal amount of depreciation expense is assigned to each year (or period) of asset use. Depreciable cost is divided by useful life in years to determine the annual depreciation expense. The equation for SL depreciation, applied to the truck data from Exhibit 10-3, is:

$$\text{Straight-line depreciation per year} = \frac{\text{Cost} - \text{Residual value}}{\text{Useful life, in years}}$$

$$= \frac{\$41,000 - \$1,000}{5}$$

$$= \$8,000$$

EXHIBIT 10-3

Data for Depreciation Computations

Data Item	Amount
Cost of truck............................	$41,000
Estimated residual value	1,000
Depreciable cost.......................	$40,000
Estimated useful life:	
Years......................................	5 years
Units of production..............	100,000 units [miles]

Date	Asset Cost	Depreciation for the Year				Accumulated Depreciation	Asset Book Value
		Depreciation Rate	Depreciable Cost		Depreciation Amount		
1- 1-19X1	$41,000						$41,000
12-31-19X1		0.20	× $40,000	=	$8,000	$ 8,000	33,000
12-31-19X2		0.20	× 40,000	=	8,000	16,000	25,000
12-31-19X3		0.20	× 40,000	=	8,000	24,000	17,000
12-31-19X4		0.20	× 40,000	=	8,000	32,000	9,000
12-31-19X5		0.20	× 40,000	=	8,000	40,000	1,000

EXHIBIT 10-4
Straight-Line Depreciation Schedule

The entry to record this depreciation is

Depreciation Expense.. 8,000
    Accumulated Depreciation... 8,000

Assume that the truck was purchased on January 1, 19X1, and that the business's fiscal year ends on December 31. A *straight-line depreciation schedule* is presented in Exhibit 10-4.

The final column in Exhibit 10-4 shows the asset's *book value*, which is its cost less accumulated depreciation. Book value is also called *carrying amount.*

As an asset is used, accumulated depreciation increases, and the book value decreases. (Compare the Accumulated Depreciation column and the Book Value column.) An asset's final book value is its *residual value* ($1,000 in the exhibit). At the end of its useful life, the asset is said to be fully depreciated.

Short Exercise: An asset with cost of $10,000, useful life of 5 years or 16,000 units, and residual value of $2,000 was purchased on 1/1. What was SL depreciation for the first year? *A:* $1,600 ($10,000 – $2,000/5)

Units-of-Production (UOP) Method

In the **units-of-production (UOP)** method, a fixed amount of depreciation is assigned to each unit of output, or service, produced by the plant asset. Depreciable cost is divided by useful life, in units of production, to determine this amount. This per-unit depreciation expense is multiplied by the number of units produced each period to compute depreciation for the period. The UOP depreciation equation for the truck data in Exhibit 10-3, in which the units are miles, is:

$$\text{Units-of-production depreciation per unit of output} = \frac{\text{Cost} - \text{Residual value}}{\text{Useful life, in units of production}}$$

$$= \frac{\$41,000 - \$1,000}{100,000 \text{ miles}}$$

$$= \$0.40$$

Assume that the truck is expected to be driven 20,000 miles during the first year, 30,000 during the second, 25,000 during the third, 15,000 during the fourth, and 10,000 during the fifth. The UOP depreciation schedule for this asset is shown in Exhibit 10-5.

The amount of UOP depreciation per period varies with the number of units the asset produces. Here the total number of units produced is 100,000, the measure of this asset's useful life. Therefore, UOP depreciation does not depend directly on time as do the other methods.

Short Exercise: The asset in the preceding Short Exercise produced 3,000 units in the first year, 4,000 in the second, 4,500 in the third, 2,500 in the fourth, and 2,000 units in the last year. What was UOP depreciation for each year?
A: Depreciation per unit ($10,000 – $2,000)/16,000 = $0.50
Yr. 1: $1,500 (3,000 × $0.50)
Yr. 2: $2,000 (4,000 × $0.50)
Yr. 3: $2,250 (4,500 × $0.50)
Yr. 4: $1,250 (2,500 × $0.50)
Yr. 5: $1,000 (2,000 × $0.50)

Date	Asset Cost	Depreciation for the Year				Accumulated Depreciation	Asset Book Value
		Depreciation per Unit	Number of Units		Depreciation Amount		
1- 1-19X1	$41,000						$41,000
12-31-19X1		$0.40	×	20,000	= $ 8,000	$ 8,000	33,000
12-31-19X2		0.40	×	30,000	= 12,000	20,000	21,000
12-31-19X3		0.40	×	25,000	= 10,000	30,000	11,000
12-31-19X4		0.40	×	15,000	= 6,000	36,000	5,000
12-31-19X5		0.40	×	10,000	= 4,000	40,000	1,000

EXHIBIT 10-5

Units-of-Production Depreciation Schedule

Double-Declining-Balance (DDB) Method

An **accelerated depreciation method** writes off a relatively larger amount of the asset's cost nearer the start of its useful life than does straight-line. *Double-declining-balance* is one of the accelerated depreciation methods. **Double-declining-balance (DDB) depreciation** computes annual depreciation by multiplying the asset's book value by a constant percentage, which is two times the straight-line depreciation rate. DDB amounts are computed as follows:

First, compute the straight-line depreciation rate per year. For example, a 5-year truck has a straight-line depreciation rate of 1/5, or 20 percent. A 10-year asset has a straight-line rate of 1/10, or 10 percent, and so on.

Second, multiply the straight-line rate by 2 to compute the DDB rate. The DDB rate for a 5-year asset is 40 percent (20% × 2 = 40%). For a 10-year asset the DDB rate is 20 percent (10% × 2 = 20%).

Short Exercise: What is DDB depreciation of the asset in the Short Exercise at the top of page 411 for each year? *A:*
Yr. 1: $4,000 ($10,000 × 40%)
Yr. 2: $2,400 ($6,000 × 40%)
Yr. 3: $1,440 ($3,600 × 40%)
Yr. 4: $160 ($2,160 − $2,000)*

---
*The asset is not depreciated below residual value.

Third, multiply the DDB rate by the period's beginning asset book value (cost less accumulated depreciation). Ignore the residual value of the asset in computing depreciation by the DDB method, except during the last year. The DDB rate for the truck in Exhibit 10-3 is:

$$\text{DDB rate per year} = \frac{1}{\text{Useful life, in years}} \times 2$$

$$= \frac{1}{5 \text{ years}} \times 2$$

$$= 20\% \times 2 = 40\%$$

Fourth, determine the final year's depreciation amount, the amount needed to reduce the asset's book value to its residual value. In the DDB depreciation schedule in Exhibit 10-6, the fifth and final year's depreciation is $4,314—the $5,314 book

EXHIBIT 10-6

Double-Declining-Balance Depreciation Schedule

Date	Asset Cost	Depreciation for the Year				Accumulated Depreciation	Asset Book Value
		DDB Rate	Asset Book Value		Depreciation Amount		
1- 1-19X1	$41,000						$41,000
12-31-19X1		0.40	×	$41,000	= $16,400	$16,400	24,600
12-31-19X2		0.40	×	24,600	= 9,840	26,240	14,760
12-31-19X3		0.40	×	14,760	= 5,904	32,144	8,856
12-31-19X4		0.40	×	8,856	= 3,542	35,686	5,314
12-31-19X5					4,314*	40,000	1,000

*Last-year depreciation is the amount needed to reduce asset book value to the residual value ($5,314 − $1,000 = $4,314).

value less the $1,000 residual value. The residual value should not be depreciated but should remain on the books until the asset's disposal.

Many companies change to the straight-line method during the next-to-last year of the asset's life. Under this plan, annual depreciation for 19X4 and 19X5 is $3,928. Depreciable cost at the end of 19X3 is $7,856 (book value of $8,856 less residual value of $1,000). Depreciable cost can be spread evenly over the last two years of the asset's life ($7,856 ÷ 2 remaining years = $3,928 per year).

The DDB method differs from the other methods in two ways. (1) The asset's residual value is ignored initially. In the first year, depreciation is computed on the asset's full cost. (2) The final year's calculation is changed in order to bring the asset's book value to the residual value.

Key Point: Rarely will the asset's book value equal its residual value in the final year. Depreciation expense in the final year is the amount that will reduce the asset's book value to the residual value.

Sum-of-Years'-Digits (SYD) Method

In the **sum-of years'-digits (SYD) method**—another accelerated method—depreciation is figured by multiplying the depreciable cost of the asset by a fraction. The *denominator* of the SYD fraction is the sum of the years' digits. For a 5-year asset, the years' digits are 1, 2, 3, 4, and 5, and their sum is 15 (1 + 2 + 3 + 4 + 5 = 15). An easy formula for computing the sum of the years' digits is:

$$\text{Sum of the years' digits} = \frac{N(N+1)}{2}$$

where N is the useful life of the asset, expressed in years. For a 10-year asset, N = 10, so the sum of the years' digits = 10(10 + 1)/2 = 55.

The *numerator* of the SYD fraction for the first year of a 5-year asset is 5. The numerator is 4 for the second year, 3 for the third year, 2 for the fourth year, and 1 for the fifth year.

The SYD depreciation equation for the truck in Exhibit 10-3 is:

$$\begin{aligned}\text{SYD depreciation per year} &= (\text{Cost} - \text{Residual value}) \times \frac{\text{Years' digits, largest first}}{\text{Sum of the years' digits}} \\ &= (\$41,000 - \$1,000) \times \frac{5}{1+2+3+4+5} \quad \text{(for the first year)} \\ &= \$40,000 \times \frac{5}{15} = \$13,333 \end{aligned}$$

Exhibit 10-7 is the SYD depreciation schedule based on our example data. Each year's fraction is multiplied by the depreciable cost ($40,000).

EXHIBIT 10-7
Sum-of-Years'-Digits Depreciation Schedule

Date	Asset Cost	Depreciation for the Year			Accumulated Depreciation	Asset Book Value
		SYD Fraction	Depreciable Cost	Depreciation Amount		
1- 1-19X1	$41,000					$41,000
12-31-19X1		5/15 ×	$40,000 =	$13,333	$13,333	27,667
12-31-19X2		4/15 ×	40,000 =	10,667	24,000	17,000
12-31-19X3		3/15 ×	40,000 =	8,000	32,000	9,000
12-31-19X4		2/15 ×	40,000 =	5,333	37,333	3,667
12-31-19X5		1/15 ×	40,000 =	2,667	40,000	1,000

Comparison of the Depreciation Methods

Compare the four methods in terms of the yearly amount of depreciation:

Amount of Depreciation Per Year

Year	Straight-Line	Units-of-Production	Accelerated Methods	
			Double-Declining-Balance	Sum-of-Years'-Digits
1	$ 8,000	$ 8,000	$16,400	$13,333
2	8,000	12,000	9,840	10,667
3	8,000	10,000	5,904	8,000
4	8,000	6,000	3,542	5,333
5	8,000	4,000	4,314	2,667
Total	$40,000	$40,000	$40,000	$40,000

The yearly amount of depreciation varies by method, but the total $40,000 depreciable cost is expensed under all four methods.

Generally accepted accounting principles (GAAP) direct a business to match the expense of an asset against the revenue that asset produces. For a plant asset that generates revenue evenly over time, the straight-line method best meets the matching principle. During each period the asset is used, an equal amount of depreciation is recorded.

The units-of-production method best fits those assets that wear out because of physical use, not obsolescence. Depreciation is recorded only when the asset is used, and the more units the asset generates in a given year, the greater the depreciation expense.

Key Point: The DDB and SYD methods are accelerated depreciation methods. Accelerated methods write off more asset cost in the early years of an asset's life than in the later years. These methods assume that an asset is more useful (productive) in its early years and therefore should be depreciated more then.

The accelerated methods (DDB and SYD) apply best to those assets that generate greater revenue earlier in their useful lives. The greater expense recorded under the accelerated methods in the earlier periods is matched against those periods' greater revenue.

Exhibit 10-8 graphs annual depreciation amounts for straight-line, units-of-production, and the accelerated depreciation methods. The graph of straight-line depreciation is flat because annual depreciation is the same in all periods. Units-of-production depreciation follows no particular pattern because annual depreciation depends on the use of the asset. The greater the use, the greater the amount of depreciation. Accelerated depreciation is greatest in the asset's first year and less in the later years.

CONCEPT HIGHLIGHT

EXHIBIT 10-8
Depreciation Patterns through Time

EXHIBIT 10-9
*Use of the Depreciation Methods
by 600 Companies*

*Most of these are probably declining-balance methods because depreciation
for income tax purposes is based on the declining-balance concept. Some
companies use the same depreciation method for financial statement purposes
and for tax purposes.

A recent survey of 600 companies indicated that the straight-line method is
most popular. Exhibit 10-9 shows the percentages of companies that use each of the
four depreciation methods.

SUMMARY PROBLEM FOR YOUR REVIEW   MID-CHAPTER

Hubbard Company purchased equipment on January 1, 19X5, for $44,000. The expected
useful life of the equipment is 10 years, and its residual value is $4,000. Under three depreciation
methods, the annual depreciation expense and the balance of accumulated depreciation at the end
of 19X5 and 19X6 are:

Year	Method A Annual Depreciation Expense	Accumulated Depreciation	Method B Annual Depreciation Expense	Accumulated Depreciation	Method C Annual Depreciation Expense	Accumulated Depreciation
19X5	$4,000	$4,000	$8,800	$ 8,800	$7,273	$ 7,273
19X6	4,000	8,000	7,040	15,840	6,545	13,818

Required

1. Identify the depreciation method used in each instance, and show the equation and computation for each. (Round off to the nearest dollar.)
2. Assume continued use of the same method through year 19X7. Determine the annual depreciation expense, accumulated depreciation, and book value of the equipment for 19X5 through
   19X7 under each method.

Requirement 1

Method A: Straight-line

Depreciable cost = $40,000 ($44,000 − $4,000)
Each year: $40,000/10 years = $4,000

Method B: Double-declining-balance

$$\text{Rate} = \frac{1}{10 \text{ years}} \times 2 = 10\% \times 2 = 20\%$$

19X5: 0.20 × $44,000 = $8,800
19X6: 0.20 × ($44,000 − $8,800) = $7,040

Method C: Sum-of-years'-digits

SYD = N(N + 1)/2 = 10(10 + 1)/2 = 55
Depreciable cost = $40,000 ($44,000 − $4,000)
19X5: 10/55 × $40,000 = $7,273
19X6: 9/55 × $40,000 = $6,545

Requirement 2

	Method A: Straight-Line			Method B: Double-Declining-Balance			Method C: Sum-of-Years'-Digits		
Year	Annual Depreciation Expense	Accumulated Depreciation	Book Value	Annual Depreciation Expense	Accumulated Depreciation	Book Value	Annual Depreciation Expense	Accumulated Depreciation	Book Value
Start			$44,000			$44,000			$44,000
19X5	$4,000	$ 4,000	40,000	$8,800	$ 8,800	35,200	$7,273	$ 7,273	36,727
19X6	4,000	8,000	36,000	7,040	15,840	28,160	6,545	13,818	30,182
19X7	4,000	12,000	32,000	5,632	21,472	22,528	5,818	19,636	24,364

Computations for 19X7:

Straight-Line	$40,000/10 years = $4,000
Double-Declining-Balance	0.20 × $28,160 = $5,632
Sum-of-Years'-Digits	8/55 × $40,000 = $5,818

Depreciation and Income Taxes

OBJECTIVE 4

Identify the best depreciation method for income tax purposes

Most companies use the straight-line depreciation method for reporting to their stockholders and creditors on their financial statements. But companies keep a separate set of depreciation records for computing their income taxes. For income tax purposes, most companies use an accelerated depreciation method.

Suppose you are a business manager. The IRS allows an accelerated depreciation method, which most managers choose in preference to straight-line depreciation. Why? Because it provides the most depreciation expense as quickly as possible, thus decreasing your immediate tax payments. The cash you save may be applied to fit your business needs. This is the strategy most businesses follow.

To understand the relationships between cash flow (cash provided by operations), depreciation, and income tax, recall our earlier depreciation example: First-year depreciation is $8,000 under straight-line and $16,400 under double-declining-balance. For illustrative purposes here, assume that DDB is permitted for reporting to the income tax authorities. Assume that the business has $400,000 in cash sales and $300,000 in cash operating expenses during the asset's first year and that the income tax rate is 30 percent. The cash flow analysis appears in Exhibit 10-10.

	Income Tax Rate 30 Percent	
	SL	Accelerated
Revenues..	$400,000	$400,000
Cash operating expenses	300,000	300,000
Cash provided by operations before income tax...........................	100,000	100,000
Depreciation expense (a noncash expense)	8,000	16,400
Income before income tax...	92,000	83,600
Income tax expense (30%)...	27,600	25,080
Net income..	$ 64,400	$ 58,520
Cash-flow analysis:		
Cash provided by operations before income tax.........................	$100,000	$100,000
Income tax expense...	27,600	25,080
Cash provided by operations...	$ 72,400	$ 74,920
Extra cash available for investment if DDB is used ($74,920 – $72,400)		$ 2,520
Assumed earnings rate on investment of extra cash....................		× 0.10
Cash advantage of using DDB over SL		$ 252

Exhibit 10-10 highlights several important business relationships. Compare the amount of cash provided by operations before income tax. Both columns show $100,000. If there were no income taxes, the total cash provided by operations would be the same regardless of the depreciation method used. Depreciation is a noncash expense and so does not affect cash from operations.

But depreciation is a tax-deductible expense. The higher the depreciation expense, the lower the before-tax income and thus the lower the income tax payment. Therefore, accelerated depreciation helps conserve cash for use in the business. Exhibit 10-10 indicates that the business will have $2,520 more cash at the end of the first year if it uses accelerated depreciation instead of SL ($74,920 against $72,400). If the company invests this money to earn a return of 10 percent during the second year, it will be better off by $252 ($2,520 × 10% = $252). The cash advantage of using the accelerated method is the $252 additional revenue.

The Tax Reform Act of 1986 created a special depreciation method—used only for income tax purposes—called the Modified Accelerated Cost Recovery System (MACRS). Under this method, assets are grouped into one of eight classes, as shown in Exhibit 10-11. Depreciation for the first four classes is computed by the double-declining-balance method. Depreciation for 15-year assets and 20-year assets is computed by the 150-percent-declining-balance method. Under this method, the annual depreciation rate is computed by multiplying the straight-line rate by 1.50 (rather than by 2.00, as for DDB). For a 20-year asset, the straight-line rate is 0.05 (1/20 = 0.05), so the annual MACRS depreciation rate is 0.075 (0.05 × 1.50 = 0.075). Most real estate is depreciated by the straight-line method.

Short Exercise: Rother Co. had cash revenues of $200,000 and cash operating expenses of $100,000. Rother uses SL depreciation of $4,000 for financial reporting and MACRS depreciation of $6,700 on its tax return. How much additional cash is available for investment by using MACRS for tax purposes?

A:
	SL	MACRS
Revenues	$200,000	$200,000
Cash oper. exp.	100,000	100,000
Operating cash	100,000	100,000
Depr. exp.	4,000	6,700
Income before tax	96,000	93,700
Income tax (30%)	28,800	28,110
Net income	$ 67,200	$ 65,590
Operating cash	$100,000	$100,000
Income tax	28,800	28,110
Cash provided by operations	$ 71,200	$ 71,890

Additional cash for investment: $690 ($71,890 – $71,200)

Class Identified by Asset Life	Representative Assets	Depreciation Method
3 years	Race horses	DDB
5 years	Automobiles, light trucks	DDB
7 years	Equipment	DDB
10 years	Equipment	DDB
15 years	Sewage-treatment plants	150% DB
20 years	Certain real estate	150% DB
27 1/2 years	Residential rental property	SL
39 years	Nonresidential rental property	SL

EXHIBIT 10-11

Details of the Modified Accelerated Cost Recovery System (MACRS) Depreciation Method

Depreciation for Partial Years

Companies purchase plant assets as needed. They do not wait until the beginning of a year or a month. Therefore, companies must develop policies to compute *depreciation for partial years*. Suppose County Line Bar-B-Q Restaurant purchases a building on April 1 for $500,000. The building's estimated life is 20 years, and its estimated residual value is $80,000. The restaurant company's fiscal year ends on December 31. Consider how the company computes depreciation for the year ended December 31.

Many companies compute partial-year depreciation by first computing a full year's depreciation. They then multiply that amount by the fraction of the year that they held the asset. Assuming the straight-line method, the year's depreciation for the restaurant building is $15,750, computed as follows:

Short Exercise: Assume that the asset in the first Short Exercise on p. 411 was acquired on 4/1. Compute SL depreciation at 12/31 for the life of the asset.
A: Yr. 1: $1,200 ($8,000/5 =
$1,600 × 9/12)
Yr. 2-5: $1,600
Yr. 6: $400 ($1,600 × 3/12)

$$\frac{(\$500,000 - \$80,000)}{20} = \$21,000 \text{ per year} \times \frac{9}{12} = \$15,750$$

What if the company bought the asset on April 18? A widely used policy directs businesses to record no depreciation on assets purchased after the 15th of the month and to record a full month's depreciation on an asset bought on or before the 15th. Thus the company would record no depreciation for April on an April 18 purchase. In this case, the year's depreciation would be $14,000 ($21,000 × 8/12).

How is partial-year depreciation computed under the other depreciation methods? Suppose this building is acquired on October 4 and the restaurant uses the double-declining-balance method. For a 20-year asset, the DDB rate is 10 percent (1/20 = 5%; 5% × 2 = 10%). The annual depreciation computations for 19X1, 19X2, and 19X3 are as shown in Exhibit 10-12.

EXHIBIT 10-12

Annual DDB Depreciation for Partial Years

Date	Asset Cost	DDB Rate	Asset Book Value— Beginning	Fraction of the Year		Depreciation Amount	Accumulated Depreciation	Asset Book Value— Ending
			Depreciation for the Year					
10- 4-19X1	$500,000							$500,000
12-31-19X1		1/20 × 2 = 0.10 × $500,000 ×	3/12	=	$12,500	$ 12,500	487,500
12-31-19X2		= 0.10 × 487,500 ×	12/12	=	48,750	61,250	438,750
12-31-19X3		= 0.10 × 438,750 ×	12/12	=	43,875	105,125	394,875

Partial-year depreciation under the sum-of-years'-digits method is computed similarly, by taking the appropriate fraction of a full year's amount. But no special computation is needed for partial-year depreciation under the units-of-production method. Simply use the number of units produced, regardless of the time period the asset is held.

Most companies use computerized systems to account for fixed assets. They identify each asset with a unique identification number and indicate the asset's cost, estimated life, residual value, and depreciation method. The system will automatically calculate the depreciation expense for each period. Both Accumulated Depreciation and book value are automatically updated.

Change in the Useful Life of a Depreciable Asset

As previously discussed, a business must estimate the useful life of a plant asset to compute depreciation on that asset. This prediction is the most difficult part of accounting for depreciation. After the asset is put into use, the business is able to refine its estimate on the basis of experience and new information. The Walt Disney Company made such a change, called a *change in accounting estimate*, to recalculate depreciation on the basis of revised useful lives of several of its theme park assets. The following note in Walt Disney's financial statement reports this change in accounting estimate:

"The Walt Disney Company made such a change, called a change in accounting estimate, to recalculate depreciation on the basis of revised useful lives of several of its theme park assets."

Note 5

. . .[T]he Company extended the estimated useful lives of certain theme park ride and attraction assets based upon historical data and engineering studies. The effect of this change was to decrease depreciation by approximately $8 million (an increase in net income of approximately $4.2 million . . .).

Such accounting changes are common because no business has perfect foresight. Generally accepted accounting principles require the business to report the nature, reason, and effect of the change on net income, as the Disney example shows. To *record* a change in accounting estimate, the remaining book value of the asset is spread over its adjusted remaining useful life. The adjusted useful life may be longer or shorter than the original useful life. With computer-based systems, depreciation calculations resulting from revised useful lives or revised residual values are automatic and accurate.

Assume that Disney's hot dog stand cost $40,000 and that the company originally believed the asset had an eight-year useful life with no residual value. Using the straight-line method, the company would record $5,000 depreciation each year ($40,000/8 years = $5,000). Suppose Disney used the asset for two years. Accumulated depreciation reached $10,000, leaving a remaining depreciable book value (cost *less* accumulated depreciation *less* residual value) of $30,000 ($40,000 − $10,000). From its experience with the asset during the first two years, management believes the asset will remain useful for an additional 10 years. The company would compute a revised annual depreciation amount and record it as follows:

Asset's Remaining Depreciable Book Value	÷	(New) Estimated Useful Life Remaining	=	(New) Annual Depreciation
$30,000	÷	10 years	=	$3,000

The yearly depreciation entry based on the new estimated useful life follows:

Depreciation Expense—Hot Dog Stand...	3,000	
Accumulated Depreciation—Hot Dog Stand...........................		3,000

Short Exercise: In 1974, ABC Co. purchased for $600,000 a building that had an estimated residual value of $100,000 and a life of 40 years. In 1994, a $200,000 addition to the building increased its residual value by $50,000. The accumulated depreciation on the building is $250,000. Calculate SL depreciation expense for 1994.

A: Calculate book value:

Cost (new)	$800,000
Acc. Depr.	250,000
Revised book value	$550,000

Revised SL depreciation

$$= \frac{\$550,000 - \$150,000}{20}$$

$$= \$20,000$$

1. Suppose Wal-Mart Stores, Inc., was having a bad year—net income below expectations and lower than last year's income. For depreciation purposes Wal-Mart extended the estimated useful lives of its depreciable assets. How would this accounting change affect Wal-Mart's (a) depreciation expense? (b) net income? (c) owners' equity?

Answer: An accounting change that lengthens the estimated useful lives of depreciable assets (a) decreases depreciation expense and (b, c) increases net income and owners' equity.

2. Suppose that Wal-Mart's accounting change turned a loss year into a profitable year. Without the accounting change, the company would have reported a net loss for the year. But the accounting change enabled Wal-Mart to report net income. Under GAAP, Wal-Mart's annual report must disclose the accounting change and its effect on net income. Would investors evaluate Wal-Mart as better or worse in response to these disclosures?

Answer: Investors' reactions are not always predictable. There is evidence, however, that companies cannot fool investors. If investors have enough information—such as the knowledge of an accounting change disclosed in the annual report—they can process the information correctly. In this case, investment advisers would *probably* subtract from Wal-Mart's reported net income the amount caused by the accounting change. Investors could then use the remaining net *loss* figure to evaluate Wal-Mart's lack of progress during the year. Investors would probably view Wal-Mart as worse for having made this accounting change.

Using Fully Depreciated Assets

Key Point: The total amount of depreciation recorded on an asset cannot exceed its depreciable cost. An asset *can* be used after it is fully depreciated.

A fully depreciated asset is an asset that has reached the end of its *estimated* useful life. No more depreciation is recorded for the asset. If the asset is no longer suitable for its purpose, it is disposed of, as discussed in the next section. However, the company may be in a cash bind and unable to replace the asset. Or the asset's useful life may have been underestimated at the outset. Foresight is not perfect. In any event, companies sometimes continue using fully depreciated assets. The asset account and its related accumulated depreciation account remain in the ledger even though no additional depreciation is recorded for the asset.

Disposal of Plant Assets

OBJECTIVE 5
Account for disposal of plant assets

Eventually, a plant asset ceases to serve a company's needs. The asset may have become worn out, obsolete, or for some other reason no longer useful to the business. In general a company disposes of a plant asset by selling or exchanging it. If the asset cannot be sold or exchanged, then the asset is junked. Whatever the method of disposal, the business should bring depreciation up to date to measure the asset's final book value properly.

To account for disposal, credit the asset account and debit its related accumulated depreciation account. Suppose the final year's depreciation expense has just been recorded for a machine that cost $6,000 and was estimated to have zero residual value. The machine's accumulated depreciation thus totals $6,000. Assuming that this asset cannot be sold or exchanged, the entry to record its disposal is

Accumulated Depreciation—Machinery..............	6,000	
Machinery		6,000
To dispose of fully depreciated machine.		

If assets are junked before being fully depreciated, the company records a loss equal to the asset's book value. Suppose Wal-Mart store fixtures that cost $4,000 are disposed of in this manner. Accumulated depreciation is $3,000, and book value is therefore $1,000. Disposal of these store fixtures is recorded as follows:

Accumulated Depreciation—Store Fixtures	3,000	
Loss on Disposal of Store Fixtures	1,000	
Store Fixtures		4,000
To dispose of store fixtures.		

Loss accounts such as Loss on Disposal of Store Fixtures decrease net income. Losses are reported on the income statement and closed to Income Summary along with expenses.

Selling a Plant Asset

Suppose the business sells furniture on September 30, 19X4, for $5,000 cash. The furniture cost $10,000 when purchased on January 1, 19X1, and has been depreciated on a straight-line basis. Managers estimated a 10-year useful life and no residual value. Prior to recording the sale of the furniture, accountants must update depreciation. Since the business uses the calendar year as its accounting period, partial-year depreciation must be recorded for the asset's expense from January 1, 19X4, to the sale date. The straight-line depreciation entry at September 30, 19X4, is:

Sep. 30 Depreciation Expense ($10,000/10 years × 9/12)	750	
Accumulated Depreciation—Furniture		750
To update depreciation.		

After this entry is posted, the Furniture account and the Accumulated Depreciation—Furniture account appear as follows. The furniture book value is $6,250 ($10,000 – $3,750).

Furniture	Accumulated Depreciation—Furniture
Jan. 1, 19X1 10,000	Dec. 31, 19X1 1,000
	Dec. 31, 19X2 1,000
	Dec. 31, 19X3 1,000
	Sep. 30, 19X4 750
	Balance 3,750

The entry to record sale of the furniture for $5,000 cash is

Sep. 30 Cash	5,000	
Accumulated Depreciation—Furniture	3,750	
Loss on Sale of Furniture	1,250	
Furniture		10,000
To sell furniture.		

When recording the sale of a plant asset, the business must remove the balances in the asset account (Furniture, in this case) and its related accumulated depreciation account and also record a gain or a loss if the amount of cash received differs from the asset's book value. In our example, cash of $5,000 is less than the book value of the furniture, $6,250. The result is a loss of $1,250.

Short Exercise: Equipment with original cost of $10,000, residual value of $2,000, and 5-year life was sold on 3/31/X3 for $6,400. Accumulated depreciation (SL method) on the asset was $2,500 as of 12/31/X2. Record the sale.
A: First, calculate depreciation from 12/31/X2 to 3/31/X3: ($10,000 – $2,000)/5 × 3/12 = $400. Add this figure to the $2,500 as of 12/31/X2 to bring accumulated depreciation as of 3/31/X3 to $2,900. Now, make the entry:

Cash	6,400	
Acc. Depr.	2,900	
Loss on Sale	700	
Equipment		10,000

If the sale price had been $7,000, the business would have had a gain of $750 (Cash, $7,000 − asset book value, $6,250). The entry to record this transaction would be:

Sep. 30	Cash	7,000	
	Accumulated Depreciation—Furniture	3,750	
	Furniture...		10,000
	Gain on Sale of Furniture		750
	To sell furniture.		

A gain is recorded when an asset is sold for a price greater than the asset's book value. A loss is recorded when the sale price is less than book value. Gains increase net income. Gains and losses are reported on the income statement and closed to Income Summary along with the revenues.

Exchanging Plant Assets

Businesses often exchange (trade in) their old plant assets for similar assets that are newer and more efficient. For example, Domino's pizzeria may decide to trade in a five-year-old delivery car for a newer model. To record the exchange, the business must remove from the books the balances for the asset being exchanged and its related accumulated depreciation account.

"Domino's pizzeria may decide to trade in its five-year-old delivery car for a newer model."

Assume that the pizzeria's old delivery car cost $9,000 and has accumulated depreciation totaling $8,000. The book value, then, is $1,000. The cash price for a new delivery car is $11,000, and the car dealer offers a $1,000 trade-in-allowance. The pizzeria pays cash for the remaining $10,000. The trade-in is recorded with this entry:

Delivery Auto (new)	11,000	
Accumulated Depreciation (old)	8,000	
Delivery Auto (old)		9,000
Cash ($11,000 − $1,000)...		10,000

In this example, the book value and the trade-in allowance are both $1,000, and so no gain or loss occurs on the exchange. Usually, however, an exchange results in a gain or a loss. If the trade-in allowance received is greater than the book value of the asset given, the business has a gain. If the trade-in allowance received is less than the book value of the asset given, the business has a loss. Generally accepted accounting principles require that losses (but not gains) be recognized on the exchange of similar assets. We now turn to the entries for gains and losses on exchanges, continuing our delivery-car example and its data.[1]

SITUATION 1 Loss recognized on asset exchange: Assume that the new delivery car has a cash price of $11,000 and that the dealer gives a trade-in allowance of $600 on the old vehicle. Domino's pays the balance, $10,400, in cash. The loss on the exchange is $400 (book value of old asset given, $1,000, minus trade-in allowance received, $600). The account Loss on Exchange of Delivery Auto is debited for $400. The entry to record this exchange is:

---

[1]GAAP rules for exchanges may differ from income tax rules. In this discussion, we are concerned with the accounting rules.

Delivery Auto (new)	11,000	
Accumulated Depreciation—Delivery Auto (old)	8,000	
Loss on Exchange of Delivery Auto	400	
Delivery Auto (old)		9,000
Cash ($11,000 – $600)		10,400

SITUATION 2 Gain *not* recognized on asset exchange: Assume that the new delivery car's cash price is $11,000 and the seller gives a $1,300 trade-in allowance. Domino's pays the balance, $9,700, in cash. The gain is $300 (trade-in allowance received, $1,300, minus book value of old asset given, $1,000). However, Domino's does not recognize the gain. Instead, it reduces the cost of the new asset by the amount of the unrecognized gain.

Delivery Auto (new) ($11,000 – gain of $300)	10,700	
Accumulated Depreciation—Delivery Auto (old)	8,000	
Delivery Auto (old)		9,000
Cash ($11,000 – $1,300)		9,700

Why are losses, but not gains, recognized? The Accounting Principles Board, the predecessor of the FASB, reasoned that a company should not record a gain merely because it has substituted one plant asset for a similar plant asset. Losses are recorded, however, because conservatism favors the recognition of losses rather than gains.

STOP & THINK Suppose Wal-Mart's comparative income statement for two years included these items:

	Billions	
	19X2	**19X1**
Net sales	$42.0	$40.0
Income from operations	$ 0.2	$ 1.0
Gain on sale of store facilities	1.2	
Income before income taxes	$ 1.4	$ 1.0

Which was a better year for Wal-Mart—19X2 or 19X1?

Answer: From a *sales* standpoint, 19X2 was better because sales were higher. But from an *income* standpoint, 19X1 was the better year. In 19X1, merchandising operations—Wal-Mart's main business—generated $1 billion of income before taxes. In 19X2, merchandising produced only $0.2 billion of pre-tax income. Most of the company's income came from selling store facilities. A business cannot hope to continue on this path very long. This example illustrates why investors and creditors are interested in the sources of a company's profits, not just the final amount of net income.

Internal Control of Plant Assets

Internal control of plant assets includes safeguarding them and having an adequate accounting system. To see the need for controlling plant assets, consider the following real situation. The home office and top managers of Symington Wayne Corporation are in New Jersey. The company manufactures gas pumps in Canada, which are sold in Europe. Top managers and owners of the company rarely see the manufacturing plant and therefore cannot control plant assets by on-the-spot management. What features does their internal control system need?

Recall from Chapter 7 the importance of a strong system of internal controls within a business.

EXHIBIT 10-13
Plant Asset Ledger Record

Asset	Clothing racks			Location	Ladies' dresses	
Employee responsible for the asset	Department manager					

Cost $190,000   Purchased From   Boone Supply Co.

Depreciation Method   SL

Useful Life   10 years   Residual Value $10,000

General Ledger Account   Store Fixtures

Date	Explanation	Asset			Accumulated Depreciation		
		Dr.	Cr.	Bal.	Dr.	Cr.	Bal.
Jul. 3, 19X4	Purchase	190,000		190,000			
Dec. 31, 19X4	Depreciation					9,000	9,000
Dec. 31, 19X5	Depreciation					18,000	27,000
Dec. 31, 19X6	Depreciation					18,000	45,000

Safeguarding plant assets includes:

1. Assigning responsibility for custody of the assets.
2. Separating custody of assets from accounting for the assets. (This item is a cornerstone of internal control in almost every area.)
3. Setting up security measures—for instance, armed guards and restricted access to plant assets—to prevent theft.
4. Protecting assets from the elements (rain, snow, and so on).
5. Having adequate insurance against fire, storm, and other casualty losses.
6. Training operating personnel in the proper use of the asset.
7. Keeping a regular maintenance schedule.

Plant assets are controlled in much the same way that high-priced inventory is controlled—with the help of subsidiary records. For plant assets, companies use a plant asset ledger. Each plant asset is represented by a record describing the asset and listing its location and employee responsibility for it. These details aid in safeguarding the asset. The ledger record also shows the asset's cost, useful life, and other accounting data. Exhibit 10-13 could be an example for the clothing racks in a Wal-Mart store.

The ledger record provides the data for computing depreciation on the asset. It serves as a subsidiary record of accumulated depreciation. The asset balance ($190,000) and accumulated depreciation amount ($45,000) agree with the balances in the respective general ledger accounts (Store Fixtures and Accumulated Depreciation—Store Fixtures).

Accounting for Natural Resources and Depletion

OBJECTIVE 6

Account for natural resource assets and depletion

Natural resources such as iron ore, petroleum (oil), natural gas, and timber are plant assets of a special type. An investment in natural resources could be described as an investment in inventories in the ground (oil) or on top of the ground (timber). As plant assets (such as machines) are expensed through depreciation, so natural resource assets are expensed through depletion. **Depletion expense** is that portion of the cost of natural resources that is used up in a particular period. Depletion expense is computed in the same way as *units-of-production* depreciation.

An oil well may cost $100,000 and contain an estimated 10,000 barrels of oil. The depletion rate would be $10 per barrel ($100,000/10,000 barrels). If 3,000 barrels are extracted during the year, depletion expense is $30,000 (3,000 barrels × $10 per barrel). The depletion entry for the year is

Depletion Expense (3,000 barrels × $10) 30,000
    Accumulated Depletion—Oil..   30,000

If 4,500 barrels are removed the next year, that period's depletion is $45,000 (4,500 barrels × $10 per barrel). Accumulated Depletion is a contra account similar to Accumulated Depreciation.

Natural resource assets can be reported as follows:

Property, Plant, and Equipment:			
Land			$120,000
Buildings	$ 800,000		
Equipment	160,000		
	960,000		
Less: Accumulated depreciation...	410,000		550,000
Oil	**$340,000**		
Less: Accumulated depletion...	**90,000***		**250,000**
Total property, plant, and equipment...			$920,000

*Includes the $30,000 recorded above.

Short Exercise: Pulp Products purchases for $500,000 land that contains an estimated 500,000 board feet of timber. The land can be sold for $100,000 after the timber has been cut. If Pulp harvests 200,000 board feet in the year of purchase, how much depletion should be recorded?

A: $160,000 ($500,000 – $100,000/500,000 = $0.80/board ft. × 200,000)

Accounting for Intangible Assets and Amortization

Intangible assets are a class of long-lived assets that are not physical in nature. Instead, these assets are special rights to current and expected future benefits from patents, copyrights, trademarks, franchises, leaseholds, and goodwill.

OBJECTIVE 7
Account for intangible assets and amortization

The acquisition cost of an intangible asset is debited to an asset account. The intangible is expensed through **amortization,** the systematic reduction of a lump-sum amount. Amortization applies to intangible assets in the same way depreciation applies to plant assets and depletion applies to natural resources. All three methods of expensing assets are conceptually the same.

Amortization is generally computed on a straight-line basis over the asset's estimated useful life—up to a maximum of 40 years, according to GAAP. But obsolescence often cuts an intangible asset's useful life shorter than its legal life. Amortization expense for an intangible asset is written off directly against the asset account rather than held in an accumulated amortization account. The residual value of most intangible assets is zero.

Assume that a business purchases a patent on a special manufacturing process. Legally, the patent may run for 17 years. The business realizes, however, that the new technologies will limit the patented process's life to four years. If the patent cost $80,000, each year's amortization expense is $20,000 ($80,000/4). The balance sheet reports the patent at its acquisition cost less amortization expense to date. After one year, the patent has a $60,000 balance ($80,000 – $20,000), after two years a $40,000 balance, and so on.

Patents are federal government grants giving the holder the exclusive right for 17 years to produce and sell an invention. Patented products include Sony compact disk players and the Dolby noise-reduction process. Like any other asset, a patent may be purchased. Suppose a company pays $170,000 to acquire a patent, and the business believes the expected useful life of the patent is only five years. Amortization expense is $34,000 per year ($170,000/5 years). The company's acquisition and amortization entries for this patent are:

Jan. 1	Patents..	170,000	
	Cash		170,000
	To acquire a patent.		
Dec. 31	Amortization Expense—Patents ($170,000/5).................	34,000	
	Patents		34,000
	To amortize the cost of a patent.		

Copyrights are exclusive rights to reproduce and sell a book, musical composition, film, or other work of art. Copyrights also protect computer software programs, such as Microsoft's Windows and Lotus's 1-2-3 spreadsheet. Issued by the federal government, copyrights extend 50 years beyond the author's (composer's, artist's, or programmer's) life. The cost of obtaining a copyright from the government is low, but a company may pay a large sum to purchase an existing copyright from the owner. For example, a publisher may pay the author of a popular novel $1 million or more for the book's copyright. The useful life of a copyright is usually no longer than two or three years, so each period's amortization amount is a high proportion of the copyright's cost.

Trademarks and **trade names** (or **brand names**) are distinctive identifications of products or services. The "eye" symbol that flashes across the television screen is a trademark that identifies the CBS television network. NBC uses the peacock as its trademark. Seven-up, Pepsi, Egg McMuffin, and Rice-a-Roni are everyday trade names. Advertising slogans that are legally protected include United Airlines' "Fly the friendly skies" and Avis Rental Car's "We try harder."

The cost of a trademark or trade name is amortized over its useful life, not to exceed 40 years. The cost of advertising and promotions that use the trademark or trade name is not a part of the asset's cost but a debit to the advertising expense account.

Franchises and **licenses** are privileges granted by a private business or a government to sell a product or service in accordance with specified conditions. The Dallas Cowboys football organization is a franchise granted to its owner, Jerry Jones, by the National Football League. McDonald's restaurants and Holiday Inns are popular franchises. Consolidated Edison Company (ConEd) holds a New York City franchise right to provide electricity to residents. The acquisition costs of franchises and licenses are amortized over their useful lives rather than over legal lives, subject to the 40-year maximum.

"The Dallas Cowboys football organization is a franchise granted to its owner, Jerry Jones, by the National Football League."

A **leasehold** is a prepayment that a lessee (renter) makes to secure the use of an asset from a lessor (landlord). For example, Wal-Mart leases many of its store buildings from other entities. Often, leases require the lessee to make this prepayment in addition to monthly rental payments. The lessee debits the monthly lease payments to the Rent Expense account. The prepayment, however, is a debit to an intangible asset account titled Leaseholds. This amount is amortized over the life of the lease by debiting Rent Expense and crediting Leaseholds. Some leases stipulate that the last year's rent must be paid in advance when the lease is signed. This prepayment is debited to Leaseholds and transferred to Rent Expense during the last year of the lease.

Sometimes lessees modify or improve the lease asset. For example, a lessee may construct a fence on leased land. The lessee debits the cost of the fence to a separate intangible asset account, Leasehold Improvements, and amortizes its cost over the term of the lease or the life of the asset, if shorter.

Goodwill in accounting is a more limited term than in everyday use, as in "good-will among men." In accounting, **goodwill** is defined as the excess of the cost of an acquired company over the sum of the market values of its net assets (assets minus liabilities). Recently Wal-Mart Stores, Inc., has been expanding into Mexico. Suppose Wal-Mart acquires Mexana Company at a cost of $10 million. The sum of the market values of Mexana's assets is $9 million, and its liabilities total $1 million. In this case, Wal-Mart paid $2 million for goodwill, computed as follows:

Purchase price paid for Mexana Company		$10 million
Sum of the market values of Mexana Company's assets	$9 million	
Less: Mexana Company's liabilities	1 million	
Market value of Mexana Company's net assets		8 million
Excess is called *goodwill*		$ 2 million

Wal-Mart's entry to record the acquisition of Mexana Company, including its good-will, would be

Assets (Cash, Receivables, Inventories, Plant Assets, all at market value)	9,000,000	
Goodwill	2,000,000	
Liabilities		1,000,000
Cash		10,000,000

Goodwill has special features, which include the following points:

1. Goodwill is recorded, at its cost, only when it is purchased in the acquisition of another company. Even though a favorable location, a superior product, or an outstanding reputation may create goodwill for a company, it is never recorded by that entity. Instead, goodwill is recorded only by the acquiring company. A purchase transaction provides objective evidence of the value of the goodwill.

2. According to generally accepted accounting principles, goodwill is amortized over a period not to exceed 40 years. In reality, the goodwill of many entities increases in value. Nevertheless, the Accounting Principles Board specified in *Opinion No. 17* that the cost of all intangible assets must be amortized as expense. The *Opinion* prohibits a lump-sum write-off of the cost of goodwill upon acquisition.

INTERNATIONAL ACCOUNTING Companies in Germany (such as Krups and Volkswagen), in Great Britain (such as British Petroleum and British Airways), and in most other European nations do not have to record goodwill when they purchase another business. Instead they may debit the cost of goodwill directly to owners' equity. These companies never have to amortize the cost of goodwill, so their net income is higher than an American company's would be. American companies often cry "foul" when bidding against a European firm to acquire another business. Why? Americans claim the Europeans can pay higher prices because their income never takes a hit for amortization expense.

> *"Companies in Germany (such as Krups and Volkswagen), in Great Britain (such as British Petroleum and British Airways), and in most other European nations do not have to record goodwill when they purchase another business."*

STOP & THINK How could companies around the world be placed on the same accounting basis?

Answer: If all companies worldwide followed the same accounting rules, they would be reporting income and other amounts computed similarly. But this is not the case. Companies must follow the accounting rules of their own nation, and there are differences, as the goodwill situation illustrates. This is why international investors keep abreast of accounting methods used in different nations—much the same as American investors care whether a company uses LIFO or FIFO for inventories. An international body, the International Accounting Standards Committee, has a set of accounting standards, but the organization has no enforcement power.

Capital Expenditures versus Revenue Expenditures

OBJECTIVE 8
Distinguish capital expenditures from revenue expenditures

When a company makes a plant asset expenditure, it must decide whether to debit an asset account or an expense account. In this context, *expenditure* refers to either a cash or credit purchase of goods or services related to the asset. Examples of these expenditures range from replacing the windshield wipers on an automobile to enlarging a Wal-Mart store building.

Expenditures that increase the capacity or efficiency of the asset or extend its useful life are called **capital expenditures.** For example, the cost of a major overhaul that extends a taxi's useful life is a capital expenditure. Repair work that generates a capital expenditure is called an **extraordinary repair.** The amount of the capital expenditure, said to be capitalized, is a debit to an asset account. For an extraordinary repair on a taxi, we would debit the asset account Automobile.

Other expenditures do not extend the asset's capacity or efficiency. Expenditures that merely maintain the asset in its existing condition or restore the asset to good working order are called **revenue expenditures** because these costs are matched against revenue. Examples include the costs of repainting a taxi, repairing a dented fender, and replacing tires. The work that creates the revenue expenditure, said to be expensed, is a debit to an expense account. For the **ordinary repairs,** or betterments, on the taxi, we would debit Repair Expense.

Costs associated with intangible assets and natural resource assets also must be identified as either a capital expenditure or a revenue expenditure. For example, a license fee paid to the state of Arkansas to mine bauxite is a capital expenditure. This cost should be debited to the Bauxite Mineral Asset account. The cost of selling the ore—sales commission paid to a broker, for example—is a revenue expenditure and should be debited to an expense account.

The distinction between capital and revenue expenditures is often a matter of opinion. Does the cost extend the life of the asset, or does it only maintain the asset in good order? When doubt exists as to whether to debit an asset or an expense, companies tend to debit an expense for two reasons. First, many expenditures are minor in amount, and most companies have a policy of debiting expense for all expenditures below a specific minimum, such as $1,000. Second, the income tax motive favors debiting all borderline expenditures to expense in order to create an immediate tax deduction. Capital expenditures are not immediate tax deductions.

Exhibit 10-14 illustrates the distinction between capital expenditures and revenue expenditures (expense) for several delivery-truck expenditures. Note also the difference between extraordinary and ordinary repairs.

Treating a capital expenditure as a revenue expenditure, or vice versa, creates errors in the financial statements. Suppose a company makes an extraordinary repair to equipment and erroneously expenses this cost. It is a capital expenditure that should have been debited to an asset account. This accounting error overstates expenses and understates net income on the income statement. On the balance sheet,

Short Exercise: Basiden Co. purchased a used truck. Identify the following truck-related expenditures as revenue or capital expenditures:
1. Purchase price of truck, $10,000
2. Painting company logo on truck when purchased, $500
3. Gasoline for truck, $20
4. Hydraulic loader for truck, $1,500
5. 30,000-mile inspection, $100

A: Capital: 1, 2, 4; Revenue: 3, 5

EXHIBIT 10-14
Delivery-Truck Expenditures

the equipment account is understated, and so is owner's (or stockholders') equity. Capitalizing the cost of an ordinary repair creates the opposite error. Expenses are then understated and net income is overstated on the income statement. And the balance sheet reports overstated amounts for assets and for owner's (or stockholders') equity.

SUMMARY PROBLEMS FOR YOUR REVIEW

PROBLEM 1

The figures that follow appear in the Solution to the Mid-Chapter Summary Problem, Requirement 2, on page 416.

	Method A: Straight-Line			Method B: Double-Declining-Balance		
Year	Annual Depreciation Expense	Accumulated Depreciation	Book Value	Annual Depreciation Expense	Accumulated Depreciation	Book Value
Start			$44,000			$44,000
19X5	$4,000	$ 4,000	40,000	$8,800	$ 8,800	35,200
19X6	4,000	8,000	36,000	7,040	15,840	28,160
19X7	4,000	12,000	32,000	5,632	21,472	22,528

Required

Suppose the income tax authorities permitted a choice between these two depreciation methods. Which method would you select for income tax purposes? Why?

PROBLEM 2

A corporation purchased a building at a cost of $500,000 on January 1, 19X3. Management has depreciated the building by using the straight-line method, a 35-year life, and a residual value of $150,000. On July 1, 19X7, the company sold the building for $575,000 cash. The fiscal year of the corporation ends on December 31.

Required

Record depreciation for 19X7 and record the sale of the building on July 1, 19X7.

PROBLEM 1

For tax purposes, most companies select the accelerated method because it results in the most depreciation in the earliest years of the equipment's life. Accelerated depreciation minimizes taxable income and income payments in the early years of the asset's life, thereby maximizing the business's cash at the earliest possible time.

PROBLEM 2

To record depreciation to date of sale and related sale of building:

19X7			
July 1	Depreciation Expense—Building		
	[($500,000 – $150,000)/35 years × 1/2 year].................................	5,000	
	Accumulated Depreciation—Building		5,000
	To update depreciation.		
July 1	Cash	575,000	
	Accumulated Depreciation—Building		
	[($500,000 – $150,000)/35 years × 4 1/2 years]	45,000	
	Building		500,000
	Gain on Sale of Building..		120,000
	To record sale of building.		

SUMMARY

1. Identify the elements of a plant asset's cost. *Plant assets* are long-lived assets that the business uses in its operation. These assets are not held for sale as inventory.

2. Explain the concept of depreciation. The process of allocating a plant asset's cost to expense over the period the asset is used is called *depreciation*. The cost of all plant assets but land is expensed through depreciation.

3. Account for depreciation by four methods. Businesses may compute the depreciation of plant assets by four methods: *straight-line*, *units-of-production*, and the *accelerated* methods: *double-declining-balance* and *sum-of-years'-digits*. To measure depreciation, the accountant subtracts the asset's estimated residual value from its cost and divides that amount by the asset's estimated useful life. Most companies use the straight-line method for financial reporting purposes.

4. Identify the best depreciation method for income tax purposes. Almost all companies use an accelerated method for income tax purposes. Accelerated depreciation results in greater tax deductions early in the asset's life. These deductions decrease income tax payments and conserve cash that the company can use in its business.

5. Account for disposal of plant assets. Before disposing of a plant asset, the business updates the asset's depreciation. Disposal is recorded by removing the book balances from both the asset account and its related accumulated depreciation account. Disposal often results in recognition of a gain or a loss.

6. Account for natural resource assets and depletion. The cost of natural resources, a special category of long-lived assets, is expensed through *depletion*. Depletion of natural resources is computed on a units-of-production basis.

7. Account for intangible assets and amortization. Long-lived assets called *intangibles* are rights that have no physical form. The cost of intangibles is expensed through *amortization*. Amortization of intangibles is computed on a straight-line basis over a maximum of 40 years. However, the useful lives of most intangibles are shorter than their legal lives. Depreciation, depletion, and amortization are identical in concept.

8. Distinguish capital expenditures from revenue expenditures. *Capital expenditures* increase the capacity or the efficiency of an asset or extend its useful life. Accordingly, they are debited to an asset account. *Revenue expenditures* merely maintain the asset's usefulness and are debited to an expense account.

SELF-STUDY QUESTIONS

Test your understanding of the chapter by marking the best answer for each of the following questions.

1. Which of the following payments is *not* included in the cost of land? *(pp. 407–408)*
    a. Removal of old building
    b. Legal fees
    c. Back property taxes paid at acquisition
    d. Cost of fencing and lighting

2. A business paid $120,000 for two machines valued at $90,000 and $60,000. The business will record these machines at *(p. 408)*
    a. $90,000 and $60,000
    b. $60,000 each
    c. $72,000 and $48,000
    d. $70,000 and $50,000

3. Which of the following definitions fits depreciation? *(p. 408)*
    a. Allocation of the asset's market value to expense over its useful life
    b. Allocation of the asset's cost to expense over its useful life
    c. Decreases in the asset's market value over its useful life
    d. Increases in the fund set aside to replace the asset when it is worn out

4. Which depreciation method's amounts are not computed on the basis of time? *(p. 411)*
    a. Straight-line
    b. Units-of-production
    c. Double-declining-balance
    d. Sum-of-years'-digits

5. Which depreciation method gives the largest amount of expense in the early years of using the asset and therefore is best for income tax purposes? *(p. 416)*
    a. Straight-line
    b. Units-of-production
    c. Accelerated
    d. All are equal

6. A company paid $450,000 for a building and depreciated it by the straight-line method over a 40-year life with estimated residual value of $50,000. After 10 years, it became evident that the building's remaining useful life would be 40 years. Depreciation for the eleventh year is *(p. 419)*
    a. $7,500
    b. $8,750
    c. $10,000
    d. $12,500

7. Labrador, Inc., scrapped an automobile that cost $14,000 and had a book value of $1,100. The entry to record this disposal is *(p. 421)*
    a. Loss on Disposal of Automobile 1,100
        Automobile.................................. 1,100
    b. Accumulated Depreciation............... 14,000
        Automobile.................................. 14,000
    c. Accumulated Depreciation............... 12,900
        Automobile.................................. 12,900
    d. Accumulated Depreciation............... 12,900
        Loss on Disposal of Automobile 1,100
        Automobile.................................. 14,000

8. Depletion is computed in the same manner as which depreciation method? *(p. 424)*
    a. Straight-line
    b. Units-of-production
    c. Double-declining-balance
    d. Sum-of-years'-digits

9. Lacy Corporation paid $550,000 to acquire Gentsch, Inc. Gentsch's assets had a market value of $900,000, and its liabilities were $400,000. In recording the acquisition, Lacy will record goodwill of *(p. 427)*
    a. $50,000
    b. $100,000
    c. $550,000
    d. $0

10. Which of the following items is a revenue expenditure? *(p. 428)*
    a. Property tax paid on land one year after it is acquired
    b. Survey fee paid during the acquisition of land
    c. Legal fee paid to acquire land
    d. Building permit paid to construct a warehouse on the land

Answers to the Self-Study Questions follow the Accounting Vocabulary.

ACCOUNTING VOCABULARY

Accelerated depreciation method. A depreciation method that writes off a relatively larger amount of the asset's cost nearer the start of its useful life than does the straight-line method *(p. 412)*.

Amortization. The systematic reduction of a lump-sum amount. Expense that applies to intangible assets in the same way depreciation applies to plant assets and depletion applies to natural resources *(p. 425)*.

Capital expenditure. Expenditure that increases the capacity or efficiency of an asset or extends its useful life. Capital expenditures are debited to an asset account *(p. 428)*.

Copyright. Exclusive right to reproduce and sell a book, musical composition, film, other work of art, or computer program. Issued by the federal government, copyrights extend 50 years beyond the author's life *(p. 426)*.

Depletion expense. That portion of a natural resource's cost that is used up in a particular period. Depletion expense is computed just as units-of-production depreciation is *(p. 424)*.

Depreciable cost. The cost of a plant asset minus its estimated residual value *(p. 410)*.

Double-declining-balance (DDB) method. An accelerated depreciation method that computes annual depreciation by multiplying the asset's decreasing book value by a constant percentage, which is two times the straight-line rate *(p. 412)*.

Estimated residual value. Expected cash value of an asset at the end of its useful life. Also called residual value, scrap value, or salvage value *(p. 410)*.

Estimated useful life. Length of service that a business expects to get from an asset, may be expressed in years, units of output, miles, or other measures *(p. 409)*.

Extraordinary repair. Repair work that generates a capital expenditure *(p. 428)*.

Franchises and licenses. Privileges granted by a private business or a government to sell a product or service in accordance with specified conditions *(p. 426)*.

Goodwill. Excess of the cost of an acquired company over the sum of the market values of its net assets (assets minus liabilities) *(p. 427)*.

Intangible asset. An asset with no physical form, a special right to current and expected future benefits *(p. 425)*.

Leasehold. Prepayment that a lessee (renter) makes to secure the use of an asset from a lessor (landlord) *(p. 426)*.

Ordinary repair. Repair work that creates a revenue expenditure, which is debited to an expense account *(p. 428)*.

Patent. A federal government grant giving the holder the exclusive right for 17 years to produce and sell an invention *(p. 425)*.

Plant asset. Long-lived assets, such as land, buildings, and equipment, used in the operation of the business *(p. 406)*.

Revenue expenditure. Expenditure that merely maintains an asset in its existing condition or restores the asset to good working order. Revenue expenditures are expensed (matched against revenue) *(p. 428)*.

Straight-line (SL) method. Depreciation method in which an equal amount of depreciation expense is assigned to each year (or period) of asset use *(p. 410)*.

Sum-of-years'-digits (SYD) method. An accelerated depreciation method in which depreciation is figured by multiplying the depreciable cost of the asset by a fraction. The denominator of the SYD fraction is the sum of the years' digits of the asset's life. The numerator starts with the asset life in years and decreases by one each year thereafter *(p. 413)*.

Trademark and trade name. Distinctive identifications of a product or service *(p. 426)*.

Units-of-production (UOP) method. Depreciation method by which a fixed amount of depreciation is assigned to each unit of output produced by the plant asset *(p. 411)*.

ANSWERS TO SELF-STUDY QUESTIONS

1. d
2. c $90,000/($90,000 + $60,000) × $120,000 = $72,000;
   $60,000/($90,000 + $60,000) × $120,000 = $48,000
3. b
4. b
5. c
6. a Depreciable cost = $450,000 − $50,000 = $400,000
   $400,000/40 years = $10,000 per year
   $400,000 − ($10,000 × 10 years) = $300,000/40 years = $7,500 per year
7. d
8. b
9. a $550,000 − ($900,000 − $400,000) = $50,000
10. a

QUESTIONS

1. To what types of long-lived assets do the following expenses apply: depreciation, depletion, and amortization?
2. Describe how to measure the cost of a plant asset. Would an ordinary cost of repairing the asset after it is placed in service be included in the asset's cost?
3. Suppose land is purchased for $100,000. How do you account for the $8,000 cost of removing an unwanted building?
4. When assets are purchased as a group for a single price and no individual asset cost is given, how is each asset's cost determined?
5. Define depreciation. Present the common misconceptions about depreciation.
6. Which depreciation method does each of the following graphs characterize—straight-line, units-of-production, or accelerated?

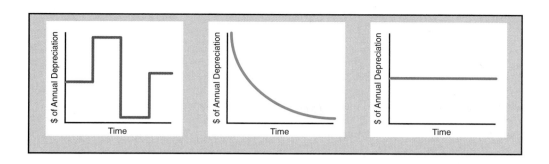

7. Which of the four depreciation methods results in the most depreciation in the first year of the asset's life?

8. Explain the concept of accelerated depreciation. Which other depreciation method is used in the definition of double-declining-balance depreciation?

9. The level of business activity fluctuates widely for Harwood Delivery Service, reaching its peak around Christmas each year. At other times, business is slow. Which depreciation method is most appropriate for the company's fleet of Ford Aerostar minivans?

10. Oswalt Computer Service Center uses the most advanced computers available to keep a competitive edge over other service centers. To maintain this advantage, Oswalt replaces its computers before they are worn out. Describe the major factors affecting the useful life of a plant asset, and indicate which factor seems most relevant to Oswalt's computers.

11. Which depreciation method does not consider estimated residual value in computing depreciation during the early years of the asset's life?

12. Which type of depreciation method is best from an income tax standpoint? Why?

13. How does depreciation affect income taxes? How does depreciation affect cash provided by operations?

14. Describe how to compute depreciation for less than a full year and how to account for depreciation for less than a full month.

15. Ragland Company paid $10,000 for office furniture. The company expected the furniture to remain in service for six years and to have a $1,000 residual value. After two years' use, company accountants believe the furniture will last an additional six years. How much depreciation will Ragland record for each of these six years, assuming straight-line depreciation and no change in the estimated residual value?

16. When a company sells a plant asset before the year's end, what must it record before accounting for the sale?

17. Describe how to determine whether a company experiences a gain or a loss when an old plant asset is exchanged for a new one. Does GAAP favor the recognition of gains or losses? Which accounting concept underlies your answer?

18. Identify seven elements of internal control designed to safeguard plant assets.

19. What expense applies to natural resources? By which depreciation method is this expense computed?

20. How do intangible assets differ from most other assets? Why are they assets at all? What expense applies to intangible assets?

21. Why is the cost of patents and other intangible assets often expensed over a shorter period than the legal life of the asset?

22. Your company has just purchased another company for $400,000. The market value of the other company's net assets is $325,000. What is the $75,000 excess called? What type of asset is it? What is the maximum period over which its cost is amortized under generally accepted accounting principles?

23. IBM Corporation is recognized as a world leader in the manufacture and sale of computers. The company's past success created vast amounts of business goodwill. Would you expect to see *this* goodwill reported on IBM's financial statements? Why or why not?

24. Distinguish a capital expenditure from a revenue expenditure. Explain the title "revenue expenditure," which is curious in that a revenue expenditure is a debit to an expense account.

25. Are ordinary repairs capital expenditures or revenue expenditures? Which type of expenditures are extraordinary repairs?

EXERCISES

Identifying the elements of a plant asset's cost
(Obj. 1)

E10-1   A company purchased land, paying $66,000 cash as a down payment and signing a $120,000 note payable for the balance. In addition, the company paid delinquent property tax of $2,000, a title fee of $500, and a $5,400 charge for leveling the land and removing an unwanted building. The company constructed an office building on the land at a cost of $410,000. It also paid $18,000 for a fence around the boundary of the property, $2,400 for the company sign near the entrance to the property, and $6,000 for special lighting of the grounds. Determine the cost of the company's land, land improvements, and building.

Allocating cost to assets acquired in a lump-sum purchase
(Obj. 1)

E10-2   Hugh McMillen Company bought three used machines in a $30,000 purchase. An independent appraisal of the machines produced the following figures:

Machine No.	Appraised Value
1	$14,000
2	18,000
3	8,000

Assuming that Hugh McMillen paid cash for the machines, record the purchase in the general journal, identifying each machine's individual cost in a separate Machine account.

Explaining the concept of depreciation
(Obj. 2)

E10-3   Greg Mendoza has just slept through the class in which Professor Conway explained the concept of depreciation. Because the next test is scheduled for Wednesday, Mendoza telephones Leah Gerbing to get her notes from the lecture. Gerbing's notes are concise: "Depreciation— Sounds like Greek to me." Mendoza next tries Ray Mellichamp, who says he thinks depreciation is what happens when an asset wears out. Sally Bower is confident that depreciation is the process of building up a cash fund to replace an asset at the end of its useful life. Explain the concept of depreciation for Mendoza. Evaluate the explanations of Mellichamp and Bower. Be specific.

Computing depreciation by four methods
(Obj. 3)

E10-4   A company delivery truck was acquired on January 2, 19X1, for $13,000. The truck was expected to remain in service four years and to last 120,000 miles. At the end of its useful life, company officials estimated that the truck's residual value would be $1,000. The truck traveled 34,000 miles the first year, 38,000 the second year, 28,000 the third year, and 20,000 in the fourth year. Prepare a schedule of *depreciation expense* per year for the truck under the four depreciation methods. Show your computations.

Recording partial-year depreciation computed by two methods
(Obj. 3)

E10-5   **Situation 1.** Arnold Industries purchased office furniture on June 3, 19X4, for $2,800 cash. Lisa Arnold expects it to remain useful for six years and to have a residual value of $400. Arnold uses the straight-line depreciation method. Record Arnold's depreciation on the furniture for the year ended December 31, 19X4.

Situation 2. Christie Company purchased equipment on October 19, 19X2, for $16,500, signing a note payable for that amount. Christie estimated that this equipment will be useful for three years and have a residual value of $1,500. Assuming Christie uses double-declining-balance depreciation, record Christie's depreciation on the machine for the year ended December 31, 19X2.

Journalizing a change in a plant asset's useful life
(Obj. 3)

E10-6   A company purchased a building for $980,000 and depreciated it on a straight-line basis over a 30-year period. The estimated residual value was $80,000. After using the building for 15 years, the company realized that wear and tear on the building would force the company to replace it before 30 years. Starting with the sixteenth year, the company began depreciating the building over a revised total life of 20 years, retaining the $80,000 estimate of residual value. Record depreciation expense on the building for years 15 and 16.

Preparing a plant ledger record, units-of-production depreciation
(Obj. 3)

E10-7   Tusa Wholesale Grocers uses a plant ledger record to account for its delivery vehicles, which are located at the company's service garage. The fleet of vehicles cost $91,000 when purchased from Steakley Chevrolet Company on September 1, 19X2. This cost is the debit balance in the Delivery Vehicles account in the general ledger. Tusa uses the units-of-production depreciation method and estimates a useful life of 400,000 miles and an $11,000 residual value for the trucks. The garage foreman is responsible for the vehicles. The company's fiscal year ends on December 31. Miles traveled were 30,000 in 19X2, 105,000 in 19X3, and 98,000 in 19X4. Complete a plant ledger record for these vehicles through December 31, 19X4.

E10-8 Using the data in Exercise 10-4, identify the depreciation method that would be most advantageous from an income tax perspective. Which depreciation method do most companies use for reporting to their stockholders and creditors on their financial statements?

Identifying depreciation methods for income tax and financial reporting purposes (Obj. 4)

E10-9 On January 2, 19X1, Gulf Coast Products purchased store fixtures for $8,700 cash, expecting the fixtures to remain in service 10 years. Gulf Coast has depreciated the fixtures on a sum-of-years'-digits basis, assuming no estimated residual value. On October 30, 19X8, Gulf Coast sold the fixtures for $950 cash. Record depreciation expense on the fixtures for the 10 months ended October 30, 19X8, and also record the sale of the fixtures.

Recording the sale of a plant asset (Obj. 5)

E10-10 A machine cost $15,000. At the end of four years, its accumulated depreciation was $4,500. For each of the following situations, record the trade-in of this old machine for a new, similar machine.

Exchanging plant assets (Obj. 5)

    Situation 1. The new machine had a cash price of $17,400; the dealer allowed a trade-in allowance of $9,000 on the old machine, and you paid the $8,400 balance in cash.

    Situation 2. The new machine had a cash price of $18,000; the dealer allowed a trade-in allowance of $10,900 on the old machine; and you signed a note payable for the $7,100 balance.

E10-11 Yosemite Mines paid $298,500 for the right to extract ore from a 200,000-ton mineral deposit. In addition to the purchase price, Yosemite also paid a $500 filing fee and a $1,000 license fee to the state of California. Because Yosemite purchased the rights to the minerals only, the company expected the asset to have zero residual value when fully depleted. During the first year of production, Yosemite removed 35,000 tons of ore. Make general journal entries to record (a) purchase of the mineral rights (debit Mineral Asset), (b) payment of fees, and (c) depletion for first-year production.

Recording natural resource assets and depletion (Obj. 6)

E10-12 **Part 1.** Mutyala Corporation manufactures high-speed printers and has recently purchased for $4.52 million a patent for the design for a new laser printer. Although it gives legal protection for 17 years, the patent is expected to provide Mutyala with a competitive advantage for only eight years. Assuming the straight-line method of amortization, use general journal entries to record (a) the purchase of the patent and (b) amortization for year 1.

Recording intangibles, amortization, and a change in the asset's useful life (Obj. 7)

    Part 2. After using the patent for four years, Mutyala learns at an industry trade show that another company is designing a more efficient printer. On the basis of this new information, Mutyala decides, starting with year 5, to amortize the remaining cost of the patent over two additional years, giving the patent a total useful life of six years. Record amortization for year 5.

E10-13 Assume that PepsiCo, Inc., purchased Chip-O Company for $10 million cash. The market value of Chip-O's assets was $14 million, and Chip-O Company had liabilities of $11 million.

Computing and recording goodwill (Obj. 7)

1. Compute the cost of the goodwill purchased by PepsiCo.
2. Record the purchase by PepsiCo.
3. Record amortization of goodwill for year 1, assuming the straight-line method and a useful life of 10 years.

E10-14 Classify each of the following expenditures as a capital expenditure or a revenue expenditure (expense) related to machinery: (a) purchase price, (b) sales tax paid on the purchase price, (c) transportation and insurance while machinery is in transport from seller to buyer, (d) installation, (e) training of personnel for initial operation of the machinery, (f) special reinforcement to the machinery platform, (g) income tax paid on income earned from the sale of products manufactured by the machinery, (h) major overhaul to extend useful life by three years, (i) ordinary recurring repairs to keep the machinery in good working order, (j) lubrication of the machinery before it is placed in service, (k) periodic lubrication after the machinery is placed in service.

Distinguishing capital expenditures from revenue expenditures (Obj. 8)

Measuring the effect of an error
(Obj. 3, 8)

E10-15 Le Coque Sportswear is a catalog merchant in France—similar to L. L. Bean and Lands' End in the United States. The company's assets consist mainly of inventory, a warehouse, and automated shipping equipment. Assume that early in year 1 Le Coque purchased equipment at a cost of 3 million francs (F 3 million). Management expects the equipment to remain in service six years. Because the equipment is so specialized, estimated residual value is negligible. Le Coque uses the straight-line depreciation method. Through an accounting error, Le Coque accidentally expensed the entire cost of the equipment at the time of purchase. The company is family-owned and operated as a partnership, so it pays no income tax.

Required

Prepare a schedule to show the overstatement or understatement in the following items at the end of each year over the six-year life of the equipment.

1. Total current assets
2. Equipment, net
3. Net income
4. Owners' equity
5. Debt ratio (Total liabilities/Total assets)

Reconstructing transactions from the financial statements
(Obj. 3, 5)

E10-16 Ford Motor Company's comparative balance sheet recently reported these amounts (in millions of dollars):

	December 31,	
Property:	**19X1**	**19X0**
Land, plant, and equipment...	$35,726.3	$34,825.1
Less accumulated depreciation	(19,422.0)	(18,486.8)
Net land, plant, and equipment	16,304.3	16,338.3
Unamortized special tools..	6,218.0	5,869.5
Net property...	$22,522.3	$22,207.8

Ford's income statement for 19X1 reported the following expenses (in millions):

Depreciation...	$2,455.8
Amortization of special tools	1,822.1

Unamortized special tools refers to the remaining asset balance after amortization expense has been subtracted. Ford uses no accumulated amortization account for special tools.

Required

1. There were no disposals of special tools during 19X1. Compute the cost of new acquisitions of special tools.
2. Assume that during 19X1 Ford sold land, plant, and equipment for $92 million and that this transaction produced a gain of $9 million. What was the book value of the assets sold?
3. Use the answer to Requirement 2 to compute the cost of land, plant, and equipment acquired during 19X1. For convenience, work with net land, plant, and equipment.

PROBLEMS

(GROUP A)

Identifying the elements of a plant asset's cost
(Obj. 1)

P10-1A Schlitterbohn Company incurred the following costs in acquiring land and a garage, making land improvements, and constructing and furnishing a home office building.

a. Purchase price of 3 1/2 acres of land, including an old building that will be used as a garage for company vehicles (land market value is $600,000; building market value is $100,000)...	$630,000
b. Delinquent real estate taxes on the land to be paid by Schlitterbohn	3,700
c. Landscaping (additional dirt and earth moving)..	3,550
d. Title insurance on the land acquisition	1,000
e. Fence around the boundary of the land	44,100
f. Building permit for the home office building	200

g. Architect fee for the design of the home office building .... $ 25,000

h. Company signs near front and rear approaches to the company property............... 23,550

i. Renovation of the garage 23,800

j. Concrete, wood, steel girders, and other materials used in the construction of the home office building.. 814,000

k. Masonry, carpentry, roofing, and other labor to construct home office building 734,000

l. Repair of vandalism damage to home office building during construction.............. 4,100

m. Parking lots and concrete walks on the property 17,450

n. Lights for the parking lot, walkways, and company signs... 8,900

o. Supervisory salary of construction supervisor (90 percent to home office building; 6 percent to fencing, parking lot, and concrete walks; and 4 percent to garage renovation) 55,000

p. Office furniture for the home office building 123,500

q. Transportation of furniture from seller to the home office building...................... 1,300

r. Landscaping (trees and shrubs).. 9,100

Schlitterbohn depreciates buildings over 40 years, land improvements over 20 years, and furniture over 8 years, all on a straight-line basis with zero residual value.

Required

1. Set up columns for Land, Land Improvements, Home Office Building, Garage, and Furniture. Show how to account for each of the foregoing costs by listing the cost under the correct account. Compute the total amount that would be debited to each account.

2. Assuming that all construction was complete and the assets were placed in service on March 19, record depreciation for the year ended December 31. Round figures to the nearest dollar.

3. How will what you learned in this problem help you manage a business?

P10-2A The board of directors of Town & Country Sales Company is having its regular quarterly meeting. Accounting policies are on the agenda, and depreciation is being discussed. A new board member, an attorney, has some strong opinions about two aspects of depreciation policy. Dirk Green argues that depreciation must be coupled with a fund to replace company assets. Otherwise, there is no substance to depreciation, he argues. He also challenges the five-year estimated life over which Town & Country is depreciating company computers. He notes that the computers will last much longer and should be depreciated over at least 10 years.

Explaining the concept of depreciation (Obj. 2)

Required

Write a paragraph or two to explain the concept of depreciation to Dirk Green and to answer his arguments.

P10-3A On January 2, 19X1, Alamo Steel Company purchased three used delivery trucks at a total cost of $63,000. Before placing the trucks in service, the company spent $2,200 painting them, $800 replacing their tires, and $4,000 overhauling their engines and reconditioning their bodies. Alamo management estimates that the trucks will remain in service for six years and have a residual value of $16,000. The trucks' combined annual mileage is expected to be 18,000 miles in each of the first four years and 14,000 miles in each of the next two years. In trying to decide which depreciation method to use, Walter Glass, the general manager, requests a depreciation schedule for each of the four generally accepted depreciation methods (straight-line, units-of-production, double-declining-balance, and sum-of-years'-digits).

Computing depreciation by four methods and the cash-flow advantage of accelerated depreciation for tax purposes (Obj. 3, 4)

Required

1. Assuming that Alamo Steel Company depreciates its delivery trucks as a unit, prepare a depreciation schedule for each of the four generally accepted depreciation methods, showing asset cost, depreciation expense, accumulated depreciation, and asset book value. Use the formats of Exhibits 10-4 through 10-7.

2. Alamo reports to stockholders and creditors in the financial statements using the depreciation method that maximizes reported income in the early years of asset use. For income tax pur-

poses, however, the company uses the depreciation method that minimizes income tax payments in those early years. Consider the first year that Alamo uses the delivery trucks. Identify the depreciation methods that meet the general manager's objectives, assuming the income tax authorities would permit the use of any of the methods.

3. Assume that cash provided by operations before income tax is $80,000 for the delivery trucks' first year. The combined federal and state income tax rate is 40 percent. For the two depreciation methods identified in Requirement 2, compare the net income and cash provided by operations (cash flow). Use the format of Exhibit 10-10 for your answer. Show which method gives the net-income advantage and which method gives the cash-flow advantage. Ignore the earnings rate in the cash-flow analysis.

Journalizing and posting plant asset transactions; capital expenditures versus revenue expenditures
(Obj. 1, 3, 5, 8)

P10-4A   Centerior Energy Company provides electrical power to the area around Cleveland, Ohio. Assume that the company completed the following transactions:

19X4

Jan. 3   Paid $16,000 cash for a used service truck.
  5   Paid $1,200 to have the truck engine overhauled.
  7   Paid $300 to have the truck modified for business use.
Oct. 3   Paid $814 for transmission repair and oil change.
Dec. 31   Used the double-declining-balance method to record depreciation on the truck. (Assume a four-year life.)
  31   Closed the appropriate accounts.

19X5

Mar. 13   Replaced the truck's broken windshield for $275 cash.
June 26   Traded in the service truck for a new truck costing $23,000. The dealer granted a $4,000 allowance on the old truck, and Centerior Energy paid the balance in cash. Recorded 19X5 depreciation for the year to date and then recorded the exchange of trucks.
Dec. 31   Used the double-declining-balance method to record depreciation on the new truck. (Assume a four-year life.)
  31   Closed the appropriate accounts.

Required

1. Open the following accounts in the general ledger: Service Trucks; Accumulated Depreciation—Service Trucks; Truck Repair Expense; Depreciation Expense—Service Trucks; and Loss on Exchange of Service Trucks.

2. Record the transactions in the general ledger and post to the ledger accounts opened.

Recording plant asset transactions, exchanges, changes in useful life
(Obj. 1, 3, 5, 8)

P10-5A   A. C. Nielsen Company surveys American television viewing trends. Nielsen's balance sheet reports the following assets under Property and Equipment: Land, Buildings, Office Furniture, Communication Equipment, Televideo Equipment, and Leasehold Improvements. The company has a separate accumulated depreciation account for each of these assets except land and leasehold improvements. Amortization on leasehold improvements is credited directly to the Leasehold Improvements account rather than to Accumulated Depreciation—Leasehold Improvements.

Assume that Nielsen completed the following transactions:

Jan. 4   Traded in communication equipment with book value of $31,000 (cost of $96,000) for similar new equipment with a cash cost of $108,000. The seller gave Nielsen a trade-in allowance of $20,000 on the old equipment, and Nielsen paid the remainder in cash.
  19   Purchased office furniture for $45,000 plus 6-percent sales tax and $300 shipping charge. The company gave a 90-day, 10-percent note in payment.
Apr. 19   Paid the furniture note and related interest.
Aug. 29   Sold a building that had cost $475,000 and had accumulated depreciation of $353,500 through December 31 of the preceding year. Depreciation is computed on a straight-line basis. The building has a 30-year useful life and a residual value of $47,500. Nielsen received $250,000 cash and a $450,000 note receivable.
Sep. 6   Paid cash to renovate leased assets at a cost of $53,000.
Nov. 10   Purchased used communication and televideo equipment from the Gallup polling organization. Total cost was $90,000 paid in cash. An independent appraisal valued the communication equipment at $75,000 and the televideo equipment at $25,000.

Dec. 31   Recorded depreciation as follows:

Equipment is depreciated by the double-declining-balance method over a five-year life with zero residual value. Record depreciation on the equipment purchased on January 4 and on November 10 separately.

Office furniture has an expected useful life of eight years with an estimated residual value of $5,000. Depreciation is computed by the sum-of-years'-digits method.

Amortization on leasehold improvements is computed on a straight-line basis over the life of the lease, which is six years, with zero residual value.

Depreciation on buildings is computed by the straight-line method. The company had assigned buildings an estimated useful life of 30 years and a residual value that is 10 percent of cost. After using the buildings for 20 years, the company has come to believe that their total useful life will be 35 years. Residual value remains unchanged. The buildings cost $96,000,000.

Required

Record the transactions in the general journal.

P10-6A   Suppose Procter and Gamble uses plant ledger records to control its service trucks, purchased from Rountree Motors. The supervisor is responsible for the trucks, which are located at the company's service garage. The following transactions were completed during 19X6 and 19X7:

Distinguishing capital expenditures from revenue expenditures; preparing a plant ledger record (Obj. 3, 5, 8)

19X6
Jan. 10   Paid $11,500 cash for a used service truck (truck no. 86).
      11   Paid $1,500 to have the truck engine overhauled.
      12   Paid $250 to have the truck modified for business use.
Aug. 3   Paid $603 for transmission repair and oil change.
Dec. 31   Recorded depreciation on the truck by the double-declining-balance method, based on a five-year life and a $1,500 residual value.

19X7
Mar. 13   Replaced a damaged bumper on truck no. 86 at a cash cost of $295.
May 12   Traded in service truck no. 86 for a new one (truck no. 103) with a cash cost of $20,500. The dealer granted a $7,000 allowance on the old truck, and Procter and Gamble paid the balance in cash. Recorded 19X7 depreciation for year to date and then recorded exchange of the trucks.
Dec. 31   Recorded depreciation on truck no. 103 by the double-declining-balance method, based on a five-year life and a $2,000 residual value.

Required

1. Identify the capital expenditures and the revenue expenditures in the transactions. Which expenditures are debited to an asset account? Which expenditures are debited to an expense account?
2. Prepare a separate plant ledger record for each of the trucks.

P10-7A   *Part 1.* Transco Energy Company operates a pipeline that provides natural gas to Atlanta; Washington, D.C.; Philadelphia; and New York City. The company's balance sheet includes the asset Oil Properties.

Recording intangibles, natural resources, and the related expenses (Obj. 6, 7)

Suppose Transco paid $8 million cash for oil and gas reserves that contained an estimated 625,000 barrels of oil. Assume that the company paid $350,000 for additional geological tests of the property and $110,000 to prepare the surface for drilling. Prior to production, the company signed a $65,000 note payable to have a building constructed on the property. Because the building provides on-site headquarters for the drilling effort and will be abandoned when the oil is depleted, its cost is debited to the Oil Properties account and included in depletion charges. During the first year of production, Transco removed 82,000 barrels of oil, which it sold on credit for $19 per barrel.

Required

Make general journal entries to record all transactions related to the oil and gas reserves, including depletion and sale of the first-year production.

Part 2. United Telecommunications, Inc. (United Telecom), provides communication services in Florida, North Carolina, New Jersey, Texas, and other states. The company's balance sheet reports the asset Cost of Acquisitions in Excess of the Fair Market Value of the Net Assets of Subsidiaries. Assume that United Telecom purchased this asset as part of the acquisition of another company, which carried these figures:

Book value of assets	$640,000
Market value of assets	920,000
Liabilities	405,000

Required

1. What is another title for the asset Cost of Acquisitions in Excess of the Fair Market Value of the Net Assets of Subsidiaries?
2. Make the general journal entry to record United Telecom's purchase of the other company for $850,000 cash.
3. Assuming United Telecom amortizes Cost of Acquisitions in Excess of the Fair Market Value of the Net Assets of Subsidiaries over 20 years, record the straight-line amortization for one year.

Part 3. Assume that United Telecom purchased a patent for $220,000. Before using the patent, United incurred an additional cost of $25,000 for a lawsuit to defend the company's right to purchase it. Even though the patent gives United legal protection for 17 years, company management has decided to amortize its cost over a five-year period because of the industry's fast-changing technologies.

Required

Make general journal entries to record the patent transactions, including straight-line amortization for one year.

(GROUP B)

Identifying the elements of a plant asset's cost
(Obj. 1)

P10-1B   Fidelity Union Insurance Company incurred the following costs in acquiring land, making land improvements, and constructing and furnishing an office building.

a.	Purchase price of four acres of land, including an old building that will be used for storage (land market value is $280,000; building market value is $20,000)...	$216,000
b.	Landscaping (additional dirt and earth moving)...	8,100
c.	Fence around the boundary of the land	17,650
d.	Attorney fee for title search on the land..	600
e.	Delinquent real estate taxes on the land to be paid by Fidelity Union	5,900
f.	Company signs at front of the company property	1,800
g.	Building permit for the office building...	350
h.	Architect fee for the design of the office building...	19,800
i.	Masonry, carpentry, roofing, and other labor to construct the office building	709,000
j.	Concrete, wood, steel girders, and other materials used in the construction of the office building..	214,000
k.	Renovation of the storage building	41,800
l.	Repair of storm damage to storage building during construction	2,200
m.	Landscaping (trees and shrubs)...	6,400
n.	Parking lot and concrete walks on the property	29,750
o.	Lights for the parking lot, walkways, and company signs...	7,300
p.	Supervisory salary of construction supervisor (85 percent to office building; 9 percent to fencing, parking lot, and concrete walks; and 6 percent to storage building renovation)..	40,000
q.	Office furniture for the office building..	107,100
r.	Transportation and installation of furniture...	1,800

Fidelity Union depreciates buildings over 40 years, land improvements over 20 years, and furniture over eight years, all on a straight-line basis with zero residual value.

Required

1. Set up columns for Land, Land Improvements, Office Building, Storage Building, and Furniture. Show how to account for each of the foregoing costs by listing the cost under the correct account. Compute the total amount that would be debited to each account.

2. Assuming that all construction was complete and the assets were placed in service on May 4, record depreciation for the year ended December 31. Round off figures to the nearest dollar.

3. How will what you learned in this problem help you manage a business?

P10-2B The board of directors of San Antonio Parking Lot Company is reviewing the 19X8 annual report. A new board member—a physician with little business experience—questions the company accountant about the depreciation amounts. The physician wonders why depreciation expense has decreased from $200,000 in 19X6 to $184,000 in 19X7 to $172,000 in 19X8. He states that he could understand the decreasing annual amounts if the company had been disposing of properties each year, but that has not occurred. Further, he notes that growth in the city is increasing the values of company properties. Why is the company recording depreciation when the property values are increasing?

Explaining the concept of depreciation
(Obj. 2)

Required

Write a paragraph or two to explain the concept of depreciation to the physician and to answer the physician's questions.

P10-3B On January 3, 19X1, Domenici Corporation paid $192,000 for equipment used in manufacturing automotive supplies. In addition to the basic purchase price, the company paid $700 transportation charges, $100 insurance for the goods in transit, $4,100 sales tax, and $3,100 for a special platform on which to place the equipment in the plant. Domenici management estimates that the equipment will remain in service five years and have a residual value of $20,000. The equipment will produce 50,000 units the first year, with annual production decreasing by 5,000 units during each of the next four years (that is, 45,000 units in year 2; 40,000 units in year 3; and so on). In trying to decide which depreciation method to use, Alfonse Domenici has requested a depreciation schedule for each of the four generally accepted depreciation methods (straight-line, units-of-production, double-declining-balance, and sum-of-years'-digits).

Computing depreciation by four methods and the cash-flow advantage of accelerated depreciation for tax purposes
(Obj. 3, 4)

Required

1. For each of the four generally accepted depreciation methods, prepare a depreciation schedule showing asset cost, depreciation expense, accumulated depreciation, and asset book value. Use the format of Exhibits 10-4 through 10-7.

2. Domenici reports to stockholders and creditors in the financial statements using the depreciation method that maximizes reported income in the early years of asset use. For income tax purposes, however, the company uses the depreciation method that minimizes income tax payments in those early years. Consider the first year Domenici uses the equipment. Identify the depreciation methods that meet Domenici's objectives, assuming the income tax authorities would permit the use of any of the methods.

3. Assume that cash provided by operations before income tax is $180,000 for the equipment's first year. The combined federal and state income tax rate is 40 percent. For the two depreciation methods identified in Requirement 2, compare the net income and cash provided by operations (cash flow). Use the format of Exhibit 10-10 for your answer. Show which method gives the net-income advantage and which method gives the cash-flow advantage. Ignore the earnings rate in the cash-flow analysis.

P10-4B Assume that a Payless drugstore completed the following transactions:

Journalizing and posting plant asset transactions; capital expenditures versus revenue expenditures
(Obj. 1, 3, 5, 8)

19X2
Jan. 6   Paid $9,000 cash for a used delivery truck.
      7   Paid $800 to have the truck engine overhauled.
      8   Paid $200 to have the truck modified for business use.
Aug. 21   Paid $156 for a minor tuneup.
Dec. 31   Recorded depreciation on the truck by the double-declining-balance method (assume a four-year life and a $2,000 residual value).
      31   Closed the appropriate accounts.

19X3

Feb. 8   Traded in the delivery truck for a new truck costing $13,000. The dealer granted a $4,000 allowance on the old truck, and the store paid the balance in cash. Recorded 19X3 depreciation for the year to date and then recorded the exchange of trucks.

July 8   Repaired the new truck's damaged fender for $625 cash.

Dec. 31   Recorded depreciation on the new truck by the double-declining-balance method. (Assume a four-year life and a residual value of $3,000.)

31   Closed the appropriate accounts.

Required

1. Open the following accounts in the general ledger: Delivery Trucks; Accumulated Depreciation—Delivery Trucks; Truck Repair Expense; Depreciation Expense—Delivery Trucks; and Loss on Exchange of Delivery Trucks.

2. Record the transaction in the general journal, and post to the ledger accounts opened.

Recording plant asset transactions, exchanges, changes in useful life
(Obj. 1, 3, 5, 8)

P10-5B   Central Freight Lines provides general freight service in the central United States. The company's balance sheet includes the following assets under Property, Plant, and Equipment: Land, Buildings, Motor-Carrier Equipment, and Leasehold Improvements. Assume that the company has a separate accumulated depreciation account for each of these assets except land and leasehold improvements. Amortization on leasehold improvements is credited directly to the Leasehold Improvements account rather than to Accumulated Amortization—Leasehold Improvements.

Assume that Central Freight Lines completed the following transactions:

Jan. 5   Traded in motor-carrier equipment with book value of $47,000 (cost of $130,000) for similar new equipment with a cash cost of $176,000. Central received a trade-in allowance of $60,000 on the old equipment and paid the remainder in cash.

Feb. 22   Purchased motor-carrier equipment for $136,000 plus 5-percent sales tax and $200 title fee. The company gave a 60-day, 12-percent note in payment.

Apr. 23   Paid the equipment note and related interest.

July 9   Sold a building that had cost $550,000 and had accumulated depreciation of $247,500 through December 31 of the preceding year. Depreciation is computed on a straight-line basis. The building has a 30-year useful life and a residual value of $55,000. Consolidated received $100,000 cash and a $600,000 note receivable.

Aug. 16   Paid cash to improve leased assets at a cost of $10,200.

Oct. 26   Purchased land and a building for a single price of $300,000. An independent appraisal valued the land at $115,000 and the building at $230,000.

Dec. 31   Recorded depreciation as follows:

Motor-carrier equipment has an expected useful life of five years and an estimated residual value of 5 percent of cost. Depreciation is computed on the double-declining-balance method. Make separate depreciation entries for equipment acquired on January 5 and February 22.

Amortization on leasehold improvements is computed on a straight-line basis over the life of the lease, which is 10 years, with zero residual value.

Depreciation on buildings is computed by the straight-line method. The company had assigned to its older buildings, which cost $200,000,000, an estimated useful life of 30 years with a residual value equal to 10 percent of the asset cost. However, management has come to believe that the buildings will remain useful for a total of 40 years. Residual value remains unchanged. The company has used all its buildings, except for the one purchased on October 26, for 10 years. The new building carries a 40-year useful life and a residual value equal to 10 percent of its cost. Make separate entries for depreciation on the building acquired on October 26 and the other buildings purchased in earlier years.

Required

Record the transactions in the general journal.

P10-6B   Suppose Illinois Power Co. uses plant ledger records to control its service trucks, purchased from Bird-Kultgen Ford. The supervisor is responsible for the trucks, which are located at the company's service garage. The following transactions were completed during 19X7 and 19X8:

Distinguishing capital expenditures from revenue expenditures; preparing a plant ledger record
(Obj. 3, 5, 8)

19X7

Jan. 6   Paid $12,420 cash for a used service truck (truck no. 117).
      7   Paid $2,500 to have the truck engine overhauled.
      8   Paid $180 to have the truck modified for business use.
Nov. 5   Paid $107 for replacement of one tire.
Dec. 31 Recorded depreciation on the truck by the double-declining-balance method, based on a four-year useful life and a $1,100 residual value.

19X8

July 16 Repaired a damaged fender on truck no. 117 at a cash cost of $877.
Sep. 6 Traded in service truck no. 117 for a new one (truck no. 182) with a cash cost of $18,000. The dealer granted a $5,500 allowance on the old truck, and Illinois Power paid the balance in cash. Recorded 19X8 depreciation for year to date and then recorded exchange of the trucks.
Dec. 31 Recorded depreciation on truck no. 182 by the double-declining-balance method, based on a four-year life and a $1,500 residual value.

Required

1. Identify the capital expenditures and the revenue expenditures in the transactions. Which expenditures are debited to an asset account? Which expenditures are debited to an expense account?

2. Prepare a separate plant ledger record for each of the trucks.

P10-7B   *Part 1.* Georgia-Pacific Corporation is one of the world's largest forest products companies. The company's balance sheet includes the assets Natural Gas, Oil, and Coal.

Recording intangibles, natural resources, and the related expenses
(Obj. 6, 7)

Suppose Georgia-Pacific paid $1.8 million cash for a lease giving the firm the right to work a mine that contained an estimated 125,000 tons of coal. Assume that the company paid $10,000 to remove unwanted buildings from the land and $45,000 to prepare the surface for mining. Further assume that Georgia-Pacific signed a $20,000 note payable to a landscaping company to return the land surface to its original condition after the lease ends. During the first year, Georgia-Pacific removed 35,000 tons of coal, which it sold on account for $17 per ton.

Required

Make general journal entries to record all transactions related to the coal, including depletion and sale of the first-year production.

Part 2. Collins Foods International, Inc., is the majority owner of Sizzler Restaurants. The company's balance sheet reports the asset Cost in Excess of Net Assets of Purchased Businesses. Assume that Collins purchased this asset as part of the acquisition of another company, which carried these figures:

Book value of assets..................	$2.4 million
Market value of assets	3.1 million
Liabilities.................................	2.2 million

Required

1. What is another title for the asset Cost in Excess of Net Assets of Purchased Businesses?

2. Make the general journal entry to record Collins's purchase of the other company for $1.7 million cash.

3. Assuming Collins amortizes Cost in Excess of Net Assets of Purchased Businesses over 20 years, record the straight-line amortization for one year.

Part 3. Suppose Collins purchased a Sizzler franchise license for $240,000. In addition to the basic purchase price, Collins also paid a lawyer $20,000 for assistance with the negotiations. Collins management believes the appropriate amortization period for its cost of the franchise license is eight years.

Required

Make general journal entries to record the franchise transactions, including straight-line amortization for one year.

EXTENDING YOUR KNOWLEDGE

DECISION PROBLEMS

Measuring profitability based on different inventory and depreciation methods
(Obj. 3)

1. Suppose you are considering investing in two businesses, Blue Bonnet Industries and Bavarian Products. The two companies are virtually identical, and both began operations at the beginning of the current year. During the year, each company purchased inventory as follows:

Jan.	4	10,000 units at	$4 =	$ 40,000
Apr.	6	5,000 units at	5 =	25,000
Aug.	9	7,000 units at	6 =	42,000
Nov. 27		10,000 units at	7 =	70,000
Totals		32,000		$177,000

Over the first year, both companies sold 25,000 units of inventory.

In early January both companies purchased equipment costing $150,000 that had a 10-year estimated useful life and a $20,000 residual value. Blue Bonnet uses the first-in, first-out (FIFO) method for its inventory and straight-line depreciation for its equipment. Bavarian uses last-in, first-out (LIFO) and double-declining-balance depreciation. Both companies' trial balances at December 31 included the following:

Sales revenue	$300,000
Operating expenses	80,000

Required

1. Prepare both companies' income statements.
2. Prepare a schedule that shows why one company appears to be more profitable than the other. Explain the schedule and amounts in your own words. What accounts for the different amounts?
3. Is one company more profitable than the other? Give your reason.

Plant assets and intangible assets
(Obj. 7, 8)

2. The following questions are unrelated except that they apply to fixed assets and intangible assets:

1. The Manager of Garden Ridge Corporation regularly buys plant assets and debits the cost to Repairs and Maintenance Expense. Why would he do that, since he knows this action violates GAAP?
2. The manager of Onassis Company regularly debits the cost of repairs and maintenance of plant assets to Plant and Equipment. Why would she do that, since she knows she is violating GAAP?
3. It has been suggested that, since many intangible assets have no value except to the company that owns them, they should be valued at $1.00 or zero on the balance sheet. Many accountants disagree with this view. Which view do you support? Why?

ETHICAL ISSUE

Village Oak Apartments purchased land and a building for the lump sum of $2.2 million. To get the maximum tax deduction, Village Oak managers allocated 90 percent of the purchase price to the building and only 10 percent to the land. A more realistic allocation would have been 70 percent to the building and 30 percent to the land.

Required

1. Explain the tax advantage of allocating too much to the building and too little to the land.
2. Was Village Oak's allocation ethical? If so, state why. If not, why not? Identify who was harmed.

FINANCIAL STATEMENT PROBLEMS

1. Refer to the Lands' End, Inc., financial statements in Appendix A, and answer the following questions.

Plant assets and intangible assets **(Obj. 4, 5, 7, 8)**

1. Which depreciation method does Lands' End use for reporting to stockholders and creditors in the financial statements? What type of depreciation method does the company probably use for income tax purposes? Why is this method preferable for tax purposes?
2. Depreciation expense is embedded in the expense amounts listed on the income statement. The statement of cash flows gives the amount of depreciation and amortization expense. Amortization expense for the year ended January 28, 1994 (fiscal 1994), was approximately $50 thousand. What was depreciation for 1994? Record depreciation expense and amortization expense for 1994.
3. The statement of cash flows also reports purchases of assets and the proceeds (sale prices) received on disposal of plant (fixed) assets. How much were Lands' End's asset acquisitions during 1994? Journalize Lands' End's acquisition of assets.
4. How much did Lands' End receive on the sale of fixed assets during 1994? Assume the fixed assets that were sold had a cost of $5,200 thousand and accumulated depreciation of $4,445 thousand. Record the sale of these fixed assets. How much was the gain or loss on the sale of fixed assets during 1994?
5. In what category on the statement of cash flows are capital expenditures included?

2. Obtain the annual report of a real company of your choosing. Answer these questions about the company. Concentrate on the current year in the annual report you select.

Plant assets and intangible assets **(Obj. 3, 5 7)**

1. Which depreciation method or methods does the company use for reporting to stockholders and creditors in the financial statements? Does the company disclose the estimated useful lives of plant assets for depreciation purposes? If so, identify the useful lives.
2. Depreciation and amortization expenses are often combined because they are similar. Many income statements embed depreciation and amortization in other expense amounts. To learn the amounts of these expenses, it often becomes necessary to examine the statement of cash flows. Where does your company report depreciation and amortization? What were these expenses for the current year? (Note: The company you selected may have no amortization—only depreciation.)
3. How much did the company spend to acquire plant assets during the current year? Journalize the acquisitions in a single entry.
4. How much did the company receive on the sale of plant assets? Assume a particular cost and accumulated depreciation of the plant assets sold. Journalize the sale of the plant assets, assuming that the sale resulted in a $700,000 loss.
5. What categories of intangible assets does the company report? What is their reported amount?

Chapter 11

Current Liabilities and Payroll Accounting

After studying this chapter, you should be able to

1. Account for current liabilities

2. Account for contingent liabilities

3. Compute payroll amounts

4. Make basic payroll entries

5. Use a payroll system

6. Report current liabilities

“Airlines with frequent-flyer programs must record as a current liability the cost of flying those who will use frequent-flyer miles over the next year. When the airline is in partnership with another organization (such as a hotel chain), the problem of determining the current liability becomes more complex.”

JOSEPH D. WESSELKAMPER, CPA, PRESIDENT OF JOSEPH D. WESSELKAMPER & ASSOCIATES, INC.

First there were the frequent-flier programs of the airlines: Fly so many miles on a particular airline, and receive a free ticket to the destination of your choice. Now some hotels—first Marriotts, then Holiday Inns and Sheratons—are offering their guests *airline* mileage that makes it easier for people to earn free air travel on such airlines as American and Delta.

Holiday Inn Worldwide, for example, offers its guests 2.5 frequent-flier miles per dollar spent on Holiday Inn rooms. Why would Holiday Inn make such an offer? To encourage travelers to stay at a Holiday Inn. To the hotel company, the cost is promotion expense. Why would American Airlines allow the hotels to make this offer? To generate revenue: The airlines charge the hotels approximately $0.015 per mile credited to a customer's account.

• • • • •

*T*his real example illustrates the challenge of accounting for liabilities. In this case the airlines have an obligation to provide travel paid for by the hotels. A *liability* is an obligation to transfer assets or to provide services in the future. The obligation may arise from a transaction with an outside party. For example, a business incurs a liability when it purchases inventory on account or when it issues a note payable to borrow money.

An obligation may arise in the absence of individual transactions. For example, interest expense accrues with the passage of time. Until this interest is paid, it is a liability. Income tax, a liability of corporations, accrues as income is earned. Proper accounting for liabilities is as important as proper accounting for assets. The failure to record an accrued liability causes the company to understate the related expense, and thus the balance sheet overstates owner's (or stockholders') equity.

Current liabilities and long-term liabilities were introduced in Chapter 4 (p. 145).

Current liabilities are obligations due within one year or within the company's operating cycle if it is longer than one year. Obligations due beyond that period of time are classified as long-term liabilities.◀

Let's focus on the airlines' transactions in this situation. Suppose that a Marriott Hotel grants 1,000,000 miles of American AAdvantage frequent-flier credit to its guests. Marriott's cost is $15,000 (1,000,000 miles at $0.015 per mile). Assume that Marriott pays American Airlines $15,000. Could you account for these transactions on the books of American Airlines?

American Airlines records a $15,000 liability for unearned service revenue when it receives cash from Marriott Corp.[1] This is a liability and not a revenue because American has not yet provided free air travel for the hotel guests. Later, as Marriott's hotel guests use their free air travel, American Airlines records the revenue.

We discuss long-term liabilities in Chapter 16. We now turn to accounting for current liabilities, including those arising from payroll expenses. Current liabilities fall into one of two categories: liabilities of a known amount and those whose amount must be estimated. We look first at current liabilities of known amount.

Current Liabilities of Known Amount

OBJECTIVE 1
Account for current liabilities

Accounts Payable

Amounts owed to suppliers for products or services that are purchased on open account are accounts payable. We have seen many accounts payable examples in previous chapters. For example, a business may purchase inventories and office supplies on an account payable.

Current liabilities arising from many similar transactions are well suited for computerized accounting. One of the most common transactions of a merchandiser is the credit purchase of inventory. It is efficient to integrate the accounts payable and perpetual inventory systems. When merchandise dips below a predetermined level, the system automatically prepares a purchase request. After the order is placed and the goods are received, inventory and accounts payable data are entered. The computer then debits Inventory and credits Accounts Payable to account for the purchase. For payments, the computer debits Accounts Payable and credits Cash. The program may also update account balances and print journals, ledger accounts, and the financial statements.

Short-Term Notes Payable

Short-term notes payable, a common form of financing, are notes payable that are due within one year. Companies often issue short-term notes payable to borrow cash or to purchase inventory or plant assets. In addition to recording the note payable and its eventual payment, the business must also accrue interest expense and interest payable at the end of the period.◀ The following entries are typical of this liability:

◀ Recall from Chapter 3, p. 101, that all adjusting entries for accrued expenses require a debit to an expense and a credit to a payable.

19X1			
Sep. 30	Inventory	8,000	
	Note Payable, Short-Term...		8,000
	Purchase of inventory by issuing a one-year 10-percent note payable.		
Dec. 31	Interest Expense ($8,000 × 0.10 × 3/12)	200	
	Interest Payable..		200
	Adjusting entry to accrue interest expense at year end.		

---

[1]See Richard A. Samuelson, "Accounting for Liabilities to Perform Services," *Accounting Horizons*, September 1993, pp. 32–45.

The balance sheet at December 31, 19X1, will report the Note Payable of $8,000 and the related Interest Payable of $200 as current liabilities. The 19X1 income statement will report interest expense of $200.

The following entry records the note's payment:

19X2

Sept. 30	Note Payable, Short-Term..	8,000	
	Interest Payable..	200	
	Interest Expense ($8,000 × 0.10 × 9/12).............................	600	
	Cash [$8,000 + ($8,000 × 0.10)]................................		8,800
	Payment of a note payable and interest at maturity.		

The cash payment entry must split the total interest on the note between the portion accrued at the end of the previous period ($200) and the current period's expense ($600).

The face amount of notes payable and their interest rates and payment dates can be stored for electronic data processing. Computer programs calculate interest, print the interest checks, journalize the transactions, and update account balances.

Short-Term Notes Payable Issued at a Discount

In another common borrowing arrangement, a company may **discount a note payable** at the bank. Discounting means that the bank subtracts the interest amount from the note's face value. The borrower receives the net amount. In effect, the borrower prepays the interest, which is computed on the principal of the note.

Suppose Procter & Gamble discounts a $100,000, 60-day note payable to its bank at 12 percent. The company will receive $98,000—that is, the $100,000 face value less interest of $2,000 ($100,000 × 0.12 × 60/360). Assume that this transaction occurs on November 25, 19X1. Procter & Gamble's entries to record discounting the note would be:

19X1

Nov. 25	Cash ($100,000 – $2,000)...	98,000	
	Discount on Note Payable ($100,000 × 0.12 × 60/360)	2,000	
	Note Payable, Short-Term		100,000
	Discounted a $100,000, 60-day, 12-percent note payable to borrow cash.		

Discount on Note Payable is a contra account to the liability Note Payable, Short-Term. A balance sheet prepared immediately after this transaction would report the note payable at its net amount of $98,000, as follows:

Current liabilities:

Note payable, short-term...	$100,000
Less: Discount on note payable	(2,000)
Note payable, short-term, net...	$ 98,000

The accrued interest at year end still must be recorded, as it would for any note payable. The adjusting entry at December 31 records interest for 36 days as follows:

19X1

Dec. 31	Interest Expense ($100,000 × 0.12 × 36/360).....................	1,200	
	Discount on Note Payable		1,200
	Adjusting entry to accrue interest expense at year end.		

Short Exercise: A $10,000, 11%, 90-day note was issued on Nov. 1. Record the accrual on Dec. 31 and the note payment on Jan 30. *A:*

12/31	
Interest Expense ($10,000 × 11% × 60/360)....	183
Interest Payable	183

1/30	
Note Payable 10,000	
Interest Payable	183
Interest Expense ...	92
Cash	10,275

Short Exercise: A company borrows $5,000 on a 60-day, 9% note on Aug. 31. Record the issuance and payment of the note with interest stated separately. *A:*

8/31	
Cash 5,000	
Note Payable	5,000

10/30	
Note Payable 5,000	
Interest Expense ...	75
Cash	5,075

Short Exercise: For the previous Short Exercise, record the issuance and payment of the note with interest deducted in advance. *A:*

8/31	
Cash 4,925	
Discount on	
Note Payable	75
Note Payable	5,000

10/30	
Int. Expense	75
Note Payable 5,000	
Cash	5,000
Discount on	
Note Payable ..	75

This entry credits the Discount account instead of Interest Payable. Why? Because the Discount balance represents future interest expense, and the accrual of interest records the current-period portion of the expense. Furthermore, crediting the Discount reduces the contra account's balance and increases the net amount of the Note Payable. After the adjusting entry, only $800 of the Discount remains, and the carrying value of the Note Payable increases to $99,200, as follows:

Current liabilities:
Note payable, short-term...	$100,000
Less: Discount on note payable ($2,000 – $1,200)...................................	(800)
Note payable, short-term, net...	$ 99,200

Finally, the business records the note's payment:

19X2		
Jan. 24	Interest Expense ($100,000 × 0.12 × 24/360).............	800
	Discount on Note Payable.................................	800
	To record interest expense.	
	Note Payable, Short-Term..	100,000
	Cash...	100,000
	To pay note payable at maturity.	

After these entries, the balances in the Note Payable account and Discount account are zero. Each period's income statement reports the appropriate interest expense.

Sales Tax Payable

Every state except Delaware, Montana, New Hampshire, and Oregon levies a sales tax on retail sales. Retailers charge their customers the sales tax in addition to the price of the item sold. Because the retailers owe the state the sales tax collected, the account Sales Tax Payable is a current liability. For example, ShowBiz Pizza Time, Inc. (known for its family restaurant/entertainment centers, home of Chuck E. Cheese), reported sales tax payable of $737,712 as a current liability. States do not levy sales tax on the sales of manufacturers, such as Procter & Gamble and General Motors.

"ShowBiz Pizza Time, Inc. (known for its family restaurant/entertainment centers, home of Chuck E. Cheese), reported sales tax payable of $737,712 as a current liability."

Such companies sell their products to wholesalers and retailers rather than to final consumers. Therefore, they have no sales tax liability.

Suppose one Saturday's sales at a ShowBiz Pizza Time totaled $2,000. The business would have collected an additional 5 percent in sales tax, which would equal $100 ($2,000 × 0.05). The business would record that day's sales as follows:

Short Exercise: Record sales of $35,650 and the related 7½% sales tax if (1) the sales tax is recorded separately and (2) the sales tax is included in Sales. *A:* (1) Only one entry is required:
    Cash.................38,324
        Sales
          Revenue.....   35,650
        Sales Tax
          Payable.......   2,674
          (cont.)

Cash ($2,000 × 1.05)..	2,100	
Sales Revenue		2,000
Sales Tax Payable ($2,000 × 0.05)		100
To record cash sales of $2,000 subject to 5-percent sales tax.		

Companies forward the collected sales tax to the taxing authority at regular intervals, at which time they debit Sales Tax Payable and credit Cash. Observe that

Sales Tax Payable does *not* correspond to any sales tax expense that the business is incurring. Nor does this liability arise from the purchase of any asset. Rather, the obligation arises because the business is collecting for the government.

Many companies consider it inefficient to credit Sales Tax Payable when recording sales. They record the sales in an amount that includes the tax. Then prior to paying tax to the state, they make a single entry for the entire period's transactions to bring Sales Revenue and Sales Tax Payable to their correct balances.

Suppose a company made July sales of $100,000, subject to a tax of 6 percent. Its summary entry to record the month's sales could be:

July 31	Cash ($100,000 × 1.06)	106,000	
	Sales Revenue		106,000
	To record sales for the month.		

The entry to adjust Sales Revenue and Sales Tax Payable to their correct balances is:

July 31	Sales Revenue [$106,000 – ($106,000 ÷ 1.06)]	6,000	
	Sales Tax Payable		6,000
	To record sales tax.		

(2) Two entries are required:

Cash	38,324	
Sales Revenue		38,324
Sales Revenue	2,674	
Sales Tax Payable		2,674

$$\left(\$2,674 = \$38,324 - \frac{\$38,324}{1.075}\right)$$

Companies that follow this procedure need to make an adjusting entry at the end of the period in order to report the correct amounts of revenue and sales tax liability on their financial statements.

Current Portion of Long-Term Debt

Some long-term notes payable and long-term bonds payable must be paid in installments. The **current portion of long-term debt**, or *current maturity*, is the amount of the principal that is payable within one year. This amount does not include the interest due. Of course, any liability for accrued interest payable must also be reported, but a separate account, Interest Payable, is used for that purpose.

"H. J. Heinz Company, best known for its ketchup, owed almost $200 million on long-term debt at April 30, the end of its fiscal year."

H. J. Heinz Company, best known for its ketchup, owed almost $200 million on long-term debt at April 30, the end of its fiscal year. Nearly $14 million was a current liability because it was due within one year. The remaining $186 million was a long-term liability. Suppose that the interest rate on the debt was 6 percent and that the interest was last paid the preceding November 30. Heinz Company's April 30 balance sheet would report these amounts:

Current Liabilities (in part)	Millions
Portion of long-term debt due within one year	$ 14
Interest payable ($200 × 0.06 × 5/12)	5
Long-Term Debt and Other Liabilities (in part)	
Long-term debt	$186

STOP & THINK Suppose that H. J. Heinz Company reported its full liability as long-term. Identify two ratios that would have been distorted by this accounting error. State whether the ratio values would be overstated or understated and whether they would report an overly positive or negative view of the company.

Answer: Reporting a liability as long-term understates current liabilities and has these effects:

Ratio	Overstated or Understated	View of the Company
Current ratio	Overstated	Overly positive
Acid-test ratio	Overstated	Overly positive

The point of this example is that accounting includes both *recording* transactions and *reporting* the information. Reporting is every bit as important as recording.

Accrued Expenses

As shown in the Heinz Company presentation, *accrued expenses*, such as interest on the note, create current liabilities because the interest is due within the year. Therefore, the interest payable (accrued interest) is reported as a current liability. Other important liabilities for accrued expenses are payroll and the related payroll taxes, which we discuss in the second half of this chapter.

Unearned Revenues

◀▥◀▥◀▥ As we saw in Chapter 3, p. 102, an unearned revenue is a liability because it represents an obligation to provide a good or service.

Unearned revenues are called *deferred revenues, revenues collected in advance*, and *customer prepayments.*◀▥ Each account title indicates that the business has received cash from its customers before it has earned the revenue. The company has an obligation to provide goods or services to the customer. The chapter-opening story provides one illustration. Let's consider another example.

The Dun & Bradstreet (D&B) Corporation provides credit evaluation services to businesses that subscribe to the D&B reports. When finance companies pay in advance to have D&B investigate the credit histories of potential customers, D&B incurs a liability to provide future service. The liability account is called Unearned Subscription Revenue (which could also be titled Unearned Subscription Income).

Assume that D&B charges $150 for a finance company's three-year subscription. D&B's entries would be:

Short Exercise: Suppose a contractor collected $300,000 in advance for the installation of special flooring in a building. At year end, one-fourth of the work is completed. What amount of Unearned Revenue should be transferred to Revenue? *A:* $300,000 × 1/4 = $75,000

19X1
Jan. 1 Cash 150
        Unearned Subscription Revenue.. 150
        To record receipt of cash at start of the three-year subscription agreement.

19X1, 19X2, 19X3
Dec. 31 Unearned Subscription Revenue.. 50
        Subscription Revenue ($150/3) 50
        To record subscription revenue earned at the end of each of three years.

D&B's financial statements would report a current liability for the unearned revenue to be earned during the next year. The remaining liability is long-term:

	December 31,		
Balance Sheet	**Year 1**	**Year 2**	**Year 3**
Current liabilities			
Unearned subscription revenue..	$50	$50	$–0–
Long-term liabilities..			
Unearned subscription revenue..	$50	–0–	–0–
Income Statement	**Year 1**	**Year 2**	**Year 3**
Revenues			
Subscription revenue	$50	$50	$50

Customer Deposits Payable

Some companies require cash deposits from customers as security on borrowed assets. These amounts are called Customer Deposits Payable because the company must refund the cash to the customer under certain conditions.

For example, telephone companies demand a cash deposit from a customer before installing a telephone. Utility companies and businesses that rent tools and appliances commonly demand a deposit as protection against damage and theft. When the customer ends service or returns the borrowed asset, the company refunds the cash deposit—if the customer has paid all the bills and has not damaged the company's property. Because the company generally must return the deposit, that obligation is a liability. The uncertainty of when the deposits will be refunded and their relatively small amounts cause many companies to classify Customer Deposits Payable as current liabilities. This practice is consistent with the concept of conservatism.

⬅||||⬅||||⬅|||| We saw in Chapter 9 (p. 381) that conservatism is a concept by which relatively pessimistic figures are presented in the financial statements.

Certain manufacturers demand *security deposits* from the merchandisers who sell their products. Stanley Home Products, Inc., for example, demands a deposit from its dealers. The security deposits, called Dealers' Security Deposits, recently came to $4 million on Stanley's balance sheet, a small amount compared with its total current liabilities of over $62 million.

Current Liabilities That Must Be Estimated

A business may know that a liability exists but not know the exact amount. The liability may not simply be ignored. The unknown amount of a liability must be estimated for reporting on the balance sheet.

Estimated current liabilities vary among companies. As an example, let's look at Estimated Warranty Payable, a liability account common among merchandisers.

Estimated Warranty Payable

Many merchandising companies guarantee their products against defects under *warranty* agreements. The warranty period may extend for any length of time. Ninety-day warranties and one-year warranties are common. The automobile companies—BMW, General Motors, and Toyota, for example—accrue liabilities for their four- or five-year, 50,000-mile warranties.

BMW accrues liabilities for the four-year, 50,000-mile warranties it offers on its cars.

Whatever the warranty's lifetime, the matching principle demands that the company record the *warranty expense* in the same period that the business recognizes sales revenue. After all, offering the warranty—and incurring any possible expense through the warranty agreement—is a part of generating revenue through sales. At the time of the sale, however, the company does not know which products are defective. The exact amount of warranty expense cannot be known with certainty, so the business must estimate its warranty expense and open the related liability account—Estimated Warranty Payable (also called Accrued Warranty Costs and Product Warranty Liability). Even though the warranty liability depends on the occurrence of future events, it is accounted for as an actual liability because the obligation for the warranty expense has occurred and its amount can be estimated.

Companies can make a reliable estimate of their warranty expense on the basis of their experience. Assume that a company made sales of $200,000, subject to product warranties. If, in past years, between 2 percent and 4 percent of products had proved defective, company management would estimate that 3 percent of the products will require repair or replacement during the one-year warranty period. The company would record warranty expense of $6,000 ($200,000 × 0.03) for the period:

Warranty Expense 6,000
    Estimated Warranty Payable   6,000
To accrue warranty expense.

A company made sales of $400,000 and estimated warranty repairs at 5% of the sales. Actual warranty outlays were $19,000. Record the sales, the warranty expense, and the warranty outlays. *A:*

Accounts Rec. 400,000
   Sales Revenue   400,000

Warranty Expense
   (400,000 × 5%).. 20,000
   Est. Warr. Pay. ...   20,000

Est. Warr. Pay. 19,000
   Cash, Inventory,
     and so on   19,000

Assume that defective merchandise totals $5,800. The company may either repair or replace it. Corresponding entries follow:

Estimated Warranty Payable...	5,800	
Cash..		5,800

To *repair* defective products sold under warranty.

Estimated Warranty Payable...	5,800	
Inventory		5,800

To *replace* defective products sold under warranty.

The expense is $6,000 on the income statement no matter what the cash payment or the cost of the replacement inventory. In future periods, the company may debit the liability Estimated Warranty Payable for the remaining $200. However, *when* the company repairs or replaces defective merchandise has no bearing on when the company records warranty expense. The business records warranty expense in the same period as the sale.

Other Estimated Current Liabilities

ESTIMATED VACATION PAY LIABILITY Most companies grant paid vacations to their employees. The employees receive this benefit when they take their vacation, but they earn the compensation by working the other days of the year. Two-week vacations are common. To match expense with revenue properly, the company accrues the vacation pay expense and liability for each of the 50 work weeks of the year. Then, the company records payment during the two-week vacation period. Employee turnover, terminations, and ineligibility force companies to estimate the vacation pay liability.

Suppose a company's January payroll is $100,000 and vacation pay adds 4 percent (2 weeks of annual vacation divided by 50 work weeks each year). Experience indicates that only 80 percent of the available vacations will be taken in any one month, so the January vacation pay estimate is $3,200 ($100,000 × 0.04 × 0.80). In January the company records vacation pay as follows:

Jan. 31	Vacation Pay Expense...	3,200	
	Estimated Vacation Pay Liability		3,200

Each month thereafter, the company makes a similar entry for 4 percent of the payroll.

If an employee takes a vacation in August, his or her $2,000 monthly salary is recorded as follows:

Aug. 31	Estimated Vacation Pay Liability	2,000	
	Cash..		2,000

ESTIMATED FREQUENT-FLIER LIABILITY OF AN AIRLINE COMPANY
The chapter-opening story describes how hotel companies are offering guests frequent-flier mileage for free air travel. In that situation the hotels prepay the airlines for the travel. Exhibit 11-1 shows how to account for the airlines' unearned service revenue, based on the chapter-opening story.

The airlines' own frequent-flier plans work differently. Usually there is no hotel operating as an intermediary. Typically, a passenger who travels a certain number of miles can take a free trip or upgrade his or her ticket from coach class to first class. The operating expense of providing this free service creates a liability for the airline. When should the expense and estimated frequent-flier liability be recorded? As the airline earns revenue from its paying customers. Under the matching principle, a company should record expense when it earns the related revenue. Because the

Panel A—Example

In 19X3, Marriott Hotel Corp. granted 1,000,000 miles of credit to its guests for free travel on American Airlines. American charges Marriott $0.015 per mile, for a total of $15,000 (1,000,000 miles × $0.015). Assume that American will earn this revenue as follows: $5,000 in 19X4 and $10,000 in 19X5.

EXHIBIT 11-1

An Airline's Accounting for Frequent-Flier Mileage Granted by a Hotel Company

Panel B—Accounting Records of American Airlines

Journal Entry	19X3	19X4	19X5
Cash	15,000		
Unearned Service Revenue	15,000		
Unearned Service Revenue		5,000	10,000
Service Revenue		5,000	10,000

	December 31,		
Balance Sheet	**19X3**	**19X4**	**19X5**
Current liabilities:			
Unearned service revenue	$ 5,000	$10,000	$ –0–
Long-term liabilities:			
Unearned service revenue	10,000	–0–	–0–

Income Statement	**19X3**	**19X4**	**19X5**
Service revenue	$ –0–	$5,000	$10,000

ultimate cost of providing the free transportation is uncertain, the airline must estimate this expense and the related liability. Suppose American Airlines records revenue of $1 million in February. American estimates that this revenue-producing travel will give customers free trips that will cost the company 3 percent of the revenue. American could record frequent-flier expense and liability as follows:

Feb. 28	Frequent-Flier Expense ($1,000,000 × 0.03)	30,000	
	Estimated Frequent-Flier Liability		30,000

In July, when a frequent flier takes a free trip costing the airlines $150, American could record the transaction as follows:

July 8	Estimated Frequent-Flier Liability	150	
	Cash, Wages Payable, and other accounts		150

The credit side of this entry would depend on the airline's particular situation. Cash is credited for expenses paid currently, Wages Payable for the cost of ticketing passengers, handling baggage, and so on.

Short Exercise: Which of the following items is a current liability at 12/31/94?

1. Note Payable due 3/31/95
2. Customer's accounts receivable with a credit balance
3. Allowance for uncollectible accounts
4. The portion of a note payable due in 1996
5. Accrued interest payable

A: Items 1, 2, and 5 are current liabilities.

Contingent Liabilities

A *contingent liability* is not an actual liability. Instead, it is a potential liability that depends on a *future* event arising out of a past transaction. For example, a town government may sue the company that installed new street lights, claiming that the electrical wiring is faulty. The past transaction is the street-light installation. The future event is the court case that will decide the suit. The lighting company thus faces a contingent liability, which may or may not become an actual obligation.

It would be unethical for the company to withhold knowledge of the lawsuit from its creditors and from anyone considering investing in the business. A person or business could be misled into thinking the company is stronger financially than it really is. The *disclosure principle* of accounting requires a company to report any information deemed relevant to outsiders of the business. The goal is to arm people with relevant, reliable information for decision making.

The Financial Accounting Standards Board (FASB) separates contingencies into two categories:

1. Contingent losses and related liabilities
2. Contingent gains and related assets

Businesses do not record contingent gains and their related assets. Accountants record only actual gains. But accountants record some contingent losses as though they had already occurred. The FASB provides these guidelines to account for contingent losses (or expenses) and their related liabilities:

1. Record a liability if it is *probable*—likely—that the loss (or expense) will occur and the amount can be reasonably estimated. Warranty expense and vacation pay expense are examples.

2. Report the contingency in a financial statement note if it is *reasonably possible* that a loss (or expense) will occur. The remainder of this section discusses contingencies of this type.

3. There is no need to report a contingent loss that is *remote*—unlikely to occur. Instead, wait until an actual transaction clears up the situation. For example, suppose an American company conducts business in Nicaragua, and the Nicaraguan government threatens to confiscate the assets of all foreign companies. The American firm will neither record a loss nor report the contingency if the probability of a loss is considered *remote*.

Sometimes the contingent liability has a definite amount. Recall from Chapter 8 that the payee of a discounted note has a contingent liability. If the maker of the note pays at maturity, the contingent liability ceases to exist. If the maker defaults, however, the payee, who sold the note, must pay its maturity value to the purchaser. In this case, the payee knows the note's maturity value, which is the amount of the contingent liability.

Another contingent liability of known amount arises from guaranteeing that another company will pay a note payable that the other company owes to a third party. This practice, called *cosigning a note*, obligates the guarantor to pay the note and interest if, and only if, the primary debtor fails to pay. Thus the guarantor has a contingent liability until the note becomes due. If the primary debtor pays off, the contingent liability ceases to exist. If the primary debtor fails to pay, the guarantor's liability becomes actual.

The amount of a contingent liability may be hard to determine. For example, companies face lawsuits, which may cause possible obligations of amounts to be determined by the courts.

Contingent liabilities may be reported in two ways. In what is called a **short presentation**, the contingent liability appears in the body of the balance sheet, after total liabilities, but with no amounts given. In general, an explanatory note accompanies a short presentation. Sears, Roebuck and Company reported contingent liabilities this way:

	Millions
Total liabilities..................................	$27,830.7
Contingent liabilities (note 10)......	—

Note 10: Various legal actions and governmental proceedings are pending against Sears, Roebuck and Co. and its subsidiaries. The consequences of these matters are not presently determinable but, in the opinion of management, the ultimate liability resulting, if any, will not have a material effect on the company.

"Various legal actions and governmental proceedings are pending against Sears, Roebuck and Co. and its subsidiaries."

Contingent liabilities do not have to be mentioned in the body of the balance sheet. Many companies use a second method of reporting, presenting the footnote only. International Business Machines Corporation (IBM) mentions its contingent liabilities in a half-page supplementary note labeled *litigation*.

The line between a contingent liability and a real liability may be hard to draw. As a practical guide, the FASB says to record an actual liability if (1) it is probable that the business has suffered a loss and (2) its amount can be reasonably estimated. If both of these conditions are met, the FASB reasons that the obligation has passed from contingent to real, even if its amount must be estimated. Suppose that at the balance sheet date, a hospital has lost a court case for uninsured malpractice, but the amount of damages is uncertain. The hospital estimates that the liability will fall between $1.0 and $2.5 million. In this case, the hospital must record a loss or expense and a liability for $1.0 million. The income statement will report the loss, and the balance sheet the liability. Also, the hospital must disclose in a note the possibility of an additional $1.5 million loss.

SUMMARY PROBLEM FOR YOUR REVIEW | MID-CHAPTER

This problem consists of three independent parts.

1. A Wendy's hamburger restaurant made cash sales of $4,000 subject to a 5 percent sales tax. Record the sales and the related sales tax. Also record Wendy's payment of the tax to the state government.

2. At April 30, 19X2, H. J. Heinz Company reported its 6-percent long-term debt:

Current Liabilities (in part)

Portion of long-term debt due within one year	$ 14,000,000
Interest payable ($200,000,000 × 0.06 × 5/12)	5,000,000

Long-Term Debt and Other Liabilities (in part)

Long-term debt...	$186,000,000

The company pays interest on its long-term debt on November 30 each year.

Show how Heinz Company would report its liabilities on the year-end balance sheet at April 30, 19X3. Assume that the current maturity of its long-term debt is $16 million.

3. What distinguishes a contingent liability from an actual liability?

1. | Cash ($4,000 × 1.05)... | 4,200 | |
    | --- | --- | --- |
    | Sales Revenue.. | | 4,000 |
    | Sales Tax payable ($4,000 × 0.05) .... | | 200 |
    | To record cash sales and related sales tax. | | |
    | | | |
    | Sales Tax Payable... | 200 | |
    | Cash... | | 200 |
    | To pay sales tax to the state government. | | |

2. H. J. Heinz Company balance sheet at April 30, 19X3:

Current Liabilities (in part)

Portion of long-term debt due within one year	$ 16,000,000
Interest payable ($186,000,000 × 0.06 × 5/12)	4,650,000

Long-Term Debt and Other Liabilities (in part)

Long-term debt..	$170,000,000

3. A contingent liability is a *potential* liability, which may or may not become an actual liability.

Accounting for Payroll

Key Point: The salaries and wages of a company are usually the single largest expense after cost of goods sold.

Payroll, also called *employee compensation*, is a major expense of many businesses. For service organizations, such as CPA firms, real estate brokers, and travel agents, payroll is *the* major expense of conducting business. Service organizations sell their personnel's services, so employee compensation is their primary cost of doing business, just as cost of goods sold is the largest expense in a merchandising company.

Employee compensation takes different forms. Some employees collect a *salary*, which is income stated at a yearly, monthly, or weekly rate. Other employees work for *wages*, which is employee pay stated at an hourly figure. Sales employees often receive a *commission*, which is a percentage of the sales the employee has made. Some companies reward excellent performance with a *bonus*, an amount over and above regular compensation.

Businesses often pay employees at a base rate for a set number of hours—called *straight time*. For working any additional hours—called *overtime*—the employee receives a higher rate.

Assume that Lucy Childres is an accountant for an electronics company. Lucy earns $600 per week straight time. The company work week runs 40 hours, so Lucy's hourly straight-time pay is $15 ($600/40). Her company pays her *time and a half* for overtime. That rate is 150 percent (1.5 times) the straight-time rate. Thus Lucy earns $22.50 for each hour of overtime she works ($15.00 × 1.5 = $22.50). For working 42 hours during a week, she earns $645, computed as follows:

Straight-time pay for 40 hours	$600
Overtime pay for 2 overtime hours: 2 × $22.50..............	45
Total pay..	$645

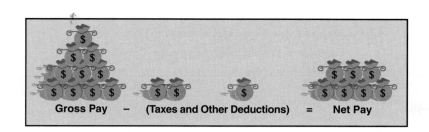

EXHIBIT 11-2
Gross Pay and Net Pay

Gross Pay   −   (Taxes and Other Deductions)   =   Net Pay

Gross Pay and Net Pay

Before withholding taxes were introduced in 1943, employees brought home all they had earned. For example, Lucy Childres would have taken home the full $645 total that she made. Payroll accounting was straightforward. Those days are long past.

The federal government, most state governments, and even some city governments require that employers act as collection agents for employee taxes, which are deducted from employee checks. Insurance companies, labor unions, and other organizations may also receive pieces of employees' pay. Amounts withheld from an employees' check are called *deductions*.

Gross pay is the total amount of salary, wages, commissions, or any other employee compensation before taxes and other deductions are taken out. **Net pay**—the "take-home pay"—equals gross pay minus all deductions. As Exhibit 11-2 shows, net pay is the amount the employee actually takes home.

Many companies also pay employee *fringe benefits*, which are a form of employee compensation. Examples include health and life insurance paid directly to the insurance companies. Other examples include retirement pay and health insurance during the retirement years, benefits that the employee does not receive immediately in cash. Payroll accounting has become quite complex. Let's turn now to a discussion of payroll deductions.

Payroll Deductions

Payroll deductions that are *withheld* from employees' pay fall into two categories: (1) *required deductions*, which include employee income tax and social security tax; and (2) *optional deductions*, which include union dues, insurance premiums, charitable contributions, and other amounts that are withheld at the employee's request. After they are withheld, payroll deductions become the liability of the employer, who assumes responsibility for paying the outside party. For example, the employer pays the government the employee income tax withheld and pays the union the employee union dues withheld.

Required Payroll Deductions

EMPLOYEE INCOME TAX   In the United States, the law requires most employers to withhold income tax from their employees' salaries and wages. Income tax is one of the largest single sources of national tax revenues. Employee income tax generates 36 percent of tax receipts in the United States, 38 percent in Sweden, and 41 percent in Canada.

The amount of income tax deducted from gross pay is called **withheld income tax**. For many employees, this deduction is the largest. The amount withheld depends on the employee's gross pay and on the number of withholding allowances the employee claims.

The employee files a Form W-4 with the employer to indicate the number of allowances claimed for withholding purposes. Each allowance lowers the amount of

EXHIBIT 11-3
Form W-4

```
............ Cut here and give the certificate to your employer. Keep the top portion for your records. ............

Form  W-4        Employee's Withholding Allowance Certificate              OMB No. 1545-0010
Department of the Treasury
Internal Revenue Service    ▶ For Privacy Act and Paperwork Reduction Act Notice, see reverse.          1994

1  Type or print your first name and middle initial   Last name              2  Your social security number
   R. C.                                              Dean                       344 86 4529
   Home address (number and street or rural route)    3 ☐ Single  ☒ Married  ☐ Married, but withhold at higher Single rate.
   4376 Palm Drive                                       Note: If married, but legally separated, or spouse is a nonresident alien, check the Single box.
   City or town, state, and ZIP code                  4  If your last name differs from that on your social security card, check
   Fort Lauderdale, FL  33317                             here and call 1-800-772-1213 for more information ▶ ☐

5  Total number of allowances you are claiming (from line G above or from the worksheets on page 2 if they apply) .   5 | 4
6  Additional amount, if any, you want withheld from each paycheck . . . . . . . . . . . .   6 $
7  I claim exemption from withholding for 1994 and I certify that I meet BOTH of the following conditions for exemption:
   • Last year I had a right to a refund of ALL Federal income tax withheld because I had NO tax liability; AND
   • This year I expect a refund of ALL Federal income tax withheld because I expect to have NO tax liability.
   If you meet both conditions, enter "EXEMPT" here . . . . . . . . . . . . . ▶  7
Under penalties of perjury, I certify that I am entitled to the number of withholding allowances claimed on this certificate or entitled to claim exempt status.

Employee's signature ▶  R. C. Dean              Date ▶              7-22 , 19 94
8  Employer's name and address (Employer: Complete 8 and 10 only if sending to the IRS)   9 Office code    10 Employer identification number
   Blumenthal's                                                         (optional)
   Crescent Square Shopping Center                                        14          83 19475
   Fort Lauderdale, FL 33310
```

tax withheld from the employee's paycheck. By varying the number of withholding allowances, the employee can adjust the amount of taxes withheld. An unmarried taxpayer can claim only one allowance; a childless married couple, up to two allowances; a married couple with one child, up to three allowances; and so on. Exhibit 11-3 shows a W-4 for R. C. Dean, who claims four allowances.

The employer sends its employees' withheld income tax to the government. The amount of the income tax withheld determines how often the employer submits tax payments. The employer must remit the taxes to the government at least quarterly. Every business must account for payroll taxes on a calendar-year basis regardless of its fiscal year.

The employer accumulates taxes in the Employee Income Tax Payable account. The word *payable* indicates that the account is the employer's liability to the government, even though the employees are the people taxed.

EMPLOYEE SOCIAL SECURITY (FICA) TAX   The *Federal Insurance Contributions Act (FICA)*, also known as the Social Security Act, created the Social Security Tax. The Social Security program provides retirement, disability, and medical benefits. The law requires employers to withhold **Social Security (FICA) tax** from employees' pay. The FICA tax has two components:

1.   Old age, survivors', and disability insurance (OASDI)
2.   Health insurance (Medicare)

The amount of tax withheld from employees' pay varies from year to year. As of 1994, the OASDI portion of the tax applies to the first $60,600 of employee earnings in a year. The taxable amount of earnings is adjusted annually depending on the rate of inflation in the U.S. economy. The OASDI tax rate is 6.2 percent. Therefore, the maximum OASDI tax that an employee paid in 1994 was $3,757 ($60,600 × 0.062).

The Medicare portion of the FICA tax applies to all employee earnings. This tax rate is 1.45 percent. An employee thus pays a combined FICA tax rate of 7.65 percent (6.2 percent + 1.45 percent) of the first $60,600 of annual earnings, plus 1.45 percent of earnings above $60,600. To ease the computational burden and focus on

Real-World Example: The IRS enforces stiff penalties for underpayment of income taxes by individuals. In 1994, the penalty was 7% of the underpayment amount.

the concepts, we assume that the FICA tax is 8 percent of the first $60,000 of employee earnings each year. For each employee who earns $60,000 or more, the employer withholds $4,800 ($60,000 × 0.08) from the employee's pay and sends that amount to the federal government. The employer records this employee tax in the account FICA Tax Payable.

Assume that Rex Jennings, an employee, earned $58,500 prior to December. Jennings' salary for December is $3,500. How much FICA tax will be withheld from his December paycheck? The computation follows:

Employee earnings subject to the tax in one year	$60,000
Employee earnings prior to the current pay period	58,500
Current pay subject to FICA tax	$ 1,500
FICA tax rate..	× 0.08
FICA tax to be withheld from current pay	$ 120

Optional Payroll Deductions

As a convenience to employees, many companies make payroll deductions and disburse cash according to employee instructions. Union dues, insurance payments, payroll savings plans, and gifts to charities are examples. The account Employees' Union Dues Payable holds employee deductions for union membership.

Many employers offer *cafeteria plans* that allow workers to select from a menu of insurance coverage. Suppose Xerox Corporation provides each employee with $250 of insurance coverage each month. One employee may use the monthly allowance to purchase only life insurance. Another employee may select only disability coverage. A third worker may take out a combination of life insurance and disability coverage. Cafeteria plans are popular because they add flexibility to a worker's total compensation package.

Employer Payroll Taxes

Employers must bear the expense of at least three payroll taxes: (1) Social Security (FICA) tax, (2) state **unemployment compensation tax**, and (3) federal unemployment compensation tax.

EMPLOYER FICA TAX In addition to being responsible for handling the employee contribution to Social Security, the employer also must pay into the program. The employer's Social Security tax is the same as the amount withheld from employee pay. Thus the Social Security system is funded by equal contributions from employees and employers. Using our 8 percent and $60,000 annual pay figures, the maximum annual employer tax on each employee is $4,800 ($60,000 × 0.08). The liability account the employer uses for this payroll tax is the same FICA Tax Payable account used for the amount withheld from employee pay. Both the tax rate and the amount of earnings subject to the tax change as Congress passes new legislation.

STATE AND FEDERAL UNEMPLOYMENT COMPENSATION TAXES These two payroll taxes are products of the Federal Unemployment Tax Act (FUTA). In recent years, employers have paid a combined tax of 6.2 percent on the first $7,000 of each employee's annual earnings. The proportion paid to the state is 5.4 percent, and 0.8 percent is paid to the federal government. The state government then uses the money to pay unemployment benefits to people who are out of

Key Point: In most states, unemployment taxes are levied only on the employer, not on the employee.

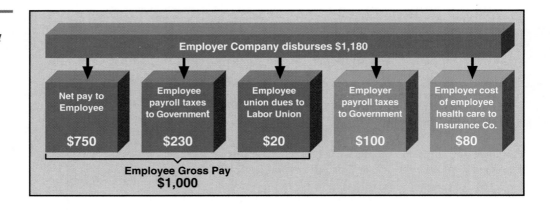

work. The employer uses the accounts Federal Unemployment Tax Payable and State Unemployment Tax Payable. Exhibit 11-4 shows a typical disbursement of payroll costs by an employer company.

Payroll Entries

OBJECTIVE 4
Make basic payroll entries

Exhibit 11-5 summarizes an employer's entries to record a monthly payroll of $10,000. All amounts are assumed for illustration only.

Entry A in Exhibit 11-5 records the employer's *salary expense*. The *gross salary* of all employees, $10,000, is their monthly pay before any deductions. The federal government imposes the two taxes. Most states and some cities also levy income taxes, which are accounted for in like manner. The union dues are optional. Employees' take-home (net) pay is $7,860. One important point about this payroll transaction is that the employees pay their own income and FICA taxes and union dues. The employer serves merely as a collecting agent and sends these amounts to the government and the union.

EXHIBIT 11-5

Payroll Accounting by the Employer

Short Exercise: Record the payroll and payroll taxes, given the following information:

Gross pay	$190,000
FICA rate	8%
Empl. fed. inc. tax withheld..........	$ 35,800
State unempl. tax rate..................	5.4%
Fed. unempl. tax rate..................	0.8%
Life insurance paid by employees........	2,000
	(cont.)

A.	Salary Expense (or Wage Expense or Commission Expense)	10,000	
	Employee Income Tax Payable		1,200
	FICA Tax Payable ($10,000 × 0.08)		800
	Employee Union Dues Payable		140
	Salary Payable to Employees [take-home pay]		7,860
	To record *salary expense*.		
B.	Payroll Tax Expense..	1,420	
	FICA Tax Payable ($10,000 × 0.08)		800
	State Unemployment Tax Payable ($10,000 × 0.054)		540
	Federal Unemployment Tax Payable ($10,000 × 0.008)		80
	To record employer's *payroll taxes*.		
C.	Health Insurance Expense for Employees	800	
	Life Insurance Expense for Employees..	200	
	Pension Expense	500	
	Employee Benefits Payable		1,500
	To record employee *fringe benefits* payable by employer.		

Entry B records the employer's *payroll taxes*. In addition to the employee's FICA tax ($800 in entry A), the employer must also pay the $800 FICA tax shown in entry B. The other two employer payroll taxes are state and federal unemployment taxes. Employees make no payments for unemployment taxes.

Entry C records employee *fringe benefits* paid by the employer. The company in the exhibit pays health and life insurance for its employees, a common practice. Also, the employer funds pensions (that is, pays cash into a pension plan) for the benefit of employees when they retire. In the exhibit, the employer's pension expense for the month is $500, and the total employer expense for fringe benefits is $1,500. The total payroll expense of the employer in Exhibit 11-5 is $12,920 (gross salary of $10,000 + employer payroll taxes of $1,420 + fringe benefits of $1,500).

A company's payments to people who are not employees—outsiders called independent contractors—are *not* company payroll expenses. Consider two CPAs, Fermi and Scott. Fermi is a corporation's chief financial officer. Scott is the corporation's outside auditor. Fermi is an employee of the corporation, and his compensation is a debit to Salary Expense. Scott, however, performs auditing service for many clients, and the corporation debits Auditing Expense when it pays her. Any payment for services performed by a person outside the company is a debit to an expense account other than payroll.

A:
Payroll entry:

Salary Expense...	190,000	
FICA Tax Pay.		15,200
Life Ins. Prem. Pay..............		2,000
Empl. Inc. Tax Pay.		35,800
Salary Payable		137,000

Payment of payroll taxes:

Payroll Tax Exp.	26,980	
FICA Tax Pay.		15,200
Fed. Unempl. Tax Pay.		10,260
State Unempl. Tax Pay.		1,520

The Payroll System

Good business means paying employees accurately and on time. Also, companies face the legal responsibility for handling employees' and their own payroll taxes, as we have seen. These demands require companies to process a great deal of payroll data. To make payroll accounting accurate and timely, accountants have developed the *payroll system*.

OBJECTIVE 5
Use a payroll system

The components of the payroll system are a *payroll register*, a special *payroll bank account*, *payroll checks*, and an *earnings record* for each employee.

Payroll Register

Each pay period, the company organizes the payroll data in a special journal called the *payroll register*, or *payroll journal*. This register lists each employee and the figures the business needs to record payroll amounts. The payroll register, which resembles the cash disbursements journal, or check register, also serves as a check register by providing a column for recording each payroll check number.

A payroll register similar to that in Exhibit 11-6 is used by companies such as Marriott Corp. The *Gross Pay* section has columns for straight-time pay, overtime pay, and total gross pay for each employee. Columns under the *Deductions* heading vary from company to company, but every employer must deduct federal income tax and FICA tax. (State income tax is left out for convenience.) Additional column headings depend on which optional deductions the business handles. In Exhibit 11-6, the employer deducts employee payroll taxes, union dues, and gifts to United Way and then sends the amounts to the proper parties. The business may add deduction columns as needed. The *Net Pay* section lists each employee's net (take-home) pay and the number of the check issued to him or her. The last two columns indicate the *Account Debited* for the employee's gross pay. (The company has office workers and salespeople.)

The payroll register in Exhibit 11-6 gives the employer the information needed to record salary expense for the pay period. Using the total amounts for columns (d) through (l), the employer records total salary expense as follows:

EXHIBIT 11-6

Payroll Register

Week ended December 27, 19X5

Employee Name	Hours	*a* Straight-Time	*b* Overtime	*c* Total	*d* Federal Income Tax	*e* FICA Tax	*f* Union Dues	*g* United Way Charities	*h* Total	*i* (c–h) Amount	*j* Check No.	*k* Office Salary Expense	*l* Sales Salary Expense
												Gross pay →	Deductions →
①Chen, W. L.	40	500.00		500.00	71.05	40.00	5.00	2.50	118.55	381.45	1621	500.00	
Dean, R. C.	46	400.00	90.00	490.00	59.94	39.20		2.00	101.14	388.86	1622		490.00
Ellis, M.	41	560.00	21.00	581.00	86.14	46.48	5.00		137.62	443.38	1623	581.00	
		1,360.00		1,360.00	463.22			15.00	478.22	881.78			1,360.00
②Trimble, E. A.	40	1,360.00		1,360.00	463.22			15.00	478.22	881.78	1641		1,360.00
Total		12,940.00	714.00	13,654.00	3,167.76	861.94	85.00	155.00	4,269.70	9,384.30		4,464.00	9,190.00

①W. L. Chen earned gross pay of $500. His net pay was $381.45, paid with check number 1621. Chen is an office worker, so his salary is debited to Office Salary Expense.

②The business deducted no FICA tax from E. A. Trimble. She has already earned more than $60,000. Any employee whose earnings exceed this annual maximum pays no additional FICA tax during that year.*

*For clarity we ignore the additional tax for Medicare benefits.

Dec. 27	Office Salary Expense	4,464.00	
	Sales Salary Expense	9,190.00	
	Employee Income Tax Payable		3,167.76
	FICA Tax Payable		861.94
	Employee Union Dues Payable		85.00
	Employee United Way Payable		155.00
	Salary Payable to Employees		9,384.30

A company may include additional information on its payroll register. The payroll register of American Airlines, for example, lists such data as year-to-date totals, hourly rates, and insurance codes. To minimize the storage requirements of the register for each employee, American Airlines uses single codes for earnings and for deductions rather than several columns for gross pay and several columns for deductions.

Payroll Bank Account

After the payroll has been recorded, the company books include a credit balance in Salary Payable to Employees for net pay of $9,384.30. (See column (i) in Exhibit 11-6.) How the business pays this liability depends on its payroll system. Many companies disburse paychecks to employees from a special *payroll bank account*. The employer draws a check for net pay ($9,384.30 in our illustration) on its regular bank account and deposits this check in the special payroll bank account. Or, as Marriott Corp. does, the company may wire the net pay amount into the payroll bank account. Then the company writes paychecks to employees out of the payroll account. When the paychecks clear the bank, the payroll account has a zero balance, ready for the activity of the next pay period. Disbursing paychecks from a separate bank account isolates net pay for analysis and control, as discussed later in the chapter.

Other payroll disbursements—for withheld taxes, union dues, and so on—are neither as numerous nor as frequent as weekly or monthly paychecks. The employer pays taxes, union dues, and charities from its regular bank account.

Payroll Checks

Most companies pay employees by check. A *payroll check* is like any other check except that its perforated attachment lists the employee's gross pay, payroll deductions, and net pay. These amounts are taken from the payroll register. Exhibit 11-7 shows payroll check number 1622, issued to R. C. Dean for net pay of $388.86 earned dur-

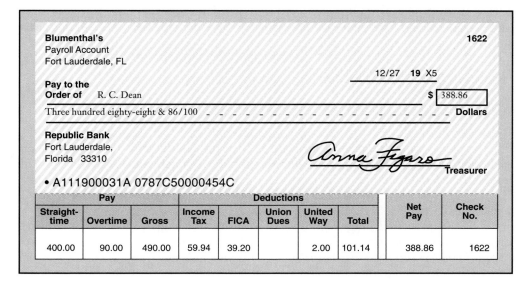

EXHIBIT 11-7
Payroll Check

ing the week ended December 27, 19X5. To enhance your ability to use payroll data, trace all amounts on the check attachment to the payroll register in Exhibit 11-6.

Increasingly, companies are paying employees by electronic funds transfer, as Marriott Corp. does. The employee can authorize the company to make all deposits directly to his or her bank. With no check to write and deliver to the employee, the company saves time and money. As evidence of the deposit, most companies, including American Airlines, issue a voided check to employees. The employee avoids the trouble of receiving, endorsing, and depositing the paycheck.

Recording Cash Disbursements for Payroll

Most employers must make at least three entries to record payroll cash disbursements: net pay to employees, payroll taxes to the government and payroll deductions, and employee fringe benefits.

NET PAY TO EMPLOYEES When the employer pays employees, the company debits Salary Payable to Employees and credits Cash. Using the data in Exhibit 11-6, the company would make the following entry to record the cash payment (column (i)) for the December 27 weekly payroll:

Dec. 27	Salary Payable to Employees	9,384.30	
	Cash...		9,384.30

PAYROLL TAXES TO THE GOVERNMENT AND PAYROLL DEDUCTIONS The employer must send to the government two sets of payroll taxes: those withheld from employees' pay and those paid by the employer. On the basis of Exhibit 11-6, columns (d) through (g), the business would record a series of cash payment entries summarized as follows (employer tax amounts are assumed):

Short Exercise: According to this journal entry, what is the total amount that the business will pay to the government on December 27 for taxes withheld and for FICA taxes?
A: $3,167.76 + $1,723.88 = $4,891.64

Dec. 27	Employee Income Tax Payable	3,167.76	
	FICA Tax Payable ($861.94 × 2)	1,723.88	
	Employee Union Dues Payable	85.00	
	Employee United Way Payable	155.00	
	State Unemployment Tax Payable............................	104.62	
	Federal Unemployment Tax Payable.........................	15.50	
	Cash...		5,251.76

FRINGE BENEFITS The employer might pay for employees' insurance coverage and pension plan. If the total cash payment for these benefits is $1,927.14, this entry for payments to third parties will be:

Dec. 27	Employee Benefits Payable	1,927.14	
	Cash...		1,927.14

Earnings Record

The employer must file payroll tax returns with the federal and state governments and must provide the employee with a wage and tax statement, Form W-2, at the end of the year. Therefore, employers maintain an *earnings record* for each employee. Exhibit 11-8 is a five-week excerpt from the earnings record of employee R. C. Dean.

The employee earnings record is not a journal or a ledger, and it is not required by law. It is an accounting tool—like the work sheet—that the employer uses to prepare payroll tax reports. Year-to-date earnings also indicate when the employee has earned $60,000, the point at which the employer can stop deducting FICA tax.

EXHIBIT 11-8

Employee Earnings Record for 19X5

EMPLOYEE NAME AND ADDRESS:

DEAN, R. C.
4376 PALM DRIVE
FORT LAUDERDALE, FL 33317

SOCIAL SECURITY NO.: 344-86-4529
MARITAL STATUS: MARRIED
WITHHOLDING EXEMPTIONS: 4
PAY RATE: $400 PER WEEK
JOB TITLE: SALESPERSON

Week Ended	Hours	Gross Pay				Federal Income Tax	FICA Tax	Deductions	United Way Charities	Total	Net Pay	Check No.
		Straight-Time	Overtime	Total	To Date			Union Dues			Amount	
Nov. 29	40	400.00		400.00	21,340.00	42.19	32.00		2.50	76.19	323.81	1525
Dec. 6	40	400.00		400.00	21,740.00	42.19	32.00		2.00	76.19	323.81	1548
Dec. 13	44	400.00	60.00	460.00	22,200.00	54.76	36.80		2.00	93.56	366.44	1574
Dec. 20	48	400.00	120.00	520.00	22,720.00	66.75	41.60		2.00	110.35	409.65	1598
Dec. 27	46	400.00	90.00	490.00	23,210.00	59.94	39.20		2.00	101.14	388.86	1622
Total		20,800.00	2,410.00	23,210.00		2,346.72	1,775.57		104.00	4,226.29	18,983.71	

EXHIBIT 11-9

Employee Wage and Tax Statement, Form W-2

a Control number	22222	Void ☐	For Official Use Only ▶ OMB No. 1545-0008		
b Employer's identification number 83-19475			1 Wages, tips, other compensation 23,210.00		2 Federal income tax withheld 2,346.72
c Employer's name, address, and ZIP code Blumenthal's Crescent Square Shopping Center Fort Lauderdale, FL 33310			3 Social security wages 23,210.00		4 Social security tax withheld 1,439.02
			5 Medicare wages and tips 23,210.00		6 Medicare tax withheld 336.55
			7 Social security tips		8 Allocated tips
d Employee's social security number 344-86-4529			9 Advance EIC payment		10 Dependent care benefits
e Employee's name (first, middle initial, last) R. C. Dean 4376 Palm Drive Fort Lauderdale, FL 33317			11 Nonqualified plans		12 Benefits included in box 1
			13 See Instrs. for box 13		14 Other

15 Statutory employee ☐	Deceased ☐	Pension plan ☐	Legal rep. ☐	942 emp. ☐	Subtotal ☐	Deferred compensation ☐

f Employee's address and ZIP code

16 State	Employer's state I.D. No.	17 State wages, tips, etc.	18 State income tax	19 Locality name	20 Local wages, tips, etc.	21 Local income tax

Cat. No. 10134D   Department of the Treasury—Internal Revenue Service

Form **W-2** Wage and Tax Statement **1994**

For Paperwork Reduction Act Notice, see separate instructions.

Copy A For Social Security Administration

Exhibit 11-9 is the Wage and Tax Statement, Form W-2, for employee R. C. Dean. The employer prepares this statement and gives copies to the employee and to the Internal Revenue Service (IRS). Dean uses the W-2 to prepare his personal income tax return. To ensure that Dean is paying income tax on all his income from that job, the IRS matches Dean's income as reported on his tax return with his earnings as reported on the W-2.

Postretirement Benefits

Employees receive some benefits, such as medical insurance, during their working years. The employer accrues this expense as it occurs to achieve a proper matching of the expense against the revenues generated by the employee's labor. Many employers also provide *postretirement benefits*—medical insurance and other benefits for retired workers.

The accounting profession has struggled to identify the appropriate accounting for the expense of postretirement benefits. Should the expense be recorded after the employee has retired, when the employer pays these expenses? Or should the expense be recorded during the employee's working years? The FASB requires that companies accrue the expense for postretirement benefits during the working years because that is when the employee's effort produces revenues. The matching principle controls this decision. Most of the liability for postretirement benefits is long-term because it accumulates over the years that an employee works to earn the postretirement medical insurance.

Pensions, which pay employees during retirement, are another postretirement benefit. Companies also accrue this expense and the related long-term liability during the employee's working years. We discuss accounting for pensions in Chapter 16, which is devoted to long-term liabilities.

Internal Control over Payrolls

The internal controls over cash disbursements discussed in Chapter 7 apply to payroll. In addition, companies adopt special controls in payroll accounting. The large number of transactions and the many different parties involved increase the risk of a control failure. Accounting systems feature two types of special controls over payroll: controls for efficiency and controls for safeguarding payroll disbursements.

Controls for Efficiency

For companies with many employees, reconciling the bank account can be time-consuming because of the large number of outstanding payroll checks. For example, a March 30 payroll check would probably not have time to clear the bank before a bank statement on March 31. This check and others in a March 30 payroll would be outstanding. Identifying a large number of outstanding checks for the bank reconciliation increases accounting expense. To limit the number of outstanding checks, many companies use two payroll bank accounts. They make payroll disbursements from one payroll account one month and from the other payroll account the next month and reconcile each account every other month. In this system, a March 30 paycheck has until April 30 to clear the bank before the account is reconciled. Outstanding checks are essentially eliminated, the time it takes to prepare the bank reconciliation is reduced, and accounting expense decreases. Also, many companies' checks become void if not cashed within a certain period of time. This constraint, too, limits the number of outstanding checks.

Payroll transactions are ideally suited for computer processing. Employee pay rates and withholding data are stored on computer. Each payroll period, computer operators enter the number of hours worked by each employee. The computer performs the calculations, prints the payroll register and paychecks, and updates the employee earnings records. The program also computes payroll taxes and prepares quarterly reports to government agencies. Expense and liability accounts are automatically updated for the payroll transactions. The payroll register is in a computer database form, which allows users to generate a wide variety of reports. At the end of an accounting period, the computerized payroll system automatically computes the amounts for the general ledger system, including any accruals of salary expense incurred but not paid.

Other payroll controls for efficiency include following established policies for hiring and firing employees and complying with government regulations. Hiring and firing policies provide guidelines for keeping a qualified, diligent work force dedicated to achieving the business's goals. Complying with government regulations avoids paying fines and penalties.

Controls for Safeguarding Payroll Disbursements

Owners and managers of small businesses can monitor their payroll disbursements by personal contact with their employees. Large corporations cannot do so. These businesses must establish controls to ensure that payroll disbursements are made only to legitimate employees and for the correct amounts. A particular danger is that payroll checks may be written to a fictitious employee and cashed by a dishonest employee. To guard against this crime and other possible breakdowns in internal control, large businesses adopt strict internal control policies.

The duties of hiring and firing employees should be separated from the duties of distributing paychecks. Requiring an identification badge bearing an employee's photograph also helps internal control. Issuing paychecks only to employees with badges ensures that only actual employees receive pay.

Key Point: A review of employers' paperwork for payrolls: *Form 941*—Employer's Quarterly Federal Tax Return. Reports FICA and income tax withheld. Must be filed quarterly and may require that taxes be deposited up to eight times a quarter.
Form 940—Federal Unemployment Tax Return. Must be filed annually. May require that unemployment taxes be deposited during the year.
State Unemployment Tax Returns—Filed quarterly in most states.
Form W-2—Must be sent to every employee by 1/31; details salary or wages, FICA taxes withheld, income taxes withheld, and other data.

A time-keeping system helps ensure that employees have actually worked the number of hours claimed. Having employees punch time cards at the start and end of the workday proves their attendance—as long as management makes sure that no employee punches in and out for others too. Some companies have their workers fill in weekly or monthly time sheets.

Again we see that the key to good internal control is separation of duties. The responsibilities of the personnel department, the payroll department, the accounting department, time-card management, and paycheck distribution should be separate.

STOP & THINK Centurion Homes of Omaha, Nebraska, builds houses and has four construction crews. The foremen hire—and fire—workers and keep their hourly records. Each Friday morning the foremen telephone their workers' hours to the home office, where accountants prepare the weekly paychecks. Around noon the foremen pick up the paychecks. They return to the construction site and pay the workers at day's end. What is the internal control weakness in this situation? Propose a way to improve the internal controls.

Answer: Construction workers often have limited contact with the home office. When the foremen control most of the information used in the payroll system, they can forge the payroll records of fictitious employees and pocket their pay. To improve internal control, Centurion could hire and fire all workers through the home office. This practice would establish the identity of all workers listed in the payroll records. Another way to improve the internal controls would be to have a home-office employee distribute paychecks on a surprise basis. Any remaining checks would arouse suspicion regarding the foreman. This system would probably prevent foremen from cheating the company.

Reporting Payroll Expense and Liabilities

OBJECTIVE 6
Report current liabilities

At the end of its fiscal year, the company reports the amount of *payroll liability* owed to all parties—employees, state and federal governments, unions, and so forth. Payroll liability is *not* the payroll expense for the year. The liability at year end is the amount of the expense that is still unpaid. Payroll expense appears on the income statement, payroll liability on the balance sheet. Kellogg Company, makers of Kellogg's Corn Flakes, Pop Tarts, and Eggo Waffles, reported salaries and wage payable of $78 million as a current liability on its year-end balance sheet; see Exhibit 11-10. However, Kellogg's payroll expense for the year far exceeded $78 million. (Exhibit 11-10 also presents other current liabilities we have discussed.)

Exhibit 11-11 summarizes all the current liabilities we have discussed in the chapter.

"Kellogg's payroll expense for the year far exceeded $78 million."

EXHIBIT 11-10
Partial Kellogg Company Balance Sheet

Current Liabilities	Millions
Current maturities of long-term debt	$ 1.9
Notes payable	210.0
Accounts payable	313.8
Accrued liabilities:	
Income taxes	104.1
Salaries and wages	78.0
Advertising and promotion	228.0
Other	135.2
Total current liabilities	**$1,071.0**

Amount of Liability Known When Recorded	Amount of Liability Estimated When Recorded
Trade accounts payable	Warranty payable
Short-term notes payable	Income tax payable
Sales tax payable	Vacation pay liability
Current portion of long-term debt	
Accrued expenses payable:	
Interest payable	
Payroll liabilities (salary payable, wages payable, and commissions payable)	
Payroll taxes payable (employee and employer)	
Unearned revenues (revenues collected in advance of being earned)	
Customer deposits payable	

EXHIBIT 11-11
Categories of Current Liabilities

SUMMARY PROBLEM FOR YOUR REVIEW

Beth Denius, Limited, a clothing store, employs one salesperson, Alan Kingsley. His straight-time pay is $360 per week. He earns time and a half for hours worked in excess of 40 per week. The owner, Beth Denius, withholds income tax (11.0 percent) and FICA tax (8.0 percent) from Kingsley's pay. She pays the following employer payroll taxes: FICA (8.0 percent) and state and federal unemployment (5.4 percent and 0.8 percent, respectively). In addition, Denius contributes to a pension plan an amount equal to 10 percent of Kingsley's gross pay.

During the week ended December 26, 19X4, Kingsley worked 48 hours. Prior to this week Kingsley had earned $5,470.

Required

1. Compute Kingsley's gross pay and net pay for the week.
2. Record the following payroll entries that Denius would make:
   a. Expense for Kingsley's salary, including overtime pay
   b. Employer payroll taxes
   c. Expense for fringe benefits
   d. Payment of cash to Kingsley
   e. Payment of all payroll taxes
   f. Payment for fringe benefits
3. How much total payroll expense did Denius incur for the week? How much cash did the business spend on its payroll?

SOLUTION TO REVIEW PROBLEM

Requirement 1

Gross Pay:	Straight-time pay for 40 hours		$360.00
	Overtime pay:		
	Rate per hour ($360/40 × 1.5)	$ 13.50	
	Hours (48 – 40)	× 8	108.00
	Total gross pay		$468.00
Net Pay:	Gross pay		$468.00
	Less: Withheld income tax ($468 × 0.11)	$ 51.48	
	Withheld FICA tax ($468 × 0.08)	37.44	88.92
	Net pay		$379.08

Requirement 2

a.	Sales Salary Expense	468.00	
	Employee Income Tax Payable		51.48
	FICA Tax Payable		37.44
	Salary Payable to Employee		379.08
b.	Payroll Tax Expense	66.45	
	FICA Tax Payable ($468 × 0.08)		37.44
	State Unemployment Tax Payable ($468 × 0.054)		25.27
	Federal Unemployment Tax Payable (468 × 0.008)		3.74
c.	Pension Expense ($468 × 0.10)	46.80	
	Employee Benefits Payable		46.80
d.	Salary Payable to Employee	379.08	
	Cash		379.08
e.	Employee Income Tax Payable	51.48	
	FICA Tax Payable ($37.44 × 2)	74.88	
	State Unemployment Tax Payable	25.27	
	Federal Unemployment Tax Payable	3.74	
	Cash		155.37
f.	Employee Benefits Payable	46.80	
	Cash		46.80

Requirement 3

Denius incurred *total payroll expense* of $581.25 (gross salary of $468.00 + payroll taxes of $66.45 + fringe benefits of $46.80). See entries (a–c).

Denius *paid cash* of $581.25 on payroll (Kingsley's net pay of $379.08 + payroll taxes of $155.37 + fringe benefits of $46.80). See entries (d–f).

SUMMARY

1. Account for current liabilities. *Current liabilities* may be divided into those of *known amount* and those that must be *estimated*. Trade accounts payable, short-term notes payable, and the related liability for accrued expenses are current liabilities of known amount. Current liabilities that must be estimated include warranties payable and corporations' income tax payable.

2. Account for contingent liabilities. *Contingent liabilities* are not actual liabilities but potential liabilities that may arise in the future. Contingent liabilities, like current liabilities, may be of known amount or an indefinite amount. A business that faces a lawsuit not yet decided in court has a contingent liability of indefinite amount.

3. Compute payroll amounts. *Payroll* accounting handles the expenses and liabilities arising from compensating employees. Employers must withhold income and FICA taxes from employees' pay and send these *employee payroll taxes* to the government. In addition, many employers allow their employees to pay for insurance and union dues and to make gifts to charities through payroll deductions. An employee's net pay is the gross pay less all payroll taxes and optional deductions.

4. Make basic payroll entries. An *employer's* payroll expenses include FICA and unemployment taxes, which are separate from the payroll taxes borne by the employees. Also, most employers provide their employees with fringe benefits, such as insurance coverage and retirement pensions.

5. Use a payroll system. A *payroll system* consists of a payroll register, a payroll bank account, payroll checks, and an earnings record for each employee. Good *internal controls* over payroll disbursements help the business to conduct payroll accounting efficiently and to safeguard the company's cash. The cornerstone of internal control is the separation of duties.

6. Report current liabilities. The company reports on the balance sheet all current liabilities that it owes.

SELF-STUDY QUESTIONS

Test your understanding of the chapter by marking the best answer for each of the following questions.

1. A $10,000, 9-percent, one-year note payable was issued on July 31. The balance sheet at December 31 will report interest payable of (p. 448)
   a. $0 because the interest is not yet due
   b. $300
   c. $375
   d. $900

2. If the note payable in the preceding question had been discounted, the cash proceeds from issuance would have been (p. 449)
   a. $9,100
   b. $9,625
   c. $9,700
   d. $10,000

3. Which of the following liabilities creates *no* expense for the company? (p. 451)
   a. Interest
   b. Sales tax
   c. FICA tax
   d. Warranty

4. Suppose Unitex Tire Company estimates that warranty costs will equal 1 percent of tire sales. Assume that November sales totaled $900,000 and that the company's outlay in tires and cash to satisfy warranty claims was $7,400. How much warranty expense should the November income statement report? (pp. 453–454)
   a. $1,600
   b. $7,400
   c. $9,000
   d. $16,400

5. Apex Sporting Company is a defendant in a lawsuit that claims damages of $55,000. On the balance sheet date, it appears likely that the court will render a judgment against Apex. How should Apex report this event in its financial statements? (pp. 456–457)
   a. Omit mention because no judgment has been rendered
   b. Disclose the contingent liability in a note
   c. Use a short presentation only
   d. Report the loss on the income statement and the liability on the balance sheet

6. Emilie Frontenac's weekly pay is $320, plus time and a half for overtime. The tax rates applicable to her earnings are 8 percent for income tax and 8 percent for FICA. What is Emilie's take-home pay for a week in which she works 50 hours? (p. 459)
   a. $369.60
   b. $392.00
   c. $404.80
   d. $440.00

7. Which payroll tax applies (or taxes apply) mainly to the employer? (pp. 461–462)
   a. Withheld income tax
   b. FICA tax
   c. Unemployment compensation tax
   d. Both b and c

8. The main reason for using a separate payroll bank account is to (p. 465)
   a. Safeguard cash by avoiding writing payroll checks to fictitious employees
   b. Safeguard cash by limiting paychecks to amounts based on time cards
   c. Increase efficiency by isolating payroll disbursements for analysis and control
   d. All of the above

9. The key to good internal control of payroll is (p. 470)
   a. Using a payroll bank account
   b. Separating payroll duties
   c. Using a payroll register
   d. Using time cards

10. Which of the following items is reported as a current liability on the balance sheet? (p. 471)
    a. Short-term notes payable
    b. Estimated warranties
    c. Accrued payroll taxes
    d. All of the above

Answers to the Self-Study Questions follow the Accounting Vocabulary.

ACCOUNTING VOCABULARY

Current portion of long-term debt. Amount of the principal that is payable within one year (p. 451).

Discounting a note payable. A borrowing arrangement in which the bank subtracts the interest amount from the note's face value. The borrower receives the net amount (p. 449).

FICA tax. Federal Insurance Contributions Act (FICA), or Social Security tax, which is withheld from employees' pay (p. 461).

Gross pay. Total amount of salary, wages, commissions, or any other employee compensation before taxes and other deductions are taken out (p. 459).

Net pay. Gross pay minus all deductions; the amount of employee compensation that the employee actually takes home (p. 459).

Payroll. Employee compensation, a major expense of many businesses (p. 458).

Short presentation. A way to report contingent liabilities in the body of the balance sheet, after total liabilities but with no amount given (p. 456).

Short-term note payable. Note payable due within one year, a common form of financing (p. 448).

Social Security tax. Another name for FICA tax (p. 460).

Unemployment compensation tax. Payroll tax paid by employers to the government, which uses the money to pay unemployment benefits to people who are out of work (p. 461).

Withheld income tax. Income tax deducted from employees' gross pay (p. 459).

1. c $10,000 \times 0.09 \times 5/12 = \$375$
2. a $\$10,000 - (\$10,000 \times 0.09) = \$9,100$
3. b
4. c $\$900,000 \times 0.01 = \$9,000$
5. d
6. a   Overtime pay: $\$320/40 = \$8 \times 1.5 = \$12$ per hour $\times 10$ hours $= \$120$
   Gross pay $= \$320 + \$120 = \$440$
   Deductions $= \$440 \times (0.08 + 0.08) = \$70.40$
   Take-home pay $= \$440 - \$70.40 = \$369.60$
7. c
8. c
9. b
10. d

QUESTIONS

1. Give a more descriptive account title for each of the following current liabilities: Accrued Interest, Accrued Salaries, Accrued Income Tax.
2. What distinguishes a current liability from a long-term liability? What distinguishes a contingent liability from an actual liability?
3. A company purchases a machine by signing a $21,000, 10-percent, one-year note payable on July 31. Interest is to be paid at maturity. What two current liabilities related to this purchase does the company report on its December 31 balance sheet? What is the amount of each current liability?
4. A company borrowed cash by discounting a $15,000, 8-percent, six-month note payable to the bank, receiving cash of $14,400. (a) Show how the amount of cash was computed. Also, identify (b) the total amount of interest expense to be recognized on this note and (c) the amount of the borrower's cash payment at maturity.
5. Explain how sales tax that is paid by consumers is a liability of the store that sold the merchandise.
6. What is meant by the term *current portion of long-term debt*, and how is this item reported in the financial statements?
7. At the beginning of the school term, what type of account is the tuition that your college or university collects from students? What type of account is the tuition at the end of the school term?
8. Why is a customer deposit a liability? Give an example.
9. Patton Company warrants its products against defects for three years from date of sale. During the current year, the company made sales of $300,000. Store management estimated that warranty costs on those sales would total $18,000 over the three-year warranty period. Ultimately, the company paid $22,000 cash on warranties. What was the company's warranty expense for the year? What accounting principle governs this answer?

10. Identify two contingent liabilities of a definite amount and two contingent liabilities of an indefinite amount.
11. Describe two ways to report contingent liabilities.
12. Why is payroll expense relatively more important to a service business such as a CPA firm than it is to a merchandising company such as Kmart?
13. Two persons are studying Allen Company's manufacturing process. One person is Allen's factory supervisor, and the other person is an outside consultant who is an expert in the industry. Which person's salary is the payroll expense of Allen Company? Identify the expense account that Allen would debit to record the pay of each person.
14. What are two elements of an employer's payroll expense in addition to salaries, wages, commissions, and overtime pay?
15. What determines the amount of income tax that is withheld from employee paychecks?
16. What are FICA taxes? Who pays them? What are the funds used for?
17. Identify two required deductions and four optional deductions from employee paychecks.
18. Identify three employer payroll taxes.
19. Who pays state and federal unemployment taxes? What are these funds used for?
20. Briefly describe a payroll accounting system's components and their functions.
21. How much Social Security tax has been withheld from the pay of an employee who has earned $52,288 during the current year? How much Social Security tax must the employer pay for this employee?
22. Briefly describe the two principal categories of internal controls over payroll.
23. Why do some companies use two special payroll bank accounts?
24. Identify three internal controls designed to safeguard payroll cash.

EXERCISES

E11-1   Make general journal entries to record the following transactions of Natural Bridge Resort Company for a two-month period. Explanations are not required.

Recording sales tax two ways
(Obj. 1)

March 31   Recorded cash sales of $92,420 for the month, plus sales tax of 5 percent collected on behalf of the state of Idaho. Recorded sales tax in a separate account.

April   6   Sent March sales tax to the state.

Journalize these transactions a second time. Record the sales tax initially in the Sales Revenue account.

E11-2   The accounting records of Town & Country, Inc., included the following balances at the end of the period:

Accounting for warranty expense and the related liability
(Obj. 1)

Estimated Warranty Payable	Sales Revenue	Warranty Expense
Beg. bal. 8,100	161,000	

In the past, Town & Country's warranty expense has been 7 percent of sales. During the current period, the business paid $10,430 to satisfy the warranty claims of customers.

Required

1. Record Town & Country's warranty expense for the period and the company's cash payments during the period to satisfy warranty claims. Explanations are not required.
2. What ending balance of Estimated Warranty Payable will Town & Country report on its balance sheet?

E11-3   Record the following note payable transactions of Montreal Development, Inc., in the company's general journal. Explanations are not required.

Recording note payable transactions
(Obj. 1)

19X2
May 1   Purchased equipment costing $14,000 by issuing a one-year, 8-percent note payable.
Dec. 31   Accrued interest on the note payable.
19X3
May 1   Paid the note payable at maturity.

E11-4   On November 1, 19X4, Garden Ridge Counseling Center discounted a six-month, $12,000 note payable to the bank at 7 percent.

Discounting a note payable
(Obj. 1)

Required

1. Prepare general journal entries to record (a) issuance of the note, (b) accrual of interest at December 31, and (c) payment of the note at maturity in 19X5. Explanations are not required.
2. Show how Garden Ridge Counseling Center would report the note on the December 31, 19X4, balance sheet.

E11-5   Villeroy Instrument Control is a defendant in lawsuits brought against the marketing and distribution of its products. Damages of $7.1 million are claimed against Villeroy, but the company denies the charges and is vigorously defending itself. In a recent press conference, the president of the company stated that he could not predict the outcome of the lawsuits. Nevertheless, he said management does not believe that any actual liabilities resulting from the lawsuits will significantly affect the company's financial position.

Reporting a contingent liability
(Obj. 2)

Required

Prepare a partial balance sheet to show how Villeroy Instrument Control would report this contingent liability in a short presentation. Total actual liabilities are $9.7 million. Also, write the disclosure note to describe the contingency.

Accruing a contingency
(Obj. 2)

E11-6 Refer to the Villeroy Instrument Control situation in Exercise 11-5. Suppose Villeroy's attorneys believe it is probable that a judgment of $2 million will be rendered against the company.

Required

Describe how to report this situation in the Villeroy Instrument Control financial statements. Journalize any entry required under GAAP. Explanations are not required.

Reporting current liabilities
(Obj. 6)

E11-7 The top management of Stattler, Inc., examines the following company accounting records at December 29, immediately before the end of the year:

Total current assets	$ 490,000
Noncurrent assets	1,230,000
	$1,720,000
Total current liabilities	$ 250,000
Noncurrent liabilities	810,000
Owners' equity	660,000
	$1,720,000

Stattler's borrowing agreements with creditors require the company to keep a current ratio of 2.0 or better. How much in current liabilities should Stattler pay off within the next two days in order to comply with its borrowing agreements?

Computing net pay
(Obj. 3)

E11-8 George Kidwell is manager of the men's department of Rich's Department Store in Atlanta. He earns a base monthly salary of $750 plus an 8 percent commission on his personal sales. Through payroll deductions, Kidwell donates $5 per month to a charitable organization, and he authorizes Rich's to deduct $22.50 monthly for his family's health insurance. Tax rates on Kidwell's earnings are 10 percent for income tax and 8 percent for FICA, subject to the maximum. During the first 11 months of the year, he earned $57,140. Compute Kidwell's gross pay and net pay for December, assuming his sales for the month are $61,300.

Computing and recording gross pay and net pay (Obj. 3, 4)

E11-9 Vidal Karlin works for a 7-Eleven store for straight-time earnings of $6 per hour, with time-and-a-half compensation for hours in excess of 40 per week. Karlin's payroll deductions include withheld income tax of 10 percent of total earnings, FICA tax of 8 percent of total earnings, and a weekly deduction of $5 for a charitable contribution to United Fund. Assuming he worked 48 hours during the week, (a) compute his gross pay and net pay for the week, and (b) make a general journal entry to record the store's wage expense for Karlin's work, including his payroll deductions. Explanations are not required. Round all amounts to the nearest cent.

Recording a payroll
(Obj. 3, 4)

E11-10 Stix Baer & Fuller Department Store incurred salary expense of $82,000 for December. The store's payroll expense includes employer FICA tax of 8 percent in addition to state unemployment tax of 5.4 percent and federal unemployment tax of 0.8 percent. Of the total salaries, $78,400 is subject to FICA tax, and $9,100 is subject to unemployment tax. Also, the store provides the following fringe benefits for employees: health insurance (cost to the store, $2,062.15), life insurance (cost to the store, $351.07), and pension benefits (cost to the store, $707.60). Record Stix Baer & Fuller's payroll taxes and its expenses for employee fringe benefits. Explanations are not required.

Reporting current and long-term liabilities
(Obj. 6)

E11-11 Suppose Lennox Air Conditioning Company borrowed $5,000,000 on December 31, 19X0, by issuing 9-percent long-term debt that must be paid in five equal annual installments plus interest each January 2. By inserting appropriate amounts in the following excerpts from the company's partial balance sheet, show how Lennox would report its long-term debt.

	December 31,				
	19X1	**19X2**	**19X3**	**19X4**	**19X5**
Current liabilities:					
Current portion of long-term debt	$_____	$_____	$_____	$_____	$_____
Interest payable	_____	_____	_____	_____	_____
Long-term liabilities:					
Long-term debt	_____	_____	_____	_____	_____

E11-12 Assume that Dunlop Sporting Goods completed these selected transactions during December 19X6:

Reporting current and long-term liabilities
(Obj. 6)

a. Sport Spectrum, a chain of sporting goods stores, ordered $40,000 of tennis and golf equipment. With its order, Sport Spectrum sent a check for $40,000. Dunlop will ship the goods on January 3, 19X7.

b. The December payroll of $195,000 is subject to employee withheld income tax of 9 percent, FICA tax of 8 percent (employee and employer), state unemployment tax of 5.4 percent, and federal unemployment tax of 0.8 percent. On December 31, Dunlop pays employees but accrues all tax amounts.

c. Sales of $2,000,000 are subject to estimated warranty cost of 1.4 percent.

d. On December 2, Dunlop signed a $100,000 note payable that requires annual payments of $20,000 plus 9-percent interest on the unpaid balance each December 2.

Required

Classify each liability, and report the amount that would appear for these items on Dunlop's balance sheet at December 31, 19X6.

CHALLENGE EXERCISES

E11-13 The balance sheets of PepsiCo, Inc., for four years reported these figures:

Accounting for and reporting current liabilities
(Obj. 1, 6)

	Millions			
	19X4	19X3	19X2	19X1
Total current assets	$ 4,842.3	$ 4,566.1	$ 4,081.4	$ 3,550.8
Noncurrent assets	16,108.9	14,209.0	13,062.0	11,575.9
	$20,951.2	$18,775.1	$17,143.4	$15,126.7
Total current liabilities	$ 4,324.4	$ 3,722.1	$ 4,770.5	$ 3,691.8
Noncurrent liabilities	11,271.1	9,507.6	7,468.7	7,543.8
Stockholders' equity	5,355.7	5,545.4	4,904.2	3,891.1
	$20,951.2	$18,775.1	$17,143.4	$15,126.7

The notes to PepsiCo's 19X4 financial statements report that during 19X3, the company reclassified $3,450 million of current liabilities as long-term. And during 19X4, PepsiCo reclassified a further $3,500 million as long-term.

Required

1. Compute PepsiCo's current ratio at the end of each year. Describe the trend that you observe.
2. Assume that PepsiCo had not reclassified current liabilities as long-term but instead had paid the current liabilities in due course. Recompute the current ratios for 19X3 and 19X4. Why do you think PepsiCo reclassified the liabilities as long-term? What could the company do to justify the reclassification?

E11-14 PepsiCo, Inc., recently reported short-term borrowings and accrued compensation and benefits as follows:

Analyzing current liability accounts (Obj. 1, 3, 6)

	December 26,	
	19X2	19X1
Current liabilities (partial):	Millions	
Short-term borrowings	$706.8	$228.2
Accrued compensation and benefits	327.0	333.8

Assume that during 19X2, PepsiCo borrowed $914.3 million on short-term debt. Also assume that PepsiCo paid $4,281.9 million for employee compensation and benefits during 19X2.

Required

1. Compute PepsiCo's payment of short-term debt during 19X2.
2. Compute PepsiCo's employee compensation and benefit expense during 19X2.

PROBLEMS

Journalizing liability-related transactions
(Obj. 1)

P11-1A   The following transactions of Econo Auto Service occurred during 19X4 and 19X5.

Required

Record the transactions in the company's general journal. Explanations are not required.

19X4

Jan. 9	Purchased a machine at a cost of $5,000, signing an 8-percent, six-month note payable for that amount.
29	Recorded the week's sales of $22,200, three-fourths on credit, and one-fourth for cash. Sales amounts are subject to an additional 6-percent state sales tax.
Feb. 5	Sent the last week's sales tax to the state.
28	Borrowed $200,000 on a 9-percent note payable that calls for annual installment payments of $50,000 principal plus interest.
Apr. 8	Received $1,427 in deposits from distributors of company products. Econo refunds the deposits after six months.
July 9	Paid the six-month, 8-percent note at maturity.
Oct. 8	Refunded security deposits to distributors.
22	Discounted a $5,000, 7-percent, 90-day note payable to the bank, receiving cash for the net amount after interest was deducted from the note's maturity value.
Nov. 30	Purchased inventory for $3,100, signing a six-month, 10-percent note payable.
Dec. 31	Accrued warranty expense, which is estimated at 3 percent of sales of $650,000.
31	Accrued interest on all outstanding notes payable. Made a separate interest accrual entry for each note payable.

19X5

Jan. 20	Paid off the 7-percent discounted note payable. Made a separate entry for the interest.
Feb. 28	Paid the first installment and interest for one year on the long-term note payable.
May 31	Paid off the 10-percent note plus interest on maturity.

Identifying contingent liabilities
(Obj. 2)

P11-2A   Covert Buick Company is the only Buick dealer in Austin, Texas, and one of the largest Buick dealers in the southwestern United States. The dealership sells new and used cars and operates a body shop and a service department. Duke Covert, the general manager, is considering changing insurance companies because of a disagreement with Doug Stillwell, Austin agent for the Travelers Insurance Company. Travelers is doubling Covert's liability insurance cost for the next year. In discussing insurance coverage with you, a trusted business associate, Stillwell brings up the subject of contingent liabilities.

Required

Write a memorandum to inform Covert Buick Company of specific contingent liabilities arising from the business. In your discussion, define a contingent liability.

Computing and recording payroll amounts
(Obj. 3, 4)

P11-3A   The partial monthly records of County Line Restaurant show the following figures:

Employee Earnings:		Accounts Debited:	
(a) Straight-time earnings	$16,431	(j) Salary Expense	$?
(b) Overtime pay	?	(k) Wage Expense	8,573
(c) Total employee earnings	?	(l) Sales Commission Expense	5,077

Deductions and Net Pay:	
(d) Withheld income tax	2,403
(e) FICA tax	?
(f) Charitable contributions	340
(g) Medical insurance	668
(h) Total deductions	5,409
(i) Net pay	17,936

Required

1. Determine the missing amounts on lines (b), (c), (e), and (j).
2. Prepare the general journal entry to record County Line Restaurant's payroll for the month. Credit Payrolls Payable for net pay. No explanation is required.

P11-4A Assume that Diane DeCastro is a vice-president of Wells Fargo Bank's leasing operations in San Francisco. During 19X6 she worked for the company all year at a $5,625 monthly salary. She also earned a year-end bonus equal to 10 percent of salary.

Computing and recording payroll amounts
(Obj. 3, 4)

DeCastro's federal income tax withheld during 19X6 was $737 per month. Also, there was a one-time federal withholding tax of $1,007 on her bonus check. State income tax withheld came to $43 per month, and there was a one-time state withholding tax of $27 on the bonus. The FICA tax withheld was 8.0 percent of the first $60,000 in annual earnings. DeCastro authorized the following payroll deductions: United Fund contribution of 1 percent of total earnings and life insurance of $19 per month.

Wells Fargo Bank incurred payroll tax expense on DeCastro for FICA tax of 8 percent of the first $60,000 in annual earnings. The bank also paid state unemployment tax of 5.4 percent and federal unemployment tax of 0.8 percent on the first $7,000 in annual earnings. In addition, the bank provides DeCastro with health insurance at a cost of $35 per month and pension benefits. During 19X6, Wells Fargo Bank paid $7,178 into DeCastro's pension program.

Required

1. Compute DeCastro's gross pay, payroll deductions, and net pay for the full year 19X6. Round all amounts to the nearest dollar.
2. Compute Wells Fargo Bank's total 19X6 payroll cost for DeCastro.
3. Prepare Wells Fargo Bank's summary general journal entries to record its expense for:
   a. DeCastro's total earnings for the year, her payroll deductions, and her net pay. Debit Salary Expense and Executive Bonus Compensation as appropriate. Credit liability accounts for the payroll deductions and Cash for net pay.
   b. Employer payroll taxes on DeCastro. Credit liability accounts.
   c. Fringe benefit provided to DeCastro. Credit a liability account. Explanations are not required.
4. How will what you learned in this problem help you manage a business?

P11-5A The general ledger of Tempo Plastics, Inc., at June 30, 19X3, the end of the company's fiscal year, includes the following account balances before adjusting entries. Parentheses indicate a debit balance.

Journalizing, posting, and reporting liabilities
(Obj. 1, 2, 4, 6)

Notes Payable, Short-Term	$ 45,000
Discount on Notes Payable	(600)
Accounts Payable	105,520
Current Portion of Long-Term Debt Payable	
Interest Payable	
Salary Payable	
Employee Payroll Taxes Payable	
Employer Payroll Taxes Payable	
Employee Benefits Payable	
Estimated Vacation Pay Liability	7,620
Sales Tax Payable	738
Customer Deposits Payable	6,950
Unearned Rent Revenue	6,000
Long-Term Debt Payable	120,000
Contingent Liabilities	

The additional data needed to develop the adjusting entries at June 30 are as follows:

a. The $45,000 balance in Notes Payable, Short-Term consists of two notes. The first note, with a principal amount of $15,000, was issued on January 31. It matures six months from date of issuance and was discounted at 8 percent. The second note was issued on April 22 for a term of 90 days. It bears interest at 9 percent. It was not discounted. Interest on this note will be paid at maturity.

b. The long-term debt is payable in annual installments of $40,000 with the next installment due on July 31. On that date, Tempo will also pay one year's interest at 7 percent. Interest was last paid on July 31 of the preceding year.

c. Gross salaries for the last payroll of the fiscal year were $5,044. Of this amount, employee payroll taxes payable were $1,088, and salary payable was $3,956.

d. Employer payroll taxes payable were $876, and Tempo's liability for employee health insurance was $1,046.

e. Tempo estimates that vacation pay expense is 4 percent of gross salaries.

f. On February 1 the company collected one year's rent of $6,000 in advance.

g. At June 30, Tempo is the defendant in a $300,000 lawsuit, which the company hopes to win. However, the outcome is uncertain. Report this contingent liability in the appropriate manner.

Required

1. Open the listed accounts, inserting their unadjusted June 30 balances.

2. Journalize and post the June 30 adjusting entries to the accounts opened. Key adjusting entries by letter.

3. Prepare the liability section of the balance sheet at June 30.

Using payroll register, recording a payroll
(Obj. 5)

P11-6A Assume that the payroll records of a district sales office of Panasonic Corporation provided the following information for the weekly pay period ended December 21, 19X5:

Employee	Hours Worked	Hourly Earnings Rate	Federal Income Tax	Union Dues	United Way Contributions	Earnings through Previous Week
Lance Blanks	42	$28	$278	$6	$5	$62,474
James English	47	8	56	4	4	23,154
Louise French	40	11	72	—	4	4,880
Roberto Garza	41	22	188	6	8	59,600

James English and Louise French work in the office, and Lance Blanks and Roberto Garza work in sales. All employees are paid time and a half for hours worked in excess of 40 per week. For convenience, round all amounts to the nearest dollar. Show computations. Explanations are not required for journal entries.

Required

1. Enter the appropriate information in a payroll register similar to Exhibit 11-6. In addition to the deductions listed, the employer also takes out FICA tax: 8 percent of the first $60,000 of each employee's annual earnings.

2. Record the payroll information in the general journal.

3. Assume that the first payroll check is number 319, paid to Lance Blanks. Record the check numbers in the payroll register. Also, prepare the general journal entry to record payment of net pay to the employees.

4. The employer's payroll taxes include FICA tax of 8 percent of the first $60,000 of each employee's earnings. The employer also pays unemployment taxes of 6.2 percent (5.4 percent for the state and 0.8 percent for the federal government on the first $7,000 of each employee's annual earnings). Record the employer's payroll taxes in the general journal.

P11-7A Following are six pertinent facts about events during the current year at Shulton, Inc.

Reporting current liabilities (Obj. 6)

a. On September 30, Shulton signed a six-month, 9-percent note payable to purchase equipment costing $50,000. The note requires payment of principal and interest at maturity.

b. On September 30, Shulton discounted a $50,000 note payable to Lake Air National Bank. The interest rate on the one-year note is 8 percent.

c. On November 30, Shulton received rent of $5,100 in advance for a lease on a building. This rent will be earned evenly over three months.

d. December sales totaled $38,000, and Shulton collected an additional state sales tax of 7 percent. This amount will be sent to the state of Arizona early in January.

e. Shulton owes $100,000 on a long-term note payable. At December 31, 6-percent interest since July 31 and $20,000 of this principal are payable within one year.

f. Sales of $430,000 were covered by Shulton's product warranty. At January 1, estimated warranty payable was $8,100. During the year, Shulton recorded warranty expense of $22,300 and paid warranty claims of $23,600.

Required

For each item, indicate the account and the related amount to be reported as a current liability on Shulton's December 31 balance sheet.

(GROUP B)

P11-1B The following transactions of Taurus Oil Company occurred during 19X2 and 19X3.

Journalizing liability-related transactions (Obj. 1)

Required

Record the transactions in the company's general journal. Explanations are not required.

19X2

Feb. 3	Purchased a machine for $6,200, signing a six-month, 8-percent note payable.
28	Recorded the week's sales of $51,000, one-third for cash, and two-thirds on credit. All sales amounts are subject to a 5-percent state sales tax.
Mar. 7	Sent the last week's sales tax to the state.
Apr. 30	Borrowed $100,000 on a 9-percent note payable that calls for annual installment payments of $25,000 principal plus interest.
May 10	Received $1,125 in security deposits from customers. Taurus refunds most deposits within three months.
Aug. 3	Paid the six-month, 8-percent note at maturity.
10	Refunded security deposits of $1,125 to customers.
Sep. 14	Discounted a $6,000, 7-percent, 60-day note payable to the bank, receiving cash for the net amount after interest was deducted from the note's maturity value.
Nov. 13	Recognized interest on the 7-percent discounted note and paid off the note at maturity.
30	Purchased inventory at a cost of $7,200, signing a 9-percent, three-month note payable for that amount.
Dec. 31	Accrued warranty expense, which is estimated at 3 percent of sales of $145,000.
31	Accrued interest on all outstanding notes payable. Made a separate interest accrual entry for each note payable.

19X3

Feb. 28	Paid off the 9-percent inventory note, plus interest, at maturity.
Apr. 30	Paid the first installment and interest for one year on the long-term note payable.

P11-2B   Windy Hill Farm provides riding lessons for girls ages 8 through 15. Most students are beginners, and none of the girls owns her own horse. Jan Wiethorn, the owner of Windy Hill, uses horses stabled at her farm and owned by the Kultgens. Most of the horses are for sale, but the economy has been bad for several years and horse sales have been slow. The Kultgens are happy that Wiethorn uses their horses in exchange for rooming and boarding them. Because of a recent financial setback, Wiethorn cannot afford insurance. She seeks your advice about her business's exposure to liabilities.

Required

Write a memorandum to inform Wiethorn of specific contingent liabilities arising from the business. It will be necessary to define a contingent liability because she is a professional horse trainer, not a businessperson. Propose a way for Wiethorn to limit her exposure to these liabilities.

P11-3B   The partial monthly records of Dellwood Pipeline Company show the following figures:

Employee Earnings:

(a) Straight-time earnings..................	$?
(b) Overtime pay	5,109
(c) Total employee earnings	?

Deductions and Net Pay:

(d) Withheld income tax	9,293
(e) FICA tax..	6,052
(f) Charitable contributions	885
(g) Medical insurance	1,373
(h) Total deductions	?
(i) Net pay	58,813

Accounts Debited:

(j) Salary Expense	31,278
(k) Wage Expense...............................	?
(l) Sales Commission Expense	27,931

Required

1. Determine the missing amounts on lines (a), (c), (h), and (k).
2. Prepare the general journal entry to record Dellwood's payroll for the month. Credit Payrolls Payable for net pay. No explanation is required.

P11-4B   Assume that Erika Kraft is a commercial lender at Swiss Credit Bank in New York City. During 19X2 she worked for the bank all year at a $5,195 monthly salary. She also earned a year-end bonus equal to 12 percent of her salary.

Kraft's federal income tax withheld during 19X2 was $822 per month. Also, there was a one-time withholding of $2,487 on her bonus check. State income tax withheld came to $61 per month, and the city of New York withheld income tax of $21 per month. In addition, Kraft paid one-time withholdings of $64 (state) and $19 (city) on the bonus. The FICA tax withheld was 8 percent of the first $60,000 in annual earnings. Kraft authorized the following payroll deductions: United Fund contribution of 1 percent of total earnings and life insurance of $17 per month.

Swiss Credit Bank incurred payroll tax expense on Kraft for FICA tax of 8 percent of the first $60,000 in annual earnings. The bank also paid state unemployment tax of 5.4 percent and federal unemployment tax of 0.8 percent on the first $7,000 in annual earnings. The bank provided Kraft with the following fringe benefits: health insurance at a cost of $48 per month, and pension benefits to be paid to Kraft during her retirement. During 19X2 Swiss Credit Bank's cost of Kraft's pension program was $8,083.

Required

1. Compute Kraft's gross pay, payroll deductions, and net pay for the full year of 19X2. Round all amounts to the nearest dollar.

2. Compute Swiss Credit Bank's total 19X2 payroll cost for Kraft.

3. Prepare Swiss Credit Bank's summary general journal entries to record its expense for:

   a. Kraft's total earnings for the year, her payroll deductions, and her net pay. Debit Salary Expense and Executive Bonus Compensation as appropriate. Credit liability accounts for the payroll deductions and Cash for net pay.

   b. Employer payroll taxes for Kraft. Credit liability accounts.

   c. Fringe benefits provided to Kraft. Credit a liability account.

   Explanations are not required.

4. How will what you learned in this problem help you manage a business?

P11-5B The Rocky Mountain Power Company general ledger at September 30, 19X7, the end of the company's fiscal year, includes the following account balances before adjusting entries. Parentheses indicate a debit balance.

Journalizing, posting, and reporting liabilities
(Obj. 1, 2, 4, 6)

Notes Payable, Short-Term	$ 49,000
Discount on Notes Payable	(1,680)
Accounts Payable	88,240
Current Portion of Long-Term Debt Payable	_____
Interest Payable	_____
Salary Payable	_____
Employee Payroll Taxes Payable	_____
Employer Payroll Taxes Payable	_____
Employee Benefits Payable	_____
Estimated Vacation Pay Liability	2,105
Sales Tax Payable	372
Property Tax Payable	1,433
Unearned Rent Revenue	3,900
Long-Term Debt Payable	220,000
Contingent Liabilities	_____

The additional data needed to develop the adjusting entries at September 30 are as follows:

a. The $49,000 balance in Notes Payable, Short-Term consists of two notes. The first note, with a principal amount of $21,000, was issued on August 31, matures one year from date of issuance, and was discounted at 8 percent. The second note was issued on September 2 for a term of 90 days and bears interest at 7 percent. It was not discounted.

b. The long-term debt is payable in annual installments of $55,000, with the next installment due on January 31, 19X8. On that date, Rocky Mountain Power will also pay one year's interest at 6.5 percent. Interest was last paid on January 31. Shift the current installment of the long-term debt to a current liability.

c. Gross salaries for the last payroll of the fiscal year were $4,319. Of this amount, employee payroll taxes payable were $958, and salary payable was $3,361.

d. Employer payroll taxes payable were $755, and Rocky Mountain Power's liability for employee life insurance was $1,004.

e. Rocky Mountain Power estimates that vacation pay is 4 percent of gross salaries.

f. On August 1 the company collected six months' rent of $3,900 in advance.

g. At September 30 Rocky Mountain Power is the defendant in a $500,000 lawsuit, which the company hopes to win. However, the outcome is uncertain. Report this contingent liability in the appropriate manner.

Required

1. Open the listed accounts, inserting their unadjusted September 30 balances.
2. Journalize and post the September 30 adjusting entries to the accounts opened. Key adjusting entries by letter.
3. Prepare the liability section of Rocky Mountain Power's balance sheet at September 30.

Using a payroll register, recording a payroll
(Obj. 5)

P11-6B Assume that payroll records of a district sales office of Kellogg Company provided the following information for the weekly pay period ended December 18, 19X3:

Employee	Hours Worked	Weekly Earnings Rate	Federal Income Tax	Health Insurance	United Way Contribution	Earnings through Previous Week
Ginny Akin	43	$ 400	$ 94	$9	$7	$17,060
Leroy Dixon	46	480	121	5	5	22,365
Karol Stastny	47	1,200	319	6	—	59,247
David Trent	40	240	32	4	2	3,413

Ginny Akin and David Trent work in the office, and Leroy Dixon and Karol Stastny work in sales. All employees are paid time and a half for hours worked in excess of 40 per week. For convenience, round all amounts to the nearest dollar. Show computations. Explanations are not required for journal entries.

Required

1. Enter the appropriate information in a payroll register similar to Exhibit 11-6. In addition to the deductions listed, the employer also takes out FICA tax: 8 percent of the first $60,000 of each employee's annual earnings.
2. Record the payroll information in the general journal.
3. Assume that the first payroll check is number 178, paid to Ginny Akin. Record the check numbers in the payroll register. Also, prepare the general journal entry to record payment of net pay to the employees.
4. The employer's payroll taxes include FICA of 8 percent of the first $60,000 of each employee's annual earnings. The employer also pays unemployment taxes of 6.2 percent (5.4 percent for the state and 0.8 percent for the federal government) on the first $7,000 of each employee's annual earnings. Record the employer's payroll taxes in the general journal.

Reporting current liabilities
(Obj. 6)

P11-7B Following are six pertinent facts about events during the current year at Misaka Tool Company.

a. On August 31, Misaka signed a six-month, 7-percent note payable to purchase a machine costing $31,000. The note requires payment of principal and interest at maturity.
b. On October 31, Misaka received rent of $2,400 in advance for a lease on a building. This rent will be earned evenly over four months.
c. On November 30, Misaka discounted a $10,000 note payable to InterBank Savings. The interest rate on the one-year note is 8 percent.
d. December sales totaled $104,000 and Misaka collected sales tax of 9 percent. This amount will be sent to the state of Washington early in January.
e. Misaka owes $75,000 on a long-term note payable. At December 31, 6-percent interest for the year plus $25,000 of this principal are payable within one year.
f. Sales of $909,000 were covered by Misaka's product warranty. At January 1 estimated warranty payable was $11,300. During the year Misaka recorded warranty expense of $27,900 and paid warranty claims of $30,100.

Required

For each item, indicate the amount and the related amount to be reported as a current liability on Misaka's December 31 balance sheet.

EXTENDING YOUR KNOWLEDGE

DECISION PROBLEMS

1. Guadalupe Builders is a large construction company in Scottsdale, Arizona. The owner and manager, Jonathan Echols, oversees all company operations. He employs 15 work crews, each made up of 6 to 10 members. Construction supervisors, who report directly to Echols, lead the crews. Most supervisors are longtime employees, so Echols trusts them. Echols's office staff consists of an accountant and an office manager.

Identifying internal control weaknesses and their solution (Obj. 5)

Because employee turnover is high in the construction industry, supervisors hire and fire their own crew members. Supervisors notify the office of all personnel changes. Also, supervisors forward to the office the employee W-4 forms, which the crew members fill out to claim tax-withholding exemptions. Each Thursday the supervisors submit weekly time sheets for their crews, and the accountant prepares the payroll. At noon on Friday the supervisors come to the office to get paychecks for distribution to the workers at 5 P.M.

Guadalupe's accountant prepares the payroll, including the payroll checks, which are written on a single payroll bank account. Echols signs all payroll checks after matching the employee name to the time sheets submitted by the foremen. Often the construction workers wait several days to cash their paychecks. To verify that each construction worker is a bona fide employee, the accountant matches the employee's endorsement signature on the back of the canceled payroll check with the signature on that employee's W-4 form.

Required

1. Identify one *efficiency* weakness in Guadalupe's payroll accounting system. How can the business correct this weakness?
2. Identify one way that a supervisor can defraud Guadalupe Builders under the present system.
3. Discuss a control feature Guadalupe Builders can use to *safeguard* against the fraud you identified in Requirement 2.

2. The following questions are not related.

Questions about liabilities (Obj. 1, 2)

a. A friend comments that he thought liabilities represented amounts owed by a company. He asks why unearned revenues are shown as a current liability. How will you respond?

b. A warranty is like a contingent liability in that the amount to be paid is not known at year end. Why are warranties payable shown as a current liability, whereas contingent liabilities are reported in the notes to the financial statements?

c. Auditors have procedures for determining whether they have discovered all of a company's contingent liabilities. These procedures differ from the procedures used for determining that accounts payable are stated correctly. How would an auditor identify a client's contingent liabilities?

ETHICAL ISSUE

The Boeing Company, manufacturer of jet aircraft, is the defendant in numerous lawsuits claiming unfair trade practices. Boeing has strong incentives not to disclose these contingent liabilities. However, generally accepted accounting principles require that companies report their contingent liabilities.

Required

1. Why would a company prefer not to disclose its contingent liabilities?
2. Describe how a bank could be harmed if a company seeking a loan did not disclose its contingent liabilities.
3. What is the ethical tightrope that each company must walk when it reports its contingent liabilities?

Current liabilities
(Obj. 1)

1. Details about a company's current and contingent liabilities and payroll costs appear in a number of places in the annual report. Use the Lands' End financial statements to answer the following questions.

Required

1. Give the breakdown of Lands' End's current liabilities at January 28, 1994. Give the February 1994 entry to record the payment of accounts payable at January 28, 1994.
2. How much was Lands' End's long-term debt at January 28, 1994? Of this amount, how much was due within one year? How much was payable beyond one year in the future?
3. Lands' End has collected cash in advance for some revenue. The company reports this liability as "Advance Payment on Orders." Journalize the transaction, which occurred after January 28, 1994, in which Lands' End satisfied this liability. Lands' End uses a perpetual inventory system, so you will also need to record the related cost of goods sold, which was approximately $335 thousand.
4. The balance sheet lists a $12,528 thousand liability for "Income Taxes Payable." Was income tax expense for the year equal to, less than, or greater than this amount? Give your reason.

Current and contingent liabilities
and payroll
(Obj. 1, 2, 6)

2. Obtain the annual report of an actual company of your choosing. Details about the company's current and contingent liabilities and payroll costs may appear in a number of places in the annual report. Use the statements of the company you select to answer the following questions. Concentrate on the current year in the annual report.

Required

1. Give the breakdown of the company's current liabilities at the end of the current year. Journalize the payment in the following year of Accounts Payable reported on the balance sheet.
2. How much of the company's long-term debt at the end of the current year was reported as a current liability? Do the notes to the financial statements identify the specific items of long-term debt coming due within the next year? If so, identify the specific liabilities.
3. Identify the current liability for income tax at the end of the current year. Give its amount, and record its payment in the next year.
4. Does the company report any unearned revenue? If so, identify the item and give its amount.
5. Where does the company report contingent liabilities—on the face of the balance sheet or in a note? Give important details about the company's contingent liabilities at the end of the current year.

Chapter 12
The Foundation for Generally Accepted Accounting Principles

After studying this chapter, you should be able to

1. Identify the basic objective of financial reporting

2. Identify and apply the underlying concepts of accounting

3. Identify and apply the principles of accounting

4. Allocate revenue to the appropriate period by four methods

5. Report information that satisfies the disclosure principle

6. Apply the materiality constraint and the conservatism constraint to accounting

❝When PepsiCo presents financial data in an annual or quarterly report or in an earnings press release, we use this question as a benchmark: What should investors in our stock know about our three businesses in order to make informed decisions about their investment in our company? And since most [of our] employees are investors in PepsiCo, we can answer that question by asking ourselves, what do we need to know?❞

LOTA ZOTH, MANAGER OF FINANCIAL REPORTING FOR PEPSICO, INC.

The foundation for generally accepted accounting principles is continually changing. A group of the American Institute of Certified Public Accountants (AICPA) is proposing changes in the data that companies report to the public. The panel was formed to improve the disclosures in financial reports.

According to panel members, specific recommendations the group is likely to suggest include (1) demanding more financial data from large companies than from small companies and (2) forcing companies to divide their financial disclosures into more categories to illuminate the financial positions of the component companies. PepsiCo's annual report, for example, reveals details about the company's three lines of business—beverages, snack foods, and restaurants. PepsiCo's annual report includes all the required data so that potential investors can compare the net sales and operating profits of each of its three divisions as well as those of its domestic operations with its international operations. PepsiCo also presents detailed data on capital spending, acquisitions and investments in affiliates, amortization of intangible assets, and depreciation expense. Not all companies are so forthcoming.

Proposals by the panel must be approved by the Financial Accounting Standards Board (FASB), the AICPA's Auditing Standards Board, and the Securities and Exchange Commission (SEC). Needless to say, the proposed recommendations are disturbing to many corporate financial officers.

● ● ● ● ●

The chapter-opening story reveals an interesting political situation that can be diagrammed as in Exhibit 12-1. The accountants are caught in the middle. As providers of information, accountants design systems to meet the needs of investors and creditors. This is the objective of financial reporting. But accountants' clients—businesses led by top managers—pay accountants' fees. Top managers are reluctant to disclose every piece of information that investors and creditors request. They also want to hold down the cost of their accounting systems. After all, the accounting department of a business brings in no revenue. The result

EXHIBIT 12-1
The Politics of Setting Accounting Standards

is an interesting political environment for accountants. To address these issues, the accounting profession has formulated a theoretical foundation. This chapter covers that foundation and illustrates each concept and principle with examples that apply to real situations.

Accounting Standards in the United States

Every technical area has professional associations and regulatory bodies that govern the practice of the profession. Accounting is no exception. In the United States generally accepted accounting principles (GAAP) are influenced most by the FASB. The FASB has seven full-time members, a large staff, and an annual budget of $14 million. Its financial support comes from professional associations such as the AICPA.

The FASB is an independent organization with no government or professional affiliation. The FASB's pronouncements, called *Statements of Financial Accounting Standards*, currently specify how to account for certain business transactions. Each new *Standard* becomes part of GAAP, the "accounting law of the land." In the same way that our laws draw authority from their acceptance by the people, GAAP depends on the general acceptance by the business community. Throughout this book, we refer to GAAP as the proper way to do financial accounting.

The U.S. Congress has given the SEC ultimate responsibility for establishing accounting rules for companies that are owned by the general investing public. However, the SEC has delegated much of its rule-making power to the FASB. Exhibit 12-2 outlines the flow of authority for developing GAAP.

Setting accounting standards is a complex process involving the FASB, the SEC, and occasionally Congress. Individuals and companies often exert pressure on all three bodies to try to shape accounting decisions to their advantage. Accountants also try to influence accounting decisions. Although overruling is rare, the SEC has the authority to overrule an FASB decision, and Congress can overrule an SEC or an FASB decision (Exhibit 12-2). But in most cases, the FASB plays the key role.

We have seen that GAAP guides companies in the preparation of their financial statements. Independent auditing firms of certified public accountants (CPAs) hold the responsibility for making sure companies do indeed follow GAAP.

The Conceptual Framework

EXHIBIT 12-2
Flow of Authority for Developing GAAP

Throughout Chapters 1 to 11, we introduced key concepts and principles as they applied to the topics under discussion. For example, Chapter 1 introduced the entity concept so that we could account for the transactions of a particular business. In

Chapter 2, we discussed the revenue and matching principles as the guidelines for measuring income. Now that you have an overview of the accounting process, we consider the full range of accounting concepts and principles. Collectively, they form the foundation for accounting practice—GAAP.

Shortly after its formation in 1973, the FASB began the Conceptual Framework Project. The FASB's goal is to develop a constitution that will define the nature and function of financial accounting. This project provides a framework for the various accounting concepts and principles that are used to prepare financial statements.

Accounting principles differ from natural laws such as the law of gravity. Accounting principles draw their authority from their acceptance in the business community rather than from their ability to explain physical phenomena. Thus they really are *generally accepted* by those people and organizations who need guidelines in accounting for their financial undertakings. Exhibit 12-3 diagrams how we move from the conceptual framework to the financial statements.

We now look at the objective of financial reporting. This objective tells what financial accounting is intended to accomplish. Thus it provides the goal for accounting information. Next, we examine particular accounting concepts and principles used to implement the objective. The difference between concepts and principles is that concepts are broader in their application; principles are more specific.

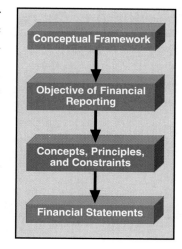

EXHIBIT 12-3
Overview of Generally Accepted Accounting Principles

Objective of Financial Reporting

The basic *objective of financial reporting* is to provide information that is useful in making investment and lending decisions. The FASB believes that accounting information can be useful in decision making only if it is *relevant, reliable,* and *comparable.*

Relevant information is useful in making predictions and for evaluating past performance—that is, the information has feedback value. For example, PepsiCo's disclosure of the profitability of each of its lines of business is relevant for investor evaluations of the company. To be relevant, information must be timely. *Reliable* information is free from significant error—that is, it has validity. Also, it is free from the bias of a particular viewpoint—that is, it is verifiable and neutral. *Comparable* and *consistent* information can be compared from period to period to help investors and creditors track the entity's progress through time. These characteristics combine to shape the concepts and principles that make up GAAP. Exhibit 12-4 summarizes the qualities that increase the value of accounting information.

OBJECTIVE 1
Identify the basic objective of financial reporting

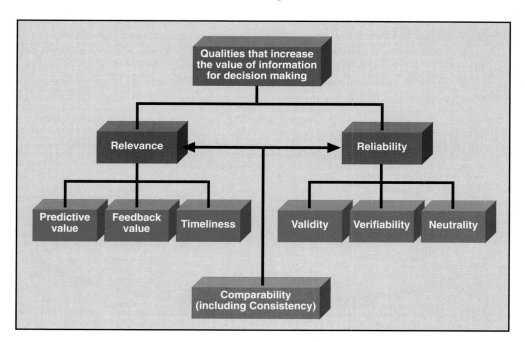

EXHIBIT 12-4
Qualities that Increase the Value of Information for Decision Making

Underlying Concepts

OBJECTIVE 2

Identify and apply the underlying concepts of accounting

Key Point: The entity concept requires that the transactions of each entity are accounted for separately from the transactions of all other organizations and persons.

Entity Concept

The **entity concept** is the most basic concept in accounting because it draws a boundary around the organization being accounted for. That is, the transactions of each entity are accounted for separately from transactions of all other organizations and persons, including the owners of the entity. This separation allows us to measure the performance and the financial position of each entity independent of all other entities.

A business entity may be a sole proprietorship (owned and operated by a single individual), a partnership of two or more persons, or a large corporation such as Exxon. The entity concept applies with equal force to all types and sizes of organizations. The proprietor of a travel agency, for example, accounts for her personal transactions separately from those of her business. This division allows her to evaluate the success or failure of the travel agency. If she were to mix her personal and business accounting records, she would lose sight of the information needed to evaluate the business alone.

At the other end of the spectrum, Exxon is a giant company with oil-refining, retail gasoline sales, and chemical operations (Exhibit 12-5). Exxon accounts for each of its divisions separately in order to know which part of the business is earning a profit, which needs to borrow money, and so on. The entity concept also provides the basis for consolidating subentities into a single set of financial statements. Exxon reports a single set of consolidated financial statements to the public.

"Exxon accounts for each of its divisions separately in order to know which part of the business is earning a profit, which needs to borrow money, and so on."

Going-Concern Concept

Key Point: The going-concern concept assumes that a business will operate long enough for it to recover the cost of its assets.

Under the **going-concern** (or **continuity**) **concept,** accountants assume that the business will continue operating for the foreseeable future. The logic behind the going-concern concept is best illustrated by considering the alternative assumption: going out of business.

When a business stops, it sells its assets, converting them to cash. This process is called *liquidation*. With the cash, the business pays off its liabilities, and the owners keep any remaining cash. In liquidation, the amount of cash for which the assets are sold measures their current value. Likewise, the liabilities are paid off at their current value. But if the business does not halt operations—if it remains a going concern—how will its assets and liabilities be reported in the balance sheet?

EXHIBIT 12-5

The Entity Exxon Corporation

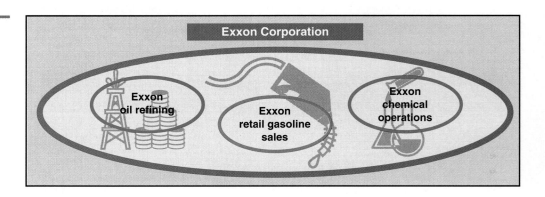

For a going concern, the balance sheet reports assets and liabilities on the basis of historical cost. To consider what the asset may be worth in the current market requires making an estimate. This estimate may or may not be made objectively. Under the going-concern concept, it is assumed that the entity will continue long enough to recover the cost of its assets.

The going-concern concept allows for the reporting of assets and liabilities as current or long-term, a distinction that investors and creditors find useful in evaluating a company. For example, a creditor wants to know the portion of the company's liabilities that are scheduled to come due within the next year and the portion payable beyond the year. The assumption is that the entity will continue in business and honor its commitments.

Time-Period Concept

The **time-period concept** ensures that accounting information is reported at regular intervals. This timely presentation of accounting data aids the comparison of business operations over time; from year to year, quarter to quarter, and so on. Managers, owners, lenders, and other people and businesses need regular reports to assess the business's success—or failure. These persons are making decisions daily. Although the ultimate success of a company cannot be known for sure until the business liquidates, decision makers cannot wait until liquidation to learn whether operations yielded a profit.

Key Point: For accounting information to be useful, it must be made available at regular intervals. The time-period concept ensures that accounting information is reported at regular intervals.

Nearly all companies use the year as their basic time period. *Annual* reports are common in business. Companies also prepare quarterly and monthly reports—called *interim* reports—to meet managers', investors', and creditors' needs for timely information.

The time-period concept underlies the use of accruals. Suppose the business's accounting year ends at December 31 and the business has accrued—but will not pay until the next accounting period—$900 in salary expense. To tie this expense to the appropriate period, the accountant enters this adjusting entry, as we have seen:

Dec. 31 Salary Expense 900
           Salary Payable 900

Accrual entries assign revenue and expense amounts to the correct accounting period and thus help produce meaningful financial statements.

Stable-Monetary-Unit Concept

Accounting information is expressed primarily in monetary terms. The monetary unit is the prime means of measuring assets. This measure is not suprising, given that money is the common denominator in business transactions. In the United States, the monetary unit is the dollar; in Great Britain, the pound sterling; in Japan, the yen. The stable-monetary-unit concept provides an orderly basis for handling account balances to produce the financial statements.

Unlike a liter, a foot, and many other measurements, the value of the monetary unit may change over time. Most of us are familiar with inflation. Groceries that cost $50 a few years ago may cost $60 today. The value of the dollar changes. In view of the fact that the dollar does not maintain a constant value, how does a business measure the worth of assets and liabilities acquired over a long span of time? The business records all assets and liabilities at cost. Each asset and each liability on the balance sheet is the sum of all the individual dollar amounts added over time. For example, if a company bought 100 acres of land in 1975 for $60,000 and another 100 acres of land in 1995 for $300,000, the asset Land on the balance sheet carries a $360,000 balance, and the change in the purchasing power of the dollar is ignored. The **stable-monetary-unit concept** is the accountant's basis for ignoring the effect of inflation and making no restatements for the changing value of the dollar (Exhibit 12-6). Let's look at the shortcomings of this concept.

| 1977 | 1996 | 1977 | 1996 |

Due to inflation, a dollar in 1996 is worth less than a dollar was in 1977.

Under the stable-monetary-unit concept, the effect of inflation is ignored.

EXHIBIT 12-6
The Stable-Monetary-Unit Concept

Suppose another company paid $600,000 for the same 200 acres of land in 1995. Its balance sheet would show a higher amount for the land. How do we compare the two companies' balance sheets? The comparison based on the stable-monetary-unit concept may not be valid because mixing dollar values at different times is like mixing apples and oranges.

Many businesspeople believe that accounting information should be restated for changes in the dollar's purchasing power. In general, however, accounting is based on historical costs.

Accounting Principles

OBJECTIVE 3
Identify and apply the principles of accounting

Reliability (Objectivity) Principle

The **reliability principle** requires that accounting information be dependable—free from significant error and bias. Users of accounting information rely on its truthfulness. To be reliable, information must be verifiable by people outside the business. Financial statement users may consider information reliable if independent experts would agree that the information is based on objective and honest measurement.

Consider the error in a company's failure to accrue interest revenue at the end of an accounting period. This error results in understated interest revenue and understated net income. Clearly, this company's accounting information is unreliable.

Biased information—data prepared from a particular viewpoint and not based on objective facts—is also unreliable. Suppose a company purchased inventory for $25,000. At the end of the accounting period, the inventory has declined in value and can be replaced for $20,000. Under the lower-of-cost-or-market rule, the company must record a $5,000 loss for the decrease in the inventory's value. Company management may believe that the appropriate value for the inventory is $22,000, but that amount is only an opinion. If management reports the $22,000 figure, total assets and owner equity will be overstated on the balance sheet. Income will be overstated on the income statement.

Recall from Chapter 9 (p. 382) that the lower-of-cost-or-market rule requires that an asset be reported at the lower of its historical cost or its market value.

To establish a *reliable* figure for the inventory's value, management could get a current price list from the inventory supplier or call in an outside professional appraiser to revalue the inventory. Evidence obtained from outside the company leads to reliable, verifiable information. The reliability principle applies to all financial accounting information—from assets to equity on the balance sheet and from revenue to net income on the income statement.

Comparability Principle

The **comparability principle** has two requirements. First, accounting information must be comparable from business to business. Second, each business's financial statements must be comparable (consistent) from one period to the next. The FASB encourages comparability to enable investors and creditors to compare business to business, period to period. Standardization of formats for financial statements promotes comparability. Using the same terms to describe the statement elements—assets, liabilities, revenues, and so on—aids the comparison process.

Even among companies that adhere to standard formats and standard terms, comparability may be less than perfect. Comparisons of companies that use different inventory methods—LIFO and FIFO, for example—are difficult. When GAAP allows a choice among acceptable accounting methods—in inventory, depreciation, and other areas—comparability may be hard to achieve.

Recall that the comparability principle directs each individual company to produce accounting information that is comparable over time. To achieve this quality—which accountants call *consistency*—companies may follow the same accounting practices from period to period. The business that uses FIFO for inventory and straight-line for depreciation in one period ought to use those same methods in the next period. Otherwise, a financial statement user could not tell whether changes in income and asset values resulted from operations or from the way the business accounts for operations.

Companies may change accounting methods in response to a change in business operations. PepsiCo may add a new product line that calls for a different inventory method. GAAP allows the company to make a change in accounting method, but the business must disclose the change, the reason for making the change, and its effect on net income. This disclosure is made in a note to the financial statements.

Short Exercise: Which of the following violates the principle of comparability (consistency)?
1. Firms in the same industry use different accounting methods for a given type of transaction.
2. A company changes from FIFO to LIFO for inventory.
3. A company fails to write down its inventory to the lower of cost or market.
4. A firm fails to adjust its financial statements for changes in the purchasing power of the dollar.

A: 2

Cost Principle

The **cost principle** states that assets and services are recorded at their purchase cost and that the accounting record of the asset continues to be based on cost rather than on current market value. By specifying that assets be recorded at cost, this principle also governs the recording of liabilities and owner equity. Suppose a land developer purchased 20 acres of land for $50,000. Additional costs included fees paid to the county ($1,500), removal of an unwanted building ($10,000), and leveling ($20,000), a total cost of $81,500. The Land account carries this balance because it is the cost of bringing the land to its intended use. Assume that the developer holds the land for one year, then offers it for sale at a price of $200,000. The cost principle requires that the accounting value of the land remain at $81,500.

The developer may wish to lure buyers by showing them a balance sheet that reports the land at $200,000. However, this value would be inappropriate under GAAP because $200,000 is merely the developer's opinion of what the land is worth.

The underlying basis for the cost principle is the reliability principle. Cost is a reliable value for assets and services because cost is supported by completed transactions between parties with opposing interests. Buyers try to pay the lowest price possible, and sellers try to sell for the highest price. The actual cost of an asset or service is objective evidence of its value.

Revenue Principle

The **revenue principle** provides guidance on the *timing* of the recording of revenue and the *amount* of revenue to record. The general rule is that revenue should be recorded when it is earned and not before.

Some revenues, such as interest and rent, accrue with the passage of time. Their timing and amount are easy to figure. The accountant records the amount of revenue earned over each period of time.

Other revenues are earned by selling goods or rendering services. Identifying *when* these revenues are earned depends on more factors than the passage of time. Under the revenue principle, three conditions must be met before revenue is recorded: (1) The seller has done everything necessary to expect to collect from the buyer; (2) the amount of revenue can be objectively measured; and (3) collectibility is reasonably assured. In most cases, these conditions are met at the point of sale or when services are performed.

The *amount* of revenue to record is the value of the assets received—usually cash or a receivable. But situations may arise in which the amount of revenue or the timing of earning the revenue is not easily determined. We turn to four methods that guide the accountant in applying the revenue principle in different situations.

We saw in Chapter 3 (p. 92) that the revenue principle is the basis for recording revenue. It is one reason why adjusting entries are needed.

Key Point: Under the revenue principle, three conditions must be met before revenue is recorded: (1) The seller has done everything necessary to expect to collect from the buyer; (2) the amount of revenue can be objectively determined; and (3) collectibility is reasonably assured.

SALES METHOD   Under the *sales method*, revenue is recorded at the point of sale. Consider a retail sale in a hardware store. When a sale occurs, the customer pays the store and takes the merchandise. The store records the sale by debiting Cash and crediting Sales Revenue. In other situations, the point of sale occurs when the seller ships the goods to the buyer. Suppose a mining company sells iron ore to Bethlehem Steel Corporation. By shipping the ore to Bethlehem Steel, the mining company has completed its duty and may expect to collect cash for the revenue earned. If the amount of revenue can be objectively measured and collection is reasonably certain, the mining company can then record revenue. The sale entry is a debit to Accounts Receivable and a credit to Sales Revenue. The sales method is used for most sales of goods and services.

"By shipping the ore to Bethlehem Steel, the mining company has completed its duty and may expect to collect cash for the revenue earned."

Short Exercise: A product that cost $500 was in the shipping room when the physical inventory was counted. It was marked "Hold for customer's shipping instructions." The customer's order was dated December 15, 1995, and was filled on December 29, 1995. The goods being held were shipped to the customer on January 5, 1996. Should the sale be recorded in 1995 or 1996? *A:* The sale should be recorded in 1995 because the company had done everything needed to complete the sale.

COLLECTION METHOD   The *collection method* is used only if the receipt of cash is uncertain. Under this method, the seller waits until cash is received to record the sale. Professionals such as physicians and attorneys use the collection method because they often find it difficult to collect their receivables. They may not reasonably assume that they can collect the revenue, so they wait until actual receipt of the cash before recording it. The collection method is conservative in that revenue is not recorded in advance of the receipt of cash.

INSTALLMENT METHOD   The *installment method* is a type of collection method that is used for installment sales. In a typical installment sale, the buyer makes a downpayment when the contract is signed and pays the remainder in installments. Real estate companies sell on the installment plan. Under this method, gross profit (sales revenue – cost of goods sold) is recorded as cash is collected.

Suppose a real estate developer sells land for a down payment of $80,000 plus three annual installments of $120,000, $140,000, and $160,000 (a total of $500,000). The developer's cost of the land is $300,000, so the gross profit is $200,000:

Installment sale	$500,000
Cost of the land sold	300,000
Gross profit	$200,000

To determine the gross profit associated with each collection under the installment method, we must compute the gross profit percentage, as follows:

$$\text{Gross profit percentage} = \frac{\text{Gross profit}}{\text{Installment sale}} = \frac{\$200,000}{\$500,000} \times 100\% = 40\%$$

We next apply the gross profit percentage to each collection. The result is the amount of gross profit recorded as revenue at the time of cash receipt:

Year	Collections	×	Gross Profit Percentage	=	Gross Profit
1	$ 80,000	×	40%	=	$ 32,000
2	120,000	×	40%	=	48,000
3	140,000	×	40%	=	56,000
4	160,000	×	40%	=	64,000
Total	$500,000	×	40%	=	$200,000

Accountants would record gross profit of $32,000 in year 1, $48,000 in year 2, and so on. The total gross profit ($200,000) is the same as under the sales method. But

	Gross Profit Percentage	**Gross Profit by Year = Cash Receipt × Gross Profit Percentage**			
		Year 1	Year 2	Year 3	Year 4
Year 1 sales	40%	$80,000 × 0.40 = $32,000	$120,000 × 0.40 = $48,000	$140,000 × 0.40 = $56,000	$160,000 × 0.40 = $64,000
Year 2 sales	45%		90,000 × 0.45 = 40,500	100,000 × 0.45 = 45,000	20,000 × 0.45 = 9,000
Year 3 sales	42%			75,000 × 0.42 = 31,500	65,000 × 0.42 = 27,300
Year 4 sales	35%				30,000 × 0.35 = 10,500
		$32,000	$88,500	$132,500	$110,800

EXHIBIT 12-7

Installment Method for Revenue

under the sales method, the full $200,000 of gross profit would be recorded at the beginning of the contract.

Of course, companies make installment sales year after year, and the gross profit percentage may change from year to year. In the preceding example, year 1 installment sales earned gross profit of 40 percent. Suppose year 2 sales earn gross profit of 45 percent, year 3 sales earn 42 percent, and year 4 sales earn 35 percent. The total gross profit for a year is the sum of all the gross profit amounts recorded on cash collections made that year.

Using assumed cash receipts on installment sales made in years 2, 3, and 4, the gross profit computations for years 1 through 4 appear in Exhibit 12-7. All year 1 amounts are taken from our computations above.

The installment method is attractive for income tax purposes: It postpones the recording of revenue and thus the payment of taxes. But it can be used only under limited circumstances, such as the sale of real estate. Under GAAP, this method is permissible only when no reasonable basis exists for estimating collections.

Short Exercise: A business sells on the installment basis: 19X3 sales are $27,500, downpayments are $2,750, and collections on installments total $8,000. Beginning inventory is $4,000, ending inventory is $3,500, and purchases are $16,000. (1) What are cost of goods sold, total gross profit, and the gross profit percentage for the year? (2) What gross profit will the business report if it uses the installment method?
A: (1)
COGS = Beg. Inv. + Pur. – End. Inv. $16,500 = $4,000 + $16,000 – $3,500
GP = Sales – COGS
$11,000 = $27,500 – $16,500
GP% = 40% ($11,000/$27,500)
(2)

Downpayment	$ 2,750
Collections	8,000
Total rec'd	10,750
	× 40%
Inst. method GP	$ 4,300

STOP & THINK *Ethical Issue:* Lincoln Savings and Loan Association of Phoenix, Arizona, went bankrupt during the 1980s. Consider the following actual business transactions:

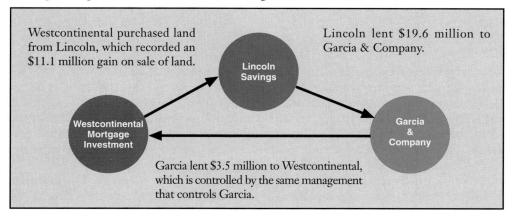

One national accounting firm approved of Lincoln's accounting. The auditors viewed Lincoln's sale of the land as authentic and the gain as real. A second CPA firm, which specializes in accounting for real estate transactions, viewed Lincoln's gain as artificial. That firm's CPAs believed that no sale took place because Westcontinental had received its cash for the purchase from Garcia, which in turn had received its cash from Lincoln. In effect, Westcontinental had none of its own money in the land. Was it ethical for Lincoln Savings to record the gain?

Answer: There is no clear answer. However, when there is a doubt about the ethics of a situation, it is safest to avoid any appearance of unethical conduct. Develop your own ethical guidelines and be prepared to use them in your career. Chances are, your ethical position *will* be challenged.

PERCENTAGE-OF-COMPLETION METHOD Construction of office buildings, bridges, dams, and other large assets often extends over several years. The construction company must decide *when* to record the revenue. The most conservative approach is to record all the revenue earned on the project in the period when the project is completed. This procedure, called the *completed-contract method*, is acceptable under limited circumstances.

Under the preferred method, called the *percentage-of-completion method*, the construction company recognizes revenue as work is performed. Each year the company estimates the percentage of project completion as construction progresses. One way to make this estimate is to compare the cost incurred for the year with the total estimated project cost. This percentage is then multiplied by the total project revenue to compute the construction revenue for the year. Construction income for the year is revenue minus cost.

Assume that General Electric (GE) Company receives a contract to build the engines for a power plant for a price of $42 million. GE estimates total costs of $36 million over the three-year construction period: $6 million in year 1, $18 million in year 2, and $12 million in year 3. Construction revenue and income during the three years are as follows (amounts in millions):

Year	Cost for Year	Total Project Cost	Percentage of Project Completion for Year	Total Project Revenue	Construction Revenue for Year	Construction Income for Year
1	$ 6	$36	$ 6/$36 = 1/6	$42	$42 × 1/6 = $ 7	$ 7 − $ 6 = $1
2	18	36	18/ 36 = 1/2	42	42 × 1/2 = 21	21 − 18 = 3
3	12	36	12/ 36 = 1/3	42	42 × 1/3 = 14	14 − 12 = 2
	$36				$42	$42 $36 $6

The percentage-of-completion method is appropriate when the company can estimate the degree of completion during the construction period, which most construction companies can do. When estimates are not possible, the completed-contract method is required. If GE had used the completed-contract method, its income statement for year 3 would have reported total project revenue of $42 million, total project expenses of $36 million, and income of $6 million. The income statements of years 1 and 2 would have reported nothing concerning this project. Most accountants believe the results under the percentage-of-completion method are more realistic.

Matching Principle

◀▥ ◀▥ ◀▥ We saw in Chapter 3 (p. 93) that the matching principle is the basis for recording expenses. It is one reason why adjusting entries are needed.

The **matching principle** governs the recording and reporting of expenses. ◀▥ This principle goes hand in hand with the revenue principle to govern income recognition in accounting. Recall that income is revenue minus expense. During any period, the company first measures its revenues by the revenue principle. The company then identifies and measures all the expenses it incurred during the period to earn the revenues. To *match* the expenses against the revenues means to subtract the expenses from the revenues. The result is the income for the period.

Some expenses are easy to match against particular revenues. For example, PepsiCo's cost of goods sold is related directly to the company's sales revenue: Without the sales, there would be no cost of goods sold. Commissions and fees paid for selling the goods and the expense of delivering soft drinks to stores, for example, are related to sales revenue for the same reason.

Other expenses are not so easily linked to particular sales because they occur whether or not any revenues arise. Depreciation, salaries, and home-office expenses of PepsiCo's headquarters in Purchase, New York, are in this category. Accountants usually match these expenses against revenue on a time basis. For example, the company's home-office building may be used for general management and marketing. Straight-line depreciation of a 40-year building assigns one-fortieth of the building's cost to expense each year, whatever the level of revenue. The annual salary expense for a warehouse employee is the person's total salary for the year, regardless of revenue.

Losses, like expenses, are matched against revenue on a time basis. For example, if an asset such as inventory loses value, the loss is recorded when it occurs, without regard for the revenues earned during the period.

Disclosure Principle

OBJECTIVE 5
Report information that satisfies the disclosure principle

The **disclosure principle** holds that a company's financial statements should report enough information for outsiders to make knowledgeable decisions about the company. In short, the company should report *relevant*, *reliable*, and *comparable* information about its economic affairs. We now discuss and illustrate different types of disclosures.

SUMMARY OF SIGNIFICANT ACCOUNTING POLICIES To evaluate a company, investors and creditors need to know how its financial statements were prepared. This consideration is especially important when the company can choose from several acceptable methods. Companies summarize their accounting policies in the first note to their financial statements. The note may include both monetary amounts and written descriptions. Companies commonly disclose revenue-recognition method, inventory method, and depreciation method.

Dresser Industries, Inc., a manufacturer of oilfield and other industrial equipment, reported the following:

NOTE A—SUMMARY OF SIGNIFICANT ACCOUNTING POLICIES [IN PART]

Long-Term Contracts
   Revenues and earnings related to products requiring long-term construction periods, principally draglines and electrostatic precipitators, are recognized for financial reporting purposes on the percentage of completion basis.
Inventories
   Substantially all the U.S. inventories of the Company are recorded on a last-in, first-out (LIFO) cost basis. Inventories not on LIFO cost valuation, principally foreign inventories, are recorded at the "lower of cost (principally average cost) or market."
Fixed Assets
   Fixed assets are depreciated over the estimated service life. Accelerated depreciation methods are used for financial statement purposes, except for U.S. fixed assets with a service life of 10 years or less, which are depreciated on a straight-line basis. Accelerated depreciation methods are also used for tax purposes wherever permitted.

PROBABLE LOSSES The disclosure principle directs a business to record and report a probable loss *before* it occurs if the loss is likely and its amount can be estimated. Phillips Petroleum Company reported such a loss in a recent financial statement. The disposal of assets has not occurred yet, but Phillips does *expect* the disposal to result in a loss.

NOTE 1—DISCONTINUED OPERATION [IN PART]

   [T]he company announced plans to discontinue its minerals operation. Assets associated with these operations were sold, abandoned, or written down…in anticipation of their future sales or abandonment, resulting in an estimated net loss on disposal…of $171 million, net of income tax….

The $171 million loss on disposal appeared on Phillips's income statement as follows:

	Millions
Income from Continuing Operations	$596
Discontinued operations (net of income taxes)	
Loss from operations	(7)
Loss on disposal	**(171)**
Net Income	$418

ACCOUNTING CHANGES   Consistent use of accounting methods and procedures is important, as we saw in discussing comparability. When a company does change from one accounting method or procedure to another, it must disclose the change, the reason for making the change, and the effect of the change on net income. Two common accounting changes are *changes in accounting principles* and *changes in accounting estimates*.

A **change in accounting principle** is a change in accounting method. A switch from the LIFO method to the FIFO method for inventories and a switch from the double-declining-balance depreciation method to the straight-line method are examples of accounting changes. Special rules that apply to changes in accounting principles are discussed in later accounting courses. Whatever the change in principle, the notes to the financial statements must inform the reader of the change and its effect on income.

A **change in accounting estimate** occurs in the normal course of business as the company alters earlier expectations. A company may record uncollectible account expense based on the estimate that bad debts will equal 2 percent of sales. If actual collections exceed this estimate, the company may lower its estimated expense to 1 1/2 percent of sales in the future.

An airline company such as American or Delta may originally estimate that a new Boeing 767 airplane will provide 15 years' service. After 10 years of using the plane, the company sees that the plane's full useful life will stretch to 18 years. The company must recompute depreciation on the basis of this new information at the start of the plane's eleventh year of service. Assume that this plane cost $80 million, has an estimated residual value of $20 million, and is depreciated by the straight-line method.

Annual depreciation for each of the first 10 years of the asset's life is $4 million, computed as follows:

$$\text{Depreciation per year} = \frac{\$80 \text{ million} - \$20 \text{ million}}{15 \text{ years}} = \$4 \text{ million}$$

Changes in estimate are accounted for by spreading the asset's remaining depreciable book value over its remaining life. Annual depreciation after the accounting change is $2.5 million, computed in the following manner:

$$\text{Depreciation per year} = \frac{\text{Remaining depreciable book value}}{\text{Remaining life}} = \frac{\$80 \text{ million} - \$20 \text{ million} - (\$4 \text{ million} \times 10)}{18 \text{ total years} - 10 \text{ years used}}$$

$$= \frac{\$20 \text{ million}}{8 \text{ years}} = \$2.5 \text{ million}$$

This revised amount of depreciation is recorded in the usual manner.

SUBSEQUENT EVENTS   A company usually takes several weeks after the end of the year to close its books and to publish its financial statements. Occasionally, events occur during this period that affect the interpretation of the information in those financial statements. Such an occurrence is called a **subsequent event** and should be disclosed in the prior period's statements. The most common examples of subsequent events are borrowing money, paying debts, making investments, selling assets, and becoming a defendant in a lawsuit.

United Merchants and Manufacturers, Inc., a maker of textiles for apparel and for home furnishings, disclosed a subsequent event that involved the sale of another business. In its financial statements for the year ended June 30, 19X6, United reported the following:

"United Merchants and Manufacturers, Inc., a maker of textiles for apparel and for home furnishings, disclosed a subsequent event that involved the sale of another business."

NOTE 17—SUBSEQUENT EVENTS

On September 11, 19X6, the Company sold 17 percent of [its investment in] Victoria Creations, Inc., which is in the costume jewelry business. The sale resulted in cash proceeds to the Company of $13,910,000, which has been used to reduce indebtedness. The sale also resulted in a gain...of approximately $6,400,000, which will be reflected in the Company's results of operations for...19X7.

BUSINESS SEGMENTS Most large companies operate in more than one product line or industry. Each industry is called a *business segment*. Sears, Roebuck, and Company, best known for its retail stores, also has real estate, investment banking, and other financial operations. Union Pacific Corporation, the railroad company, is also active in the oil and gas business. Diversification like this is not limited to large international companies. A realtor may also own a restaurant. A farmer may sell farm implements. An automobile dealer may also own a furniture store.

Suppose you are considering investing in a company that is active in the steel industry but also owns a meat packer and several leisure resorts. The American steel industry is losing income because of intense foreign competition. With income and asset data broken down by business segments, you can determine how much of the company's assets are committed to each segment and which lines of businesses are most (and least) profitable. Companies disclose segment data in notes to their financial statements.

The PepsiCo, Inc., data in Exhibit 12-8 illustrate the disclosure of business segments. These data reveal that in 19X2, PepsiCo's restaurants generated the most sales revenue. But snack foods were the most profitable.

The chapter-opening story refers to a proposal for companies to disclose more information about their business segments. It would be difficult to improve on the PepsiCo data presented here.

DISCLOSURE TECHNIQUES Companies use parenthetical notes in the financial statements. An example is the allowance for uncollectibles, reported as follows by RJR Nabisco, Inc. (in millions):

| | December 31, | |
	19X7	19X6
Accounts and notes receivable (less allowances of $61 and $67, respectively)	$1,745	$1,675

Industry Segment ($ in millions)	Net Sales			Operating Profits		
	19X2	19X1	19X0	19X2	19X1	19X0
Beverages	$ 7,605.6	$ 6,915.2	$ 6,523.0	$ 798.6	$ 863.3	$ 767.6
Snack foods	6,132.1	5,250.1	4,766.8	984.7	756.7	892.6
Restaurants	8,232.3	7,126.9	6,225.7	718.5	575.6	522.4
Total	$21,970.0	$19,292.2	$17,515.5	$2,501.8	$2,195.6	$2,182.6

EXHIBIT 12-8
PepsiCo Annual Report Data for Its Business Segments

Other companies, including CPC International, Inc., list the allowance on a separate line of the balance sheet, as follows (in millions):

	December 31,	
	19X7	19X6
Notes and accounts receivable [summarized]	$549.9	$592.5
Allowances for doubtful accounts.................................	(12.5)	(14.2)

Both disclosure techniques provide adequate information on the total amount receivable and the net amount expected to be collected.

MARKET VALUE FOR FINANCIAL INSTRUMENTS   Companies must report the current market value of their *financial instruments* (mainly cash, receivables, investments, and payables).[1] The balance sheet reports these assets and liabilities at carrying value, which, except for some investments, is tied to historical cost.

The market value of a long-term receivable may differ significantly from its historical cost. Suppose that a bank lent $100,000 to a customer. The bank received a $100,000 note receivable from the customer. But market conditions have changed and have caused the note's market value to drop to $96,000. The customer could pay off the note, in which case the bank would receive only $96,000—a $4,000 loss. For this reason the FASB requires companies to disclose (in notes to the financial statements) the current market value of their notes receivable and other financial instruments. With this information, investors and creditors can evaluate a company's financial position realistically in view of current market conditions. In this example, a stockholder in the bank would compare the note receivable's $96,000 current market value to its carrying value of $100,000. The stockholder would learn instantly that the bank would suffer a loss if the customer paid off the loan today.

Constraints on Accounting

OBJECTIVE 6

Apply the materiality constraint and the conservatism constraint to accounting

Do financial statements report every detail, no matter how small, to meet the need for relevant, reliable, and comparable information? The result would be an avalanche of data. To address this problem, accountants use the *materiality concept*. Also, a company's top managers are responsible for its financial statements. To balance managers' optimism—which could bias the statements and present too favorable a picture of company operations—accountants follow the *conservatism* concept. We now discuss these constraints on accounting information.

Materiality Concept

Short Exercise: Which of the following principles or concepts directs a business to record as an expense all items that cost $50 or less, even if the item will be used for more than one accounting period?
1. Disclosure
2. Matching
3. Objectivity
4. Materiality
5. Going-concern
A: 4

The **materiality concept** states that a company must perform strictly proper accounting only for items and transactions that are significant to the business's financial statements. Information is significant—accountants call it *material*—when its inclusion and correct presentation in the financial statements would cause a statement user to change a decision because of that information. *Immaterial*—insignificant—items justify less-than-perfect accounting. The inclusion and proper presentation of immaterial items would not affect a statement user's decision. The materiality concept frees accountants from having to compute and report every last item in strict accordance with GAAP. Thus the materiality concept reduces the cost of accounting.

------

[1]*FASB Statement No. 107, Disclosures about Fair Value of Financial Instruments,* December 1991.

How does a business decide where to draw the line between what is material and what is immaterial? This decision rests to a great degree on how large the business is. Wendy's, for example, has over $500 million in assets. Management would likely treat as immaterial a $100 purchase of wastebaskets. These wastebaskets may well remain useful for 10 years, and strictly speaking, Wendy's should capitalize their cost and depreciate the wastebaskets. However, this treatment is not practical. The accounting costs of computing, recording, and properly reporting this asset outweigh the benefits of any information provided. No Wendy's statement user—a potential investor or lender, for example—would change a decision on the basis of so insignificant (immaterial) an amount. The cost of accounting in this case outweighs the benefit of the resulting information.

"No Wendy's statement user—a potential investor or lender, for example—would change a decision on the basis of so insignificant (immaterial) an amount."

Large companies may draw the materiality line at as high a figure as $10,000 and expense any smaller amount. Smaller firms may choose to expense only those items less than $50. Materiality varies from company to company. An amount that is material to the local service station may not be material to General Motors.

The materiality concept does not free a business from having to account for every item. Wendy's, for example, must still account for the wastebaskets. Wendy's would credit Cash (or Accounts Payable) to record their purchase, of course, but what account would the company debit? Because the amount is immaterial, management may decide to debit Supplies Expense. No matter what account receives the debit, no statement-user's decision would be changed by the information.

Conservatism Concept

Business managers are often optimists. Asked how well the company is doing, its president would likely answer, "Great, we're having our best year ever." Without constraints, this optimism could find its way into the company's reported assets and profits. Managers may try to present too favorable a view of the company. For example, they may pressure accountants to capitalize a cost associated with fixed assets that should be expensed. Doing so would result in less immediate expense and higher current income on the income statement. The balance sheet would report unduly high fixed asset values and owner equity. The overall result would be that the managers' performance would appear to be better than it actually was. Traditionally, accountants have been conservative to counter management's optimism.

Conservatism has been interpreted as

"Anticipate no profits, but anticipate all losses."

A clear-cut example is the lower-of-cost-or-market (LCM) method for inventories. Under LCM, inventory is reported at the *lower* of its cost or market value, which results in higher cost of goods sold and lower net income. Thus profits and assets are reported at their lowest reasonable amount. Other conservative accounting practices include the LIFO method for inventories when inventory costs are increasing, accelerated depreciation, and the completed-contract method for construction revenues. These methods result in earlier recording of expenses or later recording of revenues. Both effects postpone the reporting of net income and therefore are conservative.

In recent years, conservatism's effect on accounting has decreased. The FASB has stated that conservatism should not mean deliberate understatement of assets, profits, and equity. However, if two different values can be used for an asset or a lia-

Short Exercise: Choose the accounting principle or concept that is best described by this statement: "Recognize that some accounting measurements take place in a context of significant uncertainty and that possible errors in measurement could occur. Financial statements should understate rather than overstate net assets and income."
1. Materiality
2. Disclosure
3. Entity
4. Reliability
5. Conservatism
A: 5

bility, the concept suggests using the less optimistic value. Conservatism is a secondary consideration in accounting. Relevant, reliable, and comparable information is the goal, and conservatism is a factor only after those primary goals are met.

STOP & THINK *Ethical Issue:* Suppose Donahue Company sales are up 20 percent. Expenses are under control, and it appears that Donahue's net income for the year will exceed expectations. Next year the company may have trouble repeating this year's success, so Donahue's board of directors is looking for ways to dampen this year's reported income. A director suggests recording a large expense and crediting a liability for estimated losses. He reasons that this accounting treatment is conservative. It also serves to shift part of this year's net income to next year, when the company may need it more. Is this practice conservative? Is it ethical?

Answer: This practice is conservative because it would overstate expenses and liabilities and understate net income. The practice is unethical, however, because it would artificially decrease reported income. "Cooking the books" to manage earnings in this manner violates the reliability principle and is therefore unacceptable.

PUTTING SKILLS TO WORK

ACCOUNTING STANDARDS THROUGHOUT THE WORLD

We have focused on the principles of accounting that are generally accepted in the United States. Most of the methods of accounting are consistent throughout the world. Double-entry bookkeeping, the accrual accounting system, and the basic financial statements are used worldwide. Differences, however, do exist among countries.

In discussing depreciation—Chapter 10—we emphasized that in the United States the methods used for reporting to tax authorities differ from the methods used for reporting to shareholders. In contrast, tax reporting and shareholder reporting are identical in many countries. For example, France has a "Plan Compatible" that specifies a National Uniform Chart of Accounts used for both tax returns and reporting to shareholders. German financial reporting is also determined primarily by tax laws. In Japan, certain principles are allowed for tax purposes only if they are also used for shareholder reporting.

A company that sells its stock through a foreign stock exchange must follow the accounting principles of the foreign country. For example, British Petroleum (BP) stock is available through the New York Stock Exchange, so BP financial statements issued in the United States follow American GAAP.

A significant difference among countries is the extent to which the financial statements account for inflation. In the 1980s the FASB experimented with requiring supplementary disclosure of inflation-adjusted numbers, but

The British oil company BP must follow American accounting principles because BP issues stock in the United States.

there is no requirement for such supplementary disclosure in the United States. In contrast, some countries have full or partial adjustments for inflation as part of their reporting to both investors and tax authorities. For example, Argentina and Brazil, which have experienced very high inflation rates, require all statements to be adjusted for changes in the general price level.

The globalization of business enterprises and capital markets is creating much interest in establishing common, worldwide accounting standards. There are probably too many cultural, social, and political differences to expect complete worldwide standardization of financial reporting in the near future. However, the number of differences is decreasing. Cooperation among accountants has been fostered by the International Federation of Accountants (IFAC), an organization of accountancy bodies from more than 75 countries. International standards are being formulated and published by the International Accounting Standards Committee (IASC).

International Accounting Differences

Country	Inventories	Goodwill	Research and Development Costs
United States	Specific unit cost, FIFO, LIFO, weighted-average	Amortized over period not to exceed 40 years.	Expensed as incurred.
Germany	Similar to U.S.	Amortized over useful life or written off immediately.	Expensed as incurred.
Japan	Similar to U.S.	Amortized over 5 years.	May be capitalized and amortized over 5 years.
United Kingdom	LIFO is unacceptable for tax purposes and is not widely used.	Amortized over useful life or written off immediately.	Expense research costs. Some development costs may be capitalized.

Note: For inventory, goodwill, and research and development costs, German accounting practices are more similar to those of the United States than to those of other countries. Despite the common heritage of the United States and the United Kingdom, American and British accounting practices vary widely.

This chapter discussed the following principles and concepts, among others:

Entity concept
Going-concern concept
Time-period concept
Reliability principle

Cost principle
Revenue principle
Matching principle

Comparability principle
Disclosure principle
Materiality concept

Indicate which of those principles or concepts is being violated in each of the following situations:

1. A construction company signs a two-year contract to build a bridge for the state of Montana. The president of the company immediately records the full contract price as revenue.

2. Competition has taken away much of the business of a small airline. The airline is unwilling to report its plans to sell half its fleet of planes.

3. After starting the business in February 19X2, a coal-mining company keeps no accounting records for 19X2, 19X3, and 19X4. The owner is waiting until the mine is exhausted to determine the success or failure of the business.

4. Assets recorded at cost by a drug store chain are written up to their fair market value at the end of each year.

5. The accountant for a manufacturing company keeps detailed depreciation records on every asset no matter how small its value.

6. A physician mixes her personal accounting records with those of the medical practice.

7. Expenses are recorded whenever the bookkeeper records them rather than when related revenues are earned.

8. The damaged inventory of a discount store is being written down. To minimize income taxes, the store manager bases the write-down entry on his own subjective opinion.

9. A quick-copy center changes accounting methods every year to report the maximum amount of net income possible under generally accepted accounting principles.

10. The owners of a private hospital base its accounting records on the assumption that the hospital might have to close at any time. The hospital has a long record of service to the community.

SOLUTION TO REVIEW PROBLEM

1. Revenue principle
2. Disclosure principle
3. Time-period concept
4. Cost principle
5. Materiality concept

6. Entity concept
7. Matching principle
8. Reliability principle
9. Comparability principle
10. Going-concern concept

SUMMARY

1. Identify the basic objective of financial reporting. The Financial Accounting Standards Board (FASB) formulates generally accepted accounting principles (GAAP) to provide relevant, reliable, and comparable accounting information. *Relevant* information allows users to make business predictions and to evaluate past decisions. *Reliable* data are free from material error and bias. Accounting information is also intended to be *comparable* from company to company and from period to period.

2. Identify and apply the underlying concepts of accounting. Four concepts underlie accounting. The most basic, the *entity concept*, draws clear boundaries around the accounting entity. The entity, based on the *going-concern concept*, is assumed

to remain in business for the foreseeable future. The *time-period concept* is the basis for reporting accounting information for particular time periods such as months, quarters, or years. Under the *stable-monetary-unit concept*, no adjustment is made for the changing value of the dollar.

3. Identify and apply the principles of accounting. Accounting principles provide detailed guidelines for recording transactions and preparing the financial statements. The *reliability* and *comparability principles* require that accounting information be based on objective data and be useful for comparing companies over different time periods. The *cost principle* governs accounting for assets and liabilities, and the *revenue principle* governs accounting for revenues.

4. Allocate revenue to the appropriate period by four methods. Different methods exist to account for revenues, depending on when the revenue has been earned, when it can be measured objectively, and whether collectibility is assured.

Matching is the basis for recording expenses.

5. Report information that satisfies the disclosure principle. The *disclosure principle* requires companies to report their accounting policies, probable future losses, accounting changes,

subsequent events, and business-segment data. They use different disclosure techniques.

6. Apply the materiality constraint and the conservatism constraint to accounting. Two constraints on accounting are materiality and conservatism. The *materiality concept* allows companies to avoid excessive cost in accounting for immaterial items. *Conservatism* constrains the optimism of managers by anticipating no profits, but anticipating all losses.

SELF-STUDY QUESTIONS

Test your understanding of the chapter by marking the best answer for each of the following questions.

1. The organization that issues accounting pronouncements that make up GAAP is the (p. 490)
   a. U.S. Congress
   b. Accounting Principles Board
   c. Financial Accounting Standards Board
   d. Securities and Exchange Commission

2. Which of the following characteristics of accounting information does the objective of financial reporting omit? (p. 491)
   a. Timeliness
   b. Relevance
   c. Reliability
   d. Comparability

3. A new business is starting. The president wishes to wait until significant contracts have been fulfilled before reporting the results of the business's operations. Which underlying concept serves as the basis for preparing financial statements at regular intervals? (p. 493)
   a. Entity
   b. Going-concern
   c. Time-period
   d. Stable-monetary-unit

4. Which of these revenue methods is the most conservative? (pp. 496–498)
   a. Sales method
   b. Collection method
   c. Percentage-of-completion method
   d. All of the above are equally conservative

5. Suppose a Montgomery Ward store sells $10,000 worth of kitchen appliances on the installment plan and collects a down payment of $1,500. Ward's cost of the appliances is $7,000. How much gross profit will the company report this period under the installment revenue method? (pp. 496–497)
   a. $450
   b. $1,500
   c. $3,000
   d. $10,000

6. A construction company spent $180,000 during the current year on a building with a contract price of $900,000. The company estimated total construction cost at $720,000. How much construction *income* will the company report under the percentage-of-completion method? (p. 498)
   a. $45,000
   b. $144,000
   c. $180,000
   d. $225,000

7. Which of the following items should be reported to satisfy the disclosure principle? (pp. 499–501)
   a. Business segment data
   b. Probable losses
   c. Accounting changes
   d. All of the above

8. Important subsequent events should be disclosed because they (p. 500)
   a. Occur immediately after the current period
   b. Describe changes in accounting methods
   c. Reveal losses that have a high probability of occurring in the future
   d. May affect the interpretation of the current-period financial statements

9. Which of the following statements is most in keeping with the materiality concept? (pp. 502–503)
   a. Accountants record material losses but are reluctant to record material gains
   b. Different companies have different materiality limits, depending on their size
   c. Business-segment data are disclosed to fulfill the materiality concept
   d. Companies report all the information needed to communicate a material view of the entity

10. Conservatism would avoid reporting (p. 503)
    a. Insignificant data
    b. Too much income
    c. Too much for liabilities
    d. Footnotes

Answers to the Self-Study Questions follow the Accounting Vocabulary.

ACCOUNTING VOCABULARY

Change in accounting estimate. A change that occurs in the normal course of business as a company alters earlier expectations (p. 500).

Change in accounting principle. A change in accounting method, such as from the LIFO method to the FIFO method for inventories and a switch from an accelerated depreciation method to the straight-line method (p. 500).

Comparability principle. Specifies that accounting information must be comparable from business to business and that a single business's financial statements must be comparable from one period to the next (p. 494).

Conservatism. Concept by which the least favorable figures are presented in the financial statements. (p. 503).

Cost principle. States that assets and services are recorded at their purchase

cost and that the accounting record of the asset continues to be based on cost rather than on current market value (p. 495).

Disclosure principle. Holds that a company's financial statements should report enough information for outsiders to make knowledgeable decisions about the company (p. 499).

Entity concept. States that the transactions of each entity are accounted for separately from the transactions of all other organizations and persons (p. 492).

Going-concern concept. Accountants' assumption that the business will continue operating in the foreseeable future (p. 492).

Matching principle. The basis for recording expenses; directs accountants to identify all expenses incurred during the period, to measure the expenses and to match them against the revenues earned during that same span of time (p. 498).

Materiality concept. States that a company must perform strictly proper accounting only for items and transactions that are significant to the business's financial statements (p. 502).

Reliability principle. Requires that accounting information be dependable (free from error and bias). Also called the objectivity principle (p. 494).

Revenue principle. The basis for recording revenues; tells accountants when to record revenue and the amount of revenue to record (p. 495).

Stable-monetary-unit concept. Ac-

countants' basis for ignoring the effect of inflation and making no restatements for the changing value of the dollar (p. 493).

Subsequent event. An event that occurs after the end of a company's accounting period but before publication of its financial statements and that may affect the interpretation of the information in those statements (p. 500).

Time-period concept. Ensures that accounting information is reported at regular intervals (p. 493).

ANSWERS TO SELF-STUDY QUESTIONS

1. c
2. a
3. c
4. b
5. a   ($10,000 – $7,000)/$10,000 = 0.30 × $1,500 = $450
6. a $180,000/$720,000 = 0.25 × $900,000 = $225,000; $225,000 – $180,000 = $45,000
7. d
8. d
9. b
10. b

QUESTIONS

1. How do accounting principles differ from natural laws?
2. State the basic objective of financial reporting.
3. What three characteristics make accounting information useful for decision making? Briefly discuss each one.
4. What is the entity concept?
5. How does the going-concern concept affect accounting? What is liquidation?
6. Identify two practical results of the time-period concept.
7. What is the shortcoming of the stable-monetary-unit concept?
8. What are the comparability principle's two requirements?
9. Why is consistency important in accounting?
10. Discuss the relationship between the cost principle and the reliability principle.
11. What three conditions must be met before revenue is recorded? What determines the amount of the revenue?
12. Which revenue recognition method is more conservative, the sales method or the collection method? Give your reason.
13. Suppose Century Realty sold land for $200,000 on an installment basis, receiving a down payment of $50,000 to be followed by 12 installments of $12,500 each. If Century's cost of the land was $120,000, how much gross profit would Century record under the installment method (a) when the down payment is received and (b) when each installment is received?
14. Briefly discuss two methods of recognizing revenue on long-term construction contracts.
15. Give two examples of expenses that are easy to relate to sales revenue and two examples of expenses that are not so easy to relate to particular sales. On what basis are the latter expenses matched against revenue?

16. Phoenix Company agreed on November 22, 19X7, to sell an unprofitable manufacturing plant. Phoenix estimates on December 31 that the company is likely to incur a $4 million loss on the sale when it is finalized in 19X8. In which year should Phoenix report the loss? What accounting principle governs this situation?
17. Identify three items commonly disclosed in a company's summary of significant accounting policies.
18. What is a subsequent event? Why should companies disclose important subsequent events in their financial statements?
19. How does information on business segments help an investor?
20. Classify each of the following as a change in accounting principle or a change in accounting estimate:
    a. Change from straight-line to double-declining-balance depreciation
    b. Change in the uncollectibility of accounts receivable
    c. Change from LIFO to FIFO for inventory
    d. Change from the percentage-of-completion method to the completed-contract method for revenue on long-term construction contracts
    e. Change from an 8-year life to a 10-year life for a machine
    f. Change in estimated warranty expense stated as a percent of sales
21. Sloan Sales Company expenses the cost of plant assets below $500 at the time of purchase. What accounting concept allows this departure from strictly proper accounting? Why would Sloan Sales follow such a policy?
22. Give three examples of conservative accounting methods, stating why the methods are conservative.

EXERCISES

Identifying the objective of financial reporting
(Obj. 1)

E12-1   As a financial analyst with Prudential Bache Securities, your job is to follow the automobile industry. Specifically, you compare companies in this industry to recommend to Prudential Bache clients which companies to invest in. What is the basic objective of financial reporting? Briefly discuss some of the predictions and related evaluations of past performance that an investment analyst would make. Also state why the analyst feels more comfortable using information that has been audited by an independent CPA.

Applying accounting concepts
(Obj. 2)

E12-2   *The Yankee Traveler* is a magazine devoted to fall foliage tours in New England. Its owner, Kellie Key, is better attuned to cultural affairs than to the business aspects of running a magazine. Readership is at an all-time high, but the financial position of the business has suffered. For each of the following items indicate the accounting action needed at December 31, the end of the accounting year. Also identify the underlying accounting concept most directly applicable to your answer.

a. On March 31, *The Yankee Traveler* had to borrow $50,000 to pay bills. The interest rate of this one-year loan is 7 percent, payable March 31.

b. Key intermingles her personal assets with those of the business. In applying for the $50,000 loan, she wanted to include on the company books her Cadillac automobile, which was worth $24,000. Her reasoning was that the business was a proprietorship and that her personal assets are available to the magazine if needed.

c. Its financial position is so dismal that *The Yankee Traveler* is in danger of failure. Assets measured at historical cost total $1.3 million, but their current market value is only $400,000, which barely exceeds liabilities of $350,000. For now it appears that the magazine will remain in business.

Reporting assets as a going concern and as a liquidating entity
(Obj. 2, 3)

E12-3   Boch International Company has the following assets:

- Cash, $9,000
- Accounts receivable, $25,600; allowance for uncollectible accounts, $4,300
- Office supplies: cost, $280; scrap value, $70
- Office machinery: cost, $72,000; accumulated depreciation, $14,000; current sales value, $47,400
- Land: cost, $45,000; current sales value, $105,000

Required

1. Assume that Boch continues as a going concern. Compute the amount of its assets for reporting on the balance sheet.
2. Assume that Boch is going out of business by liquidating its assets. Compute the amount of its assets at liquidation value.

Applying the revenue and matching principles
(Obj. 3)

E12-4   Burleson, Inc., introduced a new laser disc in December 19X2 and received $100,000 from customers in advance. During 19X3, Burleson shipped the products to customers and received an additional $400,000. In 19X4 Burleson received $300,000 as the final payment for the 19X3 shipments.

Burleson spent $90,000 in 19X2 to advertise the laser discs during 19X3. Cost of goods sold was $160,000. Burleson paid an additional $230,000 during 19X4 for expenses accrued at the end of 19X3.

Required

Show revenues, expenses, and net income for 19X2, 19X3, and 19X4.

Reporting assets under GAAP
(Obj. 3)

E12-5   Identify the amount at which each of the following assets should be reported in the financial statements of Loew's Company. Cite the concept, principle, or constraint that is most applicable to each answer.

a. Loew's purchased a machine for $16,000 less a $1,300 cash discount. To ship the machine to the office, Loew's paid transportation charges of $500 and insurance of $200 while in transit. After using the machine for one month, Loew's purchases lubricating oil costing $150 for use in operating the machine.

b. Inventory has a cost of $42,000, but its current market value is $39,400.

c. Loew's purchased land for $222,000 and paid $2,500 to have the land surveyed, $15,400 to have old buildings removed, and $40,300 for grading land. Loew's is offering the land for sale at $225,000 and has received a $200,000 offer.

$280,200
COST PRINCIPLE

E12-6 San Marcos Electronics failed to record the following items at December 31, 19X4, the end of its fiscal year:

Reporting income under GAAP (Obj. 3)

- Accrued salary expense, $1,100
- Prepaid insurance, $700
- Accrued interest expense, $600
- Depreciation expense, $400

Instead of recording the accrued expenses at December 31, 19X4, San Marcos recorded the expenses when it paid them in 19X5. The company recorded the insurance as expense when it was prepaid for one year, late in 19X4. Depreciation expense for 19X5 was correctly recorded.

San Marcos incorrectly reported net income of $10,000 in 19X4 and $7,400 in 19X5 because of the above errors.

Required

Compute San Marcos's correct net income for 19X4 and 19X5. Compare the trend in net income, as corrected, with the reported trend.

E12-7 For each of the folllowing situations, indicate the amount of revenue to report for the current year ended December 31 and for the following year:

Reporting revenues under GAAP (Obj. 4)

a. Sold gift certificates, collecting $4,000 in advance. At December 31, $1,400 of the gifts had been claimed. The remainder were claimed during the next year.

b. Sold merchandise for $4,400, receiving a down payment of $1,100 and the customer's receivable for the balance. The company accounts for these sales by the sales method.

c. On April 1 loaned $35,000 at 12 percent on a three-year note.   ?

d. Performed $900 of services for a high-risk customer on August 18, accounting for the revenue by the collection method. At December 31 the company had received $200 of the total; $550 was received the following year.

e. On September 1 collected one year's rent of $12,000 in advance on a building leased to another company.

E12-8 Pellegrini Appliances sells on the installment plan. The store's installment sales figures for 19X7 follow:

Computing gross profit under the sales method and the installment method (Obj. 4)

Sales	$420,000
Down payment received on the sales	80,000
Collections on installments	170,000
Inventory at beginning of 19X7	60,000
Inventory at end of 19X7	42,000
Purchases	216,000

Required

Compute the store's gross profit if it uses (a) the sales method of revenue recognition and (b) the installment method. Round gross profit percentage to three decimal places.

E12-9 Weinstein Construction Company builds bridges for the state of Montana. The construction period typically extends for several years. During 19X5 Weinstein completed a bridge with a contract price of $1,000,000. Weinstein's $640,000 cost of the bridge was incurred as follows: $40,000 in 19X3, $360,000 in 19X4, and $240,000 in 19X5. Compute Weinstein's revenue for each year 19X3 through 19X5 if the company uses (a) the completed-contract method and (b) the percentage-of-completion method. Which method better matches expense with revenue?

Computing construction revenue under the completed-contract method and the percentage-of-completion method (Obj. 4)

E12-10 Weinstein Construction Company uses a crane on its construction projects. The company purchased the crane early in January 19X3 for $600,000. For 19X3 and 19X4 depreciation was taken by the straight-line method on the basis of an eight-year life and an estimated residual

Changing the useful life of a depreciable asset (Obj. 5)

value of $80,000. In early 19X5 it became evident that the crane would be useful beyond the original life of eight years. Therefore, beginning in 19X5, Weinstein changed the depreciable life of the crane to a total life of 10 years. The company retained the straight-line method and did not alter the residual value.

Required

Prepare Weinstein's depreciation entries for 19X4 and 19X5. Identify the accounting principles most important in this situation.

Identifying subsequent events for the financial statements (Obj. 5)

E12-11 Tri-State Bindery experienced the following events after May 31, 19X8, the end of the company's fiscal year, but before publication of its financial statements on July 12:

a. Tri-State sales personnel received a contract to supply Bronson Company with laser equipment.

b. Increased demand for Tri-State products suggests that the next fiscal year will be the best in the company's history.

c. On July 6 Tri-State is sued for $1 million. Loss of the lawsuit could lead to Tri-State's bankruptcy.

d. Tri-State collected $210,000 of the $480,000 accounts receivable reported on the May 31 balance sheet. Tri-State expects to collect the remainder in the course of business during the next fiscal year.

e. A major customer, who owed Tri-State $140,000 at May 31, declared bankruptcy on June 21.

Required

Identify the subsequent events that Tri-State should disclose in its May 31, 19X8, financial statements.

Using accounting concepts and principles (Obj. 2, 6)

E12-12 Identify the accounting concept or principle, if any, that is violated in each of the following situations. Choose among *disclosure, conservatism, cost, entity,* and *matching.*

a. A manufacturer records depreciation during years when net income is high but fails to record depreciation when net income is low. Revenues are relatively constant.

b. The inventory of a pharmacy has a current market value of $163,000. The store reports the inventory at its cost of $181,000.

c. The owner of a court reporting service used the business bank account to pay her family's household expenses, making no note that the expenses were personal.

d. A manufacturing company changed from the FIFO inventory method to the LIFO method and failed to report the accounting change in the financial statements.

e. A paper company that purchased 1,000 acres of timberland at $800 per acre in 1982 reports the land at its current market value of $3,000 per acre.

Using accounting concepts and principles (Obj. 2, 6)

E12-13 Indicate the accounting concept or principle that applies to the following situations. Choose among *comparability, materiality, reliability, revenue,* and *time-period.*

a. Although Ikeda Company could increase its reported income by changing depreciation methods, Ikeda management has decided not to make the change.

b. Uncle Dan's Barbecue was recently sued for $200,000, but the plaintiff has indicated a willingness to settle for less than that amount. Uncle Dan's hopes to settle for $50,000, but its attorneys believe the settlement will be between $90,000 and $100,000. Uncle Dan's auditor reports the settlement as a real liability on the balance sheet. The only remaining issue is whether to report the liability at $50,000 or at $95,000.

c. Econo Leasing Company is considering publishing quarterly financial statements to provide more current information about its affairs.

d. Corbin, Inc., is negotiating the sale of $500,000 of inventory. Corbin has been in financial difficulty and desperately needs to report this sale on its income statement of the current year. At December 31, the end of the company's accounting year, the sale has not been closed.

e. Lancer Distributors expenses the cost of plant assets that cost less than $300.

CHALLENGE EXERCISE

E12-14   Littlefield Corporation's income statement follows:

Applying generally accepted accounting principles
(Obj. 2, 3, 6)

LITTLEFIELD COMPANY
INCOME STATEMENT
DECEMBER 31, 19X9

Revenues:	
Sales revenue, including sales taxes of $40,000	$820,000
Discount earned on high-quantity purchases of merchandise inventory (all the goods have been sold)	19,000
Recoveries of accounts receivable previously written off as uncollectible	24,000
Increase in the market value of land	62,000
Interest revenue	9,000
Total revenue	$934,000
Expenses:	
Cost of goods sold, including sales taxes of $18,000	$462,000
Salary and related payroll expense	183,000
Depreciation expense	64,000
Reserve for contingent losses	18,000
Household expenses of owner	59,000
Property tax expense	26,000
Utilities expense	17,000
Distributions to owner	61,000
Purchases of property, plant, and equipment	85,000
Loss on sale of investments	12,000
Additional depreciation due to inflation	6,000
Total expenses and losses	$993,000
Net income (loss) for the year	$(59,000)

This income statement has 10 errors. Identify each, and prepare a corrected income statement.

PROBLEMS

(GROUP A)

P12-1A   The following practices are in accord with GAAP. Identify all the accounting concepts and principles that form the basis for each accounting practice. More than one may apply.

Identifying the basis for good accounting practices
(Obj. 2, 3, 6)

a. A real estate developer paid $1.3 million for land and held it for three years before selling it for $2 million. There was significant inflation during this period, but the developer reported the $0.7 million gain on sale with no adjustment for the change in the value of the dollar.

b. Liabilities are reported in two categories: current and long-term.

c. TGI Friday's, a restaurant, makes such small payments for fire insurance that TGI expenses them and makes one year-end adjustment for prepaid insurance.

d. The inventory of a personal computer store declined substantially in value because of changing technology. The store wrote its computer inventory down to the lower of cost or market.

e. A construction company changed from the completed-contract method to the percentage-of-completion method of recording revenue on its long-term construction contracts. The company disclosed this accounting change in the notes to its financial statements.

f. A mining company recorded an intangible asset at the cost of the mineral lease and all other costs necessary to bring the mine to the point of production. After the mine was in operation, the company amortized the asset's cost as expense in proportion to the revenues from sale of the minerals.

g. Because of a downturn in the economy, a jeweler increased his business's allowance for doubtful accounts.

h. The personal residence of the owner of a freight company is not disclosed in the financial statements of the business.

i. A manufacturing company's plant assets are carried on the books at cost under the assumption that the company will remain in operation for the foreseeable future.

j. A clothing store discloses in notes to its financial statements that it uses the FIFO method.

Identifying the concepts and principles violated by bad accounting practices
(Obj. 2, 3, 6)

P12-2A The following accounting practices are *not* in accord with generally accepted accounting principles. Identify the single accounting concept or principle that is most clearly violated by each accounting practice.

a. A flood on July 2 caused $150,000 in damage to Tyler Construction property. The company did not report the flood as a subsequent event in the June 30 financial statements.

b. Hernandez, Inc., overstates depreciation expense to report low amounts of net income.

c. The balance sheet of Jean-Paul Pascal's medical practice includes significant receivables that he will probably never collect. Nevertheless, Pascal's accountant refuses to use the collection method to account for revenue.

d. The current market value of Miska Electronics's inventory is $119,000, but the company reports its inventory at cost of $134,000. The decline in value is permanent.

e. The liabilities of Waco Jet Company exceed the company's assets. To get a loan from the bank, Waco Jet's owner, Slade McQueen, includes his personal investments as assets on the balance sheet of the business.

f. Lancer Corporation increases the carrying value of its land on the basis of recent sales of adjacent property.

g. Mission Ford Sales records expenses on an irregular basis without regard to the pattern of the company's revenues.

h. Frisco Software Company omits the significant accounting policies note from its financial statements because the company uses the same accounting methods that its competitors use.

i. National Seed Supply regularly changes accounting methods in order to report a target amount of net income each year.

j. Texas Land Company reports land at its market value of $820,000, which is greater than the cost of $400,000.

Using the installment revenue method
(Obj. 4)

P12-3A Jefferson Office Furniture makes all sales on the installment basis but uses the sales method to record revenue. The company's income statements for the most recent three years follow:

	Year 1	Year 2	Year 3
Sales	$240,000	$210,000	$290,000
Cost of goods sold	144,000	121,800	179,800
Gross profit	96,000	88,200	110,200
Operating expenses	26,400	28,300	37,300
Net income	$ 69,600	$ 59,900	$ 72,900
Collections from sales of year 1	$100,000	$ 75,000	$ 60,000
Collections from sales of year 2		68,000	120,000
Collections from sales of year 3			145,000

Required

Compute the amount of net income Jefferson would have reported if it had used the installment method for revenue. Ignore the effect of uncollectible accounts, and use the following format:

Installment-method net income:	Year 1	Year 2	Year 3
Gross profit	$?	$?	$?
Operating expenses	26,400	28,300	37,300
Net income (net loss)	$?	$?	$?

Accounting for construction income (Obj. 4)

P12-4A Seaboard Contractors participates in the construction of small ships under long-term contracts. During 19X7 Seaboard began three projects that progressed according to the following schedule during 19X7, 19X8, and 19X9:

			19X7		19X8		19X9	
Project	Contract Price	Total Project Cost	Cost for Year	% Completed during Year	Cost for Year	% Completed during Year	Cost for Year	% Completed during Year
1	$2,100,000	$1,200,000	$ 500,000	42%	$ 700,000	58%	—	—
2	1,200,000	740,000	740,000	100	—	—	—	—
3	7,400,000	6,300,000	1,260,000	20	$2,205,000	35	$2,835,000	45%

Required

1. Assume that Seaboard Contractors uses the completed-contract method for construction revenue. Compute the company's construction revenue and income to be reported in 19X7, 19X8, and 19X9.

2. Compute Seaboard Contractor's construction revenue and income to be reported in the three years by the percentage-of-completion method.

P12-5A Sara Cloud established Sara's Boutique in January 19X4 to import woolens from Scotland. During 19X4 and 19X5 Cloud kept the company's books and prepared the financial statements, although she had no training or experience in accounting. As a result, the accounts contain numerous errors. Cloud recorded revenue from sales on the collection method, which is not appropriate for the company. She should have been using the sales method for revenues. She also recorded inventory purchases as the cost of goods sold.

Accounting for revenues and expenses according to GAAP (Obj. 2, 3, 4)

When the value of the store building increased by $50,000 in 19X6, Cloud recorded an increase in the Building account and credited Revenue. On January 2, 19X4, she borrowed $30,000 on a 9-percent, three-year note. She intended to wait until 19X7, when the note was due, to record the full amount of interest expense for three years. The company's records reveal the following:

	19X4	19X5	19X6
Reported net income (net loss)	$(19,200)	$ 48,600	$ 72,100
Sales	256,700	303,500	366,800
Cash collections from customers	210,400	309,000	317,800
Purchases of inventory	141,000	187,400	202,300
Ending inventory	35,800	59,900	73,400
Accrued expenses not recorded at year end; these expenses were recorded during the next year, when paid	13,500	22,600	30,100
Interest expense recorded	–0–	–0–	–0–
Revenue recorded for increase in the value of the store building			50,000

Required

1. In early 19X7 Cloud employed you as an accountant. Apply the concepts and principles of GAAP to compute the correct net income of Sara's Boutique for 19X4, 19X5, and 19X6.

2. How will what you learned in this problem help you manage a business?

(GROUP B)

P12-1B The following accounting practices are in accord with generally accepted accounting principles. Identify all the accounting concepts and principles that form the basis for each accounting practice. More than one concept or principle may apply.

Identifying the basis for good accounting practices (Obj. 2, 3, 6)

a. A fire destroyed the company garage after December 31, 19X7, but before the financial statements were published in early February 19X8. Although the fire loss is insured, reconstruction of the garage will disrupt the company's operations. This subsequent event will be reported in the 19X7 financial statements.

b. A paint company accounts for its operations by dividing the business into four separate units. This division enables the company to evaluate each unit apart from the others.

c. A theater company accrues employee salaries at year end even though the salaries will be paid during the first few days of the new year.

d. Assets are reported at liquidation value on the financial statements of a company that is going out of business.

e. The cost of machinery is being depreciated over a five-year life because independent engineers believe the machinery will become obsolete after that time. (The company had hoped to depreciate the machinery over 10 years to report lower depreciation and higher net income in the early years of the asset's life.)

f. A manufacturing firm built some specialized equipment for its own use. The equipment would have cost $110,000 if purchased from an outside company, but the cost of constructing the equipment was only $89,000. The firm recorded the equipment at cost of $89,000.

g. Depreciation of the home-office building is difficult to relate to particular sales. Therefore, the company records depreciation expense on a time basis.

h. A company wishes to change its method of accounting for revenue. However, the company does not switch because it wants to use the same accounting method that other companies in the industry use.

i. Because it is often difficult to collect installment receivables, a realtor uses the installment method of revenue recognition rather than the sales method.

j. The cost of office equipment such as staplers and wastebaskets is not capitalized and depreciated because of their relative insignificance.

Identifying the concepts and principles violated by bad accounting practices
(Obj. 2, 3, 6)

P12-2B   The following accounting practices are *not* in accord with generally accepted accounting principles. A few of the practices violate more than one concept or principle. Identify all the accounting concepts and principles not followed in each situation.

a. Tapes Unlimited is continuing in business, but its owner accounts for assets as though the store were liquidating.

b. Major Construction Company recognizes all revenue on long-term construction projects at the start of construction.

c. All amounts on the balance sheet and income statement of Cleveland Consulting Company have been adjusted for changes in the value of the dollar during the period.

d. Waterloo Wheat Processor records half the depreciation of its grain silos when it purchases them and the other half over their estimated useful lives.

e. Linda's Threads sells high-fashion clothing to customers on credit. Thus far, collection losses on receivables have been very small. Nevertheless, Linda Vela, the owner, uses the collection method to recognize revenue. The entity's revenue is understated because credit sales are not accounted for properly.

f. Canton Importers changed from the FIFO method to the LIFO method for inventory but did not report the accounting change in the financial statements.

g. Quebec Fisheries, Inc., applied the lower-of-cost-or-market method to account for its inventory. Quebec used an estimate of the inventory value developed by its management. This estimate differed widely from estimates supplied by two independent appraisers. The estimates of the two appraisers were similar.

h. Butler Manufacturing does not report a lawsuit in which it is the defendant. Alvin Butler, the president, argues that the outcome of the case is uncertain and that to report the lawsuit would introduce subjective data into the financial statements.

i. Todd Department Store records cost of goods sold in a predetermined amount each month regardless of the level of sales.

j. Tim Ihnacek is having difficulty evaluating the success of his advertising firm because he fails to separate business assets from personal assets.

Using the installment revenue method
(Obj. 4)

P12-3B   High Point Realty Company makes all sales on the installment basis but uses the sales method to record revenue. The company's income statements for the most recent three years are as follows:

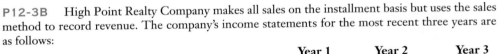

	Year 1	Year 2	Year 3
Sales	$380,000	$404,000	$370,000
Cost of goods sold	190,000	181,800	199,800
Gross profit	190,000	222,200	170,200
Operating expenses	104,000	121,700	115,100
Net income (net loss)	$ 86,000	$100,500	$ 55,100
Collections from sales of year 1	$140,000	$151,000	$ 72,000
Collections from sales of year 2		143,000	209,000
Collections from sales of year 3			163,000

Required

Compute the amount of net income High Point would have reported if the company had used the installment method for revenue. Ignore the effect of uncollectible accounts, and present your answer in the following format:

Installment-method net income:	Year 1	Year 2	Year 3
Gross profit	$?	$?	$?
Operating expenses	104,000	121,700	115,100
Net income	$?	$?	$?

P12-4B   Great Lakes Bridge Company constructs bridges under long-term contracts. During 19X5, Great Lakes began three projects that progressed according to the following schedule during 19X5, 19X6, and 19X7.

Accounting for construction income
(Obj. 4)

| | | Total | 19X5 | | 19X6 | | 19X7 | |
| | Contract | Project | Cost | % Completed | Cost | % Completed | Cost | % Completed |
Project	Price	Cost	for Year	during Year	for Year	during Year	for Year	during Year
1	$2,400,000	$1,600,000	$1,600,000	100%	—	—	—	—
2	3,100,000	2,200,000	528,000	24	$1,672,000	76%	—	—
3	1,900,000	1,400,000	280,000	20	840,000	60	$280,000	20%

Required

1. Assume that Great Lakes Bridge Company uses the completed-contract method for construction revenue. Compute the company's construction revenue and income to be reported in 19X5, 19X6, and 19X7.

2. Compute Great Lakes's construction revenue and income to be reported in the three years if the company uses the percentage-of-completion method.

P12-5B   Robin Forge established Forge Home Furnishings in January 19X7. During 19X7, 19X8, and most of 19X9, Forge kept the company's books and prepared its financial statements, although she had no training or experience in accounting. As a result, the accounts and statements contain numerous errors. For example, Forge recorded only cash receipts from customers as revenue. The sales method is appropriate for the business. She recorded inventory purchases as the cost of goods sold. When the current market value of her company's equipment increased by $6,200 in 19X7 and by $1,700 in 19X9, Forge debited the Equipment account and credited Revenue. She recorded no depreciation during 19X7, 19X8, and 19X9.

Accounting for revenues and expenses according to GAAP
(Obj. 2, 3, 4)

Late in 19X9 Forge employed an accountant, who determined that depreciable assets of the firm cost $150,000 on June 30, 19X7, and had an expected residual value of $10,000 and a total useful life of eight years. The accountant believes the straight-line depreciation method is appropriate for Forge's plant assets. The company's fiscal year ends December 31. At the end of 19X9 the company's records reveal the amounts in the accompanying table.

	19X7	19X8	19X9
Reported net income (net loss)	$ 39,300	$(18,200)	$ 51,900
Sales	131,800	164,700	226,100
Cash collections from customers	106,500	151,300	239,600
Purchases of inventory	100,600	136,000	191,700
Ending inventory	20,800	47,400	83,700
Accrued expenses not recorded at year end; these expenses were recorded during the next year, when paid	3,800	2,700	6,800
Depreciation expense recorded	–0–	–0–	–0–
Revenue recorded for increase in the value of equipment	6,200		1,700

Required

1. Apply the concepts and principles of GAAP to compute the correct net income of Forge Home Furnishings for 19X7, 19X8, and 19X9.

2. How will what you learned in this problem help you manage a business?

EXTENDING YOUR KNOWLEDGE

DECISION PROBLEMS

1.   Multivision Camera Shop was founded in January 19X5 by Mike and Edrena Smith, who share the management of the business. The Smiths believe the store has prospered, but they are uncertain about precisely how well it has done. It is now December 31, 19X5, and they are trying to decide whether to borrow a substantial sum in order to expand the business.

Measuring income according to GAAP
(Obj. 2, 3, 4)

They have asked for your help because of your accounting knowledge. You learn that the Smiths opened the store with an initial investment of $51,000 cash and a building valued at

$100,000. The cash receipts totaled $180,000, which included collections; $15,000 invested by the Smiths; $50,000 borrowed from the bank in the name of the camera shop; and $7,500 of earnings from a family inheritance. The store made credit sales of $105,000 that have not been collected at December 31. The Smiths purchased camera and film inventory on credit for $160,000, and inventory at December 31, 19X5, was $75,000. The store paid $90,000 on account.

The 19X5 cash expenses were $92,000. Additional miscellaneous expenses totaled $2,700 at year's end. These expenses included the Smiths' household costs of $15,000 and interest on the business debt. The $5,000 of depreciation on the store building was omitted.

The Smiths have decided to proceed with the expansion plan only if net income for the first year was $40,000 or more. Their analysis of the cash account leads them to believe that net income was $49,000, so they are ready to expand. You are less certain than they of the wisdom of this decision primarily because the Smiths have mixed personal and business assets.

Required

1. Use a Cash T-account to show how the Smiths arrived at the $49,000 amount for net income.
2. Prepare the income statement of the camera shop for 19X5.
3. Should the Smiths borrow to expand their business?
4. Which accounting concept or principle is most fundamental to this problem situation?

Examining the disclosure principle (Obj. 3, 5)

2. Consider the disclosure principle.

Required

1. It has been suggested that the disclosure principle is perhaps one of the most important concepts and principles underlying financial reporting. Why is it so important?
2. Accounting researchers are studying the understandability of financial statements. Why are they doing this? What contribution might their research make?
3. The text suggests that *subsequent events* and *long-term commitments* should be disclosed in the notes to the financial statements. What about these two items makes their disclosure so important to users?

ETHICAL ISSUE

Some real estate companies sold land under terms that permitted low down-payments by purchasers and stretched payments over many years. In many cases, the land had not yet been divided into the individual lots that would be sold. Also, the land often had not been landscaped. Estimating the cost of preparing the land for eventual use was difficult. Under accounting practices widespread in the 1960s and 1970s, real estate companies could record the full amount of the revenue in the year of the sale. These companies were thus able to report unusually high net incomes even though their cash collections were quite low.

Required

1. What three conditions must a company meet in order to record revenue on a sale? Which conditions did the real estate companies meet? Which condition(s) did they not meet?
2. Which revenue method were companies using during the 1960s and 1970s? In your opinion, was it ethical for these companies to use this method? Give your reason.
3. Which collection method is well suited for this situation? Give your reason.

COMPREHENSIVE PROBLEMS FOR PART TWO

1. COMPARING TWO BUSINESSES

At age 25, you created a software package that is now being sold worldwide. You recently sold the business to a large company. Now you are ready to invest in a small resort property. Several locations look promising: Branson, Missouri; Newport, Rhode Island; and Scottsdale, Arizona. Each place has its appeal, but Branson wins out. The main allure is that prices there are low, so a dollar will stretch further. Two small resorts are available. The property owners provide the following data:

	Branson Resorts	Bear Creek Hideaway
Cash	$ 34,100	$ 63,800
Accounts receivable	20,500	18,300
Inventory	74,200	68,400
Land	270,600	669,200
Buildings	1,800,000	1,960,000
Accumulated depreciation—buildings	(105,000)	(822,600)
Furniture and fixtures	750,000	933,000
Accumulated depreciation—furniture and fixtures	(225,000)	(535,300)
Total assets	$2,619,400	$2,354,800
Total liabilities	$1,124,300	$1,008,500
Owner equity	1,495,100	1,346,300
Total liabilities and owner equity	$2,619,400	$2,354,800

Income statements for the last three years report total net income of $531,000 for Branson Resorts and $283,000 for Bear Creek Hideaway.

INVENTORIES Branson uses the FIFO inventory method, and Bear Creek uses the LIFO method. If Branson had used LIFO, its reported inventory would have been $7,000 lower. If Bear Creek had used FIFO, its reported inventory would have been $6,000 higher. Three years ago there was little difference between LIFO and FIFO amounts for either company.

PLANT ASSETS Branson uses the straight-line depreciation method and an estimated useful life of 40 years for buildings and 10 years for furniture and fixtures. Estimated residual values are $400,000 for buildings, and $0 for furniture and fixtures. Branson's buildings are 3 years old.

Bear Creek uses the double-declining-balance method and depreciates buildings over 30 years with an estimated residual value of $460,000. The furniture and fixtures, now 3 years old, are being depreciated over 10 years with an estimated residual value of $85,000.

ACCOUNTS RECEIVABLE Branson uses the direct write-off method for uncollectibles. Bear Creek uses the allowance method. The Branson owner estimates that $2,000 of the company's receivables are doubtful. Prior to the current year, uncollectibles were insignificant. Bear Creek's receivables are already reported at net realizable value.

Required

1. Puzzled at first by how to compare the two resorts, you decide to convert Branson's balance sheet to the accounting methods and the estimated useful lives used by Bear Creek. Round all depreciation amounts to the nearest $100. The necessary revisions will not affect Branson's total liabilities.

2. Convert Branson's total net income for the last three years to reflect the accounting methods used by Bear Creek. Round all depreciation amounts to the nearest $100.

3. Compare the two resorts' finances after you have revised Branson's figures. Which resort looked better at the outset? Which looks better when they are placed on equal footing?

2. GROUP PROJECT: REFINING YOUR BUSINESS PLAN FOR CURRENT ASSETS AND CURRENT LIABILITIES

Review your business plan for an audio/video store (or other business) that you developed at the end of Part 1 (after Chapter 6). Since then, you have learned about internal controls, cash, receivables, inventories, plant assets, and current liabilities (including payrolls). Now revise your business plan to include refinements that apply to cash, receivables, inventories, plant assets, and current liabilities. Include specific internal control procedures that you will undertake to safeguard assets, to encourage employees to follow company policies, and to promote operational efficiency. If required by your instructor, prepare a presentation for class. Direct your report to the employees of your store in order to gain their support for your plan.

Turbulent Times for the Airline Industry

In recent years, the airline industry has dominated headlines as airline companies have adjusted to government deregulation of fares and routes. Fare wars, bankruptcies, and new "no-frills" carriers are signs of an industry fighting to survive. Many airlines cannot fill the planes they own. Fierce competition has resulted in bargain fares that fail to cover the airlines' operating costs. And the government has repeatedly raised fuel and excise taxes.

To date, the consumer has been the big winner. As competing airlines lower fares to fill seats, consumers have learned to shop around for the lowest rates. The carriers have also lured customers with frequent-flyer programs, which award free flights to passengers who accumulate specified miles of travel. Some years ago, the business community (and the accounting profession) recognized that unredeemed frequent-flyer mileage represents a liability that airlines must include on their balance sheets.

Industry executives believe that, to succeed, airlines must reduce operating costs and offer various levels of service at different prices—such as the hotel chains do.

Southwest Airlines, a profitable, no-frills carrier based in Dallas, has been a notable exception to this industry's ills. Southwest controls costs by flying to smaller, less expensive airports; using only one model of aircraft; serving no meals; increasing staff efficiency; and having a shorter aircraft turnaround time between flights. And the fact that most of the cities served by Southwest have predictable weather maximizes its on-time arrival record.

Industry executives predict that, in the long run, the weaker airlines will go out of business. The supply of passenger seats will adjust to match consumer demand better. The resulting decrease in competition will put an end to the bargain fares.

CASE QUESTIONS

1. Many of the aircraft purchased by airlines in the "booming" 1980s now sit idle. When purchased, the aircraft represented major amounts of depreciable assets for those companies. What accounting considerations arise when a company is strapped with significant amounts of nonproductive equipment? How might an airline achieve more flexibility in the number of aircraft in service?

2. Frequent-flyer programs have grown into significant obligations for airlines. Why should a liability be recorded for those programs? Discuss how you might calculate the amount of this liability. Can you think of other industries that offer similar incentives that create a liability?

3. One of Southwest Airlines' strategies for success is shortening stops at airport gates between flights. The company's chairman has stated, "What [you] produce is lower fares for the customers, because you generate more revenue from the same fixed cost in that airplane." What is the "fixed cost" of an airplane? How can better utilization of assets improve a company's profits?

PART THREE

Accounting for Partnerships and Corporate Transactions

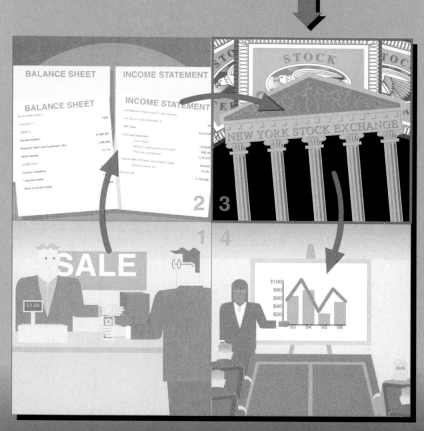

FINANCIAL ACCOUNTING

Chapter 13
Accounting for Partnerships

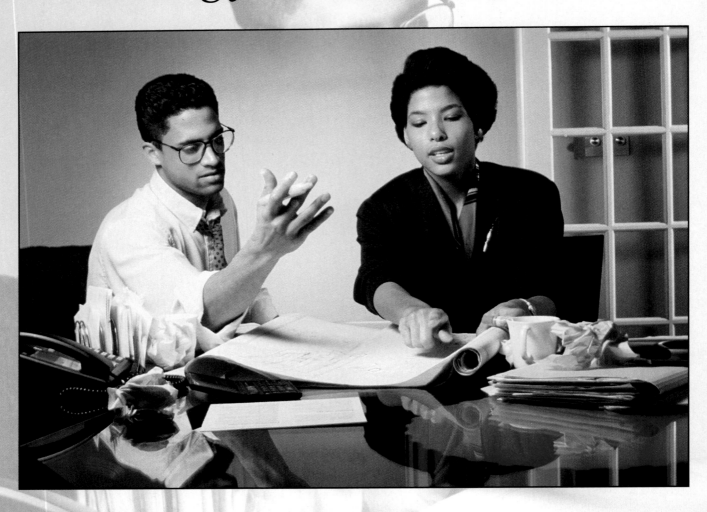

Chapter Objectives

After studying this chapter, you should be able to

1. Identify the characteristics of a partnership

2. Account for partners' initial investments in a partnership

3. Allocate profits and losses to the partners by different methods

4. Account for the admission of a new partner to the business

5. Account for the withdrawal of a partner from the business

6. Account for the liquidation of a partnership

7. Prepare partnership financial statements

Marva Turner's accounting practice grew rapidly. After three years, the firm's revenue topped $150,000, and net income reached $85,000. After taking the business this far while working alone, Turner faced a tough decision. Should she continue as a sole proprietorship or incorporate the business? She decided that neither option was ideal and chose instead to take on a partner.

Turner's closest friend at Louisiana State University, Brad Lail, had recently retired from the San Francisco 49ers and moved back to New Orleans. Like Turner, Lail had majored in accounting at LSU. During the off season he passed the CPA exam and worked as a consultant for an accounting firm in San Francisco. Together, the pair formed the partnership of Turner & Lail, Certified Public Accountants. Turner would specialize in tax matters, and Lail would attract consulting clients.

• • • • •

The partnership form of business introduced some complexities that Turner's proprietorship had avoided. How much cash should Lail contribute to the business? He was buying into the client base developed by Turner. How should the partners divide profits and losses? How should a partner who leaves the firm be compensated for his or her share of the business? Turner and Lail had to iron out these and many other details.

A partnership is an association of two or more persons who co-own a business for profit. This definition stems from the Uniform Partnership Act, which nearly every state in the United States has adopted to regulate partnership practice.

Forming a partnership is easy. It requires no permission from government authorities and involves no legal procedures. When two persons decide to go into business together, a partnership is automatically formed.

Rank 1993	Firm	City	1993 Revenue Millions	Percentage Revenue Change 1992–1993
1	Arthur Andersen & Co., S.C.	Chicago	$2,912.9	9
2	Ernst & Young	New York	2,400.0	5
3	Deloitte & Touche	Wilton, Conn.	2,055.0	5
4	KPMG Peat Marwick	New York	1,822.0	1
5	Coopers & Lybrand	New York	1,642.0	5
6	Price Waterhouse	New York	1,430.0	4
7	Grant Thornton	Chicago	224.0	1
8	McGladrey & Pullen	Davenport, Iowa	196.6	4
9	Kenneth Leventhal & Co.	Los Angeles	192.7	2
10	BDO Seidman	New York	182.3	0

Source: Accounting Today, December 13, 1993, Special Section.

A partnership brings together the capital, talents, and experience of the partners. Business opportunities closed to an individual may open up to a partnership. Suppose neither Turner nor Lail has enough capital individually to buy a small office building in which to practice. They may be able to afford it together in a partnership. Or they may pool their talents and know-how. Their partnership may offer a fuller range of accounting services than either person could offer alone.

Partnerships come in all sizes. Many partnerships have fewer than 10 partners. Some medical and law firms have 20 or more partners. The largest CPA firms have almost 2,000 partners. Exhibit 13-1 lists the 10 largest CPA firms in the United States, their revenues in 1993, and their percentage change in revenues from 1992.

Characteristics of a Partnership

OBJECTIVE 1

Identify the characteristics of a partnership

Recall from Chapter 1 that a sole proprietorship has a single owner whereas a corporation usually has more owners, with ownership evidenced by shares of stock.

Key Point: A partnership is not required to have a formal written agreement. But a written agreement prevents confusion as to the sharing of profits and losses, partners' responsibilities, admission of new partners, how the partnership will be liquidated, and so on. A written agreement does not preclude discord, however.

Starting a partnership is voluntary. A person cannot be forced to join a partnership, and partners cannot be forced to accept another person as a partner. Although the partnership agreement may be oral, a written agreement between the partners reduces the chance of a misunderstanding. The following characteristics distinguish partnerships from sole proprietorships and corporations.

THE WRITTEN PARTNERSHIP AGREEMENT A business partnership is like a marriage. To be successful, the partners must cooperate. But business partners do not vow to remain together for life. Business partnerships come and go. To make certain that each partner fully understands how a particular partnership operates and to lower the chances that any partner might misunderstand how the business is run, partners may draw up a **partnership agreement**, also called the **articles of partnership.** This agreement is a contract between the partners, so transactions involving the agreement are governed by contract law. The articles of partnership should make the following points clear:

1. Name, location, and nature of the business
2. Name, capital investment, and duties of each partner
3. Method of sharing profits and losses by the partners
4. Withdrawals of assets allowed to the partners
5. Procedures for settling disputes between the partners
6. Procedures for admitting new partners
7. Procedures for settling up with a partner who withdraws from the business
8. Procedures for liquidating the partnership—selling the assets, paying the liabilities, and disbursing any remaining cash to the partners

LIMITED LIFE   A partnership has a life limited by the length of time that all partners continue to own the business. If Marva Turner of the chapter-opening story withdraws from the business, the partnership of Turner & Lail will cease to exist. A new partnership may emerge to continue the same business, but the old partnership will have been *dissolved*. **Dissolution** is the ending of a partnership. The addition of a new partner dissolves the old partnership and creates a new partnership.

MUTUAL AGENCY   **Mutual agency** in a partnership means that every partner can bind the business to a contract within the scope of the partnership's regular business operations. If Brad Lail enters into a contract with a business to provide accounting service, then the firm of Turner & Lail—not only Lail—is bound to provide that service. If Lail signs a contract to purchase lawn services for his home, however, the partnership will not be bound to pay. Contracting for personal services is not a regular business operation of the partnership.

UNLIMITED LIABILITY   Each partner has an **unlimited personal liability** for the debts of the partnership. When a partnership cannot pay its debts with business assets, the partners must use their personal assets to meet the debt.

Key Point: All partners are personally liable for any debt of the business. It is extremely important to choose a partner carefully.

Suppose the Turner & Lail firm has had an unsuccessful year and the partnership's liabilities exceed its assets by $20,000. Turner and Lail must pay this amount with their personal assets. Because each partner has *unlimited* liability, if a partner is unable to pay his or her part of the debt, the other partner (or partners) must make payment. If Lail can pay only $5,000 of the liability, Turner must pay $15,000.

Unlimited liability and mutual agency are closely related. A dishonest partner or a partner with poor judgment may commit the partnership to a contract under which the business loses money. In turn, creditors may force *all* the partners to pay the debt from personal assets. Hence, a business partner should be chosen with care.

Partners can avoid unlimited personal liability for partnership obligations by forming a *limited partnership*. In this form of business organization, one or more general partners assume the unlimited liability for business debts. In addition there is another class of owners, limited partners, who can lose only as much as their investment in the business. In this sense limited partners have limited liability that is similar to the limited liability that stockholders of a corporation have. Some of the large accounting firms in Exhibit 13-1 have reorganized as limited partnerships.

CO-OWNERSHIP OF PROPERTY   Any asset—cash, inventory, machinery, and so on—that a partner invests in the partnership becomes the joint property of all the partners. Also, each partner has a claim to his or her share of the business's profits.

NO PARTNERSHIP INCOME TAXES   A partnership pays no income tax on its business income. Instead, the net income of the partnership is divided and becomes the taxable income of the partners. Suppose Turner & Lail, Certified Public Accountants, earned net income of $180,000, shared equally by the partners. The firm would pay no income tax *as a business entity*. Turner and Lail, however, would pay income tax as individuals on their $90,000 shares of partnership income.

PARTNERS' OWNER'S EQUITY ACCOUNTS   Accounting for a partnership is much like accounting for a proprietorship. We record buying and selling, collecting and paying for a partnership just as we do for a business with only one owner. But because a partnership has more than one owner, the partnership must have more than one owner's equity account. Every partner in the business—whether the firm has two or two thousand partners—has an individual owner's equity account. Often these accounts carry the name of the particular partner and the word *capital*. For example, the owner's equity account for Brad Lail would read "Lail, Capital." Similarly, each partner has a withdrawal account. If the number of partners is large, the general ledger may contain the single account Partners' Capital, or Owners' Equity. A subsidiary ledger can be used for individual partner accounts.

Exhibit 13-2 lists the advantages and disadvantages of partnerships (compared with proprietorships and corporations).

Partnership Advantages	Partnership Disadvantages
Versus Proprietorships: 1. Can raise more capital. 2. Brings together the expertise of more than one person. 3. 1+1 > 2 in a good partnership. If they work well together, the partners can achieve more than by working alone. *Versus Corporations*: 4. Less expensive to organize than a corporation, which requires a charter from the state. 5. No taxation of partnership income, which is taxed to the partners as individuals.	1. Partnership agreement may be difficult to formulate. Each time a new partner is admitted or a partner withdraws, the business needs a new partnership agreement. 2. Relationships among partners may be fragile. 3. Mutual agency and unlimited personal liability create personal obligations for each partner.

Initial Investments by Partners

Let's see how to account for the multiple owner's equity accounts—and learn how they appear on the balance sheet—by looking at how to account for starting up a partnership.

Partners in a new partnership may invest assets and liabilities in the business. These contributions are entered in the books in the same way that a proprietor's assets and liabilities are recorded. Subtraction of each person's liabilities from his or her assets yields the amount to be credited to the capital account for that person. Often the partners hire an independent firm to appraise their assets and liabilities at current market value at the time a partnership is formed. This outside evaluation assures an objective accounting for what each partner brings into the business.

Assume that Dave Benz and Joan Hanna form a partnership to manufacture and sell computer software. The partners agree on the following values based on an independent appraisal:

Benz's contributions:
- Cash, $10,000; inventory, $70,000; and accounts payable, $85,000 (the appraiser believes that the current market values for these items equal Benz's values)
- Accounts receivable, $30,000, less allowance for doubtful accounts of $5,000
- Computer equipment: cost, $600,000; market value, $450,000

Hanna's contributions:
- Cash, $5,000
- Computer software: cost, $18,000; market value, $100,000

The partners record their initial investments at the current market values:

Benz's investment:

June 1	Cash	10,000	
	Accounts Receivable	30,000	
	Inventory	70,000	
	Computer Equipment	450,000	
	Allowance for Doubtful Accounts		5,000
	Accounts Payable		85,000
	Benz, Capital		470,000
	To record Benz's investment in the partnership.		

BENZ AND HANNA BALANCE SHEET JUNE 1, 19X5					
Assets			**Liabilities**		
Cash....................................		$ 15,000	Accounts payable..................		$ 85,000
Accounts receivable	$30,000				
Less Allowance for					
doubtful accounts........	5,000	25,000	**Capital**		
Inventory.............................		70,000	Benz, capital..........................		470,000
Computer equipment		450,000	Hanna, capital........................		105,000
Computer software		100,000	Total liabilities		
Total assets		$660,000	and capital.........................		$660,000

EXHIBIT 13-3
Partnership Balance Sheet

Key Point: The major difference in accounting for a proprietorship versus a partnership is the number of capital and drawing accounts. The partnership balance sheet shows a separate capital account for each partner, and there is a separate drawing account for each partner. The asset and liability sections on the balance sheet and the income statement are the same for a proprietorship and a partnership.

Hanna's investment:

June 1	Cash	5,000	
	Computer Software	100,000	
	Hanna, Capital		105,000
	To record Hanna's investment in the partnership.		

The initial partnership balance sheet reports the amounts as shown in Exhibit 13-3.

Sharing Partnership Profits and Losses

How to allocate profits and losses among partners is one of the most challenging aspects of managing a partnership. If the partners have not drawn up an agreement or if the agreement does not state how the partners will divide profits and losses, then, by law, the partners must share profits and losses equally. If the agreement specifies a method for sharing profits but not losses, then losses are shared in the same proportion as profits. For example, a partner who was allocated 75 percent of the profits would likewise absorb 75 percent of any losses.

In some cases, an equal division is not fair. One partner may perform more work for the business than the other partner, or one partner may make a larger capital contribution. In the preceding example, Joan Hanna might agree to work longer hours for the partnership than Dave Benz to earn a greater share of profits. Benz could argue that he should share in more of the profits because he contributed more net assets ($470,000) than Hanna did ($105,000). Hanna might contend that her computer software program is the partnership's most important asset and that her share of the profits should be greater than Benz's share. Agreeing on a fair sharing of profits and losses in a partnership may be difficult. We now discuss options available in determining partners' shares.

OBJECTIVE 3
Allocate profits and losses to the partners by different methods

Sharing Based on a Stated Fraction

Partners may agree to any profit-and-loss-sharing method they desire. They may, for example, state a particular fraction of the total profits and losses that each individual partner will share. Suppose the partnership agreement of Ian Cagle and Justin Dean allocates two-thirds of the business profits and losses to Cagle and one-third to Dean. If net income for the year is $90,000 and all revenue and expense accounts have been closed, the Income Summary account has a credit balance of $90,000:

Income Summary	
	Bal. 90,000

Not all partners share profits and losses equally.

The entry to close this account and allocate the profit to the partners' capital accounts is

Dec. 31	Income Summary	90,000	
	Cagle, Capital ($90,000 × 2/3)		60,000
	Dean, Capital ($90,000 × 1/3)		30,000
	To allocate net income to partners.		

Consider the effect of this entry. Does Cagle get cash of $60,000 and Dean cash of $30,000? No. The increase in the capital accounts of the partners cannot be linked to any particular asset, including cash. Instead, the entry indicates that Cagle's ownership in *all* the assets of the business increased by $60,000 and Dean's by $30,000.

If the year's operations resulted in a net loss of $66,000, the Income Summary account would have a debit balance of $66,000. In that case, the closing entry to allocate the loss to the partners' capital accounts would be

Dec. 31	Cagle, Capital ($66,000 × 2/3)..	44,000	
	Dean, Capital ($66,000 × 1/3)	22,000	
	Income Summary...		66,000
	To allocate net loss to partners.		

Short Exercise: Ash, Black, and Cole share profits in a 30:40:30 ratio. Compute each partner's share of net income if the partnership income is $50,000. *A:*
Ash:
($50,000 × 30%) = $15,000
Black:
($50,000 × 40%) = 20,000
Cole:
($50,000 × 30%) = 15,000
$50,000

Sharing Based on Capital Contributions

Profits and losses are often allocated in proportion to the partners' capital contributions in the business. Suppose that Jim Antoine, Erika Barber, and Rico Cabañas are partners in ABC Company. Their capital accounts have the following balances at the end of the year, before the closing entries:

Antoine, Capital	$ 40,000
Barber, Capital	60,000
Cabañas, Capital........................	50,000
Total capital balances	$150,000

Assume that the partnership earned a profit of $120,000 for the year. To allocate this amount on the basis of capital contributions, compute each partner's percentage share of the partnership's total capital balance. Simply divide each partner's contribution by the total capital amount. These figures, multiplied by the $120,000 profit amount, yield each partner's share of the year's profits:

Short Exercise: Ash, Black, and Cole share profits on the basis of capital account balances of $10,000, $20,000, and $70,000, respectively. Compute each partner's share of net income if the partnership net income is $50,000. *A:*
Ash:
($10,000/$100,000
× $50,000) = $ 5,000
Black:
($20,000/$100,000
× $50,000) = 10,000
Cole:
($70,000/$100,000
× $50,000) = 35,000
$50,000

Antoine: ($40,000/$150,000) × $120,000 =	$ 32,000
Barber: ($60,000/$150,000) × $120,000 =	48,000
Cabañas: ($50,000/$150,000) × $120,000 =	40,000
Net income allocated to partners =	$120,000

The closing entry to allocate the profit to the partners' capital accounts is

Dec. 31	Income Summary..	120,000	
	Antoine, Capital		32,000
	Barber, Capital		48,000
	Cabañas, Capital		40,000
	To allocate net income to partners.		

After this closing entry, the partners' capital balances are:

Antoine, Capital ($40,000 + $32,000)	$ 72,000
Barber, Capital ($60,000 + $48,000)	108,000
Cabañas, Capital ($50,000 + $40,000)	90,000
Total capital balances after allocation of net income	$270,000

Sharing Based on Capital Contributions and on Service

One partner, regardless of his or her capital contribution, may put more work into the business than the other partners do. Even among partners who log equal service time, one person's superior experience and knowledge may command a greater share of income. To reward the harder-working or more valuable person, the profit-and-loss-sharing method may be based on a combination of contributed capital *and* service to the business. The Chicago-based law firm Baker & McKenzie, for example, which has nearly 500 partners, takes seniority into account in determining partner compensation.

Assume that Debbie Randolph and Nancy Scott formed a partnership in which Randolph invested $60,000 and Scott invested $40,000, a total of $100,000. Scott devotes more time to the partnership and earns the larger salary. Accordingly, the two partners have agreed to share profits as follows:

1. The first $50,000 of partnership profits is to be allocated on the basis of partners' capital contributions to the business.
2. The next $60,000 of profits is to be allocated on the basis of service, with Randolph receiving $24,000 and Scott receiving $36,000.
3. Any remaining amount is to be allocated equally.

If net income for the first year is $125,000, the partners' shares of this profit are computed as follows:

	Randolph	Scott	Total
Total net income			$125,000
Sharing of first $50,000 of net income, based on capital contributions:			
Randolph ($60,000/$100,000 × $50,000)	$30,000		
Scott ($40,000/$100,000 × $50,000)		$ 20,000	
Total			50,000
Net income remaining for allocation			75,000
Sharing of next $60,000, based on service:			
Randolph	24,000		
Scott		36,000	
Total			60,000
Net income remaining for allocation			15,000
Remainder shared equally:			
Randolph ($15,000 × 1/2)	7,500		
Scott ($15,000 × 1/2)		7,500	
Total			15,000
Net income remaining for allocation			$ –0–
Net income allocated to the partners	$61,500	$ 63,500	$125,000

On the basis of this allocation, the closing entry is:

Dec. 31	Income Summary	125,000	
	Randolph, Capital		61,500
	Scott, Capital		63,500
	To allocate net income to partners.		

Short Exercise: Ash, Black, and Cole have capital balances of $10,000, $20,000, and $70,000, respectively. The partners share profits and losses as follows: (1) The first $25,000 is allocated on the basis of partners' capital balances. (2) The next $19,000 is allocated on the basis of service, with Ash, Black, and Cole receiving $5,000, $6,000, and $8,000, respectively. (3) The remainder is divided equally.

Compute each partner's share of net income if the partnership earns $50,000. *A:*

Ash:
($10,000/$100,000 × $25,000) + $5,000 + $2,000* = $9,500

Black:
($20,000/$100,000 × $25,000) + $6,000 + $2,000* = $13,000

Cole:
($70,000/$100,000 × $25,000) + $8,000 + $2,000* = $27,500

*Remainder shared equally: ($50,000 – $25,000 – $19,000 = $6,000)

Sharing Based on Salaries and on Interest

Partners may be rewarded for their service and their capital contributions to the business in other ways. In one sharing plan, the partners are allocated salaries plus interest on their capital balances. Assume that Randy Lewis and Gerald Clark form an oil-exploration partnership. At the beginning of the year, their capital balances are $80,000 and $100,000, respectively. The partnership agreement allocates annual salary of $43,000 to Lewis and $35,000 to Clark. After salaries are allocated, each partner earns 8-percent interest on his beginning capital balance. Any remaining net income is divided equally. Partnership profit of $96,000 will be allocated as follows:

Short Exercise: Ash, Black, and Cole have capital balances of $10,000, $20,000, and $70,000, respectively. The partners share profits and losses as follows: (1) Ash and Cole receive salaries of $6,000 and $7,000, respectively. (2) Interest of 10% is paid on the capital balances. (3) The remainder is divided equally.

Compute each partner's share of net income if the partnership earns $50,000. *A:*
Ash: $6,000 + (10% × $10,000) + $9,000* = $16,000
Black: (10% × $20,000) + $9,000* = $11,000
Cole: $7,000 + (10% × $70,000) + $9,000* = $23,000

---

*Remainder = [$50,000 – $6,000 – $7,000 – (10% × $100,000)] = $27,000

	Lewis	Clark	Total
Total net income			$96,000
First, salaries:			
Lewis	$43,000		
Clark		$35,000	
Total			78,000
Net income remaining for allocation			18,000
Second, interest on beginning capital balances:			
Lewis ($80,000 × 0.08)	6,400		
Clark ($100,000 × 0.08)		8,000	
Total			14,400
Net income remaining for allocation			3,600
Third, remainder shared equally:			
Lewis ($3,600 × 1/2)	1,800		
Clark ($3,600 × 1/2)		1,800	
Total			3,600
Net income remaining for allocation			$ –0–
Net income allocated to the partners	$51,200	$44,800	$96,000

In the preceding illustration, net income exceeded the sum of salary and interest. If the partnership profit is less than the allocated sum of salary and interest, a negative remainder will occur at some stage in the allocation process. Even so, the partners use the same method for allocation purposes. For example, assume that Lewis and Clark Partnership earned only $82,000:

	Lewis	Clark	Total
Total net income			$82,000
First, salaries:			
Lewis	$43,000		
Clark		$35,000	
Total			78,000
Net income remaining for allocation			4,000
Second, interest on beginning capital balances:			
Lewis ($80,000 × 0.08)	6,400		
Clark ($100,000 × 0.08)		8,000	
Total			14,400
Net income remaining for allocation			(10,400)
Third, remainder shared equally:			
Lewis ($10,400 × 1/2)	(5,200)		
Clark ($10,400 × 1/2)		(5,200)	
Total			(10,400)
Net income remaining for allocation			$ –0–
Net income allocated to the partners	$44,200	$37,800	$82,000

A net loss would be allocated to Lewis and Clark in the same manner outlined for net income. The sharing procedure would begin with the net loss and then allocate salary, interest, and any other specified amounts to the partners.

STOP & THINK Are these salaries and interest amounts business expenses in the usual sense? Explain your answer.

Answer: No, partners do not work for their own business to earn a salary, as an employee does. They do not loan money to their own business to earn interest. Their goal is for the partnership to earn a profit. Therefore, salaries and interest in partnership agreements are simply ways of expressing the allocation of profits and losses to the partners. For example, the salary component of partner income rewards service to the partnership. The interest component rewards a partner's investment of cash or other assets in the business. But the partners' salary and interest amounts are *not* salary expense and interest expense in the partnership's accounting or tax records.

We see that partners may allocate profits and losses on the basis of a stated fraction, contributed capital, service, interest on capital, or any combination of these factors. Each partnership shapes its profit-and-loss-sharing ratio to fit its own needs.

Partner Drawings

Like anyone else, partners need cash for personal living expenses. Partnership agreements usually allow partners to withdraw cash or other assets from the business. Drawings from a partnership are recorded exactly as for a proprietorship. Assume that both Randy Lewis and Gerald Clark are allowed a monthly withdrawal of $3,500. The partnership records the March withdrawals with this entry:

Mar. 31	Lewis, Drawing..	3,500	
	Clark, Drawing	3,500	
	Cash		7,000
	Monthly partner withdrawals.		

During the year, each partner drawing account accumulates 12 such amounts, a total of $42,000 ($3,500 × 12). At the end of the period, the general ledger shows the following account balances immediately after net income has been closed to the partners' capital accounts. Assume these beginning balances for Lewis and Clark at the start of the year and that $82,000 of profit has been allocated on the basis of the preceding illustration.

Real-World Example: According to the Internal Revenue Code, partners are taxed on their share of partnership income, not on the amount of their withdrawals.

Lewis, Capital		
	Jan. 1 Bal.	80,000
	Dec. 31 Net. inc.	44,200

Clark, Capital		
	Jan. 1 Bal.	100,000
	Dec. 31 Net. inc.	37,800

Lewis, Drawing	
Dec. 31 Bal.	42,000

Clark, Drawing	
Dec. 31 Bal.	42,000

The withdrawal accounts must be closed at the end of the period, exactly as for a proprietorship: The closing entry credits each partner's drawing account and debits each capital account.

Admission of a Partner

A partnership lasts only as long as its partners remain in the business. The addition of a new member or the withdrawal of an existing member dissolves the partnership. We turn now to a discussion of how partnerships dissolve—and how new partnerships arise.

Often a new partnership is formed to carry on the former partnership's business. In fact, the new partnership may retain the dissolved partnership's name. Price Waterhouse, for example, is an accounting firm that retires and hires partners during the year. Thus the former partnership dissolves and a new partnership begins many times. But the business retains the name and continues operations. Other partnerships may dissolve and then re-form under a new name. Let's look now at the ways that a new member may gain admission into an existing partnership.

"Price Waterhouse . . . is an accounting firm that retires and hires partners during the year."

Admission by Purchasing a Partner's Interest

A person may become a member of a partnership by gaining the approval of the other partner (or partners) for entrance into the firm *and* by purchasing a present partner's interest in the business. Let's assume that Beverly Fisher and Renata Garcia have a partnership that carries these figures:

Cash	$ 40,000	Total liabilities	$120,000
Other assets	360,000	Fisher, capital	110,000
		Garcia, capital	170,000
		Total liabilities and	
Total assets	$400,000	capital	$400,000

Business is going so well that Fisher receives an offer from Barry Dynak, an outside party, to buy her $110,000 interest in the business for $150,000. Fisher agrees to sell out to Dynak, and Garcia approves Dynak as a new partner. The firm records the transfer of capital interest in the business with this entry:

Apr. 16	Fisher, Capital	110,000	
	Dynak, Capital		110,000
	To transfer Fisher's equity in the business to Dynak.		

The debit side of the entry closes Fisher's capital account because she is no longer a partner in the firm. The credit side opens Dynak's capital account because Fisher's equity has been transferred to Dynak. The entry amount is Fisher's capital balance ($110,000) and not the $150,000 price that Dynak paid Fisher to buy into the business. The full $150,000 goes to Fisher, including the $40,000 difference between her capital balance and the price received from Dynak. In this example, the partnership receives no cash because the transaction was between Dynak and Fisher, not between Dynak and the partnership. Suppose Dynak pays Fisher less than Fisher's capital balance. The entry on the partnership books is not affected. Fisher's equity is transferred to Dynak at book value ($110,000).

The old partnership has dissolved. Garcia and Dynak draw up a new partnership agreement with a new profit-and-loss-sharing ratio and continue business operations. If Garcia does not accept Dynak as a partner, Dynak gets no voice in management of the firm. However, under the Uniform Partnership Act, the purchaser shares in the profits and losses of the firm and in its assets at liquidation.

Short Exercise: Ted and Fred are partners with capital balances of $16,000 and $24,000, respectively. Profits and losses are shared on the basis of capital balances. Ann offers Fred $60,000 for his interest in the business. What is the entry to record the transfer of capital?

A:

Fred, Capital	24,000	
Ann, Capital		24,000

Admission by Investing in the Partnership

As Brad Lail did in our chapter-opening story, a person may be admitted as a partner by investing directly in the partnership rather than by purchasing an existing partner's interest. The new partner contributes assets—for example, cash, inventory, or equipment—to the business. Assume that the partnership of Robin Ingel and Michael Jay has the following assets, liabilities, and capital:

Cash...............................	$ 20,000	Total liabilities................................	$ 60,000
Other assets...................................	200,000	Ingel, capital...................................	70,000
		Jay, capital.....................................	90,000
Total assets	$220,000	Total liabilities and capital	$220,000

Laureen Kahn offers to invest equipment and land (Other Assets) with a market value of $80,000 to persuade the existing partners to take her into the business. Ingel and Jay agree to dissolve the existing partnership and to start up a new business, giving Kahn one-third interest—($70,000 + $90,000 + $80,000)/$240,000 = 1/3—in exchange for the contributed assets. The entry to record Kahn's investment is

July 18	Other Assets...	80,000	
	Kahn, Capital		80,000
	To admit L. Kahn as a partner with a one-third interest in the business.		

After this entry, the partnership books show:

Cash....................................	$ 20,000	Total liabilities................................	$ 60,000
Other assets ($200,000 + $80,000) .	280,000	Ingel, capital...................................	70,000
		Jay, capital.....................................	90,000
		Kahn, capital	80,000
Total assets	$300,000	Total liabilities and capital	$300,000

Kahn's one-third interest in the partnership does not necessarily entitle her to one-third of the profits. The sharing of profits and losses is a separate element in the partnership agreement.

ADMISSION BY INVESTING IN THE PARTNERSHIP—BONUS TO THE OLD PARTNERS   The more successful a partnership, the higher the payment the partners may demand from a person entering the business. Partners in a business that is doing quite well might require an incoming person to pay them a bonus. The bonus increases the current partners' capital accounts.

Suppose that Hiro Nagasawa and Ralph Osburn's partnership has earned above-average profits for 10 years. The two partners share profits and losses equally. The partnership balance sheet carries these figures:

Cash....................................	$ 40,000	Total liabilities................................	$100,000
Other assets...................................	210,000	Nagasawa, capital............................	70,000
		Osburn, capital................................	80,000
Total assets	$250,000	Total liabilities and capital	$250,000

The partners agree to admit Glen Parker to a one-fourth interest with his cash investment of $90,000. Parker's capital balance on the partnership books is $60,000, computed as follows:

Short Exercise: Ted and Fred are partners with capital balances of $16,000 and $24,000, respectively. Profits and losses are shared on the basis of capital balances. Ted and Fred admit Jill to a 20% interest with a $12,000 investment. What is the entry to record Jill's admission to the partnership: *A:*

Cash	12,000	
Jill, Capital		10,400
Ted, Capital....		640
Fred, Capital ..		960

Jill: $10,400 = ($16,000 + $24,000 + $12,000) × 0.2
Ted: $640 = $16,000/$40,000 × ($12,000 − $10,400)
Fred: $960 = $24,000/$40,000 × ($12,000 − $10,400)

Partnership capital before Parker is admitted ($70,000 + $80,000)...............	$150,000
Parker's investment in the partnership	90,000
Partnership capital after Parker is admitted	$240,000
Parker's capital in the partnership ($240,000 × 1/4)......................................	$ 60,000

The entry on the partnership books to record Parker's investment is:

Mar. 1	Cash	90,000	
	Parker, Capital..		60,000
	Nagasawa, Capital ($30,000 × 1/2)		15,000
	Osburn, Capital ($30,000 × 1/2)		15,000
	To admit G. Parker as a partner with a one-fourth interest in the business.		

Parker's capital account is credited for his one-fourth interest in the partnership. The other partners share the $30,000 difference between Parker's investment ($90,000) and his equity in the business ($60,000). This difference is called a *bonus*. It is accounted for as income to the old partners and is, therefore, allocated to them on the basis of their profit-and-loss ratio.

The new partnership's balance sheet reports these amounts:

Cash ($40,000 + $90,000)...............	$130,000	Total liabilities	$100,000
Other assets...................................	210,000	Nagasawa, capital ($70,000 + $15,000).....................	85,000
		Osburn, capital ($80,000 + $15,000).....................	95,000
		Parker, capital.................................	60,000
Total assets	$340,000	Total liabilities and capital	$340,000

ADMISSION BY INVESTING IN THE PARTNERSHIP—BONUS TO THE NEW PARTNER A potential new partner may be so important that the existing partners offer him or her a partnership share that includes a bonus. A law firm may strongly desire a former governor or other official as a partner because of the person's reputation and connections. A restaurant owner may want to go into partnership with a famous sports personality, movie star, or model. The growing chain Planet Hollywood, for example, opened its first restaurant in 1991 in New York City. Planet Hollywood, whose majority owner is Robert Earl, has prospered with the help of celebrity partners Sylvester Stallone, Arnold Schwarzenegger, Bruce Willis, and Don Johnson.

"Planet Hollywood, whose majority owner is Robert Earl, has prospered with the help of celebrity partners Sylvester Stallone, Arnold Schwarzenegger, Bruce Willis, and Don Johnson."

Suppose that Allan Page and Miko Osuka have a law partnership. The firm's balance sheet appears as follows:

Cash..	$140,000	Total liabilities................................	$120,000
Other assets..................................	360,000	Page, capital	230,000
		Osuka, capital.................................	150,000
Total assets	$500,000	Total liabilities and capital	$500,000

Page and Osuka admit Martin Schiller, a former attorney general, as a partner with a one-third interest in exchange for his cash investment of $100,000. At the time of

Schiller's admission, the firm's capital is $380,000—Page, $230,000, and Osuka, $150,000. Page and Osuka share profits and losses in the ratio of two-thirds to Page and one-third to Osuka. The computation of Schiller's equity in the partnership is:

Partnership capital before Schiller is admitted ($230,000 + $150,000)	$380,000
Schiller's investment in the partnership..	100,000
Partnership capital after Schiller is admitted..	$480,000
Schiller's capital in the partnership ($480,000 × 1/3)	$160,000

The capital accounts of Page and Osuka are debited for the $60,000 difference between the new partner's equity ($160,000) and his investment ($100,000). The existing partners share this decrease in capital, which is accounted for as though it were a loss, on the basis of their profit-and-loss ratio. The entry to record Schiller's investment is:

Aug. 24	Cash	100,000	
	Page, Capital ($60,000 × 2/3).............................	40,000	
	Osuka, Capital ($60,000 × 1/3)	20,000	
	Schiller, Capital...		160,000
	To admit M. Schiller as a partner with a one-third interest in the business.		

The new partnership's balance sheet reports these amounts:

Cash ($140,000 + $100,000)	$240,000	Total liabilities	$120,000	
Other assets....................................	360,000	Page, capital		
		($230,000 – $40,000)...................	190,000	
		Osuka, capital		
		($150,000 – $20,000)...................	130,000	
		Schiller, capital	160,000	
Total assets	$600,000	Total liabilities and capital	$600,000	

Withdrawal of a Partner

A partner may withdraw from the business for many reasons, including retirement or a dispute with the other partners. The withdrawal of a partner dissolves the old partnership. The partnership agreement should contain a provision to govern how to settle with a withdrawing partner. In the simplest case, as illustrated on page 530, a partner may withdraw and sell his or her interest to another partner in a personal transaction. The only entry needed to record this transfer of equity debits the withdrawing partner's capital account and credits the purchaser's capital account. The dollar amount of the entry is the capital balance of the withdrawing partner, regardless of the price paid by the purchaser. The accounting when one current partner buys a second partner's interest is the same as when an outside party buys a current partner's interest.

If the partner withdraws in the middle of an accounting period, the partnership books should be updated to determine the withdrawing partner's capital balance. The business must measure net income or net loss for the fraction of the year up to the withdrawal date and allocate profit or loss according to the existing ratio. After the books have been closed, the business then accounts for the change in partnership capital.

The withdrawing partner may receive his or her share of the business in partnership assets other than cash. The question arises as to what value to assign the partnership assets: book value or current market value. The settlement procedure may specify an independent appraisal of assets to determine their current market value. If market values have changed, the appraisal will result in revaluing the partnership assets. Thus the partners share in any market value changes that their efforts caused.

Suppose that Keith Isaac is retiring in midyear from the partnership of Green, Henry, and Isaac. After the books have been adjusted for partial-period income but before the asset appraisal, revaluation, and closing entries, the balance sheet reports:

Short Exercise: Jane, Wayne, and Lane are partners with capital account balances of $20,000, $30,000, and $50,000, respectively. They share profits in a 2:3:5 ratio. Wayne is withdrawing from the business, so the partners have the assets appraised. The building's market value is $4,000 more than its book value. The inventory's market value is $6,000 less than cost. What are the journal entries to revalue these assets? *A:*
Building 4,000
   Jane, Capital 800
   Wayne, Capital.. 1,200
   Lane, Capital 2,000
Jane, Capital 1,200
Wayne, Capital 1,800
Lane, Capital 3,000
   Inventory 6,000

Cash...		$ 39,000	Total liabilities.................................		$ 80,000
Inventory...		44,000	Green, capital...................................		54,000
Land		55,000	Henry, capital...................................		43,000
Building	$95,000		Isaac, capital		21,000
Less accum. depr.	35,000	60,000	Total liabilities and		
Total assets		$198,000	capital...		$198,000

An independent appraiser revalues the inventory at $38,000 (down from $44,000) and the land at $101,000 (up from $55,000). The partners share the differences between these assets' market values and their prior book values on the basis of their profit-and-loss ratio. The partnership agreement has allocated one-fourth of the profits to Susan Green, one-half to Charles Henry, and one-fourth to Isaac. (This ratio may be written 1:2:1 for one part to Green, two parts to Henry, and one part to Isaac.) For each share that Green or Issac has, Henry has two. The entries to record the revaluation of the inventory and land are:

July 31	Green, Capital ($6,000 × 1/4)	1,500	
	Henry, Capital ($6,000 × 1/2)	3,000	
	Issac, Capital ($6,000 × 1/4)	1,500	
	Inventory ($44,000 − $38,000)...................................		6,000
	To revalue the inventory and allocate the loss in value		
	to the partners.		
31	Land ($101,000 − $55,000)..	46,000	
	Green, Capital ($46,000 × 1/4)................................		11,500
	Henry, Capital ($46,000 × 1/2)................................		23,000
	Isaac, Capital ($46,000 × 1/4).................................		11,500
	To revalue the land and allocate the gain in value		
	to the partners.		

After the revaluations, the partnership balance sheet reports:

Short Exercise: What are the partners' capital account balances after the revaluations in the previous Short Exercise? *A:*
Jane: ($20,000 + $800
   − $1,200) = $19,600
Wayne: ($30,000 + $1,200
   − $1,800) = $29,400
Lane: ($50,000 + $2,000
   − $3,000) = $49,000

Cash...		$ 39,000	Total liabilities.................................	$ 80,000
Inventory...		38,000	Green, capital	
Land		101,000	($54,000 − $1,500 + $11,500)	64,000
Building	$95,000		Henry, capital	
Less accum. depr............	35,000	60,000	($43,000 − $3,000 + $23,000)......	63,000
			Isaac, capital	
			($21,000 − $1,500 + $11,500)......	31,000
Total assets		$238,000	Total liabilities and capital	$238,000

The books now carry the assets at current market value, which becomes the new book value, and the capital accounts have been adjusted accordingly. Isaac has a claim to $31,000 in partnership assets. How is his withdrawal from the business accounted for?

Withdrawal at Book Value

If Keith Isaac withdraws by receiving cash equal to the book value of his owner's equity, the entry will be:

July 31	Isaac, Capital..	31,000	
	Cash		31,000
	To record withdrawal of K. Isaac from the partnership.		

This entry records the payment of partnership cash to Isaac and the closing of his capital account upon his withdrawal from the business.

Withdrawal at Less Than Book Value

The withdrawing partner may be so eager to leave the business that he or she is willing to take less than his or her equity. This situation has occurred in real estate and oil-drilling partnerships. Assume that Keith Isaac withdraws from the business and agrees to receive partnership cash of $10,000 and the new partnership's note for $15,000. This $25,000 settlement is $6,000 less than Isaac's $31,000 equity in the business. The remaining partners share this $6,000 difference—which is a bonus to them—according to their profit-and-loss ratio. However, because Isaac has withdrawn from the partnership, a new agreement—and a new profit-and-loss ratio—must be drawn up. Henry and Green, in forming a new partnership, may decide on any ratio that they see fit. Let's assume they agree that Henry will earn two-thirds of partnership profits and losses and Green one-third. The entry to record Isaac's withdrawal at less than book value is:

Short Exercise: Refer to the Short Exercises on p. 534. Assume that Wayne is willing to accept $20,000 for his partnership interest. What is the journal entry to record his retirement? *A:*

Wayne, Capital....29,400
  Cash 20,000
  Jane, Capital 2,686*
  Lane, Capital ... 6,714†

*$9,400 × 2/7 = $2,686
†$9,400 × 5/7 = $6,714

Jane and Lane will now share profits in a 2:5 ratio.

July 31	Isaac, Capital..	31,000	
	Cash		10,000
	Note Payable to K. Isaac		15,000
	Green, Capital ($6,000 × 1/3)		2,000
	Henry, Capital ($6,000 × 2/3)		4,000
	To record withdrawal of K. Isaac from the partnership.		

Isaac's account is closed, and Henry and Green may or may not continue the business.

Withdrawal at More Than Book Value

The settlement with a withdrawing partner may allow him or her to take assets of greater value than the book value of that partner's capital. Also, the remaining partners may be so eager for the withdrawing partner to leave the firm that they pay him or her a bonus to withdraw from the business. In either case, the partner's withdrawal causes a decrease in the book equity of the remaining partners. This decrease is allocated to the partners on the basis of their profit-and-loss ratio.

The accounting for this situation follows the pattern illustrated for withdrawal at less than book value—with one exception. The remaining partners' capital accounts are debited because the withdrawing partner receives more than his or her book equity.

Short Exercise: Refer to the Short Exercises on p. 534. Assume that Jane and Lane agree to pay Wayne $40,000 for his partnership interest. What is the journal entry to record his retirement? *A:*

Jane, Capital 3,029*
Wayne, Capital ... 29,400
Lane, Capital ...... 7,571†
  Cash 40,000

*$10,600 × 2/7 = $3,029
†$10,600 × 5/7 = $7,571

Death of a Partner

Death of a partner, like any other form of partnership withdrawal, dissolves a partnership. The partnership accounts are adjusted to measure net income or loss for the fraction of the year up to the date of death, then closed to determine the partners' capital balances on that date. Settlement with the deceased partner's estate is based on the partnership agreement. The estate commonly receives partnership assets equal to the partner's capital balance. The partnership closes the deceased partner's capital account with a debit. This entry credits a payable to the estate.

Alternatively, a remaining partner may purchase the deceased partner's equity. The deceased partner's equity is debited, and the purchaser's equity is credited. The amount of this entry is the ending credit balance in the deceased partner's capital account.

Liquidation of a Partnership

OBJECTIVE 6

Account for the liquidation of a partnership

Admission of a new partner or withdrawal or death of an existing partner dissolves the partnership. However, the business may continue operating with no apparent change to outsiders such as customers and creditors. Business **liquidation**, however, is the process of going out of business by selling the entity's assets and paying its liabilities. The final step in liquidation of a business is the *distribution of the remaining cash to the owners*. Before the business is liquidated, its books should be adjusted and closed. After closing, only asset, liability, and partners' capital accounts remain open.

Liquidation of a partnership includes three basic steps:

1. Sell the assets. Allocate the gain or loss to the partners' capital accounts on the basis of the profit-and-loss ratio.
2. Pay the partnership liabilities.
3. Disburse the remaining cash to the partners on the basis of their capital balances.

In practice, the liquidation of a business can stretch over weeks or months. Selling every asset and paying every liability of the entity takes time. After the 80 partners of Shea & Gould, one of New York's best-known law firms, voted to dissolve their partnership in January 1994, the firm remained open for an extra year to collect bills and pay off liabilities.

"After the 80 partners of Shea & Gould . . . voted to dissolve their partnership in January 1994, the firm remained open for an extra year to collect bills and pay off liabilities."

To avoid excessive detail in our illustrations, we include only two asset categories—Cash and Noncash Assets—and a single liability category—Liabilities. Our examples assume that the business sells the noncash assets in a single transaction and pays the liabilities in a single transaction.

Assume that Jane Aviron, Elaine Bloch, and Mark Crane have shared profits and losses in the ratio of 3:1:1. (This ratio is equal to 3/5, 1/5, 1/5, or a 60-percent, 20-percent, 20-percent sharing ratio.) They decide to liquidate their partnership. After the books are adjusted and closed, the general ledger contains the following balances:

Cash	$ 10,000	Liabilities	$ 30,000
Noncash assets	90,000	Aviron, capital	40,000
		Bloch, capital	20,000
		Crane, capital	10,000
Total assets	$100,000	Total liabilities and capital	$100,000

Sale of Noncash Assets at a Gain

Assume that the Aviron, Bloch, and Crane partnership sells its noncash assets (shown on the balance sheet at $90,000) for cash of $150,000. The partnership realizes a gain of $60,000, which is allocated to the partners on the basis of their profit-and-loss-sharing ratio. The entry to record this sale and allocation of the gain is:

Oct. 31   Cash   150,000
        Noncash Assets   90,000
        Aviron, Capital ($60,000 × 0.60)......................   36,000
        Bloch, Capital ($60,000 × 0.20)   12,000
        Crane, Capital ($60,000 × 0.20)......................   12,000
        To sell noncash assets in liquidation and allocate gain
        to partners.

The partnership must next pay off its liabilities:

Oct. 31   Liabilities   30,000
        Cash   30,000
        To pay liabilities in liquidation.

In the final liquidation transaction, the remaining cash is disbursed to the partners. *The partners share in the cash according to their capital balances.* (In contrast, *gains and losses* on the sale of assets are shared by the partners on the basis of their profit-and-loss-sharing ratio.) The amount of cash left in the partnership is $130,000—the $10,000 beginning balance plus the $150,000 cash sale of assets minus the $30,000 cash payment of liabilities. The partners divide the remaining cash according to their capital balances:

Oct. 31   Aviron, Capital ($40,000 + $36,000)   76,000
        Bloch, Capital ($20,000 + $12,000)..............................   32,000
        Crane, Capital ($10,000 + $12,000)   22,000
        Cash   130,000
        To disburse cash to partners in liquidation.

A convenient way to summarize the transactions in a partnership liquidation is given in Exhibit 13-4.

After the disbursement of cash to the partners, the business has no assets, liabilities, or owners' equity. All the balances are zero. By the accounting equation, partnership assets *must* equal partnership liabilities plus partnership capital.

Sale of Noncash Assets at a Loss

Liquidation of a business often includes the sale of noncash assets at a loss. When this occurs, the partners' capital accounts are debited as they share the loss in their profit-and-loss-sharing ratio. Otherwise, the accounting follows the pattern illustrated for the sale of noncash assets at a gain.

Short Exercise: Kelly and Keith are partners in a partnership with cash of $10,000 and noncash assets of $50,000. The capital balances of Kelly and Keith are $40,000 and $20,000, respectively. The partners share profits and losses 60:40. The noncash assets are sold for $56,000. All liabilities have been paid. What journal entries record sale of the assets and distribution of cash to the partners? *A:*

Cash 56,000
  Noncash
    Assets............   50,000
  Kelly, Capital .   3,600*
  Keith, Capital   2,400†

*$6,000 gain × 60% = $3,600
†$6,000 × 40% = $2,400

Kelly, Capital
($40,000
+ $3,600) 43,600
Keith, Capital
($20,000
+ $2,400) 22,400
    Cash........   66,000

EXHIBIT 13-4
Partnership Liquidation—Sale of Assets at a Gain

	Cash	+	Noncash Assets	=	Liabilities	+	Capital		
							Aviron (60%)	+ Bloch (20%)	+ Crane (20%)
Balance before sale of assets.....................	$ 10,000		$ 90,000		$ 30,000		$ 40,000	$ 20,000	$ 10,000
Sale of assets and sharing of gain.......	150,000		(90,000)				36,000	12,000	12,000
Balances.....................	160,000		–0–		30,000		76,000	32,000	22,000
Payment of liabilities	(30,000)				(30,000)				
Balances.....................	130,000		–0–		–0–		76,000	32,000	22,000
Disbursement of cash to partners	(130,000)						(76,000)	(32,000)	(22,000)
Balances....................	$ –0–		$ –0–		$ –0–		$ –0–	$ –0–	$ –0–

STOP & THINK The liquidation of the Dirk & Cross partnership included the sale of assets at a $150,000 loss. Lorraine Dirk's Capital balance of $45,000 was less than her $60,000 share of the loss. Allocation of losses to the partners created a $15,000 deficit (debit balance) in Dirk's Capital account. Identify ways that the partnership could deal with the negative balance (a capital deficiency) in Dirk's Capital account.

Answer: Two possibilities are:
1. Dirk could contribute assets to the partnership in an amount equal to her capital deficiency.
2. Joseph Cross, Lorraine Dirk's partner, could absorb Dirk's capital deficiency by decreasing his own capital balance.

Partnership Financial Statements

Partnership financial statements are much like those of a proprietorship. However, a partnership income statement includes a section showing the division of net income to the partners. For example, the partnership of Leslie Gray and DeWayne Hayward might report its statements for the year ended December 31, 19X6, as shown in Panel A of Exhibit 13-5. A proprietorship's statements are presented in Panel B for comparison.

EXHIBIT 13-5
Financial Statements of a Partnership and a Proprietorship

PANEL A—Partnership

GRAY AND HAYWARD CONSULTING INCOME STATEMENT FOR THE YEAR ENDED DECEMBER 31, 19X6		
Revenues		$ 460
Expenses		(270)
Net income		$ 190
Allocation of net income:		
To Gray	$114	
To Hayward	76	$ 190

GRAY AND HAYWARD CONSULTING STATEMENT OF OWNERS' EQUITY FOR THE YEAR ENDED DECEMBER 31, 19X6		
	Gray	**Hayward**
Capital, December 31, 19X5	$ 50	$ 40
Additional investments	10	—
Net income	114	76
Subtotal	174	116
Drawings	(72)	(48)
Capital, December 31, 19X6	$102	$ 68

GRAY AND HAYWARD CONSULTING BALANCE SHEET DECEMBER 31, 19X6	
Assets	
Cash and other assets	$170
Owners' Equity	
Gray, capital	$102
Hayward, capital	68
Total capital	$170

PANEL B—Proprietorship

GRAY CONSULTING INCOME STATEMENT FOR THE YEAR ENDED DECEMBER 31, 19X6	
Revenues	$ 460
Expenses	(270)
Net income	$ 190

GRAY CONSULTING STATEMENT OF OWNER'S EQUITY FOR THE YEAR ENDED DECEMBER 31, 19X6	
Capital, December 31, 19X5	$ 90
Additional investment	10
Net income	190
Subtotal	290
Drawings	(120)
Capital, December 1, 19X6	$170

GRAY CONSULTING BALANCE SHEET DECEMBER 31, 19X6	
Assets	
Cash and other assets	$170
Owner's Equity	
Gray, capital	$170

EXHIBIT 13-6
Reporting Net Income for a Large Partnership

MAIN PRICE & ANDERS
COMBINED STATEMENT OF EARNINGS
FOR THE YEAR ENDED AUGUST 31, 19X7

Dollar amounts in thousands

Fees for professional services	$914,492

Earnings for the year	$297,880
Allocation of earnings:	
To partners active during the year—	
Resigned, retired, and deceased partners	$ 19,901
Partners active at year end	253,270
To retired and deceased partners—retirement and death benefits...............	8,310
Not allocated to partners—retained for specific	
partnership purposes..	16,399
	$297,880
Average earnings per partner active at year end (1,336 partners)	$ 223

Large partnerships may not find it feasible to report the net income of every partner. Instead, the firm may report the allocation of net income to active and retired partners and average earnings per partner. For example, Exhibit 13-6 shows how the CPA firm Main Price & Anders reported its earnings.

SUMMARY PROBLEM FOR YOUR REVIEW

The partnership of Taylor & Uvalde is considering admitting Steven Vaughn as a partner on January 1, 19X8. The partnership general ledger includes the following balances on that date:

Cash...	$ 9,000	Total liabilities..................................	$ 50,000
Other assets......................................	110,000	Taylor, capital...................................	45,000
		Uvalde, capital...................................	24,000
Total assets	$119,000	Total liabilities and capital	$119,000

Ross Taylor's share of profits and losses is 60 percent, and Thomas Uvalde's share is 40 percent.

Required (Items 1 and 2 are independent)

1. Suppose that Vaughn pays Uvalde $31,000 to acquire Uvalde's interest in the business. Taylor approves Vaughn as a partner.
   a. Record the transfer of owner's equity on the partnership books.
   b. Prepare the partnership balance sheet immediately after Vaughn is admitted as a partner.

2. Suppose that Vaughn becomes a partner by investing $31,000 cash to acquire a one-fourth interest in the business.
   a. Compute Vaughn's capital balance, and record his investment in the business.
   b. Prepare the partnership balance sheet immediately after Vaughn is admitted as a partner. Include the heading.

3. Which way of admitting Vaughn to the partnership increases its total assets? Give your reason.

SOLUTION TO REVIEW PROBLEM

Requirement 1

a.

Jan. 31	Uvalde, Capital	24,000	
	Vaughn, Capital		24,000
	To transfer Uvalde's equity in the partnership to Vaughn.		

b. The balance sheet for the partnership of Taylor and Vaughn is identical to the balance sheet given for Taylor and Uvalde in the problem, except that Vaughn's name replaces Uvalde's name in the title and in the listing of capital accounts.

Requirement 2

a. Computations of Vaughn's capital balance:

Partnership capital before Vaughn is admitted ($45,000 + $24,000)	$ 69,000
Vaughn's investment in the partnership	31,000
Partnership capital after Vaughn is admitted	$100,000
Vaughn's capital in the partnership ($100,000 × 1/4)	$ 25,000

Jan. 1	Cash	31,000	
	Vaughn, Capital		25,000
	Taylor, Capital		
	[($31,000 − $25,000) × 0.60]		3,600
	Uvalde, Capital		
	[($31,000 − $25,000) × 0.40]		2,400
	To admit Vaughn as a partner with a one-fourth interest in the business.		

b.

TAYLOR, UVALDE, & VAUGHN BALANCE SHEET JANUARY 1, 19X8			
Cash ($9,000 + $31,000)	$ 40,000	Total liabilities	$ 50,000
Other assets	110,000	Taylor, capital	
		($45,000 + $3,600)	48,600
		Uvalde, capital	
		($24,000 + $2,400)	26,400
		Vaughn, capital	25,000
Total assets	$150,000	Total liabilities and capital....	$150,000

Requirement 3

Vaughn's investment in the partnership increases its total assets by the amount of his contribution. Total assets of the business are $150,000 after his investment, compared with $119,000 before. In contrast, Vaughn's purchase of Uvalde's interest in the business is a personal transaction between the two individuals. It does not affect the assets of the partnership regardless of the amount Vaughn pays Uvalde.

SUMMARY

1. **Identify the characteristics of a partnership.** A *partnership* is a business co-owned by two or more persons for profit. The characteristics of this form of business organization are its *ease of formation, limited life, mutual agency, unlimited liability,* and *no partnership income taxes.* In a *limited partnership,* the limited partners have limited personal liability for the obligations of the business.

A written *partnership agreement,* or *articles of partnership,* establishes procedures for admission of a new partner, withdrawals of a partner, and the sharing of profits and losses among the partners. When a new partner is admitted to the firm or an existing partner withdraws, the old partnership is *dissolved,* or ceases to exist. A new partnership may or may not emerge to continue the business.

2. **Account for partners' initial investments in a partnership.** Accounting for a partnership is similar to accounting for a proprietorship. However, a partnership has more than one owner. Each partner has an individual capital account and a withdrawal account.

3. **Allocate profits and losses to the partners by different methods.** Partners share net income or loss in any manner they choose. Common sharing agreements base the *profit-and-loss ratio* on a stated fraction, partners' capital contributions, and/or their service to the partnership. Some partnerships call the cash drawings of partners *salaries* and *interest,* but these amounts are not expenses of the business. Instead, they are merely ways of allocating partnership net income to the partners.

4. **Account for the admission of a new partner to the business.** An outside person may become a partner by purchasing a current partner's interest or by investing in the partnership. In some cases the new partner must pay the current partners a bonus to join. In other situations the new partner may receive a bonus to join.

5. **Account for the withdrawal of a partner from the business.** When a partner withdraws, partnership assets may be reappraised. Partners share any gain or loss on the asset revaluation on the basis of their profit-and-loss ratio. The withdrawing partner may receive payment equal to, greater than, or less than his or her capital book value, depending on the agreement with the other partners.

6. **Account for the liquidation of a partnership.** In *liquidation* a partnership goes out of business by selling the assets, paying the liabilities, and disbursing any remaining cash to the partners.

7. **Prepare partnership financial statements.** Partnership *financial statements* are similar to those of a proprietorship. However, the partnership income statement commonly reports the allocation of net income to the partners, and the balance sheet has a capital account for each partner.

SELF-STUDY QUESTIONS

Test your understanding of the chapter by marking the best answer for each of the following questions.

1. Which of these characteristics does *not* apply to a partnership? (p. 523)
   a. Unlimited life   c. Unlimited liability
   b. Mutual agency   d. No business income tax

2. A partnership records a partner's investment of assets in the business at (p. 524)
   a. The partner's book value of the assets invested
   b. The market value of the assets invested
   c. A special value set by the partners
   d. Any of the above, depending upon the partnership agreement

3. The partnership of Lane, Murdock, and Nu divides profits in the ratio of 4:5:3. During 19X6 the business earned $40,000. John Nu's share of this income is (pp. 525–526)
   a. $10,000   b. $13,333   c. $16,000   d. $16,667

4. Suppose that the partnership of Lane, Murdock, and Nu of Self-Study Question 3 lost $40,000 during 19X6. Frank Murdock's share of this loss is (p. 525)
   a. Not determinable because the ratio applies only to profits
   b. $13,333
   c. $16,000
   d. $16,667

5. The partners of Placido, Quinn, & Rolfe share profits and losses 1/5, 1/6, and 19/30. During 19X3, the first year of their partnership, the business earned $120,000, and each partner had drawings of $50,000 for personal use. What is the balance in Carol Rolfe's capital account after all closing entries? (p. 529)
   a. Not determinable because Rolfe's investment in the business is not given
   b. Minus $10,000
   c. $26,000
   d. $70,000

6. Bob Fuller buys into the partnership of Graff and Harrell by purchasing a one-third interest for $55,000. Prior to Fuller's entry, Ted Graff's capital balance was $46,000 and Lena Harrell's balance was $52,000. The entry to record Fuller's buying into the business is (p. 531)

a.	Cash	55,000	
	Fuller, Capital.................		55,000
b.	Graff, Capital............................	27,500	
	Harrell, Capital........................	27,500	
	Fuller, Capital.................		55,000
c.	Cash	55,000	
	Fuller, Capital.................		51,000
	Graff, Capital..................		2,000
	Harrell, Capital		2,000
d.	Cash	51,000	
	Graff, Capital............................	2,000	
	Harrell, Capital........................	2,000	
	Fuller, Capital.................		55,000

7. The partners of Thomas, Valik, & Wollenberg share profits and losses equally. Their capital balances are $40,000, $50,000, and $60,000, respectively, when Brenda Wollenberg sells her interest in the partnership to Brett Valik for $90,000. Dionne Thomas and Valik continue the business. Immediately after Wollenberg's retirement, the total assets of the partnership are *(pp. 530–531)*
   a. Increased by $30,000
   b. Increased by $90,000
   c. Decreased by $60,000
   d. The same as before Wollenberg sold her interest to Valik

8. Prior to Ward Hogg's withdrawal from the partnership of Hogg, Hamm, and Bacon, the partners' capital balances were $140,000, $110,000 and $250,000, respectively. The partners share profits and losses 1/3, 1/4, and 5/12. The appraisal indicates that assets should be written down by $36,000. Sam Hamm's share of the write-down is *(p. 534)*
   a. $7,920   b. $9,000   c. $12,000   d. $18,000

9. The process of closing the business, selling the assets, paying the liabilities, and disbursing remaining cash to the owners is called *(p. 536)*
   a. Dissolution   c. Withdrawal
   b. Forming a new partnership d. Liquidation

10. Eric Huber and Beth Hudson have shared profits and losses equally. Immediately prior to the final cash disbursement in a liquidation of their partnership, the books show:

Cash	= Liabilities +	Huber, Capital +	Hudson, Capital
$100,000	$ –0–	$60,000	$40,000

How much cash should Huber receive? *(p. 536)*
   a. $40,000   c. $60,000
   b. $50,000   d. None of the above

Answers to the Self-Study Questions follow the Accounting Vocabulary.

ACCOUNTING VOCABULARY

Articles of partnership. Agreement that is the contract between partners specifying such items as the name, location, and nature of the business; the name, capital investment, and duties of each partner; and the method of sharing profits and losses by the partners. Also called the partnership agreement *(p. 522)*.

Dissolution. Ending of a partnership *(p. 523)*.

Liquidation. The process of going out of business by selling the entity's assets and paying its liabilities. The final step in liquidation of a business is the distribution of any remaining cash to the owners *(p. 536)*.

Mutual agency. Every partner can bind the business to a contract within the scope of the partnership's regular business operations *(p. 523)*.

Partnership. An association of two or more persons who co-own a business for profit *(p. 522)*.

Partnership agreement. Another name for the articles of partnership *(p. 522)*.

Unlimited personal liability. When a partnership (or a proprietorship) cannot pay its debts with business assets, the partners (or the proprietor) must use personal assets to meet the debt *(p. 523)*.

ANSWERS TO SELF-STUDY QUESTIONS

1. a
2. b
3. a   ($40,000 × 3/12 = $10,000)
4. d   ($40,000 × 5/12 = $16,667)
5. a
6. c   [($46,000 + $52,000 + $55,000) × 1/3 = $51,000; $55,000 – $51,000 = $4,000; $4,000 ÷ 2 = $2,000 each to Graff and Harrell]
7. d
8. b   ($36,000 × 1/4 = $9,000)
9. d
10. c

QUESTIONS

1. What is another name for a partnership agreement? List eight items that the agreement should specify.
2. Ron Montgomery, who is a partner in M&N Associates, commits the firm to a contract for a job within the scope of its regular business operations. What term describes Montgomery's ability to obligate the partnership?
3. If a partnership cannot pay a debt, who must make the payment? What term describes this obligation of the partners?
4. How is the income of a partnership taxed?
5. Identify the advantages and disadvantages of the partnership form of business organization.
6. Rex Randall and Ken Smith's partnership agreement states that Randall gets 60 percent of profits and Smith gets 40 percent. If the agreement does not discuss the treatment of losses, how are losses shared? How do the partners share profits and losses if the agreement specifies no profit-and-loss-sharing ratio?

7. What determines the amount of the credit to a partner's capital account when the partner contributes assets other than cash to the business?

8. Do partner withdrawals of cash for personal use affect the sharing of profits and losses by the partner? If so, explain how. If not, explain why not.

9. Name two events that can cause the dissolution of a partnership.

10. Briefly describe how to account for the purchase of an existing partner's interest in the business.

11. Jeff Malcolm purchases Nona Brown's interest in the Brown & Kareem partnership. What right does Malcolm obtain from the purchase? What is required for Malcolm to become Paula Kareem's partner?

12. Both Sal Assissi and Cal Carter have capital of $75,000 in their business. They share profits in the ratio of 55:45. Kathy Denman acquires a one-fifth share in the partnership by investing cash of $50,000. What are the capital balances of the three partners immediately after Denman is admitted?

13. When a partner resigns from the partnership and receives assets greater than his or her capital balance, how is the excess shared by the other partners?

14. Distinguish between dissolution and liquidation of a partnership.

15. Name the three steps in liquidating a partnership.

16. The partnership of Ralls and Sauls is in the process of liquidation. How do the partners share (a) gains and losses on the sale of noncash assets and (b) the final cash disbursement?

17. Compare and contrast the financial statements of a proprietorship and a partnership.

18. Summarize the situations in which partnership allocations are based on (a) the profit-and-loss-sharing ratio and (b) the partners' capital balances.

EXERCISES

E13-1 Rhonda Puente, a friend from college, approaches you about forming a partnership to export software. Since graduating, Puente has worked for the Export-Import Bank, developing important contacts among government officials and business leaders in Eastern Europe. Puente believes she is in a unique position to capitalize on the growing market in Eastern Europe for American computers. With expertise in finance, you would have responsibility for accounting and finance in the partnership.

Organizing a business as a partnership
(Obj. 1)

Required
Discuss the advantages and disadvantages of organizing the export business as a partnership rather than a proprietorship. Comment on how partnership income is taxed.

E13-2 Rebecca Stepanik has operated an apartment-location service as a proprietorship. She and Kristen Clem have decided to reorganize the business as a partnership. Stepanik's investment in the partnership consists of cash, $2,100; accounts receivable, $10,600, less allowance for uncollectibles, $800; office furniture, $2,700, less accumulated depreciation, $1,100; a small building, $55,000, less accumulated depreciation, $27,500; accounts payable, $3,300; and a note payable to the bank, $10,000.

Recording a partner's investment
(Obj. 2)

To determine Stepanik's equity in the partnership, she and Clem hire an independent appraiser. This outside party provides the following market values of the assets and liabilities that Stepanik is contributing to the business: cash, accounts receivable, office furniture, accounts payable, and note payable—the same as Stepanik's book value; allowance for uncollectible accounts, $2,900; building, $71,000; and accrued expenses payable (including interest on the note payable), $1,200.

Required
Make the entry on the partnership books to record Stepanik's investment.

E13-3 Matt Looney and Dave Briseño form a partnership, investing $40,000 and $70,000, respectively. Determine their shares of net income or net loss for each of the following situations:

Computing partners' shares of net income and net loss
(Obj. 3)

a. Net loss is $44,000, and the partners have no written partnership agreement.

b. Net income is $66,000, and the partnership agreement states that the partners share profits and losses on the basis of their capital contributions.

c. Net loss is $77,000, and the partnership agreement states that the partners share profits on the basis of their capital contributions.

d. Net income is $125,000. The first $60,000 is shared on the basis of partner capital contributions. The next $45,000 is based on partner service, with Looney receiving 30 percent and Briseño receiving 70 percent. The remainder is shared equally.

Computing partners' capital balances
(Obj. 3)

E13-4 Matt Looney withdrew cash of $62,000 for personal use, and Dave Briseño withdrew cash of $50,000 during the year. Using the data from situation (d) in Exercise 13-3, journalize the entries to close the (a) income summary account and (b) the partners' drawing accounts. Explanations are not required. Indicate the amount of increase or decrease in each partner's capital balance. What was the overall effect on partnership capital?

Admitting a new partner
(Obj. 4)

E13-5 Clay Brown is admitted to a partnership. Prior to his admission, the partnership books show Bob Reitmeier's capital balance at $100,000 and Lisa Jayne's capital balance at $50,000. Compute each partner's equity on the books of the new partnership under the following plans:

a. Brown pays $60,000 for Jayne's equity. Brown's payment is not an investment in the partnership but instead goes directly to Jayne.

b. Brown invests $50,000 to acquire a one-fourth interest in the partnership.

c. Brown invests $70,000 to acquire a one-fourth interest in the partnership.

Recording the admission of a new partner *(Obj. 4)*

E13-6 Make the partnership journal entry to record the admission of Brown under plans (a), (b), and (c) in Exercise 13-5. Explanations are not required.

Withdrawal of a partner
(Obj. 5)

E13-7 After the books are closed, Allen & Bowden's partnership balance sheet reports capital of $60,000 for Allen and $70,000 for Bowden. Allen is withdrawing from the firm. The partners agree to write down partnership assets by $40,000. They have shared profits and losses in the ratio of one-third to Allen and two-thirds to Bowden. If the partnership agreement states that a withdrawing partner will receive assets equal to the book value of his owner's equity, how much will Allen receive? Bowden will continue to operate the business as a proprietorship. What is Bowden's beginning capital on the proprietorship books?

Liquidation of a partnership
(Obj. 6)

E13-8 The partnership of Lee, Molnari, and Nix is dissolving. Business assets, liabilities, and partners' capital balances prior to dissolution follow. The partners share profits and losses as follows: Kim Lee, 25 percent; Sandra Molnari, 55 percent; and Ray Nix, 20 percent.

Required

Create a spreadsheet or solve manually—as directed by your instructor—to show the ending balances in all accounts after the noncash assets are sold for $145,000 and for $95,000. Determine the unknown amounts (?):

	A	B	C	D	E	F
1			Lee, Molnari, and Nix			
2			Sale of Noncash Assets			
3			(For $145,000)			
4						
5		Noncash		Lee	Molnari	Nix
6	Cash	Assets	Liabilities	Capital	Capital	Capital
7						
8	$ 6,000	$126,000	$77,000	$12,000	$37,000	$6,000
9	145,000	(126,000)		?	?	?
10						
11	$151,000	$ 0	$77,000	$?	$?	$?
12						
13						($A9–$B8) * .25
14			(For $95,000)			
15						
16						
17		Noncash		Lee	Molnari	Nix
18	Cash	Assets	Liabilities	Capital	Capital	Capital
19						
20	$ 6,000	$126,000	$77,000	$12,000	$37,000	$6,000
21	95,000	(126,000)		?	?	?
22						
23	$101,000	$ 0	$77,000	$?	$?	$?
24						
						($A21–$B20)*.25

Identify two ways the partners can deal with the negative ending balance in Nix's capital account.

E13-9   On October 31, 19X9, Jill Crabtree and Don Evelyn agree to combine their proprietorships as a partnership. Their balance sheets on October 31 are as follows:

Preparing a partnership balance sheet
(Obj. 7)

	Crabtree's Business		Evelyn's Business	
Assets	Book Value	Current Market Value	Book Value	Current Market Value
Cash	$ 3,700	$ 3,700	$ 8,000	$ 8,000
Accounts receivable (net)	22,000	20,200	8,000	6,300
Inventory	51,000	46,000	34,000	35,100
Plant assets (net).........................	121,800	123,500	53,500	57,400
Total assets...................................	$198,500	$193,400	$103,500	$106,800
Liabilities and Capital				
Accounts payable	$ 23,600	$ 23,600	$ 9,100	$ 9,100
Accrued expenses payable	2,200	2,200	1,400	1,400
Notes payable	75,000	75,000	—	—
Crabtree, capital	97,700	—	—	—
Evelyn, capital	—	—	93,000	—
Total liabilities and capital..........	$198,500	$193,400	$103,500	$106,800

Required

Prepare the partnership balance sheet at October 31, 19X9.

PROBLEMS

(GROUP A)

P13-1A   Dolores Sanchez and Leticia Gaitan are discussing the formation of a partnership to import dresses from Guatemala. Sanchez is especially artistic, so she will travel to Central America to buy merchandise. Gaitan is a super salesperson and has already lined up several large stores to which she can sell the dresses.

Writing a partnership agreement
(Obj. 1)

Required

Write a partnership agreement to cover all elements essential for the business to operate smoothly. Make up names, amounts, profit-and-loss-sharing percentages, and so on as needed.

P13-2A   Jo Ringle and Mel LeBlanc formed a partnership on March 15. The partners agreed to invest equal amounts of capital. LeBlanc invested his proprietorship's assets and liabilities (credit balances in parentheses):

Investments by partners
(Obj. 2, 7)

	LeBlanc's Book Value	Current Market Value
Accounts receivable	$ 12,000	$ 12,000
Allowance for doubtful accounts...	(740)	(1,360)
Inventory	43,850	31,220
Prepaid expenses	2,400	2,400
Store equipment...	36,700	26,600
Accumulated depreciation...	(9,200)	(–0–)
Accounts payable..	(22,300)	(22,300)

On March 15 Ringle invested cash in an amount equal to the current market value of LeBlanc's partnership capital. The partners decided that LeBlanc would earn 70 percent of partnership profits because he would manage the business. Ringle agreed to accept 30 percent of profits. During the period ended December 31, the partnership earned $80,000. Ringle's drawings were $32,000, and LeBlanc's drawings were $36,000.

Required

1. Journalize the partners' initial investments.
2. Prepare the partnership balance sheet immediately after its formation on March 15.
3. Journalize the December 31 entries to close the Income Summary account and the partner drawing accounts.

Computing partners' shares of net income and net loss
(Obj. 3, 7)

P13-3A   Robin Dewey, Kami Karlin, and Dean DeCastro, have formed a partnership. Dewey invested $20,000; Karlin, $40,000; and DeCastro, $60,000. Dewey will manage the store, Karlin will work in the store three-quarters of the time, and DeCastro will not work in the business.

Required

1. Compute the partners' shares of profits and losses under each of the following plans.
    a. Net income is $87,000, and the articles of partnership do not specify how profits and losses are shared.
    b. Net loss is $47,000, and the partnership agreement allocates 45 percent of profits to Dewey, 35 percent to Karlin, and 20 percent to DeCastro. The agreement does not discuss the sharing of losses.
    c. Net income is $104,000. The first $50,000 is allocated on the basis of salaries of $34,000 for Dewey and $16,000 for Karlin. The remainder is allocated on the basis of partner capital contributions.
    d. Net income for the year ended September 30, 19X4, is $91,000. The first $30,000 is allocated on the basis of partner capital contributions. The next $30,000 is based on service, with $20,000 going to Dewey and $10,000 going to Karlin. Any remainder is shared equally.
2. Revenues for the year ended September 30, 19X4, were $572,000, and expenses were $481,000. Under plan (d), prepare the partnership income statement for the year.
3. How will what you learned in this problem help you manage a partnership?

Recording changes in partnership capital
(Obj. 4, 5)

P13-4A   Airborne Systems is a partnership owned by three individuals. The partners share profits and losses in the ratio of 30 percent to Eve Koehn, 40 percent to Earl Neiman, and 30 percent to Ivana Marcus. At December 31, 19X6, the firm has the following balance sheet:

Cash		$ 25,000	Total liabilities		$103,000
Accounts receivable	$ 16,000				
Less allowance for					
uncollectibles	1,000	15,000			
Inventory		92,000	Koehn, capital.................		38,000
Equipment........................	130,000		Nieman, capital		49,000
Less accumulated			Marcus, capital		42,000
depreciation	30,000	100,000	Total liabilities and		
Total assets........................		$232,000	capital.........................		$232,000

Koehn withdraws from the partnership on this date.

Required

Record Koehn's withdrawal from the partnership under the following plans:

1. Koehn gives her interest in the business to Lynn Albelli, her cousin.
2. In personal transactions, Koehn sells her equity in the partnership to Matt Bullock and Shelley Jones, who each pay Koehn $15,000 for half her interest. Neiman and Marcus agree to accept Bullock and Jones as partners.
3. The partnership pays Koehn cash of $5,000 and gives her a note payable for the remainder of her book equity in settlement of her partnership interest.
4. Koehn receives cash of $20,000 and a note payable for $20,000 from the partnership.
5. The partners agree that the equipment is worth $150,000 and that accumulated depreciation should remain at $30,000. After the revaluation, the partnership settles with Koehn by giving her cash of $10,000 and inventory for the remainder of her book equity.

Liquidation of a partnership
(Obj. 6)

P13-5A   The partnership of Whitney, Kosse, & Itasca has experienced operating losses for three consecutive years. The partners, who have shared profits and losses in the ratio of Fran Whitney, 15 percent; Walt Kosse, 60 percent; and Emil Itasca, 25 percent, are considering the liquidation of the business, They ask you to analyze the effects of liquidation under various possibilities regarding the sale of the noncash assets. They present the following condensed partnership balance sheet at December 31, end of the current year:

Cash	$ 7,000	Liabilities	$ 63,000
Noncash assets	163,000	Whitney, capital	24,000
		Kosse, capital	66,000
		Itasca, capital	17,000
		Total liabilities and	
Total assets	$170,000	capital	$170,000

Required

1. Prepare a summary of liquidation transactions (as illustrated in the chapter) for each of the following situations:
   a. The noncash assets are sold for $175,000.
   b. The noncash assets are sold for $141,000.
2. Make the journal entries to record the liquidation transactions in Requirement 1b.

(GROUP B)

P13-1B Rudy Aceves and Mary Keim are discussing the formation of a partnership to install payroll accounting systems. Aceves is skilled in systems design, and he is convinced that his designs will draw large sales volumes. Keim is a super salesperson and has already lined up several clients.

Writing a partnership agreement
(Obj. 1)

Required

Write a partnership agreement to cover all elements essential for the business to operate smoothly. Make up names, amounts, profit-and-loss-sharing percentages, and so on as needed.

P13-2B On June 30 Joshua Axtell and Zack Riesel formed a partnership. The partners agreed to invest equal amounts of capital. Axtell invested his proprietorship's assets and liabilities (credit balances in parentheses).

Investments by partners
(Obj. 2, 7)

On June 30 Riesel invested cash in an amount equal to the current market value of Axtell's partnership capital. The partners decided that Axtell would earn two-thirds of partnership profits because he would manage the business. Riesel agreed to accept one-third of the profits. During the remainder of the year, the partnership earned $60,000. Axtell's drawings were $35,200, and Riesel's drawings were $23,000.

	Axtell's Book Value	Current Market Value
Accounts receivable	$ 7,200	$ 7,200
Allowance for doubtful accounts	(–0–)	(1,050)
Inventory	22,340	24,100
Prepaid expenses	1,700	1,700
Office equipment	45,900	27,600
Accumulated depreciation	(15,300)	–0–
Accounts payable	(19,100)	(19,100)

Required

1. Journalize the partners' initial investments.
2. Prepare the partnership balance sheet immediately after its formation on June 30.
3. Journalize the December 31 entries to close the Income Summary account and the partner drawing accounts.

P13-3B Larry Collins, Elinor Davis, and Paul Chiu have formed a partnership. Collins invested $15,000, Davis $18,000, and Chiu $27,000. Collins will manage the store, Davis will work in the store half-time, and Chiu will not work in the business.

Computing partners' shares of net income and net loss
(Obj. 3, 7)

Required

1. Compute the partners' shares of profits and losses under each of the following plans.
   a. Net loss is $42,900, and the articles of partnership do not specify how profits and losses are shared.

b. Net loss is $60,000, and the partnership agreement allocates 40 percent of profits to Collins, 25 percent to Davis, and 35 percent to Chiu. The agreement does not discuss the sharing of losses.

c. Net income is $92,000. The first $40,000 is allocated on the basis of salaries, with Collins receiving $28,000 and Davis receiving $12,000. The remainder is allocated on the basis of partner capital contributions.

d. Net income for the year ended January 31, 19X8, is $180,000. The first $75,000 is allocated on the basis of partner capital contributions, and the next $36,000 is based on service, with Collins receiving $28,000 and Davis receiving $8,000. Any remainder is shared equally.

2. Revenues for the year ended January 31, 19X8, were $870,000, and expenses were $690,000. Under plan (d), prepare the partnership income statement for the year.

3. How will what you learned in this problem help you manage a partnership?

Recording changes in partnership capital
(Obj. 4, 5)

P13-4B   Personal Financial Services is a partnership owned by three individuals. The partners share profits and losses in the ratio of 28 percent to Dan Smythe, 38 percent to Max Lark, and 34 percent to Emily Spahn. At December 31, 19X7, the firm has the following balance sheet:

Cash		$ 12,000	Total liabilities	$ 75,000
Accounts receivable	$ 22,000			
Less allowance for				
uncollectibles	4,000	18,000	Smythe, capital	83,000
Building	$310,000		Lark, capital	50,000
Less accumulated			Spahn, capital	62,000
depreciation	70,000	240,000	Total liabilities and	
Total assets		$270,000	capital..........................	$270,000

Lark withdraws from the partnership on December 31, 19X7, to establish his own consulting practice.

Required

Record Lark's withdrawal from the partnership under the following plans:

1. Lark gives his interest in the business to Terry Boyd, his nephew.

2. In personal transactions, Lark sells his equity in the partnership to Bea Patell and Al Bruckner, who each pay Lark $40,000 for half his interest. Smythe and Spahn agree to accept Patell and Bruckner as partners.

3. The partnership pays Lark cash of $15,000 and gives him a note payable for the remainder of his book equity in settlement of his partnership interest.

4. Lark receives cash of $10,000 and a note for $70,000 from the partnership.

5. The partners agree that the building is worth only $280,000 and that its accumulated depreciation should remain at $70,000. After the revaluation, the partnership settles with Lark by giving him cash of $14,100 and a note payable for the remainder of his book equity.

Liquidation of a partnership
(Obj. 6)

P13-5B   The partnership of Monet, Blair, & Trippi has experienced operating losses for three consecutive years. The partners, who have shared profits and losses in the ratio of Mindy Monet, 10 percent; Burt Blair, 30 percent; and Toni Trippi, 60 percent, are considering the liquidation of the business. They ask you to analyze the effects of liquidation under various possibilities regarding the sale of the noncash assets. They present the following condensed partnership balance sheet at December 31, end of the current year:

Cash...	$ 27,000	Liabilities..	$131,000
Noncash assets	202,000	Monet, capital.................................	21,000
		Blair, capital...................................	39,000
		Trippi, capital	38,000
Total assets	$229,000	Total liabilities and capital	$229,000

Required

1. Prepare a summary of liquidation transactions (as illustrated in the chapter) for each of the following situations:
   a. The noncash assets are sold for $212,000.
   b. The noncash assets are sold for $182,000.
2. Make the journal entries to record the liquidation transactions in Requirement 1b.

EXTENDING YOUR KNOWLEDGE

DECISION PROBLEMS

1. Becky Jones invested $20,000 and Imelda Nichols invested $10,000 in a public relations firm that has operated for 10 years. Neither partner has made an additional investment. They have shared profits and losses in the ratio of 2:1, which is the ratio of their investments in the business. Jones manages the office, supervises the 16 employees, and does the accounting. Nichols, the moderator of a television talk show, is responsible for marketing. Her high profile generates important revenue for the business. During the year ended December 19X4 the partnership earned net income of $87,000, shared in the 2:1 ratio. On December 31, 19X4, Jones's capital balance was $150,000, and Nichols's capital balance was $100,000.

Disagreements among partners
(Obj. 3)

Required

Respond to each of the following situations:

1. What explains the difference between the ratio of partner capital balances at December 31, 19X4, and the 2:1 ratio of partner investments and profit sharing?
2. Nichols believes that the profit-and-loss-sharing ratio is unfair. She proposes a change, but Jones insists on keeping the 2:1 ratio. What two factors may underlie Nichols's unhappiness?
3. During January 19X5 Jones learned that revenues of $16,000 were omitted from the reported 19X4 income. She brings this omission to Nichols's attention, pointing out that her share of this added income is three-fourths, or $12,000, and Nichols's share is one-fourth, or $4,000. Nichols believes that they should share this added income on the basis of their capital balances—60 percent, or $9,600, to Jones and 40 percent, or $6,400, to herself. Which partner is correct? Why?
4. Assume that the 19X4 $16,000 omission was an account payable for an operating expense. How would the partners share this amount?

2. Answer the following independent questions.

Questions about partnerships
(Obj. 1, 5)

1. The text suggests that a written partnership agreement should be drawn up between the partners in a partnership. One benefit of an agreement is that it provides a mechanism for resolving disputes between the partners. List five areas of dispute that might be resolved by a partnership agreement.
2. The statement has been made that "If you must take on a partner, make sure the partner is richer than you are." Why is this statement valid?
3. Willis, Boone, and Hill is a law partnership. Andrew Hill is planning to move to Canada. What options are available to Hill to enable him to convert his share of the partnership assets to cash?

ETHICAL ISSUE

Gail LaRue and Ben Loo operate The Office Center, an office supply store in Atlanta. The partners split profits and losses equally, and each takes an annual salary of $50,000. To even out the work load, Loo does the buying and LaRue serves as the accountant. From time to time they use small amounts of store merchandise for personal use. In preparing for a large private party, LaRue took engraved invitations, napkins, place mats, and other goods that cost $1,000. She recorded the transaction as follows:

Cost of Goods Sold	1,000	
Inventory.....................		1,000

Required

1. How should LaRue have recorded this transaction?
2. Discuss the ethical dimensions of LaRue's action.

Chapter 14

Corporate Organization, Paid-in Capital, and the Balance Sheet

After studying this chapter, you should be able to

1. Identify the characteristics of a corporation

2. Record the issuance of stock

3. Prepare the stockholders' equity section of a corporation balance sheet

4. Account for the incorporation of a going business

5. Account for cash dividends

6. Compute two profitability measures: return on assets and return on stockholders' equity

7. Distinguish among market value, redemption value, liquidation value, and book value

8. Account for a corporation's income tax

❝ *"Going public is a good way for a company to raise needed capital. Being publicly traded gets the company more attention in the financial pages and in brokerage-firm research reports. This allows the company, when it's doing well, to raise money more easily and cheaply. These benefits come at the cost of intense scrutiny from stockholders, who expect the company to continue to do well.* **❞**

Malcolm P. Appelbaum, Private Equity Investor, Wand Partners, Inc.

Started in 1958 and based in Glendale, California, IHOP Corporation develops, franchises, and operates International House of Pancakes family restaurants. There are almost 600 IHOPs (fewer than 60 of them owned by the company) in 35 states, Canada, and Japan—with big concentrations of IHOP restaurants in California, New York, New Jersey, Florida, and Texas.

IHOP still serves up stacks of great pancakes, but now you can buy the stock as well. IHOP Corp. went public in July 1991, offering 6.2 million shares at $10 apiece. The shares got off to a strong start and have performed well. IHOP's stock lately has traded at about $28 per share, down slightly from its 52-week high of $31.25. "For people who bought this [IHOP Corp. stock] at the offering," said Sandy Mehta, a vice-president with Ariel Capital Management, "this has been a really good investment." *Sources: Adapted from "Stacked Stock,"* Forbes, *July 6, 1992, p. 128, and "Looking at IHOP: Not Just Pancakes,"* The New York Times, *November 6, 1992.*

• • • • •

What does it mean to "go public," as IHOP did? A corporation *goes public* when it issues its stock to the general public. Instead, the owners of the corporation—the stockholders—can keep the stock *closely held*, that is, owned by a few insiders. A common reason for going public is to raise money for expansion. By offering its stock to the public, a company can hope to raise more money than if the stockholders are a limited group. IHOP probably went public for that reason. In its public offering of stock, IHOP hoped to receive cash of $62 million (6.2 million shares of stock at $10 each).

If you were a creditor of IHOP, would you look with favor or disfavor on IHOP's going public? You would probably be pleased, because by raising $62 million of owners' equity, IHOP would improve its ability to pay its debts to you. Immediately, IHOP's debt ratio (total liabilities divided by the total stockholders' equity) would drop. This change would indicate a decrease in IHOP's financial risk. Issuance of the stock would improve the company's ability to pay existing liabilities.

Characteristics of a Corporation

OBJECTIVE 1

Identify the characteristics of a corporation

The corporation is the dominant form of business organization in the United States. International House of Pancakes is an example. Although proprietorships and partnerships are more numerous, corporations transact more business and are larger in terms of total assets, sales revenue, and number of employees. Most well-known companies, such as PepsiCo, CBS, General Motors, IBM, and Boeing, are corporations. Their full names include *Corporation* or *Incorporated* (abbreviated *Corp.* and *Inc.*) to indicate that they are corporations—for example, CBS, Inc., and General Motors Corporation. This chapter and Chapters 15 through 17 discuss corporations.

Why is the corporation form of business so attractive? We now look at the features that distinguish corporations from proprietorships and partnerships.

Separate Legal Entity

A *corporation* is a business entity formed under state law. The state grants a **charter**, which is the document that gives a business the state's permission to form a corporation.

A corporation is a distinct entity from a legal perspective. We may consider the corporation as an artificial person that exists apart from its owners, who are called **stockholders** or **shareholders.** The corporation has many of the rights that a person has. For example, a corporation may buy, own, and sell property. Assets and liabilities in the business belong to the corporation rather than to its owners. The corporation may enter into contracts, sue, and be sued.

The owners' equity of a corporation is divided into shares of **stock.** A person becomes a stockholder by purchasing the stock of the corporation. The corporate charter specifies how much stock the corporation can issue (sell) and lists the other details of the corporation's relationship with the state.

Continuous Life and Transferability of Ownership

Most corporations have *continuous lives* regardless of changes in the ownership of their stock. The stockholders of IHOP or any corporation may transfer stock as they wish. They may sell or trade the stock to another person, give it away, bequeath it in a will, or dispose of it in any other way. The transfer of the stock does not affect the continuity of the corporation. Proprietorships and partnerships, on the other hand, terminate when their ownership changes.

No Mutual Agency

Mutual agency is an arrangement whereby all owners act as agents of the business. A contract signed by one owner is binding for the whole company. Mutual agency operates in partnerships but *not* in corporations. ◄▦ A stockholder of IHOP Corp. cannot commit the corporation to a contract (unless he or she is also an officer in the business). For this reason, a stockholder need not exercise the care that partners must in selecting co-owners of the business.

◄▦◄▦◄▦ We introduced the idea of mutual agency, which applies only to partnerships, in Chapter 13 (p. 523).

Limited Liability of Stockholders

A stockholder has **limited liability** for corporation debts. He or she has no personal obligation for corporation liabilities. The most that a stockholder can lose on an investment in a corporation's stock is the cost of the investment. Conversely, proprietors and partners are personally liable for all the debts of their businesses.

The combination of limited liability and no mutual agency means that persons can invest limited amounts in a corporation without fear of losing all their personal wealth because of a business failure. This feature enables a corporation to raise more capital from a wider group of investors than proprietorships and partnerships.

Separation of Ownership and Management

Stockholders own the business, but a *board of directors*—elected by the stockholders—appoints corporate officers to manage the business. Thus stockholders may invest $1,000 or $1 million in the corporation without having to manage the business or disrupt their personal affairs.

The theory of finance states that the goal of management is to maximize the value of the firm for the benefit of the stockholders. However, the separation between owners—stockholders—and management may create problems. Corporate officers may decide to run the business for their own benefit and not to the stockholders' advantage. Stockholders may find it difficult to lodge an effective protest against management policy because of the distance between them and management.

Corporate Taxation

Corporations are separate taxable entities. They pay a variety of taxes not borne by proprietorships or partnerships. These taxes include an annual franchise tax levied by the state. The franchise tax is paid to keep the corporation charter in force and enables the corporation to continue in business. Corporations also pay federal and state income taxes. Corporate earnings are subject to **double taxation**. First, corporations pay their own income taxes on corporate income. Then, stockholders pay personal income tax on the cash dividends (distributions) that they receive from corporations. This feature is different from taxation of proprietorships and partnerships, which pay no business income tax. Instead, the tax falls solely on the owners.

Government Regulation

Strong government regulation is an important disadvantage to the corporation. Because stockholders have only limited liability for corporation debts, outsiders doing business with the corporation can look no further than the corporation itself for any claims that may arise against the business. To protect persons who loan money to a corporation or who invest in its stock, states monitor the affairs of corporations. This government regulation consists mainly of ensuring that corporations disclose the business information that investors and creditors need to make informed decisions. For many corporations, this government regulation is expensive. Exhibit 14-1 lists the advantages and disadvantages of the corporation form of business organization.

Corporation Advantages	Corporation Disadvantages
1. Can raise more capital than a proprietorship or partnership can	1. Separation of ownership and management
2. Continuous life	2. Corporate taxation
3. Ease of transferring ownership	3. Government regulation
4. No mutual agency of stockholders	
5. Limited liability of stockholders	

CONCEPT HIGHLIGHT

EXHIBIT 14-1
Advantages and Disadvantages of a Corporation

Organization of a Corporation

Key Point: Most corporations are authorized to issue many more shares of stock than they intend to issue originally. The corporation can raise additional capital by selling stock in the future without having to request state authorization of more shares.

Creation of a corporation begins when its organizers, called the **incorporators**, obtain a charter from the state. The charter includes the authorization for the corporation to issue a certain number of shares of stock, which are shares of ownership in the corporation. The incorporators pay fees, sign the charter, and file required documents with the state. Then the corporation comes into existence. The incorporators agree to a set of **bylaws**, which act as the constitution for governing the corporation.

The ultimate control of the corporation rests with the stockholders, who receive one vote for each share of stock they own. The stockholders elect the members of the **board of directors**, which sets policy for the corporation and appoints the officers. The board elects a **chairperson**, who usually is the most powerful person in the corporation. The board also designates the **president**, who is the chief operating officer in charge of day-to-day operations. Most corporations also have vice-presidents in charge of sales, manufacturing, accounting and finance, and other key areas. Often the president and one or more vice-presidents are also elected to the board of directors. Exhibit 14-2 shows the authority structure in a corporation.

The structure of proprietorships, partnerships, and corporations is similar in that all three types of business have owners, managers, and employees. In proprietorships and partnerships, policy decisions are usually made by the owners—the proprietor or the partners. In a corporation, however, the managers who set policy—the board of directors—may or may not be owners (stockholders).

Most corporations have an annual meeting at which the stockholders elect directors and make other stockholder decisions. Stockholders unable to attend this annual meeting may vote on corporation matters by use of a *proxy*, which is a legal document that expresses the stockholder's preference and appoints another person to cast the vote.

EXHIBIT 14-2

Authority Structure in a Corporation

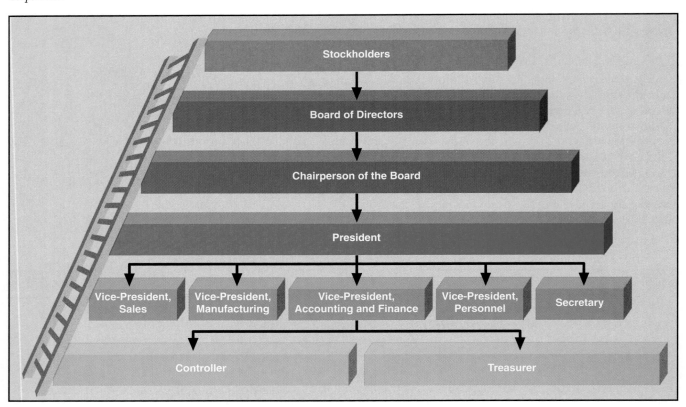

A corporation keeps a record of its stockholders. The business must notify the stockholders of the annual stockholder meeting and mail them dividend payments (which we discuss later in this chapter). Large companies use a registrar to maintain the stockholder list and a transfer agent to issue stock certificates. Banks provide these registration and transfer services. The transfer agent handles the change in stock ownership from one shareholder to another.

Capital Stock

A corporation issues *stock certificates* to its owners in exchange for their investments in the business. Because stock represents the corporation's capital, it is often called *capital stock*. The basic unit of capital stock is called a *share*. A corporation may issue a stock certificate for any number of shares it wishes—one share, one hundred shares, or any other number. (But we shall see that the total number of *authorized* shares is limited by charter.) Exhibit 14-3 depicts an actual stock certificate for 288 shares of common stock. The certificate shows the company name, the stockholder name, the number of shares, and the par value of the stock (which we discuss later).

Stock in the hands of a stockholder is said to be **outstanding**. The total number of shares of stock outstanding at any time represents 100 percent ownership of the corporation.

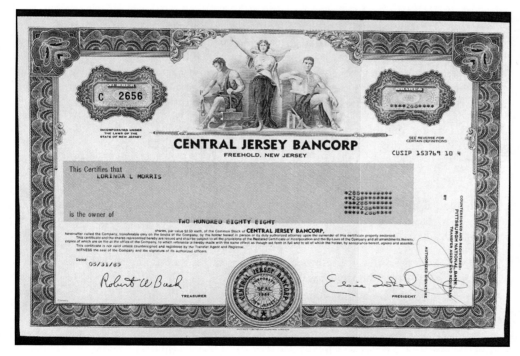

EXHIBIT 14-3
Stock Certificate

Key Point: Note the differences among the following terms: *Authorized stock*—the number of shares the corporation can issue. This number is specified in the charter but can be increased.
Issued stock—stock that has been sold to a stockholder and for which a stock certificate has been issued.
Outstanding stock—stock that is in the hands of a stockholder. Not all issued stock is outstanding. Corporations may buy their stock back; this stock, treasury stock, has been issued but is not outstanding.

Stockholders' Equity

The balance sheet of a corporation reports assets and liabilities in the same way as a proprietorship or a partnership. However, owners' equity of a corporation—called **stockholders' equity**—is reported differently. State laws require corporations to report the sources of their capital. The two most basic sources of capital are invest-

Assets	$20,565	Liabilities	$11,806
		Stockholders' Equity	
		Paid-in capital:	
		Common stock.........................	**756**
		Retained earnings......................	**8,003**
		Total stockholders'equity...........	**8,759**
		Total liabilities and	
Total assets..............	$20,565	stockholders' equity	$20,565

ments by the stockholders, called **paid-in capital** or **contributed capital**, and capital earned through profitable operation of the business, called **retained earnings**. Exhibit 14-4 outlines a summarized version of the balance sheet of Wal-Mart Stores, Inc., to show how to report these categories of stockholders' equity.

Common stock is paid-in capital. It is regarded as the permanent capital of the business because it is *not* subject to withdrawal by the stockholders.

An investment of cash or any other asset in a corporation increases its assets and stockholders' equity. Wal-Mart's entry for receipt of a $20,000 stockholder investment in the business is:

Oct. 20	Cash	20,000	
	Common Stock......................................		20,000
	Investment by stockholders.		

Profitable operations produce income, which increases stockholders' equity through an account called Retained Earnings. At the end of the year, the balance of the Income Summary account is closed to Retained Earnings. For example, if Wal-Mart's net income is $19,995 million, Income Summary will have a $19,995 million credit balance. Wal-Mart's closing entry will debit Income Summary to transfer net income to Retained Earnings as follows (in millions of dollars):

Dec. 31	Income Summary...	19,995	
	Retained Earnings....................................		19,995
	To close Income Summary by transferring net *income* to Retained Earnings.		

If operations produce a net *loss* rather than net income, the Income Summary account will have a debit balance. Income Summary must be credited to close it. With a $60,000 loss, the closing entry is the following:

Dec. 31	Retained Earnings...	60,000	
	Income Summary......................................		60,000
	To close Income Summary by transferring net *loss* to Retained Earnings.		

A large loss may cause a debit balance in the Retained Earnings account. This condition—called a Retained Earnings **deficit**, or accumulated deficit—is reported on the balance sheet as a negative amount in stockholders' equity. HAL, INC., which owns Hawaiian Airlines, Inc., reported this deficit:

Stockholders' Equity	
Paid-in capital:	
Common stock	$ 50,101,203
Deficit...	(192,821,668)
Total stockholders' equity	$(142,720,465)

HAL's deficit was so large that it produced a negative amount of stockholders' equity. This situation is unusual for a going concern.

If the corporation has been profitable and has sufficient cash, a distribution of cash may be made to the stockholders. Such distributions—called **dividends**—decrease both the assets and the retained earnings of the business. The balance of the Retained Earnings account at any time is the sum of earnings accumulated since incorporation, minus any losses and minus all dividends distributed to stockholders. Retained Earnings is reported separately from paid-in capital because retained earnings is used for dividends. Most states prohibit the practice of using paid-in capital for dividends. Accountants use the term *legal capital* to refer to the portion of stockholders' equity that *cannot* be used for dividends.

Some people think of Retained Earnings as a fund of cash. It is not, because Retained Earnings is an element of stockholders' equity, representing a claim against all assets resulting from cumulative earnings minus cumulative dividends since the corporation's beginning. In short, remember that dividends are *paid* out of assets, not out of retained earnings.

Stockholders' Rights

The ownership of stock entitles stockholders to four basic rights, unless specific rights are withheld by agreement with the stockholders:

1. *Vote*. The right to participate in management by voting on matters that come before the stockholders. This is the stockholder's sole right to a voice in the management of the corporation. A stockholder is entitled to one vote for each share of stock owned.
2. *Dividends*. The right to receive a proportionate part of any dividend. Each share of stock in a particular class receives an equal dividend.
3. *Liquidation*. The right to receive a proportionate share (based on number of shares held) of any assets remaining after the corporation pays its liabilities in liquidation.
4. *Preemption*. The right to maintain one's proportionate ownership in the corporation. Suppose you own 5 percent of a corporation's stock. If the corporation issues 100,000 new shares of stock, it must offer you the opportunity to buy 5 percent (5,000) of the new shares. This right, called the *preemptive right*, is usually withheld from the stockholders.

Classes of Stock

Corporations issue different types of stock to appeal to a wide variety of investors. The stock of a corporation may be either common or preferred and par or no-par.

Common and Preferred Stock

Every corporation issues *common stock*, the most basic form of capital stock. Unless designated otherwise, the word *stock* is understood to mean "common stock." Common stockholders have the four basic rights of stock ownership, unless a right is specifically withheld. For example, some companies issue Class A common stock, which usually carries the right to vote, and Class B common stock, which may be nonvoting. (Classes of common stock may also be designated Series A, Series B, and so on.) The general ledger has a separate account for each class of common stock. In describing a corporation, we would say the common stockholders are the owners of the business.

Investors who buy common stock take the ultimate risk with a corporation. The corporation makes no promises to pay them. If the corporation succeeds, it will pay dividends to its stockholders, but if net income and cash are too low, the stockholders may receive no dividends. The stock of successful corporations increases in value, and investors enjoy the benefit of selling the stock at a gain. But stock prices can decrease, leaving the investors holding worthless stock certificates. Because common stockholders take a risky investment position, they demand increases in stock prices, high dividends, or both. If the corporation does not deliver, the stockholders sell the stock, and its market price falls. Short of bankruptcy, this is one of the worst things that can happen to a corporation because it means that the company cannot raise capital as needed.

Short Exercise: For the following list of characteristics of capital stock, indicate whether each characteristic applies to preferred and common stock:
1. Stated dividend
2. Voting rights
3. Preemptive right
4. Priority to receive assets in the event of liquidation
5. Cumulative
6. Callable

A:	Preferred	Common
1.	Yes	No
2.	Yes	Yes
3.	Maybe	Maybe
4.	Yes	No
5.	Yes	No
6.	Maybe	No

Preferred stock gives its owners certain advantages over common stockholders. These benefits include the priority to receive dividends before the common stockholders and the priority to receive assets before the common stockholders if the corporation liquidates. Because of the preferred stockholders' priorities, common stock represents the residual ownership in the corporation's assets after the liabilities and the claims of preferred stockholders have been subtracted. Owners of preferred stock also have the four basic stockholder rights, unless a right is specifically denied. Often the right to vote is withheld from preferred stockholders. Companies may issue different classes of preferred stock. (Class A and Class B or Series A and Series B, for example). Each class is recorded in a separate account.

Investors who buy preferred stock take less risk than do common stockholders. Why? Because corporations pay a fixed amount of dividends on preferred stock. Investors usually buy preferred stock to earn those dividends. An increase in the market value of preferred stock is less important than an increase in the market value of common stock because preferred stocks' values do not fluctuate much.

Preferred stock operates as a hybrid somewhere between common stock and long-term debt. Like debt, preferred stock pays a fixed dividend. But like stock, the dividend becomes a liability only after the board of directors has declared the dividend. Also, there is no obligation to pay back true preferred stock in the manner required by debt. Preferred stock that must be redeemed (paid back) by the corporation is a liability masquerading as a stock. Experienced investors treat mandatorily redeemable preferred stock as part of total liabilities, not as part of owners' equity. Preferred stock that must be redeemed is rare.

Preferred stock is rarer than you might think. A recent survey of 600 corporations revealed that only 147 of them (less than 25 percent) had some preferred stock outstanding (Exhibit 14-5). All corporations have common stock.

Why is preferred stock so unpopular? Mainly because dividend payments are not tax-deductible. Dividends are a distribution of assets created by earnings. Dividends are *not* an expense. If companies are going to commit to pay a fixed amount (of preferred dividends) each year, they want a tax deduction for the payment. Therefore, most companies would rather borrow money and get a tax deduction for the interest expense. Exhibit 14-6 summarizes the similarities and differences among common stock, preferred stock, and long-term debt.

EXHIBIT 14-5

Preferred Stock

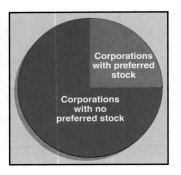

EXHIBIT 14-6

Comparison of Common Stock, Preferred Stock, and Long-Term Debt

	Common Stock	Preferred Stock	Long-Term Debt
Investment risk	High	Medium	Low
Corporate obligation to repay principal	No	No	Yes
Dividends/interest	Dividends	Dividends	Tax-deductible interest expense
Corporate obligation to pay dividends/interest	Only after declaration	Only after declaration	At fixed dates
Fluctuations in market value under normal conditions	High	Medium	Low

Par Value and No-Par Stock

Stock may be par value stock or no-par stock. **Par value** is an arbitrary amount assigned to a share of stock. Most companies set the par value of their common stock quite low. The *common* stock par value of Kimberly-Clark, best known for its Kleenex tissues, is $1.25 per share. Of 300 million shares of stock, Kimberly-Clark has issued 161.9 million shares at that par

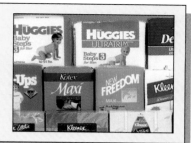

"The common stock par value of Kimberly-Clark, best known for its Kleenex tissues, is $1.25 per share."

value. J. C. Penney's common stock par value is 50¢ per share, and Bethlehem Steel's common stock par value is $8 per share. Par value of preferred stock is often higher; $100 per share is typical, but some preferred stocks have par value of $25 and $10. Par value is used to compute dividends on preferred stock, as we shall see.

No-par stock does not have par value. Kimberly-Clark has 20 million shares of *preferred* stock with no par value. But some no-par stock has a *stated value*, which makes it similar to par value stock. The stated value is also an arbitrary amount that accountants treat as though it were par value.

Issuing Stock

Large corporations such as PepsiCo, Xerox, and British Petroleum need huge quantities of money to operate. They cannot expect to finance all their operations through borrowing. They need capital that they raise by issuing stock. The charter that the incorporators receive from the state includes an **authorization of stock**—that is, a provision giving the state's permission for the business to issue—to sell—a certain number of shares of stock. Corporations may sell the stock directly to the stockholders or use the service of an *underwriter*, such as the brokerage firms Merrill Lynch and Dean Witter. An underwriter agrees to buy all the stock it cannot sell to its clients.

> **OBJECTIVE 2**
> **Record the issuance of stock**

The corporation need not issue all the stock that the state allows. Management may hold some stock back and issue it later if the need for additional capital arises. The stock that the corporation does issue to stockholders is called *issued stock*. Only by issuing stock—not by receiving authorization—does the corporation increase the asset and stockholders' equity amounts on its balance sheet.

The price that the stockholder pays to acquire stock from the corporation is called the *issue price*. Often the issue price far exceeds the stock's par value because the par value was intentionally set quite low. A combination of market factors, including the company's comparative earnings record, financial position, prospects for success, and general business conditions, determines issue price. Investors will not pay more than market value for the stock. The following sections show how to account for the issuance of stock.

Key Point: Owners invest in a corporation by buying stock. Issuance of stock increases the corporation's assets and stockholders' equity.

Issuing Common Stock

Companies often advertise the issuance of their stock to attract investors. *The Wall Street Journal* is the most popular medium for the advertisements, which are also called *tombstones*. Exhibit 14-7 is a reproduction of IHOP's tombstone that appeared in *The Wall Street Journal* on July 15, 1991, with the data given in the chapter-opening story.

The lead underwriter of IHOP's public offering was The First Boston Corporation. Twenty-one other domestic brokerage firms and investment bankers sold IHOP's stock to their clients. Outside the United States, six investment bankers assisted with the offering. Altogether, IHOP hoped to raise approximately $62 million

EXHIBIT 14-7

Announcement of Public Offering of IHOP Stock

July 15, 1991

6,200,000 Shares

IHOP CORP.

Common Stock
($.01 par value)

Price $10 Per Share

These securities are being offered in the United States and internationally.

United States Offering
4,960,000 Shares

The First Boston Corporation

Alex. Brown & Sons Incorporated	Donaldson, Lufkin & Jenrette Securities Corporation	A. G. Edwards & Sons, Inc.
Goldman, Sachs & Co.	Lehman Brothers	Montgomery Securities
PaineWebber Incorporated		Prudential Securities Incorporated
Smith Barney, Harris Upham & Co. Incorporated		Wertheim Schroder & Co. Incorporated
William Blair & Company	J.C. Bradford & Co.	D.A. Davidson & Co. Incorporated
Ladenburg, Thalmann & Co. Inc.		C.J. Lawrence Inc.
McDonald & Company Securities, Inc.		Morgan Keegan & Company, Inc.
Ragen MacKenzie Incorporated		Raymond James & Associates, Inc.
The Robinson-Humphrey Company, Inc.		Stephens Inc.

International Offering
1,240,000 Shares

Credit Suisse First Boston Limited

ABN AMRO	Banque Indosuez
Dresdner Bank Aktiengesellschaft	County NatWest Limited
Yamaichi International (Europe) Limited	

of capital. As it turned out, IHOP issued only 3.2 million of the shares and received cash of approximately $32 million.

ISSUING COMMON STOCK AT PAR   Suppose IHOP's common stock carried a par value of $10 per share. The stock issuance entry would be:

Jan. 8	Cash (3,200,000 × $10)	32,000,000	
	Common Stock...		32,000,000
	To issue common stock at par.		

The amount invested in the corporation, $32 million in this case, is called paid-in capital or contributed capital. The credit to Common Stock records an increase in the paid-in capital of the corporation.

ISSUING COMMON STOCK AT A PREMIUM   Many corporations set par value at a low amount. They usually issue common stock for a price above par value. The excess amount above par is called a *premium*. IHOP's common stock has a par value of $0.01 (1 cent) per share. The $9.99 difference between issue price ($10) and par value ($0.01) is a premium. This sale of stock increases the corporation's paid-in capital by the full $10, the total issue price of the stock. Both the par value of the stock and the premium are part of paid-in capital. A premium on the sale of stock is not gain, income, or profit to the corporation, because the entity is dealing with its own stockholders. This situation illustrates one of the fundamentals of accounting: A company can neither earn a profit nor incur a loss when it sells its stock to, or buys its stock from, its own stockholders.

With a par value of $0.01, IHOP's entry to record the issuance of the stock is

July 23	Cash (3,200,000 × $10)...	32,000,000	
	Common Stock (3,200,000 × $0.01)		32,000
	Paid-in Capital in Excess of Par—		
	Common (3,200,000 × $9.99)		31,968,000
	To issue common stock at a premium.		

Account titles that could be used in place of Paid-in Capital in Excess of Par—Common are Additional Paid-in Capital—Common and Premium on Common Stock. Since both par value and premium amounts increase the corporation's capital, they appear in the stockholders' equity section of the balance sheet.

At the end of the year, IHOP Corp. would report stockholders' equity on its balance sheet as follows, assuming that the corporate charter authorizes 40,000,000 shares of common stock and retained earnings is $26,000,000.

<table>
<tr><td colspan="2" align="center">Stockholders' Equity</td></tr>
<tr><td>Paid-in capital:</td><td></td></tr>
<tr><td>Common stock, $0.01 par, 40 million shares
   authorized, 3.2 million shares issued.........................</td><td>$ 32,000</td></tr>
<tr><td>Paid-in capital in excess of par ....</td><td>31,968,000</td></tr>
<tr><td>   Total paid-in capital...</td><td>32,000,000</td></tr>
<tr><td>Retained earnings...</td><td>26,000,000</td></tr>
<tr><td>Total stockholders' equity ....</td><td>$58,000,000</td></tr>
</table>

We determine the dollar amount reported for common stock by multiplying the total number of shares *issued* (3.2 million) by the par value per share. The *authorization* reports the maximum number of shares the company may issue under its charter.

Short Exercise: Answer the following questions on the basis of this journal entry for stock issued at $23 per share:

Cash	276,000
Common Stock	180,000
Paid-in Cap. in	
Excess of Par—	
Common.......	96,000

(1) How many shares of stock were issued? (2) What is the par value? (3) What is the excess over par value ("premium") per share? *A:* (1) $276,000/$23 = 12,000 shares (2) $180,000/12,000 shares = $15 (3) $23 − $15 = $8 per share

STOP & THINK IHOP Corp. actually had total liabilities of $92 million on the balance-sheet date just given. What was IHOP's debt ratio?

Answer: The debt ratio is 0.61:

$$\frac{\text{Total liabilities}}{\text{Total assets}} = \frac{\$92{,}000{,}000}{\$92{,}000{,}000 + \$58{,}000{,}000} = 0.61$$

ISSUING NO-PAR COMMON STOCK   When a company issues stock that has no par value, there can be no premium. A recent survey of 600 companies revealed that they had 66 issues of no-par stock.

When no-par stock is issued, the asset received is debited, and the stock account is credited. Glenwood Corporation, which manufactures skateboards, issues 300 shares of no-par common stock for $20 per share. The stock issuance entry is:

Aug. 14	Cash (300 × $20)	6,000	
	Common Stock		6,000
	To issue no-par common stock.		

Regardless of the stock's price, Cash is debited and Common Stock is credited for the amount of cash received. There is no Paid-in Capital in Excess of Par for true no-par stock.

Assume that the charter authorizes Glenwood to issue 5,000 shares of no-par stock and that the company has $3,000 in retained earnings. The corporation will report stockholders' equity as follows:

Stockholders' Equity	
Paid-in capital:	
Common stock, no par, 5,000 shares authorized, 300 shares issued	$6,000
Retained earnings	3,000
Total stockholders' equity	$9,000

ISSUING NO-PAR COMMON STOCK WITH A STATED VALUE   Accounting for no-par stock with a stated value is identical to accounting for par value stock. The premium account for no-par common stock with a stated value is entitled Paid-in Capital in Excess of Stated Value—Common.

ISSUING COMMON STOCK FOR ASSETS OTHER THAN CASH   When a corporation issues stock in exchange for assets other than cash, it debits the assets received for their current market value and credits the capital accounts accordingly. The assets' prior book value does not matter because the stockholder will demand stock equal to the market value of the asset given. Kahn Corporation issued 15,000 shares of its $1-par common stock for equipment worth $4,000 and a building worth $120,000. The entry is:

Nov. 12	Equipment	4,000	
	Building	120,000	
	Common Stock (15,000 × $1)		15,000
	Paid-in Capital in Excess of Par—Common ($124,000 – $15,000)		109,000
	To issue common stock in exchange for equipment and a building.		

Short Exercise: Prepare journal entries for each situation: A company issues

1. 100,000 shares of no-par common stock for $35 per share. *A:*

Cash 3,500,000
  Common Stock
    (100,000 × $35) . 3,500,000

2. 50,000 shares of $10-par common stock for $15 per share. *A:*

Cash
($50,000 × $15)........750,000
  Common Stock
    (50,000 × $10) ...   500,000
  Paid-in Cap. in Exc.
    of Par—Com.
    (50,000 × $5)......... 250,000

3. 160,000 shares of $1-par common stock in exchange for land valued at $55,000, a building valued at $125,000, and a computer valued at $5,000. *A:*

Equipment   5,000
Building............. 125,000
Land 55,000
  Common Stock .   160,000
  Paid-in Cap. in Exc.
    of Par—Com. ...   25,000

4. 20,000 shares of no-par common stock with a $2 stated value for $3.50 per share. *A:*

Cash (20,000
  × $3.50).............70,000
  Common Stock
    (20,000 × $2).   40,000
  Paid-in Cap. in Exc.
    of Stated Val.—Com.
    (20,000 × $1.50)   30,000

STOP & THINK How did this transaction affect Kahn Corporation's paid-in capital? Retained earnings? Total stockholders' equity?

Answer:

Paid-in Capital	Effect on Retained Earnings	Total Stockholders' Equity
Increase $124,000	None	Increase $124,000

Issuing Preferred Stock

Accounting for preferred stock follows the pattern illustrated for common stock. The charter of Brown-Forman Corporation, a distilling company, authorizes issuance of 1,177,948 shares of 4-percent, $10 par preferred stock. Assume that on July 31 the company issued all the shares at a price equal to the par value. (Preferred stock usually sells at its par value or at a premium.) The issuance entry is:

July 31	Cash	11,779,480	
	Preferred Stock (1,177,948 × $10)		11,779,480
	To issue preferred stock at par.		

If Brown-Forman had issued the preferred stock at a premium, the entry would have also credited an account titled Paid-in Capital in Excess of Par—Preferred. A corporation lists separate accounts for Paid-in Capital in Excess of Par on Preferred Stock and on Common Stock to differentiate the two classes of equity.

Accounting for *no-par preferred stock* follows the pattern illustrated for no-par common stock.

Short Exercise: From this list, calculate total paid-in capital and total stockholders' equity:

Common Stock........... $12,500
Preferred Stock........... 6,000
Paid-in Cap. in Exc.
  of Stated Val.—Com. 3,755
Paid-in Capital—
  Preferred................. 836
Retained Earnings...... 18,934

A: Total paid-in capital =
$23,091 ($12,500 + $6,000 + $3,755 + $836)
Total stockholder's equity = $42,025 ($23,091 + $18,934)

Review of Accounting for Stock

Let's review the first half of this chapter by showing the stockholders' equity section of Medina Corporation's balance sheet in Exhibit 14-8. (Assume that all figures, which are arbitrary, are correct.) Note the two sections of stockholders' equity: paid-in capital and retained earnings. Also observe the order of the equity accounts: preferred stock at par value, paid-in capital in excess of par on preferred stock, common stock at par value, and paid-in capital in excess of par on common stock.

OBJECTIVE 3

Prepare the stockholders' equity section of a corporation balance sheet

Stockholders' Equity	
Paid-in capital:	
Preferred stock, 5%, $100 par, 5,000 shares authorized, 400 shares issued	$ 40,000
Paid-in capital in excess of par—preferred	14,000
Common stock, $10 par, 20,000 shares authorized, 4,500 shares issued...	45,000
Paid-in capital in excess of par—common	72,000
Total paid-in capital..	171,000
Retained earnings..	85,000
Total stockholders' equity	$256,000

EXHIBIT 14-8
Part of Medina Corporation's Balance Sheet

1. Test your understanding of the first half of this chapter by answering whether each of the following statements is true or false.

   a. A stockholder may bind the corporation to a contract.
   b. The policy-making body in a corporation is called the board of directors.
   c. The owner of 100 shares of preferred stock has greater voting rights than the owner of 100 shares of common stock.
   d. Par value stock is worth more than no-par stock.
   e. Issuance of 1,000 shares of $5 par value stock at $12 increases contributed capital by $12,000.
   f. The issuance of no-par stock with a stated value is fundamentally different from issuing par value stock.
   g. A corporation issues its preferred stock in exchange for land and a building with a combined market value of $200,000. This transaction increases the corporation's owners' equity by $200,000 regardless of the assets' prior book value.
   h. Preferred stock is a riskier investment than common stock.

2. The brewery Adolph Coors Company has two classes of common stock. Only the Class A common stockholders are entitled to vote. The company's balance sheet included the following presentation:

Shareholders' Equity

Capital stock	
Class A common stock, voting, $1 par value,	
authorized and issued 1,260,000 shares	$ 1,260,000
Class B common stock, nonvoting, no-par value,	
authorized and issued 46,200,000 shares	11,000,000
	12,260,000
Additional paid-in capital...	2,011,000
Retained earnings...	872,403,000
	$886,674,000

Required

a. Record the issuance of the Class A common stock. Assume that the additional paid-in capital amount is related to the Class A common stock. Use the Coors account titles.
b. Record the issuance of the Class B common stock. Use the Coors account titles.
c. Rearrange the Coors stockholders' equity section to correspond to the following format:

Shareholders' Equity

Paid-in capital:	
Class A common stock...	$
Paid-in capital in excess of par—Class A	
common stock...	
Class B common stock...	
Total paid-in capital..	
Retained earnings...	
Total shareholders' equity	$

d. What is the total paid-in capital of the company?
e. How did Coors withhold the voting privilege from their Class B common stockholders?

1. Answers to true/false statements:

    a. False   **b.** True   **c.** False   **d.** False   **e.** True

    f. False   **g.** True   **h.** False

2. **a.** Cash 3,271,000

        Class A Common Stock   1,260,000

        Additional Paid-in capital   2,011,000

    To record issuance of Class A common stock

    at a premium.

    b. Cash 11,000,000

        Class B Common Stock   11,000,000

    To record issuance of Class B common stock.

    c. Shareholders' Equity

      Paid-in capital:

      Class A common stock, voting, $1 par value,

          authorized and issued 1,260,000 shares .... $ 1,260,000

      Paid-in capital in excess of par—Class A common stock ..   2,011,000

      Class B common stock, nonvoting, no par

          value, authorized and issued 46,200,000 shares   11,000,000

        Total paid-in capital   14,271,000

      Retained earnings   872,403,000

      Total shareholders' equity $886,674,000

    d. Total paid-in capital is $14,271,000, as shown in the answer to (c).

    e. The voting privilege was withheld from stockholders by specific agreement with them.

Donations Received by a Corporation

Corporations occasionally receive gifts, or *donations*. For example, city council members may offer a company free land to encourage it to locate in their city. Cities in the southern United States have lured some companies away from the North with such an offer. The free land is a donation. For example, J. C. Penney Co. and American Airlines moved corporate headquarters from New York City to the Dallas-Fort Worth area because of concessions granted

"American Airlines moved corporate headquarters from New York City to the Dallas-Fort Worth area because of concessions granted by the Texas cities."

by the Texas cities. Also, a stockholder may make a donation to the corporation in the form of cash, land or other assets, or stock.

A donation increases the assets of the corporation, but the donor (giver) receives no ownership interest in the company in return. A donation increases the corporation's revenue and thus affects income and retained earnings. The corporation records a donation by debiting the asset received at its current market value and by crediting Revenue from Donations, which is reported as Other Revenue on the income statement. But a donation received from a governmental entity is recorded as a credit to Donated Capital. For example, American Airlines would credit Donated Capital for the value of any land it receives from a city or county government.[1]

---

[1]FASB, *Statement of Financial Accounting Standards No. 116, Accounting for Contributions Received and Contributions Made* (June 1993).

Incorporation of a Going Business

OBJECTIVE 4

Account for the incorporation of a going business

You may dream of having your own business some day, or you may currently be a business proprietor or partner. Businesses that begin as a proprietorship or a partnership often incorporate at a later date. By incorporating a going business (a "going concern"), the proprietor or partners avoid the unlimited liability for business debts. And, as we discussed earlier, incorporating makes it easier to raise capital.

To account for the incorporation of a going business, we close the owner equity accounts of the prior entity and set up the stockholders' equity accounts of the corporation. Suppose Santa Fe Travel Associates is a partnership owned by Joe Brown and Monica Lee. The partnership balance sheet, after all adjustments and closing entries have been made, reports Joe Brown, Capital, of $50,000, and Monica Lee, Capital, of $70,000. The travel agency is incorporated as Santa Fe Travel Company, Inc., with an authorization to issue 200,000 shares of $1-par common stock. Brown and Lee agree to receive common stock equal in par value to their partnership owner's equity balances. The entry to record the incorporation of the business is:

Feb. 1	Joe Brown, Capital...	50,000	
	Monica Lee, Capital...	70,000	
	Common Stock		120,000
	To incorporate the business, close the capital accounts of the partnership, and issue common stock to the incorporators.		

Organization Cost

The costs of organizing a corporation, such as the Dallas-based Mary Kay Cosmetics, Inc., include legal fees, taxes and fees paid to the state, and charges by promoters for selling the stock. These costs are grouped in an account titled Organization Cost, which is an asset because these costs contribute to a business's start-up. Suppose Mary Kay pays legal fees of $15,000 and the state of Texas incorporation fee of $500 to organize the corporation. In addition, a promoter charges a fee of $24,000 for selling the stock and receives the corporation's no-par stock as payment. Mary Kay's journal entries to record these organization costs are:

"The costs of organizing a corporation, such as the Dallas-based Mary Kay Cosmetics, Inc., include legal fees, taxes and fees paid to the state, and charges by promoters for selling the stock."

Mar. 31	Organization Cost ($15,000 + $500)...............................	15,500	
	Cash		15,500
	Legal fees and state incorporation fee to organize the corporation.		
Apr. 3	Organization Cost	24,000	
	Common Stock...		24,000
	Promoter fee for selling stock in organization.		

Organization cost is an *intangible asset*, reported on the balance sheet along with patents, trademarks, goodwill, and any other intangibles. We know that an intangible asset should be amortized over its useful life, and organization costs will benefit the corporation for as long as the corporation operates. But how long will that be? We cannot know in advance, but we still must expense these costs over some period of time. GAAP allows a maximum 40-year useful life. Companies amortize organization costs over a period of between 5 and 40 years. If we assume a 10-year life, the preceding organization cost of $39,500 ($15,500 + $24,000) would be amortized by a debit to Amortization Expense and a credit to Organization Cost for $3,950 ($39,500/10) each year.

Dividend Dates

A corporation must declare a dividend before paying it. The board of directors alone has the authority to declare a dividend. The corporation has no obligation to pay a dividend until the board declares one, but once declared, the dividend becomes a legal liability of the corporation. Three relevant dates for dividends are:

1. *Declaration date.* On the declaration date, the board of directors announces the intention to pay the dividend. The declaration creates a liability for the corporation. Declaration is recorded by debiting Retained Earnings and crediting Dividends Payable.
2. *Date of record.* The corporation announces the record date, which follows the declaration date by a few weeks, as part of the declaration. The corporation makes no journal entry on the date of record because no transaction occurs. Nevertheless, much work takes place behind the scenes to properly identify the stockholders of record on this date because the stock is being traded continuously. Only the people who own the stock on the date of record receive the dividend.
3. *Payment date.* Payment of the dividend usually follows the record date by two to four weeks. Payment is recorded by debiting Dividends Payable and crediting Cash.

Key Point: A stock will sell "ex-dividend" (without the dividend) three business days before the date of record. This three-day period gives the registrar time to update all stock transactions.

Dividends on Preferred and Common Stock

Declaration of a cash dividend is recorded by debiting Retained Earnings and crediting Dividends Payable as follows:

OBJECTIVE 5

Account for cash dividends

June 19	Retained Earnings	XXX	
	Dividends Payable...		XXX
	To declare a cash dividend.		

Payment of the dividend, which usually follows declaration by a few weeks, is recorded by debiting Dividends Payable and crediting Cash:

July 2	Dividends Payable	XXX	
	Cash...		XXX
	To pay a cash dividend.		

Dividends Payable is a current liability. When a company has issued both preferred and common stock, the preferred stockholders receive their dividends first. The common stockholders receive dividends only if the total declared dividend is large enough to pay the preferred stockholders first.

In addition to its common stock, Pine Industries, Inc., has 9,000 shares of preferred stock outstanding. Preferred dividends are paid at the annual rate of $1.75 per share. Assume that Pine declares an annual dividend of $150,000. The allocation to preferred and common stockholders is as follows:

Short Exercise: Georgia Corporation was organized on 1/1/X1 with 100,000 shares of stock authorized; 50,000 shares were issued on 1/5/X1. Georgia earned $50,000 during 19X1 and declared a dividend of $0.40 per share on 11/30/X1 payable to stockholders on 1/1/X2. (1) Journalize the declaration and payment of the dividend. (2) Compute the balance of retained earnings on 12/31/X1. *A:*

(1) 11/30/X1 declaration
Retained Earnings .   20,000
    Div. Payable   20,000
      (50,000 shares × $0.40)

1/1/X2 payment
Div. Payable   20,000
    Cash   20,000
(2) The balance in retained earnings is $30,000 ($50,000 – $20,000). The declaration on 11/30/X1—not the payment on 1/1/X2—reduced retained earnings.

	Total Dividend of $150,000
Preferred dividend (9,000 shares × $1.75 per share).................	$ 15,750
Common dividend (remainder: $150,000 – $15,750)...............	134,250
Total dividend	$150,000

If Pine declares only a $20,000 dividend, preferred stockholders receive $15,750, and the common stockholders receive $4,250 ($20,000 – $15,750).

This example illustrates an important relationship between preferred stock and common stock. To an investor, the preferred stock is safer because it receives dividends first. For example, if Pine Industries earns only enough net income to pay the preferred stockholders' dividends, the owners of common stock receive no dividends. However, the earnings potential from an investment in common stock is much greater than from an investment in preferred stock. Preferred dividends are usually limited to the specified amount, but there is no upper limit on the amount of common dividends.

We noted that preferred stockholders enjoy the advantage of priority over common stockholders in receiving dividends. The dividend preference is stated as a percentage rate or a dollar amount. For example, preferred stock may be "6 percent preferred," which means that owners of the preferred stock receive an annual dividend of 6 percent of the par value of the stock. If par value is $100 per share, preferred stockholders receive an annual cash dividend of $6 per share (6 percent of $100). The preferred stock may be "$3 preferred," which means that stockholders receive an annual dividend of $3 per share regardless of the preferred stock's par value. The dividend rate on no-par preferred stock is stated in a dollar amount per share.

Cumulative and Noncumulative Preferred Stock

The allocation of dividends may be complex if the preferred stock is *cumulative*. Corporations sometimes fail to pay a dividend to their preferred stockholders. This occurrence is called *passing the dividend*, and the passed dividends are said to be *in arrears*. The owners of **cumulative preferred stock** must receive all dividends in arrears plus the current year's dividend before the corporation pays dividends to the common stockholders.

The preferred stock of Pine Industries is cumulative. Suppose the company passed the 19X4 preferred dividend of $15,750. Before paying dividends to its common stockholders in 19X5, the company must first pay preferred dividends of $15,750 for both 19X4 and 19X5, a total of $31,500. *Preferred stock is cumulative in the eyes of the law unless it is labeled as noncumulative.*

Assume that Pine Industries passes its 19X4 preferred dividend. In 19X5 the company declares a $50,000 dividend. The entry to record the declaration is:

Sep. 6	Retained Earnings..	50,000	
	Dividends Payable, Preferred ($15,750 × 2)		31,500
	Dividends Payable, Common ($50,000 – $31,500).		18,500
	To declare a cash dividend.		

If the preferred stock is *noncumulative*, the corporation is not obligated to pay dividends in arrears. Suppose that the Pine Industries preferred stock was noncumulative and the company passed the 19X4 preferred dividend of $15,750. The preferred stockholders would lose the 19X4 dividend forever. Of course, the common stockholders would not receive a 19X4 dividend either. Before paying any common dividends in 19X5, the company would have to pay the 19X5 preferred dividend of $15,750.

Having dividends in arrears on cumulative preferred stock is *not* a liability to the corporation. (A liability for dividends arises when the board of directors declares the dividend.) Nevertheless, a corporation must report cumulative preferred dividends in arrears. This information alerts common stockholders as to how much in cumulative preferred dividends must be paid before any dividends will be paid on the common stock. This information gives the common stockholders an idea about the likelihood of receiving dividends and satisfies the disclosure principle. ◀▥ ◀▥ ◀▥

Dividends in arrears are often disclosed in notes, as follows (all dates and amounts assumed). Observe the two references to Note 3 in this section of the balance sheet. The "6 percent" after "Preferred stock" is the dividend rate.

Preferred stock, 6 percent, par $50, 2,000 shares issued (Note 3)...............	$100,000
Retained earnings (Note 3)...	414,000

Note 3—Cumulative preferred dividends in arrears. At December 31, 19X2, dividends on the company's 6 percent preferred stock were in arrears for 19X1 and 19X2, in the amount of $12,000 (6% × $100,000 × 2 years).

◀▥ ◀▥ ◀▥ Recall from Chapter 12, p. 499, that, by the disclosure principle, a company's financial statements must report enough data for outsiders to make informed decisions about the company.

Participating and Nonparticipating Preferred Stock

The owners of *participating preferred stock* may receive—that is, *participate in*—dividends beyond the stated amount or stated percentage. Assume that the corporation declares a dividend. First, the preferred stockholders receive their dividends. If the corporation has declared a large enough dividend, then the common stockholders receive their dividends. If an additional dividend amount remains to be distributed, common stockholders and participating preferred stockholders share it. For example, the owners of a $4 preferred stock must receive the specified annual dividend of $4 per share before the common stockholders receive any dividends. Then a $4 dividend is paid on each common share. The participation feature takes effect only after the preferred and common stockholders have received the specified $4 rate. Payment of an extra *common* dividend of, say, $1.50 is accompanied by a $1.50 dividend on each preferred share.

Participating preferred stock is rare. In fact, preferred stock is nonparticipating unless it is specifically described on the stock certificate and in the financial statements as participating. Therefore, if the preferred stock in our example is nonparticipating, the largest annual dividend that a preferred stockholder will receive is $4.

Short Exercise: Wheeler Corp. has outstanding 15,000 shares of $20-par common stock and 5,000 shares of $30-par, 6%, cumulative preferred stock. The company has declared no dividends for the past two years but plans to pay $56,250 this year. Compute the dividends for preferred and common stock if the preferred is nonparticipating. *A:*

Preferred Stock:	
Dividends in arrears (6% × $150,000 × 2)........	$18,000
Current dividend.........	9,000
Total to Preferred	$27,000
Common Stock:	
Remainder of dividend ($56,250 – $27,000).	29,250
Total dividend	$56,250

Convertible Preferred Stock

Convertible preferred stock may be exchanged by the preferred stockholders, if they choose, for another class of stock in the corporation. For example, the Pine Industries preferred stock may be converted into the company's common stock. A note to Pine's balance sheet describes the conversion terms as follows:

The...preferred stock is convertible at the rate of 6.51 shares of common stock for each share of preferred stock outstanding.

If you owned 100 shares of Pine's convertible preferred stock, you could convert it into 651 (100 × 6.51) shares of Pine common stock. Under what condition would you exercise the conversion privilege? You would do so if the market value of the common stock that you could receive from conversion exceeded the market value of the preferred stock that you presently held. This way, you as an investor could increase your personal wealth.

Key Point: Convertible preferred stock may be exchanged for common stock at the shareholder's option.

Short Exercise: Record the conversion of 100 shares of $100-par, 9% convertible preferred stock that was originally issued at par. Each preferred stock is convertible into 4 shares of $10-par value common stock. *A:*

Preferred Stock
(100 × $100) 10,000
   Common Stock
   (400 × $10)   4,000
   Paid-in Cap. in Excess
     of Par—Common   6,000

Pine Industries preferred stock has par value of $100 per share, and par value of the common stock is $1. The company would record conversion of 100 shares of preferred stock, issued previously at par, into 651 shares of common stock as follows:

Mar. 7	Preferred Stock (100 × $100)...	10,000	
	Common Stock (651 × $1)		651
	Paid-in Capital in Excess of Par—Common		9,349
	Conversion of preferred stock into common.		

If the preferred stock was issued at a premium, Paid-in Capital in Excess of Par—Preferred must also be debited to remove its balance from the books.

Preferred stock, we see, offers alternative features not available to common stock. Preferred stock is cumulative or noncumulative, participating or nonparticipating, and convertible or not convertible.

Evaluating Operations: Rate of Return on Total Assets and Rate of Return on Common Stockholders' Equity

OBJECTIVE 6

Compute two profitability measures: return on assets and return on stockholders' equity

Investors and creditors are constantly evaluating the ability of managers to earn profits. Investors search for companies whose stocks are likely to increase in value. Creditors are interested in profitable companies that can pay their debts. Investment and credit decisions often include a comparison of companies. But a comparison of IHOP Corp.'s net income with the net income of a new company in the restaurant industry simply is not meaningful. IHOP's profits may run into the millions of dollars, which far exceed a new company's net income. Does that automatically make IHOP a better investment? Not necessarily. To make relevant comparisons between companies different in size, scope of operations, or any other measure, investors, creditors, and managers use some standard profitability measures, including rate of return on total assets and rate of return on stockholders' equity.

The **rate of return on total assets**, or simply **return on assets**, measures a company's success in using its assets to earn income for the persons who are financing the business. Creditors have loaned money to the corporation and earn interest. Stockholders have invested in the corporation's stock and expect the company to earn net income. The sum of interest expense and net income is the return to the two groups that have financed the corporation's activities, and this is the numerator of the return on assets ratio. The denominator is average total assets. Return on assets is computed as follows, using actual data from the 1992 annual report of IHOP Corp. (amounts in thousands of dollars):

Short Exercise: The financial statements of Reeder Co. reported:

	19X2	19X1
Net income	$ 40,000	$ 45,000
Interest expense	10,000	12,000
6% Pfd. stock	50,000	50,000
Common stock	100,000	100,000
Retained earnings	90,000	80,000
Total assets	420,000	380,000

Dividends of $27,000 were declared and paid to common

$$\text{Rate of return on total assets} = \frac{\text{Net income} + \text{interest expense}}{\text{Average total assets}} = \frac{\$7,931 + \$4,762}{(\$112,800 + \$149,822)/2} = \frac{\$12,693}{\$131,311} = 0.097$$

Net income and interest expense are taken from the income statement. Average total assets is computed from the beginning and ending balance sheets. How is this profitability measure used in decision making? To compare companies in terms of how well their management earns a return for the people who finance the corporation. By relating the sum of net income and interest expense to average total assets, we have a standard measure that describes the profitability of all types of companies. Brokerage companies such as Merrill Lynch and Kidder Peabody often single out particular industries as good investments. For example, brokerage analysts may believe that the steel industry is in a growth phase. These analysts would identify specific steel companies whose profitabilities are likely to lead the industry and so be sound investments. Return on assets is one measure of profitability.

What is a good rate of return on total assets? There is no single answer to this question because rates of return vary widely by industry. For example, high-technology companies earn much higher returns than do utility companies, groceries, and manufacturers of consumer goods such as toothpaste.

Rate of return on common stockholders' equity, often called **return on equity**, shows the relationship between net income and average common stockholders' equity. The numerator is net income minus preferred dividends, information taken from the income statement. The denominator is average common stockholders' equity—total stockholders' equity minus preferred equity. IHOP Corp.'s rate of return on common stockholders' equity for 1992 is computed as follows (amounts in thousands of dollars):

$$\begin{array}{c}\text{Rate of return}\\ \text{on common}\\ \text{stockholders'}\\ \text{equity}\end{array} = \begin{array}{c}\text{Net income} -\\ \text{preferred dividends}\\ \hline \text{Average common}\\ \text{stockholders' equity}\end{array} = \frac{\$7,931 - \$0}{(\$48,660 + \$58,000)/2} = \frac{\$7,931}{\$53,330} = 0.149$$

IHOP Corp. has no preferred stock, so preferred dividends are zero. With no preferred stock outstanding, average *common* stockholders' equity is the same as average *total* equity—the average of the beginning and ending amounts.

IHOP's return on equity (14.9 percent) is higher than its return on assets (9.7 percent). This difference results from the interest expense component of return on assets. Companies such as IHOP borrow at one rate, say, 7 percent, and invest the funds to earn a higher rate, say, 15 percent. Borrowing at a lower rate than the return on investments is called *leverage*. During good times, leverage produces high returns for the stockholders. But too much leverage can make it difficult to pay the interest on the debt. The company's creditors are guaranteed a fixed rate of return on their loans. The stockholders, conversely, have no guarantee that the corporation will earn net income, so their investments are riskier. Consequently, stockholders demand a higher rate of return than do creditors, and this explains why return on equity should exceed return on assets. If return on assets is higher than return on equity, the company is in trouble.

Investors and creditors use return on common stockholders' equity in much the same way they use return on total assets—to compare companies. The higher the rate of return, the more successful the company. IHOP's 15 percent return on common stockholders' equity would be considered quite good in most industries. Investors also compare a company's return on stockholders' equity with interest rates available in the market. If interest rates are almost as high as return on equity, many investors will lend their money to earn interest. They choose to forgo the extra risk of investing in stock when the rate of return on equity is too low.

Different Values of Stock

The business community refers to several different *stock values* in addition to par value. These values include market value, redemption value, liquidation value, and book value.

Market Value

A stock's **market value,** or *market price*, is the price for which a person could buy or sell a share of the stock. The issuing corporation's net income, financial position, and future prospects and the general economic conditions determine market value. Daily newspapers report the market price of many stocks. Corporate financial statements report the high and the low market values of the company's common stock for each quarter of the year. *In almost all cases, stockholders are more concerned about the market value of a stock than about any of the other values discussed next.* In the chapter-opening story, IHOP's most recent stock price was quoted at 28, which means that the stock

stockholders in 19X2. Compute (1) the return on assets and (2) the return on common stockholders' equity for 19X2.
A:
(1) 12.5%:

$$\frac{\$40,000 + \$10,000}{(\$420,000 + \$380,000)/2}$$
$$= 0.125$$

(2) 20%:

$$\frac{\$40,000 - (6\% \times \$50,000)}{(\$190,000 + \$180,000)/2}$$
$$= 0.20$$

OBJECTIVE 7

Distinguish among market value, redemption value, liquidation value, and book value

Real-World Example: If you buy stock in IBM from another investor, IBM gets no cash. The transaction is a sale between investors. IBM records only the change in stockholder name.

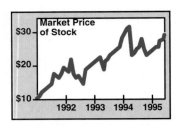

EXHIBIT 14-9
IHOP's Market Value

Key Point: The difference between the par (issue) price of preferred stock and the redemption value reduces Retained Earnings (which is not an expense). A corporation never records gains or losses on its own stock transactions because it cannot earn income or suffer a loss in transactions with its owners.

could be sold for, or bought for, $28 per share. The purchase of 100 shares of IHOP stock would cost $2,800 ($28.00 × 100), plus a commission. If you were selling 100 shares of IHOP stock, you would receive cash of $2,800 less a commission. The commission is the fee an investor pays to a stockbroker for buying or selling the stock. In this real situation the price of a share of IHOP stock has fluctuated from $10 at issuance to a recent high of $31.25 (Exhibit 14-9).

Redemption Value

Companies may wish to buy back, or redeem, their preferred stock to avoid paying the dividends. Preferred stock that provides for redemption at a set price is called redeemable preferred stock. In some cases, the company has the *option* of redeeming its preferred stock at a set price. In other cases, the company is *obligated* to redeem the preferred stock. The price the corporation agrees to pay for the stock, which is set when the stock is issued, is called the *redemption value*.

The preferred stock of Pine Industries, Inc., is "redeemable at the option of the Company at $25 per share." Beginning in 1995, Pine is "required to redeem annually 6,765 shares of the preferred stock ($169,125 annually)." Pine's annual redemption payment to the preferred stockholders will include this redemption value plus any dividends in arrears.

 STOP & THINK Suppose you are a financial analyst who follows Pine Industries as a potential investment. In computing Pine's debt ratio, how will you treat the preferred stock in 1994? How will you treat the preferred stock in 1995 and beyond? Give your reason.

Answer: In 1994, you should treat Pine Industries' preferred stock as owners' equity because there is no obligation to redeem the stock. In 1995 and beyond, Pine's preferred stock becomes a liability because the company is *required* to pay the stockholders in order to redeem the stock.

Liquidation Value

The *liquidation value*, which applies only to preferred stock, is the amount the corporation agrees to pay the preferred stockholder per share if the company liquidates. Dividends in arrears are added to liquidation value in determining the payment to the preferred stockholders if the company liquidates. Consider the BF Goodrich Company, which makes chemicals and aerospace components and sells tires under the Michelin label. BF Goodrich has 2.2 million shares of convertible preferred stock that is stated at "a liquidation value of $50 per share." The balance in BF Goodrich's preferred stock account is $110 million (2.2 million shares × $50).

"BF Goodrich has 2.2 million shares of convertible preferred stock that is stated at 'a liquidation value of $50 per share.'"

Book Value

The **book value** of a stock is the amount of owners' equity on the company's books for each share of its stock. Corporations often report this amount in their annual reports. If the company has only common stock outstanding, its book value is computed by dividing total stockholders' equity by the number of shares outstanding. A company with stockholders' equity of $180,000 and 5,000 shares of common stock outstanding has book value of $36 per share ($180,000/5,000 shares).

If the company has both preferred and common stock outstanding, the preferred stockholders have the first claim to owners' equity. Ordinarily, preferred stock has a specified liquidation or redemption value. The book value of preferred is its redemption value plus any cumulative dividends in arrears on the stock. Its book value *per share* equals the sum of redemption value and any cumulative dividends in arrears divided by the number of preferred shares outstanding. After the corporation figures the preferred shares' book value, it computes the common stock book value per share. The corporation divides the common equity (total stockholders' equity minus preferred equity) by the number of common shares outstanding.

Assume that the company balance sheet reports the following amounts:

Stockolders' Equity

Paid-in capital:	
Preferred stock, 6%, $100 par, 5,000 shares authorized,	
400 shares issued..	$ 40,000
Paid-in capital in excess of par—preferred	4,000
Common stock, $10 par, 20,000 shares authorized,	
5,500 shares issued...	55,000
Paid-in capital in excess of par—common	72,000
Total paid-in capital	171,000
Retained earnings	85,000
Total stockholders' equity	$256,000

Suppose that four years' (including the current year) cumulative preferred dividends are in arrears and that preferred stock has a redemption value of $130 per share. The book-value-per-share computations for this corporation follow:

Preferred:	
Redemption value (400 shares × $130)..	$ 52,000
Cumulative dividends ($40,000 × 0.06 × 4)................................	9,600
Stockholders' equity allocated to preferred................................	$ 61,600
Book value per share ($61,600/400 shares)	$ 154.00
Common:	
Total stockholders' equity..	$256,000
Less stockholders' equity allocated to preferred........................	61,600
Stockholders' equity allocated to common	$194,400
Book value per share ($194,400/5,500 shares)	$ 35.35

BOOK VALUE AND DECISION MAKING   How is book value per share used in decision making? Companies negotiating the purchase of a corporation may wish to know the book value of its stock. The book value of stockholders' equity may figure into the negotiated purchase price. Corporations—especially those whose stock is not publicly traded—may buy out a retiring executive, agreeing to pay the book value of the person's stock in the company.

Some investors have traditionally compared the book value of a share of a company's stock with the stock's market value. The idea was that a stock selling below its book value was underpriced and thus was a good buy. The relationship between book value and market value is far from clear, however. Book value is a product of the accounting system, which is based on historical costs. Market value, conversely, depends on investors' subjective outlook for dividends and appreciation in the stock's value. Exhibit 14-10 contrasts the book values and ranges of market values for the common stocks of three well-known companies.

Only IBM's stock was trading at a price near book value. At the time, IBM was experiencing great difficulty. Therefore, it was unclear that IBM's stock price was undervalued.

	Year-End Book Value	Fourth-Quarter Market-Value Range
IHOP Corp..................	$ 6.54	$13.75 – $31.25
Eli Lilly and Company.	16.71	57.75 – 65.50
IBM............................	48.34	48.75 – 81.13

EXHIBIT 14-10
Book Value and Market Value

Accounting for Income Taxes by Corporations

OBJECTIVE 8

Account for a corporation's income tax

Corporations pay taxes on their income in the same way that individuals do. Corporate and personal tax rates differ, however. At the time of this writing the federal tax rate on most corporate income is 35 percent. In addition, most states also levy income taxes on corporations.

For each period, the corporation measures income tax expense and the related income tax payable. Corporate strategy is directed more at minimizing the income tax payable because that is the amount of cash the company must pay the government. But the main accounting issue centers on the measurement of net income. Therefore accountants strive for a reasonable measure of income tax expense. Total revenues minus total expenses, including income tax expense, produces net income.

Income Tax Expense is based on **pretax accounting income**, or income before income tax, from the income statement. Income Tax Payable is based on **taxable income** from the income tax return filed with the Internal Revenue Service. Taxable income is the basis for computing the amount of tax to *pay* the government. Pretax accounting income and taxable income are rarely the same amount.

$$\begin{array}{c}\text{Income}\\\text{tax}\\\text{expense}\end{array}=\begin{array}{c}\text{Pretax acount-}\\\text{ing income}\\\text{(from income}\\\text{statement)}\end{array}\times\begin{array}{c}\text{Income}\\\text{tax}\\\text{rate}\end{array}\quad\Bigg|\Bigg|\quad\begin{array}{c}\text{Income}\\\text{tax}\\\text{payable}\end{array}=\begin{array}{c}\text{Taxable}\\\text{income}\\\text{(from tax}\\\text{return)}\end{array}\times\begin{array}{c}\text{Income}\\\text{tax}\\\text{rate}\end{array}$$

The authors are indebted to Jean Marie Hudson for this presentation.

Some revenues and expenses enter the determination of accounting income in periods different from the periods in which they enter the determination of taxable income. Over a period of several years, total pretax accounting income may equal total taxable income, but for any one year the two income amounts are likely to differ.

The most important difference between pretax accounting income and taxable income occurs when a corporation uses the straight-line method to compute depreciation for the financial statements and a special tax depreciation method for the tax return and the payment of taxes. The tax depreciation method is called the *modified accelerated cost recovery system*, abbreviated as MACRS. ◄▥ For any one year, MACRS depreciation listed on the tax return may differ from accounting depreciation on the income statement.

◄▥ ◄▥ ◄▥ We learned in Chapter 10, p. 417, that the MACRS depreciation method is used only for income tax purposes. It groups assets into eight classes by years of asset life.

Suppose IHOP Corp. has pretax accounting income of $12,200,000 in each of two years. The accounting issue is, What is the correct amount of income tax expense for the two years? By answering this question, we can complete IHOP's income statement:

Income Statement (partial)

	19X1	19X2
Income before income tax................	$12,200,000	$12,200,000
Income tax expense.........................	?	?
Net income.....................................	$?	$?

IHOP's income tax expense for both years is $4,270,000 ($12,200,000 × 0.35) regardless of the amount of income tax payable to the government each year. IHOP uses straight-line depreciation to compute income for the income statement. On the tax return, IHOP and most other corporations use MACRS depreciation, and so the tax returns report taxable income of $12,000,000 in 19X1 and $12,400,000 in 19X2. Exhibit 14-11 gives IHOP's entries to record income tax during 19X1 and 19X2.

19X1	Income Tax Expense ($12,200,000 × 0.35)...................	4,270,000	
	Income Tax Payable ($12,000,000 × 0.35)		4,200,000
	Deferred Income Tax ($200,000 × 0.35)		70,000
19X2	Income Tax Expense ($12,200,000 × 0.35)...................	4,270,000	
	Deferred Income Tax ($200,000 × 0.35)	70,000	
	Income Tax Payable ($12,400,000 × 0.35)		4,340,000

EXHIBIT 14-11

Income Tax Entries for a Corporation

Total *taxable* income for the two years combined—$24,400,000—is the same as total *pretax accounting* income for the two years. However, each year shows a difference between taxable income and pretax accounting income. With a 35 percent tax rate, income tax payable to the government is $4,200,000 ($12,000,000 × 0.35) in 19X1 and $4,340,000 ($12,400,000 × 0.35) in 19X2.

Corporations account for income tax expense and all other expenses on the basis of when the expense occurs, not when it is paid. The process of accruing income taxes during the period that the related income occurs is called *income tax allocation*. The goal of income tax allocation is to match the period's expenses against its revenues. In this case, IHOP Corp. will record the same amount of income tax expense in both years because pretax accounting income is the same ($12,200,000 each year).

Corporations generally record Income Tax Expense based on the amount of *pretax accounting income* multiplied by the tax rate. Income Tax Payable is credited for an amount equal to *taxable income* multiplied by the tax rate. When these two amounts differ, a new account, Deferred Income Tax, is credited or debited to balance the entry. In Exhibit 14-11, Deferred Income Tax is credited in 19X1 because pretax accounting income ($12,200,000) exceeds taxable income ($12,000,000). The reverse is true in 19X2, and Deferred Income Tax is debited. The 19X2 entry eliminates the preceding credit balance in Deferred Income Tax.

For other corporations, the 19X1 entry may include a debit to Deferred Income Tax. This occurs if taxable income exceeds pretax accounting income. In that case, the credit to Income Tax Payable is greater than the debit to Income Tax Expense, and the balancing amount is a debit to Deferred Income Tax. Entries in later years will include credits to eliminate the debit balance in Deferred Income Tax. Here is a way to remember whether to debit or credit Deferred Income Tax:

- Debit: Income Tax Expense for the amount equal to *pretax accounting income* multiplied by the income tax rate.
- Credit: Income Tax Payable for the amount equal to *taxable income* multiplied by the income tax rate.
- Debit or Credit: Deferred Income Tax for the amount needed to balance the entry.

Exhibit 14-12 shows IHOP's partial comparative financial statements for 19X1 and 19X2. Income Tax Expense, Income Tax Payable, and Deferred Income Tax come directly from the entries recorded in Exhibit 14-11.

Income Tax Payable and Deferred Income Tax are reported as liabilities on the balance sheet. Income Tax Payable is a current liability because it must be paid within a few months. Deferred income tax is usually a long-term liability, as it is for IHOP Corp. Why long-term? Because the asset that caused the deferred tax (depreciable property) is classified as long-term.

Study the entries in Exhibit 14-11. Observe that the $70,000 Deferred Income Tax amount for 19X1 was eliminated in 19X2. This is why Deferred Income Tax has a zero balance in Exhibit 14-12.

Short Exercise: Sellers Corp. reported $135,000 of income (income statement) before depreciation. Straight-line (book) depreciation was $16,000, and MACRS (tax) depreciation was $19,000. Assume a 35% tax rate. (1) Calculate Sellers' income tax expense, income tax payable, and deferred taxes for the year. (2) Is the deferred tax amount a debit or a credit?
A:
(1) Inc. tax expense: ($135,000 − $16,000) × 0.35 = $41,650
Inc. tax payable: ($135,000 − $19,000) × 0.35 = $40,600
Deferred inc. taxes:
$41,650 − $40,600 = $1,050
(2) A credit because the expense exceeds the payable.

EXHIBIT 14-12
Income Tax on Corporate Financial Statements

IHOP CORP.
PARTIAL INCOME STATEMENT
FOR THE YEARS ENDED DECEMBER 31, 19X1 AND 19X2

	19X1	19X2
Income before income tax	$12,200,000	$12,200,000
Income tax expense ($12,200,000 × 0.35 both years)	4,270,000	4,270,000
Net income	$ 7,930,000	$ 7,930,000

IHOP CORP.
PARTIAL BALANCE SHEET
DECEMBER 31, 19X1 AND 19X2

Liabilities	19X1	19X2
Current:		
Income tax payable	$4,200,000	$4,340,000
Long-term:		
Deferred income tax	70,000	—

SUMMARY PROBLEMS FOR YOUR REVIEW

1. Use the following accounts and related balances to prepare the classified balance sheet of Whitehall, Inc., at September 30, 19X4. Use the account format of the balance sheet.

Common stock, $1 par, 50,000 shares authorized, 20,000 shares issued	$ 20,000	Long-term note payable	$ 74,000
		Inventory	85,000
Dividends payable	4,000	Property, plant, and equipment, net	225,000
Cash	9,000	Revenue from donations	18,000
Accounts payable	28,000	Accounts receivable, net	23,000
Retained earnings	75,000	Preferred stock, $3.75, no-par 10,000 shares authorized,	
Paid-in capital in excess of par—common	115,000	2,000 shares issued	24,000
Organization cost, net	1,000	Accrued liabilities	3,000

2. The balance sheet of Trendline Corporation reported the following at March 31, 19X6, the end of its fiscal year. Note that Trendline reports paid-in capital in excess of par or stated value after the stock accounts.

Stockholders' Equity

Preferred stock, 4%, $10 par, 10,000 shares authorized (redemption value, $110,000)	$100,000
Common stock, no-par, $5 stated value, 100,000 shares authorized	250,000
Paid-in capital in excess of par or stated value:	
Common stock	231,500
Retained earnings	395,000
Total stockholders' equity	$976,500

Required

a. Is the preferred stock cumulative or noncumulative? Is it participating or nonparticipating? How can you tell?

b. What is the total amount of the annual preferred dividend?

c. How many shares of preferred and common stock has the company issued?

d. Compute the book value per share of the preferred and the common stock. No prior year preferred dividends are in arrears, but Trendline has not declared the current-year dividend.

SOLUTIONS TO REVIEW PROBLEMS

1.

WHITEHALL, INC. BALANCE SHEET SEPTEMBER 30, 19X4				
Assets			**Liabilities**	
Current:			Current:	
Cash	$ 9,000		Accounts payable	$ 28,000
Accounts receivable, net	23,000		Dividends payable	4,000
Inventory	85,000		Accrued liabilities	3,000
Total current assets	117,000		Total current liabilities	35,000
Property, plant and equipment, net	225,000		Long-term note payable	74,000
Intangible assets:			Total liabilities	109,000
Organization cost, net	1,000		**Stockholders' Equity**	
			Paid-in capital:	
			Preferred stock, $3.75, no-par, 10,000 shares authorized, 2,000 shares issued	$ 24,000
			Common stock, $1 par, 50,000 shares authorized, 20,000 shares issued	20,000
			Paid-in capital in excess of par—common	115,000
			Total paid-in capital	159,000
			Retained earnings	75,000
			Total stockholders' equity	234,000
			Total liabilities and	
Total assets	$343,000		stockholders' equity	$343,000

2. Answers to Trendline Corporation questions:

a. The preferred stock is cumulative and nonparticipating because it is not specifically labeled otherwise.

b. Total annual preferred dividend: $4,000 ($100,000 × 0.04).

c. Preferred stock issued: 10,000 shares
   Common stock issued: 50,000 shares ($250,000/$5 stated value).

d. Book values per share of preferred and common stock:

Preferred:
Redemption value	$110,000
Cumulative dividend for current year ($100,000 × 0.04)	4,000
Stockholders' equity allocated to preferred	$114,000
Book value per share ($114,000/10,000 shares)	$11.40

Common:
Total stockholders' equity	$976,500
Less stockholders' equity allocated to preferred	114,000
Stockholders' equity allocated to common	$862,500
Book value per share ($862,500/50,000 shares)	$17.25

SUMMARY

1. Identify the characteristics of a corporation. A corporation is a separate legal and business entity. *Continuous life*, the *ease of raising large amounts of capital and transferring ownership*, and *limited liability* are among the advantages of the corporate form of organization. An important disadvantage is *double taxation*. Corporations pay *income taxes*, and stockholders pay tax on dividends. *Stockholders* are the owners of the corporations. They elect a *board of directors*, which elects a chairperson and appoints the officers to manage the business.

2. Record the issuance of stock. Corporations may issue different classes of stock: *par value, no-par value, common*, and *preferred*. Stock is usually issued at a *premium*—an amount above par value.

3. Prepare the stockholders' equity section of a corporation balance sheet. The balance sheet carries the capital raised through stock issuance under the heading Paid-in Capital or Contributed Capital in the stockholders' equity section.

4. Account for the incorporation of a going business. Close the owner's equity accounts of the prior entity, and open the stockholders' equity accounts of the corporation.

5. Account for cash dividends. Only when the board of directors declares a *dividend* does the corporation incur the liability to pay dividends. Preferred stock has priority over common stock as to dividends, which may be stated as a percentage of par value or as a dollar amount per share. In addition, preferred stock has a claim to dividends in arrears if it is *cumulative* and a claim to further dividends if it is *participating*. *Convertible* preferred stock may be exchanged for the corporation's common stock.

6. Compute two profitability measures: return on assets and return on stockholders' equity. *Return on assets* and *return on stockholders' equity* are two standard measures of profitability. A healthy company's return on equity will exceed its return on assets.

7. Distinguish among market value, redemption value, liquidation value, and book value. A stock's *market value* is the price for which a share may be bought or sold. *Redemption value, liquidation value*, and *book value*—the amount of owners' equity per share of company stock—are other values that may apply to stock.

8. Account for a corporation's income tax. Corporations pay income tax and must account for the income tax expense and income tax payable. A difference between the expense and the payable creates another account, Deferred Income Tax.

SELF-STUDY QUESTIONS

Test your understanding of the chapter by marking the best answer for each of the following questions.

1. Which of the following is a *disadvantage* of the corporate form of business organization? *(pp. 554–555)*
   a. Limited liability of stockholders
   b. Government regulation
   c. No mutual agency
   d. Transferability of ownership

2. The person with the most power in a corporation is the *(p. 556)*
   a. Incorporator
   b. Chairman of the board
   c. President
   d. Vice-president

3. The dollar amount of the stockholder investments in a corporation is called *(pp. 557–558)*
   a. Outstanding stock
   b. Total stockholders' equity
   c. Paid-in capital
   d. Retained earnings

4. The arbitrary value assigned to a share of stock is called *(p. 561)*
   a. Market value
   b. Liquidation value
   c. Book value
   d. Par value

5. Which is the most widely held class of stock? *(pp. 559–561)*
   a. Par value common stock
   b. No-par common stock
   c. Par value preferred stock
   d. No-par preferred stock

6. Mangum Corporation receives a building in exchange for 1,000 shares of Mangum's $100 par value stock. The building's book value is $385,000, and its current market value is $640,000. How much stockholders' equity does this transaction create? *(p. 564)*
   a. $0 because the corporation received no cash
   b. $100,000
   c. $385,000
   d. $640,000

7. Organization cost is classified as a (an) *(p. 568)*
   a. Operating expense
   b. Current asset
   c. Contra item in stockholders' equity
   d. None of the above

8. Trade Days, Inc., has 10,000 shares of $3.50, $50 par preferred stock, and 100,000 shares of $4 par common stock outstanding. Two years' preferred dividends are in arrears. Trade Days declares a cash dividend large enough to pay the preferred dividends in arrears, the preferred dividends for the current period, and a $1.50 dividend to common. What is the total amount of the dividend? *(pp. 569–570)*
   a. $255,000
   b. $220,000
   c. $150,000
   d. $105,000

9. The preferred stock of Trade Days, Inc., in Question 8 was issued at $55 per share. Each preferred share can be converted into 10 common shares. The entry to record the conversion of this preferred stock into common is *(p. 572)*

   a.
Cash	550,000	
Preferred Stock		500,000
Paid-in Capital in Excess of Par—Preferred Stock		50,000

   b.
Preferred Stock	500,000	
Paid-in Capital in Excess of Par—Preferred Stock	50,000	
Common Stock		550,000

   c.
Preferred Stock	500,000	
Paid-in Capital in Excess of Par—Preferred Stock	50,000	
Common Stock		400,000
Paid-in Capital in Excess of Par—Common Stock		150,000

d.	Preferred Stock	550,000	
	Common Stock		400,000
	Paid-in Capital in		
	Excess of Par—		
	Common Stock		150,000

10. When an investor is buying stock as an investment, the value of most direct concern is *(p. 573)*

a. Par value   c. Liquidation value
b. Market value   d. Book value

Answers to the Self-Study Questions follow the Accounting Vocabulary.

ACCOUNTING VOCABULARY

Authorization of stock. Provision in a corporate charter that gives the state's permission for the corporation to issue—that is, to sell—a certain number of shares of stock *(p. 561)*.

Board of directors. Group elected by the stockholders to set policy for a corporation and to appoint its officers *(p. 556)*.

Book value. Amount of owners' equity on the company's books for each share of its stock *(p. 574)*.

Bylaws. Constitution for governing a corporation *(p. 556)*.

Chairperson. Elected by a corporation's board of directors, usually the most powerful person in the corporation *(p. 556)*.

Charter. Document that gives the state's permission to form a corporation *(p. 554)*.

Common stock. The most basic form of capital stock. In a description of a corporation, the common stockholders are the owners of the business *(p. 558)*.

Contributed capital. Another name for paid-in capital *(p. 558)*.

Convertible preferred stock. Preferred stock that may be exchanged by the preferred stockholders, if they choose, for another class of stock in the corporation *(p. 571)*.

Cumulative preferred stock. Preferred stock whose owners must receive all dividends in arrears before the corporation pays dividends to the common stockholders *(p. 570)*.

Deficit. Debit balance in the Retained Earnings account *(p. 558)*.

Dividends. Distributions by a corpora-

tion to its stockholders *(p. 559)*.

Double taxation. Corporations pay their own income taxes on corporate income. Then, the stockholders pay personal income tax on the cash dividends that they receive from corporations *(p. 555)*.

Incorporators. Persons who organize a corporation *(p. 556)*.

Limited liability. No personal obligation of a stockholder for corporation debts. A stockholder can lose no more on an investment in a corporation's stock than the cost of the investment *(p. 555)*.

Market value. Price for which a person could buy or sell a share of stock *(p. 573)*.

Organization cost. The costs of organizing a corporation, including legal fees, taxes and fees paid to the state, and charges by promoters for selling the stock. Organization cost is an intangible asset *(p. 568)*.

Outstanding stock. Stock in the hands of stockholders *(p. 557)*.

Paid-in capital. A corporation's capital from investments by the stockholders. Also called contributed capital *(p. 558)*.

Par value. Arbitrary amount assigned to a share of stock *(p. 561)*.

Preferred stock. Stock that gives its owners certain advantages over common stockholders, such as the priority to receive dividends before the common stockholders and the priority to receive assets before the common stockholders if the corporation liquidates *(p. 560)*.

President. Chief operating officer in

charge of managing the day-to-day operations of a corporation *(p. 556)*.

Pretax accounting income. Income before income tax from the income statement *(p. 576)*.

Rate of return on common stockholders' equity. Net income minus preferred dividends, divided by average common stockholders' equity. A measure of profitability. Also called return on equity *(p. 573)*.

Rate of return on total assets. The sum of net income plus interest expense divided by average total assets. This ratio measures the success a company has in using its assets to earn income for the persons who finance the business. Also called return on assets *(p. 572)*.

Retained earnings. A corporation's capital that is earned through profitable operation of the business *(p. 558)*.

Return on assets. Another name for rate of return on total assets *(p. 572)*.

Return on equity. Another name for rate of return on common stockholders' equity *(p. 573)*.

Shareholder. Another name for stockholder *(p. 554)*.

Stock. Shares into which the owners' equity of a corporation is divided *(p. 554)*.

Stockholder. A person who owns the stock of a corporation *(p. 554)*.

Stockholders' equity. Owners' equity of a corporation *(p. 557)*.

Taxable income. Income from the income tax return filed with the Internal Revenue Service; the basis for computing the amount of tax to pay the government *(p. 576)*.

ANSWERS TO SELF-STUDY QUESTIONS

1. b   6. d
2. b   7. d Intangible asset
3. c   8. a [(10,000 × $3.50 × 3 = $105,000) + (100,000 × $1.50 = $150,000) = $255,000]
4. d   9. c
5. a   10. b

QUESTIONS

1. Why is a corporation called a creature of the state?
2. Identify the characteristics of a corporation.
3. Explain why corporations face a tax disadvantage.
4. Briefly outline the steps in the organization of a corporation.
5. How are the structures of a partnership and a corporation similar, and how are they different?
6. Name the four rights of a stockholder. Is preferred stock automatically nonvoting? Explain how a right may be withheld from a stockholder.
7. Dividends on preferred stock may be stated as a percentage rate or a dollar amount. What is the annual dividend on these preferred stocks: 4-percent, $100-par; $3.50, $20-par; and 6-percent, no-par with $50 stated value?
8. Which event increases the assets of the corporation: authorization of stock or issuance of stock? Explain.
9. Suppose H. J. Heinz Company issued 1,000 shares of its 3.65-percent, $100-par preferred stock for $120. How much would this transaction increase the company's paid-in capital? How much would it increase Heinz's retained earnings? How much would it increase Heinz's annual cash dividend payments?
10. Give two alternative account titles for Paid-in Capital in Excess of Par—Common Stock.
11. How does issuance of 1,000 shares of no-par stock for land and a building, together worth $150,000, affect paid-in capital?
12. Journalize the incorporation of the Barnes & Connally partnership. The partners' capital account balances exceed the par value of the new corporation's common stock. (Omit amounts.)
13. Rank the following accounts in the order they would appear on the balance sheet: Common Stock, Organization Cost, Preferred Stock, Retained Earnings, Dividends Payable. Also, give each account's balance sheet classification.
14. What type of account is Organization Cost? Briefly describe how to account for organization cost.
15. Briefly discuss the three important dates for a dividend.
16. Mancini, Inc., has 3,000 shares of its $2.50, $10-par preferred stock outstanding. Dividends for 19X1 and 19X2 are in arrears, and the company has declared no dividends on preferred stock for the current year, 19X3. Assume that Mancini declares total dividends of $35,000 at the end of 19X3. Show how to allocate the dividends to preferred and common if preferred is (a) cumulative or (b) noncumulative.
17. As a preferred stockholder, would you rather own cumulative or noncumulative preferred? If all other factors are the same, would the corporation rather the preferred stock be cumulative or noncumulative? Give your reason.
18. How are cumulative preferred dividends in arrears reported in the financial statements? When do dividends become a liability of the corporation?
19. Distinguish between the market value of stock and the book value of stock. Which is more important to investors?
20. How is book value per share of common stock computed when the company has both preferred stock and common stock outstanding?
21. Why should a healthy company's rate of return on stockholders' equity exceed its rate of return on total assets?
22. Explain the difference between the income tax expense and the income tax payable of a corporation.

EXERCISES

Organizing a corporation
(Obj. 1)

E14-1 Carena Datig and Jennifer Robertson are opening a limousine service to be named C&J Transportation Enterprises. They need outside capital, so they plan to organize the business as a corporation. Because your office is in the same building, they come to you for advice. Write a memorandum informing them of the steps in forming a corporation. Identify specific documents used in this process, and name the different parties involved in the ownership and management of a corporation.

Issuing stock
(Obj. 2)

E14-2 Ford Corporation made the following stock issuance transactions:

Feb. 19 Issued 1,000 shares of $1.50 par common stock for cash of $10.50 per share.
Mar. 3 Sold 300 shares of $4.50, no-par Class A preferred stock for $12,000 cash.
      11 Received inventory valued at $20,000 and equipment with market value of $11,000 for 3,300 shares of the $1.50 par common stock.
      15 Issued 1,000 shares of 5-percent, no-par Class B preferred stock with stated value of $50 per share. The issue price was cash of $60 per share.

Required

1. Journalize the transactions. Explanations are not required.
2. How much paid-in capital did these transactions generate for Ford Corporation?

Recording issuance of stock
(Obj. 2)

E14-3 The actual balance sheet of Gulf Resources & Chemical Corporation, as adapted, reported the following stockholders' equity. Gulf has two separate classes of preferred stock, labeled Series A and Series B. All dollar amounts, except for per-share amounts, are given in thousands.

Stockholders' Investment
[same as stockholders' equity]

Preferred stock, $1 par, authorized 4,000,000 shares (Note 7)	
Series A	$ 58
Series B..	376
Common stock, $0.10 par, authorized 20,000,000, [issued and] outstanding	
9,130,000 shares	913
Capital in excess of par...	75,542

Note 7. Preferred Stock:

	Shares [Issued and] Outstanding
Series A..............	58,000
Series B..............	376,000

Required

Assume that the Series A preferred stock was issued for $5 cash per share, the Series B preferred was issued for $10 cash per share, and the common was issued for cash of $72,839. Make the summary journal entries to record issuance of all the Gulf Resources stock. Explanations are not required. After you record these entries, what is the balance of Capital in Excess of Par?

E14-4 Alexanians, located in Lansing, Michigan, is an importer of European furniture and Oriental rugs. The corporation issues 2,000 shares of no-par common stock for $50 per share. Record issuance of the stock if the stock (a) is true no-par stock and (b) has stated value of $5 per share.

Recording issuance of no-par stock (Obj. 2)

E14-5 The charter of Equinox Corporation authorizes the issuance of 5,000 shares of Class A preferred stock, 1,000 shares of Class B preferred stock, and 10,000 shares of common stock. During a two-month period, Equinox completed these stock-issuance transactions:

Stockholders' equity section of a balance sheet (Obj. 3)

June 23	Issued 1,000 shares of $1 par common stock for cash of $12.50 per share.
July 2	Sold 300 shares of $4.50, no-par Class A preferred stock for $20,000 cash.
12	Received inventory valued at $25,000 and equipment with market value of $16,000 for 3,300 shares of the $1 par common stock.
17	Issued 1,000 shares of 5-percent, no-par Class B preferred stock with stated value of $50 per share. The issue price was cash of $60 per share.

Required

Prepare the stockholders' equity section of the Equinox balance sheet for the transactions given in this exercise. Retained earnings has a balance of $91,000.

E14-6 Zhang Corp. recently organized. The company issued common stock to an attorney who gave Susan Zhang legal services of $5,000 to help her in organizing the corporation. It issued common stock to another person in exchange for his patent with a market value of $40,000. In addition, Zhang received cash both for 2,000 shares of its preferred stock at $110 per share and for 26,000 shares of its common stock at $15 per share. The city of Sacramento donated 50 acres of land to the company as a plant site. The market value of the land was $600,000. Without making journal entries, determine the total paid-in capital created by these transactions.

Paid-in capital for a corporation (Obj. 2)

E14-7 Pay-n-Sav, Inc., has the following selected account balances at June 30, 19X7. Prepare the stockholders' equity section of the company's balance sheet.

Stockholders' equity section of a balance sheet (Obj. 3)

Inventory..	$112,000	Common stock, no-par with	
Machinery and equipment..............	109,000	$1 stated value, 500,000 shares	
Preferred stock, 5%, $20		authorized, 120,000 shares issued	$120,000
par, 20,000 shares authorized,		Accumulated depreciation—	
11,000 shares issued	220,000	machinery and equipment	62,000
Paid-in capital in excess		Retained earnings.............................	119,000
of par—preferred stock...............	88,000	Organization cost, net......................	3,000
		Revenue from donations..................	81,000

E14-8 The Barlow Flashes are a semiprofessional baseball team that has been operated as a partnership by J. Barlow and B. Hearn. In addition to their management responsibilities, Barlow plays second base and Hearn sells hot dogs. Journalize the following transactions in the first month of operation as a corporation:

Incorporating a partnership (Obj. 4)

May 14   The incorporators paid legal fees of $840 and state taxes and fees of $500 to obtain a corporate charter.

   14   Issued 2,500 shares of $5 par common stock to Barlow and 1,000 shares to Hearn. Barlow's capital balance on the partnership books was $20,000, and Hearn's capital balance was $12,000.

   18   The city of Mineola donated 20 acres of land to the corporation for a stadium site. The land's market value was $80,000.

Computing dividends on preferred and common stock
(Obj. 5)

E14-9   The following elements of stockholders' equity are adapted from the balance sheet of Gulf Resources & Chemical Corporation. All dollar amounts, except the dividends per share, are given in thousands.

Stockholders' Equity	
Preferred stock, cumulative and nonparticipating, $1 par (Note 7)	
Series A, 58,000 shares issued	$ 58
Series B, 376,000 shares issued	376
Common stock, $0.10 par, 9,130,000 shares issued	913

Note 7. Preferred Stock:	**Designated Annual Cash Dividend per Share**
Series A...............	$0.20
Series B...............	1.30

Assume that the Series A preferred has preference over the Series B preferred and that the company has paid all preferred dividends through 19X4.

Required

Compute the dividends to both series of preferred and to common for 19X5 and 19X6 if total dividends are $0 in 19X5 and $1,100,000 in 19X6. Round to the nearest dollar.

Evaluating profitability
(Obj. 6)

E14-10   Tempo Services, Inc., reported these figures for 19X7 and 19X6:

	19X7	**19X6**
Income statement:		
Interest expense	$ 7,400,000	$ 7,100,000
Net income	22,000,000	18,700,000
Balance sheet:		
Total assets	351,000,000	317,000,000
Preferred stock, $1.30, no-par, 100,000 shares issued and outstanding	2,500,000	2,500,000
Common stockholders' equity	164,000,000	151,000,000
Total stockholders' equity	166,500,000	153,500,000

Compute rate of return on total assets and rate of return on common stockholders' equity for 19X7. Do these rates of return suggest strength or weakness? Give your reason.

Book value per share of preferred and common stock
(Obj. 7)

E14-11   The balance sheet of Delta Corporation reported the following, with all amounts, including shares, in thousands:

Redeemable preferred stock; redemption value $6,362		$ 4,860
Common stockholders' equity, 10,120 shares issued and outstanding		216,788
Total stockholders' equity		$221,648

Assume that Delta has paid preferred dividends for the current year and all prior years (no dividends in arrears) and that the company has 100 shares of preferred stock outstanding.

Required

Compute the book value per share of the preferred stock and the common stock.

Book value per share of preferred and common stock; preferred dividends in arrears (Obj. 5, 7)

E14-12   Refer to Exercise 14-11. Compute the book value per share of the preferred stock and the common stock, assuming that three years' preferred dividends (including dividends for the current year) are in arrears. The preferred stock dividend rate is 6 percent.

E14-13 Chrysler Manufacturing Company of Texas has pretax accounting income of $420,000 in 19X6 and $470,000 in 19X7. Taxable income is $380,000 in 19X6 and $510,000 in 19X7. Texas has no corporate income tax, and the federal income tax rate is 35 percent. Record Chrysler's income taxes for both years. What is the balance in the Deferred Income Tax account at the end of each year?

Accounting for income tax by a corporation (Obj. 8)

CHALLENGE EXERCISES

E14-14 Wal-Mart Stores, Inc., reported these comparative stockholders' equity data (amounts in thousands except par value per share):

Accounting for stockholders' equity transactions (Obj. 2, 5)

	January 31,	
	19X2	**19X1**
Common stock ($0.10 par value per share)...............	$ 114,903	$ 114,228
Capital in excess of par value	625,669	415,586
Retained earnings..	6,249,138	4,835,710

During 19X2, Wal-Mart completed these transactions and events:

a. Net income, $1,608,476.
b. Cash dividends, $195,048.
c. Issuance of stock for cash, 914 shares, $21,025.
d. Issuance of stock to purchase other companies (Wal-Mart debited the Investments account), 5,832 shares, $189,733.

Required

Without making journal entries, show how Wal-Mart's 19X2 transactions and events accounted for the changes in the stockholders' equity accounts. For each stockholders' equity account, start with the January 31, 19X1, balance and work toward the balance at January 31, 19X2.

E14-15 Case A—The income statement of Hewitt Corp. reports

Accounting for income tax by a corporation (Obj. 8)

	19X1	**19X2**
Income before income tax...............	$25,000	$30,000

The combined federal and state income tax rate is 40 percent.

1. How much net income will Hewitt Corp. report each year?
2. Compute the amount of income tax payable from each year's operations.

Case B—Keep all facts as they were in Case A, except that Hewitt uses straight-line depreciation for accounting purposes and MACRS depreciation for income tax purposes. During 19X1, MACRS depreciation exceeds straight-line depreciation by $6,000. In 19X2, MACRS depreciation exceeds straight-line by $4,000.

1. How much net income will Hewitt Corp. report each year?
2. Compute the amount of income tax payable from each year's operations.
3. Assume that Hewitt began operations in 19X1. What will be the balance of Deferred Income Tax at the end of 19X1 and at the end of 19X2? Explain the desirable feature of the deferred income taxes.

PROBLEMS

(GROUP A)

P14-1A Anthony Krystofnik and Lou Hersch are opening a Shoney's Restaurant in a growing section of Columbia, South Carolina. There are no competing family restaurants in the immediate vicinity. Their most fundamental decision is how to organize the business. Krystofnik thinks the partnership form is best for their business. Hersch favors the corporate form of organization. They seek your advice.

Organizing a corporation (Obj. 1)

Required

Discuss the advantages and the disadvantages of organizing the business as a corporation.

P14-2A The partnership of Gomez and Salazar needed additional capital to expand into new markets, so the business incorporated as Tiempo Grande, Inc. The charter from the state of Arizona authorizes Tiempo Grande to issue 50,000 shares of 6-percent, $100-par preferred stock and 100,000 shares of no-par common stock with a stated value of $5 per share. In its first month, Tiempo Grande completed the following transactions:

Dec. 1 Paid a charter fee of $200 and incorporation taxes of $6,100 to the state of Arizona and paid legal fees of $4,000 to organize as a corporation.

2 Issued 300 shares of common stock to the promoter for assistance with issuance of the common stock. The promotional fee was $1,800.

2 Issued 9,000 shares of common stock to Gomez and 12,000 shares to Salazar in return for the net assets of the partnership. Gomez's capital balance on the partnership books was $54,000, and Salazar's capital balance was $72,000.

8 Received a parcel of land valued at $92,000 as a donation from the city of Tucson.

10 Issued 400 shares of preferred stock to acquire a patent with a market value of $50,000.

16 Issued 2,000 shares of common stock for cash of $12,000.

Required

1. Record the transactions in the general journal.
2. Prepare the stockholders' equity section of the Tiempo Grande, Inc., balance sheet at December 31. The ending balance of Retained Earnings is $42,100.

P14-3A The following summaries for Millett Corp. and Structural Castings, Inc., provide the information needed to prepare the stockholders' equity section of the company balance sheet. The two companies are independent.

Millett Corp. Millett Corp. is authorized to issue 50,000 shares of $1-par common stock. All the stock was issued at $12 per share. The company incurred net losses of $30,000 in 19X1 and $14,000 in 19X2. It earned net incomes of $23,000 in 19X3 and $71,000 in 19X4. The company declared no dividends during the four-year period.

Structural Castings, Inc. Structural Castings's charter authorizes the company to issue 5,000 shares of 5-percent, $100-par preferred stock and 500,000 shares of no-par common stock. Structural Castings issued 1,000 shares of the preferred stock at $105 per share. It issued 100,000 shares of the common stock for $400,000. The company's retained earnings balance at the beginning of 19X4 was $120,000. Net income for 19X4 was $80,000, and the company declared a 5-percent preferred dividend for 19X4. Preferred dividends for 19X3 were in arrears.

Required

For each company, prepare the stockholders' equity section of its balance sheet at December 31, 19X4. Show the computation of all amounts. Entries are not required.

P14-4A The purpose of this problem is to familiarize you with the financial statement information of a real company. Bethlehem Steel Corporation is one of the nation's largest steel companies. Bethlehem included the following stockholders' equity on its balance sheet:

Stockholders' Equity	($ Millions)
Preferred stock—	
Authorized 20,000,000 shares in each class; issued:	
$5.00 Cumulative Convertible Preferred Stock, at $50.00	
stated value, 2,500,000 shares	$ 125
$2.50 Cumulative Convertible Preferred Stock, at $25.00	
stated value, 4,000,000 shares	100
Common stock—$8 par value—	
Authorized 80,000,000 shares; issued 48,308,516 shares..............	621
Retained earnings	529
	$1,375

Observe that Bethlehem reports no Paid-in Capital in Excess of Par or Stated Value. Instead, the company reports those items in the stock accounts.

Required

1. Identify the different issues of stock Bethlehem has outstanding.
2. Which class of stock did Bethlehem issue at par or stated value, and which class did it issue above par or stated value?
3. Rearrange the Bethlehem Steel stockholders' equity section to correspond, as appropriate, to the terminology and format illustrated on page 575. Report dollar amounts in millions, as Bethlehem does.
4. Suppose Bethlehem passed its preferred dividends for one year. Would the company have to pay these dividends in arrears before paying dividends to the common stockholders? Give your reason.
5. What amount of preferred dividends must Bethlehem declare and pay each year to avoid having preferred dividends in arrears?
6. Assume preferred dividends are in arrears for 19X5.
   a. Write Note 6 of the December 31, 19X5, financial statements to disclose the dividends in arrears.
   b. Journalize the declaration of a $60 million dividend for 19X6. An explanation is not required.

P14-5A The following accounts and related balances of Surgical Products, Inc., are arranged in no particular order.

Preparing a corporation balance sheet; measuring profitability (Obj. 3, 6)

Required

1. Prepare the company's classified balance sheet in the account format at November 30, 19X7.
2. Compute rate of return on total assets and rate of return on common stockholders' equity for the year ended November 30, 19X7.
3. Do these rates of return suggest strength or weakness? Give your reason.
4. How will what you learned in this problem help you evaluate an investment?

Dividends payable	$ 3,000	Inventory	$181,000
Total assets, November 30, 19X6	781,000	Property, plant, and	
Net income	36,200	equipment, net	378,000
Common stockholders' equity,		Organization cost, net	6,000
November 30, 19X6	483,000	Prepaid expenses	13,000
Interest expense	12,800	Patent, net	31,000
Additional paid-in capital—		Accrued liabilities	17,000
common	140,000	Long-term note payable	104,000
Accounts payable	31,000	Accounts receivable, net	102,000
Retained earnings	?	Preferred stock, 4%, $10 par,	
Common stock, $5 par,		25,000 shares authorized,	
100,000 shares authorized,		3,700 shares issued	37,000
42,000 shares issued	210,000	Cash	32,000

P14-6A MacLayne Corporation has 5,000 shares of 5-percent, $10 par value preferred stock and 100,000 shares of $1.50 par common stock outstanding. During a three-year period, MacLayne declared and paid cash dividends as follows: 19X1, $1,500; 19X2, $12,000; and 19X3, $31,000.

Computing dividends on preferred and common stock (Obj. 5)

Required

1. Compute the total dividends to preferred stock and common stock for each of the three years if:
   a. Preferred is noncumulative and nonparticipating.
   b. Preferred is cumulative and nonparticipating.
2. For case (1b), record the declaration of the 19X3 dividends on December 22, 19X3, and the payment of the dividends on January 14, 19X4.

Analyzing the stockholders' equity
of an actual corporation
(Obj. 5, 7)

P14-7A The balance sheet of Oak Manufacturing, Inc., reported the following:

Stockholders' Investment [same as stockholders' equity]	($ Thousands)
Cumulative convertible preferred stock..	$ 45
Common stock, $1 par value, authorized 40,000,000 shares; issued 16,000,000 shares...	16,000
[Additional] paid-in capital...	176,000
Retained earnings	(77,165)
Total stockholders' investment...	$114,880

Notes to the financial statements indicate that 9,000 shares of $1.60 preferred stock with a stated value of $5 per share were issued and outstanding. The preferred stock has a redemption value of $25 per share, and preferred dividends are in arrears for two years, including the current year. The additional paid-in capital was contributed by the common stockholders. On the balance sheet date, the market value of the Oak Manufacturing common stock was $7.50 per share.

Required

1. Is the preferred stock cumulative or noncumulative, participating or nonparticipating? How can you tell?
2. What is the amount of the annual preferred dividend?
3. What is the total paid-in capital of the company?
4. What was the total market value of the common stock?
5. Compute the book value per share of the preferred stock and the common stock.

Computing and recording a
corporation's income tax
(Obj. 8)

P14-8A The accounting (not the income tax) records of Valley View Corporation provide the comparative income statement for 19X7 and 19X8:

	19X7	19X8
Total revenue	$930,000	$990,000
Expenses:		
Cost of goods sold	$430,000	$460,000
Operating expenses.........................	270,000	280,000
Total expenses before tax...............	700,000	740,000
Pretax accounting income	$230,000	$250,000

Total revenue of 19X8 includes revenue of $15,000 that was received late in 19X7. This revenue is included in 19X8 total revenue because it was earned in 19X8. However, revenue that is collected in advance is included in the taxable income of the year when the cash is received. In calculating taxable income on the tax return, this revenue belongs in 19X7.

Also, the operating expenses of each year include depreciation of $50,000 computed on the straight-line method. In calculating taxable income on the tax return, Valley View Corporation uses the modified accelerated cost recovery system (MACRS). MACRS depreciation was $80,000 for 19X7 and $20,000 for 19X8.

Required

(Assume a corporate income tax rate of 35 percent.)

1. Compute taxable income for each year.
2. Journalize the corporation's income taxes for each year.
3. Prepare the corporation's single-step income statement for each year.

(GROUP B)

P14-1B Ursula Williams and Stephanie Magursky are opening an Office Depot store in a shopping center in Santa Fe, New Mexico. The area is growing, and no competitors are located nearby. Their most basic decision is how to organize the business. Williams thinks the partnership form is best. Magursky favors the corporate form of organization. They seek your advice.

Required

Discuss the advantages and the disadvantages of organizing the business as a corporation.

P14-2B The partners who own LeClerc & Duvalle wished to avoid the unlimited personal liability of the partnership form of business, so they incorporated the partnership as L&D Exploration, Inc. The charter from the state of Louisiana authorizes the corporation to issue 10,000 shares of 6-percent, $100-par preferred stock and 250,000 shares of no-par common stock with a stated value of $5 per share. In its first month, L&D Exploration completed the following transactions:

Journalizing corporation transactions and preparing the stockholders' equity section of the balance sheet
(Obj. 2, 3)

Dec. 1   Paid incorporation taxes of $1,500 and a charter fee of $2,000 to the state of Louisiana and paid legal fees of $1,900 to organize as a corporation.

3   Issued 500 shares of common stock to the promoter for assistance with issuance of the common stock. The promotional fee was $5,000.

3   Issued 5,100 shares of common stock to LeClerc and 3,800 shares to Duvalle in return for the net assets of the partnership. LeClerc's capital balance on the partnership books was $51,000, and Duvalle's capital balance was $38,000.

7   Received land valued at $160,000 as a donation from the city of Lafayette.

12   Issued 1,000 shares of preferred stock to acquire a patent with a market value of $110,000.

22   Issued 1,500 shares of common stock for $10 cash per share.

Required

1.   Record the transactions in the general journal.
2.   Prepare the stockholders' equity section of the L&D Exploration, Inc., balance sheet at December 31. The ending balance of Retained Earnings is $91,300.

P14-3B Stockholders' equity information is given for Premier Computing Corp. and Ensenada, Inc. The two companies are independent.

Stockholders' equity section of the balance sheet
(Obj. 3)

Premier Computing Corp. Premier Computing Corp. is authorized to issue 50,000 shares of $5 par common stock. All the stock was issued at $12 per share. The company incurred a net loss of $12,000 in 19X1. It earned net income of $60,000 in 19X2 and $90,000 in 19X3. The company declared no dividends during the three-year period.

Ensenada, Inc. Ensenada's charter authorizes the company to issue 10,000 shares of $2.50 preferred stock with par value of $100 and 120,000 shares of no-par common stock. Ensenada issued 1,000 shares of the preferred stock at $104 per share. It issued 40,000 shares of the common stock for a total of $220,000. The company's retained earnings balance at the beginning of 19X3 was $72,000, and net income for the year was $90,000. During 19X3 the company declared the specified dividend on preferred and a $0.50 per share dividend on common. Preferred dividends for 19X2 were in arrears.

Required

For each company, prepare the stockholders' equity section of its balance sheet at December 31, 19X3. Show the computation of all amounts. Entries are not required.

P14-4B The purpose of this problem is to familiarize you with the financial statement information of a real company, U and I Group. U and I, which makes food products and livestock feeds, included the following stockholders' equity on its year-end balance sheet at February 28:

Analyzing the stockholders' equity of an actual corporation
(Obj. 3, 5)

Stockholders' Equity	($ Thousands)
Voting Preferred stock, 5.5% cumulative—par value $23 per share; authorized 100,000 shares in each class:	
Class A—issued 75,473 shares	$ 1,736
Class B—issued 92,172 shares	2,120
Common stock—par value $5 per share; authorized 5,000,000 shares; issued 2,870,950 shares...	14,355
[Additional] Paid-in Capital	5,548
Retained earnings	8,336
	$32,095

Required

1. Identify the different issues of stock U and I has outstanding.
2. Give the summary entries to record issuance of all the U and I stock. Assume that all the stock was issued for cash and that the additional paid-in capital applies to the common stock. Explanations are not required.
3. Rearrange the U and I stockholders' equity section to correspond, as appropriate, to the format and terminology illustrated on page 575.
4. Suppose U and I passed its preferred dividends for one year. Would the company have to pay those dividends in arrears before paying dividends to the common stockholders? Give your reason.
5. What amount of preferred dividends must U and I declare and pay each year to avoid having preferred dividends in arrears?
6. Assume that preferred dividends are in arrears for 19X8.
   a. Write Note 5 of the February 28, 19X8, financial statements to disclose the dividends in arrears.
   b. Record the declaration of a $450,000 dividend in the year ended February 28, 19X9. An explanation is not required.

Preparing a corporation balance sheet; measuring profitability (Obj. 3, 6)

P14-5B   The following accounts and related balances of Yeltsin Art Supply, Inc., are arranged in no particular order.

Required

1. Prepare the company's classified balance sheet in the account format at June 30, 19X2.
2. Compute rate of return on total assets and rate of return on common stockholders' equity for the year ended June 30, 19X2.
3. Do these rates of return suggest strength or weakness? Give your reason.
4. How will what you learned in this problem help you evaluate an investment?

Cash	$ 13,000	Interest expense	$ 6,100
Accounts receivable, net	46,000	Property, plant, and	
Paid-in capital in excess		equipment, net	247,000
of par—common	19,000	Common stock, $1 par,	
Accrued liabilities	26,000	500,000 shares authorized,	
Long-term note payable	72,000	236,000 shares issued	236,000
Inventory	139,000	Prepaid expenses	10,000
Dividends payable	9,000	Revenue from donation	6,000
Retained earnings	?	Common stockholders' equity,	
Accounts payable	31,000	June 30, 19X1	322,000
Trademark, net	9,000	Net income	31,000
Organization cost, net	14,000	Total assets, June 30, 19X1	504,000
Preferred stock, $0.20, no-par,			
10,000 shares authorized and			
issued	27,000		

Computing dividends on preferred and common stock (Obj. 5)

P14-6B   Dhaliwal Corporation has 10,000 shares of $3.50, no-par preferred stock and 50,000 shares of no-par common stock outstanding. Dhaliwal declared and paid the following dividends during a three-year period: 19X1, $30,000; 19X2, $80,000; and 19X3, $215,000.

Required

1. Compute the total dividends to preferred stock and common stock for each of the three years if:
   a. Preferred is noncumulative and nonparticipating.
   b. Preferred is cumulative and nonparticipating.
2. For case (1b), record the declaration of the 19X3 dividends on December 28, 19X3, and the payment of the dividends on January 17, 19X4.

P14-7B The balance sheet of Elsimate, Inc., reported the following:

Analyzing the stockholders' equity of an actual corporation (Obj. 5, 7)

Stockholders' Investment
[same as stockholders' equity]

Redeemable nonvoting preferred stock, no-par (Redemption value, $358,000).............	$320,000
Common stock, $1.50 par value, authorized 75,000 shares; issued 36,000 shares..........	54,000
[Additional] paid-in capital	231,000
Retained earnings..	119,000
Total stockholders' investment	$724,000

Notes to the financial statements indicate that 8,000 shares of $2.60 preferred stock with a stated value of $40 per share were issued and outstanding. Preferred dividends are in arrears for three years, including the current year. The additional paid-in capital was contributed by the common stockholders. On the balance sheet date, the market value of the Elsimate common stock was $7.50 per share.

Required

1. Is the preferred stock cumulative or noncumulative, participating or nonparticipating? How can you tell?
2. What is the amount of the annual preferred dividend?
3. Which class of stockholders controls the company? Give your reason.
4. What is the total paid-in capital of the company?
5. What was the total market value of the common stock?
6. Compute the book value per share of the preferred stock and the common stock.

P14-8B The accounting (not the income tax) records of Waterhouse Microfilms, Inc., provide the comparative income statement for 19X3 and 19X4:

Computing and recording a corporation's income tax (Obj. 8)

	19X3	19X4
Total revenue	$680,000	$720,000
Expenses:		
Cost of goods sold	$290,000	$310,000
Operating expenses........................	180,000	190,000
Total expenses before tax...............	470,000	500,000
Pretax accounting income	$210,000	$220,000

Total revenue of 19X4 includes rent of $10,000 that was received late in 19X3. This rent is included in 19X4 total revenue because the rent was earned in 19X4. However, rent revenue that is collected in advance is included in taxable income when the cash is received. In calculating taxable income on the tax return, this rent revenue belongs in 19X3.

Also, the operating expenses of each year include depreciation of $40,000 computed under the straight-line method. In calculating taxable income on the tax return, Waterhouse uses the modified accelerated cost recovery system (MACRS). MACRS depreciation was $60,000 for 19X3 and $20,000 for 19X4.

Required

Assume a corporate income tax rate of 35 percent.

1. Compute taxable income for each year.
2. Journalize the corporation's income taxes for each year.
3. Prepare the corporation's single-step income statement for each year.

EXTENDING YOUR KNOWLEDGE

DECISION PROBLEMS

Evaluating alternative ways of raising capital
(Obj. 2, 3)

1. Dave Den Herder and J. J. Joe have written a computer program for a video game that they believe will rival Nintendo. They need additional capital to market the product, and they plan to incorporate their partnership. They are considering alternative capital structures for the corporation. Their primary goal is to raise as much capital as possible without giving up control of the business. The partners plan to receive 110,000 shares of the corporation's common stock in return for the net assets of the partnership. After the partnership books are closed and the assets adjusted to current market value, Den Herder's capital balance will be $60,000, and Joe's balance will be $50,000.

The corporation's plans for a charter include an authorization to issue 5,000 shares of preferred stock and 500,000 shares of $1-par common stock. Den Herder and Joe are uncertain about the most desirable features for the preferred stock. Prior to incorporating, the partners are discussing their plans with two investment groups. The corporation can obtain capital from outside investors under either of the following plans:

Plan 1. Group 1 will invest $105,000 to acquire 1,000 shares of $5, no-par preferred stock and $70,000 to acquire 70,000 shares of common stock. Each preferred share receives 50 votes on matters that come before the stockholders.

Plan 2. Group 2 will invest $160,000 to acquire 1,400 shares of 6-percent, $100-par nonvoting, noncumulative, participating preferred stock.

Required

Assume that the corporation is chartered.

1. Journalize the issuance of common stock to Den Herder and Joe.
2. Journalize the issuance of stock to the outsiders under both plans.
3. Assume that net income for the first year is $150,000 and total dividends are $19,100. Prepare the stockholders' equity section of the corporation balance sheet under both plans.
4. Recommend one of the plans to Den Herder and Joe. Give your reasons.

Questions about corporations
(Obj. 2, 6)

2. Answer the following questions.

1. Why do you think capital stock and retained earnings are shown separately in the shareholders' equity section?
2. Lynn Liu, major shareholder of L-S, Inc., proposes to sell some land she owns to the company for common shares in L-S. What problem does L-S, Inc., face in recording the transaction?
3. Preferred shares generally are preferred with respect to dividends and on liquidation. Why would investors buy common stock when preferred stock is available?
4. What does it mean if the liquidation value of a company's preferred stock is greater than its market value?
5. If you owned 100 shares of stock in Carta Corporation and someone offered to buy the stock for its book value, would you accept the offer? Why or why not?

ETHICAL ISSUE

Note: This case is based on a real situation.

George Campbell paid $50,000 for a franchise that entitled him to market Success Associates software programs in the countries of the European Common Market. Campbell intended to sell individual franchises for the major language groups of western Europe—German, French, English, Spanish, and Italian. Naturally, investors considering buying a franchise from Campbell asked to see the financial statements of his business.

Believing the value of the franchise to be greater than $50,000, Campbell sought to capitalize his own franchise at $500,000. The law firm of McDonald & LaDue helped Campbell form a corporation chartered to issue 500,000 shares of common stock with par value of $1 per share. Attorneys suggested the following chain of transactions:

a. A third party borrows $500,000 and purchases the franchise from Campbell.
b. Campbell pays the corporation $500,000 to acquire all its stock.
c. The corporation buys the franchise from the third party, who repays the loan.

In the final analysis, the third party is debt-free and out of the picture. Campbell owns all the corporation's stock, and the corporation owns the franchise. The corporation balance sheet lists a franchise acquired at a cost of $500,000. This balance sheet is Campbell's most valuable marketing tool.

Required

1. What is unethical about this situation?
2. Who can be harmed? How can they be harmed? What role does accounting play?

FINANCIAL STATEMENT PROBLEMS

1. The Lands' End, Inc., financial statements appear in Appendix A. Answer the following questions about the company's common stock.

Stockholders' equity
(Obj. 2, 3)

1. What does Lands' End call its stockholders' equity?
2. Solely on the basis of the balance sheet, how much common stock did Lands' End issue during the year ended January 28, 1994? Give your reason.
3. An investor or creditor should not jump to a premature conclusion in analyzing a company's financial statements. It is often necessary to analyze different parts of the statements to reach a correct conclusion. Refer to the statement of shareholders' investment for the year ended January 28, 1994 (the bottom panel of the statement), and answer Question 2 again. Give your reason.
4. On the basis of the statement of shareholders' investment, what is the par value per share of Lands' End common stock? Where besides the statement of shareholders' investment can you obtain the answer to this question?
5. As of January 28, 1994, what was the average issue price per share of common stock? In other words, how much had the Lands' End stockholders paid, on average, for each share of Lands' End stock that the company had issued through January 28, 1994? How does the average issue price per share compare to the par value per share?
6. Lands' End's Donated Capital arose prior to the FASB statement that requires companies to report donations as revenues. What asset was donated to the company, and who made the donation? How does donated capital differ from the other paid-in capital?

2. Obtain the annual report of an actual company of your choosing. Answer the following questions about the company. Concentrate on the current year in the annual report you select.

Stockholders' equity
(Obj. 2, 3, 7)

1. What classes of stock does the company have outstanding? What is its par value? How many shares are authorized? How many shares were outstanding on the most current balance sheet date?
2. Under what title does the company report additional paid-in capital?
3. How much is total stockholders' equity? If the total is not labeled, compute total stockholders' equity.
4. Using the company's terminology, journalize the issuance of 100,000 shares of the company's common stock at $55 per share. Recompute all account balances to include the effect of this transaction.
5. Compute the average amount paid in per share of the company's common stock. Then examine the recent market prices of the company's stock in the multiyear summary of financial data. Compare the average amount paid in per share with recent market prices to determine whether the bulk of the company's stock was issued within the recent past. Give the reason for your answer.

Chapter 15

Retained Earnings, Dividends, Treasury Stock, and the Income Statement

After studying this chapter, you should be able to

1. Account for stock dividends

2. Distinguish stock splits from stock dividends

3. Account for treasury stock

4. Report restrictions on retained earnings

5. Identify the elements of a corporation income statement

6. Account for prior-period adjustments

7. Prepare a statement of stockholders' equity

> *Corporations often restructure their operations and take large one-time losses to enhance future results. Sophisticated managers simultaneously sell other assets at a gain to offset the impact of the loss. There is usually a small net effect on financial statements but a substantial rise in the price of the stock.*

WILBUR L. ROSS, JR.,
SENIOR MANAGING
DIRECTOR OF THE
INVESTMENT BANKING
FIRM ROTHSCHILD, INC.

Limited, Inc., is a major clothing retailer based in Columbus, Ohio. The corporation owns nearly 4,500 specialty stores, including The Limited, Lerner, Victoria's Secret, Henri Bendel, and Express. In August 1993 a spokesperson for Limited, Inc., announced that the company would restructure its operations. Limited had already sold its Brylane catalog division for $285 million in cash. This transaction alone was expected to result in a pretax gain of $203 million.

The restructuring plan included closing or downsizing about 360 The Limited and Lerner stores by late 1995 and buying back $500 million, or some 6 percent, of the company's stock. To reduce the carrying amount of some of its assets to current market value, Limited announced its intention to take a $200 million loss in the third quarter.

What does Limited, Inc., hope to accomplish by restructuring? Rapid growth of the company's retail operations. Said Vice-Chairman Kenneth B. Gilman, "Going forward, we believe this effort will bear fruit as we emphasize our best performing stores and shed those assets that do not perform to our expectations." The day after the announcement, Limited, Inc., stock rose in price $1.375, or 6.2 percent, to $23.625 on the New York Stock Exchange. So far, so good. *Source: Adapted from Teri Agins, "Limited Plans Reorganization, Stock Buyback," The Wall Street Journal, August 31, 1993, pp. A3, A12.*

• • • • •

*B*usinesses like Limited, Inc., take actions to increase shareholder value. Apparently, Limited succeeded, because the company's stock price increased by $1.375 per share in one day. If you had owned 1,000 shares of Limited stock before the announcement, your one-day gain would have been $1,375. An increase in its stock price helps a company raise additional capital if the need arises.

In this case Limited, Inc., is shrinking—closing unprofitable stores—rather than expanding. The loss from closing or downsizing stores and the gain from selling its catalog division will appear on Limited's income statement, as illustrated in this chapter. Limited purchased some of its own stock. Stock that a company issues and buys back is called *treasury stock*. This chapter also shows how corporations account for their treasury stock. First, however, we continue the discussion of retained earnings and corporate dividends begun in Chapter 14.

Retained Earnings and Dividends

We have seen that the equity section on the corporation balance sheet is called stockholders' equity or shareholders' equity. The paid-in capital accounts and retained earnings make up the stockholders' equity section.

Retained Earnings is the corporation account that carries the balance of the business's net income less its net losses from operations and less any declared dividends accumulated over the corporation's lifetime. *Retained* means "held onto." Retained Earnings is the shareholders' claim against total assets arising from accumulated income. Successful companies grow by reinvesting the assets they generate by profitable operations.

A debit balance in Retained Earnings, which arises when a corporation's expenses exceed its revenues, is called a *deficit*. This amount is subtracted from the sum of the credit balances in the other equity accounts on the balance sheet to determine total stockholders' equity. In a recent survey, 71 of 600 companies (11.8 percent) had a retained earnings deficit (Exhibit 15-1).

At the end of each accounting period, the Income Summary account—which carries the balance of net income for the period—is closed to the Retained Earnings account. Assume that the following amounts are drawn from a corporation's temporary accounts:

EXHIBIT 15-1
Retained Earnings of the Accounting Trends & Techniques *600 Companies*

			Income Summary		
Dec. 31, 19X6	Expenses	750,000	Dec. 31, 19X6	Revenues	850,000
			Dec. 31, 19X6	Bal.	100,000

This final closing entry transfers net income from Income Summary to Retained Earnings:

19X6			
Dec. 31	Income Summary..	100,000	
	Retained Earnings		100,000
	To close net income to Retained Earnings.		

STOP & THINK Assume that the beginning balance of Retained Earnings was $720,000. What will Retained Earnings's balance be after this net income?

Answer:

		Retained Earnings		
		Jan. 1, 19X6	Bal.	720,000
		Dec. 31, 19X6	Net inc.	100,000
		Dec. 31, 19X6	Bal.	820,000

Remember that the account title includes the word *earnings. Credits to the Retained Earnings account arise only from net income.* When we examine a corporation's financial statements and want to learn how much net income the corporation has earned and retained in the business, we turn to Retained Earnings.

The Retained Earnings account is not a reservoir of cash waiting for the board of directors to pay dividends to the stockholders. Instead, Retained Earnings is an owners' equity account representing a claim on all assets in general and not on any asset in particular. Its balance is the cumulative, lifetime earnings of the company less its cumulative losses and dividends. In fact, the corporation may have a large balance in Retained Earnings but not have the cash to pay a dividend. Why? Because the company purchased a building. To *declare* a dividend, the company must have an adequate balance in Retained Earnings. To *pay* the dividend, it must have the cash. Cash and Retained Earnings are two separate accounts with no particular relationship.

Key Point: Retained Earnings is *not* a bank account. A $500,000 balance in Retained Earnings means that $500,000 of capital has been created by profits reinvested in the business.

Stock Dividends

A **stock dividend** is a proportional distribution by a corporation of its own stock to its stockholders. Stock dividends are fundamentally different from cash dividends because stock dividends do not transfer the assets of the corporation to the stockholders. Cash dividends are distributions of the asset cash, but stock dividends affect *only* the accounts within stockholders' equity. Stock dividends have *no* affect on total stockholders' equity. Stock dividends increase the stock account and decrease Retained Earnings. Because both these accounts are elements of stockholders' equity, total stockholders' equity is unchanged. There is merely a transfer from one stockholders' equity account to another, and no asset or liability is affected by a stock dividend.

OBJECTIVE 1
Account for stock dividends

The corporation distributes stock dividends to stockholders in proportion to the number of shares they already own. For example, suppose you owned 300 shares of Xerox Corporation common stock. If Xerox distributed a 10-percent common stock dividend, you would receive 30 (300 × 0.10) additional shares. You would now own 330 shares of the stock. All other Xerox stockholders would receive additional shares equal to 10 percent of their prior holdings. You would all be in the same relative position after the dividend as you were before.

Reasons for Stock Dividends

In distributing a stock dividend, the corporation gives up no assets. Why, then, do companies issue stock dividends? A corporation may choose to distribute stock dividends for these reasons:

1. To continue dividends but conserve cash. A company may want to keep cash in the business in order to expand, buy inventory, pay off debts, and so on. Yet the company may wish to continue dividends in some form. To do so, the corporation may distribute a stock dividend. The debit to Retained Earnings indirectly conserves cash by decreasing the Retained Earnings available for the declaration of future cash dividends. Stockholders pay tax on cash dividends but not on stock dividends.

2. To reduce the market price per share of its stock. Many companies pay low cash dividends and grow by reinvesting their earnings in operations. As they grow, the company's stock price increases. If the price gets high enough, some potential investors may be prevented from purchasing the stock. Distribution of a stock dividend may cause the market price of a share of the company's stock to decrease because of the increased supply of the stock. Suppose the market price of a share of stock is $50. Doubling the number of shares of stock outstanding by issuing a stock dividend would drop the stock's market price by approximately half, to $25 per share. The objective is to make the stock less expensive and thus attractive to a wider range of investors.

Real-World Example: In *The Wall Street Journal,* you can read "Dividend News" to discover interesting facts about corporations' dividend actions. On 5/9/94, Sun Bancorp reported a 5% (small) stock dividend to shareholders of record on 5/27/94, payable on 6/10/94. Also on 5/9/94, Johnson & Johnson increased its quarterly cash dividend from $0.26 to $0.29 per share, payable on 6/7/94 to shareholders of record on 5/17/94.

Entries for Stock Dividends

◀▥◀▥◀▥ Recall from Chapter 14, p. 569, that the date of record is the date on which a stock's owners are identified and that the payment date is when the dividend is paid.

The board of directors announces stock dividends on the declaration date. The date of record and the payment date follow. ◀▥ (This is the same sequence of dates used for a cash dividend.) The declaration of a stock dividend does *not* create a liability because the corporation is not obligated to pay assets. (Recall that a liability is a claim on *assets*.) Instead, the corporation has declared its intention to distribute its stock. Assume that General Lumber Corporation has the following stockholders' equity prior to the dividend:

Stockholders' Equity

Paid-in capital:	
Common stock, $10 par, 50,000 shares authorized,	
20,000 shares issued	$200,000
Paid-in capital in excess of par—common	70,000
Total paid-in capital	270,000
Retained earnings	85,000
Total stockholders' equity	$355,000

The entry to record a stock dividend depends on the size of the dividend. Generally accepted accounting principles distinguish between *small stock dividends* (less than 25 percent of the corporation's issued stock) and *large stock dividends* (25 percent or more of issued stock). Stock dividends between 20 percent and 25 percent are rare.

Assume that General Lumber Corporation declares a 10-percent (small) common stock dividend on November 17. The company will distribute 2,000 (20,000 × 0.10) shares in the dividend. On November 17 the market value of its common stock is $16 per share. GAAP requires small stock dividends to be accounted for at market value. Therefore, Retained Earnings is debited for the market value of the 2,000 dividend shares. Common Stock Dividend Distributable is credited for par value, and Paid-in Capital in Excess of Par is credited for the remainder. General Lumber makes the following entry on the declaration date:[1]

Nov. 17	Retained Earnings (20,000 × 0.10 × $16)	32,000	
	Common Stock Dividend Distributable		
	(20,000 × 0.10 × $10)		20,000
	Paid-in Capital in Excess of Par—		
	Common		12,000
	To declare a 10-percent common stock dividend.		

On the distribution (payment) date, the company records issuance of the dividend shares as follows:

Dec. 12	Common Stock Dividend Distributable	20,000	
	Common Stock		20,000
	To issue common stock in a stock dividend.		

Common Stock Dividend Distributable is an owners' equity account. (It is *not* a liability because the corporation has no obligation to pay assets.) If the company prepares financial statements after the declaration of the stock dividend but before the dividend has been issued, Common Stock Dividend Distributable is reported in the

---

[1]Committee on Accounting Procedure, "Accounting Research Bulletin No. 43," *Restatement and Revision of Accounting Research Bulletins* (New York: AICPA, 1961), Chap. 7, Sec. B, pars. 10–14.

stockholders' equity section of the balance sheet immediately after Common Stock and before Paid-in Capital in Excess of Par—Common. However, this account holds the par value of the dividend shares only from the declaration date to the date of distribution.

The following tabulation shows the changes in stockholders' equity caused by the stock dividend:

Stockholders' Equity	Before the Dividend	After the Dividend	Change
Paid-in capital:			
Common stock, $10 par,			
50,000 shares authorized,			
20,000 shares issued	$200,000		
22,000 shares issued		$220,000	Up by $20,000
Paid-in capital in excess of par—			
common..	70,000	82,000	Up by $12,000
Total paid-in capital...........................	270,000	302,000	Up by $32,000
Retained earnings	85,000	53,000	Down by $32,000
Total stockholders' equity	$355,000	$355,000	Unchanged

Compare stockholders' equity before and after the stock dividend. Observe the increase in the balances of Common Stock and Paid-in Capital in Excess of Par—Common and the decrease in Retained Earnings. Also observe that total stockholders' equity is unchanged from $355,000.

AMOUNT OF RETAINED EARNINGS TRANSFERRED IN A STOCK DIVIDEND Stock dividends are said to be *capitalized retained earnings* because they transfer an amount from retained earnings to paid-in capital. The paid-in capital accounts are more permanent than retained earnings because they are not subject to reduction by dividends. As we saw in the preceding example, the amount transferred from Retained Earnings in a *small* stock dividend is the market value of the dividend shares because the effect of the market price of each share of the company's stock is likely to be small. Therefore, many stockholders view small stock dividends as distributions similar to cash dividends.

A *large* stock dividend, though, significantly increases the number of shares available in the market and so is likely to decrease the stock price significantly. Because of the drop in market price per share, a large stock dividend is not likely to be perceived as a dividend. GAAP does not require that large stock dividends be accounted for at a specific amount. A common practice is to use the par value of the dividend shares.

Suppose General Lumber declared a 50-percent common stock dividend. The declaration entry is as follows:

Dec. 7	Retained Earnings (20,000 × 0.50 × $10 par)	100,000	
	Common Stock Dividend Distributable		100,000
	To declare a 50-percent common stock dividend.		

Issuance of the dividend shares on the payment date is recorded by this entry:

Dec. 22	Common Stock Dividend Distributable........................	100,000	
	Common Stock		100,000
	To issue common stock in a stock dividend.		

Once again, total stockholders' equity is unchanged. For a large stock dividend, the increase in Common Stock is exactly offset by the decrease in Retained Earnings.

Short Exercise: A corporation issued 1,000 shares of its $15-par common stock as a stock dividend when the stock's market price was $25 per share. Record the declaration and distribution. Assume that the 1,000 shares issued are (1) 10% of the outstanding shares and (2) 100% of the outstanding shares. *A:*

(1) *Date of declaration:*
Retained Earnings
(1,000 × $25)........ 25,000
    Com. Stock Dividend Distributable
    (1,000 × $15)   15,000
    Paid-in Capital in Excess of Par—Common....... 10,000

Date of distribution:
Com. Stock Dividend Distributable 15,000
    Com. Stock...... 15,000

(2) *Date of declaration:*
Retained Earnings
(1,000 × $15)........ 15,000
    Com. Stock Dividend Distributable   15,000

Date of distribution:
Com. Stock Dividend Distributable.... 15,000
    Com. Stock.. 15,000

Stock Splits

A large stock *dividend* may decrease the market price of the stock. A stock *split* also decreases the market price of stock—with the intention of making the stock more attractive. A **stock split** is an increase in the number of authorized, issued, and outstanding shares of stock, coupled with a proportionate reduction in the par value of the stock. For example, if the company splits its stock 2 for 1, the number of outstanding shares is doubled and each share's par value is halved. Most leading companies in the United States—IBM, Ford Motor Company, Giant Food, Inc., and others—have split their stock. Honeywell, Inc., split its stock 2 for 1 twice in a three-year period. The board of directors for the company, which makes electronic controls for the home, industry, and space and aviation markets, authorized the stock splits as dividends distributable to stockholders.

"*Honeywell, Inc., split its stock 2 for 1 twice in a three-year period.*"

The market price of a share of IBM common stock has been approximately $40. Assume that the company wishes to decrease the market price to approximately $10. IBM decides to split the common stock 4 for 1 to reduce the stock's market price from $40 to $10. A 4-for-1 stock split means that the company would have four times as many shares of stock outstanding after the split as it had before and that each share's par value would be quartered. Assume that IBM had 150 million shares of $5 par common stock issued and outstanding before the split.

Stockholders' Equity [Before Stock Split]	($ Millions)
Paid-in capital:	
Common stock, **$5 par**, 900 million shares authorized,	
150 million shares issued	$ 750
Paid-in capital in excess of par—common	5,200
Total paid-in capital...	5,950
Retained earnings	20,000
Total stockholders' equity	$25,950

After the 4-for-1 stock split, IBM would have 3,600 million shares authorized and 600 million shares (150 million shares × 4) of $1.25 par ($5/4) common stock issued and outstanding. Total stockholders' equity would be exactly as before the stock split. Indeed, the balance in the Common Stock account does not even change. Only the par value of the stock and the number of shares authorized and issued change. Compare the highlighted figures in the two stockholders' equity presentations.

Short Exercise: Answer these questions to review stock and cash dividends:
1. How is a stock dividend like a cash dividend? *A:* Both are a distribution to shareholders; both reduce Retained Earnings.
2. What happens to total paid-in capital as a result of cash and stock dividends? *A:* No change with a cash dividend;

Stockholders' Equity [After Stock Split]	($ Millions)
Paid-in capital:	
Common stock, **$1.25 par, 3,600 million shares authorized,**	
600 million shares issued	$ 750
Paid-in capital in excess of par—common	5,200
Total paid-in capital...	5,950
Retained earnings	20,000
Total stockholders' equity	$25,950

Because the stock split affects no account balances, no formal journal entry is necessary. Instead, the split is recorded in a memorandum entry such as the following:

Aug. 19   Called in the outstanding $5 par common stock and distributed four shares of $1.25 par common stock for each old share previously outstanding.

A company may engage in a reverse split to decrease the number of shares of stock outstanding. For example, IBM could split its stock 1 for 4. After the split, par value would be $20 ($5 × 4), shares authorized would be 225 million (900 million/4), and shares issued and outstanding would be 37.5 million (150 million/4). Reverse splits are unusual.

Stock Dividends and Stock Splits

Both a stock dividend and a stock split increase the number of shares of stock owned per stockholder. Also, neither a stock dividend nor a stock split changes the investor's total cost of the stock owned. Consider Avon Products, Inc., whose beauty products are sold in 119 countires primarily by independent sales representatives. Assume that you paid $3,000 to acquire 150 shares of Avon common stock. If Avon distributes a 100-percent stock dividend, your 150 shares increase to 300, but your total cost is still $3,000. Likewise, if Avon distributes a 2-for-1 stock split, your shares increase in number to 300, but your total cost is unchanged. Neither type of stock action creates taxable income for the investor.

"Consider Avon Products, Inc., whose beauty products are sold in 119 countries primarily by independent sales representatives."

Both a stock dividend and a stock split increase the corporation's number of shares of stock outstanding. For example, a 100-percent stock dividend and a 2-for-1 stock split both double the number of outstanding shares and cut the stock's market price per share in half. They differ in that a stock *dividend* shifts an amount from retained earnings to paid-in capital, leaving the par value per share unchanged. A stock *split* affects no account balances whatsoever. Instead a stock split changes the par value of the stock. It also increases the number of shares of stock authorized.

Exhibit 15-2 summarizes the effects of dividends and stock splits on total stockholders' equity.

increase with a stock dividend (by the same amount that Retained Earnings decreases).

3. What happens to total stockholders' equity as a result of cash and stock dividends? *A:* Decrease with cash dividend; no change with stock dividend.

4. Which type of dividend gives taxable income to the shareholder? *A:* Cash dividend only.

OBJECTIVE 2
Distinguish stock splits from stock dividends

EXHIBIT 15-2
Effects of Dividends and Stock Splits on Total Stockholders' Equity

| | Effect on Total Stockholders' Equity | |
	Declaration	Payment of Cash or Distribution of Stock
Cash dividend..............	Decrease	None
Stock dividend..............	None	None
Stock split.....................	None	None

Source: Adapted from Beverly Terry.

Treasury Stock

OBJECTIVE 3
Account for treasury stock

Key Point: Treasury stock is issued stock, but it is *not* outstanding.

Corporations may purchase their own stock from their shareholders for several reasons: (1) The company has issued all its authorized stock and needs the stock for distributions to officers and employees under bonus plans or stock purchase plans. (2) The purchase helps support the stock's current market price by decreasing the supply of stock available to the public. This could be Limited's motivation for purchasing its own stock in the chapter-opening story. (3) The business is trying to increase net assets by buying its shares low and hoping to sell them for a higher price later. (4) Management wants to avoid a takeover by an outside party.

Stock that a corporation has issued and later reacquired is called **treasury stock**.[2] (In effect, the corporation holds the stock in its treasury.) Treasury stock is like unissued stock: Neither category of stock is outstanding in the hands of shareholders. The company does not receive cash dividends on its treasury stock, and treasury stock does not entitle the company to vote or to receive assets in liquidation. The difference between unissued stock and treasury stock is that treasury stock has been issued and bought back by the company itself.

The purchase of treasury stock decreases the company's assets and its stockholders' equity. The size of the company literally decreases, as shown on the balance sheet. This appears to be occurring as Limited, Inc., is closing some stores and scaling back the size of other stores. Overall, Limited is downsizing its operations. Purchasing treasury stock is consistent with a corporate strategy of downsizing.

The Treasury Stock account has a debit balance, which is the opposite of the other owners' equity accounts. Therefore, Treasury Stock is a contra stockholders' equity account.

Purchase of Treasury Stock

We record the purchase of treasury stock by debiting Treasury Stock and crediting the asset given in exchange—usually Cash. Suppose that Southwest Drilling Company had the following stockholders' equity before purchasing treasury stock:

Stockholders' Equity [*Before* Purchase of Treasury Stock]	
Paid-in capital:	
Common stock, $1 par, 10,000 shares authorized, 8,000 shares issued	$ 8,000
Paid-in capital in excess of par—common	12,000
Total paid-in capital	20,000
Retained earnings	14,600
Total stockholders' equity	$34,600

On November 22 Southwest purchases 1,000 shares of its $1-par common as treasury stock, paying cash of $7.50 per share. Southwest records the purchase of treasury stock as follows:

Nov. 22	Treasury Stock, Common (1,000 × $7.50)	7,500	
	Cash		7,500
	Purchased 1,000 shares of treasury stock at $7.50 per share.		

---

[2]In this book we illustrate the *cost* method of accounting for treasury stock because it is used most widely. Alternative methods are presented in intermediate accounting courses.

Treasury stock is recorded at cost, without reference to the par value of the stock. The Treasury Stock account appears beneath Retained Earnings on the balance sheet, and its balance is subtracted from the sum of total paid-in capital and retained earnings, as follows:

Stockholders' Equity [*After* Purchase of Treasury Stock]

Paid-in capital:	
Common stock, $1 par, 10,000 shares authorized,	
8,000 shares issued, 7,000 shares outstanding...................	$ 8,000
Paid-in capital in excess of par—common	12,000
Total paid-in capital	20,000
Retained earnings	14,600
Subtotal	34,600
Less treasury stock (1,000 shares at cost)...........................	**(7,500)**
Total stockholders' equity..	$27,100

The purchase of treasury stock does not decrease the number of shares issued. The Common Stock, Paid-in Capital in Excess of Par, and Retained Earnings accounts remain unchanged. However, total stockholders' equity decreases by the cost of the treasury stock. Also, shares of stock *outstanding* decrease from 8,000 to 7,000. To compute the number of outstanding shares, subtract the treasury shares (1,000) from the shares issued (8,000). Although the number of outstanding shares is not required to be reported on the balance sheet, this figure is important. Only outstanding shares have voting rights, receive cash dividends, and share in assets if the corporation liquidates.

STOP & THINK *Ethical Issue:* Treasury stock transactions have a serious ethical and legal dimension. A company buying its own shares as treasury stock must be extremely careful that its disclosures of information are complete and accurate. Otherwise, a stockholder who sold shares back to the company may claim that he or she was deceived into selling the stock at too low a price. What would happen if a company purchased treasury stock at $17 per share and one day later announced a technological breakthrough that would generate millions of dollars of new business?

Answer: The stock would likely increase in response to the new information. If it could be proved that management withheld the information, a shareholder selling stock back to the company may file a lawsuit to gain the difference per share. The stockholder would claim that with knowledge of the technological advance, he or she would have held the stock until after the price increase. Companies strive to avoid such situations.

Short Exercise: Jackson Products, Inc., issued 100,000 shares of $10-par common stock. Later, when the market price was $15 per share, Jackson distributed a 10% stock dividend. Then Jackson purchased 500 shares of stock, at $20 a share, to hold in the treasury. What is the Common Stock balance? *A:* $1,100,000:

$$\begin{aligned} 100{,}000 \text{ shares} \times \$10 \\ = \$1{,}000{,}000 \\ + 10\% \times 100{,}000 \times \$10 \\ = \underline{\quad 100{,}000} \\ \$1{,}100{,}000 \end{aligned}$$

The treasury stock was not used in the calculation—it does not affect Common Stock.

Sale of Treasury Stock

SALE OF TREASURY STOCK AT COST Treasury stock may be sold at any price agreeable to the corporation and the purchaser. If the stock is sold for the same price that the corporation paid to reacquire it, the entry is a debit to Cash and a credit to Treasury Stock for the same amount.

SALE OF TREASURY STOCK ABOVE COST If the sale price is greater than the reacquisition cost, the difference is credited to the account Paid-in Capital from Treasury Stock Transactions. Suppose Southwest Drilling Company resold 200 of its treasury shares for $9 per share. The entry is:

Dec. 7	Cash (200 × $9)...	1,800	
	Treasury Stock, Common (200 × $7.50—		
	the purchase cost per share)		1,500
	Paid-in Capital from Treasury Stock		
	Transactions..		300
	To sell 200 shares of treasury stock at $9 per share.		

Paid-in Capital from Treasury Stock Transactions is reported with the other paid-in capital accounts on the balance sheet, beneath the Common Stock and Capital in Excess of Par accounts.

SALE OF TREASURY STOCK BELOW COST   At times the resale price is less than cost. The difference between these two amounts is debited to Paid-in Capital from Treasury Stock Transactions if this account has a credit balance, as in our example. If the difference between resale price and cost is greater than the credit balance in Paid-in Capital from Treasury Stock Transactions, or if Paid-in Capital from Treasury Stock Transactions has a zero balance, then the company debits Retained Earnings for the remaining amount. For example, Southwest Drilling records the sale of 400 shares of treasury stock at $5 per share in the following entry:

Dec. 23	Cash (400 × $5)...	2,000	
	Paid-in Capital from Treasury Stock		
	Transactions...	300	
	Retained Earnings	700	
	Treasury Stock, Common (400 × $7.50—		
	the purchase cost per share)		3,000
	To sell 400 shares of treasury stock at $5 per share.		

Paid-in Capital from Treasury Stock Transactions receives only a $300 debit because that is the extent of this account's credit balance. (See the preceding example illustrating the sale of treasury stock above cost.) The remaining $700 is debited to Retained Earnings.

Short Exercise: (1) Record the purchase of 1,500 shares of $5-par common stock as treasury stock for $15 per share. (2) Record the sale of treasury stock, 500 shares for $20 per share. (3) Record the sale of the remaining 1,000 shares for $12 per share. *A:*

(1)
Treasury Stock, Com.
    (1,500 × $15)........ 22,500
        Cash 22,500
(2)
Cash (500 × $20) 10,000
    Treasury Stock, Com.
        (500 × $15)... 7,500
    Paid-in Cap. from Treas.
        Stock Trans.. 2,500
(3)
Cash (1,000 × $12) .. 12,000
    Paid-in Cap. from Treas.
        Stock Trans...... 2,500
    Retained Earnings 500
        Treas. Stock, Com. 15,000

PUTTING SKILLS TO WORK

TREASURY STOCK TRANSACTIONS

Neither the purchase nor the sale of treasury stock affects net income. Sale of treasury stock above cost is an increase in paid-in capital, not income. Likewise, sale of treasury stock below cost is a decrease in paid-in capital or retained earnings, not a loss. Treasury stock transactions take place between the business and its owners, the stockholders. Because a company cannot earn a profit in dealing in its own stock with its owners, we credit Paid-in Capital from Treasury Stock Transactions for sale above cost and debit that account (and, if necessary, Retained Earnings) for a sale below cost. These accounts appear on the balance sheet, not on the income statement.

Does this mean that a company cannot increase its net assets by buying treasury stock low and selling it high? Not at all. Management often buys treasury stock because it believes that the market price of its stock is too low. For example, Limited, Inc., purchased $500 million of its own stock in the chapter-opening story. Suppose Limited holds the stock as the market price rises and resells the stock for $600 million. Net assets of the company increase by $100 million. This increase is reported as paid-in capital, not as income.

  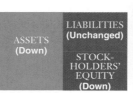

1. Limited, Inc., before the purchase of its own stock

2. Limited, Inc., after the purchase of its own stock

3. Limited, Inc., after the resale of its own stock

Limited, Inc., bought back about 6 percent of its own stock.

Simplicity Pattern Co., Inc., a well-known maker of sewing patterns, reported the following shareholder's equity:

Shareholders' Equity	($ Thousands)
Preferred stock, $1.00 par value	
Authorized—10,000,000 shares	
Issued—None	$ —
Common stock, 8 1/3 cents par value	
Authorized, 30,000,000 shares	
Issued 13,733,229 shares	1,144
Capital in excess of par value...	48,122
Earnings retained in business	89,320
	138,586
Less treasury stock, at cost (1,919,000 common shares)........	14,742
	$123,844

Required

1. What was the average issue price per share of the common stock?

2. Journalize the issuance of 1,200 shares of common stock at $4 per share. Use Simplicity's account titles.

3. How many shares of Simplicity's common stock are outstanding?

4. How many shares of common stock would be outstanding after Simplicity split its common stock 3 for 1?

5. Using Simplicity account titles, journalize the declaration of a stock dividend when the market price of Simplicity common stock is $3 per share. Consider each of the following stock dividends independently:

   a. Simplicity declares a 10-percent common stock dividend on the shares outstanding, computed in Requirement 3.

   b. Simplicity declares a 100-percent common stock dividend on the shares outstanding, computed in Requirement 3.

6. Journalize the following treasury stock transactions, assuming they occur in the order given:

   a. Simplicity purchases 500 shares of treasury stock at $8 per share.

   b. Simplicity sells 100 shares of treasury stock for $9 per share.

   c. Simplicity sells 100 shares of treasury stock for $5 per share.

SOLUTION TO REVIEW PROBLEM

1. Average issue price of common stock was $3.59 per share
   [($1,144,000 + $48,122,000)/13,733,229 shares = $3.59].

2.
Cash (1,200 × $4)...	4,800	
Common Stock (1,200 × $0.08 1/3).....................................		100
Capital in Excess of Par Value..		4,700

   To issue common stock at a premium.

3. Shares outstanding = 11,814,229 (13,733,229 shares issued minus 1,919,000 shares of treasury stock)

4. Shares outstanding after a 3-for-1 stock split = 35,442,687
   (11,814,229 shares outstanding × 3)

5a.
Earnings Retained in Business		
(11,814,229 × 0.10 × $3)	3,544,269	
Common Stock Dividend Distributable		
(11,814,229 × 0.10 × $0.08 1/3)....................................		98,452
Capital in Excess of Par Value..		3,445,817

   To declare a 10-percent common stock dividend.

b. Earnings Retained in Business		
(11,814,229 × $0.08 1/3)..	984,519	
Common Stock Dividend Distributable................................		984,519
To declare a 100-percent common stock dividend.		
6a. Treasury Stock (500 × $8)..	4,000	
Cash		4,000
To purchase 500 shares of treasury stock at $8 per share.		
b. Cash (100 × $9)...	900	
Treasury Stock (100 × $8)..		800
Paid-in Capital from Treasury Stock Transactions................		100
To sell 100 shares of treasury stock at $9 per share.		
c. Cash (100 × $5)...	500	
Paid-in Capital from Treasury Stock		
Transactions (balance from answer 6b)..	100	
Earnings Retained in Business	200	
Treasury Stock (100 × $8)..		800
To sell 100 shares of treasury stock at $5 per share.		

Retirement of Stock

A corporation may purchase its own common stock or preferred stock and *retire* it by canceling the stock certificates. The retired stock cannot be reissued. Retiring stock, like purchasing treasury stock, decreases the outstanding stock of the corporation. Unlike a treasury stock purchase, stock retirement decreases the number of shares issued. In retiring stock, the corporation removes the balances from all paid-in capital accounts related to the retired shares, such as Capital in Excess of Par.

A corporation may repurchase shares for retirement for a price that is below the stock's issue price (par value plus any capital in excess of par). This difference between purchase price and issue price is a credit to Paid-in Capital from Retirement of Common Stock (or Preferred Stock). If the corporation must pay more than the stock's issue price, the excess is debited to Retained Earnings.

Retiring stock, like purchasing stock, is a transaction that does not affect net income. No gain or loss arises from stock retirement because the company is doing business with its owners. Stock retirement affects *balance sheet accounts*, not income statement accounts.

Restrictions on Retained Earnings

OBJECTIVE 4

Report restrictions on retained earnings

Dividends, purchases of treasury stock, and retirements of stock require payments by the corporation to its stockholders. In fact, treasury stock purchases and stock retirements are returns of paid-in capital to the stockholders. These outlays decrease the corporation's assets, so fewer assets are available to pay liabilities. Therefore, its creditors seek to restrict a corporation's dividend payments and treasury stock purchases. For example, a bank may agree to loan $500,000 only if the borrowing corporation limits dividend payments and purchases of its stock.

To ensure that corporations maintain a minimum level of stockholders' equity for the protection of creditors, state laws restrict the amount of its own stock that a corporation may purchase. The maximum amount a corporation can pay its stockholders without decreasing paid-in capital is its balance of retained earnings. Therefore, restrictions on dividends and stock purchases focus on the balance of retained earnings.

Companies usually report their retained earnings restrictions in notes to the financial statements. The following disclosure by RTE Corporation, a manufacturer of electronic transformers, is typical:

NOTES TO CONSOLIDATED FINANCIAL STATEMENTS
NOTE F—LONG-TERM DEBT

The...loan agreements...restrict cash dividends and similar payments to shareholders. Under the most restrictive of these provisions, retained earnings of $4,300,000 were unrestricted as of December 31, 19X3.

Alberto-Culver Company—maker of Molly McButter butter substitute, Static Guard antistatic spray, and Alberto VO5 hair products—also had restrictions on retained earnings. These restrictions are indicated in Alberto-Culver's Note 3, part of which follows:

"Alberto-Culver Company—maker of Molly McButter butter substitute, Static Guard antistatic spray, and Alberto VO5 hair products—also had restrictions on retained earnings."

NOTES TO CONSOLIDATED FINANCIAL STATEMENTS
NOTE 3: LONG-TERM DEBT

Various borrowing arrangements impose restrictions on such items as total debt, working capital, dividend payments, treasury stock purchases, and interest expense. At September 30, 19X3, the company was in compliance with these arrangements and $73 million of consolidated retained earnings was not restricted as to the payment of dividends and purchases of treasury stock.

STOP & THINK   Why would a borrower such as Alberto-Culver Company agree to restrict dividends as a condition for receiving a loan?

Answer: To get a lower interest rate. Other things being equal, the greater the borrower's concessions, the more favorable the terms offered by the lender.

Appropriations of Retained Earnings

Appropriations are restrictions on Retained Earnings that are recorded by formal journal entries. A corporation may *appropriate*—segregate in a separate account—a portion of Retained Earnings for a specific use. For example, the board of directors may appropriate part of Retained Earnings for building a new manufacturing plant or for meeting possible future liabilities. A debit to Retained Earnings and a credit to a separate account—Retained Earnings Appropriated for Plant Expansion—records the appropriation. This appropriated retained earnings account appears directly above the regular Retained Earnings account on the balance sheet.

Retained earnings appropriations are rare. Corporations generally disclose any retained earnings restrictions in the notes to the financial statements as illustrated in the preceding section.

Key Point: Most restrictions are reported in the notes to the financial statements, but a company may also choose to journalize the restriction. This journalizing approach is called appropriating retained earnings. It is rare.

Variations in Reporting Stockholders' Equity

Real-world accounting and business practices may use terminology and formats in reporting stockholders' equity that differ from our general examples. We use a more detailed format in this book to help you learn the components of the stockholders' equity section. Companies assume that readers of their statements already understand the details they omit.

General Teaching Format		Real-World Format	
Stockholders' equity		**Stockholders' equity**	
Paid-in capital:		Preferred stock, 8%, $10 par, 30,000	
		shares authorized and issued	$ 310,000
Preferred stock, 8%, $10 par, 30,000 shares		Common stock, $1 par, 100,000	
authorized and issued	$ 300,000	shares authorized, 60,000 shares	
Paid-in capital in excess of par—preferred	10,000	issued..	60,000
		Additional paid-in capital	2,160,000
Common stock, $1 par, 100,000 shares		Retained earnings (Note 7)	1,565,000
authorized, 60,000 shares issued	60,000	Less treasury stock, common	
		(1,400 shares at cost).................................	(42,000)
Paid-in capital in excess of par—common	2,140,000		$4,053,000
Paid-in capital from treasury stock			
transactions, common..............................	9,000		
Paid-in capital from retirement of		*Note 7—Restriction on retained earnings.*	
preferred stock	11,000	At December 31, 19XX, $400,000 of retained earnings is restricted by the company's board of directors to absorb the effect of any contingencies that may arise. Accordingly, possible dividend declarations are restricted to a maximum of $1,165,000 ($1,565,000 − $400,000).	
Total paid-in capital.....................................	2,530,000		
Retained earnings appropriated for			
contingencies..	400,000		
Retained earnings—unappropriated...............	1,165,000		
Total retained earnings................................	1,565,000		
Subtotal...	4,095,000		
Less treasury stock, common			
(1,400 shares at cost)	(42,000)		
Total stockholders' equity	$4,053,000		

EXHIBIT 15-3

Formats for Reporting Stockholders' Equity

One of the most important skills you will learn in this course is the ability to understand the financial statements of real companies. Thus we present in Exhibit 15-3 a side-by-side comparison of our general teaching format and the format that you are more likely to encounter in real-world balance sheets. Note the following points in the real-world format:

1. The heading Paid-in Capital does not appear. It is commonly understood that Preferred Stock, Common Stock, and Additional Paid-in Capital are elements of paid-in capital.

2. Preferred stock is often reported in a single amount that combines its par value and premium.

3. For presentation in the financial statements, all additional paid-in capital—from capital in excess of par on common stock, treasury stock transactions, and stock retirement—appears as a single amount labeled Additional Paid-in Capital. Additional Paid-in Capital belongs to the common stockholders, and so it follows Common Stock in the real-world format.

4. Often, total stockholders' equity ($4,053,000 in Exhibit 15-3) is not specifically labeled.

Corporation Income Statement

OBJECTIVE 5

Identify the elements of a corporation income statement

A corporation's net income receives more attention than any other item in the financial statements. In fact, net income is probably the most important piece of information about a company. Net income measures the business's ability to earn a profit and indicates how successfully the company has managed its operations. To stockholders, the larger the corporation's profit, the greater the likelihood of dividends. To creditors, the larger the corporation's profit, the better able it is to pay its debts. Net income builds up a company's assets and owners' equity. It also helps to attract capital from new investors who hope to receive dividends from future successful operations.

Suppose you are considering investing in the stock of two manufacturing companies. In reading their annual reports and examining their past records, you learn that the companies showed the same net income figure for last year and that each company has increased its net income by 15 percent annually over the last five years.

The two companies, however, have generated income in different ways. Company A's income has resulted from the successful management of its central operations (manufacturing). Company B's manufacturing operations have been flat for two years. Its growth in net income has resulted from selling off segments of its business at a profit. Which company would you invest in?

Company A holds the promise of better future earnings. This corporation earns profits from continuing operations. We may reasonably expect the business to match its past earnings in the future. Company B shows no growth from operations. Its net income results from one-time transactions, the selling off of its operating assets. Sooner or later, Company B will have sold off the last of its assets used in operations. When that occurs, the business will have no means of generating income. On the basis of this reasoning, your decision is to invest in the stock of Company A. Investors would say that Company A's earnings were of *higher quality* than Company B's earnings.

This example points to two important investment considerations: the *trend* of a company's earnings and the *makeup* of its net income. More intelligent investment decisions are likely if the income statement separates the results of central, continuing operations from special, one-time gains and losses. We now discuss the components of the corporation income statement. We will see how the income statement reports the results of operations in a manner that allows statement users to get a good look at the business's operations. Exhibit 15-4 will be used throughout these discussions. The items of primary interest are highlighted for emphasis.

Continuing Operations

We have seen that income from a business's continuing operations helps financial statement users make predictions about the business's future earnings. In the income statement of Exhibit 15-4, the topmost section reports income from continuing operations. This part of the business is expected to continue from period to period. We may use this information to predict that Electronics Corporation will earn income of approximately $54,000 next year.

The continuing operations of Electronics Corporation include two items deserving explanation. First, during 19X5, the company restructured operations at a loss of $10,000. This loss is similar to the $200 million loss that Limited, Inc., announced in the chapter-opening story. Restructuring costs include severance pay to laid-off workers, moving expenses for employees transferred to other locations, and environmental cleanup expenses. The restructuring loss is part of continuing operations because Electronics is remaining in the same line of business. But the restructuring loss is highlighted as an "other" item on the income statement because its cause—restructuring—falls outside Electronics Corporation's main business endeavor, which is selling electronics products.

Second, income tax expense has been deducted in arriving at income from continuing operations. The tax that corporations pay on their income is a significant expense. The federal income tax rate for corporations varies over time, and the current maximum rate is 35 percent. For computational ease, we will use an income tax rate of 40 percent in our illustrations. This is a reasonable estimate of combined federal and state income taxes. The $36,000 income tax expense in Exhibit 15-4 equals the pretax income from continuing operations multiplied by the tax rate ($90,000 \times 0.40 = $36,000).

EXHIBIT 15-4

Corporation Income Statement

ELECTRONICS CORPORATION INCOME STATEMENT FOR THE YEAR ENDED DECEMBER 31, 19X5		
Sales revenue		$ 500,000
Cost of goods sold		240,000
Gross margin		260,000
Operating expenses (detailed)		181,000
Operating income		79,000
Other gains (losses):		
Loss on restructuring operations		(10,000)
Gain on sale of machinery		21,000
Income from continuing operations before income tax		90,000
Income tax expense		36,000
Income from continuing operations		54,000
Discontinued operations:		
Operating income, $30,000, less income tax of $12,000	$18,000	
Gain on disposal, $5,000, less income tax of $2,000	3,000	21,000
Income before extraordinary item and cumulative effect of change in depreciation method		75,000
Extraordinary flood loss, $20,000, less income tax saving of $8,000		(12,000)
Cumulative effect of change in depreciation method, $10,000, less income tax of $4,000		6,000
Net income		$ 69,000
Earnings per share of common stock (20,000 shares outstanding):		
Income from continuing operations		$ 2.70
Income from discontinued operations		1.05
Income before extraordinary item and cumulative effect of change in depreciation method		3.75
Extraordinary loss		(0.60)
Cumulative effect of change in depreciation method		0.30
Net income		$ 3.45

Short Exercise: On 9/1/X9, American Equipment Corp. sells its division that manufactures mobile homes. The assets are sold at a gain of $850,000. The loss from operations for the year up to the date of sale was $480,000. Tax rate is 30%. How would you present the loss for the year and the sale of the division on the 19X9 income statement? *A:* In the Discontinued Operations section you would list two items:

Operating loss, $480,000, less income tax savings, $144,000............$(336,000)

Gain on disposal, $850,000, less income tax, $255,000............ 595,000

$ 259,000

Real-World Example: Segments represent major lines of business or geographic areas. McDonald's derives most of its revenues from the sale of menu items at restaurants, so it reports its segments only for geographic areas. The U.S. provides its greatest revenues, followed by Europe/Africa. Procter and Gamble reports geographical segments as well as product groups—laundry and cleaning, personal care, food and beverage, and pulp and chemicals. Personal care is the largest segment.

Discontinued Operations

Most large corporations engage in several lines of business. For example, General Mills, Inc., best known for its food products, also has retailing and restaurant operations. Sears, Roebuck & Co., in addition to its retail stores, has a real estate development company (Homart) and an insurance company (Allstate). We call each identifiable division of a company a **segment of the business**.

A company may sell a segment of its business. For example, Limited, Inc., sold its catalog division. Such a sale is not a regular source of income because a company cannot keep on selling its segments indefinitely. The sale of a business segment is viewed as a one-time transaction. The income statement carries information on the segment that has been disposed of under the heading Discontinued Operations. This section of the income statement is divided into two components: (1) operating income or (loss) on the segment that is disposed of and (2) any gain (or loss) on the disposal. Income and gain are taxed at the 40-percent rate and reported as follows:

Discontinued operations:		
Operating income, $30,000, less income tax, $12,000	$18,000	
Gain on disposal, $5,000, less income tax, $2,000	3,000	$21,000

Trace this presentation to Exhibit 15-4.

It is necessary to separate discontinued operations into these two components because the company may operate the discontinued segment for part of the year. This is the operating income (or loss) component. Then, the disposal of the segment results in a gain (or loss).

Discontinued operations are common in business. RJR Nabisco sold Kentucky Fried Chicken to PepsiCo, Inc., because of disappointing returns. The Black and Decker Manufacturing Company disposed of its gasoline chain-saw business, and Purolator, Inc., sold its armored-car segment. Each of these items was disclosed as discontinued operations in the company's income statement.

"RJR Nabisco sold Kentucky Fried Chicken to PepsiCo, Inc., because of disappointing returns."

Extraordinary Gains and Losses

Extraordinary gains and losses, also called *extraordinary items*, are both unusual for the company and infrequent. Losses from natural disasters (such as earthquakes, floods, and tornadoes), and the taking of company assets by a foreign government (expropriation), are extraordinary.

Extraordinary items are reported along with their income tax effect. During 19X5 Electronics Corporation lost $20,000 of inventory in a flood. This flood loss, which reduces income, also reduces the company's income tax. The tax effect of the loss is computed by multiplying the amount of the loss by the tax rate. The tax effect decreases the net amount of the loss in the same way that the tax effect of income reduces the amount of net income. An extraordinary loss can be reported along with its tax effect as follows:

Extraordinary flood loss.................	$(20,000)	
Less income tax saving...............	8,000	$(12,000)

Trace this item to the income statement in Exhibit 15-4. An extraordinary gain is reported in the same way, net of the income tax on the gain.

Gains and losses due to employee strikes, the settlement of lawsuits, discontinued operations, and the sale of plant assets are *not* extraordinary items. They are considered normal business occurrences. However, because they are outside the business's central operations, they are reported on the income statement as other gains and losses. Examples include the gain on sale of machinery and the restructuring loss in Exhibit 15-4.

Cumulative Effect of a Change in Accounting Principle

Companies sometimes change from one accounting method to another, such as from double-declining-balance (DDB) to straight-line depreciation, or from FIFO to weighted-average cost for inventory. An accounting change makes it difficult to compare one period's financial statements with the statements of preceding periods. Without detailed information, investors and creditors can be led to believe that the current year is better or worse than the preceding year when in fact the only difference is a change in accounting method. To help investors separate the effects of business operations from those effects generated by a change in accounting method, companies report the effect of the accounting change in a special section of the income statement. The section usually appears after extraordinary items.

Short Exercise: How would you report on an income statement: (1) $70,000 extraordinary gain, 30% tax rate, and (2) $120,000 extraordinary loss, 35% tax rate? *A:*

(1) Extraordinary gain $70,000
   Less income taxes   21,000
   Extraordinary gain,
     net of tax $49,000

(2) Extraordinary loss $120,000
   Less tax savings   42,000
   Extraordinary loss,
     net of tax $ 78,000

We need to know what cumulative effect an accounting change would have had on net income of prior years. GAAP requires companies that change accounting methods to disclose the difference between net income actually reported under the old method being discontinued and the net income that the company would have experienced if it had used the new method all along.

Suppose Electronics Corporation changes from DDB to straight-line depreciation at the beginning of 19X5. How will this change in depreciation method affect the 19X5 financial statements? First, it will affect income from continuing operations, which will include the effect of 19X5 depreciation expense by the new method, straight-line. Second, the change will affect cumulative amounts from previous years. If the company had been using straight-line depreciation every year, net income would have been $6,000 higher ($10,000 less the additional income tax of $4,000). In this case the cumulative effect of the change increases net income. A change from straight-line to double-declining-balance usually produces a negative cumulative effect.

Changes in inventory methods and changes in revenue methods are also generally reported in this manner. Numerous exceptions make changes in accounting principle—usually a change in accounting method—a complicated area. Details are covered in later accounting courses.

Earnings per Share (EPS)

The final segment of a corporation income statement presents the company's earnings per share, abbreviated as EPS. In fact, GAAP requires that corporations disclose EPS figures on the income statement. **Earnings per share** is the amount of a company's net income per share of its outstanding common stock. EPS is a key measure of a business's success:

$$\text{Earnings per share} = \frac{\text{Net income}}{\text{Shares of common stock outstanding}}$$

$$\text{EPS} = \frac{\$200,000}{100,000} = \$2$$

Corporation A
Net income: $200,000
Shares of common
  stock outstanding: 100,000

$$\text{EPS} = \frac{\$200,000}{50,000} = \$4$$

Corporation B
Net income: $200,000
Shares of common
  stock outstanding: 50,000

Just as the corporation lists separately its different sources of income—from continuing operations, discontinued operations, and so on—it lists separately the EPS figure based on different income sources. Consider the following EPS calculations for Electronics Corporation:

Earnings per share of common stock (20,000 shares outstanding):	
Income from continuing operations ($54,000/20,000)	$2.70
Income from discontinued operations ($21,000/20,000)	1.05
Income before extraordinary item and cumulative effect of change in depreciation method ($75,000/20,000)	3.75
Extraordinary loss ($12,000/20,000)	(0.60)
Cumulative effect of change in depreciation method ($6,000/20,000)	0.30
Net income ($69,000/20,000)	$3.45

Exhibit 15-4 shows how the EPS figures would actually be reported on the income statement.

WEIGHTED-AVERAGE NUMBER OF SHARES OF COMMON STOCK OUTSTANDING

Computing EPS is straightforward if the number of common shares outstanding does not change over the entire accounting period. For many corporations, however, this figure varies over the course of the year. Consider a corporation that had 100,000 shares outstanding from January through November, then purchased 60,000 shares as treasury stock. This company's EPS would be misleadingly high if computed using 40,000 (100,000 – 60,000) shares. To make EPS as meaningful as possible, corporations use the weighted-average number of common shares outstanding during the period.

Let's assume the following figures for Diskette Demo Corporation. From January through May the company had 240,000 shares of common stock outstanding; from June through August, 200,000 shares; and from September through December, 210,000 shares. We compute the weighted average by considering the outstanding shares per month as a fraction of the year:

Short Exercise: The net income of Hart Corp. amounted to $3,750,000. Hart had 200,000 shares of 9%, 100-par preferred stock and 310,000 shares of common stock at the end of the year. At the beginning of the year, Hart had 270,000 shares outstanding and issued 40,000 shares on April 1. Calculate Hart's EPS. *A:*
Weighted average:
$270,000 \times 3/12 = 67,500$
$310,000 \times 9/12 = \underline{232,500}$
$300,000$ shares

$$EPS = \frac{\$3,750,000 - (200,000 \times \$100 \times 9\%)}{300,000 \text{ shares}}$$

$$= \frac{\$3,750,000 - \$1,800,000}{300,000}$$

$$= \$6.50$$

Number of Common Shares Outstanding		Fraction of Year			Weighted-Average Number of Common Shares Outstanding
240,000	×	5/12	(January through May)	=	100,000
200,000	×	3/12	(June through August)	=	50,000
210,000	×	4/12	(September through December)	=	70,000
			Weighted-average number of common shares outstanding during the year		220,000

The 220,000 weighted average would be divided into net income to compute the corporation's EPS.

PREFERRED DIVIDENDS Throughout the EPS discussion we used only the number of shares of common stock outstanding. Holders of preferred stock have no claim to the business's income beyond the stated preferred dividend. But preferred dividends do affect the EPS figure. Recall that EPS is earnings per share of *common* stock. Recall also that dividends on preferred stock are paid first. Therefore, preferred dividends must be subtracted from income subtotals (income from continuing operations, income before extraordinary items, and net income) in the computation of EPS. Preferred dividends are not subtracted from income or loss from discontinued operations, and they are not subtracted from extraordinary gains and losses.

If Electronics Corporation had 10,000 shares of preferred stock outstanding, each with a $1.50 dividend, the annual preferred dividend would be $15,000 (10,000 × $1.50). The $15,000 would be subtracted from each of the different income subtotals, resulting in the following EPS computations for the company:

Earnings per share of common stock (20,000 shares outstanding):
Income from continuing operations ($54,000 – $15,000)/20,000	$1.95
Income from discontinued operations ($21,000/20,000)	1.05
Income before extraordinary item and cumulative effect of change in depreciation method ($75,000 – $15,000)/20,000	3.00
Extraordinary loss ($12,000/20,000)	(0.60)
Cumulative effect of change in depreciation method ($6,000/20,000)	0.30
Net income ($69,000 – $15,000)/20,000	$2.70

DILUTION Some corporations make their preferred stock more attractive to investors by offering convertible preferred stock. Holders of convertible preferred may exchange the preferred stock for common stock. When preferred stock is converted to common stock, the EPS is *diluted*—reduced—because more common stock shares are divided into net income. Because convertible preferred can be traded in for common stock, the common stockholders want to know the amount of the decrease in EPS if the preferred stock is converted into common. To provide this information, corporations present two sets of EPS amounts: EPS based on outstanding common shares (primary EPS) and EPS based on outstanding common shares plus the number of additional common shares that would arise from conversion of the preferred stock into common (diluted EPS).

EPS is the most widely used accounting figure. Many income statement users place top priority on EPS. Also, a stock's market price is related to the company's EPS. By dividing the market price of a company's stock by its EPS, we compute a statistic called the price-to-earnings ratio. *The Wall Street Journal* reports the price/earnings ratio (listed as P/E) daily for more than 3,000 companies.

Statement of Retained Earnings

Retained earnings may be a significant portion of a corporation's owners' equity. The year's income increases the retained earnings balance, and dividends decrease it. Retained earnings are so important that corporations prepare a financial statement to report the major changes in this equity account, much as the statement of owner's equity presents information on changes in the equity of a proprietorship. The statement of retained earnings for Electronics Corporation appears in Exhibit 15-5.

Some companies report income and retained earnings on a single statement. Exhibit 15-6 illustrates how Electronics would combine its income statement and its statement of retained earnings.

EXHIBIT 15-5
Statement of Retained Earnings

ELECTRONICS CORPORATION STATEMENT OF RETAINED EARNINGS FOR THE YEAR ENDED DECEMBER 31, 19X5	
Retained earnings balance, December 31, 19X4.............	$130,000
Net income for 19X5	69,000
	199,000
Dividends for 19X5..	(21,000)
Retained earnings balance, December 31, 19X5.............	$178,000

EXHIBIT 15-6
Statement of Income and Retained Earnings

ELECTRONICS CORPORATION STATEMENT OF INCOME AND RETAINED EARNINGS FOR THE YEAR ENDED DECEMBER 31, 19X5	
Sales revenue..	$500,000
Cost of goods sold	240,000
Net income for 19X5..	$ 69,000
Retained earnings, December 31, 19X4	130,000
	199,000
Dividends for 19X5	(21,000)
Retained earnings, December 31, 19X5	$178,000
Earnings per share of common stock (20,000 shares outstanding):	
Income from continuing operations..	$2.70
Income from discontinued operations...	1.05
Income before extraordinary item and cumulative effect of change in	
depreciation method	3.75
Extraordinary loss	(0.60)
Cumulative effect of change in depreciation method	0.30
Net income...	$3.45

Prior-Period Adjustments

What happens when a company makes an error in recording revenues or expenses? Detecting the error in the period in which it occurs allows the company to make a correction before that period's financial statements have been prepared. But failure to detect the recording error until a later period means that the business will have reported an incorrect amount of income on its income statement. After the revenue and expense accounts are closed, the company's Retained Earnings account will absorb the effect of the error. The balance of Retained Earnings will be wrong until the error is corrected.

Corrections to the beginning balance of Retained Earnings for errors of an earlier period are called **prior-period adjustments**. The correcting entry includes a debit or credit to Retained Earnings for the error amount and a credit or debit to the asset or liability account that was misstated. The prior-period adjustment appears on the corporation's statement of retained earnings to indicate to readers the amount and the nature of the change in the Retained Earnings balance.

Assume that De Graff Corporation recorded income tax expense for 19X4 as $30,000. The correct amount was $40,000. This error resulted in understating 19X4 expenses by $10,000 and overstating net income by $10,000. A bill from the government in 19X5 for the additional $10,000 in taxes alerts the De Graff management to the mistake. The entry to record this prior-period adjustment in 19X5 is the following:

19X5			
June 19	Retained Earnings	10,000	
	Income Tax Payable		10,000
	Prior-period adjustment to correct error in		
	recording income tax expense of 19X4.		

The debit to Retained Earnings keeps the error correction from being reported on the income statement of 19X5. Recall the matching principle. ◀ If Income Tax Expense is debited when the prior-period adjustment is recorded in 19X5, then this $10,000 in taxes will appear on the 19X5 income statement. Its appearance there would not be proper, because the income tax expense arose from 19X4 operations.

This prior-period adjustment would appear on the statement of retained earnings, as follows:

◀▥◀▥◀▥ The matching principle introduced in Chapter 3, p. 93, directs the accountant to record in the same period both expenses incurred (to generate revenues) and the related revenues.

DE GRAFF CORPORATION STATEMENT OF RETAINED EARNINGS FOR THE YEAR ENDED DECEMBER 31, 19X5	
Retained earnings balance, December 31, 19X4, **as**	
originally reported	$390,000
Prior-period adjustment—debit to correct error in	
recording income tax expense of 19X4	(10,000)
Retained earnings balance, December 31, 19X4, **as adjusted**	380,000
Net income for 19X5	114,000
	494,000
Dividends for 19X5	(41,000)
Retained earnings balance, December 31, 19X5	$453,000

ELECTRONICS CORPORATION
STATEMENT OF STOCKHOLDERS' EQUITY
FOR THE YEAR ENDED DECEMBER 31, 19X5

	Common Stock	Additional Paid-in Capital	Retained Earnings	Treasury Stock	Total
Balance, December 31, 19X4	$ 80,000	$160,000	$130,000	$(25,000)	$345,000
Issuance of stock	20,000	65,000			85,000
Net income			69,000		69,000
Cash dividends			(21,000)		(21,000)
Stock dividends—8%	8,000	26,000	(34,000)	–0–	
Purchase of treasury stock				(9,000)	(9,000)
Sale of treasury stock		13,000		4,000	17,000
Balance, December 31, 19X5	$108,000	$264,000	$144,000	$(30,000)	$486,000

EXHIBIT 15-7
Statement of Stockholders' Equity

Statement of Stockholders' Equity

OBJECTIVE 7

Prepare a statement of stockholders' equity

Many companies report a statement of stockholders' equity, which is more comprehensive than a statement of retained earnings. The statement of stockholders' equity is formatted exactly as a statement of retained earnings but with columns for each element of stockholders' equity. The **statement of stockholders' equity** thus reports the changes in all categories of equity during the period: the stock accounts, additional paid-in capital, retained earnings, treasury stock, and the total.

Exhibit 15-7 uses assumed figures for Electronics Corporation to illustrate the statement of stockholders' equity. Negative amounts—debits—appear in parentheses.

Like the retained earnings statement, the statement of stockholders' equity is less important than the income statement or the balance sheet. However, it reports stock transactions, dividends, and the effects of treasury stock transactions in the interest of full disclosure.

SUMMARY PROBLEM FOR YOUR REVIEW

The following information was taken from the ledger of Kraft Corporation:

Loss on sale of discontinued operations	$ 5,000	Treasury stock, common (5,000 shares at cost)	$ 25,000
Prior-period adjustments—credit to Retained Earnings	5,000	Dividends	16,000
		Selling expenses	78,000
Gain on sale of plant assets	21,000	Common stock, no-par, 45,000	
Cost of goods sold	380,000	shares issued	180,000
Income tax expense (saving):		Sales revenue	620,000
Continuing operations	32,000	Interest expense	30,000
Discontinued operations:		Extraordinary gain	26,000
Operating income	10,000	Operating income, discontinued	
Loss on sale	(2,000)	operations	25,000
Extraordinary gain	10,000	Loss due to lawsuit	11,000
Cumulative effect of change in inventory method	(4,000)	General expenses	62,000

| Preferred stock, 8%, $100 par, 500 shares issued | $ 50,000 | Retained earnings, beginning, as originally reported | $103,000 |
| Paid-in capital in excess of par—preferred | 7,000 | Cumulative effect of change in inventory method (debit) | (10,000) |

Required

Prepare a single-step income statement and a statement of retained earnings for Kraft Corporation for the current year ended December 31. Include the earnings-per-share presentation and show computations. Assume no changes in the stock accounts during the year.

SOLUTION TO REVIEW PROBLEM

KRAFT CORPORATION
INCOME STATEMENT
FOR THE YEAR ENDED DECEMBER 31, 19XX

Revenue and gains:		
Sales revenue		$620,000
Gain on sale of plant assets		21,000
Total revenues and gains		641,000
Expenses and losses:		
Cost of goods sold	$380,000	
Selling expenses	78,000	
General expenses	62,000	
Interest expense	30,000	
Loss due to lawsuit	11,000	
Income tax expense	32,000	
Total expenses and losses		593,000
Income from continuing operations		48,000
Discontinued operations:		
Operating income, $25,000, less income tax, $10,000	15,000	
Loss on sale of discontinued operations, $5,000, less income tax saving, $2,000	(3,000)	12,000
Income before extraordinary item and cumulative effect of change in inventory method		60,000
Extraordinary gain, $26,000, less income tax, $10,000		16,000
Cumulative effect of change in inventory method, $10,000, less income tax saving, $4,000		(6,000)
Net income		$ 70,000
Earnings per share:		
Income from continuing operations [($48,000 – $4,000)/40,000 shares]		$1.10
Income from discontinued operations ($12,000/40,000 shares)		0.30
Income before extraordinary item and cumulative effect of change in inventory method [($60,000 – $4,000)/40,000 shares]		1.40
Extraordinary gain ($16,000/40,000 shares)		0.40
Cumulative effect of change in inventory method ($6,000/40,000)		(0.15)
Net income [($70,000 – $4,000)/40,000 shares]		$1.65

Computations:

$$EPS = \frac{Income - Preferred\ dividends}{Common\ shares\ outstanding}$$

Preferred dividends: $50,000 × 0.08 = $4,000
Common shares outstanding:
45,000 shares issued – 5,000 treasury shares = 40,000 shares outstanding

---

KRAFT CORPORATION
STATEMENT OF RETAINED EARNINGS
FOR THE YEAR ENDED DECEMBER 31, 19XX

Retained earnings balance, beginning, as originally reported	$103,000
Prior-period adjustment—credit	5,000
Retained earnings balance, beginning, as adjusted............................	108,000
Net income for current year	70,000
	178,000
Dividends for current year...	(16,000)
Retained earnings balance, ending	$162,000

SUMMARY

1. Account for stock dividends. *Retained Earnings* carries the balance of the business's net income accumulated over its lifetime, less its declared dividends and any net losses. *Cash dividends* are distributions of corporate assets made possible by earnings. *Stock dividends* are distributions of the corporation's own stock to its stockholders.

2. Distinguish stock splits from stock dividends. Stock dividends shift amounts from retained earnings to paid-in capital. *Stock splits* do not change any account balance. Stock splits change the par value of the stock, whereas stock dividends do not. Both increase the number of shares outstanding and lower the market price per share of stock.

3. Account for treasury stock. *Treasury stock* is the corporation's own stock that has been issued and reacquired and is currently held by the company. The corporation may sell treasury stock for its cost or for more or less than cost.

4. Report restrictions on retained earnings. Retained earnings may be *restricted* by law or contract or by the corpora-

tion itself. An *appropriation* is a restriction of retained earnings that is recorded by formal journal entries.

5. Identify the elements of a corporation income statement. The corporate *income statement* lists separately the various sources of income—*continuing operations*, which include other gains and losses, *discontinued operations*, and *extraordinary gains and losses*. The bottom line of the income statement reports *net income* or *net loss* for the period. *Income tax expense* and *earnings-per-share* figures also appear on the income statement, likewise divided into different categories based on the nature of income.

6. Account for prior-period adjustments. The *statement of retained earnings* reports the causes for changes in the Retained Earnings account, including any prior-period adjustments. This statement may be combined with the income statement.

7. Prepare a statement of stockholders' equity. A statement of stockholders' equity reports the changes in all the equity accounts, including Retained Earnings.

SELF-STUDY QUESTIONS

Test your understanding of the chapter by marking the best answer for each of the following questions.

1. A corporation has total stockholders' equity of $100,000, including retained earnings of $19,000. The cash balance is $35,000. The maximum cash dividend the company can declare and pay is *(p. 597)*
   a. $19,000   **c.** $65,000
   b. $35,000   **d.** $100,000

2. A stock dividend *(pp. 597, 599)*
   a. Decreases stockholders' equity
   b. Decreases assets
   c. Leaves total stockholders' equity unchanged
   d. None of the above

3. Meyer's Thrifty Acres has 100,000 shares of $20 par common stock outstanding. The stock's market value is $37 per share. Meyer's board of directors declares and distributes a 1-percent common stock dividend. Which of the following entries shows the full effect of declaring and distributing the dividend? *(p. 598)*

a. Retained Earnings	37,000	
Common Stock Dividend		
Distributable		20,000
Paid-in Capital in Excess of		
Par—Common......................		17,000
b. Retained Earnings	20,000	
Common Stock........................		20,000
c. Retained Earnings	17,000	
Paid-in Capital in Excess of		
Par—Common......................		17,000
d. Retained Earnings	37,000	
Common Stock........................		20,000
Paid-in Capital in Excess of		
Par—Common......................		17,000

4. Lang Real Estate Investment Corporation declared and distributed a 50-percent stock dividend. Which of the following stock splits would have the same effect on the number of Lang shares outstanding? *(p. 600)*

a. 2 for 1   **c.** 4 for 3
b. 3 for 2   **d.** 5 for 4

5. A company purchased 10,000 of its $1.50-par common stock as treasury stock, paying $6 per share. This transaction (pp. 602–603)

    a. Has no effect on company assets   **c.** Decreases owners' equity by $15,000

    b. Has no effect on owners' equity   **d.** Decreases owners' equity by $60,000

6. A restriction on retained earnings (p. 607)

    a. Has no effect on total retained earnings

    b. Reduces retained earnings available for the declaration of dividends

    c. Can be reported by a note or by appropriation of retained earnings, or both

    d. All of the above

7. Which of the following items is not reported on the income statement? (p. 610)

    a. Premium on stock   **c.** Income tax expense

    b. Extraordinary gains and losses   **d.** Earnings per share

8. The income statement item that is likely to be most useful for predicting income from year to year is (pp. 608–611)

    a. Extraordinary items   **c.** Income from continuing operations

    b. Discontinued operations   **d.** Net income

9. When earnings per share is computed, dividends on preferred stock are (p. 613)

    a. Added because they represent earnings to the preferred stockholders

    b. Subtracted because they represent earnings to the preferred stockholders

    c. Ignored because they do not pertain to the common stock

    d. Reported separately on the income statement

10. A corporation accidentally overlooked an accrual of property tax expense at December 31, 19X4. Accountants for the company detect the error early in 19X5 before the expense is paid. The entry to record this prior-period adjustment is

    a. Retained Earnings....................... XXX
             Property Tax Expense XXX

    b. Property Tax Expense XXX
             Property Tax Payable XXX

    c. Retained Earnings....................... XXX
             Property Tax Payable XXX

    d. Property Tax Payable XXX
             Property Tax Expense XXX

Answers to the Self-Study Questions follow the Accounting Vocabulary.

ACCOUNTING VOCABULARY

Appropriation of retained earnings. Restriction of retained earnings that is recorded by a formal journal entry (p. 607).

Earnings per share (EPS). Amount of a company's net income per share of its outstanding common stock (p. 612).

Extraordinary item. A gain or loss that is both unusual for the company and infrequent (p. 611).

Prior-period adjustment. A correction to retained earnings for an error of an earlier period (p. 615).

Segment of a business. One of various separate divisions of a company (p. 610).

Statement of stockholders' equity. Reports the changes in all categories of stockholders' equity during the period (p. 616).

Stock dividend. A proportional distribution by a corporation of its own stock to its stockholders (p. 597).

Stock split. An increase in the number of outstanding shares of stock coupled with a proportionate reduction in the par value of the stock (p. 600).

Treasury stock. A corporation's own stock that it has issued and later reacquired (p. 602).

ANSWERS TO SELF-STUDY QUESTIONS

1. a   **2.** c   **3.** d   **4.** b   **5.** d

6. d   **7.** a   **8.** c   **9.** b   **10.** c

QUESTIONS

1. Identify the two main parts of stockholders' equity.

2. Identify the account debited and the account credited from the last closing entry a corporation makes each year. What is the purpose of this entry?

3. Ametek, Inc., reported a cash balance of $73 million and a retained earnings balance of $162.5 million. Explain how Ametek can have so much more retained earnings than cash. In your answer, identify the nature of retained earnings and state how it ties to cash.

4. A friend of yours receives a stock dividend on an investment. He believes that stock dividends are the same as cash dividends. Explain why the two are not the same.

5. Give two reasons for a corporation to distribute a stock dividend.

6. A corporation declares a stock dividend on December 21 and reports Stock Dividend Payable as a liability on the December 31 balance sheet. Is this correct? Give your reason.

7. What percentage distinguishes a small stock dividend from a large stock dividend? What is the main difference in accounting for small and large stock dividends?

8. To an investor, a stock split and a stock dividend have essentially the same effect. Explain the similarity and difference to the corporation between a 100-percent stock dividend and a 2-for-1 stock split.

9. Give four reasons why a corporation might purchase treasury stock.

10. What effect does the purchase of treasury stock have on the (a) assets, (b) issued stock, and (c) outstanding stock of the corporation?

11. What is the normal balance of the Treasury Stock account? What type of account is Treasury Stock? Where is Treasury Stock reported on the balance sheet?

12. Revell Inc. purchased treasury stock for $25,000. If Revell sells half the treasury stock for $15,000, what account should it credit for the $2,500 difference? If Revell later sells the remaining half of the treasury stock for $9,000, what accounts should be debited for the $3,500 difference?

13. What effect does the purchase and retirement of common stock have on the (a) assets, (b) issued stock, and (c) outstanding stock of the corporation?

14. Why do creditors wish to restrict a corporation's payment of cash dividends and purchases of treasury stock?

15. What are two ways to report a retained earnings restriction? Which way is more common?

16. Identify three items on the income statement that generate income tax expense. What is an income tax saving, and how does it arise?

17. Why is it important for a corporation to report income from continuing operations separately from discontinued operations and extraordinary items?

18. Give two examples of extraordinary gains and losses and four examples of gains and losses that are *not* extraordinary.

19. What is the most widely used of all accounting statistics? What is the price-to-earnings ratio? Compute the price-to-earnings ratio for a company with EPS of $2 and market price of $12 per share of common stock.

20. What is the earnings per share of a company with net income of $5,500, issued common stock of 12,000 shares, and treasury common stock of 1,000 shares?

21. What account do all prior-period adjustments affect? On what financial statement are prior-period adjustments reported?

EXERCISES

Journalizing dividends and reporting stockholders' equity (Obj. 1)

E15-1 Thornton, Inc., is authorized to issue 100,000 shares of $1-par common stock. The company issued 50,000 shares at $4 per share, and all 50,000 shares are outstanding. When the retained earnings balance was $150,000, Thornton declared and distributed a 50-percent stock dividend. Later, Thornton declared and paid a $0.20 per share cash dividend.

Required

1. Journalize the declaration and distribution of the stock dividend.
2. Journalize the declaration and payment of the cash dividend.
3. Prepare the stockholders' equity section of the balance sheet after both dividends.

Journalizing a stock dividend and reporting stockholders' equity (Obj. 1)

E15-2 The stockholders' equity for Cohen Jewelry Corporation on September 30, 19X4—end of the company's fiscal year—follows:

Stockholders' Equity	
Common stock, $10 par, 100,000 shares authorized,	
50,000 shares issued	$500,000
Paid-in capital in excess of par—common...............................	50,000
Retained earnings..	340,000
Total stockholders' equity	$890,000

On November 16, the market price of Cohen's common stock was $14 per share and the company declared a 10-percent stock dividend. Cohen issued the dividend shares on November 30.

Required

1. Journalize the declaration and distribution of the stock dividend.
2. Prepare the stockholders' equity section of the balance sheet after the issuance of the stock dividend.

E15-3 Kiefer Showbiz, Inc., had the following stockholders' equity at May 31:

Common stock, $2 par, 200,000 shares authorized,	
50,000 shares issued	$100,000
Paid-in capital in excess of par...	180,000
Retained earnings...	210,000
Total stockholders' equity	$490,000

Reporting stockholders' equity after a stock split
(Obj. 2)

On June 7, Kiefer split its $2 par common stock 4 for 1. Make the necessary entry to record the stock split, and prepare the stockholders' equity section of the balance sheet immediately after the split.

E15-4 Identify the effects of these transactions on total stockholders' equity. Each transaction is independent.

Effects of stock issuance, dividends, and treasury stock transactions
(Obj. 1, 2, 3)

a. Purchase of 1,500 shares of treasury stock (par value $0.50) at $4.25 per share.

b. Fifty-percent stock dividend. Before the dividend, 1,000,000 shares of $2 par common stock were outstanding; market value was $13.75 at the time of the dividend.

c. Issuance of 50,000 shares of $10 par common at $16.50.

d. Ten-percent stock dividend. Before the dividend, 500,000 shares of $1 par common stock were outstanding; market value was $7.625 at the time of the dividend.

e. Sale of 600 shares of $5 par treasury stock for $9.00 per share. Cost of the treasury stock was $6.00 per share.

f. Three-for-one stock split. Prior to the split, 60,000 shares of $4.50 par common were outstanding.

E15-5 Journalize the following transactions of Shoe Renewry, Inc., a national chain of shoe repair shops:

Journalizing treasury stock transactions
(Obj. 3)

May 19	Issued 10,000 shares of no-par common stock at $15 per share.
Aug. 22	Purchased 900 shares of treasury stock at $14 per share.
Nov. 11	Sold 200 shares of treasury stock at $16 per share.
Dec. 28	Sold 100 shares of treasury stock at $13 per share.

E15-6 College Book Sales, Inc., had the following stockholders' equity on November 30:

Journalizing treasury stock transactions and reporting stockholders' equity
(Obj. 3)

Stockholders' Equity

Common stock, $5 par, 500,000 shares authorized,	
50,000 shares issued	$250,000
Paid-in capital in excess of par...	150,000
Retained earnings...	220,000
Total stockholders' equity	$620,000

On December 19 the company purchased 1,000 shares of treasury stock at $6 per share. Journalize the purchase of the treasury stock, and prepare the stockholders' equity section of the balance sheet at December 31.

E15-7 The agreement under which Yung Corporation issued its long-term debt requires the restriction of $250,000 of the company's retained earnings balance. Total retained earnings is $270,000, and total paid-in capital is $820,000.

Reporting a retained earnings restriction
(Obj. 4)

Required

Show how to report stockholders' equity (including retained earnings) on Yung's balance sheet, assuming:

a. Yung discloses the restriction in a note. Write the note.

b. Yung appropriates retained earnings in the amount of the restriction and includes no note in its statements.

c. Yung's cash balance is $85,000. What is the maximum amount of dividends Yung can declare?

Preparing a multiple-step income statement
(Obj. 5)

E15-8 The ledger of Vienna Corporation contains the following information for 19X4 operations:

Cost of goods sold............................	$45,000
Loss on discontinued operations	50,000
Income tax expense—	
extraordinary gain	4,800
Income tax saving —change	
in depreciation method	2,000
Income tax saving—loss	
on discontinued operations	20,000
Extraordinary gain	12,000
Sales revenue	130,000
Operating expenses	
(including income tax)................	43,000
Cumulative effect of change in	
depreciation method (debit)........	(6,000)

Required

Prepare a multiple-step income statement for 19X4. Omit earnings per share. Was 19X4 a good year or a bad year for Vienna Corporation? Explain your answer in terms of the outlook for 19X5.

Computing earnings per share
(Obj. 5)

E15-9 Swingline Corporation earned net income of $56,000 for the second quarter of 19X6. The ledger reveals the following figures:

Preferred stock, $1.75 per year, no-par, 1,600 shares issued and	
outstanding..	$ 70,000
Common stock, $10 par, 52,000 shares issued..	520,000
Treasury stock, common, 2,000 shares at cost	36,000

Required

Compute EPS for the quarter, assuming no changes in the stock accounts during the quarter.

Computing earnings per share
(Obj. 5)

E15-10 Connecticut Supply had 40,000 shares of common stock and 10,000 shares of $10 par, 5-percent preferred stock outstanding on December 31, 19X8. On April 30, 19X9, the company issued 9,000 additional common shares and ended 19X9 with 49,000 shares of common stock outstanding. Income from continuing operations of 19X9 was $115,400, and loss on discontinued operations (net of income tax) was $8,280. The company had an extraordinary loss (net of tax) of $55,200.

Required

Compute Connecticut Supply's EPS amounts for 19X9, starting with income from continuing operations.

Preparing a statement of retained earnings with a prior-period adjustment
(Obj. 6)

E15-11 Big Red, Inc., a soft-drink company, reported a prior-period adjustment in 19X9. An accounting error caused net income of prior years to be overstated by $3.8 million. Retained earnings at January 1, 19X9, as previously reported, stood at $395.3 million. Net income for 19X9 was $92.1 million, and dividends were $39.8 million.

Required

Prepare the company's statement of retained earnings for the year ended December 31, 19X9.

E15-12 The Kroger Company, a large grocery company, had retained earnings of $792.6 million at the beginning of 19X7. The company showed these figures at December 31, 19X7:

Preparing a combined statement of income and retained earnings (Obj. 5, 6)

	($ Millions)
Increases in retained earnings:	
Net income	$127.1
Decreases in retained earnings:	
Cash dividends—preferred	2.3
common	85.2
Debit to retained earnings due to purchase of preferred stock	11.3

Required

Beginning with net income, prepare a combined statement of income and retained earnings for The Kroger Company for 19X7. What type of transaction caused the $11.3 million debit to Retained Earnings?

E15-13 At December 31, 19X5, NOVA Corp. of Melbourne, Florida, reported this stockholders' equity:

Preparing a statement of stockholders' equity (Obj. 7)

Common stock, $5 par, 200,000 shares authorized,	
120,000 shares issued	$ 600,000
Additional paid-in capital	3,100,000
Retained earnings	1,700,000
Treasury stock, 2,500 shares at cost	(78,000)
	$5,322,000

During 19X6, NOVA completed these transactions and events (listed in chronological order):

a. Declared and issued a 50-percent stock dividend. At the time, NOVA's stock was quoted at a market price of $31 per share.

b. Sold 1,000 shares of treasury stock for $36 per share (cost was $31).

c. Issued 500 shares of common stock to employees at the discount price of $28 per share.

d. Net income for the year, $340,000.

e. Declared cash dividends of $180,000, to be paid early in 19X7.

Required

Prepare NOVA Corp.'s statement of stockholders' equity for 19X6.

CHALLENGE EXERCISE

E15-14 Universal Syndicates, Inc., began 19X8 with 3 million shares of $1 par common stock issued and outstanding. Beginning capital in excess of par was $6.4 million, and retained earnings was $9.7 million. In March 19X8 Universal issued 50,000 shares of stock at $50 per share. 19X8 was an exceptional year for Universal. The company's stock price reached an all-time high of $95 late in October. Universal split the stock two for one. Then in December, when the stock's market price was $45 per share, the board of directors declared a 2-percent stock dividend, distributable in January 19X9.

Analyzing the effects of a stock dividend and a stock split (Obj. 1, 2)

Required

Without making journal entries, show the balance in each stockholders' equity account at December 31, 19X8.

Journalizing stockholders' equity transactions
(Obj. 1, 3)

P15-1A   Assume that IHOP Corp. completed the following selected transactions during the current year:

Jan.   9   Discovered that income tax expense of the preceding year was overstated by $7,000. Recorded a prior-period adjustment to correct the error.

Feb. 10   Split common stock 2 for 1 by calling in the 100,000 shares of $10 par common and issuing new stock in its place.

April 18   Declared a cash dividend on the 5-percent, $100 par preferred stock (1,000 shares outstanding). Declared a $0.20 per share dividend on the common stock outstanding. The date of record was May 2, and the payment date was May 23.

May 23   Paid the cash dividends.

July 30   Declared a 10-percent stock dividend on the common stock to holders of record August 21, with distribution set for September 11. The market value of the common stock was $15 per share.

Sep. 11   Issued the stock dividend shares.

Oct. 26   Purchased 2,500 shares of the company's own common stock at $14 per share.

Nov. 8   Sold 1,000 shares of treasury common stock for $17 per share.

Dec. 13   Sold 500 shares of treasury common stock for $13 per share.

Required

Record the transactions in the general journal.

Journalizing dividend and treasury stock transactions and reporting stockholders' equity
(Obj. 1, 2, 3)

P15-2A   The balance sheet of Bayview Amusements, Inc., at December 31, 19X5, reported 100,000 shares of no-par common stock authorized, with 30,000 shares issued and a Common Stock balance of $180,000. Bayview also had 5,000 shares of 6-percent, $10 par preferred stock authorized and outstanding. The preferred stock was issued in 19X1 at par. Retained Earnings had a credit balance of $104,000. During the two-year period ended December 31, 19X7, the company completed the following selected transactions:

19X6

Mar. 15   Purchased 4,000 shares of the company's own common stock for the treasury at $5 per share.

July   2   Declared the annual 6-percent cash dividend on the preferred stock and a $0.75 per share cash dividend on the common stock. The date of record was July 16, and the payment date was July 31.

July 31   Paid the cash dividends.

Nov. 30   Declared a 20-percent stock dividend on the *outstanding* common stock to holders of record December 21, with distribution set for January 11, 19X7. The market value of Bayview common stock was $10 per share.

Dec. 31   Earned net income of $104,000 for the year.

19X7

Jan. 11   Issued the stock dividend shares.

June 30   Declared the annual 6-percent cash dividend on the preferred stock. The date of record was July 14, and the payment date was July 29.

July 29   Paid the cash dividends.

Aug. 2   Purchased and retired all the preferred stock at $14 per share.

Oct. 8   Sold 2,800 shares of treasury common stock for $12 per share.

Dec. 19   Split the no-par common stock 2 for 1 by issuing two new no-par shares for each old no-par share previously issued. Prior to the split, the corporation had issued 35,200 shares. Stock splits affect all issued stock, including treasury stock as well as stock that is outstanding.

31   Earned net income of $117,000 during the year.

Required

1.   Record the transactions in the general journal. Explanations are not required.

2.   Prepare the stockholders' equity section of the balance sheet at two dates: December 31, 19X6, and December 31, 19X7.

P15-3A Weberg Corporation is positioned ideally in the clothing business. Located in Scranton, Pennsylvania, Weberg is the only company with a distribution network for its imported goods. The company does a brisk business with specialty stores such as Bloomingdale's, I. Magnin, and Bonwit Teller. Weberg's recent success has made the company a prime target for a takeover. Against the wishes of Weberg's board of directors, an investment group from Boston is attempting to buy 51 percent of Weberg's outstanding stock. Board members are convinced that the Boston investors would sell off the most desirable pieces of the business and leave little of value.

At the most recent board meeting, several suggestions were advanced to fight off the hostile takeover bid. One suggestion is to increase the stock outstanding by distributing a 100-percent stock dividend.

Required

As a significant stockholder of Weberg Corporation, write a short memo to explain to the board whether distributing the stock dividend would make it more difficult for the investor group to take over Weberg Corporation. Include in your memo a discussion of the effect that the stock dividend would have on assets, liabilities, and total stockholders' equity—that is, the dividend's effect on the size of the corporation.

P15-4A The balance sheet of Hamilton Corporation at December 31, 19X6, reported the following stockholders' equity:

Paid-in capital:	
Common stock, $10 par, 100,000 shares	
authorized, 20,000 shares issued	$200,000
Paid-in capital in excess of par-common	300,000
Total paid-in capital..	500,000
Retained earnings...	190,000
Total stockholders' equity	$690,000

During 19X7 Hamilton completed the following selected transactions:

Feb.	7	Discovered that income tax expense of 19X6 was understated by $24,000. Recorded a prior-period adjustment to correct the error.
Apr.	30	Declared a 10-percent stock dividend on the common stock. The market value of Hamilton common stock was $24 per share. The record date was May 21, with distribution set for June 5.
June	5	Issued the stock dividend shares.
July	29	Purchased 2,000 shares of the company's own common stock at $21 per share.
Nov.	13	Sold 400 shares of treasury common stock for $22 per share.
	27	Declared a $0.30 per share dividend on the common stock outstanding. The date of record was December 17, and the payment date was January 7, 19X8.
Dec.	31	Closed the $62,000 credit balance of Income Summary to Retained Earnings.

Required

1. Record the transactions in the general journal.
2. Prepare a retained earnings statement at December 31, 19X7.
3. Prepare the stockholders' equity section of the balance sheet at December 31, 19X7.

P15-5A The following information was taken from the ledger and other records of Kahama, Inc., at September 30, 19X6.

Cost of goods sold...........................	$424,000
Cumulative effect of change in	
depreciation method (debit)........	(3,000)
Loss on sale of plant assets..............	8,000
Sales returns	9,000

Income tax expense (saving):	
Continuing operations...............................	$ 72,000
Discontinued segment:	
Operating loss	(6,000)
Gain on sale...	8,000
Extraordinary loss	(12,000)
Cumulative effect of change in	
depreciation method	(1,000)
Gain on sale of discontinued	
segment	20,000
Prior-period adjustment—debit to	
Retained Earnings.......................................	6,000
Contributed capital from treasury	
stock transactions	7,000
Sales discounts	18,000
Interest expense...	11,000
General expenses..	113,000
Preferred stock, $2	
no-par, 10,000 shares	
authorized, 5,000 shares issued...................	200,000
Paid-in capital in excess of	
par—common	20,000
Retained earnings, beginning, as	
originally reported	88,000
Selling expenses	136,000
Common stock, $10 par, 25,000	
shares authorized and issued......................	250,000
Sales revenue...	860,000
Treasury stock, common	
(1,000 shares at cost)	11,000
Dividends	35,000
Interest revenue	4,000
Extraordinary loss	30,000
Operating loss, discontinued	
segment	15,000
Loss on insurance settlement	12,000

Required

1. Prepare a single-step income statement, including earnings per share, for Kahama, Inc., for the fiscal year ended September 30, 19X6. Evaluate income for the year ended September 30, 19X6, in terms of the outlook for 19X7. Assume that 19X6 was a typical year and that Kahama managers hoped to earn income from continuing operations equal to 10 percent of net sales.

2. Prepare the statement of retained earnings for the year ended September 30, 19X6.

3. Prepare the stockholders' equity section of the balance sheet at that date.

4. How will what you learned in this problem help you evaluate an investment?

Preparing a corrected combined statement of income and retained earnings
(Obj. 5, 6)

P15-6A Lane Collins, accountant for Santa Rosa Book Distributors, was injured in a skiing accident. Another employee prepared the accompanying income statement for the fiscal year ended December 31, 19X3.

    The individual amounts listed on the income statement are correct. However, some accounts are reported incorrectly, and others do not belong on the income statement at all. Also, income tax (40 percent) has not been applied to all appropriate figures. Santa Rosa issued 52,000 shares of common stock in 19X1 and held 2,000 shares as treasury stock during 19X3. The retained earnings balance, as originally reported at December 31, 19X2, was $111,000.

```
                    SANTA ROSA BOOK DISTRIBUTORS
                         INCOME STATEMENT
                              19X3

Revenue and gains:
  Sales ...........................................................      $362,000
  Gain on retirement of preferred stock
    (issued for $81,000; purchased for $71,000) ..................        10,000
  Paid-in capital in excess of par—common ........................        80,000
  Total revenues and gains ......................................        452,000
Expenses and losses:
  Cost of goods sold ............................    $105,000
  Selling expenses...............................      56,000
  General expenses...............................      61,000
  Sales returns..................................      11,000
  Dividends......................................       7,000
  Sales discounts ...............................       6,000
  Income tax expense.............................      20,000
    Total expenses and losses....................                        266,000
Income from operations...........................                        186,000
Other gains and losses:
  Gain on sale of discontinued operations........    $ 10,000
  Extraordinary flood loss .......................    (20,000)
  Operating loss on discontinued segment..........    (13,000)
  Prior-period adjustment—understated
    income tax for 19X2 .........................     (14,000)
    Total other losses ...........................                       (37,000)
Net income.......................................                       $149,000
Earnings per share...............................                       $   2.98
```

Required

Prepare a corrected combined statement of income and retained earnings for 19X3; include earnings per share. Prepare the income statement in single-step format.

P15-7A The capital structure of Lockridge-Priest Air Conditioning, Inc., at December 31, 19X6, included 20,000 shares of $1.25 preferred stock and 44,000 shares of common stock. Common shares outstanding during 19X7 were 44,000 January through May, 50,000 June through August, and 60,500 September through December. Income from continuing operations during 19X7 was $81,100. The company discontinued a segment of the business at a gain of $6,630, and an extraordinary item generated a loss of $33,660. Lockridge-Priest's board of directors restricts $80,000 of retained earnings for contingencies.

Computing earnings per share and reporting a retained earnings restriction
(Obj. 4, 5, 6)

Required

1. Compute Lockridge-Priest's earnings per share. Start with income from continuing operations. Income and loss amounts are net of income tax.

2. Show two ways of reporting Lockridge-Priest's retained earnings restriction. Retained earnings at December 31, 19X6, was $107,000, and total paid-in capital at December 31, 19X7, is $314,000. Lockridge-Priest declared cash dividends of $29,000 during 19X7.

P15-8A DenHerder, Inc., reported the following statement of stockholders' equity for the year ended October 31, 19X4:

Using a statement of stockholders' equity
(Obj. 7)

DenHerder, Inc. STATEMENT OF STOCKHOLDERS' EQUITY YEAR ENDED OCTOBER 31, 19X4					
(Dollar amounts in millions)	Common Stock	Additional Paid-in Capital	Retained Earnings	Treasury Stock	Total
Balance, Nov. 1, 19X3..........................	$427	$1,622	$904	$(117)	$2,836
Net income...			336		336
Cash dividends			(194)		(194)
Issuance of stock (10,000,000 shares) ..	8	41			49
Stock dividend.....................................	22	113	(135)		—
Sale of treasury stock............................		9		19	28
Balance, Oct. 31, 19X4.........................	$457	$1,785	$911	$ (98)	$3,055

Required

Answer these questions about DenHerder's stockholders' equity transactions.

1. The income tax rate is 40 percent. How much income before income tax did DenHerder, Inc., report on the income statement?
2. What is the par value of the company's common stock?
3. At what price per share did DenHerder issue its common stock during the year?
4. What was the cost of treasury stock sold during the year? What was the selling price of the treasury stock sold? What was the increase in total stockholders' equity?
5. DenHerder's statement lists the stock transactions in the order they occurred. What was the percentage of the stock dividend? Round to the nearest percentage.

(GROUP B)

Journalizing stockholders' equity transactions
(Obj. 1, 3)

P15-1B Career Planning, Inc., completed the following selected transactions during 19X6:

Jan. 13 Discovered that income tax expense of 19X5 was understated by $6,000. Recorded a prior-period adjustment to correct the error.

21 Split common stock 3 for 1 by calling in the 10,000 shares of $15 par common and issuing new stock in its place.

Feb. 6 Declared a cash dividend on the 10,000 shares of $2.25, no-par preferred stock. Declared a $0.20 per share dividend on the common stock outstanding. The date of record was February 27, and the payment date was March 20.

Mar. 20 Paid the cash dividends.

Apr. 18 Declared a 50-percent stock dividend on the common stock to holders of record April 30, with distribution set for May 30. The market value of the common stock was $15 per share.

May 30 Issued the stock dividend shares.

June 18 Purchased 2,400 shares of the company's own common stock at $12 per share.

Nov. 14 Sold 800 shares of treasury common stock for $10 per share.

Dec. 22 Sold 700 shares of treasury common stock for $16 per share.

Required

Record the transactions in the general journal.

P15-2B   The balance sheet of Video Library, Inc., at December 31, 19X7, reported 10,000 shares of $0.50, no-par preferred stock authorized and outstanding. The preferred was issued in 19X1 at $8 per share. Video Library also had 500,000 shares of $1 par common stock authorized with 100,000 shares issued. Paid-in Capital in Excess of Par—Common had a balance of $300,000. Retained Earnings had a balance of $18,000, and the preferred dividend for 19X7 was in arrears. During the two-year period ended December 31, 19X9, the company completed the following selected transactions:

Journalizing dividend and treasury stock transactions and reporting stockholders' equity (Obj. 1, 2, 3)

19X8

Feb. 15	Purchased 5,000 shares of the company's own common stock for the treasury at $4 per share.
Apr. 2	Declared the cash dividend on the preferred stock in arrears for 19X7 and the current cash dividend on preferred. The date of record was April 16, and the payment date was May 1.
May 1	Paid the cash dividends.
2	Purchased and retired all the preferred stock at $7.50 per share.
Dec. 31	Earned net income of $61,000 for the year.

19X9

Mar. 8	Sold 2,000 shares of treasury common stock for $7 per share.
Sep. 28	Declared a 10-percent stock dividend on the *outstanding* common stock to holders of record October 15, with distribution set for October 31. The market value of Video Library's common stock was $5 per share.
Oct. 31	Issued the stock dividend shares.
Nov. 5	Split the common stock 2 for 1 by calling in the 109,700 shares of old $1 par common stock and issuing twice as many shares of $0.50 par common. (Stock splits affect all issued stock, including treasury stock and stock that is outstanding.)
Dec. 31	Earned net income of $73,000 during the year.

Required

1. Record the transactions in the general journal. Explanations are not required.
2. Prepare the stockholders' equity section of the balance sheet at two dates: December 31, 19X8, and December 31, 19X9.

P15-3B   Nogales Corporation is positioned ideally in its business. Located in Yuma, Arizona, Nogales is the only company between Texas and California with reliable sources for its imported gifts. The company does a brisk business with specialty stores such as Pier 1 Imports. Nogales's recent success has made the company a prime target for a takeover. An investment group from Toronto is attempting to buy 51 percent of Nogales's outstanding stock against the wishes of Nogales's board of directors. Board members are convinced that the Toronto investors would sell the most desirable pieces of the business and leave little of value.

Purchasing treasury stock to fight off a takeover of the corporation (Obj. 3)

At the most recent board meeting, several suggestions were advanced to fight off the hostile takeover bid. The suggestion with the most promise is to purchase a huge quantity of treasury stock. Nogales has the cash to carry out this plan.

Required

1. As a significant stockholder of Nogales Corporation, write a memorandum to explain for the board how the purchase of treasury stock would make it more difficult for the Toronto group to take over Nogales. Include in your memo a discussion of the effect that purchasing treasury stock would have on stock outstanding and on the size of the corporation.
2. Suppose Nogales management is successful in fighting off the takeover bid and later sells the treasury stock at prices greater than the purchase price. Explain what effect these sales will have on assets, stockholders' equity, and net income.

Journalizing prior-period adjustments and dividend and treasury stock transactions, reporting retained earnings and stockholders' equity
(Obj. 1, 3, 6)

P15-4B   The balance sheet of Puebla Corporation at December 31, 19X3, presented the following stockholders' equity:

Paid-in capital:	
Common stock, $1 par, 250,000 shares authorized,	
50,000 shares issued	$ 50,000
Paid-in capital in excess of par—common	350,000
Total paid-in capital..	400,000
Retained earnings	110,000
Total stockholders' equity...	$510,000

During 19X4, Puebla completed the following selected transactions:

Jan. 7 Discovered that income tax expense of 19X3 was overstated by $12,000. Recorded a prior-period adjustment to correct the error.

Mar. 29 Declared a 50-percent stock dividend on the common stock. The market value of Puebla common stock was $5 per share. The record date was April 19, with distribution set for May 19.

May 19 Issued the stock dividend shares.

July 13 Purchased 2,000 shares of the company's own common stock at $6 per share.

Oct. 4 Sold 1,600 shares of treasury common stock for $8 per share.

Dec. 27 Declared a $0.20 per share dividend on the common stock outstanding. The date of record was January 17, 19X5, and the payment date was January 31.

     31 Closed the $71,000 credit balance of Income Summary to Retained Earnings.

Required

1. Record the transactions in the general journal.
2. Prepare the retained earnings statement at December 31, 19X4.
3. Prepare the stockholders' equity section of the balance sheet at December 31, 19X4.

Preparing a single-step income statement and a statement of retained earnings and reporting stockholders' equity on the balance sheet
(Obj. 5, 6)

P15-5B   The following information was taken from the ledger and other records of Sundem Sales Corporation at June 30, 19X5:

General expenses	$ 71,000
Loss on sale of discontinued	
segment..	8,000
Prior-period adjustment—debit	
to Retained Earnings	4,000
Cost of goods sold	319,000
Income tax expense (saving):	
Continuing operations.............................	28,000
Discontinued segment:	
Operating income	3,600
Loss on sale	(3,200)
Extraordinary gain	10,800
Cumulative effect of change in	
depreciation method.............................	3,000
Interest expense	23,000
Gain on settlement of lawsuit......................	8,000
Sales returns...	15,000
Paid-in capital from retirement of	
preferred stock	16,000
Dividend revenue	11,000
Treasury stock, common	
(2,000 shares at cost)...............................	28,000
Sales discounts	7,000
Extraordinary gain.......................................	27,000
Loss on sale of plant assets	10,000
Operating income, discontinued	
segment..	9,000
Dividends on preferred stock	?

Preferred stock, 6%, $25 par, 20,000 shares authorized, 4,000 shares issued	$100,000
Cumulative effect of change in depreciation method (credit)	7,000
Dividends on common stock......................	12,000
Sales revenue..	589,000
Retained earnings, beginning, as originally reported	63,000
Selling expenses	87,000
Common stock, no-par, 22,000 shares authorized and issued	350,000

Required

1. Prepare a single-step income statement, including earnings per share, for Sundem Sales Corporation for the fiscal year ended June 30, 19X5. Evaluate income for the year ended June 30, 19X5, in terms of the outlook for 19X6. Assume that 19X5 was a typical year and that Sundem's managers hoped to earn income from continuing operations equal to 8 percent of net sales.

2. Prepare the statement of retained earnings for the fiscal year ended June 30, 19X5.

3. Prepare the stockholders' equity section of the balance sheet at that date.

4. How will what you learned in this problem help you evaluate an investment?

P15-6B Brandi Gilbert, accountant for The Software Connection, Inc., was injured in a sailing accident. Another employee prepared the following income statement for the fiscal year ended June 30, 19X4:

Preparing a corrected combined statement of income and retained earnings
(Obj. 5, 6)

THE SOFTWARE CONNECTION, INC.
INCOME STATEMENT
JUNE 30, 19X4

Revenues and gains:		
Sales		$733,000
Gain on retirement of preferred stock (issued for $70,000; purchased for $59,000)		11,000
Paid-in capital in excess of par—common		100,000
Total revenues and gains.....................................		844,000
Expenses and losses:		
Cost of goods sold	$383,000	
Selling expenses...................................	103,000	
General expenses	74,000	
Sales returns..	22,000	
Prior-period adjustment—understated income tax for 19X3	4,000	
Dividends..	15,000	
Sales discounts....................................	10,000	
Income tax expense..............................	32,000	
Total expenses and losses...................		643,000
Income from operations..........................		201,000
Other gains and losses:		
Extraordinary gain................................	$ 30,000	
Operating income on discontinued segment......................	25,000	
Loss on sale of discontinued operations	(40,000)	
Total other gains................................		15,000
Net income..		$216,000
Earnings per share................................		$10.80

The individual amounts listed on the income statement are correct. However, some accounts are reported incorrectly, and others do not belong on the income statement at all. Also, income tax (40 percent) has not been applied to all appropriate figures. The Software Connection, Inc., issued 24,000 shares of common stock in 19X1 and held 4,000 shares as treasury stock during the fiscal year 19X4. The retained earnings balance, as originally reported at June 30, 19X3, was $209,000.

Required

Prepare a corrected combined statement of income and retained earnings for fiscal year 19X4; include earnings per share. Prepare the income statement in single-step format.

Computing earnings per share and reporting a retained earnings restriction
(Obj. 4, 5, 6)

P15-7B   Pellegrini Construction's capital structure at December 31, 19X2, included 5,000 shares of $2.50 preferred stock and 130,000 shares of common stock. Common shares outstanding during 19X3 were 130,000 January through February; 119,000 during March; 121,000 April through October; and 128,000 during November and December. Income from continuing operations during 19X3 was $371,885. The company discontinued a segment of the business at a gain of $69,160, and an extraordinary item generated a gain of $49,510. The board of directors of Pellegrini Construction has restricted $280,000 of retained earnings for expansion of the company's office facilities.

Required

1. Compute Pellegrini's earnings per share. Start with income from continuing operations. Income and loss amounts are net of income tax.
2. Show two ways of reporting Pellegrini's retained earnings restriction. Retained earnings at December 31, 19X2, was $127,800, and total paid-in capital at December 31, 19X3, is $524,610. Pellegrini declared cash dividends of $264,500 during 19X3.

Using a statement of stockholders' equity
(Obj. 7)

P15-8B   Mutyala, Inc., reported the following statement of stockholders' equity for the year ended June 30, 19X6:

MUTYALA, INC.					
STATEMENT OF STOCKHOLDERS' EQUITY					
YEAR ENDED JUNE 30, 19X6					

(Dollar amounts in millions)	Common Stock	Additional Paid-in Capital	Retained Earnings	Treasury Stock	Total
Balance, July 1, 19X5	$173	$2,118	$1,706	$ (18)	$3,979
Net income................................			520		520
Cash dividends			(117)		(117)
Issuance of stock					
(5,000,000 shares)..................	3	46			49
Stock dividend...........................	18	272	(290)		—
Sale of treasury stock		5		11	16
Balance, June 30, 19X6	$194	$2,441	$1,819	$ (7)	$4,447

Required

Answer these questions about Mutyala's stockholders' equity transactions.

1. The income tax rate is 35 percent. How much income before income tax did Mutyala, Inc., report on the income statement?

2. What is the par value of the company's common stock?

3. At what price per share did Mutyala issue its common stock during the year?

4. What was the cost of treasury stock sold during the year? What was the selling price of the treasury stock sold? What was the increase in total stockholders' equity?

5. Mutyala's statement of stockholders' equity lists the stock transactions in the order in which they occurred. What was the percentage of the stock dividend? Round to the nearest percentage.

EXTENDING YOUR KNOWLEDGE

DECISION PROBLEMS

1. Perez Fabrics, Inc., had the following stockholders' equity amounts on June 30 of the current year:

Analyzing cash dividends and stock dividends
(Obj. 1)

Common stock, no-par, 100,000 shares issued	$ 750,000
Retained earnings	830,000
Total stockholders' equity..	$1,580,000

In the past, Perez has paid an annual cash dividend of $1.50 per share. Despite the large retained earnings balance, the board of directors wished to conserve cash for expansion. The board delayed the payment of cash dividends by one month and in the meantime distributed a 10-percent stock dividend. During the following year, the company's cash position improved. The board declared and paid a cash dividend of $1.364 per share.

Suppose you own 10,000 shares of Perez common stock, acquired three years ago. The market price of the stock was $30 per share before any of the above dividends.

Required

1. How does the stock dividend affect your proportionate ownership in Perez Fabrics, Inc.? Explain.

2. What amount of cash dividends did you receive last year? What amount of cash dividends will you receive after the above dividend action?

3. Immediately after the stock dividend was distributed, the market value of Perez stock decreased from $30 per share to $27.273 per share. Does this decrease represent a loss to you? Explain.

4. Suppose Perez announces at the time of the stock dividend that the company will continue to pay the annual $1.50 cash dividend per share, even after the stock dividend. Would you expect the market price of the stock to decrease to $27.27 per share as in Requirement 3 above? Explain.

2. Answer the following independent questions.

Earnings and dividends
(Obj. 1, 3, 5)

1. An investor noted that the market price of stocks seemed to decline after the date of record. Why do you think that would be the case?

2. The treasurer of Larson Shoe Company wanted to disclose a large loss as an extraordinary item because Larson produced too much product just before a very cool summer. Why do you think the treasurer wanted to use that particular disclosure? Would such disclosure be acceptable?

3. Corporations sometimes purchase their own stock. When asked why they do so, management often responds that it feels that the stock is undervalued. What advantage would the company gain by buying and selling its own stock under these circumstances?

4. Mensa, Inc., earned a significant profit in the year ended November 30, 19X2, because land it held was expropriated for a new highway. The company proposes to treat the sale of land to the government as other revenue. Why do you think Mensa is proposing such treatment? Is this disclosure appropriate?

ETHICAL ISSUE

Anadarko Petroleum Company is an independent oil producer in Anadarko, Oklahoma. In February, company geologists discovered a pool of oil that tripled the company's proven reserves. Prior to disclosing the new oil to the public, top managers of the company quietly bought most of Anadarko's stock as treasury stock. After the discovery was announced, Anadarko's stock price increased from $13 to $40.

Required

1. Did Anadarko managers behave ethically? Explain your answer.
2. Identify the accounting principle relevant to this situation.
3. Who was helped and who was harmed by management's action?

FINANCIAL STATEMENT PROBLEMS

Treasury stock, retained earnings, and earnings per share
(Obj. 3, 5)

1. Use the Lands' End, Inc., financial statements in Appendix A to answer the following questions.

 1. Lands' End reports stock *issued* on the balance sheet and gives details in the statement of shareholders' investment. At January 28, 1994, how many shares of common stock had Lands' End issued? How many shares were in the treasury? How many shares were outstanding at January 28, 1994?

 2. Examine the Lands' End balance sheet. Did the company purchase any treasury stock during the year ended January 28, 1994? Give your reason. Now refer to the statement of shareholders' investment, and journalize the purchase of treasury stock. What was the average price per share that Lands' End paid to acquire treasury stock during the year ended January 28, 1994?

 3. Prepare a T-account for Retained Earnings to show the beginning and ending balances and all activity in the account during the year ended January 28, 1994. How could the treasury stock transaction cause the debit to Retained Earnings?

 4. Show how to compute net income *per share* for the year ended January 28, 1994.

Treasury stock, retained earnings, and earnings per share
(Obj. 3, 5)

2. Obtain the annual report of an actual company of your choosing. Answer the following questions about the company. Concentrate on the current year in the annual report you select.

 1. How many shares of common stock had the company issued through the end of the current year? How many shares were in the treasury? How many shares were outstanding on the date of the current balance sheet?

 2. Compute average cost per share of treasury stock (common). Compare this figure to book value per share of common stock. Does it appear that the company was able to purchase treasury stock at book value?

 Note: This question can be answered only if the company reports the cost of treasury stock.

3. Prepare a T-account for Retained Earnings to show the beginning and ending balances and all activity in the account during the current year.

4. Did the company have any prior-period adjustments during any year reported in the annual report? How can you tell?

5. Show how to compute net income (or net loss) *per share* for the current year.

Chapter 16
Long-Term Liabilities

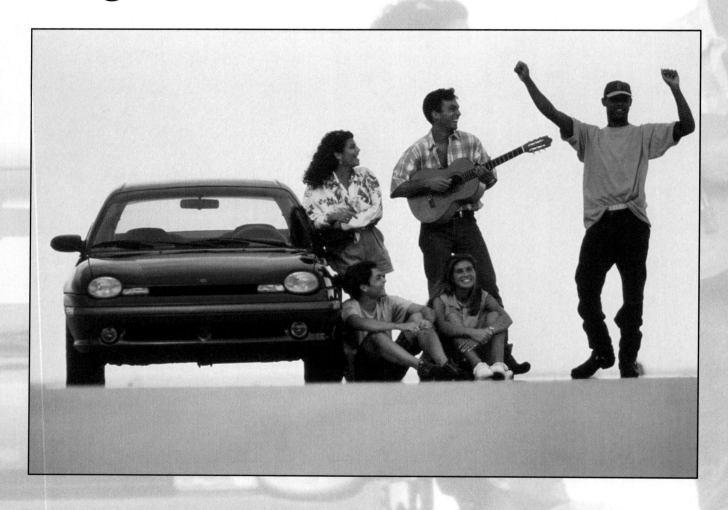

How do investors assess the risk of a bond? Two main rating agencies, Moody's Investors Service and Standard & Poor's Corp. (S&P) evaluate the risk of—that is, they *rate*—corporate bonds. To make this very subjective judgment, these organizations study the company's management, operations, finances, and outlook for the future. They then assign the bond to a rating category that indicates its risk. The higher the risk, the higher the interest rate on the bond, and vice versa. A central truth of business is that return on investment depends on the risk of the investment. Stated differently,

> To earn a high rate of return, an investor must take a high degree of risk. An investor who is unwilling to take much risk cannot expect to earn a high rate of return on the investment.

This is equally true whether the investment is a bond, a stock, real estate, a start-up business, an established organization, or any other venture.

In 1991 Chrysler Corp. experienced some financial difficulty, and the automaker's bonds were downgraded to junk-bond status—that is, rated as highly risky. What was the result? Chrysler's interest expense shot up, and this increase hurt the company's profits. Since then Chrysler Corp. has worked hard to improve its bond rating. The company has enhanced product quality, redesigned its successful minivans and Jeep Grand Cherokee, and introduced the Neon subcompact and a new Ram pickup truck. Moody's has taken note of these operational improvements and has upgraded the Chrysler bonds. The result? "It cut our interest rate payments by half a point, or $5 million annually," according to a Chrysler spokesperson. Not only will these savings greatly improve reported income, but the stock market responded to the bond-rating news by increasing the price of Chrysler stock by 37.5 cents per share.

• • • • •

Chapter Objectives

After studying this chapter, you should be able to

1. Account for basic bonds payable transactions by the straight-line amortization method

2. Amortize bond discount and premium by the effective-interest method

3. Account for retirement of bonds payable

4. Account for conversion of bonds payable

5. Explain the advantages and disadvantages of borrowing

6. Account for lease transactions

A1. Compute the future value of an investment made in a single amount

A2. Compute the future value of an annuity-type investment

A3. Compute the present value of a single future amount

A4. Compute the present value of an annuity

A5. Determine the cost of an asset acquired through a capital lease

*L*arge companies such as Chrysler Corp. cannot borrow billions from a single lender because no lender will risk that much money on a single company. Banks and other lenders diversify their risk by loaning smaller amounts to numerous customers. That way if a borrower cannot repay, the lender is not devastated. How then do large corporations borrow a huge amount? They issue bonds to the public. **Bonds payable** are groups of notes payable issued to multiple lenders, called bondholders. The idea is that Chrysler can borrow large amounts from thousands of individual investors, each buying a modest amount of Chrysler bonds. Chrysler receives the amount it needs, and each investor limits his or her risk by diversifying investments—not putting all the "eggs in one basket."

Chapters 14 and 15 covered two ways of financing operations: contributed capital (the stock accounts and additional paid-in capital) and profitable operations (retained earnings). This chapter discusses the third way to finance a company—long-term liabilities, including bonds payable (and notes payable), lease liabilities, and pension liabilities. We treat bonds payable and long-term notes payable together because their accounting is the same. The chapter appendix provides background on the valuation of long-term liabilities.

The Nature of Bonds

Key Point: The following comparison will help you "jump" from equity to debt.

Stocks
1. Stocks represent ownership (equity) of corporation.
2. Shareholder is an owner.
3. Shareholder has the right to receive dividends, if declared.
4. Dividends are optional to corporation.
5. Dividends are not tax-deductible for corporation.
6. Common stock does not have a fixed cost (to corporation) or a fixed return (to shareholder).
7. Corporation is not obligated to repay amount invested by shareholders.

Bonds
1. Bonds represent a debt (liability).
2. Bondholder is a creditor.
3. Bondholder has the right to receive interest.
4. Interest is a contractual obligation of corporation.
5. Interest is a tax-deductible expense of corporation.
6. Bonds have a fixed cost (to corporation) and a fixed return (to bondholder).
7. Corporation must repay bond payable at maturity.

To gain access to large amounts of cash, a company may issue bonds. Each bond is, in effect, a long-term note payable that bears interest. Bonds are debts of the company for the amounts borrowed from the investors.

Purchasers of bonds receive a bond certificate, which carries the issuing company's name. The certificate also states the *principal*, which is the amount that the company has borrowed from the bondholder. This figure, typically stated in units of $1,000, is also called the bond's face value, maturity value, or par value. The bond obligates the issuing company to pay the holder the principal amount at a specific future date, called the maturity date, which also appears on the certificate.

Bondholders loan their money to companies for a price: interest on the principal. The bond certificate states the interest rate that the issuer will pay the holder and the dates that the interest payments are due (generally twice a year). Some bond certificates name the bondholder (the investor). When the company pays back the principal, the holder returns the certificate, which the company retires (or cancels). Exhibit 16-1 shows an actual bond certificate.

The board of directors may authorize a bond issue. In some companies the stockholders—as owners—may also have to vote their approval. Issuing bonds usually requires the services of a securities firm, such as Merrill Lynch, to act as the *underwriter* of the bond issue. The **underwriter** purchases the bonds from the issuing company and resells them to its clients, or it may sell the bonds for a commission from the issuer, agreeing to buy all unsold bonds.

Types of Bonds

All the bonds in a particular issue may mature at a specified time (**term bonds**), or they may mature in installments over a period of time (**serial bonds**). By issuing serial bonds, the company spreads its principal payments over time and avoids paying the entire principal at one time. Serial bonds are like installment notes payable.

Secured, or *mortgage*, *bonds* give the bondholder the right to take specified assets of the issuer if the company *defaults*, that is, fails to pay interest or principal. *Unsecured bonds*, called **debentures**, are backed only by the good faith of the borrower.

A secured bond is not necessarily more attractive to an investor than is a debenture. The primary motive of a person investing in bonds is to receive the interest

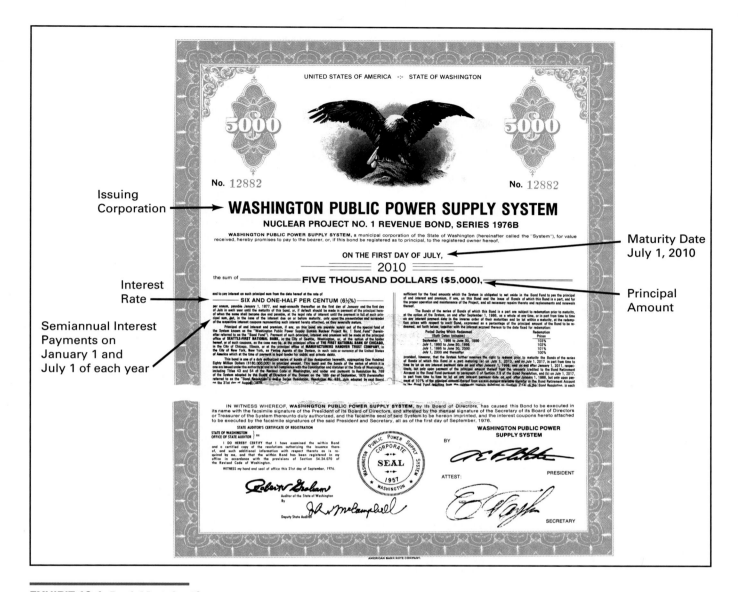

Issuing Corporation

Interest Rate

Semiannual Interest Payments on January 1 and July 1 of each year

Maturity Date July 1, 2010

Principal Amount

EXHIBIT 16-1 *Bond (Note) Certificate*

amounts and the bonds' maturity value on time. Thus a debenture from a business with an excellent record in meeting obligations may be more attractive to an investor than a secured bond from a business that is new or that has a bad credit record.

Bond Prices

Investors may transfer bond ownership through bond markets. The most famous bond market is the New York Exchange, which lists several thousand bonds. Bond prices are quoted at a percentage of their maturity value. For example, a $1,000 bond quoted at 100 is bought or sold for $1,000, which is 100 percent of its par value. The same bond quoted at 101 1/2 has a market price of $1,015 (101.5 percent of par value, or $1,000 × 1.015). Prices are quoted to one-eighth of 1 percent. A $1,000 bond quoted at 88 3/8 is priced at $883.75 ($1,000 × 0.88375).

Exhibit 16-2 contains real price information for the bonds of Ohio Edison Company, taken from *The Wall Street Journal*. On this particular day, 12 of Ohio Edison's 9 1/2 percent, $1,000 par value bonds maturing in the year 2006 (indicated

Short Exercise: Bonds are quoted in eighths of a percent. Calculate these issue prices: (1) 98⅛ quote on a $1,000 bond; (2) 104 3/8 quote on a $10,000 bond.

A:

(1)	$ 1,000	(2)	$ 10,000
	× 0.98125		× 1.04375
	$981.25		$10,437.50

EXHIBIT 16-2

*Bond Price Information for Ohio
Edison Company (OhEd)*

Bonds	Volume	High	Low	Close	Net Change
OhEd $9\frac{1}{2}$ 06	12	$79\frac{1}{2}$	$78\frac{1}{2}$	$79\frac{1}{2}$	+2

by 06) were traded. The bonds' highest price on this day was $795 ($1,000 × 0.795). The lowest price of the day was $785 ($1,000 × 0.785). The closing price (last sale of the day) was $795. This price was 2 points higher than the closing price of the preceding day. What was the bonds' closing price the preceding day? It was 77 1/2 (79 1/2 – 2).

The length of time until the bond matures is one factor that affects the market price of a bond. The earlier the maturity date, the more attractive the bond, and the more an investor is willing to pay for it. Also, the bonds issued by a company with a proven ability to meet all payments commands a higher price than an issue from a company with a poor record. Bond price hinges too on the rates of other available investment plans. Is a 9-percent bond the best way to invest $1,000, or does another investment strategy pay a higher rate? Of course, the higher the percentage rate, the higher the market price. Buying a 9-percent bond will cost you more than buying an 8-percent bond, given that both issues have the same maturity date and have been issued by equally sound businesses.

A bond issued at a price above its maturity (par) value is said to be issued at a **premium**, and a bond issued at a price below maturity (par) value has a **discount**. As a bond nears maturity, its market price moves toward par value. On the maturity date the market value of a bond exactly equals its par value because the company that issued the bond pays that amount to retire the bond.

Present Value[1]

A dollar received today is worth more than a dollar received in the future. You may invest today's dollar and earn income from it. Likewise, deferring any payment gives your money a longer period to grow. Money earns income over time, a fact called the *time value of money*. Let's examine how the time value of money affects the pricing of bonds.

Assume that a bond with a face value of $1,000 reaches maturity three years from today and carries no interest. Would you pay $1,000 to purchase the bond? No, because the payment of $1,000 today to receive the same amount in the future provides you with no income on the investment. You would not be taking advantage of the time value of money. Just how much would you pay today in order to receive $1,000 at the end of three years? The answer is some amount *less* than $1,000. Let's suppose that you feel $750 is a good price. By investing $750 now to receive $1,000 later, you earn $250 interest revenue over the three years. The issuing company sees the transaction this way: It pays you $250 interest for the use of your $750 for three years.

The amount that a person would invest *at the present time* to receive a greater amount at a future date is called the **present value** of a future amount. In our example, $750 is the present value of the $1,000 amount to be received three years later.

Our $750 bond price is a reasonable estimate. The exact present value of any future amount depends on (1) the amount of the future payment (or receipt), (2) the length of time from the investment to the date when the future amount is to be received (or paid), and (3) the interest rate during the period. Present value is always

---

[1]The chapter appendix covers present value in more detail.

EXHIBIT 16-3
Price of a Bond

Key Point: Present value is always less than future value. You should be able to invest today's money (present value) so that it will increase (future value). The difference between present value and future value is interest.

less than the future amount. We discuss the method of computing present value in the appendix that follows this chapter. We need to be aware of the present-value concept, however, in the discussion of bond prices that follows. Therefore, please study the appendix now.

Bond Interest Rates

Bonds are sold at market price, which is the amount that investors are willing to pay at any given time. Market price is the bond's present value, which equals the present value of the principal payment plus the present value of the cash interest payments (which are made semiannually, annually, or quarterly over the term of the bond).

Two interest rates work to set the price of a bond. The **contract interest rate**, or **stated interest rate**, is the interest rate that determines the amount of cash interest the borrower pays—and the investor receives—each year. For example, Chrysler's 8-percent bonds have a contract interest rate of 8 percent. Thus Chrysler pays $8,000 of interest annually on each $100,000 bond. Each semi-annual interest payment is $4,000 ($100,000 × 0.08 × 1/2).

The **market interest rate**, or **effective interest rate**, is the rate that investors demand for loaning their money. The market rate varies, sometimes daily. A company may issue bonds with a contract interest rate that differs from the prevailing market interest rate. Chrysler may issue its 8-percent bonds when the market rate has risen to 9 percent. Will the Chrysler bonds attract investors in this market? No, because investors can earn 9 percent on other bonds of similar risk. Therefore, investors will purchase Chrysler bonds only at a price less than par value. The difference between the lower price and face value is a *discount* (Exhibit 16-3). Conversely, if the market interest rate is 7 percent, Chrysler's 8-percent bonds will be so attractive that investors will pay more than face value for them. The difference between the higher price and face value is a *premium*.

Exhibit 16-4 summarizes the effects of the various factors on bond prices.

Key Point: Because market interest rates fluctuate daily, the contract interest rate will seldom equal the market interest rate on the date the bonds are sold. Bonds sell at a premium if the market rate drops below the bonds' contract rate and at a discount if the market rate rises above the contract rate.

Factor	Effects on Bond Price	
Risk of the issuing corporation	High-risk company———————→	Low price
	Low-risk company———————→	High price
Length of time to maturity	Long time to maturity———————→	Low price
	Short time to maturity———————→	High price
Contract interest rate paid by the bond	High contract interest rate———————→	High price
	Low contract interest rate———————→	Low price
Market interest rate when the bonds are issued	High market interest rate———————→	Low price
	Low market interest rate———————→	High price

EXHIBIT 16-4
Factors Affecting Bond Prices

Issuing Bonds Payable

Short Exercise: The following data will be used to illustrate various points covered in the next several Short Exercises: Assume that Quill Corp. issues, at par, $300,000 of 9%, 10-year bonds on May 31, 1996. The bonds pay interest each May 31 and November 30. What entries record issuance, first semi-annual interest payment, and retirement at maturity? *A:*

Issuance: 5/31/96
Cash...................... 300,000
   Bonds Payable ..   300,000
First interest payment:
11/30/96
Interest Expense... 13,500
   Cash..................   13,500
Maturity: 5/31/96
Bonds Payable...... 300,000
   Cash..................   300,000

Suppose Chrysler Corporation has $50 million in 8-percent bonds that mature in 10 years. Assume that Chrysler issues these bonds at par on January 1, 1995. The issuance entry is

1995			
Jan. 1	Cash	50,000,000	
	Bonds Payable..............................		50,000,000
	To issue 8%, 10-year bonds at par.		

The corporation that is borrowing money makes a one-time entry similar to this to record the receipt of cash and the issuance of bonds. Afterward, investors buy and sell the bonds through the bond markets. The buy-and-sell transactions between investors do *not* involve the corporation that issued the bonds. It keeps no records of these transactions, except for the names and addresses of the bondholders. This information is needed for mailing the interest and principal payments.

Interest payments occur each January 1 and July 1. Chrysler's entry to record the first semiannual interest payment is

1995			
July 1	Interest Expense ($50,000,000 × 0.08 × 6/12)	2,000,000	
	Cash..		2,000,000
	To pay semiannual interest on bonds payable.		

At maturity, Chrysler will record payment of the bonds as follows:

2005			
Jan. 1	Bonds Payable	50,000,000	
	Cash		50,000,000
	To pay bonds payable at maturity.		

Issuing Bonds and Notes Payable between Interest Dates

The foregoing entries to record Chrysler's bond transactions are straightforward because the company issued the bonds on an interest payment date (January 1). However, corporations often issue bonds between interest dates.

MGM Grand, Inc., which runs the MGM Grand Hotel and Theme Park in Las Vegas, issued $230 million of 12-percent notes payable due in the year 2002. These notes were dated 1992 and carry the price "100 plus accrued interest from date of original issue." An investor purchasing the MGM Grand, Inc., notes after the issue date must pay market value *plus accrued interest*. The issuing company will pay the full semiannual interest amount to the bondholder at the next interest payment date. Companies do not split semiannual interest payments among two or more investors who happen to hold the bonds during a particular six-month interest period.

Assume that MGM Grand, Inc., sold $100,000,000 of its notes on July 15, 1992, one month after the date of original issue on June 15. The market price of the notes on July 15 is the face value. MGM Grand receives one month's accrued interest in addition to the notes' face value. MGM Grand's entry to record issuance of the notes payable is as follows:

PUTTING SKILLS TO WORK

SALE OF BONDS AND NOTES BETWEEN INTEREST DATES— "PLUS ACCRUED INTEREST"

Selling bonds and notes between interest dates at market value plus accrued interest simplifies the borrower's accounting. MGM Grand, Inc., pays the same amount of interest on each note regardless of the length of time the investor has held the note. MGM Grand need not compute each noteholder's interest payment on an individual basis.

When an investor sells bonds or notes to another investor, the price is always "plus accrued interest." Suppose you hold MGM Grand, Inc., notes as an investment for two months of a semiannual interest period and sell the notes to another investor before you receive your interest. The person who buys the notes will receive your two months of interest on the next specified interest date. Business practice dictates that you must collect your share of the interest from the buyer when you sell your investment. For this reason, all bond or note transactions are "plus accrued interest."

An entrance of the MGM Grand Hotel.

1992
July 15 Cash 101,000,000
  Bonds Payable   100,000,000
  Interest Payable ($100,000,000 × 0.12 × 1/12)   1,000,000
  To issue 12%, 10-year notes at par, one month
  after the original issue date.

MGM Grand's entry to record the first semiannual interest payment is:

1992
Dec. 15 Interest Expense ($100,000,000 × 0.12 × 5/12) 5,000,000
  Interest Payable... 1,000,000
  Cash ($100,000,000 × 0.12 × 6/12)..............   6,000,000
  To pay semiannual interest on notes payable.

The debit to Interest Payable eliminates the credit balance in that account (from July 15). MGM Grand, Inc., has now paid off that liability.

Note that MGM Grand, Inc., pays a full six months' interest on December 15. After subtracting the one month's accrued interest received at the time of issuing the note, MGM Grand has recorded interest expense for five months ($5,000,000). This interest expense is the correct amount for the five months that the notes have been outstanding.

Short Exercise: Assume that Quill Corp. issues its $300,000, 9%, 10-year bonds at par on September 30, 1996 (four months after the interest date, May 31). What are the entries for the original issuance and the first interest payment? *A:*
Issuance: 9/30/96
Cash...................... 309,000
  Bonds Payable ..   300,000
  Interest Payable   9,000
($300,000 × 9% × 4/12
                             = $9,000)
Interest payment: 11/30/96
Interest Expense...   4,500
Interest Payable....   9,000
  Cash.................   13,500

Six months' interest has been paid in cash, but only two months of interest expense has been incurred by Quill. This is correct because the bonds have been outstanding only two months.

Issuing Bonds Payable at a Discount

Unlike stocks, bonds are often issued at a discount. We know that market conditions may force the issuing corporation to accept a discount price for its bonds. Suppose Chrysler issues $100,000 of its 8-percent, 10-year bonds when the market interest rate is slightly above 8 percent. The market price of the bonds drops to 98, which means 98 percent of par value. Chrysler receives $98,000 ($100,000 × 0.98) at issuance. The entry is the following:

Short Exercise: Assume that Quill Corp. issues its $300,000, 9% bonds on May 31, 1996, when the market rate of interest is just under 10%. The bonds are issued at 97 1/2. What entry records the issuance? *A:* 5/31/96

Cash...................... 292,500
Discount on
   Bonds Payable .. 7,500
     Bonds Payable   300,000
($300,000 × 0.975 = $292,500)
The carrying amount on the balance sheet on 5/31/96 is:
Bonds payable......... $300,000
Less: Discount on
  bonds payable   7,500
Carrying amount.... $292,500

1995
Jan. 1   Cash ($100,000 × 0.98) 98,000
        Discount on Bonds Payable 2,000
           Bonds Payable..   100,000
     To issue 8%, 10-year bonds at a discount.

After posting, the bond accounts have the following balances:

Bonds Payable	Discount on Bonds Payable
100,000	2,000

Chrysler's balance sheet immediately after issuance of the bonds reports:

Long-term liabilities:
  Bonds payable, 8%, due 2005 .... $100,000
  Less: Discount on bonds payable..............   2,000 $98,000

Discount on Bonds Payable is a contra account to Bonds Payable. Subtracting its balance from Bonds Payable yields the book value, or carrying amount, of the bonds. The relationship between Bonds Payable and the Discount account is similar to the relationships between Equipment and Accumulated Depreciation and between Accounts Receivable and Allowance for Uncollectible Accounts. Thus Chrysler's liability is $98,000, which is the amount the company borrowed. If Chrysler were to pay off the bonds immediately (an unlikely occurrence), Chrysler's required outlay would be $98,000 because the market price of the bonds is $98,000.

INTEREST EXPENSE ON BONDS ISSUED AT A DISCOUNT We earlier discussed the difference between the contract interest rate and the market interest rate. Suppose the market rate is 8 1/4 percent when Chrysler issues its 8-percent bonds. The 1/4-percent interest-rate difference creates the $2,000 discount on the bonds. Investors are willing to pay only $98,000 for a $100,000, 8-percent bond when they can purchase similar bonds and earn 8 1/4 percent on the investment. Chrysler borrows $98,000 cash but must pay $100,000 cash when the bonds mature, 10 years later. What happens to the $2,000 balance of the discount account over the life of the bond issue? The $2,000 discount is really an additional interest expense to the issuing company. That amount is a cost—beyond the stated interest rate—that the business pays for borrowing the investors' money. The discount has the effect of raising the interest expense on the bonds to the market interest rate of 8 1/4 percent.

The discount amount is an interest expense not paid until the bond matures. However, the borrower—the bond issuer—benefits from the use of the investors' money each accounting period over the full term of the bond issue. The matching principle directs the business to match expense against its revenues on a period-by-period basis. Each accounting period over the life of the bonds, the discount is allocated to interest expense through amortization.

OBJECTIVE 1
Account for basic bonds payable transactions by the straight-line amortization method

STRAIGHT-LINE AMORTIZATION OF DISCOUNT We may amortize a bond discount by dividing it into equal amounts for each interest period. This method is called *straight-line amortization*. In our example, the initial discount is $2,000, and there are 20 semiannual interest periods during the bonds' 10-year life. Therefore 1/20 of the $2,000 ($100) of bond discount is amortized each interest period. Chrysler's semiannual interest entry on July 1, 1995 is as follows:

1995
July 1   Interest Expense.. 4,100

          Cash ($100,000 × 0.08 × 6/12)..   4,000

          Discount on Bonds Payable ($2,000/20).....................   100

         To pay semiannual interest and amortize discount on
bonds payable.

Interest expense of $4,100 is the sum of the contract interest ($4,000, which is paid in cash) plus the amount of discount amortized ($100). Discount on Bonds Payable is credited to amortize (reduce) the account's debit balance. Because Discount on Bonds Payable is a contra account, each reduction in its balance increases the book value of Bonds Payable. Twenty amortization entries will decrease the discount balance to zero, which means that the carrying amount of Bonds Payable will have increased by $2,000 to its face value of $100,000. The entry to pay off the bonds at maturity is the following:

2005
Jan. 1   Bonds Payable... 100,000

          Cash   100,000

         To pay bonds payable at maturity.

Issuing Bonds Payable at a Premium

Why are bonds issued at a premium less common than bonds issued at a discount? Because companies prefer to issue bonds that pay a lower cash interest rate. To illustrate issuing bonds at a premium, let's change the Chrysler example. Assume that the market interest rate is 7 1/2 percent when the company issues its 8-percent, 10-year bonds. Because 8-percent bonds are attractive in this market, investors pay a premium price to acquire them. If the bonds are priced at 103 1/2 (103.5 percent of par value), Chrysler receives $103,500 cash upon issuance. The entry is as follows:

1995
Jan. 1   Cash ($100,000 × 1.035)... 103,500

          Bonds Payable..   100,000

          Premium on Bonds Payable   3,500

         To issue 8%, 10-year bonds at a premium.

After posting, the bond accounts have the following balances:

Bonds Payable	Premium on Bonds Payable
100,000	3,500

Chrysler's balance sheet immediately after issuance of bonds reports:

Long-term liabilities:

     Bonds payable, 8%, due 2005 .... $100,000

     Premium on bonds payable...................   3,500 $103,500

Premium on Bonds Payable is added to Bonds Payable to show the book value, or carrying amount, of the bonds. Chrysler's liability is $103,500, which is the amount that the company borrowed. Immediate payment of the bonds would require an outlay of $103,500 because the market price of the bonds at issuance is $103,500. The investors would be unwilling to give up the bonds for less than their market value.

Short Exercise: For the $300,000 of 10-year bonds issued by Quill Corp. on May 31, 1996, at 97 1/2, what entry on November 30, 1996, records the first semiannual interest payment and amortization of the discount? *A:*

11/30/96

Interest Expense...   13,875

   Cash.................   13,500

   Discount on

     Bonds Payable   375

($300,000 × 0.09 × 6/12 = $13,500 interest paid in cash, $7,500 ÷ 20 = $375 amortization)

Discount on Bonds Payable is reduced equally in each of the 20 periods until its balance reaches zero at maturity. The recording of discount amortization *increases* Interest Expense each period. That is, Interest Expense is greater than the cash paid for interest.

Short Exercise: Assume that Quill Corp.'s $300,000 of 9%, 10-year bonds are issued on May 31, 1996, when the market rate of interest is just over 8%. The bonds are issued at 102. (1) What is the entry to record the issuance? (2) What is the entry on November 30, 1996, to record the first semiannual interest payment and amortize the premium? *A:*   *(cont.)*

(1) 5/31/96

Cash 306,000
  Bonds Payable.... 300,000
  Premium on
    Bonds Payable 6,000
($300,000 × 1.02 = $306,000)
The carrying amount on the
balance sheet on 5/31/96 is:
Bonds payable........... $300,000
Plus: Premium on
  bonds payable .... <u>6,000</u>
Carrying amount ...... <u>$306,000</u>

(2) 11/30/96

Interest Expense 13,200
Premium on
  Bonds Payable 300
    Cash 13,500
($300,000 × 0.09 × 6/12 =
  $13,500 interest paid in cash;
  $6,000 ÷ 20 = $300 amortiz.)

Premium on Bonds Payable is
reduced equally in each of the
20 periods until the balance is
fully amortized. The recording
of the premium amortization
decreases Interest Expense each
period. Interest Expense is less
than the cash paid for interest.

INTEREST EXPENSE ON BONDS ISSUED AT A PREMIUM The 1/2-percent difference between the 8-percent contract rate on the bonds and the 7 1/2-percent market interest rate creates the $3,500 premium. Chrysler borrows $103,500 cash but must pay only $100,000 cash at maturity. We treat the premium as a savings of interest expense to Chrysler. The premium cuts Chrysler's cost of borrowing the money and reduces Chrysler's interest expense to an effective interest rate of 7 1/2 percent, the market rate. We account for the premium much as we handled the discount. We amortize the bond premium as a decrease in interest expense over the life of the bonds.

STRAIGHT-LINE AMORTIZATION OF PREMIUM In our example, the beginning premium is $3,500, and there are 20 semiannual interest periods during the bonds' 10-year life. Therefore, 1/20 of the $3,500 ($175) of bond premium is amortized each interest period. Chrysler's semiannual interest entry on July 1, 1995, is the following:

1995
July 1 Interest Expense 3,825
      Premium on Bonds Payable ($3,500/20) 175
        Cash ($100,000 × 0.08 × 6/12)..................................... 4,000
    To pay semiannual interest and amortize premium
    on bonds payable.

Interest expense of $3,825 is the remainder of the contract cash interest ($4,000) less the amount of premium amortized ($175). The debit to Premium on Bonds Payable reduces its credit balance.

STOP & THINK Consider bonds issued at a discount. Which will be greater, the cash interest paid per period or the amount of interest expense? Answer the same question for bonds issued at a premium.

Answer: For bonds issued at a *discount*, interest expense will be greater than cash interest paid, by the amount of the discount amortized for the period. For bonds issued at a *premium*, cash interest paid will be greater than interest expense, by the amount of the premium amortized for the period.

Reporting Bonds Payable

Bonds payable are reported on the balance sheet at their maturity amount plus any unamortized premium or minus any unamortized discount. For example, at December 31, Chrysler in the preceding example would have amortized Premium on Bonds Payable for two semiannual periods ($175 × 2 = $350). The Chrysler balance sheet would show these bonds payable as follows:

Long-term liabilities:
  Bonds payable, 8%, due 2005 .... $100,000
  Premium on bonds payable [$3,500 − (2 × $175)] .... <u>3,150</u> $103,150

Over the life of the bonds, 20 amortization entries will decrease the premium balance to zero. The payment at maturity will debit Bonds Payable and credit cash for $100,000.

Adjusting Entries for Interest Expense

Companies issue bonds when they need cash. The interest payments seldom occur on December 31 (or the end of the fiscal year). Nevertheless, interest expense must be accrued at the end of the period to measure income accurately. ⇐ The accrual entry may often be complicated by the need to amortize a discount or a premium for only a partial interest period.

Xenon Corporation issued $100,000 of its 8-percent, 10-year bonds at a $2,000 discount on October 1, 1995. The interest payments occur on March 31 and September 30 each year. On December 31 Xenon records interest for the three-month period (October, November, and December) as follows:

⇐ ⇐ ⇐ The adjusting entry for bond interest expense is the same as the adjusting entries for other accrued liabilities as in Chapters 3 (p. 100) and 11 (p. 458) except for the addition of the amortization of the premium or discount.

```
1995
Dec. 31    Interest Expense.........................................    2,050
                Interest Payable ($100,000 × 0.08 × 3/12)...............         2,000
                Discount on Bonds Payable ($2,000/10 × 3/12).......              50
           To accrue three months' interest and amortize discount
           on bonds payable for three months.
```

Interest Payable is credited for the three months of cash interest that have accrued since September 30. Discount on Bonds Payable is credited for three months of amortization.

Xenon's balance sheet at December 31, 1995, reports Interest Payable of $2,000 as a current liability. Bonds Payable appears as a long-term liability, presented as follows:

```
Long-term liabilities:
    Bonds payable, 8%, due 2005 ...........................................    $100,000
    Less: Discount on bonds payable ($2,000 – $50) ...............       1,950     $98,050
```

Observe that the balance of Discount on Bonds Payable decreases by $50. The bonds' carrying amount also increases by $50. The bonds' carrying amount continues to increase over its 10-year life, reaching $100,000 at maturity, when the discount will be fully amortized.

The next semiannual interest payment occurs on March 31, 1996:

```
1996
Mar. 31    Interest Expense.........................................    2,050
           Interest Payable.........................................    2,000
                Cash ($100,000 × 0.08 × 6/12) .................................         4,000
                Discount on Bonds Payable ($2,000/10 × 3/12)........              50
           To pay semiannual interest, part of which was accrued,
           and amortize three months' discount on bonds
           payable.
```

Short Exercise: For the previous Short Exercise, (1) what year-end adjusting entry is required on 12/31/96? (2) What entry will follow on 5/31/97? *A:*

(1) 12/31/96
Interest Expense... 2,200
Premium on
    Bonds Payable ..   50
    Interest Pay...   2,250
($13,500 × 1/6 = $2,250 and $300 × 1/6 = $50, both for 1 month) The amounts recorded are 1/6 of the usual semiannual amortization and interest amounts.
(2) 5/31/97
Interest Expense... 11,000
Interest Payable....   2,250
Premium on
    Bonds Payable   250
        Cash...............   13,500

This entry represents 5 months of interest expense and of amortization and 6 months of interest paid in cash. Interest expense and amortization for the remaining month have been recorded in the 12/31/96 adjusting entry.

Amortization of a premium over a partial interest period is similar except that Premium on Bonds Payable is debited.

Assume that Alabama Power Company has outstanding an issue of 9-percent bonds that mature on May 1, 2016. The bonds are dated May 1, 1996, and Alabama Power pays interest each April 30 and October 31.

Required

1. Will the bonds be issued at par, at a premium, or at a discount if the market interest rate is 8 percent at date of issuance? If the market interest rate is 10 percent?

2. Assume that Alabama Power issued $1,000,000 of the bonds at 104 on May 1, 1996.

   a. Record issuance of the bonds.

   b. Record the interest payment and amortization of premium or discount on October 31, 1996.

   c. Accrue interest and amortize premium or discount on December 31, 1996.

   d. Show how the company would report the bonds on the balance sheet at December 31, 1996.

   e. Record the interest payment on April 30, 1997.

SOLUTION TO REVIEW PROBLEM

Requirement 1

If the market interest rate is 8 percent, 9-percent bonds will be issued at a *premium*. If the market rate is 10 percent, the 9-percent bonds will be issued at a *discount*.

Requirement 2

```
1996
a. May  1    Cash ($1,000,000 × 1.04).................................     1,040,000
                 Bonds Payable.......................................................              1,000,000
                 Premium on Bonds Payable...................................                 40,000
             To issue 9%, 20-year bonds at a premium.

b. Oct. 31   Interest Expense ...............................................        44,000
             Premium on Bonds Payable ($40,000/40) ......................         1,000
                 Cash ($1,000,000 × 0.09 × 6/12)............................                 45,000
             To pay semiannual interest and amortize premium
             on bonds payable.

c. Dec. 31   Interest Expense ...............................................        14,667
             Premium on Bonds Payable ($40,000/40 × 2/6)............           333
                 Interest Payable ($1,000,000 × 0.09 × 2/12).........                 15,000
             To accrue interest and amortize bond premium
             for two months.

d. Long-term liabilities:
                 Bonds payable, 9%, due 2016...............   $1,000,000
                 Premium on bonds payable
                 ($40,000 – $1,000 – $333) ...................        38,667    $1,038,667

1997
e. Apr. 30   Interest Expense ...............................................        29,333
             Interest Payable .................................................        15,000
             Premium on Bonds Payable ($40,000/40 × 4/6) ...........           667
                 Cash ($1,000,000 × 0.09 × 6/12) ..........................                 45,000
             To pay semiannual interest, part of which was
             accrued, and amortize four months' premium on
             bonds payable.
```

Bond problems include many details. You may find it helpful to check your work. We verify the answers to the Summary Problem in this supplement.

On April 30, 1997, the bonds have been outstanding for one year. After the entries have been recorded, the account balances should show the results of one year's cash interest payments and one year's bond premium amortization.

Fact 1:	Cash interest payments should be $90,000 ($100,000 × 0.09).
Accuracy check:	Two credits to Cash of $45,000 each = $90,000. Cash payments are correct.
Fact 2:	Premium amortization should be $2,000 ($40,000/40 semiannual periods × 2 semiannual periods in 1 year).
Accuracy check:	Three debits to Premium on Bonds Payable ($1,000 + $333 + $667) = $2,000. Premium amortization is correct.
Fact 3:	Also we can check the accuracy of interest expense recorded during the year ended December 31, 1996. The bonds in this problem will be outstanding for a total of 20 years, or 240 (that is, 20 × 12) months. During 1996 the bonds are outstanding for 8 months (May through December). Interest expense for 8 months *equals* payment of cash interest for 8 months minus premium amortization for 8 months. Interest expense should therefore be ($1,000,000 × 0.09 × 8/12 = $60,000) minus [($40,000/240) × 8 = $1,333], or ($60,000 − $1,333 = $58,667).
Accuracy check:	Two debits to Interest Expense ($44,000 + $14,667) = $58,667. Interest expense for 1996 is correct.

Effective-Interest Method of Amortization

The straight-line amortization method was explained first to introduce the concept of amortizing bond discount and premium. However, it has a theoretical weakness. Each period's amortization amount for a premium or discount is the same dollar amount over the life of the bonds. Over that time, however, the bonds' carrying amount continues to increase (with a discount) or decrease (with a premium). Thus the fixed dollar amount of amortization changes as a percentage of the bonds' carrying amount, making it appear that the bond issuer's interest rate changes over time. This appearance misleads because in fact the issuer locked in a fixed interest rate when the bonds were issued. The interest *rate* on the bonds does not change.

OBJECTIVE 2
Amortize bond discount and premium by the effective-interest method

GAAP (*Accounting Principles Board Opinion No. 21*) requires that discounts and premiums be amortized using the *effective-interest method* unless the difference between the straight-line method and the effective-interest method is immaterial. In that case, either method is permitted. We will see how the effective-interest method keeps each interest expense amount at the same percentage of the bonds' carrying amount for every interest payment over the bonds' life. The total amount amortized over the life of the bonds is the same under both methods.

Effective-Interest Method of Amortizing Discount

Assume that Bethlehem Steel Corporation issues $100,000 of its 9-percent bonds at a time when the market rate of interest is 10 percent. Assume also that these bonds mature in five years and pay interest semiannually, so there are 10 semiannual inter-

EXHIBIT 16-5
Effective-Interest Method of Amortizing Bond Discount

PANEL A—Bond Data

Maturity value—$100,000
Contract interest rate—9%
Interest paid—4 1/2% semiannually, $4,500 ($100,000 × 0.045)
Market interest rate at time of issue—10% annually, 5% semiannually
Issue price—$96,149

PANEL B—Amortization Table

	A	B	C	D	E
Semiannual Interest Period	Interest *Payment* (4 1/2% of Maturity Value)	Interest *Expense* (5% of Preceding Bond Carrying Amount)	Discount Amortization (B – A)	Discount Account Balance (D – C)	Bond Carrying Amount ($100,000 – D)
Issue Date				$3,851	$ 96,149
1	$4,500	$4,807	$307	3,544	96,456
2	4,500	4,823	323	3,221	96,779
3	4,500	4,839	339	2,882	97,118
4	4,500	4,856	356	2,526	97,474
5	4,500	4,874	374	2,152	97,848
6	4,500	4,892	392	1,760	98,240
7	4,500	4,912	412	1,348	98,652
8	4,500	4,933	433	915	99,085
9	4,500	4,954	454	461	99,539
10	4,500	4,961*	461	–0–	100,000

*Adjusted for effect of rounding.

Notes

- *Column A* The semiannual interest payments are constant—fixed by the contract interest rate and the bonds' maturity value.
- *Column B* The interest expense each period is computed by multiplying the preceding bond carrying amount by the market interest rate. The effect of this *effective interest rate* determines the interest expense each period. The amount of interest each period increases as the effective interest rate, a constant, is applied to the increasing bond carrying amount (E).
- *Column C* The excess of each interest expense amount (B) over each interest payment amount (A) is the discount amortization for the period.
- *Column D* The discount balance decreases by the amount of amortization for the period (C), from $3,851 at the bonds' issue date to zero at their maturity. Balance of discount + bonds' carrying amount = bonds' maturity value.
- *Column E* The bond's carrying amount increases from $96,149 at issuance to $100,000 at maturity.

Short Exercise: Back to Quill Corp. and the $300,000, 9%, 10-year bonds dated 5/31/96. Assume that the bonds are sold on 5/31/96 for $281,337 to yield an effective rate of 10%. Using the effective-interest method, what entry is required on 11/30/96, the first interest payment date? *A:*

11/30/96
Interest Expense... 14,067*
   Discount on
      Bonds Payable   567†
   Cash.................. 13,500

*$281,337 × 5% = $14,067
†$14,067 – $13,500 = $567

The Discount account has been reduced by $567 and has a new balance of $18,096 ($18,663 – $567). The bonds' new carrying value is $281,904 ($300,000 – $18,096).

Key Point: The amount of cash paid each semiannual interest period is calculated with the formula:
Interest paid = Par value × (Contract rate/2)
This amount does not change over the term of the bond.

---

est payments. The issue price of the bonds is $96,149.[2] The discount on these bonds is $3,851 ($100,000 – $96,149). Exhibit 16-5 illustrates amortization of the discount by the effective-interest method.

Recall that we want to present interest expense amounts over the full life of the bonds at a fixed percentage of the bonds' carrying amount. The 5-percent rate—the effective interest rate—*is* that percentage. We have figured the cost of the money borrowed by the bond issuer—the interest expense—as a constant percentage of the carrying amount of the bonds. The dollar *amount* of interest expense varies from period to period, but the interest percentage remains the same.

---

[2]We compute this present value by using the tables that appear in this chapter's appendix.

The *accounts* debited and credited under the effective-interest amortization method and the straight-line method are the same. Only the *amounts* differ. We may take the amortization *amounts* directly from the table in Exhibit 16-5. We assume that the first interest payment occurs on July 1 and use the appropriate amounts from Exhibit 16-5, reading across the line for the first interest payment date:

July 1   Interest Expense (column B) 4,807
          Discount on Bonds Payable (column C)....................... 307
          Cash (column A)... 4,500
      To pay semiannual interest and amortize discount on bonds payable.

Key Point: The amount of semiannual interest expense is calculated with the formula:
Interest expense = Bond carrying value × (Market interest rate/2)
This amount will change each period as carrying value changes over the term of the bond.

STOP & THINK Over the life of a bond issued at a *discount*, will the periodic amount of interest expense increase or decrease under the effective-interest amortization method?

Answer: The periodic amount of interest expense *increases* because the carrying amount of the bond *increases* toward maturity value. To see this, refer to columns B and E of Exhibit 16-5.

Effective-Interest Method of Amortizing Premium

Let's modify the Bethlehem Steel example to illustrate the interest method of amortizing bond premium. Assume that Bethlehem Steel issues $100,000 of five-year, 9-percent bonds that pay interest semiannually. If the bonds are issued when the market interest rate is 8 percent, their issue price is $104,100.[3] The premium on these bonds is $4,100, and Exhibit 16-6 illustrates amortization of the premium by the effective-interest method.

Assuming that the first interest payment occurs on October 31, we read across the line in Exhibit 16-6 for the first payment date and get the appropriate amounts:

Oct. 31   Interest Expense (column B)... 4,164
          Premium on Bonds Payable (column C)............................ 336
          Cash (column A) 4,500
      To pay semiannual interest and amortize premium on bonds payable.

STOP & THINK How does the method of amortizing bond premium or discount affect the amount of cash interest paid on a bond?

Answer: The amortization method for bond premium or discount has *no effect* on the amount of cash interest paid on a bond. The amount of cash interest paid depends on the contract interest rate stated on the bond. That interest rate, and the amount of cash interest paid, are fixed and therefore remain constant over the life of the bond. To see this, examine column A of Exhibits 16-5 and 16-6.

At year end it is necessary to make an adjusting entry for accrued interest and amortization of the bond premium for a partial period. In our example, the last interest payment occurred on October 31. The adjustment for November and December must cover two months, or one-third of a semiannual period. The entry, with amounts drawn from Exhibit 16-6, line 2, is as follows:

Dec. 31   Interest Expense ($4,151 × 1/3) 1,384
          Premium on Bonds Payable ($349 × 1/3) 116
          Interest Payable ($4,500 × 1/3)................................... 1,500
      To accrue two months' interest and amortize premium
      on bonds payable for two months.

The second interest payment occurs on April 30 of the following year. The payment of $4,500 includes interest expense for four months (January through April), the interest payable at December 31, and premium amortization for four months. The payment entry is the following:

---

[3]Again we compute the present value of the bonds from the tables in this chapter's appendix.

EXHIBIT 16-6
Effective-Interest Method of Amortizing Bond Premium

PANEL A—Bond Data

Maturity value—$100,000
Contract interest rate—9%
Interest paid—4 1/2% semiannually, $4,500 ($100,000 × 0.045)
Market interest rate at time of issue—8% annually, 4% semiannually
Issue price—$104,100

PANEL B—Amortization Table

Semiannual Interest Period	A — Interest *Payment* (4 1/2% of Maturity Value)	B — Interest *Expense* (4% of Preceding Bond Carrying Amount)	C — Premium Amortization (A – B)	D — Premium Account Balance (D – C)	E — Bond Carrying Amount ($100,000 + D)
Issue Date				$4,100	$104,100
1	$4,500	$4,164	$336	3,764	103,764
2	4,500	4,151	349	3,415	103,415
3	4,500	4,137	363	3,052	103,052
4	4,500	4,122	378	2,674	102,674
5	4,500	4,107	393	2,281	102,281
6	4,500	4,091	409	1,872	101,872
7	4,500	4,075	425	1,447	101,447
8	4,500	4,058	442	1,005	101,005
9	4,500	4,040	460	545	100,545
10	4,500	3,955*	545	–0–	100,000

*Adjusted for effect of rounding.

Notes

- *Column A* The semiannual interest payments are constant—fixed by the contract interest rate and the bonds' maturity value.
- *Column B* The interest expense each period is computed by multiplying the preceding bond carrying amount by the effective interest rate. The amount of interest decreases each period as the bond carrying amount decreases.
- *Column C* The excess of each interest payment (A) over the period's interest expense (B) is the premium amortization for the period.
- *Column D* The premium balance decreases by the amount of amortization for the period (C) from $4,100 at issuance to zero at maturity. Bonds' carrying amount – premium balance = bonds' maturity value.
- *Column E* The bonds' carrying amount decreases from $104,100 at issuance to $100,000 at maturity.

Apr. 30	Interest Expense ($4,151 × 2/3)	2,767	
	Interest Payable	1,500	
	Premium on Bonds Payable ($349 × 2/3)	233	
	Cash		4,500

To pay semiannual interest, some of which was accrued, and amortize premium on bonds payable for four months.

If these bonds had been issued at a discount, procedures for these interest entries would be the same, except that Discount on Bonds Payable would be credited.

STOP & THINK For a bond issued at a *premium*, will the periodic amount of interest expense increase or decrease? Assume the effective-interest method.

Answer: The periodic amount of interest expense *decreases* because the carrying amount of the bond *decreases* toward maturity value. To see this, study columns B and E of Exhibit 16-6.

Retirement of Bonds Payable

Normally companies wait until maturity to pay off, or retire, their bonds payable. All bond discount or premium has been amortized, and the retirement entry debits Bonds Payable and credits Cash for the bonds' maturity value. But companies sometimes retire their bonds payable prior to maturity. The main reason for retiring bonds early is to relieve the pressure of making interest payments. Interest rates fluctuate. The company may be able to borrow at a lower interest rate and then use the proceeds from new bonds to pay off the old bonds, which bear a higher interest rate.

Some bonds are **callable**, which means that the bonds' issuer may *call*, or pay off, those bonds at a specified price whenever the issuer so chooses. The call price is usually a few percent above the par value, perhaps 104 or 105. Callable bonds give the issuer the benefit of being able to take advantage of low interest rates by paying off the bonds whenever it is most favorable to do so. An alternative to calling the bonds is to purchase them in the open market at their current market price. Whether the bonds are called or purchased in the open market, the journal entry is the same.

Air Products and Chemicals, Inc., a producer of industrial gases and chemicals, has $70 million of debentures outstanding with unamortized discount of $350,000. Lower interest rates in the market may convince management to pay off these bonds now. Assume that the bonds are callable at 103. If the market price of the bonds is 99 1/4, will Air Products and Chemicals call the bonds or purchase them in the open market? The market price is lower than the call price, so market price is the better choice. Retiring the bonds at 99 1/4 results in a gain of $175,000, computed as follows:

Par value of bonds being retired	$70,000,000
Unamortized discount	350,000
Book value	69,650,000
Market price ($70,000,000 × 0.9925)	69,475,000
Gain on retirement	$ 175,000

The following entry records retirement of the bonds, immediately after an interest date:

June 30	Bonds Payable	70,000,000	
	Discount on Bonds Payable		350,000
	Cash ($70,000,000 × 0.9925)		69,475,000
	Extraordinary Gain on Retirement of Bonds Payable		175,000
	To retire bonds payable before maturity.		

The entry removes the bonds payable and the related discount from the accounts and records a gain on retirement. Any existing premium would be removed with a debit. If Air Products and Chemicals retired only half these bonds, the accountant would remove half the discount or premium. Likewise, if the price paid to retire the bonds exceeded their carrying amount, the retirement entry would record a loss with a debit to the account Extraordinary Loss on Retirement of Bonds. GAAP identifies gains and losses on early retirement of debts as *extraordinary*, and they are reported separately on the income statement, net of tax.

OBJECTIVE 3

Account for retirement of bonds payable

Key Point: Callable bonds may be paid off at the corporation's option. The bondholder does not have the choice of refusing but must surrender the bond for retirement.

Key Point: When bonds are retired before maturity, these steps must be followed: (1) Record partial period amortization of premium or discount, if date is other than an interest payment date. (2) Write off the portion of Premium or Discount that relates to the portion of bonds being retired. (3) Calculate extraordinary gain or loss on retirement.

Short Exercise: Quill Corp. has sold $300,000 of 10-year bonds at a discount. Interest has just been paid, and the remaining carrying value of the bonds is $299,000. Half the bonds are retired when the market price is 96 1/2. What entry is required? *A:*

Bonds Payable.........150,000*
    Discount on
        Bonds Pay. .... 500†
    Cash.................... 144,750‡
    Extraordinary Gain
        on Retirement. 4,750§

*$300,000 par value × ½ = $150,000
†$1,000 unamortized discount × ½ = $500
‡$150,000 × 0.965 = $144,750
§($150,000 − $500) − $144,750 = $4,750 gain

Convertible Bonds and Notes

Many corporate bonds and notes payable may be converted into the common stock of the issuing company at the option of the investor. These bonds and notes, called **convertible bonds** (or **notes**), combine the safety of assured interest receipts and receipt of principal on the bonds with the opportunity for large gains on the stock. The conversion feature is so attractive that investors usually accept a lower contract, or stated, interest rate than they would on nonconvertible bonds. The lower cash interest payments benefit the issuer. Convertible bonds are recorded like any other debt at issuance.

If the market price of the issuing company's stock gets high enough, the bondholders will convert the bonds into stock. The corporation records conversion by debiting the bond accounts and crediting the stockholders' equity accounts. The carrying amount of the bonds becomes the book value of the newly issued stock. No gain or loss is recorded.

"Prime Western, Inc., which operates hotels, had convertible notes outstanding carried on the books at $12.5 million."

Prime Western, Inc., which operates hotels, had convertible *notes* outstanding carried on the books at $12.5 million. Assume that the maturity value of the notes was $13 million. Also assume that Prime Western's stock rose significantly so that noteholders converted the notes into 400,000 shares of the company's $1 par common stock. Prime Western's entry to record conversion is as follows:

May 14	Notes Payable	13,000,000	
	Discount on Notes Payable......................		500,000
	Common Stock (400,000 × $1)		400,000
	Paid-in Capital in Excess of		
	Par—Common		12,100,000
	To record conversion of notes payable.		

The carrying amount of the notes ($13,000,000 – $500,000) becomes the amount of increase in stockholders' equity ($400,000 + $12,100,000). The entry closes the notes (or bonds) payable account and its related discount or premium account.

Current Portion of Long-Term Debt

Serial bonds and serial notes are payable in serials, or installments. The portion payable within one year is a current liability, and the remaining debt is long-term. At July 3, 1993, Sara Lee Corporation had $1,590 million of long-term debt maturing in various amounts in future years. The portion payable in the next year was $426 million. Therefore, $426 million was a current liability at July 3, 1993, and $1,164 million was a long-term liability. Sara Lee Corporation reported the following among its liabilities at July 3, 1993:

	$ Millions
Current liabilities:	
Current maturities of long-term debt..............	$ 426
Long-term debt less current maturities	1,164

Mortgage Notes Payable

You have probably heard of mortgage payments. Many notes payable are mortgage notes, which actually contain two agreements. The *note* is the borrower's promise to pay the lender the amount of the debt. The **mortgage**—a security agreement related to the note—is the borrower's promise to transfer to the lender the legal title to certain assets if the debt is not paid on schedule. The borrower is said to pledge these assets as security for the note. Often the asset that is pledged was acquired with the borrowed money. For example, most homeowners sign mortgage notes to purchase their residence, pledging that property as security for the loan. Businesses sign mortgage notes to acquire buildings, equipment, and other long-term assets. Mortgage notes are usually serial notes that require monthly or quarterly payments.

Advantage of Financing Operations with Bonds versus Stock

Businesses have different ways to acquire assets. Management may decide to purchase or to lease equipment. The money to finance the asset may be financed by the business's retained earnings, a stock issue, a note payable, or a bond issue. Each financing strategy has its advantages, as follows:

OBJECTIVE 5

Explain the advantages and disadvantages of borrowing

Advantages of Financing Operations By

Issuing Stock	Issuing a Note or Bonds
• Creates no liabilities or interest expense, which must be paid even during bad years. Less risky to the issuing corporation.	• Does not dilute stock ownership or control of the corporation. • Results in higher earnings per share because interest expense is tax-deductible and ownership is not diluted.

Exhibit 16-7 shows the earnings-per-share (EPS) advantage of borrowing. Suppose that a corporation with net income of $300,000 and with 100,000 shares of common stock outstanding needs $500,000 for expansion. Management is considering two financing plans. Plan 1 is to issue $500,000 of 10-percent bonds payable, and plan 2 is to issue 50,000 shares of common stock for $500,000. Management believes the new cash can be invested in operations to earn income of $200,000 before interest and taxes.

Earnings per share (EPS) is a company's net income per share of outstanding common stock (Chapter 15, p. 612). EPS may be the most important figure on the income statement.

EXHIBIT 16-7
Earnings-per-Share Advantage of Borrowing

	Plan 1 Borrow $500,000 at 10%		Plan 2 Issue $500,000 of Common Stock
Net income before expansion......................		$300,000	$300,000
Project income before interest and income tax	$200,000		$200,000
Less interest expense ($500,000 × 0.10)	50,000		–0–
Project income before income tax................	150,000		200,000
Less income tax expense (40%)	60,000		80,000
Project net income...		90,000	120,000
Total company net income............................		$390,000	$420,000
Earnings per share including expansion:			
Plan 1 ($390,000/100,000 shares).............		$3.90	
Plan 2 ($420,000/150,000 shares).............			$2.80

The earnings-per-share amount is higher if the company borrows. The business earns more on the investment ($90,000) than the interest it pays on the bonds ($50,000). Earning more income on borrowed money than the related interest expense increases the earnings for common stockholders and is called **trading on the equity**. It is widely used in business to increase earnings per share of common stock.

Borrowing has its disadvantages. Interest expense may be high enough to eliminate net income and lead to a cash crisis or even bankruptcy. Also, borrowing creates liabilities that accrue during bad years as well as during good years. In contrast, a company that issues stock can omit its dividends during a bad year.

The following quotation from *Business Week* (July 2, 1990, p. 38) describes how a major company overextended its financial capabilities. A *leveraged buyout* is a debt-financed acquisition of another company, often with so-called junk bonds. These bonds bear high interest rates because their probability of repayment is relatively low.

Was it only last year that financier Henry Kravis and his partners borrowed a whopping $28 billion to buy RJR Nabisco in the biggest leveraged buyout in history? It seems like an age—namely, the age of excessive debt. Now, only 17 months

"Was it only last year that financier Henry Kravis and his partners borrowed a whopping $28 billion to buy RJR Nabisco in the biggest leveraged buyout in history?"

later, the landscape is littered with casualties of overborrowing—Robert Campeau, Merv Griffin, Donald Trump. Kravis, whose name became synonymous with leveraged buyouts in the go-go 1980s, seems determined to avoid the same fate. Adapting to the pay-as-you-go 1990s, Kohlberg Kravis Roberts is planning to put RJR on a sounder financial footing. The firm indicated that it would plow $1.7 billion of new equity into the food and tobacco giant and retire some $4 billion of high-yield junk bonds. Said a Shearson Lehman Hutton trader, "It's the official end of the junk-bond era."

Computer spreadsheets are useful in evaluating financing alternatives: issuing common stock, preferred stock, or bonds. This assessment is often called "what if" analysis—for instance, "what if we finance with common stock?" The answers to "what if" questions can be modeled on a spreadsheet to project the company's financial statements over the next few years.

A preferred stock issue would probably mean higher dividend payments than would a common stock issue. Likewise, long-term borrowing would involve interest expense, but the interest charge is tax-deductible, unlike dividend payments to stockholders. The use of a spreadsheet facilitates such analysis, especially when you are considering the effects of a combination of stocks and bonds.

Nonmonetary considerations, such as the dilution of control of current shareholders by the issuance of more stock, cannot be easily modeled on a spreadsheet. The effects of such considerations are qualitative, and computers are less well suited to answering qualitative questions.

Lease Liabilities

OBJECTIVE 6
Account for lease transactions

A **lease** is a rental agreement in which the tenant (**lessee**) agrees to make rent payments to the property owner (**lessor**) in exchange for the use of the asset. Leasing allows the lessee to acquire the use of a needed asset without having to make the large initial cash down payment that purchase agreements require. Accountants divide leases into two types: operating and capital.

Operating Leases

Operating leases are usually short-term or cancelable. Many apartment leases and most car-rental agreements are for a year or less. These operating leases give the lessee the right to use the asset but provide the lessee with no continuing rights to the asset. The lessor retains the usual risks and rewards of owning the leased asset. To account for an operating lease, the lessee debits Rent Expense (or Lease Expense) and credits Cash for the amount of the lease payment. The lessee's books do not report the leased asset or any lease liability (except perhaps a prepaid rent amount or a rent accrual at the end of the period).

Capital Leases

Most businesses use capital leasing to finance the acquisition of some assets. A capital lease is a long-term and noncancelable financing obligation that is a form of debt. How would you distinguish a capital lease from an operating lease? *FASB Statement No. 13* provides the guidelines. To be classified as a **capital lease**, a particular lease agreement must meet any *one* of the following criteria:

1. The lease transfers title of the leased asset to the lessee at the end of the lease term. Thus the lessee becomes the legal owner of the leased asset.
2. The lease contains a *bargain purchase option*. The lessee can be expected to purchase the leased asset and become its legal owner.
3. The lease term is 75 percent or more of the estimated useful life of the leased asset. The lessee uses up most of the leased asset's service potential.
4. The present value of the lease payments is 90 percent or more of the market value of the leased asset. In effect, the lease payments operate as installment payments for the leased asset.

Only those leases that fail to meet *all* these criteria may be accounted for as operating leases.

ACCOUNTING FOR A CAPITAL LEASE Accounting for a capital lease is much like accounting for a purchase. The lessor removes the asset from its books. The lessee enters the asset into its own accounts and records a lease liability at the beginning of the lease term. Thus the lessee capitalizes the asset in its own financial statements even though the lessee may never take legal title to the property.

Most companies lease some of their plant assets rather than buy them. *A recent survey of 600 companies indicates that they have more leases than any other type of long-term debt.*

Walgreen Co. operates drug stores in buildings that it leases from other companies. Suppose that Walgreen leases a building, agreeing to pay $10,000 annually for a 20-year period, with the first payment due immediately. This arrangement is similar to purchasing the building on an installment plan. In an installment purchase, Walgreen would debit Building and credit Cash and Installment Note Payable. The company would then pay interest and principal on the note payable and record depreciation on the building. Accounting for a capital lease follows this pattern.

"Walgreen Co. operates drug stores in buildings that it leases from other companies."

Walgreen records the building at cost, which is the sum of the $10,000 initial payment plus the present value of the 19 future lease payments of $10,000 each.[4] The company credits Cash for the initial payment and credits Lease Liability for the present value of the future lease payments. Assume that the interest rate on Walgreen's lease is 10 percent and that the present value (PV) of the future lease payments is $83,650.[5] At the beginning of the lease term, Walgreen makes the following entry:

19X1			
Jan. 2	Building ($10,000 + $83,650)..	93,650	
	Cash...		10,000
	Lease Liability (PV of future lease payments)............		83,650
	To acquire a building and make the first annual lease payment on a capital lease.		

Because Walgreen Co. has capitalized the building, the company records depreciation. Assume that the building has an expected life of 25 years. It is depreciated over the lease term of 20 years because the lessee has the use of the building only for that period. No residual value enters into the depreciation computation because the lessee will have no residual asset when the building is returned to the lessor at the expiration of the lease. Therefore, the annual depreciation entry is as follows:

19X1			
Dec. 31	Depreciation Expense ($93,650/20)	4,683	
	Accumulated Depreciation—Building		4,683
	To record depreciation on leased building.		

At year end Walgreen must also accrue interest on the lease liability. Interest expense is computed by multiplying the lease liability by the interest rate on the lease. The following entry credits Lease Liability (not Interest Payable) for this interest accrual:

19X1			
Dec. 31	Interest Expense ($83,650 × 0.10)......................................	8,365	
	Lease Liability...		8,365
	To accrue interest on the lease liability.		

The balance sheet at December 31, 19X1 reports:

Assets

Plant assets:		
Building..	$93,650	
Less: Accumulated depreciation	4,683	$88,967

Liabilities

Current liabilities:		
Lease liability (next payment due on Jan. 2, 19X2)............	$10,000	
Long-term liabilities:		
Lease liability [beginning balance ($83,650) + interest accrual ($8,365) – current portion ($10,000)]	82,015	

---

[4]The chapter appendix explains present value.
[5]The formula for this computation appears in the chapter appendix.

The lease liability is split into current and long-term portions because the next payment ($10,000) is a current liability and the remainder is long-term.

The January 2, 19X2, lease payment is recorded as follows:

19X2
Jan. 2   Lease Liability.. 10,000
                  Cash..   10,000
          To make second annual lease payment on building.

Off-Balance-Sheet Financing

An important part of business is obtaining the funds needed to acquire assets. To finance operations a company may issue stock, borrow money, or retain earnings in the business. All three of these financing plans affect the right-hand side of the balance sheet. Issuing stock affects preferred or common stock. Borrowing creates notes or bonds payable. Internal funds come from profitable operations (represented by retained earnings) that generate cash.

Off-balance-sheet financing is the acquisition of assets or services with debt that is not reported on the balance sheet. A prime example is an operating lease. The lessee has the use of the leased asset, but neither the asset nor any lease liability is reported on the balance sheet. In the past, most leases were accounted for by the operating method. However, *FASB Statement No. 13* has required businesses to account for an increasing number of leases by the capital lease method. Also, *FASB Statement No. 13* has brought about detailed reporting of operating lease payments in the notes to the financial statements. Much useful information is reported only in the notes. Experienced investors study them carefully.

Pension and Postretirement Benefits Liabilities

PENSIONS Most companies have a pension plan for their employees. A **pension** is employee compensation that will be received during retirement. Employees earn the pensions by their service, so the company records pension expense while employees work for the company. To record the company's payment into a pension plan, the company debits Pension Expense and credits Cash. Insurance companies and pension trusts manage pension plans. They receive the employer payments and any employee contributions, then invest those amounts for the employees' future benefit. The goal is to have the funds available to meet any obligations to retirees.

Pensions are perhaps the most complex area of accounting. As employees earn their pensions and the company pays into the pension plan, the assets of the plan grow. The obligation for future pension payments to employees also accumulates. At the end of each period, the company compares the fair market value of the assets in the pension plan—cash and investments—with the accumulated benefit obligation of the pension plan. The *accumulated benefit obligation* is the present value of promised future pension payments to retirees. If the plan assets exceed the accumulated benefit obligation, the plan is said to be *overfunded*. In this case, the asset and obligation amounts need be reported only in the notes to the financial statements. However, if the accumulated benefit obligation exceeds plan assets, the plan is *underfunded*, and the company must report the excess liability amount as a long-term pension liability in the balance sheet.

The pension plan of Mainstream Manufacturing & Sales, Inc., has assets with a fair market value of $3 million on December 31, 19X0. On this date the accumulated pension benefit obligation to employees is $4 million. Mainstream's balance sheet will report Long-Term Pension Liability of $1 million. This liability will be listed, in no particular order, along with Bonds Payable, Long-Term Notes Payable, Lease Liabilities, and other long-term liabilities.

Key Point: A pension plan is a contract between a business and its employees. The contract's terms outline the retirement benefits the company will pay to retired employees.

Real-World Example: There are two types of pension plans: (1) Defined Contribution Plan: The employee, employer, or both must contribute a certain amount each period to the pension fund. The retirement benefits depend on how much is in the fund. (2) Defined Benefit Plan: The amount of the retirement benefit is defined by, say, 80% of salary in the year of retirement. The amount to be contributed to this type of pension fund requires a complex calculation and the services of an actuary.

FASB Statement No. 87 started requiring companies to report pension liabilities in this manner in 1987. Before that date, pensions were another example of off-balance-sheet financing. Companies received the benefit of their employees' service but could avoid reporting pension liabilities on the balance sheet.

POSTRETIREMENT BENEFITS In 1993 the FASB began requiring accrual-basis accounting for the expense and liability of providing benefits, mainly for health care, to retirees. The concept is the same as for pensions. As employees work, the company accrues the expense and the liability of providing health benefits during retirement. This practice satisfies the matching principle. Before *FASB Statement No. 106*, many companies accounted for these costs on a pay-as-you-go basis. Under that system, companies report no liability. The long-term liability for postretirement benefits other than pensions can be substantial, as these figures show for several well-known companies:

Company	(Millions) Liability for Postretirement Benefits Other Than Pensions	Total Stockholders' Equity
IBM	$4,129	$27,624
H. J. Heinz Company	222	2,321
PepsiCo, Inc.	637	5,356

IBM's liability is almost 15 percent of total stockholders' equity. Heinz's and Pepsi-Co's nonpension liabilities are a smaller percentage of stockholders' equity.

SUMMARY PROBLEM FOR YOUR REVIEW

The Cessna Aircraft Company has outstanding an issue of 8-percent convertible bonds that mature in 2012. Suppose the bonds were dated October 1, 1992, and pay interest each April 1 and October 1.

Required

1. Complete the following effective-interest amortization table through October 1, 1994:

Bond Data:

Maturity value—$100,000
Contract interest rate—8%
Interest paid—4% semiannually, $4,000 ($100,000 × 0.04)
Market interest rate at the time of issue—9% annually, 4 1/2% semiannually
Issue price—90 3/4

Amortization Table:

Semiannual Interest Date	A Interest Payment (4% of Maturity Amount)	B Interest Expense (4 1/2% of Preceding Bond Carrying Amount)	C Discount Amortization (B – A)	D Discount Account Balance (D – C)	E Bond Carrying Amount ($100,000 – D)
10-1-92					
4-1-93					
10-1-93					
4-1-94					
10-1-94					

2. Using the amortization table, record the following transactions:
  a. Issuance of the bonds on October 1, 1992.
  b. Accrual of interest and amortization of discount on December 31, 1992.
  c. Payment of interest and amortization of discount on April 1, 1993.
  d. Conversion of one-third of the bonds payable into no-par stock on October 2, 1994.
  e. Retirement of two-thirds of the bonds payable on October 2, 1994. Purchase price of the bonds was 102.

SOLUTION TO REVIEW PROBLEM

Requirement 1

	A	B	C	D	E
Semiannual Interest Date	Interest Payment (4% of Maturity Amount)	Interest Expense (4 ½% of Preceding Bond Carrying Amount)	Discount Amortization (B – A)	Discount Account Balance (D – C)	Bond Carrying Amount ($100,000 – D)
10-1-92				$9,250	$90,750
4-1-93	$4,000	$4,084	$84	9,166	90,834
10-1-93	4,000	4,088	88	9,078	90,922
4-1-94	4,000	4,091	91	8,987	91,013
10-1-94	4,000	4,096	96	8,891	91,109

Requirement 2

1992

a. Oct. 1

Cash ($100,000 × 0.9075)	90,750	
Discount on Bonds Payable	9,250	
Bonds Payable		100,000

To issue 8%, 20-year bonds at a discount.

b. Dec. 31

Interest Expense ($4,084 × 3/6)	2,042	
Discount on Bonds Payable ($84 × 3/6)		42
Interest Payable ($4,000 × 3/6)		2,000

To accrue interest and amortize bond discount for three months.

1993

c. Apr. 1

Interest Expense	2,042	
Interest Payable	2,000	
Discount on Bonds Payable ($84 × 3/6)		42
Cash		4,000

To pay semiannual interest, part of which was accrued, and amortize three months' discount on bonds payable.

1994

d. Oct. 2

Bonds Payable ($100,000 × 1/3)	33,333	
Discount on Bonds Payable ($8,891 × 1/3)		2,964
Common Stock ($91,109 × 1/3)		30,369

To record conversion of bonds payable.

e. Oct. 2

Bonds Payable ($100,000 × 2/3)	66,667	
Extraordinary Loss on Retirement Bonds	7,260	
Discount on Bonds Payable ($8,891 × 2/3)		5,927
Cash ($100,000 × 2/3 × 1.02)		68,000

To retire bonds payable before maturity.

SUMMARY

1. *Account for basic bonds payable transactions by the straight-line amortization method.* A corporation may borrow money by issuing long-term notes and *bonds payable*. A bond contract specifies the maturity value of the bonds, the *contract interest rate*, and the dates for paying interest and principal. Bonds may be secured (*mortgage* bonds) or unsecured (*debenture* bonds).

Bonds are traded through organized markets, such as the New York Exchange. Bonds are typically divided into $1,000 units. Their prices are quoted at a percentage of face value. *Market interest rates* fluctuate and may differ from the contract rate on a bond. If a bond's contract rate exceeds the market rate, the bond sells at a *premium*. A bond with a contract rate below the market rate sells at a *discount*.

Money earns income over time, a fact that gives rise to the *present-value concept*. An investor will pay a price for a bond equal to the present value of the bond principal plus the present value of the bond interest.

Straight-line amortization allocates an equal amount of premium or discount to each interest period.

2. *Amortize bond discount and premium by the effective-interest method.* In the *effective-interest method* of amortization, the market rate at the time of issuance is multiplied by the bonds' carrying amount to determine the interest expense each period and to compute the amount of discount or premium amortization.

3. *Account for retirement of bonds payable.* Companies may retire their bonds payable before maturity. *Callable* bonds give the borrower the right to pay off the bonds at a specified call price, or the company may purchase the bonds in the open market. Any gain or loss on early extinguishment of debt is classified as *extraordinary*.

4. *Account for conversion of bonds payable.* *Convertible bonds* and notes give the investor the privilege of trading the bonds in for stock of the issuing corporation. The carrying amount of the bonds becomes the book value of the newly issued stock.

5. *Explain the advantages and disadvantages of borrowing.* A key advantage of raising money by borrowing versus issuing stock is that interest expense on debt is tax-deductible. Thus borrowing is less costly than issuing stock. Borrowing's disadvantage results from the fact that the company *must* repay the loan and its interest.

6. *Account for lease transactions.* A *lease* is a rental agreement between the *lessee* and the *lessor*. In an *operating lease* the lessor retains the usual risks and rights of owning the asset. The lessee debits Rent Expense and credits Cash when making lease payments. A *capital lease* is long-term, noncancelable, and similar to an installment purchase of the leased asset. In a capital lease, the lessee capitalizes the leased asset and reports a lease liability.

Companies also report a *pension liability* on the balance sheet if the accumulated benefit obligation exceeds the market value of pension plan assets.

SELF-STUDY QUESTIONS

Test your understanding of the chapter by marking the best answer for each of the following questions.

1. An unsecured bond is called a (*p. 638*)
    - **a.** Serial bond
    - **b.** Callable bond
    - **c.** Debenture bond
    - **d.** Mortgage bond

2. How much will an investor pay for a $100,000 bond priced at 101⅞, plus a brokerage commission of $1,100? (*p. 639*)
    - **a.** $100,000
    - **b.** $101,100
    - **c.** $101,875
    - **d.** $102,975

3. A bond with a stated interest rate of 9 1/2 percent is issued when the market interest rate is 9 3/4 percent. This bond will sell at (*p. 641*)
    - **a.** Par value
    - **b.** A discount
    - **c.** A premium
    - **d.** A price minus accrued interest

4. Ten-year, 11-percent bonds payable of $500,000 were issued for $532,000. Assume that the straight-line amortization method is appropriate. The total annual interest expense on these bonds is (*p. 642*)
    - **a.** $51,800
    - **b.** $55,000
    - **c.** $58,200
    - **d.** A different amount each year because the bonds' book value decreases as the premium is amortized

5. Repeat Question 4, but use the effective-interest method of amortization. (*p. 652*)
    - **a.** $51,800
    - **b.** $55,000
    - **c.** $58,200
    - **d.** A decreasing amount each year because the bonds' book value decreases as the premium is amortized

6. Bonds payable with face value of $300,000 and carrying amount of $288,000 are retired before their scheduled maturity with a cash outlay of $292,000. Which of the following entries correctly records this bond retirement? (*p. 653*)

    a.

Bonds Payable............................	300,000	
Discount on Bonds Payable	12,000	
Cash		292,000
Extraordinary Gain...................		20,000

    b.

Bonds Payable............................	300,000	
Extraordinary Loss	4,000	
Discount on Bonds Payable......		12,000
Cash		292,000

    c.

Bonds Payable............................	300,000	
Discount on Bonds Payable......		6,000
Cash		292,000
Extraordinary Gain...................		2,000

    d.

Bonds Payable............................	288,000	
Discount on Bonds Payable	12,000	
Extraordinary Gain...................		8,000
Cash		292,000

7. An advantage of financing operations with debt versus stock is *(pp. 655–656)*
   a. The tax-deductibility of interest expense on debt
   b. The legal requirement to pay interest and principal
   c. Lower interest payments compared with dividend payments
   d. All of the above

8. In a capital lease, the lessee records *(pp. 657–659)*
   a. A leased asset and a lease liability
   b. Depreciation on the leased asset
   c. Interest on the lease liability
   d. All of the above

9. Which of the following is an example of off-balance-sheet financing? *(p. 659)*
   a. Operating lease
   b. Current portion of long-term debt
   c. Debenture bonds
   d. Convertible bonds

10. A corporation's pension plan has accumulated benefit obligations of $830,000 and assets that are worth $790,000. What will this company report for its pension plan? *(p. 659)*
   a. Accumulated benefit obligation of $830,000
   b. Note disclosure of the $40,000 excess of accumulated benefit obligation over plan assets
   c. Long-term pension liability of $40,000
   d. Nothing

Answers to the Self-Study Questions follow the Accounting Vocabulary.

ACCOUNTING VOCABULARY

Bond discount. Excess of a bond's maturity (par) value over its issue price *(p. 640)*.

Bond premium. Excess of a bond's issue price over its maturity (par) value *(p. 640)*.

Bonds payable. Groups of notes payable (bonds) issued to multiple lenders called bondholders *(p. 638)*.

Callable bonds. Bonds that the issuer may call or pay off at a specified price whenever the issuer wants *(p. 653)*.

Capital lease. Lease agreement that meets any one of four criteria: (1) The lease transfers title of the leased asset to the lessee. (2) The lease contains a bargain purchase option. (3) The lease term is 75 percent or more of the estimated useful life of the leased asset. (4) The present value of the lease payments is 90 percent or more of the market value of the leased asset *(p. 657)*.

Contract interest rate. Interest rate that determines the amount of cash interest the borrower pays and the investor receives each year. Also called the stated interest rate *(p. 641)*.

Convertible bonds. (or **notes**). Bonds (or notes) that may be converted into the common stock of the issuing company at the option of the investor *(p. 654)*.

Debentures. Unsecured bonds, backed only by the good faith of the borrower *(p. 638)*.

Effective interest rate. Another name for market interest rate *(p. 641)*.

Lease. Rental agreement in which the tenant (lessee) agrees to make rent payments to the property owner (lessor) in exchange for the use of the asset *(p. 656)*.

Lessee. Tenant in a lease agreement *(p. 656)*.

Lessor. Property owner in a lease agreement *(p. 656)*.

Market interest rate. Interest rate that investors demand in order to loan their money. Also called the effective interest rate *(p. 641)*.

Mortgage. Borrower's promise to transfer the legal title to certain assets to the lender if the debt is not paid on schedule *(p. 655)*.

Off-balance-sheet financing. Acquisition of assets or services with debt that is not reported on the balance sheet *(p. 659)*.

Operating lease. Usually a short-term or cancelable rental agreement *(p. 657)*.

Pension. Employee compensation that will be received during retirement *(p. 659)*.

Premium. Excess of a bond's issue price over its maturity (par) value *(p. 640)*.

Present value. Amount a person would invest now to receive a greater amount at a future date *(p. 640)*.

Serial bonds. Bonds that mature in installments over a period of time *(p. 638)*.

Stated interest rate. Another name for the contract interest rate *(p. 641)*.

Term bonds. Bonds that all mature at the same time for a particular issue *(p. 638)*.

Trading on the equity. Earning more income on borrowed money than the related interest expense, thereby increasing the earnings for the owners of the business *(p. 656)*.

Underwriter. Organization that purchases the bonds from an issuing company and resells them to its clients or sells the bonds for a commission, agreeing to buy all unsold bonds *(p. 638)*.

ANSWERS TO SELF-STUDY QUESTIONS

1. c
2. d [($100,000 × 1.01875) + $1,100 = $102,975]
3. b
4. a [($500,000 × 0.11) – ($32,000/10) = $51,800]
5. d
6. b
7. a
8. d
9. a
10. c

QUESTIONS

1. Identify three ways to finance the operations of a corporation.
2. How do bonds payable differ from notes payable?
3. How does an underwriter assist with the issuance of bonds?
4. Compute the price to the nearest dollar for the following bonds with a face value of $10,000:
   a. 93   d. 122 1/2
   b. 88 3/4   e. 100
   c. 101 3/8
5. In which of the following situations will bonds sell at par? At a premium? At a discount?
   a. 9% bonds sold when the market rate is 9%
   b. 9% bonds sold when the market rate is 10%
   c. 9% bonds sold when the market rate is 8%
6. Identify the accounts to debit and credit for transactions (a) to issue bonds at *par*, (b) to pay interest, (c) to accrue interest at year end, and (d) to pay off bonds at maturity.
7. Identify the accounts to debit and credit for transactions (a) to issue bonds at a *discount*, (b) to pay interest, (c) to accrue interest at year end, and (d) to pay off bonds at maturity.
8. Identify the accounts to debit and credit for transactions (a) to issue bonds at a *premium*, (b) to pay interest, (c) to accrue interest at year end, and (d) to pay off bonds at maturity.
9. Why are bonds sold for a price "plus accrued interest"? What happens to accrued interest when the bonds are sold by an individual?
10. How does the straight-line method of amortizing bond discount (or premium) differ from the effective-interest method?

11. A company retires 10-year bonds payable of $100,000 after five years. The business issued the bonds at 104 and called them at 103. Compute the amount of gain or loss on retirement. How is this gain or loss reported on the income statement?
12. Bonds payable with a maturity value of $100,000 are callable at 102 ½. Their market price is 101¼. If you are the issuer of these bonds, how much will you pay to retire them before maturity?
13. Why are convertible bonds attractive to investors? Why are they popular with borrowers?
14. Describe how to report serial bonds payable on the balance sheet.
15. Contrast the effects on a company of issuing bonds versus issuing stock.
16. Identify the accounts a lessee debits and credits when making operating lease payments.
17. What characteristics distinguish a capital lease from an operating lease?
18. A business signs a capital lease for the use of a building. What accounts are debited and credited (a) to begin the lease term and make the first lease payment, (b) to record depreciation, (c) to accrue interest on the lease liability, and (d) to make the second lease payment?
19. Show how a lessee reports on the balance sheet any leased equipment and the related lease liability under a capital lease.
20. What is off-balance-sheet financing? Give two examples.
21. Distinguish an overfunded pension plan from an underfunded plan. Which situation requires the company to report a pension liability on the balance sheet? How is this liability computed?

EXERCISES

Issuing bonds payable and paying interest
(Obj. 1)

E16-1 Chevrolet, Inc., issues $300,000 of 8-percent, 20-year bonds payable that are dated April 30. Record (a) issuance of bonds at par on May 31 and (b) the next semiannual interest payment on October 31.

Issuing bonds payable, paying and accruing interest, and amortizing discount by the straight-line method
(Obj. 1)

E16-2 On February 1, Rose Corp. issues 20-year, 7-percent bonds payable with a face value of $1,000,000. The bonds sell at 98 and pay interest on January 31 and July 31. Rose amortizes bond discount by the straight-line method. Record (a) issuance of the bonds on February 1, (b) the semiannual interest payment on July 31, and (c) the interest accrual on December 31.

Issuing bonds payable, paying and accruing interest, and amortizing premium by the straight-line method
(Obj. 1)

E16-3 Memorex Corporation issues 20-year, 8-percent bonds payable with a face value of $5,000,000 on March 31. The bonds sell at 101½ and pay interest on March 31 and September 30. Assume that Memorex amortizes bond premium by the straight-line method. Record (a) issuance of the bonds on March 31, (b) payment of interest on September 30, and (c) accrual of interest on December 31.

Issuing bonds payable between interest dates (Obj. 1)

E16-4 Refer to the data for Memorex Corporation in Exercise 16-3. If Memorex issued the bonds payable on June 30, how much cash would Memorex receive upon issuance of the bonds?

E16-5   Klingler Co. is authorized to issue $500,000 of 7-percent, 10-year bonds payable. On January 2, when the market interest rate is 8 percent, the company issues $400,000 of the bonds and receives cash of $372,660. Klingler amortizes bond discount by the effective-interest method.

Preparing an effective-interest amortization table; recording interest payments and the related discount amortization
(Obj. 2)

Required

1. Prepare an amortization table for the first four semiannual interest periods. Follow the format of Exhibit 16-5, Panel B.
2. Record the first semiannual interest payment on June 30 and the second payment on December 31.

E16-6   On September 30, 1995, the market interest rate is 7 percent. Staedtner, Inc., issues $300,000 of 8-percent, 20-year bonds payable at 110 5/8. The bonds pay interest on March 31 and September 30. Staedtner amortizes bond premium by the effective-interest method.

Preparing an effective-interest amortization table; recording interest accrual and payment and the related premium amortization
(Obj. 2)

Required

1. Prepare an amortization table for the first four semiannual interest periods. Follow the format of Exhibit 16-6, Panel B.
2. Record issuance of the bonds on September 30, 1995, the accrual of interest at December 31, 1995, and the semiannual interest payment on March 31, 1996.

E16-7   Home Health Surgical Supply issued $600,000 of 8 3/8-percent (0.08375), 5-year bonds payable when the market interest rate was 9 1/2 percent (0.095). Home Health pays interest annually at year end. The issue price of the bonds was $574,082.

Debt payment and discount amortization schedule
(Obj. 2)

Required

Create a spreadsheet model to prepare a schedule to amortize the discount on these bonds. Use the effective-interest method of amortization. Round to the nearest dollar, and format your answer as follows:

	A	B	C	D	E	F
1						
2						**Bond**
3		**Interest**	**Interest**	**Discount**	**Discount**	**Carrying**
4	**Date**	**Payment**	**Expense**	**Amortization**	**Balance**	**Amount**
5	1-1-X1				$ ☐	$574,082
6	12-31-X1	$ ☐	$ ☐	$ ☐		☐
7	12-31-X2					
8	12-31-X3					
9	12-31-X4					
10	12-31-X5					
		600000*.08375	+F5*.095	+C6–B6	600000–F5	+F5+D6

E16-8   Ernst Corp. issued $1,000,000 of 8-percent bonds payable at 97 on October 1, 19X0. These bonds mature on October 1, 19X8, and are callable at 101. Ernst pays interest each April 1 and October 1. On October 1, 19X5, when the bonds' market price is 104, Ernst retires the bonds in the most economical way available.

Recording retirement of bonds payable
(Obj. 3)

Required

Record the payment of the interest and amortization of bond discount at October 1, 19X5, and the retirement of the bonds on that date. Ernst uses the straight-line amortization method.

E16-9 Hersch Bonding Company issued $400,000 of 8 1/2-percent bonds payable on July 1, 19X4, at a price of 98 1/2. After five years the bonds may be converted into the company's common stock. Each $1,000 face amount of bonds is convertible into 40 shares of $20 par stock. The bonds' term to maturity is 15 years. On December 31, 19X9, bondholders exercised their right to convert the bonds into common stock.

Required

1. What would cause the bondholders to convert their bonds into common stock?
2. Without making journal entries, compute the carrying amount of the bonds payable at December 31, 19X9. Hersch Bonding Company uses the straight-line method to amortize bond premium and discount.
3. All amortization has been recorded properly. Journalize the conversion transaction at December 31, 19X9.

E16-10 Shanghai Industries reported the following at September 30:

Long-term liabilities:		
Convertible bonds payable, 9%, 8 years to maturity.....	$300,000	
Discount on bonds payable	6,000	$294,000

Required

1. Record retirement of half the bonds on October 1 at the call price of 101.
2. Record conversion of one-fourth of the bonds into 4,000 shares of Shanghai's $5-par common stock on October 1. What would cause the bondholders to convert their bonds into stock?

E16-11 Consider the following situations.

a. A note to the financial statements of Mapco, Inc., reported (in thousands):

Note 5: Long-Term Debt	
Total	$537,888
Less—Current portion	22,085
Unamortized discount...............	1,391
Long-term debt	$514,412

Assume that none of the unamortized discount is related to the current portion of long-term debt. Show how Mapco's balance sheet would report these liabilities.

b. El Campo Incorporated's pension plan has assets with a market value of $720,000. The plan's accumulated benefit obligation is $770,000. What amount of long-term pension liability, if any, will El Campo report on its balance sheet?

E16-12 Liu Curtain Rod Company is considering two plans for raising $1,000,000 to expand operations. Plan A is to borrow at 8 percent, and plan B is to issue 200,000 shares of common stock. Before any new financing, Liu has net income of $600,000 and 200,000 shares of common stock outstanding. Management believes the company can use the new funds to earn additional income of $420,000 before interest and taxes. The income tax rate is 40 percent.

Required

Prepare an analysis like Exhibit 16-7 to determine which plan will result in higher earnings per share.

E16-13 A capital lease agreement for equipment requires 10 annual payments of $8,000, with the first payment due on January 2, 19X5. The present value of the 9 future lease payments at 10 percent is $51,831.

Required

1. Journalize the following lessee transactions:

19X5
Jan.   2   Beginning of lease term and first annual payment.
Dec. 31   Depreciation of equipment.
      31   Interest expense on lease liability.

19X6
Jan.   2   Second annual lease payment.

2. Show how to report on the 19X5 income statement and the balance sheet at December 31, 19X5, all accounts (but Cash) affected by the 19X5 capital lease transactions.

3. Journalize the January 2, 19X5, lease payment if this is an operating lease.

CHALLENGE EXERCISES

E16-14   This (partial) advertisement appeared in *The Wall Street Journal*.

Analyzing bond transactions
(Obj. 1, 2)

This announcement is neither an offer to sell nor a solicitation of an offer to buy any of these securities. The offering is made only by the Prospectus.

New Issue

$200,000,000

MARK IV INDUSTRIES INC.

13⅜% Subordinated Debentures due March 15, 1999
Interest payable March 15 and September 15

Price 98.50%

Required

Answer these questions:

1. Suppose investors purchased these securities at their offering price on March 15, 1989. Describe the transaction in detail, indicating who received cash, who paid cash, and how much.
2. Why is the contract interest rate on these bonds so high?
3. Compute the annual cash interest payment on the bonds.
4. Compute the annual interest expense under the straight-line amortization method.
5. Compute both the first-year (from March 15, 1989) and the second-year interest expense under the effective-interest amortization method. The market rate of interest at the date of issuance was approximately 13.65 percent.
6. Suppose you purchased $100,000 of these bonds on March 15, 1989. How much cash did you pay? If you had purchased $100,000 of these bonds on March 31, 1989, how much cash would you have paid?

E16-15   Refer to the real bond situation of Mark IV Industries in Exercise 16-14. Assume Mark IV Industries issued the bonds at the advertised price and that the company uses the effective-interest amortization method and reports financial statements on a calendar-year basis.

Analyzing bond transactions
(Obj. 1, 2)

Required

Journalize all of Mark IV Industries' bond transactions for the period March 15, 1989, through March 15, 1990.

PROBLEMS

Journalizing bond transactions (at par) and reporting bonds payable on the balance sheet
(Obj. 1)

P16-1A   The board of directors of Carter Nashville Corp. authorizes the issue of $3 million of 7-percent, 10-year bonds payable. The semiannual interest dates are May 31 and November 30. The bonds are issued through an underwriter on June 30, 19X5, at par plus accrued interest.

Required

1. Journalize the following transactions:
   a. Issuance of the bonds on June 30, 19X5.
   b. Payment of interest on November 30, 19X5.
   c. Accrual of interest on December 31, 19X5.
   d. Payment of interest on May 31, 19X6.
2. Check your recorded interest expense for 19X5, using as a model the supplement to the summary problem on page 649.
3. Report interest payable and bonds payable as they would appear on the Carter Nashville Corp. balance sheet at December 31, 19X5.

Issuing bonds at a discount, amortizing by the straight-line method, and reporting bonds payable on the balance sheet
(Obj. 1, 2)

P16-2A   On March 1, 19X4, Rushlikon Corp. issues 8 1/2-percent, 20-year bonds payable with a face value of $500,000. The bonds pay interest on February 28 and August 31. Rushlikon amortizes premium and discount by the straight-line method.

Required

1. If the market interest rate is 7 3/8 percent when Rushlikon issues its bonds, will the bonds be priced at par, at a premium, or at a discount? Explain.
2. If the market interest rate is 8 7/8 percent when Rushlikon issues its bonds, will the bonds be priced at par, at a premium, or at a discount? Explain.
3. Assume that the issue price of the bonds is 96. Journalize the following bond transactions:
   a. Issuance of the bonds on March 1, 19X4.
   b. Payment of interest and amortization of discount on August 31, 19X4.
   c. Accrual of interest and amortization of discount on December 31, 19X4.
   d. Payment of interest and amortization of discount on February 28, 19X5.
4. Check your recorded interest expense for the year ended February 28, 19X5, using as a model the supplement to the summary problem on page 649.
5. Report interest payable and bonds payable as they would appear on the Rushlikon balance sheet at December 31, 19X4.

Analyzing a company's long-term debt, journalizing its transactions, and reporting long-term debt on the balance sheet
(Obj. 2)

P16-3A   The notes to Baker Magnetic's financial statements recently reported the following data on September 30, Year 1 (the end of the fiscal year):

NOTE 4. INDEBTEDNESS
Long-Term debt at September 30, Year 1, included the following:

6.00% debentures due Year 20 with an effective-interest rate of 9.66%, net of unamortized discount of $58,695,000	$166,305,000
Other indebtedness with an interest rate of 8.30%, due $12,108,000 in Year 5 and $19,257,000 in Year 6	31,365,000

Baker amortizes discount by the effective-interest method.

Required

1. Answer the following questions about Baker's long-term liabilities:
   a. What is the maturity value of the 6.00% debenture bonds?
   b. What are Baker's annual cash interest payments on the 6.00% debenture bonds?
   c. What is the carrying amount of the 6.00% debenture bonds at September 30, Year 1?

2. Prepare an amortization table through September 30, Year 4, for the 6.00% debenture bonds. Round all amounts to the nearest thousand dollars, and assume that Baker pays interest annually on September 30.

3. Record the September 30, Year 3 and Year 4, interest payments on the 6.00% debenture bonds.

4. There is no premium or discount on the other indebtedness. Assuming that annual interest is paid on September 30 each year, record Baker's September 30, Year 2, interest payment on the other indebtedness. Round interest to the nearest thousand dollars.

5. Show how Baker would report the debenture bonds payable and other indebtedness of September 30, Year 4.

P16-4A   On December 31, 19X1, Advantage, Inc., issues 9-percent, 10-year convertible bonds with a maturity value of $300,000. The semiannual interest dates are June 30 and December 31. The market interest rate is 8 percent, and the issue price of the bonds is 106. Advantage amortizes bond premium and discount by the effective-interest method.

Issuing convertible bonds at a premium, amortizing by the effective-interest method, retiring bonds early, converting bonds, and reporting the bonds payable on the balance sheet
(Obj. 2, 3, 4)

Required

1. Prepare an effective-interest method amortization table for the first four semiannual interest periods.

2. Journalize the following transactions:

  a. Issuance of the bonds on December 31, 19X1. Credit Convertible Bonds Payable.

  b. Payment of interest on June 30, 19X2.

  c. Payment of interest on December 31, 19X2.

  d. Retirement of bonds with face value of $100,000 on July 1, 19X3. Advantage pays the call price of 102.

  e. Conversion by the bondholders on July 1, 19X3, of bonds with face value of $150,000 into 10,000 shares of Advantage's $10 par common stock.

3. Prepare the balance sheet presentation of the bonds payable that are outstanding at December 31, 19X3.

P16-5A   Journalize the following transactions of Sequoia Forest Products, Inc.:

Journalizing bonds payable and capital lease transactions
(Obj. 1, 6)

19X1

Jan.	1	Issued $500,000 of 8-percent, 10-year bonds payable at 97.
	1	Signed a 5-year capital lease on equipment. The agreement requires annual lease payments of $20,000, with the first payment due immediately. At 12 percent, the present value of the four future lease payments is $60,750.
July	1	Paid semiannual interest and amortized discount by the straight-line method on our 8-percent bonds payable.
Dec. 31		Accrued semiannual interest expense, and amortized discount by the straight-line method on our 8-percent bonds payable.
	31	Recorded depreciation on leased equipment.
	31	Accrued interest expense on the lease liability.

19X11

Jan.	1	Paid the 8-percent bonds at maturity.

P16-6A   Two businesses must consider how to raise $10 million.

Financing operations with debt or with stock
(Obj. 5)

Milwaukee Corporation is in the midst of its most successful period since it began operations in 1952. For each of the past 10 years, net income and earnings per share have increased by 15 percent. The outlook for the future is equally bright, with new markets opening up and competitors unable to manufacture products of Milwaukee's quality. Milwaukee Corporation is planning a large-scale expansion.

Green Bay Company has fallen on hard times. Net income has remained flat for five of the last six years, even falling by 10 percent from last year's level of profits. Top management has experienced unusual turnover, and the company lacks strong leadership. To become competitive again, Green Bay Company desperately needs $10 million for expansion.

Required

1. Propose a plan for each company to raise the needed cash. Which company should borrow? Which company should issue stock? Consider the advantages and the disadvantages of raising money by borrowing and by issuing stock, and discuss them in your answer.
2. How will what you learned in this problem help you manage a business?

Reporting liabilities on the balance sheet
(Obj. 6)

P16-7A The accounting records of LP Gas, Inc., include the following items:

Bonds payable, long-term	$180,000	Interest expense.............................	$ 47,000
Premium on bonds		Pension plan assets	
payable (all long-term)	13,000	(market value)	190,000
Interest payable	14,200	Bonds payable, current	
Interest revenue...........................	5,300	portion	20,000
Capital lease liability,		Accumulated depreciation,	
long-term...................................	73,000	building.......................................	108,000
Accumulated pension		Mortgage note payable,	
benefit obligation	207,000	long term	67,000
Building acquired under			
capital lease................................	190,000		

Required

Show how these items would be reported on LP Gas's balance sheet, including headings and totals for current liabilities, long-term liabilities, and so on. Note disclosures are not required.

(GROUP B)

Journalizing bond transactions (at par) and reporting bonds payable on the balance sheet
(Obj. 1)

P16-1B The board of directors of Dina Fragrances Company authorizes the issue of $2 million of 8-percent, 20-year bonds payable. The semiannual interest dates are March 31 and September 30. The bonds are issued through an underwriter on April 30, 19X7, at par plus accrued interest.

Required

1. Journalize the following transactions:
    a. Issuance of the bonds on April 30, 19X7.
    b. Payment of interest on September 30, 19X7.
    c. Accrual of interest on December 31, 19X7.
    d. Payment of interest on March 31, 19X8.
2. Check your recorded interest expense for 19X7, using as a model the supplement to the summary problem on page 649.
3. Report interest payable and bonds payable as they would appear on the Dina Fragrances balance sheet at December 31, 19X7.

Issuing notes at a premium, amortizing by the straight-line method, and reporting notes payable on the balance sheet
(Obj. 1, 2)

P16-2B On March 1, 19X6, Hi-Tech Recording Studio issues 7 3/4-percent, 10-year notes payable with a face value of $300,000. The notes pay interest on February 28 and August 31, and Hi-Tech amortizes premium and discount by the straight-line method.

Required

1. If the market interest rate is 8 1/2 percent when Hi-Tech issues its notes, will the notes be priced at par, at a premium, or at a discount? Explain.
2. If the market interest rate is 7 percent when Hi-Tech issues its notes, will the notes be priced at par, at a premium, or at a discount? Explain.
3. Assume that the issue price of the notes is 101. Journalize the following note payable transactions:
    a. Issuance of the notes on March 1, 19X6.
    b. Payment of interest and amortization of premium on August 31, 19X6.
    c. Accrual of interest and amortization of premium on December 31, 19X6.
    d. Payment of interest and amortization of premium on February 28, 19X7.

4. Check your recorded interest expense for the year ended February 28, 19X7, using as a model the supplement to the summary problem on page 649.

5. Report interest payable and notes payable as they would appear on the Hi-Tech balance sheet at December 31, 19X6.

P16-3B   The notes to Golden Fried Chicken's financial statements reported the following data on September 30, Year 1 (the end of the fiscal year):

Analyzing a company's long-term debt, journalizing its transactions, and reporting the long-term debt on the balance sheet
(Obj. 2)

NOTE E—LONG-TERM DEBT

5% debentures due Year 14, net of unamortized discount of $31,645,000 (effective interest rate of 7.50%)	$119,855,000
Notes payable, interest of 8.67%, due in annual amounts of $22,840,000 in Years 5 through 16................................	274,080,000

Golden amortizes discount by the effective-interest method.

Required

1. Answer the following questions about Golden's long-term liabilities:
   a. What is the maturity value of the 5% debenture bonds?
   b. What are Golden's annual cash interest payments on the 5% debenture bonds?
   c. What is the carrying amount of the 5% debenture bonds at September 30, Year 1?

2. Prepare an amortization table through September 30, Year 4, for the 5% debenture bonds. Round all amounts to the nearest thousand dollars, and assume that Golden pays interest annually on September 30.

3. Record the September 30, Years 3 and 4, interest payments on the 5% debenture bonds.

4. There is no premium or discount on the notes payable. Assuming that annual interest is paid on September 30 each year, record Golden's September 30, Year 2, interest payment on the notes payable. Round interest to the nearest thousand dollars.

5. Show how Golden Fried Chicken would report the debenture bonds payable and notes payable at September 30, Year 4.

P16-4B   On December 31, 19X1, Oriental Credit Corp. issues 8-percent, 10-year convertible bonds with a maturity value of $500,000. The semiannual interest dates are June 30 and December 31. The market interest rate is 9 percent, and the issue price of the bonds is 94. Oriental amortizes bond premium and discount by the effective-interest method.

Issuing convertible bonds at a discount, amortizing by the effective-interest method, retiring bonds early, converting bonds, and reporting the bonds payable on the balance sheet
(Obj. 2, 3, 4)

Required

1. Prepare an effective-interest method amortization table for the first four semiannual interest periods.

2. Journalize the following transactions:
   a. Issuance of the bonds on December 31, 19X1. Credit Convertible Bonds Payable.
   b. Payment of interest on June 30, 19X2.
   c. Payment of interest on December 31, 19X2.
   d. Retirement of bonds with face value of $100,000 July 1, 19X3. Oriental purchases the bonds at 96 in the open market.
   e. Conversion by the bondholders on July 1, 19X3, of bonds with face value of $200,000 into 50,000 shares of Oriental $1-par common stock.

3. Prepare a balance sheet presentation of the bonds payable that are outstanding at December 31, 19X3.

P16-5B   Journalize the following transactions of Roget Laminating, Inc.:

Journalizing bonds payable and capital lease transactions
(Obj. 1, 6)

19X1
Jan. 1   Issued $2,000,000 of 8-percent, 10-year bonds payable at 97.
      1   Signed a 5-year capital lease on machinery. The agreement requires annual lease payments of $16,000, with the first payment due immediately. At 12 percent, the present value of the four future lease payments is $48,590.

July 1 Paid semiannual interest and amortized discount by the straight-line method on our 8-percent bonds payable.

Dec. 31 Accrued semiannual interest expense and amortized discount by the straight-line method on our 8-percent bonds payable.

    31 Recorded depreciation on leased machinery.

    31 Accrued interest expense on the lease liability.

19X11

Jan. 1 Paid the 8-percent bonds at maturity.

Financing operations with debt or with stock
(Obj. 5)

P16-6B Marketing studies have shown that consumers prefer upscale stores, and recent trends in industry sales have supported the research. To capitalize on this trend, Visual Images, Inc., is embarking on a massive expansion. Plans call for opening 50 new stores within the next 18 months. Each store is scheduled to be 30 percent larger than the company's existing stores, furnished more elaborately, and stocked with more expensive merchandise. Management estimates that company operations will provide $10 million of the cash needed for expansion. Visual Images must raise the remaining $8.5 million from outsiders. The board of directors is considering obtaining the $8.5 million either through borrowing or by issuing common stock.

Required

1. Discuss for company management the advantages and disadvantages of borrowing and of issuing common stock to raise the needed cash. Which method of raising the funds would you recommend?

2. How will what you learned in this problem help you manage a business?

Reporting liabilities on the balance sheet
(Obj. 6)

P16-7B The accounting records of Army-Navy Surplus Company include the following items:

Capital lease liability, long-term	$ 81,000	Accumulated depreciation, equipment	$ 46,000
Discount on bonds payable (all long-term)	7,000	Capital lease liability, current	18,000
Interest revenue	5,000	Mortgage note payable, current	23,000
Equipment acquired under capital lease	137,000	Accumulated pension benefit obligation	419,000
Pension plan assets (market value)	382,000	Bonds payable, long-term	400,000
Interest payable	13,000	Mortgage note payable, long-term	82,000
Interest expense	57,000		
Bonds payable, current portion	75,000		

Required

Show how these items would be reported on the Army-Navy Surplus Company balance sheet, including headings and totals for current liabilities, long-term liabilities, and so on. Note disclosures are not required.

EXTENDING YOUR KNOWLEDGE

DECISION PROBLEMS

Analyzing alternative ways of raising $5 million
(Obj. 5)

1. Business is going well for Carolina Mills, Inc. The board of directors of this family-owned company believes that Carolina could earn an additional $1,500,000 income before interest and taxes by expanding into new markets. However, the $5 million that the business needs for growth cannot be raised within the family. The directors, who strongly wish to retain family control of Carolina, must consider issuing securities to outsiders. They are considering three financing plans.

Plan A is to borrow at 9 percent. Plan B is to issue 100,000 shares of common stock. Plan C is to issue 100,000 shares of nonvoting, $3.75 preferred stock. Carolina presently has net income of $6,000,000 and 500,000 shares of common stock outstanding. The income tax rate is 40 percent.

Required

1. Prepare an analysis similar to Exhibit 16-7 to determine which plan will result in the highest earnings per share of common stock.
2. Recommend one plan to the board of directors. Give your reasons.

2. The following questions are not related.

a. Why do you think corporations prefer operating leases over capital leases? How do you think a wise shareholder would view an operating lease?

b. Companies like to borrow for longer terms when interest rates are low and for shorter terms when interest rates are high. Why is this statement true?

c. If you were to win $2 million from a Canadian lottery, you would receive the $2 million at once, whereas if you won $2 million in a U.S. lottery, you would receive 20 annual payments of $100,000. Are the prizes equivalent? If not, why not?

Questions about long-term debt
(Obj. 6 and Appendix)

ETHICAL ISSUE

Ling-Temco-Vought, Inc. (LTV), manufacturer of aircraft and aircraft-related electronic devices, borrowed heavily during the 1970s to exploit the advantage of financing operations with debt. At first, LTV was able to earn operating income much higher than its interest expense and was therefore quite profitable. However, when the business cycle turned down, LTV's debt burden pushed the company to the brink of bankruptcy. Operating income was less than interest expense.

Required

Is it unethical for managers to saddle a company with a high level of debt? Or is it just risky? Who could be hurt by a company's taking on too much debt? Discuss.

FINANCIAL STATEMENT PROBLEMS

1. The Lands' End, Inc., income statement, balance sheet, and statement of cash flows in Appendix A provide details about the company's long-term debt. Use those data to answer the following questions.

Long-term debt
(Obj. 1, 3)

1. How much cash did Lands' End borrow on short-term and long-term debt during the year ended January 28, 1994? Journalize this transaction.
2. Journalize in a single entry Lands' End's interest expense for the year ended January 28, 1994. Assume that Lands' End paid 90 percent of its interest expense and accrued the remainder at year end.
3. How can Lands' End's interest expense be so much greater than the company's short-term and long-term debt?
4. Examine the statement of cash flows for the year ended January 31, 1992. Journalize the two transactions that affected short-term and long-term debt. There was no premium or discount.

2. Obtain the annual report of an actual company of your choosing. Answer the following questions about the company. Concentrate on the current year in the annual report you select.

Long-term debt
(Obj. 2, 3)

1. Examine the statement of cash flows. How much long-term debt did the company pay off during the current year? How much new long-term debt did the company incur during the year? Journalize these transactions, using the company's actual account balances.
2. Prepare a T-account for the Long-Term Debt account to show the beginning and ending balances and all activity in the account during the year. If there is a discrepancy, insert this amount in the appropriate place. Note: Do not expect to be able to explain all details in real financial statements!
3. Study the notes to the financial statements. Is any of the company's retained earnings balance restricted as a result of borrowings? If so, indicate the amount of the retained earnings balance that is restricted and the amount that is unrestricted. How will the restriction affect the company's dividend payments in the future?
4. Journalize in a single entry the company's interest expense for the current year. If the company discloses the amount of amortization of premium or discount on long-term debt, use the real figures. If not, assume the amortization of discount totaled $700,000 for the year.

Appendix

Time Value of Money: Future Value and Present Value

The following discussion of future value lays the foundation for present value but is not essential. For the valuation of long-term liabilities, some instructors may wish to begin on page 678.

The term *time value of money* refers to the fact that money earns interest over time. Interest is the cost of using money. To borrowers, interest is the expense of renting money. To lenders, interest is the revenue earned from lending. When funds are used for a period of time, we must recognize the interest. Otherwise we overlook an important part of the transaction. Suppose you invest $4,545 in corporate bonds that pay 10-percent interest each year. After one year, the value of your investment has grown to $5,000. The difference between your original investment ($4,545) and the future value of the investment ($5,000) is the amount of interest revenue you will earn during the year ($455). If you ignored the interest, you would fail to account for the interest revenue you have earned. Interest becomes more important as the time period lengthens because the amount of interest depends on the span of time the money is invested.

Let's consider a second example, but from the borrower's perspective. Suppose you purchase a machine for your business. The cash price of the machine is $8,000, but you cannot pay cash now. To finance the purchase, you sign an $8,000 note payable. The note requires you to pay the $8,000 plus 10-percent interest one year from date of purchase. Is your cost of the machine $8,000, or is it $8,800 [$8,000 plus interest of $800 ($8,000 × 0.10)]? The cost is $8,000. The additional $800 is interest expense and not part of the cost of the machine. If you ignored the interest, you would overstate the cost of the machine and understate the amount of interest expense.

Future Value

OBJECTIVE A1

Compute the future value of an investment made in a single amount

The main application of future value is the accumulated balance of an investment at a future date. In our first example above, the investment earned 10 percent per year. After one year, $4,545 grew to $5,000, as shown in Exhibit 16A-1. If the money were invested for five years, you would have to perform five such calculations. You would also have to consider the compound interest that your investment is earning. Compound interest is the interest you earn not only on your principal amount but also on the interest you receive on the interest you have already earned. Most business appli-

EXHIBIT 16A-1
Future Value

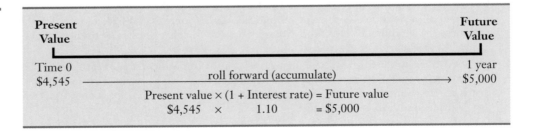

cations include compound interest. The following table shows the interest revenue earned each year at 10 percent:

End of Year	Interest	Future Value
0	—	$4,545
1	$4,545 × 0.10 = $455	5,000
2	5,000 × 0.10 = 500	5,500
3	5,500 × 0.10 = 550	6,050
4	6,050 × 0.10 = 605	6,655
5	6,655 × 0.10 = 666	7,321

Earning 10 percent, a $4,545 investment grows to $5,000 at the end of one year, to $5,500 at the end of two years, and so on. Throughout this discussion we round off to the nearest dollar.

Future Value Tables

The process of computing a future value is called *accumulating* because the future value is *more* than the present value. Mathematical tables ease the computational burden. Exhibit 16A-2, Future Value of $1, gives the future value for a single sum (a present value), $1, invested to earn a particular interest rate for a specific number of periods. Future value depends on three factors: (1) the amount of the investment, (2) the length of time between investment and future accumulation, and (3) the interest rate.

The heading in Exhibit 16A-2 states $1. Future value tables and present value tables are based on $1 because unity (the value 1) is so easy to work with. Observe

EXHIBIT 16A-2
Future Value of $1

FUTURE VALUE OF $1

Periods	4%	5%	6%	7%	8%	9%	10%	12%	14%	16%
1	1.040	1.050	1.060	1.070	1.080	1.090	1.100	1.120	1.140	1.160
2	1.082	1.103	1.124	1.145	1.166	1.188	1.210	1.254	1.300	1.346
3	1.125	1.158	1.191	1.225	1.260	1.295	1.331	1.405	1.482	1.561
4	1.170	1.216	1.262	1.311	1.360	1.412	1.464	1.574	1.689	1.811
5	1.217	1.276	1.338	1.403	1.469	1.539	1.611	1.762	1.925	2.100
6	1.265	1.340	1.419	1.501	1.587	1.677	1.772	1.974	2.195	2.436
7	1.316	1.407	1.504	1.606	1.714	1.828	1.949	2.211	2.502	2.826
8	1.369	1.477	1.594	1.718	1.851	1.993	2.144	2.476	2.853	3.278
9	1.423	1.551	1.689	1.838	1.999	2.172	2.358	2.773	3.252	3.803
10	1.480	1.629	1.791	1.967	2.159	2.367	2.594	3.106	3.707	4.411
11	1.539	1.710	1.898	2.105	2.332	2.580	2.853	3.479	4.226	5.117
12	1.601	1.796	2.012	2.252	2.518	2.813	3.138	3.896	4.818	5.936
13	1.665	1.886	2.133	2.410	2.720	3.066	3.452	4.363	5.492	6.886
14	1.732	1.980	2.261	2.579	2.937	3.342	3.797	4.887	6.261	7.988
15	1.801	2.079	2.397	2.759	3.172	3.642	4.177	5.474	7.138	9.266
16	1.873	2.183	2.540	2.952	3.426	3.970	4.595	6.130	8.137	10.748
17	1.948	2.292	2.693	3.159	3.700	4.328	5.054	6.866	9.276	12.468
18	2.026	2.407	2.854	3.380	3.996	4.717	5.560	7.690	10.575	14.463
19	2.107	2.527	3.026	3.617	4.316	5.142	6.116	8.613	12.056	16.777
20	2.191	2.653	3.207	3.870	4.661	5.604	6.727	9.646	13.743	19.461

the Periods column and the interest rate columns 4% through 16%. In business applications interest rates are always stated for the annual period of one year unless specified otherwise. In fact, an interest rate can be stated for any period, such as 3 percent per quarter or 5 percent for a six-month period. The length of the period is arbitrary. For example, an investment may promise a return (income) of 3 percent per quarter for six months (two quarters). In that case you would be working with 3-percent interest for two periods. It would be incorrect to use 6 percent for one period because the interest is 3 percent compounded quarterly, and that amount differs somewhat from 6 percent compounded semiannually. Take care in studying future value and present value problems to align the interest rate with the appropriate number of periods.

Let's use Exhibit 16A-2. The future value of $1.00 invested at 8 percent for one year is $1.08 ($1.00 × 1.080, which appears at the junction under the 8% column and across from 1 in the Periods column). The figure 1.080 includes both the principal (1.000) and the compound interest for one period (0.080).

Suppose you deposit $5,000 in a savings account that pays annual interest of 8 percent. The account balance at the end of one year will be $5,400. To compute the future value of $5,000 at 8 percent for one year, multiply $5,000 by 1.080 to get $5,400. Now suppose you invest in a 10-year, 8-percent certificate of deposit (CD). What will be the future value of the CD at maturity? To compute the future value of $5,000 at 8 percent for 10 periods, multiply $5,000 by 2.159 (from Exhibit 16A-2) to get $10,795. This future value of $10,795 indicates that $5,000 earning 8-percent interest compounded annually, grows to $10,795 at the end of 10 years. In this way you can find any present amount's future value at a particular future date. Future value is especially helpful for computing the amount of cash you will have on hand for some purpose in the future.

Future Value of an Annuity

In the preceding example, we made an investment of a single amount. Other investments, called annuities, include multiple investments of an equal periodic amount at fixed intervals over the duration of the investment. Consider a family investing for a child's education. The Dietrichs can invest $4,000 annually to accumulate a college fund for 15-year-old Helen. The investment can earn 7 percent annually until Helen turns 18—a three-year investment. How much will be available for Helen on the date of the last investment? Exhibit 16A-3 shows the accumulation—a total future value of $12,860.

The first $4,000 invested by the Dietrichs grows to $4,580 over the investment period. The second amount grows to $4,280, and the third amount stays at $4,000 because it has no time to earn interest. The sum of the three future values ($4,580 + $4,280 + $4,000) is the future value of the annuity ($12,860), which can be computed as follows:

EXHIBIT 16A-3
Future Value of an Annuity

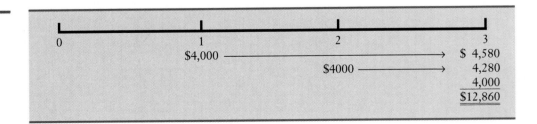

End of Year	Annual Investment	Interest	Increase for the Year	Future Value of Annuity
0	—	—	—	0
1	$4,000	—	$4,000	$ 4,000
2	4,000 + ($4,000 × 0.07 = $280) =		4,280	8,280
3	4,000 + ($8,280 × 0.07 = $580) =		4,580	12,860

These computations are laborious. As with the Future Value of $1 (a lump sum), mathematical tables ease the strain of calculating annuities. Exhibit 16A-4, Future Value of Annuity of $1, gives the future value of a series of investments, each of equal amount, at regular intervals.

What is the future value of an annuity of three investments of $1 each that earn 7 percent? The answer 3.215 can be found in the 7% column and across from 3 in the Periods column of Exhibit 16A-4. This amount can be used to compute the future value of the investment for Helen's education, as follows:

Amount of each periodic investment × Future value of annuity of $1 **(Exhibit 16A-4)** = Future value of investment

$4,000 × 3.215 = $12,860

This one-step calculation is much easier than computing the future value of each annual investment and then summing the individual future values. In this way you can compute the future value of any investment consisting of equal periodic amounts at regular intervals. Businesses make periodic investments to accumulate funds for equipment replacement and other uses—an application of the future value of an annuity.

EXHIBIT 16A-4
Future Value of Annuity of $1

FUTURE VALUE OF ANNUITY OF $1

Periods	4%	5%	6%	7%	8%	9%	10%	12%	14%	16%
1	1.000	1.000	1.000	1.000	1.000	1.000	1.000	1.000	1.000	1.000
2	2.040	2.050	2.060	2.070	2.080	2.090	2.100	2.120	2.140	2.160
3	3.122	3.153	3.184	3.215	3.246	3.278	3.310	3.374	3.440	3.506
4	4.246	4.310	4.375	4.440	4.506	4.573	4.641	4.779	4.921	5.066
5	5.416	5.526	5.637	5.751	5.867	5.985	6.105	6.353	6.610	6.877
6	6.633	6.802	6.975	7.153	7.336	7.523	7.716	8.115	8.536	8.977
7	7.898	8.142	8.394	8.654	8.923	9.200	9.487	10.089	10.730	11.414
8	9.214	9.549	9.897	10.260	10.637	11.028	11.436	12.300	13.233	14.240
9	10.583	11.027	11.491	11.978	12.488	13.021	13.579	14.776	16.085	17.519
10	12.006	12.578	13.181	13.816	14.487	15.193	15.937	17.549	19.337	21.321
11	13.486	14.207	14.972	15.784	16.645	17.560	18.531	20.655	23.045	25.733
12	15.026	15.917	16.870	17.888	18.977	20.141	21.384	24.133	27.271	30.850
13	16.627	17.713	18.882	20.141	21.495	22.953	24.523	28.029	32.089	36.786
14	18.292	19.599	21.015	22.550	24.215	26.019	27.975	32.393	37.581	43.672
15	20.024	21.579	23.276	25.129	27.152	29.361	31.772	37.280	43.842	51.660
16	21.825	23.657	25.673	27.888	30.324	33.003	35.950	42.753	50.980	60.925
17	23.698	25.840	28.213	30.840	33.750	36.974	40.545	48.884	59.118	71.673
18	25.645	28.132	30.906	33.999	37.450	41.301	45.599	55.750	68.394	84.141
19	27.671	30.539	33.760	37.379	41.446	46.018	51.159	63.440	78.969	98.603
20	29.778	33.066	36.786	40.995	45.762	51.160	57.275	72.052	91.025	115.380

Present Value

OBJECTIVE A3

Compute the present value of a single future amount

Often a person knows a future amount and needs to know the related present value. Recall Exhibit 16A-1, in which present value and future value are on opposite ends of the same time line. Suppose an investment promises to pay you $5,000 at the *end* of one year. How much would you pay *now* to acquire this investment? You would be willing to pay the present value of the $5,000 future amount.

Present value also depends on three factors: (1) the amount of payment (or receipt), (2) the length of time between investment and future receipt (or payment), and (3) the interest rate. The process of computing a present value is called *discounting* because the present value is *less* than the future value.

In our investment example, the future receipt is $5,000. The investment period is one year. Assume that you demand an annual interest rate of 10 percent on your investment. With all three factors specified, you can compute the present value of $5,000 at 10 percent for one year:

$$\frac{\text{Future value}}{(1 + \text{Interest rate})} = \frac{\$5,000}{1.10} = \$4,545$$

By turning the data around into a future-value problem, we verify the present-value computation:

Amount invested (present value)...	$4,545
Expected earnings ($4,545 × 0.10)...	455
Amount to be received one year from now (future value)..............	$5,000

This example illustrates that present value and future value are based on the same equation:

$$\text{Present value} \times (1 + \text{Interest rate}) = \text{Future value}$$

$$\frac{\text{Future value}}{(1 + \text{Interest rate})} = \text{Present value}$$

If the $5,000 is to be received two years from now, you will pay only $4,132 for the investment, as shown in Exhibit 16A-5. By turning the data around, we verify that $4,132 accumulates to $5,000 at 10 percent for two years:

EXHIBIT 16A-5

Two-Year Investment

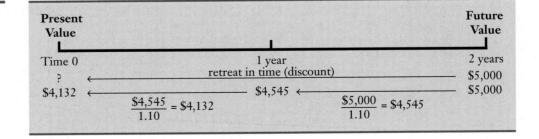

Amount invested (present value)...	$4,132
Expected earnings for first year ($4.132 × 0.10)............................	413
Value of investment after one year...	4,545
Expected earnings for second year ($4,545 × 0.10)........................	455
Amount to be received two years from now (future value).............	$5,000

You would pay $4,132—the present value of $5,000—to receive the $5,000 future amount at the end of two years at 10 percent per year. The $868 difference between the amount invested ($4,132) and the amount to be received ($5,000) is the return on the investment, the sum of the two interest receipts: $413 + $455 = $868.

Present-Value Tables

We have shown the simple formula for computing present value. However, figuring present value "by hand" for investments spanning many years becomes drawn out. The "number crunching" presents too many opportunities for arithmetical errors. Present-value tables ease our work. Let's reexamine our examples of present value by using Exhibit 16A-6: Present Value of $1.

For the 10-percent investment for one year, we find the junction in the 10% column and across from 1 in the Periods column. The figure 0.909 is computed as follows: 1/1.10 = 0.909. This work has been done for us, and only the present values are given in the table. The heading in Exhibit 16A-6 states $1. To figure present value for $5,000, we multiply 0.909 by $5,000. The result is $4,545, which matches the result we obtained by hand.

For the two-year investment, we read down the 10% column and across the Period 2 row. We multiply 0.826 (computed as 0.909/1.10 = 0.826) by $5,000 and get $4,130, which confirms our earlier computation of $4,132 (the difference is due to rounding in the present-value table). Using the table, we can compute the present value of any single future amount.

Short Exercise: What is the present value of $1,000 to be received at the end of 5 years at 10%? *A:* Look in Exhibit 16A-6 at the factor for 5 periods and 10%: 0.621. The present value is: $1,000 × 0.621 = $621. The amount of interest that could be earned over 5 years with an initial investment of $621 is $379 ($1,000 – $621).

EXHIBIT 16A-6
Present Value of $1

PRESENT VALUE OF $1

Periods	4%	5%	6%	7%	8%	10%	12%	14%	16%
1	0.962	0.952	0.943	0.935	0.926	0.909	0.893	0.877	0.862
2	0.925	0.907	0.890	0.873	0.857	0.826	0.797	0.769	0.743
3	0.889	0.864	0.840	0.816	0.794	0.751	0.712	0.675	0.641
4	0.855	0.823	0.792	0.763	0.735	0.683	0.636	0.592	0.552
5	0.822	0.784	0.747	0.713	0.681	0.621	0.567	0.519	0.476
6	0.790	0.746	0.705	0.666	0.630	0.564	0.507	0.456	0.410
7	0.760	0.711	0.665	0.623	0.583	0.513	0.452	0.400	0.354
8	0.731	0.677	0.627	0.582	0.540	0.467	0.404	0.351	0.305
9	0.703	0.645	0.592	0.544	0.500	0.424	0.361	0.308	0.263
10	0.676	0.614	0.558	0.508	0.463	0.386	0.322	0.270	0.227
11	0.650	0.585	0.527	0.475	0.429	0.350	0.287	0.237	0.195
12	0.625	0.557	0.497	0.444	0.397	0.319	0.257	0.208	0.168
13	0.601	0.530	0.469	0.415	0.368	0.290	0.229	0.182	0.145
14	0.577	0.505	0.442	0.388	0.340	0.263	0.205	0.160	0.125
15	0.555	0.481	0.417	0.362	0.315	0.239	0.183	0.140	0.108
16	0.534	0.458	0.394	0.339	0.292	0.218	0.163	0.123	0.093
17	0.513	0.436	0.371	0.317	0.270	0.198	0.146	0.108	0.080
18	0.494	0.416	0.350	0.296	0.250	0.180	0.130	0.095	0.069
19	0.475	0.396	0.331	0.277	0.232	0.164	0.116	0.083	0.060
20	0.456	0.377	0.312	0.258	0.215	0.149	0.104	0.073	0.051

Present Value of an Annuity

Return to the investment example beginning near the bottom of page 678. That investment provided the investor with only a single future receipt ($5,000 at the end of two years). Annuity investments provide multiple receipts of an equal amount at fixed intervals over the investment's duration.

Consider an investment that promises *annual* cash receipts of $10,000 to be received at the end of each of three years. Assume that you demand a 12-percent return on your investment. What is the investment's present value? What would you pay today to acquire the investment? The investment spans three periods, and you would pay the sum of three present values. The computation is as follows:

Year	Annual Cash Receipt	Present Value of $1 at 12% (Exhibit 16A-6)	Present Value of Annual Cash Receipt
1	$10,000	0.893	$ 8,930
2	10,000	0.797	7,970
3	10,000	0.712	7,120
Total present value of investment			$24,020

Short Exercise: What is the present value of $1,000 to be received at the end of each of the next five years at 10%? *A:* Look in Exhibit 16A-7 at 5 periods and 10%. The factor is 3.791. The present value of *all five* $1,000 receipts is $1,000 × 3.791 = $3,791.

The present value of this annuity is $24,020. By paying this amount today, you will receive $10,000 at the end of each of the three years while earning 12 percent on your investment.

The example illustrates repetitive computations of the three future amounts, a time-consuming process. One way to ease the computational burden is to add the three present values of $1 (0.893 + 0.797 + 0.712) and multiply their sum (2.402) by the annual cash receipt ($10,000) to obtain the present value of the annuity ($10,000 × 2.402 = $24,020).

An easier approach is to use a present value of an annuity table. Exhibit 16A-7 shows the present value of $1 to be received periodically for a given number of peri-

EXHIBIT 16A-7

Present Value of Annuity of $1

	PRESENT VALUE OF ANNUITY OF $1								
Periods	4%	5%	6%	7%	8%	10%	12%	14%	16%
1	0.962	0.952	0.943	0.935	0.926	0.909	0.893	0.877	0.862
2	1.886	1.859	1.833	1.808	1.783	1.736	1.690	1.647	1.605
3	2.775	2.723	2.673	2.624	2.577	2.487	2.402	2.322	2.246
4	3.630	3.546	3.465	3.387	3.312	3.170	3.037	2.914	2.798
5	4.452	4.329	4.212	4.100	3.993	3.791	3.605	3.433	3.274
6	5.242	5.076	4.917	4.767	4.623	4.355	4.111	3.889	3.685
7	6.002	5.786	5.582	5.389	5.206	4.868	4.564	4.288	4.039
8	6.733	6.463	6.210	5.971	5.747	5.335	4.968	4.639	4.344
9	7.435	7.108	6.802	6.515	6.247	5.759	5.328	4.946	4.607
10	8.111	7.722	7.360	7.024	6.710	6.145	5.650	5.216	4.833
11	8.760	8.306	7.887	7.499	7.139	6.495	5.938	5.453	5.029
12	9.385	8.863	8.384	7.943	7.536	6.814	6.194	5.660	5.197
13	9.986	9.394	8.853	8.358	7.904	7.103	6.424	5.842	5.342
14	10.563	9.899	9.295	8.745	8.244	7.367	6.628	6.002	5.468
15	11.118	10.380	9.712	9.108	8.559	7.606	6.811	6.142	5.575
16	11.652	10.838	10.106	9.447	8.851	7.824	6.974	6.265	5.669
17	12.166	11.274	10.477	9.763	9.122	8.022	7.120	6.373	5.749
18	12.659	11.690	10.828	10.059	9.372	8.201	7.250	6.467	5.818
19	13.134	12.085	11.158	10.336	9.604	8.365	7.366	6.550	5.877
20	13.590	12.462	11.470	10.594	9.818	8.514	7.469	6.623	5.929

ods. The present value of a three-period annuity at 12 percent is 2.402 (the junction of the Period 3 row and the 12% column). Thus $10,000 received annually at the end of each of three years, discounted at 12 percent, is $24,020 ($10,000 × 2.402), which is the present value.

Present Value of Bonds Payable

The present value of a bond—its market price—is the present value of the future principal amount at maturity plus the present value of the future contract interest payments. The principal is a single amount to be paid at maturity. The interest is an annuity because it occurs periodically.

Let's compute the present value of the 9-percent, five-year bonds of Bethlehem Steel. The face value of the bonds is $100,000, and they pay 4 1/2-percent contract (cash) interest semiannually. At issuance the market interest rate is expressed as 10 percent, but it is computed at 5 percent semiannually. Therefore, the effective interest rate for each of the 10 semiannual periods is 5 percent. We use 5 percent in computing the present value (PV) of the maturity and of the interest. The market price of these bonds is $96,149, as follows:

The market price of the Bethlehem Steel bonds show a discount because the contract interest rate on the bonds (9 percent) is less than the market interest rate (10 percent). We discuss these bonds in more detail on pages 649–651.

Let's consider a premium price for the Bethlehem Steel bonds. Assume that the market interest rate is 8 percent at issuance. The effective interest rate is 4 percent for each of the 10 semiannual periods:

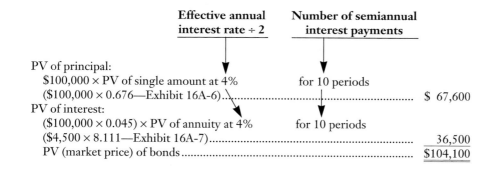

We discuss accounting for these bonds on pages 651 and 652.

Short Exercise: What is the present value of a $100,000, 12%, 10-year bond priced to yield 14% interest? Interest is paid semiannually. *A:*
PV of principal:
$100,000 × 0.258 = $25,800
PV of interest:
$6,000 × 10.594 = 63,564
PV of bond $89,364

The factors are for 20 interest periods, since the 10-year bond pays interest semiannually. The interest rate used to compute the semiannual receipts of cash interest is the bond's stated rate (12%). The interest rate used in the present-value table is the effective rate (14%). How would the issue price of this bond be quoted? *A:* $89,364/$100,000 = 89 3/8 approximately.

Capital Leases

How does a lessee compute the cost of an asset acquired through a capital lease? Consider that the lessee gets the use of the asset but does *not* pay for the leased asset in full at the beginning of the lease. A capital lease is therefore similar to an installment purchase of the leased asset. The lessee must record the leased asset at the present value of the lease liability. The time value of money must be weighed.

The cost of the asset to the lessee is the sum of any payment made at the beginning of the lease period plus the present value of the future lease payments. The lease payments are equal amounts occurring at regular intervals—that is, they are annuity payments.

Consider the 20-year building lease of Walgreen Co. The lease requires 20 annual payments of $10,000 each, with the first payment due immediately. The interest rate in the lease is 10 percent, and the present value of the 19 future payments is $83,650 ($10,000 × PV of annuity at 10 percent for 19 periods, or 8.365 from Exhibit 16A-7). Walgreen's cost of the building is $93,650 (the sum of the initial payment, $10,000, plus the present value of the future payments, $83,650). The entries for a capital lease are illustrated on pages 657–659.

APPENDIX PROBLEMS

Computing the future value of an investment
(Obj. A1, A2)

P16A-1   For each situation, compute the required amount.

a.   Langefeld Enterprises is budgeting for the acquisition of land over the next several years. Langefeld can invest $300,000 today at 9 percent. How much cash will Langefeld have for land acquisitions at the end of five years? At the end of six years?

b.   Mercer Associates is planning to invest $10,000 each year for five years. The company's investment adviser believes that Mercer can earn 6-percent interest without taking on too much risk. What will be the value of Mercer's investment on the date of the last deposit if Mercer can earn 6 percent? If Mercer can earn 8 percent?

Relating the future and present values of an investment
(Obj. A1, A3)

P16A-2   For each situation, compute the required amount.

a.   Eastman Kodak's operations are generating excess cash that will be invested in a special fund. During 19X2, Kodak invests $11,287,000 in the fund for a planned advertising campaign for a new product to be released six years later, in 19X8. If Kodak's investments can earn 10 percent each year, how much cash will the company have for the advertising campaign in 19X8?

b.   Eastman Kodak Company will need $20 million to advertise a new type of photo film in 19X8. How much must Kodak invest in 19X2 to have the cash available for the advertising campaign? Kodak's investments can earn 10 percent annually.

c.   Explain the relationship between your answers to (a) and (b).

Computing the present values of various notes and bonds
(Obj. A2, A3)

P16A-3   Determine the present value of the following notes and bonds:

1. $40,000, five-year note payable with contract interest rate of 11 percent, paid annually. The market interest rate at issuance is 12 percent.

2.   Ten-year bonds payable with maturity value of $100,000 and contract interest rate of 12 percent, paid semiannually. The market rate of interest is 10 percent at issuance.

3.   Same bonds payable as in number 2, but the market interest rate is 8 percent.

4.   Same bonds payable as in number 2, but the market interest rate is 12 percent.

P16A-4 On December 31, 19X1, when the market interest rate is 8 percent, Interstate Express Co. issues $300,000 of 10-year, 7.25-percent bonds payable. The bonds pay interest semiannually.

Computing a bond's present value, recording its issuance at a discount and interest payments
(Obj. A3, A4)

Required

1. Determine the present value of the bonds at issuance.
2. Assume that the bonds are issued at the price computed in requirement 1. Prepare an effective-interest method amortization table for the first two semiannual interest periods.
3. Using the amortization table prepared in requirement 2, journalize issuance of the bonds and the first two interest payments.

P16A-5 Yokohama Children's Home needs a fleet of vans to transport the children to singing engagements throughout Japan. Nissan offers the vehicles for a single payment of 6,300,000 yen due at the end of four years. Toyota prices a similar fleet of vans for four annual payments of 1,500,000 yen each. The children's home could borrow the funds at 6 percent, so this is the appropriate interest rate. Which company should get the business, Nissan or Toyota? Base your decision on present value, and give your reason.

Deciding between two payment plans
(Obj. A3, A4)

P16A-6 Goldblatt Institute acquired equipment under a capital lease that requires six annual lease payments of $10,000. The first payment is due when the lease begins, on January 1, 19X6. Future payments are due on January 1 of each year of the lease term. The interest rate in the lease is 16 percent.

Computing the cost of equipment acquired under a capital lease and recording the lease transactions
(Obj. A5)

Required

1. Compute Goldblatt's cost of the equipment.
2. Journalize the (a) acquisition of the equipment, (b) depreciation for 19X6, (c) accrued interest at December 31, 19X6, and (d) second lease payment on January 1, 19X7.

Chapter 17

Investments and Accounting for International Operations

"Combining Viacom and Paramount made enormous strategic, operational, and financial sense. The combined company has the critical mass to build a worldwide entertainment and publishing company with unmatched programming, distribution, and technological depth. It has the financial resources to enhance our core businesses while extending into new product areas, emerging distribution outlets, and untapped geographic markets."

FRANK J. BIONDI, JR.,
PRESIDENT AND CEO
OF VIACOM, INC.

In one of the biggest investment events of 1994, Viacom, Inc., the owner of the Nickelodeon, Showtime, MTV, and VH-1 cable television networks, purchased Paramount Communications, which includes Paramount Pictures, Simon & Schuster publishing, and Paramount Parks amusement centers. Viacom paid about $10 billion to Paramount stockholders to buy Paramount Communications. What Viacom was buying, according to John Greenwald in *Time* magazine, were "some of the crown jewels of entertainment, including the Paramount film and television studios and a library of 890 movies ranging from *Wayne's World* and *The Firm* to *Sunset Boulevard*."

Sumner M. Redstone, the chairperson and controlling shareholder of Viacom, Inc., took charge of the combined new company. "We have put together the No. 1 software company in the world—a monster entertainment company," said Redstone about the merger. "We've succeeded in changing the faces of our own companies and in changing the face of the media business." *Source: Adapted in part from "The Deal That Forced Diller to Fold,"* Time, *February 28, 1994, pp. 50, 53.*

• • • • •

*I*nvestments come in all sizes and shapes—from the purchase of an entire company to the purchase of a few shares of a company's stock, to investment in bonds. In earlier chapters we discussed stocks and bonds from the perspective of the company that issued the securities. In this chapter we examine stocks and bonds from the investor's viewpoint.

Why do individuals and corporations invest in stocks and bonds? You would probably make an investment in order to earn dividends and to sell the stock at a higher price than you paid for it. Investment companies such as brokerage firms, mutual funds, insurance companies, and bank trust departments buy stocks and bonds for this same reason.

Most other companies invest in stocks and bonds for a second reason: to influence or to control the other company. Top managers of Viacom and Paramount envisioned changes in the media business, and they hoped to remain competitive in their industry.

In one sense, your purchase of a few shares of stock is similar to Viacom's purchase of Paramount Communications. In both cases, the stockholder—an individual or Viacom—is an owner of Paramount. But the purchase of an entire company raises questions about how the parent company should account for its investment. We address these questions in this chapter. We also consider the challenging area of accounting for international operations. First, however, let's review how investment transactions take place.

ACCOUNTING FOR INVESTMENTS

Stock Prices

Investors buy more stock in transactions among themselves than from the issuing company. Each share of stock is issued only once, but it may be traded among investors many times thereafter. People and businesses buy and sell stocks from each other in markets, such as the New York Stock Exchange and the American Stock Exchange. Brokers such as Merrill Lynch and Prudential Bache handle stock transactions for a commission.

A broker may "quote a stock price," which means to state the current market price per share. The financial community quotes stock prices in dollars and one-eighth fractions. A stock selling at 32 1/8 costs $32.125 per share. A stock listed at 55 3/4 sells at $55.75. Financial publications and many newspapers carry daily information on the stock issues of thousands of corporations. These one-line summaries carry information as of the close of trading the previous day.

Exhibit 17-1 presents information for the common stock of The Boeing Com-

"During the previous day, 1,055,700 . . . shares of Boeing common stock were traded."

pany, a large aircraft manufacturer, just as this information appears in newspaper listings. During the previous 52 weeks, Boeing common stock reached a high of $41 and a low of $33.125 per share. The annual cash dividend is $1.00 per share. During the previous day, 1,055,700 (10,557 × 100) shares of Boeing common stock were traded. The prices of these transactions ranged from a high of $38.50 to a low of $37.25 per share. The day's closing price of $37.625 was $1 lower than the closing price of the preceding day.

EXHIBIT 17-1
Stock Price Information

52 Weeks								
High	Low	Stock	Dividend	Sales 100s	High	Low	Close	Net Change
41	$33\frac{1}{8}$	Boeing	1.00	10557	$38\frac{1}{2}$	$37\frac{1}{4}$	$37\frac{5}{8}$	−1

What causes a change in a stock's price? The company's net income trend, the development of new products, court rulings, new legislation, business success, and upward market trends drive a stock's price up, and business failures and bad economic news pull it down. The market sets the price at which a stock changes hands.

Investments in Stock

To begin the discussion of investments in stock, we need to define two key terms. The person or company that owns stock in a corporation is the *investor*. The corporation that issued the stock is the *investee*. If you own shares of Boeing common stock, you are an investor and Boeing is the investee.

A business may purchase another corporation's stock simply to put extra cash to work in the hope of earning dividends and gains on the sale of the stock. These investments are rare, however. Most entities prefer to invest in inventory, employees, and plant assets in their own line of business. More likely, the entity may make the investment to gain a degree of control over the investee's operation. An investor holding 25 percent of the outstanding stock of the investee owns one-fourth of the business. This one-quarter voice in electing the directors of the corporation is likely to give the investor a lot of say in how the investee conducts its business. An investor holding more than 50 percent of the outstanding shares controls the investee.

Let's consider why one corporation might want to gain a say in another corporation's business. The investor may want to exert some control over the level of dividends paid by the investee. Or perhaps the investee has products closely linked to the investor's own line of business. This is the case with Viacom and Paramount. By influencing the investee's business, the investor may be able to exert some control on product distribution, product-line improvements, pricing strategies, and other important business considerations. A swimming-pool manufacturer might want to purchase stock in a diving-board company, a swimsuit maker, or some other corporation with related business.

Why doesn't the investor simply diversify its own operations? Why didn't Viacom start producing movies and publishing books? In those industries, Paramount and other companies were already established. To start competing with industry giants would have been too expensive and too risky.

PORTFOLIO DIVERSIFICATION Investments are not without risk. To offset the ill effects of a sudden downturn in the operations of any one investee, smart investors hold a *portfolio* of stocks. The portfolio holds investments in different companies. By diversifying its holdings, the investor gains protection from losing too much if any one investee runs into problems and its stock price plummets.

Classifying Stock Investments

Investments in stock are assets to the investor. The investments may be short-term or long-term. **Short-term investments**—sometimes called **marketable securities**—are current assets. To be listed on the balance sheet as short-term, investments must be liquid (readily convertible to cash). Also, the investor must intend either to convert the investments to cash within one year or to use them to pay a current liability. Investments not meeting these two requirements are classified on the balance sheet as **long-term investments,** a category of noncurrent assets.

Short-term investments include certificates of deposit and the stocks and bonds of other companies. *Long-term investments* include stocks and bonds that the investor expects to hold longer than one year or that are not readily marketable—for instance, real estate not used in the operations of the business. Exhibit 17-2 shows the positions of short-term and long-term investments on the balance sheet.

EXHIBIT 17-2

*Reporting Investments on the
Balance Sheet*

Current Assets		
Cash	$X	
Short-term investments	X	
Accounts receivable	X	
Inventories	X	
Prepaid expenses	X	
Total current assets		$X
Long-term investments [or simply Investments]		X
Property, plant, and equipment		X
Intangible assets		X
Other assets		X

Key Point: FASB 115 requires that investments for which there is less than 20% of outstanding stock or debt be categorized as follows:

Trading: Stock or debt securities purchased for short-term profit potential. Adjusted to current market value for financial statement purposes with holding gains or losses reported on the income statement. Reported as current assets only.

Held to Maturity: Debt that is expected to be held to maturity. Can be current (if maturing within one year) or noncurrent. Reported on the balance sheet at amortized cost. (Market value is not used here.)

Available for Sale: Both stock and debt securities that have no significant influence and do not fit into the other groups. The basis for reporting is current market value, but gains and losses are reported as a separate item in stockholders' equity, not in net income (which is included in retained earnings). Can be current or long-term.

We report assets in the order of their liquidity. Cash is the most liquid asset, followed by Short-Term Investments, Accounts Receivable, and so on. Long-Term Investments are less liquid than Current Assets but more liquid than Property, Plant, and Equipment.

Accounting for Stock Investments

Investments in stock are classified as either trading securities or as available-for-sale securities. **Trading securities** are stock investments that are to be sold in the very near future—days, weeks, or only a few months—with the intent of generating profits on price changes. Trading securities are therefore classified as *current assets* (see short-term investments in Exhibit 17-2). **Available-for-sale securities** are all stock investments other than trading securities. They are classified as current assets if the business expects to sell the investments within the next year or within the business's normal operating cycle if longer than a year. Otherwise the available-for-sale securities are classified as *long-term investments* (Exhibit 17-2).

After classifying an investment as a trading security or as an available-for-sale security, the investor accounts for the two categories separately. We begin by illustrating the accounting for trading security investments.

Trading Investments—The Market Value Method

OBJECTIVE 1

Account for trading investments in stock by the market value method

The **market value method** is used to account for all trading investments in stock because the stock will be sold in the near term at market value. *Cost* is used only as the initial amount for recording trading investments. These investments are reported on the balance sheet at their current *market* value.

All investments are recorded initially at cost. Suppose that Dade, Inc., purchases 1,000 shares of Hewlett-Packard Company common stock at the market price of 35 3/4. Dade intends to sell this investment within a few months and, therefore, classifies it as a trading investment. Dade's entry to record the investment is:

19X1			
Oct. 23	Trading Investment in Hewlett-Packard		
	Common Stock (1,000 × $35.75)	35,750	
	Cash		35,750
	Purchased 1,000 shares of Hewlett-Packard common stock at $35.75.		

Assume that Dade receives a $0.22 per share cash dividend on the Hewlett-Packard stock. Dade's entry to record receipt of the dividend is

19X1

Nov. 14	Cash (1,000 × $0.22)...	220	
	Dividend Revenue		220
	Received a $0.22 per share cash dividend on Hewlett-Packard common stock.		

Unlike interest, dividends do not accrue with the passage of time. In this example, Hewlett-Packard has no liability for dividends until the dividends are declared. An investor makes no accrual entry for dividend revenue at year end in anticipation of a dividend declaration.

Reporting Trading Investments at Fair Market Value

Because of the relevance of market values for decision making, trading investments in stock are reported at their market value. This reporting requires an adjustment of the trading investments from their last carrying amount to current market value. Assume that the market value of Dade's investment in Hewlett-Packard's common stock is $36,400 on December 31, 19X1. In this case Dade, Inc., the investor, makes the following adjustment:

19X1

Dec. 31	Trading Investment in Hewlett-Packard Common Stock ($36,400 – $35,750).............................	650	
	Holding Gain on Trading Investments....................		650
	Adjusted trading investment to market value.		

A **holding gain or loss** arises from changes in the market value of the asset, not from a sale transaction. Another name for Holding Gain or Loss is Unrealized Gain or Loss.

The income statement reports the Holding Gain among the Other Revenues and Gains, and the balance sheet reports the investments at market value as follows:

Current Assets	
Cash	$ XXX
Short-term investments—trading securities, at market value	**36,400**
Accounts receivable, net...	XXX

The process of adjusting the Trading Investment account and reporting the investments at current market value is repeated each period. For example, suppose the Hewlett-Packard stock's market value falls to $34,900 on December 31, 19X2, the end of the next year. In this case, Dade, Inc., would adjust the investment balance to current market value as follows:

19X2

Dec. 31	Holding Loss on Trading Investments..............................	1,500	
	Trading Investment in Hewlett-Packard Common Stock ($36,400 – $34,900)		1,500
	Adjusted trading investment to market value.		

The balance sheet would then report the investment at its current market value of $34,900.

The market value method is a radical departure from historical cost accounting. The cost of an investment becomes irrelevant, except at acquisition, when cost and market value are the same. In the market value method, the only gains and losses the investor reports are holdings gains and losses. The sale of an investment does not

Short Exercise: The cost, market value, and number of shares of stock in the March Corp. trading investment portfolio are:

	Shares	Cost	Market
A Co.	1,000	$20	$22
B Co.	1,500	10	8

Journalize the adjusting entry needed at December 31. *A:*

Trading Investment in A (1,000 × $2).	2,000	
Holding Loss	1,000	
Trading Investment in B (1,500 × $2)		3,000

include a gain or a loss because the investment is always adjusted to market value.[2] In a sale transaction, the investor simply debits Cash and credits Trading Investments, both at the same amount—the current market value of the investment that is sold.

Receipt of a Stock Dividend on a Trading Investment

Key Point: Receipt of stock dividends and stock splits is recorded in a memorandum entry. The Trading Investment should be adjusted to the stock's current market value if the market value of the investment has been affected by the dividend or split.

The receipt of a stock dividend on a trading investment increases the number of shares of stock held. Upon receipt of the dividend shares, the investor makes a memorandum entry of the number of shares received. This entry enables the investor to keep a record of the total number of shares of stock held as an investment.

The stock dividend may or may not affect the market value of the investment. If a change in market value occurs, the investor should adjust the Trading Investment account to the current market value of the stock held. As a practical matter, the investor would probably wait until the next financial statement date and then adjust to current market value according to the procedures outlined earlier.

Available-for-Sale Securities—The Cost and Market Value Method

Available-for-sale investments are accounted for by a combination of the cost and market value methods. Cost is maintained in the Investment account, but the investments are reported at current market value. Holding gains and losses are reported as a separate element of owners' equity. Realized gains and losses—the difference between the selling price of an investment and its cost—are reported on the income statement. This advanced topic is covered in intermediate accounting courses.

Long-Term Investments Accounted for by the Equity Method

OBJECTIVE 2
Use the equity method for stock investments

Key Point: An investor with 20% of a company's stock can usually elect 20% of the board of directors and influence company decisions. With more than 50% control (majority ownership), the investor can control the company's affairs.

An investor who holds less than 20 percent of the investee's voting stock usually plays no important role in the investee's operations. However, an investor with a larger stock holding—between 20 percent and 50 percent of the investee's voting stock—may *significantly influence* how the investee operates the business. Such an investor can likely affect the investee's decisions on dividend policy, product lines, sources of supply, and other important matters.

Investments in the range of 20–50 percent of the other company's stock are common. For example, General Motors owns nearly 40 percent of Isuzu Motors Overseas Distribution Corporation. Similarly, Chrysler Corporation owns 50 percent of a partnership with Renault of France. Because the investor has a voice in shaping business policy and operations, accountants believe that some measure of the investee's success and failure should be included in accounting for the investment. We use the **equity method** to account for investments in which the investor can significantly influence the decisions of the investee. A recent survey of 600 companies by *Accounting Trends & Techniques* indicated that 233 (38.8 percent) of the corporations held investments that they accounted for by the equity method.

"General Motors owns nearly 40 percent of Isuzu Motors Overseas Distribution Corporation."

Investments accounted for by the equity method are recorded initially at cost. Suppose Phillips Petroleum Company pays $400,000 for 30 percent of the common stock of White Rock Corporation. Phillips's entry to record the purchase of this investment is as follows:

---

[2] *FASB Statement No. 115, Accounting for Certain Investments in Debt and Equity Securities*, May 1993. Confirmed by direct communication with the FASB.

Jan. 6   Investment in White Rock Common Stock   400,000

　　　　 Cash   400,000

　　　 To purchase 30% investment in White Rock common stock.

Under the equity method, Phillips, as the investor, applies its percentage of ownership—30 percent, in our example—in recording its share of the investee's net income and dividends. If White Rock reports net income of $250,000 for the year, Phillips records 30 percent of this amount as an increase in the investment account and as equity-method investment revenue, as follows:

Dec. 31 Investment in White Rock Common Stock

　　　　 ($250,000 × 0.30)   75,000

　　　　　　 Equity-Method Investment Revenue   75,000

　　　 To record 30% of White Rock net income.

Short Exercise: P Co. purchased 40% of S Co.'s stock for $750,000. S Co. reported $100,000 income and paid $40,000 dividends during the next year. (1) On P Co.'s books, record the purchase, the net income of S, and dividends of S. (2) What is the carrying amount of P Co.'s investment in S Co.? *A:*
(1) Purchase:
　Investment in S ..750,000
　　Cash   750,000
　Net income of S:
　Investment in S .. 40,000
　　Equity-Method
　　　Invest. Rev. .   40,000
　Dividends of S:
　Cash 16,000
　　Invest. in S   16,000
(2) $774,000 ($750,000 + $40,000 – $16,000)

The Investment Revenue account carries the Equity-Method label to identify its source. This labeling is similar to distinguishing Sales Revenue from Service Revenue.

The investor increases the Investment account and records Investment Revenue when the investee reports income because of the close relationship between the two companies. As the investee's owner equity increases, so does the Investment account on the books of the investor.

Phillips records its proportionate part of cash dividends received from White Rock. Assuming that White Rock declares and pays a cash dividend of $100,000, Phillips receives 30 percent of this dividend, recorded as follows:

Jan. 17   Cash ($100,000 × 0.30)   30,000

　　　　　 Investment in White Rock Common Stock   30,000

　　　 To record receipt of 30% of White Rock cash dividend.

The Investment account is credited for the receipt of a dividend on an equity-method investment. Why? Because the dividend decreases the investee's owner equity, and so it also reduces the investor's investment. The investor received cash for this portion of the investment and reduced the investor's claim against the investee.

After the above entries are posted, Phillips's Investment account reflects its equity in the net assets of White Rock:

Key Point: A simple T-account illustrates how to account for equity-method investments:

Investment in White Rock Common Stock

19X1			19X2		
Jan. 6	Purchase	400,000	Jan. 17	Dividends	30,000
Dec. 31	Net income	75,000			
19X2					
Jan. 17	Balance	445,000			

Equity Method

Original cost	Share of losses
Share of income	Share of dividends

Gain or loss on the sale of an equity-method investment is measured as the difference between the sale proceeds and the carrying amount of the investment. For example, sale of one-tenth of the White Rock common stock for $41,000 would be recorded as follows:

Feb. 13   Cash   41,000

　　　　 Loss on Sale of Investment   3,500

　　　　　 Investment in White Rock Common Stock

　　　　　　 ($445,000 × 1/10)   44,500

　　　 Sold one-tenth of investment in White Rock common stock.

The appliance manufacturer Whirlpool has numerous investments in foreign affiliates, which are accounted for by the equity method.

Companies with investments accounted for by the equity method often refer to the investee as an *affiliated company*. The account title Investment in Affiliated Companies refers to investments that are accounted for by the equity method. Consider Whirlpool Corporation, manufacturer of refrigerators, washing machines, and other appliances. Whirlpool reported a $13 million equity-method loss on its investments in Brazilian and Mexican affiliated companies, which include Brastemp S.A., Consul S.A., (both in Brazil) and Vitromatic S.A. (in Mexico). Whirlpool recorded the transaction as follows:

	$ Millions
Equity-Method Investment Loss	13
Investment in Brazilian	
and Mexican Companies	13

Joint Ventures—Accounted for by the Equity Method

A *joint venture* is a separate entity or project owned and operated by a small group of businesses. Joint ventures are common in risky endeavors such as the petroleum and construction industries. Moreover, they are widely used in regions with developing economies, such as China, eastern Europe, and the Middle East. Most U.S. companies that do business abroad enter into joint ventures. Rather than risk a huge investment in uncertain oil exploration, the large oil companies form joint ventures with foreign entities that have known oil sources. For example, Aramco, which stands for Arabian American Oil Company, is a joint venture owned 50 percent by Saudi Arabia. Several multinational oil companies (Exxon, Chevron, and others) own the remaining 50 percent. Despite the risks of operating in the volatile Middle East, Aramco's partners have enjoyed big profits. The company earned $15 billion during the Persian Gulf War alone.

"Aramco ... is a joint venture owned 50 percent by Saudi Arabia. Several multinational oil companies (Exxon, Chevron, and others) own the remaining 50 percent."

A joint venturer such as Exxon accounts for its investment in a joint venture by the equity method even when the investor may own less than 20 percent of the venture. The equity method is used for accounting purposes because a joint venturer is presumed to have a significant influence on the investee company.

Long-Term Investments Accounted for by the Consolidation Method

OBJECTIVE 3
Consolidate parent and subsidiary balance sheets

Most large corporations own controlling interests in other corporations. A **controlling** (or **majority**) **interest** is the ownership of more than 50 percent of the investee's voting stock. Such an investment enables the investor to elect a majority of the investee's board of directors and so control the investee. The investor is called the **parent company**, and the investee company is called the **subsidiary**. For example, Paramount Communications, Inc., is a subsidiary of Viacom, Inc., the parent. The stockholders of Viacom control Viacom. Because Viacom owns Paramount Communications, its stockholders also control Paramount, as diagrammed in Exhibit 17-3.

Why have subsidiaries? Why not have the corporation take the form of a single legal entity? Subsidiaries may enable the parent to save on income taxes, may limit the parent's liabilities in a risky venture, and may ease expansion into foreign countries. For example, IBM finds it more feasible to operate in France through a French-based subsidiary company than through the American parent company. Ex-

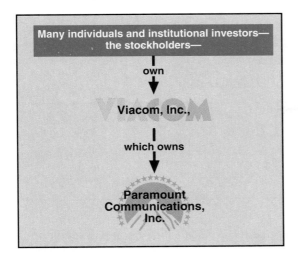

EXHIBIT 17-3
Ownership Structure of Viacom, Inc.

Parent Company	Selected Subsidiaries
General Motors Corporation Total assets $184 billion	Saturn Corporation Electronic Data Systems Corporation Hughes Aircraft Company General Motors Acceptance Corporation (GM's financing subsidiary, which makes up 43 percent of GM's total assets)
Ford Motor Company Total assets $174 billion	Ford Aerospace Corporation Jaguar, Ltd. Ford Motor Credit Company (Ford's financing subsidiary, which makes up 70 percent of Ford's total assets)
Chrysler Corporation Total assets $43 billion	Jeep/Eagle Corporation Thrifty Rent-a-Car System, Inc. Chrysler Credit Corporation (Chrysler's financing subsidiary, which makes up 29 percent of Chrysler's total assets)

hibit 17-4 shows some of the more interesting subsidiaries of the "Big-Three" U.S. auto makers.

Consolidation accounting is a method of combining the financial statements of two or more companies that are controlled by the same owners. This method implements the entity concept by reporting a single set of financial statements for the consolidated entity, which carries the name of the parent company. Exhibit 17-5 illustrates the accounting method for stock investments according to the percentage of the investor's ownership in the investee company.

Almost all published financial reports include consolidated statements. To understand the statements you are likely to encounter, you need to know the basic concepts underlying consolidation accounting. **Consolidated statements** combine the balance sheets, income statements, and other financial statements of the parent company with those of majority-owned subsidiaries into an overall set as if the parents and its subsidiaries were a single entity. The goal is to provide a better perspective on total operations than could be obtained by examining the separate reports of each individual company. The assets, liabilities, revenues, and expenses of each subsidiary are added to the parent's accounts. The consolidated financial statements present the combined account balances. For example, the balance in the Cash account of Paramount Communications is added to the balance in the Viacom Cash account, and the sum of the two amounts is presented as a single amount in the consolidated balance sheet of Viacom, Inc. Each account balance of a subsidiary loses its identity in

EXHIBIT 17-6

Parent Company with Consolidated Subsidiaries and an Equity-Method Investment

the consolidated statements. The subsidiary companies' names may be listed in the parent company's annual report. A reader of corporate annual reports cannot hope to understand them without knowing how consolidated statements are prepared. Exhibit 17-6 diagrams a corporate structure whose parent corporation owns controlling interests in five subsidiary companies and an equity-method investment in another investee company.

CONSOLIDATED BALANCE SHEET—PARENT CORPORATION OWNS ALL OF SUBSIDIARY'S STOCK Suppose that Parent Corporation has purchased all the outstanding common stock of Subsidiary Corporation at its book value of $150,000. In addition, Parent Corporation loaned Subsidiary Corporation $80,000. The $150,000 is paid to the *former owners* of Subsidiary Corporation as private investors. The $150,000 is *not* an addition to the existing assets and stockholders' equity of Subsidiary Corporation. *That is, the books of Subsidiary Corporation are completely unaffected by Parent Corporation's initial investment and Parent's subsequent accounting for that investment. Subsidiary Corporation is not dissolved. It lives on as a separate legal entity but with a new owner, Parent Corporation.*

As we saw in Chapter 14 (p. 574), the book value of a corporation is its stockholders' equity or its net assets (assets minus liabilities).

Parent Corporation Books[3]			Subsidiary Corporation Books		
Investment in Subsidiary					
Corporation......................	150,000		No entry		
Cash...........................		150,000			
Note Receivable from			Cash.......................................	80,000	
Subsidiary	80,000		Note Payable		
Cash...........................		80,000	to Parent		80,000

Each legal entity has its individual set of books. The consolidated entity does not keep a separate set of books. Instead, a work sheet is used to prepare the consolidated statements. A major concern in consolidation accounting is this: Do not double-count—that is, do not include the same item twice.

Companies may prepare a consolidated balance sheet immediately after the acquisition. The consolidated balance sheet shows all the assets and liabilities of both the parent and the subsidiary. The Investment in Subsidiary Corporation account on the parent's books represents all the assets and liabilities of Subsidiary. The consolidated statements cannot show both the investment amount *plus* the amounts for the subsidiary's assets and liabilities. Doing so would count the same resources twice. To avoid this double-counting, we eliminate the $150,000 Investment in Subsidiary on

---

[3]The parent company may use either the cost method or the equity method for work sheet entries to the Investment account. Regardless of the method used, the consolidated statements are the same. Advanced accounting courses deal with this topic.

the parent's books and the $150,000 stockholders' equity on the subsidiary's books ($100,000 Common Stock and $50,000 Retained Earnings).

EXPLANATION OF ELIMINATION—ENTRY (a) Exhibit 17-7 shows the work sheet for consolidating the balance sheet. Consider the elimination entry for the parent-subsidiary ownership accounts. Entry (a) credits the parent Investment account to eliminate its debit balance. It also eliminates the subsidiary stockholder's equity accounts by debiting Common Stock for $100,000 and Retained Earnings for $50,000. The resulting consolidated balance sheet reports no Investment in Subsidiary account, and the consolidated totals for Common Stock and Retained Earnings are those of Parent Corporation only. The consolidated amounts appear in the final column of the consolidation work sheet.

EXPLANATION OF ELIMINATION—ENTRY (b) Parent Corporation loaned $80,000 to Subsidiary Corporation, and Subsidiary signed a note payable to Parent. Therefore, Parent's balance sheet includes an $80,000 note receivable, and Subsidiary's balance sheet reports a note payable, for this amount. This loan was entirely within the consolidated entity and so must be eliminated. Entry (b) accomplishes this. The $80,000 credit in the elimination column of the work sheet offsets Parent's debit balance in Notes Receivable from Subsidiary. After this work sheet entry, the consolidated amount for notes receivable is zero. The $80,000 debit in the elimination column offsets the credit balance of Subsidiary's notes payable, and the resulting consolidated amount for notes payable is the amount owed to those outside the consolidated entity.

STOP & THINK Examine Exhibit 17-7. Why does the consolidated stockholders' equity ($176,000 + $155,000) exclude the equity of Subsidiary Corporation?

Answer: Because the stockholders' equity of the consolidated entity is that of the parent only. Also, the subsidiary's equity and the parent company's investment balance represent the same resources. Therefore, including them both would amount to double-counting.

PARENT CORPORATION BUYS SUBSIDIARY'S STOCK AND PAYS FOR GOODWILL A company may acquire a subsidiary by paying a price in excess of the market value of the subsidiary's net assets (assets minus liabilities). By definition, this excess is *goodwill*.◄■■■ What drives a company's market value up? The company may create goodwill through its superior products, service, or location.

◄■■■◄■■■◄■■■ In Chapter 10, p. 427, we described goodwill as the excess of the cost of an acquired company over the sum of the market values of its net assets.

EXHIBIT 17-7

Work Sheet for Consolidated Balance Sheet—Parent Corporation Owns All of Subsidiary's Stock

Assets	Parent Corporation	Subsidiary Corporation	Eliminations Debit	Eliminations Credit	Consolidated Amounts
Cash	12,000	18,000			30,000
Notes receivable from					
Subsidiary................................	80,000	—		(b) 80,000	—
Inventory......................................	104,000	91,000			195,000
Investment in Subsidiary	150,000	—		(a) 150,000	—
Other assets.................................	218,000	138,000			356,000
Total...	564,000	247,000			581,000
Liabilities and Stockholders' Equity					
Accounts payable	43,000	17,000			60,000
Notes payable	190,000	80,000	(b) 80,000		190,000
Common stock..............................	176,000	100,000	(a) 100,000		176,000
Retained earnings	155,000	50,000	(a) 50,000		155,000
Total...	564,000	247,000	230,000	230,000	581,000

The subsidiary does not record goodwill. The goodwill is identified in the process of consolidating the parent and subsidiary financial statements.

Suppose Parent Corporation paid $450,000 to acquire 100 percent of the common stock of Subsidiary Corporation, which had Common Stock of $200,000 and Retained Earnings of $180,000. Parent's payment included $70,000 for goodwill ($450,000 – $200,000 – $180,000 = $70,000).[4] The following entry eliminates Parent's Investment account against Subsidiary's equity accounts:

Dec. 31	Common Stock, Subsidiary	200,000	
	Retained Earnings, Subsidiary	180,000	
	Goodwill	70,000	
	Investment in Subsidiary		450,000

To eliminate cost of investment in subsidiary against Subsidiary's equity balances and to recognize Subsidiary's unrecorded goodwill.

In practice, this entry would be made only on the consolidation work sheet. Here we show it in general journal form for instructional purposes.

The asset goodwill is reported on the consolidated balance sheet among the intangible assets, after plant assets. For example, the last asset on Coca-Cola's consolidated balance sheet is Goodwill and Other Intangible Assets of $383.3 million. Goodwill is amortized to expense over its useful life.

CONSOLIDATED BALANCE SHEET—PARENT COMPANY OWNS LESS THAN 100 PERCENT OF SUBSIDIARY'S STOCK

When a parent company owns more than 50 percent (a majority) of the subsidiary's stock but less than 100 percent of it, a new category of owners' equity, called *minority interest*, must appear on the balance sheet. Suppose Parent Company buys 75 percent of Subsidiary's common stock. The minority interest is the remaining 25 percent of Subsidiary's equity. Thus **minority interest** is the subsidiary's equity that is held by stockholders other than the parent company. Most companies report minority interest as a liability, while a few show it as a separate element of stockholders' equity. To be consistent with actual practice, in this book we list minority interest as a liability. Exhibit 17-8 is the consolidation work sheet. Again, focus on the Eliminations columns and the Consolidated Amounts.

Entry (a) in Exhibit 17-8 eliminates P Company's Investment balance of $120,000 against the $160,000 owners' equity of S Company. All of S's equity is eliminated even though P holds only 75 percent of S's stock. The outside 25 percent interest in S's equity is credited to Minority Interest ($160,000 × 0.25 = $40,000). Thus entry (a) reclassifies 25 percent of S Company's equity as minority interest. Entry (b) in Exhibit 17-8 eliminates S Company's $50,000 note receivable against P's note payable of the same amount. The consolidated amount of notes payable ($42,000) is the amount that S Company owes to outsiders.

The consolidated balance sheet of P Company in Exhibit 17-9 is based on the work sheet of Exhibit 17-8. The consolidated balance sheet reveals that ownership of P Company and its consolidated subsidiary is divided between P's stockholders (common stock and retained earnings totaling $338,000) and the minority interest of S Company ($40,000).

INCOME OF A CONSOLIDATED ENTITY

The income of a consolidated entity is the net income of the parent plus the parent's proportion of the subsidiaries' net income. Suppose Parent Company owns all the stock of Subsidiary S-1 and 60

Key Point: The elimination entry requires, at most, five steps: (1) Eliminate intercompany receivables and payables. (2) Eliminate the stockholders' equity accounts of the subsidiary. (3) Eliminate the Investment in Subsidiary account. (4) Record goodwill. (5) Record minority interest.

Short Exercise: P Co. purchases 80% of S Co. for $280,000. Their balance sheets immediately afterward are:

Assets

	P Co.	S Co.
Cash	$ 200,000	$ 50,000
Accounts rec...	275,000	60,000
Inventory	300,000	80,000
Invest. in S	280,000	
Plant & equip.	500,000	170,000
	$1,555,000	$360,000

Liabilities and Stockholders' Equity

Accounts pay..	$ 350,000	$ 60,000
Com. stock.....	500,000	120,000
Ret. earnings..	705,000	180,000
	$1,555,000	$360,000

P Co. owes S Co. $10,000 on account. Prepare the elimination entry in general journal form and the consolidated balance sheet. *A:*

Accounts Payable......	10,000	
Common Stock.........	120,000	
Retained Earnings	180,000	
Goodwill	40,000	
[$280,000 – ($300,000 × 80%)]		
Investment in S..........		280,000
Minority Interest		
($300,000 × 20%) ..		60,000
Accounts Receivable..		10,000

Assets

Cash............................	$ 250,000
Accounts rec.	325,000
Inventory.....................	380,000
Plant & equip.	670,000
Goodwill.....................	40,000
Total..........................	$1,665,000

Liabilities & Stockholders' Equity

Accounts pay................	$ 400,000
Minority interest........	60,000
Common stock...........	500,000
Ret. earnings	705,000
Total..........................	$1,665,000

---

[4]For simplicity, we are assuming that the fair market value of the subsidiary's net assets (assets minus liabilities) equals the book value of the company's owners' equity. Advanced courses consider other situations.

Assets	P Company	S Company	Eliminations Debit	Eliminations Credit	Consolidated Amounts
Cash.........................	33,000	18,000			51,000
Notes receivable from P	—	50,000		(b) 50,000	—
Accounts receivable, net	54,000	39,000			93,000
Inventory......................	92,000	66,000			158,000
Investment in S	120,000	—		(a) 120,000	—
Plant and equipment, net..............	230,000	123,000			353,000
Total	529,000	296,000			655,000
Liabilities and Stockholders' Equity					
Accounts payable	141,000	94,000			235,000
Notes payable	50,000	42,000	(b) 50,000		42,000
Minority interest.........................	—	—		(a) 40,000	40,000
Common stock.............................	170,000	100,000	(a) 100,000		170,000
Retained earnings	168,000	60,000	(a) 60,000		168,000
Total	529,000	296,000	210,000	210,000	655,000

EXHIBIT 17-8
Work Sheet for Consolidated Balance Sheet—Parent Company Owns Less Than 100 Percent of Subsidiary's Stock

percent of the stock of Subsidiary S-2. During the year just ended, Parent earned net income of $330,000, S-1 earned $150,000, and S-2 had a net loss of $100,000. Parent Company would report net income of $420,000, computed as follows:

	Net Income (Net Loss)	Parent Stockholders' Ownership	Parent Net Income (Net Loss)
Parent Company	$330,000	100%	$330,000
Subsidiary S-1................................	150,000	100	150,000
Subsidiary S-2................................	(100,000)	60	(60,000)
Consolidated net income			$420,000

The parent's net income is the same amount that would be recorded under the equity method. However, the equity method stops short of reporting the investees' assets and liabilities on the parent's balance sheet because with an investment in the range of 20 to 50 percent, the investor owns less than a controlling interest in the investee company.

P COMPANY AND CONSOLIDATED SUBSIDIARY
CONSOLIDATED BALANCE SHEET
DECEMBER 31, 19XX

Assets

Cash	$ 51,000
Accounts receivable, net..	93,000
Inventory	158,000
Plant and equipment, net	353,000
Total assets..	$655,000

Liabilities and Stockholders' Equity

Accounts payable	$235,000
Notes payable	42,000
Minority interest	40,000
Common stock	170,000
Retained earnings...	168,000
Total liabilities and stockholders' equity..............	$655,000

EXHIBIT 17-9
Consolidated Balance Sheet of P Company

The procedures for preparation of a consolidated income statement parallel those outlined above for the balance sheet. The consolidated income statement is discussed in an advanced course.

Computers and Consolidations

Consider diversified companies such as W. R. Grace & Co., the world's largest specialty chemicals company. Grace includes nearly 30 subsidiary firms, with more than 100 different product lines—from food packaging to construction materials to health-care products. A company such as Grace can prepare its consolidated financial statements automatically with a fully integrated accounting information system. But many wholly-owned subsidiaries retain their own accounting systems. If the subsidiaries have adopted the parent company's standard chart of accounts, a supplementary system can automatically combine the accounts of the parent and subsidiary companies and prepare the consolidated statements. If each subsidiary maintains its own unique chart of accounts, the consolidation must be performed manually. A computer spreadsheet program may still ease the preparation of the consolidated statements. Each subsidiary can enter its statements in a spreadsheet that is electronically linked to a central spreadsheet that automatically updates the consolidated statements. The advantage of the computer spreadsheet becomes clear when you prepare consolidated statements.

Investments in Bonds and Notes

OBJECTIVE 4
Account for investments in bonds

Industrial and commercial companies invest far more in stocks than they invest in bonds. The major investors in bonds are financial institutions, such as pension plans, bank trust departments, mutual funds, and insurance companies. The relationship between the issuing corporation and the investor (bondholder) may be diagrammed as follows:

Issuing Corporation	Investor (Bondholder)
Bonds payable	Investment in bonds
Interest expense	Interest revenue

The dollar amount of a bond transaction is the same for issuer and investor, but the accounts debited and credited differ. However, the accounts are parallel. For example, the issuing corporation's interest expense is the investor's interest revenue.

An investment in bonds is classified either as short-term (a current asset) or as long-term. Investments in bonds and notes are further classified as either trading securities, available-for-sale securities, or as held-to-maturity securities. Trading securities and available-for-sale securities have the same meaning for bond investments as they do for stock investments. **Held-to-maturity securities** is a special category of investments in bonds, notes, and other debt securities that the investor expects to hold until the maturity date of the bonds. Most held-to-maturity-securities are classified as long-term investments.

Accounting for Bond Investments

Accounting for bond investments held as trading securities follows a pattern similar to that illustrated for stock investments. Bond investments are recorded at cost. The investments are reported on the balance sheet at current market value. We begin by illustrating the accounting for a bond investment held as a *trading security*—a short-term investment and therefore a current asset.

Trading Investments—The Market Value Method

Bond investments are recorded at cost. The amortization of bond premium or discount is *not* recorded on trading investments because the investor plans to hold the bonds for so short a period that any amortization would be immaterial.

Suppose that an investor purchases $10,000 of CBS bonds on April 1, 19X2, paying a price of 95.2. The annual contract interest rate is 6 percent, paid semiannually on April 1 and October 1. The cost of the bonds is $9,520 ($10,000 × 0.952). The investor records the purchase on April 1 as follows:

Apr. 1	Trading Investment in CBS Bonds ($10,000 × 0.952)	9,520	
	Cash		9,520
	To purchase bond investment.		

The investor's entry for receipt of the first semiannual interest amount on October 1 is:

Oct. 1	Cash ($10,000 × 0.06 × 6/12)	300	
	Interest Revenue		300
	To receive semiannual interest.		

At December 31 the investor accrues interest revenue for three months (October, November, and December), debiting Interest Receivable and crediting Interest Revenue for $150 ($10,000 × 0.06 × 3/12). The investor's December 31 balance sheet reports the investment as follows (we assume that the market price of the bonds is 96):

Current Assets	
Cash	$ XXX
Trading investments, at market value	**9,600**
Interest receivable	150

Accounting for changes in the market value of trading investments in bonds follows the pattern illustrated earlier for trading investments in stock. At each financial statement date, the investment carrying amount is adjusted to current market value, and the investor records a Holding Gain or a Holding Loss.

Held-to-Maturity Investments—The Amortized Cost Method

Accounting for held-to-maturity investments in bonds follows a different pattern because the bonds will be held until their maturity date. At maturity the investor will receive the face value of the bonds. For held-to-maturity investments, discount or premium is amortized to account more precisely for interest revenue over the period the bonds will be held. The amortization of discount or premium on a bond investment affects Interest Revenue and the carrying amount of the bonds in the same way as for the company that issued the bonds. Held-to-maturity investments in bonds are reported at their *amortized cost*, which determines the carrying amount.

The accountant records amortization on the cash interest dates and at year end, along with the accrual of interest receivable. Accountants rarely use separate discount and premium accounts for investments. Amortization of a discount is recorded by directly *debiting* the Held-to-Maturity Investment in Bonds account and *crediting* Interest Revenue. Amortization of a premium is recorded by directly crediting the Held-to-Maturity Investment account. This entry debits Interest Revenue. These entries bring the investment balance to the bonds' face value on the maturity date. They also record the correct amount of interest revenue each period.

Short Exercise: Assume that Quill Corp. is buying bonds as a trading investment. Quill buys $300,000 of 9%, 10-year bonds at 104. The bonds pay interest on February 1 and August 1. What are the entries to record (1) the purchase on 8/1/96, (2) the year-end accrual, and (3) the first semiannual receipt of interest? *A:*

(1) Purchase on 8/1/96:

Trading Investment in Bonds	312,000	
Cash ($300,000 × 1.04)		312,000

(2) Accrual on 12/31/96:

Interest Receivable	11,250	
Interest Revenue		11,250
($300,000 × 9% × 5/12)		

(3) Interest receipt on 2/1/97:

Cash ($300,000 × 0.045)	13,500	
Interest Receivable		11,250
Interest Revenue		2,250

Suppose the $10,000 of 6-percent CBS bonds in the preceding example were purchased on April 1, 19X2, as a long-term investment to be held to maturity. Interest dates are April 1 and October 1. These bonds mature on October 1, 19X6, so they will be outstanding for 48 months. Assume amortization of the discount by the straight-line method. ◄▥▥ The following entries for a long-term investment highlight the accounts that differ between accounting for a trading bond investment and for a bond investment to be held to maturity:

◄▥▥ ◄▥▥ ◄▥▥ Straight-line amortization of premium or discount on a bond investment is calculated the same way as for bonds payable (Chapter 16, pp. 644, 646).

Apr. 1	**Held-to-Maturity Investment in CBS Bonds**	
	($10,000 × 0.952) 9,520	
	Cash	9,520
	To purchase bond investment.	
Oct. 1	Cash ($10,000 × 0.06 × 6/12) 300	
	Interest Revenue	300
	To receive semiannual interest.	
Oct. 1	**Held-to-Maturity Investment in CBS Bonds**	
	[($10,000 – $9,520)/(48 × 6)] 60	
	Interest Revenue	60
	To amortize discount on bond investment for six months.	

At December 31, the year-end adjustments are:

Dec. 31	Interest Receivable ($10,000 × 0.06 × 3/12) 150	
	Interest Revenue	150
	To accrue interest revenue for three months.	
Dec. 31	**Held-to-Maturity Investment in CBS Bonds**	
	[($10,000 – $9,520)/(48 × 3)] 30	
	Interest Revenue	30
	To amortize discount on bond investment for three months.	

The financial statements at December 31, 19X2, report the following effects of this investment in bonds (assume that the bonds' market price is 102):

Short Exercise: Refer to the previous Short Exercise but assume that Quill Corp. bought the bonds to hold to maturity. What entries record (1) the purchase on 8/1/96, (2) the year-end accrual, and (3) the first semiannual interest receipt and straight-line amortization of the premium? *A:*

(1) Purchase on 8/1/96:
Held-to-Maturity
  Invest. in Bonds..... 312,000
Cash ($300,000 ×
  1.04).................. 312,000

(2) Accrual on 12/31/96:
Interest Receivable.... 11,250
  Interest Revenue ... 11,250
($300,000 × 9% × 5/12)

Interest Revenue 500
  Held-to-Maturity
  Invest. in Bonds. 500
[($12,000 prem./20 semiann.
int. periods) = $600 × 5/6]

(3) Interest receipt on 2/1/97:
Cash ($300,000 ×
  0.045)..................... 13,500
  Interest Receivable 11,250
  Interest Revenue ... 2,250

Interest Revenue 100
  Held-to-Maturity
  Invest. in Bonds. 100
($600 × 1/6)

Balance sheet at December 31, 19X2:

Current assets:	
Interest receivable..	$ 150
Total current assets	X,XXX
Held-to-maturity investments in bonds ($9,520 + $60 + $30)—Note 6..............	**9,610**
Property, plant, and equipment	X,XXX

Note 6: Long-term investments:
Bond investments that will be held to maturity are reported at *amortized cost*. At December 31, 19X2, the market value of long-term investments in bonds was $10,200.

Income statement (multiple-step) for the year ended December 31, 19X2:

Other revenues:	
Interest revenue ($300 + $60 + $150 + $30)...	$ 540

Type of Investment	Accounting Method
Short-term investment in stock or bonds	
Trading investment _____	Market value
Available-for-sale investment classified as current asset _____	Cost and market value
Long-term investment:	
Investor owns less than 20 percent of investee stock	
(Available-for-sale investment classified as noncurrent asset) _____	Cost and market value
Investor owns between 20 and 50 percent of investee stock _____	Equity
Investment in a joint venture _____	Equity
Investor owns more than 50 percent of investee stock _____	Consolidation
Long-term investment in bonds (Held-to-maturity investment) _____	Amortized cost

In particular, note that the investments in bonds to be held to maturity are reported by the *amortized cost* method. Where discount or premium is amortized by the effective-interest method, accounting for long-term investments follows the pattern illustrated here.◀▥

Exhibit 17-10 summarizes the accounting methods for investments.

EXHIBIT 17-10
Accounting Methods for Investments

◀▥◀▥◀▥ Effective-interest amortization amounts are calculated the same way as for bonds payable (Chapter 16, p. 649).

SUMMARY PROBLEM FOR YOUR REVIEW   MID-CHAPTER

This problem consists of four independent items.

1. Identify the appropriate accounting method for each of the following situations:
   a. Investment in 25 percent of investee's stock
   b. Trading investment in stock
   c. Investment in more than 50 percent of investee's stock

2. At what amount should the following trading investment portfolio be reported on the December 31 balance sheet? All the investments are less than 5 percent of the investee's stock and were purchased late in the current year.

Stock	Investment Cost	Current Market Value
Eastman Kodak.................	$ 5,000	$ 5,500
Exxon	61,200	53,000
General Motors	3,680	6,230

Journalize any adjusting entry required by these data.

3. Investor paid $67,900 to acquire a 40-percent equity-method investment in the common stock of Investee. At the end of the first year, Investee's net income was $80,000, and Investee declared and paid cash dividends of $55,000. Journalize Investor's (a) purchase of the investment, (b) share of Investee's net income, (c) receipt of dividends from Investee, and (d) sale of Investee stock for $80,100.

4. Parent Company paid $100,000 for all the common stock of Subsidiary Company, and Parent owes Subsidiary $20,000 on a note payable. Complete the following consolidation work sheet:

Assets	Parent Company	Subsidiary Company	Eliminations Debit	Eliminations Credit	Consolidated Amounts
Cash	7,000	4,000			
Note receivable from Parent.....................	—	20,000			
Investment in Subsidiary	100,000	—			
Goodwill.............................	—	—			
Other assets	108,000	99,000			_____
Total...................................	215,000	123,000			_____

Liabilities and Stockholders' Equity

Accounts payable	15,000	8,000			
Notes payable	20,000	30,000			
Common stock	135,000	60,000			
Retained earnings...............	45,000	25,000	_____	_____	_____
Total...................................	215,000	123,000			_____

SOLUTION TO REVIEW PROBLEM

1. (a) Equity   (b) Market value   (c) Consolidation
2. Report the investments at market value, $64,730.

Stock	Investment Cost	Current Market Value
Eastman Kodak................	$ 5,000	$ 5,500
Exxon	61,200	53,000
General Motors	3,680	6,230
Totals...............................	$69,880	$64,730

Adjusting entry:

Holding Loss on Trading Investments	5,150	
Trading Investments ($69,880 – $64,730)		5,150
To adjust investments to current market value.		

3. a.
Investment in Investee Common Stock..	67,900	
Cash..		67,900
To purchase 40% investment in Investee common stock.		

b.
Investment in Investee Common Stock ($80,000 × 0.40)...	32,000	
Equity-Method Investment Revenue		32,000
To record 40% of Investee net income.		

c.
Cash ($55,000 × 0.40)..	22,000	
Investment in Investee Common Stock		22,000
To record receipt of 40% of Investee cash dividend.		

d.
Cash	80,100	
Investment in Investee Common Stock ($67,900 + $32,000 – $22,000)...		77,900
Gain on Sale of Investment..		2,200
Sold investment in Investee common stock.		

4. Consolidation work sheet:

Assets	Parent Company	Subsidiary Company	Eliminations Debit	Eliminations Credit	Consolidated Amounts
Cash.........................	7,000	4,000			11,000
Note receivable from Parent...................	—	20,000		(a) 20,000	—
Investment in Subsidiary.....................	100,000	—		(b) 100,000	—
Goodwill.........................	—	—	(b) 15,000		15,000
Other assets....................	108,000	99,000			207,000
Total.................................	215,000	123,000			233,000
Liabilities and Stockholders' Equity					
Accounts payable.............	15,000	8,000			23,000
Notes payable.................	20,000	30,000	(a) 20,000		30,000
Common stock................	135,000	60,000	(b) 60,000		135,000
Retained earnings.............	45,000	25,000	(b) 25,000		45,000
Total.................................	215,000	123,000	120,000	120,000	233,000

ACCOUNTING FOR INTERNATIONAL OPERATIONS

Did you know that Exxon and Bank of America earn most of their revenue outside the United States? It is common for American companies to do a large part of their business abroad. IBM, Eli Lilly, PepsiCo, Sara Lee, and Whirlpool, among many others, are very active in other countries. Exhibit 17-11 shows these companies' percentages of international sales and pretax income.

Accounting for business activities across national boundaries makes up the field of *international accounting*. As communications and transportation improve and trade barriers fall, global integration makes international accounting more important.

Economic Structures and Their Impact on International Accounting

The business environment varies widely across the globe. New York reflects the diversity of the market-driven economy of the United States. Japan's economy is similar to ours, although Japanese business activity focuses more on imports and exports. The central government controls the economy of China, so private business decisions are only beginning to take root there. In Brazil, extremely high rates of inflation have made historical-cost amounts meaningless. Accounting amounts are altered periodically to measure changes in the purchasing power of the cruzeiro, Brazil's monetary unit. International accounting deals with such differences in economic structures.

Company	Percent of International Sales	Percent of International Pretax Income (Loss)
IBM	62%	(21)%
Eli Lilly	34	40
PepsiCo	25	21
Sara Lee	34	48
Whirlpool	39	25

EXHIBIT 17-11
Extent of International Business

Foreign Currencies and Foreign-Currency Exchange Rates

Each country uses its own national currency. If Boeing, a U.S.-owned company, sells a 747 jet to Air France, will Boeing receive U.S. dollars or French francs? If the transaction takes place in dollars, Air France must exchange its francs for dollars to pay Boeing in U.S. currency. If the transaction takes place in francs, Boeing will receive francs, which it must exchange for dollars. In either case, a step has been added to the transaction: One company must convert domestic currency into foreign currency, or the other company must convert foreign currency into domestic currency.

The price of one nation's currency may be stated in terms of another country's monetary unit. This measure of one currency against another currency is called the **foreign-currency exchange rate**. In Exhibit 17-12, the dollar value of a French franc is $0.17. This means that one French franc could be bought for seventeen cents. Other currencies, such as the pound and the yen (also listed in Exhibit 17-12), are similarly bought and sold.

We use the exchange rate to convert the cost of an item given in one currency to its cost in a second currency. We call this conversion a *translation*. Suppose an item costs 200 French francs. To compute its cost in dollars, we multiply the amount in francs by the conversion rate: 200 French francs × $0.17 = $34.

To aid the flow of international business, a market exists for foreign currencies. Traders buy and sell U.S. dollars, French francs, and other currencies in the same way that they buy and sell other commodities such as beef, cotton, and automobiles. And just as supply and demand cause the prices of these other commodities to shift, so supply and demand for a particular currency cause exchange rates to fluctuate daily. When the demand for a nation's currency exceeds the supply of that currency, its exchange rate rises. When supply exceeds demand, the currency's exchange rate falls.

Two main factors determine the supply and demand for a particular currency: (1) the ratio of a country's imports to its exports and (2) the rate of return available in the country's capital markets.

THE IMPORT/EXPORT RATIO   Japanese exports far surpass Japan's imports. Customers of Japanese companies must buy yen (the Japanese unit of currency) in the international currency market to pay for their purchases. This strong demand drives up the price—the foreign exchange rate—of the yen. France, however, imports more goods than it exports. French businesses must sell francs to buy the foreign currencies needed to acquire the foreign goods. The supply of the French franc increases, and so its price decreases.

THE RATE OF RETURN   The rate of return available in a country's capital markets affects the amount of investment funds flowing into the country. When rates of return are high in a politically stable country such as the United States, international investors buy stocks, bonds, and real estate in that country. This activity increases the demand for the nation's currency and drives up its exchange rate.

Currencies are often described as "strong" or "weak." The exchange rate of a **strong currency** is rising relative to other nations' currencies. The exchange rate of a **weak currency** is falling relative to other currencies.

EXHIBIT 17-12

Foreign-Currency Exchange Rates

Country	Monetary Unit	Dollar Value	Country	Monetary Unit	Dollar Value
Canada	Dollar	$0.73	Great Britain	Pound	$ 1.48
European Common Market	European Currency Unit	1.15	Italy	Lira	0.0006
France	Franc	0.17	Japan	Yen	0.0097
Germany	Mark	0.60	Mexico	Peso	0.298

Source: *The Wall Street Journal*, March 31, 1994, p. C15.

Suppose *The Wall Street Journal* listed the exchange rate for the British pound as $1.52 on October 14. On October 15 that rate has changed to $1.50. We would say that the dollar has risen against—is stronger than—the British pound because the pound has become less expensive, and so the dollar now buys more pounds. A stronger dollar would make travel to England more attractive to Americans.

Assume that *The Wall Street Journal* reports a rise in the exchange rate of the Japanese yen from $0.0097 to $0.0099. This change indicates that the yen is stronger than the dollar. Japanese automobiles, cameras, and electronic products are more expensive because each dollar buys fewer yen.

In our examples—in which the pound has dropped relative to the dollar and the yen has risen relative to the dollar—we would describe the yen as the strongest currency, the pound as the weakest currency. The dollar would be said to lie somewhere between the other two currencies.

Real-World Example: Only three years ago the Mexican peso was worth $0.0003. Since then the Mexican government has revalued the peso.

Accounting for International Transactions

When an American company transacts business with a foreign company, the transaction price can be stated either in dollars or in the national currency of the other company. If the price is stated in dollars, the American company has no special accounting difficulties. The transaction is recorded and reported in dollars exactly as though the other company were also American.

OBJECTIVE 5

Account for transactions stated in a foreign currency

Purchases on Account

If the transaction price is stated in units of the foreign currency, the American company encounters two accounting steps. First, the transaction price must be translated into dollars for recording in the accounting records. Second, credit transactions (the most common international transaction) usually cause the American company to experience a **foreign-currency transaction gain** or **loss**. This type of gain or loss occurs when the exchange rate changes between the date of the purchase on account and the date of the subsequent payment of cash.

The credit purchase creates an Account Payable that is recorded at the prevailing exchange rate. Later, when the buyer pays cash, the exchange rate has almost certainly changed. Accounts Payable is debited for the amount recorded earlier, and Cash is credited for the amount paid at the current exchange rate. A debit difference is a loss, and a credit difference is a gain.

Suppose that on April 1, Macy's Department Store imports Ralph Lauren's Polo fragrance from the French supplier L'Oreal at a price of 200,000 francs. The exchange rate is $0.19 per French franc. Macy's records this credit purchase of inventory as follows:

"Suppose that on April 1, Macy's Department Store imports Ralph Lauren's Polo fragrance from the French supplier L'Oreal at a price of 200,000 francs."

Apr. 1	Inventory	38,000	
	Accounts Payable (200,000 × $0.19).....................		38,000

Macy's translates the French franc price of the merchandise (200,000 Fr) into dollars ($38,000) for recording the purchase and the related account payable.

If Macy's were to pay this account immediately—which is unlikely in international commerce—Macy's would debit Accounts Payable and credit Cash for $38,000. Suppose, however, that the credit terms specify payment within 60 days. On May 20, when Macy's pays this debt, the exchange rate has fallen to $0.18 per French franc. Macy's payment entry is the following:

Short Exercise: (1) On May 13, the exchange rate for German marks was DM = $0.59. International Corp. (a U.S. company) purchased inventory from a German company at a cost of 50,000 DM. Record the purchase in dollars. (2) Record the payment on May 31 for a current exchange rate of DM = $0.58. **A:**

(1) Inventory 29,500
    Accounts Payable .. 29,500
    (50,000 DM × $0.59 = $29,500)
(2) Accounts Payable....... 29,500
    Foreign-Currency
      Transaction
      Gain 500
    Cash 29,000
    (50,000 DM × $0.58 = $29,000)

May 20	Accounts Payable	38,000	
	Cash (200,000 × $0.18).............................		36,000
	Foreign-Currency Transaction Gain		2,000

Macy's has a gain because the company has settled the debt with fewer dollars than the amount of the original account payable. If on the payment date the exchange rate of the French franc had exceeded $0.19, Macy's would have paid more dollars than the original $38,000. The company would have recorded a loss on the transaction as a debit to Foreign-Currency Transaction Loss.

Sales on Account

International sales on account also may be measured in foreign currency. Suppose IBM sells a small computer to the German government on December 9. The price of the computer is 140,000 German marks, and the exchange rate is $0.64 per German mark. IBM's sale entry is as follows:

| Dec. 9 | Accounts Receivable (140,000 × $0.64) .... | 89,600 | |
| | Sales Revenue... | | 89,600 |

Assume that IBM collects from Germany on December 30, after the exchange rate has fallen to $0.63 per German mark. IBM receives fewer dollars than the recorded amount of the receivable and so experiences a foreign-currency transaction loss. The following is the collection entry:

Dec. 30	Cash (140,000 × $0.63)	88,200	
	Foreign-Currency Transaction Loss	1,400	
	Accounts Receivable		89,600

Foreign-Currency Transaction Gains and Losses are combined for each accounting period. The net amount of gain or loss can be reported as Other Revenue and Expense on the income statement.

UNREALIZED FOREIGN-CURRENCY TRANSACTION GAINS AND LOSSES Foreign-currency transaction gains and losses are *realized* when cash is paid or received. In our examples thus far, cash receipts and cash payments occurred in the same period as the related sale or purchase. This will not always be so. Suppose IBM collects from the German government in January. At December 31, the German mark is worth only $0.63, $0.01 less than the exchange rate at which IBM recorded the receivable. In this case IBM will record a foreign-currency transaction loss for the decrease in the dollar value of the account receivable. The adjusting entry is:

Short Exercise: On December 1, when the exchange rate for French francs (F) was $0.15, International Corp. sold goods to a French company on account for F45,000. The account is due January 2. What journal entry should International make on December 31 if the value of the franc is $0.16? **A:**

Accounts Receivable
[F45,000 × ($0.16 –
   $0.15)] 450
  Foreign-Currency
   Transaction Gain 450

International will collect $450 more because the exchange rate has increased. Hence the gain.

Dec. 31	Foreign-Currency Transaction Loss		
	[140,000 × ($0.64 – $0.63)]	1,400	
	Accounts Receivable		1,400

This loss is *unrealized* in the sense that IBM has not yet received cash from the customer. If IBM collects on January 9, when the exchange rate is $0.62 per mark, the cash receipt entry records a further loss:

Jan. 9	Cash (140,000 × $0.62)...	86,800	
	Foreign-Currency Transaction Loss		
	[140,000 × ($0.63 – $0.62)]..	1,400	
	Accounts Receivable ($89,600 – $1,400)		88,200

IBM would have recorded a foreign-currency transaction gain on January 9 if the exchange rate had exceeded $0.63 per mark. In that case the cash collection would have been greater than the carrying amount of Accounts Receivable.

Hedging—A Strategy to Avoid Foreign-Currency Transaction Losses

One approach to avoiding foreign-currency transaction losses for U.S. companies is to insist that international transactions be settled in dollars, which puts the burden of currency translation on the foreign party. However, that strategy may alienate customers and lose sales, or it may cause suppliers to demand unreasonable credit terms. Another way for a company to insulate itself from the effects of fluctuating foreign-currency exchange rates is called hedging.

Hedging means to protect oneself from losing money in one transaction by engaging in a counterbalancing transaction. An American company selling goods measured in Mexican pesos expects to receive a fixed number of pesos in the future. If the peso is weak, the American company would expect the pesos to be worth fewer dollars than the amount of the receivable—an expected loss situation.

The American company may have accumulated payables stated in Mexican pesos in the normal course of its business. Losses on the receipt of pesos would be approximately offset by gains on the payment of pesos to Mexican suppliers. Most companies do not have equal amounts of receivables and payables in the same foreign currency. However, buying foreign currencies to be received in the future effectively creates a payable to offset a receivable and vice versa. Many companies that do business internationally use hedging techniques.

STOP & THINK Suppose you manage a division of Sara Lee Corporation that makes lots of sales to Mexico. Which hedging strategy would you prefer—(1) counterbalancing peso-denominated receivables against an equal amount of peso-denominated payables or (2) purchasing futures contracts for pesos? Give your reason.

Answer: You would prefer to counterbalance peso-denominated receivables and payables. That strategy avoids the cost of paying a commission to the seller of the futures contracts.

Consolidation of Foreign Subsidiaries

An American company with a foreign subsidiary must consolidate the subsidiary's financial statements into its own statements for reporting to the public. The consolidation of a foreign subsidiary poses two special challenges. Many countries outside the United States specify accounting treatments that differ from American accounting principles. For the purpose of reporting to the American public, accountants for the parent company must first bring the subsidiary's statements into conformity with American GAAP.

OBJECTIVE 6
Compute a foreign-currency translation adjustment

The second accounting challenge arises when the subsidiary statements are expressed in a foreign currency. A preliminary step in the consolidation process is to translate the subsidiary statements into dollars. Then the dollar-value statements of the subsidiary can be combined with the parent's statements in the usual manner, as illustrated in the first half of this chapter.

The process of translating a foreign subsidiary's financial statements into dollars may create a *foreign-currency translation adjustment*. This item appears in the financial statements of most multinational companies and is reported as part of stockholders' equity on the consolidated balance sheet. A translation adjustment arises because of changes in the foreign exchange rate over time. In general, *assets* and *liabilities* in the foreign subsidiaries' financial statements are translated into dollars at the exchange rate in effect on the date of the statements. However, *stockholders' equity* is translated into dollars at older, historical exchange rates. This difference in exchange rates creates an out-of-balance condition on the balance sheet. The translation adjustment amount brings the balance sheet back into balance.

Italian Imports, Inc., Amounts	Lire	Exchange Rate	Dollars
Assets	800,000,000	$0.00060	$480,000
Liabilities...	500,000,000	0.00060	$300,000
Stockholders' equity:			
Common stock	100,000,000	0.00070	70,000
Retained earnings................................	200,000,000	0.00067	134,000
Translation adjustment........................	—		(24,000)
	800,000,000		$480,000

Suppose U.S. Express Corporation owns Italian Imports, Inc., whose financial statements are expressed in lire. U.S. Express consolidates the Italian subsidiary's financial statements into its own financial statements. When U.S. Express acquired Italian Imports in 19X1, a lira was worth $0.00070. When Italian Imports earned its retained income during 19X1 through 19X6, the average exchange rate was $0.00067. On the balance sheet date in 19X6, a lira is worth only $0.00060. Exhibit 17-13 shows how to translate Italian Imports' balance sheet into dollars and illustrates how the translation adjustment arises.

The **foreign-currency translation adjustment** is the balancing amount that brings the dollar amount of the total liabilities and stockholders' equity of a foreign subsidiary into agreement with the dollar amount of its total assets ($480,000). Only after the translation adjustment do total liabilities and stockholders' equity equal total assets stated in dollars. In this case the translation adjustment is negative, and total stockholders' equity becomes $180,000 ($70,000 + $134,000 – $24,000).

What in the economic environment caused the negative translation adjustment? A weakening of the lira since the acquisition of Italian Imports brought about the need for this adjustment. When U.S. Express acquired the foreign subsidiary in 19X1, a lira was worth $0.00070. When Italian Imports earned its retained income during 19X1 through 19X6, the average exchange rate was $0.00067. On the balance sheet date in 19X6, a lira is worth only $0.00060, so Italian Imports' net assets (assets minus liabilities) are translated into only $180,000 ($480,000 – $300,000).

To bring stockholders' equity to $180,000 requires a $24,000 negative amount. In a sense, a negative translation adjustment is like a loss. But it is reported as a contra item in the stockholders' equity section of the balance sheet, not on the income statement. The Italian Imports dollar figures in Exhibit 17-13 are the amounts that U.S. Express Corporation would include in its consolidated balance sheet. The consolidation procedures would follow those illustrated beginning on page 692.

The translation adjustment can be positive—a gain—as well as negative, depending on the movement of foreign currency exchange rates. Consider Schlumberger Limited, a multinational industrial firm that explores for oil and gas and measures and manages electricity, water, and gas services. The following excerpt from Schlumberger Limited's actual balance sheet shows a positive translation adjustment:

Short Exercise: Assume that a subsidiary of a U.S. enterprise uses the French franc as its currency. During the year, the franc weakens against the dollar. (It takes more francs to make up one dollar). Will there be a positive or a negative translation adjustment? *A:* The subsidiary's assets are recorded in francs. The weakening of the franc means that when the asset's value is translated into U.S. dollars, that value is reduced. This situation creates a negative translation adjustment.

Stockholders' Equity	(Stated in Thousands)
Common Stock............................	$ 660,129
Income retained for use in the business..........................	6,106,461
Treasury stock at cost	(2,283,743)
Translation adjustment...............	(76,507)
	$ 4,406,340

Almost 60 percent of the 600 companies surveyed by *Accounting Trends & Techniques* report a translation adjustment on their balance sheet.

STOP & THINK Does Schlumberger's negative translation adjustment indicate a strong dollar or a weak dollar, relative to the foreign currencies of the countries where Schlumberger does business?

Answer: A negative translation adjustment indicates a *strong dollar*—weak foreign currencies relative to the dollar. It is as though Schlumberger has invested in the foreign currencies. When the foreign-currency amounts are translated into dollars, their current value in dollars is less than their historical cost. Thus Schlumberger has a loss on its net investment in foreign-currency-denominated assets. A *weak dollar*—strong foreign currencies—would produce a positive translation adjustment.

International Accounting Standards

For the most part, accounting principles are similar from country to country, but some important differences exist. For example, some countries, such as Italy, require financial statements to conform closely to income tax laws. In other countries, such as Brazil and Argentina, high inflation rates dictate that companies make price-level adjustments to report amounts in units of common purchasing power. Neither practice is followed as closely in the United States.

Several organizations are working to achieve worldwide harmony of accounting standards. Chief among these is the International Accounting Standards Committee (IASC). Headquartered in London, the IASC operates much as the Financial Accounting Standards Board in the United States. It has the support of the accounting professions in the United States, most of the British Commonwealth countries, Japan, France, Germany, the Netherlands, and Mexico. The IASC, however, has no authority to require compliance with its accounting standards. It must rely on cooperation by the various national accounting professions. Since its creation in 1973, the IASC has succeeded in narrowing some differences in international accounting standards.

SUMMARY PROBLEMS FOR YOUR REVIEW

PROBLEM 1

Journalize the following transactions of American Corp.:

19X5
Nov. 16   Purchased equipment on account for 40,000 Swiss francs when the exchange rate was $0.63 per Swiss franc.
   27   Sold merchandise on account to a Belgian company for 700,000 Belgian francs. Each franc is worth $0.0305.
Dec. 22   Paid the Swiss company when the franc's exchange rate was $0.625.
   31   Adjusted for the change in the exchange rate of the Belgian franc. Its current exchange rate is $0.0301.

19X6
Jan.   4   Collected from the Belgian company. The exchange rate is $0.0307.

PROBLEM 2

Translate the balance sheet of the Spanish subsidiary of American Corp. into dollars. When American acquired this subsidiary, the exchange rate of the peseta was $0.0101. The average exchange rate applicable to retained earnings is $0.0108. The peseta's current exchange rate is $0.0111.

Before performing the translation, predict whether the translation adjustment will be positive or negative. Does this situation generate a translation gain or a translation loss? Give your reasons.

	Pesetas
Assets...	200,000,000
Liabilities...................................	110,000,000
Stockholders' equity:	
Common stock....................	20,000,000
Retained earnings................	70,000,000
	200,000,000

SOLUTION TO REVIEW PROBLEMS

PROBLEM 1

Entries for transactions stated in foreign currencies:

19X5			
Nov. 16	Equipment (40,000 × $0.63)	25,200	
	Accounts Payable		25,200
27	Accounts Receivable (700,000 × $0.0305)	21,350	
	Sales Revenue..		21,350
Dec. 22	Accounts Payable	25,200	
	Cash (40,000 × $0.625)		25,000
	Foreign-Currency Transaction Gain		200
31	Foreign-Currency Transaction Loss		
	[700,000 × ($0.0305 – $0.0301)]	280	
	Accounts Receivable		280
19X6			
Jan. 4	Cash (700,000 × $0.0307)	21,490	
	Accounts Receivable ($21,350 – $280)............................		21,070
	Foreign-Currency Transaction Gain		420

PROBLEM 2

Translation of foreign-currency balance sheet:

This situation will generate a *positive* translation adjustment, which is like a gain. The gain occurs because the peseta's current exchange rate, which is used to translate net assets (assets minus liabilities), exceeds the historical exchange rates used for stockholders' equity.

	Pesetas	Exchange Rate	Dollars
Assets..	200,000,000	$0.0111	$2,220,000
Liabilities	110,000,000	0.0111	$1,221,000
Stockholders' equity:			
Common stock............................	20,000,000	0.0101	202,000
Retained earnings	70,000,000	0.0108	756,000
Translation adjustment...............	—		41,000
	200,000,000		$2,220,000

SUMMARY

1. **Account for trading investments in stock by the market value method.** Investments are classified as short-term or long-term. *Short-term investments* are liquid, and the investor intends to convert them to cash within one year or less or to use them to pay a current liability. All other investments are *long-term*.

Different methods are used to account for stock investments. All investments are recorded initially at *cost*. *Trading investments* are accounted for by the *market value method*—reported on the balance sheet at current market value with holding gains and losses shown on the income statement. *Available-for-sale investments* are accounted for by a combination of the cost and market value methods.

2. **Use the equity method for stock investments.** The *equity* method is used to account for investments of between 20 and 50 percent of the investee company's stock. Such an investment enables the investor to influence significantly the investee's activities. Investee income is recorded by the investor by debiting the Investment account and crediting an account entitled Equity-Method Investment Revenue. The investor records receipt of dividends from the investee by crediting the Investment account.

3. **Consolidate parent and subsidiary balance sheets.** Ownership of more than 50 percent of the voting stock creates a *parent-subsidiary* relationship, and the *consolidation* method must be used. Because the parent has control over the subsidiary, the subsidiary's financial statements are included in the consolidated statements of the parent company. Two features of consolidation accounting are (1) addition of the parent and subsidiary accounts to prepare the parent's consolidated statements and (2) elimination of intercompany items. When a parent owns less than 100 percent of the subsidiary's stock, the portion owned by outside investors is called *minority interest*. Purchase of a controlling interest at a cost greater than the market value of the subsidiary creates an intangible asset called *goodwill*. A consolidation work sheet is used to prepare the consolidated financial statements.

4. **Account for investments in bonds.** Trading investments in bonds are accounted for by the market value method. *Held-to-maturity investments* are accounted for at amortized cost.

5. **Account for transactions stated in a foreign currency.** *International accounting* deals with accounting for business activities across national boundaries. A key issue is the translation of foreign-currency amounts into dollars, accomplished through a *foreign-currency exchange rate*. Changes in exchange rates cause companies to experience *foreign-currency transaction gains* and *losses* on credit transactions.

6. **Compute a foreign-currency translation adjustment.** Consolidation of a foreign subsidiary's financial statements into the parent company's statements requires adjusting the subsidiary statements to American accounting principles and then translating the foreign-company statements into dollars. The translation process creates a *translation adjustment* that is reported in stockholders' equity. The International Accounting Standards Committee is working to harmonize accounting principles worldwide.

SELF-STUDY QUESTIONS

Test your understanding of the chapter by marking the best answer for each of the following questions.

1. Short-term investments are reported on the balance sheet (*p. 688*)
   a. Immediately after cash
   b. Immediately after accounts receivable
   c. Immediately after inventory
   d. Immediately after current assets

2. Byforth, Inc., distributes a 10-percent stock dividend. An investor who owns Byforth stock should (*p. 690*)
   a. Debit Investment and credit Dividend Revenue for the par value of the stock received in the dividend distribution
   b. Debit Investment and credit Dividend Revenue for the market value of the stock received in the dividend distribution
   c. Debit Cash and credit Investment for the market value of the stock received in the dividend distribution
   d. Make a memorandum entry to record the new number of shares of Byforth stock held

3. Trading investments are reported at the (*p. 688*)
   a. Total cost of the investment
   b. Total market value of the investment
   c. Lower of total cost or total market value of the investment
   d. Total equity value of the investment

4. Putsch Corporation owns 30 percent of the voting stock of Mazelli, Inc. Mazelli reports net income of $100,000 and declares and pays cash dividends of $40,000. Which method should Putsch use to account for this investment? (*p. 690*)
   a. Cost (with LCM)   c. Equity
   b. Market value   d. Consolidation

5. In Self-Study Question 4, what effect do Mazelli's income and dividends have on Putsch's net income? (*pp. 691–692*)
   a. Increase of $12,000   c. Increase of $30,000
   b. Increase of $18,000   d. Increase of $42,000

6. In applying the consolidation method, elimination entries are (*p. 695*)
   a. Necessary
   b. Required only when the parent has a receivable from, or a payable to, the subsidiary
   c. Required only when there is a minority interest
   d. Required only for the preparation of the consolidated balance sheet

7. Parent Company has separate net income of $155,000. Subsidiary A, of which Parent owns 90 percent, reports net income of $60,000, and Subsidiary B, of which Parent owns 60 percent, reports net income of $80,000. What is Parent Company's consolidated net income? (*p. 696*)
   a. $155,000   c. $263,000
   b. $257,000   d. $295,000

8. On May 16, the exchange rate of a German mark was $0.58. On May 20, the exchange rate is $0.57. Which of the following statements is true? *(pp. 703–704)*
   a. The dollar has risen against the mark.
   b. The dollar has fallen against the mark.
   c. The dollar is weaker than the mark.
   d. The dollar and the mark are equally strong.

9. A strong dollar encourages *(p. 705)*
   a. Travel to the United States by foreigners
   b. Purchase of American goods by foreigners
   c. Americans to travel abroad
   d. Americans to save dollars

10. Ford Motor Company purchased auto accessories from an English supplier at a price of 500,000 British pounds. On the date of the credit purchase, the exchange rate of the British pound was $1.50. On the payment date, the exchange rate of the pound is $1.52. If payment is in pounds, Ford experiences *(pp. 705–706)*
    a. A foreign-currency transaction gain of $10,000
    b. A foreign-currency transaction loss of $10,000
    c. Neither a transaction gain nor a loss because the debt is paid in dollars
    d. A translation adjustment to stockholders' equity

Answers to the Self-Study Questions follow the Accounting Vocabulary.

ACCOUNTING VOCABULARY

Available-for-sale securities. Stock investments other than trading securities and bond investments other than trading securities and held-to-maturity securities *(p. 688)*.

Consolidated statements. Financial statements of the parent company plus those of majority-owned subsidiaries as if the combination were a single legal entity *(p. 693)*.

Controlling (majority) interest. Ownership of more than 50 percent of an investee company's voting stock *(p. 692)*.

Equity method for investments. The method used to account for investments in which the investor has 20 to 50 percent of the investee's voting stock and can significantly influence the decisions of the investee. The investment account is debited for ownership in the investee's net income and credited for ownership in the investee's dividends *(p. 690)*.

Foreign-currency exchange rate. The measure of one currency against another currency *(p. 704)*.

Foreign-currency transaction gain or loss. A gain or loss that occurs when the exchange rate changes between the date of a purchase or sale on account and the subsequent payment or receipt of cash *(p. 705)*.

Foreign-currency translation adjustment. The balancing figure that brings the dollar amount of the total liabilities and stockholders' equity of a foreign subsidiary into agreement with the dollar amount of its total assets *(p. 708)*.

Hedging. Protecting oneself from losing money in one transaction by engaging in a counterbalancing transaction *(p. 707)*.

Held-to-maturity securities. Investment in bonds, notes, and other debt securities that the investor expects to hold until their maturity date *(p. 698)*.

Holding gain. A gain that arises from a change in the market value of an asset, not from a sale transaction *(p. 689)*.

Holding loss. A loss that arises from a change in the market value of an asset, not from a sale transaction *(p. 689)*.

Long-term investment. Separate asset category reported on the balance sheet between current assets and plant assets *(p. 687)*.

Marketable security. Another name for short-term investment *(p. 687)*.

Market value method for investments. Used to account for all trading investments in stocks and bonds. These investments are reported at their current market value *(p. 688)*.

Minority interest. A subsidiary company's equity that is held by stockholders other than the parent company *(p. 696)*.

Parent company. An investor company that owns more than 50 percent of the voting stock of a subsidiary company *(p. 692)*.

Short-term investment. Investment that is readily convertible to cash and that the investor intends either to convert to cash within one year or to use to pay a current liability; also called a marketable security, a current asset *(p. 687)*.

Strong currency. A currency that is rising relative to other nations' currencies *(p. 704)*.

Subsidiary company. An investee company in which a parent company owns more than 50 percent of the voting stock *(p. 692)*.

Trading securities. Investments that are to be sold in the very near future with the intent of generating profits on price changes *(p. 688)*.

Weak currency. A currency that is falling relative to other nations' currencies *(p. 704)*.

ANSWERS TO SELF-STUDY QUESTIONS

1. a
2. d
3. b
4. c
5. c ($100,000 × 0.30 = $30,000; dividends have *no* effect on investor net income under the equity method)
6. a
7. b [$155,000 + ($60,000 × 0.90) + ($80,000 × 0.60) = $257,000]
8. a
9. c
10. b [500,000 × ($1.52 − $1.50) = $10,000]

QUESTIONS

1. How are stock prices quoted in the securities market? What is the investor's cost of 1,000 shares of Ford Motor Company stock at 55 3/4, with a brokerage commission of $1,350?
2. What distinguishes a short-term investment from a long-term investment?
3. Show the positions of short-term investments and long-term investments on the balance sheet.
4. Outline the accounting methods for the different types of investments.
5. How does an investor record the receipt of a cash dividend on a trading investment? How does this investor record receipt of a stock dividend?
6. An investor paid $11,000 for 1,000 shares of stock—a trading investment—and later received a 10-percent stock dividend. At December 31, the investment's market value is $11,800. Compute the holding gain or loss on the investment.
7. At what amount are short-term investments reported on the balance sheet? What two categories can make up total short-term investments?
8. When is an investment accounted for by the equity method? Outline how to apply the equity method. Mention how to record the purchase of the investment, the investor's proportion of the investee's net income, and receipt of a cash dividend from the investee. Describe how to measure gain or loss on sale of this investment.
9. Identify three transactions that cause debits or credits to an equity-method investment account.
10. What are two special features of the consolidation method for investments?
11. Why are intercompany items eliminated from consolidated financial statements? Name two intercompany items that are eliminated.
12. Name the account that expresses the excess of cost of an investment over the market value of the subsidiary's owners' equity. What type of account is this, and where in the financial statements is it reported?
13. When a parent company buys less than 100 percent of a subsidiary's stock, a certain amount is created. What is it called, and how do most companies report it?
14. How would you measure the net income of a parent company with three subsidiaries? Assume that two subsidiaries are wholly (100 percent) owned and that the parent owns 60 percent of the third subsidiary.
15. What is the difference between accounting for a trading bond investment and accounting for a bond investment that will be held to maturity?
16. Explain the difference between a foreign-currency transaction gain or loss and a translation adjustment. Indicate the specific location in the financial statements where each item is reported.
17. Which of the following situations results in a foreign-currency transaction gain for an American business? Which situation results in a loss?
    a. Credit purchase denominated in pesos, followed by weakness in the peso
    b. Credit purchase denominated in pesos, followed by weakness in the dollar
    c. Credit sale denominated in pesos, followed by weakness in the peso
    d. Credit sale denominated in pesos, followed by weakness in the dollar
18. Explain the concept of hedging against foreign-currency transaction losses.
19. What is the difference between a realized foreign-currency transaction gain and an unrealized foreign-currency transaction gain?
20. McVey, Inc., acquired a foreign subsidiary when the foreign currency's exchange rate was $0.32. Over the years the foreign currency has steadily risen against the dollar. Will McVey's balance sheet report a positive or a negative translation adjustment?
21. Describe the computation of a foreign-currency translation adjustment.

EXERCISES

E17-1   Journalize the following trading investment transactions of Wonnacott, Inc.:

Journalizing transactions for a trading investment
(Obj. 1)

a. Purchased 400 shares (8 percent) of Advanced Corporation common stock at $44 per share, with the intent of selling the stock in the very near future.
b. Received cash dividend of $1 per share on the Advanced Corporation investment.
c. Sold the Advanced Corporation stock for the market price of $49 per share.

E17-2   Late in the current year, Nafta Corporation bought 3,000 shares of Boeing common stock at $37.375, 600 shares of Anheuser-Busch stock at $46.75, and 1,400 shares of Hitachi stock at $79—all as trading investments. At December 31, *The Wall Street Journal* reports Boeing stock at $39.125, Anheuser-Busch at $48.50, and Hitachi at $68.25.

Accounting for short-term investment transactions
(Obj. 1)

Required

1. Compute the cost and the market value of the short-term investment portfolio at December 31.
2. Journalize any adjusting entry needed at December 31.
3. Report the balance sheet and the income statement effects of the information given.

Journalizing transactions under the equity method (Obj. 2)

E17-3 Sears, Roebuck and Co. owns equity-method investments in several companies. Suppose Sears paid $2 million to acquire a 25-percent investment in All-Star Company. Assume that All-Star Company reported net income of $640,000 for the first year and declared and paid cash dividends of $420,000. Record the following in Sears's general journal: (a) purchase of the investment, (b) Sears's proportion of All-Star's net income, and (c) receipt of the cash dividends.

Recording equity-method transactions directly in the accounts (Obj. 2)

E17-4 Without making journal entries, record the transactions of Exercise 17-3 directly in the Investment in All-Star Company Common Stock account. Assume that after all the above transactions took place, Sears sold its entire investment in All-Star common stock for cash of $2,400,000. Journalize the sale of the investment.

Comparing the equity and market value methods (Obj. 1, 2)

E17-5 Mellon Corporation paid $160,000 for a 40-percent investment in the common stock of Kahn, Inc. For the first year, Kahn reported net income of $84,000 and at year end declared and paid cash dividends of $16,000. On the balance sheet date, the market value of Mellon's investment in Kahn stock was $134,000.

Required

1. On Mellon's books, journalize the purchase of the investment, recognition of Mellon's portion of Kahn's net income, and receipt of dividends from Kahn under the method appropriate for these circumstances.
2. Repeat Requirement 1 but follow the market value method for comparison purposes only.
3. Show the amount that Mellon would report for the investment on its year-end balance sheet under the two methods.

Completing a consolidation work sheet with minority interest (Obj. 3)

E17-6 Lyle Gas Corp. owns a 90-percent interest in Gore, Inc. Complete the following consolidation work sheet.

Assets	Lyle Gas Corp.	Gore, Inc.
Cash	$ 49,000	$ 14,000
Accounts receivable, net	82,000	53,000
Note receivable from Lyle Gas	—	12,000
Inventory	114,000	77,000
Investment in Gore	90,000	—
Plant assets, net	186,000	129,000
Other assets	22,000	8,000
Total	$543,000	$293,000

Liabilities and Stockholders' Equity		
Accounts payable	$ 44,000	$ 26,000
Notes payable	47,000	36,000
Other liabilities	82,000	131,000
Minority interest	—	—
Common stock	210,000	80,000
Retained earnings	160,000	20,000
Total	$543,000	$293,000

Elimination entries under the consolidation method (Obj. 3)

E17-7 Assume that on December 31 Shearson Financial Consultants, a 100-percent-owned subsidiary of American Express Company, had the following owners' equity:

Common Stock	$2,000,000
Retained Earnings	4,100,000

Assume further that American Express's cost of its investment in Shearson was $6,100,000 and that Shearson owed American Express $319,000 on a note.

Required

Give the work sheet entry in general journal form to eliminate (a) the investment of American Express and the stockholders' equity of Shearson and (b) the note receivable of American Express and note payable of Shearson.

E17-8   On March 31 Petrol Corporation paid 92 1/4 for 7-percent bonds of Keating Company as a trading investment. The maturity value of the bonds is $20,000, and they pay interest on March 31 and September 30. Record Petrol's purchase of the bond investment, the receipt of semi-annual interest on September 30, and the accrual of interest revenue on December 31. At December 31, the bonds' market value is 93. Show how the investment would be reported on the balance sheet at December 31.

Recording trading bond investment transactions (Obj. 4)

E17-9   Assume that the Keating Company bonds in Exercise 17-8 are purchased as a long-term investment on March 31, 19X3, to be held to maturity on September 30, 19X7.

Recording long-term bond investment transactions (Obj. 4)

Required

1. Using the straight-line method of amortizing the discount, journalize all transactions on the bonds for 19X3.
2. How much more interest revenue would the investor record in 19X3 for a long-term investment than for a trading investment in these bonds? What accounts for this difference?
3. Show how the investment would be reported on the balance sheet at December 31.

E17-10   Journalize the following foreign-currency transactions:

Journalizing foreign-currency transactions (Obj. 5)

Nov. 17   Purchased goods on account from a Japanese company. The price was 200,000 yen, and the exchange rate of the yen was $0.0090.

Dec. 16   Paid the Japanese supplier when the exchange rate was $0.0091.

   19   Sold merchandise on account to a French company at a price of 60,000 French francs. The exchange rate was $0.16.

   31   Adjusted for the drop in value of the franc, which had an exchange rate of $0.155.

Jan. 14   Collected from the French company when the exchange rate was $0.17.

E17-11   Translate into dollars the balance sheet of Illinois Tool Company's Italian subsidiary. When Illinois acquired the foreign subsidiary, an Italian lira was worth $0.00080. The current exchange rate is $0.00085. During the period when retained earnings were earned, the average exchange rate was $0.00088.

Translating a foreign-currency balance sheet into dollars (Obj. 6)

   Before you perform the translation operation, predict whether the translation adjustment will be positive (a gain) or negative (a loss). Explain your answer.

	Lire
Assets	500,000,000
Liabilities	300,000,000
Stockholders' equity:	
Common stock	100,000,000
Retained earnings	100,000,000
	500,000,000

CHALLENGE EXERCISES

E17-12   Whirlpool Corporation is a leading manufacturer of household appliances. In Brazil and Mexico Whirlpool operates through affiliated companies, whose stock Whirlpool owns in various percentages between 20 and 50 percent. Whirlpool's financial statements reported these items:

Analyzing an actual company's financial statements (Obj. 2)

	Millions of Dollars	
	19X2	19X1
Balance Sheet		
Investment in affiliated companies	$282	$296
Statement of Cash Flows		
Increase in investment in affiliated companies	12	2
Statement of Earnings		
Equity in net earnings (losses) of affiliated companies	(13)	4

Whirlpool's financial statements reported no sales of investments in affiliated companies during 19X2 or 19X1.

Required

Compute the amount of dividends Whirlpool Corporation received from affiliated companies during 19X2. Show your work.

E17-13   Whirlpool Corporation reported the following stockholders' equity:

Stockholders' Equity	Millions of Dollars 19X2	19X1
Capital stock	$ 76	$ 75
Paid-in capital	47	37
Retained earnings	1,721	1,593
Other..	(18)	(12)
Cumulative translation adjustments..............	(49)	(1)
Treasury stock—at cost.................................	(177)	(177)
	$1,600	$1,515

Whirlpool owns controlling interests in several subsidiary companies that are incorporated in foreign countries, mainly in Europe. During 19X2, was the U.S. dollar strong or weak relative to the monetary currencies of these European countries? Explain your answer.

PROBLEMS   (GROUP A)

P17-1A   Toyota Motor Company owns numerous investments in the stock of American companies. Assume that Toyota completed the following investment transactions:

19X4

May   1   Purchased 8,000 shares, which exceeds 20 percent, of the common stock of MIC Company at total cost of $720,000.

July   1   Purchased 1,600 additional shares of MIC Company common stock at cost of $140,000.

Sep. 15   Received semiannual cash dividend of $1.40 per share on the MIC investment.

Oct. 12   Purchased 1,000 shares of JAX Corporation common stock as a short-term investment, paying $22 1/2 per share.

Dec. 14   Received semiannual cash dividend of $0.75 per share on the JAX investment.

Dec. 31   Received annual report from MIC Company. Net income for the year was $350,000. Of this amount, Toyota's proportion is 21.25 percent.

The current market value of the JAX stock is $20,700.

19X5

Feb.   6   Sold 1,920 shares of MIC stock for net cash of $169,700.

Required

Record the transactions in the general journal of Toyota Motor Company.

P17-2A   The beginning balance sheet of Four Seasons, Inc., included:

Investments in Affiliates $1,057,000

The company completed the following investment transactions during the year:

Mar.   3   Purchased 5,000 shares of common stock as a trading investment, paying $9 1/4 per share.

        4   Purchased new long-term investment in affiliate at cost of $408,000.

May 14   Received semiannual cash dividend of $0.82 per share on the trading investment purchased March 3.

June 15   Received cash dividend of $27,000 from affiliated company.

Aug. 28   Sold the trading investment (purchased on March 3) for $10 1/2 per share. Adjusted the entire investment to current market value and then recorded the sale.

Oct. 24   Purchased trading investments for $226,000.

Dec. 15   Received cash dividend of $29,000 from affiliated company.

      31   Received annual reports from affiliated companies. Their total net income for the year was $620,000. Of this amount, Four Seasons' proportion is 30 percent.

The market value of trading investments is $219,000.

Required

1. Record the transactions in the general journal of Four Seasons.
2. Post entries to the Investments in Affiliates T-account, and determine its balance at December 31. Do likewise for the Trading Investments T-account.
3. Show how to report the Trading Investments and the Investments in Affiliates at December 31.

P17-3A Walesa Corporation paid $179,000 to acquire all the common stock of Ritz, Inc., and Ritz owes Walesa $55,000 on a note payable. Immediately after the purchase on May 31, 19X7, the two companies' balance sheets were as follows:

Preparing a consolidated balance sheet
(Obj. 3)

Assets	Walesa Corporation	Ritz, Inc.
Cash...................................	$ 18,000	$ 32,000
Accounts receivable, net	64,000	43,000
Note receivable from Ritz	55,000	—
Inventory....................................	93,000	153,000
Investment in Ritz...........................	179,000	—
Plant assets, net	205,000	138,000
Total	$614,000	$366,000

Liabilities and Stockholders' Equity		
Accounts payable...........................	$ 76,000	$ 37,000
Notes payable................................	118,000	123,000
Other liabilities	44,000	27,000
Common stock..............................	282,000	90,000
Retained earnings...........................	94,000	89,000
Total	$614,000	$366,000

Required

1. Prepare a consolidation work sheet.
2. Prepare the consolidated balance sheet on May 31, 19X7. Show total assets, total liabilities, and total stockholders' equity. It is not necessary to classify assets and liabilities as current and long-term.

P17-4A On August 17, 19X8, Kenya Printing Corp. paid $229,000 to purchase all the common stock of Travelers, Inc., and Travelers owes Kenya Printing $42,000 on a note payable. Immediately after the purchase, the two companies' balance sheets were as follows:

Preparing a consolidated balance sheet
(Obj. 3)

Assets	Kenya Printing Corp.	Travelers, Inc.
Cash	$ 23,000	$ 37,000
Accounts receivable, net........................	71,000	54,000
Note receivable from Travelers	42,000	—
Inventory	213,000	170,000
Investment in Travelers...........................	229,000	—
Plant assets, net	197,000	175,000
Goodwill..	—	—
Total..	$775,000	$436,000

Liabilities and Stockholders' Equity		
Accounts payable	$119,000	$ 77,000
Notes payable	190,000	71,000
Other liabilities..................................	33,000	88,000
Common stock	219,000	113,000
Retained earnings...............................	214,000	87,000
Total..	$775,000	$436,000

Required

1. Prepare a consolidation work sheet.
2. Prepare the consolidated balance sheet on August 17, 19X8. Show total assets, total liabilities, and total stockholders' equity. It is not necessary to classify assets and liabilities as current and long-term.

Accounting for a bond investment purchased at a discount
(Obj. 4)

P17-5A Financial institutions such as insurance companies and pension plans hold large quantities of bond investments. Suppose The Prudential Insurance Company purchases $500,000 of 8-percent bonds of General Motors Corporation for 92 on January 31, 19X0. These bonds pay interest on January 31 and July 31 each year. They mature on July 31, 19X8. At December 31, 19X0, the market price of the bonds is 93.

Required

1. Journalize Prudential's purchase of the bonds as a long-term investment on January 31, 19X0 (to be held to maturity), receipt of cash interest and amortization of discount on July 31, 19X0, and accrual of interest revenue and amortization of discount at December 31, 19X0. Assume that the straight-line method is appropriate for amortizing discount.
2. Show all financial statement effects of this long-term bond investment at December 31, 19X0. Assume a multiple-step income statement.
3. Repeat Requirement 2 under the assumption that Prudential purchased these bonds as a trading investment.

Note: Problem 17-6A is based on the appendix in Chapter 16.

Computing the cost of a bond investment and journalizing its transactions
(Obj. 4)

P17-6A On December 31, 19X1, when the market interest rate is 10 percent, an investor purchases $400,000 of Tepotzlan, Inc., 10-year, 9.5-percent bonds at issuance. Determine the cost (present value) of this bond investment, which the investor expects to hold to maturity. Journalize the purchase on December 31, 19X1, the first semiannual interest receipt on June 30, 19X2, and the year-end interest receipt on December 31, 19X2. The investor uses the effective-interest amortization method. Prepare a schedule for amortizing the premium on the bond investment through December 31, 19X2. If necessary, refer to Chapter 16 and its appendix.

Journalizing foreign-currency transactions and reporting the transaction gain or loss, translating a foreign-currency balance sheet
(Obj. 5, 6)

P17-7A *Part A.* Suppose United Mining Corporation completed the following transactions:

Dec. 1 Sold iron ore on account to Pirelli Tire Company for $19,000. The exchange rate of the Italian lira is $0.0007, and Pirelli agrees to pay in dollars.
       10 Purchased supplies on account from a Canadian company at a price of Canadian $50,000. The exchange rate of the Canadian dollar is $0.80, and payment will be in Canadian dollars.
       17 Sold inventory on account to an English firm for 100,000 British pounds. Payment will be in pounds, and the exchange rate of the pound is $1.50.
       22 Collected from Pirelli.
       31 Adjusted the accounts for changes in foreign-currency exchange rates. Current rates: Canadian dollar, $0.82; English pound, $1.58.
Jan. 18 Paid the Canadian company. The exchange rate of the Canadian dollar is $0.77.
       24 Collected from the English firm. The exchange rate of the British pound is $1.57.

Required

1. Record these transactions in United's general journal, and show how to report the transaction gain or loss on the income statement.
2. How will what you learned in this problem help you structure international transactions?

Part B. Suppose that Alaskan, Inc., owns a subsidiary based in Denmark.

Required

1. Translate the foreign-currency balance sheet of the Danish subsidiary of Alaskan, Inc., into dollars. When Alaskan acquired this subsidiary, the Danish krone was worth $0.17. The current exchange rate is $0.16. During the period when the subsidiary earned its income, the average exchange rate was $0.18 per krone.

Before you perform the translation calculations, indicate whether Alaskan has experienced a positive or a negative translation adjustment. State whether the adjustment is a gain or a loss. Explain your answer.

	Krone
Assets	3,000,000
Liabilities................................	1,000,000
Stockholders' equity:	
Common stock	300,000
Retained earnings................	1,700,000
	3,000,000

2. How will what you learned in this problem help you understand published financial statements?

(GROUP B)

P17-1B   Segovia Packing Company owns numerous investments in the stock of other companies. Assume that Segovia completed the following investment transactions:

Journalizing transactions under the market value and equity methods
(Obj. 1, 2)

19X2

Feb. 12   Purchased 20,000 shares, which exceeds 20 percent, of the common stock of Agribusiness, Inc., at total cost of $715,000.
July   1   Purchased 8,000 additional shares of Agribusiness common stock at cost of $300,000.
Aug. 9   Received annual cash dividend of $0.90 per share on the Agribusiness investment.
Oct. 16   Purchased 800 shares of Apex Company common stock as a trading investment, paying $41 1/2 per share.
Nov. 30   Received semiannual cash dividend of $0.60 per share on the Apex investment.
Dec. 31   Received annual report from Agribusiness, Inc. Net income for the year was $510,000. Of this amount, Segovia's proportion is 35 percent.

The current market value of the Apex stock is $34,100.

19X3

Mar. 3   Sold 4,000 shares of Agribusiness stock for net cash of $141,000.

Required

Record the transactions in the general journal of Segovia Packing Company.

P17-2B   The beginning balance sheet of Picadilly Incorporated included:

Applying the market value method and the equity method
(Obj. 1, 2)

Investments in Affiliates $6,344,000

The company completed the following investment transactions during the year:

Mar   2   Purchased 2,000 shares of common stock as a trading investment, paying $12 1/4 per share.
       5   Purchased new long-term investment in affiliate at cost of $540,000.
Apr. 21   Received semiannual cash dividend of $0.75 per share on the trading investment purchased March 2.
May 17   Received cash dividend of $47,000 from affiliated company.
July 16   Sold the trading investment (purchased on March 2) for $10 1/8 per share. Adjusted the entire investment to current market value and then recorded the sale.
Oct. 8   Purchased trading investments in stock for $136,000.
      17   Received cash dividend of $49,000 from affiliated company.
Dec. 31   Received annual reports from affiliated companies. Their total net income for the year was $550,000. Of this amount, Picadilly's proportion is 22 percent.

The market value of trading investments is $142,000.

Required

1. Record the transactions in the general journal of Picadilly Incorporated.
2. Post entries to the Investments in Affiliates T-account, and determine its balance at December 31. Do likewise for the Trading Investments T-account.
3. Show how to report the Trading Investments and the Investments in Affiliates at December 31.

Preparing a consolidated balance sheet
(Obj. 3)

P17-3B Ben Silver Corp. paid $266,000 to acquire all the common stock of Massada, Inc., and Massada owes Ben Silver $81,000 on a note payable. Immediately after the purchase on June 30, 19X3, the two companies' balance sheets were as follows:

Assets	Ben Silver Corp.	Massada, Inc.
Cash	$ 24,000	$ 20,000
Accounts receivable, net	91,000	42,000
Note receivable from Massada	81,000	—
Inventory	145,000	214,000
Investment in Massada	266,000	—
Plant assets, net	178,000	219,000
Total	$785,000	$495,000

Liabilities and Stockholders' Equity		
Accounts payable	$ 57,000	$ 49,000
Notes payable	177,000	149,000
Other liabilities	129,000	31,000
Common stock	274,000	118,000
Retained earnings	148,000	148,000
Total	$785,000	$495,000

Required

1. Prepare a consolidation work sheet.
2. Prepare the consolidated balance sheet on June 30, 19X3. Show total assets, total liabilities, and total stockholders' equity. It is not necessary to classify assets and liabilities as current and long-term.

Preparing a consolidated balance sheet
(Obj. 3)

P17-4B On March 22, 19X4, Viking Travel Corp. paid $280,000 to purchase 80 percent of the common stock of Seaboard Cruise Line, and Seaboard owes Viking $67,000 on a note payable. Immediately after the purchase, the two companies' balance sheets were as follows:

Assets	Viking Travel Corp.	Seaboard Cruise Line
Cash	$ 41,000	$ 43,000
Accounts receivable, net	86,000	75,000
Note receivable from Seaboard	67,000	—
Inventory	128,000	206,000
Investment in Seaboard	280,000	—
Plant assets, net	277,000	168,000
Total	$879,000	$492,000

Liabilities and Stockholders' Equity		
Accounts payable	$ 72,000	$ 65,000
Notes payable	301,000	67,000
Other liabilities	11,000	10,000
Minority interest	—	—
Common stock	141,000	160,000
Retained earnings	354,000	190,000
Total	$879,000	$492,000

Required

1. Prepare a consolidation work sheet.
2. Prepare the consolidated balance sheet on March 22, 19X4. Show total assets, total liabilities, and total stockholders' equity. It is not necessary to classify assets and liabilities as current and long-term.

P17-5B Financial institutions such as insurance companies and pension plans hold large quantities of bond investments. Suppose Ostway Insurance Co. purchases $600,000 of 9-percent bonds of Royal Corporation for 103 on March 1, 19X1. These bonds pay interest on March 1 and September 1 each year. They mature on March 1, 19X8. At December 31, 19X1, the market price of the bonds is 103 1/2.

Accounting for a bond investment purchased at a premium (Obj. 4)

Required

1. Journalize Ostway's purchase of the bonds as a long-term investment on March 1, 19X1 (to be held to maturity), receipt of cash interest, and amortization of premium at December 31, 19X1. Assume that the straight-line method is appropriate for amortizing premium.
2. Show all financial statement effects of this long-term bond investment at December 31, 19X1. Assume a multiple-step income statement.
3. Repeat Requirement 2 under the assumption that Ostway purchased these bonds as a trading investment.

Note: Problem 17-6B is based on the appendix in Chapter 16.

P17-6B On December 31, 19X1, when the market interest rate is 8 percent, an investor purchases $500,000 of Bali Corp. 6-year, 7.4-percent bonds at issuance. Determine the cost (present value) of this long-term bond investment, which the investor expects to hold to maturity. Journalize the purchase on December 31, 19X1, the first semiannual interest receipt on June 30, 19X2, and the year-end interest receipt on December 31, 19X2. The investor uses the effective-interest amortization method. Prepare a schedule for amortizing the discount on bond investment through December 31, 19X2. If necessary, refer to Chapter 16 and its appendix.

Computing the cost of a bond investment to be held to maturity and journalizing its transactions (Obj. 4)

P17-7B *Part A.* Suppose PepsiCo, Inc., completed the following transactions:

Journalizing foreign-currency transactions and reporting the transaction gain or loss, translating a foreign-currency balance sheet (Obj. 5, 6)

May 4	Sold soft-drink syrup on account to a Mexican company for $71,000. The exchange rate of the Mexican peso is $0.0004, and the customer agrees to pay in dollars.
13	Purchased inventory on account from a Canadian company at a price of Canadian $100,000. The exchange rate of the Canadian dollar is $0.75, and payment will be in Canadian dollars.
20	Sold goods on account to an English firm for 70,000 British pounds. Payment will be in pounds, and the exchange rate of the pound is $1.50.
27	Collected from the Mexican company.
31	Adjusted the accounts for changes in foreign-currency exchange rates. Current rates: Canadian dollar, $0.76; English pound, $1.49.
June 21	Paid the Canadian company. The exchange rate of the Canadian dollar is $0.72.
July 17	Collected from the English firm. The exchange rate of the British pound is $1.47.

Required

1. Record these transactions in PepsiCo's general journal, and show how to report the transaction gain or loss on the income statement.
2. How will what you learned in this problem help you structure international transactions?

Part B. Suppose that Cunard, Inc., has a subsidiary company based in Japan.

Required

1. Translate into dollars the foreign-currency balance sheet of the Japanese subsidiary of Cunard, Inc. When Cunard acquired this subsidiary, the Japanese yen was worth $0.0064. The current exchange rate is $0.0093. During the period when the subsidiary earned its income, the average exchange rate was $0.0089 per yen.

Before you perform the translation calculations, indicate whether Cunard has experienced a positive or a negative translation adjustment. State whether the adjustment is a gain or a loss and show where it is reported in the financial statements.

	Yen
Assets	300,000,000
Liabilities	80,000,000
Stockholders' equity:	
Common stock	20,000,000
Retained earnings	200,000,000
	300,000,000

2. How will what you learned in this problem help you understand published financial statements?

EXTENDING YOUR KNOWLEDGE

DECISION PROBLEMS

Understanding the cost and equity methods of accounting for investments
(Obj. 1, 2)

1. Leann Masai is the accountant for AAdvantage Corp., whose year end is December 31. The company made two investments during the first week of January 19X7. Both investments are to be held for at least five years. Information about the investments follows:

a. AAvantage purchased 30 percent of the common stock of Rotary Motor Co. for its book value of $200,000. During the year ended December 31, 19X7, Rotary earned $106,000 and paid a total dividend of $53,000.

b. One thousand shares of the common stock of Oxford Medical Corporation was purchased as a trading investment for $95,000. During the year ended December 31, 19X7, Oxford paid AAdvantage a dividend of $3,000. Oxford earned a profit of $317,000 for that period, and at year end the market value of AAdvantage's investment in Oxford stock was $107,000.

Masai has come to you, her auditor, to ask how to account for the investments. AAvantage has never had such investments before. You attempt to explain the proper accounting to her by indicating that different accounting methods apply to different situations.

Required

Help Masai understand by:

1. Describing the methods of accounting applicable to these investments.
2. Identifying which method should be used to account for the investments in Rotary Motor Co. and Oxford Medical Corporation.

Understanding the consolidation method for investments and for international accounting
(Obj. 3, 6)

2. Vijay Karan inherited some investments, and he has received the annual reports of the companies in which the funds are invested. The financial statements of the companies are puzzling to Karan, and he asks you the following questions:

a. The companies label their financial statements as *consolidated* balance sheet, *consolidated* income statement, and so on. What are consolidated financial statements?

b. Notes to the statements indicate that "certain intercompany transactions, loans, and other accounts have been eliminated in preparing the consolidated financial statements." Why does a company eliminate transactions, loans, and accounts? Karan states that he thought a transaction was a transaction and that a loan obligated a company to pay real money. He wonders if the company is juggling the books to defraud the IRS.

c. The balance sheet lists the asset Goodwill. What is Goodwill? Does this mean that the company's stock has increased in value?

d. The stockholders' equity section of the balance sheet reports Translation Adjustments. Karan asks what is being translated and why this item is negative.

Required

Respond to each of Karan's questions.

ETHICAL ISSUE

Dover Corporation owns 18 percent of the voting stock of Hassan, Inc. The remainder of the Hassan stock is held by numerous investors with small holdings. Monica Kurtz, president of Dover and a member of Hassan's board of directors, heavily influences Hassan's policies.

Under the market value method of accounting for investments, Dover's net income increases as it receives dividends from Hassan. Dover pays President Kurtz a bonus computed as a percentage of Dover's net income. Therefore, Kurtz can control her personal bonus to a certain extent by influencing Hassan's dividends.

A recession occurs in 19X0, and corporate income is low. Kurtz uses her power to have Hassan, Inc., pay a large cash dividend. The action requires Hassan to borrow so heavily that it may lead to financial difficulty.

Required

1. In getting Hassan to pay the large cash dividend, is Kurtz acting within her authority as a member of the Hassan board of directors? Are Kurtz's actions ethical? Whom can her actions harm?

2. Discuss how using the equity method of accounting for investments would decrease Kurtz's potential for manipulating her bonus.

FINANCIAL STATEMENT PROBLEMS

1. Use the Lands' End, Inc., financial statements in Appendix A to answer the following questions about Lands' End's investments in the stock of other companies.

Investments in stock
(Obj. 3)

1. Lands' End's last asset on its balance sheet is Intangibles, Net (of Accumulated Amortization). Note 1 states that goodwill is the company's main intangible asset. Explain the nature of Lands' End's goodwill, and tell how the goodwill arose during the year ended January 28, 1994. Note 9 gives additional details.

2. During the year ended January 28, 1994, Lands' End's intangibles increased dramatically. Assume for this requirement that goodwill is the company's only intangible asset. During the year, Lands' End's amortization of goodwill was approximately $50,000. Analyze the Intangibles (Goodwill) account to compute the amount of goodwill Lands' End purchased during the year. A T-account helps.

3. Lands' End's last liability on its balance sheet is Minority Interest in Equity of Consolidated Affiliate. Explain the nature of this item, and tell why it is a liability. Note 9 gives the details.

2. Obtain the annual report of an actual company of your choosing. Answer the following questions about the company. Concentrate on the current year in the annual report you select.

Investments in stock
(Obj. 1, 2, 3)

1. Many companies refer to other companies in which they own equity-method investments as *affiliated companies*. This signifies the close relationship between the two entities even though the investor does not own a controlling interest.

   Does the company have equity-method investments? Cite the evidence. If present, what were the balances in the investment account at the beginning and the end of the current year? If the company had no equity-method investments, skip the next question.

2. Scan the income statement. If equity-method investments are present, what amount of revenue (or income) did the company earn on the investments during the current year? Scan the statement of cash flows. What amount of dividends did the company receive during the current year from companies in which it held equity-method investments? Note: The amount of dividends received may not be disclosed. If not, you can still compute the amount of dividends received, from the following T-account:

Investments, at Equity			
Beg. bal. (from balance sheet)	W		
Equity-method revenue (from income statement)	X	Dividends received (unknown; must compute)	Y
End. bal. (from balance sheet)	Z		

3. The company probably owns some consolidated subsidiaries. You can tell whether the parent company owns 100 percent or less of the subsidiaries. Examine the income statement and the balance sheet to determine whether there are any minority interests. If so, what does that fact indicate?

4. The stockholders' equity section of most balance sheets lists Foreign Currency Translation Adjustment or a similar account title. A positive amount signifies a gain, and a negative amount indicates a loss. The change in this account balance from the beginning of the year to the end of the year signals whether the U.S. dollar was strong or weak during the year in comparison to the foreign currencies. For the company you are analyzing, was the dollar strong or weak during the current year?

COMPREHENSIVE PROBLEMS FOR PART THREE

1. ACCOUNTING FOR CORPORATE TRANSACTIONS

Gateway International's corporate charter authorizes the company to issue 1 million shares of $1-par value common stock and 200,000 shares of 5-percent, $10-par value preferred stock. During the first quarter of operations, Gateway completed the following selected transactions:

Oct. 1   Issued 75,000 shares of common stock for cash of $6 per share.

     2   Signed a capital lease for equipment. The lease requires a down payment of $50,000, plus 20 quarterly lease payments of $10,000. Present value of the future lease payments is $135,900 at an annual interest rate of 16 percent.

     5   Issued 2,000 shares of preferred stock to attorneys who helped organize the corporation. Their bill listed legal services of $22,000.

     22   Received land from the county as an incentive for locating in Augusta. Fair market value of the land was $260,000.

     30   Purchased 5,000 shares (20 percent) of the outstanding common stock of Newbold Corp. as a long-term investment, $85,000.

Nov. 1   Issued $200,000 of 9-percent, 10-year bonds payable at 94.

     14   Purchased trading investments in the common stocks of PepsiCo, $22,000, and Data General, $31,000.

     19   Experienced an extraordinary flood loss of inventory that cost $21,000. Cash received from the insurance company was $8,000.

     20   Purchased 10,000 shares of Gateway common stock for the treasury at $5 per share.

Dec. 1   Received cash dividends of $1,100 on the PepsiCo investment.

     16   Sold 1,000 shares of the treasury stock for cash of $6.25 per share.

     29   Received a report from Newbold Corp. indicating that net income for November and December was $70,000.

     30   Sold merchandise on account, $716,000. Cost of the goods was $439,000. Operating expenses totaled $174,000, with $166,000 of this amount paid in cash. Gateway uses a perpetual inventory system.

     31   Accrued interest and amortized discount (straight-line method) on the bonds payable.

     31   Accrued interest on the capital lease liability.

     31   Depreciated the equipment acquired by the capital lease. The company uses the double-declining-balance method.

     31   Market values of the trading investments: PepsiCo stock, $24,000, and the Data General stock, $30,000.

     31   Accrued income tax expense of $136,000.

     31   Closed all revenues, expenses, and losses to Retained Earnings in a single closing entry.

     31   Declared a quarterly cash dividend of $0.125 per share on the preferred stock. Record date is January 11, with payment scheduled for January 19.

Required

1. Record these transactions in the general journal. Explanations are not required.

2. Prepare a single-step income statement, including earnings per share, for the quarter ended December 31. Income tax expense of $136,000 should be reported as follows: Income tax expense of $141,000 applies to income before extraordinary items. The tax effect of the extraordinary loss is an income tax saving of $5,000.

3. Report the liabilities and the stockholders' equity as they would appear on the balance sheet at December 31.

2. GROUP PROJECT: REFINING YOUR BUSINESS PLAN TO INCLUDE CORPORATE TRANSACTIONS

Review the business plan for an audio/video store (or other business) that you developed at the end of Part 1 and refined at the end of Part 2. Since that time you have learned about partnerships and more about corporations and international operations.

Revise your business plan to include refinements that apply to stockholders' equity, long-term debt, investments, and international operations. For example, consider the classes of stock you may wish to issue, the amount of long-term debt financing your business may use, and your business's policies on dividends and treasury stock. Will international operations affect your business? Be as specific as possible, and identify all the factors you consider important for success.

Wal-Mart Stores, Inc.

The acknowledged giant in the retail sector of the U.S. economy is Wal-Mart. Behind its carefully groomed image of homespun values and low prices lies a high-technology, high-powered organization that has succeeded in reaping huge rewards for its shareholders over time.

From its beginnings as a single store opened by Sam Walton in Arkansas almost 50 years ago, Wal-Mart has grown to a $32.6 billion retailing empire today. Its strategies for success include the following:

- Wal-Mart is a leader in the effective use of computers to manage inventory levels, monitor product sales information, and control purchasing. Optimizing the use of resources for billions of dollars in inventory purchased and sold helps Wal-Mart maximize the profits earned on its shareholders' investments.
- As one of the first department stores to use bar code scanning, Wal-Mart created information systems that permit instantaneous exchanges of inventory data. Even its suppliers can access by computer information on inventory levels and sales of their products at Wal-Mart locations.
- Wal-Mart motivates its employees with programs such as profit-sharing plans and a team approach that encourages and values suggestions from staff on improving service.
- Customers are lured with low prices and amenities such as knowledgeable in-store greeters. Wal-Mart also conducts extensive market-research surveys to identify consumer needs and desires.

Combining traditional, down-to-earth values with state-of-the-art information and management techniques has paid off. The Waltons are now the wealthiest family in the United States. And an investor wise enough to purchase 100 shares of Wal-Mart stock for $1,650 in 1974 would now hold stock worth more than $2 million. Analysts credit Wal-Mart's knack at managing inventory "on the shelves" with making its stock so attractive to investors.

The company's continued expansion with new stores has recently begun to meet resistance. Residents of some communities are organizing to prevent planned construction of Wal-Mart stores, claiming that local retailers will be forced out of business and that the small-town atmosphere they value will suffer.

CASE QUESTIONS

1. Suppose Wal-Mart issued 100 shares of common stock in 1974 for $1,650. How would the company have recorded the issuance of those shares? If the same shares are now worth $2 million, how much equity is reflected on Wal-Mart's books today for those shares? Do you think the 100 shares now sell for $20,000 each ($2 million divided by 100)? Why or why not?
2. Why are publicly traded companies intent on increasing the value of their shares if doing so has no effect on the companies' financial position?
3. Explain why effective management of inventory on the shelves makes a retailer especially attractive to investors.
4. The Walton family's wealth is attributable mainly to the value of their ownership of Wal-Mart stock. Explain how that acquisition of wealth happened.

PART FOUR

Analysis of Accounting Information

Chapter 18
Statement of Cash Flows

After studying this chapter, you should be able to

1. Identify the purposes of the statement of cash flows

2. Distinguish among operating, investing, and financing activities

3. Prepare a statement of cash flows by the direct method

4. Use the financial statements to compute the cash effects of a wide variety of business transactions

5. Prepare a statement of cash flows by the indirect method

A1. Prepare a work sheet for the statement of cash flows

❝Historically the Company's financing capability has produced sufficient cash to support hotel operations and expansion. Lodging [companies'] . . . principal investment is in fixed assets rather than inventories. The . . . operations also generate cash flow sufficient to support current needs.❞

PRIME MOTOR INNS, INC.,
ANNUAL REPORT, P. 16,
1989 [ONE YEAR BEFORE
BANKRUPTCY]

For decades we've made the most fundamental and far-reaching economic decisions on the basis of that supposedly magic number, the bottom line.

As investors, we buy and sell stocks depending on whether a company's earnings are growing or shrinking. As managers, we decide what investments to make based largely on what earnings the projects will yield.

We're making a big mistake. Reported earnings have become virtually worthless in terms of their ability to tell us what's really going on in a company.

Take Prime Motor Inns, until [recently] the world's second-largest hotel operator. Last year Prime reported a healthy net income of $77 million—18 percent of revenues—up nearly 15 percent from the year before. In September Prime filed for Chapter 11 bankruptcy.

What happened? Could the bankruptcy filing have been foreseen? Prime's problem was that it didn't have enough cash coming in. . . . According to banking consultants Financial Proformas, Inc., Prime had a $15 million cash *outflow* from operations in 1989—the year it reported a $77 million profit—compared with a positive cash flow of $58 million the year before. Source: *Adapted from D. Wechsler Linden,* Forbes, *November 12, 1990, p. 106. Used with permission of Forbes, Inc.*

• • • • •

Ｈow can a company such as Prime Motor Inns generate a large profit and yet have an outflow of cash? The company could be making sales but not collecting its receivables. A merchandiser could be stockpiling inventory that it cannot sell. Or the business could be paying off huge amounts of current liabilities that drain cash. What is the significance of Prime Motor Inns' cash-flow problems? The company ran out of cash.

◀‖‖ ◀‖‖ ◀‖‖ We learned in
Chapter 1 (Exhibit 1-8) that
the statement of cash flows is
one of the four required financial statements.

The statement of cash flows, a required financial statement, reports where cash came from and how it was spent.◀‖‖ The objective of the three major financial reports—income statement, balance sheet, and statement of cash flows—is to enable investors and creditors to make informed decisions about a company. The income statement of Prime Motor Inns presented one picture of the company: relatively high net income. The cash-flow statement gave a different, more penetrating view: not enough cash. This example underscores the challenge of financial analysis, that a company's signals may point in different directions. Astute investors and creditors know what to look for; increasingly, they are focusing on cash flows.

This chapter discusses the statement of cash flows. **Cash flows** are cash receipts and cash payments (disbursements). The **statement of cash flows** reports cash receipts and cash disbursements classified according to the entity's major activities: operating, investing, and financing. What information does it provide? What decisions does it aid? We address these questions and then show how to prepare the statement. If you understand how to prepare the statement of cash flows, you will be in a good position to use the information it provides.

Basic Concept of the Statement of Cash Flows

The balance sheet reports the cash balance at the end of the period. By examining two consecutive balance sheets, you can tell whether cash increased or decreased during the period. However, the balance sheet does not indicate *why* the cash balance changed. The income statement reports revenues, expenses, and net income—clues about the sources and uses of cash—but it does not tell *why* cash increased or decreased.

The statement of cash flows reports the entity's cash receipts and cash payments during the period—where cash came from and how it was spent. It explains the *causes* for the change in the cash balance. This information cannot be learned solely from the other financial statements. The statement of cash flows covers a span of time and therefore is dated "For the Year Ended XXX" or "For the Month Ended XXX." Exhibit 18-1 illustrates the timing of the statements.

EXHIBIT 18-1
Timing of the Financial Statements

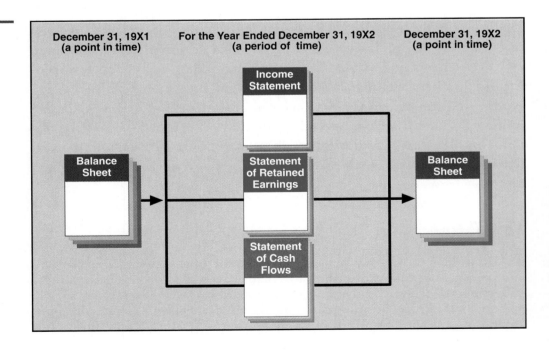

Overview of the Statement of Cash Flows

The statement of cash flows is designed to fulfill the following purposes:

1. *To predict future cash flows.* Cash, not reported accounting income, pays the bills. Prime Motor Inns illustrates this fact. In many cases, past cash receipts and disbursements are a reasonably good predictor of future cash receipts and disbursements.

2. *To evaluate management decisions.* If managers make wise investment decisions, their businesses prosper. If they make unwise decisions, the businesses suffer. The statement of cash flows reports the company's investment in plant assets and thus gives investors and creditors cash-flow information for evaluating managers' decisions. A classic example is Montgomery Ward's decision shortly after World War II *not* to expand the business. Montgomery Ward's top management expected a recession and decided to play it safe until the U.S. economy settled down after the war. Conversely, Sears, Roebuck predicted a strong economy and went full speed ahead. Sears invested heavily in new stores, and Montgomery Ward fell significantly behind Sears. Investors can analyze cash-flow statements to see which businesses are expanding and which are cutting back.

"*Montgomery Ward's top management expected a recession and decided to play it safe until the U.S. economy settled down after the war.*"

3. *To determine the ability to pay dividends to stockholders and interest and principal to creditors.* Stockholders are interested in receiving dividends on their investments. Creditors want to receive their interest and principal amounts on time. The statement of cash flows helps investors and creditors predict whether the business can make these payments.

4. *To show the relationship of net income to changes in the business's cash.* Usually, cash and net income move together. High levels of income tend to lead to increases in cash, and vice versa. However, a company's cash balance can decrease when net income is high, and cash can increase when income is low. The failures of companies such as Prime Motor Inns, which was earning net income but had insufficient cash, have pointed to the need for cash-flow information.

OBJECTIVE 1

Identify the purposes of the statement of cash flows

Cash and Cash Equivalents

On a statement of cash flows, *Cash* has a broader meaning than just cash on hand and cash in the bank. It includes **cash equivalents**, which are highly liquid short-term investments that can be converted into cash with little delay. Because their liquidity is one reason for holding these investments, they are treated as cash. Examples include money-market investments and investments in U.S. Government Treasury bills. Businesses invest their extra cash in these types of liquid assets rather than let it remain idle. Throughout this chapter, the term *cash* refers to cash and cash equivalents.

Operating, Investing, and Financing Activities

A business may be evaluated in terms of three types of business activities. After the business is up and running, operations are the most important activity, followed by investing activities and financing activities. The statement of cash flows in Exhibit 18-2 shows how cash receipts and disbursements are divided into operating activities, investing activities, and financing activities for Anchor Corporation, a small

OBJECTIVE 2

Distinguish among operating, investing, and financing activities

ANCHOR CORPORATION STATEMENT OF CASH FLOWS FOR THE YEAR ENDED DECEMBER 31, 19X2 (AMOUNTS IN THOUSANDS)			
Cash flows from operating activities:			
Receipts:			
Collections from customers..		$ 271	
Interest received on notes receivable		10	
Dividends received on investments in stock		9	
Total cash receipts.......................................			$290
Payments:			
To suppliers...		$(133)	
To employees		(58)	
For interest..		(16)	
For income tax		(15)	
Total cash payments...................................			(222)
Net cash inflow from operating activities			68
Cash flows from investing activities:			
Acquisition of plant assets		$(306)	
Loan to another company		(11)	
Proceeds from sale of plant assets		62	
Net cash outflow from investing activities..................			(255)
Cash flows from financing activities:			
Proceeds from issuance of common stock		$ 101	
Proceeds from issuance of long-term debt		94	
Payment of long-term debt..		(11)	
Payment of dividends		(17)	
Net cash inflow from financing activities..................			167
Net decrease in cash			**$(20)**
Cash balance, December 31, 19X1			42
Cash balance, December 31, 19X2			$ 22

Key Point: If the revenues and
expenses on the income statement are converted to the cash
basis, then cash flow from operations is complete. Operating
activities include all cash inflows and outflows not associated with investing or
financing.

manufacturer of glass products. As Exhibit 18-2 illustrates, each set of activities includes both cash inflows—receipts—and cash outflows—payments. Outflows are shown in parentheses to indicate that payments must be subtracted. Each section of the statement reports a net cash inflow or a net cash outflow.

Operating activities create revenues and expenses in the entity's major line of business. Therefore, operating activities affect the income statement, which reports the accrual-basis effects of operating activities. The statement of cash flows reports their impact on cash. The largest cash inflow from operations is the collection of cash from customers. Less important inflows are receipts of interest on loans and dividends on stock investments. The operating cash outflows include payments to suppliers and to employees and payments for interest and taxes. Exhibit 18-2 shows that Anchor's net cash inflow from operating activities is $68,000. A large positive operating cash flow is a good sign. In the long run, operations must be the main source of a business's cash.

OPERATING ACTIVITIES ARE RELATED TO THE TRANSACTIONS THAT MAKE UP NET INCOME.[1]

Investing activities increase and decrease the long-term assets available to the business. A purchase or sale of a plant asset such as land, a building, or equipment is

---

[1]The authors thank Alfonso Oddo for suggesting this display.

an investing activity, as is the purchase or sale of an investment in stock or bonds of another company. On the statement of cash flows, investing activities include more than the buying and selling of assets that are classified as investments on the balance sheet. Making a loan—an investing activity because the loan creates a receivable for the lender—and collecting on the loan are also reported as investing activities on the statement of cash flows. The acquisition of plant assets dominates Anchor Corporation's investing activities, which produce a net cash outflow of $255,000.

> **INVESTING ACTIVITIES ARE RELATED TO THE LONG-TERM ASSET ACCOUNTS.**[1]

Investments in plant assets lay the foundation for future operations. A company that invests in plant and equipment appears stronger than one that is selling off its plant assets. Why? The latter company may have to sell income-producing assets to pay the bills. Its outlook is bleak.

Financing activities obtain from investors and creditors the cash needed to launch and sustain the business. Financing activities include issuing stock, borrowing money by issuing notes and bonds payable, selling treasury stock, and making payments to the stockholders—dividends and purchases of treasury stock. Payments to the creditors include principal payments only. The payment of interest is an operating activity. Financing activities of Anchor Corporation brought in net cash of $167,000. One thing to watch among financing activities is whether the business is borrowing heavily. Excessive borrowing has been the downfall of many companies.

> **FINANCING ACTIVITIES ARE RELATED TO THE LONG-TERM LIABILITY ACCOUNTS AND THE OWNERS' EQUITY ACCOUNTS.**[1]

Overall, Anchor's cash decreased by $20,000 during 19X2. The company began the year with cash of $42,000 and ended with $22,000.

Each of these categories of activities includes both cash receipts and cash disbursements, as shown in Exhibit 18-3. The exhibit lists the more common cash receipts and cash disbursements that appear on the statement of cash flows.

STOP & THINK Reread the chapter-opening story. Which of the following statements is the most likely explanation of Prime Motor Inns' cash outflow from operations? Give your reason.

a. Prime's cash drain resulted from investing too heavily in new properties.

b. Payments to suppliers and employees exceeded collections from customers.

c. Prime did not borrow enough money to finance operations during the year.

d. Net income was too low.

Answer: (b). The chapter-opening story says nothing about (a), an investing activity, or (c), a financing activity, and (d) contradicts the true income situation of Prime Motor Inns.

Interest and Dividends

You may be puzzled by the listing of receipts of interest and dividends as operating activities. After all, these cash receipts result from investing activities. Interest comes from investments in loans, and dividends come from investments in stock. Equally puzzling is listing the payment of interest as part of operations. Interest expense results from borrowing money—a financing activity. After much debate, the FASB decided to include these items as part of operations. Why? Mainly because they affect the computation of net income. Interest revenue and dividend revenue increase net

---

[1]The authors thank Alfonso Oddo for suggesting this display.

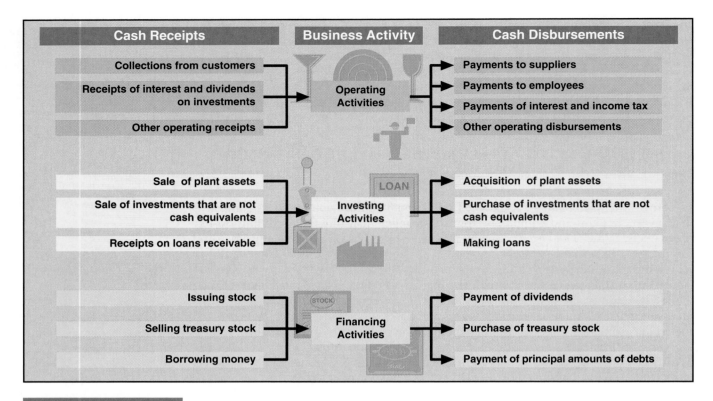

Cash Receipts	Business Activity	Cash Disbursements
Collections from customers		Payments to suppliers
Receipts of interest and dividends on investments	Operating Activities	Payments to employees
		Payments of interest and income tax
Other operating receipts		Other operating disbursements
Sale of plant assets		Acquisition of plant assets
Sale of investments that are not cash equivalents	Investing Activities	Purchase of investments that are not cash equivalents
Receipts on loans receivable		Making loans
Issuing stock		Payment of dividends
Selling treasury stock	Financing Activities	Purchase of treasury stock
Borrowing money		Payment of principal amounts of debts

CONCEPT HIGHLIGHT

EXHIBIT 18-3

Cash Receipts and Disbursements on the Statement of Cash Flows

income, and interest expense decreases income. Therefore, cash receipts of interest and dividends and cash payments of interest are reported as operating activities on the cash-flow statement.

In contrast, dividend payments are not listed among the operating activities of Exhibit 18-3. Why? Because they do not enter the computation of income. Dividend payments are reported in the financing activities section of the cash-flow statement because they go to the entity's owners, who finance the business by holding its stock.

Format of the Statement of Cash Flows

Short Exercise: Is net income the amount of cash received from operations? *A:* No, net income is computed by the accrual basis. Revenues are recorded when earned, and expenses when incurred. Included in accrual-basis net income are some noncash expenses such as depreciation. "Net cash inflow from operations" measures cash-basis net income.

In *FASB Statement No. 95* (1988), the FASB approved two formats for reporting cash flows from operating activities. The **direct method**, illustrated in Exhibit 18-2, lists cash receipts from specific operating activities and cash payments for each major operating activity. *FASB Statement No. 95* expresses a clear preference for the direct method because it reports where cash came from and how it was spent on operating activities. The direct method is required for some insurance companies, and most governmental entities use the direct method.

Companies' accounting systems are designed for accrual, rather than cash-basis, accounting. This format makes it easier for companies to compute cash flows from operating activities by a short-cut method. The **indirect method** starts with net income and reconciles to cash flows from operating activities. Exhibit 18-4 gives an overview of the process of converting from accrual-basis income to the cash basis for the statement of cash flows.

The direct method is easier to understand, it provides more information for decision making, and the FASB prefers it. By learning how to compute the cash-flow amounts for the direct method, you will be learning something far more important: how to determine the cash effects of business transactions. That is a critical skill for analyzing financial statements because accrual-basis accounting often hides cash effects. (Prime Motor Inns in the chapter-opening story illustrates this point and underscores the importance of cash flows to a business.) Then, after you have a firm foundation in cash-flow analysis, it is easier to learn the indirect method. But if your

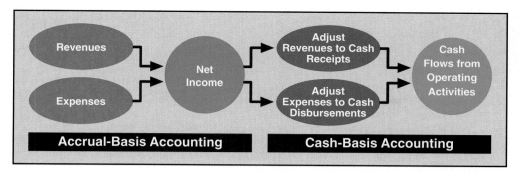

instructor focuses solely on the indirect method, you can study that method, which begins on page 747, with a minimum of references to earlier sections of the chapter.

The two basic ways of presenting the statement of cash flows arrive at the same subtotals for operating activities, investing activities, financing activities, and the net change in cash for the period. They differ only in the manner of showing the cash flows from operating activities.

Preparing the Statement of Cash Flows: The Direct Method

Let's see how to prepare the statement of cash flows by the direct method in Exhibit 18-2. Suppose Anchor Corporation has assembled the summary of 19X2 transactions in Exhibit 18-5. These summary transactions give the data for both the income statement and the statement of cash flows. Some transactions affect one statement, some the other. Sales, for example, are reported on the income statement, but cash collections appear on the cash-flow statement. Other transactions, such as the cash receipt of dividend revenue, affect both. *The statement of cash flows reports only those transactions with cash effects* (those with an asterisk in Exhibit 18-5).

OBJECTIVE 3
Prepare a statement of cash flows by the direct method

Preparation of the statement of cash flows follows these steps: (1) Identify the activities that increased cash or decreased cash—those items with asterisks in Exhibit 18-5; (2) classify each cash increase and each cash decrease as an operating activity, an investing activity, or a financing activity; and (3) identify the cash effect of each transaction. Preparing the statement is discussed next.

CASH FLOWS FROM OPERATING ACTIVITIES Operating cash flows are listed first because they are the largest and most important source of cash for most businesses. The failure of a company's operations to generate the bulk of its cash inflows for an extended period may signal trouble. But Exhibit 18-2 shows that Anchor is sound; its operating activities were the largest source of cash receipts, $290,000.

Cash Collections from Customers. Cash sales bring in cash immediately. Credit sales, however, increase Accounts Receivable but not Cash. Receipts of cash on account are a separate transaction, and only cash receipts are reported on the statement of cash flows. "Collections from customers" on the statement include both cash sales and collections of accounts receivable from credit sales—$271,000— in Exhibit 18-2.

Cash Receipts of Interest. Interest revenue is earned on notes receivable. The income statement reports interest revenue. As the clock ticks, interest accrues, but cash interest is received only on specific dates. Only the cash receipts of interest appear on the statement of cash flows—$10,000 in Exhibit 18-2.

Cash Receipts of Dividends. Dividends are earned on investments in stock. Dividend revenue is ordinarily recorded as an income statement item when cash is received. This cash receipt is reported on the statement of cash flows—$9,000 in Exhibit 18-2. (Dividends *received* are part of operating activities, but dividends *paid* are a financing activity.)

EXHIBIT 18-5

Summary of Anchor Corporation's 19X2 Transactions

Key Point: After you have listed all the accounts used to convert income statement items to the cash basis, notice that changes in the remaining asset accounts signal an *investing* activity. Changes in the remaining liability and stockholders' equity accounts signal *financing* activities.

Operating Activities:
1. Sales on credit, $284,000
*2. Collections from customers, $271,000
3. Interest revenue on notes receivable, $12,000
*4. Collection of interest receivable, $10,000
*5. Cash receipt of dividend revenue on investments in stock, $9,000
6. Cost of goods sold, $150,000
7. Purchases of inventory on credit, $147,000
*8. Payments to suppliers, $133,000
9. Salary and wage expense, $56,000
*10. Payments of salary and wages, $58,000
11. Depreciation expense, $18,000
12. Other operating expense, $17,000
*13. Interest expense and payments, $16,000
*14. Income tax expense and payments, $15,000

Investing Activities:
*15. Cash payments to acquire plant assets, $306,000
*16. Loan to another company, $11,000
*17. Proceeds from sale of plant assets, $62,000, including $8,000 gain

Financing Activities:
*18. Proceeds from issuance of common stock, $101,000
*19. Proceeds from issuance of long-term debt, $94,000
*20. Payment of long-term debt, $11,000
*21. Declaration and payment of cash dividends, $17,000

*Indicates a cash-flow transaction to be reported on the statement of cash flows.

Payments to Suppliers. Payments to suppliers include all cash disbursements for inventory and operating expenses except employee compensation, interest, and income taxes. Suppliers are those entities that provide the business with its inventory and essential services. For example, a clothing store's payments to Levi Strauss, Liz Claiborne, and Reebok are listed as payments to suppliers. A grocery store makes payments to suppliers such as Nabisco, Campbell's, and Coca-Cola. Other suppliers provide advertising, utility, and other services that are classified as operating expenses. This category *excludes* payments to employees, payments for interest, and payments for income taxes because these are separate categories of operating cash payments. In Exhibit 18-2, Anchor Corporation reports payments to suppliers of $133,000.

Payments to Employees. This category includes disbursements for salaries, wages, commissions, and other forms of employee compensation. Accrued amounts are excluded because they have not yet been paid. The income statement reports the expense, including accrued amounts. The statement of cash flows reports only the payments ($58,000) in Exhibit 18-2.

Payments for Interest Expense and Income Tax Expense. These cash payments are reported separately from the other expenses. Interest payments show the cash cost of borrowing money. Excessive borrowing can lead to a large amount of interest payments that could result in financial trouble. Macy's and Donald Trump's casinos are examples of businesses that have faced problems because of too much borrowing. Income tax payments also deserve emphasis because of their significant amount. In the Anchor Corporation example, interest and income tax expenses equal the cash payments. Therefore, the same

"Macy's and Donald Trump's casinos are examples of businesses that have faced problems because of too much borrowing."

amount appears on the income statement and the statement of cash flows. In practice, this is rarely the case. Year-end accruals and other transactions usually cause the expense and cash payment amounts to differ. The cash-flow statement reports the cash payments for interest ($16,000) and income tax ($15,000).

Depreciation, Depletion, and Amortization Expense. These expenses are *not* listed on the statement of cash flows in Exhibit 18-2 because they do not affect cash. For example, depreciation is recorded by debiting the expense and crediting Accumulated Depreciation. No debit or credit to the Cash account occurs.

CASH FLOWS FROM INVESTING ACTIVITIES

Many analysts regard investing as a critical activity because a company's investments determine its future course. Large purchases of plant assets signal expansion, which is usually a good sign about the company. Low levels of investing activities over a lengthy period indicate that the business is not replenishing its capital assets. Knowing these cash flows helps investors and creditors evaluate the direction that managers are charting for the business.

Cash Payments to Acquire Plant Assets and Investments, and Loans to Other Companies. These cash payments are similar because they acquire a noncash asset. The first transaction of Anchor Corporation purchases plant assets, such as land, buildings, and equipment ($306,000) in Exhibit 18-2. In the second transaction, Anchor makes an $11,000 loan and obtains a note receivable. These are investing activities because the company is investing in assets for use in the business rather than for resale. These transactions have no effect on revenues or expenses and thus are not reported on the income statement. Another transaction in this category—not shown in Exhibit 18-2—is a purchase of an investment in the stocks or bonds of another company.

Proceeds from the Sale of Plant Assets and Investments, and Collections of Loans. These transactions are the opposites of acquisitions of plant assets and investments, and making loans. They are cash receipts from investment transactions.

The sale of the plant assets needs explanation. The statement of cash flows reports that Anchor Corporation received $62,000 cash on the sale of plant assets. The income statement shows an $8,000 gain on this transaction. What is the appropriate amount to show on the cash-flow statement? It is $62,000, the cash proceeds from the sale. If we assume that Anchor sold equipment that cost $64,000 and had accumulated depreciation of $10,000, the following journal entry would record the sale:

Cash	62,000	
Accumulated Depreciation	10,000	
Equipment		64,000
Gain on Sale of Plant Assets (from income statement)		8,000

The analysis indicates that the book value of the equipment was $54,000 ($64,000 – $10,000). However, the book value of the asset sold is not reported on the statement of cash flows. Only the cash proceeds of $62,000 are reported on the statement. For the income statement, only the gain is reported. Since a gain occurred, you may wonder why this cash receipt is not reported as part of operations. Operations consist of buying and selling merchandise or rendering services to earn revenue. Investing activities are the acquisition and disposition of assets used in operations. Therefore, the FASB views the sale of plant assets and the sale of investments as cash inflows from investing activities.

STOP & THINK Suppose Scott Paper Company sold timberland at a $35 million gain. The land cost Scott Paper $9 million when it was purchased in 1969. What amount will Scott Paper Company report as an investing activity on the statement of cash flows?

Answer: Cash receipt of $44 million (cost of $9 million plus the gain of $35 million).

"*Despite the downsizing, Grumman could no longer compete and was taken over by Martin Marietta.*"

Investors and creditors are often critical of a company that sells large amounts of its plant assets. Such sales may signal an emergency. Because of budget cuts in the defense industry, the defense contractor Grumman Corp. shed almost one-third of its facilities worldwide in 1994. The closing of Grumman's aircraft manufacturing plant on Long Island, laboratories, and other facilities, plus massive employee lay-offs, promised to save the company $600 million in operating expenses. Despite the downsizing, Grumman could no longer compete and was taken over by Martin Marietta.

Short Exercise: Collins Corp. sold at a $3,000 loss an investment that had cost $25,000. Make the journal entry to help you identify the cash receipt (the number for the cash-flow statement). *A:*

Cash 22,000
Loss on Sale of
    Investment 3,000
       Investment ..   25,000

In other situations, selling off fixed assets may be good news about the company if it is getting rid of an unprofitable division. Whether sales of plant assets are good news or bad news should be evaluated in light of a company's operating and financing characteristics.

CASH FLOWS FROM FINANCING ACTIVITIES Cash flows from financing activities include the following:

Proceeds from Issuance of Stock and Debt. Readers of the financial statements want to know how the entity obtains its financing. Issuing stock (preferred and common) and debt are two common ways to finance operations. In Exhibit 18-2, Anchor Corporation issued common stock of $101,000 and long-term debt of $94,000.

Payment of Debt and Purchases of the Company's Own Stock. The payment of debt decreases Cash, which is the opposite effect of borrowing money. Anchor Corporation reports debt payments of $11,000. Other transactions in this category are purchases of treasury stock and payments to retire the company's stock.

Payment of Cash Dividends. The payment of cash dividends decreases Cash and is therefore reported as a cash payment, as illustrated by Anchor's $17,000 payment in Exhibit 18-2. A dividend in another form—a stock dividend, for example—has no effect on Cash and is *not* reported on the cash-flow statement.

When the statement of cash flows became a required financial statement, computerized accounting systems were changed so that they could generate this statement as easily as they do the balance sheet and the income statement. Consider the direct method for preparing the statement of cash flows (see Exhibit 18-3). The amounts for the operating section can be obtained by drawing cash inflows and outflows (grouped by related revenue and expense category) from the posted accounts. Specifically, the cash receipts postings to Accounts Receivable provide the information necessary to show Cash Collections from Customers. The computer adds the monthly postings to reach the yearly total. All other cash flows for operating activities, as well as cash flows for financing and investing activities, are handled similarly.

MID-CHAPTER SUMMARY PROBLEM FOR YOUR REVIEW

Drexel Corporation's accounting records include the following information for the year ended June 30, 19X8:

a. Salary expense, $104,000

b. Interest revenue, $8,000

c. Proceeds from issuance of common stock, $31,000

d. Declaration and payment of cash dividends, $22,000

e. Collection of interest receivable, $7,000

f. Payments of salaries, $110,000

g. Credit sales, $358,000

h. Loan to another company, $42,000

i. Proceeds from sale of plant assets, $18,000, including $1,000 loss

j. Collections from customers, $369,000

k. Cash receipt of dividend revenue on stock investments, $3,000

l. Payments to suppliers, $319,000

m. Cash sales, $92,000

n. Depreciation expense, $32,000

o. Proceeds from issuance of short-term debt, $38,000

p. Payments of long-term debt, $57,000

q. Interest expense and payments, $11,000

r. Loan collections, $51,000

s. Proceeds from sale of investments, $22,000, including $13,000 gain

t. Amortization expense, $5,000

u. Purchases of inventory on credit, $297,000

v. Income tax expense and payments, $16,000

w. Cash payments to acquire plant assets, $83,000

x. Cost of goods sold, $284,000

y. Cash balance: June 30, 19X7—$83,000
June 30, 19X8—$54,000

Required

Prepare Drexel Corporation's statement of cash flows and income statement for the year ended June 30, 19X8. Follow the cash-flow statement format of Exhibit 18-2 and the single-step format for the income statement (as shown in Exhibit 18-6).

SOLUTION TO REVIEW PROBLEM

DREXEL CORPORATION
STATEMENT OF CASH FLOWS
FOR THE YEAR ENDED JUNE 30, 19X8
(AMOUNTS IN THOUSANDS)

Item (Reference Letter)			
	Cash flows from operating activities:		
	Receipts:		
j, m	Collections from customers ($369 + $92)................	$ 461	
e	Interest received on notes receivable......................	7	
k	Dividends received on investments in stock............	3	
	Total cash receipts		$ 471
	Payments:		
l	To suppliers	$(319)	
f	To employees...	(110)	
q	For interest..	(11)	
v	For income tax	(16)	
	Total cash payments		(456)
	Net cash inflow from operating activities............		15
	Cash flows from investing activities:		
w	Acquisition of plant assets...	$ (83)	
h	Loan to another company..	(42)	
s	Proceeds from sale of investments.............................	22	
i	Proceeds from sale of plant assets.............................	18	
r	Collection of loans	51	
	Net cash outflow from investing activities		(34)
	Cash flows from financing activities:		
o	Proceeds from issuance of short-term debt.................	$ 38	
c	Proceeds from issuance of common stock...................	31	
p	Payments of long-term debt	(57)	
d	Dividends declared and paid......................................	(22)	
	Net cash outflow from financing activities		(10)
	Net decrease in cash		$ (29)
y	Cash balance, June 30, 19X7		83
y	Cash balance, June 30, 19X8		$ 54

Revenue and gains:		
Sales revenue ($358 + $92)................	$450	
Gain on sale of investments..............	13	
Interest revenue.................................	8	
Dividend revenue	3	
Total revenues and gains		$474
Expenses and losses:		
Cost of goods sold.............................	$284	
Salary expense	104	
Depreciation expense........................	32	
Income tax expense	16	
Interest expense.................................	11	
Amortization expense........................	5	
Loss on sale of plant assets...............	1	
Total expenses.............................		453
Net income		$ 21

Computing Individual Amounts for the Statement of Cash Flows

OBJECTIVE 4

Use the financial statements to compute the cash effects of a wide variety of business transactions

How do accountants compute the amounts for the statement of cash flows? Many accountants prepare the statement of cash flows from the income statement amounts and from *changes* in the related balance sheet accounts. For the *operating* cash-flow amounts, the adjustment process follows this basic approach:

Revenue or expense from the income statement → **Adjustment for the change in the related balance sheet account(s)** → **Amount for the statement of cash flows**

Accountants label this the T-account approach.[2] Learning to analyze T-accounts in this manner is one of the most useful accounting skills you will acquire. It will enable you to identify the cash effects of a wide variety of transactions. It will also strengthen your grasp of the accrual basis of accounting.

The following discussions use Anchor Corporation's income statement in Exhibit 18-6 and comparative balance sheet in Exhibit 18-7. For continuity, trace the $22,000 and $42,000 cash amounts on the balance sheet in Exhibit 18-7 to the bottom part of the cash-flow statement in Exhibit 18-2.

Computing the Cash Amounts of Operating Activities

Key Point: A decrease in Accounts Receivable indicates that cash collections were greater than sales. The decrease is added to Sales.

An increase in Accounts Receivable indicates that sales were greater than cash collections. The increase is subtracted from Sales.

COMPUTING CASH COLLECTIONS FROM CUSTOMERS Collections can be computed by converting sales revenue (an accrual-basis amount) to the cash basis. Anchor Corporation's income statement (Exhibit 18-6) reports sales of $284,000. Exhibit 18-7 shows that Accounts Receivable increased from $80,000 at the beginning of the year to $93,000 at year end, a $13,000 increase. Based on those amounts, Collections equals $271,000, as shown in the Accounts Receivable T-account:

---

[2]The chapter appendix covers the work sheet approach to preparation of the statement of cash flows.

EXHIBIT 18-6

Income Statement

ANCHOR CORPORATION
INCOME STATEMENT
FOR THE YEAR ENDED DECEMBER 31, 19X2
(AMOUNTS IN THOUSANDS)

Revenues and gains:		
Sales revenue	$284	
Interest revenue.................................	12	
Dividend revenue	9	
Gain on sale of plant assets	8	
Total revenues and gains		$313
Expenses:		
Cost of goods sold............................	$150	
Salary and wage expense	56	
Depreciation expense........................	18	
Other operating expense...................	17	
Interest expense................................	16	
Income tax expense	15	
Total expenses.............................		272
Net income..		$ 41

Accounts Receivable

Beginning balance	80,000			
Sales	284,000	Collections		271,000
Ending balance	93,000			

Another explanation: Because Accounts Receivable increased by $13,000, we can say that Anchor Corporation received $13,000 less cash than sales revenue for

EXHIBIT 18-7

Comparative Balance Sheet

ANCHOR CORPORATION
COMPARATIVE BALANCE SHEET
DECEMBER 31, 19X2 AND 19X1
(AMOUNTS IN THOUSANDS)

Assets	19X2	19X1	Increase (Decrease)	
Current:				
Cash	$ 22	$ 42	$ (20)	
Accounts receivable	93	80	13	⎫
Interest receivable	3	1	2	⎬ Changes in current assets—**Operating**
Inventory	135	138	(3)	⎪
Prepaid expenses.......................................	8	7	1	⎭
Long-term receivable from another company	11	—	11	⎱ Changes in noncurrent assets—
Plant assets, net	453	219	234	⎰ **Investing**
Total	$725	$487	$238	
Liabilities				
Current:				
Accounts payable	$ 91	$ 57	$ 34	⎱ Changes in current liabilities—
Salary and wage payable	4	6	(2)	⎰ **Operating**
Accrued liabilities	1	3	(2)	
Long-term debt..	160	77	83	⎱ Changes in long-term liabilities and paid-in capital accounts—**Financing**
Stockholders' Equity				
Common stock	359	258	101	⎰
Retained earnings......................................	110	86	24	⎱ Change due to net income—**Operating** and change due to dividends—**Financing**
Total	$725	$487	$238	

EXHIBIT 18-8
Direct Method of Determining Cash Flows from Operating Activities

RECEIPTS / PAYMENTS	From Income Statement	Change in Account Balance From Balance Sheet	
RECEIPTS:			
From customers	Sales Revenue	+ Decrease in Accounts Receivable − Increase in Accounts Receivable	
Of interest	Interest Revenue	+ Decrease in Interest Receivable − Increase in Interest Receivable	
Of dividends	Dividend Revenue	+ Decrease in Dividends Receivable − Increase in Dividends Receivable	
PAYMENTS:			
To suppliers	Cost of Goods Sold	+ Increase in Inventory − Decrease in Inventory	+ Decrease in Accounts Payable − Increase in Accounts Payable
	Operating Expense	+ Increase in Prepaids − Decrease in Prepaids	+ Decrease in Accrued Liabilities − Increase in Accrued Liabilities
To employees	Salary (Wage) Expense	+ Decrease in Salary (Wage) Payable − Increase in Salary (Wage) Payable	
For interest	Interest Expense	+ Decrease in Interest Payable − Increase in Interest Payable	
For income tax	Income Tax Expense	+ Decrease in Income Tax Payable − Increase in Income Tax Payable	

We thank Barbara Gerrity for suggesting this exhibit.

Key Point: An increase in Inventory indicates more inventory has been purchased than sold. An increase in inventory is added to COGS.

A decrease in Inventory indicates that less merchandise has been purchased than sold. The decrease is subtracted from COGS.

A decrease in Accounts Payable indicates that the cash payments for merchandise were greater than what was purchased. The decrease is added to COGS.

An increase in Accounts Payable indicates that more merchandise was purchased than was paid for. The increase is deducted from COGS.

the period. A decrease in Accounts Receivable would mean that the company received more cash than the amount of sales revenue. This computation is given as the first item in Exhibit 18-8.

All collections of receivables are computed in the same way. In our example, Anchor Corporation's income statement, Exhibit 18-6, reports interest revenue of $12,000. Interest Receivable's balance in Exhibit 18-7 increased by $2,000. Cash receipts of interest must be $10,000 (Interest Revenue of $12,000 minus the $2,000 increase in Accounts Receivable). Exhibit 18-8 shows this computation.

COMPUTING PAYMENTS TO SUPPLIERS This computation includes two parts, payments for inventory and payments for expenses other than interest and income tax.

Payments for inventory are computed by converting cost of goods sold to the cash basis. We accomplish this by analyzing Cost of Goods Sold and Accounts Payable. Many companies also purchase inventory on short-term notes payable. In that case, we would analyze Short-Term Notes Payable in the same manner as Accounts Payable. The computation of Anchor Corporation's cash payments for inventory is given by this analysis of the T-accounts:

Cost of Goods Sold			
Beg. inventory	138,000	End. inventory	135,000
Purchases	147,000		
Cost of goods sold	150,000		

Accounts Payable			
Payments for inventory	113,000	Beg. bal.	57,000
		Purchases	147,000
		End bal.	91,000

Beginning and ending inventory amounts are taken from the balance sheet, and Cost of Goods Sold from the income statement. We must solve for purchases, which affect both Cost of Goods Sold and Accounts Payable. *Payments for inventory* show up as a debit to Accounts Payable.

By another explanation, payments for inventory appear in the Accounts Payable account. But we must first work through Cost of Goods Sold and the change in the Inventory account, as shown in Exhibit 18-8 under Payments to Suppliers.

Payments to suppliers ($133,000 in Exhibit 18-2) equal the sum of payments for inventory ($113,000) plus payments for operating expenses ($20,000), as explained next.

COMPUTING PAYMENTS FOR OPERATING EXPENSES

Payments for operating expenses other than interest and income tax can be computed by analyzing Prepaid Expenses and Accrued Liabilities, as follows for Anchor Corporation:

Prepaid Expenses					Accrued Liabilities				Operating Expenses (other than Salaries, Wages, and Depreciation)	
Beg. bal.	7,000	Expiration		Payment of		Beg. bal.	3,000	Accrual of		
Payments	8,000	of prepaid		beg. bal.	3,000	Accrual of		expense at		
		expense	7,000			expense at		year end	1,000	
End. bal.	8,000					year end	1,000	Expiration of		
						End. bal.	1,000	prepaid		
								expense	7,000	
								Payments	9,000	
								End. bal.	17,000	

Total payments for operating expenses = $20,000 ($8,000 + $3,000 + $9,000)

By another explanation: Increases in prepaid expenses require cash payments, and decreases indicate that payments were less than expenses. Decreases in accrued liabilities can occur only from cash payments, and increases mean that cash was *not* paid. Exhibit 18-8 shows a streamlined version of this computation.

COMPUTING PAYMENTS TO EMPLOYEES

The company may have separate accounts for salaries, wages, and other forms of cash compensation to employees. Payments to employees can be computed conveniently by combining them into one account. Anchor's calculation adjusts Salary and Wage Expense for the change in Salary and Wage Payable, as shown in the Salary and Wage Payable T-account:

Salary and Wage Payable			
		Beginning balance	6,000
Payments to employees	58,000	Salary and wage expense	56,000
		Ending balance	4,000

Exhibit 18-8 gives this computation under Payments to Employees.

COMPUTING PAYMENTS OF INTEREST AND INCOME TAXES

In our example, the expense and payment amounts are the same for each expense. Therefore, no analysis is required to determine the payment amount. If the expense and the payment differ, the payment can be computed by analyzing the related liability account. The payment computation follows the pattern illustrated for payments to employees.

Computing the Cash Amounts of Investing Activities

Investing activities affect asset accounts, such as Plant Assets, Investments, and Notes Receivable. The cash amounts of investing activities can be identified by analyzing those accounts. Most data for the computations are taken directly from the income statement and the beginning and ending balance sheets. Other amounts come from analysis of accounts in the ledger.

Key Point: Increases and decreases in Salary Payable are treated in the same way as increases and decreases in Accounts Payable and Accrued Liabilities.

A decrease in Salary Payable indicates that salaries paid exceeded salary expense. The decrease is added to Salary Expense.

An increase in Salary Payable indicates that salary expense exceeded salaries paid. The increase is subtracted from Salary Expense.

Key Point: A decrease in Interest Payable or Income Tax Payable indicates that interest or income taxes paid exceeded interest expense or income tax expense. The decrease is added to Interest Expense or Income Tax Expense. An increase in Interest Payable or Income Taxes Payable indicates that interest expense or income tax expense exceeded interest or income taxes paid. The increase is subtracted from Interest Expense or Income Tax Expense.

COMPUTING ACQUISITIONS AND SALES OF PLANT ASSETS Most companies have separate accounts for Land, Buildings, Equipment, and other plant assets. It is helpful to combine these accounts into a single summary for computing the cash flows from acquisitions and sales of these assets. Also, we subtract accumulated depreciation from the assets' cost and get a net figure for plant assets. This approach allows us to work with a single plant asset account as opposed to a large number of plant asset and related accumulated depreciation accounts.

To illustrate, observe that Anchor Corporation's balance sheet (Exhibit 18-7) reports beginning plant assets, net of depreciation, of $219,000 and an ending net amount of $453,000. The income statement shows depreciation of $18,000 and an $8,000 gain on sale of plant assets. Further, the acquisitions total $306,000. How much are the proceeds from the sale of plant assets? First, we must determine the book value of plant assets sold from the Plant Assets T-account, as follows:

Plant Assets (net)			
Beginning balance	219,000	Depreciation	18,000
Acquisitions	306,000	Book value of assets sold	54,000
Ending balance	453,000		

Key Point: Proceeds from the sale of an asset need not equal the asset's book value. Remember:

Now we can compute the sale proceeds as follows:

Book value + Gain = Proceeds
Book value − Loss = Proceeds

The book value information comes from the balance sheet, the gain or loss from the income statement.

$$\textbf{Sale proceeds = Book value sold + Gain − Loss}$$

$$= \$54,000 \qquad + \$8,000 − \$0 = \$62,000$$

Trace the sale proceeds of $62,000 to the statement of cash flows in Exhibit 18-2. If the sale resulted in a loss of $3,000, the sale proceeds would be $51,000 ($54,000 − $3,000), and the statement would report $51,000 as a cash receipt from this investing activity.

COMPUTING ACQUISITIONS AND SALES OF ASSETS CLASSIFIED AS INVESTMENTS, AND LOANS AND THEIR COLLECTIONS Accountants use a separate category of assets for investments in stocks, bonds, and other types of assets. The cash amounts of transactions involving these assets can be computed in the manner illustrated for plant assets. Investments are easier to analyze, however, because there is no depreciation to account for, as shown in the following T-account:

Short Exercise: Greene Corp. reported the following:

Retirement of preferred
   stock.......................... $ 45
Sale of bonds issued by
   Blue Co...................... 112
Payment of interest on
   mortgage note 11
Purchase of land 158
Payment of income taxes   38
Sale of treasury stock
   (common) 105
Collection of note
   receivable 63
Payment of dividends... 150

What is Greene's net change in cash from investing activities?
A:
($112 − $158 + $63) = $17, a net increase. Categorize the other items. *Operating:* Payment of interest, payment of taxes. *Financing:* Retirement of preferred stock, sale of treasury stock, payment of dividends.

Investments			
Beginning balance	XXX		
Purchases	XXX	Cost of investments sold	XXX
Ending balance	XXX		

Loan transactions follow the pattern described on pages 740–742 for collections from customers. New loans cause a debit to a receivable and an outflow of cash. Collections increase cash and cause a credit to the receivable:

Loans and Notes Receivable			
Beginning balance	XXX		
New loans made	XXX	Collections	XXX
Ending balance	XXX		

Computing the Cash Amounts of Financing Activities

Financing activities affect liability and stockholders' equity accounts, such as Notes Payable, Bonds Payable, Long-Term Debt, Common Stock, Paid-in Capital in Excess of Par, and Retained Earnings. The cash amounts of financing activities can be computed by analyzing these accounts.

COMPUTING ISSUANCES AND PAYMENTS OF LONG-TERM DEBT

The beginning and ending balances of Long-Term Debt, Notes Payable, or Bonds Payable are taken from the balance sheet. If either the amount of new issuances or the amount of the payments is known, the other amount can be computed. New debt issuances total $94,000. The computation of debt payments follows from analysis of the Long-Term Debt T-account, using amounts from Anchor Corporation's balance sheet, Exhibit 18-7:

	Long-Term Debt		
		Beginning balance	77,000
Payments	11,000	Issuance of new debt	94,000
		Ending balance	160,000

COMPUTING ISSUANCES AND RETIREMENTS OF STOCK AND PURCHASES AND SALES OF TREASURY STOCK

The cash effects of these financing activities can be determined by analyzing the various stock accounts. For example, the amount of a new issuance of common stock is determined by combining the Common Stock and any related Capital in Excess of Par account. It is convenient to work with a single summary account for stock as we do for plant assets. Using Exhibit 18-7 data, we have:

	Common Stock		
		Beginning balance	258,000
Retirements of stock	0	Issuance of new stock	101,000
		Ending balance	359,000

Cash flows affecting Treasury Stock, a debit balance account, can be analyzed by using the Treasury Stock T-account:

Treasury Stock			
Beginning balance	XXX		
Purchases of treasury stock	XXX	Cost of treasury stock sold	XXX
Ending balance	XXX		

If either the purchase amount or the cost of treasury stock sold is known, the other amount can be computed. For a sale of treasury stock, the amount to report on the cash flow statement is the sale proceeds. Suppose a sale brought in cash that was $2,000 less than the $14,000 cost of the treasury stock sold. In this case, the statement of cash flows would report a cash receipt of $12,000 ($14,000 − $2,000).

COMPUTING DIVIDEND PAYMENTS

If the amount of the dividends is not given elsewhere (for example, in a statement of retained earnings), it can be computed as follows:

	Retained Earnings					Dividends Payable		
Dividend declarations	17,000	Beg. bal.	86,000				Beg. bal.	XXX
		Net income	41,000				Dividend declarations	XXX
		End. bal.	110,000		Dividend payments	XXX	End. bal.	XXX

First, we compute dividend declarations by analyzing the Retained Earnings T-account. Then we solve for dividend payments with the Dividends Payable T-account. Anchor Corporation has no Dividends Payable account, so dividend payments are the same as declarations.

Short Exercise: In the previous Short Exercise, what is Greene's net change in cash from financing activities? *A:* (−$45 + $105 − $150) = $90, a net decrease.

Noncash Investing and Financing Activities

Companies make investments that do not require cash. They also obtain financing other than cash. Our example included none of these transactions. Now suppose that Anchor Corporation issued no-par common stock valued at $320,000 to acquire a warehouse. Anchor would journalize this transaction as follows:

Warehouse Building..	320,000	
Common Stock...		320,000

This transaction would not be reported on the cash-flow statement because Anchor paid no cash. But the importance of the investment in the warehouse and the financing aspect of issuing stock require that the transaction be reported. Noncash investing and financing activities like this transaction are reported in a separate schedule that accompanies the statement of cash flows. Exhibit 18-9 illustrates how to report noncash investing and financing activities (all amounts are assumed). This information is required in a schedule immediately after any cash-flow statement or in a note.

EXHIBIT 18-9 *Noncash Investing and Financing Activities (amounts in thousands)*

Acquisition of building by issuing common stock	$320
Acquisition of land by issuing note payable	72
Payment of long-term debt by transferring investment assets to the creditor..............	104
Acquisition of equipment by issuing short-term note payable	37
Total noncash investing and financing activities...	$533

Reconciliation of Net Income to Net Cash Flow from Operating Activities

The FASB requires companies that format operating activities by the direct method to report a reconciliation from net income to net cash inflow (or outflow) from operating activities. Exhibit 18-10 shows the reconciliation for Anchor Corporation.

EXHIBIT 18-10

Reconciliation of Net Income to Net Cash Inflow from Operating Activities

ANCHOR CORPORATION RECONCILIATION OF NET INCOME TO NET CASH INFLOW FROM OPERATING ACTIVITIES		
Net income		$41
Add (subtract) items that affect net income and cash flow differently:		
Depreciation	$ 18	
Gain on sale of plant assets......................................	(8)	
Increase in accounts receivable.................................	(13)	
Increase in interest receivable..................................	(2)	
Decrease in inventory	3	
Increase in prepaid expenses....................................	(1)	
Increase in accounts payable....................................	34	
Decrease in salary and wage payable	(2)	
Decrease in accrued liabilities..................................	(2)	27
Net cash inflow from operating activities..............		$68

The end result—net cash inflow from operating activities of $68,000—is the same as the result we derived earlier under the *direct* method (see Exhibit 18-2). The reconciliation is the same as the *indirect* method of computing operating cash flows. We now turn our attention to the indirect method.

Preparing the Statement of Cash Flows: The Indirect Method

An alternative to the direct method of computing cash flows from *operating* activities is the *indirect method*, or the **reconciliation method**, as shown in Exhibit 18-10. This method starts with net income and shows the reconciliation from net income to operating cash flows. For example, the consolidated cash-flow statement of the Washington Post Company lists first "Net income" and then "Adjustments to recon-

OBJECTIVE 5
Prepare a statement of cash flows by the indirect method

cile net income to net cash provided by operating activities." The indirect method shows the link between net income and cash flow from operations better than the direct method. That is why the Washington Post Company, which publishes the *Washington Post* and *Newsweek* and owns several television stations, chooses the indirect method over the direct method. In fact, 585 companies (97.5 percent) of a 600-firm survey (*Accounting Trends and Techniques, 1993*) use the

"*The consolidated cash-flow statement of the Washington Post Company lists first 'Net income' and then 'Adjustments to reconcile net income to net cash provided by operating activities.'*"

indirect method even though the FASB recommends the direct method. The main drawback of the indirect method is that it does not report the detailed operating cash flows—collections from customers and other cash receipts, payments to suppliers, payments to employees, and payments for interest and taxes.

These two methods of preparing the cash-flow statement affect only the operating activities section of the statement. No difference exists in the reporting of investing activities or financing activities.

Exhibit 18-11 is Anchor Corporation's statement prepared by the indirect method. Only the operating section of the statement differs from the direct method format in Exhibit 18-2. The new items are keyed to their explanations, which follow. One reason companies prefer the indirect method is its ease of preparation from the income statement and the beginning and ending balance sheets. For convenience, we repeat Anchor Corporation's income statement and balance sheet here as Exhibits 18-12 and 18-13.

Logic behind the Indirect Method

The operating section of the statement begins with net income, taken from the income statement. Additions and subtractions follow. These are labeled "Add (subtract) items that affect net income and cash flow differently." In this section, we discuss those items.

DEPRECIATION, DEPLETION, AND AMORTIZATION EXPENSES These expenses are added back to net income when we go from net income to cash flow from operations. Let's see why.

Depreciation is recorded as follows:Ⓐ

Depreciation Expense..	18,000	
Accumulated Depreciation		18,000

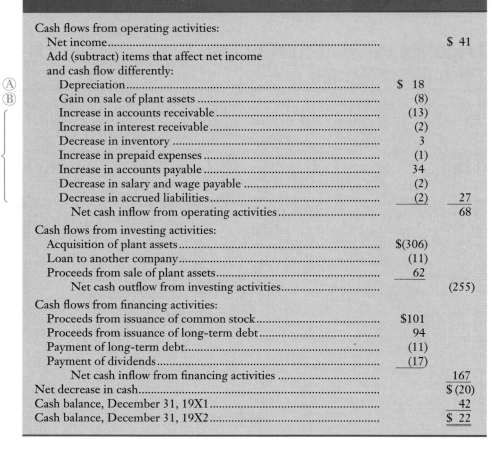

ANCHOR CORPORATION
STATEMENT OF CASH FLOWS
FOR THE YEAR ENDED DECEMBER 31, 19X2
(AMOUNTS IN THOUSANDS)

Cash flows from operating activities:		
Net income		$ 41
Add (subtract) items that affect net income and cash flow differently:		
(A) Depreciation	$ 18	
(B) Gain on sale of plant assets	(8)	
Increase in accounts receivable	(13)	
Increase in interest receivable	(2)	
(C) Decrease in inventory	3	
Increase in prepaid expenses	(1)	
Increase in accounts payable	34	
Decrease in salary and wage payable	(2)	
Decrease in accrued liabilities	(2)	27
Net cash inflow from operating activities		68
Cash flows from investing activities:		
Acquisition of plant assets	$(306)	
Loan to another company	(11)	
Proceeds from sale of plant assets	62	
Net cash outflow from investing activities		(255)
Cash flows from financing activities:		
Proceeds from issuance of common stock	$101	
Proceeds from issuance of long-term debt	94	
Payment of long-term debt	(11)	
Payment of dividends	(17)	
Net cash inflow from financing activities		167
Net decrease in cash		$ (20)
Cash balance, December 31, 19X1		42
Cash balance, December 31, 19X2		$ 22

EXHIBIT 18-12

Income Statement (repeated from Exhibit 18-6)

ANCHOR CORPORATION
INCOME STATEMENT
FOR THE YEAR ENDED DECEMBER 31, 19X2
(AMOUNTS IN THOUSANDS)

Revenues and gains:		
Sales revenue	$284	
Interest revenue	12	
Dividend revenue	9	
Gain on sale of plant assets	8	
Total revenues and gains		$313
Expenses:		
Cost of goods sold	$150	
Salary and wage expense	56	
Depreciation expense	18	
Other operating expense	17	
Interest expense	16	
Income tax expense	15	
Total expenses		272
Net income		$ 41

EXHIBIT 18-13

*Comparative Balance Sheet
(repeated from Exhibit 18-7)*

ANCHOR CORPORATION
COMPARATIVE BALANCE SHEET
DECEMBER 31, 19X2 AND 19X1
(AMOUNTS IN THOUSANDS)

Assets	19X2	19X1	Increase (Decrease)
Current:			
Cash	$ 22	$ 42	$ (20)
Accounts receivable	93	80	13
Interest receivable	3	1	2
Inventory	135	138	(3)
Prepaid expenses	8	7	1
Long-term receivable from another company	11	—	11
Plant assets, net	453	219	234
Total	$725	$487	$238
Liabilities			
Current:			
Accounts payable	$ 91	$ 57	$ 34
Salary and wage payable	4	6	(2)
Accrued liabilities	1	3	(2)
Long-term debt	160	77	83
Stockholders' Equity			
Common stock	359	258	101
Retained earnings	110	86	24
Total	$725	$487	$238

This entry contains no debit or credit to Cash, so depreciation expense has no cash effect. However, depreciation is deducted from revenues in the computation of income. Therefore, in going from net income to cash flow from operations, we add depreciation back to net income. The addback cancels the earlier deduction. The following example should help: Suppose a company had only two transactions during the period, a $1,000 cash sale and depreciation expense of $300. Net income is $700 ($1,000 – $300). Cash flow from operations is $1,000. To show how net income ($700) is related to cash flow ($1,000), we must add the depreciation amount of $300.

> All expenses with no cash effects are added back to net income on the cash-flow statement.

Depletion and amortization are also added back.

> Likewise, revenues that do not provide cash are subtracted from net income.

An example is equity-method investment revenue.

GAINS AND LOSSES ON THE SALE OF ASSETS® Sales of plant assets are investing activities on the cash-flow statement. A gain or loss on the sale is an adjustment to income. Exhibit 18-11 includes an adjustment for a gain. Recall that Anchor sold for $62,000 equipment with a book value of $54,000, producing a gain of $8,000. You can learn how to treat an item on the cash-flow statement by examining the journal entry that recorded it, as shown on page 737.

The $8,000 gain is reported on the income statement and, therefore, is included in net income. However, the cash receipt from the sale is $62,000, which includes the gain. To avoid counting the gain twice, we need to remove its effect from income and report the cash receipt of $62,000 in the investing activities section of the statement. Starting with net income, we subtract the gain. This deduction removes the gain's earlier effect on income. The sale of plant assets is reported as a $62,000 cash receipt from an investing activity, as shown in Exhibits 18-2 and 18-11.

A loss on the sale of plant assets is also an adjustment to net income on the statement of cash flows. However, a loss is added back to income to compute cash flow from operations. The proceeds from selling the plant assets are reported under investing activities.

CHANGES IN THE CURRENT ASSET AND CURRENT LIABILITY ACCOUNTS©
Most current assets and current liabilities result from operating activities. Changes in the current accounts are reported as adjustments to net income on the cash-flow statement. The following rules apply:

Key Point: These rules may help with the indirect method: (1) An *increase* in a current asset is subtracted from net income. (2) A *decrease* in a current asset is added to net income. (3) An *increase* in a current liability is added to net income. (4) A *decrease* in a current liability is subtracted from net income.

1. **An *increase* in a current asset other than cash is subtracted from net income to compute cash flow from operations**. Suppose a company makes a sale. Income is increased by the sale amount. However, collection of less than the full amount leaves Accounts Receivable with an increase. For example, Exhibit 18-13 reports that Anchor Corporation's Accounts Receivable increased by $13,000 during 19X2. To compute the impact of revenue on Anchor's cash-flow amount, we must subtract the $13,000 increase in Accounts Receivable from net income in Exhibit 18-11. The same logic applies to the other current assets. If they increase during the period, subtract the increase from net income.

2. **A *decrease* in a current asset other than cash is added to net income.** For example, suppose Anchor's Accounts Receivable balance decreased by $4,000 during the period. Cash receipts cause the Accounts Receivable balance to decrease, so decreases in Accounts Receivable and the other current assets are added to net income.

3. **A *decrease* in a current liability is subtracted from net income**. The payment of a current liability causes it to decrease, so decreases in current liabilities are subtracted from net income. For example, in Exhibit 18-11, the $2,000 decrease in Accrued Liabilities is subtracted from net income to compute net cash inflow from operating activities.

4. **An *increase* in a current liability is added to net income**. Accounts Payable increased during the year. This increase can occur only if cash is not spent to pay this liability, which means that cash payments are less than the related expense. In this case, increases in current liabilities are added to net income.

The computation of net cash inflow or net cash outflow from *operating* activities by the indirect method takes a path that is very different from the computation by the direct method. However, the two methods arrive at the same amount of net cash flow from operating activities, as shown in Exhibits 18-2 and 18-11, both of which report a net cash inflow of $68,000.

Exhibit 18-14 summarizes the adjustments needed to convert net income to net cash inflow (or net cash outflow) from operating activities by the indirect method.

If you are studying *only* the indirect method for operating cash flows, please turn to page 743 for coverage of investing and financing activities.

EXHIBIT 18-14
Indirect Method of Determining Cash Flows from Operating Activities

Net Income

| Add (subtract) items that affect net income and cash flow differently | + Depreciation
+ Depletion
+ Amortization
+ Loss on disposal or exchange of long-term asset or early extinguishment of debt
− Gain on disposal of long-term asset or early extinguishment of debt
+ Decrease in current asset other than cash
− Increase in current asset other than cash
+ Increase in current liability*
− Decrease in current liability* |

Net cash inflow (or outflow) from operating activities

*Short-term notes payable for general borrowing, and current portion of long-term notes payable, are related to financing activities, not to operating activities.

We thank Barbara Gerrity and Jean Marie Hudson for suggesting this exhibit.

PUTTING SKILLS TO WORK

NIKE'S STATEMENT OF CASH FLOWS FOR OPERATING ACTIVITIES—INDIRECT METHOD

NIKE, INC.
STATEMENT OF CASH FLOWS
(INDIRECT METHOD FOR OPERATING ACTIVITIES)
FOR THE YEAR ENDED MAY 31, 19X7
(IN THOUSANDS)

Cash provided (used) by operations:	
Net income	$ 35,879
Income charges (credits) not affecting cash:	
Depreciation	12,078
Deferred income taxes	8,486
Other	2,494
Changes in certain working capital components:	
Decrease in inventory	59,542
Decrease in accounts receivable	1,174
Decrease in other current assets	4,331
Increase in accounts payable, accrued liabilities, and income taxes payable	8,462
Cash provided by operations	132,446
Cash provided (used) by investing activities:	
Additions to property, plant, and equipment	(11,874)
Disposals of property, plant, and equipment	1,728
Additions to other assets	(930)
Cash used by investing activities	(11,076)
Cash provided (used) by financing activities:	
Additions to long-term debt	30,332
Reductions in long-term debt including current portion	(10,678)
Decrease in notes payable to banks	(18,489)
Proceeds from exercise of options	1,911
Dividends—common and preferred	(15,188)
Cash used by financing activities	(12,112)
Effect of exchange-rate changes on cash	(529)
Net increase (decrease) in cash	108,729
Cash and equivalents, beginning of year	18,138
Cash and equivalents, end of year	$126,867

Nike, Inc., is a well-known maker of athletic shoes and clothing. Nike uses the indirect method to report cash flows from operating activities. Most of the items in Nike's statement of cash flows have been discussed earlier, but three need clarification. First, deferred income taxes are added back to net income in the operating section. These taxes do not require current cash payments and are, therefore, similar to accrued liabilities. Second, financing activities include proceeds from exercise of options. This is the amount of cash received from issuance of stock to executives. Third, changes in exchange rates show the cash effect of fluctuations in foreign currencies, a topic that is beyond the scope of this course. Nike's reporting of this item agrees with GAAP.

EVALUATION OF NIKE'S 19X7 CASH-FLOW RESULTS

Nike's cash flows for 19X7 look very strong. Cash increased from $18 million to almost $127 million. Virtually all the cash increase came from operations—a sign of strength. During 19X7, Nike invested in new plant and equipment ($11.9 million) and paid off more than $29 million ($10.7 million + $18.5 million) of debt. The company issued only $30 million of new debt. Nike's board of directors was so confident of the future that the board paid $15 million of dividends, almost half of net income.

Nike, Inc., reports cash flows by the indirect method.

STOP & THINK Examine Anchor Corporation's statement of cash flows, Exhibit 18-11.

a. Does Anchor Corporation appear to be growing or shrinking? How can you tell?

b. Where did Anchor's cash for expansion come from?

c. Suppose Accounts Receivable increased by $40,000 (instead of $13,000) during the current year. What would this increase signal about the company?

Answers:

a. This is an *INVESTING* question. Anchor appears to be growing. The company acquired more plant assets ($306,000) than it sold during the year, and current assets changed very little.

b. This is a *FINANCING* question. The cash for expansion came from the issuance of common stock ($101,000) and from borrowing ($94,000).

c. This is an *OPERATING* question. If accounts receivable had increased by $40,000, Anchor Corporation would have $27,000 less cash ($40,000 minus $13,000). A large increase in accounts receivable may signal difficulty in collecting cash from customers or a sharp increase in sales. A manager, stockholder, or creditor of Anchor Corporation should compare current-year sales with sales revenue for the preceding year. If sales are up, higher accounts receivable are good news. If sales are down, higher receivables may signal a cash shortage.

Computers and the Indirect Method of Generating the Statement of Cash Flows

The computer can generate the statement of cash flows by the indirect method with ease. After the income statement is prepared, the computer picks up net income, depreciation, and the other noncash expenses. Changes in the current assets and the current liabilities and the data for the investing activities and the financing activities are obtained from the specific account balances in the general ledger.

The statement of cash flows created from a computer's general ledger files is not automatically correct from a GAAP point of view. For example, noncash financing and investing activities of a large corporation, such as Abbott Laboratories, a manufacturer of pharmaceuticals, might be incorrectly combined with the company's cash flows. The computerized system must be sophisticated enough to distinguish among the various categories of cash activities. Most important, accountants must analyze the information fed into the computer and check that its output adheres to generally accepted accounting principals. Revisions to a company's computer accounting system are common.

SUMMARY PROBLEM FOR YOUR REVIEW

Prepare the 19X3 statement of cash flows for Robins Corporation, using the indirect method to report cash flows from operating activities. In a separate schedule, report Robins's noncash investing and financing activities.

	December 31,	
	19X3	**19X2**
Current assets:		
Cash and cash equivalents	$19,000	$ 3,000
Accounts receivable	22,000	23,000
Inventories	34,000	31,000
Prepaid expenses	1,000	3,000
Current liabilities:		
Notes payable (for inventory purchases)	$11,000	$ 7,000
Accounts payable	24,000	19,000
Accrued liabilities	7,000	9,000
Income tax payable	10,000	10,000

Transaction data for 19X3:

Purchase of equipment	$98,000	Depreciation expense	$ 7,000
Payment of cash dividends	18,000	Issuance of long-term note payable	
Net income	26,000	to borrow cash	7,000
Issuance of common stock to		Issuance of common stock for cash	19,000
retire bonds payable	13,000	Sale of building	74,000
Purchase of long-term investment	8,000	Amortization expense	3,000
Issuance of long-term note payable		Purchase of treasury stock	5,000
to purchase patent	37,000	Loss on sale of building	2,000

SOLUTION TO REVIEW PROBLEM

ROBINS CORPORATION
STATEMENT OF CASH FLOWS
YEAR ENDED DECEMBER 31, 19X3
INCREASE (DECREASE) IN CASH AND CASH EQUIVALENTS

Cash flows from operating activities:		
Net income		$26,000
Add (subtract) items that affect net income and cash flow differently:		
Depreciation	$ 7,000	
Amortization	3,000	
Loss on sale of building	2,000	
Decrease in accounts receivable	1,000	
Increase in inventories	(3,000)	
Decrease in prepaid expenses	2,000	
Increase in notes payable, short-term	4,000	
Increase in accounts payable	5,000	
Decrease in accrued liabilities	(2,000)	19,000
Net cash inflow from operating activities		45,000
Cash flows from investing activities:		
Purchase of equipment	$(98,000)	
Sale of building	74,000	
Purchase of long-term investment	(8,000)	
Net cash outflow from investing activities		(32,000)
Cash flows from financing activities:		
Issuance of common stock	$ 19,000	
Payment of cash dividends	(18,000)	
Issuance of long-term note payable	7,000	
Purchase of treasury stock	(5,000)	
Net cash inflow from financing activities		3,000
Net increase in cash and cash equivalents		$16,000
Noncash investing and financing activities:		
Issuance of long-term note payable to purchase patent		$37,000
Issuance of common stock to retire bonds payable		13,000
Total noncash investing and financing activities		$50,000

SUMMARY

1. Identify the purposes of the statement of cash flows.
The *statement of cash flows* reports a business's cash receipts, cash disbursements, and net change in cash for the accounting period. It shows *why* cash increased or decreased during the period. A required financial statement, it gives a different view of the business from that given by accrual-basis statements. The cash-flow statement helps financial statement users predict the future cash flows of the entity. Cash includes cash on hand, cash in bank, and *cash equivalents* such as liquid, short-term investments.

2. Distinguish among operating, investing, and financing activities. The statement is divided into *operating activities*, *investing activities*, and *financing activities*. Operating activities create revenues and expenses; investing activities affect long-term assets; and financing activities obtain the cash needed to launch and sustain the business. Each section of the statement includes cash receipts and cash payments and concludes with a net cash increase or decrease. In addition, *noncash investing and financing activities* are reported in an accompanying schedule.

3. Prepare a statement of cash flows by the direct method. Two formats are used to report operating activities—the direct method and the indirect method. The *direct method* lists the major sources of cash receipts and disbursements—for example, cash collections from customers and cash payments to suppliers and to employees.

4. Use the financial statements to compute the cash effects of a wide variety of business transactions. The analysis of T-accounts aids the computation of the cash effects of business transactions.

5. Prepare a statement of cash flows by the indirect method. The *indirect method* shows the reconciliation from net income to cash flow from operations. Although the FASB permits both the indirect and the direct methods, it prefers the direct method. The indirect method, however, is more widely used in practice.

SELF-STUDY QUESTIONS

Test your understanding of the chapter by marking the best answer for each of the following questions.

1. The income statement and the balance sheet (p. 730)
   a. Report the cash effects of transactions
   b. Fail to report why cash changed during the period
   c. Report the sources and uses of cash during the period
   d. Are divided into operating, investing, and financing activities

2. The purpose of the statement of cash flows is to (p. 731)
   a. Predict future cash flows
   b. Evaluate management decisions
   c. Determine the ability to pay dividends and interest
   d. All of the above

3. A successful company's major source of cash should be (pp. 731–732)
   a. Operating activities
   b. Investing activities
   c. Financing activities
   d. A combination of the above

4. Dividends paid to stockholders are reported on the statement of cash flows as a (an) (p. 734)
   a. Operating activity
   b. Investing activity
   c. Financing activity
   d. Combination of the above

5. Which of the following items appears on a cash-flow statement prepared by the direct method? (p. 732)
   a. Depreciation expense
   b. Decrease in accounts receivable
   c. Loss on sale of plant assets
   d. Cash payments to suppliers

6. Interest Receivable's beginning balance is $18,000, and its ending amount is $14,000. Interest revenue earned during the year is $43,000. How much cash interest was received? (pp. 740–742)

a. $39,000   c. $45,000
b. $43,000   d. $47,000

7. McGrath Company sold an investment at a gain of $22,000. The Investment account reports a beginning balance of $104,000 and an ending balance of $91,000. During the year, McGrath purchased new investments costing $31,000. What were the proceeds from the sale of investments? (p. 744)
   a. $22,000   c. $66,000
   b. $44,000   d. $186,000

8. Noncash investing and financing activities (p. 746)
   a. Are reported in the cash-flow statement itself
   b. Are reported in a separate schedule that accompanies the cash-flow statement
   c. Are reported on the income statement
   d. Are not reported in the financial statements

9. The indirect method does a better job than the direct method of (p. 747)
   a. Reporting the cash effects of financing activities
   b. Reporting why the cash balance changed
   c. Showing the link between net income and cash flow from operations
   d. Reporting the separate components of operating cash flows such as collections from customers and payments to suppliers and employees

10. Net income is $17,000, depreciation is $9,000, and amortization is $3,000. In addition, the sale of a plant asset generated a $4,000 gain. Current assets other than cash increased by $6,000, and current liabilities increased by $8,000. What was the amount of cash flow from operations? (p. 748)
    a. $23,000   c. $31,000
    b. $27,000   d. $35,000

Answers to the Self-Study Questions follow the Accounting Vocabulary.

ACCOUNTING VOCABULARY

Cash equivalents. Highly liquid short-term investments that can be converted into cash with little delay (p. 731).

Cash flows. Cash receipts and cash payments (disbursements) (p. 730).

Direct method. Format of the operating activities section of the statement of cash flows that lists the major cate-gories of operating cash receipts (collections from customers and receipts of interest and dividends) and cash disbursements (payments to suppliers, to employees, for interest and income taxes) (p. 734).

Financing activity. Activity that obtains the funds from investors and creditors needed to launch and sustain the busi-ness; a section of the statement of cash flows (p. 733).

Indirect method. Format of the operating activities section of the statement of cash flows that starts with net income and shows the reconciliation from net income to operating cash flows. Also called the reconciliation method (p. 734).

Investing activity. Activity that increases and decreases the long-term assets available to the business; a section of the statement of cash flows (p. 732).

Operating activity. Activity that creates revenue or expense in the entity's major line of business; a section of the statement of cash flows. Operating activities affect the income statement (p. 732).

Reconciliation method. Another name for the indirect method (p. 747).

Statement of cash flows. Reports cash receipts and cash disbursements classified according to the entity's major activities: operating, investing, and financing (p. 730).

ANSWER TO SELF-STUDY QUESTIONS

1. b
2. d
3. a
4. c
5. d
6. d ($43,000 + $4,000 decrease in Interest Receivable = $47,000)
7. c ($104,000 + $31,000 – Cost of investment sold = $91,000; Cost = $44,000; Proceeds = Cost, $44,000 + Gain, $22,000 = $66,000)
8. b
9. c
10. b ($17,000 + $9,000 + $3,000 – $4,000 – $6,000 + $8,000 = $27,000)

QUESTIONS

1. What information does the statement of cash flows report that is not shown on the balance sheet, the income statement, or the statement of retained earnings?

2. Identify four purposes of the statement of cash flows.

3. Identify and briefly describe the three types of activities that are reported on the statement of cash flows.

4. How is the statement of cash flows dated, and why?

5. What is the check figure for the statement of cash flows? Where is it obtained, and how is it used?

6. What is the most important source of cash for most successful companies?

7. How can cash decrease during a year when income is high? How can cash increase during a year when income is low? How can investors and creditors learn these facts about the company?

8. DeBerg, Inc., prepares its statement of cash flows by the *direct* method for operating activities. Identify the section of DeBerg's statement of cash flows where each of the following transactions will appear. If the transaction does not appear on the cash-flow statement, give the reason.

   a. Cash 14,000
          Note Payable, Long-Term   14,000
   b. Salary Expense 7,300
          Cash   7,300
   c. Cash... 28,400
          Sales Revenue   28,400
   d. Amortization Expense................. 6,500
          Goodwill...........................   6,500
   e. Accounts Payable 1,400
          Cash   1,400

9. Why are depreciation, depletion, and amortization expenses *not* reported on a cash-flow statement that reports operating activities by the direct method? Why and how are these expenses reported on a statement prepared by the indirect method?

10. Mainline Distributing Company collected cash of $92,000 from customers and $6,000 interest on notes receivable. Cash payments included $24,000 to employees, $13,000 to suppliers, $6,000 as dividends to stockholders, and $5,000 as a loan to another company. How much was Mainline's net cash inflow from operating activities?

11. Summarize the major cash receipts and cash disbursements in the three categories of activities that appear on the cash-flow statement.

12. Kirchner, Inc., recorded salary expense of $51,000 during a year when the balance of Salary Payable decreased from $10,000 to $2,000. How much cash did Kirchner pay to employees during the year? Where on the statement of cash flows should Kirchner report this item?

13. Marshall Corporation's beginning plant asset balance, net of accumulated depreciation, was $193,000, and the ending amount was $176,000. Marshall recorded depreciation of $37,000 and sold plant assets with a book value of $9,000. How much cash did Marshall pay to purchase plant assets during the period? Where on the statement of cash flows should Marshall report this item?

14. How should issuance of a note payable to purchase land be reported in the financial statements? Identify three other transactions that fall in this same category.

15. Which format of the cash-flow statement gives a clearer description of the individual cash flows from operating activities? Which format better shows the relationship between net income and operating cash flow?

16. An investment that cost $65,000 was sold for $80,000, resulting in a $15,000 gain. Show how to report this transaction on a statement of cash flows prepared by the indirect method.

17. Identify the cash effects of increases and decreases in current assets other than cash. What are the cash effects of increases and decreases in current liabilities?

18. Milano Corporation earned net income of $38,000 and had depreciation expense of $22,000. Also, noncash current assets decreased $13,000, and current liabilities decreased $9,000. What was Milano's net cash flow from operating activities?

19. What is the difference between the direct method and the indirect method of reporting investing activities and financing activities?

20. Milgrom Company reports operating activities by the direct method. Does this method show the relationship between net income and cash flow from operations? If so, state how. If not, how can Milgrom satisfy this purpose of the cash-flow statement?

EXERCISES

Identifying the purposes of the statement of cash flows
(Obj. 1)

E18-1 Prime Hotel Properties, a real estate partnership, has experienced an unbroken string of 10 years of growth in net income. Nevertheless, the business is facing bankruptcy! Creditors are calling all of Prime's outstanding loans for immediate payment, and the cash is simply not available. Attempts to explain where Prime went wrong make it clear that managers placed undue emphasis on net income and gave too little attention to cash flows.

Required

Write a brief memo, in your own words, to explain to the managers of Prime Hotel Properties the purposes of the statement of cash flows.

Identifying activities for the statement of cash flows
(Obj. 2)

E18-2 Identify each of the following transactions as an operating activity (O), an investing activity (I), a financing activity (F), a noncash investing and financing activity (NIF), or a transaction that is not reported on the statement of cash flows (N). Assume that the direct method is used to report cash flows from operating activities.

_____ **a.** Payment of account payable
_____ **b.** Issuance of preferred stock for cash
_____ **c.** Payment of cash dividend
_____ **d.** Sale of long-term investment
_____ **e.** Amortization of bond discount
_____ **f.** Collection of account receivable
_____ **g.** Issuance of long-term note payable to borrow cash
_____ **h.** Depreciation of equipment
_____ **i.** Purchase of treasury stock
_____ **j.** Issuance of common stock for cash
_____ **k.** Purchase of long-term investment
_____ **l.** Payment of wages to employees
_____ **m.** Collection of cash interest
_____ **n.** Cash sale of land
_____ **o.** Distribution of stock dividend
_____ **p.** Acquisition of equipment by issuance of note payable
_____ **q.** Payment of long-term debt
_____ **r.** Acquisition of building by issuance of common stock
_____ **s.** Accrual of salary expense

Classifying transactions for the statement of cash flows
(Obj. 2)

E18-3 Indicate where, if at all, each of the following transactions would be reported on a statement of cash flows prepared by the *direct* method and the accompanying schedule of noncash investing and financing activities.

a. Salary Expense	4,300	
Cash		4,300
b. Equipment	18,000	
Cash		18,000
c. Cash	7,200	
Long-Term Investment		7,200
d. Bonds Payable	45,000	
Cash		45,000

e.	Building...	164,000	
	Note Payable, Long-Term		164,000
f.	Cash...	1,400	
	Accounts Receivable		1,400
g.	Dividends Payable..	16,500	
	Cash..		16,500
h.	Furniture and Fixtures..	22,100	
	Note Payable, Short-Term		22,100
i.	Accounts Payable	8,300	
	Cash..		8,300
j.	Cash...	81,000	
	Common Stock..		12,000
	Paid-in Capital in Excess of Par—Common.............		69,000
k.	Treasury Stock...	13,000	
	Cash..		13,000
l.	Retained Earnings...	36,000	
	Common Stock..		36,000
m.	Cash...	2,000	
	Interest Revenue		2,000
n.	Land	87,700	
	Cash..		87,700

E18-4   Analysis of the accounting records of Beaufain Corporation reveals:

Computing cash flows from operating activities—direct method **(Obj. 3)**

Cash sales...............................	$ 9,000	Increase in current assets	
Loss on sale of land	5,000	other than cash...............	$17,000
Acquisition of land	37,000	Payment of dividends	7,000
Payment of accounts		Collection of accounts	
payable	48,000	receivable	93,000
Net income..............................	21,000	Payment of salaries and	
Payment of income tax.............	13,000	wages	34,000
Collection of dividend		Depreciation	12,000
revenue..............................	7,000	Decrease in current	
Payment of interest	16,000	liabilities.......................	23,000

Compute cash flows from operating activities by the direct method. Use the format of the operating section of Exhibit 18-2.

E18-5   Selected accounts of Indigo Investments, Inc., show:

Identifying items for the statement of cash flows—direct method **(Obj. 3)**

Dividends Receivable

Beginning balance	9,000	Cash receipts of dividends	38,000
Dividend revenue	40,000		
Ending balance	11,000		

Investment in Land

Beginning balance	90,000	Cost of investments sold	109,000
Acquisitions	127,000		
Ending balance	108,000		

Long-Term Debt

Payments	69,000	Beginning balance	273,000
		Issuance of debt for cash	83,000
		Ending balance	287,000

For each account, identify the item or items that should appear on a statement of cash flows prepared by the direct method. State where to report the item.

Preparing the statement of cash flows—direct method
(Obj. 3)

E18-6 The income statement and additional data of Nebraska Milling Company follow.

NEBRASKA MILLING COMPANY
INCOME STATEMENT
YEAR ENDED SEPTEMBER 30, 19X2

Revenues:		
Sales revenue............................	$229,000	
Dividend revenue.....................	8,000	$237,000
Expenses:		
Cost of goods sold	103,000	
Salary expense..........................	45,000	
Depreciation expense...............	29,000	
Advertising expense	11,000	
Interest expense	2,000	
Income tax expense..................	9,000	199,000
Net income		$ 38,000

Additional data:

a. Collections from customers are $7,000 more than sales.
b. Payments to suppliers are $9,000 less than the sum of cost of goods sold plus advertising expense.
c. Payments to employees are $1,000 more than salary expense.
d. Dividend revenue, interest expense, and income tax expense equal their cash amounts.
e. Acquisition of plant assets is $116,000. Of this amount, $101,000 is paid in cash, $15,000 by signing a note payable.
f. Proceeds from sale of land, $14,000.
g. Proceeds from issuance of common stock, $30,000.
h. Payment of long-term note payable, $15,000.
i. Payment of dividends, $11,000.
j. Increase in cash balance, $?

Prepare Nebraska Milling Company's statement of cash flows and accompanying schedule of non-cash investing and financing activities. Report operating activities by the *direct* method.

Computing amounts for the statement of cash flows
(Obj. 3, 4)

E18-7 Compute the following items for the statement of cash flows:

a. Cost of goods sold is $82,000. Beginning Inventory balance is $25,000, and ending Inventory balance is $21,000. Beginning and ending Accounts Payable are $11,000 and $8,000, respectively. How much are cash payments for inventory?
b. Beginning and ending Accounts Receivable are $22,000 and $26,000, respectively. Credit sales for the period total $81,000. How much are cash collections?

Computing investing and financing amounts for the statement of cash flows
(Obj. 4)

E18-8 Compute the following items for the statement of cash flows:

a. Beginning and ending Plant Assets, net, are $103,000 and $107,000, respectively. Depreciation for the period is $16,000, and acquisitions of new plant assets are $27,000. Plant assets were sold at a $1,000 gain. What were the cash proceeds of the sale?
b. Beginning and ending Retained Earnings are $45,000 and $73,000, respectively. Net income for the period is $62,000, and stock dividends are $22,000. How much are cash dividend payments?

Computing cash flows from operating activities—indirect method
(Obj. 5)

E18-9 The accounting records of Beaufain Corporation reveal the following:

Cash sales...	$ 9,000	Payment of accounts payable	$48,000
Loss on sale of land	5,000	Net income	21,000
Acquisition of land	37,000	Payment of income tax	13,000

Collection of dividend revenue........	$ 7,000	Collection of accounts receivable	$93,000
Payment of interest	16,000	Payment of salaries and	
Increase in current assets		wages	34,000
other than cash	17,000	Depreciation	12,000
Payment of dividends	7,000	Decrease in current liabilities......	23,000

Compute cash flows from operating activities by the indirect method. Use the format of the operating section of Exhibit 18-11.

E18-10 Two transactions of Battery Amusement Co. are recorded as follows:

Classifying transactions for the statement of cash flows
(Obj. 3, 5)

a. Cash	59,000	
Accumulated Depreciation....................	83,000	
Equipment		135,000
Gain on Sale of Equipment..............		7,000
b. Land...	290,000	
Cash		130,000
Note Payable		160,000

Required

1. Indicate where, how, and in what amount to report these transactions on the statement of cash flows and accompanying schedule of noncash investing and financing activities. Battery Amusement Co. reports cash flows from operating activities by the *direct* method.

2. Repeat Requirement 1, assuming that Battery reports cash flows from operating activities by the *indirect* method.

E18-11 Use the income statement of Nebraska Milling Company in Exercise 18-6, plus these additional data:

Preparing the statement of cash flows by the indirect method
(Obj. 5)

a. Collections from customers are $7,000 more than sales.

b. Payments to suppliers are $9,000 less than the sum of cost of goods sold plus advertising expense.

c. Payments to employees are $1,000 more than salary expense.

d. Dividend revenue, interest expense, and income tax expense equal their cash amounts.

e. Acquisition of plant assets is $116,000. Of this amount, $101,000 is paid in cash, $15,000 by signing a note payable.

f. Proceeds from sale of land, $14,000.

g. Proceeds from issuance of common stock, $30,000.

h. Payment of long-term note payable, $15,000.

i. Payment of dividends, $11,000.

j. Increase in cash balance, $?

k. From the balance sheet:

	September 30,	
	19X2	**19X1**
Current Assets:		
Accounts receivable...	$51,000	$58,000
Inventory	83,000	77,000
Prepaid expenses	9,000	8,000
Current Liabilities:		
Notes payable (for inventory purchases)	$20,000	$20,000
Accounts payable..	35,000	22,000
Accrued liabilities..	23,000	21,000

Prepare Nebraska Milling Company's statement of cash flows for the year ended September 30, 19X2, using the indirect method.

Computing cash flows from operating activities—indirect method
(Obj. 5)

E18-12 The accounting records of Chen Restaurant Supply include these accounts:

Cash			
Mar. 1	5,000		
Receipts	47,000	Payments	48,000
Mar. 31	4,000		

Accounts Receivable			
Mar. 1	18,000		
Sales	43,000	Collections	47,000
Mar. 31	14,000		

Inventory			
Mar. 1	19,000		
Purchases	37,000	Cost of sales	35,000
Mar. 31	21,000		

Equipment			
Mar. 1	93,000		
Acquisition	6,000		
Mar. 31	99,000		

Accumulated Depreciation—Equipment			
		Mar. 1	52,000
		Depreciation	3,000
		Mar. 31	55,000

Accounts Payable			
Payments	32,000	Mar. 1	14,000
		Purchases	37,000
		Mar. 31	19,000

Accrued Liabilities			
		Mar. 1	9,000
Payments	14,000	Expenses	11,000
		Mar. 31	6,000

Retained Earnings			
Quarterly		Mar. 1	64,000
dividend	18,000	Net income	19,000
		Mar. 31	65,000

Compute Chen's net cash inflow or outflow from operating activities during March. Does Chen have trouble collecting receivables or selling inventory? How can you tell?

Interpreting a cash-flow statement—indirect method
(Obj. 5)

E18-13 Consider three independent cases for the cash-flow data of Prime Motor Company:

	Case A	Case B	Case C
Cash flows from operating activities:			
Net income...	$ 30,000	$ 30,000	$ 30,000
Depreciation and amortization............	11,000	11,000	11,000
Increase in current assets	(19,000)	(7,000)	(1,000)
Decrease in current liabilities	(6,000)	(8,000)	–0–
	$ 16,000	$ 26,000	$ 40,000
Cash flows from investing activities:			
Acquisition of plant assets....................	$(91,000)	$ (91,000)	$(91,000)
Sales of plant assets	97,000	4,000	8,000
	$ 6,000	$ (87,000)	$(83,000)
Cash flows from financing activities:			
New borrowing	$ 16,000	$104,000	$ 50,000
Payment of debt	(21,000)	(29,000)	(9,000)
	$ (5,000)	$ 75,000	$ 41,000
Net increase (decrease in cash)	$ 17,000	$ 14,000	$ (2,000)

For each case, identify from the cash-flow statement how Prime generated the cash to acquire new plant assets.

CHALLENGE EXERCISE

Analyzing an actual company's statement of cash flows
(Obj. 5)

E18-14 PepsiCo's statement of cash flows for 1992 is reproduced on page 761.

Required

1. Which format does PepsiCo use for reporting cash flows from operating activities?
2. What was PepsiCo's largest source of cash during 1992? 1991? 1990?
3. The operating activities section of the statement lists (millions):

Consolidated Statement of Cash Flows

(in millions)
PepsiCo, Inc. and Subsidiaries
Fifty-two weeks ended December 26, 1992, December 28, 1991 and December 29, 1990

	1992	1991	1990
Cash Flows — Continuing Operations:			
Income from continuing operations before cumulative effect of accounting changes	$1,301.7	$1,080.2	$1,090.6
Adjustments to reconcile income from continuing operations before cumulative effect of accounting changes to net cash provided by continuing operations:			
Depreciation and amortization	1,214.9	1,034.5	884.0
Deferred income taxes	(52.0)	98.0	86.4
Gain on joint venture stock offering	—	—	(118.2)
Other noncash charges and credits, net	315.6	227.2	120.3
Changes in operating working capital, excluding effect of acquisitions:			
Accounts and notes receivable	(45.7)	(55.9)	(124.8)
Inventories	(11.8)	(54.8)	(20.9)
Prepaid expenses, taxes and other current assets	(27.4)	(75.6)	(41.9)
Accounts payable	(102.0)	57.8	25.4
Income taxes payable	(16.9)	(3.4)	136.3
Other current liabilities	135.2	122.3	72.8
Net change in operating working capital	(68.6)	(9.6)	46.9
Net Cash Provided by Continuing Operations	2,711.6	2,430.3	2,110.0
Cash Flows — Investing Activities:			
Acquisitions and investments in affiliates	(1,209.7)	(640.9)	(630.6)
Purchases of property, plant and equipment	(1,549.6)	(1,457.8)	(1,180.1)
Proceeds from sales of property, plant and equipment	89.0	69.6	45.3
Short-term investments, by original maturity:			
More than three months — purchases	(1,174.8)	(1,849.2)	(2,093.2)
More than three months — sales	1,371.8	1,873.2	2,139.4
Three months or less, net	(249.4)	(164.9)	(228.0)
Proceeds from joint venture stock offering	—	—	129.6
Other, net	(30.8)	(105.8)	(119.7)
Net Cash Used for Investing Activities	(2,753.5)	(2,275.8)	(1,937.3)
Cash Flows — Financing Activities:			
Proceeds from issuances of long-term debt	1,092.7	2,799.6	777.3
Payments of long-term debt	(616.3)	(1,348.5)	(298.0)
Short-term borrowings, by original maturity:			
More than three months — proceeds	911.2	2,551.9	4,041.9
More than three months — payments	(2,062.6)	(3,097.4)	(2,647.4)
Three months or less, net	1,075.3	(467.1)	(1,480.7)
Cash dividends paid	(395.5)	(343.2)	(293.9)
Purchases of treasury stock	(32.0)	(195.2)	(147.7)
Proceeds from exercises of stock options	82.8	15.8	9.3
Other, net	(30.9)	(47.0)	(37.9)
Net Cash Provided by (Used for) Financing Activities	24.7	(131.1)	(77.1)
Effect of Exchange Rate Changes on Cash and Cash Equivalents	0.4	(7.5)	(1.0)
Net Increase (Decrease) in Cash and Cash Equivalents	(16.8)	15.9	94.6
Cash and Cash Equivalents — Beginning of Year	186.7	170.8	76.2
Cash and Cash Equivalents — End of Year	$ 169.9	$ 186.7	$ 170.8

See accompanying Notes to Consolidated Financial Statements, including Note 4 — Supplemental Cash Flow Information.

Accounts and notes receivable.............. ($45.7)
Accounts payable................................. ($102.0)

Did these accounts' balances increase or decrease during 1992? How can you tell?

4. During 1992, PepsiCo sold property, plant, and equipment. The gain or loss on this transaction is included in "Other noncash charges and credits, net" of $315.6 million. Assume that the book value of the plant assets that PepsiCo sold during 1992 was $104.3 million. Journalize the sale of the property, plant, and equipment.

5. During the three-year period 1990 through 1992, PepsiCo engaged in much activity with its long-term debt and short-term borrowings. On the basis of this activity, does PepsiCo appear to be growing or shrinking? Also consider the company's trends of income from continuing operations, cash provided by operations, and investing activities.

PROBLEMS

(GROUP A)

Using cash-flow information to evaluate performance
(Obj. 1)

P18-1A Top managers of LTV Broadcasting, Inc., are reviewing company performance for 19X4. The income statement reports a 15-percent increase in net income, the fifth consecutive year with an income increase above 10 percent. The income statement includes a nonrecurring loss without which net income would have increased by 16 percent. The balance sheet shows modest increases in assets, liabilities, and stockholders' equity. The assets posting the largest increases are plant and equipment because the company is halfway through a five-year expansion program. No other assets and no liabilities are increasing dramatically. A summarized version of the cash-flow statement reports the following:

Net cash inflow from operating activities................	$310,000
Net cash outflow from investing activities...............	(290,000)
Net cash inflow from financing activities	70,000
Increase in cash during 19X4..................................	$ 90,000

Required

Write a memo to give top managers of LTV Broadcasting your assessment of 19X4 and your outlook for the future. Focus on the information content of the cash-flow data.

Preparing the statement of cash flows—direct method
(Obj. 2, 3)

P18-2A Outback Outfitters, Inc., accountants have developed the following data from the company's accounting records for the year ended July 31, 19X9:

a. Salary expense, $105,300
b. Cash payments to purchase plant assets, $181,000
c. Proceeds from issuance of short-term debt, $44,100
d. Payments of long-term debt, $18,800
e. Proceeds from sale of plant assets, $59,700, including $10,600 gain
f. Interest revenue, $12,100
g. Cash receipt of dividend revenue on stock investments, $2,700
h. Payments to suppliers, $673,300
i. Interest expense and payments, $37,800
j. Cost of goods sold, $481,100
k. Collection of interest revenue, $11,700
l. Acquisition of equipment by issuing short-term note payable, $35,500
m. Payments of salaries, $104,000
n. Credit sales, $608,100
o. Loan to another company, $35,000
p. Income tax expense and payments, $56,400
q. Depreciation expense, $27,700
r. Collections on accounts receivable, $673,100
s. Loan collections, $74,400
t. Proceeds from sale of investments, $34,700, including $3,800 loss
u. Payment of long-term debt by issuing preferred stock, $107,300

v. Amortization expense, $23,900

w. Cash sales, $146,000

x. Proceeds from issuance of common stock, $116,900

y. Payment of cash dividends, $50,500

z. Cash balance: July 31, 19X8—$53,800
　　　　　　July 31, 19X9—$?

Required

Prepare Outback's statement of cash flows for the year ended July 31, 19X9. Follow the format of Exhibit 18-2, but do *not* show amounts in thousands. Include an accompanying schedule of non-cash investing and financing activities. Evaluate 19X9 in terms of cash flow. Give your reasons.

P18-3A　　The 19X3 comparative balance sheet and income statement of Silverado, Inc., follow:

Preparing the statement of cash flows—direct method
(Obj. 2, 3, 4)

COMPARATIVE BALANCE SHEET

	19X3	19X2	Increase (Decrease)
Current assets:			
Cash and cash equivalents	$ 13,700	$ 15,600	$ (1,900)
Accounts receivable	41,500	43,100	(1,600)
Interest receivable	600	900	(300)
Inventories	94,300	89,900	4,400
Prepaid expenses	1,700	2,200	(500)
Plant assets:			
Land	35,100	10,000	25,100
Equipment, net	100,900	93,700	7,200
Total assets	$287,800	$255,400	$32,400
Current liabilities:			
Accounts payable	$ 16,400	$ 17,900	$ (1,500)
Interest payable	6,300	6,700	(400)
Salary payable	2,100	1,400	700
Other accrued liabilities	18,100	18,700	(600)
Income tax payable	6,300	3,800	2,500
Long-term liabilities:			
Notes payable	55,000	65,000	(10,000)
Stockholders' equity:			
Common stock, no-par	131,100	122,300	8,800
Retained earnings	52,500	19,600	32,900
Total liabilities and stockholders' equity	$287,800	$255,400	$32,400

INCOME STATEMENT FOR 19X3

Revenues:		
Sales revenue		$438,000
Interest revenue		11,700
Total revenues		449,700
Expenses:		
Cost of goods sold	$205,200	
Salary expense	76,400	
Depreciation expense	15,300	
Other operating expense	49,700	
Interest expense	24,600	
Income tax expense	16,900	
Total expenses		388,100
Net income		$ 61,600

Silverado had no noncash investing and financing transactions during 19X3. During the year there were no sales of land or equipment, no issuances of notes payable, no retirements of stock, and no treasury stock transactions.

Required

1. Prepare the 19X3 statement of cash flows, formating operating activities by the direct method.
2. How will what you learned in this problem help you evaluate an investment?

Preparing the statement of cash flows—indirect method
(Obj. 2, 3, 5)

P18-4A   Use the Silverado data from Problem 18-3A.

Required

1. Prepare the 19X3 statement of cash flows by the indirect method. If your instructor also assigned Problem 18-3A, prepare only the operating activities section.
2. How will what you learned in this problem help you evaluate an investment?

Preparing the statement of cash flows—indirect method
(Obj. 2, 5)

P18-5A   Accountants for Maplewood Manufacturing have assembled the following data for the year ended December 31, 19X4:

	December 31,	
	19X4	**19X3**
Current accounts (all result from operations):		
Current assets:		
Cash and cash equivalents	$38,600	$34,800
Accounts receivable	70,100	73,700
Inventories	90,600	96,500
Prepaid expenses..	3,200	2,100
Current liabilities:		
Notes payable (for inventory purchases)........	$36,300	$36,800
Accounts payable	72,100	67,500
Income tax payable	5,900	6,800
Accrued liabilities	28,300	23,200

Transaction data for 19X4:

Stock dividends	$ 12,600	Payment of cash dividends	$48,300
Collection of loan	10,300	Issuance of long-term debt	
Depreciation expense......................	19,200	to borrow cash	71,000
Acquisition of equipment	69,000	Net income	50,500
Payment of long-term debt		Issuance of preferred stock	
by issuing common stock............	89,400	for cash	36,200
Acquisition of long-term		Sale of long-term	
investment..................................	44,800	investment..................................	12,200
Acquisition of building by		Amortization expense	1,100
issuing long-term note		Payment of long-term debt............	47,800
payable...	118,000	Gain on sale of investment.............	3,500

Required

Prepare Maplewood Manufacturing's statement of cash flows, using the *indirect* method to report operating activities. Include an accompanying schedule of noncash investing and financing activities.

Preparing the statement of cash flows—indirect method
(Obj. 2, 5)

P18-6A   The comparative balance sheet of Sumter Enterprises, Inc., at December 31, 19X5, reported the following:

	December 31,	
	19X5	**19X4**
Current assets:		
Cash and cash equivalents	$10,600	$12,500
Accounts receivable	28,600	29,300
Inventories	51,600	53,000
Prepaid expenses	4,200	3,700
Current liabilities:		
Notes payable (for inventory purchases)...................	$ 9,200	$ –0–
Accounts payable	21,900	28,000
Accrued liabilities..	14,300	16,800
Income tax payable	11,000	14,300

Sumter's transactions during 19X5 included the following:

Amortization expense..........................	$ 5,000	Cash acquisition of building...........	$124,000
Payment of cash dividends	17,000	Net income	31,600
Cash acquisition of equipment.........	55,000	Issuance of common stock	
Issuance of long-term note		for cash	105,600
payable to borrow cash	32,000	Stock dividend	13,000
Retirement of bonds payable		Sale of long-term investment	6,000
by issuing common stock.............	55,000	Depreciation expense	15,000

Required

Prepare the statement of cash flows of Sumter Enterprises for the year ended December 31, 19X5. Use the *indirect* method to report cash flows from operating activities. Report noncash investing and financing activities in an accompanying schedule. All current account balances result from operating transactions.

P18-7A   To prepare the statement of cash flows, accountants for Ball State Corp. have summarized 19X8 activity in two accounts as follows:

Preparing the statement of cash flows—direct and indirect methods (Obj. 3, 5)

Cash

Beginning balance	87,100	Payments of operating	
Issuance of common stock	34,600	expenses	46,100
Receipts of dividends	1,900	Payment of long-term debt	78,900
Collection of loan	18,500	Purchase of treasury stock	10,400
Sale of investments	9,900	Payment of income tax	8,000
Receipts of interest	12,200	Payments on accounts	
Collections from		payable	101,600
customers	298,100	Payment of dividends	1,800
Sale of treasury stock	26,200	Payments of salaries	
		and wages	67,500
		Payments of interest	21,800
		Purchase of equipment	79,900
Ending balance	72,500		

Common Stock

	Beginning balance	103,500
	Issuance for cash	34,600
	Issuance to acquire land	62,100
	Issuance to retire	
	long-term debt	21,100
	Ending balance	221,300

Required

1. Prepare Ball State's statement of cash flows for the year ended December 31, 19X8, using the *direct* method to report operating activities. Also prepare the accompanying schedule of noncash investing and financing activities.

Ball State's 19X8 income statement and selected balance sheet data follow.

BALL STATE CORP. INCOME STATEMENT FOR THE YEAR ENDED DECEMBER 31, 19X8		
Revenues and gains:		
Sales revenue..................................		$281,800
Interest revenue		12,200
Dividend revenue.........................		1,900
Gain on sale of investments..........		700
Total revenues and gains...........		296,600
Expenses:		
Cost of goods sold........................	$103,600	
Salary and wage expense	66,800	
Depreciation expense....................	10,900	
Other operating expense..............	44,700	
Interest expense............................	24,100	
Income tax expense	2,600	
Total expenses		252,700
Net income		$ 43,900

BALL STATE CORP. BALANCE SHEET DATA	
	Increase (Decrease)
Current assets:	
Cash and cash equivalents	$?
Accounts receivable	(16,300)
Inventories	5,700
Prepaid expenses..........................	(1,900)
Loan receivable.............................	(18,500)
Investments...................................	(9,200)
Equipment, net..............................	69,000
Land...	62,100
Current liabilities:	
Accounts payable	$ 7,700
Interest payable............................	2,300
Salary payable	(700)
Other accrued liabilities	(3,300)
Income tax payable	(5,400)
Long-term debt	(100,000)
Common stock	117,800
Retained earnings	42,100
Treasury stock................................	(15,800)

2. Use these data to prepare a supplementary schedule showing cash flows from operating activities by the *indirect* method. All activity in the current accounts results from operations.

Preparing the statement of cash flows—indirect and direct methods (Obj. 3, 4, 5)

P18-8A   Seaman-Young Corporation's comparative balance sheet at September 30, 19X4, included the following balances:

```
                    SEAMAN-YOUNG CORPORATION
                          BALANCE SHEET
                 SEPTEMBER 30, 19X4 AND 19X3
```

	19X4	19X3	Increase (Decrease)
Current assets:			
Cash..	$ 48,700	$ 17,600	$ 31,100
Accounts receivable.........................	41,900	44,000	(2,100)
Interest receivable...........................	4,100	2,800	1,300
Inventories	121,700	116,900	4,800
Prepaid expenses.............................	8,600	9,300	(700)
Long-term investments	51,100	13,800	37,300
Equipment, net.................................	131,900	92,100	39,800
Land...	47,100	74,300	(27,200)
	$455,100	$370,800	$ 84,300
Current liabilities:			
Notes payable, short-term...............	$ 22,000	$ –0–	$ 22,000
Accounts payable..............................	61,800	70,300	(8,500)
Income tax payable...........................	21,800	24,600	(2,800)
Accrued liabilities.............................	17,900	29,100	(11,200)
Interest payable................................	4,500	3,200	1,300
Salary payable..................................	1,500	1,100	400
Long-term note payable.....................	123,000	121,400	1,600
Common stock...................................	113,900	62,000	51,900
Retained earnings	88,700	59,100	29,600
	$455,100	$370,800	$ 84,300

Transaction data for the year ended September 30, 19X4:

a. Net income, $93,900.
b. Depreciation expense on equipment, $8,500.
c. Acquired long-term investments, $37,300.
d. Sold land for $38,100, including $10,900 gain.
e. Acquired equipment by issuing long-term note payable, $26,300.
f. Paid long-term note payable, $24,700.
g. Received cash of $51,900 for issuance of common stock.
h. Paid cash dividends, $64,300.
i. Acquired equipment by issuing short-term note payable, $22,000.

Required

1. Prepare Seaman-Young's statement of cash flows for the year ended September 30, 19X4, using the *indirect* method to report operating activities. Also prepare the accompanying schedule of noncash investing and financing activities. All current accounts except short-term notes payable result from operating transactions.

2. Prepare a supplementary schedule showing cash flows from operations by the *direct* method. The income statement reports the following: sales, $370,600; gain on sale of land, $10,900; interest revenue, $7,300; cost of goods sold, $161,500; salary expense, $63,400; other operating expenses, $29,600; income tax expense, $18,400; interest expense, $13,500; depreciation expense, $8,500.

(GROUP B)

P18-1B Top managers of Charter Flight Service, Inc., are reviewing company performance for 19X7. The income statement reports a 20-percent increase in net income over 19X6. However, most of the increase resulted from an extraordinary gain on insurance proceeds covering fire damage to an airplane. The balance sheet shows a large increase in receivables. The cash-flow statement, in summarized form, reports the following:

Using cash-flow information to evaluate performance (Obj. 1)

Net cash outflow from operating activities................	$(80,000)
Net cash inflow from investing activities.................	40,000
Net cash inflow from financing activities	50,000
Increase in cash during 19X7.................................	$ 10,000

Required

Write a memo to give Charter managers your assessment of 19X7 operations and your outlook for the future. Focus on the information content of the cash-flow data.

Preparing the statement of cash flows—direct method
(Obj. 2, 3)

P18-2B   Pueblo Contractors, Inc., accountants have developed the following data from the company's accounting records for the year ended April 30, 19X5:

a.   Credit sales, $583,900
b.   Loan to another company, $12,500
c.   Cash payments to acquire plant assets, $59,400
d.   Cost of goods sold, $382,600
e.   Proceeds from issuance of common stock, $8,000
f.   Payment of cash dividends, $48,400
g.   Collection of interest, $4,400
h.   Acquisition of equipment by issuing short-term note payable, $16,400
i.   Payments of salaries, $93,600
j.   Proceeds from sale of plant assets, $22,400, including $6,800 loss
k.   Collections on accounts receivable, $462,600
l.   Interest revenue, $3,800
m.   Cash receipt of dividend revenue on stock investments, $4,100
n.   Payments to suppliers, $368,500
o.   Cash sales, $171,900
p.   Depreciation expense, $59,900
q.   Proceeds from issuance of short-term debt, $19,600
r.   Payments of long-term debt, $50,000
s.   Interest expense and payments, $13,300
t.   Salary expense, $95,300
u.   Loan collections, $12,800
v.   Proceeds from sale of investments, $9,100, including $2,000 gain
w.   Payment of short-term note payable by issuing long-term note payable, $63,000
x.   Amortization expense, $2,900
y.   Income tax expense and payments, $37,900
z.   Cash balance: April 30, 19X4—$39,300
                  April 30, 19X5—$?

Required

Prepare Pueblo's statement of cash flows for the year ended April 30, 19X5. Follow the format of Exhibit 18-2, but do *not* show amounts in thousands. Include an accompanying schedule of non-cash investing and financing activities. Evaluate 19X5 from a cash-flow standpoint. Give your reasons.

Preparing the statement of cash flows—direct method
(Obj. 2, 3, 4)

P18-3B   The 19X5 comparative balance sheet and income statement of Loco Taco Corp. follow on page 769.

Loco Taco had no noncash investing and financing transactions during 19X5. During the year there were no sales of land or equipment, no issuances of notes payable, no retirements of stock, and no treasury stock transactions.

Required

1.   Prepare the 19X5 statement of cash flows, formating operating activities by the direct method.
2.   How will what you learned in this problem help you evaluate an investment?

	19X5	19X4	Increase (Decrease)
Current assets:			
Cash and cash equivalents	$ 7,200	$ 5,300	$ 1,900
Accounts receivable	28,600	26,900	1,700
Interest receivable...	1,900	700	1,200
Inventories..	83,600	87,200	(3,600)
Prepaid expenses...	2,500	1,900	600
Plant assets:			
Land..	89,000	60,000	29,000
Equipment, net..	53,500	49,400	4,100
Total assets...	$266,300	$231,400	$34,900
Current liabilities:			
Accounts payable	$ 31,400	$ 28,800	$ 2,600
Interest payable...	4,400	4,900	(500)
Salary payable	3,100	6,600	(3,500)
Other accrued liabilities	13,700	16,000	(2,300)
Income tax payable	8,900	7,700	1,200
Long-term liabilities:			
Notes payable	75,000	100,000	(25,000)
Stockholders' equity:			
Common stock, no-par	88,300	64,700	23,600
Retained earnings	41,500	2,700	38,800
Total liabilities and stockholders' equity..............	$266,300	$231,400	$34,900

INCOME STATEMENT FOR 19X5

Revenues:		
Sales revenue....................................		$213,000
Interest revenue		8,600
Total revenues		221,600
Expenses:		
Cost of goods sold...........................	$70,600	
Salary expense	27,800	
Depreciation expense......................	4,000	
Other operating expense..............	10,500	
Interest expense...............................	11,600	
Income tax expense	29,100	
Total expenses		153,600
Net income		$ 68,000

P18-4B   Use the Loco Taco Corp. data from Problem 18-3B.

Preparing the statement of cash flows—indirect method (Obj. 2, 3, 5)

Required

1. Prepare the 19X5 statement of cash flows by the indirect method. If your instructor also assigned Problem 18-3B, prepare only the operating activities section of the statement.
2. How will what you learned in this problem help you evaluate an investment?

P18-5B   NavStar Corporation accountants have assembled the following data for the year ended December 31, 19X7:

Preparing the statement of cash flows—indirect method (Obj. 2, 5)

	December 31,	
	19X7	19X6

Current accounts (all result from operations):

Current assets:

Cash and cash equivalents.....................................	$55,700	$22,700
Accounts receivable...	69,700	64,200
Inventories	88,600	83,000
Prepaid expenses	5,300	4,100

Current liabilities:

Notes payable (for inventory purchases)..............	$22,600	$18,300
Accounts payable...	52,900	55,800
Income tax payable..	18,600	16,700
Accrued liabilities...	15,500	27,200

Transaction data for 19X7:

Acquisition of land by issuing long-term note payable.......................................	$107,000	Purchase of treasury stock..............	$14,300
		Loss on sale of equipment..............	11,700
Stock dividends	31,800	Payment of cash dividends	18,300
Collection of loan	8,700	Issuance of long-term note payable to borrow cash..	34,400
Depreciation expense....................	26,800		
Acquisition of building	125,300		
Retirement of bonds payable by issuing common stock	65,000	Net income	57,100
		Issuance of common stock for cash	41,200
Acquisition of long-term investment.................................	31,600	Sale of equipment..........................	58,000
		Amortization expense	5,300

Required

Prepare NavStar Corporation's statement of cash flows, using the *indirect* method to report operating activities. Include an accompanying schedule of noncash investing and financing activities.

Preparing the statement of cash flows—indirect method (Obj. 2, 5)

P18-6B The comparative balance sheet of Caterpillar Company at March 31, 19X7, reported the following:

	March 31,	
	19X7	19X6

Current assets:

Cash and cash equivalents	$13,600	$ 4,000
Accounts receivable	14,900	21,700
Inventories	63,200	60,600
Prepaid expenses	1,900	1,700

Current liabilities:

Notes payable (for inventory purchases)..................	$ 4,000	$ 4,000
Accounts payable	30,300	27,600
Accrued liabilities...	10,700	11,100
Income tax payable	8,000	4,700

Caterpillar's transactions during the year ended March 31, 19X7, included the following:

Acquisition of land by issuing note payable......................	$76,000	Sale of long-term investment...................................	$13,700
Amortization expense	2,000	Depreciation expense	9,000
Payment of cash dividend................	30,000	Cash acquisition of building..........	47,000
Cash acquisition of equipment.....................................	78,700	Net income	70,000
Issuance of long-term note payable to borrow cash	50,000	Issuance of common stock for cash	11,000
		Stock dividend	18,000

Required

Prepare Caterpillar's statement of cash flows for the year ended March 31, 19X7, using the *indirect* method to report cash flows from operating activities. Report noncash investing and financing activities in an accompanying schedule. All current account balances resulted from operating transactions.

P18-7B To prepare the statement of cash flows, accountants for Pentech, Inc., have summarized 19X3 activity in two accounts as follows:

Preparing the statement of cash flows—direct and indirect methods (Obj. 3, 5)

Cash

Beginning balance	53,600	Payments on accounts	
Collection of loan	13,000	payable	399,100
Sale of investment	8,200	Payments of dividends	27,200
Receipts of interest	12,600	Payments of salaries	
Collections from		and wages	143,800
customers	678,700	Payments of interest	26,900
Issuance of common		Purchase of equipment	31,400
stock	47,300	Payments of operating	
Receipts of dividends	4,500	expenses	34,300
		Payment of long-term	
		debt	41,300
		Purchase of treasury	
		stock	26,400
		Payment of income tax	18,900
Ending balance	68,600		

Common Stock

Beginning balance	84,400
Issuance for cash	47,300
Issuance to acquire land	80,100
Issuance to retire	
long-term debt	19,000
Ending balance	230,800

Required

1. Prepare the statement of cash flows of Pentech, Inc., for the year ended December 31, 19X3, using the *direct* method to report operating activities. Also prepare the accompanying schedule of noncash investing and financing activities.

2. Use the following data from Pentech's 19X3 income statement and (selected) balance sheet, on page 772, to prepare a supplementary schedule showing cash flows from operating activities by the *indirect* method. All activity in the current accounts results from operations.

```
                    PENTECH, INC.
                 INCOME STATEMENT
        FOR THE YEAR ENDED DECEMBER 31, 19X3
```

Revenues:		
Sales revenue		$706,300
Interest revenue		12,600
Dividend revenue		4,500
Total revenues		723,400
Expenses and losses:		
Cost of goods sold	$402,600	
Salary and wage expense	150,800	
Depreciation expense	24,300	
Other operating expense	44,100	
Interest expense	28,800	
Income tax expense	16,200	
Loss on sale of investments	1,100	
Total expenses		667,900
Net income		$ 55,500

PENTECH, INC. BALANCE SHEET DATA	
	Increase (Decrease)
Current assets:	
Cash and cash equivalents	$?
Accounts receivable	27,600
Inventories	(11,800)
Prepaid expenses.........................	600
Loan receivable............................	(13,000)
Long-term investments.................	(9,300)
Equipment, net..............................	7,100
Land..	80,100
Current liabilities:	
Accounts payable	$ (8,300)
Interest payable............................	1,900
Salary payable	7,000
Other accrued liabilities	10,400
Income tax payable	(2,700)
Long-term debt.............................	(60,300)
Common stock, no-par	146,400
Retained earnings	28,300
Treasury stock................................	26,400

Preparing the statement of cash flows—indirect and direct methods (Obj. 3, 4, 5)

P18-8B   The comparative balance sheet of Bosco Bolt Co. at June 30, 19X7, included the following balances:

BOSCO BOLT CO. BALANCE SHEET JUNE 30, 19X7 AND 19X6			
	19X7	19X6	Increase (Decrease)
Current assets:			
Cash..	$ 16,500	$ 8,600	$ 7,900
Accounts receivable...........................	45,900	48,300	(2,400)
Interest receivable.............................	2,900	3,600	(700)
Inventories	68,600	60,200	8,400
Prepaid expenses	3,700	2,800	900
Long-term investment........................	10,100	5,200	4,900
Equipment, net	82,500	73,600	8,900
Land	42,400	96,000	(53,600)
	$272,600	$298,300	$(25,700)
Current liabilities:			
Notes payable, short-term (for general borrowing)................	$ 13,400	$ 18,100	$ (4,700)
Accounts payable...............................	42,400	40,300	2,100
Income tax payable...........................	13,800	14,500	(700)
Accrued liabilities.............................	8,200	9,700	(1,500)
Interest payable.................................	3,700	2,900	800
Salary payable...................................	900	2,600	(1,700)
Long-term note payable......................	47,400	94,100	(46,700)
Common stock..................................	59,800	51,200	8,600
Retained earnings	83,000	64,900	18,100
	$272,600	$298,300	$(25,700)

Transaction data for the year ended June 30, 19X7:

a. Net income, $56,200.
b. Depreciation expense on equipment, $5,400.
c. Purchased long-term investment, $4,900.
d. Sold land for $46,900, including $6,700 loss.
e. Acquired equipment by issuing long-term note payable, $14,300.
f. Paid long-term note payable, $61,000.
g. Received cash for issuance of common stock, $3,900.
h. Paid cash dividends, $38,100.
i. Paid short-term note payable by issuing common stock, $4,700.

Required

1. Prepare the statement of cash flows of Bosco Bolt Co. for the year ended June 30, 19X7, using the *indirect* method to report operating activities. Also prepare the accompanying schedule of noncash investing and financing activities. All current accounts except short-term notes payable result from operating transactions.

2. Prepare a supplementary schedule showing cash flows from operations by the *direct* method. The income statement reports the following: sales, $237,300; interest revenue, $10,600; cost of goods sold, $82,800; salary expense, $38,800; other operating expenses, $42,000; depreciation expense, $5,400; income tax expense, $9,900; loss on sale of land, $6,700; interest expense, $6,100.

EXTENDING YOUR KNOWLEDGE

DECISION PROBLEMS

1. The 19X6 comparative income statement and the 19X6 comparative balance sheet of Navasota, Inc., have just been distributed at a meeting of the company's board of directors. The members of the board of directors raise a fundamental question: Why is the cash balance so low? This question is especially troublesome to the board members because 19X6 showed record profits. As the controller of the company, you must answer the question.

Preparing and using the statement of cash flows to evaluate operations (Obj. 4, 5)

NAVASOTA, INC. COMPARATIVE INCOME STATEMENT YEARS ENDED DECEMBER 31, 19X6 AND 19X5 (AMOUNTS IN THOUSANDS)		
	19X6	**19X5**
Revenues and gains:		
Sales revenue	$444	$310
Gain on sale of equipment (sale price, $33)	—	18
Totals	$444	$328
Expenses and losses:		
Cost of goods sold	$221	$162
Salary expense	48	28
Depreciation expense	46	22
Interest expense	13	20
Amortization expense on patent	11	11
Loss on sale of land (sale price, $61)	—	35
Totals	339	278
Net income	$105	$ 50

NAVASOTA, INC.
COMPARATIVE BALANCE SHEET
DECEMBER 31, 19X6 AND 19X5
(AMOUNTS IN THOUSANDS)

Assets	19X6	19X5
Cash	$ 33	$ 63
Accounts receivable, net...........................	72	61
Inventories	194	181
Long-term investments.............................	31	–0–
Property, plant, and equipment...............	361	259
Accumulated depreciation........................	(244)	(198)
Patents	177	188
Totals..	$624	$554

Liabilities and Owners' Equity		
Notes payable, short-term		
(for general borrowing)	$ 32	$101
Accounts payable	63	56
Accrued liabilities	12	17
Notes payable, long-term..........................	147	163
Common stock, no-par	149	61
Retained earnings	221	156
Totals..	$624	$554

Required

1. Prepare a statement of cash flows for 19X6 in the format that best shows the relationship between net income and operating cash flow. The company sold no plant assets or long-term investments and issued no notes payable during 19X6. The changes in all current accounts except short-term notes payable arose from operations. There were *no* noncash investing and financing transactions during the year. Show all amounts in thousands.

2. Answer the board members' question: Why is the cash balance so low? In explaining the business's cash flows, identify two significant cash receipts that occurred during 19X5 but not in 19X6. Also point out the two largest cash disbursements during 19X6.

3. Considering net income and the company's cash flows during 19X6, was it a good year or a bad year? Give your reasons.

Using cash-flow data to evaluate an investment (Obj. 1, 2)

2. Magna Corp. and Altex, Inc., have requested that you recommend that your clients invest in their stock. Magna and Altex earn about the same net income and have similar financial positions, so your decision depends on their cash-flow statements, summarized as follows:

	Magna		Altex	
Net cash inflows from operating activities......................		$70,000		$ 30,000
Net cash inflows (outflows) from investing activities:				
Purchase of plant assets	$(100,000)		$(20,000)	
Sale of plant assets	10,000	(90,000)	40,000	20,000
Net cash inflows (outflows) from financing activities:				
Issuance of common stock...		30,000		—
Paying off long-term debt		—		(40,000)
Net increase in cash...		$10,000		$ 10,000

On the basis of the cash flows of Magna and Altex, which company represents the better investment? Give your reasons.

ETHICAL ISSUE

Jarvis Travel Agency is experiencing a bad year. Net income is only $65,000. Also, two important clients are falling behind in paying the amounts they owe Jarvis, and Jarvis's accounts receivable are ballooning. The company desperately needs a loan. The Jarvis board of directors is considering ways to put the best face on the company's financial statements. Jarvis's bank emphasizes cash flow from operations. Gwen Morris, the controller, suggests reclassifying as long-term the receivables from the slow-paying clients. She explains to the board that removing the $30,000 rise in accounts receivable will increase net cash inflow from operations. This approach will increase the company's cash balance and may help Jarvis get the loan.

Required

1. Using only the amounts given, compute net cash inflow from operations both without and with the reclassification of the receivables. Which reporting makes Jarvis look better?
2. Where else in Jarvis's cash-flow statement will the reclassification of the receivable be reported? What cash-flow effect will this item report? Evaluate Morris's reasoning.
3. Under what condition would the reclassification of the receivables be ethical? Unethical?

FINANCIAL STATEMENT PROBLEMS

1. Use the Lands' End, Inc., statement of cash flows along with the company's other financial statements, all in Appendix A, to answer the following questions.

Using the statement of cash flows
(Obj. 1, 2, 3, 4, 5)

1. By which method does Lands' End report net cash flows from *operating* activities? How can you tell?
2. Suppose Lands' End reported net cash flows from operating activities by the direct method. Compute these amounts for the year ended January 28, 1994:
   a. Collections from customers.
   b. Payments to employees. Assume that Employee Compensation (Salary) Expense totaled $65 million for the year. The last sentence of Note 7 gives an important detail.
   c. Payments for inventory.
3. Evaluate the year ended January 28, 1994, in terms of net income, cash flows, balance sheet position, and overall results. Be specific.

2. Obtain the annual report of an actual company of your choosing. Answer the following questions about the company. Concentrate on the current year in the annual report you select.

Computing cash-flow amounts and using cash-flow data for analysis
(Obj. 1, 2, 3, 4, 5)

1. By which method does the company report net cash flows from *operating activities?* How can you tell?
2. Suppose the company reported net cash flows from operating activities by the direct method. Compute these amounts for the current year.
   a. Collections from customers.
   b. Payments to employees. Assume that the sum of Salary Expense, Wage Expense, and other payroll expenses for the current year make up 60 percent of Selling, General, and Administrative Expenses (or expense of similar title).
   c. Payments for income tax.
3. Evaluate the current year in terms of net income (or net loss), cash flows, balance sheet position, and overall results. Be specific.

Appendix

The Work Sheet Approach to Preparing the Statement of Cash Flows

OBJECTIVE A1

Prepare a work sheet for the statement of cash flows

The main body of the chapter discusses the use of the statement of cash flows in decision making and shows how to prepare the statement by using T-accounts. The T-account approach works well as a learning device, especially for simple situations. In practice, however, most companies face complex situations. In these cases, a work sheet can help accountants prepare the statement of cash flows. This appendix shows how to prepare that statement by using a specially designed work sheet.

The basic task in preparing the statement of cash flows is to account for all the cash effects of transactions that took the business from its beginning financial position to its ending financial position. Like the T-account approach, the work sheet approach helps the accountant identify the cash effects of all transactions of the period. The work sheet starts with the beginning balance sheet and concludes with the ending balance sheet. Two middle columns—one for debit amounts and the other for credit amounts—complete the work sheet. These columns, labeled Transaction Analysis, contain the data for the statement of cash flows. Exhibit 18A-1 presents the basic framework of the work sheet. Accountants can prepare the statement directly from the lower part of the work sheet (Panel B in Exhibit 18A-1). The advantage of the work sheet approach is that it organizes in one place all relevant data for the statement's preparation. All the exhibits in this appendix are based on the Anchor Corporation data in the chapter.

The work sheet can be used with either the direct method or the indirect method for operating activities. As with the T-account approach, cash flows from investing activities and cash flows from financing activities are unaffected by the method used for operating activities.

EXHIBIT 18A-1 *The Work Sheet for Preparing the Statement of Cash Flows*

	Balances Dec. 31, 19X1	Transaction Analysis Debit	Transaction Analysis Credit	Balances Dec. 31, 19X2
ANCHOR CORPORATION WORK SHEET FOR STATEMENT OF CASH FLOWS FOR THE YEAR ENDED DECEMBER 31, 19X2				
PANEL A—Account Titles				
Cash				
Accounts receivable				
Retained earnings				
PANEL B—Statement of Cash Flows				
Cash flows from operating activities:				
Cash flows from investing activities:				
Cash flows from financing activities:				
Net increase (decrease) in cash				

Preparing the Work Sheet—Direct Method for Operating Activities

The direct method separates operating activities into cash receipts and cash payments. Exhibit 18A-2 is the work sheet for preparing the statement of cash flows by the direct method. The work sheet can be prepared by following these steps:

Step 1. In Panel A, insert the beginning and ending balances for Cash, Accounts Receivable, and all other balance sheet accounts through Retained Earnings. The amounts are taken directly from the beginning and ending balance sheets in Exhibit 18-7.

Step 2. In Panel B, lay out the framework of the statement of cash flows as shown in Exhibit 18A-1—that is, enter the headings for cash flows from operating activities, investing activities, and financing activities. Exhibit 18A-2 is based on the direct method and splits operating activities into Receipts and Payments.

Step 3. At the bottom of the work sheet, write Net Increase in Cash or Net Decrease in Cash, as the case may be. This final amount on the work sheet is the difference between ending cash and beginning cash, as reported on the balance sheet. Fundamentally, the statement of cash flows is designed to explain *why* this change in cash occurred during the period.

Step 4. Analyze the period's transactions in the middle columns of the work sheet. Transaction analysis is the most challenging part of preparing the work sheet. The remainder of this appendix explains this crucial step.

Step 5. Prepare the statement of cash flows directly from Panel B of the work sheet.

Transaction Analysis on the Work Sheet

For your convenience, we repeat the Anchor Corporation transaction data from Exhibit 18-5. Transactions with cash effects are denoted by an asterisk.

Operating Activities:
 (a) Sales on credit, $284,000
*(b) Collections from customers, $271,000
 (c) Interest revenue earned, $12,000
*(d) Collection of interest receivable, $10,000
*(e) Cash receipt of dividend revenue, $9,000
 (f) Cost of goods sold, $150,000
 (g) Purchases of inventory on credit, $147,000
*(h) Payments to suppliers, $133,000
 (i) Salary and wage expense, $56,000
*(j) Payments of salaries and wages, $58,000
 (k) Depreciation expense, $18,000
 (l) Other operating expense, $17,000
*(m) Interest expense and payments, $16,000
*(n) Income tax expense and payments, $15,000

Investing Activities:
*(o) Cash payments to acquire plant assets, $306,000
*(p) Loan to another company, $11,000
*(q) Proceeds from sale of plant assets, $62,000, including $8,000 gain

Financing Activities:
*(r) Proceeds from issuance of common stock, $101,000
*(s) Proceeds from issuance of long-term debt, $94,000
*(t) Payment of long-term debt, $11,000
*(u) Declaration and payment of cash dividends, $17,000

The transaction analysis on the work sheet appears in the form of journal entries. Only balance sheet accounts appear on the work sheet. There are no income statement accounts. Therefore, revenue transactions are entered on the work sheet as credits to Retained Earnings. For example, in transaction (a), sales on account are entered on the work sheet by debiting Accounts Receivable and crediting Retained Earnings. Cash is neither debited nor credited because credit sales do not affect cash. Nevertheless, all transactions should be entered on the work sheet to identify all the cash effects of the period's transactions. In transaction (c), the earning of interest

ANCHOR CORPORATION
WORK SHEET FOR STATEMENT OF CASH FLOWS (DIRECT METHOD)
FOR THE YEAR ENDED DECEMBER 31, 19X2

PANEL A—Account Titles	Balances Dec. 31, 19X1	(Amounts in thousands) Transaction Analysis Debit		(Amounts in thousands) Transaction Analysis Credit		Balances Dec. 31, 19X2
Cash	42			(v)	20	22
Accounts receivable	80	(a)	284	(b)	271	93
Interest receivable	1	(c)	12	(d)	10	3
Inventory	138	(g)	147	(f)	150	135
Prepaid expenses	7	(h3)	1			8
Long-term receivable from another company	—	(p)	11			11
Plant assets, net	219	(o)	306	(k)	18	
				(q)	54	453
Totals	487					725
Accounts payable	57	(h1)	113	(g)	147	91
Salary and wage payable	6	(j)	58	(i)	56	4
Accrued liabilities	3	(h2)	19	(l)	17	1
Long-term debt	77	(t)	11	(s)	94	160
Common stock	258			(r)	101	359
Retained earnings	86	(f)	150	(a)	284	110
		(l)	17	(c)	12	
		(i)	56	(e)	9	
		(k)	18	(q)	8	
		(m)	16			
		(n)	15			
		(u)	17			
Totals	487		1,251		1,251	725

PANEL B—Statement of Cash Flows					
Cash flows from operating activities:					
Receipts:					
Collections from customers		(b)	271		
Interest received		(d)	10		
Dividends received		(e)	9		
Payments:					
To suppliers				(h1)	113
				(h2)	19
				(h3)	1
To employees				(j)	58
For interest				(m)	16
For income tax				(n)	15
Cash flows from investing activities:					
Acquisition of plant assets				(o)	306
Proceeds from sale of plant		(q)	62		
Loan to another company				(p)	11
Cash flows from financing activities:					
Proceeds from issuance of common stock		(r)	101		
Proceeds from issuance of long-term debt		(s)	94		
Payment of long-term debt				(t)	11
Payment of dividends				(u)	17
			547		567
Net decrease in cash		(v)	20		
Totals			567		567

revenue is entered by debiting Interest Receivable and crediting Retained Earnings. The revenue transactions that generate cash are also recorded by crediting Retained Earnings.

Expense transactions are entered on the work sheet as debits to Retained Earnings. In transaction (f), cost of goods sold is entered by debiting Retained Earnings and crediting Inventory. Transaction (m) is a cash payment of interest expense. The work sheet entry debits Retained Earnings and credits Payments for Interest under operating activities. The remaining expense transactions follow a similar pattern.

NET INCREASE (DECREASE) IN CASH   The net increase or net decrease in cash for the period is the balancing amount needed to equate the total debits and total credits ($567,000) on the statement of cash flows. In Exhibit 18A-2, Anchor Corporation experienced a $20,000 decrease in cash. This amount is entered as a credit to Cash, transaction (v), at the top of the work sheet and a debit to Net Decrease in Cash at the bottom. Totaling the columns completes the work sheet.

Preparing the Statement of Cash Flows from the Work Sheet

To prepare the statement of cash flows, Exhibit 18-2 of the text, the accountant has only to rewrite Panel B of the work sheet and add subtotals for the three categories of activities.

Preparing the Work Sheet—Indirect Method for Operating Activities

The indirect method shows the reconciliation from net income to net cash inflow (or net cash outflow) from operating activities. Exhibit 18A-3 is the work sheet for preparing the statement of cash flows by the indirect method.

The steps in completing the work sheet by the indirect method are the same as those taken in the direct method. The analysis of investing activities and financing activities uses the information presented in Exhibit 18-5 and given on page 777 of this appendix. As mentioned previously, there is no difference for investing activities or financing activities between the direct-method work sheet and the indirect-method work sheet. Therefore, the analysis that follows focuses on cash flows from operating activities. The Anchor Corporation data come from the income statement (Exhibit 18-6) and the comparative balance sheet (Exhibit 18-7).

Transaction Analysis under the Indirect Method

Net income, transaction (a), is the first operating cash inflow. Net income is entered on the work sheet as a debit to Net Income under cash flows from operating activities and a credit to Retained Earnings. Next come the additions to, and subtractions from, net income, starting with depreciation, transaction (b), which is debited to Depreciation on the work sheet and credited to Plant Assets, Net. Transaction (c) is the sale of plant assets. The $8,000 gain on the sale is entered as a credit to Gain on Sale of Plant Assets under operating cash flows—a subtraction from net income. This credit removes the $8,000 amount of the gain from cash flow from operations because the cash proceeds from the sale were not $8,000. The cash proceeds were $62,000, so this amount is entered on the work sheet as a debit under investing activities. Entry (c) is completed by crediting the plant assets' book value of $54,000 ($62,000 – $8,000) to the Plant Assets, Net account.

Entries (d) through (j) reconcile net income to cash flows from operations for increases and decreases in the current assets other than Cash and for increases and decreases in the current liabilities. Entry (d) debits Accounts Receivable for its $13,000 increase during the year. This decrease in cash flows is credited to Increase

EXHIBIT 18A-3

Work Sheet for Statement of Cash Flows—Indirect Method

ANCHOR CORPORATION
WORK SHEET FOR STATEMENT OF CASH FLOWS (INDIRECT METHOD)
FOR THE YEAR ENDED DECEMBER 31, 19X2

PANEL A—Account Titles	Balances Dec. 31, 19X1	(Amounts in thousands) Transaction Analysis Debit		(Amounts in thousands) Transaction Analysis Credit		Balances Dec. 31, 19X2
Cash	42			(q)	20	22
Accounts receivable	80	(d)	13			93
Interest receivable	1	(e)	2			3
Inventory	138			(f)	3	135
Prepaid expenses	7	(g)	1			8
Long-term receivable from another company	—	(l)	11			11
Plant assets, net	219	(k)	306	(b)	18	
				(c)	54	453
Totals	487					725
Accounts payable	57			(h)	34	91
Salary and wage payable	6	(i)	2			4
Accrued liabilities	3	(j)	2			1
Long-term debt	77	(o)	11	(n)	94	160
Common stock	258			(m)	101	359
Retained earnings	86	(p)	17	(a)	41	110
Totals	487		365		365	725

PANEL B—Statement of Cash Flows		Debit		Credit		
Cash flows from operating activities:						
Net income		(a)	41			
Add (subtract) items that affect net income and cash flow differently:						
Depreciation		(b)	18			
Gain on sale of plant assets				(c)	8	
Increase in accounts receivable				(d)	13	
Increase in interest receivable				(e)	2	
Decrease in inventory		(f)	3			
Increase in prepaid expenses				(g)	1	
Increase in accounts payable		(h)	34			
Decrease in salary and wage payable				(i)	2	
Decrease in accrued liabilities				(j)	2	
Cash flows from investing activities:						
Acquisition of plant assets				(k)	306	
Proceeds from sale of plant assets		(c)	62			
Loan to another company				(l)	11	
Cash flows from financing activities:						
Proceeds from issuance of common stock		(m)	101			
Proceeds from issuance of long-term debt		(n)	94			
Payment of long-term debt				(o)	11	
Payment of dividends				(p)	17	
			353		373	
Net decrease in cash		(q)	20			
Totals			373		373	

ANCHOR CORPORATION
WORK SHEET FOR STATEMENT OF CASH FLOWS
FOR THE YEAR ENDED DECEMBER 31, 19X2

	Balances Dec. 31, 19X1	Transaction Analysis Debit	Transaction Analysis Credit	Balances Dec. 31, 19X2
PANEL A—Account Titles				
Cash..				
Accounts receivable				
Building.......................................	650,000	(t1) 320,000		970,000
Common stock............................	890,000		(t2) 320,000	1,210,000
Retained earnings				
PANEL B—Statement of Cash Flows				
Cash flows from operating activities:				
Net increase (decrease) in cash.......				
Noncash investing and financing transactions:				
Purchase of building by issuance of common stock.........................		(t2) 320,000	(t1) 320,000	

EXHIBIT 18A-4
Noncash Investing and Financing Activities on the Work Sheet

in Accounts Receivable under operating cash flows. Entries (e) and (g) are similar for Interest Receivable and Prepaid Expenses.

The final item in Exhibit 18A-3 is the Net Decrease in Cash—transaction (q) on the work sheet—a credit to Cash and a debit to Net Decrease in Cash, exactly as in Exhibit 18A-2. To prepare the statement of cash flows from the work sheet, the accountant merely rewrites Panel B of the statement, adding subtotals for the three categories of activities.

NONCASH INVESTING AND FINANCING ACTIVITIES ON THE WORK SHEET Noncash investing and financing activities can also be analyzed on the work sheet. Because this type of transaction includes both an investing activity and a financing activity, it requires two work sheet entries. For example, suppose Anchor Corporation purchased a building by issuing common stock of $320,000. Exhibit 18A-4 illustrates the transaction analysis of this noncash investing and financing activity. Cash is unaffected.

Work sheet entry (t1) records the purchase of the building, and entry (t2) records the issuance of the stock. The order of these entries is unimportant.

APPENDIX PROBLEMS

P18A-1 The 19X3 comparative balance sheet and income statement of Silverado, Inc., follow on page 782. Silverado had no noncash investing and financing transactions during 19X3.

Preparing the work sheet for the statement of cash flows—direct method
(Obj. A1)

Required

Prepare the work sheet for the 19X3 statement of cash flows. Format cash flows from operating activities by the *direct* method.

COMPARATIVE BALANCE SHEET

	19X3	19X2	Increase (Decrease)
Current assets:			
Cash and cash equivalents	$ 13,700	$ 15,600	$ (1,900)
Accounts receivable	41,500	43,100	(1,600)
Interest receivable	600	900	(300)
Inventories	94,300	89,900	4,400
Prepaid expenses	1,700	2,200	(500)
Plant assets:			
Land	35,100	10,000	25,100
Equipment, net	100,900	93,700	7,200
Total assets	$287,800	$255,400	$32,400
Current liabilities:			
Accounts payable	$ 16,400	$ 17,900	$ (1,500)
Interest payable	6,300	6,700	(400)
Salary payable	2,100	1,400	700
Other accrued liabilities	18,100	18,700	(600)
Income tax payable	6,300	3,800	2,500
Long-term liabilities:			
Notes payable	55,000	65,000	(10,000)
Stockholders' equity:			
Common stock, no-par	131,100	122,300	8,800
Retained earnings	52,500	19,600	32,900
Total liabilities and stockholders' equity	$287,800	$255,400	$32,400

INCOME STATEMENT FOR 19X3

Revenues:		
Sales revenue		$438,000
Interest revenue		11,700
Total revenues		449,700
Expenses:		
Cost of goods sold	$205,200	
Salary expense	76,400	
Depreciation expense	15,300	
Other operating expense	49,700	
Interest expense	24,600	
Income tax expense	16,900	
Total expenses		388,100
Net income		$ 61,600

Preparing the work sheet for the statement of cash flows—indirect method (Obj. A1)

P18A-2 Using the Silverado, Inc., data from Problem 18A-1, prepare the work sheet for Silverado's 19X3 statement of cash flows. Format cash flows from operating activities by the *indirect* method.

Preparing the work sheet for the statement of cash flows—indirect method (Obj. A1)

P18A-3 Seaman-Young Corporation's comparative balance sheet at September 30, 19X4, follows.

SEAMAN-YOUNG CORPORATION
BALANCE SHEET
SEPTEMBER 30, 19X4 AND 19X3

	19X4	19X3	Increase (Decrease)
Current assets:			
Cash...	$ 48,700	$ 17,600	$31,100
Accounts receivable........................	41,900	44,000	(2,100)
Interest receivable..........................	4,100	2,800	1,300
Inventories	121,700	116,900	4,800
Prepaid expenses............................	8,600	9,300	(700)
Long-term investments	55,400	18,100	37,300
Plant assets:			
Land	65,800	93,000	(27,200)
Equipment, net	89,500	49,700	39,800
Total assets	$435,700	$351,400	$84,300
Current liabilities:			
Notes payable, short-term...............	$ 22,000	$ –0–	$22,000
Accounts payable............................	61,800	70,300	(8,500)
Income tax payable.........................	21,800	24,600	(2,800)
Accrued liabilities..........................	17,900	29,100	(11,200)
Interest payable	4,500	3,200	1,300
Salary payable.................................	1,500	1,100	400
Note payable, long-term	62,900	61,300	1,600
Stockholders' equity:			
Common stock................................	142,100	90,200	51,900
Retained earnings...........................	101,200	71,600	29,600
Total liability and stockholders' equity..	$435,700	$351,400	$84,300

Transaction data for the year ended September 30, 19X4, are as follows:

a. Net income, $93,900.

b. Depreciation expense on equipment, $8,500.

c. Acquired long-term investments, $37,300.

d. Sold land for $38,100, including $10,900 gain.

e. Acquired equipment by issuing long-term note payable, $26,300.

f. Paid long-term note payable, $24,700.

g. Received cash of $51,900 for issuance of common stock.

h. Paid cash dividends, $64,300.

i. Acquired equipment by issuing short-term note payable, $22,000.

Required

Prepare Seaman-Young's work sheet for the statement of cash flows for the year ended September 30, 19X4, using the *indirect* method to report operating activities. Include on the work sheet the noncash investing and financing activities.

P18A-4 Refer to the data of Problem 18A-3.

Required

Prepare Seaman-Young's work sheet for the statement of cash flows for the year ended September 30, 19X4, using the *direct* method for operating activities. The income statement reports the following: sales, $370,600; gain on sale of land, $10,900; interest revenue, $7,300; cost of goods sold, $161,500; salary expense, $63,400; other operating expenses, $29,600; income tax expense, $18,400; interest expense, $13,500; depreciation expense, $8,500. Include on the work sheet the noncash investing and financing activities.

Preparing the work sheet for the statement of cash flows—direct method
(Obj. A1)

Chapter 19

Financial Statement Analysis for Decision Making

> **"** *Comptronix shareholders were wronged by the fraudulent actions of previous management. The new management has . . . implemented new planning and analysis tools for our customer-oriented business teams to use to understand the economic consequences of their business decisions. This has improved business operations and has positioned the company to increase shareholder value.* **"**
>
> MARK A. ZORKO,
> VICE-PRESIDENT, CFO,
> AND SECRETARY OF
> COMPTRONIX
> CORPORATION

After studying this chapter, you should be able to

1. Perform a horizontal analysis of comparative financial statements

2. Perform a vertical analysis of financial statements

3. Prepare common-size financial statements

4. Use the statement of cash flows in decision making

5. Compute the standard financial ratios used for decision making

6. Use ratios in decision making

In late 1992, *The Huntsville Times* featured this headline: "Comptronix Fires CEO, Cites Accounting Fraud." Three years earlier, that same newspaper had cited Comptronix's record sales and earnings. Comptronix, an electronics manufacturer, was founded in 1984 and went public in 1989. Its stock jumped to $22.75 a share in 1992. After the disclosure that Comptronix had been overstating profits by using improper accounting practices, the stock plummeted to $3.75 a share.

The three fired Comptronix executives had allegedly concocted a sophisticated scheme. According to *The Wall Street Journal*, Comptronix's profits were inflated by "improperly recording certain assets on the company's balance sheet, and either overstating current sales or understating current cost of sales on the company's income statement." The goal was to increase sales and gross profits. The officers inflated inventory and decreased the cost of sales by equal amounts to exaggerate profits.

Periodically some of the improper amounts added to inventory were shifted to the equipment account because it was easier to hide them there for a long time. To increase sales, the executives recorded phony sales out of the company's growing—but bogus—inventory. Along with the phony sales, they created phony accounts receivable.

The scheme was complex, but it was full of "red flags." A comparison of Comptronix's financial statements with those of competitors reveals that the company's sales grew far faster than its receivables, and its ratio of sales to receivables was out of line with the industry. The sales figures were unusually low in relation to plant and equipment—making its plant and equipment number suspect. Also, inventory turnover was far slower than that of Comptronix's competitors and, therefore, suspect for a company reporting such rapid growth. *Source: Adapted from G. L. Porter and S. H. Michelini, "The Rise and Fall of Comptronix,"* Management Accounting, *August 1993, p. 60.*

• • • • •

*R*eread the last paragraph of this excerpt. Let's consider the *red flags*, or warning signals, in Comptronix's financial statements.

1. Sales grew far faster than receivables.
2. Sales were unusually low in relation to plant and equipment.
3. Inventory turnover was far slower than that of competitors.

Under normal circumstances, certain accounts should stand in reasonable relationship to each other. For example, sales and receivables should grow at approximately the same rate because a credit sale transaction increases both accounts. A fast-growing company, as Comptronix appeared to be, should have above-average inventory turnover.

Red flags arise when financial statements report unreasonable relationships among the accounts. The business may be better or worse than other companies in its industry. For several years Comptronix's top management deceived investors into believing that the company was unusually successful. But top managers were *cooking the books*—recording bogus transactions in the accounting records. In time the truth came out.

This unfortunate situation shows the analytical potential of the accounting model. The intertwined nature of the accounts in a double-entry accounting system makes it very difficult to keep a fraud going. At some point the accounts will indicate odd relationships.

Instances of cooking the books are rare, so uncovering fraud is a secondary role of financial analysis. The analysis is designed to aid decision making by managers, investors, and creditors. This chapter discusses some of the basic relationships—expressed as trends, percentages, and ratios—in financial statements. Investors, creditors, managers, auditors, and others use these ratios to make decisions—for example, when managers set inventory policies and when banks lend money. The extensive informational value of these ratios is one reason accounting is called the language of business.

Financial Statement Analysis

Financial statement analysis focuses on techniques used by analysts external to the organization and by managers. Outside analysts rely on publicly available information. A major source of such information is the annual report. In addition to the financial statements (income statement, balance sheet, and statement of cash flows), annual reports usually contain

1. Footnotes to the financial statements
2. A summary of the accounting methods used
3. Management's discussion and analysis of the financial results
4. The auditor's report
5. Comparative financial data for a series of years

Management's discussion and analysis (MD&A) of financial results is especially important because top management is in the best position to know how well or how poorly the company is performing. The SEC requires the MD&A from public corporations. For example, the 1993 annual report of Bristol-Myers Squibb Company, which makes Excedrin, Ban deodorant, and Clairol hair products, includes six pages of MD&A. The report's Financial Review begins as follows:

Summary

During 1993, Bristol-Myers Squibb's worldwide sales of $11.4 billion increased 2% over the prior year. Domestic sales increased 4%, while international sales remained at prior year levels. . . .

Bristol-Myers Squibb management also discusses its sales and profits in various industry segments—pharmaceuticals, medical devices, toiletries, and beauty aids. Each discussion is accompanied by graphical representation of important financial data, such as the graphs in Exhibit 19-1.

What have these facts and predictions to do with the use of accounting information to make decisions about a company such as Bristol-Myers Squibb or Comptronix? Everything, because they help investors and creditors interpret the financial statements. The balance sheet, income statement, and statement of cash flows are based on historical data. The management discussion offers top management's glimpses into the company's future. Investors and creditors are primarily interested in where the business is headed.

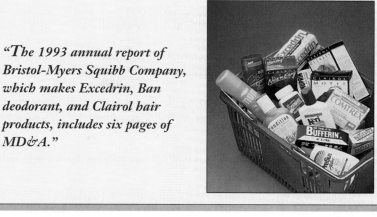

"The 1993 annual report of Bristol-Myers Squibb Company, which makes Excedrin, Ban deodorant, and Clairol hair products, includes six pages of MD&A."

Objective of Financial Statement Analysis

Investors who purchase capital stock expect to receive dividends and an increase in the value of the stock. Creditors make loans with the expectation of receiving interest and principal. Both groups bear the risk that they will not receive their expected returns. They use financial statement analysis to (1) predict the amount of expected returns and (2) assess the risks associated with those returns.

Creditors generally expect to receive specific fixed amounts and have the first claim on assets, so they are most concerned with assessing short-term liquidity and long-term solvency. **Short-term liquidity** is an organization's ability to meet current payments as they become due. **Long-term solvency** is the ability to generate

EXHIBIT 19-1
Representative Financial Data of Bristol-Myers Squibb Company

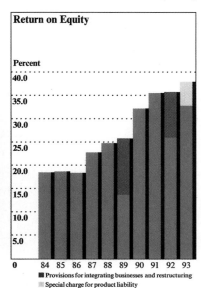

enough cash to pay long-term debts as they mature.

In contrast, *investors* are more concerned with profitability, dividends, and future security prices. Why? Because dividend payments depend on profitable operations, and stock-price appreciation depends on the market's assessment of the company's prospects. Creditors also assess profitability because profitable operations are the prime source of cash to repay loans.

We divide the tools and techniques that the business community uses in evaluating financial statement information into three broad categories: horizontal analysis, vertical analysis, and ratio analysis.

Horizontal Analysis

Key Point: Horizontal analysis often involves a percentage calculated as

$$\frac{\$ \text{ change}}{\text{base year } \$} = \% \text{ change}$$

It is important to use both dollar changes and percentage changes in horizontal analysis. The dollar increase may be growing, but the percentage change may be declining because the base is greater each year.

Many business decisions hinge on whether the numbers—in sales, income, expenses, and so on—are increasing or decreasing over time. Has the sales figure risen from last year? From two years ago? By how much? We may find that the net sales figure has risen by $20,000. This fact may be interesting, but considered alone it is not very useful for decision making. An analysis of the *percentage change* in the net sales figure over time improves our ability to use the dollar amounts. It is more useful to know that sales have increased by 20 percent than to know that the increase in sales is $20,000.

The study of percentage changes in comparative statements is called **horizontal analysis**. Computing a percentage change in comparative statements requires two steps: (1) Compute the dollar amount of the change from the base (earlier) period to the later period, and (2) divide the dollar amount of change by the base-period amount.

Horizontal analysis is illustrated for Bristol-Myers Squibb Company:

	(Dollar amounts in millions)		Increase (Decrease)	
	1993	**1992**	**Amount**	**%**
Sales............................	$11,413	$11,156	$257	2.3%
Net income	1,959	1,962	(3)	(0.2%)

The percentage change in Bristol-Myers Squibb's sales during 1993 is computed as follows:

Step 1. Compute the dollar amount of change in sales during 1993:

1993		1992		Increase
$11,413	**–**	**$11,156**	**=**	**$257**

Step 2. Divide the dollar amount of change by the base-period amount to compute the percentage change during the later period:

$$\text{Percentage change} = \frac{\text{Dollar amount of change}}{\text{Base-year amount}} = \frac{\$257}{\$11,156} = 2.3\%$$

During 1993, Bristol-Myers Squibb's sales increased by 2.3 percent.

Detailed horizontal analyses of comparative income statements and comparative balance sheets are shown in the two right-hand columns of Exhibits 19-2 and 19-3 (pages 789, 790), the financial statements of Bristol-Myers Squibb Company. The income statements (statements of earnings) reveal that net sales increased by 2.3 percent during 1993. But cost of goods sold grew even more. As a result, gross profit rose by only 1.0 percent. Overall, net income decreased slightly—a bad sign.

Other analysts would take a different view of Bristol-Myers Squibb's operations during 1993. The company's earnings from continuing operations—viewed by many

(Dollar amounts in millions)	1993	1992	Increase (Decrease) Amount	Percent
BRISTOL-MYERS SQUIBB COMPANY **STATEMENT OF EARNINGS (ADAPTED)** **YEARS ENDED DECEMBER 31, 1993 AND 1992**				

(Dollar amounts in millions)	1993	1992	Amount	Percent
Net sales	$11,413	$11,156	$257	2.3%
Cost of products sold	3,029	2,857	172	6.0
Gross profit	8,384	8,299	85	1.0
Operating expenses:				
Marketing, selling and administrative	3,098	3,075	23	0.7
Advertising and product promotion	1,255	1,291	(36)	(2.8)
Research and development	1,128	1,083	45	4.2
Other	332	863	(531)	(61.5)
Total operating expenses	5,813	6,312	(499)	(7.9)
Earnings from Continuing Operations **Before Income Taxes**	2,571	1,987	584	29.4
Income tax expense	612	449	163	36.3
Earnings from Continuing Operations	1,959	1,538	421	27.4
Discontinued Operations, net	—	670	(670)	(100.0)
Earnings before Cumulative Effect of Accounting Change	1,959	2,208	(249)	(11.3)
Cumulative Effect of Accounting Change, net	—	(246)	246	100.0
Net Earnings	$ 1,959	$ 1,962	$ (3)	0.2%

EXHIBIT 19-2
Comparative Income Statement—Horizontal Analysis

as the best indicator of future earning potential—increased dramatically during 1993. Many investors would therefore view 1993 as a better year than 1992. Moreover, the only reason 1992 net income exceeded net income for 1993 was the large gain on discontinued operations during 1992. This gain cannot be expected to recur.

The comparative balance sheet in Exhibit 19-3 shows that 1993 was a year of expansion for Bristol-Myers Squibb. Total assets increased by $1,297 million, or 12.0 percent. The bulk of this growth occurred as a result of the receivable from an insurance recovery. Total liabilities increased by 28.8 percent, and total stockholders' equity dropped by 1.3 percent. No percentage increase is computed for the insurance recovery because dividing the $1,000 million increase by zero would produce no result. Also, some percentages can be hard to interpret. Bristol-Myers's product liability rose from $63 million to $1,370 million, an increase of 2074.6 percent. Because the base-year amount is so low, the percentage increase is hard to interpret.

STOP & THINK Reconsider the chapter-opening story. Which items would be misstated in a horizontal analysis of Comptronix's income statement? Which items would be misstated in a horizontal analysis of Comptronix's balance sheet? Indicate the direction of the misstatement—overstated or understated—in both cases.

Answer:

Income Statement Analyzed Overstated	Understated	Balance Sheet Analyzed Overstated
Sales	Cost of goods sold	Accounts receivable (due to the overstatement of sales)
Gross profit		Inventory (causes the understatement of cost of goods sold)
All income amounts, including net income		Equipment (the story said Equipment was overstated)
Income tax expense		Accrued liabilities (income tax payable—due to the overstatement of income before tax)
		Retained earnings (due to the overstatement of net income)

EXHIBIT 19-3
*Comparative Balance Sheet—
Horizontal Analysis*

BRISTOL-MYERS SQUIBB COMPANY
BALANCE SHEET
DECEMBER 31, 1993 AND 1992

(Dollar amounts in millions)	1993	1992	Increase (Decrease) Amount	Percent
Assets				
Current Assets:				
Cash and cash equivalents............................	$ 2,421	$ 2,137	$ 284	13.3%
Time deposits and marketable securities......	308	248	60	24.2
Receivables, net of allowances	1,859	1,984	(125)	(6.3)
Inventories...	1,322	1,490	(168)	(11.3)
Prepaid expenses	660	762	(102)	(13.4)
Total Current Assets..................................	6,570	6,621	(51)	(0.8)
Property, Plant, and Equipment—net......	3,374	3,141	233	7.4
Insurance Recoverable..............................	1,000	—	1,000	—
Other Assets	966	889	77	8.7
Excess of cost over net tangible assets received in business acquisitions [Goodwill]	191	153	38	24.8
	$12,101	$10,804	$1,297	12.0%
Liabilities				
Current Liabilities:				
Short-term borrowings	$ 177	$ 375	$ (198)	(52.8)
Accounts payable...	649	562	87	15.5
Accrued expenses [payable].........................	1,550	1,422	128	9.0
U.S. and foreign income taxes payable.........	689	941	(252)	(26.8)
Total Current Liabilities	3,065	3,300	(235)	(7.1)
Product Liability	1,370	63	1,307	2074.6
Other Liabilities......................................	1,138	1,245	(107)	(8.6)
Long-Term Debt	588	176	412	234.1
Total Liabilities..	6,161	4,784	1,377	28.8
Stockholders' Equity				
Common stock	53	53	0	0.0
Capital in excess of par value of stock...........	353	435	(82)	(18.9)
Cumulative translation adjustments	(332)	(208)	(124)	(59.6)
Retained earnings..	7,243	6,769	474	7.0
Less cost of treasury stock...........................	(1,377)	(1,029)	(348)	(33.8)
Total Stockholders' Equity......................	5,940	6,020	(80)	(1.3)
	$12,101	$10,804	$1,297	12.0%

Trend Percentages

Trend percentages are a form of horizontal analysis. Trends are important indicators of the direction a business is taking. How have sales changed over a five-year period? What trend does gross profit show? These questions can be answered by an analysis of trend percentages over a representative period, such as the most recent five or ten years. To gain a realistic view of the company, we often must examine more than just a two- or three-year period.

Trend percentages are computed by selecting a base year whose amounts are set equal to 100 percent. The amounts of each following year are expressed as a percent of the base amount. To compute trend percentages, divide each item for years after the base year by the corresponding amount during the base year. Bristol-Myers Squibb Company showed sales, cost of goods sold, and gross profit for the past six years as follows:

Key Point: Trend percentages indicate the change between a base year and any later year:

$$\text{Trend \%} = \frac{\text{Any year \$}}{\text{Base year \$}}$$

(Amounts in millions)						
	1993	1992	1991	1990	1989	1988
Net Sales...............................	$11,413	$11,156	$10,571	$9,741	$8,578	$7,986
Cost of products sold	3,029	2,857	2,717	2,665	2,418	2,255
Gross profit	8,384	8,299	7,854	7,076	6,160	5,731

We want trend percentages for a five-year period starting with 1989. We use 1988 as the base year. Trend percentages for net sales are computed by dividing each net sales amount by the 1988 amount of $7,986 million, and likewise for the other accounts. The resulting trend percentages follow (1988, the base year = 100%):

	1993	1992	1991	1990	1989	1988
Net Sales...............................	143%	140%	132%	122%	107%	100%
Cost of products sold	134	127	120	118	107	100
Gross profit	146	145	137	123	107	100

Bristol-Myers Squibb's sales and cost of goods sold have trended upward. Gross profit has increased steadily, with the most dramatic growth during 1990. This information suggests that gross profit is increasing but at slower rates each year.

Vertical Analysis

Horizontal analysis highlights changes in an item over time. However, no single technique provides a complete picture of a business. Another way to analyze a company is called vertical analysis.

Vertical analysis of a financial statement reveals the relationship of each statement item to a specified base, which is the 100-percent figure. For example, when an income statement is subjected to vertical analysis, net sales is usually the base. Suppose under normal conditions a company's gross profit is 70 percent of net sales. A drop in gross profit to 60 percent may cause the company to report a net loss on the income statement. Management, investors, and creditors view a large decline in gross profit with alarm. Exhibit 19-4 shows the vertical analysis of Bristol-Myers

OBJECTIVE 2

Perform a vertical analysis of financial statements

BRISTOL-MYERS SQUIBB COMPANY
STATEMENT OF EARNINGS (ADAPTED)
YEARS ENDED DECEMBER 31, 1993 AND 1992

	1993		1992	
(Dollar amounts in millions)	Amount	Percent	Amount	Percent
Net sales	$11,413	100.0%	$11,156	100.0%
Cost of products sold...............................	3,029	26.5	2,857	25.6
Gross profit................................	8,384	73.5	8,299	74.4
Operating expenses:				
Marketing, selling and administrative.......	3,098	27.1	3,075	27.6
Advertising and product promotion..........	1,255	11.0	1,291	11.6
Research and development.......................	1,128	9.9	1,083	9.7
Other.......................................	332	2.9	863	7.7
Total operating expenses	5,813	50.9	6,312	56.6
Earnings from Continuing Operations				
before Income Taxes...........................	2,571	22.6	1,987	17.8
Income tax expense................................	612	5.4	449	4.0
Earnings from Continuing Operations....	1,959	17.2	1,538	13.8
Discontinued Operations, net....................	—	—	670	6.0
Earnings before Cumulative Effect				
of Accounting Change..............................	1,959	17.2	2,208	19.8
Cumulative Effect of Accounting Change, net	—	—	(246)	(2.2)
Net Earnings....................................	$ 1,959	17.2%	$ 1,962	17.6%

EXHIBIT 19-4
Comparative Income Statement—Vertical Analysis

Squibb's income statement as a percentage of net sales. Exhibit 19-5 shows the vertical analysis of the balance sheet amounts as a percentage of total assets.

The vertical analysis of Bristol-Myers Squibb's income statement (Exhibit 19-4) shows no unusual relationships. The gross profit percentage declined a bit in 1993, as did net income's percentage of sales. But there is a positive sign: 1993 earnings from continuing operations rose to 17.2 percent of sales—up from 13.8 percent of sales in 1992. Investors would view this information favorably.

The vertical analysis of Bristol-Myers Squibb's balance sheet (Exhibit 19-5) yields few surprises. Current assets' percentage of total assets declined in 1993, but so did current liabilities' percentage. The worst news on the balance sheet is the increase in product liability. The Management Discussion and Analysis explained that the large product liability in 1993 resulted from claims against the company for its breast-implant products.

Key Point: To show the relative importance of each item on the income statement, vertical analysis presents everything on that statement as a percentage of net sales:

$$\text{Vertical analysis \%} = \frac{\text{Each income statement item}}{\text{Net sales}}$$

EXHIBIT 19-5

Comparative Balance Sheet—Vertical Analysis

BRISTOL-MYERS SQUIBB COMPANY
BALANCE SHEET
DECEMBER 31, 1993 AND 1992

(Dollar amounts in millions)	1993 Amount	1993 Percent	1992 Amount	1992 Percent
Assets				
Current Assets:				
Cash and cash equivalents	$ 2,421	20.0%	$ 2,137	19.8%
Time deposits and marketable securities	308	2.5	248	2.3
Receivables, net of allowances	1,859	15.4	1,984	18.4
Inventories	1,322	10.9	1,490	13.8
Prepaid expenses	660	5.5	762	7.0
Total Current Assets	6,570	54.3	6,621	61.3
Property, Plant, and Equipment—net	3,374	27.9	3,141	29.1
Insurance Recoverable	1,000	8.3	—	—
Other Assets	966	8.0	889	8.2
Excess of cost over net tangible assets received in business acquisitions [Goodwill]	191	1.5	153	1.4
	$12,101	100.0%	$10,804	100.0%
Liabilities				
Current Liabilities:				
Short-term borrowings	$ 177	1.5%	$ 375	3.5%
Accounts payable	649	5.3	562	5.2
Accrued expenses [payable]	1,550	12.8	1,422	13.1
U.S. and foreign income taxes payable	689	5.7	941	8.7
Total Current Liabilities	3,065	25.3	3,300	30.5
Product Liability	1,370	11.3	63	0.6
Other Liabilities	1,138	9.4	1,245	11.5
Long-Term Debt	588	4.9	176	1.6
Total Liabilities	6,161	50.9	4,784	44.2
Stockholders' Equity				
Common stock	53	0.4	53	0.5
Capital in excess of par value of stock	353	2.9	435	4.0
Cumulative translation adjustments	(332)	(2.7)	(208)	(1.9)
Retained earnings	7,243	59.9	6,769	62.7
Less cost of treasury stock	(1,377)	(11.4)	(1,029)	(9.5)
Total Stockholders' Equity	5,940	49.1	6,020	55.8
	$12,101	100.0%	$10,804	100.0%

Common-Size Statements

The percentages in Exhibits 19-4 and 19-5 can be presented as a separate statement that reports only percentages (no dollar amounts). Such a statement is called a **common-size statement.**

On a common-size income statement, each item is expressed as a percentage of the net sales amount. Net sales is the "common size" to which we relate the statement's other amounts. In the balance sheet, the "common size" is the total on each side of the accounting equation (total assets *or* the sum of total liabilities and stockholders' equity). A common-size statement eases the comparison of different companies because their amounts are stated in percentages.

Common-size statements may identify the need for corrective action. Exhibit 19-6 is the common-size analysis of current assets taken from Exhibit 19-5. Exhibit 19-6 shows cash as a very high percentage of total assets at the end of each year. Receivables are a smaller percentage of total assets. Suppose receivables had increased dramatically in 1993. What could have caused such an increase? Bristol-Myers Squibb may have been lax in collecting accounts receivable, a policy that may lead to a cash shortage and reveal that the company needs to pursue collection more vigorously. Or the company may have sold to less-creditworthy customers. In any event, the company should monitor its cash position and collection of receivables to avoid a cash shortage. Common-size statements provide information useful for this purpose.

OBJECTIVE 3
Prepare common-size financial statements

BRISTOL-MYERS SQUIBB COMPANY
ANALYSIS OF CURRENT ASSETS
DECEMBER 31, 1993 AND 1992

	Percent of Total Assets	
	1993	**1992**
Current Assets:		
Cash and cash equivalents	20.0%	19.8%
Time deposits and marketable securities	2.5`	2.3
Receivables, net of allowances	15.4	18.4
Inventories	10.9	13.8
Prepaid expenses	5.5	7.0
Total Current Assets	54.3%	61.3%

Percent of Total Assets

Total Current Assets 54.3%

Receivables, net of allowances 15.4%
Cash & Cash Equivalents 20.0%
Inventories 10.9%
Long-Term Assets 45.7%
Prepaid Expenses 5.5%
Time Deposits & Marketable Securities 2.5%
1993

Total Current Assets 61.3%

Receivables, net of allowances 18.4%
Cash & Cash Equivalents 19.8%
Inventories 13.8%
Long-Term Assets 38.7%
Prepaid Expenses 7.0%
Time Deposits & Marketable Securities 2.3%
1992

EXHIBIT 19-6
Common-Size Analysis of Current Assets

Short Exercise: Calculate the common-size percentages for the following income statement:

Net sales	$150,000
COGS	60,000
Gross margin	90,000
Operating exp.	40,000
Operating income	50,000
Income tax exp.	15,000
Net income	$ 35,000

A:

Net sales	100%
COGS	40
Gross margin	60
Operating exp.	27
Operating income	33
Income tax exp.	10
Net income	23%

Industry Comparisons

We study the records of a company to help us understand past results and predict future performance. Still, the knowledge that we can develop from a company's records is limited to that one company. We may learn that gross profit has decreased and that net income has increased steadily for the last 10 years. This information is helpful, but it does not consider how businesses in the same industry have fared over this time. Have other companies in the same line of business increased their sales? Is there an industrywide decline in gross profit? Has cost of goods sold risen steeply for other businesses that sell the same products? Managers, investors, creditors, and other interested parties need to know how one company compares with other companies in the same line of business.

Exhibit 19-7 gives the common-size income statement of Bristol-Myers Squibb Company compared with the average for the pharmaceuticals industry. This analysis compares Bristol-Myers Squibb with all other companies in its line of business. The industry averages were adapted from Robert Morris Associates' *Annual Statement Studies*. Analysts specialize in a particular industry and make such comparisons in deciding which companies' stocks to buy or sell. For example, financial-ser-

EXHIBIT 19-7

Common-Size Income Statement Compared with the Industry Average

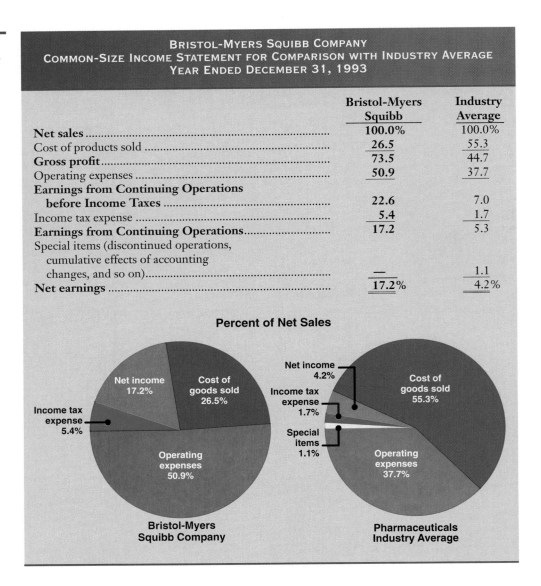

BRISTOL-MYERS SQUIBB COMPANY COMMON-SIZE INCOME STATEMENT FOR COMPARISON WITH INDUSTRY AVERAGE YEAR ENDED DECEMBER 31, 1993	Bristol-Myers Squibb	Industry Average
Net sales	100.0%	100.0%
Cost of products sold	26.5	55.3
Gross profit	73.5	44.7
Operating expenses	50.9	37.7
Earnings from Continuing Operations before Income Taxes	22.6	7.0
Income tax expense	5.4	1.7
Earnings from Continuing Operations	17.2	5.3
Special items (discontinued operations, cumulative effects of accounting changes, and so on)	—	1.1
Net earnings	17.2%	4.2%

Percent of Net Sales

Bristol-Myers Squibb Company

Net income 17.2%
Cost of goods sold 26.5%
Income tax expense 5.4%
Operating expenses 50.9%

Pharmaceuticals Industry Average

Net income 4.2%
Income tax expense 1.7%
Special items 1.1%
Cost of goods sold 55.3%
Operating expenses 37.7%

vice companies such as Merrill Lynch have health-care industry specialists, airline-industry specialists, and so on. Boards of directors evaluate top managers on the basis of how well the company compares with other companies in the industry. Exhibit 19-7 shows that Bristol-Myers Squibb compares favorably with competing companies in the pharmaceuticals industry. Its gross profit percentage is much higher than the industry average. The company does a good job of controlling total expenses, and as a result, its percentage of income from continuing operations and net income percentage are significantly higher than the industry average.

Another use of common-size statements is to aid the comparison of different-sized companies. Suppose you are considering an investment in the stock of a manufacturer of health-care products, and you are choosing between Bristol-Myers Squibb and a much smaller company. A direct comparison of their financial statements in dollar amounts is not meaningful because their amounts are so different. However, you can convert the two companies' income statements to common size and compare the percentages. You may find that one company has a higher percentage of its assets in inventory and that the other company has a higher percentage of its liabilities in long-term debt.

The Statement of Cash Flows in Decision Making

The chapter so far has centered on the income statement and balance sheet. We may also perform horizontal and vertical analysis on the statement of cash flows. In Chapter 18, we discussed how to prepare the statement. To discuss its role in decision making, let's use Exhibit 19-8.

Some analysts use cash-flow analysis to identify danger signals about a company's financial situation. For example, the statement in Exhibit 19-8 reveals what may be a weakness in DeMaris Corporation.

First, operations provided a net cash inflow of $52,000, which is much less than the $91,000 generated by the sale of fixed assets. An important question arises: Can the company remain in business by generating the majority of its cash by selling its

OBJECTIVE 4

Use the statement of cash flows in decision making

DEMARIS CORPORATION STATEMENT OF CASH FLOWS FOR THE CURRENT YEAR		
Operating activities:		
Income from operations		$ 35,000
Add (subtract) noncash items:		
Depreciation...	$ 14,000	
Net increase in current assets other than cash	(5,000)	
Net increase in current liabilities.........................	8,000	17,000
Net cash inflow from operating activities		52,000
Investing activities:		
Sale of property, plant, and equipment	$ 91,000	
Net cash inflow from investing activities		91,000
Financing activities:		
Issuance of bonds payable..	$ 72,000	
Payment of long-term debt	(170,000)	
Purchase of treasury stock	(9,000)	
Payment of dividends...	(33,000)	
Net cash outflow from financing activities................		(140,000)
Increase in cash		$ 3,000

EXHIBIT 19-8
Statement of Cash Flows

property, plant, and equipment? No, because these assets will be needed to manufacture the company's products in the future. Note also that borrowing by issuing bonds payable brought in $72,000. No company can long survive living on borrowed funds. DeMaris must eventually pay off the bonds. Indeed, the company paid $170,000 on older debt. Successful companies such as General Mills, DuPont, and Colgate-Palmolive generate the greatest percentage of their cash from operations, not from selling their fixed assets or from borrowing money. For example, General Mills, Inc., took in $859.9 million from operating activities but only $5.2 million from the disposal of land, buildings, and equipment. These conditions may be only temporary for DeMaris Corporation, but they are worth investigating.

"General Mills, Inc., took in $859.9 million from operating activities but only $5.2 million from the disposal of land, buildings, and equipment."

The most important information that the statement of cash flows provides is a summary of the company's use of cash. How a company spends its cash today determines its sources of cash in the future. The company may wisely use its cash to purchase assets that will generate income in the years ahead. If a company invests unwisely, however, cash will eventually run short.

DeMaris's statement of cash flows reveals problems. Exhibit 19-8 indicates that DeMaris invested in no fixed assets to replace those that it sold. The company may in fact be going out of business. Also, DeMaris paid dividends of $33,000, an amount that is very close to its net income. Is the company retaining enough cash to finance future operations—especially in light of the large amount of long-term debt that DeMaris paid off? Analysts seek answers to questions such as this. They analyze the information from the statement of cash flows along with the information from the balance sheet and the income statement to form a well-rounded picture of the business.

A popular measure of cash flows is called *free cash flow*, which is net cash inflow from operations minus net cash outflow from investing activities. The Coca-Cola Company discussed its use of free cash flow analysis as follows:

Liquidity and Capital Resources

One of the Company's financial strengths is its ability to generate cash from operations in excess of requirements for capital reinvestment and dividends.

"Free Cash Flow": Free Cash Flow is the cash from operations remaining after the Company has satisfied its business reinvestment opportunities. Management focuses on growing Free Cash Flow to achieve management's primary objective, maximizing shareowner value. The Company uses Free Cash Flow, along with borrowings, to make share repurchases and dividend payments. The consolidated statements of cash flows are summarized as follows (in millions):

Year Ended December 31,	**1992**	1991
Cash flows provided by (used in):		
Operations	**$2,232**	$2,084
Investment activities	**(1,359)**	(1,124)
"Free Cash Flow"	**873**	960

Cash-flow analysis of Comptronix would have revealed that cash flow from operations was too low. A company showing high income should also have generated more cash from operations. The company's bogus sales, profits, and receivables generated no cash receipts.

Perform a horizontal analysis and a vertical analysis of the comparative income statement of TRE Corporation, which makes metal detectors. State whether 19X3 was a good year or a bad year, and give your reasons.

TRE CORPORATION
COMPARATIVE INCOME STATEMENT
MONTHS ENDED DECEMBER 31, 19X3 AND 19X2

	19X3	19X2
Total revenues	$275,000	$225,000
Expenses:		
Cost of products sold	$194,000	$165,000
Engineering, selling, and administrative expenses	54,000	48,000
Interest expense	5,000	5,000
Income tax expense	9,000	3,000
Other expense (income)	1,000	(1,000)
Total expenses	263,000	220,000
Net earnings	$ 12,000	$ 5,000

SOLUTION TO REVIEW PROBLEM

TRE CORPORATION
HORIZONTAL ANALYSIS OF COMPARATIVE INCOME STATEMENT
MONTHS ENDED DECEMBER 31, 19X3 AND 19X2

			Increase (Decrease)	
	19X3	19X2	Amount	Percent
Total revenues	$275,000	$225,000	$50,000	22.2%
Expenses:				
Cost of products sold	$194,000	$165,000	$29,000	17.6
Engineering, selling, and administrative expenses	54,000	48,000	6,000	12.5
Interest expense	5,000	5,000	—	—
Income tax expense	9,000	3,000	6,000	200.0
Other expense (income)	1,000	(1,000)	2,000	—
Total expenses	263,000	220,000	43,000	19.5
Net earnings	$ 12,000	$ 5,000	$ 7,000	140.0%

TRE Corporation
Vertical Analysis of Comparative Income Statement
Months Ended December 31, 19X3 and 19X2

	19X3		19X2	
	Amount	Percent	Amount	Percent
Total revenue	$275,000	100.0%	$225,000	100.0%
Expenses:				
Cost of products sold	$194,000	70.5	$165,000	73.3
Engineering, selling, and				
administrative expenses..........	54,000	19.6	48,000	21.3
Interest expense	5,000	1.8	5,000	2.2
Income tax expense	9,000	3.3	3,000	1.4
Other expense (income).............	1,000	0.4	(1,000)	(0.4)
Total expenses	263,000	95.6	220,000	97.8
Net earnings	$ 12,000	4.4%	$ (5,000)	2.2%

The horizontal analysis shows that total revenues increased 22.2 percent. This percentage increase was greater than the 19.5-percent increase in total expenses, resulting in a 140-percent increase in net earnings.

The vertical analysis shows decreases in the percentages of net sales consumed by the cost of products sold (from 73.3 percent to 70.5 percent) and by the engineering, selling, and administrative expenses (from 21.3 percent to 19.6 percent). These two items are TRE's largest dollar expenses, so their percentage decreases are quite important. The relative reduction in expenses raised December 19X3 net earnings to 4.4 percent of sales, compared with 2.2 percent the preceding December. The overall analysis indicates that December 19X3 was significantly better than December 19X2.

Using Ratios to Make Business Decisions

OBJECTIVE 5

Compute the standard financial ratios used for decision making

The heart of financial analysis is the calculation and interpretation of ratios. A ratio expresses the relationship of one number to another number. For example, if the balance sheet shows current assets of $100,000 and current liabilities of $25,000, the ratio of current assets to current liabilities is $100,000 to $25,000. We simplify this numerical expression to the ratio of 4 to 1, which may also be written 4:1 and 4/1. Other acceptable ways of expressing this ratio include (1) "current assets are 400 percent of current liabilities," (2) "the business has four dollars in current assets for every one dollar in current liabilities," or simply, (3) "the current ratio is 4.0."

We often reduce the ratio fraction by writing the ratio as one figure over the other, for example, 4/1, and then dividing the numerator by the denominator. In this way, the ratio 4/1 may be expressed simply as 4. The 1 that represents the denominator of the fraction is understood, not written. Consider the ratio $175,000:$165,000. After dividing the first figure by the second, we come to 1.06:1, which we state as 1.06. The second part of the ratio, the 1, again is understood. Ratios provide a convenient and useful way of expressing a relationship between numbers. For example, the ratio of current assets to current liabilities gives information about a company's ability to pay its current debts with existing current assets.

A manager, lender, or financial analyst may use any ratio that is relevant to a particular decision. Many companies include ratios in a special section of their annual financial reports. Rubbermaid Incorporated, a manufacturer of plastic products for the home and garden, office, and industry, displays ratio data in the consolidated financial summary section of its annual report. Exhibit 19-9 shows a sampling of that summary section. Investment services—Moody's, Standard & Poor's, Robert Morris Associates, and others—report these ratios for companies and industries.

> *"Rubbermaid Incorporated, a manufacturer of plastic products for the home and garden, office, and industry, displays ratio data in the consolidated financial summary section of its annual report."*

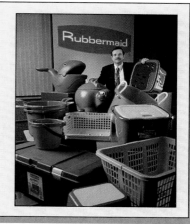

Exhibit 19-10 shows some widely used ratios that we discuss here. The ratios may be classified as follows:

1. Ratios that measure the ability to pay current liabilities
2. Ratios that measure the ability to sell inventory and collect receivables
3. Ratios that measure the ability to pay long-term debt
4. Ratios that measure profitability
5. Ratios used to analyze stock as an investment

How much can a computer help in analyzing financial statements for investment purposes? Time yourself as you perform one of the financial-ratio problems in this chapter. Multiply your efforts by, say, 100 companies that you are comparing by means of this ratio. Now consider ranking these 100 companies on the basis of four or five additional ratios.

On-line financial databases, such as Lexis/Nexis and the Dow Jones News Retrieval Service, offer quarterly financial figures for thousands of public corporations going back as much as 10 years. Assume that you wanted to compare companies' recent earnings histories. You might have the computer compare hundreds of companies on the basis of price/earnings ratio and rates of return on stockholders' equity and total assets. The computer could then give you the names of the 20 (or however many) companies that appear most favorable in terms of these ratios. Alternatively, you could have the computer download financial statement data to your spreadsheet (that is, place the data in the appropriate cells of your spreadsheet) and compute the ratios yourself.

Key Point: We must learn how to understand relationships among the numbers on a financial statement. Horizontal and vertical analyses were our first attempt at studying such relationships. We now learn to use ratios, which help even more in analyzing the statements. We compare financial statement amounts to other items to assess what the ratio indicates about the company. How do we assess a ratio? We must consider prior years, industry averages, budgeted ratios, and so on—only then does a ratio have meaning.

EXHIBIT 19-9 *Consolidated Financial Summary of Rubbermaid Incorporated*
(Dollars in thousands except per-share amounts)

Years Ended December 31,	1993	1992	1991	1990
Operating Results				
Net earnings	$211,413	$164,095	$162,650	$143,520
Per Common Share	$1.32	$ 1.02	$ 1.02	$ 0.90
Percent to sales	10.8%	9.1%	9.8%	9.4%
Return on average shareholders' equity	20.0%	17.5%	19.7%	20.2%
Financial Position				
Current assets	$829,744	$699,650	$663,999	$602,697
Current liabilities	$259,314	$223,246	$245,500	$235,300
Working capital	$570,430	$476,404	$418,499	$367,397
Current ratio	3.20	3.13	2.70	2.56

EXHIBIT 19-10 *Ratios Used in Financial Statement Analysis*

Ratio	Computation	Information Provided
Measuring the ability to pay current liabilities:		
1. Current ratio	$\dfrac{\text{Current assets}}{\text{Current liabilities}}$	Measures ability to pay current liabilities from current assets.
2. Acid-test (quick) ratio	$\dfrac{\text{Cash + short-term investments + net current receivables}}{\text{Current liabilities}}$	Shows ability to pay current liabilities from the most liquid assets.
Measuring the ability to sell inventory and collect receivables:		
3. Inventory turnover	$\dfrac{\text{Cost of goods sold}}{\text{Average inventory}}$	Indicates saleability of inventory.
4. Accounts receivable turnover	$\dfrac{\text{Net credit sales}}{\text{Average net accounts receivable}}$	**Measures collectibility of receivables.**
5. Days' sales in receivables	$\dfrac{\text{Average net accounts receivable}}{\text{One day's sales}}$	Shows how many days it takes to collect average receivables.
Measuring the ability to pay long-term debt:		
6. Debt ratio	$\dfrac{\text{Total liabilities}}{\text{Total assets}}$	Indicates percentage of assets financed through borrowing.
7. Times-interest-earned ratio	$\dfrac{\text{Income from operations}}{\text{Interest expense}}$	Measures coverage of interest expense by operating income.
Measuring profitability:		
8. Rate of return on net sales	$\dfrac{\text{Net income}}{\text{Net sales}}$	Shows the percentage of each sales dollar earned as net income.
9. Rate of return on total assets	$\dfrac{\text{Net income + interest expense}}{\text{Average total assets}}$	Gauges how profitably assets are used.
10. Rate of return on common stockholders' equity	$\dfrac{\text{Net income − preferred dividends}}{\text{Average common stockholders' equity}}$	Gauges how profitably the assets financed by the common stockholders are used.
11. Earnings per share of common stock	$\dfrac{\text{Net income − preferred dividends}}{\text{Number of shares of common stock outstanding}}$	Gives the amount of earnings per one share of common stock.
Analyzing stock as an investment:		
12. Price/earnings ratio	$\dfrac{\text{Market price per share of common stock}}{\text{Earnings per share}}$	Indicates the market price of one dollar of earnings.
13. Dividend yield	$\dfrac{\text{Dividend per share of common stock}}{\text{Market price per share of common stock}}$	Shows the proportion of the market price of each share of stock returned as dividends to stockholders each period.
14. Book value per share of common stock	$\dfrac{\text{Total stockholders' equity − preferred equity}}{\text{Number of shares of common stock outstanding}}$	Indicates the recorded accounting value of each share of common stock outstanding.

Accountants use computerized financial analysis a great deal. CPAs focus on the individual client. They want to know how the client is doing compared with the previous year and compared with other firms in the industry. Auditors want to detect any emerging trends in the company's ratios and compare the results of actual operations with expected results. To do so, an auditor can download monthly financial statistics on a spreadsheet and compute the financial ratios to gain insight into the client's situation.

Measuring the Ability to Pay Current Liabilities

Working capital is defined by the following equation:

Working capital = Current assets – Current liabilities

Working capital is widely used to measure a business's ability to meet its short-term obligations with its current assets. In general, the larger the working capital, the better able the business is to pay its debts. Recall that capital, or owners' equity, is total assets minus total liabilities. Working capital is like a "current" version of total capital. The working capital amount considered alone does not give a complete picture of the entity's working capital position, however. Consider two companies with equal working capital:

	Company A	Company B
Current assets.	$100,000	$200,000
Current liabilities...............	50,000	150,000
Working capital	$ 50,000	$ 50,000

Both companies have working capital of $50,000, but Company A's working capital is as large as its current liabilities. Company B's working capital is only one-third as large as its current liabilities. Which business has a better working capital position? Company A, because its working capital is a higher percentage of current assets and current liabilities. To use working-capital data in decision making, it is helpful to develop ratios. Two decision-making tools based on working capital data are the *current ratio* and the *acid-test ratio*.

Current Ratio

The most common ratio using current asset and current-liability data is the **current ratio,** which is current assets divided by current liabilities. ◄▬ Recall the makeup of current assets and current liabilities. Inventory is converted to receivables through sales, the receivables are collected in cash, and the cash is used to buy inventory and pay current liabilities. A company's current assets and current liabilities represent the core of its day-to-day operations.

◄▥◄▥◄▥ The current ratio was introduced in Chapter 4 (p. 148) along with the concept of analyzing liquidity.

Exhibit 19-11 gives the comparative income statement and balance sheet of Palisades Furniture, Inc. The current ratios of Palisades Furniture, Inc., at December 31, 19X7 and 19X6, follow, along with the average for the retail furniture industry:

Formula	Current Ratio of Palisades Furniture, Inc.		Retail Furniture Industry Average
	19X7	**19X6**	
Current ratio = $\dfrac{\text{Current assets}}{\text{Current liabilities}}$	$\dfrac{\$262,000}{\$142,000} = 1.85$	$\dfrac{\$236,000}{\$126,000} = 1.87$	1.80

EXHIBIT 19-11
Comparative Financial Statements

PANEL A—Comparative Income Statement of Palisades Furniture, Inc.

PALISADES FURNITURE, INC. COMPARATIVE INCOME STATEMENT YEARS ENDED DECEMBER 31, 19X7 AND 19X6		
	19X7	**19X6**
Net sales	$858,000	$803,000
Cost of goods sold	513,000	509,000
Gross profit	345,000	294,000
Operating expenses:		
Selling expenses	126,000	114,000
General expenses	118,000	123,000
Total operating expenses	244,000	237,000
Income from operations	101,000	57,000
Interest revenue	4,000	—
Interest expense	24,000	14,000
Income before income taxes	81,000	43,000
Income tax expense	33,000	17,000
Net income	$ 48,000	$ 26,000

Short Exercise: Use the following income statements and balance sheets for A Co. and B Co.:

	A Co.	B Co.
Cash	$ 31	$ 20
Acc. rec.	45	75
Inventory	21	102
Prepaid expenses	3	3
Plant & equip. (net)	200	350
Total assets	$300	$550
Current liabilities	$ 50	$150
Long-term debt	100	240
10% Preferred stock		10
Common stock	125	100
Retained earnings	25	50
Total liabilities & stock equity	$300	$550
Net sales	$160	$270
COGS	100	135
Oper. exp.	22	30
Interest exp.	6	30
Income tax exp.	12	25
Net income	$ 20	$ 50

Calculate (1) working capital, (2) the current ratio, and (3) the acid-test ratio. *A:* (1) A Co.: $50 ($31 + $45 + $21 + $3 − $50); B Co.: $50 ($20 + $75 + $102 + $3 − $150); (2) A Co.: 2:1 ($100/$50); B Co.: 1.33:1 ($200/$150); (3) A Co.: 1.52:1 ($76/$50); B Co.: 0.63:1 ($95/$150)

PANEL B—Comparative Balance Sheet of Palisades Furniture, Inc.

PALISADES FURNITURE, INC. COMPARATIVE BALANCE SHEET DECEMBER 31, 19X7 AND 19X6		
Assets	**19X7**	**19X6**
Current assets:		
Cash	$ 29,000	$ 32,000
Accounts receivable, net	114,000	85,000
Inventories	113,000	111,000
Prepaid expenses	6,000	8,000
Total current assets	262,000	236,000
Long-term investments	18,000	9,000
Property, plant, and equipment, net	507,000	399,000
Total assets	$787,000	$644,000
Liabilities		
Current liabilities:		
Notes payable	$ 42,000	$ 27,000
Accounts payable	73,000	68,000
Accrued liabilities	27,000	31,000
Total current liabilities	142,000	126,000
Long-term debt	289,000	198,000
Total liabilities	431,000	324,000
Stockholders' Equity		
Common stock, no-par	186,000	186,000
Retained earnings	170,000	134,000
Total stockholders' equity	356,000	320,000
Total liabilities and stockholders' equity	$787,000	$644,000

The current ratio decreased slightly during 19X7. Lenders, stockholders, and managers closely monitor changes in a company's current ratio. In general, a higher current ratio indicates a stronger financial position. A higher current ratio suggests that the business has sufficient liquid assets to maintain normal business operations. Compare Palisades Furniture's current ratio of 1.85 with the 1.80 average for the retail furniture industry and with the current ratios of some well-known companies:

Company	Current Ratio
Chesebrough-Pond's, Inc.	2.50
Wal-Mart Stores, Inc.	1.51
General Mills, Inc.	1.05
The Superior Oil Company	1.46

What is an acceptable current ratio? The answer to that question depends on the nature of the industry. The norm for companies in most industries is between 1.60 and 1.90, as reported by Robert Morris Associates. Palisades Furniture's current ratio of 1.85 is within the range of those values. In most industries a current ratio of 2.0 is considered good.

Acid-Test Ratio

The **acid-test** (or *quick*) **ratio** tells us whether the entity could pay all its current liabilities if they came due immediately. ◀▥ That is, could the company pass this *acid test?* The company would convert its most liquid assets to cash. To compute the acid-test ratio, we add cash, short-term investments, and net current receivables (accounts and notes receivable, net of allowances) and divide by current liabilities. Inventory and prepaid expenses are the two current assets not included in the acid-test computations because they are the least liquid of the current assets. A business may not be able to convert them to cash immediately to pay current liabilities. The acid-test ratio uses a narrower asset base to measure liquidity than the current ratio does.

Palisades Furniture's acid-test ratios for 19X7 and 19X6 follow:

◀▥◀▥◀▥ We saw in Chapter 8 (p. 347) that the higher the acid-test ratio, the better able is the business to pay its current liabilities.

Formula	Acid-Test Ratio of Palisades Furniture, Inc.		Retail Furniture Industry Average
	19X7	19X6	
Acid-test ratio = $\dfrac{\text{Cash + short-term investments + net current receivables}}{\text{Current liabilities}}$	$\dfrac{\$29,000 + \$0 + \$114,000}{\$142,000} = 1.01$	$\dfrac{\$32,000 + \$0 + \$85,000}{\$126,000} = 0.93$	0.60

The company's acid-test ratio improved considerably during 19X7 and is significantly better than the industry average. Compare Palisades Furniture's 1.01 acid-test ratio with the acid-test values of some well-known companies:

Company	Acid-Test Ratio
Chesebrough-Pond's, Inc.	1.25
Whirlpool Corporation..................	0.92
General Motors	0.91
Wal-Mart Stores, Inc.	0.08

Short Exercise: A Co. and B Co. of the Short Exercise on page 802 have equal amounts of working capital, but their current and acid-test ratios differ. Explain. *A:* A Co. has a higher ratio of current assets to current liabilities than B Co., as shown by A's higher current ratio. A Co. should be able to meet current obligations more easily as they come due. A Co. has a higher ratio of quick (liquid) assets to current liabilities than B Co., as indicated by the quick ratio—A is more "liquid" than B. Inventory and prepaid expenses are not "quick" assets. B Co. has more current liabilities than quick assets. B may have trouble paying off current debts because it must convert inventory to receivables or to cash to pay these debts. A Co. appears to have adequate quick assets to meet its debts. A seems to be in a stronger current financial position than B.

How can a leading company such as Wal-Mart function with so low an acid-test ratio? Wal-Mart has almost no receivables. Its inventory is priced low to turn over very quickly. The norm ranges from 0.20 for shoe retailers to 1.00 for manufacturers of paperboard containers and certain other equipment, as reported by Robert Morris Associates. An acid-test ratio of 0.90 to 1.00 is acceptable in most industries.

Measuring the Ability to Sell Inventory and Collect Receivables

The ability to sell inventory and collect receivables is fundamental to business success. Recall the operating cycle of a merchandiser: cash to inventory to receivables and back to cash. ◄▏▏▏ This section discusses three ratios that measure the ability to sell inventory and collect receivables.

◄▏▏▏◄▏▏▏◄▏▏▏ If you need to, refer to the discussion of the operating cycle in Chapter 5, page 177.

Inventory Turnover

Companies generally seek to achieve the quickest possible return on their investments. A return on an investment in inventory—usually a substantial amount—is no exception. The faster inventory sells, the sooner the business creates accounts receivable, and the sooner it collects cash.

Short Exercise: Refer to the Short Exercise on page 802. Take the beginning inventories for A Co. and B Co. to be $19 and $98, respectively. Compute each company's rate of inventory turnover. *A:*

A Co. $\dfrac{\$100}{(\$21 + \$19)/2} = 5.0$

B Co. $\dfrac{\$135}{(\$102 + \$98)/2} = 1.35$

Inventory turnover is a measure of the number of times a company sells its average level of inventory during a year. A high rate of turnover indicates relative ease in selling inventory, whereas a low turnover indicates difficulty in selling. In general, companies prefer a high inventory turnover. A value of 6 means that the company's average level of inventory has been sold six times during the year and is generally better than a turnover of 3 or 4. However, a high value can mean that the business is not keeping enough inventory on hand, and inadequate inventory can result in lost sales if the company cannot fill a customer's order. Therefore, a business strives for the most profitable rate of inventory turnover, not necessarily the highest.

To compute the inventory turnover ratio, we divide cost of goods sold by the average inventory for the period. We use the cost of goods sold—not sales—in the computation because both cost of goods sold and inventory are stated *at cost*. Sales is stated at the sales value of inventory and therefore is not comparable with inventory cost.

Palisades Furniture's inventory turnover for 19X7 is:

Formula	Inventory Turnover of Palisades Furniture, Inc.	Retail Furniture Industry Average
Inventory turnover $= \dfrac{\text{Cost of goods sold}}{\text{Average inventory}}$	$\dfrac{\$513,000}{\$112,000} = 4.58$	2.70

Short Exercise: Evaluate the inventory turnovers of the previous Short Exercise. *A:* A Co. turns its inventory more quickly than B Co., which sells its inventory less than twice a year. The ratio varies widely from industry to industry, but it appears that B is carrying goods that are hard to sell. Or B may be carrying too much inventory for its level of sales.

Cost of goods sold appears in the income statement (Exhibit 19-11). Average inventory is figured by averaging the beginning inventory ($111,000) and ending inventory ($113,000). (See the balance sheet, Exhibit 19-11.) If inventory levels vary greatly from month to month, compute the average by adding the 12 monthly balances and dividing the sum by 12.

Inventory turnover varies widely with the nature of the business. For example, most manufacturers of farm machinery have an inventory turnover close to three times a year. In contrast, companies that remove natural gas from the ground hold their inventory for a very short period of time and have an average turnover of 30. Palisades Furniture's turnover of 4.58 times a year is high for its industry, which has an average turnover of 2.70. Palisades Furniture's high inventory turnover results from its policy of keeping little inventory on hand. The company takes customer orders and has its suppliers ship directly to customers.

Inventory turnover rates can vary greatly within a company. At Toys "R" Us, an international retailer of toys and childcare products, diapers and formula turn over more than 12 times a year, whereas seasonal toys turn over less than three times a year. The entire Toys "R" Us inventory turns over an average of three times a year. That inventory is at its lowest point on January 31 and at its highest point around October 31.

"The entire Toys 'R' Us inventory turns over an average of three times a year."

To evaluate fully a company's inventory turnover, compare the ratio over time. A sudden sharp decline or a steady decline over a long period suggests the need for corrective action. Analysts also compare a company's inventory turnover with that of other companies in the same industry and with the industry average.

STOP & THINK Reread the chapter-opening story. Explain why Comptronix's inventory turnover was too low.

Answer: Cost of goods sold was understated, and inventory was overstated. The low numerator divided by the high denominator produced an inventory turnover value that was too low.

Accounts Receivable Turnover

Accounts receivable turnover measures a company's ability to collect cash from credit customers. In general, the higher the ratio, the more successfully the business collects cash, and the better off its operations are. However, too high a receivable turnover may indicate that credit is too tight, causing the loss of sales to good customers. To compute the accounts receivable turnover, we divide net credit sales by average net accounts receivable. The resulting ratio indicates how many times during the year the average level of receivables was turned into cash.

Palisades Furniture's accounts receivable turnover ratio for 19X7 is computed as follows:

Formula	Accounts Receivable Turnover of Palisades Furniture, Inc.	Retail Furniture Industry Average
Accounts receivable turnover = $\dfrac{\text{Net credit sales}}{\text{Average net accounts receivable}}$	$\dfrac{\$858,000}{\$99,500} = 8.62$	22.2

The sales figure comes from the income statement. Palisades Furniture makes all sales on credit. If the company makes both cash and credit sales, this ratio is best computed by using only net credit sales. Average net accounts receivable is figured by using the beginning accounts receivable balance ($85,000) and the ending balance ($114,000). If the accounts receivable balances exhibit a seasonal pattern, compute the average by using the 12 monthly balances.

Palisades Furniture's receivable turnover of 8.62 is much lower than the industry average. This results because the company is a home-town store that sells to local people who tend to pay their bills over a period of time. Many larger furniture stores sell their receivables to other companies called factors. This practice keeps receiv-

Short Exercise: In the Short Exercise on page 802, take the beginning account receivable balances to be $40 and $70, respectively. Compute (1) accounts receivable turnover; (2) days' sales in receivables. *A:*

(1) A Co.: $\dfrac{\$160}{(\$45 + \$40)/2} = 3.76$

   B Co.: $\dfrac{\$270}{(\$75 + \$70)/2} = 3.72$

(2) A: $160/365 = $0.44;
      $42.5/$0.44 = 96.6 days
   B: $270/365 = $0.74;
      $72.5/$0.74 = 98 days

Short Exercise: Evaluate the receivable ratios of the previous Short Exercise. *A:* Both companies' receivables turn over between three and four times a year—it takes about 1/3 to 1/4 of the year to collect the receivables. Compare the 96 and 98 days' sales in receivables with the company's credit terms. If A Co.'s credit terms are 2/10 n/30, then its collection department is doing a poor job of collecting. Or credit is being extended to uncreditworthy customers. A Co. should sell to those customers only on the cash basis.

ables low and receivable turnover high. But companies that factor (sell) their receivables receive less than face value on their sale. Palisades Furniture follows a different strategy.

STOP & THINK Comptronix's sales grew far faster than its receivables. Would this situation create an unusually high or an unusually low accounts receivable turnover?

Answer: Receivable turnover would be too high. This high ratio would look strange in relation to the company's past measures of receivable turnover.

Days' Sales in Receivables

Businesses must convert accounts receivable to cash. All else equal, the lower the Accounts Receivable balance, the more successful the business has been in converting receivables into cash, and the better off the business.

The **days'-sales-in-receivables** ratio tells us how many days' sales remain in Accounts Receivable. We express the money amount in terms of an average day's sales. This relation becomes clearer as we compute the ratio, a two-step process. First, divide net sales by 365 days to figure the average sales amount for one day. Second, divide this average day's sales amount into the average net accounts receivable.

◀▥◀▥◀▥ Recall from Chapter 8 (p. 347) that days' sales in receivables indicates the average collection period.

The data to compute this ratio for Palisades Furniture, Inc., for 19X7 are taken from the income statement and the balance sheet (Exhibit 19-11):

Formula	Days' Sales in Accounts Receivable of Palisades Furniture, Inc.	Retail Furniture Industry Average
Days' Sales in AVERAGE Accounts Receivable:		
1. One day's sales = $\dfrac{\text{Net sales}}{365 \text{ days}}$	$\dfrac{\$858,000}{365 \text{ days}} = \$2,351$	
2. Days' sales in average accounts receivable $= \dfrac{\text{Average net accounts receivable}}{\text{One day's sales}}$	$\dfrac{\$99,500}{\$2,351} = 42 \text{ days}$	16 days

The computation in two steps is designed to increase your understanding of the meaning of the ratio. We can compute days' sales in average receivables in one step: $\$99,500/(\$858,000/365 \text{ days}) = 42$ days.

Palisades Furniture's ratio tells us that 42 average days' sales remain in accounts receivable and need to be collected. The company will increase its cash inflow if it can decrease this ratio. To detect any changes over time in the firm's ability to collect its receivables, let's compute the days'-sales-in-receivables ratio at the beginning and the end of 19X7:

Days' Sales in ENDING 19X6 Accounts Receivable:

$\text{One day's sales} = \dfrac{\$803,000}{365 \text{ days}} = \$2,200$ $\text{Days' sales in ending 19X6 accounts receivable} = \dfrac{\$85,000}{\$2,200} = \begin{array}{l}39 \text{ days at} \\ \text{beginning} \\ \text{of 19X7}\end{array}$

Days' Sales in ENDING 19X7 Accounts Receivable:

$\text{One day's sales} = \dfrac{\$858,000}{365 \text{ days}} = \$2,351$ $\text{Days' sales in ending 19X7 accounts receivable} = \dfrac{\$114,000}{\$2,351} = \begin{array}{l}48 \text{ days} \\ \text{at end} \\ \text{of 19X7}\end{array}$

This analysis shows a drop in Palisades Furniture's collection of receivables; days' sales in accounts receivable has increased from 39 at the beginning of the year to 48 at year end. The credit and collection department should strengthen its collection efforts. Otherwise, the company may experience a cash shortage in 19X8 and beyond.

Palisades Furniture's days' sales in receivables is higher (worse) than the industry average because the company collects its own receivables. Many other furniture stores sell their receivables and carry fewer days' sales in receivables. Palisades Furniture remains competitive because of the personal relationship with customers. Without their good paying habits, the company's cash flow would suffer.

Comptronix had a high receivable turnover, which indicates strong sales and quick collection of receivables. But the company also had a low inventory turnover, which suggests difficulty in selling merchandise. The combination of high receivable turnover, low inventory turnover, and high profits suggests an irregularity.

Measuring the Ability to Pay Long-Term Debt

The ratios discussed so far give us insight into current assets and current liabilities. They help us measure a business's ability to sell inventory, to collect receivables, and to pay current liabilities. Most businesses also have long-term debts. Bondholders and banks that loan money on long-term notes payable and bonds payable take special interest in a business's ability to meet long-term obligations. Two key indicators of a business's ability to pay long-term liabilities are the *debt ratio* and the *times-interest-earned ratio*.

Debt Ratio

Suppose you are a loan officer at a bank and you are evaluating loan applications from two companies with equal sales revenue and total assets. Sales and total assets are the two most common measures of firm size. Both companies have asked to borrow $500,000, and each has agreed to repay the loan over a 10-year period. The first firm already owes $600,000 to another bank. The second owes only $250,000. Other things equal, which company is likely to get the loan at the lower interest rate? Company Two, because the bank faces less risk by loaning to Company Two. That company owes less to creditors than Company One owes.

This relationship between total liabilities and total assets—called the **debt ratio**—tells us the proportion of the company's assets that it has financed with debt. If the debt ratio is 1, then debt has been used to finance all the assets. A debt ratio of 0.50 means that the company has used debt to finance half its assets and that the owners of the business have financed the other half. The higher the debt ratio, the higher the strain of paying interest each year and the principal amount at maturity. The lower the ratio, the less the business's future obligations. Creditors view a high debt ratio with caution. If a business seeking financing already has many liabilities, then additional debt payments may be too much for the business to handle. To help protect themselves, creditors generally charge higher interest rates on new borrowing to companies with an already-high debt ratio.

Palisades Furniture's debt ratios at the end of 19X7 and 19X6 follow:

Formula	Debt Ratio of Palisades Furniture, Inc.		Retail Furniture Industry Average
	19X7	19X6	
Debt ratio = $\dfrac{\text{Total liabilities}}{\text{Total assets}}$	$\dfrac{\$431,000}{\$787,000} = 0.55$	$\dfrac{\$324,000}{\$644,000} = 0.50$	0.61

Short Exercise: Evaluate the ratios of the previous Short Exercise in relation to the ability to repay long-term debt. *A:* A Co. has a smaller percentage of total assets tied up in debt; 50% is a low debt ratio. B Co. may have more trouble paying its debts because a larger percentage of its assets are financed by liabilities as compared to equity. B Co. is earning only enough operating income to cover its interest 3.5 times. The lower this ratio, the more difficult it will be for B to pay its interest. A Co. has a much stronger financial position than B Co.

Recall from our vertical and horizontal analyses that Palisades Furniture expanded operations by financing the purchase of property, plant, and equipment through borrowing, which is common. This expansion explains the firm's increased debt ratio.

Even after the increase in 19X7, the company's debt is not very high. Robert Morris Associates reports that the average debt ratio for most companies ranges around 0.57 to 0.67, with relatively little variation from company to company. Palisades Furniture's 0.55 debt ratio indicates a fairly low-risk debt position in comparison with the retail furniture industry average of 0.61.

Times-Interest-Earned Ratio

The debt ratio measures the effect of debt on the company's *financial position* (balance sheet) but says nothing about its ability to pay interest expense. Analysts use a second ratio—the **times-interest-earned ratio**—to relate income to interest expense. To compute this ratio, we divide income from operations by interest expense. This ratio measures the number of times that operating income can *cover* interest expense. For this reason, the ratio is also called the *interest-coverage ratio*. A high times-interest-earned ratio indicates ease in paying interest expense; a low value suggests difficulty.

Palisades Furniture's times-interest-earned ratios follow:

Formula		Times-Interest-Earned Ratio of Palisades Furniture, Inc.		Retail Furniture Industry Average
		19X7	19X6	
Times-interest-earned ratio	$= \dfrac{\text{Income from operations}}{\text{Interest expense}}$	$\dfrac{\$101,000}{\$24,000} = 4.21$	$\dfrac{\$57,000}{\$14,000} = 4.07$	2.00

Short Exercise: Refer to the Short Exercise on page 802. Compute (1) the debt ratio and (2) the times-interest-earned ratio. *A:*
(1) A Co.: 50% ($150/$300)
    B Co.: 71% ($390/$550)
(2) A Co.: 6.3 times
    ($160 − $100 − $22)/$6
    B Co.: 3.5 times
    ($270 − $135 − $30)/30

The company's time-interest-earned ratio increased in 19X7. That is a favorable sign, especially since the company's short-term notes payable and long-term debt rose substantially during the year. Palisades Furniture's new plant assets, we conclude, have earned more in operating income than they have cost the business in interest expense. The company's times-interest-earned ratio of around 4.00 is significantly better than the 2.00 average for furniture retailers. The norm for American business, as reported by Robert Morris Associates, falls in the range of 2.0 to 3.0 for most companies.

On the basis of its debt ratio and its times-interest-earned ratio, Palisades Furniture appears to have little difficulty paying its liabilities, also called *servicing its debt*.

Measuring Profitability

The fundamental goal of business is to earn a profit. Ratios that measure profitability play a large role in decision making. These ratios are reported in the business press, by investment services, and in the annual financial reports of companies.

Suppose you are a personal financial planner who helps clients select stock investments. One client has $100,000 to invest in a chemical company. Over the next few years, you expect Dow Chemical Company to earn higher rates of return on its investments than analysts are forecasting for the chemicals manufacturer Monsanto Company. Which company's stock will you recommend? Probably Dow's—for reasons you will better understand after studying three rate-of-return measurements.

Rate of Return on Net Sales

In business, the term *return* is used broadly and loosely as an evaluation of profitability. Consider a ratio called the **rate of return on net sales**, or simply *return on sales*. (The word *net* is usually omitted for convenience, even though the net sales figure is used to compute the ratio.) Palisades Furniture's rate-of-return-on-sales ratios follow:

Formula		Rate of Return on Sales of Palisades Furniture, Inc.		Retail Furniture Industry Average
		19X7	19X6	
Rate of return on sales	$= \dfrac{\text{Net income}}{\text{Net sales}}$	$\dfrac{\$48,000}{\$858,000} = 0.056$	$\dfrac{\$26,000}{\$803,000} = 0.032$	0.008

The increase in Palisades Furniture's return on sales is significant and identifies the company as more successful than the average furniture store. Companies strive for a high rate of return. The higher the rate of return, the more net sales dollars are providing income to the business and the fewer net sales dollars are absorbed by expenses. See how Palisades Furniture's rate of return on sales compares with the rates of some other companies:

Company	Rate of Return on Sales
Chesebrough-Ponds, Inc.	0.076
General Motors	0.054
Kraft, Inc.	0.047
Wal-Mart Stores, Inc.	0.036

The premium price of Häagen-Dazs products results in a high rate of return on sales.

As these rates of return on sales indicates, this ratio varies widely from industry to industry.

One strategy for increasing the rate of return on sales is to develop a product that commands a premium price, such as Häagen-Dazs ice cream, Sony products, and Maytag appliances. Another strategy is to control costs. If successful, either strategy converts a higher proportion of sales into net income and increases the rate of return on net sales.

A return measure can be computed on any revenue and sales amount. Return on net sales, as we have seen, is net income divided by net sales. Return on total revenues is net income divided by total revenues. A company can compute a return on other specific portions of revenue as its information needs dictate.

Rate of Return of Total Assets

The **rate of return on total assets**, or simply *return on assets*, measures the success a company has in using its assets to earn a profit. Creditors have loaned money to the company, and the interest they receive is the return on their investment. Shareholders have invested in the company's stock, and net income is their return. The sum of interest expense and net income is the return to the two groups that have financed the company's operations, and this amount is the numerator of the return-on-assets ratio. Average total assets is the denominator. Palisades Furniture's return-on-assets ratio follows:

Formula		Rate of Return on Total Assets of Palisades Furniture, Inc.	Retail Furniture Industry Average
		19X7	
Rate of return on assets	$=\dfrac{\text{Net income} + \text{interest expense}}{\text{Average total assets}}$	$\dfrac{\$48,000 + \$24,000}{\$715,500} = 0.101$	0.049

Net income and interest expense are taken from the income statement. To compute average total assets, we use beginning and ending total assets from the comparative balance sheet. See how Palisades Furniture's rate of return on assets compares with the rates of some other companies:

Company	Rate of Return on Assets
The Gap, Inc.	0.170
Wal-Mart Stores, Inc................	0.129
General Mills, Inc.....................	0.124
Superior Oil..............................	0.080

Rate of Return on Common Stockholders' Equity

A popular measure of profitability is **rate of return on common stockholders' equity**, which is often shortened to **return on stockholders' equity**, or simply *return on equity*. This ratio shows the relationship between net income and common stockholders' investment in the company. To compute this ratio, we first subtract preferred dividends from net income. This calculation leaves only net income available to the common stockholders, which is needed to compute the ratio. We then divide net income available to common stockholders by the average stockholders' equity during the year. Common stockholders' equity is total stockholders' equity minus preferred equity. Palisades Furniture's rate of return on common stockholders' equity follows:

Formula		Rate of Return on Common Stockholders' Equity of Palisades Furniture, Inc.	Retail Furniture Industry Average
		19X7	
Rate of return on common stockholders' equity	$=\dfrac{\text{Net income} - \text{preferred dividends}}{\text{Average common stockholders' equity}}$	$\dfrac{\$48,000 - \$0}{\$338,000} = 0.142$	0.093

We compute average equity by using the beginning and ending balances [($356,000 + $320,000)/2 = $338,000]. Common stockholders' equity includes Retained Earnings and any Paid-in Capital in Excess of Par on Common Stock.

Compare Palisades Furniture's rate of return on common stockholders' equity with the rates of some leading companies:

Company	Rate of Return on Common Equity
Wal-Mart Stores, Inc.	0.25
Chesebrough-Pond's, Inc..............	0.20
General Motors	0.20

Observe that Palisades Furniture's return on equity (0.142) is higher than its return on assets (0.101). This difference results from borrowing at one rate—say, 0.08, or 8 percent—and investing the funds to earn a higher rate, such as the firm's 0.142, or 14.2-percent, return on stockholders' equity. This practice is called **trading on the equity,** or the use of **leverage.** It is directly related to the debt ratio. The higher the debt ratio, the higher the leverage. Companies that finance operations with debt are said to *lever* their positions. Leverage increases the risk to common stockholders.

For Palisades Furniture, and for many other companies, leverage increases profitability. That is not always the case, however. Leverage can also have a negative impact on profitability. If revenues drop, debt and interest expense still must be paid. Therefore, leverage is a double-edged sword, increasing profits during good times but compounding losses during bad times.

Earnings per Share of Common Stock

Earnings per share of common stock, or simply **earnings per share (EPS),** is perhaps the most widely quoted of all financial statistics. ◀▥◀▥◀▥ EPS is the only ratio that must appear on the face of the income statement. EPS is the amount of net income per share of the company's outstanding *common* stock. Earnings per share is computed by dividing net income available to common stockholders by the number of common shares outstanding during the year. Preferred dividends are subtracted from net income because the preferred stockholders have a prior claim to their dividends. Palisades Furniture, Inc., has no preferred stock outstanding and so has no preferred dividends. The firm's EPS for 19X7 and 19X6 follow (the company had 10,000 shares of common stock outstanding throughout 19X6 and 19X7):

◀▥◀▥◀▥ Recall from Chapter 15, page 612, that GAAP requires that corporations disclose EPS figures on the income statement.

	Formula	Earnings per Share of Palisades Furniture, Inc.	
		19X7	**19X6**
Earnings per share of common stock (EPS)	=	Net income – preferred dividends / Number of shares of common stock outstanding	$\frac{\$48,000 - \$0}{10,000} = \$4.80$	$\frac{\$26,000 - \$0}{10,000} = \$2.60$

Palisades Furniture's EPS increased 85 percent. Its stockholders should not expect such a significant boost in EPS every year. Most companies strive to increase EPS by 10 to 15 percent annually, and the more successful companies do so. But even the most dramatic upward trends include an occasional bad year.

Analyzing Stock as an Investment

Investors purchase stock to earn a return on their investment. This return consists of two parts: (1) gains (or losses) from selling the stock at a price that is different from the investors' purchase price and (2) dividends, the periodic distributions to stockholders. The ratios we examine in this section help analysts evaluate stock in terms of market price or dividend payments.

Price/Earnings Ratio

The **price/earnings ratio** is the ratio of the market price of a share of common stock to the company's earnings per share. This ratio, abbreviated P/E, appears in *The Wall Street Journal* stock listings. P/E plays an important part in evaluating decisions to buy, hold, and sell stocks.

Short Exercise: In the Short Exercise on page 802, use the following information:

	A Co.	B Co.
Market price per share	$20	30
Par value of common stock	5	10
Dividend per share	0.75	1.50

Compute the (1) EPS, (2) P/E, and (3) dividend yield. *A:*

(1) A Co.: $\dfrac{\$20 - \$0}{25 \text{ shares}} = \$0.80$

  B Co.: $\dfrac{\$50 - \$1}{10 \text{ shares}} = \$4.90$

(2) A Co.: 25 ($20/$0.80)
    B Co.: 6.1 ($30/$4.90)
(3) A Co.: 3.75% ($0.75/$20)
    B Co.: 5% ($1.50/$30)

The price/earnings ratios of Palisades Furniture, Inc., follow. The market price of its common stock was $50 at the end of 19X7 and $35 at the end of 19X6. These prices can be obtained from a financial publication, a stockbroker, or some other source outside the accounting records.

		Price/Earnings Ratio of Palisades Furniture, Inc.	
Formula		19X7	19X6
Price/earnings ratio	$=\dfrac{\text{Market price per share of common stock}}{\text{Earnings per share}}$	$\dfrac{\$50.00}{\$4.80} = 10.4$	$\dfrac{\$35.00}{\$2.60} = 13.5$

Given Palisades Furniture's 19X7 price/earnings ratio of 10.4, we would say that the company's stock is selling at 10.4 times earnings. The decline from the 19X6 P/E ratio of 13.5 is not a cause for alarm because the market price of the stock is not under Palisades Furniture's control. The net income is more controllable, and it increased during 19X7. Like most other ratios, P/E ratios vary from industry to industry. P/E ratios range from 8 to 10 for electric utilities (Pennsylvania Power and Light, for example) to 40 or more for "glamour stocks" such as Auto Zone, an auto parts chain, and Oracle Systems, which develops computer software.

The higher a stock's P/E ratio, the higher its *downside risk*—the risk that the stock's market price will fall. Many investors interpret a sharp increase in a stock's P/E ratio as a signal to sell the stock.

Dividend Yield

Dividend yield is the ratio of dividends per share of stock to the stock's market price per share. This ratio measures the percentage of a stock's market value that is returned annually as dividends, an important concern of stockholders. *Preferred* stockholders, who invest primarily to receive dividends, pay special attention to this ratio.

Palisades Furniture paid annual cash dividends of $1.20 per share in 19X7 and $1.00 in 19X6, and market prices of the company's common stock were $50 in 19X7 and $35 in 19X6. The firm's dividend yields follow:

		Dividend Yield on Common Stock of Palisades Furniture, Inc.	
Formula		19X7	19X6
Dividend yield on common stock	$=\dfrac{\text{Dividend per share of common stock}}{\text{Market price per share of common stock}}$	$\dfrac{\$1.20}{\$50.00} = 0.024$	$\dfrac{\$1.00}{\$35.00} = 0.029$

An investor who buys Palisades Furniture common stock for $50 can expect to receive almost 2 1/2 percent of the investment annually in the form of cash dividends. Dividend yields vary widely, from 5 to 8 percent for older, established firms (such as Procter & Gamble and General Motors) down to the range of 0 to 3 percent for young, growth-oriented companies. Palisades Furniture's dividend yield places the company in the second group.

Book Value per Share of Common Stock

Book value per share of common stock is simply common stockholders' equity divided by the number of shares of common stock outstanding. Common shareholders' equity equals total stockholders' equity less preferred equity. Palisades Furniture has no preferred stock outstanding. Its book-value-per-share-of-common-stock ratios follow. Recall that 10,000 shares of common stock were outstanding at the ends of years 19X7 and 19X6.

		Book Value per Share of the Common Stock of Palisades Furniture, Inc.	
	Formula	19X7	19X6
Book value per share of common stock	= $\dfrac{\text{Total stockholders' equity} - \text{preferred equity}}{\text{Number of shares of common stock outstanding}}$	$\dfrac{\$356,000 - \$0}{10,000} = \$35.60$	$\dfrac{\$320,000 - \$0}{10,000} = \$32.00$

Many experts argue that book value is not useful for investment analysis. ◀ It bears no relationship to market value and provides little information beyond stockholders' equity reported on the balance sheet. But other investors base their investment decisions on book value. For example, some investors rank stocks on the basis of the ratio of market price to book value. To these investors, the lower the ratio, the more attractive the stock. These investors are called "value" investors, as contrasted with "growth" investors, who focus more on trends in a company's net income.

◀◀◀ Recall from Chapter 14, pages 573–574, that book value depends on historical costs, whereas market value depends on investors' outlook for dividends and appreciation in the stock's value.

Limitations of Financial Analysis: The Complexity of Business Decisions

Business decisions are made in a world of uncertainty. As useful as ratios may be, they have limitations. We may liken their use in decision making to a physician's use of a thermometer. A reading of 101.6 degrees Fahrenheit indicates that something is wrong with the patient, but the temperature alone does not indicate what the problem is or how to cure it.

OBJECTIVE 6
Use ratios in decision making

In financial analysis, a sudden drop in a company's current ratio signals that *something* is wrong, but this change does not identify the problem or show how to correct it. The business manager must analyze the figures that go into the ratio to determine whether current assets have decreased, current liabilities have increased, or both. If current assets have dropped, is the problem a cash shortage? Are accounts receivable down? Are inventories too low? Only by analyzing the individual items that make up the ratio can the manager determine how to solve the problem. The manager must evaluate data on all ratios in the light of other information about the company and about its particular line of business, such as increased competition or a slowdown in the economy.

Legislation, international affairs, competition, scandals, and many other factors can turn profits into losses and vice versa. To be most useful, ratios should be analyzed over a period of years to take into account a representative group of these factors. Any one year, or even any two years, may not be representative of the company's performance over the long term.

Efficient Markets, Management Action, and Investor Decisions

Much research in accounting and in finance has focused on whether the stock markets are "efficient." An **efficient capital market** is one in which market prices fully reflect all information available to the public. Stocks are priced in full recognition of all publicly accessible data.

That a market is efficient has implications for management action and for investor decisions. It means that managers cannot fool the market with accounting gimmicks. As long as sufficient information is available, the market as a whole can translate accounting data into a "fair" price for the company's stock.

Suppose you are the president of Anacomp Company. Reported earnings per share are $4, and the stock price is $40—so the price/earnings ratio is 10. You believe the corporation's stock is underpriced in comparison with other companies in the same industry. To correct this situation you are considering changing your depreciation method from accelerated to straight-line. The accounting change will increase earnings per share to $5. Will the stock price then rise to $50? Probably not. The company's stock price will probably remain at $40 because the market can understand the accounting change. After all, the company merely changed its method of computing depreciation. There is no effect on the company's cash flows, and its economic position is unchanged.

In an efficient market the search for "underpriced" stock is fruitless unless the investor has relevant private information. Moreover, it is unlawful to invest on the basis of inside information—information that is available only to corporate managers. For outside investors in an efficient market, an appropriate investment strategy seeks to manage risk, to diversify, and to minimize transaction costs. The role of financial statement analysis consists mainly of identifying the risks of various stocks to manage the risk of the overall investment portfolio.

SUMMARY PROBLEM FOR YOUR REVIEW

The following financial data are adapted from the annual report of The Gap, Inc., which operates The Gap and Banana Republic clothing stores:

THE GAP, INC.
FIVE-YEAR SELECTED FINANCIAL DATA

Operating Results	19X5	19X4	19X3	19X2	19X1
(Dollar amounts in thousands)					
Net sales...	$2,960	$2,519	$1,934	$1,587	$1,252
Cost of goods sold and occupancy expenses, excluding depreciation and amortization.......................................	1,856	1,496	1,188	1,007	814
Interest expense (net)..................................	4	4	1	3	3
Income from operations.............................	340	371	237	163	126
Income taxes	129	141	92	65	52
Net earnings	211	230	145	98	74
Cash dividends..	44	41	30	23	18
Financial Position					
Merchandise inventory...............................	366	314	247	243	193
Total assets...	1,379	1,147	777	579	481
Working capital	355	236	579	129	434
Current ratio..	2.06:1	1.71:1	1.39:1	1.69:1	1.70:1
Stockholders' equity	888	678	466	338	276
Average number of shares of common stock outstanding (in thousands)...	144	142	142	141	145

Required

Compute the following ratios for 19X5 through 19X2, and evaluate The Gap's operating results. Are operating results strong or weak? Did they improve or deteriorate during the four-year period?

1. Gross profit percentage
2. Net income as a percent of sales
3. Earnings per share
4. Inventory turnover
5. Times-interest-earned ratio
6. Rate of return on stockholders' equity

SOLUTION TO REVIEW PROBLEM

	19X5	19X4	19X3	19X2
1. Gross profit percentage	$\dfrac{\$2,960 - \$1,856}{\$2,960}$	$\dfrac{\$2,519 - \$1,496}{\$2,519}$	$\dfrac{\$1,934 - \$1,188}{\$1,934}$	$\dfrac{\$1,587 - \$1,007}{\$1,587}$
	= 37.3%	= 40.6%	= 38.6%	= 36.5%
2. Net income as a percent of sales	$\dfrac{\$211}{\$2,960} = 7.1\%$	$\dfrac{\$230}{\$2,519} = 9.1\%$	$\dfrac{\$145}{\$1,934} = 7.5\%$	$\dfrac{\$98}{\$1,587} = 6.2\%$
3. Earnings per share	$\dfrac{\$211}{144} = \$1.47$	$\dfrac{\$230}{142} = \$1.62$	$\dfrac{\$145}{142} = \$1.02$	$\dfrac{\$98}{141} = \$0.70$
4. Inventory turnover	$\dfrac{\$1,856}{(\$366 + \$314)/2}$	$\dfrac{\$1,496}{(\$314 + \$247)/2}$	$\dfrac{\$1,188}{(\$247 + \$243)/2}$	$\dfrac{\$1,007}{(\$243 + \$193)/2}$
	= 5.5 times	= 5.3 times	= 4.8 times	= 4.6 times
5. Times-interest-earned ratio	$\dfrac{\$340}{\$4} = 85$ times	$\dfrac{\$371}{\$4} = 93$ times	$\dfrac{\$237}{\$1} = 237$ times	$\dfrac{\$163}{\$3} = 54$ times
6. Rate of return on stockholders' equity	$\dfrac{\$211}{(\$888 + \$678)/2}$	$\dfrac{\$230}{(\$678 + \$466)/2}$	$\dfrac{\$145}{(\$466 + \$338)/2}$	$\dfrac{\$98}{(\$338 + \$276)/2}$
	= 26.9%	= 40.2%	= 36.1%	= 31.9%

Evaluation: During this four-year period The Gap's operating results were outstanding. Operating results improved, with all ratio values but return on stockholders' equity higher in 19X5 than in 19X2. Moreover, all the performance measures indicate high levels of income and return to investors.

SUMMARY

1. Perform a horizontal analysis of comparative financial statements. Accounting provides information for decision making. Banks loan money, investors buy stocks, and managers run businesses on the basis of the analysis of accounting information. *Horizontal analysis* shows the dollar amount and the percentage change in each financial statement item from one period to the next.

2. Perform a vertical analysis of financial statements. *Vertical analysis* shows the relationship of each item in a financial statement to its total: total assets on the balance sheet and net sales on the income statement.

3. Prepare common-size financial statements. *Common-size statements*—a form of vertical analysis—show the component percentages of the items in a statement. Investment advisory services report common-size statements for various in-dustries, and analysts use them to compare a company with its competitors and with the industry averages.

4. Use the statement of cash flows in decision making. The *statement of cash flows* shows the net cash inflow or outflow caused by a company's operating, investing, and financing activities. By analyzing the inflows and outflows of cash listed on this statement, an analyst can see where a business's cash comes from and how it is being spent.

5. Compute the standard financial ratios used for decision making. *Ratios* play an important part in business decision making because they show relationships between financial statement items.

6. Use ratios in decision making. Analysis of ratios over a period of time is an important way to track a company's progress.

SELF-STUDY QUESTIONS

Test your understanding of the chapter by marking the best answer for each of the following questions.

1. Net income was $240,000 in 19X4, $210,000 in 19X5, and $252,000 in 19X6. The change from 19X5 to 19X6 is a (an) (p. 788)
   - a. Increase of 5 percent
   - b. Increase of 20 percent
   - c. Decrease of 10 percent
   - d. Decrease of 12.5 percent

2. Vertical analysis of a financial statement shows (p. 791)
   - a. Trend percentages
   - b. The percentage change in an item from period to period
   - c. The relationship of an item to its total on the statement
   - d. Net income expressed as a percentage of stockholders' equity

3. Common-size statements are useful for comparing (pp. 793–795)
   - a. Changes in the makeup of assets from period to period
   - b. Different companies
   - c. A company with its industry
   - d. All of the above

4. The statement of cash flows is used for decision making by (pp. 795–796)
   - a. Reporting where cash came from and how it was spent
   - b. Indicating how net income was earned
   - c. Giving the ratio relationships between selected items
   - d. Showing a horizontal analysis of cash flows

5. Cash is $10,000, net accounts receivable amount to $22,000, inventory is $55,000, prepaid expenses total $3,000, and current liabilities are $40,000. What is the acid-test ratio? (p. 803)
   - a. 0.25   c. 2.18
   - b. 0.80   d. 2.25

6. Inventory turnover is computed by dividing (p. 804)
   - a. Sales revenue by average inventory
   - b. Cost of goods sold by average inventory
   - c. Credit sales by average inventory
   - d. Average inventory by cost of goods sold

7. Capp Corporation is experiencing a severe cash shortage due to inability to collect accounts receivable. The decision tool most likely to help identify the appropriate corrective action is the (p. 806)
   - a. Acid-test ratio
   - b. Inventory turnover
   - c. Times-interest-earned ratio
   - d. Days' sales in receivables

8. Analysis of the Mendoza Company financial statements over five years reveals that sales are growing steadily, the debt ratio is higher than the industry average and is increasing, interest coverage is decreasing, return on total assets is declining, and earnings per share of common stock is decreasing. Considered together, these ratios suggest that (pp. 807–810)
   - a. Mendoza should pursue collections of receivables more vigorously
   - b. Competition is taking sales away from Mendoza
   - c. Mendoza is in a declining industry
   - d. The company's debt burden is hurting profitability

9. Which statement is most likely to be true? (pp. 809–810)
   - a. Return on common equity exceeds return on total assets.
   - b. Return on total assets exceeds return on common equity.
   - c. Return on total assets equals return on common equity.
   - d. None of the above.

10. How are financial ratios used in decision making? (p. 813)
    - a. They remove the uncertainty of the business environment.
    - b. They give clear signals about the appropriate action to take.
    - c. They can help identify the reasons for success and failure in business, but decision making requires information beyond the ratios.
    - d. They aren't useful because decision making is too complex.

Answers to the Self-Study Questions follow the Accounting Vocabulary.

ACCOUNTING VOCABULARY

Accounts receivable turnover. Ratio of net credit sales to average net accounts receivable. Measures ability to collect cash from credit customers (p. 805).

Acid-test ratio. Ratio of the sum of cash plus short-term investments plus net current receivables to current liabilities. Tells whether the entity could pay all its current liabilities if they came due immediately. Also called the quick ratio (p. 803).

Book value per share of common stock. Common stockholders' equity divided by the number of shares of common stock outstanding (p. 812).

Common-size statement. A financial statement that reports only percentages (no dollar amounts); a type of vertical analysis (p. 793).

Current ratio. Current assets divided by current liabilities. Measures the ability to pay current liabilities from current assets (p. 801).

Days' sales in receivables. Ratio of average net accounts receivable to one day's sales. Tells how many days' sales remain in Accounts Receivable awaiting collection (p. 806).

Debt ratio. Ratio of total liabilities to total assets. Tells the proportion of a company's assets that it has financed with debt (p. 807).

Dividend yield. Ratio of dividends per share of stock to the stock's market price per share. Tells the percentage of a stock's market value that the company pays to stockholders as dividends (p. 812).

Earnings per share (EPS). Amount of a company's income per share of its outstanding common stock (p. 811).

Efficient capital market. A capital market in which market prices fully reflect all information available to the public (p. 813).

Horizontal analysis. Study of percentage changes in comparative financial statements (p. 788).

Inventory turnover. Ratio of cost of goods sold to average inventory. Measures the number of times a company sells its average level of inventory during a year (p. 804).

Leverage. Another name for trading on the equity (p. 811).

Long-term solvency. Ability to generate enough cash to pay long-term debts as they mature (p. 787).

Price/earnings ratio. Ratio of the market price of a share of common stock to the company's earnings per share. Measures the value that the stock market places on $1 of a company's earnings (p. 811).

Rate of return on common stockholders' equity. Net income minus preferred dividends, divided by average common stockholders' equity. A measure of profitability. Also called return on common stockholders' equity (p. 810).

Rate of return on net sales. Ratio of net income to net sales. A measure of profitability. Also called return on sales (p. 809).

Rate of return on total assets. The sum of net income plus interest expense divided by average total assets. This ratio measures the success a company has in using its assets to earn income for the persons who finance the business. Also called return on assets (p. 809).

Return on stockholders' equity. Another name for rate of return on common stockholders' equity (p. 810).

Short-term liquidity. Ability to meet current payments as they come due (p. 787).

Times-interest-earned ratio. Ratio of income from operations to interest expense. Measures the number of times that operating income can cover interest expense. Also called the interest-coverage ratio (p. 808).

Trading on the equity. Earning more income on borrowed money than the related expense, thereby increasing the earnings for the owners of the business (p. 811).

Vertical analysis. Analysis of a financial statement that reveals the relationship of each statement item to the total, which is 100 percent (p. 791).

Working capital. Current assets minus current liabilities; measures a business's ability to meet its short-term obligations with its current assets (p. 801).

ANSWERS TO SELF-STUDY QUESTIONS

1. b $252,000 − $210,000 = $42,000; $42,000/$210,000 = 0.20
2. c
3. d
4. a
5. b ($10,000 + $22,000)/$40,000 = 0.80
6. b
7. d
8. d
9. a
10. c

QUESTIONS

1. Identify two groups of users of accounting information and the decisions they base on accounting data.
2. What are three analytical tools that are based on accounting information?
3. Briefly describe horizontal analysis. How do decision makers use this tool of analysis?
4. What is vertical analysis, and what is its purpose?
5. What use is made of common-size statements?
6. State how an investor might analyze the statement of cash flows. How might the investor analyze investing-activities data?
7. Why are ratios an important tool of financial analysis? Give an example.
8. Identify two ratios used to measure a company's ability to pay current liabilities. Show how they are computed.
9. Why is the acid-test ratio given that name?
10. What does the inventory turnover ratio measure?
11. Suppose the days'-sales-in-receivables ratio of Gomez, Inc., increased from 36 at January 1 to 43 at December 31. Is this a good sign or a bad sign about the company? What would Gomez management do in response to this change?
12. Company A's debt ratio has increased from 0.50 to 0.70. Identify a decision maker to whom this increase is important, and state how the increase affects this party's decisions about the company.
13. Which ratio measures the *effect of debt* on (a) financial position (the balance sheet) and (b) the company's ability to pay interest expense (the income statement)?
14. Company A is a chain of grocery stores, and Company B is a computer manufacturer. Which company is likely to have the higher (a) current ratio, (b) inventory turnover, and (c) rate of return on sales? Give your reasons.
15. Identify four ratios used to measure a company's profitability. Show how to compute these ratios and state what information each ratio provides.
16. The price/earnings ratio of General Motors was 6, and the price/earnings ratio of American Express was 45. Which company did the stock market favor? Explain.
17. McDonald's Corporation paid cash dividends of $0.78 2/3 (78 and 2/3 cents) per share when the market price of the company's stock was $58. What was the dividend yield on McDonalds' stock? What does dividend yield measure?
18. Hold all other factors constant and indicate whether each of the following situations generally signals good or bad news about a company:
    a. Increase in current ratio
    b. Decrease in inventory turnover
    c. Increase in debt ratio
    d. Decrease in interest-coverage ratio
    e. Increase in return on sales
    f. Decrease in earnings per share
    g. Increase in price/earnings ratio
    h. Increase in book value per share
19. Explain how an investor might use book value per share of stock in making an investment decision.
20. Describe how decision makers use ratio data. What are the limitations of ratios?

EXERCISES

Computing year-to-year changes in working capital
(Obj. 1)

E19-1 What were the amount of change and the percentage change in Western Bell Corporation's working capital during 19X6 and 19X7? Is this trend favorable or unfavorable?

	19X7	19X6	19X5
Total current assets	$312,000	$290,000	$280,000
Total current liabilities	150,000	117,000	140,000

Horizontal analysis of an income statement
(Obj. 1)

E19-2 Prepare a horizontal analysis of the following comparative income statement of Syntex Incorporated. Round percentage changes to the nearest one-tenth percent (three decimal places):

SYNTEX INCORPORATED COMPARATIVE INCOME STATEMENT YEARS ENDED DECEMBER 31, 19X9 AND 19X8		
	19X9	**19X8**
Total revenue	$410,000	$373,000
Expenses:		
Cost of goods sold	$202,000	$188,000
Selling and general expenses	98,000	93,000
Interest expense	7,000	4,000
Income tax expense	42,000	37,000
Total expenses	349,000	322,000
Net income	$ 61,000	$ 51,000

Why did net income increase by a higher percentage than total revenues increased during 19X9?

Computing trend percentages
(Obj. 1)

E19-3 Compute trend percentages for net sales and net income for the following five-year period, using year 1 as the base year:

	Year 5	Year 4	Year 3	Year 2	Year 1
	(amounts in thousands)				
Net sales	$1,410	$1,187	$1,106	$1,009	$1,043
Net income	117	114	83	71	85

Which grew faster during the period, net sales or net income?

Vertical analysis of a balance sheet
(Obj. 2)

E19-4 Copy World, Inc., has requested that you perform a vertical analysis of its balance sheet to determine the component percentages of its assets, liabilities, and stockholders' equity.

COPY WORLD, INC. BALANCE SHEET DECEMBER 31, 19X3	
Assets	
Total current assets	$ 72,000
Long-term investments	35,000
Property, plant, and equipment, net	217,000
Total assets	$324,000
Liabilities	
Total current liabilities	$ 58,000
Long-term debt	118,000
Total liabilities	$176,000
Stockholders' Equity	
Total stockholders' equity	148,000
Total liabilities and stockholders' equity	$324,000

E19-5 Prepare a comparative common-size income statement for Syntex Incorporated, using the 19X9 and 19X8 data of Exercise 19-2 and rounding percentages to one-tenth percent (three decimal places).

Preparing a common-size income statement (Obj. 3)

E19-6 Identify any weaknesses in the company revealed by the statement of cash flows of Nemmer Electric, Inc.

Analyzing the statement of cash flows (Obj. 4)

NEMMER ELECTRIC, INC.
STATEMENT OF CASH FLOWS
FOR THE CURRENT YEAR

Operating activities:		
Income from operations..		$ 52,000
Add (subtract) noncash items:		
Depreciation...	$ 23,000	
Net increase in current assets other than cash	(15,000)	
Net increase in current liabilities exclusive of		
short-term debt	11,000	19,000
Net cash inflow from operating activities.......................		71,000
Investing activities:		
Sale of property, plant, and equipment............................		101,000
Financing activities:		
Issuance of bonds payable	$114,000	
Payment of short-term debt	(171,000)	
Payment of long-term debt...	(79,000)	
Payment of dividends...	(42,000)	
Net cash outflow from financing activities		(178,000)
Decrease in cash...		$ (6,000)

E19-7 The financial statements of Alamo Iron Works include the following items:

Computing five ratios (Obj. 5)

	Current Year	Preceding Year
Balance sheet:		
Cash..	$ 17,000	$ 22,000
Short-term investments	11,000	26,000
Net receivables...........................	64,000	73,000
Inventory....................................	87,000	71,000
Prepaid expenses	6,000	8,000
Total current assets	185,000	200,000
Total current liabilities...............	121,000	91,000
Income statement:		
Net credit sales...........................	$454,000	
Cost of goods sold.......................	257,000	

Required

Compute the following ratios for the current year: (a) current ratio, (b) acid-test ratio, (c) inventory turnover, (d) accounts receivable turnover, and (e) days' sales in average receivables.

E19-8 Academy Control Systems has requested that you determine whether the company's ability to pay its current liabilities and long-term debts has improved or deteriorated during 19X2. To answer this question, compute the following ratios for 19X2 and 19X1: (a) current ratio, (b) acid-test ratio, (c) debt ratio, and (d) times-interest-earned ratio. Summarize the results of your analysis.

Analyzing the ability to pay current liabilities (Obj. 5, 6)

	19X2	19X1
Cash	$ 21,000	$ 47,000
Short-term investments	28,000	—
Net receivables	102,000	116,000
Inventory	226,000	263,000
Prepaid expenses	11,000	9,000
Total assets	503,000	489,000
Total current liabilities	205,000	241,000
Total liabilities	261,000	273,000
Income from operations	165,000	158,000
Interest expense	36,000	39,000

Analyzing profitability
(Obj. 5, 6)

E19-9 Compute four ratios that measure ability to earn profits for New York Packaging, Inc., whose comparative income statement follows:

NEW YORK PACKAGING, INC.
COMPARATIVE INCOME STATEMENT
YEARS ENDED DECEMBER 31, 19X6 AND 19X5

	19X6	19X5
Net sales	$174,000	$158,000
Cost of goods sold	93,000	86,000
Gross profit	81,000	72,000
Selling and general expenses	48,000	41,000
Income from operations	33,000	31,000
Interest expense	21,000	10,000
Income before income tax	12,000	21,000
Income tax expense	4,000	8,000
Net income	$ 8,000	$ 13,000

Additional data:

	19X6	19X5
Average total assets	$204,000	$191,000
Average common stockholders' equity	$ 96,000	$ 89,000
Preferred dividends	$ 3,000	$ 3,000
Shares of common stock outstanding	20,000	20,000

Did the company's operating performance improve or deteriorate during 19X6?

Evaluating a stock as an
investment
(Obj. 5, 6)

E19-10 Evaluate the common stock of Stroud Security Systems as an investment. Specifically, use the three stock ratios to determine whether the stock has increased or decreased in attractiveness during the past year.

	19X8	19X7
Net income	$ 58,000	$ 55,000
Dividends (half on preferred stock)	28,000	28,000
Common stockholders' equity at year end (80,000 shares)	530,000	500,000
Preferred stockholders' equity at year end	200,000	200,000
Market price per share of common stock at year end	$10.12	$7.75

E19-11 The following data are from the financial statements of McDonald's Corporation, operator of more than 13,000 restaurants in 65 countries.

Using ratio data to reconstruct a real company's income statement (Obj. 2, 3, 5)

	Dollars in Millions
Average stockholders' equity	$3,605
Interest expense	$ 413
Preferred stock	–0–
Operating income as a percent of sales	24.04%
Rate of return on sales	11.13%
Rate of return on stockholders' equity	20.50%
Income tax rate	37.53%

Required

Complete the following condensed income statement. Report amounts to the nearest million dollars.

Sales	$?
Operating expense	?
Operating income	?
Interest expense	?
Pretax income	?
Income tax expense	?
Net income	$?

E19-12 The following data are from the financial statements of Wal-Mart Stores, Inc., the largest retailer in the world:

Using ratio data to reconstruct a real company's balance sheet (Obj. 2, 3, 5)

	Dollars in Millions
Total liabilities	$11,806
Preferred stock	$ –0–
Total current assets	$10,196
Accumulated depreciation	$ 448
Debt ratio	57.408%
Current ratio	1.51

Required

Complete the following condensed balance sheet. Report amounts to the nearest million dollars.

Current assets		$?
Property, plant, and equipment	$?	
Less Accumulated depreciation	?	?
Total assets		$?
Current liabilities		$?
Long-term liabilities		?
Stockholders' equity		?
Total liabilities and stockholders' equity		$?

PROBLEMS

Trend percentages, return on common equity, and comparison with the industry
(Obj. 1, 5, 6)

P19-1A   Net sales, net income, and common stockholders' equity for Bear Utilities, Inc., for a six-year period follow.

	19X7	19X6	19X5	19X4	19X3	19X2
			(amounts in thousands)			
Net sales	$761	$714	$641	$662	$642	$634
Net income...	61	45	32	48	41	40
Ending common stockholders' equity ...	386	354	330	296	272	252

Required

1. Compute trend percentages for each item for 19X3 through 19X7. Use 19X2 as the base year.

2. Compute the rate of return on average common stockholders' equity for 19X3 through 19X7, rounding to three decimal places. In this industry, rates of 13 percent are average, rates above 16 percent are considered good, and rates above 20 percent are viewed as outstanding.

3. How does Bear's return on common stockholders' equity compare with the industry?

Common-size statements, analysis of profitability, and comparison with the industry
(Obj. 2, 3, 5, 6)

P19-2A   Alto Auto Glass has asked your help in comparing the company's profit performance and financial position with the average for the auto parts retail industry. The proprietor has given you the company's income statement and balance sheet and also the industry average data for retailers of auto parts.

ALTO AUTO GLASS INCOME STATEMENT COMPARED WITH INDUSTRY AVERAGE YEAR ENDED DECEMBER 31, 19X6		
	Alto	**Industry Average**
Net sales	$781,000	100.0%
Cost of goods sold	497,000	65.8
Gross profit............................	284,000	34.2
Operating expenses	163,000	19.7
Operating income	121,000	14.5
Other expenses	5,000	0.4
Net income.............................	$116,000	14.1%

ALTO AUTO GLASS BALANCE SHEET COMPARED WITH INDUSTRY AVERAGE DECEMBER 31, 19X6		
	Alto	**Industry Average**
Current assets	$350,000	70.9%
Fixed assets, net.......................	74,000	23.6
Intangible assets, net	4,000	0.8
Other assets	22,000	4.7
Total...	$450,000	100.0%
Current liabilities	$207,000	48.1%
Long-term liabilities	62,000	16.6
Stockholders' equity................	181,000	35.3
Total...	$450,000	100.0%

Required

1. Prepare a two-column common-size income statement and a two-column common-size balance sheet for Alto. The first column of each statement should present Alto's common-size statement, and the second column should show the industry averages.

2. For the profitability analysis, compute Alto's (a) ratio of gross profit to net sales, (b) ratio of operating income to net sales, and (c) ratio of net income to net sales. Compare these figures with the industry averages. Is Alto's profit performance better or worse than the industry average?

3. For the analysis of financial position, compute Alto's (a) ratio of current assets to total assets and (b) ratio of stockholders' equity to total assets. Compare these ratios with the industry averages. Is Alto's financial position better or worse than the industry averages?

Using the statement of cash flows for decision making
(Obj. 4)

P19-3A   You have been asked to evaluate two companies as possible investments. The two companies, similar in size, buy computers, airplanes, and other high-cost assets to lease to other businesses. Assume that all other available information has been analyzed, and the decision on which company's stock to purchase depends on the data in their statements of cash flows (page 823).

Required

Discuss the relative strengths and weaknesses of each company. Conclude your discussion by recommending one company's stock as an investment.

822   PART 4   ANALYSIS OF ACCOUNTING INFORMATION

ALLIED ASSETS FOR LEASE, INC.
STATEMENTS OF CASH FLOWS
FOR THE YEARS ENDED SEPTEMBER 30, 19X5 AND 19X4

	19X5		19X4	
Operating activities:				
Income from operations......		$ 37,000		$ 74,000
Add (subtract) noncash items:				
Total...		14,000		(4,000)
Net cash inflow from operating activities...		51,000		70,000
Investing activities:				
Purchase of property, plant, and equipment...	$ (13,000)		$ (3,000)	
Sale of property, plant, and equipment...	86,000		79,000	
Sale of long-term investments...	13,000		—	
Net cash inflow from investing activities...		86,000		76,000
Financing activities:				
Issuance of short-term notes payable...	$ 73,000		$ 19,000	
Issuance of long-term notes payable...	31,000		42,000	
Payment of short-term notes payable...	(181,000)		(148,000)	
Payment of long-term notes payable...	(55,000)		(32,000)	
Net cash outflow from financing activities...		(132,000)		(119,000)
Increase in cash...		$ 5,000		$ 27,000
Cash summary from balance sheet:				
Cash balance at beginning of year...		$ 31,000		$ 4,000
Increase in cash during the year...		5,000		27,000
Cash balance at end of year...		$ 36,000		$ 31,000

NORTHERN LEASING CORPORATION
STATEMENTS OF CASH FLOWS
FOR THE YEARS ENDED SEPTEMBER 30, 19X5 AND 19X4

	19X5		19X4	
Operating activities:				
Income from operations.......		$ 79,000		$ 71,000
Add (subtract) noncash items:				
Total...		19,000		—
Net cash inflow from operating activities...		98,000		71,000
Investing activities:				
Purchase of property, plant, and equipment...	$(121,000)		$(91,000)	
Sale of long-term investments...	13,000		18,000	
Net cash outflow from investing activities...		(108,000)		(73,000)
Financing activities:				
Issuance of long-term notes payable...	$ 46,000		$ 43,000	
Payment of short-term notes payable...	(15,000)		(40,000)	
Payment of cash dividends...	(12,000)		(9,000)	
Net cash inflow (outflow) from financing activities...		19,000		(6,000)
Increase (decrease) in cash...		$ 9,000		$ (8,000)
Cash summary from balance sheet:				
Cash balance at beginning of year...		$ 72,000		$ 80,000
Increase (decrease) in cash during the year...		9,000		(8,000)
Cash balance at end of year...		$ 81,000		$ 72,000

P19-4A Financial statement data of Mennonite Industries, Inc., include the following items:

Cash..	$ 22,000
Short-term investments...	19,000
Accounts receivable, net	83,000
Inventories	141,000
Prepaid expenses...	8,000
Total assets	657,000
Short-term notes payable	49,000
Accounts payable	103,000
Accrued liabilities...	38,000
Long-term notes payable.......................................	160,000
Other long-term liabilities....................................	31,000
Net income	71,000
Number of common shares outstanding..............	40,000

Required

1. Compute Mennonite's current ratio, debt ratio, and earnings per share.
2. Compute each of the three ratios after evaluating the effect of each transaction that follows. Consider each transaction *separately*.
   a. Purchased merchandise of $26,000 on account, debiting Inventory.
   b. Paid off long-term liabilities, $31,000.
   c. Declared, but did not pay, a $22,000 cash dividend on common stock.
   d. Borrowed $85,000 on a long-term note payable.
   e. Sold short-term investments for $18,000 (cost, $11,000); assume no income tax on the gain.
   f. Issued 5,000 shares of common stock, receiving cash of $120,000.
   g. Received cash on account, $19,000.
   h. Paid short-term notes payable, $32,000.

Use the following format for your answer:

		Current Ratio	**Debt Ratio**	**Earnings per Share**
Requirement 1				

	Transaction (letter)	**Current Ratio**	**Debt Ratio**	**Earnings per Share**
Requirement 2				

P19-5A Comparative financial statement data of Wahl Furniture Co. follow.

WAHL FURNITURE CO.
COMPARATIVE INCOME STATEMENT
YEARS ENDED DECEMBER 31, 19X4 AND 19X3

	19X4	19X3
Net sales	$462,000	$427,000
Cost of goods sold	229,000	218,000
Gross profit...	233,000	209,000
Operating expenses	136,000	134,000
Income from operations.........................	97,000	75,000
Interest expense	11,000	12,000
Income before income tax......................	86,000	63,000
Income tax expense................................	30,000	27,000
Net income...	$ 56,000	$ 36,000

WAHL FURNITURE CO.
COMPARATIVE BALANCE SHEET
DECEMBER 31, 19X4 AND 19X3
(SELECTED 19X2 AMOUNTS GIVEN FOR COMPUTATION OF RATIOS)

	19X4	19X3	19X2
Current assets:			
Cash	$ 96,000	$ 97,000	
Current receivables, net	112,000	116,000	$103,000
Inventories......................................	172,000	162,000	207,000
Prepaid expenses...............................	16,000	7,000	
Total current assets	396,000	382,000	
Property, plant, and equipment, net	189,000	178,000	
Total assets..	$585,000	$560,000	598,000
Total current liabilities	$206,000	$223,000	
Long-term liabilities	119,000	117,000	
Total liabilities	325,000	340,000	
Preferred stockholders' equity, 6%,			
$100 par	100,000	100,000	
Common stockholders' equity,			
no-par	160,000	120,000	90,000
Total liabilities and stockholders'			
equity	$585,000	$560,000	

Other information:

a. Market price of Wahl common stock: $49 at December 31, 19X4, and $32.50 at December 31, 19X3.

b. Common shares outstanding: 10,000 during 19X4 and 9,000 during 19X3.

c. All sales on credit.

Required

1. Compute the following ratios for 19X4 and 19X3:
   a. Current ratio
   b. Inventory turnover
   c. Accounts receivable turnover
   d. Times-interest-earned ratio
   e. Return on assets
   f. Return on common stockholders' equity
   g. Earnings per share of common stock
   h. Price/earnings ratio
   i. Book value per share of common stock

2. Decide (a) whether Wahl's financial position improved or deteriorated during 19X4 and (b) whether the investment attractiveness of its common stock appears to have increased or decreased.

3. How will what you learned in this problem help you evaluate an investment?

P19-6A   Assume that you are purchasing an investment and have decided to invest in a company in the air-conditioning and heating business. You have narrowed the choice to Smajstrla, Inc., and DuBois Corp. You have assembled the following selected data:

Using ratios to decide between two stock investments
(Obj. 5, 6)

Selected income statement data for current year:

	Smajstrla, Inc.	DuBois Corp.
Net sales (all on credit)...	$497,000	$371,000
Cost of goods sold	258,000	209,000
Income from operations	138,000	79,000
Interest expense	19,000	—
Net income	72,000	48,000

Selected balance sheet and market price data at end of current year:

	Smajstrla, Inc.	DuBois Corp.
Current assets:		
Cash..	$ 19,000	$ 22,000
Short-term investments	18,000	20,000
Current receivables, net......................................	46,000	42,000
Inventories	100,000	87,000
Prepaid expenses...	3,000	2,000
Total current assets	186,000	173,000
Total assets	328,000	265,000
Total current liabilities	98,000	108,000
Total liabilities	131,000	108,000
Preferred stock: 5%, $100 par..............................	20,000	
Common stock, $1 par (10,000 shares).................		10,000
$2.50 par (5,000 shares)..............	12,500	
Total stockholders' equity.....................................	197,000	157,000
Market price per share of common stock...............	$112	$51

Selected balance sheet data at beginning of current year:

	Smajstrla, Inc.	DuBois Corp.
Current receivables, net	$ 48,000	$ 40,000
Inventories	88,000	93,000
Total assets	270,000	259,000
Preferred stock, 5%, $100 par...............................	20,000	—
Common stock, $1 par (10,000 shares)..................		10,000
$2.50 par (5,000 shares)..............	12,500	
Total stockholders' equity......................................	126,000	118,000

Your investment strategy is to purchase the stocks of companies that have low price/earnings ratios but appear to be in good shape financially. Assume that you have analyzed all other factors and your decision depends on the results of the ratio analysis to be performed.

Required

Compute the following ratios for both companies for the current year, and decide which company's stock better fits your investment strategy.

1. Current ratio
2. Acid-test ratio
3. Inventory turnover
4. Days' sales in average receivables
5. Debt ratio
6. Times-interest-earned ratio
7. Return on net sales
8. Return on total assets
9. Return on common stockholders' equity
10. Earnings per share of common stock
11. Book value per share of common stock
12. Price/earnings ratio

P19-1B Net sales, net income, and total assets for Monica Hearn, Inc., for a six-year period follow:

Trend percentages, return on sales, and comparison with the industry (Obj. 1, 5, 6)

	19X6	19X5	19X4	19X3	19X2	19X1
			(amounts in thousands)			
Net sales	$347	$313	$266	$281	$245	$241
Net income..............................	27	21	11	18	14	13
Total assets.............................	296	254	209	197	181	166

Required

1. Compute trend percentages for each item for 19X2 through 19X6. Use 19X1 as the base year.

2. Compute the rate of return on net sales for 19X2 through 19X6, rounding to three decimal places. In this industry, rates above 5 percent are considered good, and rates above 7 percent are viewed as outstanding.

3. How does Hearn's return on net sales compare with that of the industry?

P19-2B Top managers of Bull's Eye Archery Company have asked your help in comparing the company's profit performance and financial position with the average for the sporting goods industry. The accountant has given you the company's income statement and balance sheet and also the following data for the sporting goods industry.

Common-size statements, analysis of profitability, and comparison with the industry (Obj. 2, 3, 5, 6)

BULL'S EYE ARCHERY
INCOME STATEMENT
COMPARED WITH INDUSTRY AVERAGE
YEAR ENDED DECEMBER 31, 19X3

	Bull's Eye	Industry Average
Net sales	$957,000	100.0%
Cost of goods sold..................	653,000	65.9
Gross profit	304,000	34.1
Operating expenses	257,000	28.1
Operating income	47,000	6.0
Other expenses......................	2,000	0.4
Net income............................	$ 45,000	5.6%

BULL'S EYE ARCHERY
BALANCE SHEET
COMPARED WITH INDUSTRY AVERAGE
DECEMBER 31, 19X3

	Bull's Eye	Industry Average
Current assets........................	$448,000	74.4%
Fixed assets, net....................	127,000	20.0
Intangible assets, net	42,000	0.6
Other assets	13,000	5.0
Total.....................................	$630,000	100.0%
Current liabilities	$246,000	35.6%
Long-term liabilities	144,000	19.0
Stockholders' equity..............	240,000	45.4
Total.....................................	$630,000	100.0%

Required

1. Prepare a two-column common-size income statement and a two-column common-size balance sheet for Bull's Eye. The first column of each statement should present Bull's Eye's common-size statement, and the second column should show the industry averages.

2. For the profitability analysis, compute Bull's Eye's (a) ratio of gross profit to net sales, (b) ratio of operating income (loss) to net sales, and (c) ratio of net income (loss) to net sales. Compare these figures with the industry averages. Is Bull's Eye's profit performance better or worse than average for the industry?

3. For the analysis of financial position, compute Bull's Eye's (a) ratio of current assets to total assets and (b) ratio of stockholders' equity to total assets. Compare these ratios with the industry averages. Is Bull's Eye's financial position better or worse than average for the industry?

P19-3B You are evaluating two companies as possible investments. The two companies, similar in size, are in the commuter airline business. They fly passengers from Minneapolis and Milwaukee to smaller cities in their area. Assume that all other available information has been analyzed and that the decision on which company's stock to purchase depends on the information given in their statements of cash flows, which appear on page 828.

Using the statement of cash flows for decision making (Obj. 4)

NORWEGIAN EXPRESS
STATEMENTS OF CASH FLOWS
FOR THE YEARS ENDED NOVEMBER 30, 19X9 AND 19X8

	19X9		19X8	
Operating activities:				
Income from operations......		$184,000		$131,000
Add (subtract) noncash items:				
Total.....		64,000		62,000
Net cash inflow from operating activities		248,000		193,000
Investing activities:				
Purchase of property, plant, and equipment......	$(303,000)		$(453,000)	
Sale of property, plant, and equipment......	46,000		39,000	
Sale of long-term investments......	—		33,000	
Net cash outflow from investing activities		(257,000)		(381,000)
Financing activities:				
Issuance of long-term notes payable	$ 131,000		$ 83,000	
Issuance of short-term notes payable	43,000		35,000	
Payment of short-term notes payable	(66,000)		(18,000)	
Net cash inflow from financing activities......		108,000		100,000
Increase (decrease) in cash		$ 99,000		$ (88,000)
Cash summary from balance sheet:				
Cash balance at beginning of year...........		$116,000		$204,000
Increase (decrease) in cash during the year		99,000		(88,000)
Cash balance at end of year		$215,000		$116,000

WISCONSIN AIRWAYS, INC.
STATEMENTS OF CASH FLOWS
FOR THE YEARS ENDED NOVEMBER 30, 19X9 AND 19X8

	19X9		19X8	
Operating activities:				
Income (loss) from operations		$ (67,000)		$154,000
Add (subtract) noncash items:				
Total.....		84,000		(23,000)
Net cash inflow from operating activities		17,000		131,000
Investing activities:				
Purchase of property, plant, and equipment......	$(120,000)		$ (91,000)	
Sale of property, plant, and equipment......	118,000		39,000	
Sale of long-term investments......	52,000		4,000	
Net cash inflow (outflow) from investing activities ...		50,000		(48,000)
Financing activities:				
Issuance of short-term notes payable	$ 122,000		$ 143,000	
Payment of short-term notes payable	(179,000)		(134,000)	
Payment of cash dividends......	(45,000)		(64,000)	
Net cash outflow from financing activities.....		(102,000)		(55,000)
Increase (decrease) in cash		$ (35,000)		$ 28,000
Cash summary from balance sheet:				
Cash balance at beginning of year		$ 131,000		$103,000
Increase (decrease) in cash during the year		(35,000)		28,000
Cash balance at end of year		$ 96,000		$131,000

Required

Discuss the relative strengths and weaknesses of Norwegian and Wisconsin. Conclude your discussion by recommending one of the company's stocks as an investment.

P19-4B   Financial statement data on TriState Optical Company include the following items:

Effects of business transactions on selected ratios
(Obj. 5, 6)

Cash...	$ 47,000
Short-term investments...	21,000
Accounts receivable, net	102,000
Inventories	274,000
Prepaid expenses..	15,000
Total assets	933,000
Short-term notes payable	72,000
Accounts payable	96,000
Accrued liabilities..	50,000
Long-term notes payable.......................................	146,000
Other long-term liabilities....................................	78,000
Net income	119,000
Number of common shares outstanding...............	22,000

Required

1. Compute TriState's current ratio, debt ratio, and earnings per share.
2. Compute each of the three ratios after evaluating the effect of each transaction that follows. Consider each transaction *separately*.
   a. Borrowed $76,000 on a long-term note payable.
   b. Sold short-term investments for $44,000 (cost, $66,000); assume no tax effect of the loss.
   c. Issued 14,000 shares of common stock, receiving cash of $168,000.
   d. Received cash on account, $6,000.
   e. Paid short-term notes payable, $51,000.
   f. Purchased merchandise of $48,000 on account, debiting Inventory.
   g. Paid off long-term liabilities, $78,000.
   h. Declared, but did not pay, a $51,000 cash dividend on the common stock.

Use the following format for your answer:

Requirement 1		**Current Ratio**	**Debt Ratio**	**Earnings per Share**
Requirement 2	Transaction (letter)	**Current Ratio**	**Debt Ratio**	**Earnings per Share**

P19-5B   Comparative financial statement data of Dunn's Brass Foundry follow.

Using ratios to evaluate a stock investment
(Obj. 5, 6)

DUNN'S BRASS FOUNDRY		
COMPARATIVE INCOME STATEMENT		
YEARS ENDED DECEMBER 31, 19X6 AND 19X5		
	19X6	**19X5**
Net sales	$667,000	$599,000
Cost of goods sold	378,000	283,000
Gross profit...	289,000	316,000
Operating expenses	129,000	147,000
Income from operations........................	160,000	169,000
Interest expense	57,000	41,000
Income before income tax.....................	103,000	128,000
Income tax expense................................	34,000	53,000
Net income..	$ 69,000	$ 75,000

```
                  DUNN'S BRASS FOUNDRY
                COMPARATIVE BALANCE SHEET
                 DECEMBER 31, 19X6 AND 19X5
         (SELECTED 19X4 AMOUNTS GIVEN FOR COMPUTATION OF RATIOS)
```

	19X6	19X5	19X4
Current assets:			
Cash	$ 37,000	$ 40,000	
Current receivables, net	208,000	151,000	$138,000
Inventories...	352,000	286,000	184,000
Prepaid expenses...............................	5,000	20,000	
Total current assets	602,000	497,000	
Property, plant, and equipment, net	287,000	276,000	
Total assets...	$889,000	$773,000	707,000
Total current liabilities	$286,000	$267,000	
Long-term liabilities	245,000	235,000	
Total liabilities	531,000	502,000	
Preferred stockholders' equity, 4%,			
$20 par	50,000	50,000	
Common stockholders' equity, no-par ..	308,000	221,000	148,000
Total liabilities and stockholders'			
equity	$889,000	$773,000	

Other information:

a. Market price of Dunn's common stock: $30.75 at December 31, 19X6, and $40.25 at December 31, 19X5.

b. Common shares outstanding: 15,000 during 19X6 and 14,000 during 19X5.

c. All sales on credit.

Required

1. Compute the following ratios for 19X6 and 19X5:
   a. Current ratio
   b. Inventory turnover
   c. Accounts receivable turnover
   d. Times-interest-earned ratio
   e. Return on assets
   f. Return on common stockholders' equity
   g. Earnings per share of common stock
   h. Price/earnings ratio
   i. Book value per share of common stock

2. Decide whether (a) Dunn's financial position improved or deteriorated during 19X6 and (b) the investment attractiveness of its common stock appears to have increased or decreased.

3. How will what you learned in this problem help you evaluate an investment?

Using ratios to decide between two stock investments (Obj. 5, 6)

P19-6B Assume that you are purchasing stock in a company in the hospital supply industry. You have narrowed the choice to Scott & White and Pediatric Supply and have assembled the following data:

Selected income statement data for current year:

	Scott & White	Pediatric Supply
Net sales (all on credit)	$519,000	$603,000
Cost of goods sold	387,000	454,000
Income from operations	72,000	93,000
Interest expense	8,000	—
Net income	38,000	56,000

Selected balance sheet and market price data at end of current year:

	Scott & White	Pediatric Supply
Current assets:		
Cash	$ 39,000	$ 25,000
Short-term investments	13,000	6,000
Current receivables, net	164,000	189,000
Inventories	183,000	211,000
Prepaid expenses	15,000	19,000
Total current assets	414,000	450,000
Total assets	938,000	974,000
Total current liabilities	338,000	366,000
Total liabilities	691,000	667,000
Preferred stock, 4%, $100 par	25,000	
Common stock, $1 par (150,000 shares)		150,000
$5 par (20,000 shares)	100,000	
Total stockholders' equity	247,000	307,000
Market price per share of common stock	$47.50	$9

Selected balance sheet data at beginning of current year:

	Scott & White	Pediatric Supply
Current receivables, net	$193,000	$142,000
Inventories	197,000	209,000
Total assets	909,000	842,000
Preferred stock, 4%, $100 par	25,000	
Common stock, $1 par (150,000 shares)		150,000
$5 par (20,000 shares)	100,000	
Total stockholders' equity	215,000	263,000

Your investment strategy is to purchase the stocks of companies that have low price/earnings ratios but appear to be in good shape financially. Assume that you have analyzed all other factors, and your decision depends on the results of the ratio analysis to be performed.

Required

Compute the following ratios for both companies for the current year and decide which company's stock better fits your investment strategy.

1. Current ratio
2. Acid-test ratio
3. Inventory turnover
4. Days' sales in average receivables
5. Debt ratio
6. Times-interest-earned ratio
7. Return on net sales
8. Return on total assets
9. Return on common stockholders' equity
10. Earnings per share of common stock
11. Book value per share of common stock
12. Price/earnings ratio

DECISION PROBLEMS

Identifying action to cut losses and establish profitability (Obj. 2, 5, 6)

1.   Suppose you manage Wheel Sports, Inc., a sporting goods and bicycle shop, which lost money during the past year. Before you can set the business on a successful course, you must analyze the company and industry data for the current year to learn what is wrong. The data appear below.

WHEEL SPORTS BALANCE SHEET DATA	Wheel Sports	Industry Average
Cash and short-term investments...........................	3.0%	6.8%
Trade receivables, net	15.2	11.0
Inventory..	64.2	60.5
Prepaid expenses	1.0	0.0
Total current assets	83.4	78.3
Fixed assets, net..	12.6	15.2
Other assets..	4.0	6.5
Total assets	100.0%	100.0%
Notes payable, short-term, 12%	17.1%	14.0%
Accounts payable	21.1	25.1
Accrued liabilities...	7.8	7.9
Total current liabilities...	46.0	47.0
Long-term debt, 11%...	19.7	16.4
Total liabilities..	65.7	63.4
Common stockholders' equity	34.3	36.6
Total liabilities and stockholders' equity	100.0%	100.0%

WHEEL SPORTS INCOME STATEMENT DATA	Wheel Sports	Industry Average
Net sales...	100.0%	100.0%
Cost of sales	(68.2)	(64.8)
Gross profit..	31.8	35.2
Operating expense	(37.1)	(32.3)
Operating income (loss)..	(5.3)	2.9
Interest expense	(5.8)	(1.3)
Other revenue	1.1	0.3
Income (loss) before income tax...........................	(10.0)	1.9
Income tax (expense) saving	4.4	(0.8)
Net income (loss)...	(5.6)%	1.1%

Required

On the basis of your analysis of these figures, suggest four courses of action Wheel Sports should take to reduce its losses and establish profitable operations. Give your reasons for each suggestion.

2. Consider the following business situations.

a. Krista Chen has asked you about the stock of a particular company. She finds it attractive because it has a high dividend yield relative to another stock she is also considering. Explain to her the meaning of the ratio and the danger of making a decision based on it alone.

b. Rocketdyne's owners are concerned because the number of days' sales in receivables has increased over the previous two years. Explain why the ratio might have increased.

c. Mark Lott is the controller of Hunan Industries, Inc., whose year end is December 31. Lott prepares checks for suppliers in December and posts them to the appropriate accounts in that month. However, he holds on to the checks and mails them to the suppliers in January. What financial ratio(s) are most affected by the action? What is Lott's purpose in undertaking this activity?

Understanding the components of accounting ratios
(Obj. 5, 6)

ETHICAL ISSUE

River Front Restaurant Company's long-term debt agreements make certain demands on the business. River Front may not purchase treasury stock in excess of the balance of Retained Earnings. Also, Long-Term Debt may not exceed Stockholder's Equity, and the current ratio may not fall below 1.50. If River Front fails to meet these requirements, the company's lenders have the authority to take over management of the corporation.

Changes in consumer demand have made it hard for River Front to attract customers. Current liabilities have mounted faster than current assets, causing the current ratio to fall to 1.47. Before releasing financial statements, River Front management is scrambling to improve the current ratio. The controller points out that an investment can be classified as either long-term or short-term, depending on management's intention. By deciding to convert an investment to cash within one year, River Front can classify the investment as short-term—a current asset. On the controller's recommendation, River Front's board of directors votes to reclassify long-term investments as short-term.

Required

1. What effect will reclassifying the investments have on the current ratio? Is River Front's financial position stronger as a result of reclassifying the investments?

2. Shortly after the financial statements are released, sales improve and so, then, does the current ratio. As a result, River Front management decides not to sell the investments it had reclassified as short-term. Accordingly, the company reclassifies the investments as long-term. Has management behaved unethically? Give your reason.

FINANCIAL STATEMENT PROBLEMS

1. Use the financial statements and the data labeled Nine-Year Consolidated Financial Summary that appear at the end of the Lands' End, Inc., financial statements (Appendix A) to answer the following questions.

Measuring profitability and analyzing stock as an investment
(Obj. 5, 6)

Required

1. From the Nine-Year Consolidated Financial Summary, chart these ratios over the three most recent fiscal years, 1994, 1993, and 1992:

a. Percent of pretax income to net sales (similar to rate of return on sales)

b. Net income per share

c. Rate of return on common stockholders' equity

d. Rate of return on total assets

2. Compute these ratios at the end of each of the three most recent fiscal years:

    a. Current ratio

    b. Debt ratio

3. Compute inventory turnover for each of the three most recent fiscal years. You will have to reconstruct ending inventory at January 31, 1992, and January 31, 1991, from the changes in the Inventory account given on the statement of cash flows.

4. Evaluate Lands' End's progress (or lack of progress) in profitability and the company's ability to turn over its inventory and to pay current and long-term liabilities during this three-year period.

Measuring profitability and analyzing stock as an investment (Obj. 5, 6)

2. Obtain the annual report of a real company of your choosing.

Required

1. Use the financial statements and the multi-year summary data to chart the company's progress during the three most recent years, including the current year. Compute the following ratios that measure profitability and are used to analyze stock as an investment:

Profitability Measures

    a. Rate of return on net sales

    b. Rate of return on common stockholders' equity

    c. Rate of return on total assets

Stock Analysis Measure

    d. Price/earnings ratio (If given, use the average of the "high" and "low" stock prices for each year.)

2. Is the trend in the profitability measures consistent with the trend in the stock analysis measure? Evaluate the company's overall outlook for the future.

COMPREHENSIVE PROBLEMS FOR PART FOUR

1. ANALYZING A COMPANY FOR ITS INVESTMENT POTENTIAL

In its 1994 annual report, Lands' End, Inc., includes a Nine-Year Consolidated Financial Summary. Analyze the company's financial statements and Nine-Year Summary for the fiscal years ended 1990 through 1994 to decide whether to invest or not to invest in the common stock of Lands' End. Include the following sections in your analysis, and fully explain your final decision.

- Trend analysis
- Profitability analysis
- Measuring ability to sell inventory
- Cash-flow analysis (net cash inflow or outflow from operating activities)
- Measuring ability to pay debts

To compute some of the items not given in the Nine-Year Summary, you will need the following data:

(Dollar Amounts in Millions)

	1992	1991	1990	1989
Cost of sales	$395	$359	$316	—
Cash	$ 1.4	$ 27.3	$ 8.3	$32.1
Inventory	$113	$ 74	$ 86	—

2. GROUP PROJECT: REFINING YOUR BUSINESS PLAN TO ANALYZE ACCOUNTING INFORMATION

In Part 4 of this book (Chapters 18 and 19) you learned how to analyze the cash effects of transactions and how to report those effects on the statement of cash flows. You also learned a number of ratios that managers, investors, and creditors use for decision making. How will you use what you have learned to (a) manage a business and (b) evaluate investments?

Beyond the Macy's Bankruptcy

One of the most widely publicized bankruptcy cases in recent times is that of Macy's department stores. In an industry hard hit by recession, Macy's has been unable to match other retailer's progress toward recovery. Macy's continues to operate under Chapter 11 of the bankruptcy laws, which allow a struggling company to freeze payments on old debts while it tries to reorganize and recover. But despite major Christmas advertising campaigns and new systems to respond more quickly to consumer demand, Macy's has not yet overcome sales declines and operating losses.

Analysts attribute Macy's decline to bloated management ranks, excessive inventory, and a substantial debt incurred to acquire two other retailers, I. Magnin and Bullock's. The same management group that "took the company private" (bought back all the outstanding stock) in 1986 remains in control. Some observers question whether the very people who led Macy's into hard times will be able to bring the company back to life.

Industry analysts predict that pre-bankruptcy suppliers will collect about 50 cents on the dollar for old balances. They question how Macy's can successfully reorganize without cutting thousands of jobs from its workforce of 68,000. Macy's reorganization plan focuses mostly on a new system to allocate inventory to stores more efficiently. New managers called *planners* track every sale recorded in Macy's stores and use the data to advise buyers on what to purchase for each of the company's 112 locations. In the past, Macy's allocation of inventory was arbitrary, and its high prices necessitated frequent markdown sales. When the company declared bankruptcy, $300 million of obsolete inventory had to be written off the books as worthless.

Macy's management believes that its new inventory control procedures will generate $800 million in cash flows by 1998, as opposed to a projected $210 million without the proposed changes. Those stores operating under the new system have reported increased revenues and profits already. And even though Macy's has fallen on hard times, suppliers still clamor to place their merchandise in its stores. Its New York City location, the largest department store in the world, is still a standard for the retailing industry.

Despite management's optimism about the company's long-term recovery, industry observers note that Macy's projects no sales growth in the next five years. Macy's will be under tremendous pressure to reduce prices and raise productivity.

CASE QUESTIONS

1. Financial statement analysis is a tool for predicting a company's future on the basis of historical financial information. Explain how such analysis may help creditors or investors predict bankruptcy. (Consider horizontal, vertical, and ratio analysis methods.)
2. From what you have learned about cash flows and accrual-basis accounting, do you believe that a profitable company can be forced into bankruptcy? Why or why not?
3. Among Macy's problems have been the large amount of debt it incurred when it bought two other retailers and excess inventory that became obsolete.
   a. Explain how ratio analysis may help discover excess inventory.
   b. Which financial statement ratios would be most affected when a company carries an unusually high amount of long-term debt?
   c. How would cash flows related to Macy's debt be reported on its statement of cash flows?

▶ PART FIVE

Management Accounting and Product Costing

Chapter 20

Introduction to Management Accounting: Manufacturing Accounting and Job Order Costing

General Motors Corporation's Saturn Division turned its first operating profit in 1993, earning bonuses for its workers. The division's profits set the stage for a struggle within GM over whether to sink another $1 billion into the corporation's small-car experiment.

For John F. Smith, Jr., GM's president, Saturn poses a dilemma. The innovative project could lose momentum unless it gets money by 1996 to expand its production capacity and redesign its cars. The division's executives want Smith and GM's board of directors to approve a second Saturn plant in order to boost capacity from 322,000 to 500,000 cars per year. But with the additional plant, Saturn may go back into the red, unable to generate its own new-product capital.

Executives at other GM divisions are skeptical that Saturn can justify a second plant, given the flood of new entries into the small-car market. And Smith cannot appear to favor Saturn at a time when divisions with greater short-term profit potential are starved for capital. *Source: Adapted from J. B. White, "GM Saturn Unit Trumpets Profit Turned in 1993," The Wall Street Journal, January 6, 1994, p. A4. Reprinted by permission. © 1994 Dow Jones & Co., Inc. All rights reserved worldwide.*

• • • • •

Should General Motors Corporation build a second Saturn plant? What price should the company charge for each body style and option package? Which projects should Saturn engineers undertake to improve the quality and lower the costs of the division's cars? General Motors executives use accounting information to help them make these and many other decisions.

Our study of accounting has focused on reporting information for decision makers *outside* the organization: investors, creditors, and government authorities. Accounting that reports to parties outside the business is called *financial accounting*. In Chapters 1 through 19, we analyzed financial accounting

Chapter Objectives

After studying this chapter, you should be able to

1. Distinguish between financial accounting and management accounting

2. Prepare the financial statements of a manufacturing company

3. Use cost of goods manufactured to compute cost of goods sold

4. Relate job cost information to inventory and expense accounts

5. Account for direct materials in a job order costing system

6. Account for direct labor in a job order costing system

7. Account for manufacturing overhead in a job order costing system reports—the income statement, the balance sheet, and the statement of cash flows. These statements report the *past* performance and position of a business.

We now shift our focus to how accounting information helps shape the business's *future*. We examine accounting through the eyes of the people who run the business. Decision makers *inside* a company are called *managers*, and accounting designed to meet their information needs is called *management accounting*.

The Functions of Management

Business managers perform two broad functions: planning and controlling (Exhibit 20-1). **Planning** means choosing goals and deciding how to achieve them. For example, one goal of ice-cream maker Baskin Robbins may be to increase operating income. The company's managers may decide to

1. Increase sale prices of ice cream
2. Increase advertising costs to generate more sales volume, or
3. Use less high-cost fruits and nuts and more low-cost flavorings

Suppose that management planning leads Baskin Robbins executives to decide on alternative 3. At that point, controlling begins. **Controlling** means acting to implement planning decisions and then evaluating the performance of operations and employees. Baskin Robbins managers communicate new ice-cream recipes to the purchasing officer who buys the ingredients and to the people who mix ingredients in the plant. The managers also budget the costs of ice cream, considering both costs per gallon and expected production quantities. A **budget** is a quantitative expression of a plan of action that helps managers to coordinate and implement the plan.

Baskin Robbins' accounting system records how many gallons of ice cream the company produces. The system also records the purchase prices and quantities of fruits, nuts, and flavorings used. After production is completed, managers compare the actual costs with the budgeted costs in order to aid performance evaluation. If actual costs fall below budgeted costs, that is good news. But if actual costs exceed budgeted amounts, corrective action may be needed. The operating costs provide feedback that helps managers evaluate their decision to change recipes.

The chapter-opening story illustrates both the long-term and short-term aspects of planning and controlling. General Motors executives must plan far into the future in order to bring exciting new automobiles to the public. Building a new Saturn plant will tie up GM's cash for years to come. In the short-term, GM managers must decide whether to work two shifts or three shifts in response to customer demand for Saturn automobiles.

EXHIBIT 20-1
The Functions of Management

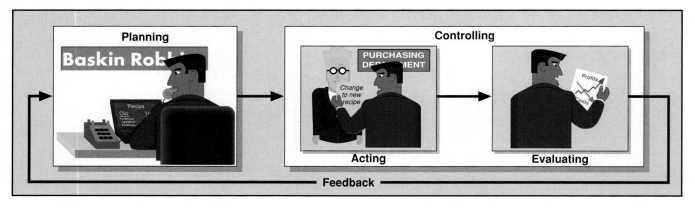

	Management Accounting	Financial Accounting
1. Primary users	Internal—managers of the business	External—investors, creditors, and government authorities
2. Time focus	Future orientation; example: 1997 budget prepared in 1996	Past orientation; example: 1997 actual performance reported in 1998
3. Reports	Not restricted by GAAP; detailed reports on parts of the company: products, departments, territories	Restricted by GAAP; summary reports primarily on the company as a whole
4. Behavioral implications	Concern about how reports will affect employee behavior	Concern about adequacy of disclosure; behavioral implications are secondary

EXHIBIT 20-2
Distinctions Between Management Accounting and Financial Accounting

Key Point: Management accounting provides managers with information needed to run the business successfully. Because the information is used only by insiders, it does not have to be reported according to GAAP.

Management Accounting and Financial Accounting

Exhibit 20-2 summarizes the distinctions between management accounting and financial accounting. Consider points 1 and 2 of the exhibit. The decision whether to build a new Saturn plant is related to General Motors' future, and the decision makers are GM managers. GM will budget (predict) the future income and cash flows generated by the plant. Managers will then compare the benefits and costs of operating the plant with the benefits and costs of alternative investments. For example, the $1 billion required for the Saturn project could be used to develop a practical battery-powered car instead. GM executives will choose the investment with the greatest expected net benefit to the company.

Now consider point 3 of Exhibit 20-2—accounting reports used by decision makers. Managers are free to choose how to plan and control their operations. But most companies largely adhere to GAAP for *internal* as well as external accounting purposes. ◄■■ Why? Because accrual accounting and the basic financial statements provide a uniform way to measure the firm's performance.

Point 4 of Exhibit 20-2 highlights another major difference between management accounting and financial accounting: The behavioral implications of budgets and other management accounting tools deserve front-and-center attention by managers and accountants. Managers' actions are heavily influenced by how their performance is measured, and the accounting system is used to measure performance. For example, the manager of a Baskin Robbins store will care about cleanliness and cheerful service if her performance evaluation is based on the store's profit. Excellent customer service leads to higher sales, which add to profit. The manager will be less concerned about customer service if she is evaluated only on her ability to control costs. In that case, she may save money by cleaning the store less often. Top executives create incentive plans very carefully due to their effects on employee behavior.

OBJECTIVE 1
Distinguish between financial accounting and management accounting

◄■■◄■■◄■■ GAAP (Chapter 12) restricts the items that are classified as assets, liabilities, and owners' equity on the balance sheet.

Management's Use of Accounting Information

Managers use accounting information for three broad purposes:

- *Purpose 1.* To plan and control routine business operations. This includes evaluating the performance of people and activities.
- *Purpose 2.* To make nonroutine decisions. Short-term decisions include what to charge for products and services, whether to accept a special order for a product, and which of several products or services to emphasize. Long-term decisions include whether to produce a new product and where to locate a new plant or store.
- *Purpose 3.* To report to external parties the company's financial position and results of operations.

We begin our study of management accounting in Chapters 20 and 21 by examining companies that manufacture goods. These companies provide a broad overview; they not only engage in the usual business functions of marketing and general administration, but also convert raw materials and parts into finished goods. Both external parties and managers need to know the costs of manufactured goods.

Management accounting is not confined to manufacturing companies such as General Motors. Chapters 22 through 27 cover diverse topics that relate to managers in all kinds of organizations, whether large or small, profit-seeking or not-for-profit. Those chapters emphasize purposes 1 and 2—how accounting information aids managers in planning, controlling, and decision making.

Merchandising versus Manufacturing

Previous chapters addressed only merchandising. The key difference between a merchandising company and a manufacturing company is the way they acquire inventory for sale. Consider the distinction between a sporting goods store—a merchandiser—and a company that manufactures athletic shoes—a manufacturer.

Footlocker specializes in selling athletic shoes. Like other merchandisers, Footlocker buys ready-made inventory for resale to customers. Determining Footlocker's cost of the shoes is relatively easy. Cost is the price that the merchandiser pays for the shoes plus the freight-in costs and any applicable customs duties.

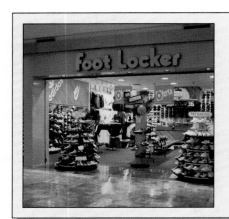

"Like other merchandisers, Footlocker buys ready-made inventory for resale to customers."

Companies that supply athletic shoes to stores such as Footlocker—Reebok, Nike, Adidas, and others—use their labor forces and factory assets to shape raw materials into finished products. Their manufacturing processes begin with materials (cloth, rubber, plastics, and so on). These materials are cut, glued, stitched, and formed into athletic shoes. The process of converting materials into finished products makes it more difficult to measure the inventory cost of a manufacturer than to measure that of a merchandiser.

The first part of this chapter introduces manufacturing accounting. The second part discusses a particular system for determining a manufacturer's product cost—job order costing.

Manufacturing and the Value Chain

Consider Apple Computer. Many people describe Apple (or IBM or Hewlett-Packard) as a manufacturing company. Apple may be described more accurately as a company that does manufacturing. Why? Because manufacturing is only one of its major business functions. Indeed, Apple's marketing costs exceed its manufacturing costs. Companies that do manufacturing also do many other things. For example, a company such as Reebok also conducts research and development to determine what new products to introduce into the market. It uses that information to design new products, which then are manufactured, marketed, and distributed. All these business functions collectively are called a **value chain**—the sequence of all business functions in which value is added to a firm's products or services (Exhibit 20-3).

In discussing the value chain, managers sometimes use the image of a river to describe the flow of value. Research, development, and product design are considered "upstream" functions because they occur prior to manufacturing. Marketing,

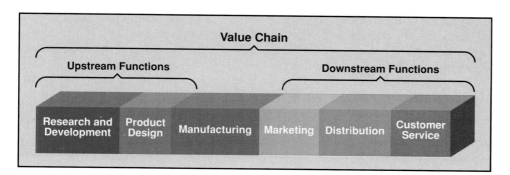

EXHIBIT 20-3
The Value Chain

distribution, and customer service are labeled "downstream" functions because they follow manufacturing.

Managers are concerned about the value chain taken as a whole. They aim to control the total costs of the entire chain. For example, companies may willingly spend more in product design to enhance product quality and thereby reduce manufacturing costs and the customer service costs of honoring product warranties. Even though product design costs are then higher, the total cost of the product—as measured by the entire value chain—may be lower.

Traditionally, cost accounting has been associated with manufacturing. Many cost accounting techniques and analyses were developed to measure the costs incurred to manufacture products. Nonetheless, the basic concepts of how to plan and control costs and how to compute the costs of products and services are applicable to the entire value chain.

Product Costs

Accountants use the term *product costs* to denote the costs that they assign to products (Exhibit 20-4). The costs assigned depend on the purpose. For external reporting, accountants assign only manufacturing costs to products. **Manufacturing product costs** are the costs of resources that are used to manufacture a product. Manufacturing product costs are reported on the income statement as cost of goods sold and on the balance sheet as the cost of product inventories.

For planning, controlling, and decision making, managers must know full product costs. **Full product costs** are the costs of all resources that are used throughout the value chain for a product. The profit that Reebok earns on a particular shoe model is the difference between its sales revenue and the total cost that Reebok incurs to research, design, manufacture, market, and distribute the model as well as to service the customers who buy it. Before launching a new model, managers must predict all these costs. Also, the company's managers must decide which of their many products to emphasize. If they determine that the profit (revenue minus

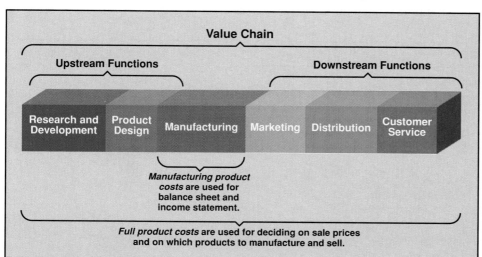

EXHIBIT 20-4
Different Meanings of the Term
Product Costs *and Their*
Relations to the Value Chain

full product costs) of a children's sneaker is less than the profit of another product, they may drop the sneaker and use the freed-up production capacity to produce additional units of the more profitable product. The more accurate the assignment of costs to individual products, the better.

Manufacturing costs are product costs that are used for both external reporting and internal decision making. We now take a closer look at manufacturing costs.

Manufacturing Costs

OBJECTIVE 2

Prepare the financial statements of a manufacturing company

Inventory Accounts—Materials, Work in Process, and Finished Goods

Accounting for inventory differs between merchandisers and manufacturers. Merchandisers need only one category of inventory for the finished goods they buy and sell. In contrast, manufacturers have three inventory accounts: Materials Inventory, Work in Process Inventory, and Finished Goods Inventory. Exhibit 20-5 compares the inventory accounts of a manufacturing company with those of a merchandising company. *The two types of business have identical balance sheets except for the inventory accounts.*

Key Point: Materials Inventory includes any material that goes into manufactured goods.

The **Materials Inventory** account holds the cost of materials on hand that are intended for use in the manufacturing process. For example, a shoe manufacturer's materials include leather, glue, plastic, cloth, and thread. Raw materials for Bethlehem Steel include iron ore, coal, and chemicals. Materials—kept in vats, bins, or other storage areas—are collectively called *stores.*

Key Point: Work in Process Inventory includes all costs associated with units started but not yet completed. Only part of their cost has been added.

The **Work in Process Inventory** account gives the cost of the goods that are in the manufacturing process but are not yet complete. For the Saturn Division, partially completed cars make up its work in process inventory. For Texaco, work in process is the crude oil being distilled into gasoline and other products. Work in process inventory also is called *work in progress* or *goods in process.*

The cost of completed goods that have not yet been sold makes up the **Finished Goods Inventory** account. Manufacturers store finished goods in warehouses, tanks, or whatever storage facilities are appropriate for their inventories. Finished goods are what the manufacturer sells to a merchandising business. For example, Procter & Gamble manufactures Tide laundry soap and Crest toothpaste, which are finished goods that it sells to Safeway, Kmart, and other stores. The finished goods inventory of a manufacturer, then, becomes the inventory of a merchandiser.

"Procter & Gamble manufactures Tide laundry soap and Crest toothpaste, which are finished goods that it sells to Safeway, Kmart, and other stores."

EXHIBIT 20-5

Inventory Accounts of a Manufacturing Firm and a Merchandising Firm

Manufacturing Firm			Merchandising Firm		
Current assets:			Current assets:		
Cash..............................		$ X,XXX	Cash		$ X,XXX
Short-term			Short-term		
investments..............		X,XXX	investments		X,XXX
Receivables..................		X,XXX	Receivables..............		X,XXX
Inventories:			**Inventories**.............		**13,000**
Materials.................	$1,000		Prepaid expenses......		X,XXX
Work in process......	4,000				
Finished goods........	8,000				
Total inventories		13,000			
Prepaid expenses		X,XXX			
Total current assets		$XX,XXX	Total current assets ..		$XX,XXX

Materials inventory, work in process inventory, and finished goods inventory are assets to the manufacturer and are reported as current assets on the balance sheet, as Exhibit 20-5 shows. We will use the Finished Goods Inventory account to compute cost of goods sold on the income statement.

Key Point: Finished Goods Inventory includes the costs of products that have been completed but not yet sold.

Definitions of Key Manufacturing Terms

Before we compute cost of goods sold, we must define some key manufacturing terms. Exhibit 20-6 illustrates these terms.

DIRECT MATERIALS To be considered **direct materials,** materials must meet two requirements: (1) They must become a physical part of the finished product, and (2) their costs must be separately and conveniently traceable through the manufacturing process to finished goods. Consider again Reebok. The leather uppers, the rubber and plastic soles, and the laces of the company's athletic shoes are among its direct materials. They become part of the finished shoe. Also, we can trace their costs directly from materials inventory through work in process to finished goods.

DIRECT LABOR **Direct labor** is the compensation of employees who physically convert materials into the company's products. For Reebok, direct labor includes the wages of the machine operators and the persons who assemble the shoes. For Saturn, direct labor is the pay of employees who work on the division's automobile production lines. The effort of these persons can be traced *directly* to finished goods.

MANUFACTURING OVERHEAD **Manufacturing overhead** includes all manufacturing costs besides direct materials and direct labor. Examples include indirect materials, indirect labor, factory utilities, repairs, maintenance, rent, insurance, property taxes, and depreciation on factory buildings and equipment. Manufacturing overhead also is called *factory overhead* or *indirect manufacturing cost.*

INDIRECT MATERIALS The glue and thread used in athletic shoes are materials that become physical parts of the finished product. But, compared with the cost of the leather uppers and rubber soles, the costs of glue and thread are minor. Measuring the costs of those low-priced materials is difficult for a single pair of shoes. How would a supervisor figure the cost of a brushful of glue? Or the cost of the thread used in a shoelace? How useful would such detailed information be? We call materials whose costs cannot conveniently be traced directly to particular finished products **indirect materials.** Indirect materials are accounted for as part of manufacturing overhead cost.

INDIRECT LABOR Some manufacturing labor costs are classified as **indirect labor.** These costs are difficult to trace to specific products. Examples include the pay of forklift operators, janitors, and plant managers. Indirect labor, like indirect materials, is a part of manufacturing overhead.

EXHIBIT 20-6
Key Manufacturing Terms

Major cost elements are sometimes combined in cost terminology as follows. **Prime costs** consist of direct materials plus direct labor. **Conversion costs** consist of direct labor plus manufacturing overhead:

$$\text{Prime costs} \left\{ \begin{array}{l} \text{Direct materials} \\ \text{Direct labor} \\ \text{Manufacturing overhead} \end{array} \right\} \text{Conversion costs}$$

Cost of Goods Manufactured

OBJECTIVE 3

Use cost of goods manufactured to compute cost of goods sold

Recall the merchandiser's computation of cost of goods sold: *beginning inventory + purchases – ending inventory = cost of goods sold.* All of a merchandiser's inventory is finished goods; a merchandiser has no materials inventory or work in process inventory. A manufacturer, however, produces its own inventory. **Cost of goods manufactured** is the manufacturer's counterpart to the merchandiser's purchases—that is, the cost that is added to finished goods inventory during the period. As Exhibit 20-7 shows, the cost of goods manufactured takes the place of purchases in computing cost of goods sold. *Otherwise, the income statement of a manufacturer is identical to the income statement of a merchandiser.*

Purchases is the total cost of all goods a merchandiser buys for resale during the period. Cost of goods manufactured is more complex. Exhibit 20-8 shows the computation of the cost of goods manufactured in a schedule prepared for the managers of Reebok.

The cost of goods manufactured is the manufacturing cost of the goods completed during a production period (the year 19X3 in Exhibit 20-8). The cost of the goods completed is transferred with the goods from the factory (represented by the Work in Process Inventory account) to finished goods storage (represented by the Finished Goods Inventory account). Therefore, computation of the cost of goods manufactured centers on Work in Process Inventory.

The computation begins with the Work in Process Inventory balance at the beginning of the year ($2,000). To this amount we add the three components of total manufacturing cost incurred during the year: direct materials used ($14,000), direct labor ($19,000), and manufacturing overhead cost ($12,000). Adding the sum of these amounts ($45,000) to the beginning Work in Process Inventory balance of $2,000 gives the total cost assigned to goods worked on during the year—$47,000. Some of these goods were completed and sent into Finished Goods Inventory during the year; the others are still in process at the end of the year. Thus, we subtract the cost of goods in process on December 31 ($5,000) to arrive at the cost of goods manufactured total of $42,000.

EXHIBIT 20-7

Cost of Goods Manufactured on the Income Statement

Manufacturing Firm		Merchandising Firm	
Sales revenue:	$XX,XXX	Sales revenue:	$XX,XXX
Cost of goods sold:		Cost of goods sold:	
Beginning finished goods inventory	$ 6,000	Beginning inventory	$ 6,000
Cost of goods manufactured	**42,000**	**Purchases**	**42,000**
Goods available for sale	48,000	Goods available for sale	48,000
Ending finished goods inventory	(8,000)	Ending inventory	(8,000)
Cost of goods sold	40,000	Cost of goods sold	40,000
Gross margin	X,XXX	Gross margin	X,XXX
Operating expenses:		Operating expenses:	
Marketing	X,XXX	Marketing	X,XXX
General	X,XXX	General	X,XXX
Total operating expenses	X,XXX	Total operating expenses	X,XXX
Net income	$ X,XXX	Net income	$ X,XXX

REEBOK
SCHEDULE OF COST OF GOODS MANUFACTURED
YEAR ENDED DECEMBER 31, 19X3

Beginning work in process inventory		$ 2,000
Add: Direct materials used:		
Beginning inventory...	$ 9,000	
Purchases of direct materials.............................	27,000	
Available for use...	36,000	
Ending inventory...	(22,000)	
Direct materials used		$14,000
Direct labor..		19,000
Manufacturing overhead:		
Indirect materials..	$ 1,500	
Indirect labor...	3,500	
Depreciation—factory building	2,000	
Depreciation—factory equipment.....................	1,000	
Utilities..	2,500	
Insurance	1,000	
Property tax...	500	12,000
Total manufacturing costs		
incurred during the year...............................		45,000
Total manufacturing costs		
to account for..		47,000
Less: Ending work in process		
inventory..		(5,000)
Cost of goods manufactured		$42,000

EXHIBIT 20-8
Schedule of Cost of Goods Manufactured

Key Point: Cost of Goods Manufactured is not the same as Manufacturing Costs.

Manufacturing Costs:
   Direct Materials
 + Direct Labor
 + Manufacturing Overhead
 = Manufacturing Costs*

Cost of Goods Manufactured:
   Beg. Work in Process Inv.
 + Manufacturing Costs
 − End. Work in Process Inv.
 = Cost of Goods Manufactured

The Cost of Goods Manufactured includes costs from the previous period (beginning work in process inventory) and current period manufacturing costs, but does not include costs for goods started but not yet finished (ending work in process inventory). Cost of Goods Manufactured refers to goods finished during the period.

Direct Materials Inventory	Work in Process Inventory	Finished Goods Inventory
Beginning inventory + Purchases	Beginning inventory + Direct materials used + Direct labor + Manufacturing overhead	Beginning inventory + Cost of goods manufactured

= Direct materials
   available for use
− Ending inventory
	= Subtotal
	
	− Ending inventory
		= Cost of goods
		   available for sale
		− Ending inventory

= Direct materials
   used
	= Cost of goods
	   manufactured
		= Cost of goods sold

The authors are indebted to Judith Cassidy for this presentation.

Exhibit 20-9 diagrams the flow of costs through a manufacturer's inventory accounts. It reveals a similar computational format at all three stages—direct materials, work in process, and finished goods. For example, the cost of direct materials used—the decrease in the Direct Materials Inventory account—is the beginning inventory plus purchases minus the ending inventory. The final amount at each stage flows into the next stage. This flow of costs through the inventory accounts can be seen in the income statement of Exhibit 20-7 and the schedule of cost of goods manufactured of Exhibit 20-8.

Inventoriable Costs and Period Costs

The rules of financial accounting have a major influence on accounting for manufacturing costs. For example, manufacturing costs are **inventoriable costs,** which are all costs of a product that are regarded as an asset for financial reporting under GAAP. Inventoriable costs become expenses (in the form of cost of goods sold) only

EXHIBIT 20-10
*Inventoriable Costs versus Period
Costs*

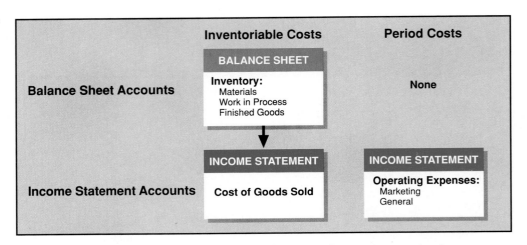

when the units in inventory are sold. Of course, sales may occur in the same accounting period as manufacture or in a subsequent period. Manufacturing costs are regarded as inventoriable because direct materials, direct labor, and manufacturing overhead costs are assigned to products and tracked through the inventory accounts.

All costs other than manufacturing costs are regarded as *immediate expenses* under GAAP. These costs often are called **period costs,** because they are expensed in the period in which they are incurred. They are never tracked through the inventory accounts. Examples include research, marketing, and distribution expenses. Exhibit 20-10 illustrates the distinction between inventoriable costs and period costs.

Exhibit 20-10 helps us distinguish between companies that manufacture products and those that do not. For example, a retailer or wholesaler buys goods for resale without changing their basic form. The *only* inventoriable cost of those companies is the cost of merchandise. All labor, depreciation, insurance, utilities, and other operating costs are period costs. In contrast, any of those costs *that are related to the manufacturing effort* are inventoriable for manufacturing companies.

STOP & THINK Goods worked on during a production period may be classified according to when they are begun and when they are completed. For example, some of the goods worked on in 19X3 were begun in 19X2 and completed in 19X3. Other goods worked on in 19X3 were both begun and completed during the year. Still others were begun late in 19X3 but not completed until 19X4. Refer to Exhibit 20-8. Suppose that $3,000 of the total manufacturing cost incurred during the year was incurred to complete the beginning work in process inventory (which was begun in 19X2). What is the total cost of the goods that were both begun and completed in 19X3?

Answer: The total manufacturing cost incurred during the year was $45,000. If $3,000 of that total was incurred to complete the beginning work in process inventory, then $42,000 was incurred to produce goods both begun and completed during 19X3 and goods begun in 19X3 but not completed as of December 31, 19X3. The cost of the incomplete goods is the ending work in process inventory cost of $5,000. Therefore $37,000 ($42,000 – $5,000) is the total cost of the goods both begun and completed during the year.

Perpetual and Periodic Inventory Systems

In Chapter 9, pp. 368–369, entries for the perpetual inventory system are compared with entries for the periodic inventory system.

Chapter 9 compared accounting for inventories under the perpetual system and the periodic system. Most manufacturers use the perpetual system because they need a continuous record of materials, work in process, and finished goods on hand. The perpetual records help managers control operations. During periods of high customer demand, a manufacturer focuses on meeting production schedules. Important accounting controls may be relaxed. As a peak production season winds down, managers may find it difficult to bring accounting information up to date. A computerized perpetual system is easier to keep current throughout the year than a manual system. But even companies that use a perpetual system take physical counts of inventories at least annually to check the accuracy of their records.

Manufacturers that use a periodic inventory system follow the general accounting procedures that merchandisers use, as discussed in Chapter 9. Here we concentrate on the perpetual system because it is more commonly used by manufacturers than the periodic system.

Key Point: An advantage to the perpetual inventory system is that it gives the current cost data needed to determine the cost of manufactured goods.

SUMMARY PROBLEMS FOR YOUR REVIEW   MID-CHAPTER

1. Show how to compute cost of goods manufactured. Use the following amounts: direct materials used ($24,000), direct labor ($9,000), manufacturing overhead ($17,000), and work in process, beginning ($5,000) and ending ($4,000).

2. Identify the following as either an inventoriable cost or a period cost:
   a. Depreciation on factory equipment
   b. Depreciation on salespersons' automobiles
   c. Insurance on factory building
   d. Marketing manager's salary

SOLUTIONS TO REVIEW PROBLEMS

1. Cost of goods manufactured:

Beginning work in process inventory		$ 5,000
Add: Direct materials used	$24,000	
Direct labor	9,000	
Manufacturing overhead	17,000	
Total manufacturing costs incurred during the period		50,000
Total manufacturing costs to account for		55,000
Less: Ending work in process inventory		(4,000)
Cost of goods manufactured		$51,000

2. a. Inventoriable cost; b. Period cost; c. Inventoriable cost; d. Period cost.

Job Order Costing

Manufacturers develop costing systems to assign to their products the costs of direct materials, direct labor, and manufacturing overhead resources. The two basic types of product costing systems are *job order costing* and *process costing*. The type of system a company uses depends on the nature of its production operations.

Job order costing is used by companies that manufacture products as individual units or in small batches that vary considerably in terms of resources consumed, time required, or complexity. These companies, which often produce goods according to customer specifications, are found in a wide range of industries, including aircraft, furniture, construction, and machinery. For example, a *job* may be production of a single bridge by a construction contractor or an order for five tractors by Caterpillar, Inc.

"A job may be production of a single bridge by a construction contractor or an order for five tractors by Caterpillar, Inc."

In a job order costing (often shortened to *job costing*) system, the job is the primary cost object. A **cost object** is anything to which costs are assigned. To assign costs to jobs accurately, accountants seek to determine the *drivers* of job costs. A **cost driver** is any factor that affects costs. When a cost driver changes, the total cost of the job (or other cost object) changes. For example, direct labor *hours* are cost drivers of direct labor *costs*. When the number of direct labor hours increases, the total direct labor cost of, say, a batch of Saturn cars increases. Because each job is distinct, the assignment of costs to jobs involves little averaging of costs across jobs.

Companies that produce large numbers of similar or identical product units use *process costing* systems. Industries in which process costing is common include oil refining, food and beverage, and pharmaceuticals. Texaco produces thousands of gallons of each grade of gasoline at a time; Bayer manufactures millions of aspirin tablets—about 158 million in one month. In process costing systems, the cost object is a manufacturing process. Costs of individual units—gallons or tablets—are computed by averaging the total costs of the process across the total number of units produced.

We discuss process costing in Chapter 21. In this chapter we cover product costing in a job costing system. We are concerned with both inventory valuation and planning and control. Careful planning and cost control are keys to earning a profit on each job. If costs are too high, profit is reduced or eliminated. Managers must monitor the progress of each job to ensure that its costs stay within budgeted limits.

Job Costing Illustrated

Consider the La-Z-Boy Furniture Company. Suppose that La-Z-Boy has a job order costing system with the following inventories on December 31, 19X4:

Materials inventory (many kinds)	$20,000
Work in process inventory (5 jobs)	29,000
Finished goods inventory (unsold units from 2 jobs)	12,000

The following is a summary of transaction data for the year 19X5:

1. Materials purchased on account	$320,000
2. Direct materials used for manufacturing	285,000
Indirect materials used for manufacturing	40,000
3. Manufacturing wages incurred	335,000
4. Direct labor on jobs	250,000
Indirect labor to support manufacturing activities	85,000
5. Manufacturing overhead (depreciation on plant and equipment)	50,000
6. Manufacturing overhead (factory utilities)	20,000
7. Manufacturing overhead (factory insurance)	5,000
8. Manufacturing overhead (property taxes—factory)	10,000
9. Manufacturing overhead assigned to jobs	200,000
10. Cost of goods manufactured	740,000
11. Sales on account	996,000
Cost of goods sold	734,000

We will explain the accounting for these transactions step by step.

Job Cost Record

OBJECTIVE 4

Relate job cost information to inventory and expense accounts

The document used to accumulate the costs of a job is called a **job cost record.** A completed job cost record for La-Z-Boy Furniture Company is shown in Exhibit 20-11. It has separate sections for the costs of direct materials, direct labor, and manufacturing overhead charged to Job 293. The total cost of the job is $1,220. The average cost of each recliner chair is $122 ($1,220 ÷ 10).

Managers use job cost data to plan and control manufacturing operations. Suppose $450 was the budgeted direct materials cost of Job 293. Then the $500 actual cost exceeds the budget by more than 10 percent. Production managers may investigate this cost overrun to gain insights that will help them improve their budgeting procedures or future performance, depending on the cause of the overrun.

Companies that use job order costing initiate a job cost record when work on a job begins. Records of jobs in process (begun but not yet completed) form a subsidiary ledger for the general ledger account Work in Process Inventory. As costs are

EXHIBIT 20-11
Job Cost Record

Job Cost Record

La-Z-Boy

Job No. 293

Customer Name and Address   Macy's New York City

Job Description   10 recliner chairs

Date Promised 7-31	Date Started 7-24	Date Completed 7-29

Date	Direct Materials		Direct Labor		Manufacturing Overhead Costs		
	Requisition Numbers	Amount	Time Ticket Numbers	Amount	Date	Rate	Amount
19X5 7-24 25 28	334 338 347	$ 90 180 230	236, 251, 258 264, 269, 273, 291 305	$150 200 50	7-29	80% of direct labor	$320
					Overall Cost Summary		
					Direct materials . . . . $ 500		
					Direct labor 400		
					Manufacturing overhead . 320		
Totals		$500		$400	**Total Job Cost** $1,220		

incurred on a job, they are added to its job cost record. Those costs eventually are totaled and transferred to Finished Goods Inventory. When the job's output is sold, its costs are moved to Cost of Goods Sold.

We now illustrate accounting procedures for a job costing system. As we do so, you will learn how management accountants assigned the direct materials, direct labor, and manufacturing overhead costs to Job 293.

Accounting for Materials in a Job Costing System

Manufacturing companies that use job order costing tend to have relatively low inventories. They purchase materials as needed to fill orders. Suppose that La-Z-Boy Furniture Company receives an order for 10 recliner chairs. If the company needs to buy additional lumber, La-Z-Boy sends a *purchase order* to a lumber supplier. ◄▥▥

In practice, general ledger entries are made monthly. To offer a sweeping overview, however, we use a summary entry for the entire year 19X5. Our first entry is for purchases of materials (data from page 852):

1. Materials Inventory 320,000
   Accounts Payable 320,000

La-Z-Boy receives the lumber and stores it. Control over materials in storage is established with a subsidiary materials ledger. This ledger holds perpetual inventory records, which list the quantity and cost of all manufacturing materials on hand. Exhibit 20-12 shows a materials ledger record for the lumber that goes into the manufacture of recliner chairs.

La-Z-Boy's materials received are logged in by receiving report number (ab-

OBJECTIVE 5

Account for direct materials in a job order costing system

◄▥ ◄▥▥ ◄▥▥   Recall from Chapter 5 (p. 179) that the purchase order is sent by the buyer to the supplier of goods, requesting that goods be sent. No journal entry is made until the buyer receives an invoice from the supplier.

"La-Z-Boy's materials received are logged in by receiving report number . . . ."

EXHIBIT 20-12
Materials Ledger Record

Materials Ledger Record

La-Z-Boy

Item No. ___B-220___   Description ___Lumber/Recliner chairs___

	Received				Used				Balance		
Date	Rec. Report No.	Units	Price	Total Price	Mat. Req. No.	Units	Price	Total Price	Units	Price	Total Price
19X5 7-20									30	$9.00	$270
7-23	678	20	$9.00	$180					50	9.00	450
7-24					334	10	$9.00	$90	40	9.00	360

breviated as *Rec. Report No.* in Exhibit 20-12). Materials used in the product are recorded by materials requisition number *(Mat. Req. No.).* Management can use these underlying data to follow the flow of materials into the production process and thereby control operations on a day-to-day basis.

The materials ledger includes a separate record for each raw material. Exhibit 20-13 illustrates the general ledger Materials Inventory account and the materials ledger for La-Z-Boy. The balance of Materials Inventory in the general ledger

EXHIBIT 20-13
Materials Inventory Accounts

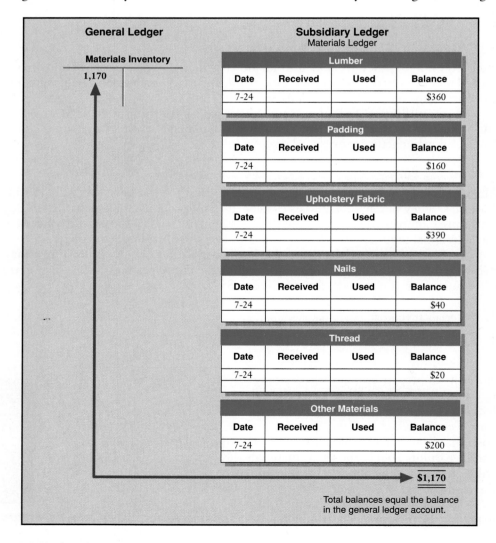

breviated — Total balances equal the balance in the general ledger account.

EXHIBIT 20-14

Materials Requisition

Materials Requisition No. 334

La-Z-Boy

Date 7-24-X5   **Job No.** 293

Item No.	Item	Quantity	Unit Price	Amount
B-220	Lumber/Recliner chairs	10	$9.00	$90

equals the sum of the balances in the subsidiary materials ledger.

Managers need a tremendous amount of information to plan manufacturing operations and to control costs. A company manufacturing hundreds of items may have a materials ledger with thousands of accounts. It is little wonder that so many manufacturers have computerized their accounting systems.

After materials are purchased and stored, the manufacturing process is set in motion by a document called a **materials requisition.** That document is a request for materials prepared by manufacturing personnel. In effect, they ask that the lumber be moved from storage to the factory so work can begin. Exhibit 20-14 illustrates a materials requisition for the lumber needed to manufacture the 10 recliner chairs that make up Job 293. (See the "Used" section in Exhibit 20-12.) Similar requisitions are used for nails and other indirect materials.

DIRECT AND INDIRECT MATERIALS   Materials Inventory is debited for the costs of all materials purchased, direct and indirect. The Materials Inventory account in Exhibit 20-13 includes the costs of direct materials—lumber, padding, and upholstery fabric—and the costs of indirect materials—nails and thread. When either direct or indirect materials are requisitioned from storage, Materials Inventory is credited.

What account is debited? The answer depends on the type of materials. For direct materials, the debit is to Work in Process Inventory. Recall that Work in Process Inventory is a control account whose balance equals the total cost of jobs in process. Exhibit 20-14 indicates that the $90 cost of requisition 334 is for Job 293. La-Z-Boy accountants enter this cost directly on the job cost record (Exhibit 20-15).

EXHIBIT 20-15

Job Cost Record Entry for Direct Materials

Job Cost Record

La-Z-Boy

Job No. 293

Customer Name and Address   Macy's New York City

Job Description   10 recliner chairs

Date Promised	7-31	Date Started	7-24	Date Completed	

Date	Direct Materials		Direct Labor		Manufacturing Overhead Costs		
	Requisition Numbers	Amount	Time Ticket Numbers	Amount	Date	Rate	Amount
19X5							
7-24	334	$90					
					Overall Cost Summary		
					Direct materials . . . . $		
					Direct labor		
					Manufacturing overhead .		
Totals					Total Job Cost . . . . $		

Short Exercise: Prepare the journal entry for the following materials-related transactions. (1) Purchased raw materials on account, $25,000. (2) Materials requisitions for the month show that $20,000 was requisitioned for jobs and that $3,000 of indirect materials were used.
A:
(1) Materials Inventory...... 25,000
    Accounts Payable   25,000

(2) Work in Process
    Inv 20,000
  Manufacturing
    Overhead.................. 3,000
        Materials Inventory   23,000

The costs of indirect materials are part of overhead. Actual manufacturing overhead costs are *neither* entered on job cost records *nor* added to Work in Process Inventory. Instead, these costs are accumulated in a separate account called Manufacturing Overhead.

La-Z-Boy Furniture Company works on many jobs over the course of the year. At regular intervals (commonly a month, but for our illustration, a year), accountants collect the data from materials requisitions to make a single journal entry. The 19X5 entry for La-Z-Boy is:

2. Work in Process Inventory 285,000
   Manufacturing Overhead.. 40,000
      Materials Inventory   325,000

The flow of materials costs may be diagrammed as follows (data from page 852):

Materials Inventory						Work in Process Inventory	
Bal.	20,000			Direct materials, $285,000	Bal.	29,000	
1. Purchased	320,000	2. Used	325,000		2. Direct materials	285,000	

Indirect materials, $40,000

Manufacturing Overhead	
2. Indirect materials	40,000

Accounting for Labor in a Job Costing System

OBJECTIVE 6
Account for direct labor in a job order costing system

Chapter 11 (pp. 463–465) defined the payroll register as a special journal that lists each employee and the data to record payroll amounts.

Control over labor costs in a job costing system is established through payroll registers and time tickets. A labor time ticket identifies the employee, the amount of time spent on a particular job, and the labor cost charged to the job. Time tickets are accumulated for each job to determine its total direct labor cost. Exhibit 20-16 illustrates a labor time ticket used in a job costing system.

In a computerized accounting system, the collection of data such as direct labor cost is much simpler than in a manual system. Computer terminals may be set up on a company's production floor. At various stages in the manufacturing process of Saturn automobiles, for example, employees insert their magnetically imprinted identification cards into the terminals. The system thus captures direct labor time and cost without detailed labor records.

La-Z-Boy's entry for 19X5 for all manufacturing wages for all jobs is:

3. Manufacturing Wages 335,000
      Wages Payable..   335,000

This entry records the actual labor costs incurred. The separation of direct labor and indirect labor is accomplished as shown in the following diagram:

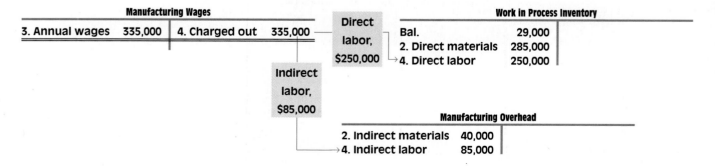

Manufacturing Wages						Work in Process Inventory	
3. Annual wages	335,000	4. Charged out	335,000	Direct labor, $250,000	Bal.	29,000	
					2. Direct materials	285,000	
					4. Direct labor	250,000	

Indirect labor, $85,000

Manufacturing Overhead	
2. Indirect materials	40,000
4. Indirect labor	85,000

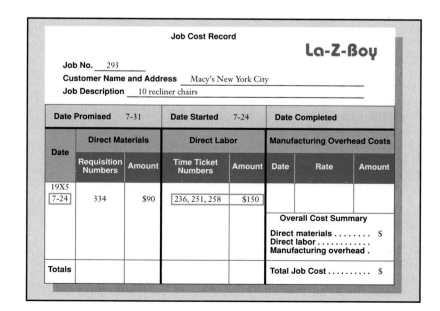

EXHIBIT 20-16
Labor Time Ticket

DIRECT AND INDIRECT LABOR   As the diagram at the bottom of page 856 indicates, direct labor is debited directly to Work in Process Inventory. Indirect labor is added to the Manufacturing Overhead account. The transfer of labor cost to production results in a credit to Manufacturing Wages. The following entry assigns manufacturing wages to Work in Process Inventory and Manufacturing Overhead:

4.	Work in Process Inventory	250,000	
	Manufacturing Overhead..	85,000	
	Manufacturing Wages		335,000

This entry brings the balance in Manufacturing Wages to zero, its transferred balance now divided between Work in Process Inventory (direct labor) and Manufacturing Overhead (indirect labor).

Assume that $150 of one day's direct labor cost is for Job 293. La-Z-Boy Furniture enters Job 293's direct labor on the job cost record. The $150 amount in the Direct Labor section of Exhibit 20-17 includes Jay Barlow's wages of $60 (from time ticket 251, Exhibit 20-16) and the labor costs entered on time tickets 236 and 258.

The Work in Process Inventory account now contains the costs of direct materials and direct labor charged to Job 293—and the costs of many other jobs as well. Work in Process Inventory serves as a control account, with the job cost records giving the supporting details for each job.

EXHIBIT 20-17
Job Cost Record Entry for Direct Labor

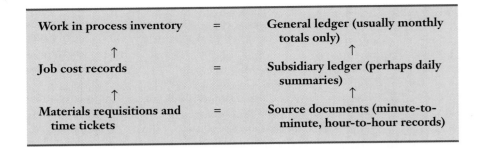

Work in process inventory	=	General ledger (usually monthly totals only)
↑		↑
Job cost records	=	Subsidiary ledger (perhaps daily summaries)
↑		↑
Materials requisitions and time tickets	=	Source documents (minute-to-minute, hour-to-hour records)

Exhibit 20-18 summarizes the accounting for materials and labor just illustrated. Accounting data are most condensed in the general ledger and most detailed in the source documents. We have discussed several documents used in a job order costing system, including job cost records. In a computerized job costing system, physical job cost records may not exist. To record the cost of direct materials used on a job, an employee simply calls up the online job cost record and records the cost. Direct labor costs are added electronically as work is performed. The computer tallies materials and labor costs and automatically posts the appropriate general ledger accounts.

Accounting for Manufacturing Overhead in a Job Order Costing System

OBJECTIVE 7

Account for manufacturing overhead in a job order costing system

As our indirect materials and indirect labor examples demonstrated, all overhead costs are debited to a single general ledger account—Manufacturing Overhead. Entries 5 through 8 below complete the recording of La-Z-Boy Furniture's overhead costs given on page 852. The account titles in parentheses indicate the specific records that are debited in an overhead subsidiary ledger. Budgeting these individual items and then analyzing the differences between budgeted and actual amounts helps managers control overhead costs.

Key Point: Review the flow of costs in a job order cost system:

5. Manufacturing Overhead
   (Depreciation—Plant andEquipment) 50,000
       Accumulated Depreciation—Plant and Equipment.....   50,000
6. Manufacturing Overhead (Factory Utilities) 20,000
       Cash   20,000
7. Manufacturing Overhead (Factory Insurance)...................... 5,000
       Prepaid Insurance—Factory   5,000
8. Manufacturing Overhead (Property Taxes—Factory) 10,000
       Property Taxes Payable   10,000

The Manufacturing Overhead account now contains all the overhead costs:

Materials Inventory

Materials purchased	Transferred to WIP (direct materials) and MOH (indirect materials)

Manufacturing Wages

Total wages	Charged out (transferred) to WIP (direct labor) and MOH (indirect labor)

Manufacturing Overhead

Total actual overhead costs	Applied MOH transferred to WIP

Notice that only actual costs are debited to these accounts. When the costs are transferred to Work in Process or Manufacturing Overhead, these accounts are credited.

Manufacturing Overhead		
2. Indirect materials	40,000	
4. Indirect labor	85,000	
5. Depreciation—plant and equipment	50,000	
6. Factory utilities	20,000	
7. Factory insurance	5,000	
8. Property taxes—factory	10,000	
Total overhead cost	**210,000**	

How are overhead costs assigned to jobs? Materials requisitions and labor time tickets make it relatively easy to identify direct materials and direct labor costs with individual jobs. But manufacturing overhead includes a variety of costs that cannot be linked to particular orders. For example, it is virtually impossible to say that a specific amount of the cost incurred to cool the factory is related to Job 293. Yet manufacturing overhead costs are as essential as direct materials and direct labor to the production of goods. We now see how accountants assign overhead costs to jobs.

Allocating Overhead Costs to Jobs

Managers want to know the costs incurred to produce each job, including manufacturing overhead costs. The total overhead cost that accountants assign to each job includes a portion of the cost of *providing* production capacity, which is represented by items such as depreciation and insurance on manufacturing plant and equipment. The assigned overhead also includes a measure of the costs incurred while *using* production capacity to produce jobs, among them indirect materials, indirect labor, and factory utilities. (We discuss differences between the costs of providing capacity and the costs of using capacity in Chapter 23.)

Accountants frequently speak of *tracing* direct costs to cost objects and *allocating* manufacturing overhead and other indirect costs. They use the general term *cost application* to refer to the assignment of both direct and indirect costs to manufactured products. Thus, direct materials, direct labor, and manufacturing overhead costs are *applied* to jobs.

We apply overhead costs to jobs using a rate per unit of a cost application base. A **cost application base** is a common denominator for systematically linking indirect costs to products. Ideally, the application base is the primary cost driver, the best available measure of the cause-and-effect relationship between overhead costs and production volume. In many companies, direct labor costs rise and fall proportionately with changes in production volume, and accountants use direct labor dollars or direct labor hours as the cost application base. In companies such as Saturn, with highly automated production processes, labor is less important. These companies often use machine-hours as the base.

Managers need timely cost information. Decisions about pricing, bidding, and product emphasis often must be made before jobs are started. For this reason, accountants compute budgeted application rates in advance of the year's production activity. The following six steps may be used to develop and apply a company's manufacturing overhead cost application rate:

1. Select a cost application base. As the Manufacturing Overhead section of Exhibit 20-11 shows, La-Z-Boy's accountants selected direct labor cost.

2. Budget the total overhead cost for the planning period, which is ordinarily a year. Assume that late in 19X4 La-Z-Boy personnel predicted overhead costs for 19X5 of $220,000.

3. Budget the total units of the cost application base. La-Z-Boy production managers expected to incur $275,000 of direct labor cost during 19X5.

4. Compute the budgeted manufacturing overhead application rate as follows:

$$\text{Budgeted manufacturing overhead rate} = \frac{\text{Total budgeted overhead}}{\text{Total budgeted application base units}}$$

$$= \frac{\text{Total budgeted overhead}}{\text{Total budgeted direct labor cost}}$$

$$= \frac{\$220,000}{\$275,000} = 0.80 \text{ or } 80\%$$

5. Obtain actual application base data, on a job-by-job basis, as the year unfolds. The total direct labor cost of Job 293 is $400.

6. Apply manufacturing overhead to jobs by multiplying the budgeted manufacturing overhead rate by the application base units that pertain to each job. For Job 293, the applied overhead cost is $320 ($400 × 0.80). This amount is added to the job cost record as shown in Exhibit 20-19.

The job cost record of Job 293 now is complete. It provides the details that support the $1,220 total cost and the $122 ($1,220 ÷ 10) unit cost of the Macy's order.

Short Exercise: Prepare the general journal entries for the following labor-related transactions. Labor time tickets for the month show direct labor of $17,000 and indirect labor of $4,000. *A:*

Manufacturing Wages 21,000
  Wages Payable 21,000

Work in Process Inv 17,000
Manufacturing Overhead ... 4,000
  Manufacturing Wages 21,000

Short Exercise: The Winslow Co. budgeted its manufacturing overhead and direct labor to be $90,000 and $60,000, respectively. The actual costs for the year are:

  Indirect labor $40,000
  Factory supplies 20,000
  Machinery repair 15,000
  Advertising 6,000
  Rent on factory 15,000
  Factory utilities 10,000
  Selling expenses 30,000
  Direct labor 64,000

(1) Calculate the predetermined overhead rate. (2) Calculate actual overhead. (3) Calculate applied overhead. *A:*
(1) Manufacturing Overhead rate = 150% of direct labor ($90,000/$60,000)
(2) Actual Manufacturing Overhead = $100,000 ($40,000 + $20,000 + $15,000 + $15,000 + $10,000)
(3) Applied Manufacturing Overhead = $96,000 ($64,000 × 150%)

EXHIBIT 20-19
*Job Cost Record Entry for
Manufacturing Overhead*

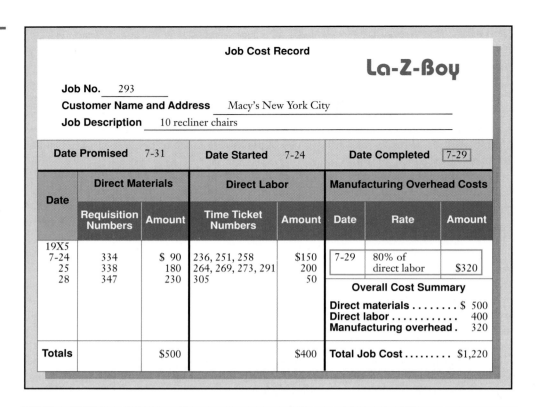

Job Cost Record						La-Z-Boy	

Job No.   293

Customer Name and Address   Macy's New York City

Job Description   10 recliner chairs

| Date Promised   7-31 | | Date Started   7-24 | | Date Completed   7-29 | | |

Date	Direct Materials		Direct Labor		Manufacturing Overhead Costs		
	Requisition Numbers	Amount	Time Ticket Numbers	Amount	Date	Rate	Amount
19X5 7-24 25 28	334 338 347	$ 90 180 230	236, 251, 258 264, 269, 273, 291 305	$150 200 50	7-29	80% of direct labor	$320
					Overall Cost Summary		
					Direct materials . . . . $ 500 Direct labor . . . . 400 Manufacturing overhead . 320		
Totals		$500		$400	Total Job Cost $1,220		

STOP & THINK Management accountants say that the assignment of costs to a job is accurate if the costs assigned represent the additional (incremental) costs incurred to produce the job—that is, the costs that are incurred only because the job is produced. In general, which do you believe is more accurate: the tracing of direct costs to jobs or the allocation of indirect costs? Why?

Answer: In general, the tracing of direct costs is more accurate. No averaging is required to determine, for example, that Saturn's cost of a car tire is $30 or that the cost of an hour of assemblyline labor is $20. In contrast, the allocation of indirect costs often involves substantial averaging. Consider La-Z-Boy's budgeted manufacturing overhead rate. The total budgeted cost of $220,000 includes indirect labor, indirect materials, depreciation, and utilities. It is unlikely that direct labor cost, the selected application base, is the only driver of each of those costs. Therefore, it is unlikely that the ratio of additional overhead costs to direct labor costs is exactly the same for every job. Rather, the 80-percent rate is an average for all jobs. Using a broadly averaged application rate to apply indirect costs results in some jobs being overcosted and others undercosted.

Overhead costs applied to jobs are debited to Work in Process Inventory and credited to Manufacturing Overhead. For 19X5, the total overhead applied to all jobs worked on is 80 percent of $250,000 direct labor, or $200,000. The summary journal entry is:

9. Work in Process Inventory 200,000
         Manufacturing Overhead   200,000

La-Z-Boy's application of manufacturing overhead may be diagrammed in this way:

Manufacturing Overhead				Work in Process Inventory	
2.	40,000	9. Applied 200,000		Bal.	29,000
4.	85,000			2.	285,000
5.	50,000		Manufacturing	4.	250,000
6.	20,000		Overhead	9.	200,000
7.	5,000		Applied		
8.	10,000				
Actual costs	210,000				
Bal.	10,000				

An additional detail exists in accounting for overhead costs: disposing of under- or overapplied overhead. First, however, we must demonstrate accounting for finished goods and for the sale of inventory.

Accounting for Finished Goods, Sales, and Cost of Goods Sold

As each job is completed, its total cost is transferred from Work in Process Inventory to Finished Goods Inventory. Sales of finished goods are recorded as they occur.

A summary entry for La-Z-Boy Furniture's goods completed in 19X5 follows:

| 10. | Finished Goods Inventory .... | 740,000 | |
| | Work in Process Inventory .... | | 740,000 |

In turn, the usual entries are made for sales and cost of goods sold:

11.	Accounts Receivable...	996,000	
	Sales Revenue		996,000
	Cost of Goods Sold	734,000	
	Finished Goods Inventory......................................		734,000

The second entry is needed to maintain the perpetual inventory records. Only the first entry is needed in a periodic inventory system.

The key accounts for La-Z-Boy's manufacturing costs now show:

Work in Process Inventory				Finished Goods Inventory			Cost of Goods Sold
Bal. 29,000	10. 740,000			Bal. 12,000	11. 734,000	→	11. 734,000
2. 285,000			→	10. 740,000			
4. 250,000				Bal. 18,000			
9. 200,000							
Bal. 24,000							

Disposing of Underapplied or Overapplied Overhead

During the year, Manufacturing Overhead is debited for actual overhead costs incurred and credited for applied amounts. The total debits rarely equal the total credits. Why? Because overhead is applied to jobs at a *budgeted* rate that represents the *anticipated* relationship between overhead costs and application base units. In our example, La-Z-Boy's accountants expected to incur 19X5 overhead at the rate of 80 percent of direct labor costs ($220,000 ÷ $275,000, page 859). But the *actual* rate was 84 percent of direct labor costs ($210,000 ÷ $250,000, pages 858 and 852). Thus, less overhead was applied to jobs than was actually incurred. Every job worked on in 19X5 was undercosted—that is, was assigned less overhead cost than if the 84 percent rate had been accurately forecasted and used.

The $10,000 debit balance of Manufacturing Overhead shown on page 860 is called *underapplied overhead* because the applied cost was less than (under) the actual cost. If the actual overhead rate had been less than 80 percent of direct labor, a credit balance of Manufacturing Overhead, called *overapplied overhead*, would have resulted. Accountants usually ignore under- and overapplied overhead during the year and dispose of it at year end, when the Manufacturing Overhead account is closed.

When overhead is underapplied, as in our example, a credit to Manufacturing Overhead brings the account balance to zero. What account(s) is (are) debited? Accountants sometimes debit Work in Process Inventory, Finished Goods Inventory, and Cost of Goods Sold, thereby allocating the underapplied amount to the three accounts in proportion to their balances. Adjusting the balances of Work in Process Inventory, Finished Goods Inventory, and Cost of Goods Sold for underapplied or overapplied overhead is known as *proration*. For La-Z-Boy, the account balances before proration total $776,000 ($24,000 + $18,000 + $734,000). Proration is accomplished as follows:

Short Exercise: Answer the following questions using these T-accounts. Assume no beginning balances.

Materials			WIP	
52,000	44,000		40,000	136,000
			60,000	
			48,000	

FG			Labor	
136,000	122,000		70,000	70,000

MOH	
4,000	48,000
10,000	
37,000	

What is (1) the cost of the direct materials used? indirect materials? (2) the cost of direct labor applied to production? indirect labor incurred? (3) the cost of goods manufactured? (4) the actual overhead? applied overhead? (5) the cost of goods sold? (6) the budgeted overhead rate, as a percentage of direct labor? (7) Is overhead over- or underapplied? By how much? *A:*
(1) $40,000; $4,000 (2) $60,000; $10,000 (3) $136,000 (4) $51,000; $48,000 (5) $122,000 (6) 80% ($48,000/$60,000) (7) Underapplied by $3,000

Work in Process Inventory (24/776 × $10,000)...........................	309
Finished Goods Inventory (18/776 × $10,000)...........................	232
Cost of Goods Sold (734/776 × $10,000)	9,459
Manufacturing Overhead	10,000

This December 31 entry adjusts the inventory and expense balances upward to approximately what they would have been if the 84-percent actual overhead application rate had been used throughout the year.

In practice, few companies prorate under- or overapplied overhead unless failure to do so would materially misstate the three affected account balances. When the amount is insignificant, as it is here, it is closed directly to the current year's Cost of Goods Sold, as shown at the top of the next page.

PUTTING SKILLS TO WORK

OVERVIEW OF LA-Z-BOY FURNITURE COMPANY EXAMPLE

The accompanying illustration provides an overview of the La-Z-Boy Furniture Company job order costing example. The ending balance sheet account balances are:

Materials Inventory	$15,000
Work in Process Inventory	24,000
Finished Goods Inventory	18,000

La-Z-Boy's condensed income statement for 19X5 reports the following through gross margin:

Sales	$996,000
Cost of goods sold	744,000
Gross margin (or gross profit)	$252,000

As mentioned in the text, the remainder of the manufacturer's income statement (operating expenses, other revenues and expenses, and net income) is the same as for a merchandising company.

Job Order Costing, General Flow of Costs for La-Z-Boy (in thousands)

12. Cost of Goods Sold 10,000
        Manufacturing Overhead 10,000

   With or without proration, the entry to close Manufacturing Overhead ensures that the total actual overhead cost incurred—$210,000 in this case—eventually will be expensed as part of Cost of Goods Sold.
   The Manufacturing Overhead balance now is zero, concluding our job order costing example:

Manufacturing Overhead					Cost of Goods Sold	
Actual	210,000	Applied	200,000		734,000	
		Closed	10,000 →		10,000	

SUMMARY PROBLEM FOR YOUR REVIEW

Hillis Incorporated had the following inventories at the end of 19X4:

Materials	$20,000
Work in Process..............	17,000
Finished Goods...............	11,000

   During January 19X5 Hillis completed the following transactions:

a. Purchased materials on account, $31,000.
b. Requisitioned (placed into production) direct materials, $39,000.
c. Manufacturing labor cost, $40,000.
d. Allocated manufacturing labor as follows: direct labor, 90 percent; indirect labor, 10 percent.
e. Requisitioned indirect materials, $3,000.
f. Incurred other manufacturing overhead, $13,000 (credit Accounts Payable).
g. Applied manufacturing overhead to production at 50 percent of direct labor.
h. Completed production, $99,000.
i. Sold goods on account, $172,000; cost of goods sold, $91,400.
j. Closed ending balance of Manufacturing Overhead to Cost of Goods Sold.

Required

1. Record the transactions in the general journal.
2. Determine the ending balances in the three inventory accounts and Cost of Goods Sold.

SOLUTION TO REVIEW PROBLEM

Requirement 1 (Journal entries)

a. Materials Inventory... 31,000
      Accounts Payable... 31,000
b. Work in Process Inventory.. 39,000
      Materials Inventory.. 39,000
c. Manufacturing Wages... 40,000
      Wages Payable.. 40,000
d. Work in Process Inventory ($40,000 × 0.90) 36,000
   Manufacturing Overhead ($40,000 × 0.10)...................................... 4,000
      Manufacturing Wages.. 40,000
e. Manufacturing Overhead.. 3,000
      Materials Inventory.. 3,000
f. Manufacturing Overhead 13,000
      Accounts Payable... 13,000
g. Work in Process Inventory ($36,000 × 0.50) 18,000
      Manufacturing Overhead... 18,000

h. Finished Goods Inventory	99,000	
Work in Process Inventory		99,000
i. Accounts Receivable	172,000	
Sales Revenue		172,000
Cost of Goods Sold	91,400	
Finished Goods Inventory		91,400
j. Cost of Goods Sold	2,000	
Manufacturing Overhead		2,000

Balance in Manufacturing Overhead for entry (j):

Manufacturing Overhead

(d)	4,000	(g)	18,000
(e)	3,000		
(f)	13,000		
Bal.	2,000		

Requirement 2 (Ending balances)

Materials Inventory

Bal.	20,000	(b)	39,000
(a)	31,000	(e)	3,000
Bal.	9,000		

Work in Process Inventory

Bal.	17,000	(h)	99,000
(b)	39,000		
(d)	36,000		
(g)	18,000		
Bal.	11,000		

Finished Goods Inventory

Bal.	11,000	(i)	91,400
(h)	99,000		
Bal.	18,600		

Cost of Goods Sold

(i)	91,400		
(j)	2,000		
Bal.	93,400		

SUMMARY

1. Distinguish between financial accounting and management accounting. Management accounting information is used by managers within an organization to plan and control operations and to help make pricing, product mix, and other decisions. In making decisions, managers compare the expected future costs and benefits of alternative courses of action. Manufacturing companies compute *manufacturing product costs* for external reporting and *full product costs* across the *value chain* for internal decision-making purposes.

2. Prepare the financial statements of a manufacturing company. Manufacturers use three inventory accounts for manufacturing product costs. The *Materials Inventory* account carries the costs of materials that are being held for use in production. The *Work in Process Inventory* account accumulates the cost of goods that are in the manufacturing process but are not yet complete. *Finished Goods Inventory* represents completed goods that have not yet been sold. These accounts hold *inventoriable costs* that are expensed as finished goods are sold. *Period costs* are expensed in the period they are incurred and are not tracked through the inventory accounts.

3. Use cost of goods manufactured to compute cost of goods sold. *Cost of goods manufactured* is the cost of finished goods that a business completes during a period. A manufacturer's cost of goods manufactured replaces a merchandiser's purchases. For a manufacturer, the beginning balance of Finished Goods Inventory plus the cost of goods manufactured minus the ending balance of Finished Goods Inventory gives the company's cost of goods sold.

4. Relate job cost information to inventory and expense accounts. In a *job order costing* system—designed to account for products manufactured as individual units or in small batches—costs are accumulated for specific jobs. A *job cost record* shows the materials, labor, and overhead costs of producing the job. This document is the basic internal management device for accumulating and controlling costs. It serves as the subsidiary record for Work in Process Inventory. Job costs eventually flow into Finished Goods Inventory and Cost of Goods Sold.

5. Account for direct materials in a job order costing system. Direct materials are the important materials used to make the product. The costs of direct materials are traced to jobs via *materials requisitions*.

6. Account for direct labor in a job order costing system. *Direct labor* is the compensation of employees who physically convert materials into the company's products. Direct labor costs are traced to jobs by labor time tickets.

7. Account for manufacturing overhead in a job order costing system. *Manufacturing overhead* is all manufacturing costs besides direct materials and direct labor. Actual manufacturing overhead costs are accumulated in the Manufacturing Overhead account. Manufacturing overhead is applied to jobs using a budgeted rate per unit of a *cost application base*. At the end of the period, any underapplied or overapplied manufacturing overhead is closed, usually to Cost of Goods Sold.

SELF-STUDY QUESTIONS

Test your understanding of the chapter by marking the best answer for each of the following questions.

1. Which of the following is an inventory account of a manufacturer but not of a merchandiser? *(p. 846)*
   a. Cost of Goods Manufactured
   b. Merchandise Inventory
   c. Work in Process Inventory
   d. Direct Labor

2. Cost of goods manufactured is used to compute *(p. 848)*
   a. Cost of goods sold
   b. Manufacturing overhead applied
   c. Direct materials used
   d. Finished goods inventory

3. Beginning Work in Process Inventory is $35,000, manufacturing costs for the period total $140,000, and ending Work in Process Inventory is $20,000. What is the cost of goods manufactured? *(pp. 848-849)*
   a. $125,000
   b. $155,000
   c. $175,000
   d. $195,000

4. Which of the following is a period cost? *(p. 850)*
   a. Materials inventory
   b. Direct labor
   c. Manufacturing overhead
   d. Selling expense

5. Job order costing would be an appropriate system to account for the manufacture of *(p. 851)*
   a. Aircraft
   b. Matches
   c. Zippers
   d. Cardboard boxes

6. What purpose does a job cost record serve? *(p. 852)*
   a. Lists total material, labor, and overhead costs charged to a job
   b. Is management's basic internal document that helps to control costs in a job costing system
   c. Both a and b
   d. Neither a nor b

7. Using direct materials in production and charging direct labor costs to a job result in debits to *(pp. 856, 857)*
   a. Direct Materials and Direct Labor
   b. Work in Process Inventory
   c. Finished Goods Inventory
   d. Materials Inventory and Manufacturing Wages

8. Which documents serve as a subsidiary ledger for the general ledger balance of Work in Process Inventory? *(p. 852)*
   a. Job cost records
   b. Material requisitions
   c. Labor time tickets
   d. Materials ledger accounts

9. Why is direct labor often used as a basis for applying overhead cost to jobs? Overhead *(p. 859)*
   a. Is very similar to direct labor
   b. Includes direct labor
   c. Occurs before direct labor is charged to a job
   d. Occurs in proportion to direct labor cost

10. At the end of a period, after overhead has been applied to all jobs, Manufacturing Overhead has a credit balance of $900. We say that overhead is *(p. 861)*
    a. Misstated
    b. Incorrectly applied
    c. Overapplied
    d. Underapplied

Answers to the Self-Study Questions follow the Accounting Vocabulary.

ACCOUNTING VOCABULARY

Budget. Quantitative expression of a plan of action that helps managers to coordinate and implement the plan *(p. 842)*.

Controlling. Acting to implement planning decisions and then evaluating the performance of operations and employees *(p. 842)*.

Conversion costs. Direct labor plus manufacturing overhead *(p. 848)*.

Cost application base. A common denominator for systematically linking indirect costs to products. Ideally, the best measure of the cause-and-effect relationship between overhead costs and production volume *(p. 859)*.

Cost driver. Any factor that affects costs *(p. 851)*.

Cost of goods manufactured. Manufacturer's counterpart to the merchandiser's purchases; the cost that is added to finished goods inventory during a period *(p. 848)*.

Cost object. Anything to which costs are assigned *(p. 851)*.

Direct labor. The compensation of employees who physically convert materials into the company's products; labor costs that are conveniently traceable to finished goods *(p. 847)*.

Direct materials. Materials that become a physical part of a finished product and whose costs are separately and conveniently traceable through the manufacturing process to finished goods *(p. 847)*.

Finished goods inventory. Completed goods that have not been sold *(p. 846)*.

Full product costs. The costs of all resources that are used throughout the value chain for a product *(p. 845)*.

Indirect labor. Manufacturing labor costs other than direct labor; labor costs that are difficult to trace to specific products *(p. 847)*.

Indirect materials. Materials whose costs cannot conveniently be traced directly to particular finished products *(p. 847)*.

Inventoriable costs. All costs of a product that are regarded as an asset for financial reporting under GAAP *(p. 849)*.

Job cost record. Document used to accumulate the costs of a job *(p. 852)*.

Job order costing. Costing system used by companies that manufacture products as individual units or in small batches that vary considerably in terms of resources consumed, time required, or complexity *(p. 851)*.

Manufacturing Overhead. All manufacturing costs besides direct materials and direct labor *(p. 847)*.

Manufacturing product costs. The costs of resources that are used to manufacture a product *(p. 845)*.

Materials inventory. Materials on hand that are intended for use in the manufacturing process *(p. 846)*.

Materials requisition. Request for materials, prepared by manufacturing personnel *(p. 855)*.

Period costs. Operating costs that are expensed in the period in which they are incurred *(p. 850)*.

Planning. Choosing goals and deciding how to achieve them *(p. 842)*.

Prime costs. Direct materials plus direct labor *(p. 848)*.

Value chain. Sequence of all business functions in which value is added to a firm's products or services *(p. 844)*.

Work in process inventory. Goods that are in the manufacturing process but are not yet complete *(p. 846)*.

1. c

2. a

3. b ($35,000 + $140,000 − $20,000 = $155,000)

4. d

5. a   8. a

6. c   9. d

7. b   10. c

QUESTIONS

1. Name three distinctions between management accounting and financial accounting.

2. How do manufacturing companies differ from merchandisers? What inventory accounts does a manufacturer use that a merchandiser does not need?

3. Identify the various business functions in the value chain of a manufacturing company. Separate the upstream functions from the downstream functions. To which functions is management accounting relevant?

4. What are the purposes of management accounting information?

5. What is the manufacturer's counterpart to the merchandiser's purchases?

6. Distinguish direct materials from indirect materials and direct labor from indirect labor. Direct materials and direct labor are debited directly to what inventory account when placed in production? What account do indirect materials and indirect labor pass through en route to this inventory account?

7. Give examples of direct materials and indirect materials for a home builder.

8. Identify at least six components of manufacturing overhead. Is Manufacturing Overhead an asset or an expense account?

9. Outline the flow of inventory costs through a manufacturing company's accounting system.

10. Distinguish between inventoriable costs and period costs. Which represents an asset, and which is used to account for expenses?

11. What costs should managers consider in deciding on the sale price of a product: manufacturing product costs or full product costs? Give your reason.

12. Name two benefits of a perpetual inventory system.

13. What do the terms *charged to a job* and *applied to a job* mean? What account is debited when a cost is applied to a job?

14. What is the essential nature of a job order costing system? How can companies that use a job order costing system operate with low levels of inventories?

15. What document is used to charge labor cost to specific jobs? Briefly describe how the document is used.

16. Is manufacturing overhead cost applied to jobs by a precise identification of the overhead cost of each job or by an estimation process? Briefly discuss the process.

17. When is manufacturing overhead underapplied? When is it overapplied?

18. Insignificant amounts of over- or underapplied overhead are closed to what account? Significant amounts are prorated to what three accounts?

19. Which of the following accounts have their balances brought to zero at the end of the period? Which keep their ending balances to start the next period: Materials Inventory, Manufacturing Overhead, Finished Goods Inventory, Manufacturing Wages.

20. Summarize the computation of cost of goods manufactured. Use any dollar amounts.

EXERCISES

Reporting current assets of a manufacturer
(Obj. 2)

E20-1   Consider the following selected amounts and account balances of Midwest Foods:

Cost of goods sold	$101,000	Prepaid expenses	$ 5,000
Direct labor	47,000	Marketing expense	39,000
Direct materials	25,000	Work in process inventory	42,000
Accounts receivable	73,000	Manufacturing overhead	26,000
Cash	9,000	Finished goods inventory	68,000
Cost of goods manufactured	94,000	Materials inventory	17,000

Show how Midwest would report current assets on the balance sheet. Not all data are used.

Computing cost of goods manufactured and cost of goods sold
(Obj. 3)

E20-2   Compute cost of goods manufactured and cost of goods sold from the following amounts:

	Beginning of Year	End of Year
Materials inventory	$22,000	$26,000
Work in process inventory	38,000	30,000
Finished goods inventory	18,000	23,000
Purchases of raw materials		75,000
Direct labor		82,000

	Beginning of Year	End of Year
Indirect labor..		15,000
Factory insurance		9,000
Depreciation—factory building and equipment		11,000
Repairs and maintenance—factory.................................		4,000
Marketing expenses...		63,000
General and administrative expenses.............................		29,000
Income tax expense		30,000

E20-3   Prepare an income statement for the company in Exercise 20-2. Assume that it sold 27,000 units of its product at a price of $14 during the current year.

Preparing a manufacturer's income statement (Obj. 2)

E20-4   Supply the missing amounts from the following computation of gross margin:

Computing gross margin for a manufacturer (Obj. 2)

Sales revenue..			$483,000
Cost of goods sold:			
Beginning finished goods inventory...		$ 91,000	
Cost of goods manufactured:			
Beginning work in process inventory.........................		$ 57,000	
Direct materials used	$84,000		
Direct labor......................................	X		
Manufacturing overhead.................	51,000		
Total manufacturing costs incurred during the period..........		226,000	
Total manufacturing costs to account for		X	
Ending work in process inventory..		(40,000)	
Cost of goods manufactured...........		X	
Goods available for sale		X	
Ending finished goods inventory........		(107,000)	
Cost of goods sold.............................			X
Gross margin			$ X

E20-5   Lee Publishing Company job cost records yielded the following information:

Analyzing job cost data (Obj. 4)

Job No.	Date Started	Date Finished	Date Sold	Total Cost of Job at July 31
1	June 19	July 14	July 15	$ 1,700
2	June 29	July 21	July 26	17,000
3	July 3	Aug. 11	Aug. 13	6,300
4	July 7	July 29	Aug. 1	6,200
5	July 9	July 30	Aug. 2	1,300
6	July 22	Aug. 11	Aug. 13	1,300
7	July 23	July 27	July 29	2,700

Required

Compute Lee's cost of (a) work in process inventory at July 31, (b) finished goods inventory at July 31, and (c) cost of goods sold for July.

E20-6   Record the following transactions in the general journal:

Journalizing manufacturing transactions (Obj. 5, 6, 7)

a.   Purchased materials on account, $11,100.

b.   Paid manufacturing wages, $14,000.

c.   Used in production: direct materials, $9,000; indirect materials, $2,000.

d.   Applied manufacturing labor to jobs: direct labor, 80 percent; indirect labor, 20 percent.

e. Recorded manufacturing overhead: depreciation, $13,000; insurance, $1,700; property tax, $4,200 (credit Property Tax Payable).

f. Applied manufacturing overhead to jobs, 200 percent of direct labor.

g. Completed production, $27,000.

h. Sold inventory on account, $22,000; cost of goods sold, $14,000.

i. Paid marketing expenses, $2,000.

Identifying manufacturing transactions (*Obj. 5, 6, 7*)

E20-7 Describe the lettered transactions in the following manufacturing accounts:

Materials Inventory	
(a)	(b)
	(e)

Work in Process Inventory	
(b)	(h)
(d)	(j)
(g)	

Finished Goods Inventory	
(h)	(i)
	(j)

Manufacturing Wages	
(c)	(d)

Manufacturing Overhead	
(d)	(g)
(e)	
(f)	
(j)	

Cost of Goods Sold	
(i)	(j)

Using the Work in Process Inventory account (*Obj. 4, 5, 6, 7*)

E20-8 August production generated the following activity in the Work in Process Inventory account of Cardenas Manufacturing Company:

Work in Process Inventory	
August 1 Bal.	10,000
Direct materials used	23,000
Direct labor charged to jobs	31,000
Manufacturing overhead applied to jobs	11,000

Completed production, not yet recorded, consists of jobs B-78, G-65, and Y-11, with total costs of $16,000, $19,000, and $33,000, respectively.

Required

1. Compute the cost of work in process at August 31.
2. Journalize completed production for August.
3. Journalize the credit sale of job G-65 for $41,000. Also make the cost-of-goods-sold entry.

Accounting for overhead cost (*Obj. 7*)

E20-9 Selected cost data for Oleksenko Co. are presented below:

Budgeted manufacturing overhead cost for the year	$105,000
Budgeted direct labor cost for the year	87,500
Actual manufacturing overhead cost for the year	96,600
Actual direct labor cost for the year	80,000

Required

1. Compute the budgeted manufacturing overhead rate per direct labor dollar.
2. Journalize the application of overhead cost for the year.
3. By what amount is manufacturing overhead over- or underapplied? Is this amount significant or insignificant?
4. On the basis of your answer to Requirement 3, journalize disposition of the overhead balance.

CHALLENGE EXERCISE

Prorating manufacturing overhead (*Obj. 7*)

E20-10 At the end of the 19X5 fiscal year, Orlando Company's manufacturing inventory and expense accounts held the following applied costs:

	Work in Process Inventory	Finished Goods Inventory	Cost of Goods Sold
Direct materials	$100,000	$170,000	$ 360,000
Direct labor	80,000	250,000	600,000
Manufacturing overhead	60,000	300,000	480,000
Total	$240,000	$720,000	$1,440,000

Orlando's accountants applied overhead during the year using a budgeted rate of $8.40 per machine hour. At year end, they computed the actual rate of $10 per machine hour. The beginning balances of both Work in Process Inventory and Finished Goods Inventory were zero.

Required

1. How many machine-hours were worked in 19X5?
2. Was manufacturing overhead over- or underapplied for the year? By how much?
3. Prorate the over- or underapplied overhead to the three accounts above. What are their balances after proration?

PROBLEMS

(GROUP A)

P20-1A Certain item descriptions and amounts are missing from the income statement of Pinatubo Manufacturing Company.

Completing a manufacturer's income statement (Obj. 2, 3)

PINATUBO MANUFACTURING COMPANY
INCOME STATEMENT
FOR THE MONTH ENDED JUNE 30, 19X9

Sales revenue			$ X
Cost of goods sold:			
Beginning _____ inventory		$101,000	
Cost of goods _____:			
Beginning _____ inventory.......................	$ 28,000		
Direct _____:			
Beginning materials inventory..............	$ X		
Purchases of materials...........................	62,000		
Available for use	79,000		
Ending materials inventory	(23,000)		
Direct _____...	$ X		
Direct_____..	X		
_____	40,000		
Total _____ costs _____	166,000		
Total _____ costs _____	X		
Ending _____ inventory	(30,000)		
Cost of goods _____	164,000		
Goods available for sale................................	X		
Ending _____ inventory	(X)		
Cost of goods _____		168,000	
Gross margin		230,000	
Operating expenses:			
Marketing	99,000		
General	X		
Total operating expenses		144,000	
Income before income tax.............................		X	
Income tax expense (40%).............................		X	
Net income..		$ X	

Required

Supply the missing item descriptions (_____) and the missing amounts (X).

P20-2A   O'Kelley Manufacturing Company job cost records yielded the following information. The company has a perpetual inventory system.

Job No.	Date Started	Date Finished	Sold	Total Cost of Job at June 30	Total Manufacturing Costs Added in July
1	5/26	6/7	6/9	$ 700	
2	6/3	6/12	6/13	1,700	
3	6/3	6/30	7/1	2,400	
4	6/17	7/24	7/27	200	$ 500
5	6/29	7/29	8/3	400	1,600
6	7/8	7/12	7/14		800
7	7/23	8/6	8/9		300
8	7/30	8/22	8/26		2,900

Required

1. Compute O'Kelley's cost of (a) work in process inventory at June 30 and July 31, (b) finished goods inventory at June 30 and July 31, and (c) cost of goods sold for June and July.
2. Make summary journal entries to record the transfer of completed units from work in process to finished goods for June and July.
3. Record the sale of Job 4 for $850.

P20-3A   Bass Shoe Company makes the Weejun loafer. Assume that Bass's accounting records include the following cost information on jobs for the manufacture of the basic brown leather Weejun.

During the most recent year Bass incurred manufacturing costs of $21.4 million for materials, labor, and manufacturing overhead, of which $4.6 million was applied overhead. Beginning balances for the year were Materials Inventory, $700,000; Work in Process Inventory, $900,000; and Finished Goods Inventory, $400,000. The company applies overhead on the basis of the relationship between overhead and direct labor costs. At year end the inventory accounts showed these balances (in millions):

	Materials	Direct Labor	Manufacturing Overhead
Materials Inventory	$600,000	$ –0–	$ –0–
Work in Process Inventory..............	400,000	450,000	150,000
Finished Goods Inventory...............	100,000	150,000	50,000

Required

1. Prepare Bass's schedule of cost of goods manufactured for the brown leather Weejun.
2. Compute the cost of goods sold for the Weejun product.
3. Compute the cost of materials purchased during the year.

P20-4A   Maple Leaf Homes, Inc., is a home builder in Toronto, Canada. Maple Leaf uses a perpetual inventory system and a job cost system in which each house represents a job. Because it constructs houses, the company uses accounts titled Construction Wages, Construction Overhead, and Supervisory Salaries (for indirect labor). The following transactions and events were completed during August:

a. Purchased materials on account, $385,600.
b. Requisitioned direct materials and used direct labor in construction:

	Direct Materials	Direct Labor
House 302...............	$36,800	$19,100
House 303...............	39,100	17,400
House 304...............	45,600	20,500
House 305...............	22,400	12,000
House 306...............	63,900	33,700
House 307...............	52,800	27,500

c. Depreciation of equipment used in construction, $5,800.

d. Other overhead costs incurred on houses 302–307:

Supervisory salaries	$17,000
Equipment rentals paid	7,300
Liability insurance expired	5,100

e. Applied overhead to jobs at the budgeted overhead rate of 30 percent of direct labor.

f. Houses completed: 302, 304, 305, 307.

g. Houses sold: 305 for $41,500; 307 for $115,000.

Required

1. Record the foregoing transactions and events in the general journal.

2. Open T-accounts for Work in Process Inventory and Finished Goods Inventory. Post the appropriate entries to these accounts, identifying each entry by letter. Determine the ending account balances, assuming that the beginning balances were zero.

3. Add the costs of unfinished houses, and show that this total amount equals the ending balance in the Work in Process Inventory account.

4. Add the costs of completed houses that have not yet been sold, and show that this total amount equals the ending balance in the Finished Goods Inventory account.

P20-5A   Park Magnetic Tape Company manufactures diskettes for use in reproducing sound. Park has a job cost system and a perpetual inventory system.

Preparing and using a job cost record
(Obj. 4, 5, 6, 7)

On November 2, Park began production of 10,000 diskettes, job number 378, to be sold to music stores for $1.25 each. The company incurred the following costs:

Date	Materials Requisition No.	Description	Amount
11-2	36	31 lb. polypropylene @ $8	$248
11-2	37	68 lb. magnetic filament @ $13	884
11-3	42	7 lb. bucylic acid @ $48	336

Date	Time Ticket No.	Description	Amount
11-2	556	12 hours @ $10	$120
11-3	557	25 hours @ $8	200

Park charges overhead to jobs on the basis of the relationship between budgeted overhead ($492,800) and budgeted direct labor ($448,000). Job 378 was completed on November 3 and shipped to music stores when ordered.

Required

1. Prepare a job cost record similar to that in Exhibit 20-11 for Job 378.

2. Journalize in summary form the requisition of direct materials and the application of direct labor and manufacturing overhead to Job 378.

3. Journalize completion of the job and the sale of 500 diskettes.

4. How will what you learned from this problem help you manage a business?

P20-6A   The Tibodeaux Company manufactures specialized parts used in its business. Initially, the company manufactured the parts for its own use, but it gradually began selling them to other companies as well. Tibodeaux's trial balance on April 1, the beginning of the current fiscal year, follows at the top of page 872.

Comprehensive accounting treatment of manufacturing transactions
(Obj. 2, 4, 5, 6, 7)

April 1 balances in the subsidiary ledgers were:

Materials ledger: steel, $1,580; petrochemicals, $2,810; electronic parts, $1,960; indirect materials, $430.

Work in process ledger: Job 145, $35,880.

Finished goods ledger: transformers, $5,310; transmission lines, $4,780; switches, $8,870.

```
                    THE TIBODEAUX CO.
                     TRIAL BALANCE
                      APRIL 1, 19XX

Cash ...........................................    $  19,160
Accounts receivable ......................          74,290
Inventories:
    Materials ...............................        6,780
    Work in process.........................        35,880
    Finished goods..........................        18,960
Plant assets.................................       244,570
Accumulated depreciation.................                        $103,680
Accounts payable .........................                        26,770
Wages payable .............................                        3,670
Common stock .............................                       120,000
Retained earnings ........................                       145,520
Sales revenues.............................                          —
Cost of goods sold ........................           —
Manufacturing wages .....................            —
Manufacturing overhead ..................            —
Marketing and general expenses ..........            —              —
                                                   $399,640       $399,640
```

April transactions are summarized as follows:

a. Materials purchased on credit: steel, $5,540; petrochemicals, $9,690; electronic parts, $15,830; indirect materials, $3,590.

b. Materials used in production (requisitioned):
    Job 145: steel, $340; petrochemicals, $1,770.
    Job 146: steel, $3,570; petrochemicals, $5,720; electronic parts, $3,980.
    Job 147: steel, $1,970; petrochemicals, $3,610; electronic parts, $3,730.
    Indirect materials, $2,380.

c. Manufacturing wages incurred during April, $32,430, of which $30,520 was paid. Wages payable at March 31 were paid during April, $3,670.

d. Labor time tickets for the month: Job 145, $3,500; Job 146, $12,050; Job 147, $9,940; Indirect labor, $6,940.

e. Manufacturing overhead incurred on account, $4,630.

f. Depreciation recorded on factory plant and equipment, $3,450.

g. Payments on account, $36,040.

h. Manufacturing overhead was applied at the budgeted rate of 70 percent of direct labor.

i. Jobs completed during the month: Job 145, two transformers at total cost of $43,940; Job 146, 200 switches at total cost of $33,755.

j. Marketing and general expenses paid, $27,470.

k. Credit sales on account: all of Job 145 for $97,640 (cost $43,940); Job 146, 120 switches for $35,100 (cost, $20,253).

l. Collections on account, $127,470.

Required

1. Open T-accounts for the general ledger, the materials ledger, the work in process ledger, and the finished goods ledger. Insert each account balance as given, and use the reference *Bal.*

2. Record the April transactions directly in the accounts, using the letters as references. Tibodeaux has a perpetual inventory system.

3. Prepare a trial balance at April 30 of the current year.

4. Prepare a multiple-step income statement through operating income for April of the current year, assuming that any balance in Manufacturing Overhead is insignificant. Take amounts directly from the trial balance, and report cost of goods sold as a single amount.

P20-1B   Certain item descriptions and amounts are missing from the income statement of Delmonico Systems.

Completing a manufacturer's income statement (Obj. 2, 3)

DELMONICO SYSTEMS
INCOME STATEMENT
FOR THE MONTH ENDED MARCH 31, 19X6

Sales revenue				$231,000
Cost of goods sold:				
Beginning ____ inventory			$ X	
Cost of goods ____:				
Beginning ____ inventory.......................		$ X		
Direct ____:				
Beginning materials inventory..........	$ 34,000			
Purchases of materials......................	70,000			
Available for use	X			
Ending materials inventory	(26,000)			
Direct ____...................................		$ X		
Direct____...................................		80,000		
____		19,000		
Total ____ costs ____			X	
Total ____ costs ____			X	
Ending ____ inventory			(45,000)	
Cost of goods ____			163,000	
Goods available for sale...............................			192,000	
Ending ____ inventory			(52,000)	
Cost of goods ____				X
Gross margin				91,000
Operating expenses:				
Marketing			23,000	
General			26,000	
Total operating expenses				X
Income before income tax..............................				X
Income tax expense (30%)...............................				X
Net income				$ X

Supply the missing item descriptions (____) and the missing amounts (X).

P20-2B   Atlantic Irrigation Company job cost records yielded the following information. The company has a perpetual inventory system.

Analyzing job cost data (Obj. 4)

Job No.	Date Started	Date Finished	Sold	Total Cost of Job at March 31	Total Manufacturing Cost Added in April
1	2/26	3/7	3/9	$2,200	
2	2/3	3/12	3/13	1,100	
3	3/29	3/31	4/3	300	
4	3/31	4/1	4/1	500	$ 400
5	3/17	4/24	4/27	1,400	2,200
6	4/8	4/12	4/14		700
7	4/23	5/6	5/9		1,200
8	4/30	5/22	5/26		600

Required

1.   Compute Atlantic's cost of (a) work in process inventory at March 31 and April 30, (b) finished goods inventory at March 31 and April 30, and (c) cost of goods sold for March and April.

2. Make summary journal entries to record the transfer of completed units from work in process to finished goods for March and April.

3. Record the sale of Job 5 for $7,000.

Computing manufacturing cost amounts for the financial statements
(Obj. 3, 5, 6, 7)

P20-3B Assume that Wrangler's accounting records include the following cost information on jobs for the manufacture of a line of jeans. During the most recent year, Wrangler incurred a total manufacturing cost of $163.2 million for materials, labor, and manufacturing overhead, of which $28.2 million was the cost of direct materials used. Beginning balances for the year were Materials Inventory, $3.4 million; Work in Process Inventory, $3.8 million; and Finished Goods Inventory, $7.4 million. The company applies overhead on the basis of the relationship between overhead and direct labor costs. At year end the inventory accounts showed these balances (in millions):

	Materials	Direct Labor	Manufacturing Overhead
Materials inventory	$0.9	$–0–	$–0–
Work in process inventory	1.5	2.0	2.5
Finished goods inventory	2.4	3.2	4.0

Required

1. Prepare Wrangler's schedule of cost of goods manufactured for the line of jeans.

2. Compute the cost of goods sold for the product.

3. Record the transfer from Work in Process Inventory to Finished Goods Inventory and the transfer from Finished Goods Inventory to Cost of Goods Sold during the year.

Accounting for manufacturing transactions
(Obj. 4, 5, 6, 7)

P20-4B Holiday Homes builds prefabricated houses in a factory. The company uses a perpetual inventory system and a job cost system in which each house represents a job. The following transactions and events were completed during May:

a. Purchased materials on account, $211,000.

b. Requisitioned direct materials and used direct labor in manufacturing:

	Direct Materials	Direct Labor
House 613	$26,100	$11,600
House 614	41,700	22,500
House 615	31,000	15,000
House 616	54,000	23,800
House 617	43,900	20,700
House 618	32,800	14,600

c. Depreciation of manufacturing equipment used on different houses, $14,300.

d. Other overhead costs incurred on houses 613–618:

Manufacturing wages	$21,600
Equipment rentals paid	6,000
Liability insurance expired	3,900

e Applied overhead to jobs at the budgeted rate of 30 percent of direct labor.

f. Houses completed: 613, 615, 616.

g. Houses sold: 615 for $59,000; 616 for $103,900.

Required

1. Record the foregoing transactions and events in the general journal.

2. Open T-accounts for Work in Process Inventory and Finished Goods Inventory. Post the appropriate entries to these accounts, identifying each entry by letter. Determine the ending account balances, assuming that the beginning balances were zero.

3. Add the costs of unfinished houses, and show that this total amount equals the ending balance in the Work in Process Inventory account.

4. Add the costs of completed houses that have not yet been sold, and show that this total amount equals the ending balance in the Finished Goods Inventory account.

P20-5B J. T. Lamont Company produces conveyor belts that are used by other companies in their manufacturing processes. Lamont has a job cost system and a perpetual inventory system.

On September 22, Lamont received an order for 50 industrial-grade belts from Ogden Jones Corporation at a price of $56 each. The job, assigned number 449, was promised for October 15. After purchasing the materials, Lamont began production on September 30 and incurred the following costs in completing the order:

Preparing and using a job cost record
(Obj. 4, 5, 6, 7)

Date	Materials Requisition No.	Description	Amount
9-30	593	20 lb. rubber @ $9	$180
10- 2	598	30 meters polyester fabric @ $8	240
10- 3	622	12 meters steel cord @ $12	144

Date	Time Ticket No.	Description	Amount
9-30	1754	10 hours @ $9	$ 90
10- 3	1805	31 hours @ $8	248

Lamont charges manufacturing overhead to jobs on the basis of the relationship between budgeted overhead ($375,000) and direct labor ($250,000). Job 449 was completed on October 3 and shipped to Ogden Jones on October 5.

Required

1. Prepare a job cost record similar to that in Exhibit 20-11 for Job 449.
2. Journalize in summary form the requisition of direct materials and the application of direct labor and manufacturing overhead to Job 449.
3. Journalize completion of the job and sale of the goods.
4. How will what you learned from this problem help you manage a business?

P20-6B Downstate Electric Company manufactures specialized parts used in the generation of power. Initially, the company manufactured the parts for its own use, but it gradually began selling them to other public utilities as well. The trial balance of Downstate Electric's manufacturing operation on January 1 of the current year follows:

Comprehensive accounting treatment of manufacturing transactions
(Obj. 2, 4, 5, 6, 7)

DOWNSTATE ELECTRIC COMPANY—MANUFACTURING OPERATIONS TRIAL BALANCE JANUARY 1, 19XX		
Cash	$ 33,000	
Accounts receivable	65,860	
Inventories:		
Materials	18,910	
Work in process	43,350	
Finished goods	78,550	
Plant assets	342,860	
Accumulated depreciation		$145,960
Accounts payable		88,650
Wages payable		5,700
Common stock		200,000
Retained earnings		142,220
Sales revenue		—
Cost of goods sold	—	
Manufacturing wages	—	
Manufacturing overhead	—	
Marketing and general expenses	—	—
	$582,530	$582,530

January 1 balances in the subsidiary ledgers were:

Materials ledger: steel, $4,730; petrochemicals, $5,280; electronic parts, $7,800; indirect materials, $1,100.

Work in process ledger: Job 86, $43,350.

Finished goods ledger: transformers, $35,770; transmission lines, $21,910; switches, $20,870. January transactions are summarized as follows:

a. Materials purchased on credit: steel, $12,660; petrochemicals, $19,570; electronic parts, $28,360; indirect materials, $6,130.

b. Materials used in production (requisitioned):
Job 86: steel, $1,580; petrochemicals, $3,400.
Job 87: steel, $10,580; petrochemicals, $9,870; electronic parts, $4,690.
Job 88: steel, $2,930; petrochemicals, $7,680; electronic parts, $29,920.
Indirect materials, $4,760.

c. Manufacturing wages incurred during January, $52,080, of which $49,560 was paid. Wages payable at December 31 were paid during January, $5,700.

d. Labor time tickets for the month: Job 86, $4,000; Job 87, $19,880; Job 88, $16,560; indirect labor, $11,640.

e. Manufacturing overhead incurred on account, $27,660.

f. Depreciation recorded on manufacturing plant and equipment, $6,710.

g. Payments on account, $79,330.

h. Manufacturing overhead was applied at the budgeted rate of 120 percent of direct labor.

i. Jobs completed during the month: Job 86, one transformer at total cost of $57,130; Job 87, 620 switches at total cost of $68,876.

j. Marketing and general expenses paid, $21,660.

k. Credit sales on account: All of Job 86 for $91,490 (cost $57,130); Job 87, 480 switches for $88,030 (cost, $53,323).

l. Collections on account, $177,880.

Required

1. Open T-accounts for the general ledger, the materials ledger, the work in process ledger, and the finished goods ledger. Insert each account balance as given, and use the reference *Bal.*

2. Record the January transactions directly in the accounts, using the letters as references. Downstate Electric has a perpetual inventory system.

3. Prepare a trial balance at January 31 of the current year.

4. Prepare a multiple-step income statement through operating income for January of the current year, assuming that any balance in Manufacturing Overhead is insignificant. Take amounts directly from the trial balance, and report cost of goods sold as a single amount.

EXTENDING YOUR KNOWLEDGE

DECISION PROBLEMS

Costing jobs and using job cost information to bid on contracts
(Obj. 5, 6, 7)

1. National Electronics Systems (NES) is a government contractor that specializes in electronics systems for military applications. The company's job order costing system has two direct cost categories: direct materials and direct labor. NES uses direct labor hours as its manufacturing overhead cost application base. For the current fiscal year, budgeted total manufacturing overhead cost was $2,300,000. Budgeted direct labor hours for all production totaled 100,000.

NES bids on government contracts (jobs) by adding 80 percent to the predicted total manufacturing cost of the contract. The 80-percent markup covers the upstream and downstream costs of the contract and provides the company's profit.

NES is preparing to bid on two new contracts. If the bids are accepted, the contracts will be produced as Job A and Job B. Budget data relating to the contracts are as follows:

	Job A	Job B
Direct materials cost	$30,000	$210,000
Direct labor cost...........................	$12,000	$160,000
Total direct labor hours................	600	8,000
Number of output units	100	1,000

Required

1. Compute NES's manufacturing overhead cost application rate for the current year.
2. Compute the budgeted (predicted) total manufacturing cost and the unit cost of Job A and of Job B.
3. Determine the amount per output unit that NES should bid on each contract.
4. Suppose that the government awards both contracts to NES. What factors will determine the actual profit that NES will earn?

2. Hoosier Chocolate Ltd. is located in Indianapolis. The company prepares gift boxes of chocolates for private parties and corporate promotions. Each order contains a selection of chocolates determined by the customer, and the box is designed according to the customer's specifications.

Costing and pricing identical products
(Obj. 4, 5, 6, 7)

One of Hoosier's largest customers is the Andrews and Ng law firm. This organization sends chocolates to its clients each Christmas and also provides them to employees at the firm's gatherings. The law firm's managing partner, Peter Andrews, placed the client gift order in September for 500 boxes of cream-filled dark chocolates. But Andrews and Ng did not place its December staff-party order until the last week of November. This order was for an additional 100 boxes of chocolates identical to the ones to be distributed to clients.

The cost per box for the original 500-box order was budgeted as follows:

Chocolate, filling, wrappers, box	$14.00
Employee time to fill and wrap the box (10 min.)	1.00
Manufacturing overhead	0.50
Total manufacturing cost..	$15.50

Joan Davison, the president of Hoosier Chocolate Ltd., priced the order at $17 per box.

In the past few months, Hoosier Chocolate Ltd. has experienced price increases for both dark chocolate and employee time. All other costs have remained the same. The cost per box for the second order was predicted to be:

Chocolate, filling, wrappers, box	$15.00
Employee time to fill and wrap the box (10 min.)	1.20
Manufacturing overhead	0.60
Total manufacturing cost..	$16.80

Required

1. Do you agree with the cost analysis for the second order? Explain your answer.
2. Should the two orders be accounted for as one job or two in Hoosier Chocolate Ltd.'s system?
3. What sale price per box should Joan Davison set for the second order? What are the advantages and disadvantages of this price?

ETHICAL ISSUE

North Carolina has the greatest concentration of furniture manufacturers in the United States. These companies dominate furniture sales in the Southeast. To break into this market, Ramirez Furniture Company is considering several options. Under one plan, Ramirez would charge no overhead cost to products destined for the Southeast market. This plan would enable Ramirez to offer its furniture at lower prices than its competitors charge and still show adequate profits on Southeast sales.

Required

1. Is Ramirez's pricing strategy ethical? Explain your answer.
2. Can Ramirez expect to follow this strategy indefinitely? Give your reason.

Chapter 21
Process Costing

After studying this chapter, you should be able to

1. Distinguish process costing from job order costing

2. Record process costing transactions

3. Compute equivalent units of production

4. Apply costs to units completed and to units in ending work in process inventory

5. Account for a second processing department by the FIFO method

6. Account for a second processing department by the weighted-average method

"Analysis, improvement, and management of the activities within our manufacturing processes allow Pace Foods to continue to provide high quality, low cost and on-schedule products for our consumers. Timely, internal reporting of product-specific manufacturing costs, by activity, is essential to accomplish our continuous improvement goals and to fulfill our mission to remain the world's best marketer and manufacturer of Mexican food sauces."

KATHLEEN K. MAXFIELD, CONTROLLER OF PACE FOODS, LTD.

Pace Foods, Ltd., is the market leader in the dynamic "Mexican sauces" food category, which has surpassed ketchup in supermarket sales in the United States. The San Antonio, Texas, company mass produces several-ton batches of mild, medium, and hot sauces in both regular and thick-and-chunky styles. In 1993, Pace Foods produced more than 150 million pounds of picante sauce and salsa.

Making picante sauce at Pace is a two-process operation. In the first process, jalapeño peppers, onions, and other fresh vegetables are chopped into small pieces shortly after they are received from suppliers. The chopped vegetables are then transferred to another facility for further processing. In the second process, the vegetables are mixed with tomato products and spices and the ingredients are cooked, bottled, and boxed for shipping. Each batch is continually inspected to ensure purity and consistency in texture and flavor.

Despite intense competition from major international food companies, Pace Foods has achieved steady double-digit growth. The company's managers have invested heavily in state-of-the-art manufacturing processes as well as employee training. Through effective communications, Pace's self-directed work teams are carrying out management's strategy of continuous improvement in quality and productivity. Managers and employees are working together to maintain their coveted market leadership position.

· · · · ·

*H*ow much does it cost Pace Foods to make a batch of hot picante sauce? What is the value of the inventory of fresh vegetables in the chopping process? How efficient was the cooking and bottling process last week? Much like their counterparts in other manufacturing companies, managers at Pace Foods use accounting information to answer these questions.

Process Costing: An Overview

OBJECTIVE 1

Distinguish process costing from job order costing

Manufacturers develop product costing systems to assign direct materials, direct labor, and overhead costs to their products. The two basic types of product costing systems are *job order costing* and *process costing*. We saw in Chapter 20 that job order costing is a system for costing custom goods. It uses job cost records to accumulate the costs of individual jobs. **Process costing**, in contrast, is a system for assigning costs to goods that are mass produced in a continuous sequence of steps, called processes. Process industries produce large numbers of identical units, such as steel rods, boxes of cereal, gallons of paint, and cases of picante sauce. Companies that use process costing are in the petroleum, food and beverage, pharmaceutical, and chemical industries, to name a few.

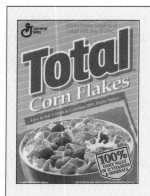

"To produce Total Corn Flakes, General Mills has one department for forming and toasting the flakes and a second department for packaging."

Whether a company uses job order costing or process costing depends on the products it produces and the nature of its production operations, as Exhibit 21-1 shows. Companies in custom industries typically divide their operations into jobs. Companies in mass-production industries typically divide their operations into departments—one for each manufacturing process. The flow of goods through the departments is continuous and repetitive. For example, to produce Total Corn Flakes, General Mills has one department for forming and toasting the flakes and a second department for packaging. The company does not use job cost records to keep track of costs. Instead, it accumulates costs in each department for each production period. At the end of processing, total manufacturing cost is the sum of all costs added in the two departments. Unit cost is computed by dividing total cost by the number of units produced. For example, if it costs $400,000 to produce 1,000,000 boxes of corn flakes, the unit cost is $0.40 ($400,000/1,000,000).

 STOP & THINK Why are job cost records used in job order costing systems but not in process costing systems?

Answer: Job cost records are used to keep track of the costs of custom goods because the unit costs of the goods differ. For example, a 2,000-square-foot house built by a contractor for one customer does not cost the same to build as a 2,000-square-foot house for another customer. The contractor uses job cost records to keep track of the costs of each house. But companies in process industries sell identical goods—with identical unit costs—to different customers. General Mills may sell 300,000 boxes of corn flakes to one customer and 100,000 boxes to another. Job cost records are not needed to determine the costs of the two orders. The company's accountants simply multiply the order quantities by the $0.40 unit cost computed previously.

Suppose that Enesco, the manufacturing company at the bottom of Exhibit 21-2, produces ceramic figurines in three steps. It mixes materials to produce liquid ceramic, injects the liquid ceramic into molds, and heats the molded figurines for

EXHIBIT 21-1
Job Order Costing versus Process Costing

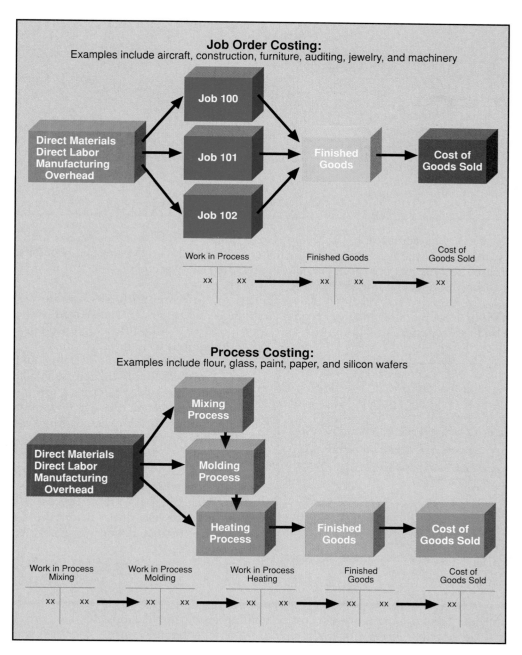

EXHIBIT 21-2
Comparison of Process Costing and Job Order Costing

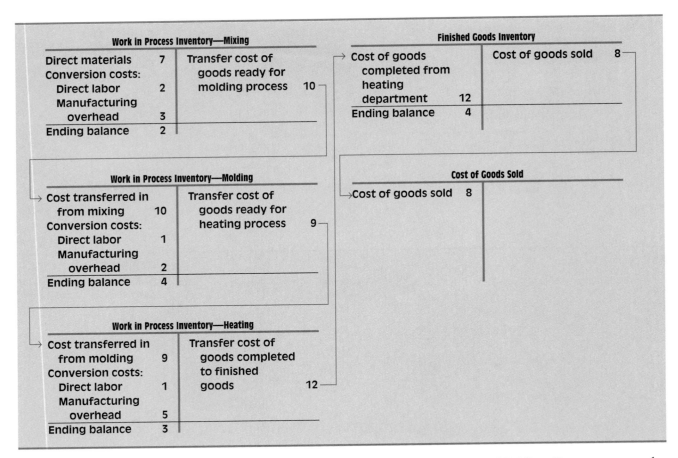

Work in Process Inventory—Mixing		
Direct materials	7	Transfer cost of goods ready for molding process 10
Conversion costs:		
Direct labor	2	
Manufacturing overhead	3	
Ending balance	2	

Finished Goods Inventory		
Cost of goods completed from heating department	12	Cost of goods sold 8
Ending balance	4	

Work in Process Inventory—Molding		
Cost transferred in from mixing	10	Transfer cost of goods ready for heating process 9
Conversion costs:		
Direct labor	1	
Manufacturing overhead	2	
Ending balance	4	

Cost of Goods Sold	
Cost of goods sold	8

Work in Process Inventory—Heating		
Cost transferred in from molding	9	Transfer cost of goods completed to finished goods 12
Conversion costs:		
Direct labor	1	
Manufacturing overhead	5	
Ending balance	3	

EXHIBIT 21-3

Flow of Costs through a Process Costing System (amounts in thousands)

hardness. The company has a Mixing Department, a Molding Department, and a Heating Department. To account for the costs that make up the finished products, Enesco accountants use three Work in Process Inventory accounts—one for mixing, one for molding, and one for heating.

In Exhibit 21-2, mixing costs accumulate in the Work in Process Inventory—Mixing account. After mixing is completed, the liquid ceramic is transferred to the Molding Department, and the costs are transferred to Work in Process—Molding. When molding is completed, product costs flow to Work in Process—Heating and then to Finished Goods Inventory. When the figurines are sold, the cost of the inventory is transferred to Cost of Goods Sold. In contrast, a job order costing system has only one Work in Process Inventory account.

Exhibit 21-3 uses dollar amounts to illustrate how costs flow through a process system. Each Enesco Work in Process Inventory account lists direct materials, direct labor, and manufacturing overhead. All amounts are assumed.

"Each Enesco Work in Process Inventory account lists direct materials, direct labor, and manufacturing overhead."

Recording Costs

The journal entries for a process cost accounting system are like those for a job order costing system. Direct materials, direct labor, and manufacturing overhead are recorded as follows (all amounts are in thousands and are assumed):

Materials Inventory	11	
Accounts Payable		11
Manufacturing Wages	4	
Wages Payable		4
Manufacturing Overhead..	10	
Accumulated Depreciation		2
Property Tax Payable		2
Accounts Payable, and so on...		6

To purchase materials and incur direct labor and manufacturing overhead.

Work in Process Inventory—Mixing..	7	
Materials Inventory...		7
Work in Process Inventory—Mixing..	2	
Manufacturing Wages...		2
Work in Process Inventory—Mixing..	3	
Manufacturing Overhead..		3

To requisition materials, assign direct labor cost, and assign manufacturing overhead cost to the Mixing Department.

Work in Process Inventory—Molding	10	
Work in Process Inventory—Mixing		10

To transfer cost from the Mixing Department to the Molding Department.

Work in Process Inventory—Molding	1	
Manufacturing Wages...		1
Work in Process Inventory—Molding	2	
Manufacturing Overhead..		2

To record the additional labor and overhead cost of the Molding Department.

Entries for the Heating Department parallel those for the Molding Department.

Finished Goods Inventory	12	
Work in Process Inventory—Heating..		12

To transfer the cost of goods completed from the Heating Department to Finished Goods Inventory.

Cost of Goods Sold	8	
Finished Goods Inventory		8

To account for the cost of goods sold.

Unlike a job order costing system, a process costing system is likely to have a separate Work in Process Inventory account for each processing department. In a job order costing system, the Work in Process Inventory account is supported by job cost records for the various jobs.

Conversion Costs

Conversion costs are all manufacturing costs other than direct materials costs. Chapter 20 introduced a threefold classification of manufacturing costs: direct materials, direct labor, and indirect manufacturing costs (manufacturing overhead). This time-honored classification still dominates practice but not as much as it once did. Many companies, particularly those using process costing and automation, have seen direct labor costs become less and less important in relation to total manufacturing costs. Thus, companies increasingly use only two categories:

Key Point: The journal entries for a *process* costing system are essentially the same as the entries for a *job order* costing system. The main difference is that in a job order costing system, goods are transferred from the Work in Process Inventory to the Finished Goods Inventory. In a process costing system, goods are transferred from one Work in Process Inventory account to another.

- Direct materials
- Conversion costs (direct labor plus overhead)

This twofold cost classification reduces accounting expense by eliminating the elaborate tracking of labor cost.

Tracking the Flow of Costs

Process costing systems must track the flow of manufacturing costs through the sequence of processes in order to compute the total cost of finished goods. At Pace Foods, the company in the chapter-opening story, the direct materials (fresh vegetables) and conversion costs of the chopping process are added to the direct materials (tomato products and packaging) and conversion costs of the cooking and bottling process. To account for costs incurred in a production period, management accountants determine the total cost of each process and then divide the cost between two groups of product units: *units completed and transferred out*—either into the next process or into finished goods—and *incomplete units* still in process at the end of the period.

Let us examine U.S. Divers, a sporting goods company that manufactures swim masks. This company's Shaping Department shapes the body of the swim masks. The Shaping Department's direct material is the plastic that is formed into the U.S. Divers masks. The partially completed masks are then moved to the Finishing Department, where the mask bodies are finished and the clear faceplates are inserted and sealed in place.

Assume that during October, the Shaping Department incurs the following costs in processing 50,000 masks:

Direct materials..................................		$140,000
Conversion costs:		
Direct labor....................................	$21,250	
Manufacturing overhead...............	46,750	68,000
Costs to account for..........................		$208,000

If the shaping process is complete for all 50,000 masks, the costs to be transferred to Work in Process Inventory—Finishing are the full $208,000. The unit cost is $4.16 ($208,000/50,000 units). But suppose that shaping is complete for only 40,000 units. At October 31, the Shaping Department still has 10,000 masks in process. How do we compute unit cost when the total cost applies to finished units *and* unfinished units? Accountants answer this question by using the concept of *equivalent units of production*.

Equivalent Units of Production

OBJECTIVE 3

Compute equivalent units of production

Equivalent units, also called *equivalent units of production*, is a measure of the amount of work done during a production period, expressed in terms of fully complete units of output.

Assume that the 10,000 unfinished units still in the Shaping Department of U.S. Divers are one-quarter complete as to conversion work. The number of partially complete units times the percentage of completion equals the number of conversion equivalent units:

Number of partially complete units	×	Percentage of completion	=	Number of conversion equivalent units
10,000 units	×	**25% complete**	=	**2,500 equivalent units**

For the Shaping Department, the number 2,500 tells us how many whole units of conversion work are represented by the incomplete units. We add the 2,500 units to the number of finished units—40,000—to arrive at the period's equivalent units of production regarding conversion: 42,500.

The idea of equivalent units is not confined to manufacturing situations. It is a basic common denominator for measuring activities, output, and workload. For example, colleges and universities measure student enrollments in "full-time equivalents." Suppose that a full-time class load is 12 hours per term. Assume that 1,000 students are taking a full load and that 1,000 other students are taking an average of six hours in classes. The school has a full-time equivalent enrollment of 1,500 students [1,000 + (1,000 × 6/12)].

Steps in Process Cost Accounting

Using the data from the swim mask example, we discuss a five-step application of process costing to each production department. Our example is the Shaping Department of U.S. Divers.

Step 1: Summarize the Flow of Production in Physical Units

Exhibit 21-4 tracks the movement of swim masks into and out of the Shaping Department. We assume for simplicity that work began October 1, so the Work in Process Inventory account had a zero balance at September 30.

Step 2: Compute Output in Terms of Equivalent Units of Production

Management accountants compute equivalent units separately for the two types of costs incurred in manufacturing: direct materials and conversion costs.

Why? Because work may progress differently for materials and for conversion. For instance, in the Shaping Department, all direct materials are added at the beginning of the process, but conversion costs are incurred evenly throughout the process. The Shaping Department has 10,000 units unfinished at October 31. We assume that all direct materials have been added (the chemicals have been added to begin shaping the bodies of the masks) but that three-quarters of the conversion work re-

Short Exercise: Data for the next few Short Exercises are summarized below.

A company using a process cost system has two departments—mixing and packaging. For the Mixing Department:

Units:
WIP, May 1 .... -0-
Started production 5,000
Transferred out—May 4,500
WIP, May 31 (45% complete as to direct materials;
10% complete as to
conversion costs) 500

Costs:
WIP, May 1 .... $ -0-
Costs added during May:
Direct Materials 15,120
Conversion Costs:
Direct Labor $11,102
Man. Overhead 16,653 27,755
Total costs added
during May $42,875

Compute the equivalent units.

SHAPING DEPARTMENT FOR THE MONTH ENDED OCTOBER 31, 19XX			
	Step 1	Step 2 Equivalent Units of Production	
Flow of Production	**Flow of Physical Units**	**Direct Materials**	**Conversion Costs**
Units to account for:			
Work in process, September 30	—		
Started in production during October	50,000		
Total physical units to account for	50,000		
Units accounted for:			
Completed and transferred out			
during October	40,000	40,000	40,000
Work in process, October 31	10,000	10,000	2,500*
Total physical units accounted for......................	50,000		
Equivalent units of production		50,000	42,500

*10,000 units each 25% complete = 2,500 equivalent units.

A:

	Equiv. Units	
	Dir. Mtls.	Conv. Costs
Trans. out	4,500	4,500
WIP, May 31	225	50
Equiv. units...	4,725	4,550

EXHIBIT 21-4

Step 1: Summarize the Flow of Production in Physical Units;
Step 2: Compute Output in Terms of Equivalent Units of Production

SHAPING DEPARTMENT
FOR THE MONTH ENDED OCTOBER 31, 19XX

Work in Process—Shaping

	Physical Units	*Dollars*		*Physical Units*	*Dollars*
Inventory, September 30	–0–	$ –0–	Transferred out	40,000	$?
Production started:	50,000				
Direct materials		140,000			
Conversion costs:					
Direct labor		21,250			
Manufacturing overhead		46,750			
Total to account for	50,000	$208,000			
Ending inventory	10,000	$?			

EXHIBIT 21-5

Step 3: Summarize Total Costs to Account For

mains to be done. Thus, all 50,000 units are finished in terms of direct materials. We must compute equivalent units for conversion costs. Because 25 percent of conversion work has been done, we multiply the 10,000 unfinished units by 0.25, which gives 2,500 equivalent units. We add that to the 40,000 finished units, so equivalent units for conversion costs total 42,500.

Exhibit 21-4 combines the data for steps 1 and 2. Note that the number of equivalent units for direct materials and conversion costs are different. This often is the case.

Step 3: Summarize Total Costs To Account For

Exhibit 21-5 summarizes the total costs to account for in the Shaping Department (cost data are from p. 884). These costs are the total debits in Work in Process Inventory—Shaping, including any beginning balance. The Shaping Department has 50,000 units and $208,000 of costs to account for. Our task is to assign these costs to the 40,000 masks completed and transferred out and to the 10,000 masks that remain in ending inventory.

Step 4: Compute Equivalent-Unit Costs

Short Exercise: Using the data from the previous Short Exercise, compute the unit cost in the Mixing Dept.

A:	Dir. Mtls.	Conv. Costs
WIP, 5/1	$ –0–	$ –0–
Costs added		
during May ...	15,120	27,755
÷ equiv. units ....÷	4,725	÷ 4,550
Cost per equiv.		
unit................	$ 3.20	$ 6.10

In step 2, we computed the number of equivalent units for direct materials (50,000) and conversion costs (42,500). Because their equivalent units differ, a separate cost per unit must be computed for each category. Exhibit 21-5 provides the data. The direct materials cost is $140,000. Conversion cost is $68,000, which is the sum of direct labor ($21,250) and manufacturing overhead ($46,750).

We now have all the data we need to compute the Shaping Department unit costs. We divide the direct materials cost by the equivalent units for direct materials: $140,000/50,000 = $2.80. This amount is the unit cost for direct materials. We compute unit conversion cost in a similar manner: $68,000/42,500 = $1.60. Exhibit 21-6 shows the computation of equivalent-unit costs.

EXHIBIT 21-6

Step 4: Compute Equivalent-Unit Costs

SHAPING DEPARTMENT
FOR THE MONTH ENDED OCTOBER 31, 19XX

	Direct Materials	Conversion Costs
Work in process, September 30	$ –0–	$ –0–
Costs added during October....................	$140,000	$68,000
Divide by equivalent units of production.........	÷50,000	÷42,500
Cost per equivalent unit	$ 2.80	$ 1.60

	Direct Materials	Conversion Costs		Total
Units completed and transferred out (40,000)........	40,000 × $4.40		=	$176,000
Units in ending work in process inventory (10,000):				
Direct materials...............................	10,000 × $2.80		=	$ 28,000
Conversion costs..............................		2,500 × $1.60	=	4,000
Total cost of work in process				32,000
Total cost accounted for.........................				$208,000

EXHIBIT 21-7
Step 5: Apply Costs to Units Completed and to Units in Ending Work in Process Inventory

Step 5: Apply Costs to Units Completed and to Units in Ending Work in Process Inventory

OBJECTIVE 4

Apply costs to units completed and to units in ending work in process inventory

Exhibit 21-7 shows how the equivalent-unit costs computed in step 4 are applied to the equivalent units computed in step 2 (Exhibit 21-4) to cost the 50,000 physical units (swim mask bodies) worked on in the Shaping Department during October.

First consider the 40,000 units completed and transferred out (that is, transferred into the Finishing Department). Exhibit 21-4 reveals 40,000 equivalent units of work for both direct materials and conversion costs. Thus, the total cost of these completed units is (40,000 × $2.80) + (40,000 × $1.60), or simply 40,000 × $4.40 = $176,000. Next consider the 10,000 units still being shaped at the end of the month. These units have 10,000 equivalent units of direct materials (at $2.80 per unit) and 2,500 equivalent units of conversion work (at $1.60 per unit). Exhibit 21-7 uses these amounts to compute the total cost of the ending inventory units as of October 31— $32,000.

The total cost accounted for in step 5, $208,000, is equal to the total cost to account for in step 3.

October production in the Shaping Department is recorded as follows:

Work in Process Inventory—Shaping..	140,000	
Materials Inventory		140,000
Work in Process Inventory—Shaping..	21,250	
Manufacturing Wages		21,250
Work in Process Inventory—Shaping..	46,750	
Manufacturing Overhead		46,750

To requisition materials and apply labor and overhead cost to the Shaping Department (Exhibit 21-5).

The entry to transfer the cost of completed units from the Shaping Department to the Finishing Department is as follows:

Work in Process Inventory—Finishing	176,000	
Work in Process Inventory—Shaping		176,000

After these entries are posted, the Work in Process Inventory—Shaping account appears as follows:

Short Exercise: Compute the total costs of mixing department units completed and ending work in process for the Short Exercise on p. 885. *A:*

Compl. (4,500 × $9.30)	$41,850
End. WIP	
Direct Mat. (225 × $3.20).....................	720
Conv. Costs (50 × $6.10)	305
Total End. WIP	1,025
Total Acc. for	$42,875

"Total [cost] accounted for" of $42,875 agrees with the amount in the previous Short Exercise for "Total costs added during May." You must account for all manufacturing costs.

Short Exercise: Using the data in the previous few Short Exercises, (1) prepare journal entries summarizing these transactions, and (2) prepare the T-account for Work in Process Inventory—Mixing. *A:*

a. To requisition materials:
WIP Inventory— Mixing................	15,120	
Materials Inventory....		15,120

b. To apply labor:
WIP Inventory— Mixing................	11,102	
Man. Wages ...		11,102

(cont.)

c. To apply overhead:
 WIP Inventory—
 Mixing................ 16,653
   Man. Overhead   16,653
d. To transfer the cost of completed units from the Mixing Dept. to the Packaging Dept.:
 WIP Inventory—
 Packaging........... 41,850
   WIP Inventory—
   Mixing........   41,850

Work in Process Inventory—Mixing

Bal., May 1	-0-	Trans. to	
Dir. mtls.	15,120	Packaging	41,850
Dir. labor	11,102		
Man. over.	16,653		
Bal., May 31	1,025		

EXHIBIT 21-8
The Five Steps of Process Costing

Work in Process Inventory—Shaping

Balance, September 30	—	Transferred to Finishing	176,000
Direct materials	140,000		
Direct labor	21,250		
Manufacturing overhead	46,750		
Balance, October 31	32,000		

Exhibit 21-8 summarizes the five steps of process costing.

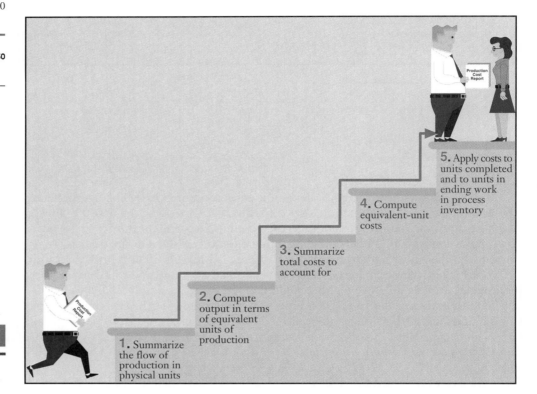

1. Summarize the flow of production in physical units
2. Compute output in terms of equivalent units of production
3. Summarize total costs to account for
4. Compute equivalent-unit costs
5. Apply costs to units completed and to units in ending work in process inventory

MID-CHAPTER SUMMARY PROBLEM FOR YOUR REVIEW

Identify the missing amounts X and Y in the following production cost report prepared by Jacobs-Webster, Inc., for May.

ASSEMBLY DEPARTMENT
PRODUCTION COST REPORT
FOR THE MONTH ENDED MAY 31, 19XX

	Physical Units	Total Costs
Work in process, April 30...	—	$ —
Started in production during May	20,000	43,200*
Total to account for	20,000	$ 43,200
Completed and transferred to Finishing Department during May .	16,000	$ X
Work in process, May 31 (25% complete as to direct materials, 55% complete as to conversion cost)	4,000	Y
Total accounted for...	20,000	$ 43,200

*Includes direct materials of $6,800 and conversion costs of $36,400.

Step 1: Summarize the Flow of Production in Physical Units;
Step 2: Compute Output in Terms of Equivalent Units of Production

ASSEMBLY DEPARTMENT
FOR THE MONTH ENDED MAY 31, 19XX

Flow of Production	Step 1 Flow of Physical Units	Step 2 Equivalent Units of Production — Direct Materials	Step 2 Equivalent Units of Production — Conversion Costs
Units to account for:			
Work in process, April 30	—		
Started in production during May...........................	20,000		
Total physical units to account for	20,000		
Units accounted for:			
Completed and transferred out during May	16,000	16,000	16,000
Work in process, May 31	4,000	1,000*	2,200*
Total physical units accounted for	20,000		
Equivalent units of production..		17,000	18,200

*Direct materials: 4,000 units each 25% complete = 1,000 equivalent units.
Conversion costs: 4,000 units each 55% complete = 2,200 equivalent units.

Step 3: Summarize Total Costs to Account For

ASSEMBLY DEPARTMENT
FOR THE MONTH ENDED MAY 31, 19XX

	Direct Materials	Conversion Costs	Total
Work in process, April 30	$ –0–	$ –0–	$ –0–
Costs added during May.................	6,800	36,400	43,200
Total cost to account for			$43,200

Step 4: Compute Equivalent-Unit Costs

ASSEMBLY DEPARTMENT
FOR THE MONTH ENDED MAY 31, 19XX

	Direct Materials	Conversion Costs
Work in process, April 30	$ –0–	$ –0–
Costs added during May..	$ 6,800	$ 36,400
Divide by equivalent units of production...............	÷17,000	÷18,200
Cost per equivalent unit	$ 0.40	$ 2.00

ASSEMBLY DEPARTMENT FOR THE MONTH ENDED MAY 31, 19XX			
	Direct Materials	Conversion Costs	Total
X Units completed and transferred out (16,000)..	16,000 × $2.40		= $38,400
Units in ending work in process inventory (4,000):			
Direct materials................................	1,000 × $0.40		= 400
Conversion costs		2,200 × $2.00	= 4,400
Y Total cost of work in process			4,800
Total cost accounted for			$43,200

Process Costing for a Second Department—FIFO Method

OBJECTIVE 5

Account for a second processing department by the FIFO method

Most manufacturing systems have multiple processing steps. In this section, we introduce a second department—the Finishing Department of U.S. Divers—to complete the picture of process costing. We also introduce beginning inventories of work in process, a complicating factor that was not present in our examples up to this point.

As in many areas of accounting, there are alternative methods of accounting for process costs. We discuss two: the first-in, first-out (FIFO) method and the weighted-average method. (A third method, standard costing, is covered in cost accounting and advanced managerial accounting texts.) FIFO and weighted-average differ in their treatment of beginning work in process inventory. When there is no beginning inventory, the two methods are identical. They use the same five steps that we applied earlier to U.S. Divers' Shaping Department.

◀▥▥ ◀▥▥ ◀▥▥ In Chapter 9, page 371, we saw that in the FIFO method of inventory costing, the first costs into inventory are the first costs out to COGS.

The **first-in, first out (FIFO) method** of process costing assigns to each period's equivalent units of production that period's costs per equivalent unit. ◀▥▥ Consider swim masks that are transferred to the Finishing Department of U.S. Divers and partially processed in September and then are completed in October. The total Finishing Department cost of the masks is the sum of September's equivalent units costed at September's equivalent-unit costs and October's equivalent units costed at October's equivalent-unit costs.

The Finishing Department smoothes and polishes the shaped swim mask bodies and adds the faceplates to them. The faceplate is the direct material added in the finishing process. Keep in mind that the label *direct materials* in the Finishing Department refers to the faceplates added *in that department* and not to the materials (the plastic) added in the previous department, Shaping. Likewise, *conversion cost* in the Finishing Department refers to all manufacturing costs (other than direct materials) of that department only.

Steps 1 and 2: Summarize the Flow of Production in Physical Units and Compute Output in Terms of Equivalent Units of Production

We assume that 5,000 units were in process in the Finishing Department on October 1. These units were 60 percent complete as to Finishing Department conversion costs but 0 percent complete as to direct materials because the faceplates are added near the end of the finishing process. These facts, used throughout our discussion of the Finishing Department, are summarized in Exhibit 21-9.

EXHIBIT 21-9

Finishing Department Data for October

Units:
  Work in process, September 30
    (0% complete as to direct materials,
    60% complete as to conversion work)............................... 5,000 units
  Transferred in from Shaping Department
    during October .... 40,000 units
  Completed during October .... 38,000 units
  Work in process, October 31 (0% complete as to direct
    materials, 30% complete as to conversion work)............... 7,000 units

Costs:
  Work in process, September 30 .... $ 24,000
    (Transferred-in cost $22,900; conversion costs, $1,100)
  Transferred in from Shaping Department
    during October 176,000
  Direct materials added during October.............................. 19,000
  Conversion costs added during October:
    Direct labor.. $ 3,710
    Manufacturing overhead................................... 11,130   14,840

FINISHING DEPARTMENT
FOR THE MONTH ENDED OCTOBER 31, 19XX

Flow of Production	Step 1 Flow of Physical Units	Step 2 Equivalent Units of Production		
		Transferred In	Direct Materials	Conversion Costs
Units to account for:				
Work in process, September 30	5,000			
Transferred in during October..........................	40,000			
Total physical units to account for	45,000			
Units accounted for:				
Completed and transferred out during October:				
From beginning inventory..............................	5,000	—	5,000*	2,000*
Transferred in and completed during October				
(38,000 – 5,000)	33,000	33,000	33,000	33,000
Work in process, October 31............................	7,000	7,000	— †	2,100†
Total physical units accounted for....................	45,000			
Equivalent units of production..........................		40,000	38,000	37,100

*Direct materials: 5,000 units each 100% completed in Finishing Department during October = 5,000 equivalent units.
 Conversion costs: 5,000 units each 40% completed in Finishing Department during October = 2,000 equivalent units.
†Direct materials: 7,000 units each 0% completed in Finishing Department during October = 0 equivalent units.
 Conversion costs: 7,000 units each 30% completed in Finishing Department during October = 2,100 equivalent units.

A major task in accounting for a second department is the computation of equivalent units of production. Exhibit 21-10 summarizes the flow of physical units (step 1) and tabulates equivalent units (step 2) for the Finishing Department. There are three categories of equivalent units. In addition to equivalent units for direct materials (faceplates) and conversion costs added in the Finishing Department, we must compute equivalent units for the shaped swim masks that are *transferred in* from the Shaping Department. All second and later departments in a production sequence have materials and costs that are transferred in from the preceding department.

The FIFO method of process costing is used in Exhibits 21-10 through 21-14. With FIFO, the focus is on the current period—October in this example. The FIFO method determines October equivalent units of work and costs those units with Oc-

EXHIBIT 21-10

FIFO Method, Step 1: Summarize the Flow of Production in Physical Units; Step 2: Compute Output in Terms of Equivalent Units of Production

Units:

WIP, May 1 (100% complete as to direct mtls.; 50% complete as to conv. costs)............	4,000
Trans. in from Mixing Dept. during May	4,500
Completed during May	7,000
WIP, May 31 (80% complete as to dir. mtls.; 40% complete as to conv. costs)............	1,500

Costs:

WIP, May 1	$ 43,100
Trans. in from Mixing Dept. during May	41,850
Dir. mtls. added—May	1,890
Conv. costs added—May Dir. labor... $10,800 Man. Over. 4,600	15,400
Total cost to acc. for.......	$102,240

Compute the equivalent units. Use FIFO.

A:

	Trans. In	Dir. Mtls.	Conv. Costs
To compl. beg. inv.	0*	0*	2,000
Trans. in & compl. in May (7,000 - 4,000)	3,000	3,000	3,000
WIP, May 31	1,500	1,200	600
Equiv. units	4,500	4,200	5,600

*Since the beginning inventory was 100% complete, no transferred-in costs or materials were added to the beginning inventory.

EXHIBIT 21-11

FIFO Method, Steps 3 and 4: Summarize Total Costs to Account For and Compute Equivalent-Unit Costs

tober unit costs. A major advantage of the FIFO method is that with these current amounts, the efficiency of October production can be judged independently of production efficiency in other months. Current-month data are important for planning and control.

As Exhibit 21-10 shows, the FIFO method distinguishes between two categories of swim masks completed during October: the 5,000 units already in the Finishing Department on October 1 and the 33,000 units that were both transferred in and completed during that month. This distinction is due to FIFO's current-month orientation. All the Finishing Department work on the 33,000 units was done in October, but some of the work on the beginning inventory units was done in September. This key difference in the timing of work affects the equivalent-unit computations in step 2.

The Transferred In column of Exhibit 21-10 shows that 40,000 shaped swim masks were transferred from the Shaping Department to the Finishing Department in October. Of these, 33,000 were completed and 7,000 remain in Finishing on October 31. The Direct Materials column shows that faceplates were added to the 38,000 units completed and transferred out during the month. These completed units include the 5,000 that were in the Finishing Department on October 1 and the 33,000 that were both transferred in and completed. Ending inventory has no direct materials equivalent units.

The equivalent-unit total for conversion costs has three components: beginning work in process inventory, units transferred in and completed during the month, and ending work in process inventory. The beginning inventory of 5,000 units was 60 percent complete as to conversion work when September ended. During October, the Finishing Department completed these 5,000 units by doing the remaining 40 percent of conversion work. For beginning inventory, equivalent production is 2,000 units (5,000 × 0.40). Units transferred in and completed during the month (33,000 units) are the second component of equivalent production. Ending inventory is the third component. At October 31 the inventory of 7,000 units still in process is 30 percent complete as to conversion work, so equivalent production is 2,100 units (7,000 × 0.30). Altogether, October equivalent production for Finishing Department conversion totals 37,100 units (2,000 + 33,000 + 2,100).

Steps 3 and 4: Summarize Total Costs to Account For and Compute Equivalent-Unit Costs

The October costs of the Finishing Department are accumulated as shown in Exhibit 21-11. The exhibit shows how to use equivalent units to compute equivalent-unit costs. The $24,000 beginning balance of work in process is kept separate from the costs incurred during the current period. That is, the $24,000 is not included in the computation of equivalent-unit costs for work done in October. The work in process beginning balance is the cost incurred in *September* on the 5,000 physical units in process on October 1. Under FIFO, each *October* cost per equivalent unit is computed by dividing an October cost by an October number of equivalent units of work.

FINISHING DEPARTMENT				
FOR THE MONTH ENDED OCTOBER 31, 19XX				
	Transferred-In Costs	Direct Materials	Conversion Costs	Total
Work in process, September 30 (from Exhibit 21-9)...............				$ 24,000
Costs added during October (from Exhibit 21-9)...................	$176,000	$ 19,000	$ 14,840	209,840
Divide by equivalent units (from Exhibit 21-10)	÷40,000	÷ 38,000	37,100	
Cost per equivalent unit...	$ 4.40	$ 0.50	$ 0.40	
Total cost to account for				$233,840

Step 5: Apply Costs to Units Completed and to Units in Ending Work in Process Inventory

Exhibit 21-12 shows how to apply the costs of the Finishing Department of U.S. Divers to units completed and transferred to finished goods and to units still in process at the end of the period.

The entries for the Shaping Department were recorded on page 887. The following entries record Finishing Department activity during October.

Work in Process Inventory—Finishing	176,000	
Work in Process Inventory—Shaping		176,000

To transfer in the cost of shaped swim masks from the Shaping Department.

Work in Process Inventory—Finishing	19,000	
Materials Inventory		19,000
Work in Process Inventory—Finishing	3,710	
Manufacturing Wages		3,710
Work in Process Inventory—Finishing	11,130	
Manufacturing Overhead		11,130

To requisition materials and apply conversion costs to the Finishing Department (amounts from Exhibit 21-9).

The entry to transfer the cost of completed units from the Finishing Department to finished goods is based on the dollar amount in Exhibit 21-12:

Finished Goods Inventory	202,200	
Work in Process Inventory—Finishing		202,200

Short Exercise: Using the data in the previous Short Exercises, compute the unit costs in the Packaging Dept. *A:*

	Trans. In	Dir. Mtls.	Conv. Costs
Costs added, May	$41,850	$1,890	$15,400
÷	÷	÷	÷
equiv. units	4,500	4,200	5,600
Cost/equiv. unit	$9.30	$0.45	$2.75

Short Exercise: Apply unit costs to (a) units completed and (b) units in ending work in process, for the previous Short Exercise.

A:

(a) Units completed and
    transferred out to FG:
    From WIP, May 1 .... $ 43,100
    Costs added—May
      Dir. mtls. .... -0-[a]
      Conv. costs .... 5,500[b]
Total completed from
    May 1 inventory 48,600
Units trans. in and
    completed—May .... 37,500[c]
Total costs trans. out 86,100
(b) WIP, May 31
    Trans.-in costs .... 13,950[d]
    Dir. mtls. .... 540[e]
    Conv. costs .... 1,650[f]
Total WIP, May 31 16,140
Total cost acc. for $102,240

[a]0 × $0.45
[b]2,000 × $2.75
[c]3,000 × [$9.30 + $0.45 + $2.75]
[d]1,500 × $9.30
[e]1,200 × $0.45
[f]600 × $2.75

EXHIBIT 21-12

FIFO Method, Step 5: Apply Total Cost to Units Completed and to Units in Ending Work in Process Inventory

FINISHING DEPARTMENT
FOR THE MONTH ENDED OCTOBER 31, 19XX

	Transferred-In Costs	Direct Materials	Conversion Costs	Total
Units completed and transferred out to Finished Goods Inventory:				
From work in process, September 30				$ 24,000
Costs added during October:				
Direct materials		5,000 × $0.50		2,500
Conversion costs			2,000 × $0.40	800
Total completed from September 30 inventory				27,300
Units transferred in and completed during October	33,000 × ($4.40 + $0.50 + $0.40)			174,900
Total cost transferred out				202,200
Work in process, October 31:				
Transferred-in costs	7,000 × $4.40			30,800
Direct materials		—		—
Conversion costs			2,100 × $0.40	840
Total work in process, October 31				31,640
Total cost accounted for				$233,840

1. To requisition materials:
   WIP Inventory—
   Pkg 1,890
       Materials Inventory.   1,890
2. To apply labor:
   WIP Inventory—
   Pkg 10,800
       Manufacturing
       Wages   10,800
3. To apply overhead:
   WIP Inventory—
   Pkg 4,600
       Man. Over.   4,600
4. To transfer complete units:
   Finished Goods
   Inventory..................... 86,100
       WIP Inventory—
       Pkg..........................   86,100

After posting, the key accounts appear as follows. Observe the accumulation of costs as debits to Work in Process Inventory and the transfer of costs from one account to the next.

Work in Process Inventory—Shaping

(Exhibit 21-5)		(Exhibit 21-7)	
Balance, September 30	—	Transferred to Finishing	176,000
Direct materials	140,000		
Direct labor	21,250		
Manufacturing overhead	46,750		
Balance, October 31	32,000		

Work in Process Inventory—Finishing

(Exhibit 21-9)		(Exhibit 21-12)	
Balance, September 30	24,000	Transferred to Finished	
Transferred in from		goods	202,200
Shaping	176,000		
Direct materials	19,000		
Direct labor	3,710		
Manufacturing overhead	11,130		
Balance, October 31	31,640		

Finished Goods Inventory

Balance, September 30	—
Transferred in from	
Finishing	202,200

Production Cost Report

A **production cost report** summarizes the operations of a processing department for the period. Exhibit 21-13 is a FIFO production cost report for the Finishing Department of U.S. Divers for October. It shows the department's beginning inventory, the number of units and the cost transferred in during the month, and the costs added. These amounts make up the totals to account for. The report also shows the units completed, the costs transferred out of the department, and the ending inventory.

Production cost reports vary from company to company, depending on the level of detail desired by the managers. If managers want more detail, some or all of the additional information in Exhibits 21-10, 21-11, and 21-12 can be included. For example, Exhibit 21-14 provides more detail about costs than does Exhibit 21-13.

EXHIBIT 21-13
FIFO Method Production Cost Report

FINISHING DEPARTMENT PRODUCTION COST REPORT FOR THE MONTH ENDED OCTOBER 31, 19XX	Physical Units	Total Costs
Work in process, September 30...	5,000	$ 24,000
Transferred in from Shaping Department during October...............	40,000	176,000
Costs added in Finishing Department during October:		
Direct materials...	—	19,000
Conversion costs ($3,710 + $11,130)...................................	—	14,840
Total to account for...	45,000	$233,840
Completed and transferred to finished goods during October	38,000	$202,200
Work in process, October 31...	7,000	31,640
Total accounted for	45,000	$233,840

EXHIBIT 21-14 *FIFO Method Production Cost Report (Expanded)*

FINISHING DEPARTMENT
PRODUCTION COST REPORT (EXPANDED)
FOR THE MONTH ENDED OCTOBER 31, 19XX

	Transferred-In Costs	Direct Materials	Conversion Costs	Total
Work in process, September 30..				$ 24,000
Costs added during October...	$176,000	$19,000	$ 14,840	209,840
Total cost to account for				$233,840
Equivalent units of production	÷40,000	÷38,000	÷37,100	
Cost per equivalent unit...	$ 4.40	$ 0.50	$ 0.40	
Application of total costs:				
Units completed during October:				
From work in process, September 30				$ 24,000
Costs added during October......................................		5,000 × $0.50 = $2,500	2,000 × $0.40 = $800	3,300
Total completed from September 30 inventory..............				27,300
Units transferred in and completed during October........	33,000 × ($4.40 + $0.50 + $0.40)			174,900
Total completed and transferred out				202,200
Work in process, October 31:				
Transferred-in costs...	7,000 × $4.40			30,800
Direct materials...		—		—
Conversion costs.			2,100 × $0.40	840
Total work in process, October 31.................................				31,640
Total cost accounted for..				$233,840

How is the production cost report used for decision making? U.S. Divers managers compare actual direct materials and conversion costs—particularly the unit costs in Exhibit 21-14—with budgeted amounts for the department. If these costs are too high, corrective action may be taken. If costs are below budget, the employees responsible may receive incentive awards.

Managers also compare the number of units produced with budgeted production. Production that is too low can be investigated and corrected. If production in excess of the budget is welcomed, such performance may lead to rewards for high-achieving employees.

"U.S. Divers managers compare actual direct materials and conversion costs . . . with budgeted amounts for the department."

Process Costing for a Second Department— Weighted-Average Method

We now rework our Finishing Department example to demonstrate the second process costing method, weighted-average. We learned that the FIFO method assigns costs to (1) physical units completed and transferred out and (2) work in process ending inventory by costing equivalent units of work done each period with that period's unit costs. In contrast, the **weighted-average method** costs all equivalent units of work to account for each period with a weighted average of that period's and the previous period's costs per equivalent unit. Exhibits 21-15 through 21-19 are the weighted-average equivalents of Exhibits 21-10 through 21-14. We apply the weighted-average method with the same five steps that we used with FIFO.

Recall from Chapter 9, page 371, that the weighted-average method of inventory costing is based on the weighted-average cost (cost of goods available for sale/units available).

Steps 1 and 2: Summarize the Flow of Production in Physical Units and Compute Output in Terms of Equivalent Units of Production

Exhibit 21-15 shows that 38,000 units were completed and transferred out of the Finishing Department in October. The full 38,000 equivalent units of production are assigned to these physical units in each step 2 cost category. Why? Because by October 31, all these units had been transferred into Finishing from Shaping, face-plates had been added to all of them, and all the finishing conversion work had been done. The equivalent units for ending inventory of work in process are the same with the weighted-average method as with FIFO. All the Finishing Department work done on these 7,000 units by October 31 was done in October, because they were among the 40,000 units transferred in from Shaping during that month.

STOP & THINK Suppose that you know the weighted-average equivalent-unit totals in Exhibit 21-15. How can you use these amounts to compute FIFO equivalent units for October?

Answer: Weighted-average equivalent units of work are the sum of the current-month (FIFO) equivalent units and equivalent units already in the process when the current month began. The Finishing Department inventory on October 1 consisted of 5,000 physical units that were 0 percent complete as to direct materials and 60 percent complete as to conversion work. Thus, on October 1, 5,000 transferred-in equivalent units, zero direct-materials equivalent units, and 3,000 (5,000 × 0.60) conversion equivalent units were in the finishing process. FIFO equivalent units can be computed as follows:

Short Exercise: Using the data from the previous Short Exercises, apply the weighted-average method to a second department. Compute equivalent units.

A:

	Trans. In	Dir. Mat.	Conv. Costs
Trans. out	7,000	7,000	7,000
WIP, end.	1,500	1,200	600
Equiv. units	8,500	8,200	7,600

Equivalent Units of Production

	Transferred In	Direct Materials	Conversion Costs
Weighted-average totals	45,000	38,000	40,100
October 1 work in process inventory	5,000	0	3,000
FIFO totals	40,000	38,000	37,100

The FIFO totals can be seen in Exhibit 21-10.

EXHIBIT 21-15

*Weighted-Average Method, Step 1: Summarize the Flow of Production in Physical Units;
Step 2: Compute Output in Terms of Equivalent Units of Production*

	Step 1	Step 2 Equivalent Units of Production		
FINISHING DEPARTMENT FOR THE MONTH ENDED OCTOBER 31, 19XX				
Flow of Production	Flow of Physical Units	Transferred In	Direct Materials	Conversion Costs
Units to account for:				
Work in process, September 30	5,000			
Transferred in during October	40,000			
Total physical units to account for	45,000			
Units accounted for:				
Completed and transferred out during October	38,000	38,000	38,000*	38,000*
Work in process, October 31	7,000	7,000	—†	2,100†
Total physical units accounted for	45,000			
Equivalent units of production		45,000	38,000	40,100

*Direct materials: 38,000 units each 100% completed in Finishing Department by October 31 = 38,000 equivalent units.
Conversion costs: 38,000 units each 100% completed in Finishing Department by October 31 = 38,000 equivalent units.
†Direct materials: 7,000 units each 0% completed in Finishing Department by October 31 = 0 equivalent units.
Conversion costs: 7,000 units each 30% completed in Finishing Department by October 31 = 2,100 equivalent units.

FINISHING DEPARTMENT
FOR THE MONTH ENDED OCTOBER 31, 19XX

	Transferred-In Costs	Direct Materials	Conversion Costs	Total
Work in process, September 30	$ 22,900	$ —	$ 1,100	$ 24,000
Costs added during October (from Exhibit 21-9)	176,000	19,000	14,840	209,840
Total cost	$198,900	$ 19,000	$ 15,940	
Divide by equivalent units (from Exhibit 21-15)	÷45,000	÷38,000	÷40,100	
Cost per equivalent unit	$ 4.42	$ 0.50	$ 0.3975	
Total cost to account for				$233,840

Step 3: Summarize Total Costs to Account For

The total cost to account for (Exhibit 21-16) is the sum of work in process beginning inventory cost ($24,000) and the costs added to the Work in Process—Finishing account during October ($209,840). The total is $233,840.

Step 4: Compute Equivalent-Unit Costs

The numerators and denominators of the weighted-average unit-cost calculations include both current-month amounts and amounts from October's beginning work in process inventory. In our example, the resulting unit costs are weighted averages of September unit costs and October unit costs. The computations are shown in Exhibit 21-16. Consider conversion costs. The $1,100 cost of the 3,000 equivalent units of conversion work in October 1 work in process is added to the $14,840 cost of the 37,100 equivalent units of October conversion work. The sum, $15,940, is divided by the sum of the equivalent units, 40,100 (3,000 + 37,100). The resulting cost of $0.3975 is a weighted average of September's unit cost of $0.3667 ($1,100/3,000) and October's unit cost of $0.40 ($14,840/37,100).

Step 5: Apply Total Cost to Units Completed and to Units in Ending Work in Process Inventory

With the weighted-average method, the 38,000 physical units completed and transferred out of the Finishing Department of U.S. Divers are costed in one step. The 38,000 equivalent units are multiplied by the full equivalent-unit cost of $5.3175 ($4.42 + $0.50 + $0.3975). The result is $202,065 (Exhibit 21-17). Equivalent units in October 31 work in process inventory also are costed at the appropriate unit amounts.

EXHIBIT 21-16
*Weighted-Average Method,
Step 3: Summarize Total Costs to
Account For;
Step 4: Compute Equivalent-Unit
Costs*

Short Exercise: Assume that
the beginning inventory for the
previous Short Exercises consisted of $1,800 of materials,
$4,100 of conversion costs, and
$37,200 of transferred-in costs.
Compute unit costs.

A:

	Trans. In	Dir. Mat.	Conv. Costs
Beg. WIP	$37,200	$1,800	$ 4,100
Costs added	41,850	1,890	15,400
Total cost	$79,050	$3,690	$19,500
Equiv. units	8,500	8,200	7,600
Unit cost	$ 9.30	$ 0.45	$2.5658

	Total
Beg. WIP	$ 43,100
Costs added	59,140
Total cost	$102,240

EXHIBIT 21-17
*Weighted-Average Method,
Step 5: Apply Costs to Units
Completed and to Units in Ending
Work in Process Inventory*

FINISHING DEPARTMENT
FOR THE MONTH ENDED OCTOBER 31, 19XX

	Transferred-In Costs	Direct Materials	Conversion Costs	Total
Units completed and transferred out to Finished Goods Inventory	38,000 × ($4.42 + $0.50 + $0.3975)			$202,065
Work in process, October 31:				
Transferred-in costs	7,000 × $4.42			30,940
Direct materials		—		—
Conversion costs			2,100 × $0.3975	835
Total work in process, October 31				31,775
Total cost accounted for				$233,840

FINISHING DEPARTMENT PRODUCTION COST REPORT FOR THE MONTH ENDED OCTOBER 31, 19XX	Physical Units	Total Costs
Work in process, September 30...	5,000	$ 24,000
Transferred in from Shaping Department during October....................	40,000	176,000
Costs added in Finishing Department during October:		
Direct materials..	—	19,000
Conversion costs ($3,710 + $11,130).................................	—	14,840
Total to account for..	45,000	$233,840
Completed and transferred to finished goods during October	38,000	$202,065
Work in process, October 31..	7,000	31,775
Total accounted for	45,000	$233,840

Short Exercise: Apply unit costs for the previous Short Exercises to (a) units completed and (b) units in End. WIP.

A:

Units completed and trans. out
[7,000 × ($9.30 +
$0.45 + $2.5658)]... $ 86,211

End. WIP
Trans. in (1,500 ×
$9.30)................ $13,950
Mat. (1,200 × $0.45)   540
Conv. costs
(600 × 2.5658).....   1,539   16,029

Total cost accounted
for........................ $102,240

The weighted-average production cost reports in Exhibit 21-18 and 21-19 are similar to their FIFO counterparts, Exhibits 21-13 and 21-14. They too may signal the need for action if actual costs or production quantities differ materially from budgeted amounts. But their reported unit costs are not as useful for evaluating the efficiency of October production because they are affected by the costs incurred in September. Even so, managers may use the weighted-average method because (1) the computations are simpler than those of the FIFO method and (2) the differences in costs assigned to units often are immaterial.

CONCEPT HIGHLIGHT

EXHIBIT 21-19
Weighted-Average Method Production Cost Report (Expanded)

FINISHING DEPARTMENT PRODUCTION COST REPORT (EXPANDED) FOR THE MONTH ENDED OCTOBER 31, 19XX	Transferred-In Costs	Direct Materials	Conversion Costs	Total
Work in process, September 30...............................	$ 22,900	$ —	$ 1,100	$ 24,000
Costs added during October.................................	176,000	19,000	14,840	209,840
Total cost to account for	$198,900	$19,000	$ 15,940	$233,840
Equivalent units of production	÷45,000	÷38,000	÷ 40,100	
Cost per equivalent unit...................................	$ 4.42	$ 0.50	$ 0.3975	
Application of total costs:				
Units completed during October		38,000 × ($4.42 + $0.50 + $0.3975)		$202,065
Work in process, October 31:				
Transferred-in costs	7,000 × $4.42			30,940
Direct materials..		—		—
Conversion costs			2,100 × $0.3975	835
Total work in process, October 31.........................				31,775
Total cost accounted for...................................				$233,840

This problem extends the Mid-Chapter Summary Problem on page 888 to a second processing department. During May, Jacobs-Webster, Inc., has the following activity in its Finishing Department:

Finishing Department Facts for May

Units:	
Work in process, April 30 (20% complete as to direct materials, 70% complete as to conversion work)...	4,000 units
Transferred in from Assembly Department during May	16,000 units
Completed during May..	15,000 units
Work in process, May 31 (36% complete as to direct materials, 80% complete as to conversion work)...	5,000 units
Costs:	
Work in process, April 30	$18,000
(Transferred-in costs, $11,982; direct materials costs, $488; conversion costs, $5,530)	
Transferred in from Assembly Department during May	38,400
Direct materials added during May...	6,400
Conversion costs added during May	24,300

Required

Show the allocation of total cost to units completed and to units in ending work in process inventory for the Finishing Department in May. Use

1. The FIFO method.
2. The weighted-average method.

SOLUTION TO REVIEW PROBLEM

1. The FIFO method

Step 1: Summarize the Flow of Production in Physical Units;
Step 2: Compute Output in Terms of Equivalent Units of Production

FINISHING DEPARTMENT
FOR THE MONTH ENDED MAY 31, 19XX

	Step 1	Step 2 Equivalent Units of Production		
Flow of Production	Flow of Physical Units	Transferred In	Direct Materials	Conversion Costs
Units to account for:				
Work in process, April 30..............................	4,000			
Transferred in during May	16,000			
Total physical units to account for	20,000			
Units accounted for:				
Completed and transferred out during May:				
From beginning inventory.............................	4,000	—	3,200*	1,200*
Transferred in and completed during May (16,000 − 5,000)	11,000	11,000	11,000	11,000
Work in process, May 31	5,000	5,000	1,800†	4,000†
Total physical units accounted for	20,000			
Equivalent units of production..........................		16,000	16,000	16,200

*Direct materials: 4,000 units each 80% completed = 3,200 equivalent units.
Conversion costs: 4,000 units each 30% completed = 1,200 equivalent units.
†Direct materials: 5,000 units each 36% completed = 1,800 equivalent units.
Conversion costs: 5,000 units each 80% completed = 4,000 equivalent units.

Step 3: Summarize Total Costs to Account For; Step 4: Compute Equivalent-Unit Costs

FINISHING DEPARTMENT
FOR THE MONTH ENDED MAY 31, 19XX

	Transferred-In Costs	Direct Materials	Conversion Costs	Total
Work in process, April 30..............				$ 18,000
Costs added during May................	$ 38,400	$ 6,400	$ 24,300	69,100
Divide by equivalent units............	÷ 16,000	÷ 16,000	÷ 16,200	
Cost per equivalent unit	$ 2.40	$ 0.40	$ 1.50	
Total cost to account for...............				$ 87,100

Step 5: Apply Costs to Units Completed and to Units in Ending Work in Process Inventory

FINISHING DEPARTMENT
FOR THE MONTH ENDED MAY 31, 19XX

	Transferred-In Costs	Direct Materials	Conversion Costs	Total
Units completed and transferred out to Finished Goods Inventory:				
From work in process, April 30...				$18,000
Costs added during May:				
Direct materials...		3,200 × $0.40		1,280
Conversion costs...			1,200 × $1.50	1,800
Total completed from April 30 inventory........................				21,080
Units transferred in and completed during May.................	11,000 × ($2.40 + $0.40 + $1.50)			47,300
Total cost transferred out..				68,380
Work in process, May 31:				
Transferred-in costs	5,000 × $2.40			12,000
Direct materials..		1,800 × $0.40		720
Conversion costs			4,000 × $1.50	6,000
Total work in process, May 31				18,720
Total cost accounted for...				$87,100

2. The weighted-average method

Step 1: Summarize the Flow of Production in Physical Units;
Step 2: Compute Output in Terms of Equivalent Units of Production

FINISHING DEPARTMENT
FOR THE MONTH ENDED MAY 31, 19XX

	Step 1	Step 2 Equivalent Units of Production		
Flow of Production	**Flow of Physical Units**	**Transferred In**	**Direct Materials**	**Conversion Costs**
Units to account for:				
Work in process, April 30............................	4,000			
Transferred in during May	16,000			
Total physical units to account for	20,000			
Units accounted for:				
Completed and transferred out during May...............	15,000	15,000	15,000	15,000
Work in process, May 31	5,000	5,000	1,800*	4,000*
Total physical units accounted for................	20,000			
Equivalent units of production........................		20,000	16,800	19,000

*Direct materials: 5,000 units each 36% completed = 1,800 equivalent units.
Conversion costs: 5,000 units each 80% completed = 4,000 equivalent units.

900

Step 3: Summarize Total Costs to Account For; Step 4: Compute Equivalent-Unit Costs

FINISHING DEPARTMENT
FOR THE MONTH ENDED MAY 31, 19XX

	Transferred-In Cost	Direct Materials	Conversion Costs	Total
Work in process, April 30.............	$ 11,982	$ 488	$ 5,530	$18,000
Costs added during May...............	38,400	6,400	24,300	69,100
Total cost......................................	$ 50,382	$ 6,888	$ 29,830	
Divide by equivalent units............	÷ 20,000	÷ 16,800	÷ 19,000	
Cost per equivalent unit	$ 2.5191	$ 0.41	$ 1.57	
Total cost to account for...............				$87,100

Step 5: Apply Costs to Units Completed and to Units in Ending Work in Process Inventory

FINISHING DEPARTMENT
FOR THE MONTH ENDED MAY 31, 19XX

	Transferred-In Cost	Direct Materials	Conversion Costs	Total
Units completed and transferred out to Finished Goods Inventory.........................	15,000 × ($2.5191 + $0.41 + $1.57)			$67,486
Work in process, May 31:				
Transferred-in costs...................	5,000 × $2.5191			12,596
Direct materials.........................		1,800 × $0.41		738
Conversion costs........................			4,000 × $1.57	6,280
Total work in process, May 31...				19,614
Total cost accounted for				$87,100

SUMMARY

1. Distinguish process costing from job order costing. *Process costing* is a system for assigning costs to goods that are produced in a continuous sequence of steps, or processes. Process costing is used by companies that mass produce identical goods in large quantities. Job order costing is for companies that produce custom goods in relatively small quantities. In process costing systems, costs are accumulated by processing departments and flow from one department to another until the product is completed. In contrast, in job order systems, costs are accumulated on job cost records.

2. Record process costing transactions. Journal entries in a process costing system are like those in a job order system, with one key exception: A job order system typically uses one Work in Process Inventory account, but a process costing system uses one such account for each processing department. Direct materials and conversion (direct labor and overhead) costs are debited to the Work in Process Inventory accounts of the individual processing departments in which the costs are incurred. As goods move from one department to the next, the Work in Process Inventory account of the receiving department is debited and the account of the transferring department is credited. After processing is completed, the cost of the goods

moves with them into Finished Goods Inventory and Cost of Goods Sold.

3. Compute equivalent units of production. The main accounting task in process costing is to determine, for each department, the costs assigned to (1) units of product completed and transferred out during a production period (either into the next process or into finished goods inventory) and (2) ending inventory of work in process. A complication arises because goods in process may be in various stages of completion. To help them assign costs to the two categories of output units, accountants compute *equivalent units of production*—the amount of work expressed in terms of fully completed units of output. Equivalent units are computed for each input cost category.

4. Apply costs to units completed and to units in ending work in process inventory. Accounting for a department's costs is a five-step procedure. First, the flow of production in physical (output) units is determined. Second, equivalent units of production are computed for units completed and transferred out and for ending work in process inventory. Third, the total cost to account for is determined by adding the beginning balance of work in process to costs incurred during the current period. Fourth, unit costs are computed for each input category. And fifth, physical units are costed by multiplying equivalent units of production from step 2 by equivalent-unit costs from step 4.

5. Account for a second processing department by the FIFO method. *FIFO*, one of two methods that are widely used for process costing, focuses on current-period work. With this method, equivalent units of work performed in the current month are costed at current-month unit costs.

6. Account for a second processing department by the weighted-average method. The *weighted-average method* costs all work to account for each month—work in process at the beginning of the month and the current month's work—with unit costs that are a weighted average of current- and prior-month costs. In both methods, the operations of processing departments are summarized in monthly *production cost reports*. Managers compare the actual costs in the reports with budgeted costs to evaluate processing performance.

SELF-STUDY QUESTIONS

Test your understanding of the chapter by marking the best answer to each of the following questions.

1. For which of the following products is a process costing system most appropriate? (*p. 880*)
   a. Breakfast cereal   c. Houses
   b. Automobiles   d. Furniture

2. A key difference between job order costing and process costing is that (*p. 883*)
   a. Costs are assigned to direct materials in job order costing and to indirect materials in process costing
   b. Job order costing uses a single Work in Process Inventory account and process costing uses a separate Work in Process Inventory account for each department
   c. Job order costing, but not process costing, accounts for conversion costs
   d. Manufacturing overhead is accounted for in process costing but not in job order costing

3. During August, the Assembly Department of Fisk Manufacturing Company completed and transferred 20,000 intercom units to the Finishing Department. The Assembly Department's August 31 inventory included 6,000 units, 90 percent complete as to direct materials and 75 percent complete as to conversion work. August equivalent units of the Assembly Department total (*p. 885*)
   a. 20,000
   b. 24,500
   c. 25,400
   d. 25,400 for direct materials and 24,500 for conversion costs

4. The concept of equivalent units is useful for (*p. 886*)
   a. Measuring the total costs of direct materials and conversion incurred in a processing department
   b. Measuring the unit costs of direct materials and conversion to compute the cost of goods transferred from one processing department to the next
   c. Separating the cost of a manufacturing *process* from the cost of a manufacturing *activity*
   d. Dividing ending inventory between finished goods and work in process

5. The entry to record the transfer of goods from the Heating Department to the Drying Department is (*p. 887*)
   a. Finished Goods XXX
         Work in Process—Drying.......... XXX
   b. Work in Process—Heating............ XXX
         Work in Process—Drying.......... XXX
   c. Work in Process—Heating............ XXX
         Finished Goods XXX

   d. Work in Process—Drying.............. XXX
         Work in Process—Heating........ XXX

6. The costs to account for in a second processing department include those associated with (*p. 892*)
   a. Beginning work in process and goods transferred in during the period
   b. Beginning work in process and costs added during the period
   c. Beginning work in process, goods transferred in, and goods transferred out
   d. Beginning work in process and ending work in process

7. Refer to the production cost report in Exhibit 21-13. The unit cost of goods completed and transferred to finished goods during October was (*p. 894*)
   a. $4.40   c. $4.90
   b. $4.80   d. $5.32

8. If you already know equivalent units for transferred-in costs, direct materials costs, and conversion costs under FIFO, what is the easiest way to compute equivalent units under the weighted-average method? (*p. 896*)
   a. Add the equivalent units in beginning work in process inventory to the FIFO equivalent units
   b. Subtract the equivalent units in beginning work in process inventory from the FIFO equivalent units
   c. Add the equivalent units in ending work in process inventory to the FIFO equivalent units
   d. Subtract the equivalent units in ending work in process inventory from the FIFO equivalent units

9. If direct materials are added at the beginning of a second processing department, direct materials equivalent units for that department are (*p. 892*)
   a. Less than transferred-in equivalent units
   b. Equal to transferred-in equivalent units
   c. Greater than transferred-in equivalent units
   d. Always equal to the number of physical units transferred in currently, regardless of whether FIFO or weighted-average is used

10. An advantage of the FIFO method over the weighted-average method is that (*p. 898*)
   a. Its computations are simpler
   b. It is more useful for income determination
   c. It is more useful for inventory valuation
   d. It is more useful for evaluating manufacturing performance

Answers to the Self-Study Questions follow the Accounting Vocabulary.

ACCOUNTING VOCABULARY

Equivalent units. A measure of the amount of work done during a production period, expressed in terms of fully complete units of output *(p. 884)*.

First-in, first-out (FIFO) method. A process costing method that assigns to each period's equivalent units of production that period's costs per equivalent unit *(p. 890)*.

Process costing. System for assigning costs to goods that are mass produced in a continuous sequence of steps *(p. 880)*.

Production cost report. Summary of the activity in a processing department for a period *(p. 894)*.

Weighted-average method. A process costing method that costs all equivalent units of work to account for each period with a weighted average of that period's and the previous period's costs per equivalent unit *(p. 895)*.

ANSWERS TO SELF-STUDY QUESTIONS

1. a
2. b
3. d   Direct materials: 20,000 + (6,000 × 0.90) = 25,400
    Conversion costs: 20,000 + (6,000 × 0.75) = 24,500
4. b
5. d

6. b
7. d $202,200/38,000 = $5.32
8. a
9. b
10. d

QUESTIONS

1. Distinguish a process cost accounting system from a job order system.
2. Which type of costing system—job order or process—would be better suited to account for manufacture of each of the following products: (a) chemicals, (b) automobiles, (c) lumber, (d) hand-held calculators, (e) custom lampshades?
3. Why does a process costing system use multiple Work in Process Inventory accounts but a job order system use only one such account?
4. Give the entries (accounts only) to record the following: (a) purchase of materials; (b) incurrence of labor; (c) incurrence of manufacturing overhead cost; (d) requisition of materials and application of labor and overhead to Work in Process Inventory—Department 1 (combine in one entry); (e) transfer of cost of work in process inventory from Department 1 to Department 2; (f) transfer of cost of completed units to finished goods; (g) cost of goods sold.
5. What is an equivalent unit of production? Give an example of equivalent units.
6. Montague Manufacturing Company completed and transferred 35,000 units of its product to a second department during the period. At the end of the period, another 10,000 units were in work in process inventory, 20 percent complete. How many equivalent units did Montague produce during the period?
7. Outline the five steps of process cost accounting.
8. How are equivalent units used in Exhibits 21-6 and 21-7?

9. Why might a company have different numbers of equivalent units for direct materials and conversion costs?
10. What information does a production cost report give? Why does the format of the report differ from company to company?
11. What is the major accounting challenge in a process costing system that has more than one processing department? Why is this such a challenge?
12. Using the FIFO method, compute the equivalent units of production for Department 2 during July:

    Units:
    Work in process, June 30 (10% complete as to direct materials, 40% complete as to conversion costs) .... 1,000 units
    Transferred in from Department 1 during July .... 25,000 units
    Completed during July .... 22,000 units
    Work in process, July 31 (20% complete as to direct materials, 70% complete as to conversion costs).............................. 4,000 units

13. Repeat Question 12, using the weighted-average method.
14. Under what conditions are FIFO equivalent-unit costs equal to weighted-average equivalent-unit costs?
15. "Unit costs in process costing are averages, but that is not true in job order costing." Do you agree or disagree? Explain.

EXERCISES

E21-1 Vines & Crocker manufactures furniture in a three-stage process that includes milling, assembling, and finishing, in that order. Direct materials are added in the Milling and Finishing Departments. Direct labor and overhead are applied in those two departments and in the Assembling Department. The company's general ledger includes the following accounts:

Diagramming flows through a process costing system
(Obj. 1)

Work in Process Inventory—Finishing
Raw Materials Inventory
Finished Goods Inventory
Manufacturing Overhead

Cost of Goods Sold
Manufacturing Wages
Work in Process Inventory—Milling
Work in Process Inventory—Assembling

Outline the flow of costs through the company's accounts. Include a T-account for each account title given.

Computing equivalent units in a single department
(Obj. 3)

E21-2 Insert the missing values:

Flow of Production	Flow of Physical Units	Equivalent Units of Production	
		Direct Materials	Conversion Costs
Units to account for:			
Work in process, November 30............................	14,000		
Started in production during December..............	X		
Total physical units to account for	67,000		
Units accounted for:			
Completed and transferred out during December:			
From beginning inventory.................................	14,000	X*	X*
Started and completed during December	47,000	X	X
Work in process, December 31	X	X†	X†
Total physical units accounted for........................	67,000		
Equivalent units of production.................................		X	X

*Direct materials: 40% completed during December.
 Conversion costs: 50% completed during December.
†Direct materials: 20% completed during December.
 Conversion costs: 30% completed during December.

Computing equivalent units and applying costs to completed units and to work in process inventory
(Obj. 3, 4, 5)

E21-3 Alioto Industries, Inc., experienced the following activity in its Finishing Department during December.

Units:
  Work in process, November 30 (60% complete as to
    direct materials, 80% complete as to conversion work)................. 8,000 units
  Transferred in from Heating Department during December............ 31,000 units
  Completed during December.. 26,000 units
  Work in process, December 31 (60% complete as to
    direct materials, 80% complete as to conversion work)................. 13,000 units
Costs:
  Work in process, November 30 .... $ 59,000
  Transferred in from Heating Department during December........... 102,300
  Direct materials added during December... 72,500
  Conversion costs added during December 102,000

Required

1. Compute the number of equivalent units produced by the Finishing Department during December. Use the FIFO method.

2. Compute unit costs, and apply total cost to (a) units completed and transferred to finished goods and (b) units in December 31 work in process inventory.

Computing equivalent units and applying costs to completed units and to work in process inventory
(Obj. 3, 4, 6)

E21-4 Repeat Exercise 21-3, using the weighted-average method. Assume that the November 30 balance of Work in Process—Finishing Department ($59,000) is composed of the following amounts: transferred-in costs, $26,050; direct materials costs, $12,676; and conversion costs, $20,274.

E21-5 The Forming Department of a chemical company began February with no work in process inventory. During the month, production that cost $36,550 (direct materials, $8,550, and conversion costs, $28,000) was started on 21,000 units. A total of 17,000 units were completed and transferred to the Heating Department. The ending work in process inventory was 50 percent complete as to direct materials and 75 percent complete as to conversion work.

Transferring costs between processing departments
(Obj, 2, 3, 4)

Required

1. Journalize the transfer of cost from the Forming Department to the Heating Department.
2. What is the balance in Work in Process Inventory—Forming on February 28?
3. Account for the total cost incurred during February.

E21-6 The following information was taken from the ledger of Jackston Products. Ending inventory is 70 percent complete as to direct materials but 40 percent complete as to conversion work.

Computing processing costs and journalizing cost transfers
(Obj. 2, 3)

Work in Process—Forming

	Physical Units	Dollars		Physical Units	Dollars
Inventory, November 30	–0–	$ –0–	Transferred to Finishing	72,000	$?
Production started:	80,000				
Direct materials		271,600			
Conversion costs		240,640			
Ending Inventory	8,000	?			

Journalize the transfer of cost to the Finishing Department.

E21-7 Selected production and cost data of Sanchez, Inc., follow for May 19X5:

Computing equivalent units in two departments
(Obj, 3, 5)

	Flow of Physical Units	
Flow of Production	**Sanding Department**	**Finishing Department**
Units to account for:		
Work in process, April 30	20,000	6,000
Transferred in during May...............................	70,000	80,000
Total physical units to account for..................	90,000	86,000
Units accounted for:		
Completed and transferred out during May:		
From beginning inventory	20,000*	6,000‡
Transferred in and completed during May	60,000	75,000
Work in process, May 31	10,000†	5,000§
Total physical units accounted for	90,000	86,000

*Direct materials: 20% completed during May.   ‡Direct materials: 2/3 completed during May.
 Conversion costs: 30% completed during May.   Conversion costs: 40% completed during May.
†Direct materials: 50% completed during May.   §Direct materials: 50% completed during May.
 Conversion costs: 40% completed during May.   Conversion costs: 60% completed during May.

Use the FIFO method to compute equivalent units for transferred-in cost, direct materials, and conversion costs for each department.

E21-8 Repeat Exercise 21-7 for the Finishing Department, using the weighted-average method.

Computing equivalent units in a second department (Obj. 3, 6)

E21-9 Record the following process cost accounting transactions in the general journal:

Journalizing process costing transactions
(Obj. 2)

a. Purchase of raw materials on account, $4,300.
b. Requisition of direct materials to Processing Department 1, $1,800.
c. Payment of manufacturing labor, $11,000.
d. Incurrence of manufacturing overhead costs: depreciation, $600; insurance, $500; utilities paid, $900.

e. Application of conversion costs to Processing Department 1: direct labor, $1,900; manufacturing overhead, $2,850.

f. Transfer of cost from Processing Department 1 to Department 2, $5,300.

g. Application of conversion costs to Processing Department 2: direct labor, $700; manufacturing overhead, $1,050.

h. Transfer of cost from Processing Department 2 to finished goods, $5,200.

Using a production cost report
(Obj. 2)

E21-10 Cost accountants for West Bank Manufacturing prepared the following production cost report for February:

FINISHING DEPARTMENT
PRODUCTION COST REPORT
FOR THE MONTH ENDED FEBRUARY 28, 19XX

	Physical Units	Total Costs
Work in process, January 31	14,000	$ 82,000
Transferred in from Grinding Department during February	90,000	400,000
Costs added in Finishing Department during February:		
Direct materials	—	58,000
Conversion costs:		
Direct labor	—	84,000
Manufacturing overhead	—	83,000
Total to account for	104,000	$707,000
Completed and transferred to finished goods during February	95,000	$658,000
Work in process, February 28	9,000	49,000
Total accounted for	104,000	$707,000

Journalize all February activity in the Finishing Department.

CHALLENGE EXERCISE

Using equivalent units to determine the physical flow of production
(Obj. 5, 6)

E21-11 The following data pertain to the Cooking Department of Green Meadow Farms, Inc., for the month of April 19X4:

	Equivalent Units		
Method	Transferred In	Direct Materials	Conversion Costs
Weighted-average	420,000	420,000	417,500
FIFO	400,000	420,000	412,500

Direct materials are added when conversion is 50-percent complete in the cooking process. The number of physical units completed and transferred out during April was 410,000.

Required

1. How many physical units were transferred in to the Cooking Department in April?
2. How many physical units were in the month's beginning work in process inventory?
3. How many physical units were both transferred in and completed in April?
4. How many physical units were in the ending work in process inventory?
5. What fraction of the total required conversion work was done on the beginning work in process inventory in March? That is, at what percentage of completion were the beginning inventory units on April 1?
6. What fraction of the total required conversion work was done on the ending work in process inventory in April?

PROBLEMS

P21-1A   Western Wildlife Specialties engraves and prints specialty books on wildlife. Production occurs in three processes: engraving, printing, and binding. The Engraving Department was idle on May 31. In mid-June, Western started production on 65,000 books. Of this number, 52,600 books were engraved during June. The June 30 work in process in the Engraving Department was 20 percent complete as to direct materials and 50 percent complete as to conversion work. Direct materials costing $137,700 were placed in production in Engraving during June, and direct labor of $43,140 and manufacturing overhead of $80,340 were applied in that department.

Computing equivalent units and applying cost to completed units and work in process; no beginning inventory or cost transferred in
(Obj. 3, 4)

Required

1. Compute the number of equivalent units of production and the unit costs in the Engraving Department for June.
2. Show the application of total cost in the Engraving Department to (a) units completed and transferred to Printing during June and (b) units still in process at June 30.
3. Prepare a T-account for Work in Process Inventory—Engraving to show its activity during June, including the June 30 balance.

P21-2A   Gotham Newsprint, Inc., manufactures the paper on which newspapers are printed by a four-stage process that includes mixing, cooking, rolling, and cutting. In the Mixing Department, wood pulp and chemicals, the basic raw materials, are blended. The resulting mix is heated in the Cooking Department in much the same way food is prepared. Then the cooked mix is rolled to produce sheets. The final process, cutting, divides the sheets into large rolled units.

Cost accumulation in the Mixing Department during August is summarized in this account:

Computing equivalent units, applying cost to completed units and work in process, and journalizing transactions; no beginning inventory or cost transferred in
(Obj 2, 3, 4)

Work in Process Inventory—Mixing	
Direct materials	26,250
Direct labor	7,400
Manufacturing overhead	13,495

August activity in the Mixing Department consisted of completion of the mixing process for 2,000 rolls of newsprint plus partial completion of 300 additional rolls. These in-process units were one-third complete with respect to both direct materials and conversion work.

Required

1. Compute the equivalent units of production and unit costs in the Mixing Department for August.
2. Prove that the sum of (a) cost of goods transferred out of the Mixing Department and (b) ending Work in Process Inventory—Mixing equals the total cost accumulated in the department during August.
3. Journalize all transactions affecting the company's mixing process during August, including those already posted.

P21-3A   Heirloom Mills manufactures broadloom carpet in seven processes: spinning, dyeing, plying, spooling, tufting, latexing, and shearing. First, fluff nylon purchased from a company such as DuPont or Monsanto is spun into yarn that is dyed the desired color. Then two or more threads of the yarn are joined together, or plied, for added strength. The plied yarn is spooled for use in actual carpet making. Tufting is the process by which yarn is added to burlap backing. After the backing is latexed to hold it together and make it skid-resistant, the carpet is sheared to give it an even appearance and feel.

Computing equivalent units for a second department with beginning inventory; applying cost to completed units and work in process; FIFO method
(Obj. 3, 4, 5)

At March 31, before recording the transfer of costs among departments, the Heirloom Mills general ledger included the following account for one of its lines of carpet:

Work in Process Inventory—Dyeing	
Feb. 28 Balance	10,900
Transferred in from Spinning	22,400
Direct materials	12,390
Direct labor	7,207
Manufacturing overhead	42,900

Work in process inventory of the Dyeing Department on February 28 consisted of 75 rolls that were 60 percent complete as to direct materials and conversion work. During March, 560 rolls were transferred in from the Spinning Department. The Dyeing Department completed 500 rolls of the carpet in March, and 135 rolls were still in process on March 31. The ending inventory was 100 percent complete as to direct materials and 80 percent complete as to conversion work.

Required

1. Compute the equivalent units of production, unit costs, and total costs to account for in the Dyeing Department for March. Use the FIFO method.
2. Show the application of total Dyeing Department cost to (a) goods transferred from Dyeing to Plying and (b) Work in Process Inventory—Dyeing on March 31.

Preparing a production cost report and recording transactions on the basis of the information in the report **(Obj. 2)**

P21-4A Refer to Problem 21–3A.

Required

1. Prepare the March production cost report for the Dyeing Department.
2. Journalize all transactions affecting the Dyeing Department during March, including the entries that have already been posted.

Computing equivalent units for a second department with beginning inventory and applying cost to completed units and work in process; FIFO method **(Obj. 3, 4, 5)**

P21-5A The manufacture of lawn mowers by Nature's Helper, Inc., includes two processes: forming the blade housing from steel and assembling the parts of the mower. Two additional operations, lubricating the moving parts and testing the completed mowers, complete their manufacture. The mowers are transferred to finished goods before being shipped to Sears, Montgomery Ward, and other department stores.

Process costing information for the Assembling Department of Nature's Helper, Inc., for a period follows. No direct materials are required.

Units:	
Work in process, beginning (60% complete as to conversion work)	2,000 units
Transferred in from the Forming Department during the period	9,000 units
Completed during the period	6,000 units
Work in process, ending (70% complete as to conversion work)	5,000 units
Costs:	
Work in process, beginning	$ 92,000
Transferred in from the Forming Department during the period	306,000
Conversion costs added during the period	66,400

The cost transferred in to the lubricating phase is the cost of the mowers transferred out of the Assembling Department. The lubricating operation is entirely automated and takes 30 seconds per mower. Testing each completed mower requires an average of five minutes of a technician's time. Conversion costs are $30 per machine hour for lubricating and $50 per labor hour for testing. There is only one work order for the mowers in each production run.

Required

1. Compute the number of equivalent units produced by the Assembling Department during the period, unit costs, and total costs to account for. Use the FIFO method.
2. Show the application of total cost to (a) units completed and transferred to the lubricating operation and (b) units in ending work in process inventory.
3. Compute the total manufacturing cost of the 6,000 mowers completed and transferred to finished goods. Also compute the unit cost of each complete mower.
4. You are the production manager of Nature's Helper, Inc. Do you want periodic production cost reports in the condensed format of Exhibit 21–13 or the expanded format of Exhibit 21–14? Why?
5. How will what you learned from this problem help you manage a business?

P21-6A   Repeat Problem 21-5A, using the weighted-average method. Assume that the $92,000 balance of Work in Process—Assembling Department at the beginning of the period was composed of $71,250 of transferred-in cost and $20,750 of conversion cost.

Computing equivalent units for a second department with beginning inventory and applying cost to completed units and work in process; weighted-average method **(Obj. 3, 4, 6)**

(GROUP B)

P21-1B   Siliconia Bay, Inc., produces component parts that are used in hand-held calculators. One part, a diode generator, is manufactured in a single processing department. No diode generators were in process on May 31, and Siliconia Bay started production on 12,000 units during June. Completed production for June totaled 9,900 units. The June 30 work in process was 20 percent complete as to direct materials and 30 percent complete as to conversion work. Direct materials costing $5,676 were placed in production during June, and direct labor of $5,100 and manufacturing overhead of $2,271 were applied to the process.

Computing equivalent units and applying cost to completed units and work in process; no beginning inventory or cost transferred in **(Obj. 3, 4)**

Required

1.   Compute the number of equivalent units of production and the unit costs for June.
2.   Show the application of total cost to (a) units completed and transferred to finished goods and (b) units still in process at June 30.
3.   Prepare a T-account for Work in Process Inventory to show its activity during June, including the June 30 balance.

P21-2B   The Inverness Wool Company produces wool fabric by a three-stage process: cleaning, spinning, and weaving. Costs incurred in the Cleaning Department during September are summarized as follows:

Computing equivalent units, applying cost to completed units and work in process, and journalizing transactions; no beginning inventory or cost transferred in **(Obj. 2, 3, 4)**

Work in Process Inventory—Cleaning	
Direct materials	70,400
Direct labor	2,580
Manufacturing overhead	8,700

September activity in the Cleaning Department included completion of 17,000 pounds of wool, which were transferred to the Spinning Department. Also, work began on 3,000 pounds of wool, which on September 30 were 100 percent complete as to direct materials and 60 percent complete as to conversion work.

Required

1.   Compute the equivalent units of production and unit costs in the Cleaning Department for September.
2.   Prove that the sum of (a) cost of goods transferred out of the Cleaning Department and (b) ending Work in Process Inventory—Cleaning equals the total cost accumulated in the department during September.
3.   Journalize all transactions affecting the company's cleaning process during September, including those already posted.

P21-3B   The Gary Motor Parts Corporation manufactures auto bumpers in a two-stage process that includes shaping and plating. Steel alloy is the basic raw material of the shaping process. The steel is molded according to the design specifications of automobile manufacturers (Chrysler, Ford, and General Motors). The Plating Department then adds a finish plate of chrome.
   At March 31, before recording the transfer of cost from the Plating Department to Finished Goods Inventory, the Gary Motor Parts general ledger included the following account:

Computing equivalent units for a second department with beginning inventory; applying cost to completed units and work in process; FIFO method **(Obj. 3, 4, 5)**

Work in Process Inventory—Plating	
Feb. 28 balance	24,600
Transferred in from Shaping	36,000
Direct materials	27,060
Direct labor	17,100
Manufacturing overhead	37,620

Work in process of the Plating Department on February 28 consisted of 600 bumpers that were 50 percent complete as to direct materials and conversion work. During March, 3,000 bumpers were transferred in from the Shaping Department. The Plating Department transferred 2,200 bumpers to finished goods in March, and 1,400 bumpers were still in process on March 31. This ending inventory was 40 percent complete as to direct materials and 70 percent complete as to conversion work.

Required

1. Compute the equivalent units of production, unit costs, and total costs to account for in the Plating Department for March. Use the FIFO method.

2. Show the application of total Plating Department cost to (a) goods transferred out of the Plating Department and (b) Work in Process Inventory—Plating on March 31.

Preparing a production cost report and recording transactions on the basis of the report's information (Obj. 2)

P21-4B   Refer to Problem 21–3B.

Required

1. Prepare the March production cost report for the Plating Department.

2. Journalize all transactions affecting the Plating Department during March, including the entries that have already been posted.

Computing equivalent units for a second department with beginning inventory and applying cost to completed units and work in process; FIFO method (Obj. 3, 4, 5)

P21-5B   The forming of hand-tool parts at Timford Tool Company occurs in four departments. Consider screwdrivers with plastic handles. The forming of the handles includes mixing the raw materials, heating the mix, shaping the mix by pouring it into molds, and drying. Production of the screwdrivers is then completed in two operations: assembling the handles and shanks and packaging for shipment to retail outlets.

Process costing information for the Drying Department of Timford Tool Company for a period follows. No direct materials are required.

Units:	
Work in process, beginning (30% complete as to conversion work)	7,000 units
Transferred in from the Molding Department during the period	32,000 units
Completed during the period	16,000 units
Work in process, ending (20% complete as to conversion work)	23,000 units
Costs:	
Work in process, beginning	$ 1,190
Transferred in from the Molding Department during the period	3,840
Conversion costs added during the period	1,665

The cost transferred in to the assembling phase is the cost of the plastic handles transferred out of the Drying Department. Assembling operation direct materials are the metal shanks, which cost $1,493 for the period. The assembling and packaging operations are automated. Assembling occurs at the rate of 400 units per hour and packaging at 200 units per hour. Conversion cost is allocated to the assembling operation at the predetermined rate of $2.50 per machine-hour and to packaging at the rate of $2.75 per machine-hour. There is only one work order for the screwdrivers.

Required

1. Compute the number of equivalent units produced by the Drying Department during the period, the unit costs, and the total costs to account for. Use the FIFO method.

2. Show the application of total cost to (a) units completed and transferred to the assembly operation and (b) units in ending work in process inventory.

3. Compute the total manufacturing cost of the 16,000 screwdrivers completed and transferred to finished goods. Also compute the unit cost of each complete screwdriver.

4. You are the production manager of Timford Tool company. Do you want periodic production cost reports in the condensed format of Exhibit 21–13 or the expanded format of Exhibit 21–14? Why?

5. How will what you learned from this problem help you manage a business?

P21-6B Repeat Problem 21-5B, using the weighted-average method. Assume that the $1,190 balance of Work in Process—Drying Department at the beginning of the period was composed of $645 of transferred-in cost and $545 of conversion cost.

Computing equivalent units for a second department with beginning inventory and applying cost to completed units and work in process; weighted-average method **(Obj. 3, 4, 6)**

EXTENDING YOUR KNOWLEDGE

DECISION PROBLEMS

1. Big Bend Manufacturing Company makes automobile parts. The following cost data for the company's Finishing Department are available for October:

Preparing a production cost report and evaluating production efficiency (Obj. 5)

		Equivalent Units of Production		
Flow of Production	**Flow of Physical Units**	**Transferred In**	**Direct Materials**	**Conversion Costs**
Units to account for:				
Beginning work in process inventory...............................	12,000			
Transferred in during October...	28,000			
Total units to account for	40,000			
Units accounted for:				
Completed and transferred out to finished goods during October:				
From beginning inventory..	12,000	—	7,200	6,000
Transferred in from Molding and completed during October	24,000	24,000	24,000	24,000
Work in process, October 31	4,000	4,000	800	1,200
Total physical units accounted for.....................................	40,000			
Equivalent units of production		28,000	32,000	31,200

Unit costs:	**Transferred-In Costs**	**Direct Materials**	**Conversion Costs**	**Total**
Work in process, September 30...				$ 59,000
Costs added during October	$ 64,400	$ 35,200	$ 49,920	149,520
Divide by equivalent units..	÷28,000	÷32,000	÷31,200	
Cost per equivalent unit	$ 2.30	$ 1.10	$ 1.60	
Total cost to account for				$208,520

Allocation of total cost:	Transferred-In Costs	Direct Materials	Conversion Costs	Total
Units completed and transferred out to finished goods:				
From work in process, September 30.............................				$ 59,000
Costs added during October:				
Direct materials...		7,200 × $1.10		7,920
Conversion costs			6,000 × $1.60	9,600
Total completed from September 30 inventory				76,520
Units transferred in from Molding and				
completed during October	24,000 × ($2.30 + $1.10 + $1.60)			120,000
Total cost transferred out...				196,520
Work in process, October 31:				
Transferred-in costs	4,000 × $2.30			9,200
Direct materials..		800 × $1.10		880
Conversion costs			1,200 × $1.60	1,920
Total work in process, October 31				12,000
Total cost accounted for...				$208,520

Required

1. Prepare a basic production cost report for the Finishing Department for the month of October.

2. Suppose that the budgeted cost per completed unit of output in October was $5.05. Were Big Bend's costs during October higher or lower than budgeted? Why might the company's production managers want more information than is revealed in the basic production cost report?

Using process costing information to make an outsourcing decision (Obj. 5)

2. Refer to the data for Decision Problem 1. Suppose that the Big Bend Manufacturing Company is approached by another manufacturer that offers to finish Big Bend's products for $2.50 per unit. If Big Bend accepts the offer to "outsource" the finishing operation, it will shut down its Finishing Department.

Required

1. What process costing information is useful in deciding whether to make or buy finishing operations?

2. What other factors should be considered by Big Bend's management before it accepts or rejects the other company's offer?

ETHICAL ISSUE

Hutch Manufacturing produces component parts for laser optic equipment. Customers include civilian companies and the U.S. government. Under most government contracts, Hutch receives reimbursement for its manufacturing costs plus a specified profit. For most civilian contracts, Hutch bids a fixed price and either earns a profit or incurs a loss, depending on how well the company controls costs. Hutch accountants allocate to government contracts any overhead whose proper allocation to a particular product is questionable.

Required

1. Is Hutch's overhead allocation practice ethical? Give your reason.
2. Who benefits and who is harmed by the Hutch practice?

COMPREHENSIVE PROBLEMS FOR PART FIVE

1. USING AND EVALUATING A PRODUCT COSTING SYSTEM

Albertson Corporation has a machine shop that specializes in the production of aircraft components. Its primary manufacturing activities are materials handling, lathe work, milling, grinding, and testing completed units of product. The milling and grinding operations are automated.

Albertson's job order costing system traces direct materials and direct labor costs directly to jobs. The system applies manufacturing overhead costs to jobs at a budgeted percentage of direct labor cost. For 1995, the company expected to incur $100,000 of direct labor cost. Albertson's budgeted manufacturing overhead totaled $450,000.

Albertson Corporation bids on jobs in order to generate business. The company's bid prices are determined in two steps. First, the full cost of each job is budgeted by adding the costs of direct materials, direct labor, and manufacturing overhead to the budgeted operating (upstream and downstream) cost. Operating cost is budgeted at 10 percent of manufacturing cost. Second, the budgeted full cost of the job is marked up by 25 percent. That is, the bid price of each job is 125 percent of the job's budgeted full cost.

Albertson recently won two bids from long-time customers. Budget data for the jobs are:

	Job 1	Job 2
Direct materials cost	$5,000	$30,000
Direct labor cost	$400	$5,600
Number of parts	250	1,000
Number of machine hours	75	125
Number of product units (all of which are tested)	5	100

Required

1. Compute Albertson Corporation's 1995 budgeted manufacturing overhead cost application rate.
2. Compute Albertson's
   a. Budgeted manufacturing product cost of Jobs 1 and 2.
   b. Budgeted full product cost of Jobs 1 and 2.
   c. Bid (sale) price of each job.
3. Evaluate Albertson Corporation's costing system. Do you believe that the manufacturing overhead cost *applied* to individual jobs is an accurate estimate of the manufacturing overhead cost *incurred* on the jobs? Why or why not?
4. On the basis of your analysis for Requirement 3, which of the two jobs is likely to be less profitable than Albertson's managers believe? Which is likely to be more profitable?
5. Suppose that Job 2 is the only job that Albertson Corporation worked on in June 1995. On June 30, the company had charged $2,800 of direct labor to the job. Estimate the equivalent units of direct labor that were worked on during the month.

2. GROUP PROJECT: MAKING PRELIMINARY PLANS FOR A CATERING BUSINESS

In Chapter 1, you studied An Extra Hand, a business that provides catering services. In this and subsequent group projects, you will make planning and control decisions for your own catering firm. You will apply, in a service setting, several management accounting techniques and analyses that were developed for manufacturers. Suppose that you have decided to start a catering business in Kansas City, Missouri. Describe your business. After naming it, answer the following:

- Who will be your customers—individuals, companies, or both?
- What categories of food servings or meals will you sell? For simplicity, name three general types of product offerings, including hors d'oeuvres.
- What type of product costing system will you use—job order or process?
- What will be the product costing system's primary cost object?
- Finally, what types of costs will you incur on an ongoing basis? List as many general categories as you can, including, for example, the costs of food and of the electricity or natural gas used in cooking. You do not have to provide dollar amounts.

In future Group Projects, you will analyze your costs, budget operating income, decide which type of catered event to emphasize, and evaluate steps that lead to high-quality operations. At the end of the course, you will better understand how to plan and operate a business.

Lawless Container Corporation—Management Accounting

The success of Lawless Container Corporation (introduced in Part 1) is due in part to its commitment to effective planning and control of manufacturing operations. The company's management knows that to survive and grow in a competitive market, Lawless must monitor and control all costs of production and distribution. This is especially important because Lawless Container's profits must be adequate to service debt incurred to buy the company and to expand its production capacity.

Working to minimize costs at each stage of the value chain has helped Lawless Container capture increased market share in a stagnant market. Package design is faster and more accurate with the use of computer-aided design (CAD) technology. Raw materials costs are minimized by the company working closely with suppliers and by maximizing the use of recycled materials. Wasted dollars are minimized by means of statistical quality control in which the product is inspected frequently during processing so that adjustments can be made on the spot.

Another major factor in Lawless Container's success has been product development. After Lawless manufactured brown corrugated boxes for many years, management realized that the most significant opportunity for growth lay in value-added print-process containers and displays. These product lines offer greater potential markets, less competition, and better returns on the advanced design and manufacturing techniques developed by the company.

Recently, Lawless achieved a 50-percent increase in production output by moving to a larger facility. This move reflects management's long-range plans for growth. Reaching long-term goals, however, can sometimes hurt short-term profits. While the move from Lawless's old, cramped factory has reduced defects and enabled the company to step up sales efforts, it has also put a strain on working capital. Management realizes that Lawless Container must continue to grow through superior customer service in order to support the increased overhead costs this new production capacity brings.

CASE QUESTIONS

1. Prepare a list of product costs likely to be incurred by Lawless Container Corporation in producing cartons for Fisher Price toys. (The cartons include color pictures of the contents.) Be sure to include indirect as well as direct costs.
2. Many of Lawless's customers are reducing their inventories by purchasing smaller amounts more frequently. Explain why this situation increases the costs incurred by Lawless Container to manufacture boxes and displays.
3. Explain how statistical quality control reduces product costs and, consequently, increases profits.
4. Lawless Container recently increased its production capacity by 50 percent when it moved to a larger plant. What effect will the move have on the company's unit product costs in the short term? In the long term?

PART SIX
Internal Decision Making, Planning, and Control

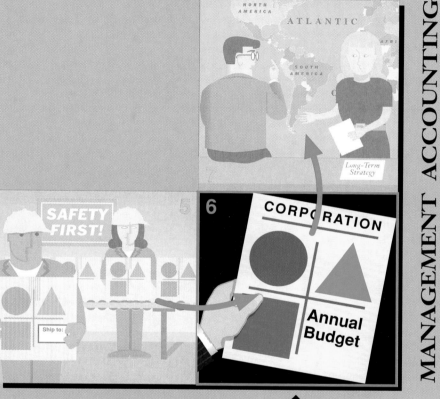

MANAGEMENT ACCOUNTING

Chapter 22

Cost-Volume-Profit Analysis and the Contribution Margin Approach to Decision Making

Apple Computer, Inc., achieved big gains in Macintosh sales during the Christmas season of 1993. This was a plus for the company, because analysts were concerned that buyers might wait for the March 1994 introduction of a new line of Macintosh computers based on the PowerPC microchip.

In the first quarter of fiscal year 1994, Apple's revenues rose to $2.47 billion, a 23-percent increase over 1993's first quarter. Unit sales were up 40 percent, to a quarterly record of more than 1 million computers.

Despite these impressive numbers, Apple's net income for the quarter plunged 75 percent from the previous year's level. The reason? Shrinking profit margins. The company had to slash Macintosh prices in order to remain competitive. According to chief executive Michael Spindler, Apple's challenge is "to continue to grow our unit shipments and revenues while we make further progress in reducing our operating expenses." *Source: J. Carlton, "Apple Computer Net Plunged 75% for Fiscal Period," The Wall Street Journal, Jan. 21, 1994, p. A3. Reprinted by permission. ©1994 Dow Jones & Company, Inc. All rights reserved worldwide.*

• • • • •

How much additional income will Apple Computer earn if it sells 10,000 more Macintosh Quadras? How many PowerPCs must the company sell to *break even* (earn enough revenue to cover expenses) on the product? How many Stylewriter printers does Apple have to sell to earn a target operating income of $1 million?

Many questions in business—on the number of computers sold, the number of airline passengers, and so on—boil down to this general question: What effect does a change in *volume* have on profit? To answer that question, managers study the links among costs, volume of products or services sold, and profit.

Cost-volume-profit (CVP) analysis expresses the relationships among costs, volume, and profit or loss. It is both an important part of the budgeting system and a key management tool for short-term operating decisions. In the first half of this chapter, you will learn how to compute *profit* in a way that is tailor-made for CVP analysis. But first we need to discuss the role of different types of *costs*.

Types of Costs

OBJECTIVE 1
Identify different cost behavior patterns

In Chapter 20, we defined a *cost driver* as any factor that affects costs. Many cost drivers exist. The most prominent cost driver is volume, which often is expressed in physical *units* produced or sold or in sales *dollars*. For example, the more T-shirts Hanes produces—that is, the greater its production volume—the greater the costs the company incurs. Nonvolume factors also act as cost drivers. An example is weight, which may affect freight costs. To emphasize basic concepts in this chapter, we focus on volume as the cost driver. **Cost behavior** describes how costs change—indeed, if they change at all—in response to a change in a cost driver. We examine three basic types of costs: variable, fixed, and mixed.

A **variable cost** is a cost that changes in total in direct proportion to a change in volume of activity. For example, sales commissions are variable costs; the higher the sales, the higher the sales commissions. Variable costs also include direct materials costs and delivery costs. These costs rise or fall directly with an increase or decrease in production or sales volume.

Exhibit 22-1 shows the graphs of three different variable costs. The slope of each line is the variable cost per unit (here, a T-shirt purchased by Target or Kmart). The higher the variable cost per unit, the steeper the slope. Every line passes through the origin, because at zero volume the total variable cost is zero.

The left-hand graph of Exhibit 22-1 is for T-shirts that cost $2 each. We see that 3,000 shirts cost $6,000 (3,000 × $2) and that 4,500 shirts cost $9,000 (4,500 × $2). A 50-percent increase in volume (4,500 − 3,000 = 1,500; 1,500/3,000 = 50%) results in a 50-percent increase in total cost ($9,000 − $6,000 = $3,000; $3,000/$6,000 = 50%). But the unit variable cost is $2 for both (and all other) volume levels.

The middle graph in Exhibit 22-1 has a steeper slope. It is for T-shirts that cost $3 each. This graph shows that 2,000 of these shirts cost $6,000 (2,000 × $3) and that 4,000 shirts cost $12,000 (4,000 × $3). When volume doubles, total cost doubles.

EXHIBIT 22-1
Variable Cost Pattern

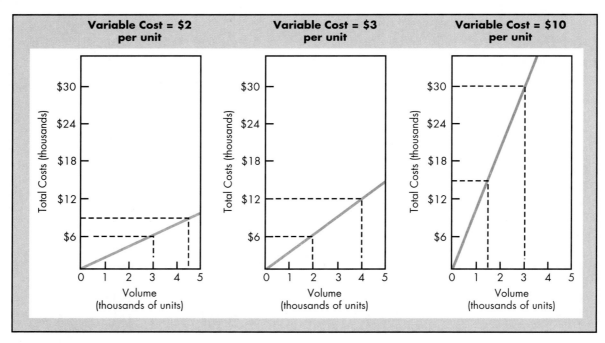

The right-hand variable cost graph relates to designer T-shirts that cost $10. Total cost increases much more rapidly with volume than it does for the less-expensive shirts.

A **fixed cost** is a cost that does not change in total despite wide changes in volume. For example, office rent usually does not change with the volume of business. A company pays the same monthly rent regardless of whether sales volume rises, falls, or stays the same. Other examples of fixed costs include depreciation, property taxes, and many executive salaries. These costs occur even if the company makes no sales. Exhibit 22-2 graphs a fixed cost, which is a horizontal line intersecting the cost axis at the level of the total cost. In such a graph, total fixed cost is the same for any volume.

A **mixed (semivariable) cost** is part variable and part fixed. Consider the costs to rent trucks, automobiles, and equipment. Rental payments often include a fixed monthly amount plus a variable amount that depends on the number of miles driven, copies made, or some other measure of volume. For example, suppose Apple rents some robotic equipment for producing Stylewriters. The rental terms are $6,000 per month plus $3 per Stylewriter produced. Exhibit 22-3 graphs this mixed cost.

The (sloped) cost behavior line in Exhibit 22–3 intersects the cost axis at the $6,000 fixed-cost point. Its slope is the $3 variable cost per unit. At any volume level, the total cost is the sum of the fixed cost and the variable cost at that volume. For example, in a month when 2,000 Stylewriters are produced, total rental cost is $12,000 [fixed cost of $6,000 plus variable cost of $6,000 (2,000 × $3)]. When 4,000 units are produced, total cost is $18,000 [fixed cost of $6,000 plus variable cost of $12,000 (4,000 × $3)]. In this case, when volume increases 100 percent, from 2,000 to 4,000 units, total cost rises only 50 percent ($18,000 − $12,000 = $6,000; $6,000/$12,000 = 50%). Thus, the total mixed cost increases with volume, but not in direct proportion as does the total variable cost.

For budgeting and CVP analysis, accountants frequently treat the fixed and variable components of mixed costs as two separate costs. They add the fixed component to other fixed costs to determine the total cost that does not vary with the vol-

Short Exercise: Fill in the blanks:

Variable Costs
(1) _____ in total amount
(2) _____ per unit
Fixed Costs
(3) _____ in total amount
(4) _____ per unit

A: (1) Vary; (2) fixed; (3) fixed; (4) vary

EXHIBIT 22-2
Fixed Cost Pattern

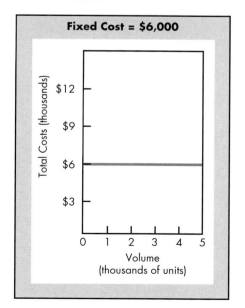

EXHIBIT 22-3
Mixed Cost Pattern

ume of goods produced or sold. Similarly, they combine the variable component with other variable costs to compute the costs that increase in direct proportion to volume. In Chapter 23, we discuss three methods that accountants use to separate mixed costs into their fixed and variable components.

Relevant Range

A **relevant range** is a band of volume in which a specific relationship exists between cost and volume. Outside the relevant range, the cost either increases or decreases. A fixed cost is fixed only in relation to a given relevant range (usually large) and a given time span (often a month or a year). Exhibit 22-4 shows a fixed cost level of $50,000 for the volume range of 0 to 10,000 units. Between 10,000 and 20,000 units, fixed costs increase to $80,000, and they increase to $120,000 for volumes above 20,000 units.

Companies use the relevant range concept in budgeting their costs. Suppose that a Thom McAn Shoe Store in Exhibit 22-4 expects sales volume of 12,000 pairs of shoes during the upcoming year. For this period, the relevant range is between 10,000 and 20,000 units, and managers budget fixed expenses of $80,000. If actual sales for the year exceed 20,000 units, Thom McAn Shoe Company will consider hiring additional employees and perhaps will expand the store, increasing rent expense. Fixed costs increase as the relevant range shifts to a higher band of volume.

Fixed costs change from year to year, and so does the relevant range. If Thom McAn expects sales of only 8,000 units next year, the company will budget fixed costs of $50,000. Its managers may have to cut back on operating hours, lay off employees, or take other actions to reduce costs.

The relevant range concept also applies to variable costs. Some variable costs behave differently at different levels of volume. For example, utility costs for water and electricity often decrease per unit as usage increases. Also, a company may pay higher sales commission rates for higher levels of sales to encourage extra selling effort. Therefore, businesses should consider cost behavior—how both fixed and variable costs change—over the full range of sales volumes that are likely to occur during the budget period.

EXHIBIT 22-4
Relevant Range

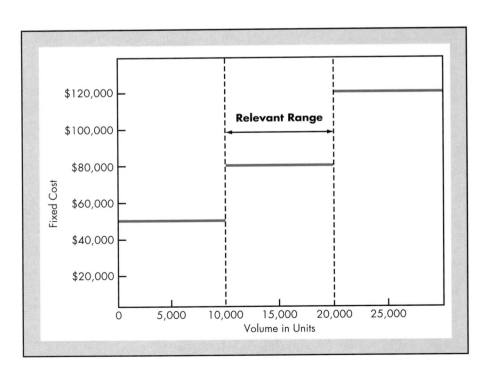

Accountants and managers analyze cost behavior to predict the profits from various courses of action. Decision alternatives often result in different volume levels. For example, Apple Computer managers may decide between (1) setting a higher price for a new Macintosh model and selling fewer units and (2) setting a lower price and selling more units. To determine the alternative with the higher expected profit, the managers must predict the total costs Apple will incur at both volume levels. Variable costs throughout the value chain will be higher at the higher volume level; fixed costs may or may not be higher, depending on their relevant ranges. Thus, an understanding of how costs vary with volume is essential for predicting profits from the two actions.

Two Approaches to Computing Profit

Earlier chapters presented the conventional income statement. That format, illustrated in Panel A of Exhibit 22-5, classifies expenses by *value chain function*. ◄▏▏▏◄▏▏▏◄▏▏▏ Manufacturing costs are expensed as cost of goods sold, and upstream and downstream costs (for example, costs of marketing and administration) are grouped as "operating expenses."

Cost of goods sold on a conventional income statement includes both variable and fixed manufacturing costs. Among the variable costs are direct materials, direct labor, and the cost of electricity used by production equipment. In contrast, such manufacturing costs as depreciation, factory rent, and property taxes are fixed. As Panel A shows, conventional income statements do not distinguish between variable and fixed expenses.

Companies use conventional income statements to report the results of operations to external parties. Managers also use the statements for budgeting and other internal purposes. But for decision making, many managers demand a different income format. To see why, let's suppose that executives want to predict the operating income that Martin Manufacturing Company will earn if sales volume increases by 10 percent.

The conventional income statement does not help Martin's managers predict the change in income. They cannot use this statement to relate variable expenses to sales volume. But consider the format in Panel B of Exhibit 22-5. This **contribution margin income statement** groups variable and fixed expenses separately. It features

◄▏▏▏◄▏▏▏◄▏▏▏ Recall from Chapter 20, p. 845, that managers are concerned with *all* costs related to a product: the costs of the entire value chain, from product design through manufacturing, distribution, and customer service.

EXHIBIT 22-5
Alternative Income Statement Formats

PANEL A—Conventional Format

MARTIN MANUFACTURING COMPANY CONVENTIONAL INCOME STATEMENT YEAR ENDED DECEMBER 31, 19X1		
Sales revenue		$2,100,000
Cost of goods sold		1,320,000
Gross margin		780,000
Operating expenses:		
Marketing	$310,000	
Other	290,000	600,000
Operating income		$ 180,000

PANEL B—Contribution Margin Format

MARTIN MANUFACTURING COMPANY CONTRIBUTION MARGIN INCOME STATEMENT YEAR ENDED DECEMBER 31, 19X1		
Sales revenue		$2,100,000
Variable expenses:		
Cost of goods sold	$840,000	
Marketing	150,000	
Other operating	210,000	1,200,000
Contribution margin		900,000
Fixed expenses:		
Manufacturing	480,000	
Marketing	160,000	
Other operating	80,000	720,000
Operating income		$ 180,000

the **contribution margin**, which is the excess of sales revenues over variable expenses.

The contribution margin is so named because the excess of revenues over variable expenses is the amount that contributes to "covering" fixed expenses and to providing operating income. Think about fixed expenses. Many fixed costs are incurred *before* any production or sales take place. These costs provide the capacity to produce and sell. For instance, machines must be purchased before goods can be produced. Their cost becomes depreciation expense. As goods are produced and sold, the contribution margin grows and covers the expense. In effect, the company recoups its machine investment. After all fixed costs are recouped by the contribution margin, additional sales provide operating income. The contribution margin is useful for decision making as well as for reporting income.

STOP & THINK   Refer to Exhibit 22-5. Suppose that Martin Manufacturing Company sold 6,000 items during the year. (a) How much did each item contribute to cover fixed expenses and provide operating income? (b) How many items were sold just to cover fixed expenses? (c) What would have been the operating income (loss) if no items had been sold?

Answer: (a) The total contribution margin is $900,000, and each item contributed $150 ($900,000 ÷ 6,000). (b) The first 4,800 items ($720,000 fixed expense/$150 contribution margin) covered fixed expenses. The final 1,200 items provided operating income (1,200 × $150 = $180,000). (c) If no items had been sold, the total contribution margin would have been zero. The company would have suffered an operating loss of $720,000, unless some fixed expenses could have been saved by moving to the lowest range of activity.

Contribution Margin Approach to Decision Making

OBJECTIVE 2

Use a contribution margin income statement to make business decisions

Suppose that Martin Manufacturing Company is considering a sales promotion that will cost $70,000. The vice-president of sales predicts that the promotion will increase sales volume by 10 percent. Should management approve the project?

Data from the contribution margin income statement may be used to compute Martin's expected increase in operating income:

Short Exercise: (1) The Allen Co. has fixed expenses of $100,000, variable expenses of $5 per unit, and a selling price of $20 per unit. Prepare a contribution margin (CM) income statement at a sales level of 15,000 units. (2) By how much would operating income increase if 25,000 units were sold? *A:* (1)

Sales	$300,000
Var. expenses	75,000
CM	225,000
Fixed expenses	100,000
Operating income	$125,000

(2) Operating income would increase by the contribution margin of the additional units sold—$150,000 (10,000 units × $15 CM).

Increase in sales revenue			$210,000
Increase in variable expenses:			
$\dfrac{\text{Increase in sales}}{\text{Current sales}} \times$ Current variable expenses			
$\dfrac{\$210,000}{\$2,100,000} \quad \times \quad \$1,200,000$			120,000
Increase in contribution margin			90,000
Increase in fixed expenses:			
Sales promotion		$70,000	
Other (current) fixed expenses		0	70,000
Increase in operating income			$ 20,000

Martin's senior managers can use this information to make their decision. If they consider the $20,000 increase in operating income to be adequate, they will go ahead with the project. If they consider $20,000 to be inadequate, they will seek another means to increase sales.

A similar analysis that uses the conventional income statement is not possible. Managers cannot use the conventional statement to predict the change in income from an increase in sales because that statement does not show which expenses are variable and which are fixed.

The 19X5 contribution margin income statement of the Country Gentleman Shirt Company is shown below. The average price of Country Gentleman's shirts is $45.

Required

1. How many shirts did Country Gentleman sell in 19X5?
2. What operating income will the company earn in 19X6 if sales volume increases by 20 percent and all sale prices, unit variable costs, and total fixed costs do not change?
3. Recast the 19X5 income statement in the conventional format.

COUNTRY GENTLEMAN SHIRT COMPANY
CONTRIBUTION MARGIN INCOME STATEMENT
YEAR ENDED DECEMBER 31, 19X5

Sales revenue		$900,000
Variable expenses:		
Cost of goods sold	$280,000	
Operating expenses	120,000	400,000
Contribution margin		500,000
Fixed expenses:		
Manufacturing	225,000	
Operating expenses	75,000	300,000
Operating income		$200,000

SOLUTION TO REVIEW PROBLEM

Requirement 1

Country Gentleman sold 20,000 shirts in 19X5:

$$\text{Shirts sold} = \frac{\text{Sales revenue}}{\text{Sale price per shirt}}$$

$$= \frac{\$900,000}{\$45} = 20,000$$

Requirement 2

Increase in sales revenue		$180,000
Increase in variable expenses:		
$\dfrac{\text{Increase in sales}}{\text{Current sales}} \times$ Current variable expenses		
$\dfrac{\$180,000}{\$900,000} \times$ $400,000		80,000
Increase in contribution margin		100,000
Increase in fixed expenses		0
Increase in operating income		100,000
19X5 operating income		200,000
19X6 operating income		$300,000

COUNTRY GENTLEMAN SHIRT COMPANY
CONVENTIONAL INCOME STATEMENT
YEAR ENDED DECEMBER 31, 19X5

Sales revenue	$900,000
Cost of goods sold*	505,000
Gross margin.............................	395,000
Operating expenses†	195,000
Operating income	$200,000

*$280,000 variable cost of goods sold + $225,000 fixed manufacturing cost from contribution margin statement.
†$120,000 variable operating expense + $75,000

Cost-Volume-Profit (CVP) Analysis

OBJECTIVE 3
Compute breakeven sales

Key Point: For CVP analysis, mixed costs must be broken down into their fixed and variable components.

Real-World Example: The breakeven point is very important. Most businesses know how many units they must sell to break even. In the chapter-opening story, Apple apparently has increased its breakeven point: Apple must sell more computers before it can become profitable.

Our Martin Manufacturing Company example showed that cost-volume-profit analysis is closely tied to the format of the contribution margin income statement. We now demonstrate two approaches that accountants use to perform CVP analysis: the equation approach and the contribution margin approach. The choice of approach is a matter of personal preference. Either may be used in any business setting—manufacturing, merchandising, or service. We consider a merchandising example to illustrate both approaches.

Kay Pak is thinking of renting a booth at a trade fair for travel agents. She plans to sell international travel posters for $3.50 each. Pak can purchase the posters for $2.10 each and can return all unsold items for a full refund. The booth rents for $700. Using this information, let's answer three questions about the business.

Question 1: What Is Pak's Breakeven Sales Level?

The **breakeven point** is the sales level at which operating income is zero: Total revenues equal total expenses. Sales below the breakeven point result in a loss. Sales above breakeven provide a profit. The breakeven point often is only incidental to managers of ongoing operations because their focus is on the sales level needed to earn a target profit. When managers are evaluating a new product or market opportunity, however, or when demand for an established product is declining, the breakeven point takes on added significance.

Equation Approach

In the equation approach, we start by dividing total expenses into variable expenses and fixed expenses. For Kay Pak, the variable cost is her cost of goods sold. This expense equals the number of posters sold multiplied by her cost of $2.10 to purchase each item. Her fixed cost is the rent expense, $700. A large company has numerous variable expenses and fixed expenses. Such a business combines all variable expenses into a single total and computes a single total for fixed expenses.

Our next step is to express income in equation form:

Key Point: One purpose of CVP analysis is to summarize results and relationships without a complicated income statement. When you prove your results by preparing an income statement, you see that CVP analysis gives the same data that the income statement gives.

$$\text{Sales} - \text{Variable expenses} - \text{Fixed expenses} = \text{Operating income}$$

At the breakeven point, sales equals expenses, so operating income is zero. Sales equals the unit sale price multiplied by the number of units sold. Variable expenses equals variable cost per unit times the number of units sold. We substitute these terms into the equation and enter the dollar amounts that we have:

Sales − Variable expenses − Fixed expenses = Operating income

$$\left(\begin{array}{c}\text{Unit}\\\text{sale}\\\text{price}\end{array} \times \text{Units sold}\right) - \left(\begin{array}{c}\text{Unit}\\\text{variable}\\\text{cost}\end{array} \times \text{Units sold}\right) - \text{Fixed expenses} = \text{Operating income}$$

($3.50 × Units sold) −	$2.10 × Units sold) −	$700 =	$0
($3.50 −	$2.10) × Units sold −	$700 =	$0
	$1.40 × Units sold	=	$700
	Units sold	=	$700/$1.40
	Breakeven sales in units	=	500 units

Kay Pak must sell 500 posters to break even. Her breakeven sales level in dollars is $1,750 (500 units × $3.50) for the travel posters.

Another form of the equation approach determines dollar sales first and unit sales second. We divide the variable expense per unit, $2.10, by the sale price, $3.50, to determine the ratio of the variable expense to the sale price:

"*Pak must sell 500 posters to break even.*"

$$\frac{\text{Variable expense}}{\text{Sale price}} = \frac{\$2.10}{\$3.50} = 0.60$$

We use this ratio in the equation, as follows:

Sales − Variable expenses − Fixed expenses = Operating income

Sales −	(0.60 × Sales)	−	$700 =	$0
Sales −	(0.60 × Sales)	=	$700	
	0.40 × Sales	=	$700	
	Sales	=	$700/0.40	
Breakeven sales in dollars	=	$1,750		
Breakeven sales in units	=	500 ($1,750/$3.50)		

Contribution Margin Approach

A second approach to CVP analysis uses the product's contribution margin. Each unit sold has a *unit contribution margin*, which is the excess of the sale price over the variable expense per unit. The unit contribution margin gives the increase in the income statement's total contribution margin, and therefore the increase in operating income, for each additional unit sold. (Remember that fixed expenses do not increase when one more unit is sold.) Each unit sold also has a **contribution margin ratio**, which is the ratio of the unit contribution margin to the sale price. The contribution margin ratio tells the increase in the total contribution margin—and operating income—for each additional dollar of sales revenue. For Kay Pak's business:

	Per Unit	Percent	Ratio
Sale price	$3.50	100%	1.00
Variable expense	−2.10	−60	−0.60
Contribution margin	$1.40	40%	0.40

The relationships expressed in the contribution margin ratio are depicted in Exhibit 22–6.

Short Exercise: The following data will be used in the next several Short Exercises. (1) Compute the breakeven point in units. (2) Prove this by preparing an income statement.

Unit sale price	$ 250
Unit variable exp.	150
Total fixed expenses	35,000

A:

(1) Let x = units sold at breakeven:

$$\$250x - \$150x = \$35,000 + \$0$$
$$\$100x = \$35,000$$
$$x = \$35,000/\$100$$
$$= 350 \text{ units}$$

(2) Revenue (350 units × $250) $87,500

Less Expenses:

Variable expenses (350 units × $150) 52,500

Fixed expenses .. 35,000

Operating income .... $ –0–

EXHIBIT 22–6

Relationships of the Contribution Margin Ratio

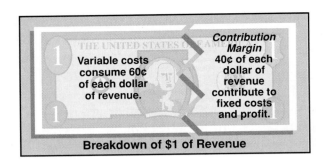

Breakdown of $1 of Revenue

Variable costs consume 60¢ of each dollar of revenue.

Contribution Margin 40¢ of each dollar of revenue contribute to fixed costs and profit.

Short Exercise: Refer to the Short Exercise on p. 925. Calculate the contribution margin per unit, contribution margin ratio, and the breakeven point in units. *A:*

	Per Unit	Ratio
Sale price	$250	1.00
Variable expense	−150	−0.60
Contribution margin	$100	0.40

$$= \frac{\$35{,}000 \text{ Fixed expenses}}{\$100 \text{ Contribution margin}}$$

$$= 350 \text{ units} = \text{Breakeven point}$$

The contribution margin approach uses a formula that is based on the contribution margin income statement. A condensed statement at the 500-unit breakeven point shows the following:

Sales revenue (500 units × $3.50)	$1,750
Variable expenses (500 units × $2.10)	1,050
Contribution margin (500 units × $1.40)	700
Fixed expenses	700
Operating income	$ 0

At any sales level, the total contribution margin may be computed by multiplying the number of units sold by the unit contribution margin:

Contribution margin = Sales in units × Unit contribution margin
$700 = 500 × $1.40

Thus, the income statement components are related in this way:

Contribution margin − Fixed expenses = Operating income
Contribution margin = Fixed expenses + Operating income
Sales in units × Unit contribution margin = Fixed expenses + Operating income

Dividing both sides of the last equation by the unit contribution margin gives the cost-volume-profit formula:

$$\text{Sales in units} = \frac{\text{Fixed expenses} + \text{Operating income}}{\text{Unit contribution margin}}$$

$$= \frac{\$700 + \$0}{\$1.40} = 500$$

The $1,750 *breakeven point in sales dollars* can be computed directly by using another form of the cost-volume-profit formula. At Kay Pak's breakeven point,

Short Exercise: Using the contribution margin ratio in the previous Short Exercises, calculate sales in dollars at the breakeven point. *A:*

$$\text{Breakeven sales} = \frac{\$35{,}000}{0.4}$$

$$= \$87{,}500 \ (350 \text{ units} \times \$250)$$

$$\text{Sales in dollars} = \frac{\text{Fixed expenses} + \text{Operating income}}{\text{Contribution margin ratio}}$$

$$= \frac{\$700 + \$0}{0.40} = \$1{,}750$$

Exhibit 22-7 shows the effects on the breakeven point of various changes to the sale price or to costs. Consider an increase in fixed expenses. Suppose that Pak can rent a booth in a better location for $1,050. With this higher fixed cost, she must sell 750 posters to break even:

$$\text{Breakeven sales in units} = \frac{\text{Fixed expenses}}{\text{Unit contribution margin}}$$

$$= \frac{\$1{,}050}{\$1.40} = 750 \text{ units}$$

Change in Factor	Change in Breakeven Sales
Increase in sale price	Decrease
Decrease in sale price	Increase
Increase in variable expenses	Increase
Decrease in variable expenses	Decrease
Increase in fixed expenses	Increase
Decrease in fixed expenses	Decrease

EXHIBIT 22-7

Effects of Changes on Breakeven Sales

Short Exercise: For the Short Exercise on p. 925: If the sale price is decreased from $250 to $240 while unit variable expenses are $150 and total fixed expenses are $35,000, what is the new breakeven point in units and in dollars? *A:*

$$\frac{\$35,000}{\$90} = 389 \text{ units}$$

The new contribution margin is $90 ($240 − $150). The new contribution margin ratio is 37.5% ($90/$240).

$$\frac{\$35,000}{0.375} = \$93,333$$

When Pak's fixed expenses increase by 50 percent, her breakeven point also goes up by 50 percent. This match in percentage increase always exists if all other factors are held constant.

In general, managers prefer a lower breakeven point to a higher one. But do not overemphasize this one aspect of CVP analysis. Decision makers are more interested in expected profits from alternative courses of action than in breakeven sales levels. In our example, Kay Pak may be willing to pay an extra $350 ($1,050 − $700) for a better location if the expected increase in sales volume provides enough contribution margin to cover the extra rent expense and to give extra operating income.

Question 2: How Many Units Must Be Sold to Earn a Target Operating Income?

OBJECTIVE 4

Compute the sales level needed to earn a target operating income

Suppose that Pak would be content with operating income of $490 for a week's work in the booth. Assuming fixed expenses of $700, how many posters must she sell to earn a profit of $490?

Until now, we have concentrated on breakeven sales, the point at which operating income is zero. How should we consider a target operating income greater than zero? The contribution margin must be sufficient to cover the fixed expenses and must also provide the profit. Our contribution margin approach is unchanged. But the numerator of our basic equation now contains both fixed expenses and the target operating income:

$$\text{Sales in units} = \frac{\text{Fixed expenses} + \text{Target operating income}}{\text{Unit contribution margin}}$$

$$= \frac{\$700 + \$490}{\$1.40} = \frac{\$1,190}{\$1.40} = 850 \text{ units}$$

$$\text{Sales in dollars} = \frac{\text{Fixed expenses} + \text{Target operating income}}{\text{Contribution margin ratio}}$$

$$= \frac{\$700 + \$490}{0.40} = \frac{\$1,190}{0.40} = \$2,975$$

The sales volume needed to earn an operating income of $490 is 850 units, or $2,975 (850 × $3.50).

Short Exercise: Use the data in the Short Exercise on p. 925. Calculate how many units must be sold to earn a target operating income of $40,000. What is the total sales revenue? *A:*

Target unit sales

$$= \frac{\$35,000 + \$40,000}{\$100} = 750 \text{ units}$$

Target dollar sales

$$= \frac{\$35,000 + \$40,000}{0.40} = \$187,500$$

Verify this by preparing an income statement.

Question 3: What Operating Income Is Expected at Various Sales Levels?

OBJECTIVE 5

Graph a set of cost-volume-profit relationships

A convenient way to determine expected operating income at various sales levels is to graph the cost-volume-profit relationships, as shown in Exhibit 22-8. To set up the graph, we place units on the horizontal axis and dollars on the vertical axis. We use Kay Pak's data (as originally given) and follow five steps:

Step 1. Choose a sales volume, such as 1,000 units. Plot the point for sales dollars at that volume: 1,000 units × $3.50 per unit = sales of $3,500. Draw the *sales line* from the origin through the $3,500 point.

Step 2. Draw the *fixed expense line*, a horizontal line that intersects the Dollars axis at $700.

EXHIBIT 22–8
Cost-Volume-Profit Graph

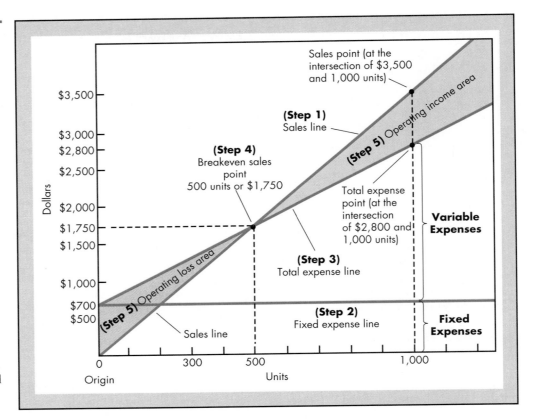

Key Point: Remember these features of a CVP graph:
1. The revenue line always passes through the origin because when no units are sold, there is no revenue.
2. The fixed expense line is parallel to the horizontal axis because fixed expenses do not change with changes in units.
3. The total expense line and the fixed expense line intersect the vertical axis in the same place.
4. The point at which the total expense line intersects the total revenue line is the breakeven point.

Step 3. Compute variable expense at the chosen sales volume: 1,000 units × $2.10 per unit = variable expense of $2,100. Add variable expense to fixed expense: $2,100 + $700 = $2,800. Plot the total expense point ($2,800) for 1,000 units. Then draw a line through this point from the $700 fixed expense intercept on the Dollars axis. This is the *total expense line.*

Step 4. Identify the *breakeven point.* The breakeven point is the spot where the sales line intersects the total expense line. The equations we used earlier told us that Pak's breakeven point is 500 units, or $1,750 in sales. The graph gives us the same information visually.

Step 5. Mark the *operating income* and the *operating loss* areas on the graph. To the left of the breakeven point, expenses exceed sales. Consider unit sales of 300, which provide dollar sales of $1,050 (300 × $3.50). Total expenses are $1,330 [(300 × $2.10) + $700]. Therefore, the axis point for sales of 300 units lies below the operating loss area. The vertical distance between the total expense line and the sales line equals the operating loss. For sales of 300 units, the loss is $280 (sales of $1,050 − total expenses of $1,330).

To the right of the breakeven point in Exhibit 22-8, Pak's business earns a profit. The vertical distance between the sales line and the total expense line equals the amount of operating income.

Computer spreadsheets are ideally suited for cost-volume-profit analysis. Spreadsheet programs can answer what-if questions such as: What will variable expenses be if sales rise by $1,000? By 200 units? If we cut fixed expenses by $20,000, how many units must we sell to earn a profit of $100,000? Computers allow managers to analyze the results of any one change or the results of several changes in the business's operations.

Many computer programs display graphs of CVP relationships. Such graphs show us whether an operating income or an operating loss will result from any particular sales volume. We can estimate the amount of the income or loss by measuring the width of the relevant area of the graph, but the equation and contribution margin approaches provide greater precision. Let's use the contribution margin approach to compute the operating income Pak will earn if she sells 900 posters:

$$\text{Sales in units} = \frac{\text{Fixed expenses} + \text{Operating income}}{\text{Unit contribution margin}}$$

$$900 = \frac{\$700 + \text{Operating income}}{\$1.40}$$

$$\$1,260 = \$700 + \text{Operating income}$$

$$\text{Operating income} = \$560$$

The first 500 posters sold provide the $700 contribution margin required to cover the rental expense. The next 400 sold add $560 to the contribution margin and give Pak $560 of profit.

Margin of Safety

The **margin of safety** is the excess of expected sales over breakeven sales. In other words, the margin of safety is the drop in sales that the company can absorb before incurring an operating loss. A high margin of safety serves as a cushion. A low margin of safety is a warning. Managers use the margin of safety to evaluate current operations or to measure the risk of a new business plan. The lower the margin, the higher the risk. The higher the margin, the lower the risk.

OBJECTIVE 6
Compute a margin of safety

Pak's breakeven point is 500 posters. Suppose she expects to sell 950 posters during the period. Her margin of safety is computed as follows:

$$\text{Margin of safety in units} = \text{Expected sales in units} - \text{Breakeven sales in units}$$

$$= 950 - 500 = 450 \text{ units}$$

$$\text{Margin of safety in dollars} = \text{Margin of safety in units} \times \text{Sale price per unit}$$

$$= 450 \times \$3.50 = \$1,575$$

Sales can drop by 450 units, or $1,575, before Pak incurs a loss.

PUTTING SKILLS TO WORK

CUTTING COSTS TO RAISE THE MARGIN OF SAFETY

In late 1994, workers at General Motors' Buick City complex in Flint, Michigan, briefly walked off the job. The issue wasn't wages, benefits or job security—the normal reasons for a strike. Their complaint: too much work. In recent years, GM had downsized repeatedly—let workers go by the thousands—in an effort to become more profitable. Now, workers at Buick City were complaining that they had to put in 60 hours a week and sometimes work on Sundays. They got generous overtime pay, but they didn't have time to enjoy it.

The strike was settled through the use of freelance part-timers, who were given no job security or benefits—just an hourly wage. GM could ill afford to add to its permanent payroll. Even after paring its hourly workforce by 100,000 people over five years, the company's productivity still lagged all other car companies. Despite record profits in 1994—nearly $5 billion on sales of $155 billion—the company's North American operations barely broke even, with a net profit margin of only 0.7%. In contrast, its newer overseas production facilities were much more profitable, unencumbered by decades of bloat.

Even so, GM had made progress. In less than two years, the average number of hours its workers spent per vehicle dropped about 25%. The corporate staff was reduced from 13,500 to 2,500. And GM negotiated $4 billion in savings from parts suppliers. All these cost-cutting moves were designed to reduce

GM has cut its costs of producing automobiles.

the company's fixed costs and raise its margin of safety.

In boom times such as the mid-1990s, GM is able to show high profits. But because of its still-massive size, investors worry about the inevitable downturn in the economy—and whether the margin of safety is sufficient for the company to remain profitable.

For any level of sales, managers can compute the margin of safety as a percentage. We divide the margin of safety in units (450) by sales in units (950), which equals 47.4 percent. We reach the same percentage by dividing the margin of safety in dollars ($1,575) by sales in dollars (950 units × $3.50 = $3,325).

Assumptions Underlying CVP Analysis

Cost-volume-profit analysis is based on the following assumptions:

1. Expenses can be classified as either variable or fixed.
2. Cost-volume-profit relationships are linear over a wide range of production and sales. Linear relationships can be graphed as straight lines (such as the lines in Exhibit 22-8).
3. Sale prices, unit variable costs, and total fixed expenses will be unchanged during the period under consideration.
4. Volume is the sole cost driver. The influences of other possible cost drivers (such as weight or size) are held constant or regarded as insignificant.
5. The relevant range of volume is specified.
6. The sales mix of products will be unchanged during the period. **Sales mix** is the combination of products that make up total sales. For example, the sales mix of a Furniture Warehouse store may be 70 percent household furniture and 30 percent office furniture. We discuss sales mix in the next section.

When these conditions are met, CVP analysis is precise. But most actual business conditions do not perfectly correspond to these assumptions. That is why managers often regard the answers to our three CVP questions as useful approximations rather than precise amounts.

Sales Mix

OBJECTIVE 7

Use the sales mix in CVP analysis

Our example thus far has focused on a single product, travel posters. Because most companies sell more than one product, sales mix must be considered in figuring CVP relationships. Sales mix has an important effect on profits. A company earns more income by selling high-margin products than by selling an equal number of low-margin items.

Managers often refer to sales mix when they are discussing the results of operations. For example, the annual report of Deere and Company, manufacturer of John Deere farm equipment, stated that profits decreased because of "a less favorable mix of products sold." What is a *less favorable mix* of products? It is a mix with a higher percentage of items that have below-average contribution margins.

"*The annual report of Deere and Company, manufacturer of John Deere farm equipment, stated that profits decreased because of 'a less favorable mix of products sold.'*"

We can perform CVP analysis for a company that sells more than one product by using the same equations that we used for a company with a single product. But first, we must compute the weighted-average contribution margin of all products. The sales mix provides the weights.

Suppose that Kay Pak plans to sell two types of posters instead of one. Recall that the regular poster costs $2.10 and sells for $3.50. Its contribution margin is $1.40 ($3.50 − $2.10). The second, larger poster costs $3.92 and sells for $6.00. Its contribution margin is $2.08 ($6.00 − $3.92).

Pak predicts that she will sell 400 regular posters and 500 large posters, a sales mix of 4:5. The total contribution margin of 9 units—4 regular and 5 large—is $16 [(4 × $1.40) + (5 × $2.08)]. The *weighted-average unit contribution margin* is $1.778 ($16/9 units). With this number, we compute the breakeven sales level as follows:

$$\text{Breakeven sales in units} = \frac{\text{Fixed expenses}}{\text{Weighted-average contribution margin per unit}} = \frac{\$700}{\$1.778} = 394 \text{ units}$$

Breakeven sales of regular posters (394 × 4/9) = 175 units
Breakeven sales of large posters (394 × 5/9) = 219 units

The breakeven point in sales dollars is $1,927—175 regular posters at $3.50 plus 219 large posters at $6.00. We can check these amounts by preparing a contribution margin income statement:

	Regular	Large	Total
Sales:			
Regular (175 units × $3.50)	$613		
Large (219 units × $6.00)		$1,314	$1,927
Variable expenses:			
Regular (175 units × $2.10)	368		
Large (219 units × $3.92)		859	1,227
Contribution margin	$245	$ 455	700
Fixed expenses			700
Operating income			$ -0-

If Pak's actual sales mix is not 4:5, her actual operating income will differ from the budgeted amount, even if she sells exactly the 900 total units she predicts. For each total number of units sold, there are as many resulting operating incomes as there are unique sales mixes. Similarly, there are as many different breakeven points—in total units and in sales dollars—as there are sales mixes. The sales-mix factor greatly complicates budgeting, especially when new products or markets are involved.

STOP & THINK Suppose that Kay Pak *budgets* the sale of 900 total posters in the 4:5 sales mix (4 regular posters sold for every 5 large posters). She *actually* sells 954 posters—530 regular and 424 large. The unit sale prices and variable expenses are exactly as predicted, and the fixed expense is the budgeted $700. Can you tell, without computations, whether Pak's actual operating income is greater than, less than, or equal to the budgeted amount?

Answer: Pak expected to sell more large, more-profitable posters than regular, less-profitable items. She did not. The actual sales mix is more heavily weighted toward regular posters, which means that the actual weighted-average contribution margin per unit is less than the budgeted amount. With everything else constant, this change decreases operating income. But total sales volume is higher than budgeted. That change increases income. Without computations, we cannot tell whether the overall effect of the two changes is positive or negative.

Companies can use CVP analysis to motivate their salespeople to emphasize high-margin products. Individuals are better equipped to generate profit when (1) they understand the separate effects of sales mix and sales volume on profit and (2) they know the contribution margin of each product they sell. Of course, compensation is a better motivator than is knowledge. Thus many companies base all or part of their sales commissions on the contribution margins produced by sales rather than on sales revenue alone.

Short Exercise: Assume that Levy Sales, Inc., sells two products, A and B:

	A	B
Sale price	$100	$80
Variable cost	60	50
Contribution margin (CM)	$ 40	$30

Levy estimates that it will sell 190 of A and 280 of B. Total fixed costs are $3,810. How many units of each product must Levy sell to break even?
A: 45 of A and 67 of B:

	A	B	Total
Sale price	$ 100	$ 80	
Variable cost	60	50	
CM per unit	$ 40	$ 30	
Est. sales in units	190	280	470
Est. CM	$7,600	$8,400	$16,000

Wtd. avg. CM/unit	= $16,000/470
	= $34.04
Breakeven sales	= $3,810/$34.04
	= 112 units
Breakeven sales of A	= 112 × 190/470
	= 45 units
Breakeven sales of B	= 112 × 280/470
	= 67 units

Prove that this is correct by preparing an income statement.

Income Effects of Alternative Approaches to Product Costing

Alternative approaches to product costing affect how companies expense costs. To understand the difference, let us revisit the Martin Manufacturing Company example of Exhibit 22-5. That exhibit shows both conventional and contribution margin income statements for 19X1, when Martin produced and sold 6,000 items. The company's average sale price was $350 ($2,100,000/6,000). Its variable costs were:

Cost of goods sold: $140 per unit ($840,000/6,000)

Marketing expense: $25 per unit ($150,000/6,000)

Other operating expense: $35 per unit ($210,000/6,000)

Exhibit 22-9 gives income statements for 19X2, when the company's operations were identical to 19X1's, with one exception: 8,000 units were produced instead of 6,000. That is, the company produced 2,000 units more than it sold. Exhibit 22-9 provides greater detail in the computation of cost of goods sold than does Exhibit 22-5. This detail aids our explanation of the difference in operating incomes.

Panel B of Exhibit 22-9 displays the contribution margin income statement of Martin Manufacturing Company. The contribution margin income statement often is called a *variable costing* statement. **Variable costing** is the costing method that assigns only variable manufacturing costs to products. Fixed overhead costs are expensed when they are incurred—as period costs—along with all nonmanufacturing costs.

In contrast, the conventional approach to computing income classifies both variable and fixed manufacturing costs as product costs. In Panel A of Exhibit 22-9, the manufacturing product cost of $200 per unit includes $140 of variable manufacturing cost (direct materials, direct labor, and variable overhead) and $60 ($480,000/8,000 units produced) of fixed manufacturing cost (fixed overhead).

The conventional approach to product costing is called *absorption costing*. **Absorption costing** is the costing method that assigns all manufacturing costs to products. It is so named because products *absorb* fixed manufacturing costs as well as variable manufacturing costs.

Martin Manufacturing Company's 19X2 operating income under absorption costing is $120,000 ($300,000 − $180,000) higher than it is under variable costing. This income difference between the two methods is due to fixed overhead cost. With variable costing, the entire amount of the fixed cost ($480,000) is expensed as a period cost. With absorption costing, only $360,000 (6,000 units sold × $60 per unit) of the fixed cost is expensed this year. The remaining $120,000 (2,000 units × $60) goes to inventory under absorption costing. This amount will be expensed as part of cost of goods sold when the final 2,000 units of 19X2 production are sold.

Now suppose that Martin produces another 8,000 units in 19X3 but sells 10,000, including the 2,000 remaining from 19X2. For 19X3, the variable costing statement will show higher income than the absorption costing statement. Variable costing will expense only the 19X3 fixed overhead cost of $480,000. But the absorption costing statement will expense $600,000 of fixed overhead (10,000 units sold × $60). The $120,000 of 19X2 fixed overhead deferred in finished goods inventory will be released to cost of goods sold in 19X3, in addition to all of 19X3's cost.

The operating income effects of the two approaches to product costing are summarized on the bottom of page 933.

Key Point: Variable costing is the same as direct costing: With this method of assigning costs, *only* direct materials, direct labor, and variable overhead are included in inventoriable cost.

Key Point: Absorption costing is the same as full costing: With this method of assigning costs, *all* manufacturing costs (direct materials, direct labor, variable overhead, *and* fixed overhead) are included in inventoriable cost.

PANEL A—Conventional Income Statement

EXHIBIT 22-9
Alternative Approaches to Computing Operating Income. Units Produced = 8,000; Units Sold = 6,000

MARTIN MANUFACTURING COMPANY
CONVENTIONAL INCOME STATEMENT (ABSORPTION COSTING)
YEAR ENDED DECEMBER 31, 19X2

Sales revenue (6,000 × $350)		$2,100,000
Cost of goods sold:		
Beginning finished goods inventory	$ 0	
Cost of goods manufactured (8,000 × $200)	1,600,000	
Cost of goods available for sale	1,600,000	
Ending finished goods inventory (2,000 × $200)	400,000	
Cost of goods sold (6,000 × $200)		1,200,000
Gross margin		900,000
Operating expenses:		
Marketing	310,000	
Other	290,000	
Total operating expenses		600,000
Operating income		$ 300,000

PANEL B—Contribution Margin Income Statement

MARTIN MANUFACTURING COMPANY
CONTRIBUTION MARGIN INCOME STATEMENT (VARIABLE COSTING)
YEAR ENDED DECEMBER 31, 19X2

Sales revenue (6,000 × $350)		$2,100,000
Variable expenses:		
Cost of goods sold:		
Beginning finished goods inventory	$ 0	
Cost of goods manufactured (8,000 × $140)	1,120,000	
Cost of goods available for sale	1,120,000	
Ending finished goods inventory (2,000 × $140)	280,000	
Cost of goods sold (6,000 × $140)	840,000	
Marketing	150,000	
Other operating	210,000	
Total variable expenses		1,200,000
Contribution margin		900,000
Fixed expenses:		
Manufacturing	480,000	
Marketing	160,000	
Other operating	80,000	
Total fixed expenses		720,000
Operating income		$ 180,000

If . . .	Then . . .
Units produced equals units sold	Absorption costing income equals variable costing income, because both methods expense the same fixed overhead cost.
Units produced exceeds units sold	Absorption costing income exceeds variable costing income, because absorption costing expenses less fixed overhead cost.
Units sold exceeds units produced	Variable costing income exceeds absorption costing income, because absorption costing expenses more fixed overhead cost.

Exhibits 22-5 and 22-9 illustrate why managers who are evaluated on absorption costing income may be tempted to produce more units of product than are needed to satisfy short-term demand. Consider the Omega Constellation, a watch that costs about $3,000. With each unit of excess production added to Omega Watch Company's inventory of watches, more of the year's fixed overhead cost is deferred to the future and less is expensed in the current year. This in turn leads to higher current income. But excessive inventory wastes money, reducing long-term profitability. For that reason, many companies use nonfinancial performance measures to motivate production managers to produce only what is needed for sales. One such measure is the number of units *produced* divided by the number of units *sold*. The higher the ratio above 1:1, the less favorable the evaluation.

"With each unit of excess production added to Omega Watch Company's inventory of watches, more of the year's fixed overhead cost is deferred to the future and less is expensed in the current year."

SUMMARY PROBLEM FOR YOUR REVIEW

PART A. Bronson Company buys jogging shorts for $6 and sells them for $10. Management budgets monthly fixed costs of $10,000 for sales volumes between zero and 12,000 pairs of shorts.

Required

1. Use both the equation approach and the contribution margin approach to compute the company's breakeven monthly sales in units and in dollars.
2. Compute the monthly sales level in units that is needed to earn a target operating income of $14,000. Use either the equation approach or the contribution margin approach.

PART B. Suppose that Bronson sells a second product—sweatpants. Each pair costs $7 and sells for $15. Fixed costs are unchanged.

Required

1. In a sales mix of 2:3 (2 pairs of jogging shorts sold for every 3 pairs of sweatpants), what operating income will Bronson Company earn if it sells a total of 11,000 items? Use the contribution margin approach.
2. In the 2:3 sales mix, Bronson's breakeven point in units sold is 1,563. What is the company's margin of safety if expected sales total 11,000 units?

SOLUTION TO REVIEW PROBLEM

PART A—Requirement 1

Equation approach:

$$\text{Sales} - \text{Variable expenses} - \text{Fixed expenses} = \text{Operating income}$$

$$\left(\begin{array}{c}\text{Unit} \\ \text{sale} \times \text{Sales in units} \\ \text{price}\end{array}\right) - \left(\begin{array}{c}\text{Unit} \\ \text{variable} \times \text{Sales in units} \\ \text{cost}\end{array}\right) - \text{Fixed expenses} = \text{Operating income}$$

$$(\$10 \times \text{Sales in units}) - (\$6 \times \text{Sales in units}) - \$10,000 = \$0$$

$$(\$10 - \$6) \times \text{Sales in units} = \$10,000$$

$$\$4 \times \text{Sales in units} = \$10,000$$

$$\text{Sales in units} = \$10,000/\$4$$

$$\text{Breakeven sales in units} = 2,500 \text{ units}$$

$$\text{Breakeven sales in dollars} = 2,500 \text{ units} \times \$10 = \$25,000$$

Contribution margin approach:

$$\text{Sales in units} = \frac{\text{Fixed expenses} + \text{Operating income}}{\text{Unit contribution margin}}$$

$$\text{Breakeven sales in units} = \frac{\$10,000 + 0}{(\$10 - \$6)} = \frac{\$10,000}{\$4} = 2,500 \text{ units}$$

$$\text{Breakeven sales in dollars} = 2,500 \text{ units} \times \$10 = \$25,000$$

Requirement 2

Equation approach:

$$\text{Sales} - \text{Variable expenses} - \text{Fixed expenses} = \text{Target operating income}$$

$$\left(\begin{matrix}\text{Unit} \\ \text{sale} \\ \text{price}\end{matrix} \times \text{Sales in units}\right) - \left(\begin{matrix}\text{Unit} \\ \text{variable} \\ \text{cost}\end{matrix} \times \text{Sales in units}\right) - \text{Fixed expenses} = \text{Target operating income}$$

$$(\$10 \times \text{Sales in units}) - (\$6 \times \text{Sales in units}) - \$10,000 = \$14,000$$
$$(\$10 - \$6) \times \text{Sales in units} = \$24,000$$
$$\$4 \times \text{Sales in units} = \$24,000$$
$$\text{Sales in units} = \$24,000/\$4$$
$$\text{Sales in units} = 6,000 \text{ units}$$
$$\text{Sales in dollars} = 6,000 \text{ units} \times \$10 = \$60,000$$

Contribution margin approach:

$$\text{Sales in units} = \frac{\text{Fixed expenses} + \text{Target operating income}}{\text{Unit contribution margin}}$$

$$\text{Sales in units} = \frac{\$10,000 + \$14,000}{(\$10 - \$6)}$$

$$= \frac{\$24,000}{\$4}$$

$$\text{Sales in units} = 6,000 \text{ units}$$
$$\text{Sales in dollars} = 6,000 \text{ units} \times \$10 = \$60,000$$

PART B—Requirement 1

	Jogging Shorts	Sweatpants	Total
Sale price per unit.....................................	$10	$15	
Variable cost per unit...............................	6	7	
Contribution margin per unit	$ 4	$ 8	
Sales mix in units	× 2	× 3	5
Contribution margin	$ 8	$24	$ 32
Weighted-average contribution margin per unit ($32/5 units)			$6.40

$$\text{Sales in units} = \frac{\text{Fixed expenses} + \text{Operating income}}{\text{Unit contribution margin}}$$

$$11,000 = \frac{\$10,000 + \text{Operating income}}{\$6.40}$$

$$\$70,400 = \$10,000 + \text{Operating income}$$
$$\text{Operating income} = \$60,400$$

Requirement 2

$$\text{Margin of safety in units} = \text{Expected sales in units} - \text{Breakeven sales}$$
$$= 11,000 - 1,563 = 9,437 \text{ units}$$

SUMMARY

1. Identify different cost behavior patterns. *Cost-volume-profit (CVP) analysis* expresses the relationships among a company's costs, volume of activity, and income. These relationships depend on *cost behavior*. We classify costs as *variable, fixed,* or *mixed.*

2. Use a contribution margin income statement to make business decisions. A *contribution margin income statement* reports variable expenses and fixed expenses separately. It features the total *contribution margin,* the excess of sales revenues over variable expenses. This format helps managers predict the operating income that will result from various decision alternatives.

3. Compute breakeven sales. Two popular ways to perform CVP analysis are the equation approach and the contribution margin approach. Both approaches use an equation or formula derived from the contribution margin income statement. The contribution margin approach uses the product's unit contribution margin or its *contribution margin ratio,* which give the increase in operating income for each additional unit sold or for each dollar of sales revenue, respectively. Either approach to CVP analysis can be used to compute a company's *breakeven point*—the sales level at which operating income is zero.

4. Compute the sales level needed to earn a target operating income. CVP analysis also can be used to compute how many units must be sold to earn a target operating income. The target operating income is added to the total fixed expense to determine the total contribution margin required to earn the income. That amount is divided by the unit contribution margin to give the number of units that must be sold.

5. Graph a set of cost-volume-profit relationships. Graphic displays of CVP relationships present information over a *relevant range* of sales levels. CVP graphs show the breakeven point and the ranges of sales volume that yield operating incomes and operating losses.

6. Compute a margin of safety. The *margin of safety* is the excess of expected sales over breakeven sales. The larger the margin, the lower the risk of a given plan.

7. Use the sales mix in CVP analysis. CVP analysis has several limitations. For example, it assumes that volume is the only cost driver and that all cost-volume-profit relationships are linear over the relevant range of activity. Also, CVP analysis assumes that the sales mix of products will be unchanged during the period under consideration. *Sales mix* is the combination of products that make up total sales.

SELF-STUDY QUESTIONS

Test your understanding of the chapter by marking the best answer for each of the following questions.

1. Cost-volume-profit analysis is most directly useful to *(p. 918)*
   a. Managers to help them predict the outcome of their decisions
   b. Investors for deciding how much to pay for a company's stock
   c. Lenders for analyzing a loan request
   d. Tax authorities for setting income tax rates

2. The graph of a mixed cost *(p. 919)*
   a. Passes through the origin and slopes upward
   b. Is horizontal from the point marking the level of fixed costs
   c. Has a steeper slope than the graph of a fixed cost or a variable cost
   d. Slopes upward from the point marking the level of fixed costs

3. Refer to Exhibit 22-5, page 921. What will operating income be if sales increase by 10 percent? *(p. 922)*
   a. $198,000   c. $390,000
   b. $270,000   d. $60,000

4. Refer to Exhibit 22-9, page 933. If sales are 8,000 units, the business can expect fixed expenses of *(p. 919)*
   a. $960,000   c. $720,000
   b. $540,000   d. $900,000

5. At the breakeven point *(p. 924),*
   a. Sales equal fixed expenses
   b. Sales equal variable expenses
   c. Sales equal total expenses
   d. Sales exactly equal operating income

6. Variable expenses consume 70 percent of sales, and fixed expenses total $420,000. The breakeven point in dollars is *(p. 925)*
   a. $140,000   c. $1,260,000
   b. $600,000   d. $1,400,000

7. What happens to the breakeven point if both variable expenses and fixed expenses increase? *(p. 927)*
   a. Breakeven sales increase
   b. Breakeven sales decrease
   c. Breakeven sales are unchanged because the two changes offset each other
   d. The effect on breakeven cannot be determined from the information given

8. William Thomas Corporation's monthly sales have averaged $480,000 for the past year. The monthly breakeven point is $400,000. The company's margin of safety percentage is *(p. 930)*
   a. 16 2/3%   c. 62 1/2%
   b. 20%   d. 100%

9. Raj Mujadeen sells handmade Oriental rugs for $1,000 each and machine-made rugs for $300 each. Customers buy five times as many machine-made rugs as handmade rugs. Variable expenses consume 80 percent of sales, and monthly fixed expenses total $2,000. How many of each type of rug must Mujadeen sell to earn a target operating income of $3,000? *(pp. 930–931)*
   a. 8 handmade and 40 machine-made rugs
   b. 10 handmade and 50 machine-made rugs
   c. 12 handmade and 60 machine-made rugs
   d. 20 handmade and 100 machine-made rugs

Answers to the Self-Study Questions follow the Accounting Vocabulary.

ACCOUNTING VOCABULARY

Absorption costing. The costing method that assigns all manufacturing costs to products (p. 932).

Breakeven point. The sales level at which operating income is zero: Total revenues equal total expenses (p. 924).

Contribution margin. The excess of sales revenues over variable expenses (p. 922).

Contribution margin income statement. Groups variable and fixed expenses separately and features the contribution margin (p. 921).

Contribution margin ratio. The ratio of the unit contribution margin to the sale price (p. 925).

Cost behavior. Description of how costs change in response to a change in a cost driver (p. 932).

Cost-volume-profit (CVP) analysis. Expresses the relationships among costs, volume, and profit or loss. An important part of the budgeting system that helps managers predict the outcome of their decisions (p. 918).

Fixed cost. Cost that does not change in total despite wide changes in volume (p. 919).

Margin of safety. Excess of expected sales over breakeven sales (p. 929).

Mixed (semivariable) cost. Cost that is part variable and part fixed (p. 919).

Relevant range. A band of volume in which a specific relationship exists between cost and volume (p. 920).

Sales mix. Combination of products that make up total sales (p. 930).

Variable cost. Cost that changes in total in direct proportion to changes in volume of activity (p. 918).

Variable costing. The costing method that assigns only variable manufacturing costs to products (p. 932).

ANSWERS TO SELF-STUDY QUESTIONS

1. a
2. d
3. b

Increase in contribution margin ($900,000 × 0.10)	$ 90,000
Operating income before sales increase	180,000
Operating income after sales increase	$270,000

4. c
5. c
6. d   Sales – 0.70 Sales = $420,000; 0.30 Sales = $420,000;
   Breakeven sales = $420,000/0.30 = $1,400,000
7. a
8. a   Margin of safety in dollars = $80,000 ($480,000 – $400,000)
   Margin of safety as a percentage = 16 2/3% ($80,000/$480,000)
9. b

	Handmade	Machine-Made	Total
Sale price per unit	$1,000	$300	
Variable expense per unit (80%)	800	240	
Contribution margin per unit	$ 200	$ 60	
Expected sales mix	× 1	× 5	6
Contribution margin	$ 200	$300	$ 500
Weighted-average contribution margin per unit ($500/6 units)			$83.333

$$\frac{\text{Sales}}{\text{in units}} = \frac{\text{Fixed expenses + Target operating income}}{\text{Weighted-average contribution margin per unit}} = \frac{\$2,000 + \$3,000}{\$83.333} = \underline{\underline{60 \text{ units}}}$$

Target sales of handmade rugs (60 units × 1/6) .... <u>10 units</u>
Target sales of machine-made rugs (60 units × 5/6) .... <u>50 units</u>

QUESTIONS

1. How is cost-volume-profit analysis used in budgeting?
2. Define the three types of cost behavior patterns.
3. Draw graphs of the three types of costs.
4. What are three questions cost-volume-profit analysis can answer?
5. How does a contribution margin income statement differ from a conventional income statement? Which income statement is more useful for predicting the income effect of a change in sales? Why?
6. Why is the concept of the relevant range important to cost-volume-profit analysis?
7. Draw a graph of fixed expenses from 0 to 50,000 units. The relevant range lies between 20,000 and 35,000 units, where fixed expenses are $300,000. Below the relevant

range, fixed expenses are $200,000. Above the relevant range, fixed expenses are $400,000.

8. What is the breakeven point? What is its significance to a business?

9. Give the cost-volume-profit formulas for breakeven sales in units and in dollars.

10. How does an increase in fixed expenses affect the breakeven point? How does a decrease in fixed expenses affect breakeven sales? Give the reason for each answer.

11. How does an increase in variable expenses affect the breakeven point? How does a decrease in variable expenses affect breakeven sales? Give the reason for each answer.

12. How does an increase in sale price affect the breakeven point? How does a decrease in sale price affect breakeven sales? Give the reason for each answer.

13. Briefly outline two ways to compute the sales in dollars needed to earn a target operating income.

14. Give the cost-volume-profit formula for sales in units needed to earn a target operating income. Do the same for sales in dollars.

15. Identify the steps in the preparation of a CVP graph.

16. What advantages does a CVP graph have over the equation approach and the contribution margin approach?

17. How does the margin of safety serve as a measure of risk?

18. Give the assumptions underlying CVP analysis.

19. Briefly describe how to perform CVP analysis when a company sells more than one product.

20. How is fixed overhead cost expensed under absorption costing? Under variable costing?

EXERCISES

Graphing cost behaviors
(Obj. 1)

E22-1 Graph each of the following cost behavior patterns over a relevant range from 0 to 10,000 units:

a. Fixed expenses of $25,000

b. Mixed expenses made up of fixed costs of $10,000 and variable costs of $3 per unit

c. Variable expenses of $10 per unit

Preparing a contribution margin
income statement
(Obj. 2, 3)

E22-2 La Vega Shirtmakers' April income statement appears as follows:

LA VEGA SHIRTMAKERS INCOME STATEMENT APRIL 19XX		
Sales revenue		$637,000
Cost of goods sold		448,000
Gross margin		189,000
Operating expenses:		
Selling	$72,000	
General and administrative	42,000	114,000
Operating income................................		$ 75,000

La Vega accounting records indicate that cost of goods sold is a variable expense. Selling expense is 20 percent fixed and 80 percent variable. General and administrative expense is half fixed and half variable. Prepare La Vega's contribution margin income statement for April. Compute the expected increase in operating income to the nearest $1,000 if sales increase by $50,000.

Using a contribution margin
income statement
(Obj. 2, 3)

E22-3 For its top managers, Star Refining Corp. formats its income statement as follows:

STAR REFINING CORP. CONTRIBUTION MARGIN INCOME STATEMENT THREE MONTHS ENDED MARCH 31, 19X3	
Sales revenue	$385,000
Variable expenses	154,000
Contribution margin	231,000
Fixed expenses	200,000
Operating income...................	$ 31,000

Star's relevant range is between sales of $310,000 and $430,000. Prepare contribution margin income statements at those volume levels. Also, compute breakeven sales in dollars.

E22-4 LENB of Santa Fe has fixed expenses $75,000 and variable expenses of $3 per unit of its product, which it sells for $5.50 per unit.

Computing breakeven sales by the contribution margin approach (Obj. 3)

Required

1. Compute the company's contribution margin per unit and its contribution margin ratio.
2. Determine the breakeven point in units and in dollars, using the contribution margin approach.

E22-5 For several years, Bratkovich's Restaurant has offered a lunch special for $4.50. Monthly fixed expenses have been $4,500. The variable cost of a meal has been $1.50. Vincent Bratkovich, the owner, believes that by remodeling the restaurant and upgrading the food services, he can increase the price of the lunch special to $5.25. Monthly fixed expenses would increase to $6,600 and the variable expenses would increase to $1.75 per meal. Use the equation approach to compute Bratkovich's monthly breakeven sales in dollars before and after remodeling.

Computing a change in breakeven sales (Obj. 3)

E22-6 Green Line Motor Freight delivers freight throughout Iowa, Nebraska, and Kansas. The company has monthly fixed expenses of $490,000 and a contribution margin of 70 percent of revenues.

Computing breakeven sales and operating income or loss under different conditions (Obj. 3, 4)

Required

1. Compute Green Line's monthly breakeven sales in dollars. Use the contribution margin approach.
2. Compute Green Line's monthly operating income or operating loss if revenues are $500,000 and if they are $800,000.

E22-7 Consider the following cases.

Computing breakeven sales and sales needed to earn a target operating income; sales-mix considerations (Obj. 3, 4, 7)

a. Honey's Auto Supply has fixed monthly expenses of $4,290 and a contribution margin ratio of 30 percent. What must monthly sales be for the business to break even? To earn operating income of $3,300?

b. Bill's Boutique sells two product lines, one with a contribution margin ratio of 50 percent, the other with a contribution margin ratio of 60 percent. Each product line makes up half of sales. If monthly fixed expenses are $4,620, what must monthly sales be for the business to break even? To earn operating income of $4,950?

E22-8 Three college friends open an off-campus shop named J. I. T-Shirts. They plan to sell a standard T-shirt for $6 and a fancier version for $7.50. The $6 shirt costs them $3, and the $7.50 shirt costs them $3.50. The friends expect to sell two fancy T-shirts for each standard T-shirt. Their monthly fixed expenses are $2,805. How many of each type of T-shirt must they sell monthly to break even? To earn $1,210?

Cost-volume-profit analysis with a sales mix (Obj. 3, 4, 7)

E22-9 Suppose that Dodger Stadium, the home of the Los Angeles Dodgers, earns total revenue that averages $18 for every ticket sold. Annual fixed expenses are $16 million, and variable expenses are $2 per ticket. Prepare the ballpark's CVP graph under these assumptions. Show the breakeven point in dollars and in tickets. Label fixed expenses, variable expenses, the operating loss area, and the operating income area on the graph.

Graphing cost-volume-profit relationships (Obj. 5)

E22-10 The top managers of Burdick Hunter, Inc., are planning the budget for 19X6. The accountant who prepared the CVP graph at the top of page 940 forgot to label the lines.

Analyzing a cost-volume-profit graph (Obj. 5)

Required

Answer the following questions asked by the managers:

1. What do the lines mean?
2. Where is the operating income area? The operating loss area?
3. What is breakeven sales in units and in dollars?
4. What will be operating income (or operating loss) if sales are 3,400 units?

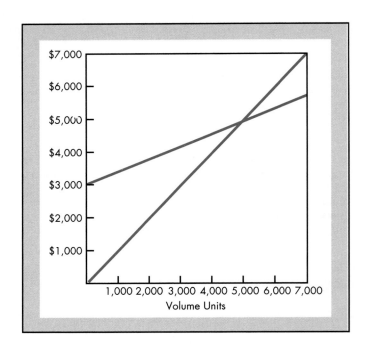

Computing a margin of safety
(Obj. 6)

E22-11 Round-the-Clock convenience store has a monthly operating income target of $5,000. Variable expenses are 60 percent of sales, and fixed monthly expenses are $8,000. Compute the monthly margin of safety in dollars if the store achieves its income goal. Express Round-the-Clock's margin of safety as a percent of target sales.

Conventional (absorption costing) and contribution margin (variable costing) income statements; business decision
(Obj. 2)

E22-12 The 19X4 data that follow pertain to the Erickson Company, manufacturer of a single product:

Sale price: $120
Variable manufacturing cost per unit: $95
Variable operating cost per unit: $15
Fixed manufacturing cost: $500,000

Fixed operating cost: $250,000
Units produced: 100,000
Units sold: 90,000

Required

1. Prepare both conventional (absorption costing) and contribution margin (variable costing) income statements for Erickson Company.
2. Which statement shows the higher operating income? Why?
3. Erickson's marketing vice-president believes that a sales promotion that costs $75,000 would increase sales to 100,000 units. Should the company go ahead with the promotion? Give your reason.

CHALLENGE EXERCISE

Computing contribution margin for one of two products
(Obj 7)

E22-13 Himalaya's, Inc., manufactures two styles of climbing shoe—the Mountaineer and the Pro Mountaineer. The following data pertain to the Mountaineer:

Sale price.. $80
Variable manufacturing cost............... 35
Variable operating cost....................... 9

Himalaya's monthly fixed expenses total $38,000. When Mountaineers and Pro Mountaineers are sold in the mix of 7:3, respectively, the sale of 2,000 total units results in an operating income of $30,000. Compute the unit contribution margin of Pro Mountaineers.

P22-1A Hunt Club Clothiers is managed as traditionally as the button-down shirts that have made it famous. Arch Huntington founded the business in 1952 and has directed operations "by the seat of his pants" ever since. Approaching retirement, he must turn the business over to his son, Ralph. Recently Arch and Ralph had this conversation:

Explaining the contribution margin approach and the margin of safety to decision makers
(Obj. 2, 6)

Ralph: Dad, I am convinced that we can increase sales by advertising. I think we can spend $600 monthly on advertising and increase monthly sales by $6,000. With our contribution margin, operating income should increase by $3,000.

Arch: You know how I feel about advertising. We've never needed it in the past. Why now?

Ralph: Two new shops have opened near us this year, and those guys are getting lots of business. I've noticed our profit margin slipping as the year has unfolded. Our margin of safety is at its lowest point ever.

Arch: Profit margin I understand, but what is the contribution margin that you mentioned? And what is this "margin of safety"?

Required

Explain for Arch Huntington the contribution margin approach to decision making. Show how Ralph Huntington computed the $3,000. (Advertising is a fixed cost.) Also, describe what Ralph means by margin of safety, and explain why the business's situation is critical.

P22-2A The budgets of four companies yield the following information:

Computing contribution margin and breakeven analysis
(Obj. 2, 3)

	E	F	G	H
Target sales...............................	$ _____	$290,000	$ _____	$500,000
Variable expenses	100,000	120,000	104,000	
Fixed expenses	82,000	138,000		
Operating income (loss)...............	$ _____	$ _____	$ 35,000	$ 60,000
Units sold	5,000			100,000
Unit contribution margin.............		$100	$12	$2
Contribution margin ratio............	0.200		0.600	

Fill in the blanks for each company. Which company has the lowest breakeven point? What causes the low breakeven point?

P22-3A The Tam O'Shanter is a schooner that sails from Annapolis, Maryland, during the spring and fall. During the summer the ship leaves from Mystic, Connecticut. The average cruise has 45 tourists on board, and each person pays $50 for a day's sail. The ship sails 80 days each year.

Computing breakeven revenue and the revenue needed to earn a target operating income; preparing a contribution margin income statement
(Obj. 2, 3, 4)

The Tam O'Shanter has a crew of 8. Each crew member earns an average of $100 per cruise. The crew is paid only when the ship sails. The other variable expense is for refreshments, which average $10 per passenger per cruise. Annual fixed expenses total $66,000.

Required

1. Compute revenue and variable expenses for each cruise.

2. Use the equation approach to compute the number of cruises the Tam O'Shanter must make each year to break even.

3. Use the contribution margin approach to compute the number of cruises needed each year to earn $70,000. Is this profit goal realistic? Give your reason.

4. Prepare the Tam O'Shanter's contribution margin income statement for 80 cruises for the year. Report only two categories of expenses: variable and fixed.

P22-4A Suppose that Specialty Ballpoints imprints ballpoint pens with company logos. The company has fixed expenses of $300,000 per year plus variable expenses of $1.60 per box of pens. For each box of pens sold, the company earns revenue of $2.90.

Analyzing CVP relationships
(Obj. 2, 3, 4)

Required

1. Use the equation approach to compute the number of boxes of pens Specialty Ballpoints must sell each year to break even.

2. Use the contribution margin approach to compute the dollar sales Specialty needs in order to earn $25,500 in operating income.

3. Prepare Specialty's contribution margin income statement for 19X5 for sales of 240,000 boxes of pens. Cost of goods sold is 80 percent of variable expenses. Operating expenses make up the rest of variable expenses and all of fixed expenses.

4. The company is considering an expansion that will increase fixed expenses by 30 percent and variable expenses by 10 cents per box of pens. Compute the new breakeven point in units and in dollars. Use either the equation approach or the contribution margin approach.

5. How will what you learned from this problem help you manage a business?

Using a contribution margin income statement for breakeven analysis; sales mix, margin of safety, and changes in CVP relationships
(Obj. 2, 3, 6, 7)

P22-5A The contribution margin income statement of Napoli Pizzeria for May 19X6 follows:

NAPOLI PIZZERIA CONTRIBUTION MARGIN INCOME STATEMENT MAY 19X6		
Sales revenue		$160,000
Variable expenses:		
Cost of goods sold	$32,000	
Selling	25,000	
General and administrative	3,000	60,000
Contribution margin		100,000
Fixed expenses:		
Selling	27,000	
General and administrative	10,500	37,500
Operating income.................................		$ 62,500

Napoli's sells three small pizzas for every large pizza. A small pizza sells for $10, with a variable expense of $4.25. A large pizza sells for $20, with a variable expense of $6.

Required

1. Determine Napoli's monthly breakeven point in the numbers of small pizzas and large pizzas. Prove the correctness of your computation by preparing a summary contribution margin income statement at breakeven. Show only two categories of expenses: variable and fixed.

2. Compute Napoli's margin of safety in dollars.

3. If Napoli's can increase monthly sales by 15 percent above $160,000, what will operating income be?

4. Napoli's hopes to decrease monthly fixed expenses by $10,000. Use the contribution margin approach to determine the new breakeven sales in dollars.

Computing breakeven sales and sales needed to earn a target operating income; graphing CVP relationships
(Obj. 3, 4, 5)

P22-6A Old Mexico Travel is opening an office in San Antonio. Fixed monthly expenses are office rent ($3,000), depreciation of office furniture ($200), utilities ($110), a special telephone line ($520), a connection with the airlines' computerized reservation service ($380), and the salary of a travel agent ($1,400). Variable expenses are utilities (2 percent of sales), incentive compensation for the employee (5 percent of sales), advertising (4 percent of sales), supplies and postage (1 percent of sales), and a usage fee for the telephone line and computerized reservation service (3 percent of sales).

Required

1. Use the contribution margin approach to compute Old Mexico's breakeven sales in dollars. If the average sale is a $600 plane ticket, how many tickets must be sold to break even?

2. Use the equation approach to compute the dollar sales needed to earn a target monthly operating income of $4,000.

3. Graph the travel agency's CVP relationships. Assume that an average sale is a $600 plane ticket. Show the breakeven point, fixed expenses, variable expenses, operating loss area, operating income area, and the sales in units and dollars when monthly operating income of $4,000 is earned. The graph should range from 0 to 25 units.

4. Assume that the average sale price decreases to $440. Use the contribution margin approach to compute the new breakeven point in tickets sold. What is the effect of the sale price decrease on the breakeven point?

P22-1B Saffron Restaurant Supply is opening early next year. The owner is considering two plans for obtaining the plant assets and employee labor needed for operations. Plan 1 calls for purchasing all equipment outright and paying employees straight salaries. Under plan 2, Saffron would lease equipment month by month and pay employees low salaries but give them a big part of their pay in commissions on sales. Discuss the effects of the two plans on variable expenses, fixed expenses, breakeven sales, and likely profits for a new business in the start-up stage. Indicate which plan you favor for Saffron.

Explaining the effects of different cost behavior patterns on the breakeven point and on likely profits
(Obj. 1)

P22-2B The budgets of four companies yield the following information:

Computing contribution margin and breakeven analysis
(Obj. 2, 3)

	W	X	Y	Z
Target sales....................................	$600,000	$280,000	$248,000	$
Variable expenses			132,000	130,000
Fixed expenses	312,000	130,000		
Operating income (loss)...................	$	$	$ 7,000	$160,000
Units sold	112,000	11,000		8,000
Unit contribution margin................		$12	$4	$40
Contribution margin ratio...............	0.30			

Fill in the blanks for each company. Which company has the lowest breakeven point? What causes the low breakeven point?

P22-3B Tradewinds Cruises sails a schooner from Maui. The average cruise has 80 tourists on board. Each person pays $75 for a day's sail in the Pacific. The ship sails 100 days each year.

Computing breakeven revenue and the revenue needed to earn a target operating income; preparing a contribution margin income statement
(Obj. 2, 3, 4)

The schooner has a crew of 12. Each crew member earns an average of $85 per cruise. The crew is paid only when the ship sails. Other variable expenses are for refreshments, which average $14 per passenger per cruise. Annual fixed expenses total $138,960.

Required

1. Compute revenue and variable expenses for each cruise.
2. Use the equation approach to compute the number of cruises needed annually to break even.
3. Use the contribution margin approach to compute the number of cruises needed annually to earn $200,000. Is this profit goal realistic? Give your reason.
4. Prepare Tradewinds' contribution margin income statement for 100 cruises each year. Report only two categories of expenses: variable and fixed.

P22-4B Suppose that Anson Advertising Associates imprints calendars with company names. The company has fixed expenses of $432,000 each month plus variable expense of $2 per carton of calendars. For each carton of calendars sold, Anson earns revenue of $3.20.

Analyzing CVP relationships
(Obj. 2, 3, 4)

Required

1. Use the equation approach to compute the number of cartons of calendars Anson must sell each month to break even.
2. Use the contribution margin approach to compute the dollar amount of monthly sales Anson needs in order to earn $60,000 in operating income.
3. Prepare Anson's contribution margin income statement for June for sales of 450,000 cartons of calendars. Cost of goods sold is 70 percent of variable expenses. Operating expenses make up the rest of the variable expenses and all of the fixed expenses.
4. The company is considering an expansion that will increase fixed expenses by 40 percent and variable expenses by 10 percent. Compute the new breakeven point in units and in dollars. Use either the equation approach or the contribution margin approach.
5. How will what you learned from this problem help you manage a business?

Using a contribution margin
income statement for breakeven
analysis; sales mix, margin of
safety, and changes in CVP
relationships
(Obj. 2, 3, 6, 7)

P22-5B The contribution margin income statement of The Working Man's Store for November 19X5 is as follows:

THE WORKING MAN'S STORE CONTRIBUTION MARGIN INCOME STATEMENT NOVEMBER 19X5		
Sales revenue		$60,000
Variable expenses:		
Cost of goods sold	$22,000	
Selling	13,000	
General and administrative	7,000	42,000
Contribution margin		18,000
Fixed expenses:		
Selling	11,000	
General and administrative	3,000	14,000
Operating income...................................		$ 4,000

The Working Man sells two ties for every belt. The ties sell for $7, with a variable expense of $4.90 per unit. The belts sell for $6, with a variable unit cost of $4.20.

Required

1. Determine The Working Man's monthly breakeven point in the numbers of ties and belts. Prove the correctness of your computation by preparing a summary contribution margin income statement at breakeven. Show only two categories of expenses: variable and fixed.
2. Compute The Working Man's margin of safety in dollars.
3. Suppose that The Working Man increases monthly sales by 15 percent above $60,000. Compute operating income.
4. The Working Man may expand the store and increase monthly fixed expenses by $4,800. Use the contribution margin approach to determine the new breakeven sales in dollars.

Computing breakeven sales and
sales needed to earn a target
operating income; graphing CVP
relationships
(Obj. 3, 4, 5)

P22-6B Overseas Travel is opening an office in San Diego. Fixed monthly expenses are office rent ($3,400), depreciation of office furniture ($190), utilities ($140), a special telephone line ($390), a connection with the airlines' computerized reservation service ($480), and the salary of a travel agent ($1,800). Variable expenses are utilities (3 percent of sales), incentive compensation of the employee (6 percent of sales), advertising (6 percent of sales), supplies and postage (1 percent of sales), and a usage fee for the telephone line and computerized reservation service (4 percent of sales).

Required

1. Use the contribution margin approach to compute the travel agency's breakeven sales in dollars. If the average sale is an $800 plane ticket, how many tickets must be sold to break even?
2. Use the equation approach to compute dollar sales needed to earn monthly operating income of $3,500.
3. Graph the travel agency's CVP relationships. Assume that an average sale is an $800 plane ticket. Show the breakeven point, fixed expenses, variable expenses, operating loss area, operating income area, and the sales in units and dollars when monthly operating income of $3,500 is earned. The graph should range from 0 to 20 units.
4. Assume that the average sale price decreases to $600. Use the contribution margin approach to compute the new breakeven point in units. What is the effect of the sale price decrease on the breakeven point?

EXTENDING YOUR KNOWLEDGE

DECISION PROBLEMS

1. Richard and Wanwipa Atkins live in Calgary, Alberta. Two years ago, they visited Thailand. Wanwipa, a professional chef, was impressed with the cooking methods and the spices used in the Thai food. Calgary has no Thai restaurant, and the Atkinses are contemplating opening one. Wan-

wipa would supervise the cooking, and Richard would leave his current job to be the maitre'd. The restaurant would serve dinner Tuesday through Saturday.

Richard has noticed a restaurant for lease. The restaurant has seven tables, each of which can seat four. Tables can be moved together for a large party. Wanwipa is planning two seatings per evening.

The Atkinses have drawn up the following estimates:

Average revenue, including beverages and dessert..............	$40 per meal
Average cost of the food, including preparation	$12 per meal
Chef's and dishwasher's salaries	$49,600 per year
Rent (premises, equipment)	$3,000 per month
Cleaning (linen and premises)	$500 per month
Replacement of dishes, cutlery, glasses	$300 per month
Utilities, advertising, telephone	$1,400 per month

Compute breakeven revenue for the restaurant. Also compute the amount of revenue needed to earn operating income of $80,000 for the year. How many meals must the Atkinses serve each night to earn their target income of $80,000? Should the couple open the restaurant?

2. Lakeshore Toy Company makes three lines of toys. Each line is manufactured in a different plant, and each line has a different set of CVP relationships. Budgeted income statements for 19X5 are:

Using a contribution margin income statement to make business decisions (Obj. 2, 3)

	Newborns	Toddlers	Preschoolers
Sales..............................	$320,000	$150,000	$270,000
Variable expenses	64,000	75,000	108,000
Contribution margin....................	256,000	75,000	162,000
Fixed expenses.............................	188,000	120,000	126,000
Operating income (loss)..............	$ 68,000	$ (45,000)	$ 36,000

Average sale prices are $2 for toys for newborns, $3 for toys for toddlers, and $5 for preschoolers' toys.

Required

1. Which product line is the least profitable?
2. How many toddler toys must be sold to break even?
3. Prepare a contribution margin income statement for 19X5 assuming that sales of toddler toys are eliminated altogether. Also assume that $120,000 is the toddler line's fixed cost for all volumes in the range of zero to 100,000 toys.
4. Would it be wise to drop the toddler toy line immediately? What would you recommend to Lakeshore's management regarding the future of the line?

ETHICAL ISSUE

In recent years, professional sports teams have shifted from paying stars straight salaries to paying them lower salaries but adding a bonus that depends on team revenues. That way, a star is motivated to play harder. The more the team wins, the greater the team revenues as more and more fans flock to the stadium and as television companies increase payments for the rights to broadcast games. If the star has a bad year, the team may win fewer games and revenues could drop, and the star's compensation would be lower. By shifting player compensation from straight salary to a bonus that is based on team revenues, these player contracts increase the team's percentage of variable costs and decrease its percentage of fixed costs.

Required

1. Why would team owners favor these contracts?
2. Are team owners taking advantage of stars? Are these contracts ethical?

Chapter 23
Cost Behavior Analysis

After studying this chapter, you should be able to

1. Identify types of fixed costs

2. Use cost behavior analysis to make business decisions

3. Identify two approaches for controlling operating labor costs

4. Compute the equal-cost volume of two cost behavior patterns

5. Graph the three major types of cost functions

6. Use three methods to estimate mixed-cost functions

7. Evaluate a mixed-cost function

❝ If successful, this technology would offer opportunity for significant cost reductions and energy savings, and also would provide substantial environmental benefits. ❞

THOMAS J. USHER, PRESIDENT AND CHIEF OPERATING OFFICER OF USX CORPORATION

In October 1994, the U.S. Steel Group of USX Corporation announced its intent to establish a joint venture with Nucor Corporation and Praxair, Inc., to develop a new technology that would produce steel directly from iron carbide. The parties announced that they would conduct a feasibility study of the iron carbide-to-steel process. If the study proved successful, the joint-venture company would construct a demonstration plant to evaluate the commercial feasibility of direct steelmaking.

Thomas J. Usher, president and chief operating officer of USX, said that U.S. Steel would contribute substantially to the development of the new technology. The company would also provide capital and technical expertise for the design, construction, and operation of the demonstration plant.

If direct steelmaking proves to be feasible, it will yield significant reductions in the cost of steel. It will also be much cleaner than conventional steelmaking processes, resulting in lower air and water emissions and fewer solid-waste byproducts. *Source: U.S. Steel Group news release, October 12, 1994.*

• • • • •

What will be U.S. Steel's cost per ton of steel in a direct steelmaking plant? What will happen to American Airlines' maintenance costs if three Boeing 757s are added to its fleet? By how much will Sears's warranty expenses decrease if lawnmower defects are reduced by 50 percent? Managers continually face questions like these. They can make better planning and control decisions if they understand how costs behave—that is, how business activities, or drivers, affect costs.

Chapter 22 considered one cost driver—total volume of activity—and introduced the two basic cost behavior patterns—fixed and variable. In this chapter we examine how another factor, management policy, affects costs. We also show how managers analyze cost behavior. Knowledge of cost behavior is essential, particularly for budgeting and evaluating performance. We begin by looking at fixed costs.

Fixed Costs

OBJECTIVE 1

Identify types of fixed costs

◄▪▪▪◄▪▪▪◄▪▪▪ Recall from Chapter 22 (p. 919) that fixed costs are costs that do not change in total despite wide changes in volume; they occur even if the company makes no sales.

Fixed costs, defined and graphed in Chapter 22, also are called *capacity costs*. They enable businesses to operate at planned levels for activities such as manufacturing, sales, administration, and research. ◄▪▪▪ Long-run sales forecasts, available technology, and management strategies affect the amounts of fixed costs that managers are willing to incur. In the short run, these costs usually are unaffected by differences between planned and actual volumes of activity. For planning and controlling, fixed costs may be categorized as either *committed* or *discretionary*.

Committed Fixed Costs

Committed fixed costs are the fixed costs that result from having property, plant, equipment, and key managerial personnel. Examples include depreciation, property taxes, and insurance on a steel mill.

Committed fixed costs usually are incurred in large, indivisible "chunks." Consider machines that mount tires onto wheels in an automobile assembly plant. Workers can mount 98,400 tires per month on each machine. If a Ford Motor Company plant needs an additional 30,000 units of tire-mounting capacity, its manager cannot buy 30 percent (30,000/98,400) of a machine. The manager can buy one machine, which will yield 68,400 more units of capacity than needed. In contrast, the manager can purchase exactly 30,000 more tires or wheels.

The amount of a company's committed fixed cost is approximately what it would incur if a strike, shortage of materials, or other problem temporarily stopped production and sales activity. These plant and basic organization costs cannot be reduced without hurting the company's ability to meet long-term goals. Indeed, many committed fixed costs cannot be altered in response to month-to-month or even year-to-year volume changes. For example, a cancer-treatment hospital must have sophisticated treatment equipment regardless of whether 5 patients or 50 patients are admitted in any particular month.

OBJECTIVE 2

Use cost behavior analysis to make business decisions

EFFECTS ON DECISIONS Should Procter & Gamble build a new plant to meet budgeted increases in demand for its soap products? Should the size of a new audio-video store in a mall be 40,000 or 80,000 square feet? To answer these and other capacity-related questions, managers take a long-term view. The goal is to tailor capacity to expected demand in order to maximize operating income over several years. Such decisions require trade-offs between operations from year to year.

Mary Harmon is considering two store sites for her Harmon's Deli restaurant and take-out business. Each of the stores must be leased for two years. Harmon's decision depends on forecasted demand for her restaurant's food. Exhibit 23-1 gives the data for the site-selection decision. Exhibit 23-2 shows forecasted contribution margin income statements, based on predicted demand levels, for both stores.

EXHIBIT 23-1
Data for Selection of Restaurant Site

PANEL A—Product-Related Data

Average revenue per order	$7
Average variable cost per order	3
Average contribution margin per order	$4
Predicted demand for orders, 19X1	25,000
Predicted demand for orders, 19X2	40,000

PANEL B—Store-Related Data

	Smaller Store	Larger Store
Capacity in orders served	25,000	50,000
Annual rent expense	$40,000	$60,000
Annual other fixed expenses	$10,000	$10,000

Smaller Store

	19X1		19X2
Sales revenue (25,000 × $7)	$175,000	(25,000 × $7)	$175,000
Variable expenses (25,000 × $3)	75,000	(25,000 × $3)	75,000
Contribution margin	100,000		100,000
Fixed expenses:			
Rent	$40,000		$40,000
Other	10,000 50,000		10,000 50,000
Operating income	$ 50,000		$ 50,000

Two-year total
$100,000

Larger Store

	19X1		19X2
Sales revenue (25,000 × $7)	$175,000	(40,000 × $7)	$280,000
Variable expenses (25,000 × $3)	75,000	(40,000 × $3)	120,000
Contribution margin	100,000		160,000
Fixed expenses:			
Rent	$60,000		$60,000
Other	10,000 70,000		10,000 70,000
Operating income	$ 30,000		$ 90,000

Two-year total
$120,000

For 19X1 only, Harmon would be better off with the smaller store. The additional 25,000 (50,000 − 25,000) orders of sales capacity of the larger store are not needed that year; the smaller store has enough capacity to satisfy predicted demand. The excess capacity of the larger store thus provides no benefit in 19X1 but costs $20,000 ($60,000 − $40,000) in additional rent. This cost accounts for the $20,000 ($50,000 − $30,000) difference in operating income between the two alternatives.

For 19X2 alone, Harmon would be worse off with the smaller store. Its lower capacity of 25,000 orders restricts sales to that number despite higher demand. Revenues, expenses, and operating income therefore are the same as in 19X1. But for 19X2, the larger store's capacity allows Harmon to satisfy all 40,000 units of predicted demand. The net benefit of the additional units of capacity is $40,000, computed as follows:

$$
\begin{array}{ccc}
\text{Additional} & \text{Additional} & \text{Additional} \\
\text{contribution} & - \quad \text{fixed} & = \text{operating} \\
\text{margin} & \text{expense} & \text{income}
\end{array}
$$

$$
\begin{array}{ccc}
\text{Additional} \times \left(\begin{array}{cc} \text{Unit} & \text{Unit} \\ \text{sale} - & \text{variable} \\ \text{price} & \text{cost} \end{array} \right) & - \quad \begin{array}{c} \text{Additional} \\ \text{fixed expense} \end{array} & = \begin{array}{c} \text{Additional} \\ \text{operating} \\ \text{income} \end{array}
\end{array}
$$

$$
\begin{array}{ccc}
(40{,}000 - 25{,}000) \times & ($7 - $3) & - ($60{,}000 - $40{,}000) = \\
15{,}000 \quad \times & $4 & - \quad $20{,}000 \quad = \\
$60{,}000 & & - \quad $20{,}000 \quad = $40{,}000
\end{array}
$$

This $40,000 of additional income appears in Exhibit 23-2 as the difference between the larger store's 19X2 income of $90,000 and the smaller store's 19X2 income of $50,000.

To decide which store to lease, Mary Harmon must consider the two years together. On the basis of her demand predictions, she should lease the larger store. Although she incurs a $20,000 cost of idle capacity in 19X1, the larger store's greater capacity yields more operating income over the two-year period.

	Low Demand 32,000 orders		High Demand 48,000 orders	
Sales revenue (32,000 × $7)		$224,000	(48,000 × $7)	$336,000
Variable expenses (32,000 × $3)		96,000	(48,000 × $3)	144,000
Contribution margin		128,000		192,000
Fixed expenses:				
Rent	$60,000		$60,000	
Other	10,000	70,000	10,000	70,000
Operating income		$ 58,000		$122,000

Many managers take this analysis one step further. They consider the possibility that actual demand for food may differ from the initial, "most-likely" predictions. Suppose Harmon believes that her restaurant's success in 19X1 may encourage someone to open a competing business nearby, resulting in 19X2 demand of only 32,000 orders. Conversely, the restaurant could be more successful than predicted. Customers might demand as many as 48,000 orders the second year. In either case, 19X2 operating income for the smaller store would remain $50,000 (Exhibit 23-2) because both the low number of 32,000 orders and the high number of 48,000 orders are above that store's 25,000-order capacity. Exhibit 23-3 shows expected operating incomes for the larger store for both the lower and the higher levels of demand.

EFFECTS OF VARIOUS PREDICTIONS Exhibits 23-2 and 23-3 together demonstrate why accurate demand predictions are crucial for determining the appropriate amount of capacity to buy or lease. If 19X2 demand is only 32,000 orders, Mary Harmon will be better off leasing the smaller store. Its two-year total operating income of $100,000 in Exhibit 23-2 is $12,000 more than the $88,000 ($30,000 + $58,000) total for the larger store. The larger store allows Harmon to fill 7,000 (32,000 − 25,000) more orders in the second year, but the $28,000 (7,000 × $4) contribution margin on those orders is insufficient to offset the extra two-year rent expense of $40,000. If 19X2 demand turns out to be 48,000 orders, the larger store is even more attractive than the initial computations indicated. This store allows Harmon to meet the additional 8,000 (48,000 − 40,000) units of 19X2 demand, adding $32,000 (8,000 × $4) to the initial $20,000 difference in total operating incomes. The two-year income for the larger store increases to $152,000 ($30,000 + $122,000), but the total for the smaller store remains $100,000.

Which store size should Mary Harmon choose? Her decision is affected by her attitudes toward risk. Because of its lower fixed cost, the smaller store has a lower breakeven point in units and a higher margin of safety each year. ◄▥ It also provides more operating income at lower volume levels, including 25,000 orders. The smaller store is the more conservative choice.

The larger store requires a higher sales volume to break even, but it provides additional capacity that could lead to higher incomes at higher volume levels, including the owner's predictions for 19X2. Regardless of her decision, Harmon's objective will be to use as much of the leased capacity as possible. For a given committed fixed cost that provides a specific amount of capacity, increased usage usually leads to increased operating income.

◄▥ ◄▥ ◄▥ In Chapter 22 we defined the breakeven point (p. 924) as the sales level at which operating income is zero and the margin of safety (p. 929) as the excess of expected sales over breakeven sales.

Discretionary Fixed Costs

Discretionary, or **managed, fixed costs** are those fixed costs that arise from periodic (usually yearly) budget decisions that reflect top-management policies. These costs have no clear relationship between inputs and outputs. Examples include advertising, public relations, employee training programs, and management salaries. In the chapter-opening story, U.S. Steel is incurring discretionary fixed costs to study the feasibility of direct steelmaking.

It is impossible to measure precisely a "correct" amount to spend on discretionary fixed costs. Many other costs have a measurable relationship between *inputs*, represented by the costs, and *outputs*, represented by production, sales, or service activity. For example, a construction contractor may specify that five gallons of paint should be used to finish the inside of a house. The contractor then may calculate the direct materials cost of the painting activity. In contrast, the proper amount to spend on an advertising campaign to sell the house is not so easy to determine. As a department store executive once said, "Fifty percent of my advertising is a total waste. The trouble is, I don't know which 50 percent is wasted." At the beginning of each budget period, managers budget discretionary fixed costs on the basis of traditions, rules of thumb, industry customs, and the anticipated behavior of competitors.

The resources acquired with discretionary budget expenditures must be carefully planned and used to produce the desired effects. Consider an employee-training program. The full amount authorized for the program may be spent for first-rate seminars, and all targeted employees may attend the presentations. The setup is perfect, but the program will have little effect on operations if the attendees are indifferent or if the seminar materials are designed for a different audience.

In addition to one-year versus multiple-year planning horizons, there is another difference between discretionary fixed costs and committed fixed costs. It is more difficult to determine whether resources acquired with discretionary costs are used effectively. The results of advertising, research, and training programs are much harder to measure than the results of using plant and equipment to make products such as steel. Thomas J. Usher of U.S. Steel might be convinced that his employees would benefit from a one-day seminar on sexual-harassment awareness. But imagine how difficult it would be for him to measure the long-term effects, both financial and interpersonal, of such a program!

There is another key difference between discretionary and committed fixed costs. Under temporarily difficult circumstances, some discretionary expenditures can be reduced for short periods of time with little damage to the organization's ability to meet long-range goals. During a year of operating losses, a company that had been spending $100,000 on labor relations programs could cut back those expenditures. The unfavorable effects of this discretionary cutback may be far less severe than the effects of selling a plant in order to reduce committed costs.

Short Exercise: Identify each of the following as either discretionary or committed fixed costs: (1) property taxes; (2) management development programs; (3) salary of president; (4) advertising; (5) lease payments on fleet vehicles. *A:* Committed: (1), (3), (5); discretionary: (2), (4).

Variable Costs

In Chapter 22, we saw that a *variable cost* is a cost that changes in direct proportion to changes in volume of activity. Variable costs are either *engineered* or *discretionary*.◀▥ ◀▥ ◀▥

◀▥ ◀▥ ◀▥ Recall from Chapter 22 (p. 918) that variable costs include sales commissions, direct material costs, delivery costs, and others.

Key Point: An engineered variable cost bears a cause-and-effect relationship to the measure of activity. For example, the direct materials cost of the food in Harmon's restaurant increases directly with sales.

Engineered Variable Costs

Engineered variable costs result from measurable, often observable, cause-and-effect relationships between inputs and outputs. These costs are most frequently found in manufacturing and distribution businesses. Examples of input-output relationships include one pound of potatoes needed to make an eight-ounce bag of potato chips, two fan belts per automobile, and one square foot of shrink-wrap material per package of bacon. Other examples are 4 hours to stain and varnish a piece of furniture, 5 minutes to sew a shirt, and 10 seconds to mount a tire onto a wheel. The efficiency of those costs can be measured by relating the quantity of inputs used to the quantity of outputs achieved.

Discretionary Variable Costs

Most variable costs are engineered, but some are discretionary. **Discretionary variable costs** change with sales or production volume simply because management has decided to spend a certain percentage of each sales dollar, or a certain dollar amount for each unit sold, for items such as research and advertising. A change in the behavior of these costs indicates a change in management's authorization to spend, which is discretionary. In contrast, a change in cause-and-effect relationships brought about by either new technology or different methods of performing tasks is engineered, not discretionary.

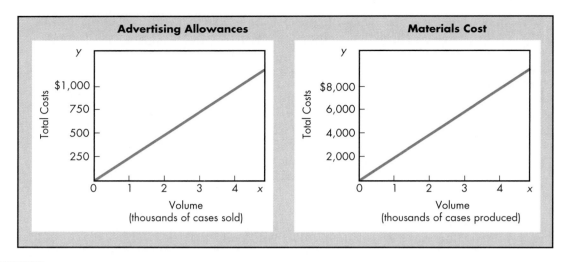

Advertising Allowances	Materials Cost

EXHIBIT 23-4
Variable Cost Behavior Patterns

Discretionary variable costs have graphical patterns similar to those of engineered material and labor costs, but for different reasons. Consider advertising allowances. Manufacturers such as Coca-Cola and PepsiCo stimulate sales by giving their retailers an advertising allowance for each unit sold. In turn, the retailers are supposed to spend the money for local advertising and sales promotions.

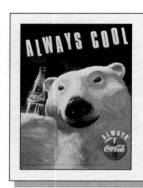

"Coca-Cola's top management could easily decide to pay the retailers a lump-sum amount (fixed cost) or both a lump-sum and a per-case allowance (mixed cost) next year."

Suppose that the costs of The Coca-Cola Company include an advertising allowance to retailers of $0.25 per case of drinks sold, and materials are used at the rate of $2 per case produced. Exhibit 23-4 graphs the costs of these advertising allowances and materials in relation to volume. The two graphs look identical, but in reality no *necessary* cause-and-effect relationship exists between cases sold and advertising allowances in the first graph. Coca-Cola's top management could easily decide to pay the retailers a lump-sum amount (fixed cost) or both a lump-sum and a per-case allowance (mixed cost) next year. In the second graph, the cost of materials varies directly with the number of cases produced. The cause-and-effect nature of this variable cost, which is engineered, is much more likely to continue from year to year than is the pattern of discretionary advertising allowances to retailers.

Real-World Example: Some state governments appropriate funds to colleges and universities on the basis of student credit hours. The appropriation rate is discretionary.

Using Cost Behavior Analysis to Budget and Control Operating Expenses

OBJECTIVE 3

Identify two approaches for controlling operating labor costs

If managers understand how costs behave, they are able to prepare useful budgets and to evaluate operating performance. Managers' approaches to budgeting depend on the traditions and management styles of their organizations. Consider a travel agency. How many agents should be employed? What should be the budgeted monthly compensation cost? Two basic budgeting approaches are available to answer these questions: the discretionary-fixed-cost approach and the engineered-variable-cost approach.

Discretionary-Fixed-Cost Approach

Most businesses manage operating labor costs as discretionary fixed costs. They tend to rely on department managers to judge the size of the necessary work force. Managers are reluctant to overhire because of the danger of having too many employees if the workload decreases. Consequently, short busy periods necessitate overtime or the hiring of temporary workers.

The **discretionary-fixed-cost approach** to managing relies on personal supervision for controlling costs. Managers control both by personal observation and by analyzing records of work activity (for example, tours booked or flights ticketed). Budgeted costs and consequent actual costs usually are very close, so variances are small. A **variance** is the difference between an actual amount and the corresponding budgeted amount.

Engineered-Variable-Cost Approach

A second approach to managing operating labor costs is to treat them as engineered variable costs. Use of the term *engineered* implies measurement. **Work measurement** is the careful analysis of a task: its size, the methods used, and its efficiency. Managers measure the workload in an operation or process to determine the number of employees needed to perform the work. To evaluate and improve performance, they quantify both inputs and outputs.

The work that is measured often is expressed in terms of cost drivers. Budgets are set for the units of cost-driver activity that occur in a given time span, such as orders packed per hour, credit applications processed per day, and phone calls answered per shift.

The **engineered-variable-cost approach** to managing applies formal work measurement to the budgeting process. Assume that 12 travel agents are employed by one branch of Carlson Travel in New York City. Suppose that each agent earns $2,400 per month. Careful analysis reveals that an agent should be able to book 24 trips in an eight-hour workday. Every agent works 20 days per month, yielding a monthly capacity of 5,760 (24 × 20 × 12) bookings.[1]

"The engineered-variable-cost approach is to develop a budget formula keyed to the unit cost of the individual trip booked by Carlson Travel."

The engineered-variable-cost approach is to develop a budget formula keyed to the unit cost of the individual trip booked by Carlson Travel. This cost may be computed as follows:

$$\text{Unit cost} = \frac{\text{Monthly salary}}{\text{Trips booked per month}}$$

$$= \frac{\$2,400}{(24 \text{ trips} \times 20 \text{ days})} = \frac{\$2,400}{480} = \$5 \text{ per trip booked}$$

Panel A of Exhibit 23-5 shows how the engineered-variable-cost approach plots the cost of each agent employed, step by step. The budget line is drawn at the end of each step to underscore the idea that each person should be working at full capacity. This tough-minded approach treats humans like water that can be turned on and off at a faucet. In contrast, Panel B of Exhibit 23-5 shows how the discretionary-fixed-cost approach plots a horizontal line for a relevant range of workload. The individuals employed are treated as a stable work force that is expected to have occasional idle time.

---

[1]This number is the approximate average or "normal" workload.

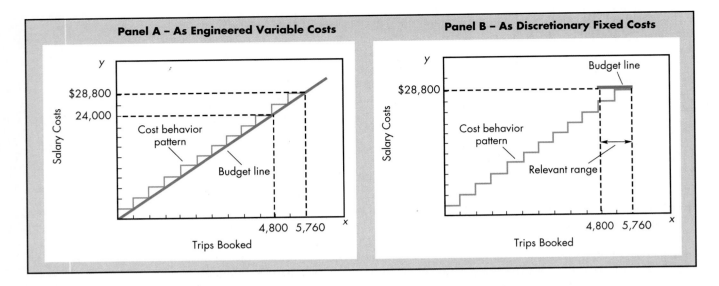

| | Panel A – As Engineered Variable Costs | Panel B – As Discretionary Fixed Costs |

EXHIBIT 23-5 *Approaches to Budgeting Operating Labor Costs*

Performance Reports

Short Exercise: An accounting firm employs 5 CPAs to prepare tax returns. Each CPA works 20 days per month, earns $3,000 a month, and is expected to prepare 5 tax returns per day. The actual labor cost for the 5 CPAs for March, when 490 tax returns were prepared, was $15,000. Compute the variance that would appear on the performance report under the (1) discretionary-fixed-cost approach and (2) engineered-variable-cost approach. *A:*

	Budget	Actual	Variance
(1)	$15,000	$15,000	0
(2)	$14,700*	$15,000	$300 U

*$15,000 salary per month/500 expected returns = $30 per return; $30 × 490 actual returns prepared = $14,700

In our example, Carlson Travel managers using the engineered-variable-cost approach would prepare the following performance report for a month in which 5,088 trips were booked:

	Budgeted as an Engineered Variable Cost	Actual Cost	Variance Amount	Variance Equivalent Persons
Travel agents' compensation	$25,440[2]	$28,800[3]	$3,360[4]	1.4[5]

The $3,360 unfavorable variance, which is equivalent to the salaries of 1.4 travel agents, is the price that management paid for one or both of the following: (1) inefficient productivity by the agents, (2) overstaffing in relation to the actual workload.

The travel agents' capacity was 5,760 bookings, not 5,088. If every customer who called or came through the door was served, management paid (consciously or unconsciously) $3,360 during the month to maintain a stable work force geared to "normal" needs. The alternative is to hire and lay off agents monthly according to expected workload. But this probably is not wise because temporary workers may lack the professionalism that customers demand.

 STOP & THINK Our discussion of the causes of variances under the engineered-variable-cost approach assumes that $5 per trip booked is an appropriate "standard," or budgeted unit cost. When should the managers of Carlson Travel change that amount?

Answer: The managers should change the budgeted cost per trip with every change in (1) the monthly salary of travel agents or in (2) the average number of trips that each travel agent should be able to book per month. The monthly quantity may change if the number of days worked per month increases or decreases or if the average time required to book one trip changes. For example, agents book both domestic and international trips. Suppose that international trips require more paperwork and thus take longer to book. If the ratio of international trips to domestic trips increases, the budgeted number of trips per month decreases, and vice versa. Carlson's managers should continually review their operations to ensure that budget data are realistic.

---

[2]5,088 trips × $5
[3]12 agents × $2,400

[4]Unfavorable (actual costs exceed budgeted costs)
[5]$3,360/$2,400 = 1.4 salaries

For comparison, consider a performance report prepared by users of the discretionary-fixed-cost approach:

	Budgeted as a Discretionary Fixed Cost	Actual Cost	Variance
Travel agents' compensation	$28,800[6]	$28,800[6]	0

The budget in this report is not based on formal work measurement. Instead, agency managers used judgment to determine the appropriate number of travel agents to employ.

Opponents of the engineered-variable-cost approach argue that it is too harsh and sometimes infeasible, because labor unions or laws restrict managements' ability to continually hire and lay off workers. Those who favor the engineered approach insist that even in those cases, consistently large variances can spur action. For example, managers may go to the bargaining table with a union to change work rules. Similarly, they may lobby legislators to change laws that hurt an industry's competitive position. Evidence from work measurement helps managers to be more persuasive.

Trade-Offs between Fixed and Variable Costs

Management strategies often include trade-offs between fixed and variable costs. Nucor and U.S. Steel may incur the fixed costs of a new plant in order to save the variable costs of energy in steelmaking. In the auto industry, increased expenditures for robotic equipment (a fixed cost) have decreased labor and other variable costs. That type of computer-controlled production equipment also has greatly improved the quality of automobiles. Higher quality means less cost incurred to repair defects. Similarly, banks, hospitals, and other service organizations have reengineered their work. Machines are processing checks, running lab tests, and typing envelopes—tasks that people once performed.

In general, when committed fixed costs increase relative to variable costs, managers lose some of their ability to respond to changes in short-term conditions. For example, consider that mail volume in the U.S. Postal Service fluctuates from month to month. It is much easier for the postmaster to adjust employee work schedules than to buy and sell mail-sorting machines. Companies must be willing to invest in fixed-cost resources, however, to take advantage of market opportunities.

In some cases, investments may be necessary just to survive. Companies are reorganizing their manufacturing processes to reduce the time it takes to make their products. If a manufacturer can ship goods to customers within one or two weeks and competitors are quoting two- to three-month deliveries, the company can charge higher prices or capture a greater market share. As long as the new technology is not too expensive, the manufacturer should be able to increase profits.

Sometimes managers choose between discretionary fixed and variable costs in order to maximize short-run income. Consider Sullivan Software Company, a new company about to launch its only product, Megaworks. President Frank Sullivan is considering two plans for paying salespeople. The mixed-cost plan is a salary of $30,000 plus a commission of $40 for each Megaworks program sold. The variable-cost plan is a straight commission of $80 per program. The average contribution margin of the company's software is $200 per unit, excluding sales commission.

Exhibit 23-6 graphs the cost behavior patterns for one salesperson under each plan. Sullivan wants the plan that will maximize the company's operating income. Other factors being equal, the plan that will minimize total compensation expense, and thereby maximize operating income, depends on the number of items each em-

OBJECTIVE 4
Compute the equal-cost volume of two cost behavior patterns
Short Exercise: Harris Creek Tree Farms has two options available to renew the lease on the land on which it grows trees: A, a flat lease payment of $2,000 per month, and B, a flat lease payment of $1,000 per month plus $10 per tree sold. At what volume would total costs under the two options be equal? *A:* 100 trees ($2,000 = $1,000 + $10x).

---

[6]12 agents × $2,400

EXHIBIT 23-6
*Alternative Sales Force
Compensation Plans*

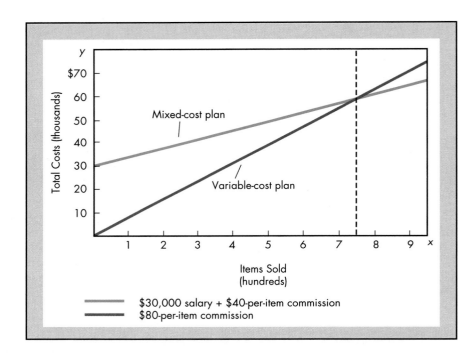

Legend:
— $30,000 salary + $40-per-item commission
— $80-per-item commission

ployee sells. At volume levels below 750 items, the variable-cost plan minimizes Sullivan's cost; the fixed salary saved is greater than the additional commission expense from the higher rate paid per item. At volume levels above 750, the mixed-cost plan is better because its savings in variable commissions exceed the fixed salary that must be paid. The point of indifference between the plans, where operating incomes are equal, is found by equating the compensation expense under the two plans:

$$\textbf{Mixed-plan compensation expense} = \textbf{Variable-plan compensation expense}$$
$$\$30,000 + (\$40 \times \textbf{items sold}) = (\$80 \times \textbf{items sold})$$
$$\$30,000 = (\$80 - \$40) \times \textbf{items sold}$$
$$\$30,000 = \$40 \times \textbf{items sold}$$
$$\frac{\$30,000}{\$40} = \textbf{items sold}$$
$$750 = \textbf{items sold}$$

The variable-cost plan may give salespeople the incentive to work harder and sell more Megaworks programs than the mixed-cost plan. In making his decision, Sullivan should consider this incentive effect in relation to the higher total cost at volume levels above 750 items. He should balance his desire to control costs with the need to keep his sales staff highly motivated.

MID-CHAPTER SUMMARY PROBLEM FOR YOUR REVIEW

PART A. Colores de Garcia makes and sells industrial paints in Monterrey, Mexico. Eduardo Garcia, the owner, is considering two alternatives for paying his four salespersons next year (19X5). Plan A is a straight commission of the equivalent of $0.40 per gallon sold. Plan B is a salary equivalent to $20,000 each plus a commission of $0.20 per gallon.

Required

1. Graph the cost behavior patterns of both plans.
2. Determine both graphically and with equations the number of gallons all four salespersons together would have to sell for Colores de Garcia to pay the same total compensation under the two plans.

PART B. In 19X4, Colores de Garcia operated at full capacity of 400,000 gallons. Each salesperson was paid according to plan A. The average sale price was $10 per gallon, and the average variable cost (excluding commission) was $6 per gallon. Fixed expenses totaled $1,000,000.

Garcia believes that his sales force can sell 500,000 gallons in 19X5 and every year thereafter if his company can produce them. He estimates that an additional committed fixed cost of $200,000 would be required to provide another 100,000 gallons of capacity.

Required

1. Compute 19X5 operating income on a contribution margin income statement if Colores de Garcia acquires the additional capacity and produces and sells 500,000 gallons. Assume that Colores de Garcia switches to plan B (a salary of $20,000 each and commission of $0.20 per gallon) to pay salespersons.

2. Repeat Requirement 1, assuming that Colores de Garcia continues to pay compensation according to plan A (a straight commission of $0.40 per gallon).

3. At production and sales volume of 500,000 gallons per year, which employee compensation plan should the company use? Why?

SOLUTION TO REVIEW PROBLEM

PART A—Requirements 1 and 2

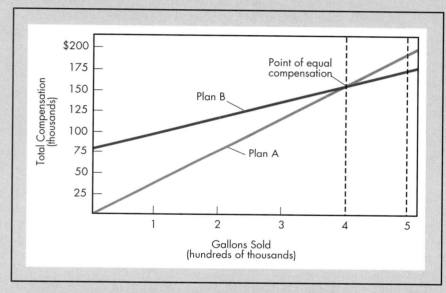

Plan A total compensation = Plan B total compensation

$$\$0.40 \times \text{gallons sold} = \$20,000 \times 4 \text{ salespersons} + (\$0.20 \times \text{gallons sold})$$
$$(\$0.40 - \$0.20) \times \text{gallons sold} = \$80,000$$
$$\$0.20 \times \text{gallons sold} = \$80,000$$
$$\text{gallons sold} = \frac{\$80,000}{\$0.20} = 400,000$$

PART B—Requirements 1 and 2

	Plan B Salary Plus Commission	Plan A Commission Only
Sales revenue (500,000 × $10)............................	$5,000,000	$5,000,000
Sales commissions (500,000 × $0.20)	100,000 (500,000 × $0.40)	200,000
Other variable expense (500,000 × $6)	3,000,000	3,000,000
Contribution margin..	1,900,000	1,800,000
Sales salary expense ($20,000 × 4)	80,000	—
Other fixed expense..	1,200,000	1,200,000
Operating income	$ 620,000	$ 600,000

PART B—Requirement 3

At production and sales volume of 500,000 gallons, Garcia should select plan B because operating income is higher under that plan.

Managers need to know how cost drivers affect costs. For many costs, a single driver can explain cost behavior. That driver usually is some measure of volume of activity. For example, the number of tons of steel produced is adequate to explain the total raw materials cost of U.S. Steel. In contrast, several cost drivers must be known in order to predict other costs accurately. For instance, materials-handling costs in a U.S. Steel warehouse might be affected by the size of materials handled, by their weight, and also by the number of individual pieces. These three drivers together provide a better understanding of cost behavior than does any single driver. In the remainder of this chapter, we demonstrate how accountants develop and evaluate mathematical functions to predict costs on the basis of their drivers.

The Cost Function

A **cost function** is a mathematical statement of the relationship between a cost and one or more cost drivers. Consider Harry and David, a mail-order business that packs and ships fresh fruit to customer order. The cost of packing materials has a single cost driver—the number of customer orders packed. In a cost function, the cost to be predicted is called the **dependent variable**, y, because its value depends on the value of the cost driver, or **independent variable**, x. The analyst's task is **cost estimation**, or **cost approximation**, which is the determination of the underlying relationship between x and y over a specified relevant range of x. After estimating the cost function, a manager may use it to predict, for example, how much packing-materials cost Harry and David will incur if it packs 8,000 orders in May 19X7.

In practice, cost approximations often are based on two major assumptions:

1. Cost behavior can be explained adequately by one cost driver alone.
2. The cost function is linear over the relevant range. That is, the function can be graphed as a straight line, with cost on the y-axis and the cost driver on the x-axis.

In many cases, these assumptions produce only rough approximations of costs. Most costs are affected by more than one cost driver. Also, many costs, because of such factors as employee learning and discounts for high-volume purchases of goods or services, are nonlinear. Managers tend to rely on rough approximations because the costs of developing and using more complex and precise estimation methods exceed their benefits (through better decisions).

An example of a nonlinear cost is shown in Exhibit 23-7. The total cost y is Harry and David's packing labor, purchased at a rate of $15 per hour. The cost driver x is customer orders packed. Each worker can pack 10 orders per hour. Packing labor

EXHIBIT 23-7

Step-Function Variable Cost

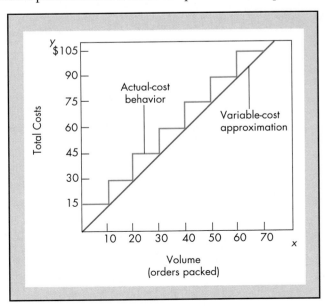

is an example of a **step-function variable cost,** which is purchased in whole quantities (hours) but used in fractional quantities (tenths of an hour per order). Because the steps are small, this step-function cost can be budgeted as a linear variable cost with little loss of accuracy.

If there is a single cost driver and the cost function is linear, each cost has a behavior pattern whose expected value, E(y), is

$$E(y) = A + Bx$$

where *A* and *B* are parameters of the relationship. (A **parameter** is a constant, such as *A*, or a coefficient, such as *B*, in a model or system of equations.) In cost-function models, *A* represents total fixed cost, and *B* represents variable cost per unit of *x*. Use caution in interpreting *A*. It is not the fixed cost at zero volume. Instead, *A* is the portion of total cost that does not vary with the level of the cost driver *within the relevant range*. If the fixed cost is discretionary, at least some of it probably can be avoided if production or sales activity completely shuts down.

The job of the cost analyst in the cost-estimation process is to estimate *a* and *b*, which are approximations of *A* and *B*, respectively. These approximations are used to predict total cost *y*,

$$y' = a + bx$$

where *y'* is the predicted or estimated cost for a specified level of the cost driver, *x*. For example, if the fixed cost *a* is $40,000 and unit variable cost *b* is $10 per customer order packed, the cost-estimation equation is

Total cost = $40,000 + ($10 × customer orders packed)

The analyst predicts total cost *y* to be $60,000 for *x* = 2,000 customer orders [$40,000 + ($10 × 2,000)] and $70,000 for *x* = 3,000 customer orders [$40,000 + ($10 × 3,000)]. Actual expenses might differ from these predicted amounts for any of four reasons: (1) The relationship between variable costs and customer orders packed may not be perfectly linear; (2) *a* and *b* are only approximations of *A* and *B*; (3) other cost drivers may affect costs; and (4) random, unpredictable factors may affect costs.

Types of Cost Functions

The three major types of cost functions—variable, fixed, and mixed—are variations of the basic cost-estimation formula *y' = a + bx*. The functions are graphed in Exhibit 23-8. Panel A shows a *variable cost*, one that changes in total in direct proportion to changes in the volume of the cost driver *x*. When volume is zero, total cost is zero. Consider Nautor's Swan, a company that makes luxury yachts in Finland. Assume that each yacht costs $100,000 to manufacture. If Swan has no sales during a particular month, the total cost of goods sold for the month is zero. If Swan sells four yachts, its cost of goods sold will total twice the amount for the sale of two yachts. Cost of goods sold for four yachts is $400,000 ($100,000 × 4), and for two yachts, $200,000 ($100,000 × 2). In this case, *b* is $100,000, the cost of goods sold per yacht.

"If Swan sells four yachts, its cost of goods sold will total twice the amount for the sale of two yachts."

Panel B of Exhibit 23-8 graphs a *fixed cost*, one that does not change in total despite changes in the volume of activity. As we have discussed, this cost behavior pattern usually is related to a specified relevant range of activity. Suppose that a Swan manager who is paid $75,000 per year can supervise the production of any number of yachts, up to 20. The manager's fixed salary cost, *a*, is $75,000. If the company produces between 21 and 40 yachts in a one-year period, two supervisors are needed. Then *a* jumps up to $150,000.

Key Point: The cost function can be expressed as
$$Ey = A + Bx$$
where *Ey*, the dependent variable, represents the expected cost (the amount of *y* depends on the amount of *x*); *x*, the independent variable, represents the activity; *A*, a parameter, represents fixed costs; and *B*, another parameter, represents variable cost per unit of activity.

Short Exercise: Prepare the cost functions for the following independent costs: (1) utility costs, $1,000 per month + $0.10 per machine-hour; (2) rent, $3,500 per month; (3) materials, $5 per unit.
A: (1) *y'* = $1,000 + $0.10*x*; (2) *y'* = $3,500; (3) *y'* = $5*x*.

OBJECTIVE 5
Graph the three major types of cost functions

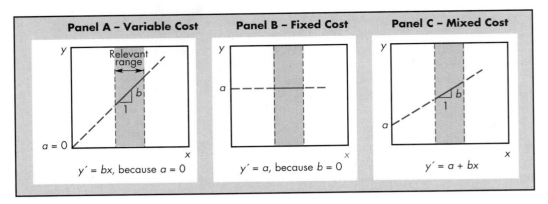

EXHIBIT 23-8
Types of Cost Functions

A *mixed cost*, which is a combination of variable and fixed elements, is graphed in Panel C of Exhibit 23-8. Total cost *y* changes as *x* changes within the relevant range, but not in direct proportion. Consider a color photocopy machine that Swan rents for $500 per month plus $0.10 per copy produced ($a$ = $500 and b = $0.10). Here, the cost-function graph originates at the fixed cost of $500 and rises according to the volume. If 2,000 copies are made in a month, the total cost is $700 [$500 + ($0.10 × 2,000)]. If twice as many copies are made, the total cost is $900 [$500 + ($0.10 × 4,000)]. The total cost at the 4,000-copy volume level is less than twice the total cost at the 2,000-copy level because the fixed cost is the same.

For planning and control purposes, mixed costs would ideally be subdivided into two accounts: one account for the fixed component and a separate account for the variable component. This action would call attention to the two different cost behavior patterns. In practice, however, mixed costs rarely are subdivided. Costs such as electrical power, equipment repairs, and shop maintenance generally are accounted for in total. Even if individual invoices could be separated into fixed and variable amounts, the benefits are not likely to outweigh the added clerical cost.

Accountants and managers rely on experience to identify mixed-cost accounts. They use past data to develop cost functions for predicting future costs. The following discussion outlines the four key steps to estimating mixed-cost functions.

Estimating Mixed-Cost Functions

To estimate a linear mixed-cost function, an analyst must first identify the total cost to be predicted. Then, he or she must proceed through the following four steps: (1) choose the cost driver, (2) collect a sample of data on the cost and the cost driver, (3) plot the data, and (4) estimate the cost function. The analyst then evaluates the func-

EXHIBIT 23-9
Examples of Cost Drivers in Different Business Function Areas

Business Function	Examples of Cost Drivers
Research and development	Number of projects
	Length of projects
	Number of personnel
Manufacturing	Materials costs
	Materials size or weight
	Labor-hours or costs
	Number of parts
	Number of items produced
Distribution	Dollar value of items distributed
	Size of items distributed
	Weight of items distributed
	Number of items distributed
Marketing	Number of advertisements
	Number of marketing personnel
Customer service	Number of service calls
	Number of products serviced

tion—that is, decides whether it is reliable for predicting the cost. Sometimes the analyst performs these steps several times before settling on an acceptable function.

Step 1: Choose the Cost Driver

Exhibit 23-9 gives examples of cost drivers in several business function areas. Costs and their drivers tend to increase and decrease together. When variables move together, they are said to be highly correlated. If a study were to show a high correlation between Eastman Kodak's cost of conducting research and the number of research projects conducted, the number of research projects would be a useful cost driver for predicting research costs. But a high correlation does not automatically identify a useful independent variable. For example, a (coincidental) high correlation between Kodak's past research costs and the number of customer service calls would not mean that service calls should be used to predict research costs in the future.

"A (coincidental) high correlation between Kodak's past research costs and the number of customer service calls would not mean that service calls should be used to predict research costs in the future."

Step 2: Collect a Sample of Data on the Cost and the Cost Driver

An ideal sample consists of numerous data *observations* for a company with stable operating methods and technology. The time period used to measure the cost and the driver should be the same. For example, the number of research projects Kodak conducts in a quarter can be used to predict quarterly, not monthly or yearly, research costs. One observation, or sample point, might be $100,000 of research cost and three projects conducted in December 19X5.

Step 3: Plot the Data

A plot of the sample points reveals the general relationship between the cost and the cost driver. It also highlights extreme observations that do not represent the normal relationship between the two variables. Extreme points may result from errors in recording the data or from an unusual event, such as a labor strike. Plotting the data also helps the analyst determine the relevant range of the cost function. Different behavior patterns may exist at different levels of volume.

Panel A of Exhibit 23-10 shows a linear relationship between research costs and number of research projects. If a straight line were drawn through the middle of the points from lower left to upper right, the points would cluster around the line. (See Exhibit 23-13, page 963, for examples of these lines.) No extreme observations

EXHIBIT 23-10

Plots of Sample Data Points for Predicting Research Costs

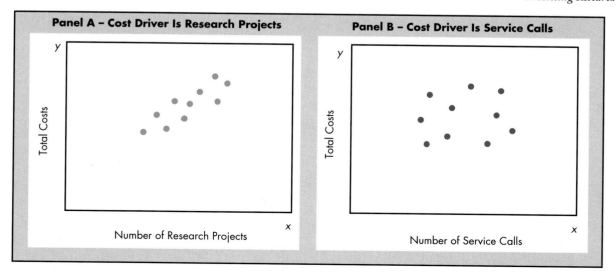

Short Exercise: Use the following data for the next few Short Exercises. The total overhead cost (OH), machine-hours (MH), and direct labor-hours (DLH) are as follows:

MH	DLH	Total OH
1,500	450	$ 7,500
2,000	510	8,500
4,500	650	13,500
2,600	500	9,700
3,000	550	10,500
3,500	575	11,500
3,100	550	10,700

Graph the total overhead cost using MH and then DLH as the independent variable. Which is a better predictor of total overhead cost? *A:* MH is better. The graph of MH in relation to total overhead is more linear than the graph of DLH and total overhead.

are apparent. The relevant range of a cost function developed from these sample points is from the lowest to the highest value of x.

Panel B reveals that no linear relationship exists between research costs and customer service calls. The points are scattered randomly, not arranged in a generally linear pattern. Analysts would conclude that customer service calls do not drive research cost and would be an inappropriate independent variable for the cost function.

Step 4: Estimate the Cost Function

In this step the analyst must separate mixed costs into their fixed and variable components. We show three methods of estimating mixed-cost functions: the high-low, visual-fit, and least-squares regression methods. We use the following example for each method.

The Boeing Company, headquartered in Seattle, Washington, is a leading manufacturer of commercial aircraft. Boeing uses sophisticated equipment that must be maintained to serve its intended purpose. For manufacturers such as Boeing, maintenance is a major expense, and maintenance employees are highly respected within the company. Suppose that Boeing accountants have observed the machinery-maintenance costs listed in Exhibit 23-11 for a recent nine-month period. They believe that machine-hours are the primary cost drivers of variable maintenance cost. Exhibit 23-11 shows nine pairs of (cost driver, cost) observations within the relevant

EXHIBIT 23-11

Data for Cost Function Estimation Procedures

Month	Cost Driver: Number of Machine-Hours (x)	Cost: Maintenance Costs Incurred (y)
January	210	$2,300
February	220	2,700
March	110	1,800
April	180	2,100
May	150	2,100
June	80	1,400
July	100	1,800
August	130	1,700
September	100	1,500

EXHIBIT 23-12

Plot of Sample Data

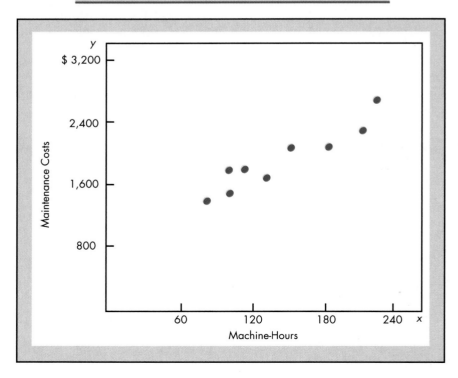

range of 80 to 220 machine-hours. The plot of the points, Exhibit 23-12, reveals a strong linear relationship between machine-hours and maintenance costs. Therefore, a linear cost function should describe the relationship well.

Three Methods of Estimating Mixed-Cost Functions

THE HIGH-LOW METHOD The **high-low method** estimates a cost function on the basis of only the highest-volume and the lowest-volume points (values of the independent variable) within the relevant range of the sample. If one of those points is an unrepresentative extreme value, or *outlier*, that has been caused by a strike, fire, or other unusual event, it is discarded. The next-highest-volume (or next-lowest-volume) point is used in its place. This action is taken because the points used in the computation of parameters *a* and *b* in the cost-estimation formula $y' = a + bx$ must represent the normal relationship between the cost and the cost driver. Otherwise, the cost function is useless.

After selecting the high and low points, the analyst connects them with a line and extends it back to the vertical axis, as in Panel A of Exhibit 23-13. The intercept becomes *a*, the fixed portion of total cost. The slope of the line becomes *b*, the variable cost per machine-hour.

The first step in computing the values of these parameters is to determine the differences between the high and low values of *x* and *y*:

EXHIBIT 23-13
Cost Function Estimations

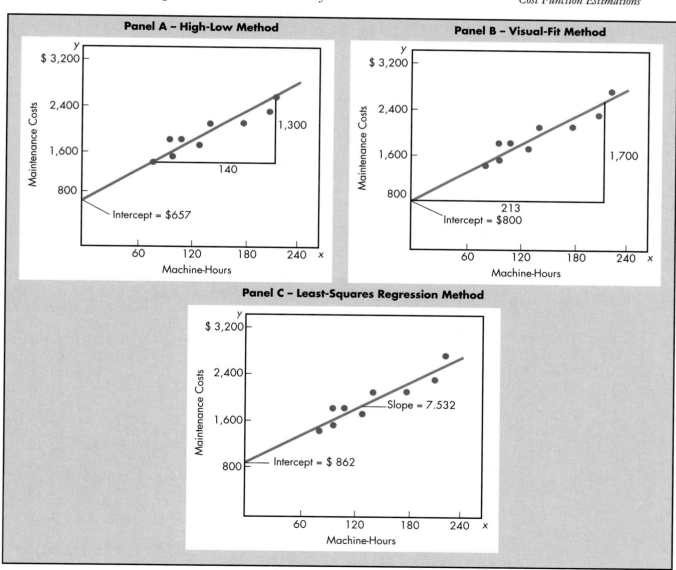

Short Exercise: Using the data from the previous Short Exercise, determine the cost function by the high-low method. Use machine-hours as the independent variable. *A:*

$y' = \$4,500^\dagger + \$2^* \times$(machine-hours)

$*\dfrac{\$13,500 - \$7,500}{4,500 - 1,500} = \$2$ per machine-hour

$\dagger\$13,500 = a + \$2 \times 4,500$

$\quad a = \$4,500$

	Number of Machine-Hours (x)	Maintenance Cost (y)
High	220	$2,700
Low	80	1,400
Difference	140	$1,300

With these results, the value of the variable cost per machine-hour, *b*, can be computed:

$$\textbf{Variable rate} = \frac{\textbf{Change in costs}}{\textbf{Change in volume}}$$

$$= \frac{\$2,700 - \$1,400}{220 - 80} = \frac{\$1,300}{140} = \$9.286 \text{ per machine-hour}$$

The value of *a* can then be found as follows:

$$\textbf{Fixed component} = \textbf{Total mixed cost less variable component}$$

$$\textbf{At high point} = \$2,700 - (\$9.286 \times 220)$$
$$= \$2,700 - \$2,043 = \$657$$

$$\textbf{At low point} = \$1,400 - (\$9.286 \times 80)$$
$$= \$1,400 - \$743 = \$657$$

Therefore, the high-low method results in the following cost function:

$$\underset{\text{Total maintenance cost}}{y'} = \underset{\text{\$657 per month plus}}{a} + \underset{\text{\$9.286 per machine-hour}}{bx}$$

The high-low method is easy to use, but it has a major defect. It uses only two data observations, regardless of the number of observations available. Because those two points may not represent the normal relationship between the cost and the cost driver, and because better estimation methods are available, the high-low method is recommended only when very few observations of past results are known.

THE VISUAL-FIT METHOD The simplest method of cost estimation that uses all available data is the **visual-fit method.** The analyst visually fits a line to the points, trying to come close to as many points as possible. Because the line represents all data points (except outliers), visual-fit usually results in approximately equal numbers of points falling above and below the line, as in Panel B of Exhibit 23-13. Inspection of the line in relation to the points gives the analyst a better understanding of the relationship than a view of the data plot only (Exhibit 23-12).

The intercept *a* of the visual-fit line is $800, taken directly from the graph. The slope can be computed from the line. For example, the line passes through $2,500 on the vertical (*y*) axis at a volume level of 213 on the horizontal (*x*) axis. The point (*x* = 213, *y* = $2,500) can be used with the *y*-intercept point (*x* = 0, *y* = $800) to determine the variable portion of the cost function formula:

$$\textbf{Variable rate} = \frac{\textbf{Change in costs}}{\textbf{Change in volume}}$$

$$= \frac{\$2,500 - \$800}{213 - 0} = \frac{\$1,700}{213} = \$7.981 \text{ per machine-hour}$$

Thus, the cost function is as follows:

$$\underset{\text{Total maintenance cost}}{y'} = \underset{\text{\$800 per month plus}}{a} + \underset{\text{\$7.981 per machine-hour}}{bx}$$

Because it uses all sample points, the visual-fit method is better than the high-low method, but visual-fit is very subjective. Two people could draw "best-fitting" lines through the same points with different intercepts and slopes. Also, this method provides no measure of how closely the line fits the plotted points. In general, the closer the sample points are to the cost-function line, the more accurate the estimation of the cost function.

THE LEAST-SQUARES REGRESSION METHOD The **least-squares regression method,** or simply **regression analysis,** is a formal model that measures the average amount of change in the dependent variable *y* that is associated with a one-unit change in the independent variable *x*. If the relationship is linear, regression analysis is the most accurate way to determine the cost behavior of a mixed cost from a sample of past observations. The regression equation is the formula for *the* best-fitting straight line through the plot of sample points. The formula's parameters can be computed by hand, but regression analysis is almost always performed on computers. Regression software programs are widely available and inexpensive.

The line in Panel C of Exhibit 23-13 was fitted by a least-squares regression program. The data in Exhibit 23-11 were used as program inputs. In addition to the Panel C graph, the program provided the following formula:

$$\underset{\textbf{Total maintenance cost}}{y'} = \underset{\textbf{\$862 per month}}{a} + \underset{\textbf{\$7.532 per machine-hour}}{bx}$$

What does this equation tell Boeing managers? For the nine months ended September 30, maintenance costs over the relevant range of 80 to 220 machine-hours averaged $862 per month plus $7.532 per machine-hour. The managers can use the equation to predict future maintenance costs accurately. Those predictions may translate into higher profits for the company.

None of the points in Panel C of Exhibit 23-13 lies on the regression line. The vertical difference between each point and the line is called a *deviation*. Each deviation is the difference between an actual amount of maintenance cost and the predicted cost (on the line) for the associated number of machine-hours. The least-squares method is so-named because the regression line minimizes the sum of the squared values of all such deviations.

Consider the month of May, when $2,100 of maintenance cost was observed at a volume of 150 machine-hours (Exhibit 23-11). The predicted maintenance cost for 150 machine-hours is

$$y' = \$862 + \$7.532x$$
$$= \$862 + \$7.532(150) = \$862 + \$1,130 = \$1,992$$

The deviation for May is $108 ($2,100 − $1,992). If accountants had used the formula to predict maintenance cost that month, the actual cost, $2,100, would have been 5.4 percent ($108/$1,992) more than the predicted cost. That amount of error in cost estimation is widely regarded as acceptable.

STOP & THINK Suppose that Boeing's executives evaluate the company's machinery-maintenance operations by comparing actual cost incurred each month with the cost predicted by the regression analysis formula for the actual number of machine-hours worked. Name one shortcoming of this approach to computing each month's budgeted cost.

Answer: The regression analysis equation gives the *average* relationship between maintenance costs and machine-hours worked within the relevant range of activity. But as Panel C of Exhibit 23-13 shows, actual costs routinely deviate from predicted costs. No actual-cost point in our sample lies on the regression line. One reason for the deviations is that other factors—such as the number of machines serviced—drive maintenance cost. That is, it may cost less to service one machine that runs for 150 hours than 10 machines that run for 15 hours each.

An ideal performance budget would be based on all factors that affect cost. The approach described here is not ideal; actual costs will differ from budgeted costs for reasons other than the efficiency of maintenance work. The approach still may be acceptable, however, because the costs of developing a multiple-cost-driver formula may outweigh the added benefits of better budgets.

Comparison of Methods of Estimating Mixed-Cost Functions

The three methods used to estimate fixed and variable costs produced different results:

	Total Fixed Cost	Variable Cost Rate
High-low method	$657	$9.286
Visual-fit method	800	7.981
Least-squares regression	862	7.532

Because the parameter values are different, predictions based on the three cost-function formulas will differ. Suppose that Boeing accountants want to predict maintenance costs for volume levels of 100, 150, and 200 machine-hours. The predictions are shown in the following table:

	Machine-Hours		
Method	100	150	200
High-low	$657 + $9.286(100) = $1,586	$657 + $9.286(150) = $2,050	$657 + $9.286(200) = $2,514
Visual-fit	$800 + $7.981(100) = $1,598	$800 + $7.981(150) = $1,997	$800 + $7.981(200) = $2,396
Regression	$862 + $7.532(100) = $1,615	$862 + $7.532(150) = $1,992	$862 + $7.532(200) = $2,368

In this sample, the high-low method generates the lowest estimate of fixed cost ($657), whereas regression analysis generates the highest ($862). Therefore, at low volume levels (100 hours), high-low produces lower total-cost predictions than does regression analysis. But the high-low method has a higher estimate of variable cost per machine-hour. Thus, at high volume levels (200 hours), high-low predicts higher total cost because the method's higher variable cost outweighs its lower fixed cost. The visual-fit method produces cost estimates between the high-low and regression-analysis methods.

Although these results apply to this sample only, they illustrate that the methods produce different predictions. The relationships among costs predicted by the three methods depend on (1) the locations of the high and low points in relation to the regression line and (2) the skill of the analyst in the visual-fit procedure. Regression analysis is the best method because it uses all available data points, is the most objective, and shows exactly how well the estimated cost function fits the data (see *goodness of fit* below). Companies such as Nucor and U.S. Steel prefer the regression method for estimating their operating costs.

Evaluating Cost Functions

OBJECTIVE 7
Evaluate a mixed-cost function

Regardless of which estimation method is used, the resulting cost function should be evaluated at the time it is determined and then periodically as it is being used. Two important criteria used in the initial evaluation are economic plausibility and goodness of fit.

Economic plausibility means that the relationship must be credible. Suppose that a regression equation for predicting equipment maintenance costs, using number of machine-hours as the independent variable, has a negative slope coefficient b. Such a result suggests that maintenance costs go down as the number of machine-hours increases. Logic tells us that the opposite is true—maintenance costs should increase as production activity increases.

What could cause such a backward-looking result? It may be that maintenance is performed on machines when production activity is low because that is the best time to take them out of service. The observed relationship between maintenance costs (recorded as incurred) and machine-hours would be due to the discretionary timing of maintenance activity and not to the underlying cause-and-effect relationship. If an unreasonable pattern emerges from a regression, accountants should rethink their assumptions. They may need to select a different cost driver. Or they simply may need to refine the way they collect their sample data.

Goodness of fit means that the relationship must explain past costs well. In effect, the regression line must come close to the plotted sample data points. Regression-analysis software programs give the analyst a goodness-of-fit statistic known as r^2, the **coefficient of determination.** It tells the percentage of variation in total cost that is explained by changes in the cost driver. If $r^2 = 0.80$ in our example, it means that 80 percent of the fluctuation in maintenance costs is explained by the volume of machine-hours. A manager can use r^2 to determine how much confidence to put in cost predictions that are based on the regression formula. The higher the r^2, the greater the confidence.

After the cost function has been used for several periods, predicted costs should be compared with actual costs. Large differences might be due to errors in the sample data that were used to determine the function. New technology may have changed the relationship between the cost and the cost driver, or current activity volumes may fall outside the relevant range of the function. Whatever the reason, the equation should be used only as long as it provides reliable estimates.

SUMMARY PROBLEM FOR YOUR REVIEW

Elizabeth Gray, purchasing manager of High-Value Stores, needs a cost function to predict purchasing department costs. She believes that the primary cost driver is the number of purchase orders placed. Gray collected the following observations for the most recent six quarters of activity:

Quarter	Number of Purchase Orders	Total Cost (thousands)
1	1,875	$312
2	1,500	225
3	3,800	380
4	2,300	275
5	3,500	312
6	2,700	325

Required

1. Plot the data observations, with total purchasing department cost as the dependent variable (y) and number of purchase orders as the independent variable (x).

2. Regression analysis reveals that the equation of the best-fitting straight line through the sample points is:

$$\text{Total cost} = \$183,160 + \$46.57 \text{ per purchase order}$$

Draw the regression-analysis line on the graph of requirement 1.

3. Use the high-low method to estimate the cost function. Draw the high-low line on the graph, and compare the high-low equation with the regression-analysis equation.

4. Use both the high-low and regression-analysis cost functions to predict purchasing department cost for a quarter in which Gray places 3,000 purchase orders with suppliers. In which prediction do you have more confidence? Give your reason.

Requirements 1, 2, and 3

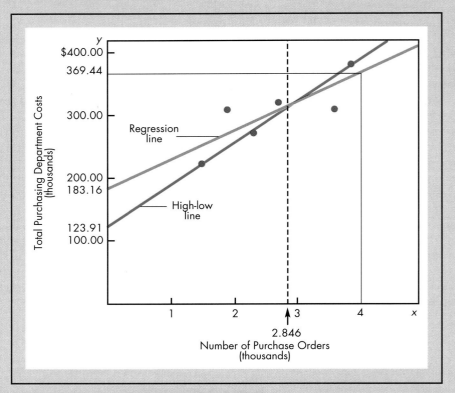

Requirement 3

$$\text{Variable rate} = \frac{\textbf{Change in costs}}{\textbf{Change in volume}}$$

$$= \frac{\$380{,}000 - \$225{,}000}{3{,}800 - 1{,}500} = \frac{\$155{,}000}{2{,}300} = \$67.391 \text{ per purchase order}$$

Fixed component = Total mixed cost less variable component
At high point = $380,000 − ($67.391 × 3,800) = $380,000 − $256,086 = $123,914
At low point = $225,000 − ($67.391 × 1,500) = $225,000 − $101,086 = $123,914

Because the high point of the sample falls above the regression line and the low point is below it, the high-low cost function has a steeper slope ($67.391 versus $46.57) and a smaller fixed-cost component ($123,914 versus $183,160). The high-low equation predicts lower costs at low volume levels (below 2,846 purchase orders) and higher costs at high volume levels.

Requirement 4

High-low prediction:

Total cost = $123,914 + ($67.391 × 3,000) = $123,914 + $202,173 = $326,087

Regression-analysis prediction:

Total cost = $183,160 + ($46.57 × 3,000) = $183,160 + $139,710 = $322,870

We have more confidence in the regression-analysis prediction. Regression analysis provides the equation of the best-fitting straight line through the sample points. The method uses all available data, not just two observations. The high-low prediction may be very accurate or very inaccurate, depending on (1) the location of the high and low points with respect to the regression line and (2) the value of the independent variable x.

SUMMARY

1. Identify types of fixed costs. Cost behavior analysis examines the relationships between costs and the activities, or cost drivers, that cause them. We classify costs as fixed, variable, or mixed. Fixed, or capacity, costs may be categorized as committed or discretionary. *Committed fixed costs* are caused primarily from having property, plant, equipment, and key managerial personnel. They cannot be changed much by month-to-month or even year-to-year management decisions.

Discretionary fixed costs arise from periodic (usually yearly) budget decisions that reflect top management policies. These costs have no clear relationship between inputs and outputs. The appropriate amounts of discretionary fixed costs are difficult to determine with precision, so budgeted amounts often are based on traditions, rules of thumb, or industry customs.

2. Use cost behavior analysis to make business decisions. Fixed costs provide the capacity to operate at a particular activity level. Variable costs result from using available capacity. *Engineered variable costs* result from measurable, often observable, cause-and-effect relationships between inputs (the costs) and outputs. Their efficiency can be measured by relating the quantity of inputs used to the quantity of outputs achieved. *Discretionary variable costs* change with production or sales activity simply because management has decided to incur the costs on a percentage or a per-unit basis. Mixed costs have both fixed and variable components that usually are not identified separately.

3. Identify two approaches for controlling operating labor costs. Managers use one of two methods to budget and control the costs of operating labor. The *discretionary-fixed-cost approach* relies on management's judgment to determine the size of the work force. The *engineered-variable-cost approach* uses *work measurement* to calibrate the workload in a process or operation in order to determine the number of employees needed to perform the work.

4. Compute the equal-cost volume of two cost behavior patterns. Managers often consider courses of action with different cost behavior patterns. They develop *cost functions*, which express the mathematical relationships between costs and their cost drivers. Decision makers can compute the equal-cost volume of cost-driver activity by setting two cost-function equations equal to one another and solving for the volume level. They can then use predictions of future volume levels to identify high-cost and low-cost actions.

5. Graph the three major types of cost functions. Fixed, variable, and mixed costs can be graphed as functions of their cost drivers. When two functions are graphed together, they intersect at the equal-cost volume of activity.

6. Use three methods to estimate mixed-cost functions. Three methods are widely used to separate mixed costs into their fixed and variable elements. All are based on samples of past data. The *high-low method* uses only the highest-volume and lowest-volume points of the sample. Because those two points may not represent normal relationships, this method is not recommended unless very few observations of past results are available.

The *visual-fit method* relies on the ability of the analyst to fit a line to the plot of sample points. It is better than the high-low method because it uses all sample points, but it is subjective and does not provide a measure of how well the line fits the points.

The most accurate method to determine the behavior pattern of a mixed cost is *least-squares regression*. Regression software programs graph the sample points and give the (cost-function) formula of the straight line that best fits the points.

7. Evaluate a mixed-cost function. To evaluate a cost function, accountants assess *economic plausibility* and *goodness of fit*. A regression equation's *coefficient of determination*, r^2, tells the percentage of variation in the cost that is explained by changes in the cost driver. The r^2 measure helps analysts determine how much confidence to put in specific cost predictions.

SELF-STUDY QUESTIONS

1. Costs caused primarily from having property, plant, equipment, and key managerial personnel are called (p. 948)
   a. Committed fixed costs
   b. Discretionary fixed costs
   c. Mixed costs
   d. Step-function variable costs

2. Refer to Exhibit 23-1 (p. 948). If demand for orders in 19X1 is 20,000, operating income for the larger store is (Exhibit 23-2) (p. 949)
   a. $30,000
   b. $80,000
   c. $10,000
   d. $70,000

3. Holmes Co. pays one salesperson a salary of $70,000 and another a salary of $40,000 plus a commission of $50 per item sold. At what sales level will the two salespersons' earnings be equal? (p. 956)
   a. 2,200
   b. 600
   c. 1,400
   d. Cannot be determined from the information given.

4. If a cost function is linear (p. 958)
   a. It can be graphed as a straight line
   b. It is either variable or fixed, but not mixed

   c. When the volume of the cost driver doubles, the amount of the cost doubles
   d. The slope coefficient of the independent variable is negative

5. For a particular cost-driver activity level, a difference between an actual cost incurred and the cost predicted by a linear equation may be caused by (p. 959)
   a. Nonlinearity in the relationship between the cost and the cost driver
   b. The effect of other cost drivers on the cost
   c. Random factors that affect the cost
   d. All of the above

6. Plotting a sample of (cost driver, cost) observations helps the analyst (p. 961)
   a. Determine the general relationship between the cost and the cost driver
   b. Identify extreme observations that do not represent the normal relationship between the cost and the cost driver
   c. Prove cause-and-effect relationships between the cost and the cost driver
   d. Both a and b

7. The high-low method of mixed-cost estimation uses only the highest and lowest observations of the *(p. 963)*
   a. Fixed-cost component
   b. Slope coefficient
   c. Independent variable (cost driver)
   d. Dependent variable (total cost)

8. The most accurate method of cost function approximation is called the *(p. 965)*
   a. High-low method
   b. Visual-fit method
   c. Least-squares regression method
   d. Mixed-cost-formula method

9. The coefficient of determination, r^2, indicates *(p. 967)*
   a. The average change in a cost function's dependent variable for each one-unit change in the independent variable

   b. The percentage of variation in total cost explained by changes in the cost driver
   c. The proportion of fixed cost to total cost at the average volume level of the relevant range
   d. The sum of the squares of deviations between observed data points and the least-squares regression line

10. If every point in a plotted sample of data observations lies very close to the least-squares regression line, we say that the cost function passes the *(p. 967)*
    a. Goodness-of-fit test
    b. Cause-and-effect test
    c. Economic-plausibility test
    d. All of the above

Answers to the Self-Study Questions follow the Accounting Vocabulary.

ACCOUNTING VOCABULARY

Coefficient of determination (r^2). The statistic that tells the percentage of variation in a cost that is explained by changes in the cost driver *(p. 967)*.

Committed fixed costs. Fixed costs that result from having property, plant, equipment, and key managerial personnel *(p. 948)*.

Cost estimation (cost approximation). Determination of the underlying relationship between a cost and its cost driver over a specified relevant range of the cost driver *(p. 958)*.

Cost function. A mathematical statement of the relationship between a cost and one or more cost drivers *(p. 958)*.

Dependent variable. The cost to be predicted in a cost function *(p. 958)*.

Discretionary (managed) fixed costs. Fixed costs that arise from periodic (usually yearly) budget decisions that reflect top-management policies. These costs have no clear relationship between inputs and outputs *(p. 950)*.

Discretionary-fixed-cost approach. An approach to managing operating labor costs that relies on personal supervision for controlling costs *(p. 953)*.

Discretionary variable costs. Variable costs that change with sales or production volume simply because management has decided to spend a certain percentage of each sales dollar or a certain dollar amount for each unit sold *(p. 951)*.

Economic plausibility. A cost function evaluation criterion that means that the relationship between the cost and the cost driver must be credible *(p. 966)*.

Engineered variable costs. Variable costs that result from measurable, often observable, cause-and-effect relationships between inputs and outputs *(p. 951)*.

Engineered-variable-cost approach. An approach to managing operating labor costs that applies formal work measurement to the budgeting process *(p. 953)*.

Goodness of fit. A cost function evaluation criterion that means that the relationship between the cost and the cost driver must explain past costs well *(p. 967)*.

High-low method. A cost-function estimation method that uses only the highest-volume and lowest-volume points within the relevant range of a sample *(p. 963)*.

Independent variable. The cost driver in a cost function *(p. 958)*.

Least-squares regression method (regression analysis). A formal model that measures the average amount of change in the dependent variable that is associated with a one-unit change in the independent variable *(p. 965)*.

Parameter. A constant or coefficient in a model or system of equations *(p. 959)*.

Step-function variable cost. A variable cost that is purchased in whole quantities (such as hours) but used in fractional quantities (such as tenths of hours) *(p. 959)*.

Variance. The difference between an actual amount and the corresponding budgeted amount *(p. 953)*.

Visual-fit method. A cost function estimation method in which the analyst visually fits a line to the plot of all sample data points *(p. 964)*.

Work measurement. The careful analysis of a task—its size, the methods used, and its efficiency *(p. 953)*.

ANSWERS TO SELF-STUDY QUESTIONS

1. a

2. c   (20,000 × contribution margin of $4 per order) – fixed expenses of $70,000 = $80,000 – $70,000 = $10,000

3. b $70,000 = $40,000 + $50 per item sold
   $30,000 = $50 per item sold
   $\dfrac{\$30,000}{\$50}$ = items sold = 600

4. a
5. d
6. d
7. c
8. c
9. b
10. a

QUESTIONS

1. Why are fixed costs also called capacity costs?
2. How do committed costs differ from discretionary costs?
3. What determines the level of committed costs? Of discretionary costs?
4. What is a cost driver? Give three examples of cost drivers.
5. How do step-function variable costs differ from strictly variable costs that change in direct proportion to changes in activity volume?
6. Give two ways committed-fixed-cost expenditures for automated equipment are helping companies compete.
7. What two assumptions frequently are made when estimating a cost function?
8. Explain the statement, "Ideally, there should be no accounts for mixed costs."
9. Describe how mixed costs are budgeted.
10. The general form of a cost-estimation equation is $y' = a + bx$. What does each of the four variables represent?
11. Why is the concept of the relevant range important in mixed-cost estimation?
12. Power cost for the Wertheim Company is $2,000 per month plus $1.00 per machine-hour. In January, 8,000 machine-hours were worked. What was the average unit cost (fixed plus variable) per machine-hour? What would

be the average unit cost at a volume of 16,000 hours in February?
13. List the four steps in estimating a cost function on the basis of past cost relationships.
14. Why is a plot of the sample data observations important when using the high-low method?
15. Why is least-squares regression analysis usually preferred over the high-low method? Over the visual-fit method?
16. "The high-low-method cost function always predicts higher cost at high volume levels than does the regression-analysis cost function." Do you agree or disagree? Explain.
17. What two criteria are important in evaluating cost functions? Which criterion can be checked with a plot of sample data?
18. Is a high coefficient of determination (close to 1.00) better than or worse than a low coefficient of determination (close to zero)? Explain.
19. Two years ago, Mahon Company accountants developed a cost function to predict machinery-maintenance cost on the basis of machine-hours (the independent variable). What might cause the function to be inaccurate today? What would indicate the need for a new function?

EXERCISES

E23-1 Ann Bolger, a hospital administrator, heard a lecture on different kinds of cost behavior. Afterward, she identified several hospital costs and presented you with the following list:

Identifying cost behavior patterns (Obj. 1)

a. Leasing cost of X-ray equipment ($10,000 per year plus $0.50 per film)
b. Training costs of an administrative resident
c. Straight-line depreciation on operating-room equipment
d. Costs incurred by Dr. Milotte in cancer research
e. Repairs to hospital furniture
f. Electricity costs
g. Nursing wages per patient (one nurse is added to a shift for every five patients)

Required

Classify each cost item on the list as one of the following: committed fixed, discretionary fixed, strictly variable, step-function variable, or mixed.

E23-2 Rod Holmes is considering the following three plans for paying his salespeople next year:

Graphing cost behavior patterns (Obj. 2, 5)

a. Discretionary-fixed-cost plan: a salary of $70,000
b. Discretionary-variable-cost plan: a commission of $175 per item sold
c. Mixed-cost plan: a salary of $40,000 plus a commission of $50 per item sold

Required

1. Graph the cost behavior pattern of each plan on a single graph.
2. From the graph, determine which plan will result in the lowest total cost to Holmes at a volume level of 500 items sold by each salesperson.

E23-3 Refer to Exercise 23-2. Now assume that Holmes is uncomfortable with graphical solutions. He much prefers to make business decisions on the basis of algebraic computations.

Computing equal-cost volume of different cost behavior patterns (Obj. 2, 4)

Required

1. Compute the point of indifference, in terms of items sold, between the discretionary-fixed-cost plan and the mixed-cost plan. If the volume level is above the point of indifference, which plan results in the lower total cost? Why?
2. Compute the point of indifference between the discretionary-variable-cost and mixed-cost plans. If the volume level is above that point, which plan yields the lower cost? Why?

Analyzing capacity costs to make
business decisions
(Obj. 1, 2)

E23-4 A. Jimmy Warren has decided to rent a store to sell college souvenir items. He will pay $25,000 to rent the space for one year. The average sale price for each item is $15; the average variable cost per item is $5. How many items must Warren sell to break even?

B. Now assume that Warren has two alternative store sites to consider. He believes he can sell 10,000 items each year if he rents the larger store for $45,000. Alternatively, expected demand with the smaller store is 8,000 items. It rents for $20,000 annually. Which store should he rent?

Analyzing cost behavior by the
high-low method
(Obj. 6)

E23-5 Maxine Baylor has been hired as a cost analyst by the plaintiff in a predatory pricing suit. She must estimate the behavior pattern of the defendant's utility costs. All she has to go on are the following sparse data:

Monthly Activity in Machine-Hours	Monthly Utility Costs Incurred
600	$3,700
1,000	4,500

Required

1. Use the high-low method to estimate the monthly fixed utility cost and the variable utility cost per machine-hour. Express the cost function in the form $y' = a + bx$.

2. What total utility expense would you expect at an activity level of 800 machine-hours? At 1,800 machine-hours?

Analyzing cost behavior by the
visual-fit method
(Obj. 6)

E23-6 Robert Keyes, president of Keyes Trucking Company, believes that total annual operating costs are a function of gross ton-miles of work. Past records show (in thousands):

	Year			
	19X1	**19X2**	**19X3**	**19X4**
Gross ton-miles	800	1,200	400	1,600
Total operating costs	$350	$350	$150	$550

Required

1. Plot the four data points.
2. Visually fit your best-fitting line to the points.
3. Using the graph, estimate the cost function for total operating costs.

Comparing the high-low and
visual-fit methods of cost function
estimation
(Obj. 6)

E23-7 Refer to Exercise 23-6. Robert Keyes has just remembered a major drawback of the visual-fit method—its subjectivity. It relies on the skill of the analyst to draw a representative best-fitting line. Keyes decides to check his visual-fit estimates of fixed operating cost and variable cost per ton-mile against estimates based on the high-low method. "At least it's objective," he thinks.

Required

1. Using the high-low method, estimate the cost function for Keyes Trucking Company.
2. Explain why differences exist between the visual-fit parameters and the high-low parameters you computed.
3. What step in the high-low method is not entirely objective?

Evaluating a cost function at the
time of estimation
(Obj. 7)

E23-8 Agnes McLeod had difficulty budgeting machinery-maintenance costs for the highly automated plant she manages. At a seminar on regression analysis, she became convinced that this "most accurate" method of cost-function estimation was the answer to her problem. After returning to work, she asked a cost analyst to run two regressions, one using production labor-hours as the independent variable and one using machine-hours. The computer program the analyst used revealed the following:

Regression-Analysis Cost Function	Coefficient of Determination (r^2)
Total maintenance cost = $1,000 per month + $2 per labor-hour	0.15
Total maintenance cost = $800 per month − $0.75 per machine-hour	0.55

Required

1. Which, if either, cost function should McLeod use to predict future machinery-maintenance costs?
2. If your answer to Requirement 1 was "neither," what should McLeod do?

E23-9 Ed Timmerman of Timmerman Appliance Repair Co. has been using the following cost-prediction equation for three years to predict the total cost of service calls each month: Total cost = $1,500 + $20 per service call. Timmerman was very pleased with the equation when it was estimated. Its coefficient of determination (r^2) was calculated to be 0.80, and he was convinced that the number of service calls was the most important driver of the variable portion of service cost.

Evaluating a cost function during use
(Obj. 7)

During the last six months, the following data were recorded:

	January	February	March	April	May	June
Service calls	120	80	100	110	85	110
Total cost	$4,500	$3,650	$3,800	$4,450	$3,450	$4,150

Required

1. Is the cost function providing reliable estimates of total service costs?
2. What might cause a once-accurate cost function to lose accuracy over time?

E23-10 All-America Insurance Co. employs 10 clerks to process insurance claims. Each clerk works 20 eight-hour days per month and is paid a monthly salary of $2,560. On the basis of a work-measurement study, All-America's senior management budgeted the efficiency of each clerk as the processing of four claims per hour. In April 19X3, the 10 clerks processed a total of 6,000 claims.

Evaluating performance of clerical labor
(Obj. 3)

Required

1. Prepare a performance report for April, using the engineered-variable-cost approach. What does the report tell management about the clerks' performance during the month?
2. Prepare a performance report, using the discretionary-fixed-cost approach. Compare the variance with the one produced by the report in Requirement 1.

CHALLENGE EXERCISE

E23-11 Refer to Exercise 23-10. Suppose that the 19X3 budgeted processing rate of four claims per hour is based on an average of five pages of information per claim. That is, each clerk was expected to process 20 pages per hour (4 claims × 5 pages per claim).

Evaluating performance of clerical labor
(Obj. 3)

It is now May 19X4. Charlotte Martin, the clerks' supervisor, has just received the following performance report for the previous month:

Budgeted as an Engineered Variable Cost	Actual Cost	Variance	
		Amount	Equivalent Persons
$22,000	$25,600	$3,600	1.41
(5,500 claims × $4)	($2,560 × 10)		($3,600/$2,560)

Martin knows that she must explain the unfavorable variance. Every manager at All-America Insurance Co. is under pressure to cut staff. Anticipating the need to defend her staffing level, Martin takes a random sample of 300 of the 5,500 claims processed in April. She counts a total of 1,800 processed pages in the sample.

Required

Prepare a brief explanation of the $3,600 unfavorable variance. Is the $4-per-claim budget appropriate? What change do you recommend, if any?

PROBLEMS

(GROUP A)

P23-1A Harold Read has decided to sell pizza in Rhode Island. He predicts that the average sale price and variable cost of his pizza will be $5 and $2, respectively. He must decide whether to open at one location, in Barrington, or at two—one in Barrington and one in nearby Bristol. Read has located two vacant stores that would serve his purposes well. Each would rent for $25,000 per year, and each would require a two-year lease. He predicts that other fixed costs would total $8,000 per store per year.

Analyzing capacity costs to make a business decision—two-year time period
(Obj. 1, 2)

Read believes that more pizzas will be demanded each year if he opens two stores. However, he does not expect the two-store demand to be twice the one-store demand, because some customers will drive from Bristol to Barrington if he opens only one store. The predicted number of pizzas sold each year under each alternative course of action is:

	One Store	Two Stores
19X4	33,000	40,000
19X5	46,000	60,000

Required

1. Prepare contribution margin income statements to determine expected operating income for 19X4 for both the one-store alternative and the two-store alternative.
2. Repeat Requirement 1 for 19X5.
3. Which course of action results in the greater expected operating income for the two-year period? Should Read rent one store or two?

Using knowledge of cost behavior patterns to evaluate different payment plans
(Obj. 2, 4)

P23-2A Gina Newton owns West Coast Marine, a power boat sales company. West Coast Marine has stores in five cities. For many years, Newton has paid her salespeople a monthly salary plus a bonus for each boat sold. In May 19X4, the monthly salary was $2,000 and the bonus was $100 per boat sold.

In June 19X4, Newton received information that Richard Hughes, one of her best salespersons, was about to resign and join the sales staff at Pacific Marine. Salespeople at Pacific Marine receive a base monthly salary of $1,000 plus 10 percent of the contribution margin on each boat (exclusive of bonus).

Prompted by this information, Newton gathered the following data on (1) Hughes and (2) the average for all 10 salespeople of West Coast Marine (including Hughes) for May 19X4:

	Hughes	Average for 10 Salespeople
Boats sold	30	20
Average contribution margin	$2,500	$1,500

Required

1. Compute the May 19X4 compensation paid by West Coast Marine to Hughes and to the average salesperson. Also compute the total compensation West Coast Marine paid.
2. Compute the May 19X4 compensation that West Coast Marine would have paid to Hughes and to the average salesperson if it had used the Pacific Marine payment plan. Compute the total compensation West Coast Marine would have paid.
3. Given an average contribution margin per boat of $1,500, at what volume level in boats sold would the West Coast Marine and Pacific Marine plans result in the same compensation paid to each salesperson?
4. Compare and contrast the two compensation plans. Which plan would be better for West Coast Marine?

Using the high-low method of cost-function estimation
(Obj. 6)

P23-3A The Helping Hand builds houses and sells them at heavily discounted prices to low-income families. The organization tries to recover about 60 percent of the cost of each house from the buyer. The remainder is provided by private donors.

The Helping Hand is preparing a budget for the coming fiscal year, 19X5. Donations for 19X4 totaled $4 million; for 19X3, $3.2 million. Total expenses for 19X4 were $9.8 million; for 19X3, $8.2 million. Donations of $5 million are expected in 19X5.

Required

1. Using donations as the cost driver (independent variable), compute The Helping Hand's total-expense cost function as implied by the observations in 19X3 and 19X4.
2. On the basis of the cost function estimated in Requirement 1, what total expense should The Helping Hand expect in 19X5?
3. Is donations the best independent variable for predicting total expense? As treasurer of the organization, what alternative independent variables would you want to investigate?

Computing cost functions with the high-low, visual-fit, and regression-analysis methods
(Obj. 6)

P23-4A The British Look manufactures and sells a line of sport coats. Mindy Bond, the company's cost accountant, is analyzing the behavior of monthly production costs for budgeting purposes. Bond has collected a sample of monthly production costs and coats produced for the most recent year, as follows:

Month	Production Cost	Coats Produced
January	$66,200	342
February	69,500	531
March	80,000	541
April	88,100	844
May	93,300	932
June	96,500	891
July	97,500	887
August	117,700	1,098
September	108,600	498
October	84,200	522
November	67,200	448
December	57,700	298

Required

1. Plot the data observations, with production cost as the dependent variable and coats produced as the independent variable.
2. Does there appear to be an outlier point? If so, what should Bond do with the observation?
3. Visually fit a line to the points. Using the graph, estimate the cost function for total production cost.
4. Using the high-low method, compute the equation of the line relating production cost and coats produced.
5. The least-squares regression method results in the following cost function: Total production cost = $50,019 + ($54 × coats produced). Use the least-squares, visual-fit, and high-low methods to predict total operating cost at a volume of 750 coats. Which is the best prediction?

P23-5A Space Manufacturing Company has been having difficulty budgeting its electricity costs. The company traditionally has regarded these costs as variable, but Dean Haun, the cost accountant, suspects that part of the cost is fixed. In recent months, whenever production volume was above average, electricity cost was less than the budgeted amount. Conversely, when volume was below average, the cost incurred was greater than budgeted.

Interpreting a least-squares regression cost function (Obj. 6, 7)

Haun decided to use least-squares regression analysis to explore this issue. He obtained the following regression results with electricity cost as the dependent variable and tools produced as the independent variable:

y intercept (a): $2,000
Slope coefficient (b): 0.05
Coefficient of determination (r^2): 0.70

Required

1. Suppose that 50,000 tools are produced in an average month. What percentage of electricity cost is variable in an average month? What percentage is fixed?
2. Are fluctuations in electricity costs caused by anything other than the number of tools produced? What percentage of the fluctuations is not explained by number of tools?
3. Assuming that both volume levels are within the relevant range of the cost function, what electricity cost would you predict in a month when 40,000 tools are produced? In a month when 80,000 are produced?
4. In addition to budget-versus-actual cost comparisons, what else would indicate that electricity is actually a mixed cost?

P23-6A Benny Carle, head of the customer-service department of Corral Electronics Company, is concerned about some cost behavior data given to him by the company's new cost analyst. The analyst's first assignment was to use regression analysis to develop a cost function for predicting total service-department cost. The service department repairs defective products when customers return them. Returns often take place four to five months after sale, and sales volume fluctuates widely from month to month.

Evaluating a mixed-cost function (Obj. 7)

The analyst ran a regression with total service-department cost as the dependent variable and number of electronics products sold as the independent variable. The cost function and coefficient of determination (r^2) were computed to be:

$$y' = \$6{,}000 - \$20x; \quad r^2 = 0.75$$

The analyst remarked that the only way to reduce service costs is to sell more products.

Required

1. Compute total service-department cost for two months—one in which 200 products are sold and one in which 250 products are sold. Comment on the results.
2. Is it logical that selling more products causes service-department costs to go down? What mistake did the cost analyst make in evaluating the cost function?
3. What could the analyst have done differently to avoid the mistake?
4. How will what you learned from this problem help you manage a business?

(GROUP B)

Analyzing capacity costs to make a business decision—two-year time period
(Obj. 1, 2)

P23-1B Julie Massey has decided to sell gourmet hamburgers in Abilene, Texas. She predicts that the average sale price and variable cost of her burgers will be $3.00 and $1.25, respectively. She must decide whether to open at one location on the north side of town or at two locations—one on the north side and one on the south side. Massey has located two vacant stores that would serve her purposes well. Each would rent for $30,000 per year, and each would require a two-year lease. She predicts that other fixed costs would total $5,000 per store per year.

Massey believes that 30,000 hamburgers will be demanded on each side of town in 19X4 and that demand will grow to 50,000 per side in 19X5. She also predicts that half the potential customers on the south side would drive to the north side if she opens only one store. The expected number of hamburgers sold each year under each alternative course of action is therefore:

	One Store	**Two Stores**
19X4	45,000	60,000
19X5	75,000	100,000

Required

1. Prepare contribution margin income statements to determine expected operating income for 19X4 for both the one-store alternative and the two-store alternative.
2. Repeat Requirement 1 for 19X5.
3. Which course of action results in the greater expected operating income for the two-year period? Should Massey rent one store or two?

Using knowledge of cost behavior patterns to evaluate different payment plans
(Obj. 2, 4)

P23-2B Walter Templin owns Western Motors, a used-car sales company. Western Motors has lots in five cities. For many years, Templin has paid his salespeople a monthly salary plus a bonus for each car sold. In March 19X4, the monthly salary was $1,600 and the bonus was $25 per car sold.

In April 19X4, Templin received information that J. D. Harrington, one of his best salespersons, was about to resign and join the sales staff at Royal Motors. Salespeople at Royal Motors receive a base monthly salary of $1,200 plus 6 percent of the gross margin on each car. The gross margin is computed as sales price less purchase cost and other costs incurred on a car before it is sold.

Prompted by this information, Templin gathered the following data on (1) Harrington and (2) the average for all 48 salespeople of Western Motors (including Harrington) for March 19X4:

	Harrington	**Average for 48 Salespeople**
Cars sold............................	37	21
Average gross margin	$1,100	$450

Required

1. Compute the March 19X4 compensation paid by Western Motors to J. D. Harrington and to the average salesperson. Also compute the total compensation Western Motors paid.
2. Compute the March 19X4 compensation that Western Motors would have paid to Harrington and to the average salesperson if it had used the Royal Motors payment plan. Compute the total compensation Western Motors would have paid.

3. Given an average gross margin per car of $450, at what volume level in cars sold would the Western Motors and Royal Motors plans result in the same compensation paid to each salesperson?

4. Compare and contrast both compensation plans. Which would be better for Western Motors?

P23-3B Like many private schools, Stanford University tries to recover about one-third of its total costs from tuition revenue. The remainder is recovered through endowment income and charitable donations. Stanford is preparing a budgeted income statement for the coming fiscal year, which will end August 31, 19X4. Tuition revenue for 19X3 was $54 million; for 19X2, $48 million. Total expenses for 19X3 were $165.6 million; for 19X2, $153.6 million. No tuition rate changes occurred in either 19X2 or 19X3. The tuition rate is not expected to change in 19X4, and tuition revenue is expected to be $60 million.

Using the high-low method of cost-function estimation (Obj. 6)

Required

1. Using tuition revenue as the cost driver (independent variable), compute Stanford's total-expense cost function as implied by the observations in 19X2 and 19X3.

2. On the basis of the cost function estimated in Requirement 1, what total expense should Stanford expect in 19X4?

3. Is tuition revenue the best independent variable for predicting total expense? As financial vice-president of the university, what two alternative independent variables would you want to investigate?

P23-4B Casey Pacioli, financial analyst at Central Railroad, is analyzing the behavior of monthly operating costs for budgeting purposes. Operating costs include such items as fuel and labor but not the costs of maintaining engines and track. Pacioli has collected a sample of monthly operating costs and track miles hauled (miles clocked by engines that pull railroad cars) for the most recent year, as follows:

Computing cost functions with the high-low, visual-fit, and regression-analysis methods (Obj. 6)

Month	Operating Cost	Track Miles Hauled
January	$47,100	3,420
February	50,400	5,310
March	60,900	5,410
April	69,000	8,440
May	74,200	9,320
June	77,400	8,910
July	78,400	8,870
August	98,600	10,980
September	89,500	4,980
October	65,100	5,220
November	48,100	4,480
December	38,600	2,980

Required

1. Plot the data observations, with operating cost as the dependent variable and track miles hauled as the independent variable.

2. Does there appear to be an outlier point? If so, what should Pacioli do with the observation?

3. Visually fit a line to the points. Using the graph, estimate the cost function for total operating cost.

4. Using the high-low method, compute the equation of the line relating operating cost and track miles hauled.

5. The least-squares regression method results in the following cost function: Total operating cost = $30,919 + ($5.40 × track miles hauled). Use the least-squares, visual-fit, and high-low methods to predict total operating cost at a volume of 8,910 track miles hauled. Which is the best prediction?

P23-5B Elliot Bay Tarp and Tent (EBTT) Company has difficulty controlling its use of heavy-duty eyelets, nylon thread, glue, and other low-cost materials. These materials are called "supplies." The company traditionally has regarded supplies as variable costs.

Over the last several months, every time production volume was above average, EBTT incurred a total supplies cost that was less than the budgeted amount. When volume was below aver-

Interpreting a least-squares regression cost function (Obj. 6, 7) age, the cost incurred was greater than budgeted. This pattern led Judy Fouhy, the new accountant, to suspect that part of the supplies cost was fixed. EBTT uses square feet of products (tarps and tents) as its production volume measure.

Fouhy decided to use least-squares regression analysis to explore this issue. She obtained the following regression results with supplies cost as the dependent variable and square feet of products as the independent variable:

$$y \text{ intercept } (a): \$1,800$$
$$\text{Slope coefficient } (b): 0.072$$
$$\text{Coefficient of determination } (r^2): 0.58$$

Required

1. Suppose that 100,000 square feet of products are produced in an average month. What percentage of supplies cost is variable in an average month? What percentage is fixed?
2. Are fluctuations in supplies cost caused by anything other than square feet of products produced? What percentage of the fluctuations is not explained by square feet of products?
3. Assuming that both volume levels are within the relevant range of the cost function, what supplies cost would you predict in a month when 75,000 square feet of products are produced? In a month when 150,000 are produced?
4. In addition to budget-versus-actual cost comparisons, what else would indicate that supplies is actually a mixed cost?

Evaluating a mixed-cost function *(Obj. 7)*

P23-6B The head of the Consumer Products Manufacturing Department of Petty Company was concerned about some cost behavior data given to him by the new cost analyst. The analyst's first assignment was to apply regression analysis to various costs in the department.

One regression on monthly data was run with building-maintenance cost as the dependent variable and production labor-hours as the independent variable. Production workers have two primary responsibilities: operate production machinery and maintain the factory buildings. The cost function and coefficient of determination (r^2) were computed to be:

$$y' = \$7,542 - \$0.54x; \quad r^2 = 0.89$$

The cost analyst suggested extensive use of the building to keep maintenance costs down.

Required

1. Compute the building-maintenance costs for two months—one in which 4,000 labor-hours are worked and one in which 6,000 hours are worked. Comment on the results.
2. Is it logical that increased use of the building causes decreased maintenance costs? What mistake did the cost analyst make in evaluating the cost function?
3. What could the analyst have done differently to avoid the mistake?
4. How will what you learned from this problem help you manage a business?

EXTENDING YOUR KNOWLEDGE

DECISION PROBLEMS

Using knowledge of cost behavior to make business decisions; trade-offs between variable and fixed costs *(Obj. 1, 2, 4)*

1. Juan Bermudez started Bermudez Marine several years ago to make specialized 21-foot sailboats. He sees an opportunity to expand and is evaluating two courses of action. He could hire additional workers and keep his operations labor-intensive. Alternatively, he could invest in machinery to automate production, making operations more capital-intensive.

Bermudez predicts that he can sell 400 boats in 19X8 and each year thereafter if he can produce that many. Annual fixed costs for the current capacity of 200 boats per year are $300,000. Variable costs are $7,500 per boat. At a sale price of $10,000 per boat, Bermudez Marine will earn $200,000 operating income on revenue of $2,000,000 and expenses of $1,800,000 in 19X7.

To make 400 boats, Bermudez could purchase robotic machines to automate several processes, increasing annual fixed costs to $2,000,000 and reducing variable costs to $4,000 per boat. Alternatively, he could hire more workers, leaving variable costs at $7,500 per boat and increasing fixed costs to only $600,000.

Required

1. Calculate the predicted operating income for 19X8 for each alternative course of action under three different predictions of production and sales volume: 300 boats, 400 boats, and 500 boats.

2. Calculate the production and sales volume at which the two alternatives yield an equal operating income.

3. How might Bermudez's confidence in his prediction of annual sales of 400 boats affect his decision?

2. Washington Electric Supply sells more than 150 electrical products. All products have a six-month guarantee of full repair or replacement. When a customer returns a product, a service report is made. The report includes details of the problem and the time and cost of resolving it.

Estimating a cost function and using it in a make-or-buy decision (Obj. 2, 5, 6, 7)

Monthly data for the most recent 10-month period are:

Month	Customer Service Department Costs	Number of Service Reports
1	$42,327	201
2	49,016	276
3	41,333	122
4	46,844	386
5	43,235	274
6	50,282	436
7	45,223	321
8	49,821	328
9	46,659	243
10	45,224	161

Required

1. Plot the relationship between customer service department costs and number of service reports. Is there a linear relationship between the two variables? Is the relationship economically plausible?

2. Using the high-low method, determine the equation of the straight line that relates service department costs to number of service reports. Does the high-low line fit the data well?

3. Washington Electric Supply averages 275 service reports (products serviced) per month. An outside service company has offered to do all of Washington's repair work for $90 per service call. If Washington accepts the offer, it will shut down its customer-service department, saving all the department's variable costs and half its fixed costs. (The remaining fixed costs are committed; they cannot be saved in the short run.) Should Washington accept or reject the outside company's offer? Support your answer with appropriate computations.

ETHICAL ISSUE

Southwestern Bell Telephone Company serves over 9 million customers in Texas, Oklahoma, Missouri, Kansas, and Arkansas. The company processes millions of customer receipts (remittances) each month with a system designed to minimize processing cost and maximize cash flow. To accomplish these objectives, the Southwestern Bell centers must quickly pick up, open, extract, sort, prepare, and deposit customer checks several times each day as they become available at local post offices. Even very short delays can result in sizable increases in the company's banking costs.

Customer envelopes are opened by high-speed machines. They are then sorted manually for appropriate treatment—either standard or some category of special handling. Suppose that a new machine can automatically extract and sort checks. Each machine costs $90,000 and lasts five years. One machine would be needed for each of Southwestern Bell's several processing centers, and each machine would replace 12 workers.

Required

1. What factors would remittance-processing managers consider in evaluating these machines?

2. Is replacement of human workers with machines ethical? Is replacement of thousands of workers by automated equipment different from replacement of a few dozen? Explain.

Chapter 24
The Master Budget and Responsibility Accounting

Chapter Objectives

Insurance giant CIGNA Corp. provides a broad range of insurance services. The corporation's largest divisions are CIGNA Healthcare and CIGNA Property/Casualty Insurance (P/C). Executives evaluate each division by comparing its actual operating income to its budget.

For 1993, Healthcare and P/C had strikingly different results. Healthcare earned $464 million of operating income, up from $327 million in 1992. The division closed strong—its fiscal fourth-quarter results exceeded the budget. In contrast, P/C lost $350 million for the second straight year. That division failed to meet its fourth-quarter budget.

CIGNA holds division presidents responsible for achieving their budget targets. To be successful in 1994, both Healthcare's Lawrence P. English and P/C's Gerald A. Isom decided to retool their operations. English eliminated 1,000 jobs; Isom overhauled the underwriting process, which determines who will be a customer and on what terms. "We're both making . . . changes," noted Isom. "One [Healthcare] to stay out front and the other [P/C] to get out of a hole." _Sources: D. Levick, "CIGNA Reports Net Profits Off 25% in 1993," Hartford (Connecticut) Courant, February 15, 1994; and C. Roush, "CIGNA Seizes the Shears," Business Week, February 21, 1994, p. 84._

• • • • •

EXHIBIT 24-1
Management's Use of Budgets and Performance Reports

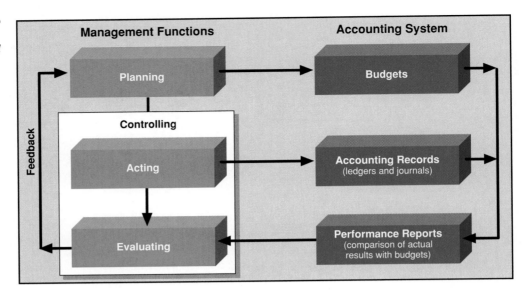

Short Exercise: Assume that a business does not budget sales. The production department produces at 100% of capacity. However, sales decline due to a foreseeable economic recession. What happens? *A:* Excess inventory is produced. The business will either keep the inventory that cannot be sold or sell it at a discount to move it. Either way the business loses money.

Managers play three key roles in organizations. First, they develop strategies—overall business goals. Second, they plan and implement specific actions to achieve the goals. Third, they evaluate operations by comparing actual results with budgets. This performance evaluation provides feedback that helps managers monitor current operations and fine-tune their planning procedures. Exhibit 24-1 shows the way managers use budgets in the process of planning and controlling. Observe that the process is continuous: plan, act, evaluate, and plan again.

In Chapter 20, we defined a *budget* as a quantitative expression of a plan of action that helps managers coordinate and implement the plan. To plan actions that will affect the company over several years, managers must predict the goods and services their customers will demand. For example, in 1994 Blockbuster Entertainment Corp. merged with Viacom Inc. What was Blockbuster's strategy? To diversify its home-video business into a media empire. Long-range budgets played a key role in the merger decisions of both Blockbuster and Viacom.

Other budgets have a short-term focus. Many companies budget their cash flows monthly, weekly, and daily to ensure that they have enough cash to meet their needs. They also budget revenues and expenses—and thus operating income—for months, quarters, and years.

The Budget Unit

Managers prepare budgets for the organization as a whole and for individual subunits. The chapter-opening story mentions two of CIGNA Corp.'s major divisions—Healthcare and Property/Casualty Insurance. Division budgets can be divided by customer, territory, or product line. A by-customer budget convinced the Property/Casualty Division to drop a customer that provided $60 million of revenue. Why? The division expected to lose money on the customer for the sixth consecutive year.

In the first part of this chapter, we examine a company's master (comprehensive) budget for a fiscal year. More than 90 percent of large industrial companies prepare these budgets. We then consider the use of budgets in evaluating the performance of subunits—such as CIGNA Healthcare—for which individual managers are responsible.

Benefits of Budgeting

Budgets are key management tools. Their preparation and use as benchmarks for judging performance get much more management attention than do actual results by themselves. Consider this comment by Carl E. Reichardt, chief executive officer of Wells Fargo Bank:

> I say our budget is the most important thing we do. I like to have all the debates over with when it is adopted. I'm not too sympathetic about hearing a lot of excuses after the fact. If budget planning is done well, there is no room for infighting and personality conflicts.

All companies, both large and small, can benefit from budgeting. The budgeting process offers the following benefits, summarized in Exhibit 24-2:

1. *Compels planning.* Budgeting helps managers set realistic goals by requiring them to plan specific actions to meet their goals. Budgeting also helps managers prepare for a range of conditions. It leads them to ask what-if questions and to plan for contingencies. Suppose that Honda assigns a plant with 3 million units of capacity to production of Accord cars. What if expected demand for a year is 2.6 million cars but actual demand turns out to be 3.2 million? To satisfy all demand, Honda must add 200,000 units of capacity. It also must buy and assemble components for 600,000 more cars than it had anticipated. If, in the budgeting process, Honda considered the possibility of such a high demand, the adjustments probably will be smoother and less costly than if Honda is forced to "manage by crisis."

> *"If, in the budgeting process, Honda considered the possibility of such a high demand, the adjustments probably will be smoother and less costly than if Honda is forced to 'manage by crisis.'"*

2. *Promotes coordination and communication.* The master budget coordinates the activities of the organization. It forces managers to consider relationships among operations across the entire value chain. Consider Cincinnati Milacron, Inc., a manufacturer

EXHIBIT 24-2
Benefits of Budgeting

1. Budgets compel managers to plan.

2. Budgets promote coordination and communication.

3. Budgets aid performance evaluation by providing a benchmark for performance.

4. Budgets motivate employees to help achieve the company's goals.

"The sales managers of Cincinnati Milacron, who are evaluated on the basis of sales volume, prefer to accept all special orders for unique machinery."

of machine tools and accessories. The sales managers of Cincinnati Milacron, who are evaluated on the basis of sales volume, prefer to accept all special orders for unique machinery. But some special orders cost the company more than the customer is willing to pay. The budget promotes coordination by encouraging sales managers to accept orders only for machines that Cincinnati Milacron can design, manufacture, and deliver at a profit.

Coordination requires effective communication. Suppose Mazda's engineers plan to redesign the Miata's brake system. By participating in the budgeting process alongside engineers, the manufacturing vice-president can see the need to change production lines. He or she communicates the plan to plant managers and production supervisors to enable them to make changes in an orderly way—and at minimal cost. Budgets are effective tools to communicate a consistent set of plans throughout the company.

3. *Aids performance evaluation.* A department or activity can be evaluated by comparing its actual results with either its budget or its past performance. In general, the budget is a better benchmark. One problem with comparisons with past results is that changes may have taken place in the company's operations or its markets. Comparing this year's results with last year's may be like comparing apples with oranges. The budget is based on the company's current status. It considers all changes from past conditions.

Suppose that Coldwell Banker's real estate agents sell 10 percent more houses in the third quarter of 19X5 than in the third quarter of 19X4. Is this good performance? Not necessarily. If nationwide sales are up 20 percent for the quarter, Coldwell Banker's results may be disappointing. But if the overall market has declined, the 10 percent increase may be viewed very favorably. The budget for 19X5's third quarter is based on that period's market conditions.

Another problem with past results is that they may represent inefficient performance. Panasonic's average production cost of $42.50 for a telephone answering machine may have been incurred when the company had problems with materials quality. An average cost of $40 the following year is an improvement. But this performance still may not be praiseworthy if the budgeted cost per machine is $36.

4. *Motivates employees.* Budgets affect behavior. The budgeting process prompts managers to look into the future. Doing so helps them foresee and avoid problems. Budgets also motivate employees to achieve the business's goals. Motivation is especially strong when employees accept budget goals as fair. For this reason, companies often ask employees to participate in preparing budgets that will be used to judge their performance.

Unrealistic budgets can hurt employee morale. Suppose Coldwell Banker's management imposed a budgeted increase of 15 percent in house sales for each territory. That budget may be acceptable to agents in areas with strong economies. They may work hard to achieve the increase. In contrast, agents in depressed areas may consider it impossible to meet the budget. They may become resentful and not work as hard. Input from agents in each territory likely will result in budgets tailored to local conditions.

The Performance Report

The comparison of budgeted amounts with actual results is a key element in evaluating operations, identifying the need for corrective action, and preparing the next period's budget. This point deserves a closer look. The performance report in Exhibit 24-3 serves as the basis for our discussion.

Actual 19X7 sales in Exhibit 24-3 are $550,000, which is $50,000 less than budgeted sales. The actual net income is half the budgeted amount. Top managers will ask what went wrong. The vice-president of sales will have to explain why sales revenue was so far below the budgeted amount. The vice-president, in turn, will meet

	Actual	Budget	Variance (Actual – Budget)
Sales revenue..............	$550,000	$600,000	$(50,000)
Total expenses.............	510,000	520,000	(10,000)
Net income..................	$ 40,000	$ 80,000	$(40,000)

EXHIBIT 24-3
Summary Income Statement Performance Report for 19X7

with the sales staff to learn why they failed to meet the budget. Three possible explanations exist in this example: (1) The budget was unrealistic; (2) the business did a poor job of selling during the period; or (3) uncontrollable factors reduced sales. Of course, all of these factors may have contributed to the poor results.

Managers use such performance reports to identify the need for corrective action. If the sales department did not perform well, managers must decide what to do. Perhaps sales staff compensation should be tied more closely to sales revenue in order to increase the incentive to sell. Or a new advertising campaign may be needed. Managers must decide if budgeted sales should be lowered for the next period—a decision that directly affects next period's budgeted net income. This situation shows how managers use a budget to plan and control operations to achieve their goals.

STOP & THINK In the performance report of Exhibit 24-3, actual sales revenue is 8.33 percent less than budgeted sales revenue ($50,000/$600,000). However, actual expenses are only 1.9 percent less than budgeted expenses ($10,000/$520,000). Give one reason why the percentage shortfall in expenses is so much lower than the percentage shortfall in revenue.

Answer: One reason why expenses did not fall as far short of the budget is that some expenses do not increase or decrease with revenue (sales volume). For example, the vice-president of sales may be paid a salary of $60,000 regardless of the revenue generated by the company. Such expenses as depreciation, rent, property taxes, and insurance are *fixed* with respect to the amount of revenue. When revenue and variable expenses decrease, fixed expenses remain the same. Thus total expense does not decrease as rapidly as revenue.

Components of the Master Budget

The **master budget** is the comprehensive budget that includes (1) the operating budget, (2) the capital expenditures budget, and (3) the financial budget. The **operating budget** sets the expected revenues and expenses—and thus operating income—for the period. The **capital expenditures budget** presents the company's plan for purchases of property, plant, equipment, and other long-term assets. The **financial budget** projects cash inflows and outflows and the period-ending balance sheet. This chapter discusses components of the operating budget and the financial budget. Chapter 27 covers budgeting for capital expenditures.

The components of the master budget are summarized as follows:

1. Operating budget
   a. Sales or revenue budget
   b. Purchases, cost of goods sold, and inventory budget
   c. Operating expenses budget
   d. Budgeted income statement
2. Capital expenditures budget
3. Financial budget
   a. Cash budget: statement of budgeted cash receipts and disbursements
   b. Budgeted balance sheet

The end result of the *operating* budget is the budgeted income statement, which shows expected revenues, expenses, and operating income for the period. The *financial* budget results in the budgeted balance sheet, which gives budgeted amounts for each asset and liability and for owners' equity. The budgeted financial statements

Short Exercise: (1) Which budget is prepared first, and why? (2) What factors influence the estimated sales volume? *A:* (1) The sales budget, because sales determines the purchases budget, the cost of goods sold budget, and so on. (2) Prior years' sales, general economic conditions, the trend of sales in that particular industry, competition, and the business's expected place in the market should be considered.

EXHIBIT 24-4
Master Budget for a Merchandising Company

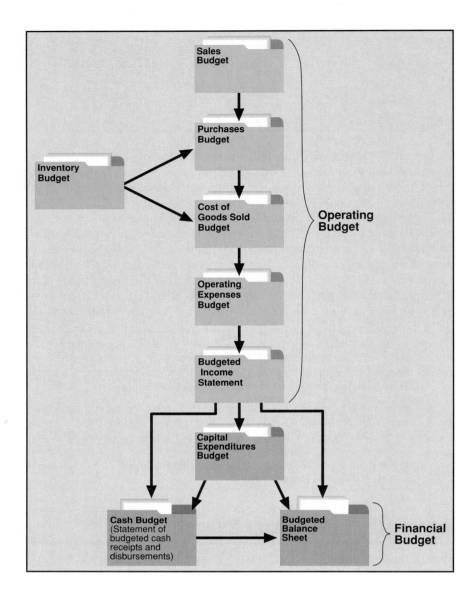

look exactly like ordinary statements. The only difference is that they list budgeted rather than actual figures. Exhibit 24-4 diagrams the various sections of the master budget for a merchandising company such as Safeway or J.C. Penney.

The sales budget is the cornerstone of the master budget. Every element on the budgeted income statement depends on sales activity. After sales and expenses are projected, the budgeted income statement can be prepared. The income statement, the capital expenditures budget, and plans for raising cash and paying debts provide information for the cash budget, which feeds into the budgeted balance sheet. Preparing the budgeted balance sheet usually is the last step in the process.

Preparing the Master Budget

To learn how to apply the concepts and methods of budgeting, you should prepare a master budget. Next we demonstrate the budgeting process.

Data for Example

1. Suppose that you manage Whitewater Sporting Goods Store No. 18, which carries a complete line of outdoor recreation gear. You are to prepare the master budget for your store for April, May, June, and July, the main selling season. The division manager

EXHIBIT 24-5
Balance Sheet

WHITEWATER SPORTING GOODS STORE NO. 18 BALANCE SHEET MARCH 31, 19X5			
Assets		**Liabilities**	
Current assets:		Current liabilities:	
Cash	$ 15,000	Accounts payable	$ 16,800
Accounts receivable	16,000	Salary and commissions	
Inventory	48,000	payable	4,250
Prepaid insurance	1,800	Total liabilities	21,050
	80,800	**Owners' Equity**	
Plant assets:			
Equipment and fixtures	32,000	Owners' equity	78,950
Accumulated depreciation	(12,800)		
	19,200	Total liabilities	
Total assets	$100,000	and owners' equity	$100,000

and the assistant controller (head of the accounting department) of the company will arrive from headquarters next week to review the budget with you.

2. Cash collections follow sales because the company sells on account. When extra cash is needed, the company borrows on six-month installment notes payable.

3. The balance sheet of your store at March 31, 19X5, the beginning of the budget period, is shown in Exhibit 24-5.

4. Sales in March were $40,000. Monthly sales are projected by sales personnel:

April	$50,000
May	80,000
June	60,000
July	50,000

Sales are 60 percent cash and 40 percent on credit. All credit sales are collected in the month following the sale. The $16,000 of accounts receivable at March 31 arose from credit sales made in March (40 percent of $40,000). Uncollectible accounts are insignificant.

5. Whitewater maintains inventory equal to $20,000 plus 80 percent of the budgeted cost of goods sold for the following month. (All these percentages are drawn from the business's past experience.) Cost of goods sold averages 70 percent of sales. These data explain why the inventory on March 31 is $48,000:

$$\text{March 31 inventory} = \$20,000 + 0.80 \times (0.70 \times \text{April sales of } \$50,000)$$

$$= \$20,000 + (0.80 \times \$35,000)$$
$$= \$20,000 + \$28,000 = \$48,000$$

Whitewater pays for inventory as follows: 50 percent during the month of purchase and 50 percent during the next month. Accounts payable consists of inventory purchases only.

6. Monthly payroll has two parts: a salary of $2,500 plus sales commissions equal to 15 percent of sales. The company pays half this amount during the month and half early in the following month. Therefore, at the end of each month Whitewater reports salary and commissions payable equal to half the month's payroll. This is why the $4,250 liability appears on the March 31 balance sheet—it is half the March payroll of $8,500:

March payroll = Salary of $2,500 + Sales commissions of $6,000 (0.15 × $40,000)
= $8,500
March 31 salary and commissions payable = 0.50 × $8,500 = $4,250

Short Exercise: In a series of Short Exercises, we are going to prepare parts of a budget for Coleman Corporation for January and February. Unit sales for January are expected to be 3,000 at $13.50 each, and for February, 4,500 at $13.75 each. Prepare the sales budget for Jan. and Feb. *A:*

Budgeted Sales	
January	**February**
3,000	4,500
× $13.50	× $13.75
$40,500	$61,875

Short Exercise: Now we can prepare Coleman's Purchases, Cost of Goods Sold, and Inventory Budget. Refer to the Sales Budget that we prepared in the previous Short Exercise. Assume that Coleman's cost of goods sold percentage is 65% of sales, and sales for March are predicted to be 4,300 units at $13.75, or $59,125. Coleman desires each month's ending inventory to be $10,000 plus 50% of the next month's cost of goods sold. *A:*

COGS (65% × ea. month's sales):
 Jan. $26,325* Feb. $40,219†
+ Desired End. Inv.
($10,000 + 50% of next month's COGS):
 Jan. 30,110** Feb. 29,216††
– Beg. Inv.:
 Jan. –23,163*** Feb. –30,110
= Purchases:
 Jan. $33,272 Feb. $39,325

*$40,500 × 65% = $26,325
†$61,875 × 65% = $40,219
**$40,219 × 50% + $10,000
 = $30,110
††($59,125 × 65% × 50%)
 + $10,000 = $29,216
***$26,325 × 50% + $10,000
 = $23,163

7. Other monthly expenses are:

Rent expense	$2,000, paid as incurred
Depreciation expense, including truck..............	500
Insurance expense	200 expiration of prepaid amount
Miscellaneous expense	5% of sales, paid as incurred

8. A used delivery truck will be purchased in April for $3,000 cash.

9. Whitewater requires each store to maintain a minimum cash balance of $10,000 at the end of each month. The store can borrow money on notes payable of $1,000 each at an annual interest rate of 12 percent. Management borrows no more than the amount needed to maintain the $10,000 minimum. Notes payable require six equal monthly payments consisting of principal plus monthly interest on the entire unpaid principal. Borrowing and all principal and interest payments occur at the end of the month.

10. Income taxes are the responsibility of corporate headquarters, so you can ignore tax for budgeting purposes.

You have studied the company guidelines on how to prepare a budget. The directions instruct you to prepare the following detailed schedules:

Schedule	
A	Sales budget
B	Purchases, cost of goods sold, and inventory budget
C	Operating expenses budget
D	Budgeted cash collections from customers
E	Budgeted cash disbursements for purchases
F	Budgeted cash disbursements for operating expenses

After compiling these schedules, you can prepare the following statements:

- Budgeted income statement for the four months ending July 31, 19X5 (see Exhibit 24-6)
- Summary statement of budgeted cash receipts and disbursements (see Exhibit 24-7)
- Budgeted balance sheet at July 31, 19X5 (see Exhibit 24-8)

Preparing the Operating Budget

As you work through the preparation of the master budget, keep in mind that you are developing the company's operating and financial plan for the next four months. The steps in this process may seem mechanical, but remember that budgeting stim-

"Preparation of the budget leads to decisions that affect the future course of Whitewater—or of any business."

ulates thoughts about pricing, product lines, job assignments, needs for additional equipment, and negotiations with banks. Preparation of the budget leads to decisions that affect the future course of Whitewater—or of any business. The operating budget—consisting of the sales budget; the purchases, cost of goods sold, and inventory budget; and the operating expenses budget—results in the budgeted income statement.

PREPARING THE BUDGETED INCOME STATEMENT There are four steps to preparing the budgeted income statement:

Step 1. Begin by preparing the sales budget (Schedule A). Sales is the key measure of business activity. The budgeted sales amount for each product is determined

EXHIBIT 24-6

Budgeted Income Statement

WHITEWATER SPORTING GOODS STORE NO. 18 BUDGETED INCOME STATEMENT FOUR MONTHS ENDING JULY 31, 19X5			
		Amount	Source
Sales...		$240,000	Schedule A
Cost of goods sold............................		168,000	Schedule B
Gross margin....................................		72,000	
Operating expenses:			
Salary and commissions	$46,000		Schedule C
Rent	8,000		
Depreciation...............................	2,000		
Insurance	800		
Miscellaneous.............................	12,000	68,800	
Operating income		3,200	
Interest expense...............................		225	Exhibit 24A-1,
Net income......................................		$ 2,975	p. 1017

Short Exercise: Look at Exhibit 24-6. Assume that the budgeted income statement projects a net loss instead of net income. What can be done? *A:* Since the sales budget is the starting point, we must first evaluate sales. Can the sale price be raised? Can we begin an advertising campaign to boost sales?

Next we evaluate cost of goods sold. Can we buy the units at a lower price from another supplier or save by buying in larger quantities?

Finally we analyze each of the operating expenses. Where can costs be cut?

The budgeted income statement often is revised and reworked until net income is an acceptable amount.

by multiplying its sale price by the predicted unit sales. The overall sales budget is the sum of the budgets for individual products.

Schedule A—Sales Budget (Item 4, page 987)

	April	May	June	July	April–July Total
Cash sales, 60%	$30,000	$48,000	$36,000	$30,000	
Credit sales, 40%..............	20,000	32,000	24,000	20,000	
Total sales, 100%	$50,000	$80,000	$60,000	$50,000	$240,000

Trace the April–July total sales to the budgeted income statement in Exhibit 24-6.

Step 2. Prepare the purchases, cost of goods sold, and inventory budget (Schedule B). This schedule determines cost of goods sold for the budgeted income statement, ending inventory for the budgeted balance sheet, and purchases for the cash budget. The relationship among these items is given by the familiar cost-of-goods-sold computation:

Beginning inventory + Purchases – Ending inventory = Cost of goods sold

Beginning inventory is known, budgeted cost of goods sold is a fixed percentage of sales, and budgeted ending inventory is a computed amount. You must solve for the budgeted purchases figure. To do this, move beginning inventory and ending inventory to the right side of the equation, isolating Purchases on the left side:

Purchases = Cost of goods sold + Ending inventory – Beginning inventory

Schedule B—Purchases, Cost of Goods Sold, and Inventory Budget   (Item 5, page 987)

	April	May	June	July	April–July Total
Cost of goods sold (0.70 × sales, from Schedule A)	$35,000	$56,000	$42,000	$35,000	$168,000
+ Desired ending inventory ($20,000 + 0.80 × Cost of goods sold for the next month)....	64,800*	53,600	48,000	42,400‡	
= Total needs	99,800	109,600	90,000	77,400	
– Beginning inventory	(48,000)†	(64,800)	(53,600)	(48,000)	
= Purchases....................................	$51,800	$44,800	$36,400	$29,400	

*$20,000 + (0.80 × $56,000) = $64,800   ‡Assumed for illustrative purposes
† Balance at March 31 (Exhibit 24-5)

To see how this information fits into the operating budget, trace the total budgeted cost of goods sold ($168,000) to the bugeted income statement in Exhibit 24-6. We will be using the budgeted inventory and purchases amounts later.

Step 3. Prepare the operating expenses budget (Schedule C). Some budgeted operating expenses, such as sales commissions and delivery expenses, fluctuate with sales. Other expenses, such as rent and insurance, are the same each month (fixed).

Schedule C—Operating Expenses Budget (Items 6 and 7, pages 987–988)

	April	May	June	July	April–July Total
Salary, fixed amount.................................	$ 2,500	$ 2,500	$ 2,500	$ 2,500	
Commission, 15% of sales from					
Schedule A	7,500	12,000	9,000	7,500	
Total salary and commissions	10,000	14,500	11,500	10,000	$46,000
Rent, fixed amount	2,000	2,000	2,000	2,000	8,000
Depreciation, fixed amount....................	500	500	500	500	2,000
Insurance, fixed amount	200	200	200	200	800
Miscellaneous, 5% of sales	2,500	4,000	3,000	2,500	12,000
Total operating expenses	$15,200	$21,200	$17,200	$15,200	$68,800

Trace the April–July totals (salary and commissions of $46,000, rent of $8,000, and so on) to the budgeted income statement in Exhibit 24-6.

Step 4. Use steps 1 through 3 to determine operating income on the budgeted income statement. We explain computation of the interest expense as part of the cash budget. (See the chapter appendix.)

Preparing the Financial Budget

The second major section of the master budget that we will discuss is the financial budget, which consists of the cash budget and the budgeted balance sheet. The **cash budget,** or *statement of budgeted cash receipts and disbursements,* details how the business expects to proceed from the beginning cash balance to the desired ending balance. Cash receipts and disbursements depend in part on revenues and expenses, which appear in the budgeted income statement. The cash budget, then, usually is prepared after the budgeted income statement.

PREPARING THE SUMMARY STATEMENT OF BUDGETED CASH RECEIPTS AND DISBURSEMENTS The cash budget has the following major parts: cash collections from customers (Schedule D), cash disbursements for purchases (Schedule E), cash disbursements for operating expenses (Schedule F), and capital expenditures. The chapter appendix shows the cash budget in month-by-month detail.

Exhibit 24-7 gives summary data for the four-month period. The cash receipt and disbursement totals in Schedules D, E, and F and the $3,000 capital expenditure to acquire the delivery truck are included. Acquisition of long-term assets such as the truck is based on a decision-making process called *capital budgeting.* We cover that management tool in Chapter 27.

Schedule D—Budgeted Cash Collections from Customers

	April	May	June	July	Total
Cash sales from Schedule A	$30,000	$48,000	$36,000	$30,000	
Collections of last month's credit sales,					
from Schedule A (Item 4, page 987)...	16,000*	20,000	32,000	24,000	
Total collections....................................	$46,000	$68,000	$68,000	$54,000	$236,000

*March 31 acounts receivable

WHITEWATER SPORTING GOODS STORE NO. 18
SUMMARY STATEMENT OF BUDGETED CASH RECEIPTS AND DISBURSEMENTS
FOUR MONTHS ENDING JULY 31, 19X5

Beginning cash balance (Item 3, page 987)		$ 15,000
Cash collections from customers (Schedule D)		236,000
Cash available before financing		251,000
Cash disbursements:		
For purchases (Schedule E)	$164,500	
For operating expenses (Schedule F)	65,250	
For purchase of delivery truck (Item 8, page 988)	3,000	232,750
Cash excess (deficiency)		18,250
Net effect of financing (Exhibit 24A-1)		4,275*
Ending cash balance		$ 22,525

*Borrowing	$9,000
Payments ($1,590 + $1,575 + $1,560)	4,725
Net effect of financing	$4,275

Schedule E—Budgeted Cash Disbursements for Purchases

	April	May	June	July	Total
50% of last month's purchases, from Schedule B	$16,800*	$25,900	$22,400	$18,200	
50% of this month's purchases, from Schedule B	25,900	22,400	18,200	14,700	
Total disbursements for purchases	$42,700	$48,300	$40,600	$32,900	$164,500

*0.50 × March purchases of $33,600 (amount assumed)

Schedule F—Budgeted Cash Disbursements for Operating Expenses

	April	May	June	July	Total
Expense amounts, from Schedule C:					
Salary and commissions:					
50% of last month's expenses, from Schedule C (Item 6, page 987)	$ 4,250*	$ 5,000	$ 7,250	$ 5,750	
50% of this month's expenses, from Schedule C	5,000	7,250	5,750	5,000	
Total salary and commissions	9,250	12,250	13,000	10,750	
Rent (Item 7, page 988)	2,000	2,000	2,000	2,000	
Miscellaneous (5% of sales, Schedule A)	2,500	4,000	3,000	2,500	
Total disbursements for operating expenses	$13,750	$18,250	$18,000	$15,250	$65,250

*March 31 salary and commissions payable

The *net effect of financing* in Exhibit 24-7 deserves special mention. Early in the four-month period ending July 31, 19X5, Whitewater expects to borrow some cash. In following months, it expects to generate excess cash and pay on the debt. The net effect is a cash inflow of $4,275. See the chapter appendix for details.

PREPARING THE BUDGETED BALANCE SHEET The final step in preparing the master budget is to complete the balance sheet. You project each asset, liability, and owners' equity account on the basis of the plans outlined in the previous schedules and exhibits. Exhibit 24-8 presents the budgeted balance sheet. If desired, you can prepare separate schedules to show the computations of accounts receivable, plant assets, and so on.

Now the *master budget* is complete. It consists of the budgeted financial statements and all supporting schedules.

Short Exercise: Assume that Coleman's sales are 25% cash and 75% on credit. Past collection history indicates that credit sales are collected:

  30% in the month of sale
  60% in the following month
   8% in the 2nd month following sale
   2% never collected
November sales were 2,900 units ($39,150) and December sales were 2,950 units ($39,825). Prepare the Budgeted Cash Collections for January and February.
A: Cash Sales (25% of each month's sales):
  Jan. $10,125 **Feb.** $15,469
Collection from current month's credit sales:
  Jan. 9,113* **Feb.** 13,922†
Collection from last month's credit sales:
  Jan. 17,921** **Feb.** 18,225††
Collection from credit sales two months previous:
  Jan. 2,349*** **Feb.** 2,390†††
Total:
  Jan. $39,508 **Feb.** $50,006

*$40,500 × 0.75 × 0.30 = $ 9,113
†$61,875 × 0.75 × 0.30 = $13,922
**$39,825 × 0.75 × 0.60 = $17,921
††$40,500 × 0.75 × 0.60 = $18,225
***$39,150 × 0.75 × 0.08 = $ 2,349
†††$39,825 × 0.75 × 0.08 = $ 2,390

EXHIBIT 24-8
Budgeted Balance Sheet

WHITEWATER SPORTING GOODS STORE NO. 18 BUDGETED BALANCE SHEET JULY 31, 19X5		
Assets		
Current assets:		
Cash (Exhibit 24-7)	$22,525	
Accounts receivable (Schedule A)	20,000	
Inventory (Schedule B)..	42,400	
Prepaid insurance (beginning balance of $1,800 – $800 for four months' expiration; Schedule C)	1,000	$ 85,925
Plant assets:		
Equipment and fixtures (beginning balance of $32,000 + $3,000 truck acquisition; Item 8, page 988)...........................	$35,000	
Accumulated depreciation (beginning balance of $12,800 + $500 depreciation for each of four months; Schedule C)..................	(14,800)	20,200
Total assets..		$106,125
Liabilities		
Current liabilities:		
Short-term note payable ($9,000 – $4,500 paid back; Exhibit 24A-1)	$ 4,500	
Accounts payable (0.50 × July purchases of $29,400; Schedule B)..	14,700	
Salary and commissions payable (0.50 × July expenses of $10,000; Schedule C)...	5,000	
Total liabilities		$ 24,200
Owners' Equity		
Owners' equity (beginning balance of $78,950 + $2,975 net income; Exhibit 24-6)..		81,925
Total liabilities and owners' equity		$106,125

Short Exercise: Assume that Coleman has $8,300 cash on hand on January 1 and requires a minimum cash balance of $7,500. January cash collections are $39,508. Total cash disbursements for January are $48,320. What is the cash excess or the cash deficiency at the end of January? *A:*

Beginning cash	$ 8,300
+ Cash collections	39,508
= Cash available	47,808
– Cash disbursements	48,320
= Ending balance before financing	(512)
– Minimum cash bal. required	7,500
= Cash deficiency ($7,500 + $512)	$ 8,012

Coleman must borrow $8,012 to bring ending cash for January up to the required $7,500.

Summary of Budgeting Procedures

The most important budget documents are the budgeted income statement (Exhibit 24-6), the summary statement of budgeted cash receipts and disbursements (Exhibit 24-7), and the budgeted balance sheet (Exhibit 24-8). Top management analyzes these statements to ensure that all the budgeted figures are consistent with company goals. As the business strives to reach those goals, management controls operations by comparing actual results with forecasted performance, as shown in the performance report (Exhibit 24-3).

Budgeting and Sensitivity Analysis

OBJECTIVE 4
Use sensitivity analysis in budgeting

The master budget is a model of the organization's *planned* activities. But actual results often deviate from plans. Thus, effective managers conduct sensitivity analyses to plan for various possibilities. **Sensitivity analysis** is a what-if technique that asks what a result will be if a predicted amount is not achieved or if an underlying assumption changes. *What* operating income will CIGNA Healthcare earn *if* sales revenue is 10 percent less than predicted? Will an equipment purchase have to be postponed? *What* will be Whitewater Store No. 18's cash balance on July 31 *if* the period's sales are 45-percent cash, not 60-percent cash? Will more cash have to be borrowed?

Sensitivity analyses may affect very specific plans. For example, suppose that Ford Motor Company executives examine different levels of car sales for May. Their analysis may lead to changes in Ford's materials purchasing plan and projected cash payments to individual suppliers, not just for May but also for June and July.

 Many companies use computer spreadsheet programs to prepare master budget schedules and statements. Managers and accountants can answer what-if questions simply by changing a number. At the press of a key, the computer prepares a new budget that includes all the effects of the change. The computer's ability to provide a nearly instant display of changes makes sensitivity analysis a very powerful planning tool.

STOP & THINK Consider two budget situations: (1) Whitewater Sporting Goods' marketing analysts produce a near-certain forecast for four-month sales of $4,500,000 for the company's 20 stores. (2) Much uncertainty exists about the period's sales. The most likely amount is $4,500,000, but analysts consider any amount between $3,900,000 and $5,100,000 to be possible. How will the budgeting process differ in these two circumstances?

Answer: Whitewater will prepare a master budget for the expected sales level of $4,500,000 in either case. Because of the great uncertainty about sales in situation 2, the company's executives will want a set of budgets covering the entire range of volume rather than a single level. Whitewater's managers may use a spreadsheet program to prepare budgets based on sales of, say, $3,900,000, $4,200,000, $4,500,000, $4,800,000, and $5,100,000. These budgets help managers plan actions for sales levels throughout the forecasted range. They also help explain differences between expected and actual amounts by showing how expenses vary with sales.

SUMMARY PROBLEM FOR YOUR REVIEW MID-CHAPTER

Review the Whitewater Sporting Goods example in the chapter. Suppose that you think that July sales might be $40,000 instead of the projected $50,000 in Schedule A, page 989. You want a new budget to learn the effects of the change in the sales amount.

Required

1. Revise Schedules A, B, and C. Prepare a revised budgeted income statement for the four months ended July 31, 19X5.
2. Revise Schedules D, E, and F. Prepare a revised summary statement of budgeted cash receipts and disbursements and a revised budgeted balance sheet at July 31, 19X5. Assume that the net effect of financing—a cash inflow of $4,275—is unchanged.

Note: You need not repeat the parts of the revised schedules that do not change.

SOLUTION TO REVIEW PROBLEM

Although not required, this solution repeats the budgeted amounts for April, May, and June. Revised figures appear in boldface type for emphasis.

Requirement 1

Revised Schedule A—Sales Budget

	April	May	June	July	Total
Cash sales, 60%	$30,000	$48,000	$36,000	**$24,000**	
Credit sales, 40%	20,000	32,000	24,000	**16,000**	
Total sales, 100%	$50,000	$80,000	$60,000	**$40,000**	$230,000

Revised Schedule B—Purchases, Cost of Goods Sold, and Inventory Budget

	April	May	June	July	Total
Cost of goods sold (0.70 × sales, from Revised Schedule A)	$35,000	$56,000	$ 42,000	**$28,000**	**$161,000**
+ Desired ending inventory ($20,000 + 0.80 × cost of goods sold for next month)	64,800	53,600	**42,400**	42,400	
= Total needs	99,800	109,600	**84,400**	70,400	
− Beginning inventory	(48,000)	(64,800)	(53,600)	**(42,400)**	
= Purchases	$51,800	$44,800	**$30,800**	**$28,000**	

Revised Schedule C—Operating Expenses Budget

	April	May	June	July	Total
Salary, fixed amount...	$ 2,500	$ 2,500	$ 2,500	$ 2,500	
Commission, 15% of sales from Revised Schedule A	7,500	12,000	9,000	6,000	
Total salary and commissions	10,000	14,500	11,500	8,500	$44,500
Rent, fixed amount..	2,000	2,000	2,000	2,000	8,000
Depreciation, fixed amount	500	500	500	500	2,000
Insurance, fixed amount...	200	200	200	200	800
Miscellaneous, 5% of sales	2,500	4,000	3,000	2,000	11,500
Total operating expenses...	$15,200	$21,200	$17,200	$13,200	$66,800

REVISED EXHIBIT 24-6

Budgeted Income Statement

WHITEWATER SPORTING GOODS STORE NO. 18
BUDGETED INCOME STATEMENT
FOUR MONTHS ENDING JULY 31, 19X5

	Amount	Source
Sales..	$230,000	Revised Schedule A
Cost of goods sold..............................	161,000	Revised Schedule B
Gross margin......................................	69,000	
Operating expenses:		
Salary and commissions $44,500		Revised Schedule C
Rent 8,000		
Depreciation.................................... 2,000		
Insurance 800		
Miscellaneous 11,500	66,800	
Operating income	2,200	
Interest expense.................................	225	Exhibit 24A-1
Net income..	$ 1,975	

Requirement 2

Revised Schedule D—Budgeted Cash Collections from Customers

	April	May	June	July	Total
Cash sales, from Revised Schedule A.........................	$30,000	$48,000	$36,000	$24,000	
Collections of last month's credit sales,					
from Revised Schedule A.......................................	16,000*	20,000	32,000	24,000	
Total collections...	$46,000	$68,000	$68,000	$48,000	$230,000

*March 31 accounts receivable

Revised Schedule E—Budgeted Cash Disbursements for Purchases

	April	May	June	July	Total
50% of last month's purchases, from					
Revised Schedule B	$16,800*	$25,900	$ 22,400	$15,400	
50% of this month's purchases, from					
Revised Schedule B	25,900	22,400	15,400	14,000	
Total disbursements for purchases..........................	$42,700	$48,300	$37,800	$29,400	$158,200

*Amount assumed for illustration

Revised Schedule F—Budgeted Cash Disbursements for Operating Expenses

	April	May	June	July	Total
Expense amounts, from Revised Schedule C:					
Salary and commissions:					
50% of last month's expenses,					
from Revised Schedule C	$ 4,250*	$ 5,000	$ 7,250	$ 5,750	
50% of this month's expenses,					
from Revised Schedule C	5,000	7,250	5,750	4,250	
Total salary and commissions	9,250	12,250	13,000	10,000	
Rent..	2,000	2,000	2,000	2,000	
Miscellaneous (5% of sales, Revised Schedule A)...............	2,500	4,000	3,000	2,000	
Total disbursements for operating expenses	$13,750	$18,250	$18,000	$14,000	$64,000

*March 31 salary and commissions payable

WHITEWATER SPORTING GOODS STORE No. 18
SUMMARY STATEMENT OF BUDGETED CASH RECEIPTS AND DISBURSEMENTS
FOUR MONTHS ENDING JULY 31, 19X5

Beginning cash balance..		$ 15,000
Cash collections from customers (Revised Schedule D)....................		230,000
Cash available before financing		$245,000
Cash disbursements:		
For purchases (Revised Schedule E)...	$158,200	
For operating expenses (Revised Schedule F)	64,000	
For purchase of delivery truck	3,000	225,200
Cash excess (deficiency)		19,800
Net effect of financing (same as Exhibit 24-7).................................		4,275
Ending cash balance..		$ 24,075

REVISED EXHIBIT 24-7
Summary Statement of Budgeted Cash Receipts and Disbursements

---

WHITEWATER SPORTING GOODS STORE No. 18
BUDGETED BALANCE SHEET
JULY 31, 19X5

Assets

Current assets:		
Cash (Revised Exhibit 24-7)...	$24,075	
Accounts receivable (Revised Schedule A).....................	16,000	
Inventory	42,400	
Prepaid insurance	1,000	$ 83,475
Plant assets:		
Equipment and fixtures	$ 35,000	
Accumulated depreciation	(14,800)	20,200
Total assets..		$103,675

Liabilities

Current liabilities:		
Short-term note payable	$ 4,500	
Accounts payable (0.50 × July purchases of **$28,000;**		
Revised Schedule B)	14,000	
Salary and commissions payable (0.50 × July		
expenses of **$8,500;** Revised Schedule C)...................	4,250	
Total liabilities		$ 22,750

Owners' Equity

Owners' equity (beginning balance of $78,950 + **$1,975**		
net income; Revised Exhibit 24-6)...............................		80,925
Total liabilities and owners' equity		$103,675

REVISED EXHIBIT 24-8
Budgeted Balance Sheet

Responsibility Accounting

OBJECTIVE 5

Distinguish among different types of responsibility centers

To achieve the goals of the master budget, a company must coordinate the actions of all its employees, from hourly wage earners to the chief executive officer. Each manager is responsible for planning and controlling some portion of the firm's activities. At lower levels, a manager's responsibility may be defined by value-chain function. For example, one manager is responsible for *design* of Ford Explorer engines; another manager for *production* of Explorers at Ford's Louisville, Kentucky, plant; and a third for *distribution* of Explorers to dealerships. Managers at higher levels are responsible for product lines. Ford's executive vice-president of light trucks is ultimately responsible for the entire Explorer line—from research and development to customer service. Lower-level managers are accountable to the executive vice-president for meeting their budget goals, just as that executive is accountable to the president of the Ford Motor Division.

"Ford's executive vice-president of light trucks is ultimately responsible for the entire Explorer line—from research and development to customer service."

How does a business evaluate the performance of managers and the activities they supervise? By comparing plans (budgets) with actions (actual results) for each responsibility center. A **responsibility center** is a part, segment, or subunit of an organization whose manager is accountable for specified activities. In the chapter-opening story, the CIGNA Healthcare and Property/Casualty Insurance divisions are responsibility centers. **Responsibility accounting** is a system for evaluating the performance of each responsibility center and its manager. Three common types of responsibility centers are cost, profit, and investment centers (Exhibit 24-9).

1. *Cost center:* a responsibility center in which a manager is accountable for costs (expenses) only. Examples include a personnel department and a shipping department. It is important for these departments to control costs; they are not responsible for generating revenues. Consequently, only costs are reported for their activities. A shipping department manager is judged, for example, on the cost of shipping a certain volume of merchandise to customers.

2. *Profit center:* a responsibility center in which a manager is accountable for revenues and costs (expenses). Examples are a Bennigan's restaurant and the appliance de-

EXHIBIT 24-9

Three Common Types of Responsibility Centers

(a) A cost center, such as a personnel department—where managers are responsible for costs

(b) A profit center, such as a Sears appliance department—where managers are responsible for generating income

(c) An investment center, such as Safeway's Nevada branch—where managers are responsible for income and invested capital

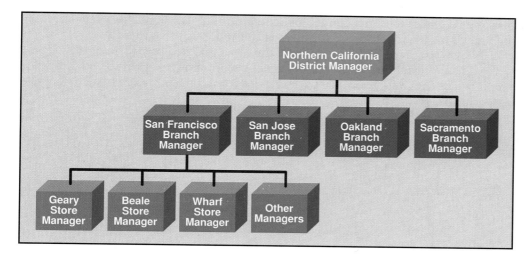

partment of a Sears store. Managers of these subunits are responsible for generating income (revenues minus expenses). Both revenues and expenses are reported to show the income of a profit center.

3. Investment center: a responsibility center in which a manager is accountable for investments, revenues, and costs (expenses). Examples are the Nevada branch of Safeway Stores and the Nutrasweet Company, which is owned by Monsanto. CIGNA Healthcare is an investment center. Investment in the business is reported in addition to revenues and expenses so that return on investment (income divided by investment) can be computed. Top managers, like investors, evaluate these projects by comparing their returns with required investments.

Short Exercise: Name the three types of responsibility centers, and give an example of each one in a department store.
1. Cost center—payroll, accounting, and personnel departments
2. Profit center—shoe, electronics, and men's clothing departments
3. Investment center—the store itself

Example of Responsibility Accounting

The simplified organization chart in Exhibit 24-10 shows how a company may assign responsibility in the fast-food industry. At the top level of O'Toole Restaurant Corporation, a district manager oversees the branch managers, who supervise the managers of the individual restaurants (called stores). Store managers have limited freedom to make operating decisions. They may decide the quantities of food items to order, the number of employees and their schedules, and store hours. Branch managers oversee several stores, evaluate store managers' performance, and set store managers' compensation levels. In turn, district managers oversee several branches, evaluate branch managers' performance and compensation, set food prices, and approve sales promotions. District managers are accountable to regional managers, who answer to home-office vice-presidents.

STOP & THINK O'Toole's store managers do not have authority to set sale prices or control advertising. Both factors affect store revenues. But despite the lack of store-manager authority, the corporation evaluates each store as a profit center instead of as a cost center. Why?

Answer: O'Toole's top management could have designated each store as a cost center. But then each store manager would be motivated to cut costs in order to keep actual costs below the budget. Excessive cost cutting can hurt quality and service. By evaluating each store as a profit center, executives give store managers the incentive to keep stores clean and to ensure that employees provide fast and friendly service. Store managers thus are more likely to work hard to increase customer value, the foundation of long-run profitability.

Exhibit 24-11 provides a more detailed view of how responsibility accounting is used to evaluate profit centers. Examine the lowest level and move to the top. Follow how the reports are related through the three levels of responsibility.

Trace the $54,000 operating income from the Beale store manager's report to the San Francisco branch manager's report. The branch manager's report summarizes the results of the stores under his supervision. In addition, charges incurred by the branch manager's office are included in this report.

Now trace the $465,000 total from the San Francisco branch manager's report to the Northern California district manager's report. The report of the district manager includes data for her own district office plus a summary of each branch's operating performance.

EXHIBIT 24-11
Responsibility Accounting at Various Levels

O'TOOLE RESTAURANT CORPORATION
RESPONSIBILITY ACCOUNTING AT VARIOUS LEVELS
(IN THOUSANDS OF DOLLARS)

Northern California District Manager
Monthly Responsibility Report

Operating income of branches and district manager office expense:	Budget This Month	Budget Year to Date	Actual This Month	Actual Year to Date	Variance Favorable (Unfavorable) This Month	Variance Favorable (Unfavorable) Year to Date
District manager office expense	$ (150)	$ (600)	$ (154)	$ (620)	$ (4)	$(20)
San Francisco branch	465	1,730	460	1,780	(5)	50
San Jose branch	500	1,800	560	1,994	60	194
Oakland branch	390	1,540	475	1,855	85	315
Sacramento branch	520	2,240	468	2,061	(52)	(179)
Operating income	$1,725	$6,710	$1,809	$7,070	$84	$360

San Francisco Branch Manager
Monthly Responsibility Report

Operating income of stores and branch manager office expense:	Budget This Month	Budget Year to Date	Actual This Month	Actual Year to Date	Variance Favorable (Unfavorable) This Month	Variance Favorable (Unfavorable) Year to Date
Branch manager office expense	$ (20)	$ (306)	$ (25)	$ (302)	$(5)	$ 4
Geary store	48	148	40	136	(8)	(12)
Beale store	54	228	61	244	7	16
Wharf store	38	160	42	170	4	10
Others	345	1,500	342	1,532	(3)	32
Operating income	$465	$1,730	$460	$1,780	$(5)	$50

Beale Store Manager
Monthly Responsibility Report

Revenues and expenses:	Budget This Month	Budget Year to Date	Actual This Month	Actual Year to Date	Variance Favorable (Unfavorable) This Month	Variance Favorable (Unfavorable) Year to Date
Revenues	$170	$690	$178	$702	$8	$12
Food expense	50	198	45	184	5	14
Paper	15	62	18	64	(3)	(2)
Wages	24	98	28	103	(4)	(5)
Repairs	5	19	4	20	1	(1)
General	12	45	12	47	—	(2)
Depreciation	10	40	10	40	—	—
Total expenses	116	462	117	458	(1)	4
Operating income	$ 54	$228	$ 61	$244	$7	$16

Management by Exception

Exhibit 24-11 stresses variances. This reporting format aids **management by exception,** the practice of directing executive attention to important deviations from budgeted amounts. Look at the district manager's report, and consider the San Francisco branch. Its actual operating income of $460,000 is very close to its budget for the current month. Under management by exception, the district manager will not waste time investigating the immaterial variance. In contrast, both the San Jose and Oakland branches substantially exceeded budgeted performance. Their large favorable variances probably will be investigated to determine their causes. For example, suppose that the Oakland manager believes that a local sales promotion was especially effective. That promotion may be repeated, and also used in other cities.

The Northern California district manager will concentrate her efforts this month on improving the Sacramento branch. Its actual income of $468,000 is 10 percent ($52,000/$520,000) lower than its budget. The district manager may ask to see the Sacramento branch manager's monthly responsibility report. That report reveals whether the income shortfall is due to excessively high office expenses, below-budget performance by individual stores, or both. The two managers will work together to identify and correct any problems that exist.

Exhibit 24-11 also shows that highly-summarized data may hide problems. Although the San Francisco branch as a whole performed well, the Geary store did not. Its actual income of $40,000 is 16.7 percent below its budgeted amount. This shortfall is offset by excellent performances by the Beale and Wharf stores. If the district manager receives only the condensed report at the top of the exhibit, she must rely on branch managers to spot and correct problems with individual stores. Some upper-level executives prefer to receive the more-detailed middle-level reports in order to keep tighter control over their responsibility centers (districts, in this example).

The format for reporting performance used in Exhibit 24-11 can be expanded to provide more information about variances. The first line of the Beale manager's report might be extended as follows:

	Budget		Actual		Variance: Favorable (Unfavorable)		Variance: Percent of Budgeted Amount	
	This Month	Year to Date	This Month	Year to Date	This Month	Year to Date	This Month	Year to Date
Revenues	$170	$690	$178	$702	$8	$12	4.7%	1.7%

What caused the Beale store's $8,000 favorable revenue variance? Perhaps it sold more meals than expected. Or perhaps the average sale price per meal was higher than budgeted. The revenue variance can be divided into the amount due to each of those factors. Similarly, the revenue variance of a Hilton hotel can be divided by cause: the difference between the budgeted and actual (1) number of rooms rented and (2) average rental rate.

No single reporting format appeals to all users. Some managers prefer greater detail, others less. The choice is a matter of personal preference.

Not a Question of Blame

Responsibility accounting is a management aid. It helps top executives delegate decision making to lower levels by assigning to managers responsibility for the actions of their units and by providing a way to evaluate their performance. Management by exception frees top managers to concentrate on strategic issues that affect the entire organization.

Responsibility accounting systems should not be misused to find fault or to place blame. The question is not, Who should be blamed for an unfavorable variance? Instead, the question is, Who is in the best position to explain why a specific variance occurred? Consider again the performance of the Sacramento branch in Exhibit 24-11. Suppose that a month of unusually nasty weather resulted in a 15-percent drop in restaurant volume. It may be that only efficient operations by the branch's stores kept the income variance as low as $52,000. Therefore, the branch manager's performance may be viewed favorably despite the unfavorable variance.

Departmental Accounting

Responsibility centers often are called *departments*. Many businesses distinguish between production departments and service departments. The main function of a **production department** is to add value to products or services sold to customers. In a manufacturing company, each production department may produce a different product. Alternatively, each department may be responsible for a different stage of production of the same product. Examples include the shaping and painting departments of a toy manufacturer.

Short Exercise: What are some examples of direct departmental costs? *A:* Department manager's salary, depreciation for furniture and equipment in the department, and delivery expense that can be traced directly to the department.

Retail companies and service firms often refer to their production departments as *operating* departments. A retailer's operating departments typically sell related product lines; examples are the housewares and appliance departments of a department store and the hardware and software departments of a computer store. A service firm's operating departments typically provide similar services. Examples are the audit, tax, and consulting departments of a CPA firm.

The primary function of a **service department** is to provide services to other departments, both production departments and other service departments. Examples include the production scheduling and power (electricity) departments of a manufacturing plant and the purchasing, payroll, and personnel departments of manufacturers and retailers. Services provided back and forth among service departments are called **reciprocal services.** Reciprocal services present special accounting problems, which we discuss in the next section.

Short Exercise: What are some examples of indirect departmental costs? *A:* Insurance, utilities, accounting, rent, and so on. These costs usually are incurred for the benefit of the business as a whole and, therefore, must be allocated to each department.

Departmental accounting systems assign both direct and indirect costs to departments. **Direct costs** are costs that are conveniently identified with and traceable to a particular department. Depreciation of a machine used in a production department and the department manager's salary are direct costs. So are the wages of salesclerks and special advertising for a shoe department of a department store. **Indirect costs** cannot be traced to a single department. Examples are building rent and the cost of a general advertising campaign that promotes an entire store. The allocated costs of service departments are indirect costs of the departments they serve.

Allocation of Service Department Costs

OBJECTIVE 7

Allocate service department costs to production departments

Labor costs and various other costs are accumulated for each service department. These costs are allocated (assigned) to the departments served, for two reasons. First, they are allocated to hold production department managers accountable for all costs, both direct and indirect, that support the activities under their supervision. Production managers have more incentive to help control service costs when they are assigned a portion of those costs. Second, in manufacturing companies, service department costs are indirect costs of producing products. Thus, these costs should be considered manufacturing overhead costs and applied to products produced. How is this accomplished? First, service department costs are allocated to the production departments that benefit from their services. Then, the allocated costs are (1) added to other overhead costs assigned to the production departments and (2) applied to products through departmental manufacturing overhead rates. Our focus here is on the first step—allocation of service department costs to production departments.

Service Department	Base for Allocating Cost to User Departments
Materials Handling Department	Number, weight, or size of items handled for each department
Power Department	Number of machine-hours worked in each department
General Plant Administration Department	Number of labor-hours or machine-hours worked in each department
Janitorial Services Department	Square feet of space in each department
Advertising Department	Separately traced if possible; otherwise, in proportion to newspaper space or radio or TV time in advertisement, or in proportion to budgeted sales or actual sales of each department
Payroll Department	Number of employees in each department
Personnel Department	Number of employees in each department
Purchasing Department	Number of orders placed for each department

EXHIBIT 24-12
Bases for Allocating Service Department Costs

To allocate a service department's cost, accountants must choose an *allocation base*, which is a logical common denominator for assigning the cost to the departments that use the services. Exhibit 24-12 offers examples of allocation bases commonly used for selected service departments. The ideal guide for choosing an allocation base is a cause-and-effect relationship. That is, What are the cost drivers, the factors that cause costs? ◄▦◄▦◄▦ As Exhibit 24-12 shows, the more square feet of space to be cleaned, the higher the cost of a janitorial service department. That relationship is relatively easy to understand. Conversely, consider the cost of a general advertising campaign for a department store. The total cost might be allocated to individual departments in relation to budgeted or actual sales, but a cause-and-effect relationship is much more difficult, if not impossible, to establish.

No one "right" allocation base exists for every cost. Managers use their experience and judgment in choosing these bases. Affected managers should participate in the choice of allocation bases; participation enhances their confidence in the reasonableness of the resulting allocations.

Two Methods of Allocating Costs

We now demonstrate the two most widely used methods of allocating the costs of service departments to production departments: the direct method and the step-down method. A third method, the reciprocal method, is covered in many cost accounting and advanced managerial accounting texts. These three methods differ in the way they treat reciprocal services.

Consider TechArt, Inc., which designs, assembles, and installs state-of-the-art integrated electronics systems for both the commercial and residential markets. TechArt has two factory service departments and two production departments in its highly automated manufacturing plant:

Factory Service Departments	Production Departments
Engineering & Maintenance	Commercial Systems
Information Systems	Residential Systems

Direct costs of departments are accumulated for planning and control purposes. Then, to determine the full cost of electronics systems, TechArt accountants allocate the costs of the two service departments to the two production departments. Data for our example are shown in Exhibit 24-13.

Exhibit 24-13 shows that $400,000 of direct cost is budgeted for Engineering & Maintenance and that $100,000 of direct cost is budgeted for Information Systems. Thus, TechArt has $500,000 of service department costs that must be allocated to its two production departments. TechArt accountants expect that Engineering &

◄▦ ◄▦ ◄▦ Recall from Chapter 20, p. 851, that a cost driver is *any* factor that affects costs.

Short Exercise: What is a reasonable basis for allocating the following costs? (1) Rent; (2) Utilities; (3) Advertising; (4) Purchasing Department costs. *A:* (1) Square feet of floor space; (2) number of machine-hours worked; (3) sales; (4) number of orders placed.

Real-World Example: Weyerhaeuser Company has developed an interesting procedure for assigning corporate overhead. Rather than allocate overhead as indirect costs, the costs of corporate services are traced directly to the departments that consume the services. Managers are free to purchase services from outsiders or from corporate service departments. Each service department must carefully price its service (preparation of payroll checks, for example) to be competitive. This new procedure for assigning overhead enabled one department to trim over 2% off its budget in the first year.

| | Factory Service Departments | | Production Departments | | |
	Engineering & Maintenance	Information Systems	Commercial Systems	Residential Systems	Total
Direct department costs.............................	$400,000	$100,000	$900,000	$750,000	$2,150,000
Services provided:					
By Engineering & Maintenance					
Budgeted labor-hours..........................	—	600	3,000	2,400	6,000
Proportion......................................	—	1/10	5/10	4/10	10/10
By Information Systems					
Budgeted computer-hours	600	—	525	375	1,500
Proportion...	40/100	—	35/100	25/100	100/100

EXHIBIT 24-13

Data for Service Department Cost Allocation at TechArt, Inc.

Maintenance employees will work 6,000 hours: 600 (1/10 of total) for Information Systems, 3,000 for Commercial Systems, and 2,400 for Residential Systems. The accountants anticipate that Information Systems employees will devote 600 computer-hours to Engineering & Maintenance, 525 to Commercial Systems, and 375 to Residential Systems.

DIRECT METHOD The **direct method** of service department cost allocation ignores all services provided by one service department to another. It allocates each service department's total cost *directly* to production departments in proportion to the services rendered to them. Exhibit 24-14 illustrates this method. The direct method ignores not only the 600 labor-hours of budgeted service provided by Engineering & Maintenance (EM) to Information Systems (IS) but also the 600 hours of computer time budgeted by IS for EM. For each service department, the base number of hours used to compute allocation percentages is the total number budgeted for Commercial Systems and Residential Systems only. That number is 5,400 (3,000 + 2,400) for EM and 900 (525 + 375) for IS.

STEP-DOWN METHOD The **step-down method** recognizes some, but not all, reciprocal services. With the step-down method, the *order* of allocation affects the amounts allocated to production departments. Exhibit 24-15 illustrates this method. For TechArt, the $500,000 of total service department cost is assigned differently to the Commercial and Residential Systems departments if the allocation procedure begins with EM than if it begins with IS.

Which department's cost should be allocated first? A popular step-down sequence is to begin with the department that renders the highest dollar amount of services to other service departments. In Exhibit 24-15 we allocate EM first.

EXHIBIT 24-14

Direct Method of Cost Allocation at TechArt, Inc.

| | Factory Service Departments | | Production Departments | | |
	Engineering & Maintenance	Information Systems	Commercial Systems	Residential Systems	Total
Direct department costs.............................	$400,000	$100,000	$ 900,000	$750,000	$2,150,000
Allocation of Engineering & Maintenance: (5/9, 4/9)*..........................	(400,000)		222,222	177,778	
	$ 0				
Allocation of Information Systems: (7/12, 5/12)†		(100,000)	58,333	41,667	
		$ 0			
Total budgeted costs of production departments......................................			$1,180,555	$969,445	$2,150,000

*Base is (3,000 + 2,400), or 5,400 hours; 3,000/5,400 = 5/9; 2,400/5,400 = 4/9
†Base is (525 + 375), or 900 hours; 525/900 = 7/12; 375/900 = 5/12

	Factory Service Departments		Production Departments		
	Engineering & Maintenance	Information Systems	Commercial Systems	Residential Systems	Total
Direct department costs............................	$400,000	$100,000	$ 900,000	$750,000	$2,150,000
Allocation of Engineering & Maintenance: (1/10, 5/10, 4/10)*............	(400,000) $ 0	40,000	200,000	160,000	
Allocation of Information Systems: (7/12, 5/12)†		(140,000) $ 0	81,667	58,333	
Total budgeted costs of production departments...			$1,181,667	$968,333	$2,150,000

*Base is (600 + 3,000 + 2,400), or 6,000 hours; 600/6,000 = 1/10; 3,000/6,000 = 5/10; 2,400/6,000 = 4/10
†Base is (525 + 375), or 900 hours; 525/900 = 7/12; 375/900 = 5/12

EM's cost is allocated to all departments served by EM, including IS. The total IS cost of $140,000 (the original $100,000 plus the $40,000 allocated from EM) is allocated to Commercial Systems and Residential Systems only. The proportions for IS are the same as those used with the direct method (Exhibit 24-14). Under the step-down method, once a service department's cost has been allocated, no other service department's cost is allocated back to it.

Which method is better? In general, the step-down, because it takes into account the most significant services provided by service departments to other service departments. However, the direct method is simpler. When the two methods produce similar results, many companies use the direct method because it is easier for managers to understand.

EXHIBIT 24-15
Step-Down Method of Cost Allocation at TechArt, Inc.

Short Exercise: Why is the direct method easy to use? **A:** Service department costs are allocated directly to production departments. There are no intermediate allocations between service departments involved.

SUMMARY PROBLEMS FOR YOUR REVIEW

Part A. Review the data for the allocation of TechArt, Inc.'s, service department costs, Exhibit 24-13. Also review Exhibit 24-15, which shows the step-down allocation of costs when the Engineering & Maintenance Department is allocated first, followed by the Information Systems Department.

Required

1. Repeat the step-down allocation of TechArt's service department costs, using the alternative sequence of Information Systems first, followed by Engineering & Maintenance.
2. If this period's results are typical for TechArt, do you expect the company to use the direct or the step-down method? Why?

Part B. Suppose that the Commercial Systems and Residential Systems departments are the two profit centers that report to TechArt's manufacturing vice-president. The current-year budget called for Commercial Systems revenue of $1,550,000 and direct costs of $900,000. Service department costs, allocated as in Part A, Requirement 1, are the only indirect costs assigned to production departments.

Assume that Commercial System's actual operating income for the year is 98 percent of the budgeted amount. Complete the following line on the vice-president's annual responsibility report:

			Variance	
	Budget	Actual	Amount	Percent of Budgeted Amount
Operating income of departments:				
Commercial Systems				2%

Part A—Requirement 1

	Factory Service Departments		Production Departments		
	Information Systems	Engineering & Maintenance	Commercial Systems	Residential Systems	Total
Direct department costs	$100,000	$ 400,000	$ 900,000	$ 750,000	$2,150,000
Allocation of Information Systems: (40/100, 35/100, 25/100)*	(100,000)	40,000	35,000	25,000	
	$ 0				
Allocation of Engineering & Maintenance: (5/9, 4/9)†		(440,000)	244,444	195,556	
		$ 0			
Total budgeted costs of production departments			$1,179,444	$ 970,556	$2,150,000

*Base is (600 + 525 + 375), or 1,500 hours; 600/1,500 = 40/100; 525/1,500 = 35/100; 375/1,500 = 25/100
†Base is (3,000 + 2,400), or 5,400 hours; 3,000/5,400 = 5/9; 2,400/5,400 = 4/9

Requirement 2

If this period's results are typical for TechArt, the company probably uses the direct method. When this method is used, the allocations to Commercial and Residential Systems are $280,555 ($222,222 + $58,333) and $219,445 ($177,778 + $41,667), respectively (Exhibit 24-14). As shown in Exhibit 24-15 and Requirement 1 above, the allocations using either sequence of the step-down method are very close to the direct-method allocations. The direct method is simpler and easier for managers to use.

Part B

			Variance	
	Budget	Actual	Amount	Percent of Budgeted Amount
Operating income of departments: Commercial Systems	$370,556*	$363,145†	$7,411‡	2%

*$1,550,000 revenue − $900,000 direct cost − $279,444 allocated service department cost
†$370,556 × 0.98
‡$370,556 − $363,145

SUMMARY

1. Identify the benefits of budgeting. A budget is a quantitative expression of a plan of action that helps managers coordinate and implement the plan. Budgets compel managers to plan, coordinate activities, and communicate plans throughout the company; aid performance evaluation; and motivate employees to achieve goals. Most companies prepare a master budget for each fiscal year. The *master budget* consists of the operating budget, the capital expenditures budget, and the financial budget.

2. Prepare an operating budget for a company. The *operating budget* sets the target revenues and expenses—and thus operating income—for the period. To budget income, accountants must budget sales, cost of goods sold, inventory, purchases, and operating expenses. Sales revenue is budgeted first because all other income statement elements—and some assets and liabilities—depend on sales volume.

3. Prepare the components of a financial budget. A *capital expenditures budget* presents plans for purchasing long-term capital assets. This budget and the budgeted income statement provide data for the *cash budget*, or *statement of budgeted cash receipts and disbursements*. All three statements are used to prepare the budgeted balance sheet.

4. Use sensitivity analysis in budgeting. Managers should make contingency plans in case actual results differ from predictions. *Sensitivity analysis* is a what-if technique for assessing the effects of changes on a company's operations and financial position. Many managers budget with spreadsheets to study a broad range of possibilities.

5. Distinguish among different types of responsibility centers. Most companies are organized by *responsibility center* to establish authority for planning and controlling activities. *Responsibility accounting* is a system for evaluating the performance of responsibility centers and their managers. Three types of responsibility centers are the cost center, the profit center, and the investment center.

6. Prepare a performance report for management by exception. Performance reports show differences between budgeted and actual amounts. By focusing on important variances, managers can direct their attention to areas that need improvement. This practice is known as *management by exception*.

7. Allocate service department costs to production departments. *Service departments* provide services to other departments. Their costs are indirect costs of the departments they serve. *Production departments* add value to products or services sold to customers. Service department costs are allocated to production departments by the *direct method* or by the *step-down method*.

SELF-STUDY QUESTIONS

1. Which of the following is *not* a benefit of budgeting? *(pp. 983–984)*
   a. Coordinates activities
   b. Automatically fires underachieving employees
   c. Aids performance evaluation
   d. Compels managers to plan

2. Chewning Corporation's actual revenues are $90,000, and operating expenses are $50,000. Budgeted revenues were $86,000 and budgeted expenses were $51,000. What is the variance in operating income? *(p. 985)*
   a. $40,000 favorable   c. $5,000 favorable
   b. $35,000 unfavorable   d. $5,000 unfavorable

3. The master budget starts with *(p. 985)*
   a. Budgeted cash   c. Budgeted sales
   b. Owners' equity   d. Inventory

4. The operating budget ends with *(p. 985)*
   a. Budgeted sales
   b. The budgeted income statement
   c. The cash budget
   d. The budgeted balance sheet

5. The master budget usually ends with *(p. 986)*
   a. Budgeted sales
   b. The budgeted income statement
   c. The cash budget
   d. The budgeted balance sheet

6. Managers can use a microcomputer along with a master budget to *(pp. 992–993)*

   a. Plan for various possibilities
   b. Eliminate uncertainty in the business environment
   c. Prepare the budget correctly on the first attempt
   d. Set ideal goals for the company

7. Which responsibility center is most likely to be a cost center? *(p. 996)*
   a. Personnel department
   b. Housewares department of a department store
   c. Audit department of a CPA firm
   d. Manufacturing plant

8. Under management by exception, which of the following variances should be investigated? *(p. 999)*
   a. Small favorable variance
   b. Small unfavorable variance
   c. Large favorable variance
   d. Large unfavorable variance

9. Responsibility accounting systems *(pp. 999–1000)*
   a. Help top managers to delegate decision making
   b. Assign responsibility for activities to managers
   c. Provide a way to evaluate performance
   d. All of the above

10. The step-down method of service department cost allocation ignores *(p. 1002)*
    a. All reciprocal services
    b. Some reciprocal services
    c. All services provided to production departments
    d. Some services provided to production departments
    Answers to the Self-Study Questions follow the Accounting Vocabulary.

ACCOUNTING VOCABULARY

Capital expenditures budget. A company's plan for purchases of property, plant, equipment, and other long-term assets *(p. 985)*.

Cash budget. Details how the business expects to go from the beginning cash balance to the desired ending balance. Also called the *statement of budgeted cash receipts and disbursements (p. 990)*.

Direct costs. Costs that are conveniently identified with and traceable to a particular department *(p. 1000)*.

Direct method. A method of service department cost allocation that ignores all services provided by one service department to another *(p. 1002)*.

Financial budget. Projects cash inflows and outflows and the period-ending balance sheet *(p. 985)*.

Indirect costs. Costs that cannot be traced to a single department; costs other than

direct costs *(p. 1000)*.

Management by exception. The practice of directing management attention to important deviations from budgeted amounts *(p. 999)*.

Master budget. The comprehensive budget that includes the operating budget, the capital expenditures budget, and the financial budget *(p. 985)*.

Operating budget. Sets the expected revenues and expenses—and thus operating income—for the period *(p. 985)*.

Production department. A department whose main function is to add value to products or services sold to customers *(p. 1000)*.

Reciprocal services. Services provided back and forth among service departments *(p. 1000)*.

Responsibility accounting. A system for evaluating the performance of each re-

sponsibility center and its manager *(p. 996)*.

Responsibility center. A part, segment, or subunit of an organization whose manager is accountable for specified activities *(p. 996)*.

Sensitivity analysis. A what-if technique that asks what a result will be if a predicted amount is not achieved or if an underlying assumption changes *(p. 992)*.

Service department. A department whose primary function is to provide services to other departments—both production departments and other service departments *(p. 1000)*.

Step-down method. A method of service department cost allocation that recognizes some, but not all, reciprocal services *(p. 1002)*.

1. b
2. c   Actual: $90,000 − $50,000 = $40,000
        Budget: 86,000 − 51,000 = 35,000
        Variance: $ 5,000 Favorable
3. c

4. b   9. d
5. d   10. b
6. a
7. a
8. c and d

QUESTIONS

1. What are four benefits of budgeting?
2. How does a manager use a performance report?
3. List the components of a master budget.
4. A Ford dealer sets a goal of selling more Ford automobiles than any other dealer in the city. Is this goal a budget? Give your reason.
5. Taft Corporation installs a budgeting system in which the president sets all the goals for the company. The vice-president checks up on all 90 employees to ensure that they are meeting the president's budget goals. What is the weakness in this budgeting system? How can the system be improved?
6. Why should the capital expenditures budget be prepared before the cash budget and the budgeted balance sheet?
7. How does a company budget inventory purchases? In your answer, show the relationships among purchases, cost of goods sold, and inventory.
8. Outline the four steps in preparing an operating budget.
9. Is sales forecasting important only to a profit-seeking business, or is it used by nonprofit organizations such as colleges and hospitals? Give your reason.
10. Why are electronic spreadsheets well suited for budgeting?
11. What three amounts are combined in the "net effect of financing" on the summary statement of budgeted cash receipts and disbursements?
12. Which manager will control expenses better: Grant, whose performance is measured by his department's sales, or Bruns, whose performance is gauged by her department's income? Why?

13. Identify three types of responsibility centers, and give examples of each. State the information they report.
14. A company owns 50 Burger King restaurants in Philadelphia, Pittsburgh, and Harrisburg. In each city, a local manager oversees operations. Starting at the individual store level, describe the likely flow of information in a responsibility accounting system. What data are reported?
15. What is the objective of management by exception?
16. What question about unfavorable variances is a responsibility accounting system designed to answer? How can such a system be abused?
17. Distinguish between direct expenses and indirect expenses of a department in a department store. Give examples of each type.
18. Name a reasonable allocation base for the following indirect expenses: heating expense, depreciation of manufacturing equipment used by three departments, and advertising expense.
19. Suppose that supplies expense is allocated to departments at the end of each period on the basis of the period's sales. In a recent month, departments X, Y, and Z had sales of $5,000, $12,000, and $8,000, respectively. How much of the month's $900 supplies expense was charged to each department?
20. A company has service departments A, B, and C and production departments X and Y. Its accountants use the step-down method of service department cost allocation, allocating the departments in alphabetical order. To which departments are A's costs allocated? B's? C's?

EXERCISES

Budgeting and performance evaluation
(Obj. 1)

E24-1 Roger Richmond owns a store that sells athletic shoes. Last year, his sales staff sold 8,000 pairs of shoes at an average sale price of $65. Variable expenses were 60 percent of sales revenue, and the total fixed expense was $100,000. This year the store sold more expensive shoe lines. Sales were 7,000 pairs at an average price of $80. The variable expense rate and the total fixed expense were the same both years. Richmond evaluates the store manager by comparing this year's income with last year's income.

Prepare a performance report for this year. Use the format of Exhibit 24-3. How would you improve Richmond's performance evaluation system to analyze this year's results better?

Budgeting purchases, cost of goods sold, and inventory
(Obj. 2)

E24-2 The sales budget of Dawson Corp. for the nine months ended September 30 is as follows:

	Quarter Ended			**Nine-Month Total**
	March 31	**June 30**	**Sep. 30**	
Cash sales, 30%...............	$ 30,000	$ 45,000	$ 33,000	$108,000
Credit sales, 70%.............	70,000	105,000	77,000	252,000
Total sales, 100%.............	$100,000	$150,000	$110,000	$360,000

In the past, cost of goods sold has been 65 percent of total sales. The director of marketing, the production manager, and the financial vice-president agree that each quarter's ending inventory should not be below $20,000 plus 10 percent of cost of goods sold for the following quarter. Dawson expects sales of $100,000 during the fourth quarter. The January 1 inventory was $22,000.

Prepare a purchases, cost of goods sold, and inventory budget for each of the first three quarters of the year. Compute cost of goods sold for the entire nine-month period. (Use Schedule B, page 989, as a model.)

E24-3 Coldwell Banker is a nationwide real estate firm. Suppose that the Boothbay Harbor, Maine, office of the firm projects that Year 2 quarterly sales will increase by 3 percent in Quarter one, 3 percent in Quarter two, 5 percent in Quarter three, and 5 percent in Quarter four. Management expects operating expenses to be 85 percent of revenues during each of the first two quarters, 86 percent of revenues during the third quarter, and 81 percent during the fourth. The office manager expects to borrow $100,000 on July 1, with quarterly principal payments of $10,000 beginning on September 30 and interest paid at the annual rate of 12 percent. Year 1 last-quarter sales were $2,000,000.

Budgeting quarterly income for a year
(Obj. 2)

Prepare a budgeted income statement for each of the four quarters of Year 2 and for the entire year. Present the Year 2 budget as follows:

Quarter 1	Quarter 2	Quarter 3	Quarter 4	Full Year

E24-4 For each of items (a) through (d), compute the amount of cash receipts or disbursements Monroe Company will budget for December. A solution to one item may depend on the answer to an earlier item.

Computing cash receipts and disbursements
(Obj. 3)

a. Management expects to sell 8,000 units in November and 8,400 in December. Each unit sells for $6. Cash sales average 30 percent of total sales, and credit sales make up the rest. Two-thirds of credit sales are collected in the month of sale, with the balance collected the following month.

b. Management has budgeted inventory purchases of $30,000 for November and $25,000 for December. Monroe Company pays for 50 percent of its inventory at the time of purchase in order to get a 2-percent discount. The business pays the balance the following month, with no discount.

c. Management expects to sell equipment that cost $14,100 at a gain of $2,000. Accumulated depreciation on this equipment is $6,000.

d. The company pays rent and property taxes of $4,000 each month. Commissions and other selling expenses average 20 percent of sales. Monroe Company pays two-thirds of selling expenses in the month incurred, with the balance paid in the following month.

E24-5 Cassell's, a family-owned furniture store, began October with $7,500 cash. Management forecasts that collections from credit customers will be $9,500 in October and $12,200 in November. The store is scheduled to receive $5,000 cash on a business note receivable in November. Projected cash disbursements include inventory purchases ($10,200 in October and $12,100 in November) and operating expenses ($3,000 each month).

Budgeting cash receipts and disbursements; sensitivity analysis
(Obj. 3, 4)

Cassell's bank requires a $7,500 minimum balance in the store's checking account. At the end of any month when the account balance goes below $7,500, the bank automatically extends credit to the store in multiples of $1,000. Cassell's borrows as little as possible and pays back these loans in quarterly installments of $3,000, plus 4.5-percent interest on the entire unpaid principal. The first payment occurs three months after the loan.

Required

1. Budget the store's cash receipts and disbursements for October and November.
2. How much cash will Cassell's borrow in November if collections from customers that month total $9,200 instead of $12,200?

E24-6 Use the following information to prepare a budgeted balance sheet for Half-Price Book Store at March 31, 19X6. Show computations for the cash and owners' equity amounts.

Preparing a budgeted balance sheet
(Obj. 3)

a. March 31 inventory balance, $16,000.
b. March payments for inventory, $5,900.

c. March payments of accounts payable and accrued liabilities, $6,100.

d. March 31 accounts payable balance, $4,900.

e. February 28 furniture and fixtures balance, $34,800; accumulated depreciation balance, $27,700.

f. March capital expenditures of $3,200 budgeted for cash purchase of furniture.

g. March operating expenses, including income tax, total $5,000; half will be paid in March and half accrued at March 31.

h. March depreciation, $300.

i. Cost of goods sold, 50 percent of sales.

j. February 28 owners' equity, $25,700.

k. February 28 cash balance, $10,300.

l. March budgeted sales, $12,400.

m. March 31 accounts receivable balance, one-fourth of March sales.

n. March cash receipts, $12,300.

Identifying different types of responsibility centers
(Obj. 5)

E24-7 Identify each responsibility center as a cost center, a profit center, or an investment center.

a. The hospital pediatrics unit reports both revenues and expenses.

b. A charter airline records revenues and expenses for each airplane each month. The airplane's performance report shows its ratio of operating income to average book value.

c. Accountants compile the cost of surgical supplies for evaluating the purchasing department of a hospital.

d. A division manager's performance is judged by the ratio of the division's operating income to the corporation's investment in the division.

e. The legal department of an insurance company prepares its budget and subsequent performance report on the basis of its expected expenses for the year.

f. The manager of an Exxon service station is evaluated on the basis of the station's revenues and expenses.

Using responsibility accounting to evaluate profit centers
(Obj. 6)

E24-8 Emmons Newspapers of Tennessee has city managers for its Martin, Jackson, and Memphis operations. These managers report to a West Tennessee manager, who reports to the manager of Tennessee operations in Nashville. The Tennessee manager has received the following data for June of the current year:

	Tennessee		
	West Tennessee		
	Martin	Jackson and Memphis	East Tennessee
Revenues, budget	$102,000	$600,000	$1,100,000
Expenses, budget	70,000	390,000	750,000
Revenues, actual	110,000	620,000	1,000,000
Expenses, actual	64,000	400,000	710,000

Arrange the data in a performance report similar to Exhibit 24-11. Show June results, in thousands of dollars, for Martin, West Tennessee, and Tennessee as a whole. As the West Tennessee manager, would you investigate the performance of Martin's operations? Why or why not?

Preparing a departmental income statement
(Obj. 3, 4)

E24-9 Timmons Northwest, Inc., has two departments, electronics and industrial. The company's income statement for 19X7 appears as follows:

Net sales	$325,000
Cost of goods sold	116,000
Gross margin	209,000
Operating expenses:	
Salaries	$ 75,000
Depreciation	15,000
Advertising	6,000
Other	10,000
Total operating expenses	106,000
Operating income	$103,000

Sales are: electronics, $136,000; industrial, $189,000. Cost of goods sold is distributed $42,000 to electronics and $74,000 to industrial products. Salaries are traced directly to departments: electronics, $33,000; industrial, $42,000. Two-thirds of advertising is spent on electronics.

Depreciation is allocated on the basis of square footage: Electronics has 28,000 square feet; industrial has 42,000 square feet. Other expenses are allocated on the basis of number of employees. An equal number work in the two departments.

Required

1. Prepare a departmental income statement that shows revenues, expenses, and operating income for the company's two departments.
2. In a departmental performance report, which are the most important of Timmons Northwest's expenses for evaluating department managers? Give your reason.

E24-10 Megasafe specializes in high-quality security systems. The company's two service departments are Engineering Support and Information Systems Support. Its two production departments are Home Security Systems and Business Security Systems. For the upcoming production period, the following hours of work are budgeted for the two service departments:

Allocating service department costs
(Obj. 7)

		Worked For		
Worked By	**Engineering Support**	**Information Systems Support**	**Home Security Systems**	**Business Security Systems**
Engineering Support	—	150	300	550
Information Systems Support	200	—	120	480

Required

1. Allocate the $1,120,000 budgeted cost of the Engineering Support Department and the $1,175,000 budgeted cost of the Information Systems Support Department to the two production departments. Use the step-down method. Allocate Information Systems Support first.
2. If Megasafe uses the direct method instead of the step-down method, will more or less cost be allocated from Information Systems Support to Home Security Systems? Explain.

CHALLENGE EXERCISE

E24-11 Freeman Engineering has two service departments—A and B—and two production departments—X and Y. The following costs are allocated from A and B to user departments under two sequences of the step-down method.

Allocating service department costs
(Obj. 7)

A first, then B:

		To	
From	B	X	Y
A	$20,000	$180,000	$200,000
B	—	66,667	53,333
		$246,667	$253,333

B first, then A:

		To	
From	A	X	Y
B	$10,000	?	?
A	—	$194,211	$215,789
		?	?

When allocating B first, then A, how much cost is allocated from B to X? From B to Y? What is the total cost allocated to X? To Y ?

PROBLEMS

(GROUP A)

P24-1A Representatives of the various departments of Honolulu Construction Co. have assembled the following data. You are the business manager, and you must prepare the budgeted income statements for July, August, and September 19X6.

Budgeting income for three months
(Obj. 2)

a. Sales in June were $184,000. You forecast that monthly sales will increase 2 percent in July, 2 percent in August, and 3 percent in September.

b. Honolulu tries to maintain inventory of $50,000 plus 20 percent of sales budgeted for the following month. Monthly purchases average 65 percent of sales. Actual inventory on June 30 is $80,000. Sales budgeted for October are $205,000.

c. Monthly salaries amount to $12,000. Sales commissions equal 6 percent of sales. Combine salaries and commissions into a single figure.

d. Other monthly expenses are:

Rent expense..............................	$14,000, paid as incurred
Depreciation expense	3,000
Insurance expense......................	1,000, expiration of prepaid amount
Miscellaneous expense..............	5% of sales
Income tax	30% of operating income

Prepare Honolulu Construction Co.'s budgeted income statements for July, August, and September. Show cost of goods sold computations. Round *all* amounts to the nearest $1,000. For example, budgeted July sales are $188,000 ($184,000 × 1.02), August sales are $192,000 ($188,000 × 1.02), and September sales are $198,000 ($192,000 × 1.03).

Budgeting cash receipts and disbursements
(Obj. 3)

P24-2A Refer to Problem 24-1A. Honolulu Construction Co.'s sales are 50 percent cash and 50 percent credit. Credit sales are collected in the month after sale. Inventory purchases are paid 60 percent in the month of purchase and 40 percent the following month. Salaries and sales commissions are paid half in the month earned and half the next month. Income tax is paid at the end of the year. Miscellaneous expenses are paid in cash in the month incurred.

The June 30, 19X6 balance sheet showed the following balances:

Cash....................................	$20,000
Accounts payable...............	48,000

Required

1. Prepare schedules of (1) budgeted cash collections from customers, (2) budgeted cash disbursements for purchases, and (3) budgeted cash disbursements for operating expenses. Show amounts for each month and totals for July through September.

2. Prepare a summary statement of budgeted cash receipts and disbursements in the format of Exhibit 24-7. Assume that no financing activity took place. What is the budgeted cash balance on September 30, 19X6?

Preparing a budgeted balance sheet; sensitivity analysis
(Obj. 3, 4)

P24-3A Hulse Supply has applied for a loan. First State Bank has requested a budgeted balance sheet at June 30, 19X4. As the controller (chief accounting officer) of Hulse, you have assembled the following information:

a. May 31 equipment balance, $60,600; accumulated depreciation, $11,700.

b. June capital expenditures of $15,800 budgeted for cash purchase of equipment.

c. June operating expenses, including income tax, total $38,800, 75 percent of which will be paid in cash and the remainder accrued at June 30.

d. June depreciation, $400.

e. Cost of goods sold, 45 percent of sales.

f. May 31 owners' equity, $97,400.

g. May 31 cash balance, $33,900.

h. June budgeted sales, $70,000, 40 percent of which is for cash. Of the remaining 60 percent, half will be collected in June and half in July.

i. June cash collections on May sales, $14,900.

j. June cash payments of liabilities, $10,700.

k. May 31 inventory balance, $10,400.

l. June purchases of inventory, $11,000 for cash and $27,400 on credit. Half the credit purchases will be paid in June and half in July.

Required

1. Prepare the budgeted balance sheet of Hulse Supply at June 30, 19X4. Show separate computations for cash, inventory, and owners' equity balances.

2. Repeat Requirement 1, assuming sales of only $50,000. Suppose Hulse has a minimum desired cash balance of $15,000. Will the company borrow cash in June?

P24-4A Identify each of the following as being most likely a cost center, a profit center, or an investment center.

Identifying different types of responsibility centers (Obj. 5)

a. Different product lines of a furniture manufacturer
b. European subsidiary of an American company
c. Proposed new office of a CPA firm
d. Lighting department in a Sears store
e. Children's nursery in a church or synagogue
f. Fast-food restaurants under the supervision of a regional manager
g. Personnel department of Coca-Cola, Inc.
h. Consumer Complaint Division of Procter & Gamble Co.
i. Service department of an automobile dealership
j. Southwest region of Pizza Inns, Inc.
k. Payroll department of a university
l. Top management of a company
m. Editorial department of *The Wall Street Journal*
n. Delta Air Lines, Inc.
o. Police department of a city
p. Branch offices of a bank
q. A small clothing boutique
r. Century 21 Real Estate Co.
s. Quality-control department of a manufacturing company
t. Job superintendents of a home builder

P24-5A Visionary, Inc., is a chain of optical shops. Each store has a manager who answers to a city manager, who in turn reports to a statewide manager. The actual income statements of Store No. 8, all stores in the Houston area (including Store No. 8), and all stores in the state of Texas (including all Houston stores) are summarized as follows for April:

Preparing a profit-center performance report for management by exception; benefits of budgeting (Obj. 1, 6)

	Store No. 8	Houston	State of Texas
Revenues and expenses:			
Sales	$39,900	$486,000	$3,264,500
Expenses:			
City/state manager office	$ —	$ 16,000	$ 44,000
Cost of goods sold	13,000	171,300	1,256,800
Salary expense	5,000	37,500	409,700
Depreciation	3,000	26,100	320,000
Utilities	2,700	19,300	245,600
Rent	1,600	16,400	186,000
Supplies	700	5,500	60,700
Total expenses	26,000	292,100	2,522,800
Operating income	$13,900	$193,900	$ 741,700

Budgeted amounts for April were as follows:

	Store No. 8	Houston	State of Texas
Revenues and expenses:			
Sales	$42,000	$468,000	$3,143,000
Expenses:			
City/state manager office	—	15,000	43,000
Cost of goods sold	$14,200	$172,800	$1,209,000
Salary expense	5,600	37,900	412,000
Depreciation	3,500	25,400	320,000
Utilities	2,100	17,000	240,000
Rent	1,600	15,700	181,000
Supplies	800	5,900	60,000
Total expenses	27,800	289,700	2,465,000
Operating income	$14,200	$178,300	$ 678,000

Required

1. Prepare a report for April that shows the performance of Store No. 8, all the stores in the Houston area, and all the stores in the state of Texas. Follow the format of Exhibit 24-11.
2. As the city manager of Houston, would you investigate Store No. 8 on the basis of this report? Why or why not?
3. Briefly discuss the benefits of budgeting. Base your discussion on Visionary's performance report.
4. How will what you learned from this problem help you manage a business?

Allocating service department costs to production departments
(Obj. 7)

P24-6A Jefferson County Hospital has two service departments and two operating (production) departments. The following data are budgeted for the upcoming fiscal year:

	Service Department		Operating Department		
	General Administration	Maintenance	Regular Admissions	Emergency Room	Total
Direct department cost.....................................	$600,000	$60,000	$2,000,000	$500,000	$3,160,000
Services provided:					
By General Administration—					
labor-hours	—	200	16,000	3,800	20,000
By Maintenance—square feet......................	5,000	—	90,000	5,000	100,000

Jefferson County has a responsibility accounting system in which the managers of the operating departments are held accountable for both direct department costs and the costs of services provided by the hospital's two service departments. Peter Schoenfeld, the accountant who designed the system, gathered input from affected managers concerning the appropriate allocation bases for assigning the service departments' costs to Regular Admissions and the Emergency Room. The consensus bases are labor-hours for General Administration and square feet of floor space for Maintenance.

Jefferson County accountants use the step-down method of service department cost allocation. They allocate first the service department that provides the highest dollar amount of services to the other service department.

Required

1. What sequence of allocation should Jefferson County Hospital follow—General Administration first, then Maintenance, or Maintenance first, then General Administration? Why?
2. Using the sequence you selected in Requirement 1, allocate the service departments' costs to Regular Admissions and the Emergency Room. Compute the total budgeted cost of each operating department.
3. Repeat Requirement 2, using the direct method. Use either sequence of allocation.

(GROUP B)

Budgeting income for three months
(Obj. 2)

P24-1B The budget committee of Laverne & Company has assembled the following data. You are the business manager, and you must prepare the budgeted income statements for April, May, and June 19X3.

a. Sales in March were $31,300. You forecast that monthly sales will increase 1.3 percent in both April and May and 1.8 percent in June.

b. The company maintains inventory of $8,000 plus 25 percent of sales budgeted for the following month. Monthly purchases average 55 percent of sales. Actual inventory on March 31 is $12,000. Sales budgeted for July are $30,600.

c. Monthly salaries amount to $4,000. Sales commissions equal 5 percent of sales. Combine salaries and commissions into a single figure.

d. Other monthly expenses are:

Rent expense...............................	$2,700, paid as incurred
Depreciation expense	500
Insurance expense......................	100, expiration of prepaid amount
Miscellaneous expense...............	3% of sales
Income tax	20% of operating income

Prepare Laverne's budgeted income statements for April, May, and June. Show cost of goods sold computations. Round *all* amounts to the nearest $100. For example, budgeted April sales are $31,700 ($31,300 × 1.013), May sales are $32,100 ($31,700 × 1.013), and June sales are $32,700 ($32,100 × 1.018).

P24-2B Refer to Problem 24-1B. Laverne's sales are 60 percent cash and 40 percent credit. Credit sales are collected in the month after sale. Inventory purchases are paid 70 percent in the month of purchase and 30 percent the following month. Salaries and sales commissions are paid half in the month earned and half the next month. Income tax is paid at the end of the year, and miscellaneous expenses are paid in cash in the month incurred.

Budgeting cash receipts and disbursements
(Obj. 3)

The March 31, 19X3 balance sheet showed the following balances:

Cash..................................	$10,000
Accounts payable...............	5,100

Required

1. Prepare schedules of (1) budgeted cash collections from customers, (2) budgeted cash disbursements for purchases, and (3) budgeted cash disbursements for operating expenses. Show amounts for each month and totals for April through June.

2. Prepare a summary statement of budgeted cash receipts and disbursements in the format of Exhibit 24-7. Assume that no financing activity took place. What is the budgeted cash balance on June 30, 19X3?

P24-3B Kramer Auto Sales Company has applied for a loan. Nation's Bank has requested a budgeted balance sheet at April 30, 19X8. As the controller (chief accounting officer) of Kramer's, you have assembled the following information:

Preparing a budgeted balance sheet; sensitivity analysis
(Obj. 3, 4)

a. March 31 equipment balance, $35,200; accumulated depreciation, $22,800.
b. April capital expenditures of $41,700 budgeted for cash purchase of equipment.
c. April operating expenses, including income tax, total $13,600, 25 percent of which will be paid in cash and the remainder accrued at April 30.
d. April depreciation, $700.
e. Cost of goods sold, 60 percent of sales.
f. March 31 owners' equity, $74,900.
g. March 31 cash balance, $26,200.
h. April budgeted sales, $80,000, 60 percent of which is for cash. Of the remaining 40 percent, half will be collected in April and half in May.
i. April cash collections on March sales, $31,200.
j. April cash payments of March 31 liabilities, $17,300.
k. March 31 inventory balance, $22,400.
l. April purchases of inventory, $9,000 for cash and $40,600 on credit. Half of the credit purchases will be paid in April and half in May.

Required

1. Prepare the budgeted balance sheet of Kramer Auto Sales Company at April 30, 19X8. Show separate computations for cash, inventory, and owners' equity balances.

2. Suppose that Kramer has become aware of more-efficient (and more-expensive) equipment than it budgeted for purchase in April. *What* is the amount of cash available for equipment purchases in April, before financing, *if* the minimum desired ending cash balance is $18,000? (For this requirement, disregard the $41,700 initially budgeted for equipment purchases.)

P24-4B Identify each of the following as being most likely a cost center, a profit center, or an investment center.

Identifying different types of responsibility centers
(Obj. 5)

a. Disneyland
b. Music director of a church or synagogue
c. Catering operation of a restaurant
d. Executive director of a United Way agency
e. Men's Clothing in a department store
f. Proposed new office of a real estate firm
g. Work crews of a painting contractor
h. The Empire State Building in New York City
i. Accounting department of a company

j. American subsidiary of a Japanese manufacturer
k. Service department of a stereo shop
l. Eastern district of a salesperson's territory
m. Assembly-line supervisors
n. Accounts payable section of an accounting department
o. Surgery unit of a privately owned hospital
p. Personnel department of Goodyear Tire and Rubber Company
q. Different product lines of a gift shop
r. Typesetting department of a printing company
s. Investments department of a bank
t. Branch warehouse of a carpet manufacturer

Preparing a profit-center performance report for management by exception; benefits of budgeting
(Obj. 1, 6)

P24-5B Shamrock Oil Company is organized with store managers reporting to a statewide manager, who in turn reports to the vice-president of marketing. The *actual* income statements of the Tulsa store, all stores in Oklahoma (including the Tulsa store), and the company as a whole (including Oklahoma stores) are summarized as follows for July 19X6:

	Tulsa	Oklahoma	Companywide
Revenues and expenses:			
Sales	$139,800	$1,647,000	$4,200,000
Expenses:			
State manager/vice-president's office	$ —	$ 59,000	$ 116,000
Cost of goods sold	57,000	671,900	1,507,000
Salary expense	38,100	415,500	1,119,000
Depreciation	7,200	91,000	435,000
Utilities	4,200	46,200	260,000
Rent	2,400	34,700	178,000
Supplies	1,100	15,600	86,000
Total expenses	110,000	1,333,900	3,701,000
Operating income	$ 29,800	$ 313,100	$ 499,000

Budgeted amounts for July were as follows:

	Tulsa	Oklahoma	Companywide
Revenues and expenses:			
Sales	$151,300	$1,769,700	$4,400,000
Expenses:			
State manager/vice-president's office	$ —	$ 65,600	$ 118,000
Cost of goods sold	61,500	763,400	1,672,000
Salary expense	38,800	442,000	1,095,000
Depreciation	7,200	87,800	449,000
Utilities	4,700	54,400	271,000
Rent	2,800	32,300	174,000
Supplies	900	16,100	93,000
Total expenses	115,900	1,461,600	3,872,000
Operating income	$ 35,400	$ 308,100	$ 528,000

Required

1. Prepare a report for July 19X6 that shows the performance of the Tulsa store, all the stores in Oklahoma, and the company as a whole. Follow the format of Exhibit 24-11.
2. As Oklahoma manager, would you investigate the Tulsa store on the basis of this report? Why or why not?
3. Briefly discuss the benefits of budgeting. Base your discussion on Shamrock's performance report.
4. How will what you learned from this problem help you manage a business?

P24-6B The Allentown Valve Company manufactures industrial valve systems in the Allentown, Pennsylvania, area. The company has two service departments, Power and General Factory Administration (GFA), and two production departments, Machining and Assembly. The following data are budgeted for the month of August, 19X4:

Allocating service department costs to production departments (Obj. 7)

	Service Department		Production Department		
	Power	**GFA**	**Machining**	**Assembly**	**Total**
Direct department cost	$10,000	$40,000	$300,000	$100,000	$450,000
Services provided:					
By Power—kilowatt-hours..............	—	60	1,020	120	1,200
Proportion		1/20	17/20	2/20	
By GFA—labors-hours..................	50	—	450	500	1,000
Proportion	1/20		9/20	10/20	

Allentown's accountants want to know the full cost of manufactured valve systems, including the cost incurred in Power and GFA. Also, the company's top management holds the two production department heads responsible for the service department costs incurred to support their departments. For these reasons, the costs of Power and GFA must be allocated to Machining and Assembly.

Required

1. Allocate the service departments' costs to production departments using the direct method. Compute the total budgeted cost of both the Machining Department and the Assembly Department.

2. Repeat Requirement 1, using the step-down method. Allocate GFA first, then Power.

EXTENDING YOUR KNOWLEDGE

DECISION PROBLEMS

1. Bonnie Bonaparte is a librarian in the Chicago City Library. Each autumn, as a hobby, she weaves cotton placemats for sale through a local craft shop. The mats sell for $20 per set of four. The shop charges 10-percent commission and remits the net proceeds to Bonaparte at the end of December. Bonaparte has woven and sold 25 sets each of the last two years. She has enough cotton in inventory to make another 25 sets. She paid $7 per set for the cotton. Bonaparte uses a four-harness loom that she purchased for cash exactly two years ago (August 31, 19X1). It is depreciated at the rate of $10 per month.

Projecting cash flows and financial statements to analyze alternatives (Obj. 2, 3)

Bonaparte is considering buying an eight-harness loom immediately so that she can weave more-intricate patterns in linen. The new loom costs $1,000; it would be depreciated at $20 per month. Her bank has agreed to lend her $1,000 at 12-percent interest, with $200 principal plus accrued interest payable each December 31. Bonaparte believes that she can weave 15 linen placemat sets in time for the Christmas rush if she does not weave any cotton mats. She predicts that each linen set will sell for $50. Linen costs $18 per set. Bonaparte's supplier will sell her linen on credit, payable December 31.

Bonaparte plans to keep her old loom whether or not she buys the new loom. The balance sheet for her weaving business at August 31, 19X3, is as follows:

BONNIE BONAPARTE, WEAVER
BALANCE SHEET
AUGUST 31, 19X3

Current assets:		Current liabilities:	
Cash..	$ 15		
Inventory of cotton	175	Accounts payable	$ 74
	190		
Fixed assets:			
Loom..	500	Owner's equity..........................	376
Accumulated depreciation	(240)		
	260	Total liabilities	
Total assets	$450	and owner's equity................	$450

Required

1. Prepare a summary statement of budgeted cash receipts and disbursements for the four months ending December 31, 19X3, for two alternatives: weaving the placemats in cotton and weaving the placemats in linen. For each alternative, prepare a budgeted income statement for the four months ending December 31, 19X3, and a budgeted balance sheet at December 31, 19X3.

2. On the basis of financial considerations only, what should Bonaparte do? Give your reason.

3. What nonfinancial factors might Bonaparte consider in her decision?

Budgeting operating expenses to analyze alternatives
(Obj. 2, 7)

2. Clemente Company has two service departments—Power and Materials Handling. The company's two production departments are Forming and Finishing. For 19X5, the budgeted number of service hours to be provided by the service departments to their "customer" departments is as follows:

	Provided to:			
Provided by:	**Materials Handling**	**Power**	**Forming**	**Finishing**
Materials Handling	—	250	625	375
Power	1,000	—	200	800

The budgeted direct costs of the service departments for 19X5 are:

	Materials Handling	**Power**
Variable costs...............	$ 70,000	$20,000
Fixed costs..................	30,000	60,000
Total costs	$100,000	$80,000

The local power company has offered to provide all the services of the present Power Department. The power company will charge Clemente $20 per kilowatt-hour. If Clemente accepts the offer, it will shut down its Power Department. Also, the workload of the Materials Handling Department will decrease by 20 percent. [Materials Handling does 250/(250 + 625 + 375), or 250/1,250 = 20% of its work for the Power Department.]

Required

1. Assume that Clemente Company rejects the power company's offer and continues to operate its Power Department. Allocate the service departments' costs to the production departments. Use the step-down method, allocating Materials Handling first.

2. On the basis of 19X5 financial considerations only, should Clemente Company accept or reject the power company's offer? To support your answer, provide budgets of Clemente's total cost of power and materials-handling services under two alternative courses of action: (1) make power and (2) buy power.

ETHICAL ISSUE

Stefan Mueller manages the men's clothing department of a Dillard's Department Store in Cedar Rapids, Iowa. Mueller buys merchandise, hires salesclerks, arranges displays, and takes inventory. His annual bonus depends on departmental operating income. The Mueller family is planning a Christmas vacation to Hawaii and is counting on his bonus. Sales for 19X4 have been below budget. Mueller overstates ending inventory for the year.

Required

1. Specify the effect of the inventory overstatement on cost of goods sold, gross margin, operating income, and Mueller's bonus.

2. Is overstating ending inventory unethical? Who is helped and who is harmed by Mueller's action?

Appendix

The Cash Budget

This appendix gives the cash budget for the Whitewater Sporting Goods example of pages 986–992. Exhibit 24-7 summarizes Whitewater's budgeted cash receipts and disbursements for the four-month period ending July 31, 19X5. Exhibit 24A-1 shows the month-by-month detail.

As the manager of Whitewater Store No. 18, you must determine on a monthly basis whether you will have less or more cash than you need for current-month requirements. If you forecast a deficiency, you must plan to borrow cash. If you have excess cash, you can repay some or all of the store's outstanding debt.

To prepare the cash budget, first forecast the cash available before financing ($61,000 for April). Then, subtract total disbursements to find the ending cash balance before financing ($1,550). Compare this amount with the minimum desired ending cash balance—$10,000—to determine the excess (deficiency) of cash available over (under) cash needed. For April, you predict an $8,450 deficiency.

You plan to borrow $9,000 on a six-month note payable. (The loan exceeds the deficiency because Whitewater borrows in even $1,000 amounts.) Compute the budgeted cash balance at the end of the month by adding the total effects of financing (the $9,000 inflow in April) to the ending cash balance before financing.

Exhibit 24A-1 shows that Store No. 18 budgets sufficient cash in May, June, and July to make its $1,500 principal payments plus pay interest on the unpaid principal. If enough cash were not available, more would have to be borrowed.

EXHIBIT 24A-1
Cash Budget

WHITEWATER SPORTING GOODS STORE NO. 18
CASH BUDGET
FOUR MONTHS ENDING JULY 31, 19X5

	April	May	June	July
Beginning cash balance	$15,000	$10,550	$10,410	$18,235
Cash collections from customers				
(Schedule D, page 990)	46,000	68,000	68,000	54,000
Cash available before financing	$61,000	$78,550	$78,410	$72,235
Cash disbursements:				
Purchases of inventory (Schedule E, page 991)	$42,700	$48,300	$40,600	$32,900
Operating expenses (Schedule F, page 991)	13,750	18,250	18,000	15,250
Purchase of delivery truck (Item 8, page 988)	3,000	—	—	—
Total disbursements	59,450	66,550	58,600	48,150
(1) Ending cash balance before financing	1,550	12,000	19,810	24,085
Minimum cash balance desired	10,000	10,000	10,000	10,000
Cash excess (deficiency)	$ (8,450)	$ 2,000	$ 9,810	$14,085
Financing of cash deficiency (see notes a–c):				
Borrowing (at end of month)	$ 9,000			
Principal payments (at end of month)		$ (1,500)	$ (1,500)	$ (1,500)
Interest expense (at 12% annually)		(90)	(75)	(60)
(2) Total effects of financing	9,000	(1,590)	(1,575)	(1,560)
Ending cash balance (1) + (2)	$10,550	$10,410	$18,235	$22,525

Note: Insurance expense is the expiration of prepaid insurance, and depreciation is the expensing of the cost of a plant asset. These expenses do not require cash outlays in the current accounting period.

a. Borrowing occurs in multiples of $1,000 and only for the amount needed to maintain a minimum cash balance of $10,000.

b. Monthly principal payments: $9,000/6 = $1,500

c. Interest expense:
May: $9,000 \times (0.12 \times 1/12) = $90
June: ($9,000 − $1,500) $\times (0.12 \times 1/12) = $75
July: ($9,000 − $1,500 − $1,500) $\times (0.12 \times 1/12) = $60
Total: $90 + $75 + $60 = $225

Chapter 25
Flexible Budgets and Standard Costs

Chapter Objectives

After studying this chapter, you should be able to

1. Prepare a flexible budget for the income statement

2. Prepare an income statement performance report

3. Identify the benefits of standard costs

4. Compute standard cost variances for direct materials and direct labor

5. Analyze overhead in a standard cost system

6. Record transactions at standard cost

7. Prepare a standard cost income statement for management

❝ Through the use of budgeting techniques such as flexible budgeting and various management information systems, the clinic manager will be able to monitor resource consumption and productivity levels more closely. With this information at hand, problem areas will be found rapidly, and more effective solutions will be implemented. ❞

CECILIA L. BAUTISTA, MASTER OF PUBLIC HEALTH

LRL Diagnostic Clinic, in the Philippines, provides a wide range of diagnostic services. The clinic's staff perform approximately 60,000 X-ray, mammography, and ultrasound procedures each year. To achieve their efficiency goals, LRL's managers must exercise tight control over expenses.

LRL executives use budgets to manage available resources. Managers forecast the costs of X-ray films, other patient supplies, printing, and maintenance. The budget for X-ray films, for example, is computed by multiplying the expected number of films to be used by the budgeted (standard) cost per film.

At the end of the month, the actual cost incurred for X-ray film is compared with the budgeted cost *for the number of procedures actually performed.* Managers follow up on large unfavorable variances between actual and budgeted amounts. For example, too-high costs for X-ray film may point to the need for more training of X-ray technicians. Once identified, such problems can be corrected before the clinic's costs race out of control. *Source: C. L. Bautista, "Meeting the Challenge of Cost Containment: A Case Study Using Variance Analysis." Hospital Cost Management and Accounting, May 1994, p. 1. © 1991 Aspen Publishers, Inc.*

• • • • •

*I*n Chapter 24, we discussed how managers quantify their plans in the form of budgets. We learned that executives compare actual revenues and expenses with budgeted amounts in order to evaluate the performance of responsibility centers and their managers. In this chapter, we explore budgeting in greater depth. The first half of the chapter shows how flexible budgets and variances help managers learn *why* actual results differed from planned performance. The insights gained into the causes of variances are useful for planning and controlling operations. The second half discusses standard costs, which many companies use to build flexible budgets. We begin by reviewing cost behavior patterns.

Cost Behavior Patterns

Cost behavior is the change in a total cost in response to a change in a cost driver. Two extremes of cost behavior are variable and fixed. *Variable costs* are those whose total amount changes in direct proportion to a change in the volume of production or sales activity. For example, to manufacture Corollas, Toyota buys steel, tires, and window glass (direct materials); pays the wages of assembly-line workers (direct labor); and incurs costs for fasteners, materials-handling labor, and the electricity that powers production equipment (variable overhead). These costs are incurred as production takes place—the more Corollas produced, the higher the total cost.

"Toyota buys steel, tires, and window glass (direct materials); pays the wages of assembly-line workers (direct labor); and incurs costs for fasteners, materials-handling labor, and . . . electricity . . . (variable overhead)."

Fixed costs are costs whose total does not change during a given time period despite wide changes in volume. Examples include depreciation, property taxes, insurance, and executives' salaries (fixed overhead). These costs often are incurred or committed before activity begins. They provide the *capacity* to produce or sell many units of output. In contrast, variable costs provide resources that are consumed on a unit-by-unit basis.◀▥

◀▥◀▥◀▥ Compare fixed costs with variable costs in Exhibits 22-1 and 22-2 (pp. 918 and 919), respectively.

Consider the LRL Diagnostic Clinic of the chapter-opening story. Exhibit 25-1 shows an analysis of two of its costs (amounts assumed). Recall that variable costs per unit do not change if the volume of activity changes ($3.75 per procedure in this example). But *unit* fixed costs do change—from $0.95 ($4,000/4,200) to $0.866 ($4,000/4,620) as LRL moves from 4,200 to 4,620 procedures per month. The relevant range of the $4,000 rental cost is 4,000 to 5,000 procedures. At 5,000 procedures, machine capacity is fully used and the unit fixed cost is only $0.80 ($4,000/5,000).

We now turn to flexible budgets and their role in planning and control.

EXHIBIT 25-1

Cost Analysis for LRL Diagnostic Clinic

Type of Cost	Volume of Procedures	
	4,200	**4,620**
Variable cost: X-ray film (3 films per X-ray procedure; $1.25 × 3 = $3.75 per procedure).....	4,200 × $3.75 = $15,750	4,620 × $3.75 = $17,325
Fixed cost: X-ray machines (5 machines rented per month, capacity 1,000 procedures per machine)	5 × $800 = $ 4,000	5 × $800 = $ 4,000

Static versus Flexible Budgets

The master budget of Chapter 24 is a **static budget**—it is prepared for only one level of volume. That volume is the organization's goal. The static budget is not altered after it is drawn up, regardless of changes in volume, sale prices, or costs. Consider a performance report of LRL Diagnostic Clinic for a month in which the expected service level was 4,200 X-ray procedures but the actual volume was 4,620 (amounts assumed):

	Actual Results	Static Budget	Variance
Procedures performed...............	4,620	4,200	420 F
Revenues....................................	$200,000	$180,000	$20,000 F
Expenses....................................	155,000	140,000	15,000 U
Operating income......................	$ 45,000	$ 40,000	$ 5,000 F

EXHIBIT 25-2
Static versus Flexible Budgets

The variances in the third column are favorable (F) if a higher actual amount increases operating income but unfavorable (U) if a higher actual result decreases operating income. The variance for procedures performed is favorable because an increase in volume (from 4,200 to 4,620 procedures) tends to increase income.

This performance report is difficult to analyze because the budget is based on one level of output volume and the actual results on another. Why did the $15,000 unfavorable expense variance occur? Were X-ray films or other resources wasted? Did the price of films unexpectedly increase? Did scheduling problems lead to excessive overtime for nurses and technicians? And how much of the additional expense was due simply to the higher-than-expected service volume? A performance report based on a static budget does not provide enough information to answer these questions.

For a detailed analysis of performance, managers often use a **flexible budget**, which is a set of budgets covering a range of volume rather than a single volume level (Exhibit 25-2). A flexible budget also is called a *variable budget* because it shows how revenues and costs vary with volume throughout the budget range. Managers use flexible budgets before the budget period to analyze cost-volume-profit relationships over the entire range of likely activity. Managers also use these budgets to help plan for contingencies. After the fact, managers use a flexible budget based on the actual output volume achieved to help answer questions raised by deviations from plans. Microcomputers and electronic spreadsheets have placed this valuable budgeting tool at the disposal of most managers in the United States.

At this point we introduce another example. Anthony Pools is a company that makes swimming pools. Exhibit 25-3 shows a condensed flexible budget for An-

Key Point: A company can use both a static and a flexible budget. The focus of the static budget is future planning. The focus of the flexible budget is evaluating past performance.

EXHIBIT 25-3
Flexible Budget

ANTHONY POOLS FLEXIBLE BUDGET EACH MONTH OF THE PERIOD APRIL–AUGUST 19X5				
	Flexible Budget Formula per Unit	Level of Volume		
Units.............................		6	8	10
Sales.............................	$12,000	$72,000	$96,000	$120,000
Variable expenses	8,000	48,000	64,000	80,000
Fixed expenses....................	(see Note)	20,000	20,000	20,000
Total expenses		68,000	84,000	100,000
Operating income		$ 4,000	$12,000	$ 20,000

Note: Fixed expenses are given as a total amount rather than as a cost per unit.

thony. Like other manufacturers, Anthony buys direct materials—cubic feet of gunite, the concrete derivative that forms the shell of each pool. It then uses labor and other resources to convert the direct materials into output—installed pools. We assume that Anthony sells and installs pools in the same month. Thus we use the terms *pools sold* and *pools installed* interchangeably.

Anthony's budgeted sale price is $12,000. Its budgeted variable costs per pool total $8,000. A more detailed budget would list individual variable costs, such as direct materials, direct labor, and supplies. It also might detail the various fixed expenses, including depreciation on equipment, insurance, and administrative overhead. Total monthly fixed expenses are $20,000 at typical volume levels.

> *"Anthony Pools' flexible budget formula for total cost is $20,000 per month for fixed expenses plus $8,000 per pool installed."*

Anthony Pools' *flexible budget formula* for total cost is $20,000 per month for fixed expenses plus $8,000 per pool installed. Exhibit 25-3 uses this formula to budget operating income for 6, 8, and 10 pools. Other columns could be added for 7, 9, or any other number of installations, as the situation warrants.

A flexible budget formula is related to a specific relevant range only. Anthony's relevant range is 0 to 11 pools. Costs are not likely to behave according to the set formula outside this range. For example, Anthony's managers will have to rent additional equipment if volume hits a monthly high of 12 pools. Thus, the flexible budget formula for the volume range that begins with 12 pools has a higher fixed cost component. The variable-cost portion of the formula also may be different, depending on the wage demands of any additional workers who are hired.

Graphing the Flexible Budget Formula

OBJECTIVE 1

Prepare a flexible budget for the income statement

A popular budgeting tool is a graph of the flexible budget formula. With such a graph, a manager can forecast the total production cost at any volume level. Exhibit 25-4 shows budgeted total expenses for the entire relevant range of 0 to 11 pools.

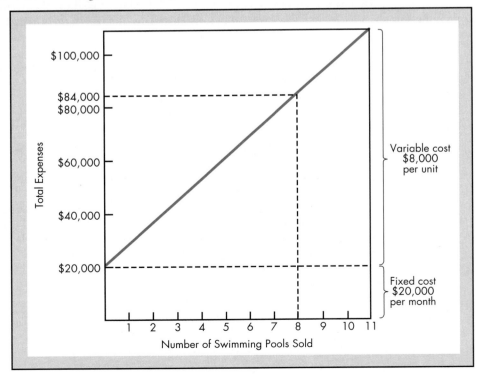

EXHIBIT 25-4

Anthony Pools Graph of Monthly Flexible Budget Formula

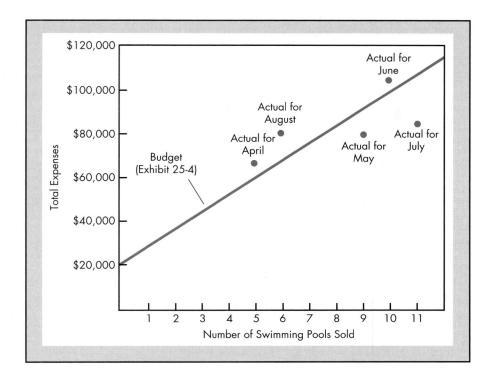

Graph labels:
- Y-axis: Total Expenses ($120,000 / $100,000 / $80,000 / $60,000 / $40,000 / $20,000)
- X-axis: Number of Swimming Pools Sold (1 2 3 4 5 6 7 8 9 10 11)
- Actual for June
- Actual for August
- Actual for April
- Actual for May
- Actual for July
- Budget (Exhibit 25-4)

We assume throughout that Anthony's managers expect to sell 8 pools per month. Hence the total expense for 8 pools ($84,000) is indicated on the graph.

A budget graph provides a visual frame of reference for management's analysis of actual results. Exhibit 25-5 is the graph of actual versus budgeted results for the peak sales season of 19X5. The graph reveals that actual expenses exceeded budgeted expenses during April, June, and August. Actual expenses were less than budgeted for May and July. Overall, the budgeted and actual amounts are close.

The Flexible Budget and Variance Analysis

Successful managers continually cycle through four key steps of planning and controlling. Such managers (1) quantify their goals in a master budget; (2) take actions to achieve their goals; (3) analyze variances between actual results and master budget amounts; and (4) make goal-directed changes called for by their analyses. Preparation of the flexible budget is an important part of step 3. We use flexible budget amounts to divide master budget variances into two broad categories: sales volume variances and flexible budget variances.

Sales volume variances are differences between amounts in the flexible budget and corresponding amounts in the static (master) budget. Unit sale prices and unit variable costs are held constant at their budgeted amounts to direct attention to sales volume effects. The master budget of Anthony Pools is based on its sales goal of 8 pools per month. In June, the company installed 10 pools. Exhibit 25-6, column 4, shows the effects on Anthony's revenues and expenses of selling 10 pools instead of 8. Both the flexible budget and the master budget are based on the budgeted sale price of $12,000 and the budgeted variable cost of $8,000 per pool. Also, both budgets show fixed expenses of $20,000, because 8 and 10 pools are within the same relevant range of activity. The sole cause of column 4's $8,000 increase in operating income was the sale of 2 pools more than the master budget number.

Flexible budget variances are differences between actual results and flexible budget amounts. This category of variances is based on the actual output level—both column 1 and column 3 in Exhibit 25-6 are based on 10 pools installed. Column 2 shows the effects on *total* revenues and variable expenses of differences between ac-

OBJECTIVE 2
Prepare an income statement performance report

Key Point: A *sales volume variance* is the difference between a flexible budget amount and a static budget amount; it is caused by a difference between the predetermined static budget volume and the actual volume. A *flexible budget variance* is the difference between a flexible budget amount and the actual result—that is, the difference between what the results should have been and what the results actually are.

EXHIBIT 25-6
*Income Statement Performance
Report*

ANTHONY POOLS
INCOME STATEMENT PERFORMANCE REPORT
FOR THE MONTH ENDED JUNE 30, 19X5

	(1) Actual Results at Actual Prices	(2) (1) – (3) Flexible Budget Variances	(3) Flexible Budget for Actual Volume Achieved*	(4) (3) – (5) Sales Volume Variances	(5) Static (Master) Budget*
Units	10	–0–	10	2 F	8
Sales.............................	$ 120,000	$ –0–	$120,000	$24,000 F	$96,000
Variable expenses	83,000	3,000 U	80,000	16,000 U	64,000
Fixed expenses..............	22,000	2,000 U	20,000	–0–	20,000
Total expenses	105,000	5,000 U	100,000	16,000 U	84,000
Operating income	$ 15,000	$5,000 U	$ 20,000	$ 8,000 F	$12,000

Flexible budget variance,
$5,000 U

Sales volume variance,
$8,000 F

Static budget variance,
$3,000 F

---

*Amounts from Exhibit 25-3.

tual and budgeted amounts *per unit*. In June, the average sale price was equal to the budgeted $12,000, but the actual variable cost exceeded the budgeted $8,000. Column 2, Flexible Budget Variances, also shows the effect on income of spending more or less than the amount budgeted for fixed expenses. Exhibit 25-6 reveals that Anthony spent an extra $2,000. The combined effect of the variable and fixed cost differences was a $5,000 reduction in operating income.

STOP & THINK Most manufacturing companies produce and sell more than one product. What two factors cause a sales volume variance for a multiple-product company?

Answer: (1) Selling more or fewer than the expected total number of units and (2) selling a mix of products different from the expected sales mix. For example, Volvo might budget the sale of 1 million cars: 500,000 four-door sedans, 400,000 two-door coupes, and 100,000 station wagons. If the company sells more or fewer than 1 million cars, or if it sells exactly 1 million but in a mix other than 5:4:1, a sales volume variance results.

In Exhibit 25-6, column 3 data are taken from Exhibit 25-3. We were able to match actual sales in units to a column of the before-the-fact flexible budget. If actual volume had been 11 pools, we could have used the budgeted sale price of $12,000 and the flexible budget formula for total cost ($20,000 plus $8,000 per pool) to prepare column 3.

The income statement performance report provides useful information to the owners of Anthony Pools. On the basis of the report, they may reward their salespersons. The sales staff's effectiveness in selling two pools more than the eight budgeted provided a 67-percent increase ($8,000/$12,000) over the master budget operating income. The report shows that none of the $3,000 favorable static budget variance (actual operating income of $15,000 minus static budget operating income of $12,000) was due to higher-than-budgeted per-pool revenues.

What does the income statement performance report say about operating efficiency? **Efficiency** is a measure of the amount of inputs used to achieve a given level of output—10 pools, in this case. Exhibit 25-6 does not tell which cost items exceeded budget. Were direct materials costs higher than expected? Direct labor costs? Travel expenses? And were *price* or *quantity* differences responsible for the higher costs? Did hourly wage rates rise unexpectedly? Or did inexperienced workers take longer than the budgeted number of hours to install each pool? A more detailed analysis of the flexible budget variances is necessary to answer these questions—that is, to provide feedback for control.

Exhibit 25-6 indicates that Anthony Pools sold and installed 10 swimming pools during June. Suppose that June sales were 7 pools instead of 10 and that the price of the pools averaged $12,500 instead of $12,000. Actual variable expenses were $57,400, and actual fixed expenses were $19,000.

Required

1. Given these new assumptions, prepare a revised income statement performance report in the form of Exhibit 25-6.
2. Show that the sum of the flexible budget variance and the sales volume variance for operating income equals the static budget variance for operating income.
3. As the company owner, what specific employees would you praise or criticize after you analyze this performance report?

SOLUTION TO REVIEW PROBLEM

Requirements 1 and 2

ANTHONY POOLS
INCOME STATEMENT PERFORMANCE REPORT—REVISED
FOR THE MONTH ENDED JUNE 30, 19X5

	(1) Actual Results at Actual Prices	(2) (1) − (3) Flexible Budget Variances	(3) Flexible Budget for Actual Volume Achieved	(4) (3) − (5) Sales Volume Variances	(5) Static (Master) Budget
Units sold	7	–0–	7	1 U	8
Sales	$87,500	$3,500 F	$84,000	$12,000 U	$96,000
Variable expenses	57,400	1,400 U	56,000	8,000 F	64,000
Fixed expenses	19,000	1,000 F	20,000	—	20,000
Total expenses	76,400	400 U	76,000	8,000 F	84,000
Operating income	$11,100	$3,100 F	$ 8,000	$ 4,000 U	$12,000

Flexible budget variance, $3,100 F   Sales volume variance, $4,000 U

Static budget variance $900 U

Requirement 3

As the company owner, you should not praise or criticize anyone until after the *causes* of the variances have been determined. Those causes may or may not be controllable by managers. For example, the large sales volume variance may be due to employee absenteeism that slowed work. Managers are responsible for having enough laborers at each job each day. But the variance may be due to a long period of heavy rains that brought work to a standstill. Also, an employee may have saved Anthony $1,000 (the flexible budget variance for fixed expenses) by finding a lower-cost source of rented equipment. But the savings may have come from delaying a needed overhaul of equipment. In the long run, this delay may increase the company's costs. The key point: Variances raise questions and guide attention. They do not fix blame or praise.

Standard Costing

We have learned that to budget a variable cost, accountants multiply a number of output units by a budgeted cost per unit. They use *budgeted* output units for the master budget and *actual* output units for the after-the-fact flexible budget. Let us continue our Anthony Pools example. We will show that the $8,000 budgeted variable cost of an installed pool is made up of direct materials, direct labor, and variable overhead costs.

Key Point: A standard cost is a cost that should be incurred under normal conditions to produce a specific product. A standard is determined by examining past experience and incorporating anticipated changes. Usually two standards are set—a price standard and a quantity standard.

Many companies—especially those that routinely produce similar or identical products—use standard costs for budgeting and control. A **standard cost** is a carefully predetermined cost that usually is expressed on a per-unit basis. In contrast, the term *budgeted cost* usually refers to a total amount. For example, suppose that the budgeted variable expenses in Exhibit 25-3 include direct materials costs as follows:

	Flexible Budget Formula per Unit	Level of Volume		
		6	8	10
Swimming pools installed				
Direct materials	$2,000	$12,000	$16,000	$20,000

The standard cost of direct materials is $2,000 *per pool*. Budgeted cost is the expected total cost of all pools sold during the month. As volume increases from 6 to 10 pools, the budgeted direct materials cost increases from $12,000 to $20,000. But the standard direct materials cost is $2,000 at all three flexible budget volumes. *Think of a standard cost as a budget for a single unit of output.*

"Thompson Consumer Electronics, which licenses the RCA brand, has a standard for the time required to solder the chassis of a VCR...."

In a standard cost system, each resource used to make a product has both a quantity standard and a price standard. Thompson Consumer Electronics, which licenses the RCA brand, has a standard for the time required to solder the chassis of a VCR and for the wage rate of workers who operate the robots that do the soldering. LRL Diagnostic Clinic has a standard for the number of X-ray films per procedure and for the price paid per film. Likewise, Anthony Pools has a standard for the cubic feet of gunite per pool and for the price per cubic foot.

Setting Standards

Accountants help managers set price standards. For direct materials, accountants consider quantity discounts, early-payment discounts, and freight and receiving costs in addition to base purchase prices. For direct labor, they take into account payroll taxes and fringe benefits as well as hourly wage rates. And for overhead, accountants help choose cost application bases and then compute application rates to use in budgeting and product costing.

Accountants are less involved in setting quantity standards than in setting price standards. Standards for direct materials and direct labor frequently are set by engineers and production managers. Boeing engineers may perform a time-and-motion study to analyze every movement in the wiring of a 747's instrument panel. Their aims are to (1) eliminate unnecessary work, (2) reduce the time and effort required for necessary work, and (3) set a standard time for the wiring activity.

Another approach to setting quantity standards is to base them on continuous improvement goals. Suppose that Frito Lay required four pounds of potatoes in 19X4 to produce one pound of potato chips. The standard for 19X5 may be set at

3.84 pounds (4 pounds × 0.96), and the standard for 19X6 at 96 percent of 19X5's actual result. By budgeting an annual 4-percent reduction in the quantity of potatoes used, Frito Lay's management signals to employees the importance of continually finding ways to reduce costs.

Whether managers use engineering studies, continuous improvement goals, or some other approach, they usually set standards at one of two levels: either perfection or what is currently attainable. *Perfection standards* allow for no waste, spoilage, or work stoppages. They represent the best possible performance under perfect operating conditions. *Currently attainable standards* allow for normal amounts of waste, spoilage, and the like. They represent very good performance that can be achieved, but with difficulty. Most companies set standards at currently attainable levels, but a growing number are using perfection standards. Why? Because many managers now believe that such standards promote continuous improvement of operating efficiency.

Benefits of Standard Costs

When standard costs are set carefully and used wisely, they yield several benefits to an organization (Exhibit 25-7):

1. They aid management planning by providing the unit amounts—the building blocks—for budgeting.
2. They aid management control by establishing expected or desired levels of operating performance. ◄▌▌▌ ◄▌▌▌ ◄▌▌▌ Significant variations from standard amounts signal the need for management attention.
3. They help motivate employees by serving as benchmarks against which their performance is measured.
4. They provide unit costs that are useful in setting the sale prices of products or services.
5. They help simplify record keeping and thereby reduce clerical costs.

Standard cost systems might appear to be costly to use. Indeed, a start-up investment is necessary to develop the standards. But *using* standards can save data-processing costs. For example, it is more economical to carry all inventories at

OBJECTIVE 3

Identify the benefits of standard costs

◄▌▌▌ ◄▌▌▌ ◄▌▌▌ We saw in Chapter 24 (p. 999) that the practice of directing management attention to important deviations from budgeted amounts is called *management by exception*.

CONCEPT HIGHLIGHT

EXHIBIT 25-7
The Benefits of Standard Costs

1. Standards aid management planning by providing unit amounts for budgeting.

2. Standards aid management control by establishing expected or desired levels of operating performance.

3. Standards motivate employees by serving as benchmarks for performance.

4. Standards provide unit costs that are useful in setting the sale prices of products or services.

5. Standards simplify record keeping, reducing clerical costs.

standard costs rather than at actual costs. In this way, accountants avoid the expense of tracking down actual unit costs and of making LIFO, FIFO, or average-cost computations.

Example of Standard Costing

Let us return to our Anthony Pools example. Recall that 10 swimming pools were sold and installed during June. Exhibit 25-8 provides cost data related to this actual level of output. To focus on the main aspects of standard costing, we assume that Anthony's system pertains to direct materials (gunite), direct labor, and manufacturing overhead but not to selling and administrative expenses. We assume also that the quantity of direct materials purchased equals the quantity used.

Exhibit 25-8 shows Anthony's flexible budget variances for direct materials ($3,100 U) and direct labor ($200 F). Accountants separate these variances into two components: a price variance and an efficiency variance.

A **price variance** is the difference between the actual unit price of an input and the standard unit price of the input, multiplied by the actual input quantity:

EXHIBIT 25-8

Data for Example of Standard Costing

ANTHONY POOLS			
DATA FOR EXAMPLE OF STANDARD COSTING			
MONTH OF JUNE			

PANEL A—Comparison of Actual Results with Flexible Budget for 10 Swimming Pools

	Actual Results at Actual Prices	Flexible Budget	Flexible Budget Variances
Variable expenses:			
Direct materials	$ 23,100*	$ 20,000‡	$3,100 U
Direct labor..	41,800†	42,000‡	200 F
Variable overhead	9,000	8,000§	1,000 U
Selling and administrative expenses	9,100	10,000	900 F
Total variable expenses...............................	83,000	80,000	3,000 U
Fixed expenses:			
Fixed overhead..	12,300	12,000‖	300 U
Selling and administrative expenses	9,700	8,000	1,700 U
Total fixed expenses..................................	22,000	20,000	2,000 U
Total expenses	$105,000	$100,000	$5,000 U

*$23,100 = 11,969 cubic feet at actual price of $1.93 per cubic foot.
†$41,800 = 3,800 hours at actual price of $11.00 per hour.
‡See Panel B.
§Variable overhead was budgeted at $2.00 per direct labor-hour: $8,000 = 4,000 direct labor-hours (10 pools × 400 direct labor-hours) × $2.00.
‖Fixed overhead was budgeted at $12,000 per month.

PANEL B—Flexible Budget for Direct Materials and Direct Labor

	(1) Standard Inputs Allowed for 10 Swimming Pools	(2) Standard Price per Unit of Input	(1) × (2) Flexible Budget for 10 Swimming Pools
Direct materials..............	1,000 cubic feet per pool × 10 pools = 10,000 cubic feet	$ 2.00	$20,000
Direct labor...................	400 hours per pool × 10 pools = 4,000 hours	10.50	42,000

$$\text{Price variance} = \begin{pmatrix} \text{Actual} \\ \text{unit} \\ \text{price of} \\ \text{input} \end{pmatrix} - \begin{pmatrix} \text{Standard} \\ \text{unit} \\ \text{price of} \\ \text{input} \end{pmatrix} \times \begin{matrix} \text{Actual quantity} \\ \text{of input} \end{matrix}$$

The standard price often is referred to as the *price that should have been paid* for input (cubic feet of gunite or direct-labor hours). If the standard price is lower than the actual price paid, the variance is unfavorable. If the standard price is higher than the actual price paid, the variance is favorable.

An **efficiency variance** is the difference between the actual quantity of an input and the standard quantity of the input, multiplied by the standard unit price:

$$\text{Efficiency variance} = \begin{pmatrix} \text{Actual} \\ \text{quantity} \\ \text{of} \\ \text{input} \end{pmatrix} - \begin{pmatrix} \text{Standard} \\ \text{quantity} \\ \text{of} \\ \text{input} \end{pmatrix} \times \begin{matrix} \text{Standard} \\ \text{unit} \\ \text{price of} \\ \text{input} \end{matrix}$$

The standard quantity often is referred to as the *quantity that should have been used*, or the standard quantity *allowed*, for the actual ouput. If the standard quantity is lower than the actual quantity used, the variance is unfavorable. If the standard quantity is higher than the actual quantity used, the variance is favorable.

We now turn our attention to computing Anthony's standard cost variances for direct materials and direct labor.

Direct Materials Variances

We begin our analysis of direct materials variances by compiling the relevant data from Exhibit 25-8 into a table, as follows:

OBJECTIVE 4
Compute standard cost variances for direct materials and direct labor

Direct Materials	Actual Amounts	Flexible Budget Standard Amounts	Flexible Budget Variance
Cubic feet	11,969	10,000	
Unit price	$1.93	× $2.00	
Total......................	$23,100	$20,000	$3,100 U

We use these data to compute the price and efficiency variances:

$$\begin{aligned} \text{Price variance} &= \begin{pmatrix} \text{Actual} \\ \text{unit} \\ \text{price of} \\ \text{input} \end{pmatrix} - \begin{pmatrix} \text{Standard} \\ \text{unit} \\ \text{price of} \\ \text{input} \end{pmatrix} \times \begin{matrix} \text{Actual quantity} \\ \text{of input} \end{matrix} \\ &= (\$1.93 - \$2.00) \times 11{,}969 \text{ cubic feet} = \$838 \text{ F} \end{aligned}$$

$$\begin{aligned} \text{Efficiency variance} &= \begin{pmatrix} \text{Actual} \\ \text{quantity} \\ \text{of} \\ \text{input} \end{pmatrix} - \begin{pmatrix} \text{Standard} \\ \text{quantity} \\ \text{of} \\ \text{input} \end{pmatrix} \times \begin{matrix} \text{Standard} \\ \text{unit} \\ \text{price of} \\ \text{input} \end{matrix} \\ &= \begin{pmatrix} 11{,}969 \\ \text{cubic feet} \end{pmatrix} - \begin{pmatrix} 10{,}000 \\ \text{cubic feet} \end{pmatrix} \times \begin{matrix} \$2.00 \text{ per} \\ \text{cubic foot} \end{matrix} = \$3{,}938 \text{ U} \end{aligned}$$

The price variance indicates that Anthony's operating income will be $838 higher because the company paid less than the standard price for gunite in June. The efficiency variance indicates that Anthony's operating income will be $3,938 lower because its workers used more gunite than the standard allowance for 10 pools.

Exhibit 25-9 shows an alternative method of computing the direct materials price and efficiency variances. Here, the price variance is determined by subtracting

Short Exercise: Use the following data for the next few Short Exercises:

Actual costs for 60,000 units:
Direct mats.	1.1 lb/unit @ $0.30/lb
Direct labor	1/4 hr @ $12/hr
Variable over.	$92,000
Fixed over.	$10,000

Standard costs:
Direct mats.	1 lb/unit @ $0.25/lb
Direct labor	1/5 hr @ $13/hr
Variable over.	1/5 hr @ $6/hr
Fixed over.	$\dfrac{\$20{,}000 \text{ budgeted}}{10{,}000 \text{ hours}}$ = $2/hr

Compute the materials variances. *A:*

Price variance
= ($0.30 − $0.25) × (60,000 × 1.1)
= $3,300 U

Efficiency variance
= (66,000 − 60,000) × $0.25
= $1,500 U

Total
= $3,300 U + $1,500 U
= $4,800 U

EXHIBIT 25-9
*Anthony Pools Direct Materials
Variance Computations*

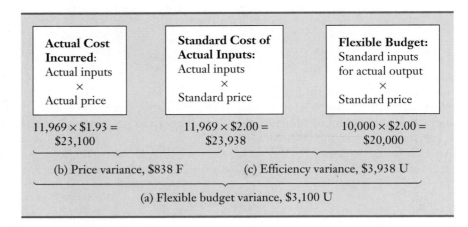

Actual Cost Incurred: Actual inputs × Actual price	Standard Cost of Actual Inputs: Actual inputs × Standard price	Flexible Budget: Standard inputs for actual output × Standard price
11,969 × $1.93 = $23,100	11,969 × $2.00 = $23,938	10,000 × $2.00 = $20,000

(b) Price variance, $838 F   (c) Efficiency variance, $3,938 U

(a) Flexible budget variance, $3,100 U

the standard cost of the actual quantity of gunite used ($23,938) from the actual cost incurred ($23,100). The efficiency variance is the difference between the standard cost of the actual quantity of gunite used ($23,938) and the standard cost of the quantity of gunite allowed for June's production of 10 pools ($20,000). The actual quantity of material is held constant in computing the price variance, and the standard price of material is held constant for the efficiency variance. The price and efficiency variances combine to account for the total direct materials flexible budget variance.

Direct Labor Variances

We begin our analysis of direct labor variances by compiling the relevant data from Exhibit 25-8 into a table, as follows:

Direct Labor	Actual Amounts	Flexible Budget Standard Amounts	Flexible Budget Variance
Hours...................	3,800	4,000	
Hourly rate	×$11.00	×$10.50	
Total.....................	$41,800	$42,000	$200 F

Short Exercise: Compute the direct labor variances for the previous Short Exercise. *A:*

Short Exercise side note continued:

Price Variance
= ($12 − $13) × (1/4 × 60,000)
= $15,000 F

Efficiency Variance
= (15,000 − 12,000) × $13
= $39,000 U

Total Variance
= $15,000 F − $39,000 U
= $24,000 U

We use the data from this table to compute the price and efficiency variances:

$$\text{Price variance} = \left(\begin{matrix} \text{Actual} \\ \text{unit} \\ \text{price of} \\ \text{input} \end{matrix} - \begin{matrix} \text{Standard} \\ \text{unit} \\ \text{price of} \\ \text{input} \end{matrix} \right) \times \begin{matrix} \text{Actual quantity} \\ \text{of input} \end{matrix}$$

$$= (\$11.00 - \$10.50) \times 3{,}800 \text{ hours} = \$1{,}900 \text{ U}$$

$$\text{Efficiency variance} = \left(\begin{matrix} \text{Actual} \\ \text{quantity} \\ \text{of} \\ \text{input} \end{matrix} - \begin{matrix} \text{Standard} \\ \text{quantity} \\ \text{of} \\ \text{input} \end{matrix} \right) \times \begin{matrix} \text{Standard} \\ \text{unit} \\ \text{price of} \\ \text{input} \end{matrix}$$

$$= (3{,}800 \text{ hours} - 4{,}000 \text{ hours}) \times \$10.50 \text{ per hour} = \$2{,}100 \text{ F}$$

Anthony's operating income will be $1,900 lower because the company paid its employees an average of $11.00 per hour in June instead of the standard rate of $10.50. But operating income will be $2,100 higher because only 3,800 hours were worked to produce 10 pools instead of the budgeted quantity of 4,000 hours.

These direct labor variances are linked together in Exhibit 25-10. As with direct materials, the price and efficiency variances sum to the flexible budget variance.

EXHIBIT 25-10
*Anthony Pools Direct Labor
Variance Computations*

Actual Cost Incurred: Actual inputs × Actual price	Standard Cost of Actual Inputs: Actual inputs × Standard price	Flexible Budget: Standard inputs for actual output × Standard price
3,800 × $11.00 = $41,800	3,800 × $10.50 = $39,900	4,000 × $10.50 = $42,000

(b) Price variance, $1,900 U   (c) Efficiency variance, $2,100 F

(a) Flexible budget variance, $200 F

Management's Use of Variance Information

Variances by themselves do not identify problems or opportunities. But large variances from standard amounts raise questions that deserve attention. Significant unfavorable variances may indicate problems that will prevent the company from accomplishing its budget goals unless the problems are corrected. Significant favorable variances may indicate opportunities for ongoing cost reductions that aid the achievement of goals. Managers usually regard small variances as normal occurrences and do not investigate them.

In June, Anthony Pools bought gunite for $1.93 per cubic foot (less than the standard price of $2.00). Most managers would consider Anthony's 3.5-percent [($1.93 – $2.00)/$2.00] direct materials price variance to be insignificant. Possible explanations of this variance are: (1) Competition among suppliers of gunite led to a small drop in prices; (2) the purchasing officer was more skillful than expected in negotiating prices with suppliers; or (3) the officer purchased a lower-than-budgeted grade of gunite. A fourth possibility is that the individual bought the material in larger lot sizes than budgeted in order to get a greater quantity discount. Because Anthony purchased only the quantity of gunite needed for June, there was no buildup of inventory. But a manager whose performance evaluation is tied to the price variance may be tempted to place a larger-than-necessary order to receive a larger discount. Then the company incurs high inventory carrying costs and suffers increased risks of obsolescence, theft, and damage. Thus the overall effect of a "favorable" variance can be unfavorable.

Anthony's 19.7-percent [(11,969 – 10,000)/10,000] unfavorable direct materials efficiency variance may indicate that the gunite used was inferior to the budgeted grade. Lower-grade materials spoil, break, or crack more often, requiring replacement. Or perhaps an uncontrollable event led to excess usage. For example, earth tremors may have cracked several pools after the gunite had hardened but before all work was completed. Some of the overstandard cubic feet may have been required to repair the damage.

Now consider Anthony's direct labor variances. The direct labor flexible budget variance is only $200. Dividing it into its two components is revealing. The 4.8-percent [($11.00 – $10.50)/$10.50] unfavorable price variance reveals that the company used more expensive labor than was budgeted. But those workers achieved greater efficiency. The average number of hours worked per pool (3,800 hours/10 pools = 380) was 5 percent less than the standard of 400 hours per pool. Anthony's managers may have decided to hire more-experienced workers and *trade off* an unfavorable price variance for an expected favorable efficiency variance. If that is so, the strategy was successful—the overall effect of their decision was favorable.

The preceding examples lead to two conclusions:

1. Executives should use caution when using standard cost variances to evaluate performance. Some variances are caused by factors that managers cannot control. Also, price and efficiency variances often are linked; in such cases, the total effect on the company's costs is more meaningful than are individual variances.

2. Executives should consider using multiple measures to evaluate performance. If managers' evaluations are based primarily on a single actual-versus-budget comparison, they may take actions that improve the variance but hurt the company. Two examples are buying excess inventory when purchase prices are below standard and postponing needed maintenance on equipment. How can upper-level managers discourage such actions? One approach is to use two *nonfinancial* measures in evaluating performance: the variance between the quantities of materials purchased and the quantities used, and the variance between maintenance procedures scheduled and maintenance procedures performed.

Manufacturing Overhead Variances

To control overhead costs, managers compare actual amounts (prices and quantities) with standard amounts. Those comparisons are made for cost categories such as indirect materials, utilities, indirect labor wages, and rent. A growing number of companies practice *activity-based management*, which we cover in Chapter 26. Such companies budget costs for each activity and then compute variances to assess the activity's performance. The activities of a swimming pool company such as Anthony Pools include site preparation, digging, forming, filter-system installation, and decking.

Instead of routinely analyzing individual overhead costs, many companies group them into a single *cost pool*. A **cost pool** is any group of individual cost items. These companies compute a total variance between actual overhead cost incurred and standard overhead cost applied to production. We will illustrate how accountants divide this total variance into two or three components to help them analyze actual results. But first let us review how overhead cost is applied.

Applying Overhead to Production

◀▦ ◀▦ ◀▦ Refer to Chapter 20, p. 859, to review the six steps used to develop and apply a company's overhead cost rate.

In a standard cost system, the overhead cost in each cost pool is applied to production at a predetermined rate. ◀▦ The company uses a predetermined rate because managers cannot wait until the end of the year to determine the overhead cost of each product. They need cost data all during the year. To compute the overhead application rate, accountants divide the budgeted total overhead cost by the budgeted units of an application base. This procedure yields, for example, a rate per direct labor-hour, per machine-hour, or per pound or cubic foot of direct material.

ANTHONY POOLS
BUDGET DATA FOR THE MONTH ENDED JUNE 30, 19X5

	Static (Master) Budget	Flexible Budget for Actual Production
Number of pools installed	8	10
Standard direct labor-hours	3,200	4,000
Budgeted overhead cost:		
Variable	$ 6,400	$ 8,000
Fixed	12,000	12,000
Total	$18,400	$20,000
Standard variable overhead rate per direct labor-hour	$ 6,400/3,200 = $2.00	
Standard fixed overhead rate per direct labor-hour	$12,000/3,200 = 3.75	
Standard total overhead rate per direct labor-hour	$18,400/3,200 = $5.75	

EXHIBIT 25-11 *Budgeted Overhead Costs*

If a cost pool contains *variable* costs, accountants seek an application base that varies in direct proportion to total cost. The ideal application base to use is the primary driver of the costs. In the case of LRL Diagnostic Clinic, the primary driver of variable overhead may be X-ray procedures performed. In the case of Anthony Pools, the primary driver of variable overhead costs is direct labor-hours. For *fixed* overhead cost pools, accountants base the application rate on some measure of capacity, often the volume level in the static budget. Anthony's accountants chose the 3,200 direct labor-hours budgeted for the output goal of 8 swimming pools per month.

Exhibit 25-11 shows the budgeted overhead costs for 8 pools. Using these data, the company computed a total overhead application rate of $5.75 per standard direct labor-hour. Of this amount, $2.00 is for variable overhead and $3.75 is for fixed overhead. The exhibit also shows flexible budget data for the 10 pools installed.

How much overhead cost did Anthony apply to the 10 pools? Exhibit 25-12 provides the answer—$23,000. This amount is the product of the standard quantity of direct labor-hours allowed for actual production (400 hours/pool × 10 pools = 4,000 hours) and the overhead application rate of $5.75 per hour. The total overhead variance of $1,700 is favorable because the actual cost incurred is less than the applied cost.

Key Point: The computation of overhead variances is different from the computation of direct materials and labor variances. Materials and labor are strictly variable, but overhead has both fixed and variable components.

EXHIBIT 25-12 *Data for Computing Overhead Cost Variances*

ANTHONY POOLS
DATA FOR COMPUTING OVERHEAD COST VARIANCES

	Actual Overhead Cost (Exhibit 25-8)	Flexible Budget for Actual Production (Exhibit 25-8)	Standard Overhead Applied to Production
Variable overhead	$ 9,000	$ 8,000	4,000 direct labor-hours × $2.00 = $ 8,000
Fixed overhead	12,300	12,000	4,000 direct labor-hours × $3.75 = 15,000
Total overhead	$21,300	$20,000	4,000 direct labor-hours × $5.75 = $23,000

Total overhead variance
$1,700 F

Two-Variance Overhead Analysis

Companies that group all their overhead costs in a single cost pool usually divide the total variance into the *overhead flexible budget (controllable) variance* and the *production volume variance.*

OVERHEAD FLEXIBLE BUDGET VARIANCE   The **overhead flexible budget variance** is the difference between the actual overhead cost and the flexible budget amount for actual production. Anthony's overhead flexible budget variance for June is computed as follows (data from Exhibit 25-12):

Actual overhead cost	$21,300
Flexible budget overhead for actual production	20,000
Overhead flexible budget variance	$ 1,300 U

The overhead flexible budget variance often is due more to variable cost differences than to fixed cost differences, and managers exercise much control over variable costs. Thus, this variance is also called the *overhead controllable variance.* But because control may not be clear-cut, we use the generic term overhead flexible budget variance.

Anthony's 6.5-percent ($1,300/$20,000) overhead flexible budget variance raises several questions. Did prices of overhead items (for example, cleaning solvents and plastic pipe) increase during June? Were excessive quantities of these items used? What was the effect on variable overhead cost of working 200 (3,800 − 4,000) fewer direct labor-hours than the budget allowed? And what was the *actual* overhead rate per hour? Many companies subdivide the overhead flexible budget variance as a first step in answering these questions. Before illustrating the resulting three-variance analysis, we turn our attention to the production volume variance.

PRODUCTION VOLUME VARIANCE   The **production volume variance** is the difference between the overhead cost in the flexible budget for actual production and the standard overhead applied to production (data from Exhibit 25-12):

Flexible budget overhead for actual production	$20,000
Standard overhead applied to production	23,000
Production volume variance	$ 3,000 F

Short Exercise: Use the two-variance method and the data from the Short Exercise on p. 1029 to compute the overhead variances. *A:*

Actual over. cost	$102,000
Flex. budget over.	92,000*
Flex. budget var.	$ 10,000 U

Flex. budget over.	$ 92,000
Standard over. applied	96,000†
Prod. volume var.	$ 4,000 F

*$20,000 + ($6 × 12,000)
†$8 × 12,000

The flexible budget variance is unfavorable because actual costs were more than the budgeted costs. The production volume variance is favorable because the predetermined volume was 10,000 hours needed to produce 50,000 units. More capacity was utilized: 60,000 units were actually produced.

A production volume variance is favorable whenever the actual production quantity (10 pools) exceeds the quantity on which the overhead application rate is based (8 pools, Exhibit 25-11). By producing 10 pools instead of 8, Anthony more fully utilized the production capacity provided by its fixed overhead costs. If Anthony had produced 7 or fewer pools, the production volume variance would have been unfavorable, because less production capacity than expected would have been used. The cost in the flexible budget would have been greater than the cost applied to production.

Exhibit 25-12 reveals that the *variable* overhead cost in the flexible budget is (always) the same as the amount applied. Thus, the production volume variance is due solely to fixed cost effects. An alternative computation of the variance clarifies this point (data from Exhibit 25-11):

Standard hours for actual production	4,000
Standard hours for static (master) budget	3,200
Flexible budget hours in excess of static budget	800
Standard *fixed* overhead rate per hour	× $3.75
Production volume variance	$ 3,000 F

Exhibit 25-13 summarizes the computations of overhead variances for a two-variance analysis. Before moving on, we must mention that the production volume variance of $3,000 is *not* the effect on Anthony's operating income of selling 2 more pools (10 instead of 8). Those additional sales increase income by $8,000:

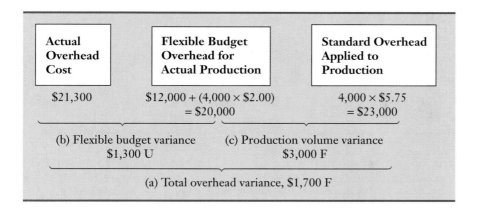

EXHIBIT 25-13
Overhead Variance Computations:
Two-Variance Analysis

Actual Overhead Cost	**Flexible Budget Overhead for Actual Production**	**Standard Overhead Applied to Production**
$21,300	$12,000 + (4,000 × $2.00) = $20,000	4,000 × $5.75 = $23,000

(b) Flexible budget variance $1,300 U   (c) Production volume variance $3,000 F

(a) Total overhead variance, $1,700 F

Increase in sales revenue (2 × $12,000)	$24,000
Increase in variable expenses (2 × $8,000)	16,000
Increase in contribution margin	8,000
Increase in fixed expenses	–0–
Increase in operating income	$ 8,000

The production volume variance is simply the portion of the total overhead variance that is not accounted for by the overhead flexible budget variance.

Three-Variance Overhead Analysis

The two-variance analysis just described is common in practice. Some companies, however, perform a three-variance analysis that splits the overhead flexible budget variance into spending and efficiency variances (Exhibit 25-14). This split helps managers explain *why* the actual overhead cost differed from the flexible budget overhead for actual production. We have discussed the production volume variance; here we address only the overhead efficiency and overhead spending variances.

OVERHEAD EFFICIENCY VARIANCE   The **overhead efficiency variance** is the difference between the flexible budget amount for actual production and the flexible budget amount for the actual units of the overhead cost application base (direct labor-hours for Anthony Pools). From Exhibit 25-15:

Flexible budget overhead for actual production	$20,000
Flexible budget overhead for actual direct labor-hours	19,600
Overhead efficiency variance	$ 400 F

The overhead efficiency variance measures the extra variable overhead cost incurred (or saved) because the actual number of cost application base units differed from the

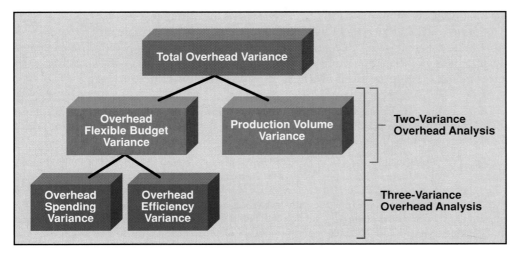

	Actual Over-head Cost (Exhibit 25-8)	Flexible Budget for Actual Direct Labor-Hours Worked	Flexible Budget for Actual Production (Exhibit 25-8)
		3,800 direct labor-hours	4,000 direct labor-hours
Variable overhead	$ 9,000	× $2.00 = $ 7,600	× $2.00 = $ 8,000
Fixed overhead..................	12,300	12,000	12,000
Total overhead	$21,300	$19,600	$20,000

EXHIBIT 25-15

Data for Computing Overhead Cost Variances: Three-Variance Analysis

standard number. Anthony Pools chose direct labor-hours to apply variable over-head to pools installed because these hours are the drivers of the company's variable overhead costs. If the number of hours worked is greater than (less than) the 4,000 that should have been worked to install 10 pools, we expect this *variable* cost to be greater than (less than) the $8,000 that should have been incurred.

Why is the efficiency variance due solely to variable cost effects? Because fixed overhead cost does not vary with direct labor-hours worked. In our example month, we would not expect any less depreciation expense or management salary cost, for example, because employees worked 3,800 hours—less than the budgeted 4,000.

An alternative computation of the efficiency variance reinforces this point:

Standard direct labor-hours for actual production.....................	4,000
Actual direct labor-hours worked	3,800
Standard hours in excess of actual hours	200
Standard variable overhead rate per direct labor-hour	× $2.00
Overhead efficiency variance...	$ 400 F

OVERHEAD SPENDING VARIANCE   The **overhead spending variance** is the difference between the flexible budget amount for the actual units of the cost application base and the actual overhead cost (data from Exhibit 25-15):

Flexible budget overhead for actual direct labor-hours	$19,600
Actual overhead cost	21,300
Overhead spending variance	$ 1,700 U

Short Exercise: Using the three-variance method and the data in the Short Exercise on p. 1029, compute the overhead variances:

	Flex. Budget Based on	
Actual Over.	Actual Dir. Labor-Hrs.	Flex. Budget Based on Actual Production
$102,000	$110,000*	$92,000
	$8,000 F	$18,000 U
	Spending	Efficiency

*$20,000 + ($6 × 15,000)

The production volume variance is $4,000 F, as before.

The overhead spending variance is the part of the overhead flexible budget variance that is not explained by the under-standard quantity of direct labor-hours. That is, it is the flexible budget variance minus the efficiency variance. The variance is called a *spending* variance rather than a *price* variance because it is caused by both price and quantity effects. Consider solvents used to clean decorative tiles installed in pool sur-faces. If the price per gallon of solvents unexpectedly increases, an unfavorable spending variance results. But an unfavorable spending variance also arises if em-ployees use more solvent per direct labor-hour than expected. Thus, non-standard *use* of supplies contributes to the overhead spending variance.

The overhead flexible budget variance includes both variable and fixed cost ef-fects. The efficiency variance—one of the two variances that make up the overhead flexible budget variance—is due solely to variable overhead. Thus the spending vari-ance includes the entire fixed overhead flexible budget variance.

 STOP & THINK Refer to Exhibit 25-15. What was the *actual* variable overhead rate per direct labor-hour in June? Besides the price and quantity factors just discussed, what other factor caused the actual rate to differ from the predetermined rate of $2.00 per hour?

Answer: The actual variable overhead rate was $2.37 per direct labor-hour ($9,000/3,800 hours). The predetermined rate of $2.00 per hour was the expected *average* rate for all of 19X5. Anthony's accountants did not expect the actual rate for each month to equal the average rate. A major reason is that direct labor-hours are not the only driver of variable overhead costs. For example, the amount of fuel consumed in digging the hole for a pool depends on the underground material that must be cleared away. The 10 holes dug in June may have been more difficult than average.

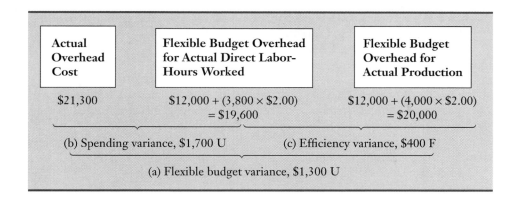

EXHIBIT 25-16
*Overhead Variance Computations:
Three-Variance Analysis*

Exhibit 25-16 summarizes the computation of the two components of the overhead flexible budget variance. The third variance in a three-variance analysis is the production volume variance. For Anthony, this variance is shown in Exhibit 25-13.

Standard Costs in the Accounts

Recall that manufacturing companies have three inventory accounts: Materials Inventory, Work in Process Inventory, and Finished Goods Inventory. Firms with standard cost accounting systems assign costs to these accounts in various ways. Some companies maintain Materials Inventory at actual cost. Others keep the account at standard cost. Most companies record individual variances in separate accounts.

OBJECTIVE 6
Record transactions at standard cost

We use the June 19X5 transactions of Anthony Pools to demonstrate standard cost accounting in a job order context. Our entries are based on an important assumption: Anthony recognizes variances from standards at the earliest opportunity. This assumption means that direct materials price variances are recorded at the time of purchase. It also means that Work in Process Inventory is debited (swimming pools are costed) at standard input quantities and prices. June's entries follow. Entry 9 is based on the two-variance approach for overhead. The entry for a three-variance analysis follows a similar pattern. A credit balance in a variance account indicates a favorable variance. A debit balance is unfavorable.

1. Materials Inventory (11,969 × $2.00).. 23,938
　　Direct Materials Price Variance.. 838
　　Accounts Payable (11,969 × $1.93) 23,100
　To record purchases of direct materials.

By maintaining Materials Inventory at the *standard* price for gunite ($2.00), Anthony accountants can record the direct materials price variance at time of purchase.

2. Work in Process Inventory (10,000 × $2.00) 20,000
　Direct Materials Efficiency Variance 3,938
　　Materials Inventory (11,969 × $2.00)................................. 23,938
　To record use of direct materials and application of direct materials costs to pools.

3. Manufacturing Wages (3,800 × $10.50)...................................... 39,900
　Direct Labor Price Variance.. 1,900
　　Wages Payable (3,800 × $11.00) 41,800
　To record direct labor costs incurred.

By maintaining Manufacturing Wages at the *standard* price for direct labor ($10.50), Anthony can record the direct labor price variance at the time work is performed.

4. Work in Process Inventory (4,000 × $10.50) 42,000

     Direct Labor Efficiency Variance 2,100

     Manufacturing Wages (3,800 × $10.50)........................... 39,900

To record application of direct labor costs to pools.

5. Manufacturing Overhead 21,300

     Accounts Payable, Accumulated Depreciation, and so on .. 21,300

To record actual overhead costs incurred.

6. Work in Process Inventory (4,000 × $5.75) 23,000

     Manufacturing Overhead 23,000

To record application of overhead costs to pools.

7. Finished Goods Inventory... 85,000

     Work in Process Inventory 85,000

To record completion of 10 pools.

8. Cost of Goods Sold 85,000

     Finished Goods Inventory 85,000

To record sale of 10 pools.

9. Manufacturing Overhead 1,700

   Overhead Flexible Budget Variance 1,300

     Production Volume Variance 3,000

To record overhead variances.

Entry 9 leaves a zero balance in Manufacturing Overhead. Many companies wait until the end of the fiscal year to close the account, which keeps a running total of under-applied (debit balance) or overapplied (credit balance) overhead during the year.

    After posting, selected Anthony accounts appear as follows:

Materials Inventory		Work in Process Inventory		Finished Goods Inventory	
(1) 23,938	23,938 (2)	(2) 20,000 (4) 42,000 (6) 23,000	85,000 (7)	(7) 85,000	85,000 (8)

Manufacturing Wages		Manufacturing Overhead		Cost of Goods Sold	
(3) 39,900	39,900 (4)	(5) 21,300 (9) 1,700	23,000 (6)	(8) 85,000	

Direct Materials Price Variance		Direct Materials Efficiency Variance		Direct Labor Price Variance	
	838 (1)	(2) 3,938		(3) 1,900	

Direct Labor Efficiency Variance		Overhead Flexible Budget Variance		Production Volume Variance	
	2,100 (4)	(9) 1,300			3,000 (9)

    At the end of the year, all variance accounts are closed to zero-out their balances. The net amount is closed to Income Summary. Anthony's total variance (the sum of all actual manufacturing costs minus the sum of all applied manufacturing costs) is $1,200 unfavorable for June. Thus, June's operating income is $1,200 lower than it would have been if all actual costs had been equal to applied amounts.

Short Exercise: Prepare journal entries to record the material and labor variances for the data in the Short Exercise on p. 1029. *A:*

Materials Inv.
(66,000 × $0.25)............. 16,500
Direct Materials
Price Var. 3,300
   Accounts Pay.
   (66,000 × $0.30)..... 19,800

WIP Inv.
(60,000 × $0.25)............. 15,000
Direct Materials
Efficiency Var. 1,500
   Materials Inv.
   (66,000 × $0.25)..... 16,500

Manufacturing Wages
(15,000 × $13)................195,000
Direct Labor
Price Var............. 15,000
   Wages Payable
   (15,000 × $12).... 180,000

WIP Inv.
(12,000 × $13)................156,000
Direct Labor
Efficiency Var. 39,000
   Manufacturing Wages
   (15,000 × $13)........ 195,000

Standard Cost Income Statement for Management

To assess overall operating performance, a company may prepare an income statement that highlights standard cost variances. The statement shows cost of goods sold at standard cost. Then, each variance is listed separately, followed by cost of goods sold at actual cost. Similar detail can be shown for selling and administrative expenses if they are subject to standard cost analysis.

Exhibit 25-17 is a standard cost income statement that the managers of Anthony Pools might use for planning and control. Recall that all pools sold in June were installed during that month and that the company had no ending inventory of gunite or work in process. Thus, the manufacturing cost variances relate solely to June's sales. If Anthony had several pools in process on June 30, its accountants might consider prorating the variances between ending inventory and cost of goods sold.

OBJECTIVE 7
Prepare a standard cost income statement for management

Key Point: A standard cost income statement helps summarize all the variances and illustrate their effect on the income of the business.

EXHIBIT 25-17
Standard Cost Income Statement

ANTHONY POOLS
STANDARD COST INCOME STATEMENT
FOR THE MONTH ENDED JUNE 30, 19X5

Sales revenue		$120,000
Cost of goods sold at standard cost	$85,000	
Manufacturing cost variances:		
Direct materials price variance	(838)	
Direct materials efficiency variance	3,938	
Direct labor price variance	1,900	
Direct labor efficiency variance	(2,100)	
Overhead flexible budget variance	1,300	
Production volume variance	(3,000)	
Cost of goods sold at actual cost		86,200
Gross margin		33,800
Selling and administrative expenses		18,800
Operating income		$ 15,000

SUMMARY PROBLEM FOR YOUR REVIEW

Exhibit 25-8 indicates that Anthony Pools installed 10 swimming pools during June. Suppose that June sales and installations were 7 pools instead of 10 and that actual expenses for the month were as follows:

Direct materials		7,400 cubic feet @ $2.00 per cubic foot
Direct labor		2,740 hours @ $10.00 per hour
Variable overhead		$ 5,400
Fixed overhead		$11,900

Required

1. Given these new data, prepare two exhibits similar to Exhibits 25-8 and 25-11. Ignore selling and administrative expenses in your first exhibit.
2. Compute direct materials and direct labor price and efficiency variances.
3. Compute the total variance, the flexible budget variance, and the production volume variance for overhead. Divide the overhead flexible budget variance into its two components, the spending variance and the efficiency variance.
4. Prepare a June income statement through operating income for the president of Anthony Pools. Report all standard cost variances; assume that selling and administrative expenses for the month were $17,700.

Requirement 1

ANTHONY POOLS
DATA FOR EXAMPLE OF STANDARD COSTING
MONTH OF JUNE

Panel A—Comparison of Actual Results with Flexible Budget
for 7 Swimming Pools

	Actual Results at Actual Prices	Flexible Budget	Flexible Budget Variances
Variable expenses:			
Direct materials	$14,800*	$14,000‡	$ 800 U
Direct labor....................................	27,400†	29,400‡	2,000 F
Variable overhead	5,400	5,600§	200 F
Total variable expenses..............	47,600	49,000	1,400 F
Fixed expenses:			
Fixed overhead..............................	11,900	12,000‖	100 F
Total expenses	$59,500	$61,000	$1,500 F

*$14,800 = 7,400 cubic feet at actual price of $2.00 per cubic foot.
†$27,400 = 2,740 hours at actual price of $10.00 per hour.
‡See Panel B.
§Variable overhead was budgeted at $2.00 per direct labor-hour:
  $5,600 = 2,800 direct labor-hours (7 pools × 400 direct labor-hours) × $2.00.
‖Fixed overhead was budgeted at $12,000 per month.

Panel B—Flexible Budget for Direct Materials and Direct Labor

	(1) Standard Inputs Allowed for 7 Swimming Pools	(2) Standard Price per Unit of Input	(1) × (2) Flexible Budget for 7 Swimming Pools
Direct materials	1,000 cubic feet × 7 = 7,000 cubic feet	$ 2.00	$14,000
Direct labor......................	400 hours × 7 = 2,800 hours	10.50	29,400

ANTHONY POOLS
BUDGET DATA FOR THE MONTH ENDED JUNE 30, 19X5

	Flexible Budget for Actual Production	Static (Master) Budget
Number of pools installed..	7	8
Standard direct labor-hours	2,800	3,200
Budgeted overhead cost:		
Variable...	$ 5,600	$ 6,400
Fixed	12,000	12,000
Total...	$17,600	$18,400
Standard variable overhead rate per direct labor-hour...........	$ 6,400/3,200 = $2.00	
Standard fixed overhead rate per direct labor-hour................	$12,000/3,200 = 3.75	
Standard total overhead rate per direct labor-hour................	$18,400/3,200 = $5.75	

Requirement 2

$$\text{Price variance} = \begin{pmatrix} \text{Actual} \\ \text{unit} \\ \text{price of} \\ \text{input} \end{pmatrix} - \begin{pmatrix} \text{Standard} \\ \text{unit} \\ \text{price of} \\ \text{input} \end{pmatrix} \times \begin{matrix} \text{Actual quantity of} \\ \text{input} \end{matrix}$$

Direct materials:
$$\text{Price variance} = (\$2.00 - \$2.00) \times 7{,}400 \text{ cubic feet} = \$ \text{ –0–}$$

Direct labor:
$$\text{Price variance} = (\$10.00 - \$10.50) \times 2{,}740 \text{ hours} = \$1{,}370 \text{ F}$$

$$\text{Efficiency variance} = \begin{pmatrix} \text{Actual} \\ \text{quantity} \\ \text{of} \\ \text{input} \end{pmatrix} - \begin{pmatrix} \text{Standard} \\ \text{quantity} \\ \text{of} \\ \text{input} \end{pmatrix} \times \begin{matrix} \text{Standard} \\ \text{unit price} \\ \text{of input} \end{matrix}$$

Direct materials:
$$\text{Efficiency variance} = \begin{pmatrix} 7{,}400 \\ \text{cubic} \\ \text{feet} \end{pmatrix} - \begin{pmatrix} 7{,}000 \\ \text{cubic} \\ \text{feet} \end{pmatrix} \times \begin{matrix} \$2.00 \\ \text{per} \\ \text{cubic foot} \end{matrix}$$
$$= 400 \times \$2.00 = \$800 \text{ U}$$

Direct labor:
$$\text{Efficiency variance} = \begin{pmatrix} 2{,}740 \\ \text{hours} \end{pmatrix} - \begin{pmatrix} 2{,}800 \\ \text{hours} \end{pmatrix} \times \begin{matrix} \$10.50 \\ \text{per} \\ \text{hour} \end{matrix}$$
$$= 60 \times \$10.50 = \$630 \text{ F}$$

Requirement 3

Actual overhead cost (variable, $5,400 + fixed, $11,900)	$17,300
Standard overhead applied to production	
(2,800 standard direct labor-hours × $5.75)	16,100
Total overhead variance	$ 1,200 U

Overhead Flexible Budget Variance:

Actual overhead cost ($5,400 + $11,900)	$17,300
Flexible budget overhead for	
actual production ($5,600 + $12,000)	17,600
Overhead flexible budget variance	$ 300 F

Overhead Spending Variance:

Flexible budget overhead for actual direct labor-hours	
[(2,740 direct labor-hours × $2.00) + $12,000]	$17,480
Actual overhead cost ($5,400 + $11,900)	17,300
Overhead spending variance	$ 180 F

Overhead Efficiency Variance:

Flexible budget overhead for actual production	
($5,600 + $12,000)	$17,600
Flexible budget overhead for actual direct labor-hours	
[(2,740 direct labor-hours × $2.00) + $12,000]	17,480
Overhead efficiency variance	$ 120 F

$\}$ $300 F

Production Volume Variance:

Flexible budget overhead for actual production	
($5,600 + $12,000)	$17,600
Standard overhead applied to production	
(2,800 direct labor-hours × $5.75)	16,100
Production volume variance	$ 1,500 U

ANTHONY POOLS
STANDARD COST INCOME STATEMENT
FOR THE MONTH ENDED JUNE 30, 19X5

Sales revenue		$84,000
Cost of goods sold at standard cost....................	$59,500	
Manufacturing cost variances:		
Direct materials price variance......................	0	
Direct materials efficiency variance	800	
Direct labor price variance............................	(1,370)	
Direct labor efficiency variance....................	(630)	
Overhead spending variance	(180)	
Overhead efficiency variance........................	(120)	
Production volume variance..........................	1,500	
Cost of goods sold at actual cost		59,500
Gross margin		24,500
Selling and administrative expenses.................		17,700
Operating income..		$ 6,800

SUMMARY

1. Prepare a flexible budget for the income statement. A *static budget* is a budget prepared for only one level of volume, which usually is the expected sales level for a period. A *flexible budget* is a set of budgets covering a range of volume. These budgets show how revenues and expenses vary—if at all—as output volume varies within the budget range. An after-the-fact flexible budget is prepared for the actual output sold.

2. Prepare an income statement performance report. Static budget variances are differences between actual results and corresponding amounts (revenues and expenses) in the static budget. Accountants prepare a flexible budget to divide static budget variances into two broad categories. *Sales volume variances* are differences between amounts in the flexible budget and amounts in the master budget. *Flexible budget variances* are differences between actual results and flexible budget amounts.

3. Identify the benefits of standard costs. *Standard costs* are carefully predetermined costs that usually are expressed on a per-unit basis. Standards represent either very good performance or the best possible performance. When used wisely, standards aid management planning and control, help motivate employees, provide unit costs, and simplify record keeping.

4. Compute standard cost variances for direct materials and direct labor. Companies divide flexible budget variances for direct materials and direct labor into price and efficiency (quantity) variances. A *price variance* reveals the effect on total cost—and thus the effect on operating income—of paying more or less for an input than the standard allows. An *efficiency variance* reveals the effect on total cost of using more or less input than

the quantity allowed by the flexible budget for actual output. Price and efficiency variances often are linked.

5. Analyze overhead in a standard cost system. Many companies compute a total variance between actual overhead cost incurred and standard overhead cost applied to production. This variance has two components: the *overhead flexible budget variance* and the *production volume variance*. A production volume variance is caused by a difference between the actual output produced and the output level on which the overhead application rate is based. Some companies divide the overhead flexible budget variance into efficiency and spending variances. The *overhead efficiency variance* measures the extra variable overhead costs incurred (or saved) because the actual number of application-base units differed from the standard number. The *overhead spending variance* tells how much more or less was spent than was budgeted for actual application-base units.

6. Record transactions at standard cost. Many companies record standard costs in their inventory and expense accounts. They also record standard cost variances. At year's end, all variance accounts are closed to zero. A net favorable (unfavorable) variance increases (decreases) operating income.

7. Prepare a standard cost income statement for management. Some companies prepare an income statement for management that highlights standard cost variances. The statement shows cost of goods sold at standard cost, lists all variances, and then shows the adjusted cost of goods sold—at actual cost. Operating expenses are treated similarly if they are part of the company's standard cost system.

SELF-STUDY QUESTIONS

Test your understanding of the chapter by marking the best answer for each of the following questions.

1. A flexible budget shows *(p. 1021)*

  a. Expected results over a range of volume levels
  b. A single target level of volume
  c. Price variances   **d.** Volume variances

2. Which is the most useful formula for budgeting expenses? (*p. 1022*)
   a. Expenses = Sales − Income
   b. Expenses = Fixed + Variable
   c. Expenses = Fixed + (Variable per unit × Number of units)
   d. Expenses = Standard + Variances

3. Flexible budget variances are differences between (*p. 1023*)
   a. Actual results and the static (master) budget
   b. Actual results and flexible budget amounts
   c. The static (master) budget and the flexible budget
   d. None of the above

4. Accountants play a major role in setting (*p. 1026*)
   a. Price standards   c. Both a and b
   b. Quantity standards   d. None of the above

5. Flexible budget variances for direct materials and direct labor are divided into (*p. 1028*)
   a. Flexible budget effects and production volume effects
   b. Efficiency effects and flexible budget effects
   c. Controllable effects and master budget effects
   d. Price effects and efficiency effects

6. Krakow, Inc., paid $3 per pound for 10,000 pounds of direct materials purchased and used. The standard price was $2.80 per pound, and standard usage for actual production was 11,000 pounds. The price variance is (*p. 1029*)
   a. $800 favorable   c. $2,800 favorable
   b. $2,000 unfavorable   d. $3,000 favorable

7. The efficiency variance in Self-Study Question 6 is (*p. 1029*)
   a. $800 favorable   c. $2,800 favorable
   b. $2,000 unfavorable   d. $3,000 favorable

8. Total variance for overhead can be divided into (*p. 1034*)
   a. Flexible budget effects and production volume effects
   b. Efficiency effects and flexible budget effects
   c. Controllable effects and master budget effects
   d. Price effects and efficiency effects

9. Actual overhead of Athens Supply Company is $540,000. Overhead for static (master) budget volume is $500,000, and flexible budget overhead for actual production is $510,000. The production volume variance is (*pp. 1034*)
   a. $10,000 unfavorable   c. $40,000 unfavorable
   b. $30,000 unfavorable   d. Not determinable. Why?

10. If direct labor-hours are used to apply overhead to output produced, the sign (favorable or unfavorable) of the overhead efficiency variance is the same as that of the (*pp. 1030, 1035*)
    a. Direct materials efficiency variance
    b. Direct labor efficiency variance
    c. Overhead spending variance
    d. Overhead flexible budget variance

11. Gonzalez Manufacturing made the following entry for the use of direct materials in production:
    Work in Process Inventory 380,000
    Direct Materials Efficiency Variance   29,000
       Materials Inventory 409,000
    Which of the following statements is true? (*p. 1036*)
    a. The actual cost of direct materials used is $380,000.
    b. The actual cost of direct materials purchased is $409,000.
    c. The actual cost of direct materials used is $409,000.
    d. The efficiency variance is unfavorable.

Answers to the Self-Study Questions follow the Accounting Vocabulary.

ACCOUNTING VOCABULARY

Cost pool. Any group of individual cost items (*p. 1032*).

Efficiency. A measure of the amount of inputs used to achieve a given level of output (*p. 1024*).

Efficiency variance. The difference between the actual quantity of an input and the standard quantity of the input, multiplied by the standard unit price (*p. 1029*).

Flexible budget. A set of budgets covering a range of volume rather than a single volume level (*p. 1021*).

Flexible budget variance. A difference between an actual result and a flexible budget amount (*p. 1023*).

Overhead efficiency variance. The difference between the flexible budget amount for actual production and the flexible budget amount for the actual units of the overhead cost application base (*p. 1035*).

Overhead flexible budget variance. The difference between the actual overhead cost and the flexible budget amount for actual production; also called *overhead controllable variance* (*p. 1034*).

Overhead spending variance. The difference between the flexible budget amount for the actual units of the cost application base and the actual overhead cost (*p. 1036*).

Price variance. The difference between the actual unit price of an input and the standard unit price of the input, multiplied by the actual input quantity (*p. 1028*).

Production volume variance. The difference between the overhead cost in the flexible budget for actual production and the standard overhead applied to production (*p. 1034*).

Sales volume variance. The difference between an amount in the flexible budget and a corresponding amount in the static (master) budget (*p. 1023*).

Standard cost. A carefully predetermined cost that usually is expressed on a per-unit basis (*p. 1026*).

Static budget. A budget prepared for only one level of volume (*p. 1020*).

ANSWERS TO SELF-STUDY QUESTIONS

1. a
2. c
3. b
4. a
5. d
6. b ($3.00 − $2.80) × 10,000 = $2,000 U
7. c (10,000 − 11,000) × $2.80 = $2,800 F
8. a
9. d Standard overhead applied to production is missing.
10. b
11. d

QUESTIONS

1. Which costs in total amount move in direct proportion to changes in volume? Which costs do not fluctuate in total amount with volume changes? How do total and unit amounts behave for these two categories of costs?
2. What is the relevant range, and why must it be considered in preparing a flexible budget?
3. How does a static budget differ from a flexible budget?
4. Identify how managers use variance information from a performance report.
5. McLaren, Inc., prepared its static (master) budget for a sales level of 35,000 for the month. Actual sales totaled 46,000. Describe the problem of using the static budget to evaluate company performance for the month. Propose a better way to evaluate McLaren's performance.
6. What advantage does a flexible budget graph offer over a columnar flexible budget with four levels of volume?
7. What do the sales volume variance and the flexible budget variance for operating income measure?
8. Describe the benefits of a standard cost system.
9. What two general categories of prime cost variances do most standard cost systems provide?
10. Identify the similarities and differences between a standard cost and a budgeted cost.
11. Your company is installing a standard cost system. What sort of standard cost is most popular? For employees, what purpose does a standard cost fulfill?
12. What does a price variance measure? How is it computed?
13. What does an efficiency variance measure? How is it computed?
14. How are the price variance and the efficiency variance related to the flexible budget variance for direct materials and direct labor?
15. Describe a trade-off a manager might make for labor cost.
16. When should a cost variance be investigated?
17. What causes an overhead flexible budget variance? What information does this variance provide?
18. What information is provided by the production volume variance? How is this variance computed?
19. Scott & White, Inc., enters standard costs in the company accounts. The standard cost of actual direct materials used to manufacture inventory was $21,600. The direct materials efficiency variance was $1,400 favorable. Make the journal entry to charge materials to production.
20. How does a standard cost income statement for management differ from an income statement reported to the public?

EXERCISES

Preparing a flexible budget for the income statement
(Obj. 1)

E25-1 Miranda Production Company sells its main product for $7 per unit. Its variable cost is $2 per unit. Fixed expenses are $200,000 per month for volumes up to 60,000 units of output. Above 60,000 units, monthly fixed expenses are $240,000.

Prepare a monthly flexible budget for the product, showing sales, variable expenses, fixed expenses, and operating income or loss for volume levels of 40,000, 50,000, and 70,000 units.

Graphing expense behavior
(Obj. 1)

E25-2 Graph the expense behavior of Miranda Production Company in Exercise 25-1. Show total expenses for volume levels of 40,000, 50,000, and 70,000 units.

Completing a performance report
(Obj. 2)

E25-3 Moreno, Inc., managers received the following incomplete performance report:

MORENO, INC.
INCOME STATEMENT PERFORMANCE REPORT
FOR THE YEAR ENDED APRIL 30, 19X3

	Actual Results at Actual Prices	Flexible Budget Variances	Flexible Budget for Actual Volume Achieved	Sales Volume Variances	Static (Master) Budget
Units..............................	24,000	_____	24,000	4,000 F	_____
Sales..............................	$192,000	_____	$192,000	$32,000 F	_____
Variable expenses	80,000	_____	72,000	12,000 U	_____
Fixed expenses................	104,000	_____	100,000	–0–	_____
Total expenses	184,000	_____	172,000	12,000 U	_____
Operating income	$ 8,000	_____	$ 20,000	$20,000 F	_____

Complete the performance report. Identify the employee group that may deserve praise and the group that may be subject to criticism. Give your reasons.

Preparing an income statement performance report (Obj. 2)

E25-4 Top managers of Yoshi Industries predicted 19X6 sales of 145,000 units of its product at a unit price of $6. Actual sales for the year were 140,000 units at $7. Variable expenses were budgeted at $2.20 per unit, and actual variable expenses were $2.25 per unit. Actual fixed expenses of

$415,000 exceeded budgeted fixed expenses by $5,000. Prepare Yoshi's income statement performance report in a format similar to Exhibit 25-6. The bracketed amounts are not required. What variance contributed most to the year's favorable results? What caused this variance?

Computing price and efficiency variances for direct materials (Obj. 4)

E25-5 The following direct materials variance computations are incomplete:

$$\text{Price variance} = (\$? - \$14) \times 14{,}500 \text{ pounds} = \$5{,}075 \text{ F}$$
$$\text{Efficiency variance} = (? - 14{,}100 \text{ pounds}) \times ? = ? \text{ U}$$
$$\text{Direct materials flexible budget variance} = \$?$$

Fill in the missing values, and identify the flexible budget variance as favorable or unfavorable.

Computing price and efficiency variances for materials and labor (Obj. 4)

E25-6 The Birch Company, which uses a standard cost accounting system, manufactured 400,000 picture frames during the year, using 1,300,000 board feet of lumber purchased at $1.50 per foot. Production required 9,500 direct labor-hours that cost $10.25 per hour. The materials standard was 3 board feet of lumber per frame, at a standard cost of $1.60 per foot. The labor standard was 0.025 direct labor-hour per frame, at a standard cost of $10.00 per hour. Compute the price and efficiency variances for direct materials and direct labor.

Journalizing standard cost transactions (Obj. 6)

E25-7 Make the journal entries to record the purchase and use of direct materials and direct labor in Exercise 25-6.

Explaining standard cost variances (Obj. 4, 5)

E25-8 Lee Corporation managers are seeking explanations for the variances in this report:

LEE CORPORATION
INCOME STATEMENT FOR MANAGERS
YEAR ENDED DECEMBER 31, 19X2

Sales revenue		$600,000
Cost of goods sold—standard	$350,000	
Manufacturing cost variances:		
Materials: price	4,000 F	
efficiency...................................	6,000 U	
Labor: price	12,000 F	
efficiency...................................	5,000 U	
Overhead: flexible budget.............................	14,000 U	
production volume	8,000 F	
Net variance..	1,000 U	
Cost of goods sold—actual.............................		351,000
Gross profit..		249,000
Selling and administrative expenses..............		209,000
Operating income...		$ 40,000

Explain the meaning of each of Lee Corporation's labor and overhead variances.

Computing overhead cost variances (Obj. 5)

E25-9 Seager Manufacturing Company charges the following standard unit costs to production on the basis of master budget volume of 30,000 units per month:

Direct materials...................	$4.50
Direct labor	2.00
Overhead	1.50
Standard unit cost	$8.00

Seager uses the following overhead flexible budget:

	Monthly Volume		
Number of units.............................	27,000	30,000	33,000
Standard machine-hours...............	2,700	3,000	3,300
Budgeted overhead cost:			
Variable.......................................	$13,500	$15,000	$16,500
Fixed	30,000	30,000	30,000

Actual values: monthly production, 27,000 units; overhead costs, variable, $14,700, and fixed, $30,500; machine-hours worked, 2,650. Compute: total variance, flexible budget variance, and production volume variance for overhead. Also compute overhead spending and efficiency variances.

E25-10 Herrara Co. revenue and expense information for the month of May follows.

	Revenue or Expense	
	Actual	**Standard**
Sales revenue	$440,000	$440,000
Cost of goods sold	?	242,000
Information regarding:		
Direct materials price variance	129,000	131,000
Direct materials efficiency variance....................	131,000	135,000
Direct labor price variance...................................	26,000	25,000
Direct labor efficiency variance	25,000	27,000
Overhead flexible budget variance.......................	77,500	75,000
Production volume variance	75,000	80,000

Prepare a standard cost income statement through gross margin. Report all standard cost variances for use by management.

CHALLENGE EXERCISE

E25-11 Huppe, Inc., repairs appliances. The company measures "production output" in terms of appliances repaired. It conducts a two-variance analysis of overhead costs. The company's combined overhead application rate is $80 per unit of output:

	Per Unit
Variable overhead rate	$30
Fixed overhead rate..................	50

In November, 19X5, Huppe "produced" 5,100 units of output. Its production volume variance was $5,000 F. Compute Huppe's budgeted fixed overhead cost per month. What monthly capacity level was used to compute the fixed overhead rate of $50 per unit?

PROBLEMS

(GROUP A)

P25-1A Carson Components Company manufactures solenoids for electronically controlled sprinkler systems. The company's master budget income statement for March 19X3 follows. It is based on expected sales volume of 9,000 units.

Carson's plant capacity is 9,500 units. If actual volume exceeds 9,500 units, Carson must rent additional space. In that case, salaries will increase by 10 percent, rent will double, and insurance expense will increase by $500. Depreciation and fixed utilities will be unaffected.

CARSON COMPONENTS COMPANY MASTER BUDGET INCOME STATEMENT MARCH 19X3	
Sales..	$189,000
Variable expenses:	
Cost of goods sold......................	72,000
Sales commissions......................	9,450
Shipping	4,500
Utilities.......................................	3,600
Fixed expenses:	
Salaries..	27,500
Depreciation...............................	13,250
Rent	11,250
Insurance	2,750
Utilities.......................................	2,250
Total operating expenses...............	146,550
Operating income	$ 42,450

Required

1. Prepare a flexible budget income statement for 7,500, 9,000, 10,000, and 11,000 units.
2. Graph the total operating expense behavior of the company.

P25-2A Refer to Carson Components Company, Problem 25-1A. The company sold 11,000 units during March 19X3, and its actual income statement was as reported below.

Preparing an income statement performance report (Obj. 2)

CARSON COMPONENTS COMPANY INCOME STATEMENT MARCH 19X3	
Sales...	$232,000
Variable expenses:	
Cost of goods sold.....................	90,250
Sales commissions.....................	11,250
Shipping	6,750
Utilities.....................................	4,500
Fixed expenses:	
Salaries.....................................	31,750
Depreciation.............................	13,250
Rent	22,000
Insurance	3,500
Utilities.....................................	2,250
Total operating expenses..............	185,500
Operating income	$ 46,500

Required

1. Prepare an income statement performance report for March.
2. What was the effect on Carson's operating income of selling 2,000 units more than the master budget level of sales?
3. How will what you learned from this problem help you manage a business?

P25-3A Modular Fabricating Company manufactures office furniture and uses flexible budgeting and a standard cost system. The company's performance report includes the following selected data:

Preparing a flexible budget and computing standard cost variances (Obj. 1, 3, 4, 5)

	Master Budget 1,000 units	Actual Results 950 units
Sales (1,000 units × $200)	$200,000	
(950 units × $192)		$182,400
Variable expenses:		
Direct materials (40,000 lb × $0.80)..................	32,000	
(41,000 lb × $0.78)..................		31,980
Direct labor (5,000 hr × $6.00).........................	30,000	
(4,825 hr × $6.03).........................		29,095
Variable overhead (40,000 lb × $0.50)...............	20,000	
(41,000 lb × $0.64)...............		26,240
Fixed expenses:		
Fixed overhead	28,000	28,500
Gross profit...	$ 90,000	$ 66,585

Required

1. Prepare a flexible budget based on actual volume.
2. Compute the price variance and the efficiency variance for direct materials and for direct labor. Compute the total variance, the flexible budget variance, and the production volume variance for overhead.
3. Show that the price variance plus the efficiency variance equals the flexible budget variance for direct materials and for direct labor. Use Exhibit 25-9 as a guide.
4. What are the benefits of standard costs? Refer to the Modular Fabricating Company data.

P25-4A The state of Florida has a shop that manufactures road signs used throughout the state. The manager of the shop uses standard costs to judge performance. Recently a clerk mistakenly threw away some of the records, and the manager has only partial data for July. The manager knows that the direct labor flexible budget variance for the month was $1,565 F and that the stan-

Using incomplete cost and variance information to determine the number of direct labor-hours worked (Obj. 4) dard labor price was $6 per hour. The shop experienced a favorable labor price variance of $0.25 per hour. The standard direct labor-hours for actual July output were 3,500.

Required

1. Find the actual number of direct labor-hours worked during July. First, find the actual direct labor price per hour. Then, determine the actual number of direct labor-hours by setting up the computation of the direct labor flexible budget variance of $1,565 F.
2. Compute the direct labor price and efficiency variances.

Computing and journalizing standard cost variances (Obj. 4, 5, 6)

P25-5A Lathrop Cotton Mills manufactures T-shirts that it sells to other companies for customizing with their own logos. Lathrop prepares flexible budgets and uses a standard cost system to control manufacturing costs. The standard unit cost of a basic white T-shirt is based on master budget volume of 40,000 T-shirts per month. The unit cost is computed as follows:

Direct materials (2 sq. yd. @ $0.15 per sq. yd.)		$0.30
Direct labor (3 minutes @ $0.12 per minute)		0.36
Overhead:		
Variable (3 minutes @ $0.08 per minute).	$0.24	
Fixed (3 minutes @ $0.14 per minute)	0.42	0.66
Total unit cost		$1.32

Transactions during May of the current year included the following:

a. Actual production and sales were 42,700 units.
b. Actual direct materials usage was 1.85 square yards per unit at cost of $0.14 per square yard.
c. Actual direct labor usage of 130,000 minutes cost $16,250.
d. Actual overhead cost was $27,500.

Required

1. Compute the price and efficiency variances for direct materials and direct labor.
2. Journalize the usage of direct materials and the application of direct labor, including the related variances.
3. Compute the total variance, the flexible budget variance, and the production volume variance for overhead. Then compute the overhead spending and efficiency variances.
4. Evaluate the performance of the plant managers in controlling overhead cost in May.

Computing standard cost variances and reporting to management (Obj. 4, 5, 7)

P25-6A Intercollegiate Academic Supplier manufactures ring binders. During August, the company produced and sold 104,000 binders and recorded the following cost data:

	Standard Unit Cost	Actual Total Cost
Direct materials:		
Standard (2 parts @ $0.15 per part)	$0.30	
Actual (209,500 parts @ $0.16 per part)		$33,520
Direct labor:		
Standard (0.02 hr @ $5.00 per hr)	0.10	
Actual (1,560 hr @ $5.50 per hr)		8,580
Overhead:		
Standard:		
Variable (0.03 machine-hr @ $6.00 per hr)	$0.18	
Fixed ($24,000 for master budget volume of 100,000 units and 3,000 machine-hours)	0.24 0.42	
Actual		45,000
Total	$0.82	$87,100

Required

1. Compute the price and efficiency variances for direct materials and direct labor.
2. Compute the total variance, the flexible budget variance, and the production volume variance for overhead.
3. Prepare a standard cost income statement through gross profit to report all variances to management. Sale price of the binders to college bookstores was $1.25 each.
4. Intercollegiate's management used more-experienced workers during August. Discuss the trade-off between the two direct labor variances.

P25-1B Hometest, Inc., produces and sells prepackaged tests for radon gas. The company's master budget income statement for June 19X7 follows. It is based on expected sales volume of 55,000 units.

Preparing a flexible budget income statement and graphing cost behavior
(Obj. 1)

HOMETEST, INC.
MASTER BUDGET INCOME STATEMENT
JUNE 19X7

Sales...	$220,000
Variable expenses:	
Cost of goods sold.....................	60,500
Sales commissions.....................	16,500
Shipping	12,100
Utilities....................................	5,500
Fixed expenses:	
Salaries....................................	36,500
Depreciation............................	24,000
Rent	11,500
Insurance	8,850
Utilities....................................	6,200
Total operating expenses..............	181,650
Operating income	$ 38,350

Hometest's plant capacity is 62,500 units. If actual volume exceeds 62,500 units, the company must expand the plant. In that case, salaries will increase by 10 percent, depreciation by 20 percent, rent by $5,500, and insurance by $1,400. Fixed utilities will be unchanged by the volume increase.

Required

1. Prepare a flexible budget income statement for the company, showing volume levels of 50,000, 55,000, 60,000, and 65,000 units.
2. Graph the total operating expense behavior of the company.

P25-2B Refer to Hometest, Inc., of Problem 25-1B. The company sold 60,000 units during June 19X7, and its actual income statement was as follows:

Preparing an income statement performance report
(Obj. 2)

HOMETEST, INC.
INCOME STATEMENT
JUNE 19X7

Sales...	$243,500
Variable expenses:	
Cost of goods sold.....................	$ 66,500
Sales commissions.....................	19,500
Shipping	13,500
Utilities....................................	6,000
Fixed expenses:	
Salaries....................................	38,000
Depreciation............................	24,000
Rent	9,500
Insurance	8,850
Utilities....................................	6,200
Total operating expenses..............	192,050
Operating income	$ 51,450

Required

1. Prepare an income statement performance report for June 19X7.

2. What accounts for most of the difference between actual operating income and master budget operating income?

3. How will what you learned from this problem help you manage a business?

Preparing a flexible budget and computing standard cost variances (Obj. 1, 3, 4, 5)

P25-3B Quadron, Inc., manufactures compact disc players and uses flexible budgeting and a standard cost system. The company's performance report includes the following selected data:

	Master Budget 20,000 units	Actual Results 21,000 units
Sales (20,000 units × $200)	$4,000,000	
(21,000 units × $210)		$4,410,000
Variable expenses:		
Direct materials (200,000 parts @ $8.00)	1,600,000	
(214,200 parts @ $7.90)		1,692,180
Direct labor (40,000 hours @ $10.00)	400,000	
(42,500 hours @ $10.25)		435,625
Variable overhead (200,000 parts @ $2.00)	400,000	
(214,200 parts @ $2.10)		449,820
Fixed expenses:		
Fixed overhead	600,000	610,000
Total cost of goods sold	3,000,000	3,187,625
Gross margin	$1,000,000	$1,222,375

Required

1. Prepare a flexible budget based on actual volume.

2. Compute the price variance and the efficiency variance for direct materials and for direct labor. Compute the total variance, the flexible budget variance, and the production volume variance for overhead.

3. Show that the price variance plus the efficiency variance equals the flexible budget variance for direct materials and for direct labor. Use Exhibit 25-9 as a guide.

4. What are the benefits of standard costs? Refer to the Quadron data in your answer.

Using incomplete cost and variance information to determine the number of direct labor-hours worked (Obj. 4)

P25-4B The city of New Orleans has a shop that manufactures lampposts. The manager of the shop uses standard costs to judge performance. Recently, a clerk mistakenly threw away some of the records, and the manager has only partial data for October. The manager knows that the direct labor flexible budget variance for the month was $1,771 U and that the standard labor price was $6.70 per hour. A recent pay raise caused an unfavorable labor price variance of $0.30 per hour. The standard direct labor-hours for actual October output were 2,870.

Required

1. Find the actual number of direct labor-hours worked during October. First, find the actual direct labor price per hour. Then, determine the actual number of direct labor-hours by setting up the computation of the direct labor flexible budget variance of $1,771 U.

2. Compute the direct labor price and efficiency variances.

Computing and journalizing standard cost variances (Obj. 4, 5, 6)

P25-5B Joseph Sohm Co. manufactures running shoes. The company prepares flexible budgets and uses a standard cost system to control manufacturing costs. The following standard unit cost of a pair of shoes is based on the master budget volume of 14,000 pairs per month:

Direct materials (2.8 sq. ft @ $2.00 per sq. ft)...............		$ 5.60
Direct labor (2 hours @ $9.50 per hour)		19.00
Overhead:		
Variable (2 hours @ $0.65 per hour).........................	$1.30	
Fixed (2 hours @ $2.20 per hour)	4.40	5.70
Total unit cost		$30.30

Data for November of the current year include:

a. Actual production was 13,600 units.

b. Actual direct materials usage was 2.70 square feet per pair of shoes at actual cost of $2.17 per square foot.

c. Actual direct labor usage of 24,480 hours cost $233,784.

d. Total actual overhead cost was $77,950.

Required

1. Compute the price and efficiency variances for direct materials and direct labor.

2. Journalize the usage of direct materials and the application of direct labor, including the related variances.

3. Compute the total variance, the flexible budget variance, and the production volume variance for overhead. Also compute the overhead spending and efficiency variances for a three-variance overhead analysis.

4. Sohm management intentionally purchased superior materials for November production. How did this decision affect the other cost variances? Overall, was the decision wise?

P25-6B Barse Manufacturing produces industrial plastics. During April the company produced and sold 42,000 sheets of plastic and recorded the following cost data:

Computing standard cost variances and reporting to management (Obj. 4, 5, 7)

	Standard Unit Cost	Actual Total Cost
Direct materials:		
Standard (3 lb @ $1.22 per lb)...	$3.66	
Actual (134,400 lb @ $1.18 per lb)......................................		$158,592
Direct labor:		
Standard (0.1 hr @ $7.00 per hr)...	0.70	
Actual (4,400 hr @ $6.90 per hr)...		30,360
Overhead:		
Standard:		
Variable (0.2 machine-hr @ $6.00 per hr)...............	$1.20	
Fixed ($64,000 for master budget volume of		
40,000 units and 8,000 machine-hours).............	1.60 2.80	
Actual...		118,680
Total...	$7.16	$307,632

Required

1. Compute the price and efficiency variances for direct materials and direct labor.

2. Compute the total variance, the flexible budget variance, and the production volume variance for overhead.

3. Prepare a standard cost income statement through gross profit to report all variances to management. Sale price of the plastic was $10.90 per sheet.

4. Barse intentionally purchased cheaper materials during April. Was the decision wise? Discuss the trade-off between the two materials cost variances.

EXTENDING YOUR KNOWLEDGE

DECISION PROBLEMS

1. The board of directors of Pro Performance, Inc., a distributor of golf clubs, is meeting to evaluate the company's performance for the year just ended. The accompanying report has been prepared for the meeting.

The directors are disappointed by the operating income results. Further, they are puzzled by the presence of so many favorable variances. After all, actual operating income for the year is only 56.5 percent of the master budget amount.

In response to the directors' initial questions, Pro Performance's controller revealed that the actual sale price of $120 per unit was equal to the budgeted price. Also, there were no changes in inventories for the year.

Preparing a performance report and using it to evaluate performance (Obj. 2)

<table>
<tr><td align="center" colspan="4">PRO PERFORMANCE, INC.
INCOME STATEMENT PERFORMANCE REPORT
FOR THE YEAR ENDED SEPTEMBER 30, 19X6</td></tr>
<tr><td></td><td align="center">Actual Results</td><td align="center">Master Budget</td><td align="center">Variances</td></tr>
<tr><td>Sales</td><td>$1,992,000</td><td>$2,430,000</td><td>$438,000U</td></tr>
<tr><td>Variable expenses:</td><td></td><td></td><td></td></tr>
<tr><td>Cost of goods sold</td><td>891,750</td><td>1,159,500</td><td>267,750 F</td></tr>
<tr><td>Sales commissions</td><td>87,675</td><td>124,500</td><td>36,825 F</td></tr>
<tr><td>Shipping</td><td>48,000</td><td>65,250</td><td>17,250 F</td></tr>
<tr><td>Utilities</td><td>9,750</td><td>10,500</td><td>750 F</td></tr>
<tr><td>Fixed expenses:</td><td></td><td></td><td></td></tr>
<tr><td>Salaries</td><td>331,200</td><td>329,250</td><td>1,950 U</td></tr>
<tr><td>Depreciation</td><td>229,500</td><td>234,750</td><td>5,250 F</td></tr>
<tr><td>Rent</td><td>128,250</td><td>128,250</td><td>–0–</td></tr>
<tr><td>Utilities</td><td>9,375</td><td>9,750</td><td>375 F</td></tr>
<tr><td>Advertising</td><td>95,100</td><td>82,500</td><td>12,600U</td></tr>
<tr><td>Total operating expenses</td><td>1,830,600</td><td>2,144,250</td><td>313,650 F</td></tr>
<tr><td>Operating income</td><td>$ 161,400</td><td>$ 285,750</td><td>$124,350U</td></tr>
</table>

Required

1. Prepare a more informative performance report than the one above. Be sure to include a flexible budget for the actual quantity of golf clubs purchased and sold.

2. A downturn in the economy was responsible for the company's inability to sell more golf clubs. In light of this information, how would you rate the company's performance? As a member of Pro Performance's top management, which variances would you want investigated? Why?

Variance analysis and reporting in a nonprofit organization (Obj. 1, 2)

2. Community Church is a congregation in suburban Chicago. At the end of 1993, the church's membership was 400 families. Each family donated an average of $500 per year to the church's operating fund and $1,000 to its mission and service fund.

For 1994, Community Church's Membership Committee budgeted a 10-percent increase in the number of families. Its Finance Committee planned a campaign to increase average donations to $525 for the operating fund and $1,050 for missions and service. On the first Sunday in 1994, the chairperson of the Finance Committee presented a budget to the congregation that incorporated the goals of the two committees. The budget called for overall receipts of $693,000.

During 1994, Community Church actually lost 10 families. The congregation's receipts totaled $629,850, including $210,600 for operations. The pastor has asked the Finance Committee if a sermon on giving is in order.

Required

1. As chairperson of the Finance Committee, prepare a thorough analysis of the congregation's donations in 1994.

2. Write a one-paragraph report to the pastor that addresses the question of a sermon on giving.

ETHICAL ISSUE

Jurgens Products, Inc., budgets from the bottom up. Production workers prepare departmental goals, which are coordinated by supervisors. Top managers combine the departmental budgets into the company's overall master budget. Standard costs developed from the budget amounts are used for the full year.

Production workers have observed that the standard costs correspond closely to their own budget amounts. Accordingly, they have built a cushion for themselves by overestimating the quantities of materials and labor needed to manufacture products.

Required

1. Are Jurgens's cost variances likely to be favorable or unfavorable? Why?
2. Whose behavior is unethical, and whose behavior is lax?
3. If this situation persists over several years, what is the likely outcome?

COMPREHENSIVE PROBLEMS FOR PART SIX

1. USING A REGRESSION EQUATION IN COST-VOLUME-PROFIT ANALYSIS

Kohl Chair Company produces two styles of chairs—the standard model, which sells for $400, and the deluxe model, which sells for $900. The unit prime costs of the chairs are:

	Direct Materials	Direct Labor
Standard model...............	$120	$ 30
Deluxe model.................	250	100

The manufacturing labor wage rate is $20 per hour.

Kohl's cost analyst used regression analysis to develop an equation to predict the company's manufacturing overhead costs. She selected two alternative independent variables: direct labor-hours and number of chairs produced. The results of the regressions follow:

Regression 1: Total overhead cost = $1,200,000 + $10 per direct labor-hour
$$r^2 = 0.85$$
Regression 2: Total overhead cost = $1,000,000 + $35 per chair produced
$$r^2 = 0.50$$

The analyst also studied the costs of the activities that are upstream (R&D and design) and downstream (marketing, distribution, and customer service) of manufacturing. The fixed costs of those nonmanufacturing activities total $625,000. The variable costs are: standard model, $60 per chair; deluxe model, $100 per chair.

Required

1. Which of the two regression equations should Kohl's managers use to predict the company's manufacturing overhead costs? Why?

2. On the basis of your answer to Requirement 1, compute the unit contribution margins of standard models and deluxe models.

3. Suppose that Kohl's sales mix for 19X5 is 7 standard models for every 2 deluxe models. How many chairs must the company sell to break even? To earn a target operating income of $200,000?

4. Kohl's cost analyst used regression analysis to develop her cost-prediction equation. Would you have used regression or some other method? Explain your answer.

2. GROUP PROJECT: ANALYZING COST BEHAVIOR, SETTING STANDARD COSTS, AND BUDGETING OPERATING INCOME FOR A CATERING BUSINESS

We now continue the Group Project that you began at the end of Part Five. There you decided on your customer market and what types of events to cater—that is, what types of meals to offer (for example, hors d'oeuvres). You also listed your cost categories. Here you must:

- Label each cost as fixed or variable. Divide variable costs into those that vary with the number of catered events and those that vary with the number of food servings.

- Assign dollar amounts to the fixed costs budgeted for the first year of operations, the standard variable costs per event, and the standard variable costs per serving. Use different variable costs for each type of event (meal served).

- Set the price per serving and predict the average number of servings for each type of event.

- Budget the total number of catered events for the year. Also, budget the mix of event types (for example, one-fourth hors d'oeuvre events, and so on).

Then, answer the following questions:

1. What is your static (master) budget operating income for the year?
2. How many events must you cater to break even?
3. What is your margin of safety in number of events?
4. Why might your firm's actual operating income differ from the static budget amount? List as many causes of the static budget variance as you can.

The Changing Movie Industry

The movie industry's formula for success has changed dramatically since the 1980s. Although the average cost to make and release a movie now exceeds $40 million, there is often little correlation between the cost of a movie and the revenues it will generate. In fact, revenues in the movie industry have not grown measurably in the last 15 years. It is no coincidence that revenues began to stagnate just as VCRs became popular. The sources of movie revenue, once confined primarily to ticket sales, have expanded to include video rentals and sales as well as consumer products such as toys and clothing.

In recent years, the video market has far outpaced ticket sales. During 1991, box-office sales were $4.8 billion while video rentals and sales totaled $11 billion. Industry analysts attribute the changing market to demographics. The baby-boom generation, which grew up with television, is opting to stay at home with their families to watch movies. Baby-boomers consider the cost of a movie ticket to be very high, whereas high-technology home entertainment systems have become more affordable. Although industry executives maintain that many consumers will always want to "get out of the house" to see movies, they also know that other sources of revenue from films are key factors in a movie studio's survival. Disney Studios is a prime example; it parlayed its children's movies such as *Beauty and the Beast* and *The Lion King* into an entire product line of toys and clothing.

From the studios' perspective, production costs have skyrocketed in response to the public's demand for big-name stars and elaborate special effects. Extensive promotion efforts increase fixed costs before revenues can be predicted with any confidence. To add to their problems, movie studios have recently undergone a spate of mergers and takeovers that resulted in significant debt service costs. Orion Studios, which produced *The Silence of the Lambs* and *Dances with Wolves*, struggles to survive despite its hit movies because of high interest payments on its debts. Some studios have tried to maximize their chances for success by focusing on remakes of old classics, such as *Miracle on 34th Street*, or sequels to recent successful films, such as *Batman*, in the hope that a "tried-and-true" approach will help produce profits.

CASE QUESTIONS

1. Describe some of the fixed costs, and costs that vary with ticket sales, incurred in the making of a movie.
2. A manufacturer's master budget begins with projected sales. Do you think a movie production company starts the same way? Why or why not?
3. What factors do you consider in deciding whether to see a movie at the theater or to wait and rent the video later? How might a studio benefit from knowledge about such consumer decisions?
4. Assume that a movie studio just finished filming its latest horror movie at a cost of $40 million and is calculating its breakeven point. The studio gets $3 for every movie theater ticket sold and $0.50 for each video rental, but it must pay 20 percent of these amounts to the stars and producers of the movie. (The cost to produce video tapes is negligible.) The studio estimates that 10 million people will see the movie in theaters.
   (a) Assuming that ticket sales and video rentals are the only sources of revenue, how many rentals are needed to break even?
   (b) Once the studio breaks even, how much profit will it realize on each $1 of sales?

PART SEVEN

Strategy and Long-Term Decision Making

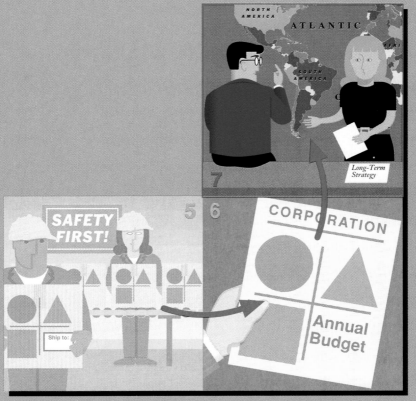

MANAGEMENT ACCOUNTING

Chapter 26
Strategy, Cost Management, and Continuous Improvement

1. Describe the distinctive features of activity-based costing (ABC)

2. Use activity-based costs to make management decisions

3. Compare the major features of a traditional production system and a just-in-time (JIT) production system

4. Record manufacturing costs for a backflush costing system

5. Prepare a life-cycle budget for a product

6. Relate target costing and kaizen costing to continuous improvement

7. Contrast the four types of quality costs

Activity-based costing (ABC) has executives at both large and small companies singing its praises. Accountants use ABC systems to determine the cost of products by adding together the costs of all activities that produce and support the products. The resulting costs generally are regarded as more accurate than costs generated by traditional accounting systems.

Engineers use ABC data to assess alternative product designs. Managers use the data to evaluate different factory layouts, reduce waste in manufacturing, and improve product and service quality.

According to Chrysler president Robert Lutz, his company "is dynamiting the old financial system" and replacing it with ABC. This major change was influenced by the company's recent experience with a very minor part, the harnesses that yoke together wires beneath minivan dashboards. Each group involved in the decision (for example, product engineers and assembly personnel) recommended a different number of distinct harnesses, ranging from one to nine. After examining the cost of each activity affected by the decision, all groups decided that the optimal number was two. *Source: Adapted from T. P. Paré, "A New Tool for Managing Costs," Fortune, June 14, 1993, pp. 124–129. © 1993 Time Inc. All rights reserved.*

• • • • •

*I*n today's international marketplace, companies prosper by implementing strategies that create a competitive advantage. A *strategy* is a set of business goals and the tactics to achieve them. Successful companies gather, organize, and use resources in ways that help them attain their goals.

A growing number of companies worldwide, including Chrysler, Boeing, and Caterpillar Tractor, are using a management process known as activity-based management (ABM). ABM focuses on the management of activities as the way to improve value delivered to customers. Providing that value generates profits. ABM strives for excellence by:

- Managing activities that advance the organization's strategy
- Eliminating activities that do not add value to customers
- Synchronizing activities within business processes
- Promoting continuous improvement of activity cost, time, and quality

The key to successful management is intelligent decision making. A successful management accounting system provides decision-making support—that is, tools and information for wise decisions and consequent actions. As the Chrysler story illustrates, activity-based management draws on activity-based costing as its major source of information. This chapter begins with activity-based costing and then discusses several other ABM techniques for continuously improving operations. Included are *just-in-time production systems*, *product life-cycle budgeting*, *target costing*, *kaizen costing*, and *total quality management*.

Activity-Based Costing

OBJECTIVE 1

Describe the distinctive features of activity-based costing (ABC)

As we have seen, one purpose of accounting information is to aid management planning and control. Managers plan and control operations in manufacturing, marketing, and other business functions by personal observation and with budgets and performance reports. Many companies split these functions into departments.

This section describes a widely acclaimed approach to measuring the costs of various cost objects. A *cost object* can be anything for which it is worthwhile to compile costs, such as an activity (polishing), a department (finishing), or a product (a table). **Activity-based costing (ABC)**, also called *activity-based accounting*, is a system that focuses on *activities* as the fundamental cost objects and uses the costs of those activities as building blocks for compiling costs. ABC is generic. It can be used in conjunction with either a job order or a process costing system and by manufacturers, merchandisers, and service firms.

If dividing companywide functions into departments helps managers, wouldn't dividing departments into activities further sharpen managers' focus? Exhibit 26-1,

EXHIBIT 26-1
Overview of Business Functions, Departments, and Activities

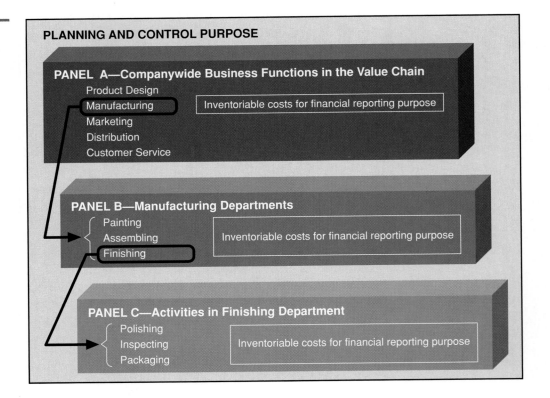

PLANNING AND CONTROL PURPOSE

PANEL A—Companywide Business Functions in the Value Chain
Product Design
Manufacturing — Inventoriable costs for financial reporting purpose
Marketing
Distribution
Customer Service

PANEL B—Manufacturing Departments
Painting
Assembling — Inventoriable costs for financial reporting purpose
Finishing

PANEL C—Activities in Finishing Department
Polishing
Inspecting — Inventoriable costs for financial reporting purpose
Packaging

Panel A, shows the different functions in the value chain of a furniture manufacturer such as Thomasville. Panel B divides the manufacturing function into departments. Panel C lists common activities in a Finishing Department. Costs are accumulated separately for each activity. Activity costs are applied to tables and other products as the products move through production. For example, if finishing a table requires polishing, the cost of that activity—polishing—is added to the cost of the table. A less expensive table may not be polished. In this case, the table bears no polishing cost. Inspecting cost and packaging cost likewise are added to the cost of the table as appropriate. *The manufacturing product cost of a table is "built up" from the cost of the specific activities undertaken to produce it.*

Exhibit 26-1 shows how cost objects can be identified ever-more-finely by dividing a particular business function into departments, and then dividing each department into activities. But how do the refinements of ABC translate into better decisions? To answer that question, we explore why managers demand ABC information.

Demand for Activity-Based Costing

Activity-based costing grew out of a need by companies to more accurately determine the costs of their products. The main difficulty in product costing is not with direct materials or direct labor. These costs are easy to trace to particular products. The difficulty is with *overhead* costs, which are difficult to relate to products. Historically, many companies have applied all overhead costs to products on the basis of a single application base, direct labor. This practice can yield inaccurate costs, for two reasons. First, in manufacturing settings that are highly automated, the bulk of overhead cost incurrence is not related to direct labor-hours or costs. Recall that a *cost driver* is any factor whose change causes a change in a related total cost. Using a cost application base that is not the driver of the cost in question results in inaccurate product costs. Second, no *single* factor drives all indirect manufacturing costs, much less all costs in the value chain. Thus, companies need a costing system that applies costs on the basis of multiple cost drivers. ABC fulfills this need. Each application base in an ABC system is selected for its causal relationship to an activity. The more-precise relationships identified by ABC yield more-accurate product costs than do traditional systems that use a single application base for overhead costs. Better cost figures help managers make wiser decisions.

Another reason managers demand ABC information is that activities cut across departmental lines. For example, consider that inspection takes place in Thomasville's painting department, its assembling department, and its finishing department. Only if detailed records of all inspection activities are kept can the company's total cost of inspection (or any other activity) be compiled and used by managers. Focusing on costs by department or product instead of by activity can obscure activity costs.

Developments in information technology make activity-based costing feasible. Optical scanning, bar coding, and robotics have reduced the cost of processing the information demanded by ABC. Before those techniques became available, it was convenient to use direct labor-hours or direct labor-dollars as the sole basis for applying overhead cost. Now, it is relatively inexpensive to obtain better cost applications with multiple cost drivers.

Product Costing in an Activity-Based System

Product costing in an ABC system is similar to product costing in a simpler system that uses a single overhead application rate. The difference is that conversion costs (labor and overhead) are applied to products from various activity cost pools with ABC. The process requires six steps. Managers must:

1. Identify manufacturing activities.
2. Budget the total cost of each activity.
3. Identify the primary cost driver as the application base for each activity.

4. Budget the total units of each application base.

5. Divide the budgeted costs in step 2 by the budgeted application base units in step 4 to compute the cost application rate for each activity.

6. Apply activity costs to products. For each product, multiply the application base units that pertain to the product by the cost application rates computed in step 5.

With an ABC system, Winston applies conversion costs to products from various activity cost pools.

Consider Winston, Inc., which manufactures lawn chairs. Assume that direct materials cost $4 per chair; each chair has eight parts and requires 15 minutes of machine time. The budgeted activity costs, cost drivers, and cost application rates for a period when Winston's managers expect to produce 1,000 chairs are:

Manufacturing Activity	Budgeted Cost of Activity	Cost Driver Chosen as Application Base	Activity Cost per Unit of Application Base
1. Materials handling	$ 800 ÷	Number of parts (8,000) =	$ 0.10
2. Machining	5,000 ÷	Machine-hours (250) =	20.00
3. Assembling	4,800 ÷	Number of parts (8,000) =	0.60
4. Inspecting	1,400 ÷	Number of finished units (1,000) =	1.40

Each chair's *manufacturing product cost* is $16, computed as follows:

Direct materials	$ 4.00
Activity costs:	
Materials handling (8 parts × $0.10)	0.80
Machining (1/4 machine-hour × $20.00)	5.00
Assembling (8 parts × $0.60)	4.80
Inspecting (1 finished unit × $1.40)	1.40
Manufacturing product cost per unit	$16.00

This detailed breakdown of costs by activity pinpoints opportunities for cost control. For example, assembling costs of $4.80 per unit may be significantly higher than the costs of a leading competitor. Knowing this, managers may work to bring costs down. A traditional costing system may keep no records of the cost of assembling chairs, and managers may be unaware that their costs are too high.

Managers also need to know *full product cost*, which includes the costs of upstream activities and downstream activities in the value chain. ◀▥ Recall that upstream activities precede manufacturing and that downstream activities follow it. Winston's full product cost per chair is $26.60, computed as follows:

◀▥◀▥◀▥ In Chapter 20 (p. 844), we described the value chain as the sequence of all activities that add value to a product—from research and development through manufacturing to customer service.

Upstream activities:	
Product design (assumed)	$ 1.40
Total manufacturing cost per unit (as before)	16.00
Downstream activities:	
Marketing, distribution, and customer service (assumed)	9.20
Full product cost per unit	$26.60

Internal decisions, such as product mix and product pricing, focus on the components of full product cost. However, the external financial statements report chairs at $16 each because that is their manufacturing (inventoriable) cost. The costs of upstream and downstream activities are expensed as incurred.

Product Costing Accuracy

A product costing system that uses a single cost application base can distort product costs. The following example demonstrates why an ABC system can lead to more-accurate product costs than a single-rate system.

Quality Instrument Company manufactures satellite instruments (one batch of 20 per month) and testing instruments (one batch of 400 per month). The company has had the same cost accounting system since its founding in 1971. A single rate based on machine-hours of running time has been used to apply all conversion costs to production. Direct materials costs and machine-hours per unit are the same for the two products. In the following tabulation, focus on conversion costs:

Product	Machine-Hours per Unit		Application Rate per Machine-Hour		Cost per Unit		Direct Materials Cost per Unit		Manufacturing Product Cost per Unit
Single Rate Conversion Cost									
Satellite instrument............	5	×	$120	=	$600	+	$200	=	$800
Testing instrument	5	×	120	=	600	+	200	=	800

STOP & THINK Why does Quality Instrument's single-rate system apply the same conversion cost to each satellite instrument that it applies to each testing instrument? Suppose that 3 machine-hours were required for each satellite instrument and 6 for each testing instrument. How much more conversion cost would be applied to testing units than to satellite units?

Answer: The single-rate system applies the same conversion cost per unit to both products because both require the same number of application-base units—5 machine-hours. If a testing instrument required twice as many hours as a satellite instrument, each testing instrument would have twice as much cost applied to it.

Quality Instrument's manufacturing process uses sophisticated machinery. It is very expensive to change machine settings from the production of satellite instruments to the production of testing instruments and vice versa. Machine setups are a substantial cost of the manufacturing process. In recent years, the cost of setting up machines has soared to $42,000. The use of a single cost application rate that is based on machine-hours of running time ignores the role of this high setup cost. To gauge the cost of each product better, management decides to use two activity cost pools—machine setups and machine running time—for conversion costs. Each batch of instruments requires one machine setup. When setup cost is subtracted from total conversion cost, the application rate for machine running time decreases to $80 per hour from the previous level of $120. The ABC computations of product costs differ significantly from the earlier figures:

ABC Conversion Cost

Product	Machine Setups		Running of Machines				Total Cost	Cost per Unit		Direct Materials Cost per Unit		Manufacturing Product Cost per Unit
			Units	Hours	Rate							
Satellite instrument	$42,000	+	(20 ×	5	× $80)	=	$ 50,000	$2,500*	+	$200	=	$2,700
Testing instrument	42,000	+	(400 ×	5	× 80)	=	202,000	505†	+	200	=	705

*$50,000/20 units = $2,500
†$202,000/400 units = $505

Compare the manufacturing product cost per unit under the two methods of applying conversion costs:

Manufacturing Product Cost per Unit

Product	Using Single Rate	Using ABC Rates
Satellite instrument...............	$800	$2,700
Testing instrument................	800	705

Use of the single rate undercosts satellite instruments ($600 conversion cost per unit instead of $2,500) and overcosts testing instruments ($600 instead of $505). In effect, the single rate applies an equal *setup cost* to each unit of both products as well as an equal amount of other conversion costs. But the ABC system provides a better application of setup costs to products:

Satellite instrument: $42,000/20   units per batch = $2,100 per unit
Testing instrument: $42,000/400 units per batch = $ 105 per unit

Short Exercise: Assume the following for an ABC system:

Activity	Cost Driver
1. Purchasing	No. parts purchased
2. Assembly	No. parts in production
3. Packaging	No. finished units

Activity Cost	Volume of Cost Driver	Activity Cost/Unit of Cost Driver
1. $24,000	12,000	$0.20
2. $60,000	15,000	4.00
3. $12,000	16,000	0.75

Each unit has four parts. These materials cost $3.00 per finished unit. What is the total manufacturing cost per unit? *A:*

Direct Materials	$ 3.00
Activity Costs:	
Purchasing (4 × $0.20) ..	0.80
Assembly (4 × $4)	16.00
Packaging (1 × $0.75)	0.75
Total mfg. cost/unit	$20.55

Activity-Based Costing and Management Decisions

Activity-based costing gives managers better information for decision making. We discuss two decisions: pricing, and make versus buy. First, consider the management task of setting the sale prices of the company's products.

The ABC system shows that Quality Instrument's average setup cost per satellite instrument is much higher than the average setup cost per testing instrument. But the single-rate system indicates that each product's conversion cost is $600, which yields a manufacturing product cost of $800. Managers use this information to decide how to price each product. A product-pricing decision based on the $800 amount can be disastrous. Suppose that the marketing department prices each satellite instrument and each testing instrument at $1,500. Managers believe each sale will yield a gross margin of $700 ($1,500 – $800). However, the company will *lose* $1,200 ($1,500 – $2,700) on each satellite instrument, plus the cost of upstream and downstream activities that support the product. In contrast, the margin on testing instruments will be higher than expected—$795 ($1,500 – $705) instead of $700.

Now consider the make-versus-buy decision. Quality Instrument Company can make its own products or buy them from an outside supplier. Suppose that an outside company offers to supply satellite instruments for $2,000 per unit. Using a single-rate system, managers will reject the offer. They believe they can make each instrument for $800. Using ABC, they may accept the outside offer. The purchase price of $2,000 is lower than Quality Instrument's manufacturing cost of $2,700.

Each of the above decisions is influenced by other factors. For example, managers should consider the contribution to profits that can be earned if the outside supplier's offer is accepted and freed-up machine time is used to produce a third product. Nonetheless, properly functioning ABC systems provide better information for decision making than do systems that use a single cost application rate.

A word of caution is in order. ABC is not easy. Describing the concept is deceptively simple: Products cause activities, and activities consume resources. However, implementing an ABC system is not simple, especially in complex organizations with many activities and multiple cost drivers. The business press has reported several failures. One problem is that some managers regard ABC as a "quick fix" for declining profitability. But ABC is not a stand-alone technique that assures success in the marketplace. Instead it is one of several activity-based management initiatives that companies are using to achieve world-class status.

Traditional versus Just-in-Time Production Systems

We now turn our attention to a second ABM technique—just-in-time (JIT) production. To aid our discussion, we contrast just-in-time production systems with traditional production systems. We begin with traditional systems.

Traditional Production Systems

Traditional production systems often produce enormous waste, in terms of both time and money. Two areas in which this waste is especially apparent are inventories and manufacturing processes.

INVENTORIES   Many businesses keep large inventories of raw materials, work in process, and finished goods. Why? First, to protect against poor quality. Poor quality in materials purchased from suppliers leads companies to purchase more materials than they need strictly for production. Also, machine breakdowns and poor-quality production *within* departments prompt managers to keep buffer stocks of work in process *between* departments. Consider the sequence of operations shown in Exhibit 26-2 for the production of drill bits from bar stock (the raw material). Work in

EXHIBIT 26-2
Sequence of Operations for Drill-Bit Production

process inventory between the thread grinding and smoothing operations allows smoothing work to continue if thread-grinding machines break down.

A second reason for large inventories is long setup times on production equipment. Some managers regard as acceptable setup times of several hours to several days, and correspondingly high setup costs. Companies make products in large batches to spread setup costs over many units of product. This minimizes the cost per unit.

A third reason for stocking large inventories is uncertainty in both deliveries from suppliers and demand from customers. Large stocks of raw materials protect against delays in deliveries; if a supplier is late in delivering materials, the company still has materials to use in production. Large stocks of finished goods protect against missed sales if customer demand is higher than expected.

Why are large inventory stocks a problem? First, inventories tie up cash. Companies either incur interest expense or forgo interest revenue on that cash. Second, inventories hide problems. Quality problems, production bottlenecks, obsolescence, and supplier unreliability often are hidden in inventories. If the drill-bit manufacturer improperly grinds threads on a batch of 1,000 bits and the problem is not discovered by the smoothing-machine operator until a week later, the company may incur costs to rework the defective bits. Alternatively, the bits may be discarded.

Key Point: JIT production eliminates excess stockpiling of inventory because products are purchased or manufactured only as needed. JIT thus reduces storage costs of raw materials, work in process, and finished goods inventories.

MANUFACTURING PROCESSES Traditionally, machines have been grouped according to function. Rough-shaping machines might be located in one area of a plant, thread-grinding machines in another area, and smoothing machines in yet another area. In many cases, raw materials and parts travel several *miles* back and forth through a factory before they are completed as finished goods, perhaps detouring to storage areas along the way. This excessive movement not only wastes time but also increases the chance that an order will be misplaced or damaged. Misplaced orders lead to delayed shipments, and delayed shipments anger customers.

Managers of traditional production processes try to keep machines busy in order to maximize output. Managers "push" materials through the manufacturing process. For example, the thread-grinding-machine operator pushes threaded bits to the smoothing-machine operator whether or not the smoothing machines are ready for them. Too often, the bits are pushed forward whether or not they meet quality standards. Thus, the desire to keep busy is another reason for high work in process inventory levels.

The time between receipt of purchased materials and completion of finished products is known as **throughput time**. Throughput time may be represented by the following equation:

$$\textbf{Throughput time} = \textbf{Processing time} + \textbf{Waiting time} + \textbf{Moving time} + \textbf{Inspection time} + \textbf{Reworking time}$$

Processing time often is called "value-added" time. Processing activity adds value to the products a company provides to its customers. The remainder of throughput time is spent on **non-value-added activities,** which do not increase customer value or satisfy a company need. In many manufacturing systems, processing time accounts for less than 10 percent of throughput time. The remainder is waste.

Just-in-Time Production Systems

Just-in-time (JIT) production systems are designed to eliminate waste. Indeed, many people regard JIT as a *general philosophy of waste elimination* instead of a particular type of manufacturing system. The production systems of companies that apply the JIT philosophy have several common characteristics:

1. *Arrangement of production activities.* JIT processes arrange machines by the sequence of operations, not by function. In our drill-bit example, a production line might manufacture a specific type of drill bit. In that line, a rough-shaping machine located near the cutting operation would be followed by a thread-grinding machine, which in turn would be followed by a smoothing machine. These machines, which perform various functions, are arranged differently from the clusters of a traditional factory layout. In some JIT cases, machines performing sequential steps are physically joined. The goal is continuous production without interruption.

Arranging machines in this sequential manner results in great reductions in throughput time. Harley-Davidson adopted JIT techniques in 1981. After six years of continuous improvement, the company had reduced the time required to produce a motorcycle by 77 percent. Two years after Hewlett-Packard adopted JIT, the throughput time of the company's thermal printers had been cut from seven days to three hours.

2. *Setup times.* JIT companies work to reduce setup times on machines that are used to make more than one product. Through a combination of employee training, preparation, and technology, the companies have achieved impressive results. For example, Toyota has reported reductions in setup times from several hours to a few minutes. Such improvements give companies greater flexibility in scheduling production to meet customer requirements. The results are increased customer satisfaction and increased profits.

3. *Production scheduling.* JIT businesses schedule production in small batches *just in time* to satisfy needs. Manufacturing usually starts from a customer order. The final operation in the production sequence (smoothing, in our drill-bit example) "pulls" parts from the preceding operation (thread grinding). The grinding-machine operator pulls shaped parts from rough shaping, and so on. This "demand-pull" system extends back to suppliers of materials. Suppliers must make frequent deliveries of small quantities of defect-free materials *just in time* to be placed into production. This arrangement coordinates efforts throughout the value chain.

Real-World Example: In 1991, Toyota implemented a JIT system in Japan whereby automobiles are produced only when ordered by customers. Not only has the finished goods inventory been reduced, but raw materials and work in process inventories also have been cut.

"JIT techniques lowered [Hewlett-Packard's] production floor-space requirements by 40 percent."

Purchasing and producing only what is demanded by customers reduces inventory quantities (and dollars tied up in inventory). As inventory quantities decrease, problems hidden by inventory are exposed. Also, floor space devoted to inventories is freed-up for more-productive use. In two years, Hewlett-Packard reduced its work in process inventory by 82 percent. JIT techniques lowered production floor-space requirements by 40 percent.

Real-World Example: Georgia Box provides boxes to Davidson Exterior Trim, a maker of bumpers for GM and Chrysler. In the past, Georgia shipped a 2-week supply to Davidson. These boxes filled a 50,000-sq.-ft. warehouse. Georgia has adopted JIT and can now ship boxes just in time for Davidson to use them, greatly reducing the space needed for storage.

JIT production yields yet another benefit. Production problems are detected quickly and can be corrected before the company produces a large number of defective units. Early detection saves rework and scrap costs.

4. *Employee roles.* Production employees in JIT systems are trained to do more than operate a single machine. They also are trained to conduct routine maintenance, to perform setups, and to operate other machines. Cross-training increases flexibility, boosts employee morale, and decreases costs.

Exhibit 26-3 compares traditional production systems with JIT production systems. The next section demonstrates how JIT techniques lead to simplified cost accounting.

Traditional Production Systems	Just-in-Time Production Systems
Arrange machines by function	Arrange machines by sequence of operations
View high machine setup costs as acceptable	Work to reduce machine setup costs
Schedule production in large batches	Schedule production in small batches
Train production workers to operate a single machine	Cross-train machine operators to do other tasks

EXHIBIT 26-3
Traditional versus Just-in-Time Production Systems

Backflush Costing

Backflush costing is a standard costing system that starts with output completed and works backward to apply manufacturing costs to units sold and to inventories. Backflush costing arose during the 1980s when JIT production systems gained popularity, but the method can be used with any production system. Businesses that use backflush costing typically (1) apply standard costs to each product and (2) have either low inventories or constant levels of direct materials and work in process.

Backflush costing differs from the more common standard costing system described in Chapter 25. ◀▥ ◀▥ ◀▥ The latter is a sequential tracking system—it traces costs through each step of the production process, from direct materials to work in process to finished goods and cost of goods sold. The simpler backflush method does not track direct materials or labor to individual processes or products. It is less time-consuming, and thus less costly to use, than traditional standard costing.

OBJECTIVE 4
Record manufacturing costs for a backflush costing system

◀▥ ◀▥ ◀▥ We introduced the sequential tracking form of standard cost accounting on p. 1026.

EXAMPLE OF BACKFLUSH COSTING The following example shows that backflush systems do not use a separate Work in Process Inventory account. Consider the Mintel Company, which buys silicon wafers and converts them into integrated circuits used in computers. Mintel uses only two inventory accounts:

- Raw and In Process (RIP) Inventory, which is a combination of direct materials and work in process
- Finished Goods Inventory, which is the usual finished goods account

Mintel has only one type of direct manufacturing product cost: silicon wafers, which are labeled "raw." All other manufacturing costs, including labor and various chemicals, are indirect costs of conversion. No cost, whether direct or indirect, is separately tracked to integrated circuits in process.

The Mintel backflush system has two **trigger points**, points in operations that prompt entries in the accounting records. The trigger points are (1) the purchase of direct materials and (2) the transfer of completed units to finished goods.

Mintel has a JIT production system with minimal inventories of $100,000 of raw and in process and $900,000 of finished goods at July 31. In August, the company's accountants:

1. Record direct materials purchases of $3,020,000:

RIP Inventory	3,020,000	
Accounts Payable		3,020,000

(RIP Inventory is carried at standard cost. Variances are discussed later.)

2. Record the actual conversion costs incurred:

Conversion Costs	18,540,000	
Various Accounts (such as payables and		
accumulated depreciation)		18,540,000

3. Determine the number of finished units manufactured. Mintel produced 3,000,000 integrated circuits in August.

4. Calculate the standard cost per finished unit. The company develops a standard conversion cost for each operation in the production process. Standard costs are "built up" for each circuit, depending on the operations that work on it. Assume that August production was limited to one type of circuit. Its standard cost is $7 ($1 direct materials + $6 conversion cost).

Short Exercise: Ace Co. manufactures a product at a standard cost of $5/unit ($3 for materials; $2 for conversion costs). In May, when 100 units were completed and 98 were sold, total materials costs were $294 and conversion costs were $210. Beginning RIP inventory was $12 and beginning finished goods inventory was $25. What are (1) the standard cost of units completed in May? (2) COGS for May? (3) the ending balances in the RIP Inventory and Finished Goods Inventory accounts? *A:* (1) $500 ($5 × 100 units); (2) $490 ($5 × 98 units); (3) RIP Inventory = $6 ($12 + $294 − $300); Finished Goods Inventory = $35 ($25 + $500 − $490).

5. Record the standard cost of goods completed during the month; 3,000,000 units × $7 per unit = $21,000,000:

Finished Goods Inventory 21,000,000		
RIP Inventory		3,000,000
Conversion Costs		18,000,000

This is the second trigger point and the essence of backflushing. The costs were not tracked as the integrated circuits moved through the various manufacturing operations. Instead, completion of the units triggered the accounting system to go back and pull costs from RIP inventory.

6. Record cost of goods sold in the usual manner. Assume that 2,930,000 units were sold; 2,930,000 units × $7 per unit = $20,510,000:

Cost of Goods Sold 20,510,000	
Finished Goods Inventory	20,510,000

The August 31 inventory balances are:

RIP inventory ($100,000 + $3,020,000 − $3,000,000).................................	$ 120,000
Finished goods inventory ($900,000 + $21,000,000 − $20,510,000)	1,390,000
Total inventory	$1,510,000

Exhibit 26-4 shows Mintel Company's major backflushing accounts. Using no work in process account eliminates detail. Physical units in process may be tracked, but costs are not assigned to units in the accounting records via materials requisitions or time records. Instead, costs are identified with physical products only at the second trigger point, when goods are completed.

Our two-trigger-point system that uses completion of goods as the second trigger point is the most popular version of backflushing, but other trigger points may be used. For example, Toyota's cost accounting system for its Kentucky plant uses the sale of units, not their completion, as the second trigger point.

The simplest version of backflush costing has only one trigger point, the completion of output. This version's accounting records do not record the purchase of direct materials. It is appropriate for manufacturing systems that have almost no direct materials inventories and minimal work in process inventories.

VARIANCES IN BACKFLUSH COSTING SYSTEMS All standard costing systems share the same fundamental approach to accounting for variances. In our Mintel Company example, assume that the direct materials were purchased for $3,145,000. Thus the materials had an unfavorable price variance of $125,000. Entry 1 then becomes:

EXHIBIT 26-4
The Mintel Company's Major Backflushing Accounts

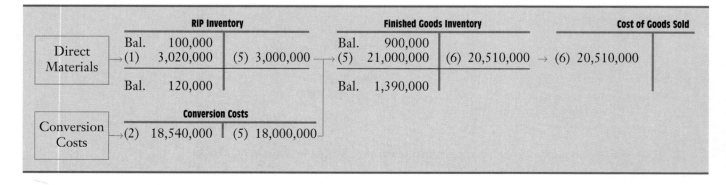

RIP Inventory	3,020,000	
Direct Materials Price Variance	125,000	
Accounts Payable		3,145,000

Direct materials efficiency variances are measured by working backward from the output units completed. Completed output is the key to determining what should remain in RIP inventory (beginning inventory plus purchases, less standard materials used for completed units). What should remain in inventory is compared with what does remain. Suppose that such a comparison for Mintel reveals an unfavorable efficiency variance of $9,000. The entry, which is linked to entry 5, is:

Direct Materials Efficiency Variance	9,000	
RIP Inventory		9,000

An unfavorable efficiency variance in backflush costing means that more direct materials were used for units *completed* during the month than the standard amount allowed. This entry pulls the cost of that over-standard material out of RIP inventory.

Conversion costs may be overapplied or underapplied in any month. Mintel's conversion costs are underapplied by $540,000 ($18,540,000 incurred – $18,000,000 applied to production) in August. Companies vary in how they write off underapplied amounts. If Mintel favors a monthly write-off, the August entry is:

Cost of Goods Sold...	540,000	
Conversion Costs		540,000

A company may close its Conversion Costs account annually instead of monthly. In that case, debits and credits accumulate throughout the year. An entry like the one above is made only at year end.

Companies that use backflush costing typically have low inventories. They therefore write off variances directly to Cost of Goods Sold.

SUMMARY PROBLEMS FOR YOUR REVIEW   MID-CHAPTER

PROBLEM 1

Indianapolis Auto Parts (IAP), a manufacturing company, uses activity-based costing. Chrysler has asked for a bid on 50,000 built-in baby seats that will be installed as an optional item on some Chrysler vans. IAP's costing system has the following features:

Activity	Cost Driver Chosen as Application Base	Activity Cost per Unit of Application Base
1. Purchasing	Number of purchase orders	$60.00
2. Assembling	Number of parts	0.50
3. Packaging	Number of finished units	0.90

Each seat has eight parts; direct materials cost per seat is $5. A total of 200 purchase orders will be necessary if Chrysler accepts IAP's bid.

Required

1. Compute the total cost that IAP will incur to purchase the needed parts and then assemble and package 50,000 baby seats. Also compute the average cost per unit.
2. Assume that for bidding purposes, IAP adds a 30-percent markup to total cost. What price will the company bid for the Chrysler order?
3. Suppose that instead of an ABC system, IAP has a traditional product costing system that applies all costs other than direct materials at the rate of $3.20 per direct labor-hour. The baby-seat order will require 100,000 direct labor-hours. What price will IAP bid on the basis of this system's total cost?

PROBLEM 2

The Flores Company manufactures telephones. Flores uses a backflush costing system with two trigger points: (1) when direct materials are purchased and (2) when completed telephones are transferred to finished goods inventory. The standard unit cost of a particular model is $37: $24 direct materials and $13 conversion costs. The standard cost of direct materials purchased during June was $2,540,000. Actual conversion costs totaled $1,295,000.

Flores completed 102,000 units of the model in June. The company sold 98,000.

Required

1. Prepare June journal entries for the transactions described.
2. Assume that the actual cost of direct materials purchased in June was $2,480,000. Record the purchase under this assumption.
3. Make the entry to close the underapplied or overapplied conversion costs to Cost of Goods Sold.

SOLUTION TO REVIEW PROBLEMS

PROBLEM 1

Requirement 1

Direct materials, 50,000 × $5.00	$250,000
Activity costs:	
Purchasing, 200 × $60.00	12,000
Assembling, 50,000 × 8 × $0.50	200,000
Packaging, 50,000 × $0.90	45,000
Total cost	$507,000
Divide by number of units	÷50,000
Average cost per unit	$ 10.14

Requirement 2

$507,000 × 130% = $659,100

Requirement 3

Direct materials, 50,000 × $5.00..............	$250,000
Other product costs, 100,000 × $3.20	320,000
Total cost	$570,000

$570,000 × 130% = $741,000

PROBLEM 2

Requirement 1

a. RIP Inventory	2,540,000	
Accounts Payable		2,540,000
b. Conversion Costs	1,295,000	
Various Accounts		1,295,000
c. Finished Goods Inventory...	3,774,000	
RIP Inventory (102,000 × $24)...		2,448,000
Conversion Costs (102,000 × $13)		1,326,000
d. Cost of Goods Sold (98,000 × $37)	3,626,000	
Finished Goods Inventory...		3,626,000

Requirement 2

a. RIP Inventory	2,540,000	
Direct Materials Price Variance		60,000
Accounts Payable		2,480,000

Requirement 3

e. Conversion Costs	31,000	
Cost of Goods Sold		31,000

Continuous Improvement and Product Life-Cycle Costs

To be competitive, businesses must continuously improve their processes and products. Many companies seek continuous improvement through cost management. The idea is for employees throughout the company's value chain to strive for cost reductions while maintaining high levels of quality, speed, and customer satisfaction.

Successful companies reduce costs at every stage of their products' life cycles. A **product life cycle** is the time from original research and development through the product's sales and on to the end of customer service. Some high-tech goods, such as disposable cameras, have life cycles of less than one year. Other products, such as automobiles and refrigerators, have much longer life cycles.

In this section we relate continuous improvement to the planning and control of new products. We use a Toyota example, because Toyota and other Japanese automobile companies pioneered the use of continuous improvement techniques.

Initial Planning

In Japan—and increasingly in the United States—a proposal to develop a new automobile model often is made by a product line's chief engineer. The initial focus is on the marketplace. What product, with what features, will have wide appeal to potential customers? At what price? How many cars will customers demand at that price?

Suppose that Toyota predicts that 400,000 units of a proposed Lexus model can be sold to retail dealers for an average price of $36,000. The company forecasts the model's life cycle to be eight years: three years in product development and five years in the marketplace.

After the sale price and production volume have been predicted, a planning committee made up of representatives of five business function areas (design, engineering, manufacturing, marketing, and accounting) calculates desired profit and allowable cost over the model's life cycle. Desired profit often is a set percentage of target sales. Allowable cost is the cost that will result in, or "allow," the desired profit. This cost includes all costs in the value chain, but we concentrate on the manufacturing function here. Thus, our measure of profit for evaluating the proposal is *life-cycle manufacturing contribution*—sales less manufacturing costs directly traceable to the product. The allowable average manufacturing cost over the Lexus model's life cycle is computed as follows:

Life-cycle average sale price	$36,000
Desired life-cycle manufacturing contribution (45%)..............	16,200
Allowable life-cycle average manufacturing cost	$19,800

Life-Cycle Budget

OBJECTIVE 5

Prepare a life-cycle budget for a product

The next step in the product development process is to prepare the initial life-cycle budget. A **life-cycle budget** compiles predicted revenues and costs of a product over its entire life cycle. The *initial* life-cycle budget is based on current technology and methods, before any cost-reduction efforts are made. The budget for our proposed Lexus model is given in Exhibit 26-5.

The life-cycle budget begins with sales minus the most prominent category of manufacturing cost—direct materials and parts. This category often is about 70 percent of the total manufacturing cost of a Japanese automobile. The Japanese industry depends heavily on its suppliers and works closely with them from early stages of design through the entire product life cycle.

The life-cycle budget shows the costs of all activities in the value chain that can be directly linked to the product. All costs in the budget are incremental. Thus, depreciation on equipment that will be purchased to produce the auto is included. Depreciation on existing equipment is excluded, because it will be the same whether the new model is produced or not.

After preparing the initial life-cycle budget, the planning committee managers decide whether the project is worth pursuing further. The budgeted average *manu-*

Sales @ $36,000	$14,400,000,000	(100%)
Direct materials and purchased parts @ $15,000	6,000,000,000	
Materials contribution margin	8,400,000,000	
Other costs direct to product:		
Variable conversion costs @ $2,425:		
Indirect materials @ $400 .... $ 160,000,000		
Direct labor @ $1,500 600,000,000		
Indirect labor @ $300 120,000,000		
Utilities @ $200 80,000,000		
Other @ $25 10,000,000	970,000,000	
Product contribution margin	7,430,000,000	
Fixed conversion costs:		
Indirect labor .... $ 200,000,000		
Depreciation on equipment 1,270,000,000		
Maintenance 200,000,000	1,670,000,000	
Life-cycle manufacturing contribution	5,760,000,000	(40%)
Other fixed costs:		
Design and engineering .... $ 760,000,000		
Marketing 900,000,000		
Customer service 450,000,000		
Other 50,000,000	2,160,000,000	
Life-cycle operating contribution	$ 3,600,000,000	(25%)

EXHIBIT 26-5
Initial Life-Cycle Budget for Proposed Lexus Model

facturing cost of the Lexus is $21,600 [($6,000,000,000 + $970,000,000 + $1,670,000,000)/400,000]. This average cost is $1,800 ($21,600 − $19,800) more than the allowable cost. Nonetheless, top management may approve the model. Why? Because cost-reduction efforts, especially in the design stage, may reduce the budgeted cost to the allowable amount.

OBJECTIVE 6
Relate target costing and kaizen costing to continuous improvement

Target Costing

To achieve allowable product costs, Japanese auto manufacturers attempt to reduce costs continuously through improvement of manufacturing, marketing, and customer service activities. However, they usually focus their cost-reduction efforts on the design stage. They have found that reductions built into the auto's design are considerably larger and more quickly realized than reductions from later efforts. **Target costing** is a cost management technique that helps managers set goals for cost reductions through product design.

Key Point: Before approving a new product, management must be convinced that the target cost is attainable.

Suppose that members of the product-planning committee believe that gradual continuous improvement *after production begins* will trim $300 from the life-cycle average cost of each car. The target unit manufacturing cost therefore is $20,100 ($19,800 allowable average cost + $300). Designers, engineers, and management accountants work together to develop a Lexus whose manufacturing cost *at the beginning of production* does not exceed the target cost of $20,100.

In the target-costing process, the planning committee budgets a currently attainable cost for each element of the proposed car. Many of these elements will be similar, if not identical, to elements in existing cars. Exhibit 26-6 shows the general approach. Then, cost planners use their experience to establish cost-reduction goals for the design teams in charge of the elements. At that point, value engineering begins.

Value engineering (VE) refers to the process of designing products that achieve cost targets and meet specified standards of quality and performance. Engineers dissect the company's processes and individual activities, rethinking their methods. After close study, they may redesign a painting process or the shape of a part. They may specify new materials or different tolerances, or substitute parts that are common to several product lines for parts designed for one product only. For example, *The Wall Street Journal* reported the following comment by an engineer whose design team was instructed to cut by 50 percent the number of unique fasten-

Cost	Product Elements					
	Engine	Body	Drive Train	Electronics	Interior	Other
Direct materials						
Purchased parts						
Indirect materials						
Direct labor						
≷						
Other						
Totals						

ers used in Nissan vehicles: "If we use fewer different screws, plant workers can save time changing the heads on their power tools. We can save 50 seconds per car. And one second equals one yen."

EXHIBIT 26-6
Initial Budget for Product Elements

STOP & THINK In what other way does reducing the number of different screws—or the number of unique parts in general—cut costs?

Answer: The number of unique parts, each with its own part number in a company's database, is a significant cost driver for many manufacturing companies. Each part must be planned, negotiated with suppliers, scheduled for use, ordered, received, stored, retrieved, and paid for. These activities are costly. Indeed, Tektronix, Inc.—a world-class producer of electronic test instruments—has reported that the number of unique parts accounts for over half of its materials-related overhead costs. In Nissan's case, using one screw instead of several similar items eliminates duplication of activities and thus reduces costs.

Through VE, design teams reduce the budgeted costs of automobile elements to their target costs. Target costing proceeds as follows (amounts assumed):

Product Element	Budgeted Cost	Value Engineering Cost Reduction	Target Cost
Engine	$ 3,000	$ 300	$ 2,700
Body	6,000	500	5,500
Drive train	2,000	150	1,850
≷	≷	≷	≷
Total	$21,600	$1,500	$20,100

Management accountants play important roles in the VE process. Accountants help engineers identify expensive activities whose costs can be reduced. Accountants also calculate the cost effects of design modifications. For example, in the chapter-opening story, accountants used activity-based cost data to help Chrysler managers evaluate dashboard-wiring alternatives for a new minivan. Target costing requires teamwork among the various functions of the business. Design engineers who lack "shop-floor" experience must work with production personnel and accountants to plan for low-cost manufacturing of products.

Kaizen Costing

The Japanese word for continuous improvement is *kaizen*. Japanese managers describe the relentless pursuit of cost reduction during the manufacturing stage of the life cycle as **kaizen costing**. In manufacturing, continuous improvement means achieving planned reductions in cost drivers such as setup times, waiting times, number of parts, and number of suppliers. Ideally, kaizen costing helps companies continuously lower the standard costs of their products—from their first months of production to the final months of their life cycles. As in target costing, accountants help to identify cost drivers and to measure the financial effects of changes.

Short Exercise: Readyever Co. is considering introducing a new battery with a budgeted sale price of $1. The desired life-cycle manufacturing contribution is $0.30 per battery. (1) Compute the allowable manufacturing cost per unit. (2) The kaizen cost reduction for the product's life cycle is expected to be $0.05 per battery; the value-engineering cost reduction goal has been set at $0.10 per battery. Compute the target cost and the original budgeted manufacturing cost. *A:* (1) $0.70 ($1 − $0.30); (2) target cost: $0.75 ($0.70 + $0.05); initial budgeted cost: $0.85 ($0.75 + $0.10).

EXHIBIT 26-7

Cost Reductions through Target Costing and Kaizen Costing

	Life-cycle sale price		$36,000
	Desired life-cycle manufacturing contribution...		16,200
Product Development and Design	Original budgeted cost	$21,600	
	Value-engineering cost reduction	1,500	
	Target cost...................................	**$20,100**	
Manufacturing	Cost reduction through **Kaizen costing**................................	300	
	Allowable life-cycle cost		$19,800

The contributions of target costing and kaizen costing to achieving the allowable life-cycle manufacturing cost of our Lexus model are shown in Exhibit 26-7.

Life-cycle budgeting, target costing, and kaizen costing are proven techniques for continuous improvement. Companies that combine these cost management tools with JIT production systems can become remarkably efficient.

Continuous Improvement and the Management of Quality

OBJECTIVE 7
Contrast the four types of quality costs

The quality of goods and services is a major feature of global competition. Businesses that deliver the best-quality products gain market share. Throughout the 1980s, Japanese automobile companies' share of the worldwide market soared, principally because of higher-quality products. Indeed, the nature of competition in many industries has been altered because of Japanese successes in using continuous improvement techniques.

Various definitions of quality exist. We define **quality** as the conformance of the attributes of a product or service to a specific set of standards. For example, Holiday Inn has standards regarding towels, soap, cleanliness, mattress firmness, light bulbs, television sets, and smoke alarms. One such standard may state that all bars of soap are to be replaced daily. Standards vary from company to company: Holiday Inn's standards may be very different from the standards of a budget chain such as Motel 6.

"Holiday Inn has standards regarding towels, soap, cleanliness, mattress firmness, light bulbs, television sets, and smoke alarms."

In today's competitive environment, customers demand ever-higher levels of quality. Managers know that if they do not provide it, their competitors will. Those managers are willing to incur costs to improve quality in order to reduce rework, scrap, and warranty costs and to minimize lost sales to dissatisfied customers. Many executives have communicated their commitment to quality improvements through *total quality management* programs.

Total Quality Management

Total quality management (TQM) is a formal effort to improve quality throughout an organization's value chain. Each business function examines its own activities and works to meet improvement goals. TQM also extends horizontally *across* business functions, from research and development to customer service. Accountants help operating managers understand how decisions in product design affect quality (and costs) in manufacturing, distribution, and customer service.

A hallmark of TQM is its emphasis on educating, training, and cross-training employees to increase and broaden their skills. Motorola's purchasing department provides an example. ◀▥ The department's managers wanted to reduce the time taken to process a requisition. Before starting the project, a departmental team took a two-day company course called High-Commitment, High-Performance Team Training. What they learned helped team members reduce the number of steps in handling a requisition from 17 to 6. They thereby slashed average processing time from 30 minutes to 3, enabling the department to process 45 percent more requisitions with no additional employees.

◀▥◀▥◀▥ The story that opens Chapter 4 (p. 133) describes how Motorola earned the Malcolm Baldrige National Quality Award for TQM.

Many managers emphasize that investments in the front end of the value chain generate savings in the back end. They want their companies to *design* and *build* quality into the product or service rather than having to *inspect* and *repair* it later. Carefully designed products and processes and high levels of employee training lead to reduced costs of inspections, rework, and warranty claims. The theme of total quality management is that superior work benefits the whole organization and inferior work hurts the whole organization. To expand this theme, we discuss the different types of quality costs.

Types of Quality Costs

Business analysts have identified four types of quality-related costs: prevention costs, appraisal costs, internal failure costs, and external failure costs.

1. Prevention costs are incurred to avoid poor-quality goods or services in the first place. For example, Arthur Andersen & Company and other accounting firms invest heavily in training personnel to use appropriate auditing and consulting procedures. Highly trained accountants are more likely to follow company policies and to make fewer errors.

2. Appraisal costs are incurred in detecting poor-quality goods or services. For example, Intel, a manufacturer of integrated circuits, incurs appraisal costs when it tests its products. One procedure, called *burn-in*, heats circuits to a temperature exceeding 2,000 degrees Centigrade. A circuit that fails the burn-in test has an unacceptably high likelihood of failing when being used by a customer.

"Intel, a manufacturer of integrated circuits, incurs appraisal costs when it tests its products."

3. Internal failure costs are incurred when poor-quality goods or services are detected before delivery to customers. An example is the labor of a BMW mechanic who reworks a faulty brake job after inspection by a supervisor. It is better to detect the problem in-house than to have it detected by the customer.

4. External failure costs are incurred when poor-quality goods or services are detected after delivery to customers. If the auto-repair shop fails to detect the faulty work, the flawed brakes will be discovered by the customer. Then the shop may have to repair the body of the car as well as the brakes. External failures can devastate a company's reputation.

Exhibit 26-8 shows additional examples of the four types of quality costs. Such costs can be difficult to measure. Cost accounting classifications often cannot identify individual components. For example, design engineers may spend only part of their time on quality-related activities. Allocating their salaries to various activities is necessarily subjective. It is especially difficult to measure the costs of external failures. Many managers believe that external failure costs dwarf the other three types. The most prominent external failure cost—profits lost because unhappy customers never come back—is not recorded in the accounts at all.

EXHIBIT 26-8
Examples of Quality Costs

Prevention Costs	Appraisal Costs
Training of company personnel and supplier personnel Improved materials Preventive maintenance Design engineering Improved equipment and processes	Inspection of incoming materials Costs of overseeing suppliers Inspection at various stages of production Inspection of final products or services
Internal Failure Costs	**External Failure Costs**
Production loss caused by quality-related downtime Rework Scrap Rejected product units Disposal of rejected units	Lost profits from lost customers Warranty costs Service costs at customer sites Sales returns and allowances due to quality problems Product liability claims

TQM programs do not necessarily compile the costs of quality. Instead, they may emphasize nonfinancial performance measures that are useful for day-to-day control purposes.

Nonfinancial Performance Measures

Nonfinancial performance measures include number of customer complaints, percentage of defective units, and first-time inspection pass rates. Companies use benchmarking to evaluate their performance on these dimensions. **Benchmarking** is the comparison of current performance with some standard. The standard often is the performance level of a leading outside organization.

Exhibit 26-9 lists examples of nonfinancial measures of quality used by the Cummins Engine Company, a manufacturer of diesel engines and trucks. The company's emphasis on continuous improvement of nonfinancial quality measures shows how businesses are broadening the scope of performance measurement. Many companies no longer are concentrating solely on financial measures such as operating income or return on investment. Companies are linking managers' compensation to performance on nonfinancial measures of quality, innovation, speed to market, and customer satisfaction. Nonetheless, the ultimate test is long-term profitability.

More and more managers believe that nonfinancial measures are the keys to profitability. They base a strategy for gaining competitive advantage on links such as those shown in Exhibit 26-10. As the exhibit indicates, continuous improvement of critical nonfinancial performance measures is essential for long-term success.

EXHIBIT 26-9
Examples of Nonfinancial Measures of Quality at Cummins Engine Company

- Percent of engines passing test first time
- Incoming supplier quality—percent of suppliers with acceptance rate of 98% or better
- Average downtime of bottleneck machines
- Number of machine breakdowns
- Number of product failures in the field
- Percent of engines delivered on time
- Average supplier delivery in percent of parts on time
- Training hours as percent of total hours worked

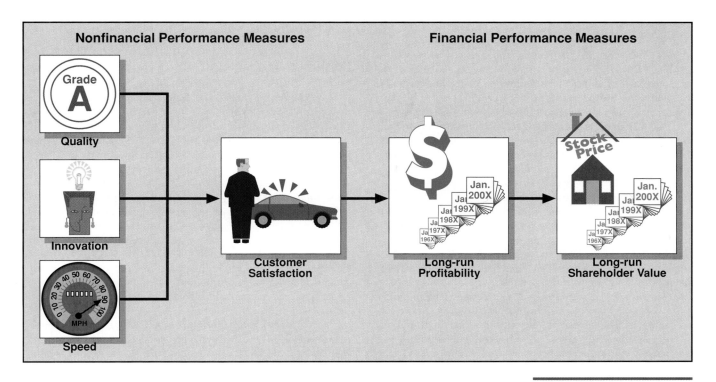

| Nonfinancial Performance Measures | Financial Performance Measures |

Quality — Grade A

Innovation

Speed — MPH

Customer Satisfaction

Long-run Profitability

Long-run Shareholder Value

EXHIBIT 26-10
Links among Performance Measures

SUMMARY PROBLEM FOR YOUR REVIEW

The Ishikawa Motorcycle Company is considering a new product line with a budgeted average sale price of $8,000. The desired life-cycle manufacturing contribution is $3,000 per motorcycle.

Required

1. Compute the allowable manufacturing cost per unit.
2. The kaizen cost reduction for the product line's life cycle is expected to be $250 per motorcycle. The value-engineering cost reduction goal has been set at $900 per unit. Compute the target cost and the budgeted unit manufacturing cost in the initial life-cycle budget.
3. Some of Ishikawa Company's costs are:

   a. Product callback repairs   c. Inspection costs of incoming materials

   b. Training of supplier personnel   d. Scrap

Identify each cost as belonging to one of the following categories of quality costs: prevention, appraisal, internal failure, or external failure.

SOLUTION TO REVIEW PROBLEM

1. Allowable cost is $8,000 − $3,000 = $5,000.
2. Target cost is $5,000 + $250 = $5,250. Initial budgeted cost is $5,250 + $900 = $6,150.
3. a. External failure
   b. Prevention
   c. Appraisal
   d. Internal failure

SUMMARY

1. *Describe the distinctive features of activity-based costing (ABC).* *Activity-based costing* focuses on activities as the fundamental cost objects. It uses the costs of activities as building blocks for compiling the costs of products and other cost objects. ABC uses multiple cost drivers to apply activity costs.

2. *Use activity-based costs to make management decisions.* ABC systems give better information for decision making than single-rate systems. Managers need to know the costs that will result from each action under consideration. ABC's more-precise relationships between costs and cost application bases produce more-accurate cost predictions.

3. *Compare the major features of a traditional production system and a just-in-time (JIT) production system.* Traditional production systems often produce enormous waste in both inventories and manufacturing processes. They have functionally arranged clusters of machines, "push" production, large inventories, long setup times, and relatively inflexible employees. *Just-in-time production systems* are designed to eliminate waste. They are characterized by sequentially arranged production activities, "demand-pull" production scheduling, minimal inventories, low setup times, and cross-trained employees. JIT systems rely on dependable suppliers to deliver materials just in time for production.

4. *Record manufacturing costs for a backflush costing system.* *Backflush costing* is a standard costing system that begins with output completed and works backward to apply manufacturing cost to units sold and to inventories. The more-common standard costing system is a sequential-tracking system that moves forward, step by step, from direct materials inventory

through cost of goods sold. Because backflush costing uses no Work in Process Inventory account, it simplifies record keeping.

5. *Prepare a life-cycle budget for a product.* Successful companies strive to reduce costs at every stage of their products' life cycles. A *life-cycle budget* compiles predicted revenues and costs of a product over its entire life. Managers compare budgeted costs with allowable life-cycle costs in order to estimate the cost reductions required to meet profitability goals.

6. *Relate target costing and kaizen costing to continuous improvement.* *Target costing* is a cost management technique that helps managers set goals for cost reductions through product design. *Value engineering* refers to design activities aimed at reducing the cost of a product without reducing its ability to satisfy the customer via high quality and performance. *Kaizen costing* is an explicit plan for cost reduction during the manufacturing stage of the product life cycle. Life-cycle budgeting, target costing, and kaizen costing are examples of continuous improvement in action.

7. *Contrast the four types of quality costs.* *Quality* is the conformance of the attributes of a product or service to a specific set of standards. *Total quality management (TQM)* is a formal effort to improve quality throughout an organization's value chain. Four types of quality costs are *prevention, appraisal, internal failure,* and *external failure.*

Nonfinancial measures are widely used to measure performance in quality management. *Benchmarking* compares current performance with some standard, often the performance level of a leading outsider.

SELF-STUDY QUESTIONS

Test your understanding of the chapter by marking the best answer for each of the following questions.

1. Activity-based product costs are likely to be more accurate than product costs computed with (*p. 1059*)
   a. A job order costing system   c. A single overhead rate
   b. A process costing system   d. Kaizen costing

2. Activity-based costing is part of an overall process known as (*p. 1058*)
   a. Activity-based management   c. Just-in-time manufacturing
   b. Total quality management   d. Backflush costing

3. Investments in activity-based costing systems are justified only if they lead to (*p. 1062*)
   a. More-accurate product costs   c. Better cost-driver analysis
   b. More-accurate inventory values d. Better management decisions

4. Which of the following is a value-added activity? (*p. 1063*)
   a. Waiting time   c. Moving time
   b. Processing time   d. Inspection time

5. Just-in-time (JIT) production systems are characterized by (*p. 1064*)
   a. Long setup times
   b. Small batch sizes

   c. Machines arranged by function
   d. Employee departments that specialize in machine setups

6. In backflush costing systems, trigger points are points in operations that prompt (*p. 1065*)
   a. Entries in the internal accounting system
   b. Collections of receivables
   c. Issuances of purchase requisitions
   d. Additions to cost of goods sold

7. Backflush costing is noteworthy because it eliminates the use of the following separate account (*p. 1065*):
   a. Work in Process Inventory   c. Finished Goods Inventory
   b. Accounts Receivable   d. Cost of Goods Sold

8. Value engineering is used to reduce costs from (*p. 1071*)
   a. Life-cycle sale price to allowable cost
   b. Initial budgeted cost to target cost
   c. Target cost to allowable cost
   d. Initial budgeted cost to allowable cost

9. Kaizen costing is a (*p. 1071*)
   a. Type of standard costing system
   b. Tool for compiling costs over a product's entire life cycle
   c. Tool that assists the product design stage
   d. Tool that assists the manufacturing stage

10. Which of the following is an example of an internal failure cost? *(p. 1074)*
  a. Inspection of services
  b. Product liability claims
  c. Rework
  d. Design engineering

Answers to the Self-Study Questions follow the Accounting Vocabulary.

ACCOUNTING VOCABULARY

Activity-based costing (ABC). A system that focuses on activities as the fundamental cost objects and uses the costs of those activities as building blocks for compiling costs *(p. 1058)*.

Activity-based management (ABM). A management process that focuses on the management of activities as the way to improve value delivered to customers *(p. 1057)*.

Appraisal costs. Costs incurred in detecting poor-quality goods or services *(p. 1073)*.

Backflush costing. A standard costing system that starts with output completed and works backward to apply manufacturing costs to units sold and to inventories *(p. 1065)*.

Benchmarking. Comparison of current performance with some standard. The standard often is the performance level of a leading outside organization *(p. 1074)*.

External failure costs. Costs incurred when poor-quality goods or services are detected after delivery to customers *(p. 1073)*.

Internal failure costs. Costs incurred when poor-quality goods or services are detected before delivery to customers *(p. 1073)*.

Just-in-time (JIT) production systems. Production systems designed to eliminate waste by such means as sequentially arranged production activities, low setup times, demand-pull production scheduling, and a high level of employee training and commitment *(p. 1064)*.

Kaizen costing. The relentless pursuit of cost reduction during the manufacturing stage of a product's life cycle *(p. 1071)*.

Life-cycle budget. A budget that compiles predicted revenues and costs of a product over its entire life cycle *(p. 1069)*.

Non-value-added activities. Activities that do not increase customer value or satisfy a company need *(p. 1063)*.

Prevention costs. Costs incurred to avoid poor-quality goods or services *(p. 1073)*.

Product life cycle. The time from original research and development through the product's sales and on to the end of customer service *(p. 1069)*.

Quality. The conformance of the attributes of a product or service to a specific set of standards *(p. 1072)*.

Strategy. A set of business goals and the tactics to achieve them *(p. 1057)*.

Target costing. A cost management technique that helps managers set goals for cost reductions through product design *(p. 1070)*.

Throughput time. The time between receipt of purchased materials and completion of finished products *(p. 1063)*.

Total quality management (TQM). A formal effort to improve quality throughout an organization's value chain *(p. 1072)*.

Trigger points. Points in operations that prompt entries in the accounting records *(p. 1065)*.

Value engineering (VE). The process of designing products that achieve cost targets and meet specified standards of quality and performance *(p. 1070)*.

ANSWERS TO SELF-STUDY QUESTIONS

1. c	3. d	5. b	7. a	9. d
2. a	4. b	6. a	8. b	10. c

QUESTIONS

1. "Activity-based costing systems provide more-accurate information than do traditional systems that use one overhead application rate. Every company should adopt ABC." Do you agree? Why or why not?

2. In what way do activity-based costing systems emphasize nonfinancial performance measures more than do traditional product costing systems?

3. "Activity-based costing systems promote coordination and communication across the various functions within a company." Do you agree? Explain.

4. "For costing-system alternatives, accountants have activity-based costing, job order costing, and process costing." True or false? Explain.

5. Give three examples of technology that have made the gathering of activity-based accounting information less expensive.

6. Contrast the traditional and just-in-time approaches to managing machine setups.

7. Describe "demand-pull" production scheduling.

8. Companies that implement JIT production systems usually reduce the number of suppliers they use. Give two benefits of doing so.

9. The backflush costing account RIP Inventory represents two accounts in a sequential-tracking system. What are they?

10. How do management accountants using a backflush costing system compute the amount of a direct materials efficiency variance?

11. "Prevention costs are the most important quality costs." Explain.

12. Why is target costing somewhat more important than kaizen costing in achieving allowable life-cycle manufacturing cost?

13. A new car's target cost is $15,000 per unit. Kaizen costing is expected to reduce its life-cycle average cost by $500. The car's life-cycle average sale price is budgeted at $43,500. If management expects the model to achieve its allowable average cost exactly, what is the desired life-cycle manufacturing contribution percentage (manufacturing contribution/sale price)?

14. "Data from an activity-based accounting system help managers evaluate prevention costs in a total quality management program." Explain.

15. "Financial performance measures are used almost exclusively in evaluating quality management efforts." Do you agree? Why or why not?

EXERCISES

Product costing in an activity-based costing system
(Obj. 1)

E26-1 Amarillo Motor Company uses activity-based costing to account for its manufacturing process. Company managers have identified four manufacturing activities: materials handling, machine setup, insertion of parts, and finishing. The budgeted activity costs for 19X5 and their cost drivers are as follows:

Manufacturing Activity	Total Budgeted Cost	Cost Driver Chosen as Application Base
Materials handling	$24,000	Number of parts
Machine setup	2,400	Number of setups
Insertion of parts	60,000	Number of parts
Finishing	9,000	Finishing direct labor-hours
	$95,400	

Amarillo Motor expects to produce 2,000 electric motors during the year. The motors are expected to use 120,000 parts, require 6 setups, and consume 500 hours of finishing time.

Required

1. Compute the four application rates for activity costs.
2. Compute the manufacturing product cost of each motor (excluding direct materials).

Product costing in activity-based and traditional systems
(Obj. 1)

E26-2 Panhandle Electric Motor Co. (PEMCO) has an activity-based costing system very similar to that of its chief rival, Amarillo Motor Company of Exercise 26-1. PEMCO's system has the same four activity categories and the same activity cost drivers. For 19X6, PEMCO's budgeted ABC application rates are:

Manufacturing Activity	Cost Driver Chosen as Application Base	Cost per Unit of Application Base
Materials handling	Number of parts	$ 0.25
Machine setup	Number of setups	300.00
Insertion of parts	Number of parts	0.75
Finishing	Finishing direct labor-hours	20.00

PEMCO produces two electric motor models: standard and deluxe. Budgeted data for 19X6 are as follows:

	Standard	Deluxe
Parts per unit	50.0	70.0
Setups per 1,000 units	3.0	3.0
Finishing direct labor-hours per unit	0.1	0.5
Total direct labor-hours per unit	2.0	4.0

The company's managers expect to produce 1,000 units of each model during the year.

Required

1. Compute the total budgeted cost for 19X6.
2. Compute the unit cost of each model.
3. Assume that PEMCO budgets conversion costs in the amount computed in Requirement 1. Assume also that PEMCO does not use an ABC system but instead applies conversion costs to products using a single rate based on total direct labor-hours. Compute the single rate, and use it to determine the cost per motor for each model.

E26-3 Refer to Exercise 26-2. For 19X7, PEMCO's managers have decided to use the same conversion costs per motor that they computed in 19X6. In addition to the unit conversion costs, the following data are budgeted for the company's standard and deluxe models for 19X7:

	Standard	Deluxe
Sale price	$110.00	$155.00
Direct materials	15.00	25.00

Suppose that because of limited machine-hour capacity, PEMCO can produce either 2,000 standard motors or 2,000 deluxe motors.

Required

1. If the company's managers rely on the ABC unit cost data computed in Exercise 26-2, which model will they decide to manufacture? (Assume that all nonmanufacturing costs are the same for both models.)
2. If the managers rely on the single-rate cost data, which model will they produce?
3. Which course of action will yield more income for PEMCO?

E26-4 Advanced MicroManufacturing (AMM) produces electronic components. AMM uses a backflush costing system with two trigger points: the purchase of direct materials and the transfer of completed units to finished goods. One of the company's products has a standard direct materials cost of $4 per unit and a standard conversion cost of $20 per unit.

During 19X3, AMM produced 500,000 units of the component and sold 480,000. It purchased direct materials whose standard cost was $2,100,000 and incurred actual conversion costs totaling $9,950,000.

Required

1. Prepare summary journal entries for 19X3.
2. Assume that AMM's January 1, 19X3, balance of the RIP Inventory account was $80,000. What is the December 31, 19X3, balance?
3. Is conversion cost overapplied or underapplied for the year? By how much?

E26-5 Ramius Engineering produces sonar components that are used on nuclear submarines. The company uses a backflush costing system with trigger points at direct materials purchase and completion of goods. In 19X4, Ramius Engineering purchased direct materials having a standard cost of $8,000,000.

Required

1. Record the journal entries that correspond to the following variances:
   a. Favorable direct materials price variance of $100,000.
   b. Unfavorable direct materials price variance of $50,000.
   c. Favorable direct materials efficiency variance of $70,000.
   d. Unfavorable direct materials efficiency variance of $40,000.
2. Conversion cost is underapplied by $60,000 in 19X4. Record the entry to close the Conversion Costs account to Cost of Goods Sold.

E26-6 Robotic Solutions produces robots for computer-controlled manufacturing systems. Sue Patrick, the engineering vice-president, is developing a proposal for a new line of robots with an expected life cycle of five years. The sales staff predicts that a total of 10,000 robots can be sold at an average sale price of $15,000. Patrick believes that with today's technology and methods, Robotic Solutions can manufacture the robots at the following product-line costs:

Fixed conversion costs............................	$34,000,000
Direct materials cost per unit	4,500
Variable conversion cost per unit.........	1,400

Required

1. Prepare an initial life-cycle budget through the life-cycle manufacturing contribution.
2. At the predicted volume level of 10,000 robots, what is the original budgeted cost per unit?
3. What percent of sales revenue is the initial life-cycle manufacturing contribution?

Using target costing and kaizen
costing to achieve cost reductions
(Obj. 6)

E26-7 The sales staff of Robotic Solutions of Exercise 26-6 is less sure of their sales volume prediction than they would like to be. They would not be surprised if life-cycle sales volume is as low as 8,000 units or as high as 12,000. Vice-president Sue Patrick is uneasy about the degree of uncertainty that exists.

The top management of Robotic Solutions has set as a goal for each product line a life-cycle manufacturing contribution of 44 percent of sales revenue. Patrick expects kaizen costing efforts to reduce the life-cycle average manufacturing cost of the robots by $100.

Required

1. Compute the allowable life-cycle average manufacturing cost of the product line.
2. Compute the target cost of the product line.
3. Determine the value engineering cost reduction per robot that is required to achieve the target cost if the life-cycle sales volume is (a) 10,000 units, (b) 8,000 units, and (c) 12,000 units.

E26-8 Household Engineering makes electronic components for microwave ovens. Fred Rogers, the president, recently instructed financial vice-president Ken Madden to develop a total quality control program. "If we don't at least match the quality improvements our competitors are making," he told Madden, "we'll soon be out of business."

Madden began his task by listing various "costs of quality" that Household Engineering incurs. The first five items that came to mind were:

a. Costs of inspecting components in one of Household's production processes.
b. Labor costs of product design engineers who work to design components that will withstand electrical overloads.
c. Costs of reworking defective components after discovery by company inspectors.
d. Costs of electronic components returned by customers.
e. Costs incurred by Household Engineering customer representatives in traveling to customer sites to inspect defective products.

Required

Classify each item as a prevention cost, an appraisal cost, an internal failure cost, or an external failure cost.

CHALLENGE EXERCISE

E26-9 Daviston Manufacturing Company completed two jobs in June 19X9. Daviston's accounting records recorded the following costs applied to the jobs with the company's activity-based costing system:

Activity	Application Base	Applied Cost Job BMW	Applied Cost Job BMX
Materials handling	Number of parts	$ 400	$ 800
Lathe work	Number of turns	4,000	12,000
Milling	Number of machine-hours	3,000	21,000
Grinding	Number of parts	400	1,600
Testing	Number of output units	150	3,000

Job BMX required 2,000 parts; 60,000 lathe turns; and 1,050 machine-hours. All 200 of the job's output units were tested, and all units of the BMW job were tested.

Required

1. How do you know that at least one of the costs recorded for the two jobs is inaccurate?
2. Disregard materials-handling costs. How many parts were used for job BMW? How many lathe turns did job BMW require? How many machine-hours? How many units were produced in the job?
3. A nearby company has offered to test all product units for $18 each. On the basis of ABC data, should Daviston accept or reject the offer? Give your reason.

PROBLEMS

P26-1A A National Semiconductor factory assembles and tests electronic components used in high-definition television sets. Consider the following data regarding component J47:

Product costing in an activity-based system
(Obj. 1)

Direct materials cost......................................	$71.00
Activity costs applied	?
Manufacturing product cost	?

The activities required to build the component follow:

Manufacturing Activity	Cost Driver	Activity Costs Applied to Each Unit
1. Start station	Number of raw component chassis	$1 \times \$ 1.30 = \$1.30$
2. Dip insertion	Number of dip insertions	$? \times 0.60 = 6.00$
3. Manual insertion	Number of manual insertions	$11 \times 0.80 = ?$
4. Wave solder	Number of components soldered	$1 \times 1.50 = 1.50$
5. Backload	Number of backload insertions	$6 \times ? = 4.20$
6. Test	Standard time each component is in test activity	$0.20 \times 90.00 = ?$
7. Defect analysis	Standard time for defect analysis and repair	$0.10 \times ? = 7.00$
Total		$\$?$

Required

1. Fill in the blanks in both the opening schedule and the list of activities.
2. How is labor cost identified with products under this product costing system?
3. Why might managers favor this activity-based accounting system instead of the older system, which applied all conversion costs on the basis of direct labor?

P26-2A Janelli, Inc., manufactures TV stands and uses an activity-based costing system. Janelli's activity areas and related data follow:

Product costing in an activity-based system
(Obj. 1, 2)

Manufacturing Activity	Budgeted Cost of Activity	Cost Driver Used as Application Base	Activity Cost per Unit of Application Base
Materials handling	$ 100,000	Number of parts	$ 0.10
Cutting	1,000,000	Number of parts	1.30
Assembling	3,000,000	Direct labor-hours	18.00
Finishing	60,000	Number of finished units	3.00

Two styles of TV stands were produced in April—the standard stand and an unfinished stand, which has fewer parts and requires no finishing. The quantities, direct materials costs, and other data follow:

Product	Units Produced	Direct Materials Costs	Number of Parts	Assembling Direct Labor-Hours
Standard TV stand	2,000	$24,000	30,000	3,000
Unfinished TV stand	3,000	27,000	36,000	2,800

Required

1. Compute the manufacturing product cost of each type of stand.
2. Suppose that upstream activities, such as product design, were analyzed and applied to the standard TV stands at $4 each and to the unfinished stands at $3 each. Similar analyses were conducted of downstream activities such as distribution, marketing, and customer service. The downstream costs applied were $18 per standard stand and $15 per unfinished stand. Compute the full product costs per unit.
3. Which product costs are reported in the external financial statements? Which costs are used for management decision making? Explain the difference.
4. What price should Janelli's managers set for unfinished stands to earn a unit profit of $10?

*Recording manufacturing costs for
a JIT backflush costing system
(Obj. 3, 4)*

P26-3A Nickoh Time Manufacturers produces precision hydraulic system components. The company uses backflush costing for its just-in-time production system. Its backflush system has two trigger points: the purchase of direct materials and the completion of hydraulic system components.

Nickoh Time has two inventory accounts: RIP Inventory and Finished Goods Inventory. On December 1, 19X3, the account balances were RIP Inventory, $3,000; Finished Goods Inventory, $5,000.

The standard cost of a component is $40: $15 direct materials plus $25 conversion costs. Data for December's activity follow.

Direct materials purchased	$227,000
Conversion costs incurred	373,000
Number of components completed	15,000
Number of components sold	14,800

Required

1. What are the major features of a just-in-time production system such as Nickoh Time's?
2. Prepare summary journal entries for December. Assume that there are no direct materials variances. Assume also that underapplied or overapplied conversion costs are closed to Cost of Goods Sold monthly.
3. Now suppose that the standard cost of direct materials purchased in December is $228,000. The actual cost remains $227,000. Nickoh Time accountants have computed the following variances: direct materials price variance, $1,000 favorable; direct materials efficiency variance, $800 favorable. Make the journal entries to record these variances.
4. Refer to Requirement 3. What is the December 31, 19X3, balance of RIP Inventory?

*Recording backflush costs, second
trigger point is sale
(Obj. 4)*

P26-4A Nickoh Time Manufacturers of Problem 26-3A has a two-trigger-point backflush costing system, but now suppose that the second trigger point is the sale, not the completion, of hydraulic system components. The company has only one inventory account, labeled simply "Inventory." Only direct materials costs are assigned to Inventory; the account balance is the sum of the costs of materials in the storeroom (if any), in process, and in finished units not yet sold.

Conversion costs are not inventoried. They are applied, at standard, to units sold. Continue to assume that the Conversion Costs account is closed to Cost of Goods Sold monthly.

Required

1. Prepare summary journal entries that correspond to the entries you prepared in Problem 26-3A, Requirement 2.
2. Why might a company use the point of sale as the second trigger point instead of the point of completion?

*Life-cycle budgeting, target
costing, and kaizen costing
(Obj. 5, 6)*

P26-5A Southwestern Telecom produces telephones. The company's *final* life-cycle budget for a new product line takes into account both expected value-engineering cost reductions and expected kaizen cost reductions from the company's new total quality management initiative:

Final Life-Cycle Budget, Proposed Telephone Product Line

Sales	$95,000,000
Direct materials	26,000,000
Materials contribution margin	69,000,000
Variable conversion costs	10,000,000
Product-line contribution margin	59,000,000
Fixed conversion costs	14,000,000
Life-cycle manufacturing contribution	$45,000,000

In this budget, the new product line achieves management's desired life-cycle manufacturing contribution exactly.

Required

1. Assume that the final life-cycle budget is based on an expected life-cycle sales volume of 1,000,000 telephones. Compute the life-cycle average sale price. Then compute the allowable life-cycle average manufacturing cost.

2. Repeat Requirement 1 for a sales volume of 2,000,000 telephones.

3. Again assume the budget is based on 1,000,000 units. Suppose that Southwestern Telecom's managers expect kaizen costing efforts to reduce variable conversion costs by $4 per unit and fixed conversion costs by a total of $2,000,000 over the product line's life cycle. Calculate the target cost.

4. If Southwestern Telecom's engineers predict a value-engineering cost reduction of $14 per unit, what is the original budgeted cost per telephone?

P26-6A Popular Electronics, Inc., is using a costs-of-quality approach to evaluate design-engineering efforts for a new laser disc player. Popular's senior managers expect the now-concluding engineering work to yield sizable savings in the costs of appraisal, internal failure, and external failure activities. The predicted reductions in activities over the two-year life cycle of the player are shown below. Also shown are the budgeted unit activity costs.

Analyzing costs of quality
(Obj. 7)

Activity	Predicted Reduction in Activity Units	Unit Activity Cost
Inspection of incoming materials	500	$ 40
Inspection of work in process	300	20
Number of defective units discovered in-house	2,000	45
Number of defective units discovered by customers	500	70
Lost sales to dissatisfied customers	150	100

Required

1. Calculate the predicted quality-cost savings from the design-engineering work.

2. Suppose that Popular spent $175,000 on design engineering for the new laser disc player. What is the net benefit of this "preventive" quality activity?

3. What major difficulty would Popular managers have in implementing this costs-of-quality approach? What alternative approach to quality improvement could they use?

4. How will what you learned from this problem help you manage a business?

(GROUP B)

P26-1B A Texas Instruments factory assembles and tests printed circuit (PC) boards. Consider the following data regarding PC Board XR1, which is used in various computers:

Product costing in an activity-based system
(Obj. 1)

Direct materials cost	$65.00
Activity costs applied	?
Manufacturing product cost	?

The activities required to build the PC boards follow:

Manufacturing Activity	Cost Driver	Activity Costs Applied to Each Unit
1. Start station	Number of raw PC boards	1 × $ 0.90 = $0.90
2. Dip insertion	Number of dip insertions	20 × 0.25 = ?
3. Manual insertion	Number of manual insertions	12 × ? = 7.20
4. Wave solder	Number of boards soldered	1 × 3.50 = 3.50
5. Backload	Number of backload insertions	? × 0.70 = 4.90
6. Test	Standard time each board is in test activity	0.25 × 80.00 = ?
7. Defect analysis	Standard time for defect analysis and repair	0.16 × ? = 8.00
Total		$?

Required

1. Fill in the blanks in both the opening schedule and the list of activities.

2. How is labor cost identified with products under this product costing system?

3. Why might managers favor this activity-based accounting system instead of the older system, which applied all conversion costs on the basis of direct labor?

Product costing in an activity-based system
(Obj. 1, 2)

P26-2B Blume Furniture Company manufactures rocking chairs in its two plants in West Virginia. The company uses activity-based costing. Its activities and related data follow.

Manufacturing Activity	Budgeted Cost of Activity	Cost Driver Used as Application Base	Activity Cost per Unit of Application Base
Materials handling	$ 200,000	Number of parts	$ 0.25
Cutting	880,000	Number of parts	1.10
Assembling	3,000,000	Direct labor-hours	15.00
Painting	70,000	Number of painted units	2.00

Two styles of chairs were produced in March—the standard chair and an unpainted chair, which has fewer parts and requires no painting. Their quantities, direct materials costs, and other data follow:

Product	Units Produced	Direct Materials Costs	Number of Parts	Assembling Direct Labor-Hours
Standard chair	5,000	$90,000	100,000	7,500
Unpainted chair	1,000	15,000	15,000	1,200

Required

1. Compute the manufacturing product cost of the standard chairs and the unpainted chairs.
2. Suppose that upstream activities, such as product design, were analyzed and applied to the standard chairs at $3 each and to the unpainted chairs at $2 each. Similar analyses were conducted of downstream activities such as distribution, marketing, and customer service. The downstream costs applied were $21 per standard chair and $16 per unpainted chair. Compute the full product costs per unit.
3. Which product costs are reported in the external financial statements? Which costs are used for management decision making? Explain the difference.
4. What price should Blume's managers set for standard chairs in order to earn a unit profit of $16.50?

Recording manufacturing costs for a JIT backflush costing system
(Obj. 3, 4)

P26-3B Hi-Tek Products produces mobile beepers. The company has a JIT production system and uses backflush costing. Its backflush system has two trigger points: the purchase of raw materials and parts and the completion of beepers.

Hi-Tek has two inventory accounts, RIP Inventory and Finished Goods Inventory. On August 1, 19X3, the account balances were RIP Inventory, $1,000; Finished Goods Inventory, $2,500.

Hi-Tek's standard cost per beeper is direct materials, $30; conversion costs, $20. The following data pertain to August manufacturing and sales activity:

Raw materials and parts purchased	$301,000
Conversion costs incurred	202,000
Number of units completed	10,000
Number of units sold	9,900

Required

1. What are the major features of a just-in-time production system such as Hi-Tek's?
2. Prepare summary journal entries for August. Assume that there are no direct materials variances and that underapplied or overapplied conversion costs are closed to Cost of Goods Sold at the end of the year.
3. Now assume that the standard cost of the raw materials and parts purchased in August is $300,700. The actual cost remains $301,000. Hi-Tek accountants have computed the following variances: direct materials price variance, $300 unfavorable; direct materials efficiency variance, $700 unfavorable. Make the journal entries to record these variances.
4. Refer to Requirement 3. What is the August 31, 19X3, balance of RIP Inventory?

P26-4B Hi-Tek Products of Problem 26-3B has a two-trigger-point backflush costing system, but now suppose that the second trigger point is the sale, not the completion, of mobile beepers. The company has only one inventory account, labeled simply "Inventory." Only direct materials costs are assigned to Inventory; the account balance is the sum of the costs of materials in the storeroom (if any), in process, and in finished units that have not been sold.

Conversion costs are not inventoried. They are applied, at standard, to units sold. Continue to assume that overapplied or underapplied conversion costs are closed to Cost of Goods Sold at the end of the year.

Recording backflush costs, second trigger point is sale
(Obj. 4)

Required

1. Prepare summary journal entries that correspond to the entries you prepared in Problem 26-3B, Requirement 2.
2. Why might a company use the point of sale as the second trigger point instead of the point of completion?

P26-5B The Computron Company makes personal computers that it sells through catalogs. The company's *final* life-cycle budget for a new product line takes into account both expected value-engineering cost reductions and expected kaizen cost reductions from the company's new total quality management initiative:

Life-cycle budgeting, target costing, and kaizen costing
(Obj. 5, 6)

Final Life-Cycle Budget, Proposed Computer Product Line

Sales	$250,000,000
Direct materials	67,500,000
Materials contribution margin	182,500,000
Variable conversion costs	22,500,000
Product-line contribution margin	160,000,000
Fixed conversion costs	60,000,000
Life-cycle manufacturing contribution	$100,000,000

In this budget, the new product line exactly achieves management's desired life-cycle manufacturing contribution.

Required

1. Assume that the final life-cycle budget is based on an expected life-cycle sales volume of 100,000 units. Compute the life-cycle average sale price. Then compute the allowable life-cycle average manufacturing cost.
2. Repeat Requirement 1 for a sales volume of 200,000 units.
3. Again assume that the budget is based on 100,000 units. Suppose that Computron's managers expect kaizen costing efforts to reduce variable conversion costs by $50 per unit and fixed conversion costs by a total of $10,000,000 over the computer line's life cycle. Calculate the target cost.
4. If Computron's engineers predict a value-engineering cost reduction of $250 per unit, what is the original budgeted cost per computer?

P26-6B Blade Close, Inc., is using a costs-of-quality approach to evaluate design-engineering efforts for a new electric shaver. The company's senior managers expect the now-concluding engineering work to yield sizable savings in the costs of appraisal, internal failure, and external failure activities. The predicted reductions in activities over the two-year life cycle of the shaver are shown below. Also shown are the budgeted unit activity costs.

Analyzing costs of quality
(Obj. 7)

Activity	Predicted Reduction in Activity Units	Unit Activity Cost
Inspection of incoming materials	300	$20
Inspection of work in process	200	25
Number of defective units discovered in-house	5,000	15
Number of defective units discovered by customers	800	30
Lost sales to dissatisfied customers	200	45

Required

1. Calculate the predicted quality-cost savings from the design-engineering work.

2. Suppose that Blade Close spent $40,000 on design engineering for the new shaver. What is the net benefit of this "preventive" quality activity?

3. What major difficulty would Blade Close managers have in implementing this costs-of-quality approach? What alternative approach to quality improvement could they use?

4. How will what you learned from this problem help you manage a business?

EXTENDING YOUR KNOWLEDGE

DECISION PROBLEMS

Costing jobs with a single overhead rate and then with ABC rates; making a decision on the basis of resulting product costs (Obj. 2)

1. National Electronics Systems is a government contractor that specializes in electronics systems for military applications. The company's current job order cost accounting system has two direct cost categories—direct materials and direct labor. Indirect manufacturing cost (overhead) is applied to jobs at the single rate of $23 per direct labor-hour.

   A task force headed by National's senior management accountant recently designed an ABC system with five activities. The ABC system retains the current system's two direct cost categories. Thus, it budgets only overhead costs for each activity. Pertinent data follow.

Activity	Cost Driver Used as Application Base	Cost per Unit of Application Base
Materials handling	Number of parts	$ 0.50
Machine setup	Number of setups	500.00
Machining	Machining hours	22.00
Assembling	Assembling direct labor-hours	18.00
Shipping	Number of shipments	1,200.00

All data necessary for both budgeting and job costing with this ABC system are collected automatically.

National Electronics Systems has been awarded two new government contracts, which will be produced as Job A and Job B. Budget data relating to the contracts follow.

	Job A	Job B
Direct materials cost	$30,000	$210,000
Direct labor cost	12,000	160,000
Number of parts	2,000	15,000
Number of setups	4	6
Number of machining hours	700	3,000
Assembling direct labor-hours	200	1,500
Number of shipments	1	1
Total direct labor-hours	600	8,000
Number of output units	100	1,000

Required

1. Compute the manufacturing product cost of each job, using the current costing system (with two direct cost categories and a single overhead application rate).

2. Suppose that National adopts the ABC system for product costing. Compute the manufacturing product cost of each job with this system, which has five activity-based overhead application rates instead of a single rate.

3. Which costing system more accurately assigns to jobs the costs of the resources consumed to produce them? Explain.

4. A dependable company has offered to produce both jobs for National for $600 per output unit. National may subcontract (buy from the outside company) either Job A only, Job B only, or both jobs. Which course of action will National managers take if they base their decision on (a) current system costs? (b) ABC system costs? Which course of action will yield more income? Explain.

2. Suppose that General Motors is using life-cycle budgeting and target costing in the development stage of a new Cadillac. The predicted average sale price of the car is $33,333. GM's senior managers desire a life-cycle manufacturing contribution of 40 percent of sales revenue. Company engineers predict that kaizen costing efforts will reduce the average cost of cars over the product life cycle by $200.

Using life-cycle budgeting and target costing to make a production decision (Obj. 6)

The original budgeted cost of the Cadillac is $23,100. Should GM managers decide to proceed with production if the value-engineering cost reduction is (a) $1,000? (b) $3,000? Explain.

ETHICAL ISSUE

Stanislav Precision Engineering manufactures complex metal products used in consumer goods. The company is under extreme pressure to reduce costs. Stanislav's managers have decided to implement a JIT production system in an effort to eliminate waste. Company accountants have decided to design a new ABC system to help identify and reduce non-value-added activities. The accountants are seeking the help of all operating personnel to identify and classify activities.

The problem? Stanislav's employees do not want to cooperate with the accounting staff. Many believe that the ABC program is just one more way to cut jobs. Specifically, they are afraid that "non-value-added activities" will be linked to "non-value-added employees," who will be fired.

Is it ethical to ask employees to participate in a management initiative that may eliminate some employees' jobs? Why or why not? What can Stanislav's management do to relieve the fears of employees and gain their cooperation?

Chapter 27
Special Business Decisions and Capital Budgeting

After studying this chapter, you should be able to

1. Identify the relevant information for a special business decision

2. Make seven types of special business decisions

3. Explain the difference between correct analysis and incorrect analysis of a particular business decision

4. Allocate joint processing costs to joint products

5. Use opportunity cost in decision making

6. Use four capital-budgeting models to make investment decisions

7. Compare and contrast popular capital-budgeting models

66We are looking at every process, every piece of property, eliminating what's not necessary or fundamental to our business. . . . These are not mindless, meat-axe cuts, however. We are . . . eliminating duplication and projects that offer little or no customer benefit. But we are also investing more in those projects that we believe will benefit our customers and create profit for IBM. 99

—LOUIS V. GERSTNER, JR., CHAIRMAN AND CEO OF IBM

When Jerome B. York became IBM's Chief Financial Officer (CFO) in 1993, he had one overriding goal: to find and root out waste. In his first year on the job, the confrontational executive made many key business decisions: He decided to eliminate 45,000 jobs, to close numerous plants, and to sell the company's unproductive real estate. The result? A savings estimated at $5 billion a year. And he was just getting started.

York's hands-on style has him criss-crossing the world to visit IBM's operating sites. One visit took him to the Austin, Texas, plant that makes glass-fiber circuit boards. The CFO observed every detail of the production process, not only asking managers to justify the way they do things, but also making suggestions for improvement.

After his visit to the Austin plant, York praised the work of plant manager Bill Amelio. Nonetheless, York issued a warning about the plant's future. "Making circuit cards is a business IBM doesn't have to be in, strategically. At some point, you'll wall out in this facility [need to expand], and when you ask for $30 million to rebuild, you'll have to show us you're highly competitive." *Source: L. Hays, "IBM's Finance Chief, Ax in Hand, Scours Empire for Costs to Cut," The Wall Street Journal, January 26, 1994, p. 1. Reprinted by permission. ©1994 Dow Jones & Company, Inc. All rights reserved worldwide.*

• • • • •

Should IBM make circuit boards or buy them from an outside supplier? If a company offers IBM a lump sum for a batch of circuit boards, should IBM accept or reject the order? Should IBM expand a circuit-board plant, convert the plant to produce another product, or sell the facility? In this chapter, we show how managers use accounting information to make these and other business decisions. We also discuss capital budgeting, a formal means of analyzing long-range investments.

Relevant Information for Decision Making

Business managers develop and implement strategies. A *strategy* is a set of business goals and the tactics to achieve them. The main financial goals in business are to earn profits and to build a strong financial position. Decisions center on how to achieve those goals.

Decision making means choosing among alternative courses of action. To choose, managers must make comparisons. After identifying alternatives, managers gather information to compare them. Then they analyze the information to determine the best action in light of their goals. Computers are ideally suited for decision analysis. They can compute the expected outcomes of alternative actions quickly and without computational error.

Managers often select the course of action that maximizes expected operating income over the period affected by the decision. To do this, they analyze relevant information. **Relevant information** is the expected future data that differ among alternative courses of action. How much *additional* revenue will IBM earn if it accepts the order for circuit boards? How much *additional* cost will the company incur if it produces and delivers the boards? These data make a difference to the decision maker. If depreciation, property taxes, and other fixed overhead costs will be the same whether the order is accepted or rejected, these items are irrelevant and may be ignored. The decision-making process is illustrated in Exhibit 27-1.

Consider an example of decision analysis that uses relevant information. Suppose that Pendleton Woolen Mills is deciding whether to use pure wool or a wool blend in the manufacture of a line of sweaters. Pendleton predicts the following costs under the two alternatives:

"Suppose that Pendleton Woolen Mills is deciding whether to use pure wool or a wool blend in the manufacture of a line of sweaters."

	Wool	Wool Blend	Cost Difference
Expected manufacturing cost per sweater:			
Direct materials	$10	$6	$4
Direct labor	2	2	0
Total cost of direct materials and direct labor	$12	$8	$4

Suppose that cost is the chief consideration in this decision. The cost of direct materials is relevant because this cost differs between alternatives (the wool costs more than the wool blend). The labor cost is irrelevant because that cost is the same for both alternatives.

We can compute the $4 cost difference between alternatives either from the cost of direct materials only or from the total cost. It helps to know that there is a $4 total-cost difference between the two alternatives. But it is more helpful for man-

EXHIBIT 27-1

How Businesses Make Special Decisions

agers to know that the $4 cost difference results from the materials, not from labor. Failure to identify the reason for the difference may lead managers to make an unwise decision.

Let us emphasize this important point about special decision analysis: Relevant information is expected *future* data that differ among alternative courses of action. Managers should base their decisions on expected future data rather than on historical data. Historical data often are supplied by the accounting system and are useful guides to predictions. However, historical data by themselves are irrelevant. They are useful only to the extent that managers can use them to predict future data.

This approach to making decisions is called the *relevant information approach*. The approach applies to a wide variety of decisions. Let us see how managers use relevant information to make seven special business decisions.

Special Sales Order

NAPA, a manufacturer of automobile parts, ordinarily sells oil filters for $3.20 each. A mail-order company has offered NAPA $35,000 for 20,000 oil filters, or $1.75 per filter ($35,000/20,000 = $1.75). This sale will not affect regular business in any way. Furthermore, it will not change fixed costs, it will not require any additional variable selling and administrative expense, and it will put to use idle manufacturing capacity. NAPA's manufacturing product cost of an oil filter is $2. Should NAPA accept the special order at a sale price of $1.75? At first glance, the answer appears to be no, because each oil filter costs $2 to make. But more thought must go into making this decision.

To set the stage for the analysis, examine NAPA's income statement. Exhibit 27-2 presents the income statement in both conventional and contribution margin formats.

Recall that the contribution margin format is based on variable costing. ◄▪▪ It categorizes expenses primarily as variable and fixed. The contribution margin format is more useful for decision analysis than the conventional format because it highlights how costs and income are affected by sales volume.

Suppose that NAPA made and sold 250,000 oil filters before considering the special order. Under absorption costing, the manufacturing cost per unit is $2 ($500,000/250,000). But the contribution margin approach shows that the *variable* manufacturing cost per unit is only $1.20 ($300,000/250,000). We now answer the

> **OBJECTIVE 2**
> Make seven types of special business decisions

◄▪▪◄▪▪◄▪▪ In Chapter 22 (p. 932) we defined variable costing as the method that assigns only variable manufacturing costs to products. See p. 921 for a comparison of conventional versus contribution margin income statements.

EXHIBIT 27-2
Conventional Format and Contribution Margin Format for NAPA's Income Statement

NAPA CORPORATION
INCOME STATEMENT
FOR THE YEAR ENDED DECEMBER 31, 19X2

Conventional Format		Contribution Margin Format		
Sales	$800,000	Sales		$800,000
Less manufacturing		Less variable expenses:		
cost of goods sold	500,000	Manufacturing	$300,000	
Gross margin	300,000	Selling and		
Less selling and		administrative	75,000	375,000
administrative		Contribution margin		425,000
expenses	200,000	Less fixed expenses:		
		Manufacturing	$200,000	
		Selling and		
		administrative	125,000	325,000
Operating income	$100,000	Operating income		$100,000

"The key question facing NAPA: What difference would the special sale make to the company's operating income?"

key question facing NAPA: What difference would the special sale make to the company's operating income?

Correct Analysis: Contribution Margin Approach

The correct analysis concentrates on the *differences* in revenues, expenses, and operating income, as Exhibit 27-3 shows. This special sale is expected to increase revenues by $35,000. The only cost affected by the sale is variable manufacturing cost, which is expected to increase by $24,000. Variable selling and administrative expenses are unchanged because NAPA makes no special effort to get the sale. Fixed expenses also do not enter the analysis because they do not change. To make the decision, NAPA should compare the additional revenues with the additional variable expenses of producing the goods. As long as the increase in revenues exceeds the increase in variable expenses, the sale contributes to profits. NAPA management predicts that the special sales order will increase operating income by $11,000.

Exhibit 27-4 gives NAPA's income statements both without the special sales order (column 1) and with it (column 2). It shows operating income under both courses of action. Column 3 repeats the summary by showing the differences that result from accepting the special order, an $11,000 increase in operating income.

EXHIBIT 27-3
Quick Summary of Special Sales Order Analysis

Expected increase in revenues—sale of 20,000 oil filters × $1.75 each.	$35,000
Expected increase in expenses—variable manufacturing costs:	
20,000 oil filters × $1.20 each	24,000
Expected increase in operating income	$11,000

EXHIBIT 27-4
Total Special Order Analysis— Income Statements without and with the Special Order

Short Exercise: What if, by accepting the special order, NAPA will have to buy a piece of stamping equipment that costs $12,000 in order to mark the oil filters with the mail-order company's logo? The equipment will then be discarded. How does this affect your decision? *A:*

Expected increase in operating income	$11,000
Less cost of equipment............	(12,000)
Loss from the special order	$(1,000)

NAPA CORPORATION
INCOME STATEMENT
FOR THE YEAR ENDED DECEMBER 31, 19X2

	(1) Without Special Order, 250,000 Units	(2) With Special Order, 270,000 Units	(3) Special Order Difference, 20,000 Units Total	Per Unit
Sales...	$800,000	$835,000	$35,000	$1.75
Variable expenses:				
Manufacturing......................	$300,000	$324,000	$24,000	$1.20
Selling and administrative...................	75,000	75,000	—	—
Total variable expenses...........................	375,000	399,000	24,000	1.20
Contribution margin	425,000	436,000	11,000	0.55
Fixed expenses:				
Manufacturing......................	200,000	200,000	—	—
Selling and administrative...................	125,000	125,000	—	—
Total fixed expenses..............	325,000	325,000	—	—
Operating income	$100,000	$111,000	$11,000	$0.55

We have shown two correct ways of deciding whether to accept or reject a special sales order at a price less than total cost per unit: (1) a quick summary of differences (Exhibit 27-3) and (2) total revenues, expenses, and operating income under both courses of action (Exhibit 27-4). Whether to use a quick summary or a total analysis depends on the question you are addressing. The summary answers this question: What will be the *difference* in revenues, expenses, and operating income if the business accepts the special order? The total analysis shows the summary of differences and answers an additional question: What will be the *total* revenues, expenses, and operating income under the alternative courses of action? Whether to accept or reject the special sales order can be decided from either analysis.

Many companies store their cost data in computers. A manager can enter the special sale price and call up the variable expenses and any fixed expenses that will change because of the special sale. The change in operating income is computed automatically. By trying different sale prices, the manager can come up with a range of acceptable options. Armed with this knowledge, the company may propose a different sale price to the buyer. More knowledge places the firm in a stronger bargaining position.

Incorrect Analysis: Ignoring the Nature of Fixed Costs

Now consider an incorrect analysis of the NAPA special sales order decision. The conventional approach, using only the left-hand side of Exhibit 27-2, leads to an incorrect measure of the change in expenses resulting from the sale.

> **OBJECTIVE 3**
>
> Explain the difference between correct analysis and incorrect analysis of a particular business decision

Total manufacturing costs	$ 500,000
Units produced	÷250,000
Manufacturing product cost per unit ($500,000/250,000)	$ 2.00
Expected increase in revenues—sale of 20,000 oil filters × $1.75 each	$ 35,000
Expected increase in expenses—*total* manufacturing expenses:	
20,000 oil filters × $2.00 each	40,000
Expected decrease in operating income	$ (5,000)

A manager who follows this approach reasons that it costs $2 to make an oil filter. In this view, it is unprofitable to sell the product for less than $2. *The flaw in this analysis arises from treating a fixed cost as though it changes in total like a variable cost does.* To manufacture one additional oil filter will cost NAPA $1.20—the variable manufacturing cost. Fixed expenses are irrelevant to the decision because NAPA will incur the fixed expenses whether or not the company accepts the special sales order. The addition of 20,000 oil filters will not add to *total* fixed expenses. As volume changes, manufacturing costs will increase at the rate of $1.20 per unit, not $2.00 per unit. In this analysis, the variable expenses are relevant, and the fixed expenses are irrelevant.

Short Run versus Long Run: Other Factors to Consider

Our special sales order analysis focused on short-run factors—the expected effect on operating income. We also must consider long-run factors. What will be the impact on customers? Will acceptance of the order at $1.75 per unit hurt NAPA's ability to sell the product at the regular price of $3.20? Will regular customers find out about the special price and balk at paying more? And how will competitors react? Will they view this sale as the start of a price war?

Accepting the order yields an $11,000 advantage in operating income. Will potential disadvantages offset this income? The sales manager may think so and reject the order. In turning away the business, the manager would say that the company is better off passing up $11,000 now to protect its long-run market position. Rejecting the special sales order is like making an $11,000 "investment" in the company's long-run future.

Deletion of Products, Departments, Territories— Fixed Costs Unchanged

To analyze whether a company should drop a product line, a department, or a territory, we modify our NAPA example. Assume that NAPA already is operating at the 270,000-unit level, as shown in column 2 of Exhibit 27-4. Suppose that the company is considering dropping the *air cleaner* product line that makes up $35,000 (20,000 units) of its sales. An income statement that is divided by product line follows:

Short Exercise: A hardware store operates three departments: paint, lumber, and tools. The paint department reports the following:

Sales........................	$ 75,000
Variable costs	60,000
Contribution margin	15,000
Fixed costs.............	25,000
Operating loss........	$ (10,000)

Should management discontinue the paint department if fixed costs will not be affected by the decision? *A:* As long as a department has a positive contribution margin, it is contributing to overall profits and should not be discontinued. Also, paint department sales may have a positive effect on sales in other departments.

Short Exercise: Spiff, Inc., sells liquid shoe polish, paste shoe polish, and saddle soap. The income statement for the saddle soap product line follows:

Sales	$81,200
Less Expenses:	
Variable costs	74,500
Fixed costs.............	14,500
Operating income (loss)	$ (7,800)

How much would Spiff's operating income change if the saddle soap line were discontinued and fixed costs would not be affected by the decision? *A:* Operating income would decrease by $6,700, the contribution margin ($81,200 – $74,500) of the saddle soap line.

		Product Line	
	Total	Oil Filters	Air Cleaners
Units...	270,000	250,000	20,000
Sales...	$835,000	$800,000	$ 35,000
Variable expenses	399,000	375,000	24,000
Contribution margin........................	436,000	425,000	11,000
Fixed expenses:			
Manufacturing..............................	200,000	185,185*	14,815*
Selling and administrative..............	125,000	115,741†	9,259†
Total fixed expenses......................	325,000	300,926	24,074
Operating income (loss)....................	$111,000	$124,074	$(13,074)

*$200,000/270,000 units = $0.74074 per unit; 250,000 units × $0.74074 = $185,185; 20,000 units × $0.74074 = $14,815

†$125,000/270,000 units = $0.46296 per unit; 250,000 units × $0.46296 = $115,741; 20,000 units × $0.46296 = $9,259

To determine product-line operating income, NAPA allocates fixed expenses in proportion to the number of units sold. Dividing the fixed manufacturing expense of $200,000 by 270,000 units yields a fixed manufacturing cost of $0.74074 per unit. Allocating this unit cost to the 250,000 units of the oil filter product line results in a fixed manufacturing cost of $185,185 for this product. The same procedure allocates $14,815 to air cleaners. Fixed selling and administrative expenses are allocated in the same manner. Using this allocation method results in an operating loss of $13,074 for air cleaners. Should the air cleaner product line be dropped?

This situation is similar to the example we studied for the special sales order. The relevant items still are the changes in revenues and expenses, but now we are considering a decrease in volume instead of an increase. The difference between the change in revenues and the change in expenses is the change in operating income, as shown in Exhibit 27-5. Again, only the variable expenses are relevant to the decision. In the short run, dropping air cleaners will decrease operating income by $11,000. This analysis suggests that NAPA should *not* drop air cleaners.

EXHIBIT 27-5

Deletion of a Product—Fixed Costs Unchanged

Expected decrease in revenues:	
Sale of 20,000 air cleaners × $1.75 each...	$35,000
Expected decrease in expenses:	
Variable manufacturing costs—20,000 air cleaners × $1.20 each	24,000
Expected decrease in operating income...	$11,000

Deletion of Products, Departments, Territories— Fixed Costs Changed

In our previous examples, total fixed expenses did not change. But do not jump to the conclusion that fixed costs always are irrelevant. Suppose that NAPA employs an engineer to improve the efficiency of the air cleaner product line. The engineer is paid $12,000, which can be avoided if the company stops producing air cleaners. Exhibit 27-6 shows how this additional savings affects the analysis.

Operating income will increase by $1,000 if NAPA drops air cleaners. In this situation, a fixed cost is relevant, so the change in the cost must be considered. Special decisions should take into account all costs affected by the choice of action. Managers must ask, What costs—variable *and* fixed—will change?

EXHIBIT 27-6

Deletion of a Product—Fixed Costs Changed

Expected decrease in revenues:		
Sale of air cleaners..		$35,000
Expected decrease in expenses:		
Variable manufacturing costs	$24,000	
Fixed expenses—engineer fee	12,000	
Expected decrease in total expenses		36,000
Expected increase in operating income..............		$ 1,000

Short Exercise: Refer to the previous Short Exercise. How much would Spiff's operating income change if $7,500 of the fixed costs could be eliminated? *A:* It would increase by $800 because the decrease in fixed costs is greater than the decrease in contribution margin ($7,500 – $6,700).

Which Product to Emphasize

Companies do not have unlimited resources. Thus, they must decide which products to emphasize and which to deemphasize. This decision has a profound impact on profits. If salespersons begin to push a product with a low profit margin, the company's operating income may decrease even though they succeed in selling the product. How should a manager decide which product to emphasize? Decisions such as this are important because of limits to production capacity, store display space, and advertising budgets.

Consider Esprit, a clothing manufacturer that produces shirts and slacks. The following data are relevant:

	Product	
	Shirts	**Slacks**
Per unit:		
Sale price	$30	$60
Variable expenses..............................	12	48
Contribution margin	$18	$12
Contribution margin ratio:		
Shirts—$18/$30	60%	
Slacks—$12/$60............................		20%

The data suggest that shirts are more profitable than slacks. But an important piece of information has been withheld—the time it takes to manufacture each product. This factor, called the *limiting factor*, or **constraint**, restricts production or sale of a product. In some companies, the constraint is production capacity. The factory or the labor force may be unable to produce more than a specified maximum number of units. This constraint—the limit to how much the company can produce—may be stated in terms of labor-hours, machine-hours, materials, or square feet of shelf

Short Exercise: A firm makes two products, a hand mixer and a can opener. It takes 1/2 hour to make a hand mixer and 2 hours to make a can opener.

	Hand Mixer	Can Opener
Sale price.........	$8	$10
Variable cost....	6	5
Contribution margin	$2	$ 5

If only 200,000 labor-hours are available, which product should be produced? *A:* Produce the mixer.

	Hand Mixer	Can Opener
Contrib. margin.	$ 2	$ 5
Hours required..	÷1/2	2
Contrib. margin per hr.............	$ 4	$2.50

Producing the mixer will yield a profit of $800,000 (200,000 × $4); producing the can opener will yield a profit of only $500,000 (200,000 × $2.50).

EXHIBIT 27-7
Which Product to Emphasize

	Product	
	Shirts	**Slacks**
(1) Units that can be produced each hour	1	2
(2) Contribution margin per unit	× $18	× $12
Contribution margin per hour (1) × (2)	$18	$24
Capacity—number of hours	× 20,000	× 20,000
Total contribution margin at full capacity..........	$360,000	$480,000

space. (For example, storage may be limited to 50,000 square feet of space in a warehouse.) These factors vary from company to company. Other companies are constrained by sales. Competition may be stiff, and the business may be able to sell only so many units.

"Suppose that Esprit can produce two pairs of slacks or one shirt per hour. . . . Which product should it emphasize?"

Suppose that Esprit can produce two pairs of slacks *or* one shirt per hour. The company has 20,000 hours of capacity. Which product should it emphasize?

The way to maximize profits for a given capacity is to obtain the highest possible contribution margin *per unit of the limiting factor*—in our example, direct labor- hours. The analysis includes two steps. First, determine the contribution margin per unit of the limiting factor. Second, multiply this unit contribution margin by the company's capacity, stated in the number of units of the limiting factor.

Exhibit 27-7 shows how to decide which product to emphasize when there is a limiting factor. Esprit should emphasize slacks. Slacks contribute more profit per hour and thus more total profit from all available hours.

Make or Buy

Short Exercise: Z Co. has been purchasing a part for $3. Z believes that it can make the part by utilizing excess capacity. Z predicts that it will need 50,000 of the parts. The unit costs have been estimated as follows:

Direct materials............ $1.25
Direct labor 0.80
Variable overhead......... 0.50
Var. cost per unit $2.55

Fixed costs will not change if the part is produced. Should Z make or buy the part? *A:* Make the part.

Var. cost to make
 ($2.55 × 50,000) $127,500
Var. cost to buy
 ($3.00 × 50,000) 150,000
Advantage to making $ 22,500

Manufactured goods often include specialized parts. Overhead garage doors, for example, are activated by electronic controls. Overhead Door Company, a garage-door manufacturer, may face this question: Should we manufacture the control device ourselves or buy it from an outsider? Tell City Furniture Company may ask, Should we stain and lacquer the furniture we manufacture or hire an outsider to do the finish work? Assuming that quality is unaffected, at the heart of the make-or-buy decision is *how best to use available facilities*.

Let us explore how to answer a make-or-buy question. NAPA's production process uses Part No. 4, which has the following manufacturing costs for 250,000 units:

	Total Cost (250,000 Units)
Part No. 4 costs:	
Direct materials...	$ 40,000
Direct labor	20,000
Variable overhead..	15,000
Fixed overhead	50,000
Total manufacturing cost	$125,000
Cost per unit ($125,000/250,000)....................................	$0.50

Another manufacturer offers to sell NAPA the same part for $0.37 per unit. Should NAPA make Part No. 4 or buy it from the outside supplier? NAPA's $0.50 unit cost of manufacturing the part is $0.13 higher than the cost of buying it outside. At first

EXHIBIT 27-8

Make or Buy

Part No. 4 costs:	Make Part	Buy Part	Cost to Make Minus Cost to Buy
Direct materials...................................	$ 40,000	$ —	$40,000
Direct labor...	20,000	—	20,000
Variable overhead...............................	15,000	—	15,000
Fixed overhead....................................	50,000	40,000	10,000
Purchase cost from outsider (250,000 × $0.37)	—	92,500	(92,500)
Total cost of Part No. 4	$125,000	$132,500	$ (7,500)
Cost per unit—250,000 units	$0.50	$0.53	$(0.03)

glance, it appears that NAPA should purchase Part No. 4. But the answer to a make-or-buy question is rarely as clear as this comparison suggests. The key to this decision lies in the difference in expected future costs between the alternatives. Which costs will differ depending on whether NAPA makes or buys Part No. 4?

Assume that by purchasing the part, NAPA can avoid all variable manufacturing costs and reduce its fixed overhead cost by $10,000. (Fixed overhead will decrease to $40,000.) Exhibit 27-8 shows the differences in costs between the make and buy alternatives.

It would cost less to make the part than to buy it outside. The net savings from making 250,000 units of Part No. 4 is $7,500, which is $0.03 per unit. This savings exists despite the make alternative's $10,000 of *incremental* fixed overhead cost.

Best Use of Facilities

The cost data in the make-or-buy decision indicate that making the part is the better course of action. The focus is on making the best use of available facilities over the planning horizon. This point is illustrated further with a make-or-buy decision that includes three alternative actions.

Suppose that buying Part No. 4 from an outside supplier will release factory facilities that can be used to manufacture another product. The expected annual profit contribution of this product is $18,000. Managers must decide among three alternatives: (1) make, (2) buy and leave facilities idle, or (3) buy and use facilities to manufacture the other product. The alternative with the lowest *net* cost indicates the best use of the facilities. A comparison of net cost under the three alternatives is given in Exhibit 27-9.

Short Exercise: Refer to the previous Short Exercise. Suppose that making the part increases fixed costs by $5,000 and that Z Co. has an opportunity to rent idle facilities to Y Co. for $20,000. How do these changes affect the decision? *A:* There is a $2,500 advantage to buying the part.

	Make	Buy
Variable costs to make	$127,000	
Fixed costs to make.............	5,000	
Cost to buy		$150,000
Rent of space ...		(20,000)
Net cost	$132,500	$130,000)

Fixed costs are relevant to this decision because they are different under the two alternatives. The fixed costs are $5,000 more if the part is made rather than purchased.

EXHIBIT 27-9

Best Use of Facilities

	Make Part	Buy Part and Leave Facilities Idle	Buy Part and Use Facilities for Other Product
Expected cost of obtaining 250,000 units of Part No. 4 (amounts from Exhibit 27-8).........	$125,000	$132,500	$132,500
Expected profit contribution from the other product	—	—	(18,000)
Expected net cost of obtaining 250,000 units of Part No. 4	$125,000	$132,500	$114,500

This analysis of net cost indicates that buying Part No. 4 outside and using the vacated facilities to manufacture the other product is the best choice. If the facilities remain idle, the company will forgo the opportunity to earn $18,000.

Special decisions often include qualitative factors—that is, factors that are difficult to quantify. For example, NAPA managers may believe they can better control the quality of Part No. 4 by manufacturing it themselves. This factor argues for NAPA's making the part. But the outside supplier may be located very close to NAPA's assembly plant. It may be able to achieve a higher on-time delivery rate than NAPA's own parts plant. This factor favors buying the part from the outside supplier. NAPA's managers should consider these qualitative factors as well as revenue and cost differences in making their decision.

Replacement of Equipment

Another business decision that requires managers to analyze relevant costs is whether to replace equipment. Many owners of equipment hold it too long because they want it to be "fully depreciated," or they want their money to be "fully recovered," before disposal. The point here is important but widely misunderstood: The book value of old equipment is irrelevant. Book value is a **sunk cost**, a past cost that is unavoidable because it cannot be changed no matter what action is taken. Book value is not an expected future cost that will differ among alternatives.

The following example shows why book value is irrelevant. The manager of a bowling alley is deciding whether to replace some old pin-setting equipment with new, more efficient equipment:

Short Exercise: Myatt Electronics purchased a machine a year ago for $30,000 but is considering replacing it with a machine that would cost $45,000. Additional information follows:

	Present Machine	Proposed Machine
Life..................	6 years	5 years
Cash oper. costs	$21,000	$7,000
Depreciation	5,000	9,000
Book value........	25,000	—
Disposal value now...............	5,000	—
Disposal value in 5 years	–0–	–0–

Should Myatt keep or replace the machine? *A:* Replace. Relevant costs will be less if Myatt replaces the machine:

	Keep	Replace
Cash oper. costs for 5 yrs	$105,000	$35,000
Disposal value now...............		(5,000)
Acquisition cost		45,000
Rel. costs...........	$105,000	$75,000

	Old Pin-Setting Equipment	Potential Replacement Equipment
Annual cash operating costs*...................................	$15,000	$ 7,000
Original cost...	35,000	22,000
Accumulated depreciation.....................................	20,000	—
Book value	15,000	—
Current disposal value in cash	3,000	—
Future disposal value in cash (in 3 years)..............	0	0
Current age in years	4	0
Useful life remaining in years	3	3

*Maintenance, power, repairs, parts, lubricants.

Exhibit 27-10 presents the relevant data for this decision. The advantage of replacement is $5,000 for the three years taken together. The time horizon is not confined to the next year only. Instead, the manager considers the full three-year life of the new equipment. In this way, he or she takes an appropriate long-run view.

The following items are *irrelevant* in equipment replacement decisions:

● *The book value of old equipment*, because it is a past (historical) cost that is common to all decision alternatives.

EXHIBIT 27-10

Cost Comparison: Replacement-Decision Relevant Items for Three Years

	Keep Old Equipment	Replace Old Equipment	Difference
Cash operating costs: $15,000 × 3 for old equipment and $7,000 × 3 for new equipment...........................	$45,000	$21,000	$24,000
Disposal value of old equipment.....................................	—	(3,000)	3,000
Acquisition cost of new equipment.................................	—	22,000	(22,000)
Total relevant costs...	$45,000	$40,000	$ 5,000

	Keep Old Equipment	Replace Old Equipment	Difference
Cash operating costs, $15,000 × 3 and $7,000 × 3	$45,000	$21,000	$24,000
Book value of old equipment:			
Periodic write-off as depreciation...................................	{ 15,000		
or			—
Lump-sum write-off...	{	15,000*	
Disposal value...	—	(3,000)*	3,000
Acquisition cost of new equipment....................................	—	22,000	(22,000)
Total costs...	$60,000	$55,000	$ 5,000

*The replacement year's income statement condenses these two items into one as "loss on disposal" of $15,000 – $3,000 = $12,000.

- *The gain or loss on disposal*, which is the difference between book value and disposal value of equipment. The book value is irrelevant, but the disposal value typically is relevant. The difference, that is, the gain or loss on disposal, combines the two, which confuses the issue.

EXHIBIT 27-11
Cost Comparison: Replacement-Decision Relevant and Irrelevant Items for Three Years

Exhibit 27-11 illustrates the irrelevance of book value. The exhibit includes both relevant and irrelevant items to reinforce the point that irrelevant items, properly analyzed, do not make a difference in the decision.

We now turn our attention to the nature of joint products. Then we discuss our final special business decision—whether to sell joint products with or without separate processing.

Joint Products

A manufacturing process that produces more than one product simultaneously is called a *joint process*. **Joint products** are the goods produced in a joint process. For example, the process of making soap produces both lanolin and other oils for cosmetics. The smelting of copper ore produces the joint products copper and ammonia. These joint products are identified as individual products only after they reach a juncture in the joint process that is known as the *split off point*.

The process of refining crude oil produces the joint products gasoline and natural gas. Exhibit 27-12 diagrams this joint process. After gasoline and natural gas are separated, further costs of the two products can be identified separately. But what

OBJECTIVE 4
Allocate joint processing costs to joint products

EXHIBIT 27-12
Joint Products

EXHIBIT 27-13
Allocation of Joint Cost to Joint Products

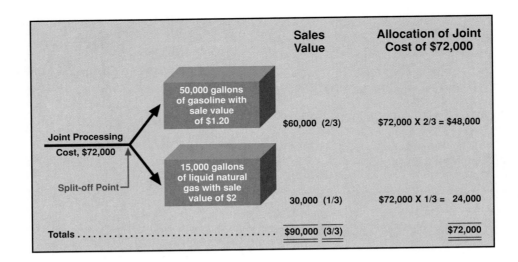

	Sales Value	Allocation of Joint Cost of $72,000
50,000 gallons of gasoline with sale value of $1.20	$60,000 (2/3)	$72,000 X 2/3 = $48,000
15,000 gallons of liquid natural gas with sale value of $2	30,000 (1/3)	$72,000 X 1/3 = 24,000
Totals	$90,000 (3/3)	$72,000

Joint Processing Cost, $72,000

Split-off Point

costs incurred *before* split-off should be assigned to the individual joint products? For example, how should we allocate the costs of exploring and drilling for oil to gasoline and natural gas? These *joint processing costs* may be allocated by using the *relative sales value* method, which most accountants consider to be the best of several available methods.

Consider the oil company Chevron. Suppose that Chevron's joint cost of processing 65,000 gallons of gasoline and liquid natural gas is $72,000. Exhibit 27-13 shows how to allocate this joint cost to the two products. The relative sales value of each joint product is computed by dividing its individual sales value by the total sales value. In the exhibit, the gasoline sales value makes up two-thirds of the total and liquid natural gas makes up one-third. Multiplying the joint cost of $72,000 by these fractions gives the two products' individual costs of $48,000 and $24,000. Any cost of processing gasoline after split-off is added to $48,000 to determine Chevron's total cost of the gasoline. The total cost of liquid natural gas is computed similarly.

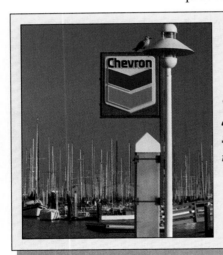

"Any cost of processing gasoline after split-off is added to $48,000 to determine Chevron's total cost of the gasoline."

Short Exercise: A company produces naphtha, jet fuel, and fuel oil from a joint process costing $240,000. Of these costs, $70,000 have been allocated to 2,000 barrels of naphtha. Each barrel of naphtha can be sold at split-off for $40 or can be processed further and sold for $65. The additional processing costs are $48,000. Should the naphtha be sold at split-off or after additional processing? *A:* There is a $2,000 advantage to processing further. *(cont.)*

Sell at Split-Off or Process Further?

Should a joint product be sold at split-off or should it be processed further? As in other decision situations, managers need to know which items are relevant. For example, let us determine whether Chevron should add a special additive to the gasoline to make it a premium product. The additional costs of materials and other resources in the subsequent process are $0.11 per gallon, resulting in an additional cost of $5,500 for 50,000 gallons. The sale price increases to $1.40 per gallon, for a total of $70,000. Processing the gasoline does not affect the liquid natural gas.

Joint processing costs are not relevant to decide whether to sell at split-off or to process further. Why? Because they do not differ between the alternatives. In contrast, separable costs are relevant. *Separable costs* are those post-split-off-point costs that can be identified exclusively with an individual product. The correct analysis focuses on the separable costs and revenues after split-off, as Exhibit 27-14 shows. The analysis favors further processing.

	Sell at Split-Off	Process Further
Expected revenue from selling 50,000 gallons of regular gasoline at $1.20 per gallon	$60,000	
Separable costs of $0.11 per gallon required to convert 50,000 gallons of regular gasoline into premium gasoline		$ (5,500)
Expected revenue from selling 50,000 gallons of premium gasoline at $1.40 per gallon		70,000
Total net revenue..	$60,000	64,500
Difference in net revenue		$ 4,500

	Sell at split-off	Process further
Expected revenue ..	$80,000	$130,000
Expected costs	-0-	48,000
Expected profit......	$80,000	$ 82,000

The joint cost of $70,000 is a sunk cost and therefore irrelevant.

EXHIBIT 27-14
Separable Costs and Revenues after Split-Off

STOP & THINK Some companies have obsolete inventories that cannot be sold at regular prices. How should managers decide whether to sell the units as-is or to incur additional manufacturing costs to rework them?

Answer: This decision is similar to the sell-at-split-off or process-further decision. Managers should predict the additional costs the company will incur to rework the inventory. Then they should forecast the additional revenues—the difference between the sales value of the units after rework and the sales value as-is. If the additional revenues that can be earned by reworking are greater than the additional costs, they should go ahead with the work. If not, they should sell the units as-is.

We have illustrated seven types of special business decisions. In each case, managers decided on one course of action—and thus rejected the opportunity to take alternative actions. When the managers rejected alternatives, their companies incurred an opportunity cost.

Opportunity Cost

An **opportunity cost** is the benefit that can be obtained from the next-best course of action in a decision. This definition indicates that opportunity cost is not an outlay cost that is recorded in accounting. An outlay cost requires a cash disbursement sooner or later, but an opportunity cost does not.

An example of an opportunity cost is the salary forgone by an engineer who may quit his job with IBM to start his own business. Suppose that this engineer analyzes his two job opportunities as follows:

OBJECTIVE 5
Use opportunity cost in decision making

Key Point: Opportunity costs are not costs that will be entered into the accounting records because they are benefits that are given up and thus are never received. However, opportunity costs are very important in decision making.

	Open an Independent Business	Remain an IBM Employee
Expected salary income from IBM		$60,000
Expected sales	$200,000	
Expected expenses	120,000	
Expected net income	$ 80,000	$60,000

The opportunity cost of staying with IBM is the forgone $80,000 of net income from the independent business. The opportunity cost of starting a new business is the $60,000 salary from IBM.

How are opportunity costs used in decision making? Consider two examples. (1) Suppose that the IBM engineer is faced with a third job opportunity—employment by Texas Instruments (TI). In order to determine the best alternative, the engineer can compare the TI salary with the $80,000 opportunity cost of not opening an independent business. If the engineer's goal is to maximize income, the IBM salary is irrelevant. (2) Refer to Exhibit 27-14. Suppose that Chevron is approached by a customer that needs 50,000 gallons of regular gasoline. The customer is willing to pay more than $1.20 per gallon. Chevron's managers can use the $64,500 opportunity cost of not further processing the gas to determine the sale price that will provide an equivalent income ($64,500/50,000 = $1.29). If the customer offers Chevron more than $1.29 per gallon, Chevron will be better off selling the regular gasoline at split-off. If the customer offers less than $1.29, Chevron will earn more net revenue by further processing the gas.

MID-CHAPTER SUMMARY PROBLEMS FOR YOUR REVIEW

PROBLEM 1

Aziz, Inc., has two products, a standard model and a deluxe model, with the following per-unit data:

	Standard	Deluxe
Sale price	$20	$30
Variable expenses	16	21

The company has 15,000 hours of capacity available. Seven units of the standard model can be produced in an hour, compared with three units of the deluxe model per hour. Which product should the company emphasize?

PROBLEM 2

Suppose that Zenith Corporation has the following manufacturing costs for 20,000 of its television cabinets:

Direct materials...	$ 20,000
Direct labor...	80,000
Variable overhead..	40,000
Fixed overhead	80,000
Total manufacturing cost	$220,000
Cost per cabinet ($220,000/20,000)	$11

Another manufacturer has offered to sell Zenith similar cabinets for $10, a total purchase cost of $200,000. By purchasing the cabinets outside, Zenith can save $50,000 of fixed overhead cost. The released facilities can be devoted to the manufacture of other products that will contribute $60,000 to profits. Identify and analyze the alternatives. What is Zenith's best course of action?

SOLUTIONS TO REVIEW PROBLEMS

PROBLEM 1

Decision: The company should emphasize the standard product because its contribution margin at full capacity is greater by $15,000:

		Product	
		Standard	Deluxe
(1)	Units per hour that can be produced	7	3
(2)	Contribution margin per unit...	× $4*	× $9*
	Contribution margin per hour	$28	$27
	Capacity—number of hours...	× 15,000	× 15,000
	Total contribution margin at full capacity..........................	$420,000	$405,000

*Contribution margins: Standard: $20 − $16 = $4; Deluxe: $30 − $21 = $9.

	Alternatives		
	Make Cabinets	Buy Cabinets and Leave Facilities Idle	Buy Cabinets and Use Facilities for Other Products
Relevant costs:			
Direct materials	$ 20,000	—	
Direct labor	80,000	—	
Variable overhead	40,000	—	
Fixed overhead	80,000	$ 30,000	$ 30,000
Purchase cost from outsider (20,000 × $10)	—	200,000	200,000
Total cost of obtaining cabinets	220,000	230,000	230,000
Profit contribution from other products			(60,000)
Net cost of obtaining 20,000 cabinets	$220,000	$230,000	$170,000

Decision: Zenith should buy the television cabinets from the outside supplier and use the released facilities to manufacture other products.

Capital Budgeting

IBM may use a circuit-board manufacturing plant for many years. Plant assets that are used over a long period of time are called *capital assets*. Examples include land, buildings, machinery, and equipment. Decisions to purchase capital assets require long-range planning. Many uncertain factors—such as consumer preferences, manufacturing technology, competition, and government regulation—must be considered in a capital-asset purchase decision. The further into the future the decision extends, the greater the likelihood that actual amounts will differ from predicted amounts. Thus, long-term decisions are riskier than short-term decisions.

IBM plant manager Bill Amelio of the chapter-opening story may need to expand his plant. He will use a **decision model**, a method or technique for evaluating alternative courses of action. In such situations, many managers are tempted to cast uncertainties in the most favorable light possible. The chief decision maker—IBM's CFO Jerome B. York—probably will be more skeptical regarding the expansion's net benefits. The point is this: Decision models do not make decisions. Instead, they help *people* make decisions. No matter how precise the calculations, decisions are based on predictions of an uncertain future. To become a successful decision maker, you must learn how to recognize and cope with uncertainty.

Capital budgeting is a formal means of analyzing long-range investment decisions. Examples include where to locate a plant, which product lines to add, and what territories to expand. Exhibit 27-15 shows where capital budgeting fits into the life cycle of long-term assets.

Key Point: Capital budgeting is a means of evaluating proposed future investments in capital assets. It is based on predictions; therefore, some uncertainty exists. But the techniques explained here provide a sound basis for analyzing predicted data.

EXHIBIT 27-15
Capital Budgeting and Long-Term Assets

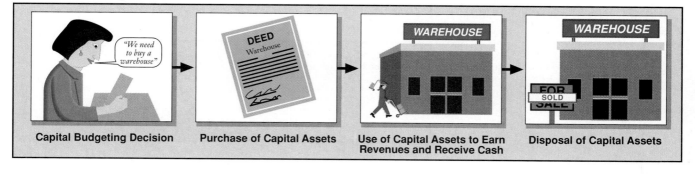

| Capital Budgeting Decision | Purchase of Capital Assets | Use of Capital Assets to Earn Revenues and Receive Cash | Disposal of Capital Assets |

The computer helps managers make capital-budgeting decisions. Suppose that Toro, which manufactures lawn-maintenance equipment, is considering building a new plant to meet demand for its lawn mowers. Company management has examined 25 sites for the plant and has narrowed the choice to five. Toro is considering six different factory designs. The computer can quickly calculate the costs of each of the 30 (5 × 6) decision alternatives. This computing power frees managers to analyze the results.

In this part of the chapter, we discuss four popular capital-budgeting decision models: payback, accounting rate of return, net present value, and internal rate of return. Three of these models examine the *net cash inflows from operations* generated by each alternative. ◄║║║ Generally accepted accounting principles are based on accrual accounting, but capital budgeting focuses on cash. The desirability of a capital asset depends on its ability to generate net cash inflows—that is, cash inflows in excess of cash outflows—over the asset's useful life.

◄║║║◄║║║◄║║║ We discuss cash flows from operating activities, often the largest source of cash, in Chapter 18 (p. 735).

Payback—Equal Annual Cash Flows

Payback is the length of time it will take to recover, in net cash inflows from operations, the dollars of a capital outlay. Suppose that Zenith Corporation pays $240,000 for an assembling machine with an estimated useful life of six years and zero predicted residual value. Managers expect use of the machine to generate net cash inflows from operations of $60,000 annually. In general, an increase in cash could result from an increase in revenues, a decrease in expenses, or a combination of the two. In this case it is a decrease in expenses.

Payback is expressed as a period of time, as shown in Exhibit 27-16. The payback model measures how swiftly investment dollars are expected to be recovered. The shorter the payback period, the more attractive the asset.

A major criticism of the payback model is that it does not consider or measure profitability. Consequently, the payback technique can lead to an unwise decision. Suppose that an alternative to the $240,000 machine is a comparable machine that also costs $240,000 but will save $80,000 annually during its three-year life. The two machines' payback periods are computed as follows:

OBJECTIVE 6

Use four capital-budgeting models to make investment decisions

$$\text{Payback period for machine 1} = \frac{\$240,000}{\$60,000} = 4 \text{ years}$$

$$\text{Payback period for machine 2} = \frac{\$240,000}{\$80,000} = 3 \text{ years}$$

Short Exercise: A company is considering a new production method that will save $130,000 a year in manufacturing costs. New equipment will cost $800,000 and will be depreciated on a straight-line basis over a 10-year life with a $40,000 salvage value. The hurdle rate is 12%. Compute the payback period. *A:*

$$\frac{\$800,000}{\$130,000} = 6.2 \text{ years}$$

The payback criterion favors the second machine because it recovers the asset's cost more quickly.

Now consider useful lives. Suppose that the useful life of machine 2 is the same as its payback period—three years. Its use will merely cover cost and provide no profits. But machine 1 has a useful life of six years. It will generate net cash inflows for two years beyond its payback period, which will give the company an additional net cash inflow of $120,000 ($60,000 × 2 years). Unlike machine 2, machine 1 will be profitable. In light of the assets' useful lives, machine 1 appears to be the better investment.

EXHIBIT 27-16
Payback—Equal Annual Net Cash Inflows

$$\text{Payback period} = \frac{\text{Amount invested}}{\text{Expected annual net cash inflow from operations}}$$

$$P = \frac{I}{O} = \frac{\$240,000}{\$60,000} = 4 \text{ years}$$

EXHIBIT 27-17

Payback—Unequal Annual Net Cash Inflows

Year	Amount Invested	Net Cash Inflow	
		Each Year	Accumulated
0	$240,000	—	—
1	—	$100,000	$100,000
2	—	80,000	180,000
3	—	50,000	230,000
3.2	—	10,000	240,000

Payback—Unequal Annual Cash Flows

The payback equation can be used only when net cash inflows are the same for each period. When periodic cash flows are unequal, the payback computation has a cumulative form. Net cash inflows are accumulated until the amount invested is recovered. Suppose that machine 1 in our example will produce net cash inflows of $100,000 in Year 1, $80,000 in Year 2, and $50,000 in Years 3 through 6. Exhibit 27-17 shows the payback computation for these unequal annual cash flows.

Years 1, 2, and 3 together bring in $230,000. Recovery of the amount invested ($240,000) occurs during Year 4. We can compute that payback occurs in 3.2 years:

$$\text{Payback} = 3 \text{ years} + \frac{\$10,000 \text{ needed to complete recovery in Year 4}}{\$50,000 \text{ net cash inflow in Year 4}} \times 1 \text{ year}$$

$$= 3 \text{ years} + 0.2 \text{ years} = 3.2 \text{ years}$$

How does a manager use the payback model in capital budgeting? Managers often compare the payback period with the asset's useful life. The asset's payback period must be shorter than its useful life. Consider an extreme example. If a machine has a payback period of five years and a useful life of three years, the company will never earn a profit from using the asset. How much shorter than the useful life the payback period must be is a matter of personal preference. When the business is deciding between two or more assets, the asset with the shortest payback period is the most profitable—*if all other factors are the same.*

The payback method highlights cash flows, a key factor in business decisions. Moreover, payback is easily understood. Advocates view it as a way to eliminate proposals that are unusually risky (projects with lengthy payback periods). A major weakness of payback is that it ignores profitability.

Accounting Rate of Return

A primary goal of business is to earn profits. One measure of profitability is the rate of return on investment. The **accounting rate of return** is computed by dividing the operating income that an asset generates by the amount of the investment in the asset:

$$\text{Accounting rate of return} = \frac{\text{Operating income}}{\text{Investment}}$$

The accounting rate of return focuses on the operating income that an asset generates. Operating income from an asset can be computed as net cash inflow minus depreciation. Accounting rate of return is computed in Exhibit 27-18 for machine 1 in the payback example. Recall that the machine costs $240,000, has a useful life of six years, and has a predicted residual value of zero. Annual straight-line depreciation is $40,000 ($240,000/6 years). The machine is expected to generate annual net cash inflows of $60,000.

The accounting rate of return is an average. It measures the average rate of return from using the asset over its entire life. Consider the average annual operating income. If operating income varies by year (as in the preceding payback example),

Recall from Chapter 10, page 410, that under straight-line depreciation, an equal amount of depreciation expense is assigned to each period of an asset's use.

EXHIBIT 27-18
Accounting Rate of Return

$$\begin{aligned}
\text{Accounting rate of return} &= \frac{\text{Average annual operating income from investment*}}{\text{Average amount invested}} = \frac{\text{Average annual net cash inflow from operations (O)} - \text{Annual depreciation (D)}}{[\text{Amount invested (I)} + \text{Residual value (RV)}]/2} \\[2mm]
&= \frac{O - D}{(I + RV)/2} \\[2mm]
&= \frac{\$60,000 - \$40,000}{(\$240,000 + \$0)/2} = \frac{\$20,000}{\$120,000} = 0.167 = 16.7\%
\end{aligned}$$

*Operating income also can be computed as revenues minus expenses.

Short Exercise: Using the data from the previous Short Exercise, compute the accounting rate of return. *A:*

$$\frac{\$130,000 - \$76,000}{(\$800,000 + \$40,000)/2} = 12.9\%$$

The accounting rate of return is greater than the hurdle rate.

compute the *total* operating income over the asset's life. Then divide the total by the number of years of life to find the *average* annual operating income. Now consider the average amount invested. The book value of the asset decreases as it is used and depreciated. Thus, the company's investment in the asset declines over time. If the asset's residual value is zero, the average investment is half the asset's cost.

If the asset's residual value is not zero, the average amount invested is greater than half the asset's cost. For example, assume that the residual value of machine 1 is $30,000. Annual depreciation is $35,000 [($240,000 − $30,000)/6]. The accounting rate of return is:

$$\text{Accounting rate of return} = \frac{\$60,000 - \$35,000}{(\$240,000 + \$30,000)/2} = \frac{\$25,000}{\$135,000} = 0.185 = 18.5\%$$

Companies that use the accounting rate of return model set a minimum acceptable rate of return on their investment projects. They invest only in assets with accounting rates of return equal to or greater than the minimum rate. Suppose that Zenith requires a rate of at least 20 percent. Would its managers approve an investment in the assembling machine, which is expected to generate an average return of 16.7 percent? No, because the machine's average annual return is less than the company's minimum acceptable rate.

Discounted Cash-Flow Models

◀▥◀▥◀▥ Recall from Chapter 16 (p. 640) that present value is the amount a person would invest now to receive a greater amount in the future.

◀▥◀▥◀▥ The time value of money is discussed in the Chapter 16 appendix (p. 674).

Chapter 16 introduced the concept of present value. ◀▥ The present value of $1 to be received in the future is less than $1 today. The logic is this: To receive $1 a year from now, we would be willing to pay less than $1 today. Why? Because if we pay $1 now to receive $1 later, we earn no income in the meantime. But if we deposit $1 in a bank and earn interest of, say, $0.06, we will have $1.06 a year from now. We would rather have $1.06 than $1.00. Thus, we would rather receive cash earlier than later. The fact that we can earn income by investing money for a period of time is called the **time value of money.** ◀▥

The timing of net cash inflows from operations is important because of the time value of money. Consider two $10,000 investments. Both investments promise future cash receipts of $11,000. Investment 1 will bring in cash of $5,500 at the end of each of the next two years. Investment 2 will return the full $11,000 at the end of the second year. Which investment is better? Investment 1, because it brings in cash sooner. Its cash can be invested for a longer period of time.

The accounting rate of return model discussed in the previous section measures profitability, but it has a major weakness. It does not recognize the time value of money. That is, it considers neither the *timing* of the cash outlay to purchase an asset nor the *timing* of its net cash inflows. *Discounted cash-flow models* overcome this weakness. These models—the net present value and the internal rate of return—are used by over 85 percent of the large industrial firms in the United States.

Net Present Value

Assume that Mitsubishi is considering the manufacture of two products, tape decks and VCRs. The products require different specialized equipment that cost the same amount, $1 million. Each machine is expected to have a five-year life and zero residual value. The two products have different patterns of predicted net cash inflows:

	Annual Net Cash Inflows	
Year	Tape Decks	VCRs
1	$ 305,450	$ 500,000
2	305,450	350,000
3	305,450	300,000
4	305,450	250,000
5	305,450	40,000
Total	$1,527,250	$1,440,000

Total net cash inflows are greater if Mitsubishi invests in the tape-deck project. However, these inflows occur in the future. The **net present value (NPV)** model computes the expected net monetary gain or loss from a project by discounting all expected future cash inflows and outflows to their present value, using a minimum desired rate of return. That is, the NPV model *discounts* all future cash flows to the present. The model thus determines the value of cash inflows and outflows at a common time so that they can be compared (added, subtracted, and so on) for decision making.

Management's minimum desired rate of return on an investment is called the **discount rate**. Synonyms are *hurdle rate, cutoff rate, required rate, cost of capital,* and *target rate*. The discount rate varies, depending on the riskiness of investments. The higher the risk, the higher the discount rate. Suppose that Mitsubishi's discount rate for these investments is 14 percent.

The manufacture and sale of tape decks is expected to generate $305,450 of net cash inflow each year. A stream of equal periodic amounts is called an **annuity**. The present value of an annuity is computed by multiplying the periodic amount ($305,450) by the present value of an annuity of $1 from Exhibit 27-19. The table indicates that the present value of an annuity of $1 for five years discounted at 14 percent per year is $3.433. Exhibit 27-20 uses this amount to compute the present value of the net cash inflows of the tape-deck project—$1,048,610.

The net cash inflows of the VCR project are unequal—$500,000 in Year 1, $350,000 in Year 2, and so on. Because these amounts vary by year, the present value of each amount is computed separately. For example:

Year	Present Value Factor from Exhibit 27-21, 14% Column	Net Cash Inflow		Present Value of Net Cash Inflow
1	0.877	× $500,000	=	$438,500
2	0.769	× 350,000	=	269,150

Exhibit 27-20 includes these present-value computations. The exhibit indicates that the VCR project has a net present value of $78,910, compared with $48,610 for the tape-deck project. The analysis favors VCRs because an investment in that project will earn the company's required rate of 14 percent plus an additional $78,910. This

Key Point: The alternative that produces the highest net present value of all cash flows is the most desirable.

EXHIBIT 27-19
Present Value of Annuity of $1

Present Value of Annuity of $1

Period	4%	5%	6%	7%	8%	10%	12%	14%	16%
1	0.962	0.952	0.943	0.935	0.926	0.909	0.893	0.877	0.862
2	1.886	1.859	1.833	1.808	1.783	1.736	1.690	1.647	1.605
3	2.775	2.723	2.673	2.624	2.577	2.487	2.402	2.322	2.246
4	3.630	3.546	3.465	3.387	3.312	3.170	3.037	2.914	2.798
5	4.452	4.329	4.212	4.100	3.993	3.791	3.605	3.433	3.274
6	5.242	5.076	4.917	4.767	4.623	4.355	4.111	3.889	3.685
7	6.002	5.786	5.582	5.389	5.206	4.868	4.564	4.288	4.039
8	6.733	6.463	6.210	5.971	5.747	5.335	4.968	4.639	4.344
9	7.435	7.108	6.802	6.515	6.247	5.759	5.328	4.946	4.607
10	8.111	7.722	7.360	7.024	6.710	6.145	5.650	5.216	4.833
11	8.760	8.306	7.887	7.499	7.139	6.495	5.938	5.453	5.029
12	9.385	8.863	8.384	7.943	7.536	6.814	6.194	5.660	5.197
13	9.986	9.394	8.853	8.358	7.904	7.103	6.424	5.842	5.342
14	10.563	9.899	9.295	8.745	8.244	7.367	6.628	6.002	5.468
15	11.118	10.380	9.712	9.108	8.559	7.606	6.811	6.142	5.575
16	11.652	10.838	10.106	9.447	8.851	7.824	6.974	6.265	5.669
17	12.166	11.274	10.477	9.763	9.122	8.022	7.120	6.373	5.749
18	12.659	11.690	10.828	10.059	9.372	8.201	7.250	6.467	5.818
19	13.134	12.085	11.158	10.336	9.604	8.365	7.366	6.550	5.877
20	13.590	12.462	11.470	10.594	9.818	8.514	7.469	6.623	5.929

Appendix B provides a fuller table for the present value of an annuity of $1.

EXHIBIT 27-20
Net Present Value

	Present Value at 14%	Net Cash Inflow	Total Present Value
Tape-Deck Project:			
Present value of equal annual net cash inflows for 5 years...............	3.433*	× $305,450 per year =	$ 1,048,610
Investment			(1,000,000)
Net present value of the tape-deck project			$ 48,610
VCR Project:			
Present value of net cash inflows by year:	Year		
	1 0.877†	× $500,000 =	$ 438,500
	2 0.769	× 350,000 =	269,150
	3 0.675	× 300,000 =	202,500
	4 0.592	× 250,000 =	148,000
	5 0.519	× 40,000 =	20,760
Total present value of net cash inflows...			1,078,910
Investment			(1,000,000)
Net present value of the VCR project ...			$ 78,910

*Present value of annuity of $1 for 5 years at 14%, Exhibit 27-19.
†Present value of $1 for 1 year, 2 years, 3 years, and so on, at 14%, Exhibit 27-21.

expected excess is greater than that of the tape-deck project, which also meets the required rate of 14 percent but returns only an additional $48,610.

This example illustrates an important point about present-value analysis. The tape-deck project promises the greater total amount of net cash inflows, but the timing of the VCR cash flows—loaded near the beginning of the project—gives the VCR investment a higher net present value. The VCR project is more attractive because of the time value of money. Its dollars, which are closer to the present, are worth more now than the more-distant dollars of the tape-deck project.

Another important point about present-value analysis is this: Either project, considered alone, is acceptable because its net present value is at least zero. A project with a negative net present value is unacceptable because it fails to earn a rate of return as high as the company's hurdle rate. In this case, both projects—tape decks and VCRs—earn at least the minimum desired rate of return of 14 percent.

NET PRESENT VALUE OF A PROJECT WITH RESIDUAL VALUE When the asset to be acquired is expected to have a residual value at the end of its useful life, that amount should be considered in the NPV analysis. The residual value is an expected cash inflow. It must be discounted to its present value to determine the total present value of the project's net cash inflows. The residual value is discounted as a single amount—not as an annuity—because it will be received only once, when the asset is sold.

Suppose that the equipment to manufacture tape decks is expected to be worth $100,000 at the end of its five-year life. To determine the tape-deck project's NPV, we discount $100,000 for five years at 14 percent—using Exhibit 27-21—and add its present value ($51,900), as shown in Exhibit 27-22.

Compare Exhibits 27-20 and 27-22. The discounted residual value raises the tape-deck project's NPV to $100,510, which is higher than that of the VCR project.

Short Exercise: Using the data from the Short Exercise on p. 1104, compute the net present value with a 12% minimum desired rate of return. *A:*

PV of manufacturing
  cost savings
  ($130,000 × 5.650).....$ 734,500
PV of residual value
  ($40,000 × 0.322).......   12,880
Initial investment .... (800,000)
NPV ....$(52,620)

The proposal should be rejected.

Present Value of $1

Period	4%	5%	6%	7%	8%	10%	12%	14%	16%
1	0.962	0.952	0.943	0.935	0.926	0.909	0.893	0.877	0.862
2	0.925	0.907	0.890	0.873	0.857	0.826	0.797	0.769	0.743
3	0.889	0.864	0.840	0.816	0.794	0.751	0.712	0.675	0.641
4	0.855	0.823	0.792	0.763	0.735	0.683	0.636	0.592	0.552
5	0.822	0.784	0.747	0.713	0.681	0.621	0.567	0.519	0.476
6	0.790	0.746	0.705	0.666	0.630	0.564	0.507	0.456	0.410
7	0.760	0.711	0.665	0.623	0.583	0.513	0.452	0.400	0.354
8	0.731	0.677	0.627	0.582	0.540	0.467	0.404	0.351	0.305
9	0.703	0.645	0.592	0.544	0.500	0.424	0.361	0.308	0.263
10	0.676	0.614	0.558	0.508	0.463	0.386	0.322	0.270	0.227
11	0.650	0.585	0.527	0.475	0.429	0.350	0.287	0.237	0.195
12	0.625	0.557	0.497	0.444	0.397	0.319	0.257	0.208	0.168
13	0.601	0.530	0.469	0.415	0.368	0.290	0.229	0.182	0.145
14	0.577	0.505	0.442	0.388	0.340	0.263	0.205	0.160	0.125
15	0.555	0.481	0.417	0.362	0.315	0.239	0.183	0.140	0.108
16	0.534	0.458	0.394	0.339	0.292	0.218	0.163	0.123	0.093
17	0.513	0.436	0.371	0.317	0.270	0.198	0.146	0.108	0.080
18	0.494	0.416	0.350	0.296	0.250	0.180	0.130	0.095	0.069
19	0.475	0.396	0.331	0.277	0.232	0.164	0.116	0.083	0.060
20	0.456	0.377	0.312	0.258	0.215	0.149	0.104	0.073	0.051

Appendix B provides a fuller table for the present value of $1.

EXHIBIT 27-21
Present Value of $1

Tape-Deck Project	Present Value at 14%		Net Cash Inflow		Total Present Value
Present value of equal annual net cash inflows for 5 years (from Exhibit 27-20)	3.433	×	$305,450 per year	=	$ 1,048,610
Present value of residual value	**0.519***	×	**$100,000**	=	**51,900**
Total present value of net cash inflows...............					1,100,510
Investment					(1,000,000)
Net present value of the tape-deck project					$ 100,510

*Present value of $1 for 5 years at 14%, Exhibit 27-21.

EXHIBIT 27-22
Net Present Value of a Project with Residual Value

If the VCR equipment is expected to have zero disposal value, then the tape-deck project is more attractive.

There is another way to use present-value analysis in capital budgeting. Suppose that Mitsubishi starts the decision-making process by computing the total present values of net cash inflows from the two projects—$1,048,610 for tape decks and $1,078,910 for VCRs. The company's managers may ask, What is the most we can invest in the tape-deck project and still earn our 14-percent target rate of return? With zero residual value, the answer is $1,048,610. Similarly, the maximum acceptable investment for VCRs is $1,078,910. The $1 million cost of both projects makes them attractive as investments.

Internal Rate of Return

Another discounted-cash-flow model for capital budgeting is the internal rate of return (IRR). The **internal rate of return (IRR)** of an investment project is the rate of return that makes the net present value of the project equal to zero. As the name implies, a project's IRR is the rate of return that a company can expect to earn by investing in the project. The higher the IRR, the more desirable the project. The lower the IRR, the less desirable.

Exhibit 27-23 shows that 16 percent is the IRR of Mitsubishi's tape-deck project. The 16-percent rate produces a net present value of zero. To evaluate the project, we:

1. Identify the expected net cash inflows ($305,450 for five years) exactly as in calculating the net present value.

2. Find the interest rate that equates the total present value of the net cash inflows

EXHIBIT 27-23
Internal Rate of Return, Tape-Deck Project

	Present Value at 16%		Net Cash Inflow		Total Present Value
Present value of equal annual net cash inflows for 5 years....................	3.274*	×	$305,450	=	$ 1,000,000[†]
Investment					(1,000,000)
Net present value of the tape-deck project					$ 0[††]

*Present value of annuity of $1 for 5 years at 16%, Exhibit 27–19.
[†]Slight rounding error.
[††]The zero difference proves that the IRR is 16%.

with the amount of the investment. Use the following equation to solve for the annuity present value (PV) factor:

$$\text{Investment} = \text{Expected annual net cash inflows} \times \text{Annuity PV factor}$$

$$\$1{,}000{,}000 = \$305{,}450 \times \text{Annuity PV factor}$$

$$\text{Annuity PV factor} = \frac{\$1{,}000{,}000}{\$305{,}450} = 3.274$$

Scan the row in Exhibit 27-19 that represents the expected life of the project, the 5-period row in our example. Choose the column with the number closest to the annuity PV factor that was calculated. The 3.274 annuity factor is in the 16-percent column. Therefore, the IRR of the tape-deck project is 16 percent. Mitsubishi expects the project to earn an annual rate of return of 16 percent over its life.

3. Compare the IRR with the minimum desired rate of return. If the IRR is equal to or greater than that minimum rate, the project is acceptable. Otherwise, it is not.

If tape decks were the only investment under consideration, managers would invest in tape decks because their 16-percent IRR exceeds the 14-percent discount rate. But recall that the VCR project has a higher net present value than does the tape-deck project. The VCR investment also has a higher IRR. Computation of the VCR's IRR requires a trial-and-error procedure. Many inexpensive calculators can perform the calculations.

Short Exercise: The Midway School District is considering the purchase of a lawn tractor. The tractor will cost $10,000 and have a 10-year life. It will save approximately $1,627 a year in operating labor costs. Compute the internal rate of return. *A:*

$$\frac{\$10{,}000}{\$1{,}627} = 6.146$$

Look in the present value of annuity table at the 10-year row; 6.145 (which is very close to the calculated 6.146) is in the 10% column. Therefore, the IRR is 10%.

Comparison of the Capital-Budgeting Models

How do the net-present-value approach and the IRR approach compare? The net-present-value method indicates the amount of the excess (or deficiency) of a project's present value of net cash inflows over (or under) its cost—for a specified rate of return. Net present value, though, does not show the project's unique rate of return. The IRR shows the project's rate but fails to indicate the dollar difference between the project's present value and its investment cost. In many cases the two methods lead to the same investment decision.

The discounted cash-flow models are conceptually better than the payback or accounting rate of return models because they are based on cash flows and they consider both the time value of money and profitability. The time value of money enters the analysis through the discounting of future dollars to present value. Profitability is built into the discounted cash-flow models. They consider all cash inflows and outflows—the determinants of profit—over the life of a project. In contrast, the payback model considers only the cash flows necessary to recover the initial cash invested.

Exhibit 27-24 summarizes the strengths and weaknesses of the payback, accounting rate of return, and discounted cash-flow models. In practice, managers

OBJECTIVE 7
Compare and contrast popular capital-budgeting models

CONCEPT HIGHLIGHT

EXHIBIT 27-24
Capital-Budgeting Decision Models

Model	Strengths	Weaknesses
Payback	Easy to understand Based on cash flows Highlights risks	Ignores profitability and the time value of money
Accounting rate of return	Based on profitability	Ignores the time value of money

Discounted cash flow models:
  Net present value
  Internal rate of return
	Based on cash flows, profitability, and the time value of money	None of the above

often use more than one model simultaneously to gain different perspectives on risks and returns.

 STOP & THINK Suppose that Merck, a pharmaceutical company, is considering two drug-research projects. Project A has a net present value of $232,000 and a 3-year payback period. Project B has a net present value of $237,000 and a payback period of 4.5 years. Which project do you think the managers will accept?

Answer: Many managers would accept Project A. Net present value is a better guide to decision making than is the payback period. But managers would consider the 2.2-percent [($237,000 − $232,000)/$232,000] difference between the NPVs to be insignificant. In contrast, the 50-percent [(4.5 years − 3.0 years)/3.0 years] difference between payback periods *is* significant. The uncertainty of receiving operating cash flows increases with each passing year. Managers often forgo small differences in expected cash inflows in order to decrease the risk of investments.

Lease or Buy

The capital-budgeting decisions that we considered focused on which investment project to acquire. Managers must also decide how to finance the acquisition. There are several possibilities. The company may be able to purchase the asset with internally generated cash or with cash obtained by borrowing. In many cases, managers can acquire the use of capital assets through leasing—that is, renting on a long-term basis.

A recent survey of 600 companies indicated that only 70 did not acquire some of their assets through leasing. Why is leasing so popular? One factor is rapid change in technology. Rather than buy a computer and risk getting stuck with an obsolete machine, a company may prefer to lease. Then if IBM, Apple, or Compaq develops a new generation of computer, the company can let its lease expire and switch to a new, more powerful machine. For similar reasons, airline companies lease some of their aircraft.

The role of leasing should be kept in perspective. There are two steps in capital budgeting: (1) deciding whether to acquire an asset, which is an investment decision, and (2) deciding whether to finance the acquisition by buying or by leasing. The second step is *not* an investment decision. It is a financing decision that is covered in textbooks on finance.

SUMMARY PROBLEM FOR YOUR REVIEW

The data for a machine follow:

Cost of machine	$48,000
Estimated residual value	6,000
Estimated annual net cash inflow	13,000
Estimated useful life	5 years
Required rate of return	16%

Required

1. Compute the machine's payback period.
2. Compute the machine's accounting rate of return.
3. Compute the machine's net present value (NPV).
4. Indicate whether reliance on each decision model leads to purchase or rejection of this investment. Would you decide to buy the machine? Give your reason.

Requirement 1

$$\text{Payback period} = \frac{\text{Amount invested}}{\text{Expected annual net cash inflow from operations}} = \frac{\$48,000}{\$13,000} = 3.7 \text{ years}$$

Requirement 2

$$\text{Accounting rate of return} = \frac{\text{Average annual operating income from investment}}{\text{Average amount invested}}$$

$$= \frac{O - D}{(I + RV)/2} = \frac{\$13,000 - \$8,400^*}{(\$48,000 + \$6,000)/2}$$

$$= \frac{\$4,600}{\$27,000} = 0.170 = 17\%$$

$$^*D = \frac{\$48,000 - \$6,000}{5 \text{ years}} = \$8,400$$

Requirement 3

Present value of equal annual net cash inflows ($13,000 × 3.274*)	$ 42,562
Present value of residual value ($6,000 × 0.476†)	2,856
Total present value of net cash inflows	45,418
Investment	(48,000)
Net present value	$ (2,582)

*Present value of annuity of $1 for 5 years at 16%, Exhibit 27-19.
†Present value of $1 for 5 years at 16%, Exhibit 27-21.

Requirement 4

Payback: Purchase the machine because its payback period (3.7 years) is less than its useful life (5 years).

Accounting rate of return: Purchase the machine because its 17-percent rate of return exceeds the target rate of 16 percent.

Net present value: Reject the machine because it has a negative net present value.

Decision: Reject the machine because of its negative net present value. The net-present-value model considers cash flows, profitability, and the time value of money. Each of the other models ignores at least one of those factors.

SUMMARY

1. ***Identify the relevant information for a special business decision.*** To make a decision, managers analyze relevant information. *Relevant information* is expected future data that differ among alternative courses of action. Historical data are irrelevant per se, but often they serve as useful guides to predictions.

2. ***Make seven types of special business decisions.*** Using relevant information, managers decide whether to accept or reject a special sales order; whether to delete a product, department, or territory; which product to emphasize when a *constraint* is present; whether to make or buy a part; how to make the best use of facilities; whether to replace equipment; and whether to sell a joint product at split-off or to process it further. Managers often select the course of action that is expected to produce the most operating income.

3. ***Explain the difference between correct analysis and incorrect analysis of a particular business decision.*** Correct analysis of a business decision focuses on differences in revenues and expenses. The conventional approach to decision making, which is based on absorption costing, may mislead managers into treating a fixed cost as a variable cost. The contribution margin approach, which is based on variable costing, often is more useful for decision analysis because it highlights how expenses and income are affected by sales volume.

4. ***Allocate joint processing costs to joint products.*** *Joint products* are identified as individual products only after the split-off point in a joint process. Costs incurred before the split-off point are allocated to joint products by the relative sales value method. Allocated joint costs are irrelevant for deciding whether to sell a joint product at split-off or to process it further.

5. ***Use opportunity cost in decision making.*** *Opportunity cost* is the benefit that can be obtained from the next-best course of action in a decision. Every business decision carries with it an opportunity cost. Opportunity cost is not an outlay cost that is recorded in accounting.

6. Use four capital-budgeting models to make investment decisions. Capital budgeting is a formal means of analyzing long-range investment decisions. Four popular capital-budgeting *decision models* are payback, accounting rate of return, net present value, and internal rate of return. *Payback* is the length of time it will take to recover the dollars of a capital outlay. The *accounting rate of return* is the average annual operating income from an investment divided by the average amount of invested capital. *Net present value (NPV)* measures the expected net monetary gain or loss from a project. The project's *internal rate of re-* *turn (IRR)* is the discount rate that makes its net present value equal to zero.

7. Compare and contrast popular capital-budgeting models. The discounted-cash-flow models, net present value and internal rate of return, are conceptually superior to the payback and accounting rate of return models. Payback ignores profitability and the *time value of money*. Accounting rate of return ignores the time value of money. NPV and IRR consider both profitability and the time value of money.

SELF-STUDY QUESTIONS

Test your understanding of the chapter by marking the best answer for each of the following questions.

1. Relevant information for decision analysis *(p. 1090)*
   a. Remains constant regardless of the alternative courses of action
   b. Is used in some but not all business decisions
   c. Varies with the alternative courses of action
   d. Excludes direct materials and direct labor because they are fixed

2. Suppose that fixed costs remain unchanged. To decide whether to make a sale at a special price, compare *(p. 1092)*
   a. Expected change in gross margin (sales minus cost of goods sold) with and without the sale
   b. Expected change in revenues with expected change in fixed expenses
   c. Expected change in revenues with expected change in selling expenses
   d. Expected change in revenues with expected change in variable expenses

3. To decide whether to delete a product, a manager should *(p. 1095)*
   a. Consider all costs that change
   b. Consider only variable costs
   c. Consider all costs that remain unchanged
   d. Consider only fixed costs

4. Pontchartrain's $0.47 manufacturing cost per unit includes fixed cost of $0.19. Acme, Inc., offers to sell the product to Pontchartrain for $0.35 per unit. The make-or-buy decision hinges on the comparison between Pontchartrain's $0.47 manufacturing cost and the total cost if the products are purchased from Acme. That total cost is *(p. 1097)*
   a. $0.28   c. $0.54
   b. $0.35   d. $0.66

5. Sunk costs are *(p. 1098)*
   a. Relevant to most business decisions

   b. The costs of the next-best alternative
   c. Equal to the residual value of a plant asset
   d. Irrelevant in business decisions

6. Capital budgeting is a (an) *(p. 1103)*
   a. Depreciation method
   b. Short-run decision
   c. Alternative to the payback method
   d. Way to analyze long-range investment decisions

7. A machine costs $45,000. It is expected to earn operating income of $6,000 and to generate a $7,500 net cash inflow annually. Expected residual value is $5,000 at the end of five years. What is the asset's payback period? *(p. 1104)*
   a. 5 years   c. 7-1/2 years
   b. 6 years   d. 9 years

8. The accounting rate of return of the machine in Self-Study Question 7 is *(p. 1106)*
   a. 15 percent   c. 26.7 percent
   b. 24 percent   d. 37.5 percent

9. The time value of money is an important part of *(p. 1111)*
   a. Payback analysis
   b. Accounting rate of return analysis
   c. Net-present-value analysis
   d. All capital-budgeting methods

10. Payback analysis and net-present-value analysis indicate that a particular investment should be rejected, but the accounting rate of return is favorable. What is the wisest investment decision? Give your reason. *(p. 1111)*
    a. Reject because of net-present-value analysis
    b. Reject because of payback analysis
    c. Accept because of favorable accounting rate of return
    d. Cannot decide because of differences among the methods' results

Answers to the Self-Study Questions follow the Accounting Vocabulary.

ACCOUNTING VOCABULARY

Accounting rate of return. A measure of profitability computed by dividing the operating income that an asset generates by the amount of the investment in the asset *(p. 1105)*.

Annuity. A stream of equal periodic amounts *(p. 1107)*.

Capital budgeting. A formal means of analyzing long-range investment decisions *(p. 1103)*.

Constraint. The factor that restricts production or sale of a product; also called the *limiting factor (p. 1095)*.

Decision model. A method or technique for evaluating and choosing among alternative courses of action *(p. 1103)*.

Discount rate. Management's minimum desired rate of return on an investment; also called the *hurdle rate, cutoff* *rate, required rate, cost of capital,* and *target rate (p. 1107).*

Internal rate of return (IRR). The rate of return that makes the net present value of a project equal to zero *(p. 1110).*

Joint products. The goods produced in a joint process *(p. 1099).*

Net present value (NVP). The decision model that computes the expected net monetary gain or loss from a project by discounting all expected future cash inflows and outflows to their present value, using a minimum desired rate of return *(p. 1107).*

Opportunity cost. The benefit that can be obtained from the next-best course of action in a decision *(p. 1101).*

Payback. The length of time it will take to recover, in net cash inflows from op-

erations, the dollars of a capital outlay *(p. 1104).*

Relevant information. The expected future data that differ among alternative courses of action *(p. 1090).*

Sunk cost. A past cost that is unavoidable because it cannot be changed no matter what action is taken *(p. 1098).*

Time value of money. The fact that income can be earned by investing money for a period of time *(p. 1106).*

ANSWERS TO SELF-STUDY QUESTIONS

1. c
2. d
3. a
4. c   Fixed cost ($0.19) + Cost of outside units ($0.35) = $0.54
5. d
6. d
7. b $45,000/$7,500 = 6 years

8. b $$\frac{\$6,000}{(\$45,000 + \$5,000)/2} = \frac{\$6,000}{\$25,000} = 24\%$$

9. c
10. a

QUESTIONS

1. How do special decisions differ from ordinary day-to-day business decisions? Give examples of special decisions.
2. Briefly describe how relevant information is used in making special decisions.
3. Discuss the roles of expected future data and historical data in decision analysis. On which data are special decisions based?
4. Identify two income statement formats. Which is more useful for deciding whether to accept a special sales order? Why?
5. Identify two long-run factors to be considered in making a special sales order decision.
6. What is the similarity between a special sales order decision and a decision to delete a product? The difference?
7. Which cost is more likely to change in a decision situation, a fixed or a variable cost? Can both costs change?
8. Outline how to decide which product to emphasize when there is a limiting factor. Give four examples of limiting factors.
9. Which is relevant to decision analysis, an asset's sunk cost or its residual value? Give your reason, including an explanation of each.
10. What is an opportunity cost? How does it differ from an ordinary accounting cost?
11. Give an example of a decision that is based on opportunity cost. Discuss the role of opportunity cost in making the decision.

12. What are decision models? Why are they helpful in capital budgeting?
13. What is capital budgeting? Are capital-budgeting decisions made before or after long-term assets are purchased?
14. Name three capital-budgeting decision models. State the strengths and the weaknesses of each model. Which model is best? Why?
15. Name the capital-budgeting model that fits each description: (a) based on operating income; (b) based on cash flows without regard for their timing or profitability; (c) based on the time value of money.
16. How is the payback period computed? How does the estimated useful life of a capital asset affect the payback computation?
17. How can managers use the accounting rate of return in capital-budgeting decisions?
18. How can the accounting rate of return be computed when the annual amounts of operating income are expected to vary?
19. State why a positive net present value indicates an attractive investment project and a negative net present value indicates an unattractive project.
20. Which capital-budgeting strategy is better? (a) Pick out the best decision model and use it exclusively. (b) Use three decision models. Support your answer.

EXERCISES

Accept or reject a special sales order
(Obj. 1, 2)

E27-1 The Tennis Hall of Fame in Newport, Rhode Island, has approached All-Sports Manufacturing Company with a special order. The Hall wishes to purchase 100,000 monogrammed tennis balls for a special promotional campaign and offers $0.75 per ball—a total of $75,000. All-Sports' total manufacturing cost per ball is $1, broken down as follows:

Variable costs:	
Direct materials..................	$0.18
Direct labor	0.09
Variable overhead...............	0.33
Total variable cost	0.60
Fixed overhead cost................	0.40
Total cost	$1.00

Prepare a quick summary to help determine whether All-Sports should accept the special sales order. Assume that All-Sports has excess capacity.

Retain or drop a product line (fixed costs unchanged)
(Obj. 1, 2, 3)

E27-2 Top managers of Panhandle Supply Co. are alarmed that operating income is so low. They are considering dropping the building materials product line. Company accountants have prepared the following analysis to help make this decision:

	Total	Hardware	Building Materials
Sales	$500,000	$290,000	$210,000
Variable expenses.................................	260,000	140,000	120,000
Contribution margin	240,000	150,000	90,000
Fixed expenses:			
Manufacturing	145,000	70,000	75,000
Selling and administrative..............	90,000	55,000	35,000
Total fixed expenses	235,000	125,000	110,000
Operating income (loss)	$ 5,000	$ 25,000	$ (20,000)

Fixed costs will not change if the company stops selling building materials.

Prepare a quick summary to show whether Panhandle should drop the building materials product line. Explain the error of concluding that dropping building materials will add $20,000 to operating income.

Retain or drop a product line (fixed costs change)
(Obj. 1, 2)

E27-3 Refer to the data of Exercise 27-2. Assume that Panhandle Supply Co. can avoid $50,000 of fixed expenses by dropping the building materials product line. Prepare a quick summary to show whether Panhandle should stop selling building materials.

Which product to emphasize
(Obj. 1, 2)

E27-4 Avant-Garde Fashions sells both designer and moderately priced women's wear. Profits have fluctuated recently, and top management is deciding which product line to emphasize. Accountants have provided the following data:

	Designer	Moderately Priced
Per item:		
Average sale price..	$200	$80
Average variable expenses...............................	70	24
Average contribution margin.........................	$130	$56
Contribution margin ratio.............................	65%	70%

The Avant-Garde store, in Portland, Oregon, has 10,000 square feet of floor space. If it emphasizes moderately priced goods, 400 items can be displayed in the store. Only 200 designer items can be displayed for sale. These numbers are also the average monthly sales in units.

Prepare an analysis to show which product to emphasize.

E27-5 Larson Company manufactures an electronic control that it uses in its final product. The electronic control has the following manufacturing costs per unit:

Make or buy
(Obj. 1, 2, 3)

Direct materials..	$ 4.90
Direct labor	1.10
Variable overhead...	1.24
Fixed overhead	4.00
Manufacturing product cost	$11.24

Another company has offered to sell Larson the electronic control for $8 per unit. If Larson buys the control from the outside supplier, the manufacturing facilities that will be idled cannot be used for any other purpose. Should Larson make or buy the electronic controls? Explain the difference between correct analysis and incorrect analysis of this decision.

E27-6 Refer to Exercise 27-5. Assume that Larson needs 90,000 of the electronic controls. By purchasing them from the outside supplier, Larson can use its idle facilities to manufacture another product that will contribute $75,000 to operating income. Identify the *net* costs that Larson will incur to acquire 90,000 electronic controls under three alternative plans. Which plan makes the best use of Larson's facilities? Support your answer.

Best use of facilities
(Obj. 1, 2)

E27-7 Catawba Paper Corporation manufactures cardboard and linerboard by a joint process that costs $300,000 each month. Cardboard sells for $32 per ton and linerboard for $12 per ton. Each month the manufacturing process generates 5,000 tons of cardboard and 20,000 tons of linerboard. Use the relative sales value method to determine the cost of each ton of the two products.

Allocating joint processing costs
(Obj. 4)

E27-8 La Garza, Inc., is considering acquiring a manufacturing plant. The purchase price is $1,700,000. The owners believe that the plant will generate net cash inflows of $265,625 annually. It will have to be replaced in five years. Use the payback model to determine whether La Garza should purchase this plant.

Payback analysis of an investment—equal cash flows
(Obj. 6)

E27-9 Wang Manufacturing is adding a new product line that will require an investment of $1,230,000. Managers estimate that this investment will generate net cash inflows of $310,000 the first year, $280,000 the second year, and $200,000 each year thereafter. What is the payback period of this investment?

Payback analysis of an investment—unequal cash flows
(Obj. 6)

E27-10 Ligon Textiles is shopping for new equipment. Managers are considering two investments. Equipment manufactured by March, Inc., costs $400,000 and will last for five years, with no residual value. The March equipment is expected to generate annual operating income of $50,000. Equipment manufactured by Gardner Controls is priced at $500,000 and will remain useful for six years. It promises annual operating income of $72,000, and its expected residual value is $30,000.

Which equipment offers the higher accounting rate of return? What is the opportunity cost of purchasing from each manufacturer? How would Ligon managers use the notion of opportunity cost in making their decision?

Accounting rate of return analysis of investments
(Obj. 5, 6)

E27-11 Use the net-present-value model to determine whether High-End Products should invest in the following projects:

Net-present-value analysis of investments
(Obj. 6)

Project A: Costs $450,000 and offers 10 annual net cash inflows of $75,000. High-End demands an annual return of 12 percent on investments of this nature.

Project B: Costs $330,000 and offers 8 annual net cash inflows of $75,000. High-End requires an annual return of 14 percent on projects like B.

What is the maximum acceptable price to pay for each project?

Internal-rate-of-return analysis of investments (Obj. 6)

E27-12 Refer to the data of Exercise 27-11. Compute the internal rate of return of each project, and use this information to identify the better investment.

CHALLENGE EXERCISE

Which product to emphasize (Obj. 1, 2)

E27-13 Olé, Inc., produces two types of youth soccer shoes, Model L and Model R. Pertinent data follow:

	Per Unit	
	Model L	**Model R**
Sale price	$110.00	$75.00
Costs:		
Direct materials	$ 33.00	$14.00
Direct labor	15.00	25.00
Variable overhead*	25.00	12.50
Fixed overhead*	10.00	5.00
Variable operating expenses	14.00	10.00
Total cost	97.00	66.50
Operating income	$ 13.00	$ 8.50

*Allocated on the basis of machine-hours.

The soccer craze is such that Olé could use all its available machine-hours producing either model. The two models are processed through the same production departments.

Which model should Olé produce? If both models should be produced, compute the mix that will maximize operating income.

PROBLEMS (GROUP A)

Accept or reject a special sales order (Obj. 1, 2)

P27-1A Allied Rubber Company's contribution margin income statement for the most recent month reports the following:

Sales in units	76,000
Sales	$190,000
Variable expenses:	
Manufacturing	$ 38,000
Selling and administrative	54,000
Total variable expenses	92,000
Contribution margin	98,000
Fixed expenses:	
Manufacturing	58,000
Selling and administrative	16,000
Total fixed expenses	74,000
Operating income	$ 24,000

Monroe Motor Company wants to buy 10,000 industrial belts from Allied. Acceptance of the order will not increase Allied's selling and administrative expenses. Allied's plant has unused capacity to manufacture the additional belts. Monroe has offered $1.60 per belt, which is considerably below the normal sale price of $2.50.

Required

1. Prepare a quick summary to help determine whether Allied should accept this special sales order.

2. Prepare a total analysis to show Allied's operating income with and without the special sales order.

3. Identify long-run factors that Allied should consider in deciding whether to accept the special sales order.

P27-2A The income statement of Salvatore's Seafood Company highlights the losses of the shellfish division:

Retain or drop a product line (Obj. 1, 2, 3)

	Total	All Other Products	Shellfish
Sales	$847,500	$630,000	$217,500
Cost of goods sold:			
Variable	$152,500	$100,000	$ 52,500
Fixed	127,500	90,000	37,500
Total cost of goods sold	280,000	190,000	90,000
Gross margin	567,500	440,000	127,500
Selling and administrative expenses:			
Variable	375,000	270,000	105,000
Fixed	132,500	80,000	52,500
Total selling and administrative expenses	507,500	350,000	157,500
Operating income (loss)	$ 60,000	$ 90,000	$ (30,000)

Franco Salvatore is considering discontinuing the shellfish product line. The company's accountants estimate that dropping shellfish will decrease fixed cost of goods sold by $25,000 and decrease fixed selling and administrative expenses by $15,000.

Required

1. Prepare a quick summary to show whether Salvatore's should drop the shellfish product line.
2. Prepare a total analysis to show Salvatore's operating income with and without the shellfish division. Prepare the income statement in contribution margin format.
3. Explain the difference between correct analysis and incorrect analysis of the decision to retain or drop the shellfish product line.

P27-3A Piziak Appliances of Los Angeles specializes in washers and dryers and in televisions. Robert and Roma Piziak, the owners, are expanding the store. They are deciding which product line to emphasize. To make this decision, they assemble the following data, which suggest that the line of washers and dryers, with the higher contribution margin, is more profitable:

Which product to emphasize (Obj. 1, 2)

	Washers/Dryers	Televisions
Per unit:		
Sale price	$500	$300
Variable expenses	260	162
Contribution margin	$240	$138
Contribution margin ratio	48%	46%

After the renovation, the store will have 6,400 square feet of floor space. By devoting the new floor space to washers/dryers, Piziak Appliances can display 25 units of merchandise. If televisions are emphasized, 50 units can be displayed. The Piziaks expect their company's merchandise to turn over once a month. That is, they expect monthly sales to equal the maximum number of units displayed.

Required

1. Identify the limiting factor for Piziak Appliances.
2. Prepare an analysis to show which product line to emphasize.

P27-4A Blue Water Corp. of America manufactures scuba equipment. Currently the company makes scuba fins. The cost of producing 2,000 pairs of fins each year is:

Make or buy; best use of facilities (Obj. 1, 2)

Direct materials	$11,000
Direct labor	15,000
Variable overhead	5,600
Fixed overhead	38,400
Total manufacturing costs	$70,000

Goodman, Inc., will sell Blue Water the fins for $30 per pair. Blue Water would pay $0.50 per pair to transport the fins to its warehouse.

Required

1. Blue Water's accountants predict that purchasing the fins from Goodman will enable the company to avoid $10,000 of fixed overhead. Prepare an analysis to show whether Blue Water should make or buy the fins.
2. Assume that the Blue Water facilities freed up by the purchase of the fins from Goodman can be used to manufacture another product. That product will contribute $32,000 to profit. Fixed costs will not change. Prepare an analysis to show which alternative makes the best use of Blue Water's facilities: (a) make fins, (b) buy fins and leave facilities idle, or (c) buy fins and make another product.

Joint-cost allocation; sell at split-off or process further; opportunity cost
(Obj. 1, 2, 4, 5)

P27-5A McLennan County Dairy purchases raw milk from area farmers and processes it until it becomes two products, cream and liquid skim. Cream can be sold at split-off for $6 per gallon and liquid skim can be sold for $3 per gallon. During August 19X4, the dairy's accountant recorded the following amounts:

Joint processing cost	$20,000
Gallons produced:	
Cream	2,000
Liquid skim	6,000

Both cream and liquid skim can be further processed past split-off: cream into butter cream and liquid skim into condensed milk. One gallon of cream, combined with other ingredients, yields one gallon of butter cream. McLennan County Dairy's cost of processing 2,000 gallons of cream into 2,000 gallons of butter cream is $3,100. Butter cream sells for $7.50 per gallon.

All the August production of cream and liquid skim was sold at split-off.

Required

1. Allocate the joint processing cost to the gallons of cream and liquid skim produced in August. Use the relative sales value method.
2. Why did the dairy's managers decide not to process cream into butter cream? Be specific.
3. Identify the opportunity cost of each alternative for cream. State how managers use the notion of opportunity cost in making decisions.

Capital-budgeting decision by three methods
(Obj. 6, 7)

P27-6A Aunt Annie's, Inc., maker of the original gourmet pretzel, is considering two possible expansion plans. Plan A is to open 12 stores at a cost of $4,000,000. This investment is expected to generate net cash inflows of $1,000,000 each year for seven years, which is the estimated life of the store properties. Estimated residual value of the stores is zero. Under Plan B, Aunt Annie's would open eight stores at a cost of $3,200,000. Expected annual net cash inflows are $700,000, with residual value of $400,000 at the end of seven years. Aunt Annie's top managers require an annual return of 14 percent.

Required

1. Compute the payback period, the accounting rate of return, and the net present value of these two plans. What are the strengths and weaknesses of these capital-budgeting models?
2. Which expansion plan should Aunt Annie's management choose? Why?
3. Estimate the internal rate of return (IRR) of Plan A. How does Plan A's IRR compare with the discount rate?
4. How will what you learned from this problem help you manage a business?

P27-1B Golden State Toy Corporation manufactures toys in San Diego, California. Golden State's contribution margin income statement for the most recent month contains the following:

Accept or reject a special sales order
(Obj. 1, 2)

Sales in units......................................	420,000
Sales...	$420,000
Variable expenses:	
Manufacturing...............................	$ 84,000
Selling and administrative..............	100,000
Total variable expenses...................	184,000
Contribution margin.........................	236,000
Fixed expenses:	
Manufacturing...............................	116,000
Selling and administrative..............	75,000
Total fixed expenses.......................	191,000
Operating income	$ 45,000

West Coast Promotions, Inc., wishes to buy 80,000 toys from Golden State. Acceptance of the order will not increase Golden State's selling and administrative expenses. Golden State's plant has unused capacity to manufacture the additional toys. West Coast has offered $0.70 per toy, which is considerably below the normal sale price of $1.

Required

1. Prepare a quick summary to help determine whether Golden State should accept this special sales order.

2. Prepare a total analysis to show Golden State's operating income with and without the special sales order.

3. Identify long-run factors that Golden State should consider in deciding whether to accept the special sales order.

P27-2B Members of the board of directors of Packard Products, Inc., have received the following income statement for the year just ended:

Retain or drop a product line
(Obj. 1, 2, 3)

	Total	Industrial Products	Household Products
Sales...	$850,000	$429,000	$421,000
Cost of goods sold:			
Variable......................................	$119,000	$ 64,000	$ 55,000
Fixed	327,000	241,000	86,000
Total cost of goods sold...............	446,000	305,000	141,000
Gross margin	404,000	124,000	280,000
Selling and administrative expenses:			
Variable......................................	178,000	86,000	92,000
Fixed	89,000	58,000	31,000
Total selling and administrative			
expenses....................................	267,000	144,000	123,000
Operating income (loss)...................	$137,000	$ (20,000)	$157,000

Members of the board are surprised that the industrial products division is losing money. They commission a study to determine whether the company should delete the industrial products line. Company accountants estimate that dropping industrial products will decrease fixed cost of goods sold by $75,000 and decrease fixed selling and administrative expenses by $20,000.

Required

1. Prepare a quick summary to show whether Packard Products should drop the industrial products line.

2. Prepare a total analysis to show Packard Products' operating income with and without industrial products. Prepare the income statement in contribution margin format.

3. Explain the difference between correct analysis and incorrect analysis of the decision to retain or drop the industrial products line.

Which product to emphasize
(Obj. 1, 2)

P27-3B Coastal Carolina Corp., located in Charleston, South Carolina, produces two lines of household appliances: deluxe and standard models. The owners are expanding the plant, and they are deciding which product line to emphasize. To make this decision, they assemble the following data, which suggest that the deluxe product line is more profitable:

	Deluxe	Standard
Per unit:		
Sale price...	$40	$30
Variable expenses	12	12
Contribution margin.........................	$28	$18
Contribution margin ratio...............	70%	60%

After the plant expansion, the factory will have a production capacity of 1,600 machine-hours per month. By devoting the machine-hours to deluxe appliances, the plant can manufacture 20 units of merchandise each hour. If standard appliances are emphasized, the plant can produce 40 units per hour.

Required

1. Identify the limiting factor for Coastal Carolina Corp.
2. Prepare an analysis to show which product line to emphasize.

Make or buy; best use of facilities
(Obj. 1, 2)

P27-4B O'Day Company manufactures sailboats. Currently the company makes the boats' seat covers. The cost of producing 1,200 seat covers is:

Direct materials...	$1,260
Direct labor	1,440
Variable overhead..	960
Fixed overhead	2,400
Total manufacturing costs for 1,200 units...............	$6,060

Claybrook Corporation will sell seat covers to O'Day for $4 each. O'Day would pay $0.20 per unit to transport the seat covers to its manufacturing plant, where it would add its own O'Day label at a cost of $0.06 per seat cover.

Required

1. O'Day's accountants predict that purchasing the seat covers from Claybrook will enable the company to avoid $900 of fixed overhead. Prepare an analysis to show whether O'Day should make or buy the seat covers.

2. Assume that the O'Day facilities freed up by the purchase of seat covers from Claybrook can be used to manufacture another product that will contribute $1,610 to profit. Fixed costs will not change. Prepare an analysis to show which alternative makes the best use of O'Day's facilities: (a) make seat covers, (b) buy seat covers and leave facilities idle, or (c) buy seat covers and make another product.

Joint-cost allocation; sell at split-off or process further; opportunity cost
(Obj. 1, 2, 4, 5)

P27-5B A BP America refinery produces two products, S and M, in a joint process. Both products are sold to manufacturers as fertilizer ingredients.

Product S sells at the split-off point for $0.50 per gallon; product M sells for $0.60 per gallon. Data for April 19X3 are:

Joint processing cost.........................	$2,800,000
Gallons produced and sold:	
S..	8,000,000
M	5,000,000

Suppose that in April the 5,000,000 gallons of M could have been processed further into 5,000,000 gallons of Super M at an additional cost of $500,000. The Super M could have been sold for $0.76 per gallon.

Required

1. Allocate the joint processing cost to product S and product M using the relative sales value method.
2. Should product M have been processed further into Super M? What is the role of the allocated joint cost (Requirement 1) in the decision to sell at split-off or to process further?
3. Identify the opportunity cost of each alternative for Product M. State how BP managers can use the notion of opportunity cost in making their decision.

P27-6B No-Chema Corp. operates a chain of grocery stores that specialize in health foods. The company is considering two possible expansion plans. Plan A is to open three stores at a cost of $6,400,000. This plan is expected to generate net cash inflows of $600,000 each year for 20 years, the estimated life of the store properties. Estimated residual value is $3,000,000. Under Plan B, No-Chema would open eight smaller stores at a cost of $7,200,000. Expected annual net cash inflows are $860,000, with zero residual value at the end of 19 years. No-Chema's top managers require an annual return of 8 percent.

Capital-budgeting decision by three methods
(Obj. 6, 7)

Required

1. Compute the payback period, the accounting rate of return, and the net present value of these two plans. What are the strengths and weaknesses of these capital-budgeting models?
2. Which expansion plan should No-Chema's owners choose? Why?
3. Estimate Plan B's internal rate of return (IRR). How does the IRR compare with the company's discount rate?
4. How will what you learned from this problem help you manage a business?

EXTENDING YOUR KNOWLEDGE

DECISION PROBLEMS

1. Jonathan Christian, a second-year business student at Pepperdine University, will graduate in two years with an accounting major and a Spanish minor. Christian is trying to decide where to work this summer. He has two choices: work full-time for a bottling plant or work part-time in the accounting department of a meat-packing plant. He probably will work the same place next summer as well. He is able to work 12 weeks during the summer.

Analyzing relevant factors in an employment decision
(Obj. 1, 5)

The bottling plant will pay Christian $330 per week this year and 7 percent more next year. At the meat-packing plant, he could work 20 hours per week at $7.25 per hour. By working only part-time, he could take two accounting courses this summer. Tuition is $225 per hour for each of the four-hour courses. Christian believes that the experience he gains this summer will qualify him for a full-time accounting position with the meat-packing plant next year. That position will pay $500 per week.

Christian sees two additional benefits of working part-time this year. First, he could reduce his workload during the fall and spring semesters by one course each term. Second, he would have the time to work as a grader in the accounting department during the 15-week fall term. Grading pays $30 per week.

Required

1. Suppose that Jonathan Christian ignores the time value of money in decisions that cover this short a time period. Suppose also that his sole goal is to make as much money as possible between now and the end of next summer. What should he do? What would *you* do if you were faced with these alternatives?
2. Now suppose that Christian considers the time value of money for all cash flows that he expects to receive one year or more in the future. Which alternative does this consideration favor? Why?

Deciding whether to purchase a new machine
(Obj. 1, 6, 7)

2. Texas Instruments (TI) is considering a new computer-controlled etching machine for etching trenches in the surfaces of silicon wafers. The company processes these wafers into semiconductor chips. The etching machine costs $820,000, and an additional $300,000 would be required for installation. Thus, $1,120,000 is the required cash outlay for the investment.

    The new etching machine would replace an existing machine that was purchased five years ago for $500,000. That machine has five years of useful life remaining. TI must either keep the old machine or replace it with the new machine. The expected useful life of the new machine is five years. TI managers believe that use of the machine would save $323,000 per year in cash operating costs. However, annual maintenance cost would be $25,000 higher with the new machine than with the old.

    Disposal values of the machines are:

	Old Machine	New Machine
Now	$20,000	—
In 5 years..............	–0–	$100,000

Texas Instruments has a minimum desired rate of return of 14 percent on assets of this type.

Required

1. Is the $500,000 cost of the old machine relevant to the decision of whether to keep or replace the old machine? Why or why not?

2. Which of the four capital-budgeting decision models is best for making this decision? Use that model to decide which course of action is better for TI.

3. Suppose that TI managers have identified several intangible benefits of the new etching machine. These include greater flexibility, improved quality, and shorter manufacturing time. What dollar amount *per year* would the managers have to assign to these intangible benefits to make the new machine an acceptable investment?

ETHICAL ISSUE

Roberta Morrison is the chief financial officer (CFO) of Standard and Smith, a diversified company with a broad range of products in the food-service and household-products industries. Morrison recently convinced Standard and Smith's top management to sell the company's old mainframe computer and replace it with a system of minicomputers and microcomputers located at the company's 20 plants and offices.

    The CFO and her task force asked two vendors to propose systems that meet Standard and Smith's operating needs. The first vendor's proposal would require a $1,000,000 up-front investment for hardware, software, and training. Its relevant net cash inflows are predicted to be $400,000 per year for the four-year decision period. The second vendor's proposal would require a $2,000,000 initial outlay. Its relevant annual net cash inflows are $750,000. Both systems would have no residual value at the end of four years.

    Standard and Smith uses the net-present-value model to evaluate investment proposals. The company's minimum desired rate of return on investments of this nature is 16 percent. However, Morrison is sure that if she were to use a 14-percent discount rate for this decision, no one would challenge her. Morrison would like to accept the proposal of the second vendor, a company owned by a close friend of hers.

Required

1. Compute the net present value of the two proposals. Use Standard and Smith's 16-percent discount rate. Which proposal should the company accept?

2. Compute the net present value of each proposal using 14 percent as the discount rate. Is this rate acceptable in this case? Would it be unethical for Morrison to make her selection on the basis of the 14-percent computations?

1. BUDGETING LIFE-CYCLE COSTS AND EVALUATING A PROPOSED PRODUCT LINE

Worldwide Container Company is evaluating a proposal to add a new product line of containers for volatile chemicals. The container line requires an investment of $3,810,000 for equipment. The equipment is expected to have a three-year life and zero disposal value.

Worldwide's managers predict that 48,000 containers can be sold in each of the next three years, at $100 per container. The company's *initial* life-cycle budget includes total cash operating costs of $9,360,000 ($3,120,000 per year) and total depreciation of $3,810,000. Worldwide Container's top managers desire a life-cycle operating contribution of 16 percent of sales for investments of this type.

Required

1. Worldwide's engineers believe that kaizen costing will reduce life-cycle average operating cost by $2 per container. For the containers, compute (a) allowable life-cycle average operating cost, (b) original budgeted cost, (c) target cost, and (d) required value-engineering cost reduction.

2. Compute the net present value of the container project, assuming that Worldwide's discount rate is 16 percent. Use the containers' allowable life-cycle average operating cost as the starting point in computing annual operating cash inflows. Should the company accept or reject the project? Why?

2. GROUP PROJECT: DECIDING WHICH PRODUCT TO EMPHASIZE AND MANAGING QUALITY IN A CATERING BUSINESS

This exercise concludes the Group Project that you worked on at the end of Parts Five and Six of this book. In the previous Group Project, you budgeted the sale price per serving and the average number of servings for each of the three types of catered events. You also budgeted the standard variable cost per event. Consider your two most profitable events (for example, hors d'oeuvres and suppers). Suppose that it takes the same amount of time *per serving* for the most profitable event as it takes for the next-most-profitable event. Time is your limiting factor. If demand for your services is greater than you can meet, which of the two events should you emphasize? Why?

Now suppose that you would like to establish a reputation as a top-quality caterer. Name three types of prevention costs that you will incur in order to improve quality. What effects will these costs have on your costs of appraisal, internal failure, and external failure? Be specific.

Reinventing Chrysler

Chrysler Corporation's successful implementation of modern organizational and operating philosophies is perhaps the most well-known turnaround for a major U.S. corporation in recent years. On the brink of bankruptcy in the 1970s, Chrysler was kept afloat with substantial loans guaranteed by the federal government. Today it is a growing, profitable auto company regarded as a leader in innovation and quality.

Behind Chrysler's success story is a major overhaul of its organizational structure—from separate, sequential operating divisions called *chimneys* to an integrated team approach called the *platform system.* Years ago, each car model went through the *design, engineering, procurement, manufacturing,* and *marketing* stages in succession. Each of these stages operated independently; each had its own vertical hierarchy and its own bureaucracy. If problems arose—for example, a bad design caused unexpected manufacturing complications—managers had to stop the process, go back and solve the problems, and then move forward again. *Finance,* on the sidelines, was prevented from developing important cost data during this process. Turf battles and frustration were the results.

Today Chrysler combines the five operating divisions and the finance division in its platform system. Four separate platform teams with representatives from each area have been assembled: small cars, large cars, minivans, and Jeeps and trucks. Individuals from design, engineering, procurement, manufacturing, marketing, and finance work together from the initial design phase through sales and distribution. This team approach identifies many problems before they occur. It also more effectively incorporates information gathered from consumers in the design and production of each new model.

Chrysler's platform system, and the use of ideas from employees at all levels of the organization, has had impressive results. Operating costs have been reduced by $3 billion, and new designs are brought to market much faster. Chrysler's LH car models and its racy Viper sports car reached the marketplace in record time. Quality has improved substantially, with major reductions in rework and repair. Suggestions from plant employees have reduced the number of stamping operations required on auto-body components. And instead of dictating materials requirements to suppliers, Chrysler listens to their ideas and coordinates production throughout the value chain.

Chrysler's total reorganization, as part of its strategic plan for the 1990s, has created an environment that fosters cooperation, creativity, and excellence. The successful strategy has allowed the auto giant to win market share by integrating the many processes that turn ideas into an automobile.

CASE QUESTIONS

1. Explain the strategic planning goals that Chrysler sought to achieve through its reorganization.
2. A Chrysler factory worker stated that under the old system, he would have performed an assembly with defective supplier parts, even if he noticed the problem and could fix it. Today he responds differently. Discuss how the changes at Chrysler have affected this man's attitude about his job and how the company benefits as a result.
3. Give an example of an auto design problem that Chrysler's platform system could prevent for (a) manufacturing and (b) customer satisfaction.

Appendix A
Published Financial Statements

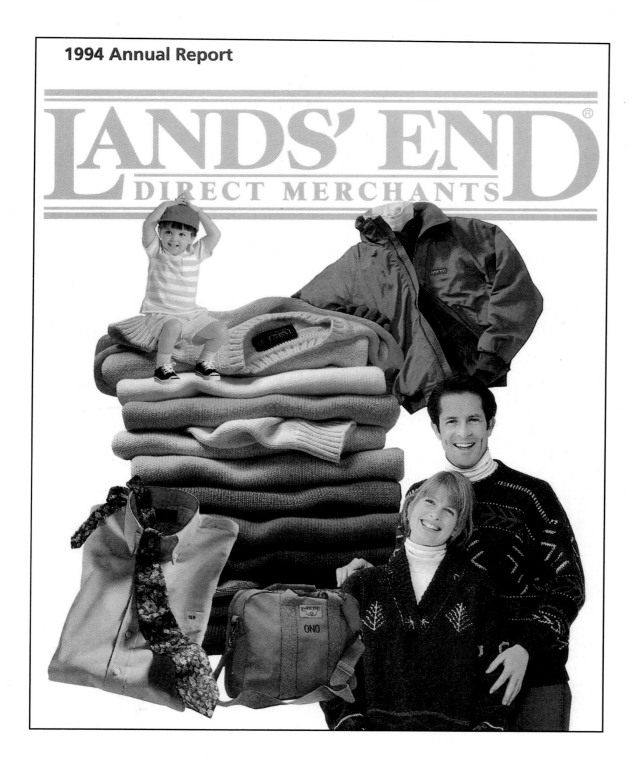

1994 Annual Report

Sales up 19% to $870 million

Pretax return on sales was 8.0%

Net income before an accounting change was $42.4 million, up 27% from the prior year

Per share earnings rose to $2.36, compared with $1.85 a year ago

Return on average shareholders' investment was 28%

Return on average assets was 18%

During our busiest season, we had 6,400 employees on hand, including temporary staff

There are almost 7.4 million Lands' End customers and 18.1 million people on our mailing list

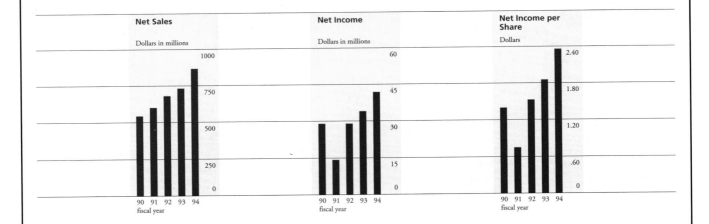

Inside this report

1

Dear Shareholder,

William T. End   David F. Dyer

Fiscal 1994 was a strong year for Lands' End. Sales reached $870 million, a 19 percent increase from fiscal 1993. Before an accounting change, net income was $42.4 million, up 27 percent from last year, and net income per share was $2.36.

Our important holiday season came in well above expectations, a nice rebound from last year. We were especially pleased to see well-balanced growth of all our businesses during fiscal 1994. Our primary and prospecting catalogs produced about half of the net sales growth. Specialty catalogs, international and our new businesses all showed sales above our expectations. We believe this can be attributed to a somewhat healthier economy and a strong catalog market, as well as better merchandising, value positioning and improvements in both product design and creative presentation.

Gross profit margin for fiscal 1994 was 41.1 percent of net sales, down from last year's 41.8 percent. This decline was due largely to the decision we made to reduce product prices and improve our value position. Value is perhaps the most important trend in retailing today. We define value as offering excellent product quality, fair prices and world-class customer service. Our customers demand value in the products they purchase, and we will continue to deliver it with prices that are generally well below those found in specialty and better department stores.

Selling, general and administrative expenses rose 14 percent, less than the rate of our sales increase. As a percentage of sales, SG&A was 33.0 percent, an improvement from fiscal 1993's 34.2 percent. Printing efficiencies and low paper costs kept the expense of catalog production well in check, and improved customer reaction to our offerings also helped our expense ratio.

We're proud of these results for fiscal 1994. We had strong sales, an improved profitability level and an enhanced quality/value offering to our customers. Additionally, we began investing for the future of Lands' End through the development of international and new businesses, in the expansion of our facilities and by making improvements in our information systems capabilities. We are also making investments in the quality and training of our most important resource, our people. Fiscal 1994 was successful because of the hard work and dedication of 6,400 Lands' End employees.

At the beginning of fiscal 1994, Dick Anderson announced his retirement as chief executive officer. Dick has been an important part of the success of Lands' End for more than 14 years and is missed by all of us. We wish him the best in his retirement and thank him for his outstanding contributions to our company.

Upon Dick's retirement, we both assumed new responsibilities, titles and challenges. Our goal is to continue to operate the company with the same commitment to our shareholders, customers, employees, suppliers, and communities as Lands' End has had since it was founded in 1963.

We are looking forward to fiscal 1995 as another exciting and challenging year. We believe Lands' End is well positioned to grow and thrive in the future because of the three key growth strategies: to grow our core U.S.

2

businesses, to expand our international businesses and to develop and grow new businesses.

Our largest and most important growth opportunity is to build our core U.S. businesses. Our product lines for men, women, children, and home are all healthy and growing. We also see the catalog industry growing and prospering as men and women have less and less free time and less time to shop. In anticipation of the January 1995 postal rate increase and the probability of higher paper costs, we will invest heavily in the acquisition of new customers during fiscal 1995.

In the international area, we plan to continue to aggressively build our relatively new catalog businesses in the U.K. and Canada. Additionally, we plan to launch a Japanese catalog business later this year.

In the new business area, we will continue to aggressively grow The Territory Ahead, a company in which we purchased a majority interest this past March, and our Corporate Sales business, launched as a separate catalog business during the year. In addition, we will actively pursue start-ups or acquisitions of direct response businesses.

There has been much discussion of the role electronic media might play in the retailing industry. While we believe this new medium will become an important factor in retailing and will cause some business shift from both stores and catalogs, it will be a number of years before this shift is significant. We continue to aggressively test electronic media to be sure we understand and realize its full potential for Lands' End.

Another important goal for us this year is to continue to improve our service to our customers. We believe this can be accomplished by being able to ship 90 percent of the items requested when an order is placed, by reducing the time it takes to deliver merchandise to our customers' homes and by improving our information systems available to our phone operators. We plan to invest heavily in all these areas in fiscal 1995.

In summary, we believe Lands' End has strong opportunities for growth in the future. As long as we continue to focus on our customer and deliver quality products, honest value and world-class service that exceed our customers' expectations, we'll continue to be successful.

Thanks for being a shareholder.

Sincerely,

William T. End
Chief Executive Officer

David F. Dyer
Vice Chairman, Merchandising & Sales

March 29, 1994

3

The Year at a Glance

February

After more than 14 years of service, Dick Anderson retires as chief executive officer, but remains vice chairman of the board. Bill End is elected chief executive officer in addition to being president, and Dave Dyer is named vice chairman of merchandising and sales.

March

Lands' End purchases a majority interest in The Territory Ahead, an upscale casualwear catalog company headquartered in Santa Barbara, California, an exciting first acquisition for our company.

April

Our popular Super-T™ shirt is featured on the cover of our April catalog at $12 as part of our value pricing strategy. Some other value programs include our $19.50 oxford dress shirt, $32.50 popular twill pants for men and our $129 cashmere sweaters.

May

Work begins on a high-bay addition to the distribution center, enabling us to store an additional 500,000 cartons of merchandise and giving us some much-needed breathing room in time for our peak holiday selling season.

June

For the first time, our primary catalog is prepared for printing in-house, using electronic desktop publishing. By the end of fiscal 1994, all our catalogs will be prepared on desktop, giving us more control and a shorter lead time for those ever-present last-minute changes.

July

We begin testing a program for multimedia interactive kiosk shopping located in Chicago. Electronic media we are testing during the year include Prodigy, GEnie, MicroMall, CompuServe, In-Flight Phone, and En Passant, a computer-based CD-ROM project developed by Apple Computer.

July

August

In Oakham, England, we celebrate the opening of our first telephone order and distribution center outside the U.S. Back at home, more than 7,000 people share a warm, sunny day at the Lands' End annual picnic on the Dodgeville campus. Good food, good times, good friends.

September

We mail two new catalogs: Textures, a collection of women's tailored clothing suitable for the work setting, and Corporate Sales, our new business-to-business catalog promoting volume sales to businesses, teams and other groups.

October

Lands' End purchases land adjacent to our Reedsburg, Wisconsin, telephone center as a site for an additional distribution center that will be built in 1994.

November

Peak is in full swing. On our busiest day, we handle 125,000 phone calls and ship 133,000 packages.

December

Our busiest month of the year. Orders received by the 22nd are in our customers' homes before the 25th — the only day we're closed. Merry Christmas!

January

Our catalogs are starting to show Spring merchandise, our photographers are shooting swimsuits, and our product development team is finalizing orders for Fall merchandise. Another new year.

4

Results of operations for fiscal 1994, compared with fiscal 1993

Consolidated statements of operations presented as a percentage of net sales

For the period ended	January 28, 1994	January 29, 1993	January 31, 1992
Net sales	100.0%	100.0%	100.0%
Cost of sales	58.9	58.2	57.8
Gross profit	41.1	41.8	42.2
Selling, general and administrative expenses	33.0	34.2	35.0
Income from operations	8.1	7.6	7.2
Interest expense	–	(0.2)	(0.2)
Other expense	(0.1)	–	–
Income before income taxes and cumulative effect of change in accounting	8.0	7.4	7.0
Income tax provision	3.1	2.8	2.8
Net income before cumulative effect of change in accounting	4.9	4.6	4.2
Cumulative effect of change in accounting for income taxes	0.1	–	–
Net income	5.0%	4.6%	4.2%

Net sales increased 19 percent to $870 million in fiscal 1994, compared with $734 million in fiscal 1993. The increase was primarily due to improved customer reaction to the catalogs and an increase in the number of regular and specialty catalogs mailed from 136 million to 155 million in fiscal 1994. About half of the net sales increase came from the main monthly catalogs and prospect catalogs, principally due to a better customer reaction to these catalogs. Other significant sources of the sales growth were four additional issues of specialty catalogs, the acquisition of a majority interest in The Territory Ahead, a California-based catalog company, and growth in our U.K. subsidiary. Specialty catalogs include the Kids catalog, featuring children's clothing; Coming Home, a catalog focusing on products for the bed and bath; Beyond Buttowndowns, a men's tailored clothing and accessories catalog; and the new Textures catalog, featuring tailored clothing for women.

Inventory at the end of fiscal 1994 totaled $150 million, a 41% increase from fiscal 1993 ending inventory of $106 million. At the end of fiscal 1993, the company had 14% lower inventory than at the end of fiscal 1992 when inventory totaled $123 million. The company believes that the fiscal 1993 year-end inventory level was lower than needed to offer the "world-class" service it attempts to give its customers and contributed to the lower than planned service levels, especially in Spring of 1994. For the year, the company was able to ship about 85 percent of items ordered by customers at the time of order placement, compared to 87 percent in fiscal 1993.

Gross profit
Gross profit increased 17% from $306 million in fiscal 1993 to $357 million in fiscal 1994 primarily due to the 19% increase in consolidated net sales partially offset by the decrease in the gross profit margin. As a percentage of net sales, gross profit decreased from 41.8% in fiscal 1993 to 41.1% in fiscal 1994 principally due to lower initial markups and steeper markdowns on liquidated merchandise. This was somewhat offset by a favorable mix of full-price sales. Liquidation of out-of-season and overstocked merchandise at reduced prices totaled approximately 10% of total net sales in fiscal 1994, compared with 11% in fiscal 1993.

Costs on inventory purchases increased approximately 0.8 percent in fiscal 1994, compared with 1.1 percent in fiscal 1993.

Selling, general and administrative expenses
Selling, general and administrative (SG&A) expenses increased 14 percent to $287.0 million, from $250.7 million in fiscal 1993, principally due to increases in fixed operating expenses, operating expenses associated with higher sales and increases in catalog mailings.

The SG&A-to-net sales ratio declined from 34.2 percent in fiscal 1993 to 33.0 percent in fiscal 1994.

8

The decrease in the ratio was primarily a result of lower catalog production expenses and relatively higher sales demand generated by the catalogs. This was partially offset by higher variable expenses due to increased package delivery costs and slightly lower first-time fulfillment, as well as somewhat higher fixed expenses. A portion of the shipping cost was offset by an increase in shipping charges to customers.

Historically, the cost of producing and mailing catalogs represents about half of total SG&A. In fiscal 1994, that portion relating to catalogs was lower due to savings in printing and lower paper costs. The company anticipates an increase in postal rates in January 1995, which could have a significant impact on SG&A. In addition, the company is unable to predict how long the soft paper market will continue.

The company is investing in information systems for the core business, expansion of its international business, acquisition of new customers, and the development of new catalog businesses. While doing so, these efforts are expected to have a negative impact on the SG&A-to-sales ratio.

Depreciation and amortization expense was up 5 percent from the prior year, to $8.3 million. Rental expense was up 15 percent to $7.3 million primarily due to increased hardware and software rentals.

Little change in utilization of credit lines
Interest expense on lines of credit was down in fiscal 1994 due to lower borrowing levels throughout the fiscal year. Inventory carried for the first five months of the year was significantly lower, resulting in less borrowing in the first half of the year. The increased level of profits and cash in the second half of the year held borrowing in check, despite rising inventory levels and capital spending increases. The lines of credit peaked at $54 million in October 1993 compared with a peak of $55 million in the prior year. At January 28, 1994, the company had no short-term debt outstanding and had $40,000 of long-term debt related to a land purchase in Reedsburg, Wisconsin.

The company plans to build a second distribution center on this land in fiscal 1995.

Net income increased 31 percent
During the first quarter of fiscal 1994, the company adopted Statement of Financial Accounting Standards No. 109, "Accounting for Income Taxes," which added $1.3 million of net income, or $0.07 per share, to the results in fiscal year 1994. Before the cumulative effect of the accounting change, net income in fiscal 1994 rose about 27 percent to $42.4 million, or $2.36 per share, compared with $33.5 million, or $1.85 per share, for the similar period a year ago.

With the inclusion of the cumulative effect of this accounting change, net income increased 31 percent in fiscal 1994 to $43.7 million, from $33.5 million in fiscal 1993. Earnings per common share increased to $2.43 from $1.85 in the prior year.

Results of operations for fiscal 1993, compared with fiscal 1992
Net sales increased 7 percent to $734 million in fiscal 1993, compared with $683 million in fiscal 1992. The increase in net sales was due principally to an increase in the smaller specialty and prospect catalogs and from increased international sales. Total catalogs mailed increased from 123 million in fiscal 1992 to 136 million in fiscal 1993.

The smaller specialty catalogs include our Kids Catalog, featuring children's clothing, Beyond Buttondowns, our men's apparel catalog, and Coming Home with Lands' End, focusing on products for bed and bath.

Inventory at the end of fiscal 1993 totaled $106 million, a 14% decrease from fiscal 1992 ending inventory. We were able to ship about 87 percent of items ordered by customers at the time of order placement, which was the same as in the previous year.

9

(Dollars in thousands, except per share data)	For the period ended		
	January 28, 1994	January 29, 1993	January 31, 1992
Net sales	**$869,975**	$733,623	$683,427
Cost of sales	**512,521**	427,292	395,302
Gross profit	**357,454**	306,331	288,125
Selling, general and administrative expenses	**287,044**	250,737	238,958
Income from operations	**70,410**	55,594	49,167
Other income (expense):			
Interest expense	**(359)**	(1,330)	(1,550)
Interest income	**346**	266	312
Other	**(527)**	(497)	(437)
Total other expense, net	**(540)**	(1,561)	(1,675)
Income before income taxes and cumulative effect of change in accounting	**69,870**	54,033	47,492
Income tax provision	**27,441**	20,533	18,760
Net income before cumulative effect of change in accounting	**42,429**	33,500	28,732
Cumulative effect of change in accounting for income taxes	**1,300**	–	–
Net income	**$ 43,729**	$ 33,500	$ 28,732
Net income per share before cumulative effect of change in accounting	**$ 2.36**	$ 1.85	$ 1.53
Cumulative effect of change in accounting	**0.07**	–	–
Net income per share	**$ 2.43**	$ 1.85	$ 1.53

The accompanying notes to consolidated financial statements are an integral part of these consolidated statements.

12

Consolidated Balance Sheets

Lands' End, Inc. & Subsidiaries

(Dollars in thousands)	January 28, 1994	January 29, 1993
Assets		
Current assets:		
Cash and cash equivalents	$ 21,569	$ 22,754
Receivables	3,644	465
Inventory	149,688	106,057
Prepaid expenses	11,787	5,496
Deferred income tax benefit	5,588	2,759
Total current assets	192,276	137,531
Property, plant and equipment, at cost:		
Land and buildings	60,866	55,371
Fixtures and equipment	57,769	53,505
Leasehold improvements	1,346	1,267
Total property, plant and equipment	119,981	110,143
Less–accumulated depreciation and amortization	40,290	35,914
Property, plant and equipment, net	79,691	74,229
Intangibles, net	1,863	43
Total assets	$273,830	$211,803
Liabilities and shareholders' investment		
Current liabilities:		
Current maturities of long-term debt	$ 40	$ —
Accounts payable	54,855	36,976
Reserve for returns	3,907	4,005
Advance payment on orders	568	1,025
Accrued liabilities	16,875	12,717
Accrued profit sharing	2,276	1,634
Income taxes payable	12,528	10,958
Total current liabilities	91,049	67,315
Long-term debt, less current maturities	40	—
Deferred income taxes	5,200	5,100
Minority interest in equity of consolidated affiliate	256	—
Shareholders' investment:		
Common stock, 20,110,294 shares issued	201	201
Donated capital	8,400	8,400
Paid-in capital	24,888	24,857
Deferred compensation	(2,001)	(1,680)
Currency translation adjustments	246	—
Retained earnings	193,460	153,324
Treasury stock, 2,154,235 and 2,082,035 shares at cost, respectively	(47,909)	(45,714)
Total shareholders' investment	177,285	139,388
Total liabilities and shareholders' investment	$273,830	$211,803

The accompanying notes to consolidated financial statements are an integral part of these consolidated balance sheets.

13

(Dollars in thousands)	Common Stock Shares	Common Stock Amount	Paid-In Capital	Donated Capital	Deferred Compensation	Accumulated Trans. Adjust.	Retained Earnings	Treasury Stock Shares	Treasury Stock Amount	Total
Balance, January 31, 1991	20,110,294	$201	$23,782	$8,400	$(1,046)	$ —	$ 98,381	892,500	$(12,892)	$116,826
Cash dividends paid to common shareholders ($0.20 per share)	—	—	—	—	—	—	(3,695)	—	—	(3,695)
Purchases of treasury stock	—	—	—	—	—	—	—	746,340	(15,391)	(15,391)
Deferred compensation expense	—	—	—	—	160	—	—	—	—	160
Net income	—	—	—	—	—	—	28,732	—	—	28,732
Balance, January 31, 1992	20,110,294	201	23,782	8,400	(886)	—	123,418	1,638,840	(28,283)	126,632
Cash dividends paid to common shareholders ($0.20 per share)	—	—	—	—	—	—	(3,589)	—	—	(3,589)
Purchases of treasury stock	—	—	—	—	—	—	—	680,195	(20,972)	(20,972)
Issuance of treasury stock	—	—	—	—	(985)	—	(5)	(237,000)	3,541	2,551
Tax benefit of stock options exercised	—	—	1,075	—	—	—	—	—	—	1,075
Deferred compensation expense	—	—	—	—	191	—	—	—	—	191
Net income	—	—	—	—	—	—	33,500	—	—	33,500
Balance, January 29, 1993	20,110,294	201	24,857	8,400	(1,680)	—	153,324	2,082,035	(45,714)	139,388
Cash dividends paid to common shareholders ($0.20 per share)	—	—	—	—	—	—	(3,592)	—	—	(3,592)
Purchases of treasury stock	—	—	—	—	—	—	—	89,800	(2,861)	(2,861)
Issuance of treasury stock	—	—	—	—	(564)	—	(1)	(17,600)	666	101
Tax benefit of stock options exercised	—	—	31	—	—	—	—	—	—	31
Deferred compensation expense	—	—	—	—	243	—	—	—	—	243
Foreign currency translation	—	—	—	—	—	246	—	—	—	246
Net income	—	—	—	—	—	—	43,729	—	—	43,729
Balance, January 28, 1994	20,110,294	$201	$24,888	$8,400	$(2,001)	$246	$193,460	2,154,235	$(47,909)	$177,285

The accompanying notes to consolidated financial statements are an integral part of these consolidated statements.

14

(Dollars in thousands)	For the period ended		
	January 28, 1994	January 29, 1993	January 31, 1992
Cash flows (used for) from operating activities:			
Net income before cumulative effect	$ 42,429	$ 33,500	$ 28,732
Adjustments to reconcile net income to net cash flows			
from operating activities–			
Depreciation and amortization	8,286	7,900	7,428
Deferred compensation expense	243	191	160
Deferred income taxes	(1,684)	(612)	(1,498)
Loss on sales of fixed assets	684	931	412
Changes in current assets and liabilities:			
Receivables	(3,179)	365	379
Inventory	(43,631)	16,501	(48,695)
Prepaid expenses	(6,291)	999	(1,007)
Accounts payable	17,879	8,625	(9,446)
Reserve for returns	(98)	552	(564)
Advance payment on orders	(457)	390	189
Accrued liabilities	4,158	(650)	3,615
Accrued profit sharing	642	400	1,234
Income taxes payable	1,570	(1,868)	5,746
Other	502	–	–
Net cash flows (used for) from operating activities	21,053	67,224	(13,315)
Cash flows (used for) from investing activities:			
Purchases of assets	(16,068)	(8,591)	(5,345)
Proceeds from sales of fixed assets	71	15	554
Net cash flows used for investing activities	(15,997)	(8,576)	(4,791)
Cash flows (used for) from financing activities:			
Proceeds from short-term and long-term debt	80	–	13,000
Payment of short-term and long-term debt	–	(16,349)	(1,682)
Tax effect of exercise of stock options	31	1,075	–
Purchases of treasury stock	(2,861)	(20,972)	(15,391)
Issuance of treasury stock	101	2,551	–
Cash dividends paid to common shareholders	(3,592)	(3,589)	(3,695)
Net cash flows used for financing activities	(6,241)	(37,284)	(7,768)
Net increase (decrease) in cash and cash equivalents	(1,185)	21,364	(25,874)
Beginning cash and cash equivalents	22,754	1,390	27,264
Ending cash and cash equivalents	$ 21,569	$ 22,754	$ 1,390
Supplemental cash flow disclosures:			
Interest paid	$ 364	$ 1,315	$ 1,533
Income taxes paid	27,475	21,905	14,489

The accompanying notes to consolidated financial statements are an integral part of these consolidated statements.

15

Note 1. Summary of significant accounting policies

Nature of business
Lands' End, Inc., (the company) is a direct marketer of traditionally styled apparel, domestics (primarily bedding and bath items), soft luggage, and other products.

Principles of consolidation
The consolidated financial statements include the accounts of the company and its subsidiaries after elimination of intercompany accounts and transactions.

Year-end
In fiscal 1993, the company adopted a fiscal year of 52-53 weeks ending on the Friday closest to January 31. Operating fiscal year 1994 ended on January 28, 1994, fiscal year 1993 ended on January 29, 1993, and fiscal year 1992 ended on January 31, 1992. This change did not have a material impact on reported results.

Fair values of financial instruments
The fair value of financial instruments does not materially differ from their carrying values.

Inventory
Inventory, primarily merchandise held for sale, is stated at last-in, first-out (LIFO) cost, which is lower than market. If the first-in, first-out (FIFO) method of accounting for inventory had been used, inventory would have been approximately $19,120,000 and $17,300,000 higher than reported at January 28, 1994, and January 29, 1993, respectively.

Catalog costs
Prepaid expenses primarily consist of catalog production and mailing costs that have not yet been fully amortized over the expected revenue stream, which is approximately three months from the date catalogs are mailed.

Depreciation and amortization
Depreciation expense is calculated using the straight-line method over the estimated useful lives of the assets, which are 20 to 30 years for buildings and land improvements and 5 to 10 years for leasehold improvements and furni-ture, fixtures, equipment, and software. The company provides one-half year of depreciation in the year of addition and retirement.

Intangibles
Intangible assets consist primarily of goodwill, the excess of cost over the fair market value of net assets of a business purchased. Goodwill is being amortized over 40 years on a straight-line basis. Other intangibles are amortized over a shorter life. Total accumulated amortization of these intangibles was $126,000 at January 28, 1994.

Net income per share
Net income per share is computed by dividing net income by the weighted average number of common shares outstanding during each period. The weighted average common shares outstanding were 17,971,187, 18,155,073 and 18,821,693 for fiscal years 1994, 1993 and 1992, respectively. Common stock equivalents consisting of awards, grants and stock options have been issued by the company. The common stock equivalents do not significantly dilute basic earnings per share.

Reserve for losses on customer returns
At the time of sale, the company provides a reserve equal to the gross profit on projected merchandise returns, based on its prior returns experience.

Forward exchange contracts and import letters of credit
At January 28, 1994, the company had no forward exchange contracts. Import letters of credit are for commitments issued through third parties to guarantee payments for merchandise within specified time periods according to terms of the agreements. Import letters of credit were approximately $5.1 million at January 28, 1994.

Foreign currency translation
Financial statements of the foreign subsidiaries are translated into U.S. dollars in accordance with the provisions of Statement of Financial Accounting Standards No. 52. Foreign currency transaction gains and losses were insignificant.

16

Postretirement benefits
The company does not currently provide any postretirement benefits for employees other than profit sharing.

Reclassifications
Certain financial statement amounts have been reclassified to be consistent with the fiscal 1994 presentation.

Note 2. Shareholders' investment

Capital stock
The company currently has authorized 30 million shares of $0.01 par value common stock. Subject to shareholder approval, the authorized shares will be increased to 160 million. In addition, the company has authorized 5,000,000 shares of the preferred stock, $0.01 par value. The company's board of directors has the authority to issue shares and to fix dividend, voting and conversion rights, redemption provisions, liquidation preferences, and other rights and restrictions of the preferred stock.

Donated capital
In 1988 and 1989, a corporation owned by the principal shareholder of the company contributed $7.0 million and $1.4 million in cash, respectively, to the company in order to fund the cost of constructing an activity center in Dodgeville for use by company employees. These transactions were recorded as donated capital.

Treasury stock
The company's board of directors has authorized the purchase of a total of 3,100,000 shares of the company's common stock. A total of 2,408,835 shares, 2,319,035 shares and 1,638,840 shares had been purchased as of January 28, 1994, January 29, 1993, and January 31, 1992, respectively, and are stated at cost. A total of 17,600 shares and 237,000 shares were reissued in fiscal 1994 and fiscal 1993, respectively.

Stock awards and grants
The shareholders of the company have approved the company's restricted stock award plan. Under the provisions of the plan, a committee of the company's board of directors can award shares of the company's common stock to its officers and key employees. Such shares generally vest over a ten-year period on a straight-line basis from the date of award.

In addition, the company has granted shares of its common stock to individuals as an inducement to enter the employ of the company. The shares granted are subject to vesting on a straight-line basis over a ten-year period.

The following table reflects the activity under the stock award and stock grant plans:

	Awards	Grants
Balance at January 31, 1991	50,000	11,000
Granted	–	–
Forfeited	1,440	–
Balance at January 31, 1992	48,560	11,000
Granted	37,000	–
Forfeited	–	–
Balance at January 29, 1993	85,560	11,000
Granted	13,600	–
Forfeited	1,800	–
Balance at January 28, 1994	**97,360**	**11,000**

A total of 27,780 and 18,900 shares awarded and granted have vested as of January 28, 1994, and January 29, 1993, respectively.

The granting of the above awards and grants has been recorded as deferred compensation based on the fair market value of the shares at the date of grant. Compensation expense under these plans is recorded as shares vest.

Stock options
The company has reserved 1,000,000 shares of common stock, either authorized and unissued shares or treasury shares, for use by the plan. On February 17, 1994, the board of directors increased the amount of shares reserved to 1,250,000, which is also subject to shareholder approval. Options are granted at the discretion of a committee of the company's board of directors to officers and key employees of the company. No option may have an exercise price less than the fair market value per share of the common stock at the date of grant.

17

Activity under the stock option plan is as follows:

	Options	Average Exercise Price
Balance at January 31, 1991	450,000	$12.75
Granted	240,000	$25.38
Exercised	–	–
Balance at January 31, 1992	690,000	$17.14
Granted	40,000	$27.91
Exercised	200,000	$12.75
Balance at January 29, 1993	530,000	$19.61
Granted	318,600	$38.24
Exercised	4,000	$25.38
Balance at January 28, 1994	**844,600**	**$26.61**

The above options outstanding vest over a five-year period from the date of grant (544,600) or on the fifth anniversary from the date of grant (300,000). A total of 170,000 and 108,000 options have vested as of January 28, 1994 and January 29, 1993, respectively. The outstanding options expire as follows:

1995	250,000
2001	236,000
2002	40,000
2003	318,600
	844,600

Note 3. Income taxes

Effective January 30, 1993, the company elected to adopt Statement of Financial Accounting Standards (SFAS) No. 109, "Accounting for Income Taxes." Under the liability method prescribed by SFAS 109, deferred taxes are provided based upon enacted tax laws and rates applicable to the periods in which the taxes become payable. The cumulative effect of adopting the standard was recorded as a change in accounting principle in the first quarter of fiscal 1994 with an increase to net income of $1,300,000 or $0.07 per common share.

The components of the provision for income taxes for each of the periods presented is as follows (in thousands):

Period ended	January 28, 1994	January 29, 1993	January 31, 1992
Current:			
Federal	$24,607	$17,800	$17,167
State	4,518	3,345	3,091
Deferred	(1,684)	(612)	(1,498)
	$27,441	$20,533	$18,760

The difference between income taxes at the statutory federal income tax rate of 35 percent for fiscal 1994, and 34 percent for fiscal 1993 and fiscal 1992 and income tax reported in the statements of operations is as follows (in thousands):

Period ended	January 28, 1994	January 29, 1993	January 31, 1992
Tax at statutory federal tax rate	$24,421	$18,371	$16,147
State income taxes, net of federal benefit	2,818	2,043	1,846
Future tax benefits not recognized under SFAS No. 96	–	67	200
Other	202	52	567
	$27,441	$20,533	$18,760

Temporary differences which give rise to deferred tax benefit and liabilities as of January 28, 1994, are as follows (in thousands):

	Current Deferred Tax Benefit	Long-term Deferred Tax Liabilities
Catalog advertising	$(1,988)	$
Inventory	5,585	
Employee benefits	673	
Reserve for returns	482	
Depreciation		5,200
Foreign operating loss carryforwards		(933)
Valuation allowance		933
Other	836	
Total	$ 5,588	$5,200

The valuation allowance required under SFAS No. 109 has been established for the deferred income tax benefits related to certain subsidiary loss carryforwards, which may not be realized.

Prior to January 30, 1993, the company followed the provisions of Statement of Financial Accounting Standards (SFAS) No. 96, "Accounting for Income Taxes." The components of the deferred tax provision is as follows (in thousands):

Period ended	January 29, 1993	January 31, 1992
Depreciation	$(255)	$ 315
Inventory	(255)	(1,205)
Other	(102)	(608)
Deferred tax provision	$(612)	$(1,498)

Note 4. Lines of credit

The company has unsecured lines of credit with various banks whereby it may borrow up to a total of $110 million. Borrowings bear interest at the banks' prime rates, or at the company's option, LIBOR plus a fixed percentage, or Federal Funds rate-based negotiated pricing or the banks' Wholesale Certificate of Deposit rate plus a fixed percentage. The company also has a $2 million unsecured bank credit line that bears interest at the bank's prime rate plus 2%. There were no amounts outstanding at January 28, 1994, and January 29, 1993. There was $13 million outstanding at January 31, 1992, at interest rates averaging 4.8%.

In addition, subsequent to year-end, the company secured lines of credit with foreign banks totaling the equivalent of $20 million for a wholly owned foreign subsidiary.

Note 5. Long-term debt

Long-term debt was $40,000 as of January 28, 1994, compared to no long-term debt outstanding as of January 29, 1993.

The company has an agreement which expires December 31, 1994, with a bank for a $20 million credit facility. Outstanding balances will bear interest at the bank's prime rate or, at the company's option, LIBOR plus a fixed percentage. The company is currently in compliance with all lending conditions and covenants related to this debt facility.

Note 6. Leases

The company leases store and office space and equipment under various leasing arrangements. The leases are accounted for as operating leases. Total rental expense under these leases was $7,281,000, $6,348,000 and $6,228,000 for the years ended January 28, 1994, January 29, 1993, and January 31, 1992, respectively.

Total future fiscal year commitments under these leases as of January 28, 1994, are as follows (in thousands):

1995	$ 6,898
1996	5,477
1997	4,160
1998	2,359
1999	691
After 1999	1,239
	$20,824

Note 7. Retirement plan and accrued compensation

The company has a retirement plan which covers most regular employees and provides for annual contributions at the discretion of the board of directors. Beginning in fiscal 1993, a 401(k) savings feature was added to the plan which enables employee contributions and a company match on a portion of those contributions. Total expense provided under this plan was $3,709,000, $1,634,000 and $1,234,000 for the years ended January 28, 1994, January 29, 1993, and January 31, 1992, respectively. Accrued liabilities include accrued compensation of $1,647,000 and $515,000 at January 28, 1994, and January 29, 1993, respectively.

Note 8. State sales and use tax

A Supreme Court decision confirmed in May 1992 that the Commerce Clause of the United States Constitution prevents a state from requiring the collection of its use tax by a mail order company unless the company has a physical presence in the state. The company believes that the decision invalidated laws adopted by a number of states including California and Tennessee, which purported to require out-of-state mail order companies to collect and remit sales and use taxes with respect to mail order sales in such states. However, the decision also established that Congress has the power to enact legislation which would permit states to require such collection by mail order companies. Congress is currently addressing a proposal which would require mail order companies to collect and remit sales and use tax in all states.

Note 9. Acquisition

In March 1993, the company purchased a majority interest in a catalog company, The Territory Ahead. Its operations were not material to the company, and as a result no pro forma data is presented. The transaction was accounted for using the purchase method. The excess of the purchase price over the fair value of net assets received was recorded as goodwill. The operating results of The Territory Ahead are included in the consolidated financial statements of the company from the date of acquisition.

Beginning in 2003, the minority shareholders have the option to require the company to purchase their shares, and the company will have the option to require the minority shareholders to sell their shares in The Territory Ahead. The price per share would be based on the fair market value of The Territory Ahead.

Note 10. Consolidated Quarterly Analysis (unaudited)

(Thousands except per share data)	Fiscal 1994				Fiscal 1993			
	1st Qtr.	2nd Qtr.	3rd Qtr.	4th Qtr.	1st Qtr.	2nd Qtr.	3rd Qtr.	4th Qtr.
Net sales	$156,256	$151,076	$215,133	$347,510	$141,413	$138,075	$174,630	$279,505
Gross profit	64,159	62,664	87,513	143,118	56,846	56,217	74,664	118,604
Pretax income	6,859	5,927	13,117	43,967	6,889	4,030	8,943	34,171
Net income before accounting change	4,239	3,554	7,976	26,660	4,271	2,499	5,544	21,186
Net income per share before accounting change	$ 0.24	$ 0.20	$ 0.44	$ 1.48	$ 0.23	$ 0.14	$ 0.31	$ 1.18
Net income	$ 5,539	$ 3,554	$ 7,976	$ 26,660	$ 4,271	$ 2,499	$ 5,544	$ 21,186
Net income per share	$ 0.31	$ 0.20	$ 0.44	$ 1.48	$ 0.23	$ 0.14	$ 0.31	$ 1.18
Cash dividends	–	–	–	$ 3,592	–	–	–	$ 3,589
Cash dividends per share	–	–	–	$ 0.20	–	–	–	$ 0.20
Common shares outstanding	17,977	17,962	17,961	17,956	18,409	18,142	17,915	18,028
Market price of shares outstanding:								
market high	29⅞	32½	44½	49¾	37⅞	34¾	33½	30¼
market low	23¼	27	29⅛	41	29	28⅞	24½	23

20

Responsibility for Consolidated Financial Statements

The management of Lands' End, Inc. and its subsidiaries has the responsibility for preparing the accompanying financial statements and for their integrity and objectivity. The statements were prepared in accordance with generally accepted accounting principles applied on a consistent basis. The consolidated financial statements include amounts that are based on management's best estimates and judgments. Management also prepared the other information in the annual report and is responsible for its accuracy and consistency with the consolidated financial statements.

The company's consolidated financial statements have been audited by Arthur Andersen & Co., independent certified public accountants. Management has made available to Arthur Andersen & Co. all the company's financial records and related data, as well as the minutes of stockholders' and directors' meetings. Furthermore, management believes that all representations made to Arthur Andersen & Co. during its audit were valid and appropriate.

Management of the company has established and maintains a system of internal control that provides for appropriate division of responsibility, reasonable assurance as to the integrity and reliability of the consolidated financial statements, the protection of assets from unauthorized use or disposition, and the prevention and detection of fraudulent financial reporting. Management believes that, as of January 28, 1994, the company's system of internal control is adequate to accomplish the objectives discussed herein.

Two directors of the company, not members of management, serve as the audit committee of the board of directors and are the principal means through which the board supervises the performance of the financial reporting duties of management. The audit committee meets with management and the company's independent auditors to review the results of external audits of the company and to discuss plans for future audits. At these meetings, the audit committee also meets privately with the independent auditors to assure its free access to them.

William T. End
Chief Executive Officer

Stephen A. Orum
Chief Financial Officer

Report of Independent Public Accountants

To the Board of Directors and Shareholders of Lands' End, Inc.:

We have audited the accompanying consolidated balance sheets of LANDS' END, INC. (a Delaware corporation) and its subsidiaries as of January 28, 1994, and January 29, 1993, and the related consolidated statements of operations, shareholders' investment and cash flows for each of the three years in the period ended January 28, 1994. These financial statements are the responsibility of the company's management. Our responsibility is to express an opinion on these financial statements based on our audits.

We conducted our audits in accordance with generally accepted auditing standards. Those standards require that we plan and perform the audit to obtain reasonable assurance about whether the financial statements are free of material misstatement. An audit includes examining, on a test basis, evidence supporting the amounts and disclosures in the financial statements. An audit also includes assessing the accounting principles used and significant estimates made by management, as well as evaluating the overall financial statement presentation. We believe that our audits provide a reasonable basis for our opinion.

In our opinion, the financial statements referred to above present fairly, in all material respects, the financial position of Lands' End, Inc. and subsidiaries as of January 28, 1994, and January 29, 1993, and the results of their operations and their cash flows for each of the three years in the period ended January 28, 1994, in conformity with generally accepted accounting principles.

As explained in the notes to the consolidated financial statements, effective January 30, 1993, the company changed its method of accounting for income taxes.

Arthur Andersen & Co.
Milwaukee, Wisconsin
March 3, 1994.

21

The following selected financial data have been derived from the company's consolidated financial statements which, except pro forma amounts, have been audited by Arthur Andersen & Co., independent public accountants. The information set forth below should be read in conjunction with "Management's Discussion and Analysis" and the consolidated financial statements and notes thereto included elsewhere herein.

(Thousands except per share data)	1994[1]	1993	1992
Income statement data:			
Net sales	$869,975	$733,623	$683,427
Pretax income	69,870	54,033	47,492
Percent to net sales	8.0%	7.4%	7.0%
Net income before accounting change	42,429	33,500	28,732
Cumulative effect of accounting change	1,300	–	–
Net income	43,729	33,500	28,732
Net income (pro forma for 1986 and 1987)	43,729	33,500	28,732
Per share of common stock:			
Net income per share before accounting change	$ 2.36	$ 1.85	$ 1.53
Cumulative effect of accounting change	.07	–	–
Net income per share	$ 2.43	$ 1.85	$ 1.53
Cash dividends per share	$ 0.20	$ 0.20	$ 0.20
Common shares outstanding	17,956	18,028	18,472
Balance sheet data:			
Current assets	$192,276	$137,531	$131,273
Current liabilities	91,049	67,315	74,548
Property, plant, equipment and intangibles, net	81,554	74,272	74,527
Total assets	273,830	211,803	205,800
Noncurrent liabilities	5,496	5,100	4,620
Shareholders' investment	177,285	139,388	126,632
Other data:			
Net working capital	$101,227	$ 70,216	$ 56,725
Capital expenditures	16,958	9,965	5,347
Depreciation and amortization expense	8,286	7,900	7,428
Return on average shareholders' investment	28%	25%	23%
Return on average assets	18%	16%	15%
Debt/equity ratio	–	–	1%

(1) Effective January 30, 1993, the company adopted Statement of Financial Accounting Standards ("SFAS") No. 109, "Accounting for Income Taxes," which was recorded as a change in accounting principle at the beginning of fiscal 1994 with an increase to net income of $1.3 million or $0.07 per share.

(2) In the fourth quarter of fiscal 1988, the company elected early adoption of the provisions of SFAS No. 96, "Accounting for Income Taxes," as recommended by the Financial Accounting Standards Board. The effect of the change for the year was to increase net income $715,000 including the cumulative effect of $685,000 or $0.03 per common share which was reflected in the first quarter.

22

| Fiscal year | | | | | |
1991	1990	1989	1988 [2]	1987 [3,4]	1986 [3]
$601,991	$544,850	$454,644	$335,740	$264,896	$226,575
24,943	47,270	52,142	38,328	28,486	21,584
4.1%	8.7%	11.4%	11.4%	10.7%	9.5%
14,743	29,071	32,282	22,120	18,650	21,584
–	–	–	685	–	–
14,743	29,071	32,282	22,805	18,650	21,584
14,743	29,071	32,282	22,805	14,605	11,270
$ 0.75	$ 1.45	$ 1.61	$ 1.11	$ 0.73	$ 0.56
–	–	–	.03	–	–
$ 0.75	$ 1.45	$ 1.61	$ 1.14	$ 0.73	$ 0.56
$ 0.20	$ 0.20	$ 0.20	$ 0.20	–	–
19,218	19,881	20,040	20,040	10,020	9,980
$107,824	$ 99,714	$103,681	$ 78,256	$ 57,660	$ 35,687
60,774	43,915	51,530	38,860	32,920	18,002
77,576	67,218	47,471	28,723	26,822	19,841
185,400	166,932	151,152	106,979	84,482	55,528
7,800	8,413	7,674	11,445	13,685	10,321
116,826	114,604	91,948	56,674	37,877	27,205
$ 47,050	$ 55,799	$ 52,151	$ 39,396	$ 24,740	$ 17,685
17,682	25,160	15,872	5,862	9,603	6,483
7,041	5,251	3,916	3,185	2,576	1,867
13%	28%	43%	48%	45%	48%
8%	18%	25%	24%	21%	22%
3%	4%	7%	15%	28%	38%

(3) Net income per share (pro forma for 1986 and 1987) was computed after giving retroactive effect to the 108-for-one stock split in August 1986 and the two-for-one stock split in August 1987, and assuming the shares sold in the October 1986 initial public offering were issued at the beginning of fiscal 1986.

(4) The company has been subject to corporate income taxes since October 6, 1986. For earlier periods shown, the company elected to be treated as an S Corporation and accordingly was not subject to corporate income taxes. The net income and net income per share for such periods reflect a pro forma tax provision as if the company had been subject to corporate income taxes.

23

Appendix B
Present-Value Tables and Future-Value Tables

This appendix provides present-value tables and future-value tables (more complete than those in the Chapter 16 appendix and in Chapter 27).

EXHIBIT B-1

Present Value of $1

Present Value

Periods	1%	2%	3%	4%	5%	6%	7%	8%	9%	10%	12%
1	0.990	0.980	0.971	0.962	0.952	0.943	0.935	0.926	0.917	0.909	0.893
2	0.980	0.961	0.943	0.925	0.907	0.890	0.873	0.857	0.842	0.826	0.797
3	0.971	0.942	0.915	0.889	0.864	0.840	0.816	0.794	0.772	0.751	0.712
4	0.961	0.924	0.888	0.855	0.823	0.792	0.763	0.735	0.708	0.683	0.636
5	0.951	0.906	0.883	0.822	0.784	0.747	0.713	0.681	0.650	0.621	0.567
6	0.942	0.888	0.837	0.790	0.746	0.705	0.666	0.630	0.596	0.564	0.507
7	0.933	0.871	0.813	0.760	0.711	0.665	0.623	0.583	0.547	0.513	0.452
8	0.923	0.853	0.789	0.731	0.677	0.627	0.582	0.540	0.502	0.467	0.404
9	0.914	0.837	0.766	0.703	0.645	0.592	0.544	0.500	0.460	0.424	0.361
10	0.905	0.820	0.744	0.676	0.614	0.558	0.508	0.463	0.422	0.386	0.322
11	0.896	0.804	0.722	0.650	0.585	0.527	0.475	0.429	0.388	0.350	0.287
12	0.887	0.788	0.701	0.625	0.557	0.497	0.444	0.397	0.356	0.319	0.257
13	0.879	0.773	0.681	0.601	0.530	0.469	0.415	0.368	0.326	0.290	0.229
14	0.870	0.758	0.661	0.577	0.505	0.442	0.388	0.340	0.299	0.263	0.205
15	0.861	0.743	0.642	0.555	0.481	0.417	0.362	0.315	0.275	0.239	0.183
16	0.853	0.728	0.623	0.534	0.458	0.394	0.339	0.292	0.252	0.218	0.163
17	0.844	0.714	0.605	0.513	0.436	0.371	0.317	0.270	0.231	0.198	0.146
18	0.836	0.700	0.587	0.494	0.416	0.350	0.296	0.250	0.212	0.180	0.130
19	0.828	0.686	0.570	0.475	0.396	0.331	0.277	0.232	0.194	0.164	0.116
20	0.820	0.673	0.554	0.456	0.377	0.312	0.258	0.215	0.178	0.149	0.104
21	0.811	0.660	0.538	0.439	0.359	0.294	0.242	0.199	0.164	0.135	0.093
22	0.803	0.647	0.522	0.422	0.342	0.278	0.226	0.184	0.150	0.123	0.083
23	0.795	0.634	0.507	0.406	0.326	0.262	0.211	0.170	0.138	0.112	0.074
24	0.788	0.622	0.492	0.390	0.310	0.247	0.197	0.158	0.126	0.102	0.066
25	0.780	0.610	0.478	0.375	0.295	0.233	0.184	0.146	0.116	0.092	0.059
26	0.772	0.598	0.464	0.361	0.281	0.220	0.172	0.135	0.106	0.084	0.053
27	0.764	0.586	0.450	0.347	0.268	0.207	0.161	0.125	0.098	0.076	0.047
28	0.757	0.574	0.437	0.333	0.255	0.196	0.150	0.116	0.090	0.069	0.042
29	0.749	0.563	0.424	0.321	0.243	0.185	0.141	0.107	0.082	0.063	0.037
30	0.742	0.552	0.412	0.308	0.231	0.174	0.131	0.099	0.075	0.057	0.033
40	0.672	0.453	0.307	0.208	0.142	0.097	0.067	0.046	0.032	0.022	0.011
50	0.608	0.372	0.228	0.141	0.087	0.054	0.034	0.021	0.013	0.009	0.003

EXHIBIT B-1

(cont'd)

Present Value

14%	15%	16%	18%	20%	25%	30%	35%	40%	45%	50%	Periods
0.877	0.870	0.862	0.847	0.833	0.800	0.769	0.741	0.714	0.690	0.667	1
0.769	0.756	0.743	0.718	0.694	0.640	0.592	0.549	0.510	0.476	0.444	2
0.675	0.658	0.641	0.609	0.579	0.512	0.455	0.406	0.364	0.328	0.296	3
0.592	0.572	0.552	0.516	0.482	0.410	0.350	0.301	0.260	0.226	0.198	4
0.519	0.497	0.476	0.437	0.402	0.328	0.269	0.223	0.186	0.156	0.132	5
0.456	0.432	0.410	0.370	0.335	0.262	0.207	0.165	0.133	0.108	0.088	6
0.400	0.376	0.354	0.314	0.279	0.210	0.159	0.122	0.095	0.074	0.059	7
0.351	0.327	0.305	0.266	0.233	0.168	0.123	0.091	0.068	0.051	0.039	8
0.308	0.284	0.263	0.225	0.194	0.134	0.094	0.067	0.048	0.035	0.026	9
0.270	0.247	0.227	0.191	0.162	0.107	0.073	0.050	0.035	0.024	0.017	10
0.237	0.215	0.195	0.162	0.135	0.086	0.056	0.037	0.025	0.017	0.012	11
0.208	0.187	0.168	0.137	0.112	0.069	0.043	0.027	0.018	0.012	0.008	12
0.182	0.163	0.145	0.116	0.093	0.055	0.033	0.020	0.013	0.008	0.005	13
0.160	0.141	0.125	0.099	0.078	0.044	0.025	0.015	0.009	0.006	0.003	14
0.140	0.123	0.108	0.084	0.065	0.035	0.020	0.011	0.006	0.004	0.002	15
0.123	0.107	0.093	0.071	0.054	0.028	0.015	0.008	0.005	0.003	0.002	16
0.108	0.093	0.080	0.060	0.045	0.023	0.012	0.006	0.003	0.002	0.001	17
0.095	0.081	0.069	0.051	0.038	0.018	0.009	0.005	0.002	0.001	0.001	18
0.083	0.070	0.060	0.043	0.031	0.014	0.007	0.003	0.002	0.001		19
0.073	0.061	0.051	0.037	0.026	0.012	0.005	0.002	0.001	0.001		20
0.064	0.053	0.044	0.031	0.022	0.009	0.004	0.002	0.001			21
0.056	0.046	0.038	0.026	0.018	0.007	0.003	0.001	0.001			22
0.049	0.040	0.033	0.022	0.015	0.006	0.002	0.001				23
0.043	0.035	0.028	0.019	0.013	0.005	0.002	0.001				24
0.038	0.030	0.024	0.016	0.010	0.004	0.001	0.001				25
0.033	0.026	0.021	0.014	0.009	0.003	0.001					26
0.029	0.023	0.018	0.011	0.007	0.002	0.001					27
0.026	0.020	0.016	0.010	0.006	0.002	0.001					28
0.022	0.017	0.014	0.008	0.005	0.002						29
0.020	0.015	0.012	0.007	0.004	0.001						30
0.005	0.004	0.003	0.001	0.001							40
0.001	0.001	0.001									50

EXHIBIT B-2

Present Value of Annuity of $1

Present Value

Periods	1%	2%	3%	4%	5%	6%	7%	8%	9%	10%	12%
1	0.990	0.980	0.971	0.962	0.952	0.943	0.935	0.926	0.917	0.909	0.893
2	1.970	1.942	1.913	1.886	1.859	1.833	1.808	1.783	1.759	1.736	1.690
3	2.941	2.884	2.829	2.775	2.723	2.673	2.624	2.577	2.531	2.487	2.402
4	3.902	3.808	3.717	3.630	3.546	3.465	3.387	3.312	3.240	3.170	3.037
5	4.853	4.713	4.580	4.452	4.329	4.212	4.100	3.993	3.890	3.791	3.605
6	5.795	5.601	5.417	5.242	5.076	4.917	4.767	4.623	4.486	4.355	4.111
7	6.728	6.472	6.230	6.002	5.786	5.582	5.389	5.206	5.033	4.868	4.564
8	7.652	7.325	7.020	6.733	6.463	6.210	5.971	5.747	5.535	5.335	4.968
9	8.566	8.162	7.786	7.435	7.108	6.802	6.515	6.247	5.995	5.759	5.328
10	9.471	8.983	8.530	8.111	7.722	7.360	7.024	6.710	6.418	6.145	5.650
11	10.368	9.787	9.253	8.760	8.306	7.887	7.499	7.139	6.805	6.495	5.938
12	11.255	10.575	9.954	9.385	8.863	8.384	7.943	7.536	7.161	6.814	6.194
13	12.134	11.348	10.635	9.986	9.394	8.853	8.358	7.904	7.487	7.103	6.424
14	13.004	12.106	11.296	10.563	9.899	9.295	8.745	8.244	7.786	7.367	6.628
15	13.865	12.849	11.938	11.118	10.380	9.712	9.108	8.559	8.061	7.606	6.811
16	14.718	13.578	12.561	11.652	10.838	10.106	9.447	8.851	8.313	7.824	6.974
17	15.562	14.292	13.166	12.166	11.274	10.477	9.763	9.122	8.544	8.022	7.120
18	16.398	14.992	13.754	12.659	11.690	10.828	10.059	9.372	8.756	8.201	7.250
19	17.226	15.678	14.324	13.134	12.085	11.158	10.336	9.604	8.950	8.365	7.366
20	18.046	16.351	14.878	13.590	12.462	11.470	10.594	9.818	9.129	8.514	7.469
21	18.857	17.011	15.415	14.029	12.821	11.764	10.836	10.017	9.292	8.649	7.562
22	19.660	17.658	15.937	14.451	13.163	12.042	11.061	10.201	9.442	8.772	7.645
23	20.456	18.292	16.444	14.857	13.489	12.303	11.272	10.371	9.580	8.883	7.718
24	21.243	18.914	16.936	15.247	13.799	12.550	11.469	10.529	9.707	8.985	7.784
25	22.023	19.523	17.413	15.622	14.094	12.783	11.654	10.675	9.823	9.077	7.843
26	22.795	20.121	17.877	15.983	14.375	13.003	11.826	10.810	9.929	9.161	7.896
27	23.560	20.707	18.327	16.330	14.643	13.211	11.987	10.935	10.027	9.237	7.943
28	24.316	21.281	18.764	16.663	14.898	13.406	12.137	11.051	10.116	9.307	7.984
29	25.066	21.844	19.189	16.984	15.141	13.591	12.278	11.158	10.198	9.370	8.022
30	25.808	22.396	19.600	17.292	15.373	13.765	12.409	11.258	10.274	9.427	8.055
40	32.835	27.355	23.115	19.793	17.159	15.046	13.332	11.925	10.757	9.779	8.244
50	39.196	31.424	25.730	21.482	18.256	15.762	13.801	12.234	10.962	9.915	8.305

EXHIBIT B-2
(cont'd)

Present Value

14%	15%	16%	18%	20%	25%	30%	35%	40%	45%	50%	Periods
0.877	0.870	0.862	0.847	0.833	0.800	0.769	0.741	0.714	0.690	0.667	1
1.647	1.626	1.605	1.566	1.528	1.440	1.361	1.289	1.224	1.165	1.111	2
2.322	2.283	2.246	2.174	2.106	1.952	1.816	1.696	1.589	1.493	1.407	3
2.914	2.855	2.798	2.690	2.589	2.362	2.166	1.997	1.849	1.720	1.605	4
3.433	3.352	3.274	3.127	2.991	2.689	2.436	2.220	2.035	1.876	1.737	5
3.889	3.784	3.685	3.498	3.326	2.951	2.643	2.385	2.168	1.983	1.824	6
4.288	4.160	4.039	3.812	3.605	3.161	2.802	2.508	2.263	2.057	1.883	7
4.639	4.487	4.344	4.078	3.837	3.329	2.925	2.598	2.331	2.109	1.922	8
4.946	4.772	4.607	4.303	4.031	3.463	3.019	2.665	2.379	2.144	1.948	9
5.216	5.019	4.833	4.494	4.192	3.571	3.092	2.715	2.414	2.168	1.965	10
5.553	5.234	5.029	4.656	4.327	3.656	3.147	2.752	2.438	2.185	1.977	11
5.660	5.421	5.197	4.793	4.439	3.725	3.190	2.779	2.456	2.197	1.985	12
5.842	5.583	5.342	4.910	4.533	3.780	3.223	2.799	2.469	2.204	1.990	13
6.002	5.724	5.468	5.008	4.611	3.824	3.249	2.814	2.478	2.210	1.993	14
6.142	5.847	5.575	5.092	4.675	3.859	3.268	2.825	2.484	2.214	1.995	15
6.265	5.954	5.669	5.162	4.730	3.887	3.283	2.834	2.489	2.216	1.997	16
6.373	6.047	5.749	5.222	4.775	3.910	3.295	2.840	2.492	2.218	1.998	17
6.467	6.128	5.818	5.273	4.812	3.928	3.304	2.844	2.494	2.219	1.999	18
6.550	6.198	5.877	5.316	4.844	3.942	3.311	2.848	2.496	2.220	1.999	19
6.623	6.259	5.929	5.353	4.870	3.954	3.316	2.850	2.497	2.221	1.999	20
6.687	6.312	5.973	5.384	4.891	3.963	3.320	2.852	2.498	2.221	2.000	21
6.743	6.359	6.011	5.410	4.909	3.970	3.323	2.853	2.498	2.222	2.000	22
6.792	6.399	6.044	5.432	4.925	3.976	3.325	2.854	2.499	2.222	2.000	23
6.835	6.434	6.073	5.451	4.937	3.981	3.327	2.855	2.499	2.222	2.000	24
6.873	6.464	6.097	5.467	4.948	3.985	3.329	2.856	2.499	2.222	2.000	25
6.906	6.491	6.118	5.480	4.956	3.988	3.330	2.856	2.500	2.222	2.000	26
6.935	6.514	6.136	5.492	4.964	3.990	3.331	2.856	2.500	2.222	2.000	27
6.961	6.534	6.152	5.502	4.970	3.992	3.331	2.857	2.500	2.222	2.000	28
6.983	6.551	6.166	5.510	4.975	3.994	3.332	2.857	2.500	2.222	2.000	29
7.003	6.566	6.177	5.517	4.979	3.995	3.332	2.857	2.500	2.222	2.000	30
7.105	6.642	6.234	5.548	4.997	3.999	3.333	2.857	2.500	2.222	2.000	40
7.133	6.661	6.246	5.554	4.999	4.000	3.333	2.857	2.500	2.222	2.000	50

EXHIBIT B-3

Future Value of $1

Future Value

Periods	1%	2%	3%	4%	5%	6%	7%	8%	9%	10%	12%	14%	15%
1	1.010	1.020	1.030	1.040	1.050	1.060	1.070	1.080	1.090	1.100	1.120	1.140	1.150
2	1.020	1.040	1.061	1.082	1.103	1.124	1.145	1.166	1.188	1.210	1.254	1.300	1.323
3	1.030	1.061	1.093	1.125	1.158	1.191	1.225	1.260	1.295	1.331	1.405	1.482	1.521
4	1.041	1.082	1.126	1.170	1.216	1.262	1.311	1.360	1.412	1.464	1.574	1.689	1.749
5	1.051	1.104	1.159	1.217	1.276	1.338	1.403	1.469	1.539	1.611	1.762	1.925	2.011
6	1.062	1.126	1.194	1.265	1.340	1.419	1.501	1.587	1.677	1.772	1.974	2.195	2.313
7	1.072	1.149	1.230	1.316	1.407	1.504	1.606	1.714	1.828	1.949	2.211	2.502	2.660
8	1.083	1.172	1.267	1.369	1.477	1.594	1.718	1.851	1.993	2.144	2.476	2.853	3.059
9	1.094	1.195	1.305	1.423	1.551	1.689	1.838	1.999	2.172	2.358	2.773	3.252	3.518
10	1.105	1.219	1.344	1.480	1.629	1.791	1.967	2.159	2.367	2.594	3.106	3.707	4.046
11	1.116	1.243	1.384	1.539	1.710	1.898	2.105	2.332	2.580	2.853	3.479	4.226	4.652
12	1.127	1.268	1.426	1.601	1.796	2.012	2.252	2.518	2.813	3.138	3.896	4.818	5.350
13	1.138	1.294	1.469	1.665	1.886	2.133	2.410	2.720	3.066	3.452	4.363	5.492	6.153
14	1.149	1.319	1.513	1.732	1.980	2.261	2.579	2.937	3.342	3.798	4.887	6.261	7.076
15	1.161	1.346	1.558	1.801	2.079	2.397	2.759	3.172	3.642	4.177	5.474	7.138	8.137
16	1.173	1.373	1.605	1.873	2.183	2.540	2.952	3.426	3.970	4.595	6.130	8.137	9.358
17	1.184	1.400	1.653	1.948	2.292	2.693	3.159	3.700	4.328	5.054	6.866	9.276	10.76
18	1.196	1.428	1.702	2.026	2.407	2.854	3.380	3.996	4.717	5.560	7.690	10.58	12.38
19	1.208	1.457	1.754	2.107	2.527	3.026	3.617	4.316	5.142	6.116	8.613	12.06	14.23
20	1.220	1.486	1.806	2.191	2.653	3.207	3.870	4.661	5.604	6.728	9.646	13.74	16.37
21	1.232	1.516	1.860	2.279	2.786	3.400	4.141	5.034	6.109	7.400	10.80	15.67	18.82
22	1.245	1.546	1.916	2.370	2.925	3.604	4.430	5.437	6.659	8.140	12.10	17.86	21.64
23	1.257	1.577	1.974	2.465	3.072	3.820	4.741	5.871	7.258	8.954	13.55	20.36	24.89
24	1.270	1.608	2.033	2.563	3.225	4.049	5.072	6.341	7.911	9.850	15.18	23.21	28.63
25	1.282	1.641	2.094	2.666	3.386	4.292	5.427	6.848	8.623	10.83	17.00	26.46	32.92
26	1.295	1.673	2.157	2.772	3.556	4.549	5.807	7.396	9.399	11.92	19.04	30.17	37.86
27	1.308	1.707	2.221	2.883	3.733	4.822	6.214	7.988	10.25	13.11	21.32	34.39	43.54
28	1.321	1.741	2.288	2.999	3.920	5.112	6.649	8.627	11.17	14.42	23.88	39.20	50.07
29	1.335	1.776	2.357	3.119	4.116	5.418	7.114	9.317	12.17	15.86	26.75	44.69	57.58
30	1.348	1.811	2.427	3.243	4.322	5.743	7.612	10.06	13.27	17.45	29.96	50.95	66.21
40	1.489	2.208	3.262	4.801	7.040	10.29	14.97	21.72	31.41	45.26	93.05	188.9	267.9
50	1.645	2.692	4.384	7.107	11.47	18.42	29.46	46.90	74.36	117.4	289.0	700.2	1,084

EXHIBIT B-4

Future Value of Annuity of $1

Future Value

Periods	1%	2%	3%	4%	5%	6%	7%	8%	9%	10%	12%	14%	15%
1	1.000	1.000	1.000	1.000	1.000	1.000	1.000	1.000	1.000	1.000	1.000	1.000	1.000
2	2.010	2.020	2.030	2.040	2.050	2.060	2.070	2.080	2.090	2.100	2.120	2.140	2.150
3	3.030	3.060	3.091	3.122	3.153	3.184	3.215	3.246	3.278	3.310	3.374	3.440	3.473
4	4.060	4.122	4.184	4.246	4.310	4.375	4.440	4.506	4.573	4.641	4.779	4.921	4.993
5	5.101	5.204	5.309	5.416	5.526	5.637	5.751	5.867	5.985	6.105	6.353	6.610	6.742
6	6.152	6.308	6.468	6.633	6.802	6.975	7.153	7.336	7.523	7.716	8.115	8.536	8.754
7	7.214	7.434	7.662	7.898	8.142	8.394	8.654	8.923	9.200	9.487	10.09	10.73	11.07
8	8.286	8.583	8.892	9.214	9.549	9.897	10.26	10.64	11.03	11.44	12.30	13.23	13.73
9	9.369	9.755	10.16	10.58	11.03	11.49	11.98	12.49	13.02	13.58	14.78	16.09	16.79
10	10.46	10.95	11.46	12.01	12.58	13.18	13.82	14.49	15.19	15.94	17.55	19.34	20.30
11	11.57	12.17	12.81	13.49	14.21	14.97	15.78	16.65	17.56	18.53	20.65	23.04	24.35
12	12.68	13.41	14.19	15.03	15.92	16.87	17.89	18.98	20.14	21.38	24.13	27.27	29.00
13	13.81	14.68	15.62	16.63	17.71	18.88	20.14	21.50	22.95	24.52	28.03	32.09	34.35
14	14.95	15.97	17.09	18.29	19.60	21.02	22.55	24.21	26.02	27.98	32.39	37.58	40.50
15	16.10	17.29	18.60	20.02	21.58	23.28	25.13	27.15	29.36	31.77	37.28	43.84	47.58
16	17.26	18.64	20.16	21.82	23.66	25.67	27.89	30.32	33.00	35.95	42.75	50.98	55.72
17	18.43	20.01	21.76	23.70	25.84	28.21	30.84	33.75	36.97	40.54	48.88	59.12	65.08
18	19.61	21.41	23.41	25.65	28.13	30.91	34.00	37.45	41.30	45.60	55.75	68.39	75.84
19	20.81	22.84	25.12	27.67	30.54	33.76	37.38	41.45	46.02	51.16	63.44	78.97	88.21
20	22.02	24.30	26.87	29.78	33.07	36.79	41.00	45.76	51.16	57.28	72.05	91.02	102.4
21	23.24	25.78	28.68	31.97	35.72	39.99	44.87	50.42	56.76	64.00	81.70	104.8	118.8
22	24.47	27.30	30.54	34.25	38.51	43.39	49.01	55.46	62.87	71.40	92.50	120.4	137.6
23	25.72	28.85	32.45	36.62	41.43	47.00	53.44	60.89	69.53	79.54	104.6	138.3	159.3
24	26.97	30.42	34.43	39.08	44.50	50.82	58.18	66.76	76.79	88.50	118.2	158.7	184.2
25	28.24	32.03	36.46	41.65	47.73	54.86	63.25	73.11	84.70	98.35	133.3	181.9	212.8
26	29.53	33.67	38.55	44.31	51.11	59.16	68.68	79.95	93.32	109.2	150.3	208.3	245.7
27	30.82	35.34	40.71	47.08	54.67	63.71	74.48	87.35	102.7	121.1	169.4	238.5	283.6
28	32.13	37.05	42.93	49.97	58.40	68.53	80.70	95.34	113.0	134.2	190.7	272.9	327.1
29	33.45	38.79	45.22	52.97	62.32	73.64	87.35	104.0	124.1	148.6	214.6	312.1	377.2
30	34.78	40.57	47.58	56.08	66.44	79.06	94.46	113.3	136.3	164.5	241.3	356.8	434.7
40	48.89	60.40	75.40	95.03	120.8	154.8	199.6	259.1	337.9	442.6	767.1	1,342	1,779
50	64.46	84.58	112.8	152.7	209.3	290.3	406.5	573.8	815.1	1,164	2,400	4,995	7,218

Appendix C

Personal Income Tax

The **income tax** is a general-purpose tax levied on the income of the taxpayer. Entirely separate from all other taxes, it is the federal government's largest source of revenue. This appendix discusses income taxes from the perspective of the taxpayer—people like you and your family and friends. Our discussion is a practical introduction to some of the steps in computing the amount of income tax that individuals pay to the government. This material provides a foundation for any future tax courses you may take.

Operation of the Income Tax

Administration of the federal tax system is the responsibility of the Internal Revenue Service (IRS), a division of the Treasury Department of the U.S. government. Congress passes tax laws, and the Treasury Department publishes Treasury Regulations—interpretations of the tax laws—and administers the tax system. The federal courts make final decisions on disputes between taxpayers and the government.

In a landmark case, Judge Learned Hand wrote that "nobody owes any public duty to pay more [taxes] than the law demands." It becomes important, therefore, for taxpayers to plan their income tax situations.

Tax planning is the legitimate reduction of, and delay in, paying taxes within the legal system. Also called **tax avoidance,** it is the structuring of transactions to pay the least amount of income tax at the latest possible time permitted by law. Tax avoidance should not be confused with **tax evasion,** which is illegal activity designed to reduce tax. An example of tax planning (tax *avoidance*) is delaying earning revenue until a later year, when tax rates are scheduled to decrease. An example of tax *evasion* is making a sale and not recording it to keep from paying tax.

In its most basic form, the amount of income tax is computed by multiplying taxable income by the tax rate. For example, a tax rate of 15 percent applied to taxable income of $20,000 results in income tax of $3,000. Income tax rates have varied over the years. The 1913 tax law set tax rates between 1 percent and 7 percent. A person with taxable income of $15,000 paid income tax of 1 percent, or $150. Today, a taxpayer with this same taxable income pays income tax of 15 percent, or $2,250. Taxpayers with higher incomes pay income tax at a higher rate. Exhibit C-1 shows some of the income tax rates that have been in effect in the United States since 1913.

Most states and some cities have an income tax that is patterned in some way after the federal income tax. Here we focus on the *federal* income tax.

	Tax Rates	
	Minimum	Maximum
1913 tax law	1%	7%
During World War II.....................	23	94
During most of the 1970s..............	14	70
Prior to 1993 tax law	15	31
1993 tax law	15	39.6

EXHIBIT C-1

Minimum and Maximum Income Tax Rates for Individual Taxpayers

Classes and Filing Status of Taxpayers

Tax law identifies four major classes of taxpayers: individuals, corporations, estates, and trusts. Here we focus on the taxation of individuals. Chapter 14 covered the basics of accounting for income tax by corporations.

Each taxpayer reports income and shows the computation of income tax on a document called a **tax return.** Submitting the completed document to the IRS is called *filing a tax return.* An individual must file his or her tax return within three and one-half months after the end of the tax year. A person who uses the calendar year must file a 1996 income tax return by April 15, 1997.

An individual taxpayer must use a particular *filing status.* This status determines the tax rates used to compute the amount of income tax. There are four filing statuses for individuals:

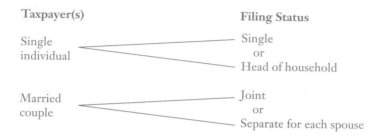

Taxpayer(s)	Filing Status
Single individual	Single or Head of household
Married couple	Joint or Separate for each spouse

A business organized as a proprietorship pays no business income tax. Business income is taxed directly to the proprietor. A partnership is taxed the same way. The business itself incurs no income tax, but each partner includes in personal taxable income his or her share of partnership income.

Income Taxation of Individuals

In general, U.S. citizens must pay tax on all income from all sources. Tax laws permit certain *exclusions, deductions,* and *exemptions* to be subtracted from total income in arriving at **taxable income**—the income amount on which income tax is based. Multiplying the amount of taxable income by the appropriate tax rate yields the amount of income tax for the year. *Tax credits* are then subtracted, and the final result is the amount of income tax liability for the year. Exhibit C-2 shows how to compute the income tax liability for an individual. Taxable income, Step 8 in Exhibit C-2, is the focal point in our discussions because its computation is complex. After taxable income is determined, computation of the amount of tax is easy.

> **OBJECTIVE 1**
> Identify the important components in determining taxable income

Total Income, Exclusions, and Gross Income—Steps 1, 2, and 3

In income taxation, **total income** is all income from any source. Salary or wage income is the most common taxable income. A business proprietor includes in total income the net income of the business (net sales less cost of goods sold and less all business expenses—salaries and wages for employees, rent, insurance, depreciation, interest, repairs, property taxes, supplies expense, and so on). Gains on the sale of business assets such as buildings and delivery vehicles are included as income, and losses are deductible in arriving at total income. In the same way, a partner pays tax on his or her share of the partnership's net income.

Also part of total income are interest earned on a savings account whether or not the interest is withdrawn, dividend revenue from a stock investment, and a gain

EXHIBIT C-2
An Individual's Income Tax Computation

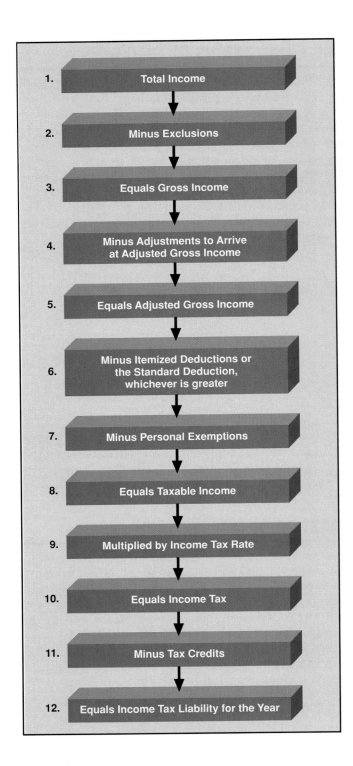

1. Total Income

2. Minus Exclusions

3. Equals Gross Income

4. Minus Adjustments to Arrive at Adjusted Gross Income

5. Equals Adjusted Gross Income

6. Minus Itemized Deductions or the Standard Deduction, whichever is greater

7. Minus Personal Exemptions

8. Equals Taxable Income

9. Multiplied by Income Tax Rate

10. Equals Income Tax

11. Minus Tax Credits

12. Equals Income Tax Liability for the Year

on the sale of an investment. Net rent income (income minus expenses) on rental property, royalties earned on minerals, commissions, bonuses, tips, and gains on the sale of assets are also included in total income. Even gambling profits and income from illegal sources appear in the tax code as taxable income.

From total income we subtract *exclusions*, which are types of income that the tax law specifically identifies as nontaxable. Common exclusions are interest revenue on tax-exempt state and municipal bonds, certain scholarships received, gifts and inheritances, life insurance benefits, and some Social Security benefits. Subtracting exclusions from total income gives us **gross income,** which is total income minus specific exclusions.

Adjustments to Arrive at Adjusted Gross Income—Step 4

The adjustments in step 4 are deductions of a wide variety. Payments into a personal retirement plan, alimony payments, and penalty on early withdrawal of savings fall into this category. The total of these adjustments is subtracted from gross income.

Adjusted Gross Income—Step 5

Gross income minus the adjustments (deductions) described in the preceding section equals an amount that exists only in the tax law—**adjusted gross income.** Often abbreviated as AGI, this amount is important in taxation because several expenses are deductible only if they exceed a certain percentage of adjusted gross income, as we discuss in the next section.

Itemized Deductions and the Standard Deduction—Step 6

An individual can take a tax deduction for the greater of two amounts: the total of itemized deductions or the standard deduction. **Itemized deductions** make up a particular category that includes the following six types of expenditures:

1. *Medical expenses* include doctor fees, hospital expenses, and the cost of eyeglasses, medicine, and special treatment. Medical expenses can be deducted only to the extent that they exceed 7½ percent (0.075) of adjusted gross income. A taxpayer with adjusted gross income of $40,000 and medical expenses of $3,300 can deduct only $300 of those expenses [$3,300 − (0.075 × $40,000)]. If this individual's medical expenses are $3,000 or less, he or she gets no medical expense deduction.

2. *Interest expense* on a home mortgage is deductible up to a maximum of interest incurred on $1 million of mortgage debt. All other interest is not deductible.

3. *Charitable contributions* are gifts to charitable and religious organizations such as United Way, the Red Cross, churches, synagogues, hospitals, and colleges and universities. The IRS keeps a list of approved charitable entities to which contributions are deductible. Gifts to friends and relatives are not.

4. *Some taxes paid* may be deducted. State income tax and local property taxes are the most common taxes deducted. Sales taxes cannot be deducted.

5. *Casualty losses* are losses of property, such as by theft or by storm damage. Casualty losses can be deducted, subject to certain limitations.

6. *Miscellaneous deductions* include such expenses as union dues, subscriptions to professional journals, investment expenses, and fees paid for the preparation of an income tax return. To get a miscellaneous deduction, the taxpayer totals the expenses in this category. If the total exceeds 2 percent of adjusted gross income (AGI), the taxpayer gets a deduction for the excess. If total miscellaneous expenses are 2 percent of AGI or less, no deduction is permitted. Suppose a taxpayer's adjusted gross income is $40,000 and miscellaneous expenses total $875. This person lists all miscellaneous expenses on the tax return and gets a miscellaneous deduction of $75 [$875 − (0.02 × $40,000)]. Miscellaneous expenses of $800 or less would not appear on the tax return because their total does not exceed 2 percent of AGI.

Personal living costs are *not* tax deductible. The cost of a home and expenditures for apartment or house rent, clothing, furniture, and an automobile may not be claimed as tax deductions.

An alternative to itemizing deductions is taking the **standard deduction,** a set amount of tax deduction that varies according to the individual's filing status. In 1994 married taxpayers filing a joint return could deduct $6,350 for the standard deduction. A head of a household could deduct $5,600, and a single taxpayer, $3,800. These amounts are adjusted for the effects of inflation. Many taxpayers favor the standard deduction because, unlike itemized deductions, it requires no receipts or other supporting documents. Thus it is much easier than itemizing. An individual who itemizes cannot take the standard deduction. Likewise, one who elects the standard deduction forgoes the opportunity to itemize.

Personal Exemptions—Step 7

Another type of income tax deduction is called a **personal exemption.** This deduction is a set amount allowed for the taxpayer, the taxpayer's spouse, and each person who qualifies as a dependent. A **dependent** is a person who receives more than half of his or her support from another individual (the taxpayer). Some examples of personal exemptions follow:

Taxpayer(s)	Number of Exemptions
Single person	1
Single person qualifying as a head of household that includes:	
1 parent as a dependent	2
2 children	3
Married couple, filing jointly:	
0 children	2
2 children	4
Married couple, filing separately, 2 children (decide which spouse claims exemptions for children):	
Total exemptions for two tax returns	4

The amount of the personal exemption was $2,450 in 1994. Each year the amount is adjusted for inflation. Taxpayers with high levels of income do not get the full benefit of the personal exemptions. For illustrative purposes and in exercises and problems, we assume a personal exemption of $2,500.

Taxable Income—Step 8

Taxable income is the earnings amount on which the income tax is based. It is the figure that is multiplied by the tax rate to compute the amount of income tax.

A special category of gains and losses—defined in the tax law—enters the determination of taxable income. These items, called **capital gains and losses,** result from the disposal of property that the tax law labels as capital assets. Common examples include investments in stocks, bonds, real estate, and personal assets such as homes, automobiles, and jewelry. A capital gain results from selling the asset for a price that exceeds its tax basis. A capital loss occurs if the sale price is less than the asset's tax basis. The *tax basis* of an asset is generally its cost (reduced by accumulated depreciation if any).

Capital gains and losses receive special treatment in a tax computation. The individual first separates capital gains and losses from other types of income, then combines capital gains and losses to calculate a net capital gain or a net capital loss for the year. A net capital gain is fully taxable. But only $3,000 of net capital losses can be deducted in any one year. Any excess may be carried forward to reduce taxes in future years.

Let's consider an example of the tax treatment of capital gains and losses. Suppose a married taxpayer has performed a partial tax computation for 19X1 and has determined that taxable income from other sources is $42,000. This taxpayer also has a capital gain of $4,000 on the sale of a stock investment and a capital loss of $9,000 on the sale of land. This person's taxable income for 19X1 is $39,000, computed as follows:

Taxable income from other sources...		$42,000
Net capital loss:		
Capital loss..	$9,000	
Capital gain..	4,000	
Net capital loss..	$5,000	
Maximum net capital loss deductible in one year		(3,000)
Taxable income		$39,000

In the determination of 19X2 taxable income, this person can deduct the net capital loss of $2,000 remaining from 19X1 ($5,000 less the $3,000 deducted in 19X1).

The tax definition of a capital asset is different from the accounting definition. For example, buildings, equipment, furniture, and other depreciable assets that are used in a business are *not* capital assets under the tax law. A loss on disposal of such *business* assets is fully deductible in the determination of taxable income. The $3,000 limit does not apply. Tax courses cover capital assets and capital gains and losses in more detail.

Income Tax Rates and the Amount of Income Tax—Steps 9 and 10

OBJECTIVE 2
Compute the income tax of an individual

Exhibit C-3 shows the tax rates that are used to compute an individual's income tax.

Exhibit C-3 shows that various tax rates apply to various levels of taxable income. Higher rates apply when income reaches specific higher levels. This is called a *progressive income tax system*. For example, a single (unmarried) person with taxable income of $16,000 is taxed at 15 percent. A single individual with income of $28,000 is taxed at 15 percent of the first $22,750 of income ($3,413) plus 28 percent of income in excess of $22,750.

A person's maximum tax rate is important for tax planning because it indicates how much of each additional dollar of income must be paid in taxes. Consider two single taxpayers. The person in the 15-percent bracket pays 15 cents of every taxable dollar earned. The person in the 28-percent bracket pays nearly double that amount, 28 cents of every additional dollar earned. Each additional dollar earned up to $55,100 is 13 cents less valuable—and less attractive—to the person in the 28-percent bracket, and so the incentive to earn additional income is less. Each dollar of a single person's income above $250,000 is taxed at 39.6 percent.

Let's work through examples to illustrate a simple and a complex tax computation. Suppose Ron and Sarah Marks have a daughter, Carmen, and they file a joint tax return. Exhibit C-4 shows their 1993 tax computation for two levels of taxable income: $44,000 and $120,000. The tax rates come from Exhibit C-3.

Single Taxpayer	
If taxable income is	The tax is
Not over $22,750	15% of taxable income
Over $22,750 but not over $55,100	$3,413 + 28% of the excess over $22,750
Over $55,100 but not over $115,000	$12,471 + 31% of the excess over $55,100
Over $115,000 but not over $250,000	$31,040 + 36% of the excess over $115,000
Over $250,000	$79,640 + 39.6% of the excess over $250,000
Married Taxpayers Filing Jointly	
If taxable income is	The tax is
Not over $38,000	15% of taxable income
Over $38,000 but not over $91,850	$5,700 + 28% of the excess over $38,000
Over $91,850 but not over $140,000	$20,778 + 31% of the excess over $91,850
Over $140,000 but not over $250,000	$35,705 + 36% of the excess over $140,000
Over $250,000	$75,305 + 39.6% of the excess over $250,000

EXHIBIT C-3
Individual Income Tax Rates

	Income Tax
Taxable Income of $44,000:	
$5,700 + [0.28($44,000 − $38,000)]	$ 7,380
Taxable Income of $120,000:	
$20,778 + [0.31($120,000 − $91,850)]	$29,505

EXHIBIT C-4
1993 Income Tax for Ron and Sarah Marks including daughter Carmen—married, filing jointly with three exemptions

Tax Credits—Step 11

Tax credits are often confused with tax deductions. The two are very different. Tax deductions are subtracted from adjusted gross income and so decrease the taxable income amount in step 8. By contrast, tax credits enter the tax computation after the amount of tax has been computed. A **tax credit** is subtracted directly from the amount of tax owed to the government. Thus a tax credit is worth more to a taxpayer because it leads to a larger decrease in the amount of tax owed. For example, a $1,000 tax *deduction* decreases income tax by $280 ($1,000 × 0.28) for a taxpayer subject to the 28 percent rate. A $1,000 tax *credit* decreases the amount of tax by the full $1,000 because the entire amount is subtracted. Two prominent tax credits are the *earned income credit*, which applies to low-income taxpayers, and the *credit for child-care expenses*, which applies to parents who work outside the home and must pay for child care.

Income Tax Liability—Step 12

The process described in the preceding paragraphs concludes with determination of the individual's income tax liability for the year. In this setting, *income tax liability* refers to the total amount of tax the person owes for the entire year. The taxpayer does not write a single check to pay this amount at the end of the year. Taxes are paid during the year, as described in the next section.

Computers have brought complex tax computations within reach of most taxpayers. Tax software, such as FasTax, TurboTax, and MacinTax, leads the taxpayer through a series of menu choices ending with the tax computation. Most professionals also use these programs.

Paying Income Tax through Withholding and Quarterly Payments

Persons who earn salaries or wages and who are not self-employed pay taxes through payroll deductions withheld from each paycheck. The employer remits the withheld taxes to the IRS on behalf of the employees. Individuals who are self-employed or who have income from sources other than their salary make quarterly tax payments directly to the IRS. All taxpayers must settle with the IRS when they file their annual tax returns. If the income tax listed on the tax return exceeds the total payments during the year, the individual must pay the difference when filing the tax return. If the amount of income tax on the tax return is less than the total payments, the taxpayer claims a refund and receives a check from the government.

SUMMARY PROBLEM FOR YOUR REVIEW

Charles Jones is a financial consultant in Kansas City. He and his wife, Becky, have a son and two daughters. During 1996 Charles's business earned gross income of $257,000 and had expenses of $62,000. Charles paid $7,600 into his retirement program. Becky worked three months as a computer consultant and received a salary of $19,000. She also received $5,000 as an inheritance. The Joneses' investments earned interest of $6,000 and dividends of $1,600. They sold a stock investment at a gain of $4,400 and land at a loss of $8,000. Their charitable contributions for the year totaled $2,700. Interest expense on their home mortgage was $13,100, and they paid property taxes of $2,400. During the year Charles made quarterly income tax payments totaling $48,200, and $3,600 was withheld from Becky's paychecks. The Joneses file a joint income tax return.

Required

Compute the Joneses' taxable income and income tax liability for the year. Show how much they must pay or will receive after they file their 1996 income tax return.

**CHARLES AND BECKY JONES
INCOME TAX COMPUTATION
1996**

Gross income (excluding inheritance):		
Charles's business gross income	$257,000	
Less: Business expenses	62,000	
Net business income		$ 195,000
Becky's salary income		19,000
Interest		6,000
Dividends		1,600
Capital gains and losses:		
Capital loss	$ 8,000	
Capital gain	4,400	
Net capital loss	3,600	
Maximum net capital loss deductible in one year		(3,000)
Gross income		218,600
Deductions to arrive at adjusted gross income:		
Payment into Charles's retirement program		7,600
Adjusted gross income		211,000
Itemized deductions or standard deduction ($6,350), whichever is greater—itemized deductions ($18,200), in this case:		
Mortgage interest	$ 13,100	
Charitable contributions	2,700	
Property tax	2,400	
Total itemized deductions	18,200	
Personal exemptions (5 × $2,500)	12,500	30,700
Taxable income		**$180,300**
Tax computation:		
$35,705 + [0.36($180,300 − $140,000)]		$ 50,213
Income tax liability for the year		50,213
Less tax payments:		
Charles's quarterly payments	$ 48,200	
Becky's withholdings	3,600	
Total payments		51,800
Tax refund to be claimed with return		$ 1,587

SUMMARY

1. Identify the important components in determining taxable income. Each individual taxpayer has a filing status: single, head of household, or joint. Determination of the person's taxable income begins with *total income*, which is all income from all sources. There are several subtractions: exclusions—income that is not taxed; adjustments, such as payments to a retirement plan and alimony payments; *itemized deductions*, which include medical expenses, certain interest expenses, charitable contributions, and some taxes paid; and *personal exemptions*, a specific amount for the taxpayer and his or her dependents. The result is *taxable income.*

2. Compute the income tax of an individual. The person's income tax equals his or her taxable income multiplied by the appropriate income tax rate. The tax rates differ according to the taxpayer's filing status. The final step in computing income tax is to subtract any *tax credits*, a special class of subtractions. People pay their income tax through withholding amounts, which are deducted from paychecks and other compensation and are sent directly to the Internal Revenue Service, and by making quarterly tax payments. On April 15 of each year the taxpayer files his or her *income tax return* and either pays the final tax due or receives a refund for the amount of taxes overpaid during the year.

ACCOUNTING VOCABULARY

Adjusted gross income. Total income minus specified adjustments (deductions) equals adjusted gross income, an amount that exists only in the tax law (*p. C-3*).

Capital gain. Special category of gain, defined in the tax law, that results from the disposal of property such as investments in stocks, bonds, real estate, and personal assets (*p. C-4*).

Capital loss. Special category of loss, defined in the tax law, that results from the disposal of property such as investments in stocks, bonds, real estate, and personal assets (*p. C-4*).

Dependent. A person who receives more than half of his or her support from another individual (the taxpayer) (*p. C-4*).

Gross income. In taxation, total income minus exclusions (*p. C-2*).

Income tax. A general-purpose tax levied on the income of a taxpayer. Separate from all other taxes, it is the federal government's largest source of revenue (*p. C-0*).

Itemized deduction. In taxation, a particular category that includes medical expenses, interest expense, charitable contributions, taxes paid, casualty losses, and miscellaneous deductions (*p. C-3*).

Personal exemption. A tax deduction that is a set amount allowed for a taxpayer, the taxpayer's spouse, and each person who qualifies as a dependent (*p. C-4*).

Standard deduction. A set amount of tax deduction that varies depending on the individual's filing status: single; married, filing jointly; married, filing separately; or head of household. The standard deduction is an alternative to itemizing tax deductions (*p. C-3*).

Tax avoidance. Structuring of transactions to pay the least amount of income tax at the latest possible time permitted by law (*p. C-0*).

Tax credit. Amount that is subtracted directly from the amount of tax owed to the government (*p. C-6*).

Tax evasion. Illegal activity designed to reduce tax (*p. C-0*).

Tax return. Document on which each taxpayer reports income and shows the computation of income tax (*p. C-1*).

Taxable income. Earnings amount on which the income tax is based, the figure that is multiplied by the tax rate to compute the amount of income tax (*p. C-1*).

Total income. In taxation, all income from any source (*p. C-1*).

EXERCISES

Classifying tax items
(Obj. 1)

EC-1 For each of the following expenditures by an individual taxpayer, indicate whether the item is a *deductible business expense*, an *adjustment to arrive at adjusted gross income*, an *itemized deduction*, or *not deductible*.

a. Contribution to a personal retirement program
b. Charitable contributions
c. Sales tax paid
d. Medical expenses less than 7½ percent of adjusted gross income
e. Cost of adding a room to personal residence
f. Interest expense paid on home mortgage note payable
g. State income taxes paid
h. Wage expense paid to employees
i. Net capital losses in excess of $3,000
j. Insurance expense on rental property

Computing adjusted gross income
(Obj. 1)

EC-2 Gabriel Koo is single with no dependents. His personal income tax records reveal the following:

Gross income of Koo Oriental Jewelers, a proprietorship	$129,000
Operating expenses of Koo Oriental Jewelers	73,000
Capital loss on sale of personal (nonbusiness) investment	7,000
Gift received from Gabriel's parents	12,500
Rent income on a building adjacent to Koo Oriental Jewelers store	19,100
Medical expenses	4,600
Interest expense:	
Home mortgage note payable	7,400
Business debt	3,100
Personal exemption	2,500

Compute Koo's adjusted gross income and taxable income.

Computing an individual's income tax (Obj. 2)

EC-3 *Case A:* Compute the income tax of Gabriel Koo in Exercise C-2.

Case B: Assume that Gabriel Koo in Exercise C-2 is married and has one child. He and his wife, Lia, file a joint income tax return. During the year, the Koos made quarterly income tax payments totaling $12,000. Compute their *income tax* for the year. Also, show the amount of *income tax they owe* or the *refund* they may claim when they file their tax return.

EC-4 Margaret Durham's architecture firm, which she operates as a proprietorship, had gross fee revenue of $255,000 for the year just ended. Business expenses included salaries of $79,000, office depreciation of $4,000, and other operating expenses of $51,000. Durham's personal investments earned dividend revenue of $4,000. She sold General Electric stock at a gain of $2,000 and another personal investment at a loss of $7,000. Her itemized deductions for the year were $4,100. She earned municipal bond interest income of $6,000. She is single and supports her two children.

Computing a single person's adjusted gross income and taxable income
(Obj. 1, 2)

Required

Compute Durham's adjusted gross income and taxable income. Assume that she files a head-of-household tax return.

EC-5 Assume that Margaret Durham of Exercise C-4 is married and has two children. Her husband's salary income is $74,900. Compute the family's taxable income and income tax for the year, assuming that she and her husband file a joint tax return.

Computing income tax for a family's joint tax return (Obj. 2)

EC-6 A taxpayer had the following capital gains and losses during a year:

Treatment of capital gains and losses
(Obj. 2)

a. Gain of $7,000; loss of $4,000
b. Gain of $3,000; loss of $1,000
c. Gain of $2,000; loss of $8,000
d. No gain; loss of $12,000

Required

For each situation, indicate the amount of net capital gain that will be included in, or the amount of net capital loss that will be deductible from, the individual's gross income.

PROBLEMS

PC-1 The tax records of Lars Dunberg, a single taxpayer with no dependents, reveal the following data for the current year:

Computing adjusted gross income, taxable income, and income tax for a single individual
(Obj. 1)

Partner interest in:				
Operating profits of Bon		Capital loss on sale of personal		
Voyage Travel Agency	$ 76,200	investment in land	7,700	
Gain on sale of travel agency		Capital gain on sale of recreational		
building	31,800	vehicle	800	
Life insurance benefits received	200,000	Medical expenses	4,775	
Contribution to a retirement		Interest expense on home		
program	5,000	mortgage note payable	3,800	
Capital gain on sale of personal		Sales tax paid	1,100	
investment in stock	3,200	Property tax paid	2,200	
		Charitable contributions	1,900	
		Personal exemption	2,500	

Compute Dunberg's adjusted gross income, taxable income, and income tax for the year.

PC-2 Betty and Larry Maddox, a married couple with two children, have income, expenses, and other expenditures for the year as follows. They file a joint tax return.

Computing income tax for a joint tax return
(Obj. 1, 2)

Salaries ($95,000 and $43,000)	$138,000	Clothing	2,600
Profit on a partnership		Food	3,800
interest in an office building	24,200	Medical expenses	1,400
Interest income on:		Interest expense on home	
Bank deposit	3,500	mortgage note payable	2,100
City of Albuquerque bonds	900	Cost of painting personal	
Gift received	2,500	residence	6,700
Contribution to retirement		State income tax paid	500
program	3,000	Property tax paid	1,800
Capital gain on sale of personal		Charitable contributions	2,200
investment in stock	2,100	Miscellaneous deductions	3,360
Unused capital loss carryover		Personal exemptions	?
from preceding year	1,900	Income tax withheld	34,300
Capital gain on sale of stereo		Total of quarterly tax payments	2,200
equipment	100		

Required

1. Compute the Maddoxes' adjusted gross income and taxable income for the year. Identify each item not used in this computation, and state why the item is not used.

2. Compute the income tax liability for the year, and show whether the Maddoxes will pay tax when they file their return or receive a refund. Show the amount.

Glossary

Absorption costing. The costing method that assigns all manufacturing costs to products (*p. 932*).

Accelerated depreciation. A depreciation method that writes off a relatively larger amount of the asset's cost nearer the start of its useful life than does the straight-line method (*p. 412*).

Account. The detailed record of the changes that have occurred in a particular asset, liability, or owner's equity during a period (*p. 44*).

Account payable. A liability backed by the general reputation and credit standing of the debtor (*p. 11*).

Account receivable. An asset, a promise to receive cash from customers to whom the business has sold goods or for whom the business has performed services (*p. 11*).

Accounting. The system that measures business activities, processes that information into reports and financial statements, and communicates the findings to decision makers (*p. 4*).

Accounting cycle. Process by which accountants produce an entity's financial statements for a specific period (*p. 134*).

Accounting equation. The most basic tool of accounting: Assets = Liabilities + Owner's Equity (*p. 11*).

Accounting information system. The combination of personnel, records, and procedures that a business uses to meet its needs for financial data (*p. 233*).

Accounting rate of return. A measure of profitability computed by dividing the operating income that an asset generates by the amount of the investment in the asset (*p. 1105*).

Accounts receivable turnover. Ratio of net credit sales to average net accounts receivable. Measures ability to collect cash from credit customers (*p. 805*).

Accrual-basis accounting. Accounting that recognizes (records) the impact of a business event as it occurs, regardless of whether the transaction affected cash (*p. 90*).

Accrued expense. An expense that has been incurred but not yet paid in cash (*p. 101*).

Accrued revenue. A revenue that has been earned but not yet received in cash (*p. 102*).

Accumulated depreciation. The cumulative sum of all depreciation expense from the date of acquiring a plant asset (*p. 99*).

Acid-test ratio. Ratio of the sum of cash plus short-term investments plus net current receivables to current liabilities. Tells whether the entity could pay all its current liabilities if they came due immediately. Also called the quick ratio (*pp. 347, 803*).

Activity-based costing (ABC). A system that focuses on activities as the fundamental cost objects and uses the costs of those activities as building blocks for compiling costs (*p. 1058*).

Activity-based management (ABM). A management process that focuses on the management of activities as the way to improve value delivered to customers (*p. 1057*).

Additional paid-in capital. Another name for paid-in capital in excess of par (*p. 558*).

Adjusted gross income. Total income minus specified adjustments (deductions) equals adjusted gross income, an amount that exists only in the tax law (*p. C-3*).

Adjusted trial balance. A list of all the ledger accounts with their adjusted balances (*p. 106*).

Adjusting entry. Entry made at the end of the period to assign revenues to the period in which they are earned and expenses to the period in which they are incurred. Adjusting entries help measure the period's income and bring the related asset and liability accounts to correct balances for the financial statements (*p. 95*).

Aging of accounts receivable. A way to estimate bad debts by analyzing individual accounts receivable according to the length of time they have been due (*p. 333*).

Allowance for doubtful accounts. A contra account, related to accounts receivable, that holds the estimated amount of collection losses. Also called allowance for uncollectible accounts. (*p. 330*).

Allowance for uncollectible accounts. Another name for allowance for doubtful accounts (*p. 330*).

Allowance method. A method of recording collection losses based on estimates prior to determining that the business will not collect from specific customers (*p. 330*)

Amortization. The systematic reduction of a lump-sum amount. Expense that applies to intangible assets in the same way depreciation applies to plant assets and depletion applies to natural resources. Another name for allowance for doubtful accounts (*p. 425*)

Annuity. A stream of equal periodic amounts (*p. 1107*).

Appraisal costs. Costs incurred in detecting poor-quality goods or services (*p. 1073*).

Appropriation of retained earnings. Restriction of retained earnings that is recorded by a formal journal entry (*p. 607*).

Articles of partnership. Agreement that is the contract between partners specifying such items as the name, location, and nature of the business; the name, capital investment, and duties of each partner; and the method of sharing profits and losses by the partners. Also called the partnership agreement (*p. 522*).

Asset. An economic resource that is expected to be of benefit in the future (*p. 11*).

Auditing. The examination of financial statements by outside accountants, the most significant service that CPAs perform.

The conclusion of an audit is the accountant's professional opinion about the financial statements (p. 39).

Authorization of stock. Provision in a corporate charter that gives the state's permission for the corporation to issue—that is, to sell—a certain number of shares of stock (p. 561).

Available-for-sale securities. Stock investments other than trading securities and bond investments other than trading securities and held-to-maturity securities (p. 688).

Backflush costing. A standard costing system that starts with output completed and works backward to apply manufacturing costs to units sold and to inventories (p. 1065).

Bad-debt expense. Another name for uncollectible-account expense (p. 329).

Balance sheet. List of an entity's assets, liabilities, and owner's equity as of a specific date. Also called the statement of financial position (p. 19).

Bank collection. Collection of money by the bank on behalf of a depositor (p. 291).

Bank reconciliation. Process of explaining the reasons for the difference between a depositor's records and the bank's records about the depositor's bank account (p. 291).

Bank statement. Document for a particular bank account showing its beginning and ending balances and listing the month's transactions that affected the account (p. 289).

Batch processing. Computerized accounting for similar transactions in a group or batch (p. 239).

Benchmarking. Comparison of current performance with some standard. The standard often is the performance level of a leading outside organization (p. 1074).

Board of directors. Group elected by the stockholders to set policy for a corporation and to appoint its officers (p. 556).

Bond discount. Excess of a bond's maturity (par) value over its issue price (p. 640).

Bond premium. Excess of a bond's issue price over its maturity (par) value (p. 640).

Bonds payable. Groups of notes payable (bonds) issued to multiple lenders called bondholders (p. 638).

Book value. Amount of owners' equity on the company's books for each share of its stock (p. 574).

Book value of a plant asset. The asset's cost less accumulated depreciation (p. 99).

Book value per share of common stock. Common stockholders' equity divided by the number of shares of common stock outstanding (p. 812).

Breakeven point. The sales level at which operating income is zero: Total revenues equal total expenses (p. 924).

Budget. Quantitative expression of a plan of action that helps managers to coordinate and implement the plan (p. 842).

Bylaws. Constitution for governing a corporation (p. 556).

Callable bonds Bonds that the issuer may call or pay off at a specified price whenever the issuer wants (p. 653).

Capital. Another name for the owner equity of a business (p. 11).

Capital budgeting. A formal means of analyzing long-range investment decisions (p. 1103).

Capital expenditure. Expenditure that increases the capacity or efficiency of an asset or extends its useful life. Capital expenditures are debited to an asset account (p. 428).

Capital expenditures budget. A company's plan for purchases of property, plant, equipment, and other long-term assets (p. 985).

Capital gain. Special category of gain, defined in the tax law, that results from the disposal of property such as investments in stocks, bonds, real estate, and personal assets (p. C-4).

Capital lease. Lease agreement that meets any one of four criteria: (1) The lease transfers title of the leased asset to the lessee. (2) The lease contains a bargain purchase option. (3) The lease term is 75 percent or more of the estimated useful life of the leased asset. (4) The present value of the lease payments is 90 percent of more of the market value of the leased asset (p. 657).

Capital loss. Special category of loss, defined in the tax law, that results from the disposal of property such as investments in stocks, bonds, real estate, and personal assets (p. C-4).

Cash budget. Details how the business expects to go from the beginning cash balance to the desired ending balance. Also called the *statement of budgeted cash receipts and disbursements* (p. 990).

Cash disbursement journal. Special journal used to record cash payments by check (p. 251).

Cash equivalents. Highly liquid short-term investments that can be converted into cash with little delay (p. 731).

Cash flows. Cash receipts and cash payments (disbursements) (p. 730).

Cash receipts journal. Special journal used to record cash receipts (p. 246).

Cash-basis accounting. Accounting that records only transactions in which cash is received or paid (p. 90).

Certified Public Accountant (CPA). A licensed accountant who serves the general public rather than one particular company (p. 6).

Chairperson. Elected by a corporation's board of directors, usually the most powerful person in the corporation (p. 556).

Change in accounting estimate. A change that occurs in the normal course of business as a company alters earlier expectations. (p. 500).

Change in accounting principle. A change in the accounting method, such as from the LIFO method to the FIFO method for inventories or a switch from an accelerated depreciation method to a straight-line method. (p. 500).

Chart of accounts. List of all the accounts and their account numbers in the ledger (p. 59).

Charter. Document that gives the state's permission to form a corporation (p. 554).

Check. Document that instructs the bank to pay the designated person or business the specified amount of money (p. 288).

Closing entries. Entries that transfer the revenue, expense, and Dividends balances from these respective accounts to the Retained Earnings account (p. 141).

Closing the accounts. Step in the accounting cycle at the end of the period that prepares the accounts for recording the transactions of the next period. Closing the accounts consists of journalizing and posting the closing entries to set the balances of the revenue, expense, and owner withdrawal accounts to zero (p. 140).

Coefficient of determination (r^2). The statistic that tells the percentage of variation in a cost that is explained by changes in the cost driver (p. 967).

Committed fixed costs. Fixed costs that result from having property, plant, equipment, and key managerial personnel (p. 948).

Common stock. The most basic form of capital stock. In a description of a corporation, the common stockholders are the owners of the business (p. 558).

Common-size statement. A financial statement that reports only percentages (no dollar amounts); a type of vertical analysis (p. 793).

Comparability principle. Specifies that accounting information must be comparable from business to business and that a single business's financial statements must be comparable from one period to the next (p. 494).

Conservatism. Concept by which the least favorable figures are presented in the financial statements (pp. 381, 503).

Consignment. Transfer of goods by the owner (consignor) to another business (consignee) that, for a fee, sells the inventory on the owner's behalf. The consignee does not take title to the consigned goods (p. 370).

Consistency principle. A business must use the same accounting methods and procedures from period to period (p. 380).

Consolidated statements. Financial statements of the parent company plus those of majority-owned subsidiaries as if the combination were a single legal entity (p. 693).

Constraint. The factor that restricts production or sale of a product; also called the *limiting factor* (p. 1095).

Contingent liability. A potential liability that will become an actual liability only if a potential event does occur. (p. 344).

Contra account. An account that always has a companion account and whose normal balance is opposite that of the companion account (p. 99).

Contract interest rate. Interest rate that determines the amount of cash interest the borrower pays and the investor receives each year. Also called the stated interest rate (p. 641).

Contributed capital. Another name for paid-in capital (p. 558).

Contribution margin income statement. Groups variable and fixed expenses separately and features the contribution margin (p. 921).

Contribution margin ratio. The ratio of the unit contribution margin to the sale price (p. 925).

Contribution margin. The excess of sales revenues over variable expenses (p. 922).

Control account. An account whose balance equals the sum of the balances in a group of related accounts in a subsidiary ledger. (p. 246).

Controlling. Acting to implement planning decisions and then evaluating the performance of operations and employees (p. 842).

Controlling (majority) interest. Ownership of more than 50 percent of an investee company's voting stock (p. 692).

Conversion costs. Direct labor plus manufacturing overhead (p. 848).

Convertible bonds (or notes) Bonds (or notes) that may be converted into the common stock of the issuing company at the option of the investor (p. 654).

Convertible preferred stock. Preferred stock that may be exchanged by the preferred stockholders, if they choose, for another class of stock in the corporation (p. 571).

Copyright. Exclusive right to reproduce and sell a book, musical composition, film, other work of art, or computer program. Issued by the federal government, copyrights extend 50 years beyond the author's life (p. 426).

Corporation. A business owned by stockholders that begins when the state approves its articles of incorporation. A corporation is a legal entity, an "artificial person," in the eyes of the law (p. 8).

Cost application base. A common denominator for systematically linking indirect costs to products. Ideally, the best measure of the cause-and-effect relationship between overhead costs and production volume (p. 859).

Cost behavior. Description of how costs change in response to a change in a cost driver (p. 932).

Cost driver. Any factor that affects costs (p. 851).

Cost estimation (cost approximation). Determination of the underlying relationship between a cost and its cost driver over a specified relevant range of the cost driver (p. 958).

Cost function. A mathematical statement of the relationship between a cost and one or more cost drivers (p. 958).

Cost object. Anything to which costs are assigned (p. 851).

Cost of goods manufactured. Manufacturer's counterpart to the merchandiser's purchases; the cost that is added to finished goods inventory during a period (p. 848).

Cost of goods sold. The cost of the inventory that the business has sold to customers, the largest single expense of most merchandising businesses. Also called cost of sales (p. 183).

Cost of sales. Another name for cost of goods sold (p. 183).

Cost pool. Any group of individual cost items (p. 1032).

Cost principle. States that assets and services are recorded at their purchase cost and that the accounting record of the asset continues to be based on cost rather than current market value (p. 495).

Cost-volume-profit (CVP) analysis. Expresses the relationships among costs, volume, and profit or loss. An important part of the budgeting system and a key management tool for short-term operating decisions (p. 918).

Credit. The right side of an account (p. 47).

Creditor. The party to a credit transaction who sells a service or merchandise and obtains a receivable (p. 329).

Cumulative preferred stock. Preferred stock whose owners must receive all dividends in arrears before the corporation pays dividends to the common stockholders. (p. 570).

Current asset. An asset that is expected to be converted to cash, sold, or consumed during the next twelve months, or within the business's normal operating cycle if longer than a year (p. 145).

Current liability. A debt due to be paid within one year or one of the entity's operating cycles if the cycle is longer than a year (p. 145).

Current portion of long-term debt. Amount of the principal that is payable within one year (p. 457).

Current ratio. Current assets divided by current liabilities. Measures the ability to pay current liabilities from current assets (pp. 148, 801).

Database program. Computer program that organizes information so that it can be systematically accessed in a variety of report forms (p. 242).

Days' sales in receivables. Ratio of average net accounts receivable to one day's sales. Tells how many days' sales remain in Accounts Receivable awaiting collection (pp. 347, 806).

Debentures. Unsecured bonds, backed only by the good faith of the borrower (p. 638).

Debit. The left side of an account (p. 47).

Debt ratio. Ratio of total liabilities to total assets. Tells the proportion of a company's assets that it has financed with debt (pp. 148, 807).

Debtor. The party to a credit transaction who makes a purchase and creates a payable (p. 328).

Decision model. A method or technique for evaluating and choosing among alternative courses of action (p. 1103).

Deficit. Debit balance in the Retained Earnings account (p. 558).

Dependent. A person who receives more than half of his or her support from another individual (the taxpayer) (p. C-4).

Dependent variable. The cost to be predicted in a cost function (p. 958).

Depletion expense. That portion of the natural resource's cost that is used up in a particular period. Depletion expense is computed in the same way as units-of-production depreciation (p. 424).

Deposit in transit. A deposit recorded by the company but not yet by its bank (p. 291).

Depreciable cost. The cost of a plant asset minus its estimated residual value (p. 410).

Depreciation. Expense associated with spreading (allocating) the cost of a plant asset over its useful life (p. 98).

Direct costs. Costs that are conveniently identified with and traceable to a particular department or other cost object (p. 1000).

Direct labor. The compensation of employees who physically convert materials into the company's products; labor costs that are conveniently traceable to finished goods (p. 847).

Direct materials. Materials that become a physical part of a finished product and whose costs are separately and conveniently traceable through the manufacturing process to finished goods (p. 847).

Direct method. Format of the operating activities section of the statement of cash flows that lists the major categories of operating cash receipts (collections from customers and receipts of interest and dividends) and cash disbursements (payments to suppliers, to employees, for interest and income taxes) (p. 734).

Direct method of service department cost allocation. The method that ignores all services provided by one service department to another (p. 1002).

Direct write-off method. A method of accounting for bad debts by which the company waits until the credit department decides that a customer's account receivable is uncollectible and then debits Uncollectible-Account Expense and credits the customer's Account Receivable (p. 335).

Disclosure principle. A company's financial statements should report enough information for outsiders to make knowledgeable decisions about the company (pp. 380, 499).

Discount rate. Management's minimum desired rate of return on an investment; also called the *hurdle rate, cutoff rate, required rate, cost of capital,* and *target rate* (p. 1107).

Discounting a note payable. A borrowing arrangement in which the bank subtracts the interest amount from the note's face value. The borrower receives the net amount (p. 449).

Discounting a note receivable. Selling a note receivable before its maturity (p. 342).

Discretionary (managed) fixed costs. Fixed costs that arise from periodic (usually yearly) budget decisions that reflect top-management policies. These costs have no clear relationship between inputs and outputs (p. 950).

Discretionary variable costs. Variable costs that change with sales or production volume simply because management has decided to spend a certain percentage of each sales dollar or a certain dollar amount for each unit sold (p. 951).

Discretionary-fixed-cost approach. An approach to managing operating labor costs that relies on personal supervision for controlling costs (p. 953).

Dishonor of a note. Failure of the maker of a note to pay a note receivable at maturity. Another name for default on a note (p. 344).

Dissolution. Ending of a partnership (p. 523).

Dividend. Distribution by a corporation to its stockholders (p. 559).

Dividend yield. Ratio of dividends per share of stock to the stock's market price per share. Tells the percentage of a stock's market value that the company pays to stockholders as dividends (p. 812).

Double taxation. Corporations pay their own income taxes on corporate income. Then, the stockholders pay personal income tax on the cash dividends that they receive from corporations (p. 555).

Double-declining-balance (DDB) method. An accelerated depreciation method that computes annual depreciation by multiplying the asset's decreasing book value by a constant percentage, which is two times the straight-line rate (p. 412).

Doubtful-account expense. Another name for uncollectible-account expense. (p. 329).

Earnings per share (EPS). Amount of a company's net income per share of its outstanding stock (*pp. 612, 811*).

Economic plausibility. A cost function evaluation criterion that means that the relationship between the cost and the cost driver must be credible (*p. 966*).

Effective interest rate. Another name for market interest rate (*p. 641*).

Efficiency. A measure of the amount of inputs used to achieve a given level of output (*p. 1024*).

Efficiency variance. The difference between the actual quantity of an input and the standard quantity of the input, multiplied by the standard unit price (*p. 1029*).

Efficient capital market. A capital market in which market prices fully reflect all information available to the public (*p. 813*).

Electronic funds transfer (EFT). System that transfers cash by electronic impulses rather than paper documents (*p. 289*).

Engineered variable costs. Variable costs that result from measurable, often observable, cause-and-effect relationships between inputs and outputs (*p. 951*).

Engineered-variable-cost approach. An approach to managing operating labor costs that applies formal work measurement to the budgeting process (*p. 953*).

Entity. An organization or a section of an organization that, for accounting purposes, stands apart from other organizations and individuals as a separate economic unit. This is the most basic concept in accounting (*p. 9*).

Entity concept. States that the transactions of each entity are accounted for separately from the transactions of all other organizations and persons (*p. 492*).

Equity method for investments. The method used to account for investments in which the investor has 20 to 50 percent of the investee's voting stock can significantly influence the decisions of the investee. The investment account is debited for ownership in the investee's net income and credited for ownership in the investee's dividends (*p. 690*).

Equivalent units. A measure of the amount of work done during a production period, expressed in terms of fully complete units of output (*p. 884*).

Estimated residual value. Expected cash value of an asset at the end of its useful life. Also called residual value, scrap value, or salvage value (*p. 410*).

Estimated useful life. Length of a service that a business expects to get from an asset, may be expressed in years, units of output, miles, or other measures (*p. 409*).

Expense. Decrease in retained earnings that results from operations; the cost of doing business; opposite of revenues (*p. 12*).

External failure costs. Costs incurred when poor-quality goods or services are detected after delivery to customers (*p. 1073*).

Extraordinary item. A gain or loss that is both unusual for the company and infrequent (*p. 611*).

Extraordinary repair. Repair work that generates a capital expenditure (*p. 428*).

FICA tax. Federal Insurance Contributions Act (FICA), or Social Security tax, which is withheld from employees' pay (*p. 460*).

Financial accounting. The branch of accounting that provides information to people outside the business (*p. 6*).

Financial budget. Projects cash inflows and outflows and the period-ending balance sheet (*p. 985*).

Financial statements. Business documents that report financial information about an entity to persons and organizations outside the business (*p. 4*).

Financing activity. Activity that obtains the funds from investors and creditors needed to launch and sustain the business; a section of the statement of cash flows (*p. 733*).

Finished goods inventory. Completed goods that have not been sold (*p. 846*).

First-in, first-out (FIFO) method. Inventory costing method by which the first costs into inventory are the first costs out to cost of goods sold. Ending inventory is based on the costs of the most recent purchases (*p. 371*).

First-in, first-out (FIFO) method of process costing. The method that assigns to each period's equivalent units of production that period's costs per equivalent unit (*p. 890*).

Fixed cost. Cost that does not change in total despite wide changes in volume (*p. 919*).

Flexible budget. A set of budgets covering a range of volume rather than a single volume level (*p. 1021*).

Flexible budget variance. A difference between an actual result and a flexible budget amount (*p. 1023*).

FOB destination. Terms of a transaction that govern when the title to the inventory passes from the seller to the purchaser —when the goods arrive at the purchaser's location (*p. 370*).

FOB shipping point. Terms of a transaction that govern when the title to the inventory passes from the seller to the purchaser—when the goods leave the seller's place of business (*p. 370*).

Foreign-currency exchange rate. The measure of one currency against another currency. (*p. 704*).

Foreign-currency transaction gain or loss. A gain or loss that occurs when the exchange rate changes between the date of a purchase or sale on account and the subsequent payment or receipt of cash (*p. 705*).

Foreign-currency translation adjustment. The balancing figure that brings the dollar amount of the total liabilities and stockholders' equity of the foreign subsidiary into agreement with the dollar amount of its total assets. (*p. 708*).

Franchises and licenses. Privileges granted by a private business or a government to sell product or service in accordance with specified conditions (*p. 426*).

Full product costs. The costs of all resources that are used throughout the value chain for a product (*p. 845*).

General journal. Journal used to record all transactions that do not fit one of the special journals (*p. 244*).

General ledger. Ledger of accounts that are reported in the financial statements (*p. 244*).

Generally accepted accounting principles (GAAP). Accounting guidelines, formulated by the Financial Accounting

Standards Board, that govern how businesses report their financial statements to the public (p. 8).

Going-concern concept. Accountants' assumption that the business will continue operating in the foreseeable future (p. 492).

Goodness of fit. A cost function evaluation criterion that means that the relationship between the cost and the cost driver must explain past costs well (p. 967).

Goodwill. Excess of the cost of an acquired company over the sum of the market values of its net assets (assets minus liabilities) (p. 427).

Gross income. In taxation, total income minus exclusions (p. C-2).

Gross margin. Excess of sales revenue over cost of goods sold. Also called gross profit (p. 176).

Gross margin method. A way to estimate inventory based on a rearrangement of the cost-of-goods-sold model: Beginning inventory + Net purchases = Cost of goods available for sale. Cost of goods available for sale − Cost of goods sold = Ending inventory. Also called gross profit method (p. 385).

Gross margin percentage. Gross margin divided by net sales revenue. A measure of profitability (p. 195).

Gross pay. Total amount of salary, wages, commission, or any other employee compensation before taxes and other deductions are taken out (p. 459).

Gross profit. Another name for gross margin (p. 176).

Hardware. Electronic equipment that includes computers, disk drives, monitors, printers, and the network that connects them (p. 235).

Hedging. Protecting oneself from losing money in one transaction by engaging in a counterbalancing transaction (p. 707).

Held-to-maturity securities. Investment in bonds, notes, and other debt securities that the investor expects to hold until their maturity date (p. 698).

High-low method. A cost-function estimation method that uses only the highest-volume and lowest-volume points within the relevant range of a sample (p. 963).

Holding gain. A gain that arises from a change in the market value of an asset, not from a sale transaction (p. 689).

Holding loss. A loss that arises from a change in the market value of an asset, not from a sale transaction. (p. 689).

Horizontal analysis. Study of percentage changes in comparative financial statements (p. 788).

Imprest system. A way to account for petty cash by maintaining a constant balance in the petty cash account, supported by the fund (cash plus disbursement tickets) totaling the same amount (p. 302).

Income from operations. Another name for operating income (p. 193).

Income statement. List of an entity's revenues, expenses, and net income or net loss for a specific period. Also called the statement of operations or the statement of earnings (p. 18).

Income summary. A temporary "holding tank" account into which the revenues and expenses are transferred prior to their final transfer to the capital account (p. 141).

Income tax. A general-purpose tax levied on the income of a taxpayer. Separate from all other taxes, it is the federal government's largest source of revenue (p. C-0).

Incorporators. Persons who organize a corporation (p. 556).

Independent variable. The cost driver in a cost function (p. 958).

Indirect costs. Costs that cannot be traced to a single department or other cost object; costs other than direct costs (p. 1000).

Indirect labor. Manufacturing labor costs other than direct labor; labor costs that are difficult to trace to specific products (p. 847).

Indirect materials. Materials whose costs cannot conveniently be traced directly to particular finished products (p. 847).

Indirect method. Format of the operating activities section of the statement of cash flows that starts with net income and shows the reconciliation from net income to operating cash flows. Also called the reconciliation method (p. 734).

Intangible asset. An asset with no physical form, a special right to current and expected future benefits (p. 425).

Itemized deduction. In taxation, a particular category that includes medical expenses, interest expense, charitable contributions, taxes paid, casualty losses, and miscellaneous deductions (p. C-3).

Interest. The revenue to the payee for loaning out the principal, and the expense to the maker for borrowing the principal (p. 339).

Interest period. The period of time during which interest is to be computed, extending from the original date of a note to the maturity date (p. 339).

Interest rate. The percentage rate that is multiplied by the principal amount to compute the amount of interest on a note (p. 340).

Internal control. Organizational plan and all the related measures adopted by an entity to safeguard assets, ensure accurate and reliable accounting records, promote operational efficiency, and encourage adherence to company policies (p. 282).

Internal failure costs. Costs incurred when poor-quality goods or services are detected before delivery to customers (p. 1073).

Internal rate of return (IRR). The rate of return that makes the net present value of a project equal to zero (p. 1110).

Inventoriable costs. All costs of a product that are regarded as an asset for financial reporting under GAAP (p. 849).

Inventory profit. Difference between gross margin figured on the FIFO basis and gross margin figured on the LIFO basis (p. 376).

Inventory turnover. Ratio of cost of goods sold to average inventory. Measures the number of times a company sells its average level of inventory during a year (pp. 196, 804).

Investing activity. Activity that increases and decreases the long-term assets available to the business; a section of the statement of cash flows (p. 732).

Job cost record. Document used to accumulate the costs of a job (p. 852).

Job order costing. Costing system used by companies that manufacture products as individual units or in small batches that vary considerably in terms of resources consumed, time required, or complexity (p. 851).

Joint products. The goods produced in a joint process (p. 1099).

Journal. The chronological accounting record of an entity's transactions (p. 50).

Just-in-time (JIT) production systems. Production systems designed to eliminate waste by such means as sequentially arranged production activities, low setup times, demand-pull production scheduling, and a high level of employee training and commitment (p. 1064).

Kaizen costing. The relentless pursuit of cost reduction during the manufacturing stage of a product's life cycle (p.1071).

Last-in, first-out (LIFO) method. Inventory costing method by which the last costs into inventory are the first costs out to cost of goods sold. This method leaves the oldest costs—those of beginning inventory and the earliest purchases of the period—in ending inventory (p. 372).

Lease. Rental agreement in which the tenant (lessee) agrees to make rent payments to the property owner (lessor) in exchange for the use of the asset (p. 656).

Leasehold. Prepayment that a lessee (renter) makes to secure the use of an asset from a lessor (landlord) (p. 426).

Least-squares regression method (regression analysis). A formal model that measures the average amount of change in the dependent variable that is associated with a one-unit change in the independent variable (p. 965).

Ledger. The book of accounts (p. 44).

Lessee. Tenant in a lease agreement (p. 656).

Lessor. Property owner in a lease agreement (p. 656).

Leverage. Another name for trading on equity (p. 811).

Liability. An economic obligation (a debt) payable to an individual or an organization outside the business (p. 11).

Life-cycle budget. A budget that compiles predicted revenues and costs of a product over its entire life cycle (p. 1069).

LIFO reserve. The difference between the LIFO cost of an inventory and what it would be under FIFO (p. 374).

Limited liability. No personal obligation of a stockholder for corporation debts. A stockholder can lose no more on an investment in a corporation's stock than the cost of the investment (p. 555).

Liquidation. The process of going out of business by selling the entity's assets and paying its liabilities. The final step in liquidation of a business is the distribution of any remaining cash to the owners (p. 536).

Liquidity. Measure of how quickly an item may be converted to cash (p. 144).

Long-term asset. An asset other than a current asset (p. 145).

Long-term investment. Separate asset category reported on the balance sheet between current assets and plant assets (p. 687).

Long-term liability. A liability other than a current liability (p. 145).

Long-term solvency. Ability to generate enough cash to pay long-term debts as they mature (p. 787).

Lower-of-cost-or-market (LCM) rule. Requires that an asset be reported in the financial statements at the lower of its historical cost or its market value (current replacement cost for inventory) (p. 382).

Maker of a note. The person or business that signs the note and promises to pay the amount required by the note agreement; the debtor (p. 339).

Management accounting. The branch of accounting that generates information for internal decision makers of a business, such as top executives (p. 6).

Management by exception. The practice of directing management attention to important deviations from budgeted amounts (p. 999).

Manufacturing overhead. All manufacturing costs besides direct materials and direct labor (p. 847).

Manufacturing product costs. The costs of resources that are used to manufacture a product (p. 845).

Margin of safety. Excess of expected sales over breakeven sales (p. 929).

Market interest rate. Interest rate that investors demand in order to loan their money. Also called effective interest rate (p. 641).

Market value method for investments. Used to account for all trading investments in stocks and bonds. These investments are reported at their current market value. (p. 688).

Market value. Price for which a person could buy or sell a share of stock (p. 573).

Marketable security. Another name for short-term investment. (p. 687).

Master budget. The comprehensive budget that includes the operating budget, the capital expenditures budget, and the financial budget (p. 985).

Matching principle. The basis for recording expenses. Directs accountants to identify all expenses incurred during the period, to measure the expenses, and to match them against the revenues earned during that same span of time (pp. 93, 498).

Materiality concept. States that a company must perform strictly proper accounting only for items and transactions that are significant to the business's financial statements (pp. 381, 502).

Materials inventory. Materials on hand that are intended for use in the manufacturing process (p. 846).

Materials requisition. Request for materials, prepared by manufacturing personnel (p. 855).

Maturity date. The date on which the final payment of the note is due. Also called the due date (p. 340).

Maturity value. The sum of the principal and interest due at the maturity date of a note (p. 340).

Menu. A list of options for choosing computer functions (p. 238).

Minority interest. A subsidiary company's equity that is held by stockholders other than the parent company (p. 696).

Mixed (semivariable) cost. Cost that is part variable and part fixed (p. 919).

Module. Separate units of an accounting package that are integrated to function together (p. 240).

Mortgage. Borrower's promise to transfer the legal title to certain assets to the lender if the debt is not paid on schedule (p. 655).

Multiple-step income statement. Format that contains subtotals to highlight significant relationships. In addition to net income, it presents gross margin and income from operations (p. 193).

Mutual agency. Every partner can bind the business to a contract within the scope of the partnership's regular business operations (p. 523).

Net earnings. Another name for net income or net profit (p. 15).

Net income. Excess of total revenues over total expenses. Also called net earnings or net profit (p. 15).

Net loss. Excess of total expenses over total revenues (p. 15).

Net pay. Gross pay minus all deductions; the amount of employee compensation that the employee actually takes home (p. 459).

Net present value (NVP). The decision model that computes the expected net monetary gain or loss from a project by discounting all expected future cash inflows and outflows to their present value, using a minimum desired rate of return (p. 1107).

Net profit. Another name for net income or net earnings (p. 15).

Net purchases. Purchases less purchase discounts and purchase returns and allowances (p. 217).

Net sales. Sales revenue less sales discounts and sales returns and allowances (p. 185).

Net sales revenue. Sales revenue less sales discounts and sales returns and allowances (p. 185).

Network. The system of electronic linkages that allow different computers to share the same information (p. 235).

Nominal account. Another name for a temporary account (p. 140).

Non-value-added activities. Activities that do not increase customer value or satisfy a company need (p. 1063).

Nonsufficient funds (NSF) check. A "hot" check, one for which the payer's bank account has insufficient money to pay the check (p. 291).

Note payable. A liability evidenced by a written promise to make a future payment (p. 11).

Note receivable. An asset evidenced by another party's written promise that entitles you to receive cash in the future (p. 11).

Off-balance-sheet financing. Acquisition of assets or services with debt that is not reported on the balance sheet (p. 659).

On-line processing. Computerized processing of related functions, such as the recording and posting of transactions, on a continuous basis (p. 239).

Operating activity. Activity that creates revenue or expense in the entity's major line of business; a section of the statement of cash flows. Operating activities affect the income statement (p. 732).

Operating budget. Sets the expected revenues and expenses—and thus operating income—for the period (p. 985).

Operating cycle. Time span during which cash is paid for goods and services that are sold to customers who then pay the business in cash (p. 145).

Operating expenses. Expenses, other than cost of goods sold, that are incurred in the entity's major line of business. Examples include rent, depreciation, salaries, wages, utilities, property tax, and supplies expense (p. 191).

Operating income. Gross margin minus operating expenses plus any other operating revenues. Also called income from operations (p. 193).

Operating lease. Usually a short-term or cancelable rental agreement (p. 657).

Opportunity cost. The benefit that can be obtained from the next-best course of action in a decision (p. 1101).

Ordinary repair. Repair work that creates a revenue expenditure, which is debited to an expense account (p. 428).

Organization cost. The costs of organizing a corporation, including legal fees, taxes and fees paid to the state, and charges by promoters for selling the stock. Organization cost is an intangible asset (p. 568).

Other expense. Expense that is outside the main operations of a business, such as a loss on the sale of plant assets (p. 193).

Other revenue. Revenue that is outside the main operations of a business, such as a gain on the sale of plant assets (p. 193).

Outstanding check. A check issued by the company and recorded on its books but not yet paid by its bank (p. 291).

Outstanding stock. Stock in the hands of stockholders (p. 557).

Overhead efficiency variance. The difference between the flexible budget amount for actual production and the flexible budget amount for the actual units of the overhead cost application base (p. 1035).

Overhead flexible budget variance. The difference between the actual overhead cost and the flexible budget amount for actual production; also called *overhead controllable variance* (p. 1034).

Overhead spending variance. The difference between the flexible budget amount for the actual units of the cost application base and the actual overhead cost (p. 1036).

Owners' equity. The claim of the owners of a business to the assets of the business. Also called capital for a proprietorship and a partnership and stockholders' equity for a corporation (p. 11).

Paid-in capital. A corporation's capital from investments by the stockholders. Also called contributed capital (*p. 558*).

Par value. Arbitrary amount assigned to a share of stock (*p. 561*).

Parameter. A constant or coefficient in a model or system of equations (*p. 959*).

Parent company. An investor company that owns more than 50 percent of the voting stock of a subsidiary company (*p. 692*).

Partnership. A business with two or more owners (*pp. 8, 522*).

Partnership agreement. Another name for the articles of partnership (*p. 522*).

Patent. A federal government grant giving the holder the exclusive right for 17 years to produce and sell an invention (*p. 425*).

Payback. The length of time it will take to recover, in net cash inflows from operations, the dollars of a capital outlay (*p. 1104*).

Payee of a note. The person or business to whom the maker of a note promises future payment; the creditor (*p. 339*).

Payroll. Employee compensation, a major expense of many businesses (*p. 458*).

Pension. Employee compensation that will be received during retirement (*p. 659*).

Percentage of sales approach. A method of estimating uncollectible receivables as a percentage of net credit sales (or net sales) (*p. 333*).

Period costs. Operating costs that are expensed in the period in which they are incurred (*p. 850*).

Periodic inventory system. The business does not keep a continuous record of the inventory on hand. Instead, at the end of the period the business makes a physical count of the on-hand inventory and applies the appropriate unit costs to determine the cost of the ending inventory (*pp. 177, 368*).

Permanent account. Another name for a real account—asset, liability, and capital—that is *not* closed at the end of the period (*p. 141*).

Perpetual inventory system. The business keeps a continuous record for each inventory item to show the inventory on hand at all times (*pp. 177, 366*).

Personal exemption. A tax deduction that is a set amount allowed for a taxpayer, the taxpayer's spouse, and each person who qualifies as a dependent (*p. C-4*).

Petty cash. Fund containing a small amount of cash that is used to pay minor expenditures (*p. 301*).

Planning. Choosing goals and deciding how to achieve them (*p. 842*).

Plant asset. Long-lived assets, such as land, buildings, and equipment, used in the operation of the business (*pp. 98, 406*).

Postclosing trial balance. List of the ledger accounts and their balances at the end of the period after the journalizing and posting of the closing entries. The last step of the accounting cycle, the postclosing trial balance ensures that the ledger is in balance for the start of the next accounting period. (*p. 143*).

Posting. Transferring of amounts from the journal to the ledger (*p. 51*).

Preferred stock. Stock that gives its owners certain advantages over common stockholders, such as the priority to receive dividends before the common stockholders and the priority to receive assets before the common stockholders if the corporation liquidates (*p. 560*).

Prepaid expense. A category of miscellaneous assets that typically expire or get used up in the near future. Examples include prepaid rent, prepaid insurance, and supplies (*p. 96*).

Present value. Amount a person would invest now to receive a greater amount at a future date (*p. 640*).

President. Chief operating officer in charge of managing the day-to-day operations of a corporation (*p. 556*).

Pretax accounting income. Income before tax from the income statement (*p. 576*).

Prevention costs. Costs incurred to avoid poor-quality goods or services (*p. 1073*).

Price variance. The difference between the actual unit price of an input and the standard unit price of the input, multiplied by the actual input quantity (*p. 1028*).

Price/earnings ratio. Ratio of the market price of a share of common stock to the company's earnings per share. Measures the value that the stock market places on $1 of a company's earnings (*p. 811*).

Prime costs. Direct materials plus direct labor (*p. 848*).

Principal amount. The amount loaned out by the payee and borrowed by the maker of a note (*p. 339*).

Prior-period adjustment. A correction to retained earnings for an error of an earlier period (*p. 615*).

Process costing. System for assigning costs to goods that are mass produced in a continuous sequence of steps (*p. 880*).

Product life cycle. The time from original research and development through the product's sales and on to the end of customer service (*p. 1069*).

Production cost report. Summary of the activity in a processing department for a period (*p. 894*).

Production department. A department whose main function is to add value to products or services sold to customers (*p. 1000*).

Production volume variance. The difference between the overhead cost in the flexible budget for actual production and the standard overhead applied to production (*p. 1034*).

Promissory note. A written promise to pay a specified amount of money at a particular future date (*p. 339*).

Proprietorship. A business with a single owner (*p. 8*).

Purchases journal. Special journal used to record all puchases of inventory, supplies, and other assets on account. (*p. 249*).

Quality. The conformance of the attributes of a product or service to a specific set of standards (*p. 1072*).

Quick ratio. Another name for the acid-test ratio (*p. 347*).

Rate of return on common stockholders' equity. Net income minus preferred dividends, divided by average common stockholders' equity. A measure of profitability. Also called return on equity (*pp. 573, 810*).

Rate of return on net sales. Ratio of net income to net sales. A measure of profitability. Also called return on sales (*p. 809*).

Rate of return on total assets. The sum of net income plus interest expense divided by average total assets. This ratio measures the success a company has in using its assets to earn income for the persons who finance the business. Also called return on assets (*pp. 572, 809*).

Real account. Another name for a permanent account (*p. 141*).

Receivable. A monetary claim against a business or an individual, acquired mainly by selling goods and services and by lending money (*p. 328*).

Reciprocal services. Services provided back and forth among service departments (*p. 1000*).

Reconciliation method. Another name for the indirect method (*p. 747*).

Relevant information. The expected future data that differ among alternative courses of action (*p. 1090*).

Relevant range. A band of volume in which a specific relationship exists between cost and volume (*p. 920*).

Reliability principle. Requires that accounting information be dependable (free from error and bias). Also called the objectivity principle (*p. 494*).

Responsibility accounting. A system for evaluating the performance of each responsibility center and its manager (*p. 996*).

Responsibility center. A part, segment, or subunit of an organization whose manager is accountable for specified activities (*p. 996*).

Retained earnings. A corporation's capital that is earned through profitable operation of the business (*pp. 12, 558*).

Return on assets. Another name for rate of return on total assets (*p. 572*).

Return on equity. Another name for rate of return on common stockholders' equity (*p. 573*).

Return on stockholders' equity. Another name for rate of return on common stockholders' equity (*p. 810*).

Revenue. Increase in retained earnings from delivering goods or services to customers or clients (*p. 12*).

Revenue expenditure. Expenditure that merely maintains an asset in its existing condition or restores the asset to good working order. Revenue expenditures are expensed (matched against revenue) (*p. 428*).

Revenue principle. The basis for recording revenues; tells accountants when to record revenue and the amount of revenue to record (*pp. 92, 495*).

Reversing entry. An entry that switches the debit and the credit of a previous adjusting entry. The reversing entry is dated the first day of the period following the adjusting entry (*p. 172*).

Sales. Another name for sales revenue (*p. 176*).

Sales discount. Reduction in the amount receivable from a customer, offered by the seller as an incentive for the customer to pay promptly. A contra account to Sales Revenue (*p. 184*).

Sales journal. Special journal used to record credit sales (*p. 243*).

Sales mix. Combination of products that make up total sales (*p. 930*).

Sales returns and allowances. Decrease in the seller's receivable from a customer's return of merchandise or from granting the customer an allowance from the amount the customer owes the seller. A contra account to Sales Revenue (*p. 184*).

Sales revenue. The amount that a merchandiser earns from selling inventory before subtracting expenses. Also called sales (*p. 176*).

Sales volume variance. The difference between an amount in the flexible budget and a corresponding amount in the static (master) budget (*p. 1023*).

Segment of a business. One of various separate divisions of a company (*p. 610*).

Sensitivity analysis. A what-if technique that asks what a result will be if a predicted amount is not achieved or if an underlying assumption changes (*p. 992*).

Serial bonds. Bonds that mature in installments over a period of time (*p. 638*).

Server. The main computer in a network where the program and data are stored (*p. 235*).

Service department. A department whose primary function is to provide services to other departments—both production departments and other service departments (*p. 1000*).

Shareholder. Another name for stockholder (*p. 554*).

Short presentation. A way to report contingent liabilities in the body of the balance sheet, after total liabilities but with no amount given (*p. 456*).

Short-term investment. Investment that is readily convertible to cash and that the investor intends either to convert to cash within one year or to use to pay a current liability; also called a marketable security, a current asset (*p. 687*).

Short-term liquidity. Ability to meet current payments as they come due (*p. 787*).

Short-term note payable. Note payable due within one year, a common form of financing (*p. 448*).

Single-step income statement. Format that groups all revenues together and then lists and deducts all expenses together without drawing any subtotals (*p. 194*).

Social Security tax. Another name for FICA tax (*p. 460*).

Software. Set of programs or instructions that cause the computer to perform the work desired (*p. 235*).

Special journal. An accounting journal designed to record one specific type of transaction (*p. 242*).

Specific unit cost method. Inventory cost method based on the specific cost of particular units of inventory (*p. 371*).

Spreadsheet. A computer program that links data by means of formulas and functions; an electronic worksheet (*p. 240*).

Stable-monetary-unit concept. Accountants' basis for ignoring the effect of inflation and making no restatements for the changing value of the dollar (*p. 493*).

Standard cost. A carefully predetermined cost that usually is expressed on a per-unit basis (*p. 1026*).

Standard deduction. A set amount of tax deduction that varies depending on the individual's filing status: single; married, filing jointly; married, filing separately; or head of household. The standard deduction is an alternative to itemizing tax deductions (p. C-3).

Stated interest rate. Another name for the contract interest rate (p. 641).

Statement of cash flows. Reports cash receipts and cash disbursements classified according to the entity's major activities: operating, investing, and financing (pp. 19, 730).

Statement of earnings. Another name for income statement (p. 18).

Statement of operations. Another name for income statement (p. 18).

Statement of stockholders' equity. Reports the changes in all categories of stockholders' equity during the period (p. 616).

Statement of owner's equity. Summary of the changes in the owner's equity of an entity during a specific period (p. 18).

Static budget. A budget prepared for only one level of volume (p. 1020).

Step-down method. A method of service department cost allocation that recognizes some, but not all, reciprocal services (p. 1002).

Step-function variable cost. A variable cost that is purchased in whole quantities (such as hours) but used in fractional quantities (such as tenths of hours) (p. 959).

Stock. Shares of ownership in a corporation (p. 554).

Stock dividend. A proportional distribution by a corporation of its own stock to its stockholders (p. 597).

Stock split. An increase in the number of outstanding shares of stock coupled with a proportionate reduction in the par value of the stock (p. 600).

Stockholder. A person who owns stock in a corporation (pp. 8, 554).

Stockholders' equity. Owners' equity of a corporation (p. 557).

Straight-line method. Depreciation method in which an equal amount of depreciation expense is assigned to each year (or period) of asset use (p. 410).

Strategy. A set of business goals and the tactics to achieve them (p. 1057).

Strong currency. A currency that is rising relative to other nations' currencies (p. 704).

Subsequent event. An event that occurs after the end of a company's accounting period but before publication of its financial statements and that may affect the interpretation of the information in those statements (p. 500).

Subsidiary company. An investee company in which a parent company owns more than 50 percent of the voting stock (p. 692).

Subsidiary ledger. Book of accounts that provides supporting details on individual balances, the total of which appears in a general ledger account (p. 245).

Sum-of-years'-digits (SYD) method. An accelerated depreciation method by which depreciation is figured by multiplying the depreciable cost of the asset by a fraction. The denominator of the SYD fraction is the sum of the years' digits of the asset's life. The numerator starts with the asset life in years and decreases by one each year thereafter (p. 413).

Sunk cost. A past cost that is unavoidable because it cannot be changed no matter what action is taken (p. 1098).

Target costing. A cost management technique that helps managers set goals for cost reductions through product design (p. 1070).

Tax avoidance. Structuring of transactions to pay the least amount of income tax at the latest possible time permitted by law (p. C-0).

Tax credit. Amount that is subtracted directly from the amount of tax owed to the government (p. C-6).

Tax evasion. Illegal activity designed to reduce tax (p. C-0).

Tax return. Document on which each taxpayer reports income and shows the computation of income tax (p. C-1).

Taxable income. Income from the income tax return filed with the Internal Revenue Service; the basis for computing the amount of tax to pay the government (pp. 576, C-1).

Temporary account. Another name for a nominal account. The revenue and expense accounts that relate to a particular accounting period and are closed at the end of the period are temporary accounts. For a proprietorship, the owner withdrawal account is also temporary (p. 140).

Term bonds. Bonds that all mature at the same time for a particular issue (p. 638).

Throughput time. The time between receipt of purchased materials and completion of finished products (p. 1063).

Time value of money. The fact that income can be earned by investing money for a period of time (p. 1106).

Time-period concept. Ensures that accounting information is reported at regular intervals (pp. 94, 493).

Times-interest-earned ratio. Ratio of income from operations to interest expense. Measures the number of times that operating income can cover interest expense. Also called the interest-coverage ratio (p. 808).

Total income. In taxation, all income from any source (p. C-1).

Total quality management (TQM). A formal effort to improve quality throughout an organization's value chain (p. 1072).

Trademarks and trade names. Distinctive identifications of a product or service (p. 426).

Trading on the equity. Earning more income on borrowed money than the related interest expense, thereby increasing the earnings for the owners of the business (pp. 656, 811).

Trading securities. Investments that are to be sold in the very near future with the intent of generating profits on price changes (p. 688).

Transaction. An event that affects the financial position of a particular entity and can be reliably recorded (p. 12).

Treasury stock. A corporation's own stock that it has issued and later reacquired (p. 602).

Trial balance. A list of all the ledger accounts with their balances (p. 54).

Trigger points. Points in operations that prompt entries in the accounting records *(p. 1065)*.

Uncollectible-account expense. Cost to the seller of extending credit. Arises from the failure to collect from credit customers *(p. 329)*.

Underwriter. Organization that purchases the bonds from an issuing company and resells them to its clients or sells the bonds for a commission, agreeing to buy all unsold bonds *(p. 638)*.

Unearned revenue. A liability created when a business collects cash from customers in advance of doing work for the customer. The obligation is to provide a product or a service in the future. Also called deferred revenue *(p. 102)*.

Unemployment compensation tax. Payroll tax paid by employers to the government, which uses the money to pay unemployment benefits to people who are out of work *(p. 461)*.

Units-of-production (UOP) method. Depreciation method by which a fixed amount of depreciation is assigned to each unit of output produced by the plant asset *(p. 411)*.

Unlimited personal liability. When a partnership (or proprietorship) cannot pay its debts with business assets, the partners (or the proprietor) must use personal assets to meet the debt *(p. 523)*.

Value chain. Sequence of all business functions in which value is added to a firm's products or services *(p. 844)*.

Value engineering (VE). The process of designing products that achieve cost targets and meet specified standards of quality and performance *(p. 1070)*.

Variable cost. Cost that changes in total in direct proportion to changes in volume of activity *(p. 918)*.

Variable costing. The costing method that assigns only variable manufacturing costs to products *(p. 932)*.

Variance. The difference between an actual amount and the corresponding budgeted amount *(p. 953)*.

Vertical analysis. Analysis of a financial statement that reveals the relationship of each statement item to the total, which is 100 percent *(p. 791)*.

Visual-fit method. A cost function estimation method in which the analyst visually fits a line to the plot of all sample data points *(p. 964)*.

Voucher. Document authorizing a cash disbursement *(p. 300)*.

Weak currency. A currency that is falling relative to other nations' currencies. *(p. 704)*.

Weighted-average cost method. Inventory costing method based on the weighted-average cost of inventory during the period. Weighted-average cost is determined by dividing the cost of goods available for sale by the number of units available. Also called the average cost method *(p. 371)*.

Weighted-average method. A process costing method that costs all equivalent units of work to account for each period with a weighted average of that period's and the previous period's costs per equivalent unit *(p. 895)*.

Withheld income tax. Income tax deducted from employees' gross pay *(p. 459)*.

Work in process inventory. Goods that are in the manufacturing process but are not yet complete *(p. 846)*.

Work measurement. The careful analysis of a task—its size, the methods used, and its efficiency *(p. 953)*.

Work sheet. A columnar document designed to help move data from the trial balance to the financial statements *(p. 134)*.

Working capital. Current assets minus current liabilities; measures a business's ability to meet its short-term obligations with its current assets *(p. 801)*.

Company Index

Prudential Insurance Company, 718
Purolator, Inc., 611

Q

Quality Instrument Company, 1060–62
Quality International, 654

R

Ralph Lauren, 705
Ralston Purina, 359
Reebok, 736, 844, 845, 847, 848
Renault of France, 690
Rich's Department Store, 476
RJR Nabisco, Inc., 501, 611, 656
Robert Morris Associates, 195, 794, 799, 803, 804, 808
Robins Corporation, 752–53
Rothschild, Inc., 595
RTE Corporation, 607
Rubbermaid Incorporated, 799
Rubinstein Jewelers, 345

S

Safeway Stores, 846, 986, 996, 997
Saks Fifth Avenue, 287
Santa Fe Travel Associates, 568
Sara Lee Corporation, 283, 297, 654, 703, 707
Sara Nichols, Attorney, Professional Corporation (P.C.), 61–65
Saturn Corporation, 693, 841, 846, 847, 859
Schlumberger Limited, 708–9
Schmidt Home Builders, 333–34
Schwinn Company, 261
Scott Paper Company, 737
Searle, 234
Sears, Roebuck, and Company, 145, 243, 367, 457, 501, 610, 714, 731, 996, 997
7-Eleven, 476
Shea & Gould, 536
Shearson Financial Consultants, 714
Shea's Research Service, Inc., 55
Sheraton, 447
ShowBiz Pizza Time, Inc., 450
Simplicity Pattern Co., Inc., 605–6
Sizzler Restaurants, 443
Sony Corporation, 175, 178, 183–85, 218, 809
Southwest Drilling Company, 602

Southwestern Bell Telephone Company, 979
Standard & Poor's Corp., 637, 799
Stanford University, 977
Stanley Home Products, Inc., 453
State Service Company, 109–12, 137–38
Stop-n-Shop, 309
Sullivan Software Company, 955–56
Sun Bancorp, 597
Sun Company, Inc., 380
Superior Oil Company, The, 803
Swingline Corporation, 622
Symington Wayne Corporation, 423

T

Taco Bell, 217
Tailwind Bicycle Shop, 261
Talon Computer Concepts, 301
Target Stores, 286, 918
Taylor & Uvalde, 539–40
TechArt, Inc., 1001–4
Tell City Furniture Company, 1096
Tennis Hall of Fame, 1116
Texaco, Inc., 7, 310, 846, 852
Texas Instruments (TI), 1083, 1102, 1124
TGI Friday's, 511
The GAP, Inc., 374, 814–15
Thomasville, 1059
Thom McAn Shoe Company, 920
Thompson Consumer Electronics, 1026
3M, 40
Thrifty Rent-a-Car System, Inc., 693
Tomassini Computer Service Center, Inc., 66–69
Toro, 1104
Toyota Motor Company, 9, 347, 453, 683, 716, 1020, 1064, 1069–70
Toys "R" Us, 805
TRE Corporation, 797–98
Trendline Corporation, 578, 579
Tupperware, 346
Turner & Lail, 521, 523

U

Ultimate Corporation, 327, 329, 347
Union Pacific Corporation, 235, 501
United Airlines, 408, 426
United Merchants and Manufacturers, Inc., 501
U.S. Divers, 882, 884–87, 890–98

U.S. Express Corporation, 707–8
U.S. Postal Service, 955
U.S. Steel, 947, 950–51, 955, 958, 966
United Technologies, 397
USX Corporation, U.S. Steel Group of, 947, 950–51, 955, 958, 966

V

Viacom, Inc., 685, 686, 687, 692, 693, 982
VISA, 234, 337
Vitromatic S.A., 692
Volkswagen, 427

W

W. R. Grace & Co., 698
Walgreen Co., 657–59, 682
Wal-Mart Stores, Inc., 194, 195, 196, 207, 307, 354, 365, 366, 367, 374–75, 380, 405, 406, 407–9, 410, 420, 421, 423, 426, 427, 558, 585, 726, 803, 804, 821
Walt Disney Company, 419
Wand Partners, Inc., 553
Washington Post Company, 747
Weberg Corporation, 625
Wells Fargo Bank, 983
Wendy's, 381, 457, 458, 503
Whirlpool Corporation, 394–95, 692, 703, 715, 716, 803
Whitehall, Inc., 578, 579
White Rock Corporation, 690–91
Whitewater Sporting Goods Store No. 18, 986–95, 1017
Winn Dixie, 309
Winston, Inc., 1060
Wrangler's, 874

X

Xenon Corporation, 647
Xerox Corporation, 103, 408, 461, 561, 597

Y

Yankelovich-Clancy-Shulman, 59

Z

Zenith Corporation, 1104, 1106

Subject Index

A

Absorption costing, 932, 933, 934
Accelerated depreciation methods, 412–13, 416, 417
Account(s), 44–46. *See also specific accounts*
  balance of, 49, 53–54
  chart of, 59–60, 85–87, 237–38
  closing the, 140–43
  control, 246, 249, 253
  grouped in ledgers, 44–46
  increases and decreases in, 47–49
  normal balance of, 60–61, 62
  open, 14
  opening the, 49
  permanent (real), 141
  temporary (nominal), 140–43
Accountants
  certified public (CPAs), 6, 7, 38, 39, 40, 490
  private vs. public, 38
  work of, 38–39
Account format
  balance sheet, 147
  four-column, 58–59
  T-account, 47
Accounting, 4
  accrual-basis, 90–92, 94, 95, 99, 138–40, 735
  for business transactions, 12–16
  career opportunities in, 38–41
  cash-basis, 90–92, 95, 735
  computers and. *See* Computerized accounting systems
  concepts and principles of. *See* Generally accepted accounting principles (GAAP)
  consolidation, 692–98
  constraints on, 502–4
  cost, 39–40
  debits and credits in, 47–49
  development of, 6–7
  ethical issues in, 7, 41, 302–5
  management, 6
  public and private, 38–40
  separation of custody of assets from, 285
  separation of duties within function of, 285–86
  separation of operations from, 285
  tax, 39
Accounting changes. *See* Changes, accounting
Accounting controls. *See* Internal control
Accounting cycle, 134, 239–40
Accounting department, 299
Accounting equation, 11–12, 65
  expansion of, 61
  rules of debit and credit and, 48
  transaction analysis and, 12–16
Accounting Horizons, 41
Accounting information
  comparable, 491, 494–95, 499, 504
  consistent, 491
  in decision making, 65–66, 148–49, 195–96, 346–48

management use of, 843–44
  relevant, 491, 499, 504, 1090–91
  reliable, 491, 494, 499, 504
  users of, 4–6
Accounting information systems, 232–77
  balancing ledgers, 252–53
  cash disbursements journal, 249, 251–52
  cash receipts journal, 246–48
  computerized vs. manual, comparison of, 236–42
  documents as journals in manual, 253
  features of effective, 234–35
  overview of, for merchandising business, 243–53
  purchases journal, 249–51
  sales journal, 243–46
  special accounting journals, 242–43, 253
Accounting organizations, 6, 7, 40–41
Accounting period, 92
Accounting Principles Board, 423
  Opinion No. 17, 427
  Opinion No. 21, 649
Accounting rate of return, 1105–6, 1111
Accounting ratios. *See* Ratios, financial
Accounting Revue, The, 41
Accounts payable, 11, 14, 448
Accounts Payable account, 45, 53, 54, 64, 65, 98
  as control account, 253
  as current liability, 145
  posting to, 252
  purchase discounts and, 180–81
  purchase returns and allowances and, 181
Accounts payable ledger, 251
Accounts payable subsidiary ledger, 249, 252
Accounts receivable, 11, 327–38. *See also* Notes receivable
  aging of, 333–35
  computers and, 348
  credit balances in, 336
  credit-card sales, 337
  defined, 328
  direct write-off method for uncollectible, 335–36
  internal control over collections of, 337–38
  reporting receivables and allowances, 345–46
  uncollectible-accounts expense, 329–35
Accounts Receivable account, 44, 64, 65, 102
  as control account, 246, 249, 253
  as current asset, 145
  dishonored note receivable transferred to, 344–45
  sales discounts and, 185
  sales returns and allowances and, 185
Accounts receivable department, 287
Accounts Receivable ledger, 244, 245, 247, 248, 250
Accounts receivable turnover, 800, 805–6
Accrual-basis accounting, 90–92
  adjusting entries in, 95, 138–40
  converting to cash-basis accounting, 735
  depreciation of plant assets in, 99

time-period concept and, 94
Accrual entry, 94
Accrued expense, 452. *See also* Payroll
  adjusting entries for, 100–102, 104
  reversing entries for, 171–72
Accrued liabilities, 45
Accrued revenues, adjusting entries for, 102, 104
Accrued Warranty Costs account, 453–54
Accumulated benefit obligation, 659
Accumulated deficit, 558
Accumulated Depletion account, 425
Accumulated depreciation, 409, 419, 420–21, 424
Accumulated Depreciation account, 99–100, 109, 421
Acid-test (quick) ratio, 347, 800, 803–4
Activity-based accounting. *See* Activity-based accounting
Activity-based costing (ABC), 1057, 1058–62
  defined, 1058
  demand for, 1059
  management decisions and, 1062
  product costing and, 1059–61
Activity-based management (ABM), 1032, 1057–67
  activity-based costing, 1057, 1058–62
  just-in-time (JIT) production systems, 1064–67
  kaizen costing, 1071–72
  product life-cycle budget, 1069–70, 1072
  target costing, 1070–71, 1072
  total quality management (TQM), 1072–75
Adjusted gross income, C:3
Adjusted trial balance, 96, 106–8, 135–36
  preparing financial statements from, 107–8
Adjusted useful life, 419
Adjusting entries, 90, 95–105
  for accrued expenses, 100–102, 104
  for accrued revenues, 102, 104
  to accrue interest revenue, 342
  alternate treatment of accounting for, 129–31
  defined, 95–96
  for depreciation of plant assets, 98–100
  for discount on note payable, 449–50
  for foreign-currency transaction loss, 706
  for interest expense, 647
  journalizing, 105, 139, 140
  for merchandising business, 188–91, 193, 194, 220–22, 224–25
  overview of, 104–5
  posting of, 105, 139, 140
  for prepaid expenses, 96–98, 104, 129–30
  recording, 138–40
  reversing entries and, 171, 172
  for Sales Revenue and Sales Tax Payable, 451
  summary of adjusting process, 104
  for uncollectible-account expense, 330, 332, 333, 334
  for unearned revenues, 102–4, 130–31
  on work sheet, 135–36

Conversion costs (cont.)
  computing equivalent units for, 885–86
  equivalent-unit total for, 892
  in process costing system, 885–86, 890, 891, 892
Convertible bonds (notes), 654
Convertible preferred stock, 571–72
Coordination, budgeting and, 983–84
Co-ownership of partnership property, 523
Copyrights, 426
Corporate codes of ethics, 303
Corporate taxation, 555
  depreciation and, 416–20
  double taxation, 555
  extraordinary gains and losses and, 611
  franchise tax, 555
  income tax, computing, 576–78, 743
  LIFO and, 373
Corporation, 8, 9, 553
  advantages and disadvantages of, 555
  capital stock of, 557
  characteristics of, 554–55
  dividends of. See Dividends
  donations received by, 567
  incorporation of a going business, 568
  manufacturing, 87
  merchandising, 86
  organizational chart of, 284
  organization cost, 568–69
  organization of, 556–57
  partnership advantages vs., 524
  profitability measures for, 572–73
  stock, classes of, 559–61
  stock, issuing of, 561–65
  stockholders' equity, 557–59, 563, 565
  stockholders' rights, 559
  stock values, 573–75
Corporation income statement, 608–14
  continued operations, 609–10
  cumulative effect of change in accounting principle, 611–12
  discontinued operations, 499–500, 610–11
  earnings per share (EPS), 612–14, 800, 811
  extraordinary gains and losses, 611, 653
Correcting entry, 144
Correlation, 961
Cosigning a note, 456
Cost(s). See also Standard costs
  budgeted, 1026
  conversion. See Conversion costs
  direct, 1000
  fixed, 919, 920, 948–51, 955–56, 1020, 1093, 1094–95
  indirect, 1000
  inventoriable, 849–50
  manufacturing, 846–49
  mixed (semivariable), 919–20
  period, 850
  prime, 848
  product, 845–46
  quality, types of, 1073–74
  separable, 1100–1101
  service department, allocation of, 1000–1003
  sunk, 1098
  trade-offs between fixed and variable, 955–56
  variable, 918–19, 920, 951–52, 955–56, 958–59, 1020
Cost accounting, 39–40
Cost and market value method, 690
Cost application base, 859
Cost behavior, 918
Cost behavior analysis. See also Cost functions
  to budget and control operating expenses, 952–55

determining how costs behave, 958–60
Cost/benefit relationship, 234–35
Cost center, 996
Cost driver, 851–52, 918, 953, 1020, 1059
  choosing allocation base and, 1001
  cost function and, 958–59
  in cost-volume-profit analysis, 930
  defined, 851
  in different business function areas, 960
  estimating mixed-cost function and, 961, 962
Cost estimation (cost approximation), 958–59
Cost functions, 958–67
  defined, 958
  evaluating, 966–67
  mixed-cost functions, estimating, 960–66
  types of, 959–60
Cost object, 851, 852, 1058–59
Cost of ending inventory, 370–71
Cost of goods manufactured, 848–49
Cost of Goods Sold account, 183
  adjustments to, 189–90
  in backflush costing, 1066
  job cost record and, 853
  in job order costing system, 861, 862, 863, 881
  in process costing system, 881, 882, 883
  standard costs in, 1038
Cost of goods sold (cost of sales), 94, 176, 183–85, 218–19, 365, 845
  computing, 186–87, 219
  on conventional vs. contribution margin income statement, 921
  effects of inventory errors on, 383–84
  estimating ending inventory and, 385–86
  inventory turnover and, 196, 804–5
Cost of product inventories, 845
Cost pool, 1032
Cost principle, 10, 370, 495
Cost-volume-profit (CVP) analysis, 924–29
  assumptions underlying, 930
  computer spreadsheets for, 928–29
  contribution margin approach, 925–29
  defined, 918
  equation approach, 924–25
  sales mix and, 930–31
CPA firms, 38
Credit, 47–49
  rules of, 47, 48, 61, 62
Credit balance, 54
  in accounts receivable, 336
  on contra asset accounts, 99
Credit-balance accounts, 60
Credit-card sales, 51, 337
Credit department, 328–29
Creditors, 11, 145, 328
  determining ability to pay, 731
  financial statement analysis by, 787–88
  as user of accounting information, 5
Credit sales, 243
Credit terms, 180, 348
Cumulative preferred stock, 570–71
Currency
  strong, 704–5, 709
  weak, 704–5, 709
Current asset accounts, changes in, 750
Current assets, 145, 146. See also Accounts receivable
  common-size analysis of, 793
  current ratio and, 148, 149, 347, 800, 801–3
  receivables as, 345–46
Current liabilities, 145, 146, 147, 446–87. See also Payroll
  accounts payable, 11, 14, 448

accrued expense, 452
categories of, 471
contingent liabilities, 344, 346, 456–57
current portion of long-term debt (current maturity), 451–52
Customer Deposits Payable, 453
estimated, 453–55
ratios measuring ability to pay, 148, 149, 347, 800, 801–4
sales tax payable, 450–51
short-term notes payable, 448–49
short-term notes payable at a discount, 449–50
unearned revenues, 145, 452
Current liability accounts, changes in, 750
Currently attainable standards, 1027
Current portion of long-term debt (current maturity), 451–52
Current ratio, 148, 149, 347, 800, 801–3
Current replacement cost, 382
Cursor, 240
Customer Deposits Payable account, 453
Customer prepayments. See Unearned revenues
Customers, cash collections from, 735
  computing, 740–42

D

Database, 235
Database programs, 242
Data processing, stages of, 236–40. See also Accounting information systems
Date of record, 569
Days' sales in receivables, 347–48, 800, 806–7
Death of partner, 535–36
Debentures, 638–39
Debit, 47–49
  rules of, 47, 48, 61, 62
Debit balance, 54
Debit-balance accounts, 60
Debt. See also Bond(s); Long-term debt
  payment of, 738
  proceeds from issuance of, 738
  servicing, 807–8
Debtor, 328
Debt ratio, 148–49, 800, 807–8
Decision makers, 4–6
Decision making. See also Financial statement analysis; Ratios, financial
  accounting information for, 65–66, 148–49, 195–96, 346–48
  activity-based costing and, 1062
  best use of facilities, 1097–98
  book value per share and, 575
  capital budgeting, 1103–6
  committed fixed costs and, 948–50
  computers for decision analysis, 1090
  contribution margin approach to, 922
  deletion of products, departments, territories, 1094–95
  joint products, 1099–1101
  lease or buy, 1112
  make-or-buy decisions, 1096–97
  opportunity cost and, 1101–2
  product emphasis, 1095–96
  qualities increasing value of information for, 491
  relevant information for, 1090–91
  replacement of equipment, 1098–99
  special sales order, 1091–93
  statement of cash flows and, role in, 795–96
Decision models, 1103
  capital-budgeting, 1104–12

Goodwill, 427, 504, 695–96
Government regulation, 555
Government regulatory agencies, 5
Greenwald, John, 685
Griffin, Merv, 656
Gross income, C:2
    adjusted, C:3
Gross margin (gross profit), 176–77
    computing, 186–87
    effects of inventory errors on, 383–84
Gross margin (gross profit) method, 385–86
Gross margin (gross profit) percentage, 195
    in installment method, 496–97
Gross margin rate, 385
Gross pay, 459
    in payroll register, 463, 464
Gross salary, 462

H

Hardware, 235
Hedging, 707
Held-to-maturity securities, 698, 699–701
    as long-term asset, 145
High-low method, 963–64, 966
Historical cost, 10
Holding gain or loss, 689
Horizontal analysis, 788–91
Hudler, Donald W., 841
Hunter, Stephen, 405

I

Iacocca, Lee, 282
Illusory profit, 376
IMA Standards of Ethical Conduct, 41
Immediate expenses, 850
Import/export ratio, 704
Imprest system, 302
Income. *See also* Net income
    adjusted gross, C:3
    alternative product costing approaches and, 932–34
    of consolidated entity, 696–98
    gross, C:2
    from operations, 193, 224
    pretax accounting, 576, 577
    taxable, 576, 577, C:1, C:4–5
    total, C:2
Income, measurement of business, 88–131.
    See also Adjusting entries
    accounting period, 92
    accrual-basis vs. cash-basis accounting, 90–92
    adjusted trial balance, 96, 106–8, 135–36
    matching principle and, 93–94
    revenue principle and, 92–93
    time-period concept and, 94
Income effects of inventory methods, 372–73
Income statement, 18, 19, 732
    from adjusted trial balance, 107, 108
    budgeted, 985, 988–90
    capital vs. revenue expenditures on, 428–29
    common-size, 793
    comparative, 789, 791–92
    computing amounts for statement of cash flows from, 740–45
    contribution margin, 921–22, 926, 932, 933, 949, 1091
    conventional, 921, 1091
    corporation, 608–14
    cost of goods manufactured on, 848
    direct write-off method and, 336
    divided by product line, 1094

example of, 20
format of, 193–95
investment in bonds on, 700
lower-of-cost-or-market (LCM) effects on, 382, 383
of merchandising business, 176, 191–93, 222–24
preparation of, 138
standard cost, 1039
statement of owners' equity and, 108
uncollectible-account expense on, 331
unearned service revenue on, 455
on work sheet, 136–37, 190, 191, 220–22
Income statement accounts, 60
Income statement performance report, 1024
Income Summary account, 141, 142, 143
    closed to Retained Earnings account, 596
Income tax, C:0–9
    classes and filing status of taxpayers, C:2
    corporate. *See* Corporate taxation
    defined, C:0
    of individuals, C:2–6
    LIFO and, 373
    operation of, C:1
    partnership and, 523
    as payroll deduction, 459–60
    quarterly payments, C:6
    withheld, 459–60, C:6
Income tax expense, 609
    in statement of cash flows, 736–37
Income Tax Expense account, 576, 577
Income tax liability, C:6
Income Tax Payable account, 576, 577
Income tax rates, C:5
Incorporation of a going business, 568
Incorporators, 556
Independent contractors, 463
Independent variable in cost function, 958, 959
Indirect costs, 1000
Indirect labor, 847
    in job order costing system, 856, 857–58
Indirect materials, 847
    in job order costing system, 855, 856
Indirect method for preparing statement of cash flows, 734, 746–52
    on work sheet, 779–81
Industry comparisons, 794–95
Inflation, 11
Information systems design, 40
Inputs, 236
Installment method, 496–97
Institute of Management Accountants (IMA), 41, 303
Insurance, prepaid, 44, 97
Insurance Expense account, 97
Intangible assets, 406, 425–28, 568–69
Integrated accounting software, 240
Interest
    compound, 674–75
    computing payments of, 743
    on notes receivable, 339, 340–41
Interest expense
    adjusting entries for, 647
    on bonds, 642, 643
    on bonds issued at discount, 644
    on bonds issued at premium, 646
    payments for, 736–37
Interest Expense account, 193
Interest Payable account, 45
    as current liability, 145
Interest period, 339, 341
Interest rate, 340, 641, 650
Interest revenue

accruing, 342
cash receipt of, 735
on checking account, 291
as operating activity, 733–34
Interest Revenue account, 45, 193
Interim periods, financial statements for, 92
Interim reports, 492
Internal auditing, 40
Internal auditors, 286
Internal control, 234, 280–325
    bank account as control device, 288–94
    cash, reporting of, 297
    over cash disbursements (payments), 299–302
    over cash receipts, 297–99
    over collections of accounts receivable, 337–38
    computerized inventory accounting systems and, 367
    defined, 282
    effective systems of, 283–87
    ethics and, 282, 302–4
    limitations of, 288
    over merchandise inventory, 386
    over payroll, 469–70
    of plant assets, 423–24
Internal failure costs, 1073, 1074
Internal rate of return (IRR), 1110–11
Internal Revenue Service (IRS), 41, 374, 416, C:0
International accounting, 427, 703–9
    consolidation of foreign subsidiaries, 707–9
    economic structures and, 703–5
    foreign currencies and foreign-currency exchange rates, 704–5
    hedging, 707
    purchases on account, 705–6
    sales on account, 706
    standards of, 504, 709
International Accounting Standards Committee (IASC), 504, 709
International Federation of Accountants (IFAC), 504
Inventoriable costs, 849–50
Inventory(ies)
    average, 196
    in merchandising vs. manufacturing, 844
    payments for, computing, 742–43
    ratios measuring ability to sell, 800, 804–6
    in traditional production systems, 1062–63
Inventory, merchandise, 175, 364–403
    adjusting, based on physical count, 188–90
    basic concept of accounting for, 366
    cost of, computing, 370
    defined, 176
    errors, effects of, 383–84
    estimating, 385–86
    internal control over, 386
    purchase of, 178–83, 217–18
    sale of, 183–85, 218–19
Inventory accounting systems, 177–78, 366–69
    periodic, 177, 178, 217–25, 243–44, 368–69, 850–51
    perpetual, 177–83, 243, 366–68, 379–80, 850–51
Inventory account (merchandising)
    closing entries to, 224–25
    as current asset, 145
    freight charge in, 182
    purchase discounts and, 180–81
    purchase returns and allowances and, 181
Inventory accounts (manufacturing), 846–47
    flow of costs through, 849

Off-balance-sheet financing, 659
Office Supplies account, 44, 52–53, 54
Old age, survivors and disability insurance (OASDI), 460
On account, 14, 15, 16
On-line processing, 239
Open account, 14
Opening the account, 49
Operating activities, 732
  cash flows from, 735–37
  computing cash amounts of, 740–43
  direct method for, 777–79
  indirect method for, 779–81
  interest and dividends revenues as, 733–34
  reconciliation from net income to net cash inflow (outflow) from, 746–51, 779–81
Operating budget, 985, 988–90
Operating cycle, 145
  of merchandising business, 177
Operating expenses, 191, 222–24
  computing payments for, 743
  cost behavior analysis to budget and control, 952–55
Operating expenses budget, 990
Operating income, 193, 224
  at breakeven point, 924
  CVP analysis and, 924–29
  product costing approaches and, 932–34
  special sales order analysis and, 1092–93
  target, 927
  at various sales levels, 927–29
Operating lease, 657, 659
Operating loss, 928
Operations, 18
  continued, 609–10
  discontinued, 499–500, 610–11
  merchandising, 176–77
  separation from accounting, 285
Opportunity cost, 1101–2
Ordinary repairs, 428
Organization cost, 568–69
Organization of corporation, 556–57
  organizational chart, 284
Organizations, accounting, 6, 7, 40–41
Other receivables, 328
Other revenue and expense, 193, 224
Outlier, 963
Outputs, 236, 239. *See also* Financial statements
Outstanding checks, 291, 293
Outstanding stock, 557
Overapplied overhead, 861–63
Overfunded pension plan, 659
Overhead
  manufacturing. *See* Manufacturing overhead
  standards for, 1026–27
Overhead efficiency variance, 1035–36
Overhead flexible budget variance, 1034
Overhead spending variance, 1036–37
Overtime, 458
Owner investment, 13
Owners' equity, 11, 12–13, 85. *See also* Stockholders' equity
  on balance sheet, 60
  as credit/debit, 47–49
  statement of. *See* Statement of owners' equity
Owners' equity accounts, 45–46
  charts of, for different types of businesses, 85
  normal balance of, 60–61, 62
  in partnership, 523
  as permanent, 141

revenues and expenses, 61–65
  in work sheet, 136
Ownership, corporate
  separation of management and, 555
  transferability of, 554

P

Paid-in-capital (contributed capital), 558, 563
Paid-in Capital from Treasury Stock Transactions account, 603–4
Paid-in Capital in Excess of Par, 563
  —Common, 598, 599
  —Preferred, 565, 572
Paid-in Capital in Excess of Stated Value—Common, 564
Paid voucher file, 324
Parameter, 959
Parent company, 692–98
Participating preferred stock, 571
Participative management style, 282
Partnership agreement, 522, 533, 535
Partnerships, 8, 9, 520–51
  admission of partner, 530–33
  advantages and disadvantages of, 524
  characteristics of, 522–24
  death of partner, 535–36
  defined, 520
  financial statements, 525, 538–39
  investments by partners, 524–25, 531–33
  liquidation of, 536–38
  partner drawings, 529
  service, 85
  sharing profits and losses in, 525–29
  withdrawal of partner, 533–35
Partner's interest, admission to partnership by purchasing, 530
Par value, issuing common stock at, 563
Passing the dividend, 570
Passwords, 235
Patents, amortization entries for, 425–26
Payables, 14. *See also* Accounts payable; Notes payable
Payback, 1104–5, 1111
  with equal annual cash flows, 1104
  with unequal annual cash flows, 1105
Payee of note, 339
Payment date of dividend, 569
Payroll, 458–72
  deductions, 459–61, 463, 464, 466
  employer payroll taxes, 461–62, 463, 466
  gross and net pay, 459, 463, 464
  internal controls over, 469–70
  recording cash disbursements for, 466–68
  reporting payroll expense and liabilities, 470–71
Payroll entries, 462–63
Payroll system, 463–66
  bank account, 465
  checks, 465–66
  register or journal, 463–65
Payroll taxes, 461–62
  entries for, 462, 463
  recording, 466
Pensions, 468, 659–60
Percentage change, analysis of, 788–89
Percentage-of-completion method, 498
Percentage of sales approach, 333, 335
Percentages, trend, 790–91
Perfection standards, 1027
Performance evaluations, budgeting and, 984
Performance measures, nonfinancial, 1074–75
Performance reports, 954–55

budgeting and, 984–85
  income statement, 1024
Period costs, 850
Periodic inventory system, 177, 178, 217–25, 243–44, 368–69, 850–51
  adjusting and closing process for merchandiser in, 220–22, 224–25
  journal entries under, 369
  purchase of inventory in, 217–18
  sale of inventory in, 218–19
Permanent (real) accounts, 141
Perpetual inventory system, 177–83, 243, 366–68, 379–80, 850–51
  journal entries under, 368, 369
  purchase of merchandise inventory in, 178–83
  records under different inventory costing methods, 379–80
Personal exemptions, C:4
Personnel
  access to accounting system, 235
  competent, reliable and ethical, 283–84
Petty cash funds, 297
  disbursements, controls for, 301–2
Petty cash ticket, 301
Phantom profit, 376
Physical system. *See* Periodic inventory system
Planning
  budgeting and, 983
  defined, 842
  product life cycle and, 1069
Plant asset(s), 98, 145, 147, 406
  on balance sheet, 99–100, 406
  capital vs. revenue expenditures, 428–29
  cash payments to acquire, 737
  computing acquisitions and sales of, 744
  cost of, 406–8
  depreciation of, 98–100, 408–15
  disposal of, 420–25
  exchanging, 422–23
  gains and losses on sale of, 749–50
  internal control of, 423–24
  natural resources and depletion, 424–25
  proceeds from sale of, 737–38
  selling, 421–22
  useful life of, determining, 409, 419
Plant asset ledger, 424
Point-of-sale terminal, 287
  internal control at, 297–98
Portfolio diversification, 687
Postclosing trial balance, 143–44
Posting, 51, 58
  accounts after, 65
  of adjusting entries, 105, 139, 140
  from cash disbursements journal, 251, 252
  closing entries, 140–43
  in computerized accounting system, 239
  to general ledger, 244–45, 247, 248
  illustrative problem of, 52–53, 62–64
  from purchases journal, 249–50
  to subsidiary ledger, 245, 247, 248
Postretirement benefits, 468, 660
Preemptive right, 559
Preferred stock, 560
  convertible, 571–72
  cumulative, 570–71
  dividends on, 569–71, 613
  issuing, 565
  liquidation value, 574
  noncumulative, 570
  nonparticipating, 571
  participating, 571
  redemption value of, 574

Valuation account, 100
Value-added time, 1063
Value chain
    defined, 844
    manufacturing and, 844–46
Value chain function, 921
Value engineering (VE), 1070–71
Variable budget. *See* Flexible budgets
Variable cost function, 959, 960
Variable costing, 932, 933
Variable costs, 918–19, 951–52, 1020
    discretionary, 951–52
    engineered, 951
    relevant range and, 920
    step-function, 958–59
    trade-off between fixed and, 955–56
Variables in cost function
    dependent, 958, 959
    independent, 958, 959
Variance(s), 1020, 1021
    in backflush costing systems, 1066–67
    defined, 953
    direct labor, 1030–31, 1037–38
    direct materials, 1029–30, 1031, 1067
    efficiency, 1029–32, 1035–36, 1067
    flexible budget, 1023–25
    investigation of, 1032
    management's use of variance information,
        1031–32
    manufacturing overhead, 1032–37
    on performance report, 954, 955
    price, 1028–32
    in responsibility report, 998, 999, 1000
    sales volume, 1023

Variance analysis, flexible budgets and,
    1023–25
Vertical analysis, 791–92
Viken, Mark, 175
Visual-fit method, 963, 964–65, 966
Volume, relevant range of, 920–21. *See also*
    Cost-volume-profit (CVP) analysis
Voting right, stockholder, 559
Voucher, 300, 321, 324
Voucher packet, 322, 324
Voucher register, 322, 323, 324
Voucher system, 321–25

W

Wage and Tax Statement (Form W–2), 466,
    468
Wages, 458
Wall Street Journal, The, 561, 614
Warranty expense, 453–54
Weak currency, 704–5, 709
Weighted-average cost, 371, 372, 373, 380
    perpetual inventory records at, 380
Weighted-average method of process costing
    for second department, 895–98
Weighted-average number of common shares
    outstanding, 613
Weighted-average unit contribution margin,
    930–31
Wesselkamper, Joseph D., 447
Withdrawal of partner from partnership,
    533–35
Withdrawals, owner, 16, 21
    as credit/debit, 62

Withdrawals (Drawing) account, 45, 53, 54,
    64, 65, 141, 142, 529
    normal balance of, 62
    as temporary account, 140
Withheld income tax, 459–60, C:6
Working capital, 801
Work in Process Inventory account, 846, 847
    cost of goods manufactured and, 848
    job cost record and, 852
    in job order costing system, 855, 856, 857,
        860, 861, 862, 881
    in process costing system, 881, 882, 883,
        886, 887–88, 893, 894
    standard costs in, 1037
Work measurement, 953
Work sheet, 106, 134–37
    for consolidated balance sheet, 694, 695
    of merchandising business, 190–91, 220–22
    for statement of cash flows, 776–83
    steps in preparation of, 135–37
    using, 138–44
Write-off entry, 331–32
Write-off method, direct, 335–36

Y

York, Jerome B., 1089, 1103

Z

Zoth, Lota, 489

Check Figures for Problems

(continued from front cover)

P15-6A RE, Dec. 31, 19X3, $179,200; EPS = $1.78

P15-7A EPS = $0.57; Total stock. equity $446,070

P15-8A 1. $560 million

P15-1B No check figure

P15-2B Total stock. equity: Dec. 31, 19X8, $454,000; Dec. 31, 19X9, $541,000

P15-3B No check figure

P15-4B Total stock. equity $578,880

P15-5B Total stock. equity $547,800

P15-6B RE, June 30, 19X4, $308,000; EPS = $5.90

P15-7B EPS = $3.87; Total stock. equity $878,465

P15-8B 1. $800 million

DP-1 No check figure

DP-2 No check figure

FSP 1 2. Average price $31.86 per share

FSP 2 No check figure

P16-1A 2. 19X5 Interest exp. $105,000

P16-2A 4. Interest exp. $43,500

P16-3A 9/30/X4 Bond carrying amount $174,768

P16-4A 12/31/X3 Bond carrying amount $314,688

P16-5A 12/31/X1 Interest exp. (bonds) $20,750

P16-6A No check figure

P16-7A Total long-term liab. $350,000

P16-1B 2. 19X7 Interest exp. $106,667

P16-2B 4. Interest exp. $22,950

P16-3B 9/30/X4 Bond carrying amount $124,423

P16-4B 12/31/X3 Bond carrying amount $474,920

P16-5B 12/31/X1 Interest exp. (bonds) $83,000

P16-6B No check figure

P16-7B Total long-term liab. $593,000

DP1 EPS Plan A $13.26

DP2 No check figure

FSP 1 No check figure

FSP 2 No check figure

P16A-1 a. $461,700 (5 yrs.)

P16A-2 a. $20,000,564

P16A-3 2. $112,472; 3. $127,140

P16A-4 12/31/X2 Bond carrying amount $285,629

P16A-5 PV Nissan 4,989,600¥; PV Toyota 5,197,500¥

P16A-6 Depr. exp. $7,123 Interest exp. $5,238

P17-1A Loss on sale, Feb. 6, 19X5, $14,487

P17-2A 2. Investment in affiliates, Dec. 31, $1,595,000

P17-3A Consol. total assets $746,000

P17-4A Consol. total assets $969,000

P17-5A 2. Held-to-maturity investments $464,314

P17-6A Cost of bond $387,578

P17-7A A. Foreign currency transaction gain $8,500; B. Foreign currency translation adj. ($37,000)

P17-1B Loss on sale Mar. 3, 19X3, $25,900

P17-2B 2. Investment in affiliates, Dec. 31, $6,909,000

P17-3B Consol. total assets $933,000

P17-4B Consol. total assets $1,024,000

P17-5B 2. Held-to-maturity investments $615,857

P17-6B Cost of bond $486,123

P17-7B A. Foreign currency transaction gain $900; B. Foreign currency translation adj. $138,000

DP 1 No check figure

DP2 No check figure

FSP 1 2. $1,870,000

FSP 2 No check figure

CP 1 3. Total liab.: Current $187,250; Long-term $289,536; Total stock. equity: $630,874

CP2 No check figure

P18-1A No check figure

P18-2A Increase in cash $6,500

P18-3A Net cash inflow from operations $75,600

P18-4A Net cash inflow from operations $75,600

P18-5A Net cash inflow from operations $84,000

P18-6A Net cash inflow from operations $50,500

P18-7A Net cash inflow from operations $67,200

P18-8A Net cash inflow from operations $67,400

P18-1B No check figure

P18-2B Increase in cash $11,300

P18-3B Net cash inflow from operations $69,600

P18-4B Net cash inflow from operations $69,600

P18-4B Net cash inflow from operations $80,200

P18-6B Net cash inflow from operations $90,600

P18-7B Net cash inflow from operations $72,800

P18-8B Net cash inflow from operations $61,100

DP 1 Net cash inflow from operations $140,000

DP 2 No check figure

FSP 1 2a. $866,796,000

FSP 2 No check figure

P18A-1 Transaction analysis total debits, Panel A $1,510,200

P18A-2 Transaction analysis total debits, Panel A $93,200

P18A-3 Transaction analysis total debits, Panel A $234,300

P18A-4 Transaction analysis total debits, Panel A $1,356,800

P19-1A 19X7: 1. Net sales 120%; 2. 0.165

P19-2A Net income 14.9%; SE 40.2%

P19-3A Invest in Northern

P19-4A 2. a. Current ratio 1.38; Debt ratio 0.60; EPS no effect

P19-5A 19X4: Inven. turnover 1.37; Return on assets 0.117; EPS $5.00

P19-6A Buy Smajstrla; Price/earnings 7.9

P19-1B 19X6: 1. Net sales 144%; 2. 0.078

P19-2B Net income 4.7%; SE 38.1%

P19-3B Invest in Norwegian

P19-4B 2. b. Current ratio 2.00; Debt ratio 0.49; EPS $4.41

P19-5B 19X6: Inven. turnover 1.18; Return on assets 0.152; EPS $4.47

P19-6B Buy Pediatric Supply; Price/earnings 24.3

DP1 No check figure

DP2 No check figure

FSP 1 3. Inventory turnover 1994, 4.01

FSP 2 No check figure

CP 1 Inventory turnover 1994, 4.0; net cash inflow 1991, $52.5 million; debt ratio 1994, 35%

CP 2 No check figure

P20-1A Net income $51,600

P20-2A July work in process inven. $3,200; July cost of goods sold $3,900

P20-3A 1. Cost of goods manuf. $21,300,000; 3. Materials purchased $2,900,000

P20-4A Fin. goods inven. bal. $133,880

P20-5A Total job cost $2,140

P20-6A Operating income $41,520

P20-1B Beg. WIP $31,000; Net income $29,400

P20-2B April work in process inven. $1,800; April cost of goods sold $5,500

P20-3B 1. Cost of goods manuf. $161 million; 2. Cost of goods sold $158.8 million

P20-4B Fin. goods inven. bal. $41,180

P20-5B Total job cost $1,409